בְּרֵאשִׁית

שִׁמְעוֹן עֵלִי
מְקוּבָּל

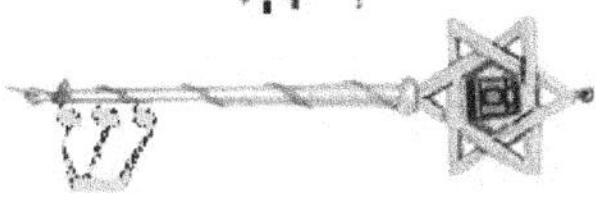

EVIDENCE *is GENESIS'* KEY

Epistemological Explanation, from the Beginning (*berēšiṯ* בְּרֵאשִׁית) to *Bāḇēl* (בָּבֶל)

Original Translation and Commentary of *Genesis*, Chapters 1 to 11

by שִׁמְעוֹן עֵלִי **SIMON ELI**

mystical traditionalist, *mekubal* מְקוּבָּל

Meditations on the Universal Timeless Gnoseology for Everyone,
agnostics, amoralists, atheists, believers, clergy, creationists, empiricists, evolutionists, freethinkers, idealists, materialists, moralists, nonreligious, pagans, philosophers, pragmatists, religious, scientists, seculars, spiritualists, unbelievers and theologians of all beliefs and opinions.

S.E.A.O., Inc.

ISBN-10: 0-692-95826-6
ISBN-13: 978-0-692-95826-1

SACER EQUESTRIS AUREUS ORDO, Inc. (S.E.A.O.), Sacred Texts Division,
West Long Branch, NJ - Charleston, SC, USA

To Bhagavan[1]

"*I am the way, the truth, and the life*
[and] *you shall realize the truth,*
and the truth shall make you free."[2]

CONTENT

ABBREVIATIONS 14
PART 1: PREMISES
PREAMBLE 16
METHODOLOGY 17
PREMISES 20
FUNDAMENTAL EPISTEMIC PREMISE 20
***GENESIS* IS AN EPISTEMIC PARABLE** 20
GRAPHIC: *AWARENESS, CONSCIOUSNESS and CERTAINTY* 23
INTRODUCTION 24
Questions 25
Names 25
Gematria values 26
Metaphor, Allegory, Symbol and Sense 26
Transcendent 30
Faith and Belief 32
GRAPHIC: *Epistemic Circularity* 35
Epistemic Loneliness 36
The Subject-Object Dichotomy 37
GRAPHIC: *Apkallu in Assyrian bas-reliefs*....37
Historicizing God 38
Epistemic Interpretation 39
Revelation 40
Oneiric studies 41
GRAPHIC: ש, *Śîn hand blessing symbol and Trident* 42
PART 2: CREATION
CHAPTER 1 GOD'S EXHALING BREATH: THE DESCENDING SIX DAYS OF CREATION 45
GRAPHIC: *Descending Centrality of Creation* 45
1-I SECTION: THE WORLD BEFORE CREATION
1 Creation out of Nothing 46
GRAPHIC: *Big Bang* 52
2 The Original Waters 52
1-II SECTION: THE SIX DAYS OF CREATION
3 I ⊙ DAY - Start of the First Day of Creation: The *Auto-Transparent* Light 55
4 I ⊙ DAY - The First Logical Rule 56
5 I ⊙ DAY - End of the First Day of Creation: Beginning of Language 58
GRAPHIC: *Day of Creation* 59
6 II ⊙ DAY - Start of the Second Day of Creation: The Pure Sky Volt 60
7 II ⊙ DAY - Logical Distinctions of the Waters 61
GRAPHIC: *The Waters* 62
8 II ⊙ DAY - End of the Second Day of Creation: I-Consciousness 62
9 III ⊙ DAY - Start of the Third Day of Creation: Converting to Physicality 63
10 III ⊙ DAY – The Physical World Acknowledged 65
11 III ⊙ DAY - From Minerals to Vegetation 66
12 III ⊙ DAY - The Vegetative Life Acknowledged 67
13 III ⊙ DAY - End of the Third Day of Creation: Individual-Consciousness 68
GRAPHIC: *The Three Levels of Consciousness* 68
14 IV ⊙ DAY - Start of the Fourth Day of Creation: Radiant Power 68
15 IV ⊙ DAY - Earth's reflected light 69

GRAPHIC: *Centrality, Light and reflection* 70
16 IV ⊙ DAY - The Subject Sun and the Object Moon 70
GRAPHIC: Sun and Moon 71
17 IV ⊙ DAY - The Light of the World 72
18 IV ⊙ DAY - Power over the Earth 73
19 IV ⊙ DAY - End of the Fourth Day of Creation: Rulership 73
20 V ⊙ DAY - Start of the Fifth Day of Creation: Biological Multiplication 74
21 V ⊙ DAY – The Reproductive Cycle 74
GRAPHIC: *The Waters of Multiplication* 75
GRAPHIC: *The Bent Serpent* 76
22 V ⊙ DAY – Flowing of the Biological Multiplication 76
23 V ⊙ DAY - End of the Fifth Day of Creation: Multiplying Impulse 76
24 VI ⊙ DAY - Start of the Sixth Day of Creation: Life 77
25 VI ⊙ DAY - Life's Generation 77
GRAPHIC: *Power, Impulse and Life, the Last Three Levels of Creation* 78
26 VI ⊙ DAY – Creation of the Human 78
GRAPHIC: *Tetragrammaton* 79
27 VI ⊙ DAY – The Image of God 80
GRAPHIC: *Articulations of Consciousness* 81
28 VI ⊙ DAY – Human Power 81
GRAPHIC: *The circle of Power*....... 82
29 VI ⊙ DAY – Human Epistemic and Biological Impulses 82
GRAPHIC: *The circle of Epistemic and Biological Impulses* 83
30 VI ⊙ DAY – Human Life 83
GRAPHIC: *The circle of Life* 84
31 VI ⊙ DAY - End of the Sixth Day of Creation: The Human Being 84
HERE ENDS THE FIRST CHAPTER OF THE EXHALING BREATH OF GOD:
THE DESCENDING SIX DAYS OF CREATION 84
CHAPTER 2 GOD'S INHALING BREATH & THE ASCENDING TREE IN THE GARDEN OF EDEN .. 85
GRAPHIC: *The Garden of Eden* 85
2-I SECTION: THE SILENCE OF AWARENESS
1 End of the Descending Process of Creation 86
2 The Centrality of the Seventh Day 86
GRAPHIC: *Descent and Ascent* 88
3 The Apnea and Inhaling of God's Breath 89
GRAPHIC: *Reversal, Ascension and the Menorah Candelabrum* 91
4 Certain Awareness 91
2-II SECTION: ADAM
5 The Barrenness of the Ideal Earth 94
6 The Mist 94
7 The Breath of Adam's Life 95
GRAPHIC: *Creation of Adam* 97
8 Adam's Garden 98
2-III SECTION: THE GARDEN OF EDEN
9 The Trees of Life and Knowledge 99
GRAPHIC: *The Tree of Life* 100
GRAPHIC: *The Tree of Knowledge-of Good and Evil* 100
10 The Rivers 102
GRAPHIC: *The Garden of Eden as the Human Body* 103

GRAPHIC: *The One River with Four Branches* 103
11 The Increasing First Branch River 104
12 Gold and Precious Stones 104
13 The Black Second Branch River 105
14 The Successful Third and Fruitful Fourth Branch Rivers 105
GRAPHIC: *The Fourth Branch River* 106
GRAPHIC: *The Third Branch River* 106
2-IV SECTION: EDEN'S GUARDIAN
15 The Appointment 108
16 Eat from All the Tree-Faculties 109
17 The Dangerous Tree 109
18 Adam's Loneliness 111
19 Animal Companions 112
20 The Human Names All Animals 113
21 The Deep Sleep 115
22 The Woman 115
GRAPHIC: *Out of the Deep Sleep* 116
23 Subject-Object 116
GRAPHIC: *Dynamo as Subject/male+ Object/female-Polarities* 117
24 One Flesh 117
25 Nakedness 118
HERE ENDS THE SECOND CHAPTER OF GOD'S INHALING BREATH AND THE ASCENDING TREE IN THE GARDEN OF EDEN 119
CHAPTER 3 THE TREE OF KNOWLEDGE AND THE TREE OF LIFE 120
GRAPHIC: *The Trees of Life & of Knowledge-of Good and Evil* 120
3-I SECTION: THE TEMPTATION
1 The Serpent 121
GRAPHIC: *The Serpent of Intentionality* 121
2 The Woman's Reply 122
3 The Forbidden Fruit 123
4 The Serpent's Reply 123
5 Ye Shall Be as Gods 124
GRAPHIC: *Before the cock crow* 125
GRAPHIC: *The Mind Pursuing the Object* 126
6 The Fruit of Desire 129
GRAPHIC: *The Tree of Knowledge-of Good and Evil* 130
7 With Opened Eyes 131
8 God's Voice 132
9 Where is Adam, the Subject? 134
10 Fear of Epistemic Loneliness 135
11 Did You Eat from That Tree? 136
12 Now We Are All Eaters from That Same Tree 138
3-II SECTION: THE PUNISHMENT
13 The Serpent's Charm 140
14 The Cursed Serpent 140
GRAPHIC: *Light's Reflection* 141
15 The Adversary 142
GRAPHIC: *The Adversity* 143
GRAPHIC: *Paterissa, Greek Orthodox Bishops' Pastoral Staff* 144

16 Sorrow and Pain 144
17 Ground Cursing 146
18 The Thorny Green Sprouts of Food 147
19 Labor and Death 147
3-III SECTION: THE EXPULSION
20 Eve 149
21 The Skin 149
22 The Tree of Life 149
GRAPHIC: *The Tree of Life* 150
23 Dismissal from Paradise 151
24 Cherubim's Sword 151
GRAPHIC: *The Cherubim's Sword* 153
HERE ENDS THE THIRD CHAPTER OF THE TREE OF KNOWLEDGE AND THE TREE OF LIFE 153
PART 3: GENEALOGICAL PARADIGMS
CHAPTER 4 THE GENERATIONS OF ADAM AND EVE & THAT OF CAIN 155
GRAPHIC: *Eve's Generations* 154
4-I SECTION: CAIN AND ABEL
1 Birth of Cain 156
2 Birth of Abel 157
3 At the End of Cain's Day 158
4 Abel's Offering 159
GRAPHIC: *Cain-Abel's functions* 159
5 Cain's Wrath 160
6 Why the distress? 164
7 Actions' Outcome 165
GRAPHIC: *Sin and Dante's dark forest* 166
8 Killing Abel 167
9 Where is Abel? 168
4-II SECTION: CAIN'S PUNISHMENT
10 Abel's Voice Cries Out 170
11 The Earth Witnesses Abel's Blood 171
12 Cain, the Grieving Wandering Wonderer 172
13 Unbearable Punishment 172
14 Fear of Being Slayed 173
15 Cain's Mark 173
16 Exile 174
GRAPHIC: *The Land of Nod* 175
4-III SECTION: CAIN'S GENERATIONS
17 Enoch 177
18 Enoch's Generation 177
19 Lamech 178
20 Farmers and Herders 179
21 Artists 179
22 Metalworkers, Wars and Beauty 179
Summary of Cain's Waking Generation 180
23 Lamech's Murderous Act 180
GRAPHIC: *in-itself & for-itself* 181
24 Lamech's Punishment 182

25 Seth ... 182
26 Seth's Generation ... 183
GRAPHIC: *The Generations of Cain* ... 184
HERE ENDS THE FOURTH CHAPTER OF THE GENERATIONS OF ADAM AND EVE & THAT OF CAIN ... 184
CHAPTER 5 THE GENERATIONS OF SETH ... 185
GRAPHIC: *The Generations of Seth* ... 185
5-I SECTION: ADAM, MALE AND FEMALE
1 Adam, the Image of Divine-Consciousness ... 186
2 Adam, Male and Female ... 186
5-II SECTION: THE GENERATIONS BEFORE THE FLOOD
3 Seth, Adam's Dream ... 188
GRAPHIC: *The waking, dreaming and sleep years* ... 189
4 Adam Conceives Offspring ... 192
5 Adam's Redemption ... 192
GRAPHIC: *Collapse of the Tree of Knowledge of Good and Evil Circle into the Tree of Life* ... 193
6 Enos ... 193
7 Seth's Offspring ... 193
8 Seth's Redemption ... 194
GRAPHIC: *Adam's wakefulness, dream, dreamless sleep and Transcendence* ... 195
9 Cainan ... 195
10 Enos' Offspring ... 196
11 Enos' Redemption ... 196
12 Mahalaleel ... 197
13 Cainan's Offspring ... 197
14 Cainan's Redemption ... 198
15 Jared ... 198
16 Mahalaleel's Offspring ... 199
17 Mahalaleel's End ... 199
18 Enoch ... 200
19 Jared's Offspring ... 200
20 Jared's Redemption ... 201
21 Methuselah ... 201
22 Enoch's Offspring ... 202
23 Enoch's Days ... 203
24 Enoch's Dreamless Sleep ... 203
25 Lamech ... 204
26 Methuselah's Offspring ... 205
27 Methuselah's Redemption ... 205
28 Lamech's Son ... 206
29 Noah ... 206
30 Lamech's Offspring ... 207
31 Lamech's Entropy ... 207
32 Shem, Ham, and Japheth ... 208
GRAPHIC: *Dream Merging in Wakefulness and in NREM* ... 209
Summary of Seth's Dreaming Generation ... 209
HERE ENDS THE FIFTH CHAPTER OF THE GENERATIONS OF SETH ... 210
PART 4: NOAH
CHAPTER 6 THE ARK ... 212

GRAPHIC: *The Ark as a skullcap on Mount Ararat* 212
6-I SECTION: DAUGHTERS' OFFSPRING
1 Subject-Object Multiplication 213
2 The Sons of God and The Daughters of Men 213
3 120 Wandering Wondering Years 214
4 The Land of Fallen Giants 216
5 Wicked Thought 218
GRAPHIC: *The Unreachable I-in-itself & Double-head Mayan mask (Guatemala).* 219
6 Compassion 219
7 Promise to Wipe Away Men 222
6-II SECTION: NOAH'S GENERATIONS
8 Noah Rested in Awareness 225
9 Noah's Generations 225
10 Noah's sons 225
GRAPHIC: *Wakefulness after Sleep* 226
11 Violence 226
12 Corrupting Flesh 227
6-III SECTION: THE FLOOD
13 The Wasteland 228
14 Build an Ark 228
GRAPHIC: *The Ark* 230
15 Ark's Measurements 231
16 The Ark's Openings 232
GRAPHIC: *Window and door of the Ark* 233
GRAPHIC: 1-*Pyramidion capstone,* 2-*Templar's Seal* 233
17 Forecasting the Deluge 234
18 Enter the Ark 235
19 All Animals in Pair 235
20 The Seminal Reasons 235
21 The Food in the Ark 237
22 Noah Follows the Orders 238
HERE ENDS THE SIXTH CHAPTER OF NOAH'S ARK 238
CHAPTER 7 THE DELUGE 238
GRAPHIC: *The Flood of Time* 238
7-I SECTION: THE ARK'S INHABITANTS
1 Enter the Ark 240
2 Clean and Unclean Animals 241
3 Birds of the Sky 242
4 Forty Days and Nights 243
5 Noah's Obedience 246
6 Noah the Righteous 247
GRAPHIC: *Salvation in the Ark* 250
7 Entering the Ark of Deep Sleep 250
8 Potential Ideal Energies 254
9 The Noetic and Noematic Aspects 254
10 The Cataclysm after the Rest 255
GRAPHIC: *The Ark as a Fish* 256
7-II SECTION: THE FLOOD
11 The Flood Begins 257

12 Forty Days and Nights of Rain 257
13 Potential Faculties and Epistemic Forms 258
14 All Ideas in their Potential State 259
GRAPHIC: *Emergence of Ideas from NREM* 260
15 Ideas in the Mental Reservoir 260
16 The Ark Closes 261
17 The Floating Ark 281
18 Above the Chaos 262
19 All Is Flooded Below Heaven 263
GRAPHIC: *The Waters Covering Everything* 263
20 Waters Founded on Perilous Calamity 264
21 We All Die in This Flood 264
GRAPHIC: *All Types of Cemeteries and or Cremation Sites Are Proof of the Current Flood* 265
22 The Shores of Death 266
23 Only in the Ark There Is Salvation 266
24 The Deluge Causes Oppressions and Afflictions 267
HERE ENDS THE SEVENTH CHAPTER OF THE DELUGE 268
CHAPTER 8 THE CURSE REVERSED 269
GRAPHIC: *Mount Ararat, the Ark and Elohim's Memory* 269
8-I SECTION: THE DRY EARTH
1 The Breath of Remembrance 270
2 The Rain Subsides 271
3 End of Attachment 272
4 The Ark Rests 272
GRAPHIC: *1 Hexagram, 2 Turtle and 3 the Head of Adam Kadmon* 273
5 Auto-Transparent Objectivity 273
6 The Window of the Eyes 275
8-II SECTION: THE BIRDS OF THE ARK
7 The Dark Raven 277
GRAPHIC: *Various Levels of Reality* 277
8 Jonah the Dove of Truth 278
9 Certainty Returns into Dreamlessness 279
GRAPHIC: *The Spiral Way of Truth and Life* 280
GRAPHIC: *Unrested Open Bent Circularity of the Consciousness-of* 282
10 The Dove Goes Out Again 282
11 Meditation as a Dove 282
GRAPHIC: *The Raven and the Doves Coming out of the Ark* 284
12 The Dove of Non-Return 286
8-III SECTION: EXIT FROM THE ARK
13 Opening of the Ark's Roof 287
GRAPHIC: *The four ways of religions* 289
14 Bright Purity 291
15 God's Command at the Exit of the Ark 292
16 Exit the Ark 292
17 Bring all the Animals with You 293
18 Noah Exits the Ark 293
19 All the Animals Exit the Ark 294
20 Noah's Offering 294
21 The Curse Is Lifted 295

22 No Rest in the Epistemic Process ... 297
HERE ENDS THE EIGHTH CHAPTER OF THE CURSE REVERSED ...298
CHAPTER 9 THE RAINBOW, THE VINEYARD AND THE BLOOD GRAPES ... 299
GRAPHIC: *The Rainbow and the Vineyard as Web* ... 299
9-I SECTION: THE EPISTEMIC FOOD
1 God's Blessing ... 300
2 All Tamed Senses ... 305
3 The Living Existence ... 307
4 You Cannot Eat the Blood ... 307
5 Divine-Consciousness Takes Care of the Blood-Life ... 309
6 The Image of Divine-Consciousness ... 310
GRAPHIC: *The Image of Divine-Consciousness* ... 311
7 Multiply Exponentially ... 312
9-II SECTION: THE COVENANT AND THE RAINBOW
8 God Spoke ... 313
9 Divine Banquet ... 313
10 All the Epistemic Modalities Move out of the Ark ... 313
11 Covenant of Immortality ... 314
12 The Sign of the Covenant ... 315
13 The Rainbow ... 316
GRAPHIC: *The Rainbow Bridge* ... 316
14 The Bow in the Concealing Cloud ... 319
15 Remembering the Covenant ... 320
GRAPHIC: *Circumcision* ... 322
16 Perceiving the Covenant ... 322
GRAPHIC: *The Ladder of Remembrance* ... 323
17 The Token of the Covenant ... 324
GRAPHIC: *Covenant Rainbow* ... 324
9-III SECTION: NOAH'S CONSCIOUSNESS-*OF* THE WORLD
18 Noah's Descendants ... 325
GRAPHIC: *Noah and His Descendants* ... 325
19 The Three Modes-of-Knowing ... 326
20 Noah's Change ... 326
21 Noah's Drunkenness ... 327
22 Ham Perceives His Father's Nakedness ... 328
GRAPHIC: *An unconceivable center without its circumference viewed as naked* ...331
23 Shem and Japheth do not Look at their Father's Nakedness ... 331
GRAPHIC: *Mirror image of someone placed between two mirrors facing each other* ... 336
24 Noah Awakes from His Intoxication ... 337
25 Canaan Cursed ... 337
GRAPHIC: *Japheth as space, Shem as time, Ham as causality and Canaan as trafficker* ... 338
The story of Isaac, Jacob and Esau ... 339
26 Canaan Is Shem's Messenger ... 342
27 Canaan Is Japheth's Messenger ... 342
28 After the Flood ... 343
29 Noah's Redemption ... 343
HERE ENDS THE NINTH CHAPTER OF RAINBOW, VINEYARD AND BLOOD GRAPES 345
PART 5: HISTORICAL AND GEOGRAPHICAL PARADIGMS

CHAPTER 10 THE GENERATIONS OF THE SONS OF NOAH 347
GRAPHIC: *Noah's Generations* 347
10-I SECTION: SPACE PARADIGMS
1 The Generations of Noah's Sons 348
2 The Sons of Japheth 348
GRAPHIC: *Unique Forms of Continuity in Space* 348
3 The Sons of Gomer 348
4 The Sons of Javan 351
5 Geographic, Ethnic and Linguistic Distinctions for Japheth's Offspring 351
GRAPHIC: *Generations of Japheth* 352
10-II SECTION: CAUSALITY PARADIGMS
6 The Sons of Ham 353
7 The Sons of Cush and Raamah 353
8 Nimrod son of Cush 354
9 Nimrod the Hunter 354
10 Nimrod's Hunting Grounds 355
11 Nimrod in the Land of Asshur 356
12 The City of the Dead 357
13 The Sons of Mizraim 358
14 And Other Sons 358
15 The Sons of Canaan 359
16 More Sons of Canaan 359
17 The Hivite, Arkite and Sinite 360
18 Canaanite Families Spread Out 360
GRAPHIC: *Generations of Ham* 361
19 Journey Through the Mind 361
GRAPHIC: *The Border of the Canaanites* 362
20 Geographic, Ethnic and Linguistic Distinctions for Ham's Offspring 363
SUMMARY OF THE CAUSE-EFFECT GENERATIONS OF HAM 365
10-III SECTION: TIME PARADIGMS
21 Eber the Time Flow 366
22 From Eternity to the Future 366
23 Uz, Hul, Gether and Mash 367
24 Salah Generates Eber 367
25 Division in days and Years 368
26 Almodad, Sheleph, Hazarmaveth and Jerah 368
27 Hadoram, Uzal and Diklah 369
28 Obal, Abimael and Sheba 369
29 Ophir, Havilah and Jobab 370
GRAPHIC: *Generations of Shem* 370
30 History 370
31 Geographic, Ethnic and Linguistic Distinctions for Shem's Offspring 371
32 Behind and after the Flood 371
SUMMARY OF THE TIME GENERATIONS OF SHEM 373
HERE ENDS THE TENTH CHAPTER OF THE GENERATIONS OF THE SONS OF NOAH ... 374
CHAPTER 11 THE TOWER OF BABEL 375
GRAPHIC: *Death and the Tower of Babel* 375
11-I SECTION: THE BUILDING OF THE TOWER
1 One Language 376

2 The Land of the Two Rivers 376
3 Purified Bricks 377
4 The Refracting Name 378
5 God Comes Down to Oversee the Work 379
6 Nothing Restrains from Thinking 380
7 The Languages Are Confused 381
8 The Lord Scattered All the People over the Face of the Earth 382
9 The City's Name Is Babel 383
11-II SECTION: SHEM'S HISTORY
10 Generations of Shem 385
11 Shem Continued in Time 386
12 Salah the Sprout 386
13 Time's Arrow 387
14 Time Goes by 387
15 As Time Passes 388
16 Disrupted Unity 388
17 The State of Anguish 389
18 Reu the companion 389
19 Peleg and the Other 389
20 Serug, the Branching Brotherhood 390
21 Reu Conscious Wakening 390
22 Nahor the Breathing Body 391
23 Nahor the Possessor of Wealth 391
24 The Bodily Station 392
25 The Breathing One Encamps in the Body 392
GRAPHIC: *The ripple effect of each noetic faculty* 393
11-III SECTION: TERAH'S HISTORY
26 Abram, Nahor and Haran 395
27 The Generations of Terah 395
28 Haran's Redemption 396
29 Terah's Epistemic Procession 397
GRAPHIC: *The Generations of Terah* 398
30 Sarai's Bareness 399
31 From the Land of the Chaldees to the Land of Canaan 400
32 The End of Terah 401
THE GENERATION OF PELAG AFTER BABEL 401
HERE ENDS THE ELEVENTH CHAPTER OF THE TOWER OF BABEL 401
PART 6: CONCLUSIONS
CONTINUING ANNOTATIONS 403
AWARENESS, CONSCIOUSNESS, APODICTICITY, UNCONSCIOUS and SUBCONSCIOUS 405
GRAPHIC: *Jacob's ladder* 405
SUMMARIZING 414
GRAPHIC: *Nothing is beyond the thinking mind conceptualizing itself* 415
TRUTH IS so dazzling EVIDENT that we easily miss it 416
LANGUAGE'S LOGICAL ANALYSIS 417
SELECTED CONCISE PHILOSOPHICAL TERMINOLOGIES 418
ALPHABETS (Greek & Hebrew) 421
SELECTED LIST OF *GENESIS'* METAPHORS 422
ARTWORK & PHOTOS INDEX 424

ABBREVIATIONS

adj. = adjective
cf. = *conferre*, compare, see
comm. = commentator or commentary
ed. = editor or edition
En. = English
ep. = epigraph
ex. = expression
f. = feminine
fol. = following
i.e. = *id est*, namely, that is
e.g. = *exempli gratia*, for example
m. = masculine
n. = noun.
tr. = translator or translation
trlt. = transliteration
viz. = videlicet = that is to say, namely.
vol. = volume

ABBREVIATIONS OF WORKS AND AUTHORS.

B = Brāhmaṇa.
BG = Bhagavad-Gītā
MB = Mahā Bhārata
ŚB = Śatapatha Brāhmaṇa
U = Upanishad
UA = Aitareya Upanishad
UAb = Amritabindu Upanishad
UB = Bṛhadāraṇyaka Upanishad
UC = Chāndogya Upanishad
UĪśa = Īśa Upanishad
UK = Kaṭha Upanishad
UKa = Kaushītaki-Brāhmaṇa Upanishad
UKai = Kaivalya Upanishad
UKe = Kena Upanishad
UM = Māṇḍūkya Upanishad
UMaitrī = Maitrī Upanishad
UMu = Muṇḍaka Upanishad
UNr = Nṛsiṃhottaratāpanī Upanishad
UP = Praśna Upanishad
UŚ = Śvetāśvatara Upanishad
UT = Taittirīya Upanishad
UV = Vajrasūcika Upanishad
UY = Yoga Darshana Upanishad
TB = Taittirīya Brāhmaṇa
V = Veda
VA = Atharva Veda
VṚ = Ṛg Veda
VS = Sāma Veda
VY = Yajur Veda
W = Monier-Williams, Sir Monier, A Sanskrit-English Dictionary

PART 1
PREMISES

PREAMBLE

Once, during a conversation with a Greek interlocutor, to highlight a point related to the topic of war, we quoted a passage from Homer's Iliad describing the Trojan Conflict. Immediately, pointlessly out of contest, our converser proudly declared,

- *I'm an atheist! -*

We felt as if, to the description of the mushroom-shaped plume of an atomic bomb's explosion, she would have stated,

- *I don't eat mushrooms! -*

Paradoxically, publicly declaring to be a-theist (with-no-god) it is like saying, 'I, non(a)-believer-in-transcendence, believe in you, who, as an I, transcends me.' In fact, it is equivalent as stating:

- *'I am not a believer in your I transcending me as other than me. In fact, transcendence does not-(a)-exist. Nevertheless, I talk to you because I believe that you are an I other than me. -*

Indeed, we know only one I, ours, and we only believe that you are a parallel I. We never know the other I as such, because it always transcends us. In fact, we do not read your mind. Communication implies necessarily the belief in the interlocutor as transcendent. Thus, no one can declare atheism without contradictorily confirming the belief in the theist-transcendence of the other, which we label "you." There could be no statement of atheism and no oral and/or written communication, if we were to bring atheism (viz. a-transcendence) to its extreme logical consequences, namely, disbelieving you as an I. To be coherent, the atheist can only say, something as, for example,

- *I do not believe in a personal creative deity, because I am the product of the impersonal power of Nature. -*

However, that would only substitute the creative transcendent god with nature or an everlasting cosmos, which, in turn, becomes a new transcendent deity.[3] *Therefore, atheism is another form of religion*[4] *in which an '**atheist**' becomes '**theist**. In fact,*

"*The Atheist's Creed* [proclaims:] I believe that the cosmos is all that is or ever was and ever will be."[5]

METHODOLOGY

The *Hebrew Bible*, *Mikra* (מקרא) meaning *that which is read*, is also called **תַנַ"ך** $T_aN_aK_h$ an , acronym designating its three subdivision, namely

<u>תוֹרה ***T**orah*</u> *Teaching*,
<u>ביאים ***N**evi'im*</u> *Prophets*, and
<u>כְּתוּבים ***K**etuvim*</u> *Writings*.

The first of the *Five Books* (*Pentateuch*)[6] of the *Torah* is *Bərēšīṯ* (בְּרֵאשִׁית) *in the Beginning*. Its Western title comes from the Greek γένεσις, *Genesis*, meaning *Origin*.

תוֹרה, *Torah*, means *teaching*. It is the blue print of the epistemic forms. It is the map for these structures to trace their origin back to Self-Awareness. Its epistemic key does not promote inactive drowsy ignorance. On the contrary, encourages and advocates the Awakening of Aware Wisdom. It is the Wondrous Rapture of Stargazing[7] pervaded by the Eternally Present Pure Shiver.[8] Similarly, evolution itself is not only a biological process but also a psychological one. In fact, Darwin states that

> "Psychology will be securely based on the foundation already well laid by Mr. Herbert Spencer,[9] that of the necessary acquirement of each mental power and capacity by gradation. Much light will be thrown on the origin of man and his history... [The] laws [of evolution are]... Growth... Inheritance... Variability... Ratio of Increase... Struggle for Life... Natural Selection... Divergence of Character and the Extinction of less improved forms. Thus, from the war of nature, from famine and death, the most exalted object which we are capable of conceiving, namely, the production of the higher animals, directly follows. There is grandeur in this view of life with its several powers, having been originally breathed by the Creator into a few forms or into one; and that, while this planet has gone circling on according to the fixed law of gravity, from so simple a beginning endless forms most beautiful and most wonderful have been, and are being evolved."[10]

We chose to write a commentary of *Genesis*, the first of the five books of the *Torah*, because it belongs to the millenary literary heritage of Humanity and, in a way or another, shaped history.[11] *In*tuited or *Re*vealed Texts belong to the ***<u>Universal Sacred Literature</u>*** expressed from the cultural language perspective of its *In*spired Author. Traditionally, literal interpreters assigned the composition, or at least, the first parts of *Genesis*, to the Patriarch Moses.[12] Traditionally, the earliest date for its writing is between the XVI and XIV centuries B.C.[13] We relate these dates without any further analysis. The controversy regarding the year/s of its composition is neither the intent of this study nor the scope of this work. By their own nature, sacred texts want to be simple timeless blueprints for a path that intends to lead beyond thought into the realization of the Transcendent.

Our culture, our perspective, our interests and/or habits always filter whatever we see, feel, hear, smell, taste, read, write and/or think. It is very difficult, if not impossible, to break away from this pattern. In fact,

> "*this people hear ... but understand not; and see ... but perceive not... Make the heart of this people fat, and make their ears heavy, and shut their eyes; lest they see with their eyes, and hear with their ears, and understand with their heart, and convert, and be healed.*"[14]

However, all perceivers have the fundamental need to reach an absolute certainty independent from any preconceived position. That same fundamental need is what motivates ascetics, prophets and mystics to renounce this world. Therefore, Job,

> "*the greatest of all the men of the east... said, 'Naked came I out of my mother's womb, and naked shall I return thither: the LORD gave, and the LORD hath taken away; blessed be the name of the LORD... Therefore have I uttered that I understood not; things too wonderful for me, which I knew not'.*"[15]

Doubt arises only within the consciousness-*of* the object. Whereas, Pure-Awareness without any objectivity, as such, is the only Certainty we may have. When and if we realize this, then we must recognize that, if other beings have explored the Pure-Depths of their Hearts,[16] then they discovered the same Univeral True Unity that joins us with no alterity.[17] This discovery has inspired their writings.

We transcribed *Genesis* in its Hebrew version known as the ***Masoretic Text***.[18] The name derives from the Masoretes Jews who, around the VII and X centuries, copied, edited and marked the writing with vowels. We transliterated the text and literally translated it word-by-word into English.

Additionally, we paralleled that text with the Ancient Greek ***Septuagint***,[19] the III century B.C. translation of the Seventy Interpreters of the Bible. Here, this text is transliterated and literally translated word-by-word in English.

Follows, the ***Vulgate***,[20] the IV century Latin translation of the *Bible*, attributed to Jerome.[21] We literally translated also this text word-by-word in English.

We further paralleled the Hebrew text with the ***King James Version***,[22] the English translation of the *Bible* authorized by King James I of England in the early beginning of the XVII century.

Our rendering follows with subsequent commentary and endnotes. All will have this format:

§:#-Title

Masoretic Hebrew text, *transliteration* (with word-by-word literal translation)
Septuagint Greek text, *transliteration* (with word-by-word literal translation)
Vulgate Latin text (with word-by-word literal translation)
King James Version English text
Our rendering

Our commentary will follow here. We will support our comments explaining our translations of the text. We will describe vocabulary and synonyms. We will indicate etymology and derivations of those terms. We will clarify the meaning of Hebrew words and we will place them in parenthesis with this format (Hebrew *transliteration*).

Endnotes will show references, clarifications, lexicon, etc.

Occasionally, we will also add dialogs with our readers.

All cross-references are with *Genesis* itself and with the *Torah* as a whole. In addition, we will reference other *Bible* versions and, when pertinent, other texts. Finally, all endnotes contain most of the references, clarifications and lexicon. To make the text understandable for contemporary reader, besides words, with their different and multilayered meanings, our translation will explain also Gematria (numerology) values, names and metaphors. For these reasons, at times and at a first glance, our translation may seem to depart quite broadly from the Greek, Latin or English renderings. However, our intent remains focused on the precise meaning of Hebrew, Greek, Latin words and on the inherent spirit of the text itself.

At first, we had resolved not to add images in this commentary, for respect to the *Biblical* injunctions.

> "*Thou shalt not make unto thee any graven image, or any likeness of any thing that is in heaven above, or that is in the earth beneath, or that is in the water under the earth.*[23]
> *Ye shall make you no idols nor graven image* (וּפֶסֶל), *neither rear you up a standing image* (וּמַצֵּבָה), *neither shall ye set up* any *image of stone* (וְאֶבֶן מַשְׂכִּית) *in your land, to bow down unto it: for I* am *the LORD your God*."[24]

However, in our contemporary world of visual arts, photos, films, television and computers, a literal reading and enforcement of those verses would paralyze all media and information, namely, the whole society, as we know it. Nevertheless, this last verse uses three different Hebrew words for the forbidden image,

1) *pecel*,[25] the sculptured image,
2) *matstsebah*,[26] the memorial image, and
3) *maskiyth*,[27] the image of stone, *'eben*.[28]

This last one, *maskiyth*, means the *petrified imagination* or *opinion*[29] as the outcome of the objectifying epistemic process of all that is in *heaven*, on *earth* and/or in the *water*. Therefore, anything, *kōl*,[30] male or female, *zāḵār 'vō nəqēḇāh*,[31] in the *land* of this entire conceptual objective world, *'erets*,[32] becomes the forbidden ideal imagery to which we daily *bow down* in worship, forgetting that I AM LORD OF AWARENESS (יְהוָה אֱלֹהֵיכֶם *yəhvāh 'ĕlōhēyḵem*) from Which we come.

For this same reason of non-conceptualization, the early Indian sculptures of the Buddha were only represented through symbols such as an aniconic empty throne. Consequently, when the Taliban's iconoclastic destructions of the Fifth Century colossal statues of Buddha, at Bamiyan, Afghanistan, left an empty alcove, they rendered the site, contrary to their intent, more Buddhist than before.[33]

As much as we can, this commentary intends to be comprehensible for everyone. Therefore, we include a number of simple, easy and clarifying GRAPHIC illustrations, related ARTWORKS and a page on LANGUAGE'S LOGICAL ANALYSIS. Furthermore, very ancient languages, as Hebrew, expressed complex concepts with a terminology different from our contemporary vocabulary. Currently, we developed new terms to convey the same philosophical, epistemic and scientific concepts, themselves not always immediately understood by the average inexpert person. Therefore, the translation of ancient texts, like *Genesis*, requires a double interpretation, first, from Hebrew to English and, second, from the ancient outlook to the contemporary mentality. It is a great mistake to assign only contemporary tangible understandings to ancient symbols. In archaic times, as an example, the brilliant *gold menorah*[34] was not only an expensive candleholder, but actually, it was a mean *to meet* and *communicate* with the Transcendent.[35] In fact, the contemplation of that symbol may have induced a reflective intuitive moment. The *menorah* traces the relationship of each light with their intercommunicating central axis, thus, prefiguring the entire creative process.

A final note, the attempt to describe the indescribable may render some passages of this book difficult to understand. In such cases, we suggest to mark the complex sentences for future reference and continue reading. The subsequent pages may clarify their meanings, enabling to reread and understand those doubtful paragraphs.

We will add succinct synopsis at the end of each chapter, section or day

FUNDAMENTAL EPISTEMIC PREMISE

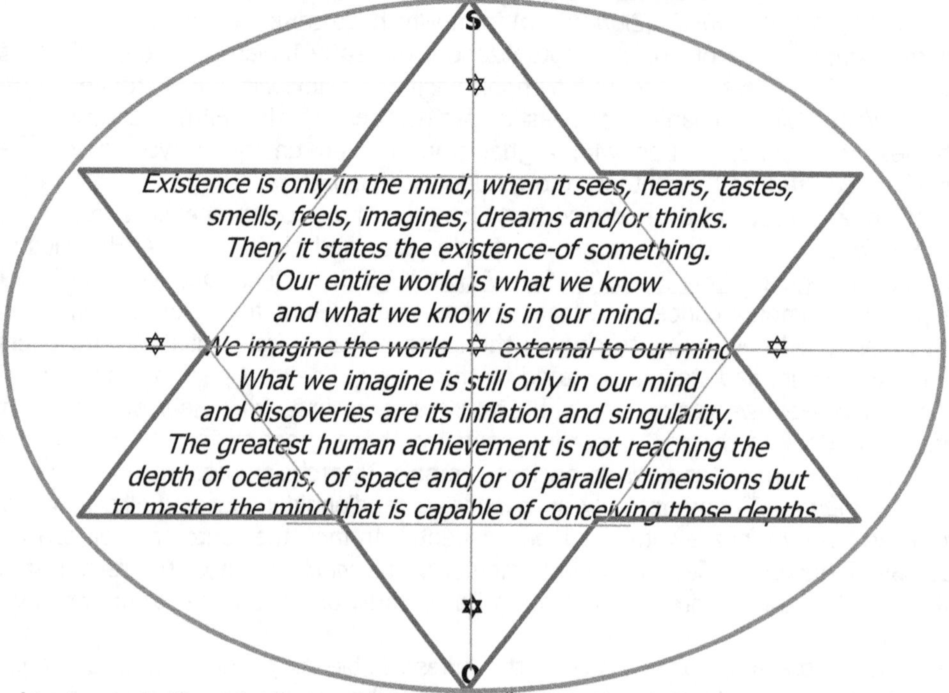

S
Existence is only in the mind, when it sees, hears, tastes,
smells, feels, imagines, dreams and/or thinks.
Then, it states the existence-of something.
Our entire world is what we know
and what we know is in our mind.
We imagine the world external to our mind
What we imagine is still only in our mind
and discoveries are its inflation and singularity.
The greatest human achievement is not reaching the
depth of oceans, of space and/or of parallel dimensions but
to master the mind that is capable of conceiving those depths.
O

Sacred texts are universal a-temporal paradigms[36] of our being here and now. Beyond any dogma, they propose a liberating path for the realization of the Unknown from which we come and to which we go.

> "*They should seek the Lord and find him, though he be not far from every one of us: For in him we live, and move, and have our being... For we are also his offspring.*"[37]

The Islamic Holy Book declares

> "*we sent down the Qur'an in Arabic so that ye may learn wisdom,*"[38]

as it is written on the original

> "tablet preserved in heaven."[39]

<u>*GENESIS* IS AN EPISTEMIC PARABLE DESCRIBING, WITH WORDS AND/OR NUMERICAL[40] TERMS, THE METAHISTORICAL *IN*-SURGE OF THE UNIVERSAL LIGHT OF CONSCIOUSNESS HAPPENING INTO THE MIND.</u>

***Genesis* is the deep introspective analytic enquiry on our modes of being and knowing**. Whether we think or discover, whether we imagine or dream or simply feel, the relationship we have with the world is through consciousness and perception. However,

> "consciousness does not come from the brain. The brain is an organ of consciousness. It focuses consciousness and pulls it in and directs it through a time and space field. But the antecedent of that is a universal consciousness of which we are all just a part."[41]

A sentient being validates the world even when does not conceptualize it. From this point of view, we extend the use of the term epistemology to include all *felt* reactions of any being in the entire universe. Experience is the foundation of any conscious and/or unconscious interaction with the world.[42] The epistemological analysis examines that relationship.

<u>EPISTEME</u> (from the Greek ἐπιστήμη *episteme*, -- *adj.* **<u>EPISTEMIC</u>**), that which is capable-of or related-to **knowledge**, **science**, **understanding**, derives from the Greek verb *epistamai* (ἐπίσταμαι) meaning **to know**. Thus, **<u>EPISTEMOLOGY</u>** (*adj.* **<u>EPISTEMOLOGICAL</u>**) is the <u>study</u> (λόγος *logos*) of **how do we know what we know and its validity**.

Here, however, we specifically use the term <u>**EPISTEMOLOGY**</u> as the study of the structure of knowledge, not of its contents, as such. Therefore, epistemology or gnoseology (study of knowledge - γνῶσις *gnōsis*) is the logical analysis of how we know. It is the form of knowledge. Finally, it investigates the validity of what we know.

Paraphrasing Thomas Aquinas, knowledge is the connection (*adaequatio*) of the objective-thing (*rei*) with (*et*) the subjective-intellect (*intellectus*).[43] However, we would never be able know what the object is independent from the mind. Universally, knowledge takes place in the presence of <u>only two</u> fundamental epistemic elements or polarities.

1) The <u>perceiver</u> is the first element. From a logical standpoint, we call it <u>**SUBJECT**</u> (**S**), *viz.* that which is *sub-jected, cast* ($_{e}$*ject*$_{ed}$) *under* (*sub*) the weight of the entire objective world.[44] The subject is the '**I**.' It is the knower, the experiencer, the thinker, the one-who-knows-and-experiences the object, *viz.* the world.

   According to Kant, the "*I-think*" is the *transcendental* subject. Different from the term transcendent, *transcendental* means

   "the manner in which objects are known, as this is possible *a-priori*."[45]

   A-priori means that we can <u>logically</u> separate the '*I*' from its object, but <u>never</u> actually divorce them. The I, then, is that which logically precedes, underlines and makes possible every act of knowledge, of consciousness and of perception. The subject is only one. It is this one reading these pages. We may think or imagine other subjects as interlocutors, but they will be known only as objects of thought, as *you*, not as knowers, the actual thinking subjects. This does not prove that there are nor are not other subjects out there. It states only that we can conjecture them but we can never know or prove them as such. In fact, when we know them they become *you*.

2) The <u>perceived</u> is the second polarity. From a logical viewpoint, we call it <u>**OBJECT**</u> (**O**),[46] *viz.* that which is *thrown* ($_{e}$*ject*$_{ed}$) *over* (*ob*$_{verse}$) the subject's shoulders. The object is the '**you**.' It is the entire world, as totality of all objects, the known-experienced-things, as lived and understood by the subject. The object is all that we think, experience, imagine, dream, feel, perceive, suffer, live, etc. In other words, they are the infinite objective possibilities that flow before our mind and flood our brain.

Nothing can exist without those two <u>inseparable-(✡)-polarities</u>, *viz.* **I**(△) as subject and **you**(▽) as object. If we remove the I-subject, the world-object would disappear. For example, without the brain the world becomes invisible and unknown. If we eliminate the '*you*' or the world-object, the I-subject would not know. Likewise, without the world the brain would see or know nothing. These two, subject/object,

"exist... only in us. What may be the nature of objects [and/or of the subject] considered as things in themselves... is quite unknown to us. We know nothing more than our own mode of perceiving them."[47]

We must clarify that the *I-think* is always the primordial-subject (*viz.* Adam). The knower is such even when it actively performs or passively suffers an action and/or when it describes an objective *you/world* as the grammatical and logical performer. As an example, if we say or write, '*the army fought the enemy*,' then, the army is the grammatical and logical subject, however it implies a fundamental primordial-subject, namely the speaker or writer who states the performer of that fighting. Consequently, the objective *you/world*, even if referred with different grammatical form/cases,[48] remains always the world-object (*viz.* Eve) as mentioned by the primordial-subject describing it. [49]⇨

In conclusion, the <u>**subject**</u> is the '*I*,' *viz.* the knower, and the <u>**object**</u> is the **known**, *viz.* the world conceived as *external* to the '*I*.' As the mythological Atlas, the subject is the one who holds on the shoulders the entire world-object and itself as object. Consequently, it is necessary for us to state precisely the meaning we give in this work to their derivate terms, like *subjective* and *objective* (including *sub/objectivity, sub/objectify, sub/objectification, sub/objectively*, and *sub/objectiveness*).[50] Popularly, the term *subjective* indicates an opinion, a statement reflecting a personal partial point of view. On the other hand, the term *objective* commonly qualifies an unbiased fact with no preconception. We define science as such. However, even an objective scientific statement needs necessarily a speaker, a scientist, namely a subject, an '*I*' who states it as an external *objectivity*. In any case, in this study, we use those terms as referring to the subject and/or the object, as we have outlined and clarified them.

We call **TRANSCENDENT** anything stated to be independent from those polarities. However, we never experience Transcendence as such. Therefore, to say that

"an objective phenomenon exists independently of human consciousness and human beliefs,"[51]

implies a *transcending belief*, a deification of the object itself. In fact, whosoever thinks, mentions or writes that something is independent *from consciousness* must still *dogmatically believe* in its independence. The phrase "*There is something out there,*" implying outside the mind, well expresses what we mean. However, it is impossible to experience anything as *truly independent* from the consciousness-*of* it. That imagined *independence* is like trying to think the unthinkable '*I*' before birth and after death without thinking of it. That in itself would have a validity but not in the field of experience or knowledge-*of* the world, as we will see. It is always and only the consciousness-*of*, which states the existence of something. The subject-object circular correlation is always the prerequisite for stating the existence of something and, subsequently, to imagine it as being external and/or independent from that circularity. In other words, when *all perceiving capabilities* end and disappear, who could know or testify the continuation of the *objective* world and write its history?

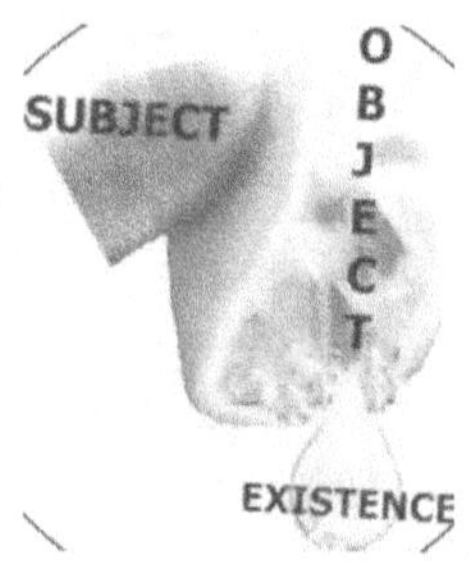

EXISTENCE, from the Latin *existere,* meaning *to out* (*ex*) *stand* (*sistere*), implies the idea of a transcendent reality conceived, but not proven, to be *ex*ternal and independent from *ex*perience itself. Therefore, it is a concept or a judgment of something expressed by and within the subject-object-inseparable✡correlation. In fact, the word "*con*cept"[52] implies the unity of the idea grasping its intended object. Subsequently, *ex*istence, *ex*tracted from that correlation, becomes a projection conceived out of that polarity. As a concept, existence is **IMMANENT**, namely, remains only within the subject-object circular correlation. Even transcendence, when expressed, as a mere thought, becomes an immanent concept. In this sense, we could say that transcendence as such does not exist. In fact, it exists only as a thought, a *noumenon,* which we can think-*of* but never know[53] as existing in-itself. However, it remains the inevitable reference of all the subject's activities. In other words, transcendence becomes the constant *transcending* projection towards a reality conceived as *ascending beyond* (*trans*) the subject-object correlation, but never known as actual Transcendence.

When we reflect on the **thinking**[54] **process**, we understand it simply as succession of ideas. However, with a deeper analysis, we realize that the integral being articulates on different levels of epistemic activities. Concisely, they are,

1) CERTAINTY, which enlightens every experience as experience,
2) the object-experienced as *physicality independent* from the experiencer,
3) the object-conceptualized as *thought internal* to the experiencer,
4) the waking-state-conscious-*of*-the-object as *external* to the ego,
5) the dreaming-state-conscious-*of*-the-idea, *internal* to the I but *dream-visualized* as *external,*
6) the dreamless-sleep-state as stillness-of-CONSCIOUSNESS without consciousness-*of*-it,
7) APODICTICITY as AWARENESS is the UNCONCEPTUALIZED-AWAKENED STATE.

Be still. Dispel your breath, without ending its flow. Stop your heart, without halting its beat. Quiet your mind, without thinking-*of* silencing it. Contemplate the object forgetting your emotional attachment to it. Identify only with the remaining Certainty. There and then, you will find Ever Present Awareness.

Ramana Maharshi states,

"After negating all of the above mentioned as 'not this', 'not this',[55] *that Awareness which alone remains — that I am."*[56]

This is what is implied by the *Biblical* injunction,

"As you desire to breathe, long after thy Transcendent Certain-True Awareness with all thine heart, and with all thy soul, and with all thy might."[57]

In this work, by AWARENESS,[58] we mean this Life as Vigilant Evident Perceiving Attention in the Stillness of Silence. By CONSCIOUSNESS,[59] we intend this Universal Light as the Way consubstantial with[60] Awareness. By CERTAINTY,[61] we connote this Ever Present Founding Blissful True Faith devoid of any objective reference. Furthermore, by consciousness-*of*, we denote the *transcending* intentional significant indication-*of* the world as object of our knowledge.

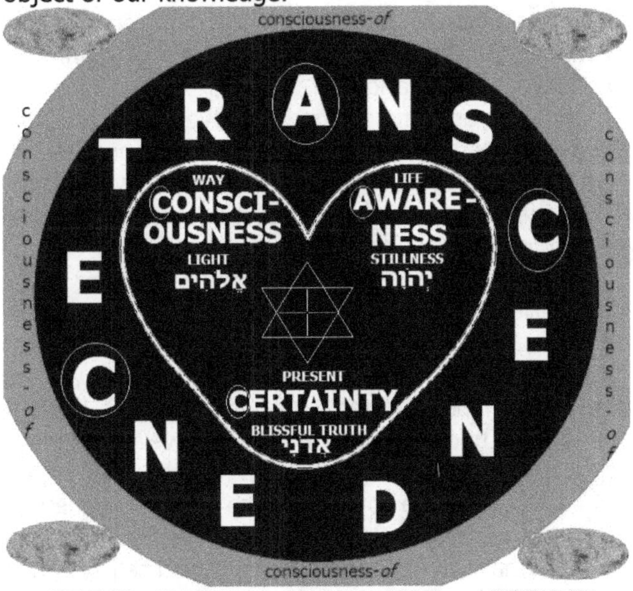

GRAPHIC: *AWARENESS, CONSCIOUSNESS and CERTAINTY*

Radical militant fundamentalists, frowning on our *Genesis'* reading, my say,

'You blaspheme by identifying the Transcendent with the individual epistemic personality.'

To put their mind at ease we reply,

*'The Transcendent is simply such, __TRANSCENDENT__. __IT__ is never individualizable or reducible to a qualified, immanent or historical object. It is spaceless, timeless, uncaused and causeless. Truthfully, nothing can be said, not even what it is not. If so, it would not be transcendent. Blasphemous and individualist is the fundamentalist who, arrogantly, believes s/he is doing the will of god by killing or fighting against perceived infidels, as if s/he were the absent hand of god. **Its** will cannot be to impose on others what **It** wants, because there cannot be anything that **It** wants, since **It** must have already always all that **It** has and wants. In fact, if it were not so __IT__ would not be __TRANSCENDENT__.'*

Inside and outside the mind are the only two fundamental elements of the world

INTRODUCTION

This commentary is NOT a confessional work. We do NOT profess any creed, NOR we intend, IN ANY WAY, to convert anyone.

We are a freethinker with no preconceived dogmas, namely, statements without demonstrations. We are spectators describing our observations. We do not impose our ideas nor we want to. We do not preach or subscribe to any religious and/or dogmatic belief. However, we are always deeply respectful of all forms of religion, belief, ideology, creed and/or opinion professed by others. Nevertheless, we do not *believe* in theism and/or a-theism. We distance ourselves from pacifists, ecologists and animalists only when they contribute to pollution and/or suffering with their taxable-incomes.[62] The real crisis today is the absence of clear values. We are apolitical.[63] We do not follow any dictatorial left, right and/or center political ideology. Furthermore, we reject blind pseudoscientific doctrinaire positivism. We regard all morals to be relative and without universal validity. On the contrary, we regard Ethic as the scientific search for the *Ius Suprēmum*, the Supreme Value. Namely, the Universal Ethic is the Will of Unattached Pure Awareness beyond any duality of good and evil. [64]

This commentary is for everyone and anyone. Believers and nonbelievers, faithful and atheists, devout and agnostic, religious and freethinkers, sceptics and everyone else are welcomed to examine this work. We are always open to their constructive logical criticism and we welcome it. We will take in serious consideration their reviews and their amendments to this commentary, which tries to explain each passage of *Genesis* on its own account. We are only an observer. We record our comments related to the oldest of the ancient *Biblical* texts.

Genesis is a three millennia old epistemic treatise. We should keep in mind that the weltanschauung, the world perspective, the philosophy and the historical context, in which *Genesis* was composed, is different from our contemporary mentality. Furthermore, we recognize that it is difficult, if not impossible, for someone, who shaped his/her entire life based on the literal interpretation of sacred texts, to accept a different way of understanding them.[65] However, the only prerequisite to read this commentary is an open critical mind not prone to preconceived bias condemnations. At times, some individuals may be reluctant to read about a topic of which they think they have already all the insights. They may have gotten them thorough old rigid clichés or may have dismissed all other interpretations as heretical. Furthermore, some may have an aversion for the topic itself because they have discharged it as a fable. They take for granted its literal reading disregarding the possibility of any other understanding of it. Fear and/or preconceptions prompt those types of attitudes.

a) Fear grips believers or creationists, when proven wrong. They may be afraid to be ostracized or damned[66] and to lose their life sustaining dogmas. This may distress them and challenge their mindset. In fact, they find comfort and life assurance from their beliefs. Therefore, they fear losing them. As an example, the *gray eminence* of the Roman Inquisition, while setting fire to Giordano Bruno's pyre in 1600, had

> "greater fear than"[67]

the *heretical* philosopher and mathematician himself, who was about to be burned alive. Bruno, the Nolan freethinker, was

> "the Academician of no academy; called the annoyed one. In sadness cheerful: in cheerfulness sad."[68]

The fear of his criminal executioners was that, by accepting Bruno's *Infinite Universe*,[69] they would have had to reject their myopic literal interpretation of the *Bible*.

Eventually, in 1633, that fear made the same Roman Inquisition condemn also Galileo Galilei to house arrest and forced him to abjure his heliocentric scientific and mathematical demonstration.[70] However, creationists, *by their own definition*, should acknowledge that, for them to exist, the Creator must always be deeper within themselves than they are to themselves. Thus, for them, Reality cannot be totally external. If so, the Maker would and could not be the creator, as we will explain.

b) Preconceptions prevent bigots, fundamentalists, atheists and ostentatious agnostics from having a critical mind. Thus, they may have pre-judged this book only by its cover and its title, without reading its content. Nevertheless, agnostics should enquire within themselves where the light of the consciousness-*of* their own agnosticism comes from.

Everyone with those qualities can stop here. They should not continue reading, since they have already publically condemned this book and its author to burn at the stake. Nonetheless, such condemnation ultimately reflects only on their fears and/or preconceptions.

Questions

This commentary addresses old controversies and questions, as

Can we reconcile faith with science? Can we resolve the dispute between creation and evolution?
Then again, what is existence? What is the meaning of the six days of creation?
Who are Adam and Eve? Was there really a Tree of Knowledge?
What was the real reason why Cain killed Abel?
Who were, Noah and the other Patriarchs? Did they really exist?
How did the penguin get to Noah's ark?
And so on.

The present writing tries to answer questions like those and others based on *Genesis*. To do so, we need a new reading and a new commentary of that text.

Names

The general theme of *Genesis* is the gradual loss of the state of grace. Following that downfall, there are numerous travails and tests to overcome in order for humans to regain the *Lost Paradise*. Throughout its narrative, the book retells the same topic repeatedly, but with different stories. To make the redeeming theme clearer for everyone, the sacred text repeats the teaching with diverse events and different *Heroes*.[71]

> "The various characters and stories in the *Bible* signify the different qualities of a person and of all people and the different stages of a person's spiritual path. The qualities and the stages are denoted by people's names, their actions, and geographical locations."[72]

It was customary, in ancient literature of different cultural backgrounds, to reinforce and elaborate concepts by using word associations, assonances and/or numerical equivalences. Many times, in those texts, personal names have archetypal meanings.[73] Just to mention a few, as we will see, *Cain* means '*possession*' and *Noah* signifies '*rest*.' The Evangelical Simon, for example, was renamed *Peter*, meaning '*solid rock*,' *petra* in Latin, on which to build Christ's Church.[74] Today's popular use of those same names refers only to the '*mythic*' personalities, not to the true archetypal meaning of the word itself. In translations, we must render those senses. We must convey the exact understanding originally intended for the ancient reader. In addition, the first textual account and use of those names meant to convey their semantic and connotative meanings. Thus, it becomes necessary to understand them, as they confer meaning and, in turn, clarify the text.

Each patriarch in the *Biblical* text becomes a real a-temporal template of epistemic functions and categories valid for every male and/or female human sharing them. Each function or form of the psyche is a patriarchal archetype. As the descending line of the prototypical patriarchs moves down in the recesses of the mind, each individual takes a new name according to its more specific and detailed function. The patriarchs are the truly internal (never external) mind-sets of this writer and/or of this reader (*if s/he is there*). For example, *Adam* is the universal male/female red land, *Abel* is the breathing function and *Seth* the sleeping one, as we will see. The individuals in the text describe the modalities of various human personalities in their diverse ways of being, knowing and behaving. Consequently, we will analyze etymologies and assonances of names and words as possible clarifications of their contextual use. For this reason and for the benefit of the readers, we will render in English all those terms and names, whose connotations and etymological derivations were readily clear to the ancient Hebrew reader. In addition, the contemporary reader can refer regularly to the original words in the transliterated texts by consulting the word-by-word translations.

Gematria values

The equivalency of word with numbers, as understood in ancient esoteric circles, will be another tool of our commentary. The number/word equivalence may cast more light on the meanings and scope of certain terms and numbers as intended originally in *Genesis*. In fact, Kabbalists[75] and ancient Gnostics[76] attributed specific meaning to numbers. They stated that

> "numbers influence the character of things that are ordered by them.... Thus, the number becomes a mediator between the Divine and the created world.... Operations with numbers... also work upon the things connected with the numbers used."[77]

Compare, as an example,

> "*The name of the beast, or the number of his name... If anyone has insight, let him calculate the number of the beast, for it is the number of a man and his number* is *666*."[78]

This is possible because all Hebrew letters, written from right to left, are, at the same time, also numbers.[79] Since

> "the Torah scroll may not be vowelized – ... we can interpret every word according to every possible reading."[80]

Each letter has a numerical value, thus, added together, each word amounts to a total. The same sum may spell more than one numerically equivalent word. As an example, the name *Adam* (אדם *'AD$_a$M*), with a value of 45 (1א*a*+4ד*d*+40ם*m*), is equivalent to the word *exact*, (מאד *M$_a$'AD*), which also corresponds to 45 (40מ*m*+1א*a*+4ד*d*). Thus, *Adam* is always this exact *selfsame* universal human being here and now. Consequently, identical numerical value may indicate different words with multiple meanings, each true in its own dimension. The ancient Hebrew Kabbalist Gematria[81] (numerology) studies the connections between those numerical *significances*. Thus, it seeks, through numbers, to reach a transcendent, deeper sense of the text, whose words express its immanence. In the course of our commentary,[82] when the text will require it or numbers are involved, we will show how this mathematical Gematria process works. Gematria will become very valuable in reference to the lifespan of the patriarchs. Then, it will clarify the meaning of their ending as paradigmatic epistemic functions.

Metaphor, Allegory, Symbol and Sense

Throughout the world, ancient minds[83] used metaphors, allegories and symbols so that everyone could understand according to their individual level and capability. Languages themselves were considered to be sacred.[84] Their written style had different levels of expression. For this reason, the Egyptians devised three different forms of writings. *E.g.* the name Ptolemy, I) was engraved in Hieroglyphics, used for official sacred texts and monuments, as , II) was inscribed in Demotic, used for popular commercial and legal purposes, as ,[85] and III) was written in Hieratic, used for priestly-writing, business and administrative purposes, as .

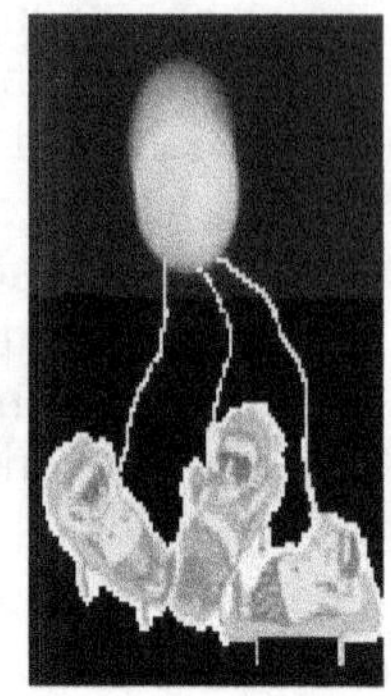

Today, we use expressions and words that try to match our inexpressible feelings. In fact, we cannot understand literally words like *honey*, when referred to a loved one, or *rival*, when indicating an opponent. Imagine a silly person insisting to [86]⇨ see the dear one's actual honeycomb and the edible sweet *honeymoon* or asking to navigate the *riv*er on which *riv*als stand competing. That gullible person will never recognize the metaphors behind the physical honey or the sense of rival beyond the river. Metaphors work when the mind extrapolates the allegorical sense rendered and connoted by the tangible physical reality of the object directly signified or denoted. The sweetness of the honey implies the sense of *delightfulness* felt towards the beloved one, but the taste buds never taste it. That *sweetness*, then, becomes an echo of the pleasurable experience of love's mystery. The animosity of contenders for *riv*er-rights becomes the sense of the opposition between enemies in all other circumstances beyond actual *rivers*. This does not mean that the words honey and river, in that contest, are meaningless. They become metaphors, senses and/or connotations of something different. As if a *dogmatic religious historical materialist*, placed before a painted likeness and constantly distracted by the design and the different choices of colors, would fail to recognize the actual physical person beyond the portrait. In addition, even historical events may be used as metaphors.[87]

Again, a metaphor does not have a physical configuration except as an object that echoes the intended ineffable concept,

"*which are unspeakable words impossible for a man to utter.*"[88]

Moreover, its idea can only suggest that which refers to it. As an example, the cipher *zero*[89] refers to *emptiness.*[90] However, no one can see or locate the void as such. A vacuum appears only in contrast or in reference with fullness as such, which, obviously, is its contrary, *viz. non-emptiness.*[91] Similarly, we can physically describe *E*, *Energy*, as a force in its driving effects, but, apart from its degrees and differences of outcomes nothing can be said of *E* as pure *Energy*. The effect alludes to the force but what that force is, as *Force*, remains unknown, in fact is named Dark Energy.[92] Similarly, the consciousness-*of* this world alludes to its awareness, but what *A*, *Awareness* is, as such, is unknown. The *Force* comparable to *Awareness*, is knowable only through and by its effects, which, we can say, become its *metaphors*. Thus, through the creatures, St. Francis sings a *Hymn of Lauds* to the Creator,[93] as the earth becomes the metaphorical *witness*[94] of Buddha's awakening.

Allegories, or parables are stories containing metaphors and symbols intended to convey meanings not immediately present. Both the words *parable* and *symbol* derive from Greek. Parable (*parabolē* παραβολή) signifies *cast*-(*bállō* βάλλω)-*alongside*-(*para* παρα) and symbol (*sumbolov* σύμβολον) means *together*-(*sŭn* σῦν)-*throw-away* (*bállō* βάλλω). An actual example of symbol is saving one half of a broken coin while *giving-away* the other half to someone else to express a

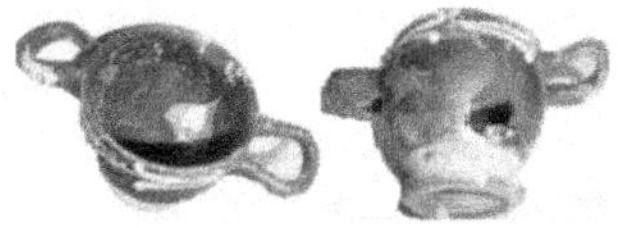

mutual bonding unity. Thus, the first half of the coin is symbol and proof of the genuineness of the other half *placed-away* elsewhere. In ancient Italic burial rituals, we find other similar examples. Then, it was customary to leave in tombs a broken vase shaped as the silhouette of a bull's face representing life.[95] The buriers kept a piece of the fragmented vessel as token-*symbol* of the connection between their living world and the transcendent realm of the dead.

Waiving patriotic flags or playing national anthems stand for ideologies that are different from the cloth composition of the banners or the musical notes of the hymns.[96] Symbols, like the sacred use of letters in Hebrew, Arabic and other languages, represent a synthesis of intended concepts called in Hebrew *sod* (סוד), the mystic-secret. They *signify*, point out an object that is present, while awakening a *meaning* that evokes qualities not immediately given by the direct original *indicated* ☞ object. A meta*phor* transports (*pherō*) beyond (*meta*)[97] its own denotation, reaching its connotation,[98] which is its sense, or its gist very different from the directly signified object.

We can read metaphors (*e.g.: honey*) both with their connotations (*i.e.: beloved one*) and/or with their denotations (*i.e.: bee product*). In either case, we have the true description of different plains of reality. The direct object never loses its physical denotation as such. Namely, in our previous examples, both honey and river remain the physical honey and river indicated. Nevertheless, at the same time, we must seek, *derash* (דרש) in Hebrew, their analogical projections towards something that the focused person may understand, while the strict empiricist may miss. Similarly, the literal account of creation may satisfy the unscientific mind, while missing the projection towards the universal quest for the Transcendent.[99] In that case, the literal accounts may translate into social behaviors unrelated to their true original connotation. Like, for example, *God's rest* on the Seventh Day of Creation obliges the religious observation of strict abstinence from physical work imposed on the Sabbath, while neglecting the implied *Stillness of* Awareness.

Someone may argue that *Genesis* expresses only that which the simple literal reading reports. Thus, we should read it, as it always has been understood (whatever that may mean), nothing more and nothing less. If that is the case, then, why bother. However, the human need for clear answers regarding fundamental existential questions remains pressing and unanswered. As an example, if the superficial conceptual and/or empirical perception of physical honey satisfies our quest for love, then, we miss the mysterious essence of its connotation. That *physical palpability* is what, metaphorically, Adam and Eve wanted to achieve by eating the forbidden fruit, which, consequently, plunged them into the time structure of the world.

"*They* [who] *read Scripture literally rather than with understanding,*"[100]

lead to contradictory and superficial views that are in contrast with the sophistication of the culture from which the text itself emerged.

"*Woe unto you, who* [literally] *interpret the law, for ye have taken away the key of knowledge: ye entered not in yourselves, and ye hindered them that were entering in.*" [101]⇨

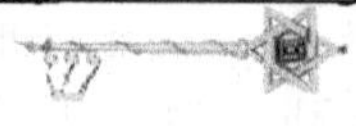

Philo of Alexandria, a first century Hellenistic Jewish Neo-platonic philosopher, recognized that the *Bible* has two meanings,

1) literal, called *simple, peshat* (פשט) in Hebrew, which satisfies the human understanding, and
2) the other *allegoric*, called *remez* (רמז) in Hebrew, which is the hinted meaning.[102]

In the Middle Ages, Dante relates that we must interpret all scriptures

"on four levels:" [103]

literal, philosophical, political and esoteric. No one level of reading will exhaust its total articulation. Adding to its complexity, the metaphoric-allegoric-symbolic interpretations rest on two different plains: cosmological, as the expression of external cosmic events (*sub specie exterioritatis*), and psychological, as the paradigm of an internal human reality (*sub specie interioritatis*).[104] Jung realized that

"no archetype can be reduced to a simple formula."[105]

Like blind men trying to describe an elephant based only on their individual vantage feeling experiences. Each may give a different partial description of it, the tail as rope, the body as rock, the leg as tree, the ear as fan, the tusk as marble, and the trunk as hose.[106] Similarly, metaphors and myths express, on each plain, the complex reality of all its faces. Just consider the wealth of insight that contemporary psychology gathered from ancient classical mythology. It was not from reading myths as factual and/or historical events that led to breakthroughs in psychology. On the contrary, it was the discovery, through them, of the inner message intrinsic to the timeless universal human mental configuration.[107] Myths, like dreams,[108] emerge from a collective unconscious,[109] the traits of which are in everyone. In fact, the ancient Indian

"*seers, searching with reflection in the heart, had found*"[110]

those inner realities. Moreover, while on his epic quest,

"*Gilgamesh said to Utnapishtim the Faraway,*[111] *'I look at you now, Utnapishtim, and your appearance is no different from mine; there is nothing strange in your feature. I thought I should find you like a hero prepared for battle, but you lie here taking your ease on your back. Tell me truly, how was it that you came to enter the company of the gods and to possess everlasting life?' Utnapishtim said to Gilgamesh, 'I will reveal to you a mystery, I will tell you a secret of the gods.'*"[112]

The literal understanding of myths and metaphors becomes valid only for those who

"*have eyes to see, and see not; they* [who] *have ears to hear, and hear not.*"[113]

Instead, to grasp the true essence of an allegory or a metaphor, one must surrender all superficial empirical reasoning. That surrender will enable the leap into a state similar to the stupor of dreamless sleep. Then, he that

"*hath ears to hear, let him hear,*"[114]

"*except ye ... become as little children, ye shall not enter into the kingdom of heaven.*"[115]

This means that the simple original stillness of Awareness is the all-encompassing intuitive state.[116]

As plants and flowers share the ground from which they grow, likewise, epistemic and psychological attributes partake of the same identical mind-*soil* from which they develop. Therefore, despite historical, geographical, cultural and semantic differences of expressions, gnoseological characters remain universal and identical in nature. In fact,

> "There is something to be learnt from Hinduism, Buddhism, Confucianism, and especially from Yoga and Zen."[117]

For this reason and to show the universal structure of the mind, we may quote other sacred texts that relate similar insights. Furthermore, we will quote ancient texts to validate the fact that modern philosophical issues were present also in ancient outlooks coeval to *Biblical* mentalities. The grip of hunger, for example, is such for everyone, every time, everywhere. It does not change, despite variances in time, latitude, longitude, language and/or species. We may express it by salivating, by pointing to the mouth, by saying *I'm hungry*, *Ho fame*, *J'ai faim*, אני רעב, أشعر بالجوع, 我餓了, πεινάω, *esurio*, *Ich habe hunger*, *Tengo hambre*, Хочу есть, मुझे भूख लगी है, etc., however it always means the same need for food.

Mythology, while using words, concomitantly tends to transcend them. It creates a new language in pictures and forms.

> "Mythology is psychology misread as cosmology, history, and biography."[118]
>
> "The wonder is that the characteristic efficacy to touch and inspire deep creative centers dwells in the smallest nursery fairy tale—as the flavor of the ocean is contained in a droplet or the whole mystery of life within the egg of a flea. For the symbols of mythology are not manufactured; they cannot be ordered, invented, or permanently suppressed. They are spontaneous productions of the psyche, and each bears within it, undamaged, the germ power of its source."[119]

We may say that it opens a door for those who have transparency of mind[120] and

> "*ears to hear.*"[121]

Our contemporary empirical merchant mentality cannot go beyond the *veil* of the strange expressions.

> "*O ye who have sound intellects / observe the doctrine that hides itself / under the veil of puzzling verses.*"[122]
>
> "RABBI SHIM'ON[123] [said,] '*Woe to the human being who says that Torah presents mere stories and ordinary words!... All the words of Torah are sublime words, sublime secrets!... The world above and the world below are perfectly balanced... Descending to this world, if...* [*the... Torah*] *did not put on the garments of this world, the world could not endure. So this story of Torah is the garment of Torah. Whosoever thinks that the garment is the real Torah and not something else... look no further. But the essence of the garment is the body; the essence of the body is the soul. So it is with Torah. She has a body... clothed in garments: the stories of this world. Fools of the world look only at that garment, the story of Torah; they know nothing more. They do not look at what is under the garment. Those who know more do not look at the garment, but rather at the body under the garment. The wise ones... look only at the soul, root of all, real Torah. In the time to come, they are destined to look at the soul of the soul of Torah... There is garment, body, soul, and soul of soul... As wine must sit in a jar, so Torah must sit in this garment. So look only at what is under the garment. All those words and all those stories are garments*'"[124]

During the Middle Ages, *Bible* teachers supported allegorical readings of sacred texts. The Egyptian Talmudic scholar Rabbi Saadia ben Yosef Gaon (882-942), in his Emunot V'Deot רסג אמונות ודיעות (*Beliefs and Opinions*),[125] argued against the literal interpretation of the *Torah*. Similarly, in favor of a metaphoric interpretation of the *Talmud* was Maimonides, the Spanish Rabbi Moshe ben Maimon (1135/8-1204).[126]

A further note is necessary to explain the reason for *Genesis'* enigmatic and cryptic expressions, which **<u>should not be taken literally</u>**. The text teaches us like in a dream, namely, the intimate solitary conversation we have with ourselves. It alerts us on some important events necessary for our life. At the insurgence of a scientific discovery of physical laws, as well as in the solution of riddles, there is a sense of enlightening wonder. Any unknotting of a mystery ushers a liberating sense of rest in a personal realization. On the other hand, like revealing in advance the ending of a mystery story, the <u>unrequested</u> final disclosure of a secret does not produce the same wondrous effect as a personal conquest. It may produce a different outcome, reducing the revealed thing to a banal meaningless cliché. This is the gist of the injunction,

"*Do not cast ye your pearls before swine, lest they trample them under their feet, and turn again and rend you.*"[127]

Metaphors are hauling vehicles. They transport the mind to an *in*tended dimension. Usually, a person envisions the world external and independent from oneself. However, its purely exteriority from the mind is unknowable. Consequently, we could say that every vision, sound, sensation, scent, flavor and thought is a metaphor. As such, they project towards the objects seen, heard, felt, smelled, tasted and thought as if they were independent from their experience. The senses, then, become bearers of fruits or gifts, but those objective donations come from the unknown land of elsewhere, namely, the unexplored land of inscrutable mysteries charted only by metaphors. The literal interpretation of metaphors, however, is their hidden danger, which may lead to institutionalized dogmatic religions, morals and political ideologies. Today's fundamentalists are those who, just by tracing their fingers over the chart of unknown regions, declare to have visited those lands. Thus, they become pompous idolatrous superficialists. In other words, they are like those fanatics that are enamored and fall in love with their own model car forgetting the only actual transporting purpose of that vehicle. The real metaphor-maker, then, is the mind itself with its five ✪ epistemic faculties, which we may also call *talents*, in the Hebrew meaning of *round circle, globe* (כִּכָּר *kikkar*)[128] *whirling and moving in a circle* (כָּרַר *karar*).[129] With them, the circularity of the mind projects itself towards the Transcendent. Therefore, the *Book of Genesis* becomes a meditative tool, an avenue leading to the realization of a recovery from the existential tragedies of this world.

Transcendent

Language, metaphors and historical references are proportionate to the times of the composition of *Genesis*. Therefore, we take in due consideration the semantic and cultural references and try to translate them in our contemporary terminology and mode of thinking. Since *Genesis* refers to the ineffable and the unthinkable *Yĕhovah* (יְהוָה), then, its language must necessarily be poetical, metaphorical and allegorical when referring to It.

"*Let no man deceive himself. If any man among you seemeth to be wise in this world, let him become a fool, that he may be wise. For the wisdom of this world is foolishness with God... The Lord knoweth the thoughts of the wise, that they are vain.*"[130]

Genesis explains in human terms that which refers to the Transcendent.

Transcendent is that which, by definition, is unexplainable, because it refers to that which goes beyond knowledge as subject/object correlation.[131] At the same time, however, is the foundation of anything we know. In fact, our knowledge refers always to an object projected towards a reality *believed* external, namely, transcendent to the epistemic act itself. However, we never know this external reality in-itself, namely, independent from our knowledge-*of* it. In fact, *Ecclesiastes* asks,

"*who knoweth the interpretation of a thing?*"[132]

We call Transcendent the Unknown *In-Itself*, the thought as such, but not mediated by our senses, by our knowledge or by our experience of it.

"*Who shall ascend into the hill of the TRANSCENDENT? or who shall stand in his holy place?*"[133]

"*There is another that beareth witness of me; and I know that the witness which he witnesseth of me is true... And the Father himself, which hath sent me, hath borne witness of me. Ye have neither heard his voice at any time, nor seen his shape. And ye have not his word abiding in you: for whom he hath sent, him ye believe not. Search the scriptures; for in them ye think ye have eternal life: and they are they which testify of me.*"[134]

"*THE UNKNOWN GOD. Whom therefore ye ignorantly worship.*"[135]

In fact, when conceived as such, it is still a concept and not the Transcendent. Then it becomes Noah's *nakedness*, as we shall see. Therefore, the Transcendent, when spoken about, it is not transcendent, but is always immanent.

Immanent, the contrary of Transcendent, is all that falls and *remains within* the correlation of the subject-knower and the object-known. Still, Transcendent refers always to something beyond thought.

<Transcendence connotes the tension of the self *in-itself*, as absolute center. The self aims beyond the circular subject-object correlation. However, only the subject-object correlation establishes that which exists, consequently, constitutes the existent in a transcendence beyond the correlation. In other words, we constantly believe that the known world persists in a reality transcending our perception of it. In truthfulness, we never experience that reality in itself. Like when we dream, we believe that the vision is independent from us, only to discover its exclusive internal truth upon awakening. We are not stating here that the world in itself is not real; we are just stating that we can never know its external reality independent from our internal insight. We are stating that we always presume that the world transcends and outlives us, but we never know that.>[136]

A reader may argue,

'If we cannot refer to the Transcendent at all, why use any metaphor to address it?'

We answer,

'Very good point, if expressed in the silence of an unrelated, non-external world. However, we always directly address someone, something and/or our self as being real beyond our thoughts of them. That someone or something can be an interlocutor, an object or our own self. In any case, we always conceive its reality as external to the concept, thus, Transcendent. That external space is unknown, except as an immanent idea-belief-feeling of exteriority.'[137]

The Transcendent

"*kingdom is not of this world,*"[138]

namely, It is not in the field of duality. Why, then, we continue to interpret the first part of *Genesis* as describing immanent historical events? Why we continue interpreting it from the realm of dualism, *viz.* the subject/object, time/space and cause/effect? The mind, like any image-maker, creates idols.

"*For as he thinketh in his heart, so is he.*"[139]

Also, sacred texts may become idols[140] for a

> "mind that had utterly hypnotized itself... on supernatural steroids... is hard to imagine a more mesmerizing object... transfixed... mind."[141]

> "If your thoughts become attached to any created thing – even something unseen or spiritual, higher than any earthly creature – it is as if you were bowing down to an idol on your hands and knees."[142]

Therefore, says the *Amritabindu Upanishad*,

> "*After studying the sacred texts, the wise one in search of realization, should get rid of them as one who seeks rice discards the husk.*"[143]

These are concepts, real only as thoughts. They assert themselves as deities and require total submission.

"The man who is not journeying towards God has made some false semblance of God his goal."[144]

The ideas of god, soul and nature are not *God, Soul* or *Nature in-themselves*, they are simply concepts. Kant calls each of them noumenon, namely, that which is thought but not known,[145] namely, not in an *a-priori synthesis* of subject and space-temporal-object. They grip our belief in three ways,

1) As dogmas, when religious and/or political indoctrination shape young minds forming uncritical dogmatic ideas;
2) As mind, when science interprets nature as an independent entity real beyond the mind studying it;
3) As philosophy, when the love for the system obscures the pure development of thought.[146]

In other words, what remains of the world when we die and there is no brain to perceive it? To exemplify further, Transcendence is like the eye not capable of seeing itself seeing, or the ear incapable to hear itself hearing. In fact,

"*neither day nor night seeth sleep with his eyes.*"[147]

Again, *what is color for a blind person?* Alternatively, *what is sound for someone who is deaf?* No one, having

"*an heart to perceive, and eyes to see, and ears to hear,*"[148]

can doubt perceiving, seeing or hearing, but no one can perceive the perceiver itself, see the seer itself or hear the hearer itself. Similarly, no one can dispute that god, soul and nature are ideas, *viz.* noumenon, which we can think but we can never know or experience as such. In fact, what are these concepts when they are not thought? They are the unknown, unexperienceable Transcendent. They do not fall in the category of existence, except as thoughts existing only as conceptualization. Namely, there cannot be any external extension of the objective things (*res extensa*) if not thought about by the perceiver's mind (*res cogitans*).[149] Thus, in all ages and in all places, the same mind needs to worship its own conceptual idols by praying, weeping and hailing in each place of cult, on all economic altars and in every political forum or sport arenas. However, the reference to the Transcendent, as such, is always present with Its Mystery shrouded in Faith.

Faith and Belief

It is necessary to explain the distinction between faith and belief.

a) **Faith** is the Undeniable-Truth. It is the **Evident**

"***Amen*** (אָמֵן *'amen*),[150] *the faithful and true witness, the beginning of Awareness' creation.*"[151]

It is the Certainty-present and evident in any experience as pure experience. It is the Faith we have in any wakefulness as wakefulness and/or in any dream as dream. It is the immediate evidence of experiencing-experience and not of its being this or that particular objective thing. It is the Apodictic-Immediate-Certitude we have here and now with all that surrounds us in life. It is the Spirit-of-Certainty (*viz. Logos-Verbum*-Word) the perfect presence of the Self-in-Itself.

"*And the Spirit of Certainty was made flesh, and dwelled among us.*"[152]

This is not *certainty-of-something*, but it is the True-Constant-Certainty Evident in the Pure-Still-Awareness. Faith is the Un-known Awareness in every consciousness-*of*-something regardless what that something is. Properly, better than Awareness, Evident-Transcendent, as we outlined it, is the term that conveys this intended sense. It is the Un-seen seer in seeing.[153] It is the Un-heard hearer in hearing. It is the Un-thinkable Thinker in thinking. It is the Non-understandable Understander in understanding.[154] That Unknown Knower is the Pure-Apodictic-Faith. Faith is synonym of Apodictical Certitude. *Faith,* in Hebrew *'emuwnah* (אמונה), in Greek *pístis* (πίστις) and in Arabic *yaqeen* (يقين), means also *certitude.*[155] Again, this *evidence* is called "*the Amen, the faithful and true witness.*" When we focus on it, that is the self-evident certitude we have, here and now, of any experience whatever it may be, without need of verification or acknowledgment.

"*Blessed are* (μακάριοι *makarioi*) *they* (οἱ *oi*) *that not* (μὴ *mē*) *have verified* (ἰδόντες *idontes*), *and* (καὶ *kai*) *yet have faith* (πιστεύσαντες *pisteusantes*)."[156]

The Hebrew *'emuwnah*, the Greek *pístis* and the Latin *fides, trust*, are terms that convey the unshakable *assurance, trust* and *certainty* inherent here and now in the foundation of Awareness. Thus,

"*If ye have certainty* (πίστις *pistis*) *as a grain of quantum-mustard seed* (σίναπι *sinapi*), *ye shall say unto this mountain, Remove hence to yonder place; and it shall remove; and nothing shall be impossible unto you.*"[157]

<In fact, the instant of *certitude* does not require thinking to be *certain*. There is no process of thought in Awareness. It is the immediate *fulguration* right here and now.>[158] in fact,

"*In the beginning was the Spirit of Certainty, and the Spirit of Certainty was with the Transcendent, and the Spirit of Certainty was the Transcendent.*"[159]

Therefore, the simple evidence of Occam's razor ensues,

"It is futile to do with more, what can be done with less."[160]

Faith is the identification with This Eternal Present here and now, which, when thought, cannot be It any longer because it becomes an idea, a belief, an object and the past, like the words in this book. An idea is like an image, a picture, a fingerprint [161]⇨ or a footprint, which, like a *true icon of the Lord* (*vera icona Domini*), conceals and hints to the Transcendent Reality without being itself That Reality. However, Faith is always the foundation of everything. Without It, we could never be certain of any experience as pure experience. It is the certainty that states the world as existing.

"*In fact, without certain-faith it is impossible to be in any acknowledgment: who comes into Awareness must be certain that It rewards them seeking it.*"[162]

Faith is the intuitive-certainty of an immediate-*eureka* moment of a mathematical-scientific discovery. It is the thoughtless-certainty the prey has of the predator, the second before it assaults it. As well as the instantaneous guarantee the slayer has before striking its victim. It is the immediate response of the samurai master to the adversary's blow. It is the adrenalin jump while facing a great danger or an intense pleasure. Faith is focusing on the Apodicticity of each event without conceiving the event itself as such.

As an example, we call ***faith*** *the certain evidence we have here and now when holding this book. If we were to say, 'You hold nothing.' You would immediately show us the book, regardless of its content. This means that your awareness is present as certainty, viz. faith, of your experience as experience not of the book as book, which follows the certain faith sustaining its experience. In fact, you may not agree or believe in the content of this book you are holding. Then, the reflected light of Awareness on the experienced object blinds us hiding the certain evidence of faith.*

b) **Belief** is an idea, a though, a concept of something, which we consider to be true in itself and to be there even when not believed. It is the contrary of faith, which we do not need to believe because it is apodictic certainty. Belief is the conceptualization-*of*-faith, which, then, becomes a dogma. It takes place when we confer to the belief the certainty we had in the moment of Awareness. However, that moment is unthinkable, but our conceptualization-*of* it reduces it to a belief. It is like fighting insomnia by thinking of sleeping. That thought will keep us awake. The consciousness-*of*-something gives the believer a sense of wellbeing. It appeases the need for security. It is a thought, an object of imagination, *viz. the forbidden fruit.* To that thought, we give a historical denotation, so that different conceptions or definitions of it will shape different belligerent ideologies and/or religions. In other words, while experiencing any event, as such, we objectify the Certain Faith we have in a mental object. Even if we believe in something proven to be objectively true, still that objectivity is destined to dissolve the moment its thought disappears. The identification of faith with belief derives from the erroneous assignment of certainty to a concept as if it were real in-itself. We do not realize that Certitude refers only to Pure-Awareness as such. The object-*of* certainty has no validity beyond the thinker, the dreamer or the believer. Awareness is the only true witness.

"*I am One that bear witness of Myself, and the Father that sent me beareth witness of me.*"[163]

Conferring independent reality to ideas or dreams in-themselves is the fabrication of dogmas and it is against Certain Faith to coerce a dogma on anyone.

As a Midas' touch,[164] <there is a drive and a need of the mind to objectify and codify the Apodictic Certitude that may have *glimpsed* in an intuitive moment, with a conceptual religious formulation or a creed or a dogma**.** This glimpse may be the product of a scientific research, a mathematical calculation, a logical analysis or simply of a real or virtual experience of any kind. On occasion, the mind, abstracting from the object, may have intuited the fundamental certitude within the experience. In every experience, the certitude of Awareness is the same. As far as Awareness goes, the correct outcome of a mathematical calculation and/or the experience of a hallucination are both the same. No one can deny witnessing an event. We may question what the perceived observation is, but we can never doubt that experience as an experience. That is certain.

The untrained mind may incorrectly superimpose an erroneous judgment on the Certitude of an experience. Therefore, it confers apodicticity and truth to the erroneous judgment. In turn, corroborated by the certainty, this error is conceptualized as a dogma in order to understand objectively that original *glimpse* of Certitude. That conceptualization, then, becomes a creed. Consequently, the mind, acting in a ***luciferous-mode***, as a mirror surface, reflects back to itself that original luminosity of Awareness. In sequence, the mind dogmatically acknowledges that reflection as having the characteristics of certitude now referred by the mind to the fabricated dogma and asserted by mere blind belief. In other words, Pure Awareness shines on a thought. The mind, centered only in the thinking process, becomes conscious-*of* the luminous thought reflecting the light of Awareness. However, it is <u>not</u> conscious-*of* Awareness because that One is obfuscated by the thought itself. The mind, mesmerized by thought, ignores Awareness that *certifies* and *sees* that idea. The idea, then, is conceived as being transcendent and self-luminous. It becomes a deified idol.[165] Therefore, it develops into a dogma.

That dogma becomes the reason for mind closures and intolerant behaviors towards any new idea that contradicts it. Atrocities, committed in the name of religious dogmas against those who do not subscribe to them, find justification in the eyes of fundamentalists.>[166]

The idea of god is a concept that, as such, cannot be the Transcendent because it is a thought, not God-in-Itself. Thus, the commandment,

> "*do not take the name* $Y_{\breve{e}}H_{o}V_{a}H$ (**יְהוָה**), *the Transcendent of 'Elohiym* (אֱלֹהִים), *Divine-Consciousness, in vain,*"[167]

becomes very understandable. In fact, the god we call "*god,*" is not the Transcendent God. When we say god, we think of the one we conceptualize, namely our idol. Therefore, silence your mind-thought and focus on your reference to the unknown reality *in-itself* without conceptualizing It.

Transcendent is the universal synonym for God. To say, *when we die, we will see and know God,* is a contradiction. This affirmation presupposes the immortality of the objectifying mind with all its epistemic modalities. The claim of Near Death Experiences (NDE)[168] remains in the immanent realm of a knower experiencing a known object. NDE is not different from the dreaming state with Rapid Eye Movement (REM), which has nothing to do with the Transcendent in-Itself. *Ecclesiastes* and *Psalm,* recognizing this impossibility, state,

> "*the dead know not anything... for there is no ... knowledge... in the grave.*"[169]
>
> "*For in death there is no remembrance of thee: in the grave who shall give thee thanks? ... Consider and hear me, o Lord my God: lighten mine eyes, lest I sleep the sleep of death.*"[170]

The Transcendent is unknown and unknowable. Any claim of the contrary is an epistemic impossibility. We can never know the Transcendent. Claiming to know It is equivalent to eating the forbidden fruit. It implies necessarily the penalty of not knowing It. This does not mean that the ultimate Truth is an occult mystery. On the contrary, nothing is occult. The practice of secret psychic empty cult rituals is another distortion of the mind. It may lead the psyche into dangerous dream-like meanders populated by dark romantic ghostly imaginations. The same can be said of drugs. They "keep you stuck in dysfunction. Their widespread use only delays... the emergence of higher consciousness... individual users... are prevented... to rise above thought and so find true liberation."[171] [172]⇨

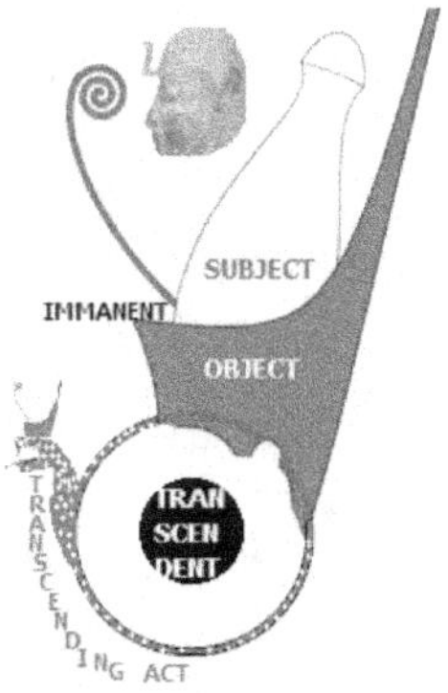

Truth is the inherent evidence shining always in the foundation of every objective occurrence. The obstacle is the seduction presented by those experiences, which distract us from the Transcendent-Central-Truth that makes them real.

The idea of transcendence and immanence are two sides of the same coin, namely, the Subject-object circularity.

1) We call *transcendence* a reality conceived and projected outside the subject-object circular correlation. We can call this mind projection *a* ***transcending act***. Thus, looking at the world *out* there, the creationist determines that a transcendent intelligence planted it there.
2) We call *immanence* a reality conceived internal to the world projected outside the subject-object circular correlation. Thus, looking at the world *out there*, the evolutionist determines that an immanent internal random blind force animates it. Then, obsolete forms, from quantum particles to the Big Bang and to the present universe with all its life, change and adapt into other ones more apt to their own environmental circumstances.

There is not a

"dual reality. On one hand, the objective reality of rivers, trees and lions; and on the other hand, the imagined reality of gods, nations and corporations."[173]

Transcending belief is the foundation of both those realities. In fact, no one knows the gods or nations objectively, *viz.* independent from our mind constructing them. Similarly, the rivers and trees cannot be thought without our mind knowing them. It would be as experiencing them without experiencing them. Created or evolved, we conceive the world *out-there* as real beyond the mind, thus, inevitably, transcendent. In any case, we consider it as *immanent-in-transcendence*. However, this conception is always internal to our epistemic circularity, which overlooks its true center or its origin. Any **S**ubject/being, insisting and living on the epistemic circumference,[174] does not realize its own center. In fact, the flooding whirlwind of the **o**bjects, before or behind the **S**ubject on that circle, distracts, seduces and makes it forget their mutual original centrality. From that center, like the seeds of a *dandelion* (*Taraxacum*) blowball, *divine radiuses* project and generate the epistemic sphere. That globe needs a deep introspection or *conversion*, a changing of the mind[175] to realize its own heart-center.[176] Here, conversion does not mean to change from one set of belief to

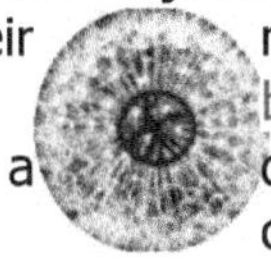

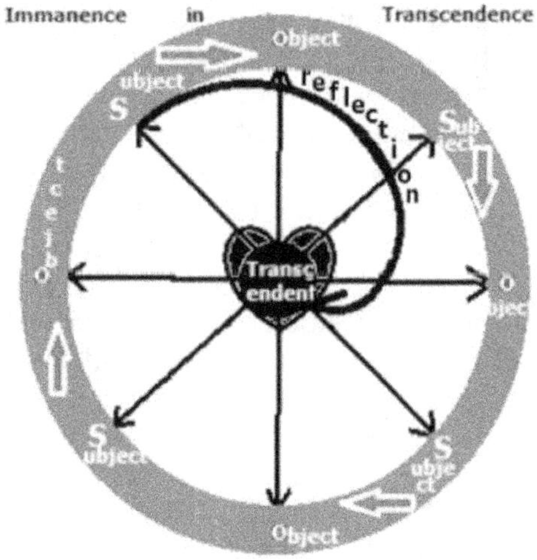

GRAPHIC: *Epistemic Circularity*

another, which may lead to wars,[177] but it is convergence, as a complete change of direction, that moves from the exteriority to the interiority of the Self. Once there, however, the flooding whirlwind subsides.

Epistemic Loneliness

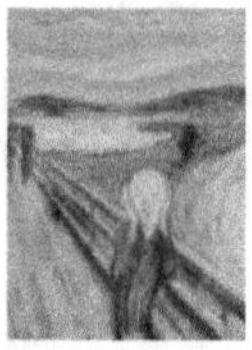

In a way, praying for a deceased one or speaking to a living person is the same thing. The difference is that, while we believe in the reality of the latter, based on physical responses, we project the departed in another dimension. Wittgenstein affirms that [178]⇨

"What the solipsist means is quite correct; only it cannot be said, but makes itself manifest. The world is my world: this is manifest in the fact that the limits of language (of that language which alone I understand) mean the limits of my world."[179]

"An individual must imagine that he is alone in the world with the Creator."[180]

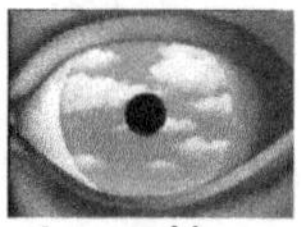

During the gnoseological act, we plunge in an epistemic solipsism, in the isolation of the 'I,' as such. We constantly project to exit this solitude. That projection is the limit of knowledge, which has its foundation in the unfathomable Transcendence. [181]⇨ The search for misplaced eyeglasses may turn out to discover that we had them always on our nose. The fundamental question that remains unanswered is, '*Who am I?* [182] Who is and/or are the *'I/Is'* we *believe* that are in-themselves *out-there* along the streets of life?' Even when we look in our self, we see, as in a mirror, only the reflection, the object of our thought that we call 'I.' In fact,

"*Man looketh on the outward appearance, but the Lord looketh on the heart.*"[183]

We can never see the seer of seeing. Namely, the *I-in-itself* is unknown to our ego. When we call someone by the first name, s/he is never the one who s/he really feels to be internally independent from us. However, what we call *'my I'* is only a conglomerate of memories held together by the string of history. Furthermore, the one who really feels internally transcends the one who declares to have internal feelings. Therefore, what we really are in-ourselves remains fundamentally unknown to us. That unknown is the Transcendent, which necessitates a transcending metaphor to describe It. The Native American

social sacred-pipe smoking is a valid example for transcending. In fact, <tobacco, very rarely employed by the early Native Americans as a recreational drug, was used as a shamanic entheogen to produce *clouds*, to connect, through the sacred pipe,[184] with the world above of the ancestors and the spirits.>[185]

If that is the case for the individual, consider how ineffable God is beyond the thought we have of god.

"*My thoughts* [are] *not your thoughts, neither* [are] *your ways my ways, saith the TRANSCENDENT LORD... so are my ways higher than your ways, and my thoughts than your thoughts.*"[186]

Transcendent is the Absolute Exteriority paradoxically coinciding with the Absolute Interiority. Even in our dream, we interact with *external* interlocutors and we *navigate* in oneiric dimensions. Only upon awakening, we realize that *exteriority* to have been only internal to the dream itself. In daily occurrences, we never experience the actual exteriority or the otherness of the '*I*' to whom we speak or write. Nevertheless, we place it in a reality that we must recognize, with careful consideration, to be unknowable, *viz.* Transcendent. The '*I,*' we speak to, becomes, inevitably, like a Japanese socializing therapeutic *Paro* robot,[187] an objective '*you.*' The great mystery is not the discovery of an alien intelligence.[188] In fact, even that alien would always necessitate the observer-observed, the subject-object correlation in order to know the world. The solution of the mystery would be the realization of *You* as *I-Self.* With critical scrutiny, we realize that the foundation and the ground of any knowledge is the Transcendent-otherness, which we can never experience as such.

In quantum physics, science investigates new directions.

"To Bohr, the observer's choice of his observing equipment had inescapable and normally unpredictable consequences for what will be found... [Thus, an] elementary quantum phenomenon"[189] becomes a phenomenon only when the <u>observer</u> registers it as a phenomenon.

"What one man calls God, another calls the laws of physics."[190]

Science preconceives the universal laws of physics as an external reality <u>independent</u> from the scientist. Its exteriority-in-itself has never been demonstrated. Belief has it that the world is *external*, *other* and *unrelated* to the knower. When we purchase a life insurance or write a book or a will, we subscribe to the *belief* in a transcendent world, which, after our death, will continue to be independent from us.

Our Latin students, Chris, Nico and Rob, argued,

'At funeral parlors, I see dead bodys, while the world still continues to go on.'

To these interlocutors we answer,

'True, but your mind is alive, still there with the dead person and the rest of the world with it. The question is, - What happens to the world when our mind is not there any longer? - No empiricist or scientist demonstrated the independent persistence of the world after his/her death. Furthermore, also all paranormal (beyond-normal) or Near Death Experiences[191] *do not prove the independence of a world in-itself because it still depends on the subjective presence of the experiencer testifying the events. However, we constantly believe in a transcending world.'*

The Subject-Object Dichotomy

Here it is necessary a very brief statement on the subject-object dichotomy. Intelligent beings conceptualize this epistemic dichotomy as *subject*, corresponding to the knower, as such, and *object*, namely, the known as such. In reality, all sentient beings, animals and/or plants included,[192] partake of that same distinction as *interiority* and *exteriority*, obviously without the necessity to logically conceptualize it.[193]

Ancient Assyrian bas-reliefs represent half-human monstrous winged Genii or Sages, named *Apkallu* (Akkadian) or *Abgal*, (Sumerian).[194] They appear holding with their left hand, the heart's side, a *container* or a *bucket* called *bandduḏû*. The *apkallu* perform a purification ritual, a sacrifice, an act of *sacred-making*[195] that putts the world into the consecrated space of existence within the subject-object correlation. The vessel is a metaphor for the mind as a "*reservoir of presences*." With the right hand, the Sages appear to grasp a cedar-cone, named the *purifier* (*mullilu*), and to zoom into something outside. With a clasping hand or with an open blessing gesture, they point out to the external world. Frequently, those Genii appear next to a plant representing the Tree of Life, namely, the whole world ruled over by the subect-king,

> "the great king, the mighty king, the king of hosts; the mighty male who tramples on the neck of his enemies."[196]

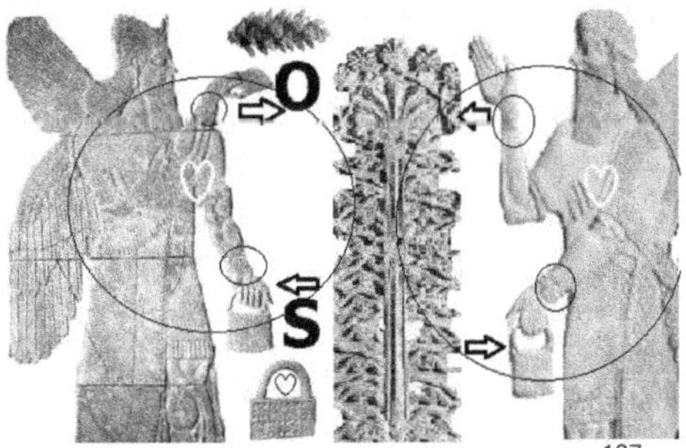

GRAPHIC: *Apkallu in Assyrian bas-reliefs.*[197]

Therefore, the *apkallu* may graphically portray the subject-object circular dichotomy. Furthermore, also the bangles, with round blossoming ornaments that they wear on both wrists, could connote that circularity. In turn, the vessel may be, metaphorically, the mental-reservoir of the *world*. Thus, the *subject's* right hand dips the *purifier* (*mullilu*) into the *bucket* (*bandduḏû*)[198] and sprinkles its content towards the objective realm projecting and establishing it into external existence.

Moreover, even if the container and the cone were  only instruments of a simple purifying-blessing ritual, like a holy water bucket with an aspergillum-sprinkler, still it would imply a subject and an object. In fact, the purifying dispenser, *i.e.* the cone, directs the content of the vessel on an *object*, which, in turn, assimilates with the fluid within the containing *subject* and reaches its purifying centrality as existence.

In other words, all beings reach out to the external world, the animal by eating their food and the plant by extracting their nutrients from the soil. Also, the *insentient* physical world exercises electromagnetic and gravitational forces on neighboring external objects. In this sense, we may loosely say that the natural interacting physical forces behave like *epistemic* structures. In fact, what is internal to a force interacts with what is external and vice versa. There is never an inside, as such, without its corresponding outside.

Historicizing God[199]

This commentary departs from the usual cosmological and historiographic understanding of Creation, which places the world in a reality *out there*, external to the reader in time and space. The problem, with this customary exegesis of sacred texts, is the literal interpretations. Following this type of reading, deluded explorers investigated and still search for the geographical location of the Garden of Eden[200] or of the relics of Noah's Ark,[201] among other things. It is like hunting for one's own shadow while searching [202]⇨ for the end-edge of the Earth. *Biblical* interpretations, commonly, place God and His Prophets in historical contests. This objectifies and codifies the text in the immanence of the past, considering the *Bible*, at the same time, a revealed book as well as a history text. To resurrect that dead past, the commentators confide in the coming of a redeeming immanent future, which is not yet done, but intends to become history. However, both past and future are thought now, but are not intended in the now, while the Present is that which is always the only living reality founded on an Intentioned Transcendence.

Historically, from East to West, most religious political authorities have fought, persecuted, opposed, and rejected gnostic interpretation of sacred texts. In fact, some, proclaiming to be religious observants, are the least prone to understand the pure call of Spiritual Silent Awareness. Furthermore, the official political-religious literal ideology, in every time, has branded as heretics and sentenced to death, for their messages, personalities like Socrates,[203] Jesus Christ,[204] Mansur al-Hallaj[205] and Giordano Bruno,[206] just to mention a few.

> "In every religion... people interpret scripture and follow particular practices according to their level of realization."[207]

Crusades[208] waged wars to exterminate entire dissident populations, like the Cathars and Albigensians (1209-1229).[209] Holy Wars fought to convert *infidels*.[210] Wars of conquest are always engaged to impose an ideology, be it for greed or fundamental blindness, they are never dictated by a truly spiritual perspective. Ancient and contemporary terrorist acts kill to impose the beliefs of their perpetrators. Like the medieval Nizari Ismailis Assassins, led by the

> "Old Man of the Mountain,"[211]

or the current *romantic* foreign legion, terrorist groups attract young minds. The interpretation of sacred texts became and becomes exclusive monopoly of political authorities camouflaged under the banner of their idolatrous conceptual worship.

> "*Not every one that saith unto me, 'Lord, Lord,' shall enter into the kingdom of heaven...* [They] *say... 'Have we not prophesied in thy name?... and ... done many wonderful works?'... Then will I profess unto them, 'I never knew you: depart from me, ye that work iniquity.'*"[212]

Starting in the IV century and with the complacency of Roman authorities, Gnostic texts were burned. Fortunately, some of them were saved, like the *Texts* found, in 1945, buried in *Nag Hammadi*,[213] Egypt. No institutionalized religious historical organized leaderships subscribed or would subscribe to an epistemic interpretation of their sacred text. That would undermine their political authority. It would reduce the validity of the texts into the confines of the readers mind. This, in fact, would destabilize the power that leaders had and have over their controlled population. Furthermore, to enforce their rulership, political and religious authorities maliciously, criminally and wickedly instill on dissident populations the fear of divine punishment and of hell.[214] However, in any case, all readings and/or interpretations of sacred texts require a new *epistemic* model to understand them.

Epistemic Interpretation

We recommend a new reading and a new interpretation of *Genesis.* We propose a gnoseological explanation. *Genesis* describes and retraces the steps of consciousness with epistemic paradigms, as they spring out in us, in our knowledge of the objective world right here and now. Let us read again from Rabbi Shim'on,

"*The world above and the world below are perfectly balanced.*"[215]

"*Whatsoever ye shall bind on earth shall be bound in heaven: and whatsoever ye shall loose on earth shall be loosed in heaven.*"[216]

Nothing is in the mind that was/is/will be not *out there* and nothing is *out there* that was/is/will be not in the mind.

"The mind is its own place, and in itself/ Can make a heav'n of hell, a hell of heav'n."[217]

Our commentary interprets the text epistemologically. Namely, *Genesis* itself describes consciousness. It details the manner in which the world happens in the mind. It describes how we know the world and the validity of this knowledge. Pure Consciousness becomes

"*the building gem stone of knowledge,*"[218]

"*the stone which the builders rejected, the same is become the head of the corner.*"[219]

This commentary interprets the act of creation in *Genesis* as a gnoseological process. If we think about it carefully, the world exists only according to the way we know it and what we know and think about it. The way we understand is different from the way other beings experience. As an example, the eyes of a hawk see the world differently from those of a human. Even among humans, there is a difference. A layperson and a scientist comprehend the world differently. In fact, the scientist searches for the Cosmos as it is without the scientist. However, this is impossible. There is no perception without the perceiver. No scientist was ever capable to self-prove the persistence of the Universe after his/her death. To understand and expand the world already conceived, new findings appear in the Present of our mind like in a progressing dream/film.[220] Any new discovery is inflation and singularity. The mind, mesmerized by the projected world, which reflects the light of Consciousness, superimposes[221] that objectivity on Awareness. Eventually, the mind, inebriated by that *fruit* of knowledge, discards and forgets the founding Transcendent Certitude.[222] We can state nothing, apart from what we consciously know, be it scientific, superficial or imaginary. These three ways may be at odds with each other, but are always only in our mind. Nothing is outside our mind that is not in our mind and nothing is in our mind that is not outside, prove the contrary if you can. Whatever you prove is still proven by you, in your mind, for the mind. The Jewish skullcap,  כ, representing God's hand,[223] the *tefillin* box,  containing Biblical verses[224] and the Muslim placing the Koran on the head,[225]  all symbolize this interiority. Worn on the head, these objects remind us of our constant mind structure. Therefore, the exhortation,

"*Thou shalt love thy Lord thy God with all thine heart, and with all thy soul, and with all thy might,*"[226]

implies that, outside that love for the Transcendent, there should be no desire left for this *seducing* world in which we live. The unknown, as such, is ultimately always an object of thought as mystery. We do not escape thought, even when we read or think of a thoughtless dimension. Therefore, the mystics renounce themselves and all emotional attachment.[227] If one wants to reach the foundation of Truth, must be still in Awareness. This is not a passive attitude, a *laissez faire,* a let it go until death parts us from this world. On the contrary, it is the active identification with Awareness and only with Awareness, which guaranties this entire world regarded as the only positive reality.

A reader may argue again,

'At this moment, in another part of the cosmos, person X may be going about its own business without necessitating our thought. In fact, that person X will persist in what it is doing regardless of our knowing it. Furthermore, is it not the repeatability of scientific experiments sufficient proof of physical laws operating independently from us?'

To that interlocutor we answer,

'True, however, person X is the imaginary object of your thought here and now. If we think and/or imagine something to be outside our thought that is still an object of our thought as being outside of it. Furthermore, there could not be physical laws without a mind recognizing them as such.'

Some literal fundamental interpreters of the text may frown on our epistemological approach and may define it fanciful, incredible and unconvincing. To them we simply answer that their naive historical and literal interpretation contradicts scientific perspectives. Moreover, it may seem that other cultural traditions converge with our commentary.[228] However, the intended universality of *Genesis* and the universal various level-degrees of epistemic structures must agree with the single unified interaction of the Universe with all its individual parts. **The Universe** itself **is the** entire multidimensional micro-macrocosmic/natural-metaphysical **articulation of Awareness**. Based on the Fundamental-Absolute-Simplicity-of-Apodictical-Awareness-In-Itself, different perspectives shed light on the very complex structure of individual perceivers.

Furthermore, readers may also argue that our epistemological approach is arbitrary. However, besides our textual, word-based and documented reading, we suggest a pragmatic proof test. If our analysis, commentary and interpretation *works*, namely, can explain all metaphors and symbols with satisfying coherent and logical explanations, without solution of continuity and without contradicting science, then it will prove to be realistically correct. We can, then, accept

"as true the simplest law that can be reconciled with our experiences,"[229]

namely, the *Astonishing-Simple-Autochthonous-Surprise* generated by the evidence of Pure-Apodictical-Awareness as such.

Revelation

Religion and science, in general, are fundamentally the same. They all postulate the belief in a reality external to the experiencer, which is never experienced as external. Revelation does not come from an external source. It is the source of the thinking process itself. Re*velation* is not a type of knowledge. It has nothing to do with knowledge. It is the *uncovering*[230] of the *veil*, which masks the Truth. It is the immediate realization, right here and now, of Reality as Apodictical-Awareness-In-Itself. Revelation is imbedded in the mind. In fact,

"*The words of the LORD are pure words:* as *silver tried in a furnace of earth, purified seven times.*"[231]

"*All Scripture is given by inspiration,*"[232]

To discover it, we must *con*vert, namely, *re*direct our *con*centration within our own consciousness with a deeply *intro*verted effort.

Nevertheless, the real question is, '*Where does thought, as such, come from?*' In *Genesis*, the whole account of Creation is the description of the process through which the world happens in the mind. It is *spiritual intro*spection,[233] or con*version*, a changing of the mind. It is the descent of consciousness in itself and through its own various levels of existence. This intimate journey manifests itself as *in*tuition.[234] This is an *in*ternal *dis*covery, which, perhaps, could account for the sense of revelation usually ascribed to it. As an example, the French mathematician and philosopher René Descartes, upon the

"*wonderful discovery* [of *existence*, in the formula] *I think therefore I am,*"[235]

perceived it as an epiphany, a revelation worthy of a thankful pilgrimage to the house of the Virgin Mary in Loreto, Italy.[236]

Oneiric studies

To be born is like a gradual awakening from nowhere. Groggy, we move in the consciousness-*of* this world. Namely, this is the three-dimensional *red land* (אֲדָמָה *'adamah*) shaped in three recurring levels, wakefulness, dream and dreamless-sleep. We travel through them as if searching for the exit back to the original state from which we came. The totality of being is all its states, namely, what we define as conscious, subconscious and unconscious. For the understanding of our translation and our epistemological commentary, it is necessary, besides the waking state, to highlight the importance of the oneiric stages. <In 1952, at the University of Chicago, Dr. Nathaniel Kleitman discovered two kinds of sleep.[237]

> "These two kinds of sleep are as different from each other as sleep is from wakefulness, [and] the essential difference between wakefulness and sleep is the loss of [wakeful] awareness,"[238]

i.e.: the state deep-unconsciousness.

> "A region of the hypothalamus... controlling sleep/wake states... mediate[s also] the sedative effects of anesthetics."[239]

The dream state is called REM, Rapid Eye Movement, so the state of sleep with no dream is called non-REM or NREM.

Let us follow the description given by Dr. William C. Dement, an American pioneer in sleep research.

> "The NREM state is often called 'quiet sleep' because of the slow regular breathing, the general absence of body movement, and the slow, regular brain activity... The body is not paralyzed ... it *can* move, but it *does not* move because the brain doesn't order it to move. The sleeper has lost contact with his environment. There is a shut-down of perception because the five senses are no longer gathering information and communicating stimuli to the brain. When gross body movements (such as rolling over) occur during NREM, the EEG[240] suggests a transient intrusion of wakefulness."[241]

Each night, there are about 4 to 6 cycles of sleep, as the EEG[242] wave pattern gradually changes from wakefulness into NREM. However, it is difficult to awaken and

> "deprive a person of stage 4."[243] In fact,

> "the intensity of the stimuli necessary to awaken the person"[244]

determines the depth of sleep. However,

> "NREM sleep is not a mental void."[245]

Further research on the oneiric or dream realm has revealed two events that more likely indicate the distinction between dream state, *i.e.*: the phasic-events, predominant in the REM stage, with

> "rapid, short-lived phenomena like twitches and the rapid eye movements,"

and deep sleep state, *i.e.*: the tonic-events, predominant in the NREM stage, with

> "slow, stable phenomena such as suppression of skeletal muscle activity"[246]

and consequent

> "breakdown of cortical effective connectivity."[247] This has led to

> "speculation and experimentation on the possibility that phasic events may be 'the building blocks of dreams.'"[248]

Researchers have found that periods of NREM with dream mentation[249] [*i.e.* recall] showed intense phasic-activity.

> "Large parts of the brain... active during waking are inactive during NREM sleep and are reactivated during REM sleep... the brain is not only a collection of passive reflex circuits, but... it actually possesses the means of regulating its own activation."[250]

Furthermore, we want to point out that every mentation takes place in the waking stage, therefore deforming, as if *translating into the language of wakefulness*, the original state in which the experience was lived by the sleeper.

> "In slow-wave NREM sleep the brain reinforces memories, while organizing them in REM sleep."[251]

Thus, in the stage of deep sleep there is unification, consolidation or reconsolidation, *i.e.:* a compact knowledge, the beginning of consciousness in which the whole world is reabsorbed. All knowledge, in fact, is contained in this stage intuitively.

"*For so he giveth his beloved sleep,*"[252]

where all contraries are unified in a solution (*coincidentia oppositorum*)[253] that establishes a state of blissful quiescence and serenity, the beginning of all possible knowledge and desires which will be actualized in the stages of dream and wakefulness.>[254] Jeremiah[255] describes these three stages as

"*a strong-fierce-lion* (אֲרִי *'ariy*)[256] *out of the sweet-thick-forest* (יַעַר *ya`ar*,[257] *i.e.* NREM) *shall slay them, and an evening-wolf* (זְאֵב *zĕ'eb*)[258] *of the dark-sterile-wilderness* (עֲרָבָה *`arabah*,[259] *i.e.* REM) *shall spoil them,* [and] *a limpid-leopard* (נָמֵר *namer*)[260] *shall watch over* (שָׁקַד *shaqad*)[261] *their cities* (עִיר *`iyr*,[262] *i.e.* wakefulness)."

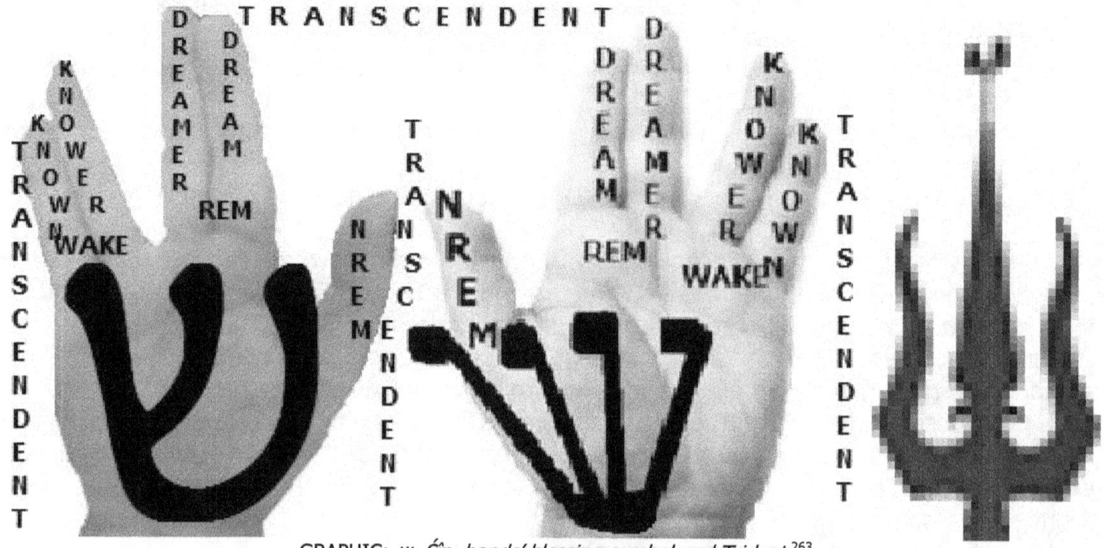

GRAPHIC: שׁ, *Śîn*, hands' blessing symbol and Trident [263]

In a way we could synthesize the three levels of waking dreaming and dreamless sleep with the three prongs of the Hebrew letter שׁ, *Śîn*. The *Śîn* hand blessing symbol seems to be more precise. In fact, the thumb may represent the singularity of the NREM state, while the index and medium finger joint together may signify the dreamer-dream duality of the REM state and the ring finger united with the pinky may indicates the knower-known duality of the waking state.[264]

The other hand symbolizes the Transcendent state, the origin and the end of the three states, represented by the Kabbalistic letter שׁ *Śîn* with four שׁ prongs . Thus,

"it is analogous to the white fire of Sinai — a sublime, hidden   Torah   that cannot be read in the usual manner."[265]

Furthermore, the *tefillin* placed on the head confirm this interpretation. In fact, **on one side of the box appears** שׁ **with three prongs, while, it has four on the other side.**

~~~~~~

A final consideration for the reader,

'If you should find this epistemological interpretation to be farfetched, compare it with the incongruity of a literal reading. Furthermore, someone, seeing all the references to different sacred texts, may accuse us of syncretic pantheism. Our defense is, THE UNIVERSAL PRINCIPLE is not only a PRINCIPLE confined to a particular portion of this Earth, but MUST BE also THE PRINCIPLE of every microscopic and/or macroscopic being PRESENT at the closest and/or farthest reaches of the entire Universe, where no Earthly language is spoken. Furthermore, wakeful exteriority, ideal-

dream interiority and bodily organic-structural unconsciousness are the three stages that constitute the integral person interwoven in Awareness. Eliminating any of these elements would seriously mutilate the individual.'

"In my Father's house are many mansions: if it were not so, I would have told you. I go to prepare a place for you."[266]

FAITH IS CERTAINTY, belief is fantasy.

PART 2

CREATION

CHAPTER 1

GOD'S EXHALING BREATH: THE DESCENDING SIX DAYS OF CREATION

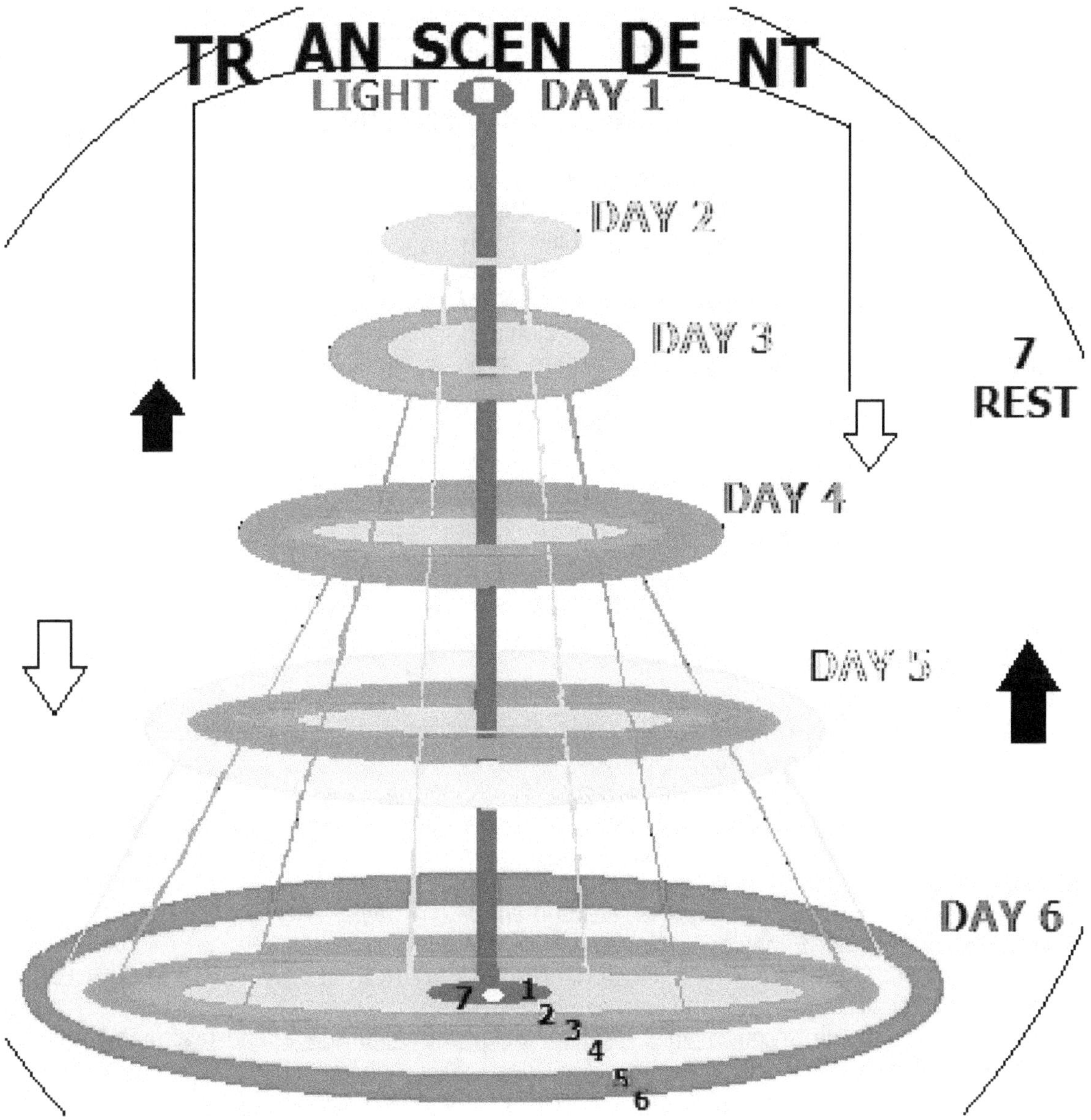

GRAPHIC: *Descending Centrality of Creation*

1-I SECTION: THE WORLD BEFORE CREATION
1:1-Creation out of Nothing

בְּרֵאשִׁית בָּרָא אֱלֹהִים אֵת הַשָּׁמַיִם וְאֵת הָאָרֶץ׃ *bare'šiyṯ* (in the beginning) *bara'* (created) *'elōhiym* (Divine-Consciousness) *ēṯ* (and) *hašāmayim* (heaven) *wa'eṯ* (together with) *ha'areṣ* (earth)
ἐν *en* (in) **ἀρχῇ** *archē* (beginning) **ἐποίησεν** *epoiēsen* (created) **ὁ** *o* (the) **θεὸς** *theos* (God) **τὸν** *ton* (the) **οὐρανὸν** *ouranon* (heaven) **καὶ** *kai* (and) **τὴν** *tēn* (the) **γῆν** *gēn* (earth)
in (in) ***principio*** (the beginning) ***creavit*** (created) ***Deus*** (God) ***caelum*** (heaven) ***et*** (and) ***terram*** (earth)
In the beginning, God created the heaven and the earth.
In the logical beginning of time, the Divine-Conscious-Awareness intentionally caused objective temporal and spatial dimensions.

The epistemic forms of <u>time</u>, <u>space</u> and <u>causality</u> take place in the logical <u>beginning of time</u> (רֵאשִׁית),[267] when the Divine-Conscious-Awareness (אֱלֹהִים)[268] <u>caused</u> (בָּרָא)[269] the objective world (אָרֶץ)[270] in <u>space</u> (שָׁמַיִם).[271]
<u>THIS IS HOW CREATION TAKES PLACE RIGHT NOW AND HERE</u>.

"From the very beginning of time... out of nothing"[272]
and *nowhere,* the **One**, *Elohim* (אֱלֹהִים), the *Divine-Consciousness,* produces the world.

"*He is Elohim-Divine-Consciousness; there is none else beside him.*"[273]

The name *Elohim* is plural of *Elowahh,*[274] *viz. God.* Elohim is The-One-Plurality, not a plural of majesty, as commonly interpreted. In fact, it is illogical for a third party, as the author of our text, to refer a powerful one with the royal-we. Only the person in authority, when speaking <u>in the first person</u>, uses the majestic plural or nosism.[275] Therefore, *Elohim,* Divine-Consciousness, means the same as the plural *Adonai* (אֲדֹנָי),[276] the *Plurality-of-the-Lord-of-Hosts.* Namely, it refers to the Supreme Transcendent together with all

"*the Judges,*"[277]

"*the Congregation of the Mighty*"[279]

278⇨

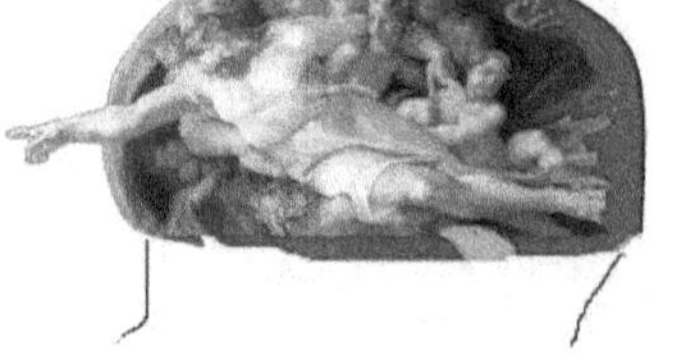

and with all the *Angelic Powers.* This implies a synthesis of Consciousness with its multiplicity of epistemic forms apt to know the universe, while retaining its singularity. It is All in all and in each one without ever losing its Plural-Singularity in-Itself, namely,

"*the Wisdom of Elohim.*"[280]

Elohim, therefore, is Divine-Conscious-Awareness, is one of the pronounceable names of God. In the *Book of Job,* God calls himself Adonai, namely

"*the Plurality of Lord that* [is] *Insightful-Wisdom.*"[281]

Then, God, together with all Its Powers, creates, produces, causes, forms and/or shapes[282] *the objective space* (אֵת' *eth*) *of heaven* (שָׁמַיִם *shamayim*) *and earth* (אֶרֶץ' *erets*) *and the Divine-Conscious-Awareness* makes the possible universe intelligible.

Many times, the proper *four-letters* (*tetra-grammaton*) *name,* **יְהוָה** [^{H}ה$_{a}$^{V}ו$_{o}$^{H}ה$_{e}$^{Y}י (Y$^{י}_{e}$H$^{ה}_{o}$V$^{ו}_{a}$H^{ה})][283] for **I AM TRANSCENDENCE**, precedes the name *Elohim*, thus,

"**יְהוָה אֱלֹהִים** *Y$_e$H$_o$V$_a$H* (I AM AWARE-EVIDENT-TRANSCENDENCE) of *El$_o$him* (CONSCIOUSNESS)."[284]

"**יְהוָה צְבָאוֹת** (*yəhvāh ṣəḇā'vōṯ*) the Lord of whole creation."[285]

Y$_e$H$_o$V$_a$H (יְהוָה), then, is the <u>Unconceivable</u>, <u>Unfathomable</u>, <u>Unpronounceable</u> and <u>Inscrutable</u> name of the <u>Ineffable One</u>. By divine injunction,

"*Thou shalt not take the name Y$_ĕ$H$_o$V$_a$H* (יְהוָה), *the Transcendent of 'Elohiym* (אֱלֹהִים), *Divine-Consciousness, in vain: for Y$_ĕ$H$_o$V$_a$H* (יְהוָה) *will not hold him guiltless that taketh his name in vain.*"[286]

In fact, when thought-*of,* it is not the one conceived, except as a transcending reference to It. **IT** is <u>Omnipresent-Eternity</u>. Actually, the *Psalm* states,

"*If I ascend up into heaven, thou <u>art there</u>: if I make my bed in hell, behold, thou <u>art there</u>.*"[287]

"Eternity isn't some later time. Eternity isn't even a long time. Eternity has nothing to do with time. Eternity is that dimension of here and now that all thinking in temporal terms cuts off."[288]

It is <u>Omniscient Omni-Aware Omnipotent *Being*</u> (הָיָה *hayah*),[289] <u>One</u>, <u>Absolute</u> and <u>Transcendent-Evident-Omni-Awareness</u>, right here and now. This is IT, *before the beginning* identical to the seventh last day of creation and beyond.

"**יְהוָה אֱלֹהֵיכֶם הוּא אֱלֹהֵי הָאֱלֹהִים וַאֲדֹנֵי הָאֲדֹנִים** *THE AWARE-TRANSCENDENT* (יְהֹוָה *yĕhovah*) *CONSCIOUSNESS* (אֱלֹהִים *'elohiym*) *is Divine-Consciousness of gods and LORD* (אֲדֹנָי *'adown*) *of lords*."[290]

Furthermore, the unutterable aspect of **יְהוָה** corresponds to the unconceivable aspect of Awareness. In fact, when we think-*of* awareness, it is not Awareness but the <u>thought</u> conscious-*of* it, which presupposes Awareness Itself. Awareness is unthinkable and unknowable in-Itself, because It precedes both the functions of thinking and knowing. We cannot describe It. It is Transcendent. Awareness is *there*, *in the beginning* (בְּרֵאשִׁית *berēšīṯ*). We cannot think of a time preceding or following Awareness, without It *Being* (הָיָה *hayah*)[291] already *here*. Try if you can.

From Transcendent Awareness proceeds the Pure-Epistemic-Structures as *Elohim-Divine-Consciousness*, namely, Pure-Consciousness, the singular totality of all the powers that puts the world into existence. By *Transcendent*, we mean the *noumenon*, namely, that which is thought but never experienced or known *in-itself*. We can think or conceive it as that which is beyond the subject-object correlation but never know it as such. In fact,

"*I appeared unto Abraham, unto Isaac, and unto Jacob, by the name of God Almighty, but by my name* יְהֹוָה (*yĕhovah*) *was I not known to them*."[292]

Therefore, the name itself cannot be pronounced[293] because, its pronunciation or the formulation of its idea transforms it into an idolatrous thought-object *immanent* in the subject/object correlation. The Singular-Plurality of Rulers, on the other hand, <u>is</u> (*hayah* היה) Pure-Consciousness, the Epistemic fundamental logical prerequisites synthesized into one. It intentions the world and without It the world would not exist. Namely, they are the Transcendent-Actuality-in-Itself, which we conceive as the *transcendental*, *viz.* the logical

"manner in which objects are known, in that is possible *a-priori*."[294]

Therefore, the fundamental gnoseological laws of the Creative Rulers are present in every being. They are present, like the act that creates the world in every one, here and now. The *Psalm* tells us,

"<u>*you are Divine-Consciousness*</u> (אלהים *'elohiym*)*; and all of you are children of the most High*,"[295]

and Jesus quotes,

"*It is written... ' <u>Ye are gods</u>.'*"[296]

Furthermore, he states,

"*behold, the kingdom of God is within you*."[297]

Thus, Awareness and its Pure-Consciousness is in you, and Paul reiterates,

"*you are the temple of God, and the Spirit of God dwelleth in you*."[298]

In fact, the world exists when known as such. The creative act is conscious <u>acknowledgement</u>. That knowledge puts the world into existence. The world exists according to the way in which we know it. The *Bṛhadāraṇyaka Upanishad* declares,

"*Indeed, he who knows this becomes a creator in this higher creation*."[299]

Outside that knowledge, we can state nothing. *Nothingness*, as such, does not exist, except as the thought of a negative term. In fact, we never experience the absence of everything, especially since that would imply also the absence of experience itself. Therefore, *Divine-Consciousness* is, at the same time, all in the totality of the world and beyond, as well as all within every individual without ever dividing itself. As an example, when we look at an object in the distance, our epistemic spatial form is all in that object without exhausting itself. However, it is also all in another object further away and so on.[300]

Existence, as such, is always *immanent*, namely, it is always built-in the circle of the inseparable *subject-object* correlation. In the epistemic process, *immanent* refers to that which persists in the relationship between the mind-*subject* and the world-*object for-itself.*

"*If I bear witness of myself, my witness is not true.*"[301]

Immanent is the relation between the 'I' and the world. However, the *way we know* is always all-in every single object of knowledge as well as it never loses its wholeness in-itself. That modality is the indispensable non-metaphysical prerequisite for everything. On the other hand, the mysterious Original-Unknown-Silence, from which a) <u>everything derives</u> and to which b) <u>everything goes</u>, is the undeniable Metaphysical-Transcendent. Even those who proclaim the void of those two states still qualify it as nothing. This claim is an unverifiable arbitrary assumption made by the mind, in the mind and for the mind. In any case, that *emptiness* is, nevertheless, still an idea generated in the field of the fullness of duality. Thus, the Mysterious-Unknowable-Transcendent, as such, is undeniable as the unsurmountable limit of life and of the world.

By its own statement, *Genesis* asserts that *Elohim*, Divine-Consciousness, creates according to the epistemic-form-dimensions of time/space/causality. However, the book is silent about what precedes that initial/vastness on which *hovers the Breath-Spirit of God.* The Silence implies that the concept of the Uncaused-Timeless-Stillness, believed to be before the origin, must be the Absolute-Transcendence. Therefore, by definition, the concept of the logical beginning of creation infers, that

1) The Unfathomable-Transcendence must be the lasting-support of all creation. In Its indivisible-totality, the Ever-Present Ineffable Foundation must be all in all and in each single aspect of creation itself. Namely, It is the Unconceivable spring from which thought itself gushes out. However, when that thought conceives it, then it becomes an idolatrous idea and not Itself any longer. Metaphorically, *Genesis* will name that spring, the waters-above, separated by those below, as we will see.
2) Creation can never be devoid of the timeless/spaceless/uncaused original formative Principle from which the creatures come. Of that unoriginated origin, we can say nothing. The *Ṛigveda* states that in the beginning

   "*there was neither being nor there was non-being.*"[302]

   Without that Ineffable Mystery, the world itself could not be. In fact, no thought establishes its own existence without again being a thought thinking of its own existence. That brings about an infinite thinking process, which still stems out from the Unknown.

Interestingly, the Hebrew term *bara'* (בָּרָא) *to create*, means also *to eat, to grow fat*, thus, *to be filled with food.*[303] This implies that the object created is also the swelling object to ingest,[304] namely, to know. Therefore, this creative inflation moves and expands. The growth takes place not only in the causal-spatial-temporal dimension, but also and above all, in the gnoseological realm, namely, in *God's-Mind*, as *epistemic food.* This expansion is as stream of consciousness-*directed-toward-something.* Therefore, Divine-Consciousness creates *heaven and earth. The One becomes two without losing Its Oneness.* Then, Creation (*bara'* בָּרָא) is Food (*bara'* בָּרָא), is the

"*Angelic Bread.*"[305]

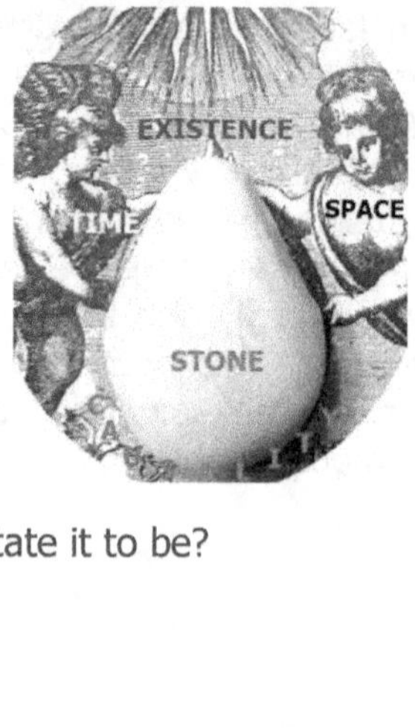

Likewise, the Angels[306] become epistemic messengers conveying the Stillness of 'Elohiym (אֱלֹהִים), the Legislative-Word (*Verbum*), the Wisdom-Logos (λόγος)[307] back to Awareness from where that Divine-Consciousness had never departed. Time, space and causality emerge as the necessary logical *a-priori* mode with which we know the world and declare it existing. Without it, no [308]⇨ knowledge would be possible. In fact, there would be only a dark formless abyss, as described in the next verse. Time, space and causality are the a-priori forms of knowledge, which, we can call messengers (ἄγγελος *aggelos*) angels that lift up the stone-object into the sun of existence. In fact, if, never in *time*, you saw in *space* a stone *caused* to roll at your feet, how would you be able to state it to be?

In general, the problem with the exegesis of *Genesis* or with the interpretation of Creation is that we tend to historicize the creative event itself. As we can never see our eye, except as an object reflected in a mirror, similarly, we can think of the Creator but we can never know it as an object. The idea of the Creator implies the creation of time. In fact, a creator subject to time would be a clear logical contradiction. If we think of the creator as ruled by time, then the real creator would be time. Therefore, time would create itself as time. Time would be creating itself at every moment in time. We can never historicize the totality of time, except in its fragmentation, which is not its entirety. However, the *origin* of its beginning moment would originate from timelessness, namely non-time, which would be a contradiction. To place creation as a historical moment or location would imply referring it to something that is not creation, but is its contrary. As a thought, creation is an act that refers to the origin from which thought itself springs into being. Therefore, that origin must be present in each historical moment and place. As a concept, creation cannot be logically placed in time, but must be creation of time, right here and right now. Augustine, describing creation and time, stated,

> "*The* [creative] *voice* [of God] *from the cloud ... spoke and moved past, began and ended. Syllables sounded and passed, the second after the first, the third after the second... and silence after the last... In the Word co-eternal with You* [God], *You at once and forever say all that you say... Everything is present... For, if there are past and future times... they are not there as future or past, but as present... 'There are three times: the present of past things, the present of present things, and the present of future things.'"*[309]

The physicist Wheeler stated,

> "We are wrong to think of the past as having a definite existence *out there*. The past only exists insofar as it is present in the records of today, and what those records are is determined by what questions we ask. There is no other history than that."[310]

Time is the present of each moment in which thought springs into life. It is impossible to conceptualize time without remembering **now** the preceding past and projecting **now** the following future. The fragmented present conceptualization of time generates history, which, however, **now** appears fleeing away. <In 1490, two years before his death, the Magnificent Lord of Florence, Lorenzo de'Medici, wrote a Carnival Ballade titled *Triumph of Bacchus and Arianna*. The recurring verses are,

> "How beautiful is youth,/ Yet, this, so swiftly flees away./ Let, whosoever wants, be joyful:/ About tomorrow there is no certainty."[311]

Lorenzo's statement is as old as life itself. One-thousand five-hundred years earlier, the Roman poet Quintus Horatius Flaccus wrote,

> "Don't ask, it is forbidden for you and me to know / what final destiny the gods have reserved... / drink wine... envious time will flee, therefore / seize the day and place little faith in tomorrow."[312]

The Bible declares that those without light encourage each other saying,

> "*Let us eat and drink; for to morrow we shall die.*"[313]>[314]

Time is always **now**. *An absolute beginning can only be logical.* There cannot be an actual beginning when there is no precedence to refer to it. There cannot be a before prior to an absolute beginning because there is no absolute beginning except NOW. When there is no preceding event, from which the new happening begins, *then*, there is only a logical beginning, which still takes place *now*. We can say that an event originates only when we refer it to an actual happening we remember as *preceding* the one from which it originates. It is like enquiring on the time preceding the Big Bang from which time and the universe originate.[315] Alternatively, it is like asking what is above an absolute summit above which there is nothing else.

Beginning (re'shiyth),[316] in the *Biblical* contest, means foundation and derives from *ro'sh,*[317] summit. In other words we may always search for physical origins beyond the latest one discovered by science. However, we may miss the act of searching itself, which is the absolute summit or the foundation of everything without any beginning. In the *Biblical* beginning, time emerges as inflation, as a logical prerequisite from the non-preceding-time before its surfacing from the timeless ocean of nowhere. In fact, there can be no time before time itself. Its beginning, therefore, is purely logical. The concept of a time considered to be before time would still be <u>in</u> time. Therefore, a pure beginning must imply timelessness. Consequently, where there is no time flow, there cannot be any beginning, as such, nor there can be any ending. What begins are objects like heaven and earth, and Earth, as such, is neither this planet nor any other one. It is this dimensional condition. Namely they are the dimensions of time, space and causality out of timeless, spaceless and unaffectedness without any historical beginning and/or end as such. In fact, the emergence of objects does not constitute an end or a beginning of Consciousness. Furthermore, for the Creator there cannot be any beginning because it would still imply a time before that beginning, which would contradict an absolute beginning. In other words, time, space and causality are only the modality with which and in which we know and rule the world, not a reality in themselves.

According to the Hebrew calendar, the world came into being 5776 years ago.[318] According to the latest scientific calculation, the universe is *about* 10 to 15 billion years old.[319] We are not suggesting that these calculations are erroneous. We are only stating that they have nothing to do with the <u>concept</u> of Creation, as such, and with its Beginning. It is *blasphemous* to historicize and place the Creator in time. In fact, it would be like asking, '*What did the creator do before creation? What is the creator doing now? What will the creator do after creation?*' The concept of Creation cannot have a before or an after. It is like establishing the beginning or the end of a circumference. Any place on it is its starting and/or its ending point. In addition, the center shapes and inflates the circle as its inherent logical projecting spring with no beginning or end. This <is the creative force, which displays itself along the entire scale of the world and in all its physical and biological bodies. Moreover, it is the energy, which becomes equal to the mass multiplied by the square of light speed ($E=mc^2$).[320] It is the force of the Big Bang, which now evolves as particle and now as wave, now as atomic structure and now as biological organism.>[321] The real beginning of a circumference or of a sphere is its center with no beginning. Actually, the center is the sphere itself, now growing into macrocosmic magnitudes, now shrinking into microcosmic dimensions, or contracting into its spaceless original central dimension.[322] The central point, like a black hole[323] at the center of a galaxy, exercises a gravitational pull on the elements projected as radiuses on its own periphery. From an epistemic perspective, the center is the reality in-itself while, on the circumference, the subject/object rotates and proceeds as relative reality for-itself.

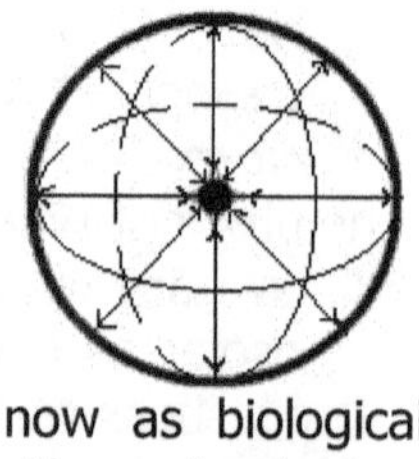

<u>The *concept* of Creation implies necessarily a *Timeless Now*</u>. Theoretically, creation is the timeless-nowhere from which Consciousness springs out right now and here. Usually, when we say '*now,*' we imply a before and an after. Inevitably, what we refer to as now comes tied with the memories of the past or the projections towards the future. However, no past can be, before its absolute '*beginning*' (ראשית *re'shiyth*) stated by *Genesis.* That beginning is this present that we encounter now, here in this consciousness. In fact, we live constantly only in this Present. Nevertheless, we know only the past.

"What's past is prologue."[324]

This is our existential condemnation. We find ourselves ignorant of our primordial origin *before* the *past.* That ignorance derives from the desire to objectify the present. In doing so, we reduce the present to a past. Thus, we condemn the present to death by projecting it now into the past, *viz. the non-present.*

The present emerges always now, as creative beginning. Paradoxically, the search for its origin, conceived as that which comes before the present itself, takes place only in the now. Nevertheless, when the mind conceives the present it immediately loses it in a past '*then.*' Every instant we conceive, as *having gone-by*, it takes us closer to death. Then, the present-instant <u>becomes</u> past, namely, that which is already dead. Try to stop the clock in your brain, if you can. Time, as we live it, is a projection toward the past-spatial dimension. True Present-Now is Eternity without any beginning or end. In fact, it is only in the present that we refer to a past or a future always experienced or thought in the now.[325] We acknowledge any time-space that we land-in as <u>this</u> time and <u>this</u> space. As a fantastic example, if we were to time-travel to attend an ancient gladiator fight in the Roman Coliseum, we would experience it as a present event not as a past one. Next year, we will acknowledge what we will be doing at that moment as this present-space, not as next year. Every time, however, we experience the present we immediately lose it by projecting it into the past, as a self-fulfilling death wish. The dead, as such, have no history. Like DNA, history itself is always the present analysis of what we conceive now to be the maker of our individuality. History, then, does not belong to the dead as such. It belongs only to the contemporary living ones who expect to die.[326] The world that we see out there is always past. It is the present one always set not less than a nanosecond to 15 billion years away in the dead past. In this sense, this universe is already a past historical one.

In this context, the idea of creation is different from the flow of time. Creation, as such, implies to put time into being, not vice versa. In the idea of God, there cannot be any distinction between past, present and future. For God, the moment of the world's creation coincides with its destructive end and this, again, with its beginning. If not so, time would be the real creator and would rule over god, making him dependent on its flow, as we are. <In a circular movement, the maximum velocity is that which covers the space of the entire circle by reaching the location of departure at the same instant in which it departed. This is the speed of auto-transparency, the time that it takes for the self to journey from the subject-for-itself to reach the self-object and return back to the subject-in-itself. Departure and arrival coincide in time and space. This a-temporal motionless-mobility, which in no time or space moves without moving, constitutes the center itself of the immobile circle and the unique smallest indivisible unit of time, even if the self perceives this process in *all* its *instants*. The journey is a reflex on the circumference of recurrent a-temporality. Thus, as rhythmic waves, the absolute central immobility reflects on its perimeter, in a linear relation that, from its center, radiates on all the infinite points of its circumference. Like a lotus flower, opening to an internal zero light source, this geometrical circle becomes the inexhaustible infinite explosive projection, never moving out of its dimensionless center point, reflecting itself as infinite radiuses on each of the infinite dimensionless points of the circumference or of the sphere. There, each point circularly chases the one before itself. Following the Big Bang singularity, time and space expanded billions of years ago. From its time-space-less origin, an infinitesimally small nucleus inflated in time and space to the current size of the Universe. Therefore, asking what took *place before* or what will take *place after* the Big Bang is a logical contradiction because *place* and *time* evolve only within it. From a quantum micro-perspective, for an observer *outside* or *external* to the Big Bang, if we can imagine such stationary-space-timelessness, no Big Bang or time-space-expansion ever takes place. S/he would see the uniform glow of its original static unity, which is exactly the uniform glow we see from within, when we gaze at the confines of the Universe, in fact,>[327]

"the origin of the universe was a quantum event."[328]

Therefore, the past affects the time ahead, as the future influences the past. When we consider the past gone and dead, then we accept it as ineluctable and unchangeable. However, if we recognize the present as the only persisting reality, then its infinite possible articulations become Reality. Nevertheless, when, we focus on only one of those articulations, then that one becomes the given past. The past, as such, is an intense reflection of the Present and that reflection obscures its source. The reason, why we cannot change the past, is that its blinding reflection of the Present mesmerizes us. It is alleged that

"According to the science of biology, people were not 'created'. They have evolved."[329]

However, **evolution does not disprove creation** and, vice versa, **creation does not disprove evolution**. They are two completely separate things. In fact, **evolution has to do with time**, while, as we saw, **creation has to do with Timeless Present. Creation is the gnoseological presence of consciousness empirically emerging now with all its psychophysical memory and history**. Evolution is the historical process[330] of the universe expanding towards the unreachable original glow at its border. Keep in mind, however, that that glow is the light of its original past singularity, namely, its Big Bang. In a way, we could say that the Whole Cosmos chases its own beginning and end.

From a historical perspective, creation and the Big Bang are both metaphysical concepts referring to the beginning of a historicized transcendent, called God by religious believers and Nature by evolutionist scientists. An absolute beginning of time is as mysterious for evolutionist scientists[331] as it is for religious creationists.

GRAPHIC: *Big Bang*

Even when certain historical-creationists accept the perspective of evolution, a new controversy emerges. Some historical-creationists accept the view of evolution as planned by a Divine Intelligent Design. This is in opposition with the evolutionists' view of Random Natural Selection. Both diatribes stem from the historical perception of events placed in time. According to the view of the Intelligent Design,[332] God, before creation, planned in time that which would evolve in the future. On the contrary, the evolutionists propose a Casual Natural Random Selection, which does not need a preplanned blueprint because all events take place randomly in the Cosmos. Therefore, the evolutionists sustain that

> "humans are the outcome of blind evolutionary processes that operate without goal or purpose."[333]

Both views need the process of time. Both perceptions recognize 1) a direction towards a particular goal or 2) a process of events driven by blind forces. The difference is that,

a) one side states that there is a Superior Being, namely, the Intelligent Designer, who wills that direction, and
b) the other side affirms that it is a Casual Randomness that runs the blind forces of Natural Selection.

What the proponents of Intelligent Design and/or Randomness fail to recognize is that only the **Intelligibility** of *randomness* and/or of *design*, as such, puts both perspectives into existence. Without that *intelligibility*, in fact, none of the two could be stated as existent nor Darwin could have written his groundbreaking book.[334] Try to think, if you can, of an intelligent design or a casual randomness without knowing the meaning of those words and without thinking of them at all. Therefore, the same axiom plagues both views. Namely, design and/or random laws are believed to be absolute in-themselves, thus, to exist as metaphysical reality independent from the subject/object correlation of the researcher as such. Furthermore, evolution means to roll*out.*[335] This implies the necessary transcending projection of *what* or *who rolls-out* of where and caused by *which* internal *force*. In other words, the random and/or designed evolution of the world or nature in-itself always transcends the mind which conceives them. Therefore, creation and/or evolution, either as design and/or as randomness, stand on the same metaphysical ground.

1:2-The Original Waters

וְהָאָ֗רֶץ הָיְתָ֥ה תֹ֙הוּ֙ וָבֹ֔הוּ וְחֹ֖שֶׁךְ עַל־פְּנֵ֣י תְה֑וֹם וְר֣וּחַ אֱלֹהִ֔ים מְרַחֶ֖פֶת עַל־פְּנֵ֥י הַמָּֽיִם׃ *vahā'āreṣ* (the earth) *hāyaṯāh* (was) *ṯōhu* (formless) *vāḇōhu* (void) *vaḥōšeḵa* (darkness) *'al* (upon) *panēy* (face) *ṯahvōm* (depth) *varuaḥ* (breath) *'ĕlōhiym* (of Divine-Consciousness) *maraḥep̄et* (floated) *'al* (upon) *panēy* (face) *hamāyim* (waters)
ἡ *ē* (the) **δὲ** *de* (furthermore) **γῆ** *gē* (earth) **ἦν** *ēn* (was) **ἀόρατος** *aoratos* (invisible) **καὶ** *kai* (and) **ἀκατασκεύαστος** *akataskeuastos* (void) **καὶ** *kai* (and) **σκότος** *skotos* (darkness) **ἐπάνω** *epanō* (over) **τῆς** *tēs* (the) **ἀβύσσου** *abussou* (abyss) **καὶ** *kai* (and) **πνεῦμα** *pneuma* (breath) **θεοῦ** *theou* (of God) **ἐπεφέρετο** *epefereto* (romed) **ἐπάνω** *epanō* (over) **τοῦ ὕδατος** *tou* (the) *udatos* (waters)
terra (the earth) ***autem*** (also) ***erat*** (was) ***inanis*** (void) ***et*** (and) ***vacua*** (empty) ***et*** (and) ***tenebrae*** (darkness) ***super*** (over) ***faciem*** (the face) ***abyssi*** (of the abyss) ***et*** (and) ***spiritus*** (the spirit) ***Dei*** (of God) ***ferebatur*** (moved) ***super*** (over) ***aquas*** (the waters)
And the earth was without form, and void; and darkness *was* upon the face of the deep.

And the Spirit of God moved upon the face of the waters.
The empty and spaceless forms of potential objectivity were void. All was unknown in that dark ocean of stillness. The Circular Breath of Divine-Consciousness hovered on the surface of those flowing waters.

What and how was the universe when, beyond *the subject/object correlation,* no intelligence was there to acknowledge it? This verse clearly states that, in the absence of perceiving epistemic dimensions, earth and heaven are void. *Then,* it was only empty and spaceless forms[336] in an ocean of dark ignorance.[337] *Then,* all was unknown. Only Conscious Breath puts the world into existence.

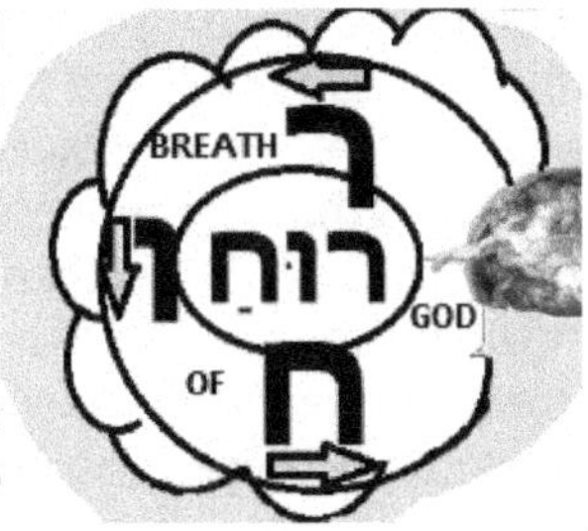

The physicist J. A. Wheeler said,

"We're all hypnotized into thinking there's something out there."[338]

He viewed the Universe, starting from the Big Bang, as

"a *self-excided circuit...* [which] gives rise to life and observers... [giving] a tangible *reality* to events that occurred long before there was any life."[339]

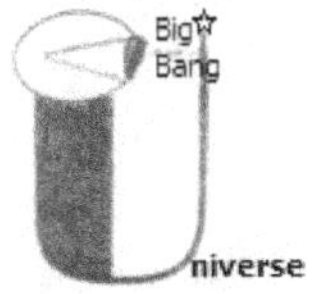

From a psychological viewpoint, Jung states that

"you looked upon it [the world] with the eye that transforms, the eye that contains the germ of what is new."[340]

Therefore, information *makes* the world. Consciousness shapes the present as well as the past. Only the Breath[341] of Divine-Consciousness moves on the surface of the timeless/spaceless ocean of waters.[342] What is that Breath and what are those waters?

Here, water cannot be the physical H_2O element, because it is not yet mentioned as created. Besides, is it the water on Earth, on Mars, on Moon Europa, comets and/or elsewhere?[343] Therefore, the waters must be a metaphor for something fluid and extensive in a dimensionless vacuity. Waters are the fluidity of Consciousness, the infinite possibilities of all the infinite Universes. Many sacred texts of different cultures give a similar description. Among them, the Indian *Ṛigveda* describes,

"*Then, there was no atmosphere, nor sky beyond it. What concealed them, where, in whose shelter? Why were the Celestial Waters of inscrutable depth? Then, there was neither death nor immortality. Nor there was knowledge of night or day. By self-power that One was breathing windless Thus, indeed no other seed was beyond it, none whatsoever... The gods, the resplendent beings of the senses came after the projection of this world.*"[344]

Similarly, Breath is a metaphor for Absolute Transcendence. To understand this Breath (רוּחַ *ruwach*), we must refer to $Y_{\breve{e}}h_o v_a h$ יְהֹוָה, the highest name of the Transcendent. That name derives from *$h_a y_a h$* (הָיָה), *to be,* further comparable to *$h_a v_a$'*הָוָה, meaning *to breathe*[345] and to אָוָה, *'$av_a h$, to hunger.*[346] Thus, the Breath of Divine-Consciousness is a metaphor for Transcendence itself and Transcendence is the Spirit or the Breath[347] that hovers[348] over (עַל *`al*) the surface (פנים *paniym*) of that ocean of waters. Thus, It is logically *before* Its descending procession through the creative progression.

Let us explain this metaphor. Breathing requires a circular flow composed of three stages,

1) Exhaling, is the internal air projected outside the lungs,
2) Inhaling, is the external air absorbed inside the lungs,[349] and
3) Apnea, is the rested air between the two previous directions.

After that, the process restarts its cycle. Breathing, therefore, like hungering, becomes a metaphor for the circular process of the mind when knowledge takes place. Thus,

1) The mind projects the object into the external world to know or to *eat* it,
2) The mind absorbs or ingests the external object into itself for the world to be known, and
3) The mind rests conscious-*of* the world assimilating it.

Then, the sequence resumes its succession. Furthermore, this circularity is present also in the three states of life, *viz.* wakefulness, REM and NREM,

1) in the waking state, the world appears outside,

2) in the REM dream state, the world is <u>inside</u>, and
3) the world <u>rests</u> in the NREM dreamless-sleep state.

In the same manner, those phases start the cycle all over again.

Hence, the Breath of Divine-Consciousness equates the circularity of the Day of Creation, as we will explain. It is

"*the spirit of wisdom,*"[350]

of the Intentional Intellect Itself. Every act of knowledge projects always toward the Unknown Knower who ratifies knowledge itself. Transcendence hovers (רחף *rachaph*) over the ocean of objectivity. Namely, we always refer the object of knowledge to a reality transcendent in itself. Nothing is outside that Transcendent Breath and even that *nothing* is in the Breath itself. That Breath is Transcendent Awareness. Divine-Consciousness is Pure-Consciousness moving over the face of the abyss of the unknown waters. That depth is like a stream of many waters. It is like a fountain from which all objectivities spring out. Eventually, those possibilities will surface as abundant-reflections[351] of the sun of Awareness that is this <u>Present</u> Omniscient, Omni-Aware, Omnipotent and Omnipresent Eternity. In turn, those waters reflect It. Divine-Consciousness will create and bring those objective reflections out of the ocean of darkness into the light of consciousness. Time, space and causality are the undefined forms of the waters logically *preceding* creation. The objective world, out of *nothingness* and *nowhere*, explodes illuminated, enlightened by Consciousness, and organized by those forms. Metaphorically, Awareness is like energy powering a computer, whereas, the mind is like a computer formatted by a software. That energy is the indispensable power without which any computer or software could ever work. From where does light come in the mind? Whosoever discovers the source of that light must realize that discover-itself is again an enlightenment of the mind. That light is the light of Consciousness, which places the world into existence.

"*The light of consciousness... is the self-luminous existence-consciousness which reveals to the seer the world of names and forms both inside and outside. The existence of this existence-consciousness can be inferred by the objects illuminated by it. It does not become the object of consciousness.*"[352]

Eventually, only consciousness-*of* the objective world establishes it as existing.

The reader may say,

'Something does not come into existence by simply thinking of it.'

We reply,

'True, however, any dream-vision comes into existence, as an image-though, only when we are in some way conscious-of it. Furthermore, how can you state the existence of something, which you have <u>never</u> imagined, dreamed-of, thought-of, heard-of and experienced directly or indirectly? If something does not enter a consciousness as such, who can state it as existing and how can it be stated to exist? Who can state what happened when no one was there? Who is the witness when there are no witnesses? We can even imagine an event, but we will still be conscious-of it as a fantasy. Then, that fancy may exist <u>as dream</u>. Even the classical tree that falls in the forest, when no one is present, still makes an imagined sound because we connect every tumbling with sound. In fact, we cannot even state the falling of a tree without the mind conceiving or imagining it.'

Instantaneously the world flows streaming into Awareness

1-II SECTION: THE SIX DAYS OF CREATION

> I ⊙ DAY >

1:3-Start of the First Day of Creation: The *Auto-Transparent* Light

וַיֹּאמֶר אֱלֹהִים יְהִי אוֹר וַיְהִי־אוֹר׃
vayō'mer (commanded) *'ĕlōhiym* (Divine-Consciousness) *yahiy* (let it be) *'vōr* (light) *vayahiy* (become)*' vōr* (light)
καὶ *kai* (and) **εἶπεν** *eipen* (said) **ὁ** *o* (the) **θεός** *theos* (God) **γενηθήτω** *genēthetō* (let it be) **φῶς** *phōs* (light) **καὶ** *kai* (and) **ἐγένετο** *egeveto* (became) **φῶς** *phōs* (light)
dixit- (said) ***que*** (and) ***Deus*** (God) ***fiat*** (let it be) ***lux*** (light) ***et*** (and) ***facta*** (made) ***est*** (was) ***lux*** (light)
And God said, Let there be light: and there was light.
The Divine-Conscious-Awareness brought forth, "*Let be there light,*" and the light of Consciousness came to exist.

This verse clearly supports an epistemic interpretation of *Genesis*. Indeed, this Light must be a non-physical light. in physics, indeed, light is any visible and/or invisible wavelength of electromagnetic radiation.[353] Photons emit and absorb visible light, whose property is a wave and a particle at the same time.[354] However, here, it cannot be the light emanating from any physical source. In fact, *then*, in the *beginning*, there was no sun, no moon, nor stars. Therefore, this must be

"*Light from Light.*"[355]

It is ***'owr* (אוֹר)**, the [356]⇨

"*light of lightening* and *lightening* itself... [the] *light of life.*"[357]

It is the light of **evidence**, emanating from the perennial unexhausting burning bush[358] illuminating itself and all other lights right here and now. The light from ***DIVI*NE**[359]**-AWARE-CONSCIOUS-CERTITUDE** is the non-physical light that illuminates the whole world and does not need eyes to see.

"With all your science can you tell how it is, and whence it is, that light comes into the soul?"[360]

When we enquire on its origin, we find no answer. Consciousness is the very essential and fundamental prerequisite for any observation of the world. Thus, the first command of the Creator is for the Light of Consciousness to come out of obscurity. This is the light of Divine-Consciousness. Its beginning is timeless and comes from nowhere. From the Autochthonous Self-Made[361] Supreme Awareness comes Pure-Consciousness as the Self-in-Itself. From It comes the Light of Consciousness, which, when conceived, *becomes* an object. It *becomes* (*hayah* הָיָה)[362] consciousness-*of*-consciousness-for-itself. Namely, that light[363] comes into existence (הָיָה *hayah*) as an object of thought. When this takes place, inevitably, consciousness is mistaken for physical matter. Some researcher even found a name for it, *perceptronium*, namely,

"conscious matter... Consciousness... understood as a state of matter."[364]

Such scientists do not acknowledge that the individual epistemic-loneliness structure impedes the determination of conscious matter in-itself. In fact, perceptronium still needs a scientist to conceive it, albeit unverified, as conscious matter different from the observer.

Any beginning[365] implies time. Namely, it refers to a before and an after. Creation is not in time,

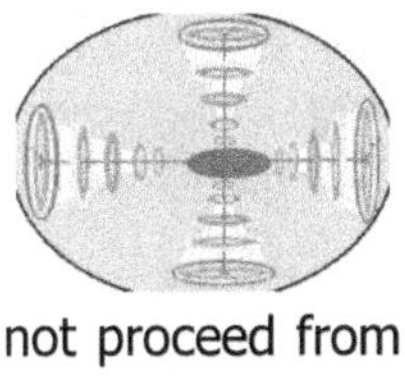

because it is always present and only present here and now. As the universal Big Bang singularity, the light stems out of Divine-Consciousness, out of Pure-Consciousness to illuminate the whole, objective world. From that light and only from it, the world events, in the sense of (e) out-comes (*venire*),[366] and exists (*ex-sistere*). If there is something by itself outside that light, we cannot and will never know. We cannot state anything if it does not proceed from that light, which, then, will become consciousness-*of*-the object. Creation, therefore, is not external to our knowledge, but is that same act, which founds and creates our epistemic process. The *Biblical* account of creation displays the entire epistemic process, which takes place right here and now while reading this page. With six steps, Creation moves, from this first insurgence of Consciousness, all the way down to its human individualization. This Light of Consciousness is at the center of the Creative Process. It descends through all the six Days of Creation without ever losing Its Centrality within each one of them. Its centrality, however, never goes out of Itself. In fact, Its Consciousness reaches Itself as Auto-Transparent Consciousness shining within Itself. As an imploding-explosion within each Day, that central Light emanates descending in every Day and generating a ripple effect producer of all Creation. Furthermore, each individual day or circularity constitutes a different and new level of consciousness. Moreover, from the Transcendent Timeless/Spaceless/Stillness proceeds Pure-Consciousness. In turn, This One creates, in its logical beginning, its light, which will illuminate the world by becoming conscious-*of* it. Therefore, *$Y_eh_ov_ah$* יְהֹוָה is the Transcendent Awareness (absurdly, the contrary would imply that God is not aware). *El_ohim* אֱלֹהִים is Its Stillness as Pure-Consciousness in-itself. *'Owr* אוֹר is the Light of the Bursting-Intuitive-Wisdom, the Fire of the Unexhausting Burning (*ba`ar* בָּעַר) Bush (*cĕnah* סְנֶה). However, when conceptualized, as we are doing here, Pure-Consciousness pauperizes (so to say, since it is impossible) becoming consciousness-*of*-consciousness, an object of thought, which is not Pure-Consciousness-in-Itself.

Divine-Consciousness commanded and bore forth[367] the light- (אוֹר *'owr*)[368] *of* consciousness, which brings the world out of the void darkness and puts it into existence. It is because of that light that we see the world. Without it, the world, even if illuminated by billions of suns, would remain in the darkness of the unseen nonexistence. In fact, as we said, existence is only when detected by the consciousness-*of* it. Imagine the existence of life on another planet. We can be conscious-*of* its existing as fantasy or we may state its existence when and if experienced as such by the direct empirical consciousness-*of* it. In either case, only consciousness determines it. If energy, *E*, is the source of life, how can we determine its existence without our consciousness-*of* it? Without consciousness, we would never be able to know or speak about it. According to Schrödinger,

> **"A physical scientist does not introduce awareness (sensation or perception) into his theories, and having thus removed the mind from nature, he cannot expect to find it there."**[369]

Therefore, the presence of Consciousness is the essential fundamental premise without which no physical formula, as Einstein's $E=mc^2$, can be expressed. In fact, how can we state existence without Consciousness? However, Consciousness finds its foundation on Certain Awareness, which is the necessary basis of everything. We are conscious-*of* our imagination, but we define it as experience-*of*-fantasy when we consciously look at it from a non-imaginative perspective. We are conscious-*of* our dream, but we define it as experience-*of*-dream when we consciously look at it from a non-dreaming perspective. We are conscious-*of* our waking-experience and we define it as real-experience when we consciously refer to it from the waking state. However, without consciousness-*of* them, we cannot state neither fantasy, nor dream, nor experience. We can define the differences between them, as consciousness-*of* that which takes place in the fantasy, or in the dream and/or in the physical-world. Nevertheless, we can never determine what they may be without any consciousness-*of* them. We can say that fantasy disappears before that which is concrete. Dream vanishes on the onset of wakefulness. Similarly, wakefulness dissolves again in the oneiric state. Each set is real as long as established by the consciousness-*of* it. When, another set superimposes on that same consciousness-*of*, then, the new disproves the later one. Each level of consciousness-*of* comes equipped with its own relative valid rules. In fact, it is possible to conceive a *jinn* on flying carpets in fairytales and/or within dreams but not in the scientific experimentation. The objective world pops into each set of consciousness and it is true only until offset by another group supported by consciousness. Without consciousness, however, we cannot state any of them.

I ⊙ DAY >>

1:4-The First Logical Rule

וַיַּרְא אֱלֹהִים אֶת־הָאוֹר כִּי־טוֹב וַיַּבְדֵּל אֱלֹהִים בֵּין הָאוֹר וּבֵין הַחֹשֶׁךְ׃   *vayara'* (saw) *'ĕlōhiym* (Divine-Consciousness) *et̲* (the) *hā'vōr* (light) *kiy* (that) *ṭvōb̲* (beautiful) *vayab̲adēl* (separated) *'ĕlōhiym* (Divine-Consciousness) *bēyn* (between) *hā'vōr* (light) *ub̲ēyn* (between) *haḥōšek̲a* (darkness)
καὶ *kai* (and) **εἶδεν** *eiden* (saw) **ὁ** *o* (the) **θεὸς** *theos* (God) **τὸ** *to* (the) **φῶς** *phōs* (light) **ὅτι** *oti* (that) **καλόν** *kalon* (good) **καὶ** *kai* (and) **διεχώρισεν** *diexhōrisen* (divided) **ὁ** *o* (the) **θεὸς** *theos* (God) **ἀνὰ** *ana* (each) **μέσον** *meson* (midst) **τοῦ** *tou* (the) **φωτὸς** *phōtos* (light) **καὶ** *kai* (and) **ἀνὰ** *ana* (each) **μέσον** *meson* (midst) **τοῦ** *tou* (the) **σκότους** *skotous* (darkness)
et (and) **vidit** (saw) **Deus** (God) **lucem** (the light) **quod** (which) **esset** (was) **bona** (good) **et** (and) **divisit** (divided) **lucem** (the light) **ac** (from) **tenebras** (the darkness)
And God saw the light, that it was good: and God divided the light from the darkness.
Then, Divine-Consciousness perceived the beauty of that light of Consciousness: and Divine-Consciousness distinguished Pure Consciousness from objective perception.

Obviously, at this moment in Creation there cannot be any sin or

"*consciousness-of the missed mark,*"[370]

because it is Awareness Itself. In God's eyes, everything must be good. There cannot be evil in Awareness. Sin, in fact, appears at the onset of judgement, when thought enters into the field of duality, when consciousness-*of* the object distinguishes this from that. Following the uttered (*'amar* אמר) command,

"יְהִי אוֹר, γενηθήτω φῶς, *fiat lux, let light be,*"

the light of **Consciousness** appears as that of **Pure Unattached Scientific Observation**.

"*God is indeed all-knowing, aware,*"[371]

states, the *Koran*. This Consciousness is the rapture of St. Francis' *Canticle of the Sun,*

"*Most high, omnipotent, all good Lord!/ All praises are Yours, the glory and the honor and all blessing./ To You, alone, Highest, they are appropriate/ and no mortal is worthy to mention You./ Be praised, my Lord with all Your creatures,/ especially noble brother Sun,/ who brings day light, and You give us light through him./ And he is beautiful and radiant with great splendor:/ of You, Most High, he bears likeness./ Be praised, my Lord, for sister Moon and the stars:/ in the sky You made them bright and precious and beautiful./ Be praised, my Lord, for brothers Wind/ and for air and clouds and serene and all weather,/ through which, You give sustenance to Your creatures./ Be praised, my Lord, for sister Water,/ she is very useful and humble and precious and pure./ Be praised, my Lord, for brother Fire,/ through whom You brighten the night:/ and he is beautiful and cheerful and robust and strong./ Be praised, my Lord, for our sister mother Earth,/ who feeds us and rules us,/ and produces various fruits with colorful flowers and herbs./ Be praised, my Lord, for those who forgive for Your love/ and endure sickness and tribulation./ Blessed are those who will endure it in peace,/ for by You, Most High, they will be crowned./ Be praised, my Lord, for our sister bodily Death,/ from whom no living person can escape:/ woe to those who will die in mortal sin;/ blessed are those that she will find in Your most holy will,/ because the second death will not harm to them./ Praise and bless my Lord and give thanks/ and serve Him with great humility.*"[372]

The first day of creation cannot be the 24 hours Earth's rotation on its axis. In fact, that planet and the Sun had not been created yet. Therefore, the rotating day of creation is a metaphor for the circularity of Consciousness.[373] Indeed, with 360° degrees, Consciousness motionlessly directs its aim towards itself to confirm the timeless presence of its own Awareness. The Light of Consciousness immediately *distinguishes* Pure Consciousness from the moment in which consciousness itself *impoverishes* by flowing into dark objectification. Obviously, Consciousness, as such, never impoverishes. However, by changing focus, consciousness moves from introspection into worldly extroversion. Then, the rapture of Consciousness become the consciousness-*of* this object, when

"*by night on my bed I sought him whom my soul loveth: I sought him, but I found him not.*"[374]

When the next oncoming consciousness-*of* objects ensues, then we miss that original *detached* and *serene* purity in-itself and we identifies with the darkness of the turbulent object as such. Pure-

Consciousness is Consciousness-in-Itself that can never be an object of thought. The consciousness-*for-itself* (συνοράω *sunoraō*), on the other hand, is the entrance into the time/space/causality dimensions. *Before the command*, at the *entrance* or at the *beginning*, there is the timeless state of non-conceptual-*being*. There reigns the serene contemplation in-itself. That is what in Japanese is named

> "*yūgen, the mysterious.*"[375]

When, however one conceptualizes that serenity, then, the *distressful* unseen black *darkness* (חשך *choshek*) sets in. Then, the pure light of Consciousness, as such, subsides in the obtuse objectivity, as such. It is like having a nightmare. Then, fear, aroused by the internal dream light, makes the dreamer forget that it is only a dream.

Divine-Consciousness *regarded*[376] the light of consciousness as being good.[377] Here, *seeing* (ראה *ra'ah*) is an act of consciousness. In fact,

> "The Hebrews (like the Greeks and others) not unfrequently use a verb of *seeing* of those things also which are not perceived by the eyes, but – by other senses, as by hearing… [or] of those things which are perceived, felt, and enjoyed by the *mind.*"[378]

Therefore, Divine-Consciousness transpires to Itself, illuminates itself without conceptualization, so that

> "*the eyes of your heart* (καρδίας *kardias*) *may be enlightened* (πεφωτισμένους *pephōtismenous*)."[379]

The light is consciousness itself. The light sees itself as light. There is an **Auto-Transparency**. However, the origin of this light remains in the ineffable, unseen realm of its own beginning-in-itself. The light, reflecting or bouncing-*of* an object, becomes, for-us, consciousness-*of*-the-illuminated-object, thus, we misplace the true Light in-itself. It is like the eye, which sees for-itself, but cannot see itself seeing, or the ear, which hears for-itself, but cannot hear itself hearing. Furthermore, this verse describes the first, primordial rational distinction.[380] The Creative-Awareness makes the logical separation between contraries, namely, between light and darkness. Alongside the principle of non-contradiction, the Unity multiplies becoming two, *viz.* the subject's-light and the object's-shade.

Divine-Consciousness *saw* and *realized* (ראה *ra'ah*)[381] that light and, thus, *consciously* intuited it as *good* and *beautiful* (טוב *towb*).[382] The Hebrew word *towb* (טוב),[383] means *good*, but it means also *beautiful*, in fact, it derives from the verb *towb* (טוב),[384] *to be beautiful.*[385] Plotinus declares,

> "*It is the good that confers beauty to all things.*"[386]

In its purity, confirms Kant, beauty is the good itself. Furthermore, he states that it is not necessary to think about beauty to recognize it. In fact,

> "the beautiful is that which apart from concepts is represented as the object of a universal satisfaction."[387]

Throughout all of the six days of Creation,[388] when Transcendent Awareness "*realized His Creation as good*" it was not an act of seeing as such. It was not as a subject perceiving the object, because it did not need the mediation of thought. It is the immediate apperception of the good in the epistemic fulgurating intuition of its beauty coming out from Itself. Hegel asserts that, while truth is the universal aspect of the idea, on the other hand,

> "beauty can be defined as the sensible appearance of the idea."[389]

In addition, Croce writes,

> "It seems to us rightful and appropriate to define beauty as a *successful expression.*"[390]

Moreover, Creation is, in fact, the supreme successful expression of Consciousness at the presence of the Goodness of Its Own Beauty. That beauty is in us when Consciousness contemplates without identifying with the consciousness-*of* the reflection of that light bouncing off the hungered object before us.

I ⊙ DAY <

1:5-End of the First Day of Creation: Beginning of Language

וַיִּקְרָא אֱלֹהִים לָאוֹר יוֹם וְלַחֹשֶׁךְ קָרָא לָיְלָה וַיְהִי־עֶרֶב וַיְהִי־בֹקֶר יוֹם אֶחָד׃ פ

vayiqarā' (called out) *'ĕlōhiym* (Divine-Consciousness) *lā'vōr* (light) *yvōm* (day) *valaḥōšeḵa* (darkness) *qārā'* (called) *lāyalāh* (night) *vayahiy* (be) *'ereḇ* (evening) *vayahiy* (became) *ḇōqer* (morning) *yvōm* (day) *'eḥāḏ* (one) *p̄* (.)

καὶ *kai* (and) **ἐκάλεσεν** *ekalesen* (called) **ὁ** *o* (the) **θεὸς** *theos* (God) **τὸ** *to* (the) **φῶς** *phōs* (light) **ἡμέραν** *ēmeran* (day) **καὶ** *kai* (and) **τὸ** *to* (the) **σκότος** *skotos* (darkness) **ἐκάλεσεν** *ekalesen* (called) **νύκτα** *nukta* (night) **καὶ** *kai* (and) **ἐγένετο** *egeneto* (arose) **ἑσπέρα** *espera* (evening) **καὶ** *kai* (and) **ἐγένετο** *egeneto* (arose) **πρωί** *prōi* (in the morning) **ἡμέρα** *ēmera* (day) **μία** *mia* (one)
appellavit-(called)***que*** (and) ***lucem*** (light) ***diem*** (day) ***et*** (and) ***tenebras*** (darkness) ***noctem*** (night) ***factum-*** (done) ***que*** (and) ***est*** (is) ***vespere*** (evening) ***et*** (and) ***mane*** (morning) ***dies*** (day) ***unus*** (one)
And God called the light Day, and the darkness he called Night. And the evening and the morning were the first day.
Then, Divine-Consciousness named Day the light of Consciousness and night the unconsciousness of objectivity. That was the first day, the evening followed by the morning.

The Day of Creation, as a *day,* has nothing to do with the actual twenty-four hours period of Earth's rotation. In fact, on the first day, the Sun and the Earth were not yet. The seasons, the days and the years appear on the fourth day, as we shall see. The Day of Creation has nothing to do with any length of time at all. The *day,*[391] as well as the year, stands for circularity. The Day of Creation is a metaphor for the circularity of the creative light of consciousness, clearly described by the Psalm as,

> "*His going forth is from the end of the heaven, and his circuit unto the ends of it: and there is nothing hid from the heat thereof.*"[392]

In fact, the Lord declares,

> "*So shall my word be that goeth forth out of my mouth: it shall not return unto me void, but it shall accomplish that which I please, and it shall prosper* [in the thing] *whereto I sent it.*"[393]

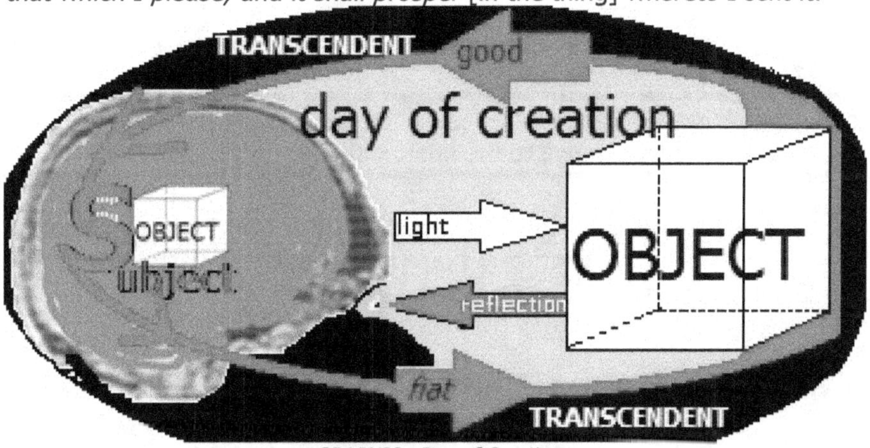

GRAPHIC: *Day of Creation*

From the *external* world, the object enters the mind of the subject to be placed immediately *outside* again only to flow back in once more. This is the circular *breath* or *light* of Consciousness. On this circumference, any point is its starting-point with no beginning and no end. The circle represents the spaceless-instantaneous flow of conscience. This is the day of Consciousness. After which creation continues with the consciousness-*of* itself or -*of* any *external* object, only to place it back again in consciousness as an existing creature. In other words, creation itself, as we will see for each of the other five days, is the epistemic process. It is how we know the objective world. The objectiveness, as such, equates to the unconscious night.[394] The term *layil, night, is the* same as *luwl,* an unused root meaning *enclosed space with folding back winding staircase.*[395] The enclosed circularity of consciousness is the same that is taking place, right here and now, in our mind winding back on its own internal self. This first day is Auto-Transparency. It is the light illuminating itself as radiant *conscious-known* and/or *unconscious-unknown* without the mediation of thought, as we will see later. That process takes no time and no space to take place. How long or how far must you go to be conscious and recognize the existence of the object under your eyes? To see and to name something one must be conscious-*of* it.

"And God saw the light… and named it."

Time and space are the deep-ocean of the waters of possibilities on which moves the circular inhaling and exhaling breath of God. The circular process of consciousness is the Breath of the Creator, which departs from the Creator, reaches the created-world to lead it back to the Creator. If this timeless and spaceless circular-day-breath-of-consciousness would not take place, there could not be any creation and no knowledge at all. In fact, if God's Consciousness were not sustaining heaven and earth now, He could not have seen or perceived (ראה *ra'ah*) them and, therefore, He could not have made them. We can explain that the Spirit-of-Breath is the Single-Center that, like a sun, simultaneously Irradiates-Itself on the circumference of the Circle-of-Creation, Now as Radiating-Subject and Now as Radial-Object, where both Subject/Object are Identical and One and the Same.

At the end of this day, Divine-Consciousness cries out the names[396] of night and day. Thus, language starts. However, while signifying the object, the name puts it also in existence. The name is the word, which becomes the essential creative idea (λόγος *logos*) *in*forming the object.

"In the beginning was the Word (λόγος logos), and the Word (λόγος logos) was with God, and the Word was God."[397]

We can say that God's *Word* or *Idea* (λόγος *logos*) is Light-Itself-In-Itself. Furthermore, the communication of a name, besides stating the essence of the object, requires the presence of a listener in whose mind the signified object lights up. In the descending process of creative hypostases, the first day is the realm of Consciousness. It is Pure-Awareness, as Pure-Love-Giving asking nothing in return for its illumination of the objects. This Love-Awareness is the watchful eye of the prodigal son's father. As the parable goes, when the dissolute son returned home,

"when he was yet a great way off, his father saw (εἶδεν *eíden was aware*) *him, and had compassion, and ran, and fell on his neck, and kissed him."*[398]

Consciousness in the stillness of dreamless-sleep is the light's daily cycle traveling from the eye to the brain and back to the eye

> II ⊙ DAY >

1:6-Start of the Second Day of Creation: The Pure Sky Volt

וַיֹּאמֶר אֱלֹהִים יְהִי רָקִיעַ בְּתוֹךְ הַמָּיִם וִיהִי מַבְדִּיל בֵּין מַיִם לָמָיִם׃   *vayō'mer* (commanded) *'ĕlōhiym* (Divine-Consciousness) *yahiy* (let there be) *rāqiya'* (firmament) *batvōka* (middle) *hamāyim* (waters) *viyhiy* (be) *mabadiyl* (divided) *bēyn* (between) *mayim* (waters) *lāmāyim* (waters)
καὶ *kai* (and) **εἶπεν** *eipen* (said) **ὁ** *o* (the) **θεός** *theos* (God) **γενηθήτω** *genēthētō* (let it be) **στερέωμα** *stereōma* (firmament) **ἐν** *en* (in) **μέσῳ** *mesō* (the middle) **τοῦ** *tou* (of the) **ὕδατος** *udatos* (waters) **καὶ** *kai* (and) **ἔστω** *estō* (it was) **διαχωρίζον** *diachōrizon* (let it be divided) **ἀνὰ** *ana* (each) **μέσον** *meson* (middle) **ὕδατος** *udatos* (waters) **καὶ** *kai* (and) **ὕδατος** *udatos* (waters) **καὶ** *kai* (and) **ἐγένετο** *egeneto* (it became) **οὕτως** *outōs* (so)
dixit (he said) ***quoque*** (also) ***Deus*** (God) ***fiat*** (let be) ***firmamentum*** (a firmament) ***in*** (in) ***medio*** (the middle) ***aquarum*** (of the waters) ***et*** (and) ***dividat*** (let it divide) ***aquas*** (waters) ***ab*** (from) ***aquis*** (the waters)
And God said, Let there be a firmament in the midst of the waters, and let it divide the waters from the waters.
And Divine-Consciousness said,   *"Let the volt of the sky-consciousness be between the waters and let it separate the Transcendent waters from the immanent waters."*

A new creative command (אמר *'amar*) from Divine-Consciousness produces the firmament or the vault of the sky.[399] This heavenly dome is the circular-arch of the day of creation, which spreads out, stretches out and overlays[400] the waters.[401] In other words, the circularity of Creative Consciousness becomes the firmament separating the waters into two realms,

1) The realm of earthly waters is this immanent flowing cascade of all the actual objects that flood us in the world of experience. Namely, like an ocean in which all thoughts, in an objective sequence, flow through the consciousness-*of* all the perceptions that actually materialize throughout the universe of our daily experiences.
2) The realm of Heavenly Waters is the Vast Silence of the Aware Transcendent Pure Consciousness without any thought mediation. However, it is the realm always referred to by the intentionality of consciousness-*of* this world. In fact, consciousness constantly aims to attribute a transcendent reality-in-itself to the objective creation.

The multiplication of the creative act continues. In this verse, there is the logical distinction between the constant universal intentional reference to the Transcendent Oneness of otherness and the flow of experiences multiplying exponentially.[402] Therefore, on one side, we have $Y_{\breve{e}}h_{o}V_{a}h$ (יְהוָה), the Infinite Foundation, the Ineffable Oceanic Unutterable Silent Stillness of Transcendence from which everything derives. On the other side, we have all the possibilities of the immanent world.

II ⊙ DAY >>

1:7-Logical Distinctions of the Waters

וַיַּעַשׂ אֱלֹהִים אֶת־הָרָקִיעַ וַיַּבְדֵּל בֵּין הַמַּיִם אֲשֶׁר מִתַּחַת לָרָקִיעַ וּבֵין הַמַּיִם אֲשֶׁר מֵעַל לָרָקִיעַ וַיְהִי־כֵן׃ *vaya'aś* (made) *'ĕlōhiym* (Divine-Consciousness) *'eṯ* (the) *hārāqiya'* (firmament) *vayaḇadēl* (divided) *bēyn* (between) *hamayim* (waters) *'ăšer* (which) *mitaḥaṯ* (out of) *lārāqiya'* (firmament) *uḇēyn* (between) *hamayim* (waters) *'ăšer* (which) *mē'al* (out of) *lārāqiya'* (firmament) *vayahiy* (is) *ḵēn* (thus)
καὶ *kai* (and) **ἐποίησεν** *epoiēsen* (made) **ὁ** *o* (the) **θεὸς** *theos* (God) **τὸ** *to* (the) **στερέωμα** *stereōma* (firmament) **καὶ** *kai* (and) **διεχώρισεν** *diechōrisen* (divided) **ὁ** *o* (the) **θεὸς** *theos* (God) **ἀνὰ** *ana* (each) **μέσον** *meson* (middle) **τοῦ** *tou* (of the) **ὕδατος** *udatos* (waters) **ὃ** *o* (it) **ἦν** *ēn* (is) **ὑποκάτω** *upokatō* (under) **τοῦ** *tou* (of the) **στερεώματος** *stereōmatos* (firmament) **καὶ** *kai* (and) **ἀνὰ** *ava* (each) **μέσον** *meson* (middle) **τοῦ** *tou* (of the) **ὕδατος** *udatos* (waters) **τοῦ** *tou* (of the) **ἐπάνω** *epanō* (over) **τοῦ** *tou* (the) **στερεώματος** *stereōmatos* (firmament)
et (and) ***fecit*** (made) ***Deus*** (God) ***firmamentum*** (the firmament) ***divisit-***(divided)***que*** (and) ***aquas*** (waters) ***quae*** (that) ***erant*** (were) ***sub*** (under) ***firmamento*** (the firmament) ***ab*** (from) ***his*** (those) ***quae*** (that) ***erant*** (were) ***super*** (over) ***firmamentum*** (the firmament) ***et*** (and) ***factum*** (done) ***est*** (is) ***ita*** (thus)
And God made the firmament, and divided the waters which *were* under the firmament from the waters which *were* above the firmament: and it was so.
Therefore, Divine-Consciousness made the vault of the sky, and separated the immanent waters that were under the sky arch from the Transcendent waters of Consciousness that were above the sky arch: and thus, it was.

As we have seen, there are four Hebrew verbs, which express the same act of creation.

1) *bara',*[403] *to create,*
2) *'amar,*[404] *to say* or *to command,*
3) *asah,*[405] *to make* or *to produce,* and
4) *qara',*[406] *to cry out* the creature's name.

The creation of Divine-Consciousness is, at the same time, an act, which projects, commands, makes the world, names it and logically distinguishes[407] its Transcendent Origin from its empirical dimension. Divine-Consciousness separates the original waters. He distinguishes the Abyss of Transcendence from the fluid ocean of time and space. Thus, it is.[408] The Aware Infinite Transcendent Creator produces an infinite creation,[409] with *"many mansions."*[410] Therefore, beyond the arch of the sky is the Transcendent Awareness, namely, all the unlimited waters of Pure-Consciousness in all the infinite possible dimensions and universes. Below the sky arch, is consciousness-*of*, namely, the unlimited waters of all the infinite actual and parallel universes populating the immanent reality.[411] When we identify with those secondary waters, then, we perish in them as in a flood, as we will see.

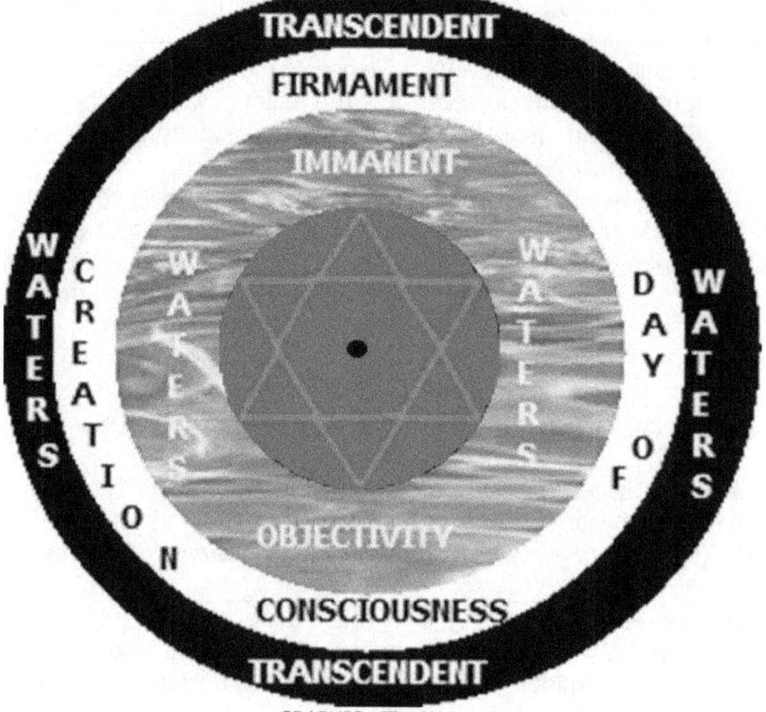

GRAPHIC: *The Waters*

II ⊙ DAY <

1:8-End of the Second Day of Creation: I-Consciousness

וַיִּקְרָא אֱלֹהִים לָרָקִיעַ שָׁמָיִם וַיְהִי־עֶרֶב וַיְהִי־בֹקֶר יוֹם שֵׁנִי׃ פ *vayiqarā '* (called) *'ĕlōhiym* (Divine-Consciousness) *lārāqiya '* (firmament) *šāmāyim* (heaven) *vayahiy* (to be) *'ereḇ* (evening) *vayahiy* (to be) *ḇōqer* (morning) *yvōm* (day) *šēniy* (second) *p̄* (.)
καὶ *kai* (and) **ἐκάλεσεν** *ekalesen* (called) **ὁ** *o* (the) **θεὸς** *theos* (God) **τὸ** *to* (the) **στερέωμα** *stereōma* (firmament) **οὐρανόν** *ouranon* (heaven) **καὶ** *kai* (and) **εἶδεν** *eiden* (saw) **ὁ** *o* (the) **θεὸς** *theos* (God) **ὅτι** *oti* (that) **καλόν** *kalon* (good) **καὶ** *kai* (and) **ἐγένετο** *egeneto* (became) **ἑσπέρα** **καὶ** *kai* (and) **ἐγένετο** *egeneto* (became) **πρωί** *prōi* (in the morning) **ἡμέρα** *ēmera* (day) **δευτέρα** *deutera* (second)
vocavit-(called)***que*** (and) ***Deus*** (God) ***firmamentum*** (firmament) ***caelum*** (heaven) ***et*** (and) ***factum*** (done) ***est*** (is) ***vespere*** (evening) ***et*** (and) ***mane*** (morning) ***dies*** (day) ***secundus*** (second)
And God called the firmament Heaven. And the evening and the morning were the second day.
Then, Divine-Consciousness named Transcendent-Heaven the highest vault of the shy. That was the second day, the evening followed by the morning.

"*Heaven's Transcendent Divine-Consciousness*"[412]
named Transcendent-Heaven the point where the vault of the sky, *shamayim* (שָׁמַיִם), becomes the threshold from which to *transit ascending* over into Transcendence in-Itself. This is
"*the gate of heaven,*[413] *the abode of Divine-Consciousness,*[414] *the Heaven of heaven.*"[415]
All this happens when Divine-Consciousness *cries out*[416] the name of Heaven, thus establishing it in consciousness. Consequently, the second day of creation concludes. Namely, He accomplishes the second circularity of consciousness.

Heaven, *shamayim*,[417] is the abode of the Transcendent. It is *the Heaven of heavens* (הַשָּׁמַיִם וּשְׁמֵי *ušəmēy hašāmāyim*), which the subject/object refers to as being beyond its correlation.

"*Behold, the heaven* (שָׁמַיִם *shamayim*) *and the Heaven* (שָׁמַיִם *shamayim*) *of heavens* (שָׁמַיִם *shamayim*) *<u>is</u> the TRANSCENDENT* (יְהוָה *Yĕhovah*) *of Divine-Consciousness* (אֱלֹהִים *'elohiym*), *the earth <u>also</u>, with all that is therein.*"[418]

Let us analyze the meaning of this. Usually, when confronted with an impending danger, both in dream and/or in wakefulness, we try to run away from it. This means that we confer to that event a reality external to and/or independent from our experience of it, thus, *transcending* us. In other words, the whole consciousness-*of* the world is always as if

"*lifted up into heaven.*"[419]

Therefore, we conceive the object as that which is real in-itself. This is because Awareness confirms what is evident and evidence confirms the existence of the object. The Indian sage Śaṅkara[420] declares,

"*In every act of perception we are conscious of some external thing corresponding to the idea... and that of which we are conscious cannot but exist...* [There is a conscious intentionality as real transcending towards the object itself that] *exists apart from consciousness... Nobody when perceiving a post or a wall is conscious of his perception only, but everyone is conscious of posts and walls and the like as objects of their perceptions...* [The intentionality of consciousness is evident since] *even those who contest the existence of external things bear witness to their existence when they say that what is an internal object of cognition appears like something external.*"[421]

In conclusion, heaven is consciousness up-lifted to the level of Transcendence. On the lower side, consciousness becomes conscious-*of* itself as consciousness. It is the thought that thinks itself as thought. This is the objective consciousness-*of* the I as an object of thought.

This is the level of I-consciousness. It is, as we will further explain, the *thought* of oneself as oneself that puts the human into transcending existence. From the Indistinct Waters of the Original Conscious-Light, *viz.* the <u>In-Itself</u>, <u>thought</u> appears as <u>thought</u> that knows itself as <u>thought for-itself</u>. Thus the Knower, *viz.* the original waters, as cogitating potentialities, thinks, distinguishes and identifies itself as the ocean of these ideas conceived here and now. In the descending process of creative hypostases, the second day is the realm of Heaven. It is the beginning, from which the physical world finds its origin.

The world flowing in the dreaming brain is separate from the one flowing in the preceding state.

> III ⊙ DAY >

1:9-Start of the Third Day of Creation: Converting to Physicality

וַיֹּאמֶר אֱלֹהִים יִקָּווּ הַמַּיִם מִתַּחַת הַשָּׁמַיִם אֶל־מָקוֹם אֶחָד וְתֵרָאֶה הַיַּבָּשָׁה וַיְהִי־כֵן׃ *vayō'mer* (uttered) *'ĕlōhiym* (Divine-Consciousness) *yiqāvu* (let gather) *hamayim* (the waters) *mitaḥaṯ* (under) *hašāmayim* (heaven) *'el* (unto) *māqvōm* (place) *'eḥāḏ* (one) *vaṯērā'eh* (perceived) *hayabāšāh* (the dry) *vayahiy* (be) *ḵēn* (thus)
καὶ *kai* (and) **εἶπεν** *eipen* (said) **ὁ** *o* (the) **θεός** *theos* (God) **συναχθήτω** *sunēchthētō* (let congregate) **τὸ** *to* (the) **ὕδωρ** *udōr* (water) **τὸ** *to* (the) **ὑποκάτω** *upokatō* (under) **τοῦ** *tou* (the) **οὐρανοῦ** *ouranou* (sky) **εἰς** *eis* (into) **συναγωγὴν** *sunagōgēn* (assembling) **μίαν** *mian* (one) **καὶ** *kai* (and) **ὀφθήτω** *ophthētō* (appear) **ἡ** *ē* (truly) **ξηρά** *xēra* (dry land) **καὶ** *kai* (and) **ἐγένετο** *egeneto* (became) **οὕτως** *outōs* (so) **καὶ** *kai* (and) **συνήχθη** *sunēxthē* (gathered) **τὸ** *to* (the) **ὕδωρ** *udōr* (water) **τὸ** *to* (the) **ὑποκάτω** *upokatō* (under) **τοῦ** *tou* (the) **οὐρανοῦ** *ouranou* (sky) **εἰς** *eis* (into) **τὰς** *tas* (the) **συναγωγὰς** *sunagōgas* (gatherings) **αὐτῶν** *autōn* (thus) **καὶ** *kai* (and) **ὤφθη** *ōphthē* (appeared) **ἡ** *ē* (truly) **ξηρά** *xēra* (dry land)
dixit (said) ***vero*** (truthfully) ***Deus*** (God) ***congregentur*** (let congregate) ***aquae*** (the waters) ***quae*** (that) ***sub*** (under) ***caelo*** (the sky) ***sunt*** (are) ***in*** (in) ***locum*** (location) ***unum*** (one) ***et*** (and) ***appareat*** (let it appear) ***arida*** (arid land) ***factum*** (done) ***que*** (that) ***est*** (is) ***ita*** (so)
And God said, Let the waters under the heaven be gathered together unto one place, and let the dry land appear: and it was so.
And Divine-Consciousness said,

'Let the immanent water fluidity of abstract thoughts within the firmament gather in one place and matter appear as the solidity of dry land.' And it was so.

Obviously, a literal reader of this verse would have difficulty explaining the water dislocations in landlocked seas (*e.g.* Dead Sea or Sea of Galilee) or on other planets like Ceres, the biggest asteroid between Mars and Jupiter.[422] Epistemically, however, the water here is a metaphor for the flowing aspect of ideas, which rests in the physicality of objects. This verse outlines two directions of that flow, a descending and an ascending one. On one side, as we saw, Consciousness projects the *transcending consciousness-of-this* physical world up into a transcendent realm. On the other end, the descending direction extends under and within the circular consciousness-*of*-this day of creation. Different names, like firmament, heaven, vault of the sky or also sub-lunar world are all metaphors for this circle of consciousness. This is the realm of the lower waters, *viz.* the actualization of all the infinite possibilities of the flowing experiences. Divine-Consciousness puts the world in order.

I) The lower waters distinguish themselves as,
   a) dream, *viz.* its *liquid* aspect (מים *mayim*) and
   b) wakefulness, *viz.* its *dry* physicality(יַבָּשָׁה *yabbashah*).[423]

   The liquidity is the state of thoughts' fluidity before they materialize in the firmness of the external objects as solid ground. In other words, it is the dry land expanse of actual objects as separated from the ocean of dreaming possibilities. All this takes place following the command and order of Divine-Consciousness. This is the level of change. The objective world appears with all its diversities. From the fluidity of ideas, the objects appear in the expanse of the concrete physicality.

II) However, the second direction is the ascending one. It is the distinction between water and dry land as in the ancient Hermetic Tradition. That lore distinguishes two paths for the achievement of the sacred Art, or *Opus*, the Humid and the Dry Way.[424]

   1) The Humid Way corresponds to being-for-itself (*viz. per-se*). It is the continuous subject/object circular correlation. <There we become emotionally involved with and in the world. It corresponds to the deadly submersion in the universal flood.
   2) The Dry Way relates to Being-in-itself (*viz. in-se*), namely, the absolute independent *transcendent* center of the *immanent* circle set apart from the inseparable *subject-object* circular correlation. There we become disengaged from the world's seductions.> [425] ⇨

This arid land corresponds to the one at the exit from the ark after the deluge, as we will see. Furthermore, the Dry Way is also the same dry land (חָרָבָה *charabah*)[426] that appeared during the exodus. Then, to make a safe passage,

"*Moses stretched out his hand over the sea; and the TRANSCENDENT caused the sea to go back by a strong east wind* (רוּחַ *ruwach*) *all that night, and made the sea dry land, and the waters were divided.*"[427]

The name Moses, *Mosheh*,[428] itself means *drawn*

"*out of the water.*"[429]

Over that dry surface, the Israelites walked to *freedom* (חפשׁ *chophshiy*)[430] from the *yoke* (עֹל *`ol*) of the *grievous* (קָשֶׁה *qashah*) *servitude* (עֲבֹדָה *`abodah*).[431] Metaphorically, the *dry pathway* means the detachment from the servile identification with the flowing passions for the objective world. [432] ⇨

"*And the children of Israel went into the midst of the sea upon the dry ground: and the waters were a wall unto them on their right hand, and on their left. And the Egyptians pursued, and went in after them to the midst of the sea, even all Pharaoh's horses, his chariots, and his horsemen."*[433]

The whole world of tragic attachments is on our pursuit. In fact, the name of the chasing Egyptians, *Mitsrayim,*[434] means *double passages,* thus they are metaphors of the world of duality. *Pharaoh,*[435] a name meaning the *great house,* is the receptacle of that duality. He chases *the children of Israel, viz.* of *the prevailing God,*[436] with all his *horses* (סוס *cuwc*), meaning, *hopping for pleasurable joy,*[437] fastened to their *burden chariots* (רכב *rekeb*)[438] and carrying the *warrior agents* of *division* (פרש *parash*).[439] The pursuing army, like apocalyptic [440]⇨ horsemen, is the combined dreadful enticements of all worldly objects, which distract and separate the mind from freedom and leads to death.

"*All the kingdoms of the world and the glory of them… I will give thee,"*[441]

says the evil seducer,

"*whatever desires, hard to satisfy in the world of mortals, all the desires you may wish: these lovely maidens, with chariots accompanied by music, such as man was never able to obtain."*[442]

Similarly, Māra-Namuci, the Evil Death the Destroyer with a strong army,[443] tempted Siddhārtha Gautama Shakyamuni urging him to indulge in his desires. [444]⇨

"*Those who find pleasure in the flesh, in it find death."*[445]

In fact, the objective world is the flood of the *already-given-coming-out-from-the-past,* thus it belongs to death. Satisfying desires means to assimilate death, to eat the forbidden fruit,

"*for in the day that thou eatest thereof thou shalt surely die."*[446]

Consequently, also all the Pharaoh's army will ultimately drown[447] in all the *plagues* (מַגֵּפָה *maggephah*),[448] like in the deluge, as we will see.

III ⊙ DAY >>

1:10-The Physical World Acknowledged.

קְרָא אֱלֹהִים לַיַּבָּשָׁה אֶרֶץ וּלְמִקְוֵה הַמַּיִם קָרָא יַמִּים וַיַּרְא אֱלֹהִים כִּי־טוֹב׃
vayiqarā' (called) *'ĕlōhiym* (Divine-Consciousness) *layabāšāh* (land) *'ereṣ* (earth) *ulamiqavēh* (reservoir) *hamayim* (of waters) *qārā'* (called) *yamiym* (sea) *vayara'* (he saw) *'ĕlōhiym* (Divine-Consciousness) *ṭvōḇ* (good)
καὶ *kai* (and) **ἐκάλεσεν** *ekalesen* (called) **ὁ** *o* (the) **θεὸς** *theos* (God) **τὴν** *tēn* (the) **ξηρὰν** *xēran* (dry land) **γῆν** *gēn* (earth) **καὶ** *kai* (and) **τὰ** *ta* (the) **συστήματα** *sustēmata* (gathering) **τῶν** *tōn* (of the) **ὑδάτων** *udatōn* (waters) **ἐκάλεσεν** *ekalesen* (named) **θαλάσσας** *thalassas* (seas) **καὶ** *kai* (and) **εἶδεν** *eiden* (he saw) **ὁ** *o* (the) **θεὸς** *theos* (God) **ὅτι** *oti* (that) **καλόν** *kalon* (good)
et (and) ***vocavit*** (called) ***Deus*** (God) ***aridam*** (dry land) ***terram*** (earth) ***congregations-***(the congregation)***que*** (and) ***aquarum*** (of the waters) ***appellavit*** (named) ***maria*** (seas) ***et*** (and) ***vidit*** (he saw) ***Deus*** (God) ***quod*** (that) ***esset*** (it was) ***bonum*** (good)
And God called the dry land Earth; and the gathering together of the waters called he Seas: and God saw that it was good.
Thus, Divine-Consciousness named Earth the dry land and the receptacle of waters He named Seas. Thus, Divine-Consciousness acknowledged that it was beautiful.

Based on what we already analyzed, once more, Divine-Consciousness generates a language to communicate and signify the world. However, this is a special verbal expression (קרא *qara'*), because its utterance not only indicates and signifies the world, but also puts creation into consciousness and, consequently, into existence. In fact, it is Consciousness that creates by setting objects into existence, namely, *to exist* (*viz.* to stay out)[449] as if unrelated to Consciousness itself. The *naming* or the *word* creates a conscious idea that realizes its own beauty. Actually, the whole world can be understood or experimented scientifically only through that Consciousness. In fact, Divine-Consciousness *saw* (ראה *ra'ah*) his creation and conceptualized it. He formulated a thought, judging it good and beautiful. Therefore,

Creation was in His Consciousness. This Consciousness generates the circularity of the third day. There the Earth[450] becomes the *firm grounding spacing element* on which the concrete object rests and the Sea becomes the *mighty river*[451] of continuously flowing time and thoughts. This Sea is the *reservoir*[452] of all the consciousness-*of* the world. Furthermore, the third day of creation is a pivotal one. In fact, it transforms the *liquidity* of the ideal world into a physical, concrete and tangible reality.

Genesis purposely offers multiple readings of its texts. So that it can be read on different levels. However, paramount above all, it intends to describe the gnoseological structure of Creation, which allows the understanding of all the other levels. Therefore, at the same time, presents the correspondence between its epistemic aspect and the development of the objective world itself. Consequently, the sea is the extended physical body of waters (יָם *yam*) and, at the same time, signifies the *roaring and foaming*[453] passion of dreams and desires. Similarly, the earth, while it is the dry land (אֶרֶץ *'erets*), it means also the *ground*[454] of objectivity on which those dreams manifest their intent.

III ⊙ DAY >>>

1:11-From Minerals to Vegetation

וַיֹּאמֶר אֱלֹהִים תַּדְשֵׁא הָאָרֶץ דֶּשֶׁא עֵשֶׂב מַזְרִיעַ זֶרַע עֵץ פְּרִי עֹשֶׂה פְּרִי לְמִינוֹ אֲשֶׁר זַרְעוֹ־בוֹ עַל־הָאָרֶץ וַיְהִי־כֵן׃ *vayō'mer* (said) *'ĕlōhiym* (Divine-Consciousness) *tadašē'* (let grow) *hā'āreṣ* (the earth) *deše'* (grass) *'ēśeb* (herb) *mazariya'* (sowing) *zera'* (seed) *'ēṣ* (tree) *pariy* (fruit) *'ōśeh* (producing) *pariy* (fruit) *lamiynvō* (of same specie) *'ăšer* (which) *zara'vō* (seed) *bvō* (in itself) *'al* (upon) *hā'āreṣ* (earth) *vayahiy* (was) *kēn* (so)
καὶ *kai* (and) **εἶπεν** *eipen* (said) **ὁ** *o* (the) **θεός** *theos* (God) **βλαστησάτω** *blastēsatō* (lel grow) **ἡ** *ē* (the) **γῆ** *gē* (eart) **βοτάνην** *botanēn* (herb) **χόρτου** *chortou* (feeding-ground) **σπεῖρον** *speiron* (plant) **σπέρμα** *sperma* (seed) **κατὰ** *kata* (down) **γένος** *genos* (kind) **καὶ** *kai* (and) **καθ'** *kath'* (down) **ὁμοιότητα** *omoiotēta* (likeness) **καὶ** *kai* (and) **ξύλον** *xulon* (tree) **κάρπιμον** *karpimon* (fruitful) **ποιοῦν** *poioun* (making) **καρπόν** *karpon* (fruit) **οὗ** *ou* (thus) **τὸ** *to* (the) **σπέρμα** *sperma* (seed) **αὐτοῦ** *autou* (whose) **ἐν** *en* (in) **αὐτῷ** *auto* (it) **κατὰ** *kata* (according to) **γένος** *genos* (kind) **ἐπὶ** *epi* (on) **τῆς** *tēs* (the) **γῆς** *gēs* (earth) **καὶ** *kai* (and) **ἐγένετο** *egeneto* (became) **οὕτως** *outos* (so)
et (and) ***ait*** (said) ***germinet*** (let sprout) ***terra*** (the earth) ***herbam*** (grass) ***virentem*** (flourishing) ***et*** (and) ***facientem*** (producing) ***semen*** (seed) ***et*** (and) ***lignum*** (tree) ***pomiferum*** (fruitful) ***faciens*** (making) ***fructum*** (fruit) ***iuxta*** (according) ***genus*** (species) ***suum*** (own) ***cuius*** (which) ***semen*** (seed) ***in*** (in) ***semet*** (seed) ***ipso*** (same) ***sit*** (be) ***super*** (on) ***terram*** (the earth) ***et*** (and) ***factum*** (done) ***est*** (was) ***ita*** (so)
And God said, Let the earth bring forth grass, the herb yielding seed, *and* the fruit tree yielding fruit after his kind, whose seed *is* in it, upon the earth: and it was so.
And Divine-Consciousness commanded, "*Let the earth grow grass, pasture producing seed, and fruit tree bearing fruit of its own species, whose seed is in-itself, on the earth.*" Therefore, it was so.

Something original and different happens now. Divine-Consciousness projects a new command, an innovative consciousness. From the *fluidity* of thoughts, the ideas sprout as objective earth-concreteness. Furthermore, that physical inertness must *bring forth* (*dasha*)[455] and produce organic *vegetation* (*deshe'*),[456] which becomes *herb* (*'eseb*)[457] meaning *the green object shining* with the reflecting light of Consciousness. Further, this new object must have *in-itself* (*bvō* בו) its own *reproducing* (*zara '*)[458] *semen* (*zera '*).[459] This semen must be the same ideal seed, which produced that objectivity in the first place. Once materialized, the objects multiply and interact. Therefore, the non-organic mineral earth generates metaphoric and organic *trees*[460]⇨ capable of reseeding themselves.[461] They produce *fruits of actions* (*pĕriy*).[462] These fruits, like computer programs, *firmly*[463] establish *exponential offspring-increases* (*parah*),[464] each one, *again reproducing*[465] new connecting actions and so on. This flora is a metaphor of the highly complex nervous systems of any creature, with all its neuronal circuits, proteins, synapses, genes, cells and sophisticated brain. The proof that herb, [466]⇨ grass and trees, here, are pure metaphors of the epistemic processes is that the creation of the sun will take place only the next day of creation. Therefore, the absence of the Sun, on this day, would impede the process of photosynthesis by which plants convert light into energy and grow (דשא *dasha*).

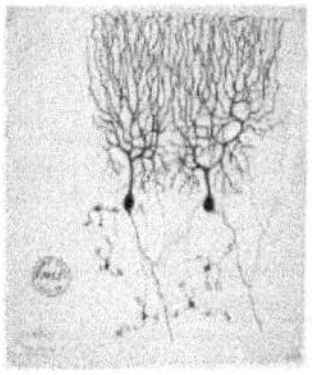

III ⊙ DAY >>>>

1:12-The Vegetative Life Acknowledged

וַתּוֹצֵא הָאָרֶץ דֶּשֶׁא עֵשֶׂב מַזְרִיעַ זֶרַע לְמִינֵהוּ וְעֵץ עֹשֶׂה־פְּרִי אֲשֶׁר זַרְעוֹ־בוֹ לְמִינֵהוּ וַיַּרְא אֱלֹהִים כִּי־טוֹב׃ *vatvōṣē'* (produced) *hā'āreṣ* (the earth) *deše'* (grass) *'ēśeb* (herb) *mazariya'* (sowing) *zera'* (seed) *lamiynēhu* (of the same kind) *va'ēṣ* (tree) *'ōśeh* (producing) *pariy* (fruit) *'ăšer* (which) *zara'vō* (seed) *bvō* (in itself) *lamiynēhu* (of the same kind) *vayara'* (saw) *'ĕlōhiym* (Divine-Consciousness) *kiy* (that) *ṭvōb* (good)
καὶ *kai* (and) **ἐξήνεγκεν** *exēnenken* (produced) **ἡ** *ē* (the) **γῆ** *gē* (earth) **βοτάνην** *botanēn* (herb) **χόρτου** *chortou* (feeding-ground) **σπεῖρον** *speiron* (plant) **σπέρμα** *sperma* (seed) **κατὰ** *kata* (down) **γένος** *genos* (kind) **καὶ** *kai* (and) **καθ'** *kath'* (down) **ὁμοιότητα** *omoiotēta* (likeness) **καὶ** *kai* (and) **ξύλον** *xulon* (tree) **κάρπιμον** *karpimon* (fruitful) **ποιοῦν** *poioun* (making) **καρπόν** *karpon* (fruit) **οὗ** *ou* (thus) **τὸ** *to* (the) **σπέρμα** *sperma* (seed) **αὐτοῦ** *autou* (whose) **ἐν** *en* (in) **αὐτῷ** *auto* (it) **κατὰ** *kata* (according to) **γένος** *genos* (kind) **ἐπὶ** *epi* (on) **τῆς** *tēs* (the) **γῆς** *gēs* (earth) **καὶ** *kai* (and) **εἶδεν** *eideno* (saw) **ὁ** *o* (the) **θεὸς** *theos* (God) **ὅτι** *oti* (thus) **καλόν** *kalon* (good)
et (and) ***protulit*** (produced) ***terra*** (the earth) ***herbam*** (grass) ***virentem*** (flourishing) ***et*** (and) ***adferentem*** (bringing) ***semen*** (seed)) ***iuxta*** (according) ***genus*** (species) ***suum*** (own) ***lignum-*** (tree)***que*** (and) ***faciens*** (making) ***fructum*** (fruit) ***et*** (and) ***habens*** (having) ***unumquodque*** (each one) ***sementem*** (seed) ***secundum*** (according to) ***speciem*** (specie) ***suam*** (own) ***et*** (and) ***vidit*** (saw) ***Deus*** (God) ***quod*** (that) ***esset*** (was) ***bonum*** (good)
And the earth brought forth grass, *and* herb yielding seed after his kind, and the tree yielding fruit, whose seed *was* in itself, after his kind: and God saw that *it was* good.
Consequently, the earth grew grass and the pasture herb producing seed according to its own kind and trees bearing fruit of its own species whose seed is in-themselves. Therefore, Divine-Consciousness intentionally saw that it was beautiful.

Following the creative intentionality, Divine-Consciousness saw, on the overall horizon of Consciousness, organic plant-life sprouting out from the non-organic world. Therefore, He was conscious that it was good and beautiful.

"That is what you see when you look from stillness without thought."[467]

It is this Consciousness that is good and beautiful. The goodness of it derives from its Pure Consciousness. Namely, it is a Consciousness that does not identify with the object created, nor is attached to it by desire. It only puts it into the serene contemplation of it. After which the consciousness-*of*-it takes place.

However, in those objects

"*there were seminal agents and there were increasing powers.*"[468]

They are the seminal agents of the object *in-itself* (*b̲vō* בוֹ). Plotinus calls them,

"*seminal* (*spermatikoí*) *reasons* (*lógoi*)."[469]

They are the potential seeds that actualize the object, the *psyche-sperm* of Plato,[470] the ideal creative seed of God that remains in the creature,

"*Whosoever is born of God doth not commit sin; for his seed* (σπέρμα *sperma*) *remaineth in him.*"[471]

III ⊙ DAY <

1:13-End of the Third Day of Creation: Individual-Consciousness

וַיְהִי־עֶרֶב וַיְהִי־בֹקֶר יוֹם שְׁלִישִׁי׃ פ
vayahiy (is) *ʽereb̲* (evening) *vayahiy* (is) *b̲ōqer* (morning) *yvōm* (day) *šaliyšiy* (third) *p̄* (.)
καὶ *kai* (and) **ἐγένετο** *egeneto* (arose) **ἑσπέρα** *espera* (evening) **καὶ** *kai* (and) **ἐγένετο** *egeneto* (arose) **πρωί** *prōi* (in the morning) **ἡμέρα** *ēmera* (day) **τρίτη** *tritē* (third)
Factum-(done)***que*** (and) ***est*** (is) ***vespere*** (evening) ***et*** (and) ***mane*** (morning) ***dies*** (day) ***tertius*** (third)
And the evening and the morning were the third day.
This was the evening and morning of the third day.

In the descending process of creative hypostases, the third day is the **Heart of Renewal**.

"*A new heart also will I give you, and a new spirit will I put within you: and I will take away the stony heart out of your flesh, and I will give you an heart of flesh.*"[472]

The physical world has changed. The Light of Consciousness reveals the inorganic physical materiality, which, in turn, produces organic reproductive life. This day concludes the third level of consciousness, the consciousness-*of* this physical world.

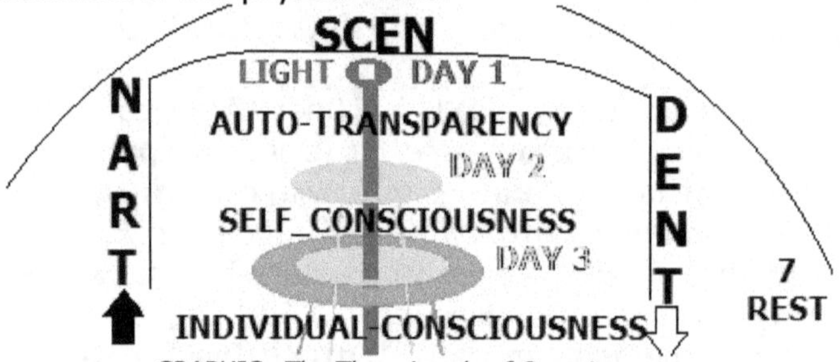

GRAPHIC: *The Three Levels of Consciousness*

1) The first level of consciousness is Auto-Transparency, Pure Consciousness and the Light of Light, as in the state of dreamless sleep.
2) The second level of consciousness is I-Consciousness, the thought of thought thinking itself as thought, as in the state of dream.
3) The third level of consciousness is Ego-Consciousness, the individual psychophysical-consciousness-*of* this world, as in the state of wakefulness.

The *roaring foaming* passionate fluid *sea* of dream images grows and renews in the waking *ground* of experience

> IV ⊙ DAY >

1:14-Start of the Fourth Day of Creation: Radiant Power

וַיֹּאמֶר אֱלֹהִים יְהִי מְאֹרֹת בִּרְקִיעַ הַשָּׁמַיִם לְהַבְדִּיל בֵּין הַיּוֹם וּבֵין הַלָּיְלָה וְהָיוּ לְאֹתֹת וּלְמוֹעֲדִים וּלְיָמִים וְשָׁנִים׃
vayōʼmer (said) *ʼĕlōhiym* (Divine-Consciousness) *yahiy* (let be) *maʼōrōt̲* (luminary) *biraqiyaʽ* (firmament) *hašāmayim* (sky above) *lahab̲adiyl* (separate) *bēyn* (between) *hayvōm* (day) *ub̲ēyn* (between) *halāyalāh* (the night) *vahāyu* (be) *laʼōt̲ōt̲* (sign) *ulamvōʽăd̲iym* (for seasons) *ulayāmiym* (for day) *vašāniym* (for year)

καὶ *kai* (and) **εἶπεν** *eipen* (said) **ὁ** *o* (the) **θεός** *theos* (God) **γενηθήτωσαν** *genēthētōsan* (let there be) **φωστῆρες** *phōstēres* (luminaries) **ἐν** *en* (in) **τῷ** *tō* (the) **στερεώματι** *stereōmati* (firmament) **τοῦ** *tou* (of the) **οὐρανοῦ** *ouranou* (sky) **εἰς** *eis* (into) **φαῦσιν** *phausin* (light) **τῆς** *tēs* (the) **γῆς** *gēs* (earth) **τοῦ** *tou* (the) **διαχωρίζειν** *dischōrizein* (disjoin) **ἀνὰ** *ana* (then) **μέσον** *meson* (in the middle) **τῆς** *tēs* (the) **ἡμέρας** *ēmeras* (days) **καὶ** *kai* (and) **ἀνὰ** *ana* (then) **μέσον** *meson* (in the middle) **τῆς** *tēs* (the) **νυκτὸς** *nuktos* (night) **καὶ** *kai* (and) **ἔστωσαν** *estōsan* (to be) **εἰς** *eis* (into) **σημεῖα** *sēmeia* (sign) **καὶ** *kai* (and) **εἰς** *eis* (into) **καιροὺς** *kairous* (season) **καὶ** *kai* (and) **εἰς** *eis* (into) **ἡμέρας** *ēmeras* (days) **καὶ** *kai* (and) **εἰς** *eis* (into) **ἐνιαυτοὺς** *enisautous* (years)
dixit (said) ***autem*** (also) ***Deus*** (God) ***fiant*** (let there be) ***luminaria*** (luminary) ***in*** (in) ***firmamento*** (firmament) ***caeli*** (of the sky) ***ut*** (so that) ***dividant*** (be divided) ***diem*** (the day) ***ac*** (from) ***noctem*** (the night) ***et*** (and) ***sint*** (let be) ***in*** (for) ***signa*** (signs) ***et*** (and) ***tempora*** (seasons) ***et*** (and) ***dies*** (days) ***et*** (and) ***annos*** (years)
And God said, Let there be lights in the firmament of the heaven to divide the day from the night; and let them be for signs, and for seasons, and for days, and years:
Also Divine-Consciousness said, "*Let lights be in the depth of the sky so that the day and night could be divided and they are for signs, for seasons, for days and for years.*

As we have analyzed, the Day of Creation connotes *only circularity* as such. Now, however, we acknowledge the creation of luminaries (מָאוֹר *ma'owr*)[473] in the sky. From the internal structure of the subject, we move to the external formation of the object. Only now, we can denote the day as a 24 hours period or as the rotation of a planet on itself and the year as the revolution around its star. These new lights are like candlesticks (מָאוֹר *ma'owr*)[474] compared to the *Light* (אוֹר *'owr*)[475] *of Consciousness* created in the First Day. In fact, the blind do not see the sun shining over them. The physical heavenly lights are only a reflection of the Light of Consciousness, without which, we would not see those astronomic luminaries. The light of Consciousness, then, becomes the midnight sun,[476] an *unseen* Light[477] illuminating everything. The new celestial lights have the power to spell out, measure and regulate time as we presently calculate it. This computation brings into existence the physical daytime, as we understand it. Therefore, Creation is the way we know the *external* object as this physical cosmos in all its articulations and the way we understand it according its geometrical/mathematical language.

This confirms that the Day of Creation does not refer to the current cycle of time, as we experience it. That Day is only a metaphor for the intrinsic Circularity of the Light of Consciousness. The mind forgetting the Circular-Conscious-Light, fixes its consciousness-*on* the object. The object, in turn, reflects that Conscious-Light that seems to lose Its Originality. From the perspective of the conscious mind, this results in:

1) an *impoverishment* of Pure-Conciseness, which, in Itself, can never impoverish, and
2) a *loss* of the Creative Act, which, in Itself, by definition, can never be lost.

Consequently, while Pure-Consciousness timelessly creates, the consciousness-*of* places objects into time. Thus, we conceive Creation as a historical act separated from the epistemic process. Then, we seek to exercise a controlling power over the object, which we call *yada'*,[478] knowledge, an euphemism for intercourse.

IV ⊙ DAY >>

1:15-Earth's reflected light

וְהָיוּ לִמְאוֹרֹת בִּרְקִיעַ הַשָּׁמַיִם לְהָאִיר עַל־הָאָרֶץ וַיְהִי־כֵן׃
vahāyu (let be) *lima'vōrōt* (luminary) *biraqiya'* (firmament) *hašāmayim* (sky) *lahā'iyr* (shine) *'al* (on) *hā'āreṣ* (earth) *vayahiy* (it was) *kēn* (so)
καὶ *kai* (and) **ἔστωσαν** *estōsan* (let be) **εἰς** *eis* (into) **φαῦσιν** *phausin* (lights) **ἐν** *en* (in) **τῷ** *tō* (the) **στερεώματι** *stereōmati* (firmament) **τοῦ** *tou* (of the) **οὐρανοῦ** *ouranou* (sky) **ὥστε** *ōste* (just) **φαίνειν** *phainein* (to enlighten) **ἐπὶ** *epi* (on) **τῆς** *tēs* (the) **γῆς** *gēs* (earth) **καὶ** *kai* (and) **ἐγένετο** *egeneto* (it came to be) **οὕτως** *outōs* (so)

ut (thus) ***luceant*** (let them shine) ***in*** (in) ***firmamento*** (the firmament) ***caeli*** (of the sky) ***et*** (and) ***inluminent*** (let them illuminate) ***terram*** (the earth) ***et*** (and) ***factum*** (done) ***est*** (is) ***ita*** (so)
And let them be for lights in the firmament of the heaven to give light upon the earth: and it was so.
Let them shine in the firmament of the sky and let them illuminate the Earth." Therefore, it was so.

Then, on the Earth's dimension, these physical lights (מָאוֹר *ma'owr*) become reflected lights. They become lights-enlightened by the Light of Consciousness. In fact, how could we mention the lights of the sky if we were not conscious of them? The Day of Creation is the circularity of Consciousness' Light. In-Itself, this Circularity reaches itself as the middle of its own centrality. However, when that circularity illuminates the object, *viz.* the Earth, *then,* its own centrality is missed and the creative process continues searching for Its Own Centrality. In other words, when the Circularity reaches and lights up the object, then it catches itself as that object. This last one is not its center from which Consciousness Originated and wants to establish its dominion over it. Thus, the Circularity continues incessantly until it recognizes its own original centrality. Therefore, the whole Process of Creation becomes the Course of Self-Consciousness Itself.

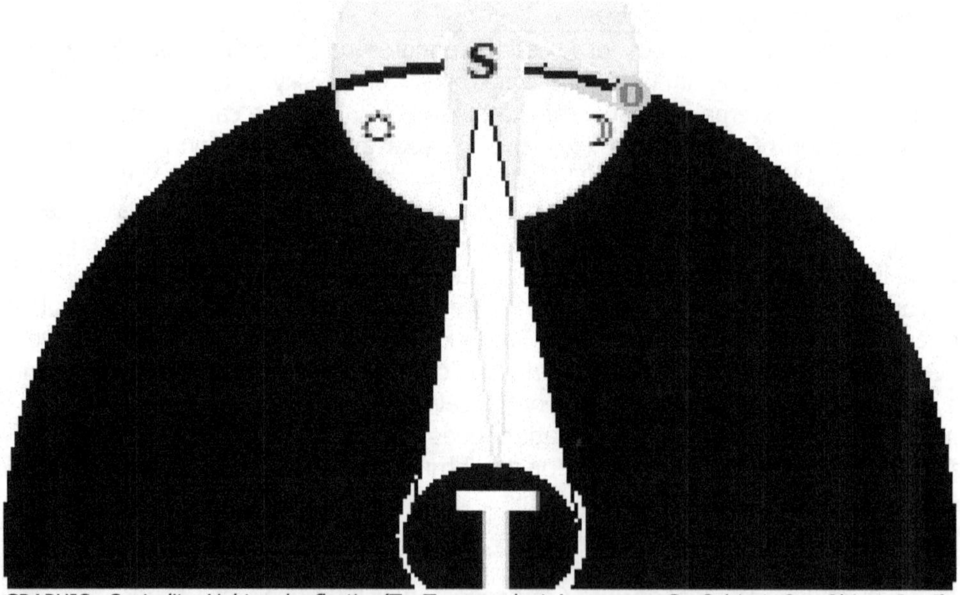

GRAPHIC: *Centrality, Light and reflection* (**T**= Transcendent-Awareness, **S**= Subject, O = Object, I = I)

IV ⊙ DAY >>>

1:16-The Subject as Sun and the Object as Moon

וַיַּעַשׂ אֱלֹהִים אֶת־שְׁנֵי הַמְּאֹרֹת הַגְּדֹלִים אֶת־הַמָּאוֹר הַגָּדֹל לְמֶמְשֶׁלֶת הַיּוֹם וְאֶת־הַמָּאוֹר הַקָּטֹן לְמֶמְשֶׁלֶת הַלַּיְלָה וְאֵת הַכּוֹכָבִים׃ *vaya'aś* (made) *'ĕlōhiym* (Divine-Consciousness) *'et̲* (the) *šanēy* (two) *hama'ōrōt̲* (luminaries) *hagad̲ōliym* (great) *'et̲* (and) *hamā'vōr* (light) *hagād̲ōl* (greatest) *lamemašelet̲* (rule) *hayvōm* (day) *va'et̲* (and) *hamā'vōr* (light) *haqāṭōn* (smaller) *lamemašelet̲* (rule) *halayalāh* (the night) *va'ēt̲* (and) *hakvōk̲āb̲iym* (star)
καὶ *kai* (and) **ἐποίησεν** *epoiēsen* (made) **ὁ** *o* (the) **θεὸς** *theos* (God) **τοὺς** *tous* (the) **δύο** *duo* (two) **φωστῆρας** *phōstēras* (lights) **τοὺς** *tous* (the) **μεγάλους** *megalos* (great) **τὸν** *ton* (the) **φωστῆρα** *phōstēra* (light) **τὸν** *tov* (the) **μέγαν** *megan* (great) **εἰς** *eis* (into) **ἀρχὰς** *archas* (rule) **τῆς** *tēs* (the) **ἡμέρας** *ēmers* (day) **καὶ** *kai* (and) **τὸν** *ton* (the) **φωστῆρα** *phōstēra* (light) **τὸν** *ton* (the) **ἐλάσσω** *elassō* (minor) **εἰς** *eis* (into) **ἀρχὰς** *archas* (rule) **τῆς** *tēs* (the) **νυκτός** *nuktos* (night) **καὶ** *kai* (and) **τοὺς** *tous* (the) **ἀστέρας** *asteras* (stars)

fecit-(made)***que*** (and) ***deus*** (God) ***duo*** (two) ***magna*** (great) ***luminaria*** (luminaries) ***luminare*** (the luminary) ***maius*** (major) ***ut*** (so that) ***praeesset*** (it presided) ***diei*** (the day) ***et*** (and) ***luminare*** (the luminary) ***minus*** (minor) ***ut*** (so that) ***praeesset*** (it presided) ***nocti*** (the night) ***et*** (and) ***stellas*** (the stars)	
And God made two great lights; the greater light to rule the day, and the lesser light to rule the night: he made the stars also.	
Furthermore, Divine-Consciousness made two great lights, 1) the greater light [the Subject/Sun], to rule over the subjectivity/day, and 2) the lesser light [the Object/Moon], to rule over the objectivity/night and made also all the objects-stars.	

A literal reader would have to decide if the sun, mentioned here, is the one illuminating this Earth or Kepler-452b, the NASA's newly discovered earth-like planet 1400 light year away.[479]

Nevertheless, to understand the universality of this verse we must consider the fundamental polarities of the epistemic process and the manner in which we know. Two aspects proceed from Divine-Consciousness,

1) the subjective-knower, metaphorically the *Sun*, and
2) the objective-known, metaphorically the *Moon*.

Nobody can know without the subject-knower. Nothing can be known without the object-known. Sun/Knower and Moon/known are the allegorical dichotomy of day and night. None of the two can be without the other. We call the knower, SUBJECT,[480] and the known, OBJECT.[481] Both are metaphoric lights. They refer to the logical structure of the process of knowledge in general. To confirm this rendering, *Genesis* does not name them *sun* (שֶׁמֶשׁ *shemesh)* or *moon* (יָרֵחַ *yareach)*. They will be mentioned, as such, only much later.[482] However, they neither are mentioned as subject nor object. The text calls these two as the greater (גָּדוֹל *qadowl*)[483] and the lesser (קָטָן *qatan*)[484] '*lights*' (מָאוֹר *ma'owr*). They are named as the greater light, *gadal* (גָּדַל), meaning *binding together*, and the lesser one, *quwt* (קוּט), meaning that *can be cut of* and segmented.

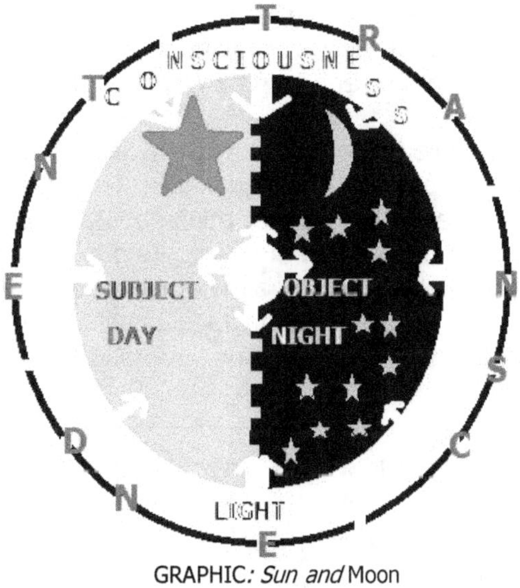

GRAPHIC*: Sun and* Moon

Following the metaphor, if we take away the Sun, we have darkness and the Moon cannot be seen. If we take away the Moon, the Sun cannot shine on it. The Sun brightens up the Moon and this one reflects back its light on the Ocean of possibilities. Similarly, the Subject illuminates the Object and this one reflects that light back into the Subject. The Subject *com*prehends that reflected light and, thus, knowledge takes place. We have, therefore, an *epistemic circularity*, *viz.* a *day*, by which the subject-knower perceives the object-known. In return, the object projects back into the subject, thus concluding

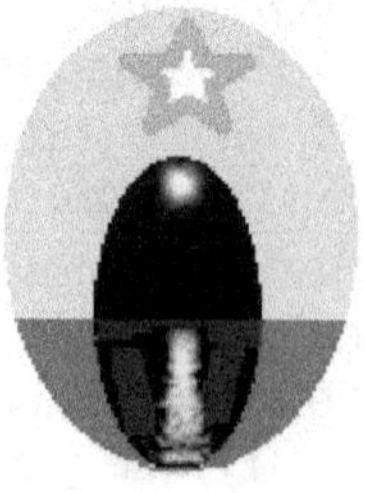

the circle of knowledge. As the function of the eye is to see, so the daylight enables seeing. Thus, the daytime is a metaphor for conscious subjectivity,[485] *viz.* the field of the subject, which is the essential light of knowledge. As the eye cannot see in darkness, so the night impedes seeing. Thus, the nighttime is a metaphor for the obscure impenetrability of objectivity,[486] *viz.* the field of the object, until it is illuminated. Then, the metaphoric *stars-objects* become visible to the subject-knower. In fact, *star, kowkab,*[487] means the *builder* who *heaps up, kabbown,*[488] the objective construction of the *scorching, kavah,*[489] world.

IV ⊙ DAY >>>>

1:17-The Light of the World

וַיִּתֵּן אֹתָם אֱלֹהִים בִּרְקִיעַ הַשָּׁמָיִם לְהָאִיר עַל־הָאָרֶץ׃ *vayitēn* (put) *'ōṯām* (them) *'ĕlōhiym* (Divine-Consciousness) *biraqiya`* (firmament) *hašāmāyim* (heaven) *lahā`iyr* (to give light) *`al* (upon) *hā'āreṣ* (earth)
καὶ *kai* (and) **ἔθετο** *etheto* (placed) **αὐτοὺς** *autos* (them) **ὁ** *o* (the) **θεὸς** *theos* (God) **ἐν** *en* (in) **τῷ** *tō* (the) **στερεώματι** *stereōmati* (firmament) **τοῦ** *tou* (of the) **οὐρανοῦ** *ouranou* (sky) **ὥστε** *ōste* (to) **φαίνειν** *phainein* (bring light) **ἐπὶ** *epi* (over) **τῆς** *tēs* (the) **γῆς** *gēs* (earth)
et (and) ***posuit*** (placed) ***eas*** (them) ***in*** (in) ***firmamento*** (the firmament) ***caeli*** (of the sky) ***ut*** (so that) ***lucerent*** (they may give light) ***super*** (over) ***terram*** (the earth)
And God set them in the firmament of the heaven to give light upon the earth,
Divine-Consciousness placed them in the firmament of the sky so that they may give light to the earth.

Divine-Consciousness places the epistemic faculties of the Subject -as Sun- and the Object -as Moon- in a logical *a-priori* sky. Metaphorically, that height is indicated as the *fundamental-firmament* (רקיע raqiya`) of the allegorical *epistemic-sky* (שָׁמַיִם shamayim). All earthly (אֶרֶץ 'erets) events take place under the firmament. This sky, obviously, must precede them all. Divine-Consciousness is the breath of Consciousness that manifests Itself by structuring the epistemic-faculties. At this level, these are not the individualized faculties of any I or of this conceived ego. They are, instead, the intrinsic structure of the light (אור 'owr) of consciousness in-itself. In turn, it manifests itself in each individual sentient being in accordance with its species. The Eternal Present *starts the beginning* of the universal state *preceding* the Big Bang or any dreamless state of mind.

We must understand that, while these verses synthetically render the universal consciousness in its fullness, on the contrary, our description of it is inadequate. The light of consciousness is the absolute essential prerequisite for every experience. We cannot think about it without its thought being something different from it. However, we cannot negate it without negating experience itself. Those lights make the experience of the objective world possible. In fact, as without eyes we cannot see the light of a million suns and moons, so, without the light of the epistemic faculties of the I-subject there is no experience of the world-object. For the human, the I is the metaphoric sun and the me is the moon, the synthesis of both lights leads to knowledge.

~~~~~~

As an example, when we look in a mirror, there are two distinct entwined circular moments,

1) *the shining-I, the Subject as the Sun and*
2) *the reflected-me, the Object as the Moon.* [490]⇨

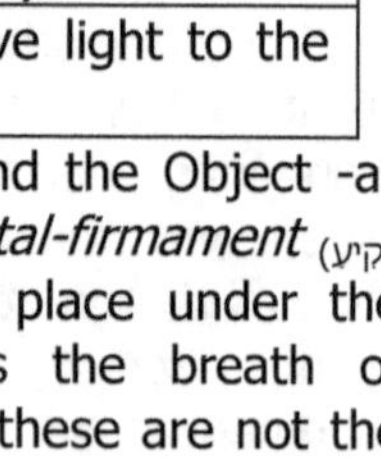

Obviously, the reflected-me is the immanent image for-the-I to see ***for-itself****. That image is not the shining-I as it is* ***in-itself*** *when not reflecting. In fact, I cannot see me without a mirror. Therefore, to explain the metaphor, the earth is the mirror on which the sunny on-looking-I observes, photographs and reflects its own image.*
~~~~~~

IV ⊙ DAY >>>>>

1:18-Power over the Earth

וְלִמְשֹׁל בַּיּוֹם וּבַלַּיְלָה וּלֲהַבְדִּיל בֵּין הָאוֹר וּבֵין הַחֹשֶׁךְ וַיַּרְא אֱלֹהִים כִּי־טוֹב׃ *valimašōl* (to rule) *bayvōm* (day) *ubalayalāh* (the night) *ulăhabadiyl* (to divide) *bēyn* (between) *hā'vōr* (day light) *ubēyn* (between) *haḥōšeka* (darkness) *vayara'* (perceived) *'ĕlōhiym* (Divine-Consciousness) *kiy* (that) *ṭvōb* (good)
καὶ *kai* (and) **ἄρχειν** *archein* (to rule) **τῆς** *tēs* (the) **ἡμέρας** *ēmeras* (day) **καὶ** *kai* (and) **τῆς** *tēs* (the) **νυκτὸς** *nuctos* (night) **καὶ** *kai* (and) **διαχωρίζειν** *diachōrizein* (to divide) **ἀνὰ** *ana* (between) **μέσον** *meson* (middle) **τοῦ** *tou* (of the) **φωτὸς** *photos* (light) **καὶ** *kai* (and) **ἀνὰ** *ana* (between) **μέσον** *meson* (middle) **τοῦ** *tou* (of the) **σκότους** *skotous* (darkness) **καὶ** *kai* (and) **εἶδεν** *eiden* (saw) **ὁ** *o* (the) **θεὸς** *theos* (God) **ὅτι** *oti* (that) **καλόν** *kalon* (good)
et (and) ***praeessent*** (preside) ***diei*** (day) ***ac*** (and) ***nocti*** (night) ***et*** (and) ***dividerent*** (be divided) ***lucem*** (light) ***ac*** (from) ***tenebras*** (darkness) ***et*** (and) ***vidit*** (divided) ***Deus*** (God) ***quod*** (that) ***esset*** (was) ***bonum*** (good)
And to rule over the day and over the night, and to divide the light from the darkness: and God saw that it was good.
Thus, to have power over the daily-subjectivity and over the nightly-objectivity, the light-subject was divided from the dark-object. And Divine-Consciousness was conscious that it was good and beautiful.

This verse validates the epistemological reading of *Genesis*. The way the mind works is the way we know the world. Namely, knowledge takes place through an *a-priori* synthesis of objective matter with the I, the transcendental subject. Here, the term transcendental is used in a Kantian sense, *i.e.*:

"the manner in which objects are known, as this is possible *a-priori*,"[491]

meaning that the 'I-subject' can be logically distinguished from its object, but never actually separated from it.

This verse describes the **field of power** and rulership over the world. In fact, the Hebrew verb *mashal*[492] (*to rule*), means also, *to assimilate* and *to make-it-like*. Therefore, this term, implies that the *creative power* (*bara'*)[493] of the *Divine Mind rules* as logical order to the world, *assimilates*, ingesting the object of knowledge, and *makes-like* a synthesis of the object and the subject.[494]

In the circular field or sphere of the fourth Day of Creation, the world is *assimilated* or *made-like* the ruling mind *of the Subject, the Knower*. Namely, it is the control exercised by the *Subject-sun-light* over the day and by the *light-reflecting-Object-moon-over* the dull night of objects. The power of this level will invest humans with the rule to exercise dominium over the whole world. This powerful rulership will shape the individuals and will spill over in the constant struggle, *jihād* (جهاد)[495] within society. Therefore, in this descending process of creative hypostases, the fourth day institutes the **Heart Center of Power**.

IV ⊙ DAY <

1:19-End of the Fourth Day of Creation: Rulership

וַיְהִי־עֶרֶב וַיְהִי־בֹקֶר יוֹם רְבִיעִי׃ פ *vayahiy* (became) *'ereb* (evening) *vayahiy* (came to pass) *bōqer* (morning) *yvōm* (day) *rabiy'iy* (fourth) *p̄* (.)
καὶ *kai* (and) **ἐγένετο** *egeneto* (arose) **ἑσπέρα** *espera* (evening) **καὶ** *kai* (and) **ἐγένετο** *egeneto* (arose) **πρωί** *prōi* (morning) **ἡμέρα** *ēmera* (day) **τετάρτη** *tetartē* (fourth)
et (and) ***factum*** (done) ***est*** (was) ***vespere*** (the evening) ***et*** (and) ***mane*** (morning) ***dies*** (day) ***quartus*** (fourth)
And the evening and the morning were the fourth day.
This was the evening and morning of the fourth day.

The term *`arab* (עָרַב) means *obscurity* and *cover*. Therefore, before discerning anything, *obscurity* (עָרַב *`arab*) with its *texture covers* and *becomes surety* (עָרַב *`arab*)[496] for all experiences. The *dark evening* (עֶרֶב *`ereb*)[497] precedes *dawn* (בֹּקֶר *boqer*)[498] as *end of night*. Explicitly, the object, obtuse in itself, reaches *intelligibility* (בָּקַר *baqar*)[499] upon completing the circular day of knowledge, *viz.* from darkness to light. Then, consciousness completes its circular day by reflecting on to the object its quality of light and beauty. This concludes the fourth Day of Creation.

Astrophysical light, as Subject/Object reflection of Consciousness, measures time, space and causality.

> V ○ DAY >

1:20-Start of the Fifth Day of Creation: Biological Multiplication

וַיֹּאמֶר אֱלֹהִים יִשְׁרְצוּ הַמַּיִם שֶׁרֶץ נֶפֶשׁ חַיָּה וְעוֹף יְעוֹפֵף עַל־הָאָרֶץ עַל־פְּנֵי רְקִיעַ הַשָּׁמָיִם׃

vayō'mer (said) *'ĕlōhiym* (Divine-Consciousness) *yišarașu* (multiply) *hamayim* (waters) *šereș* (swarmer) *nep̄eš* (creatures) *ḥayāh* (living) *va'vōp̄* (birds) *ya'vōp̄ēp̄* (flying) *'al* (over) *hā'āreș* (earth) *'al* (on) *panēy* (corner) *raqiya'* (expanse) *hašāmāyim* (sky)

καὶ *kai* (and) **εἶπεν** *eipen* (said) **ὁ** *o* (the) **θεός** *theos* (God) **ἐξαγαγέτω** *exagagetō* (let bring forth) **τὰ** *ta* (the) **ὕδατα** *udata* (waters) **ἑρπετὰ** *erpeta* (crawling) **ψυχῶν** *psuchōn* (creature) **ζωσῶν** *zōsōn* (living) **καὶ** *kai* (and) **πετεινὰ** *peteiva* (bird) **πετόμενα** *petomena* (to fly) **ἐπὶ** *epi* (on) **τῆς** *tēs* (the) **γῆς** *gēs* (earth) **κατὰ** *kata* (under) **τὸ** *to* (the) **στερέωμα** *stereōma* (firmament) **τοῦ** *tou* (of the) **οὐρανοῦ** *ouranou* (sky) **καὶ** *kai* (and) **ἐγένετο** *egeneto* (it became) **οὕτως** *outōs* (so)

dixit (said) ***etiam*** (also) ***Deus*** (God) ***producant*** (let produce) ***aquae*** (the waters) ***reptile*** (crawling) ***animae*** (animals) ***viventis*** (living) ***et*** (and) ***volatile*** (flying) ***super*** (over) ***terram*** (the earth) ***sub*** (under) ***firmamento*** (the firmament) ***caeli*** (of the sky)

And God said, Let the waters bring forth abundantly the moving creature that hath life, and fowl that may fly above the earth in the open firmament of heaven.

Furthermore, Divine-Consciousness said,
"*Let the waters multiply living creatures crawling and flying over the earth in the expanse of the sky.*"

As we have seen, all objectiveness springs out from the infinite possibilities named the *secondary waters* producing all different objective living beings. From the watery depth of infinite possibilities, the living faculties of the senses emerge like tentacles reaching out to envelope the objective world. All creatures, including the flying ones, come out from those metaphoric and/or physical waters. The one ocean of pure thought-possibility reflects in each of the infinite individual ideas, which form the actual flowing sea of experience. The ideal level coincides with what takes place on the evolutionary process of the physical realm. If that were not the case, nothing could be known or recorded. Evolution takes place not only on the biological and physical levels, but also on the mental states, which comprehend them. Like in a dream, the faculties of the senses adapt to the multitude of forms springing out and each one implements its own individual impulsiveness.

Furthermore, **this verse describes the process of evolution** not as a preordained design but as the observed multiplication (שָׁרַץ *sharats*)[500] of **random spontaneous acts** of survival of the fittest adapting to its environment.[501] Then, in the physiobiological world, the first aquatic sentient forms (נֶפֶשׁ *nephesh*)[502] that had organic life (חַי *chay*)[503] moved out of the waters (מַיִם *mayim*) seeking their own experiential intention. These are the pristine faculties of the senses, which crawl (שֶׁרֶץ *sherets*)[504] on heights above (עַל *'al*) the objective *earth* (אֶרֶץ *'erets*) and some become airborne (עוֹף *'uwph*)[505] as psychological oneiric faculties.

V ⊙ DAY >>

1:21-The Reproductive Cycle

וַיִּבְרָא אֱלֹהִים אֶת־הַתַּנִּינִם הַגְּדֹלִים וְאֵת כָּל־נֶפֶשׁ הַחַיָּה הָרֹמֶשֶׂת אֲשֶׁר שָׁרְצוּ הַמַּיִם לְמִינֵהֶם וְאֵת כָּל־עוֹף כָּנָף לְמִינֵהוּ וַיַּרְא אֱלֹהִים כִּי־טוֹב׃

vayib̲arā' (created) *'ĕlōhiym* (Divine-Consciousness) *'et̲* (the) *hataniynim* (sea serpents) *hagad̲ōliym* (great) *va'ēt̲* (and the) *nep̄*eš (animals) *'ăšer* (which) *šārașu* (multipy) *hamayim* (waters) *lamiynēhem* (species) *va'ēt̲* (and the) *kāl* (all) *'vōp̄* (birds) kānāp̄ (winged) *lamiynēhu* (kind) *vayara'*

(saw) *'ĕlōhiym* (Divine-Consciousness) *kiy* (that) *ṭvōḇ* (good)
καὶ *kai* (and) **ἐποίησεν** *epoiēsen* (created) **ὁ** *o* (the) **θεὸς** *theos* (God) **τὰ** *ta* (the) **κήτη** *kētē* (whale) **τὰ** *ta* (the) **μεγάλα** *megala* (great) **καὶ** *kai* (and) **πᾶσαν** *pasan* (all) **ψυχὴν** *psuchēn* (living) **ζῴων** *zōōn* (animals) **ἑρπετῶν** *erpetōn* (moving) **ἃ** *a* (that) **ἐξήγαγεν** *ezēgagen* (produced) **τὰ** *ta* (the) **ὕδατα** *udata* (waters) **κατὰ** *kata* (upon) **γένη** *gene* (species) **αὐτῶν** *autōn* (same) **καὶ** *kai* (and) **πᾶν** *pan* (pan) **πετεινὸν** *peteinon* (bird) **πτερωτὸν** *pterōton* (flying) **κατὰ** *kata* (upon) **γένος** *genos* (race) **καὶ** *kai* (and) **εἶδεν** *eiden* (saw) **ὁ** *o* (the) **θεὸς** *theos* (God) **ὅτι** (that) **καλά** *kala* (good)
creavit-(created)***que*** (and) ***Deus*** (God) ***cete*** (whales) ***grandia*** (great) ***et*** (and) ***omnem*** (all) ***animam*** (the animals) ***viventem*** (living) ***atque*** (and) ***motabilem*** (moving) ***quam*** (that) ***produxerant*** (produced) ***aquae*** (the waters) ***in*** (in) ***species*** (species) ***suas*** (their) ***et*** (and) ***omne*** (all) ***volatile*** (flying) ***secundum*** (according to) ***genus*** (kind) ***suum*** (its) ***et*** (and) ***vidit*** (saw) ***Deus*** (God) ***quod*** (that) ***esset*** (it was) ***bonum*** (good)
And God created great whales, and every living creature that moveth, which the waters brought forth abundantly, after their kind, and every winged fowl after his kind: and God saw that it was good.
Subsequently, Divine-Consciousness crated the great sea serpents and all the living and moving beings that the waters produced in abundance after their species and all the flying being according to its kind. Consequently, Divine-Consciousness was conscious of its goodness.

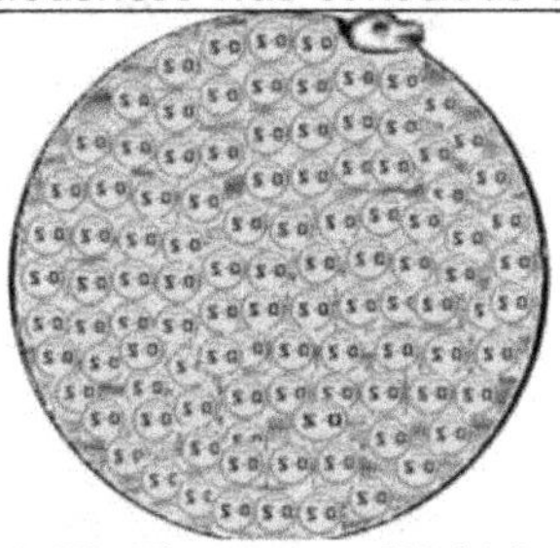

GRAPHIC: *The Waters of Multiplication*

This is the realm of the reproductive cycle, the realm of waters and the domain of all the flowing actual objects of the world of experience. It is like the dark matter on which the cosmos floats or snakes about.[506] It is like a river flooding through the consciousness-*of* perceptions. It is the consciousness-*of* all objectivities. It is intentionality. It is the hunger of the mind for representations. In this dynamic world, the senses like tentacles snake around all objectivities, which multiply before the eyes of Consciousness. This multiplication of individuals is the scanning process of consciousness-*of* aiming to find its own Awareness. It is like an intangible computer software seeking, within Its hardware, to process the power source that activates it.

Metaphorically, the great

"*serpent*[507] *in the* sea (יָם *yam*)... *is the crooked* (עֲקַלָּתוֹן *`aqallathown*) *serpent*."[508]

Like the hermetic symbol of Ouroboros,[509] the crooked or bent serpent is the one biting his own tail. It represents consciousness in its circular process eating itself as well as the consciousness-*of* others. It is like when, at the Pharaoh's presence, Aaron's rod

"*became a serpent* (תַּנִּין *tanniyn)* [which] *swallowed up* ... [the other] *serpent-rods*."[510]

On this day of creation, Divine-Consciousness was positively conscious that the circular production of the biological drive was good and beautiful. Thus, in the world, as such, there is no evil in-itself.

GRAPHIC: *The Bent Serpent*

V ☉ DAY >>>
1:22-Flowing of the Biological Multiplication

וַיְבָרֶךְ אֹתָם אֱלֹהִים לֵאמֹר פְּרוּ וּרְבוּ וּמִלְאוּ אֶת־הַמַּיִם בַּיַּמִּים וְהָעוֹף יִרֶב בָּאָרֶץ׃
vayab̲āreka (blessed) *ʾōt̲ām* (them) *ʾĕlōhiym* (Divine-Consciousness) *lēʾmōr* (saying) *paru* (be fruitful) *urab̲u* (grow) *umilaʾu* (fill) *ʾet̲* (and the) *hamayim* (birds) *yireb̲* (grow) *bāʾāreṣ* (on earth)
καὶ *kai* (and) **ηὐλόγησεν** *ēulogēsen* (blessed) **αὐτὰ** *auta* (them) **ὁ** *o* (the) **Θεὸς** *theos* (God) **λέγων** *legōn* (said) **αὐξάνεσθε** *auxanesthe* (grow) **καὶ** *kai* (and) **πληθύνεσθε** *plēthunesthe* (multiply) **καὶ** *kai* (and) **πληρώσατε** *plērōsate* (replenish) **τὰ** *ta* (the) **ὕδατα** *udata* (waters) **ἐν** *en* (in) **ταῖς** *tais* (of the) **θαλάσσαις** *thalassais* (seas) **καὶ** *kai* (and) **τὰ** *ta* (the) **πετεινὰ** *peteina* (birds) **πληθυνέσθωσαν** *plēthunesthōsan* (let multiply) **ἐπὶ** *epi* (on) **τῆς** *tēs* (the) **γῆς** *gēs* (earth)
benedixit (blessed) ***que*** (and) ***eis*** (them) ***dicens*** (saying) ***crescite*** (grow) ***et*** (and) ***multiplicamini*** (multiply) ***et*** (and) ***replete*** (fill) ***aquas*** (the waters) ***maris*** (of the seas) ***aves-*** (birds) ***que*** (and) ***multiplicentur*** (let them multiply) ***super*** (on) ***terram*** (the earth)
And God blessed them, saying, Be fruitful, and multiply, and fill the waters in the seas, and let fowl multiply in the earth.
Consequently, Divine-Consciousness blessed them by saying, *"Grow and multiply and fill the sea waters and let the birds multiply on earth."*

    In the Subject, the biological multiplying drive continues. Like the exponential speed of computers' technological reproduction, the mind flows multiplying[511] its mental interconnections at the presence of Divine-Consciousness' Approving-Dispassionate-Consciousness. This is the serene observation of the reproducing flowing objects on the river of life.

    Again, our reader may say,
'You always explain every verse with the same returning refrain of the mind's interaction.'
    We reply,
'And you are still engaging your mind while reading this commentary! Realize that, without it, you would not be able to read, accept or reject our epistemic interpretation.'

V ☉ DAY <
1:23-End of the Fifth Day of Creation: Multiplying Impulse

וַיְהִי־עֶרֶב וַיְהִי־בֹקֶר יוֹם חֲמִישִׁי׃ פ
vayahiy (was) *ʿereb̲* (evening) *vayahiy* (was) *b̲ōqer* (morning) *yvōm* (day) *hămiyšiy* (fifth) *p̲* (.)
καὶ *kai* (and) **ἐγένετο** *egeneto* (arose) **ἑσπέρα** *espera* (evening) **καὶ** *kai* (and) **ἐγένετο** *egeneto* (arose) **πρωί** *prōi* (in the morning) **ἡμέρα** *ēmera* (day) **πέμπτη** *pemptē* (fifth)
et (and) ***factum*** (done) ***est*** (was) ***vespere*** (the evening) ***et*** (and) ***mane*** (morning) ***dies*** (day) ***quintus*** (fifth)
And the evening and the morning were the fifth day.
The evening and the morning concluded of the fifth day.

    The evening is the objective aspect closing the ring of knowledge. The morning is the intentioning subjective aspect starting the cycle of knowledge. Both conclude the fifth descending circularity of consciousness in which the **field of the biological multiplying impulse** pops into existence.

Life multiplies from and within this ocean of conceptual scanning for its own origin.

> VI ⊙ DAY >

1:24-Start of the Sixth Day of Creation: Life

וַיֹּאמֶר אֱלֹהִים תּוֹצֵא הָאָרֶץ נֶפֶשׁ חַיָּה לְמִינָהּ בְּהֵמָה וָרֶמֶשׂ וְחַיְתוֹ־אֶרֶץ לְמִינָהּ וַיְהִי־כֵן׃
vayō'mer (said) *'ĕlōhiym* (Divine-Consciousness) *tvōṣē* (go forth from) *hā'āreṣ* (earth) *nep̄eš* (animals) *ḥayāh* (living) *lamiynāh* (species) *bahēmāh* (cattle) *vāremeś* (creeping things) *vaḥayat̲vō* (beasts) *'ereṣ* (of the land) *lamiynāh* (species) *vayahiy* (was) *k̲ēn* (thus)
καὶ *kai* (and) **εἶπεν** *eipen* (said) **ὁ** *o* (the) **θεός** *theos* (God) **ἐξαγαγέτω** *exagagetō* (let bring forth) **ἡ** *ē* (the) **γῆ** *gē* (earth) **ψυχὴν** *psuchēn* (living) **ζῶσαν** *zōsan* (animals) **κατὰ** *kata* (according to) **γένος** *genos* (species) **τετράποδα** *tetrapanoda* (cattle) **καὶ** *kai* (and) **ἑρπετὰ** *erpeta* (serpents) **καὶ** *kai* (and) **θηρία** *thēria* (beasts) **τῆς** *tēs* (of the) **γῆς** *gēs* (earth) **κατὰ** *kata* (according to) **γένος** *genos* (kind) **καὶ** *kai* (and) **ἐγένετο** *egeneto* (was) **οὕτως** *outōs* (so)
dixit (said) ***quoque*** (also) ***Deus*** (God) ***producat*** (let produce) ***terra*** (the earth) ***animam*** (animals) ***viventem*** (living) ***in*** (according to) ***genere*** (kind) ***suo*** (its own) ***iumenta*** (cattle) ***et*** (and) ***reptilia*** (reptiles) ***et*** (and) ***bestias*** (beasts) ***terrae*** (of the land) ***secundum*** (according to) ***species*** (species) ***suas*** (its) ***factum-***(done)***que*** (and) ***est*** (is) ***ita*** (so)
And God said, Let the earth bring forth the living creature after his kind, cattle, and creeping thing, and beast of the earth after his kind: and it was so.
Continuing, Divine-Consciousness said, "*Let the earth produce life in animals according to their species, domestic, crawling creature and wild ones of earth according to their species.*" And so it was.

We have reached the bottom of the Creative Epistemic Descent. Here, the breath of life[512] *vivifies*[513] and puts **life** (חי *chay*), as we know and experience it, *into existence*; and so (כֵן *k̲ēn*) it was (וַיְהִי־ *vayahiy*). Each living species has its own collective epistemic structure, more or less different from that of other ones. It is like interconnected different types of computer systems intended for different tasks.

VI ⊙ DAY >>

1:25-Life's Generation

וַיַּעַשׂ אֱלֹהִים אֶת־חַיַּת הָאָרֶץ לְמִינָהּ וְאֶת־הַבְּהֵמָה לְמִינָהּ וְאֵת כָּל־רֶמֶשׂ הָאֲדָמָה לְמִינֵהוּ וַיַּרְא אֱלֹהִים כִּי־טוֹב׃
vaya'aś (made) *'ĕlōhiym* (Divine-Consciousness) *'et̲* (the) *ḥayat̲* (living) *hā'āreṣ* (of earth) *lamiynāh* (according to species) *va'et̲* (and) *habahēmāh* (mute cattle) *lamiynāh* (species) *va'ēt̲* (and) *kāl* (all) *remeś* (creeping things) *hā'ăd̲āmāh* (of the red earth) *lamiynēhu* (kind) *vayara'* (saw) *'ĕlōhiym* (Divine-Consciousness) *kiy* (that) *ṭvōb̲* (good)
καὶ *kai* (and) **ἐποίησεν** *epoiēsen* (made) **ὁ** *o* (the) **θεός** *theos* (God) **τὰ** *ta* (the) **θηρία** *thēria* (beasts) **τῆς** *tēs* (of the) **γῆς** *gēs* (earth) **κατὰ** *kata* (according to) **γένος** *genos* (species) **καὶ** *kai* (and) **τὰ** *ta* (the) **κτήνη** *ktēnē* (cattle) **κατὰ** *kata* (according to) **γένος** *genos* (species) **καὶ** *kai* (and) **πάντα** *panta* (all) **τὰ** *ta* (the) **ἑρπετὰ** *erpeta* (serpents) **τῆς** *tēs* (of the) **γῆς** *gēs* (earth) **κατὰ** *kata* (according to) **γένος** *genos* (species) **αὐτῶν** *autōn* (thus) **καὶ** *kai* (and) **εἶδεν** *eiden* (saw) **ὁ** *o* (the) **θεός** *theos* (God) **ὅτι** *oti* (that) **καλά** *kala* (good)
et (and) ***fecit*** (made) ***Deus*** (God) ***bestias*** (the beasts) ***terrae*** (of the earth) ***iuxta*** (according to) ***species*** (species) ***suas*** (its) ***et*** (and) ***iumenta*** (cattle) ***et*** (and) ***omne*** (all) ***reptile*** (reptiles) ***terrae*** (of the earth) ***in*** (according to) ***genere*** (genre) ***suo*** (its) ***et*** (and) ***vidit*** (saw) ***Deus*** (God) ***quod*** (that) ***esset*** (it was) ***bonum*** (good)
And God made the beast of the earth after his kind, and cattle after their kind, and every thing that creepeth upon the earth after his kind: and God saw that it was good.
Therefore, Divine-Consciousness made the living animal of the earth each according to its specie and mute-cattle and all the creeping-reptiles of the earth each according to its specie. And Divine-

Consciousness was conscious that it was good.

This is the last level of the Epistemic Creation, namely, it is **the circle of life**. Here, Divine-Consciousness produces the living (חַיָּה chayah)[514] animal (חַי chay). The word *chay* (חַי)[515] means *animal*, and *green*, when referred to vegetation.[516] Also, it means *flowing*, like water, *active*, as for man, and, in general, *flourishing* and *appetite*. The name derives from *chayah*,[517] *to live prosperously, to grow*. Compare to *chavah*,[518] *to tell, to declare, to show, to make known* and *to breath*. Parallel it to the Aramaic *chava'*,[519] meaning, *to interpret, to explain, to inform, to tell, to declare* and *to show*. Therefore, the animal-metaphor connotes the sense of sentient activity. However, this activity is pure projection towards a *hungered* exteriority to which no feeling has yet been attributed. Thus, as such, it is *mute*. Life proceeds with a creative crescendo. From the mute-creatures or *běhemah* (בְּהֵמָה), the

"*beast* (so called from being unable to speak),"[520]

through the creeping (רֶמֶשׂ remes)[521] ones projecting on the red-earth (אדמה 'adamah),[522] life will reach, in the next verse, the redden (אָדם 'adam)[523] human Adam (אָדם 'adam).[524] S/he will confer sense to the objects by naming them.

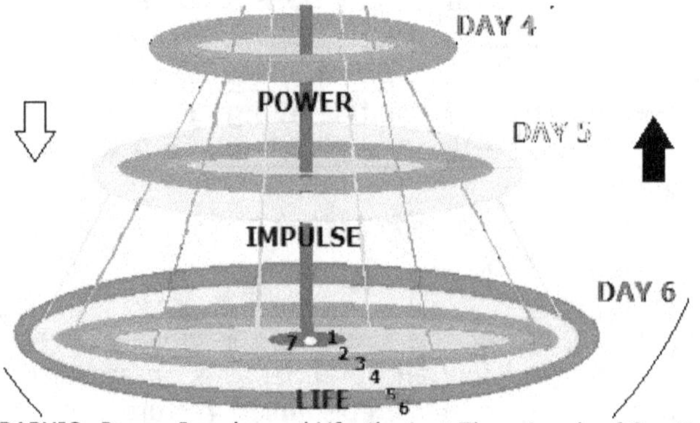

GRAPHIC: *Power, Impulse and Life, the Last Three Levels of Creation*

Once more, Divine-Consciousness was intentionally positive about this circular conscious creation of life. Again, in the world, as such, there is no evil in-itself. In fact, it never loses the mark and the centrality of Awareness itself.

VI ⊙ DAY >>>

1:26-Creation of the Human

וַיֹּאמֶר אֱלֹהִים נַעֲשֶׂה אָדָם בְּצַלְמֵנוּ כִּדְמוּתֵנוּ וְיִרְדּוּ בִדְגַת הַיָּם וּבְעוֹף הַשָּׁמַיִם וּבַבְּהֵמָה וּבְכָל־הָאָרֶץ וּבְכָל־הָרֶמֶשׂ הָרֹמֵשׂ עַל־הָאָרֶץ׃ *vayō'mer* (said) *'ĕlōhiym* (Divine-Consciousness) *na'ăśeh* (let us make) *'āḏām* (humans) *baṣalamēnu* (image) *kiḏamuṯēnu* (likeness) *vayiradu* (let them rule) *ḇiḏāḡaṯ* (fish) *hayām* (sea) *uḇa'vōp̄* (birds) *hašāmayim* (sky) *uḇabahēmāh* (beast) *uḇaḵāl* (all) *hā'āreṣ* (earth) *uḇaḵāl* (all) *harems* (creeping things) *hārōmēś* (creeping) *'al* (over) *hā'āreṣ* (earth)
καὶ *kai* (and) **εἶπεν** *eipen* (said) **ὁ** *o* (the) **θεός** *theos* (God) **ποιήσωμεν** *poiēsōmen* (let us make) **ἄνθρωπον** *avthrōpon* (man) **κατ'** *kat'* (in) **εἰκόνα** *eikona* (image) **ἡμετέραν** *emeteran* (our) **καὶ** *kai* (and) **καθ'** *kath'* (in) **ὁμοίωσιν** *omoiōsin* (likeness) **καὶ** *kai* (and) **ἀρχέτωσαν** *archetōsan* (let him dominate over) **τῶν** *tōn* (the) **ἰχθύων** *ichthuōn* (fish) **τῆς** *tēs* (of the) **θαλάσσης** *thalassēs* (seas) **καὶ** *kai* (and) **τῶν** *tōn* (the) **πετεινῶν** *peteinōn* (birds) **τοῦ** *tou* (of the) **οὐρανοῦ** *ouranou* (sky) **καὶ** *kai* (and) **τῶν** *tōn* (the) **κτηνῶν** *ktēvōn* (cattle) **καὶ** *kai* (and) **πάσης** *pasēs* (entire) **τῆς** *tēs* (the) **γῆς** *gēs* (earth) **καὶ** *kai* (and) **πάντων** *pantōn* (all) **τῶν** *tōn* (the) **ἑρπετῶν** *erpetōv* (serpents) **τῶν** *tōn* (the) **ἑρπόντων** *erpontōn* (crawling) **ἐπὶ** *epi* (on) **τῆς** *tēs* (the) **γῆς** *gēs* (earth)
et (and) ***ait*** (said) ***faciamus*** (let us make) ***hominem*** (man) ***ad*** (in) ***imaginem*** (image) ***et*** (and) ***similitudinem*** (likeness) ***nostram*** (ours) ***et*** (and) ***praesit*** (let him preside over) ***piscibus*** (the fish) ***maris*** (of the sea) ***et*** (and) ***volatilibus*** (the birds) ***caeli*** (of the sky) ***et*** (and) ***bestiis*** (the beasts) ***universae-***(all)***que*** (and) ***terrae*** (earth) ***omni-***(all)***que*** (and) ***reptili*** (the reptile) ***quod***

(that) ***movetur*** (move) ***in*** (on) ***terra*** (the earth)
And God said, Let us make man in our image, after our likeness: and let them have dominion over the fish of the sea, and over the fowl of the air, and over the cattle, and over all the earth, and over every creeping thing that creepeth upon the earth.
Again Divine-Consciousness said, *"Let us make the human in our image and likeness. Let them rule over the fish of the sea, the birds of the sky, the beasts, the entire earth, and all the crawlers that move on the earth."*

This verse and the following ones are proof that *Genesis* describes the creative development as an epistemic process. First, we must clarify that here the word *'adam*[525] is collective for humans with no gender differentiation. Since, by definition, Divine-Consciousness is Transcendent and Ineffable, then, the intention to make humans in Its own image (צֶלֶם *tselem*) and likeness (דְּמוּת *dĕmuwth*) cannot refer to a physical aspect. In fact, all physicality follows creation, does not precede it.

However, only as a graphic expedient, the Kabbalistic rendering of the ineffable proper name of the Transcendent places vertically the *Four Letters* (*viz. Tetragrammaton*) of $Y_{ĕ}H_{o}V_{a}H$ (**יְהוָה**).[526] Then, י Y becomes the head, ה H the arms, ו V the torso and ה H the legs. The effect of this graphic style produces an anthropomorphic image.[527] Obviously, this is not the image referred to in these verses.

GRAPHIC: *Tetragrammaton*

Nevertheless, how must we understand the image or likeness of Divine-Consciousness? The Hebrew word for image is *tselem*[528] and for likeness is *dĕmuwth.*[529] This last word derives from the verb *damah,*[530] to imagine, to remember, to think. Therefore, the likeness of Divine-Consciousness is the thought-reflection of His light of Consciousness, which, creating, places the world into existence. Consequently, the image or the likeness of that Consciousness is the reflection of God's light, which shines right here and now in the Human as Pure-Consciousness. Thus, to be made in God's image means that the fundamental essence of the human being is epistemic and it works in the same manner in which Divine-Consciousness works. As we saw, Pure-Consciousness is the foundation of the world, without which nothing could be. Let it be clear, this is not yet the consciousness-*of* the world, as such. Chapter 3 will address this last point.

Jalal-ad-din Rumi writes,

> "*God slept in the mineral kingdom, dreamed in the vegetable kingdom, awakened to consciousness in the animal kingdom, and became manifest in His own image in the human being.*"[531]

Figuratively speaking, as an Infinite scanning possibility, Pure Consciousness, searching for its own Awareness, timelessly and immovably enters the waking states, passes through the dream stage and reached the deep-sleep realm, <only to recognize Itself as never having left Its own Conscious-Awareness in the All-pervading Transcendence from which we come. This is not a dogmatic affirmation. It does not matter if one defines itself theist, atheist or agnostic, in each of these cases one envisions and defines its prenatal>[532] and/or postmortem condition to be beyond thought. This is, inevitably, a tacit silent declaration of Transcendence. If, at the question '*Where were you before you were born and where will you be after death?*' there is no answer that is an affirmation of the Transcendent state that rests beyond the subject-object correlation, which, once thought, cannot be Transcendent.

Making the human-consciousness, *'adam* (אָדם), in His image means that God confers on it the same epistemic modalities and control that Divine-Consciousness has on all the objects of the world. Thus, the human-consciousness equates the Awareness of Divine-Consciousness. Human-consciousness *sparkles* (אָדָם *'adam*)[533] epistemically *subduing* and *subjugating* (רָדָה *radah*)[534] *the entire known world* with its epistemic rules, namely, the plurality-of-its-perceiving-structural Certainty with which it establishes knowledge.

VI ⊙ DAY >>>>

1:27-The Image of God

וַיִּבְרָא אֱלֹהִים אֶת־הָאָדָם בְּצַלְמוֹ בְּצֶלֶם אֱלֹהִים בָּרָא אֹתוֹ זָכָר וּנְקֵבָה בָּרָא אֹתָם׃
vayiḇarā̄ (made) *'ĕlōhiym* (Divine-Consciousness) *'eṯ* (thus) *hā'āḏām* (human) *baṣalamvō* (image) *baṣelem* (image) *'ĕlōhiym* (Divine-Consciousness) *bārā̄* (created) *'ōṯvō* (with) *zāḵār* (male) *unaqēḇāh* (female) *bārā̄* (created) *'ōṯām* (together with)
καὶ *kai* (and) **ἐποίησεν** *epoiēsen* (created) **ὁ** *o* (the) **θεὸς** *theos* (God) **τὸν** *tov* (the) **ἄνθρωπον** *anthrōpov* (man) **κατ'** *kat'* (in) **εἰκόνα** *eikona* (image) **θεοῦ** *theou* (of God) **ἐποίησεν** *epoiēsen* (created) **αὐτόν** *auton* (he) **ἄρσεν** *arsen* (male) **καὶ** *kai* (and) **θῆλυ** *thēlu* (female) **ἐποίησεν** *epoiēsen* (created) **αὐτούς** *autous* (he)
et (and) ***creavit*** (created) ***Deus*** (God) ***hominem*** (man) ***ad*** (in) ***imaginem*** (the image) ***suam*** (his) ***ad*** (in) ***imaginem*** (the image) ***Dei*** (of God) ***creavit*** (created) ***illum*** (he) ***masculum*** (male) ***et*** (and) ***feminam*** (female) ***creavit*** (created) ***eos*** (them)
So God created man in his own image, in the image of God created he him; male and female created he them.
Therefore, Divine-Consciousness made the human in His own image. In the image of Divine-Consciousness He created. He created them male and female.

In this verse, the word *tselem* (צֶלֶם) means *image shadowing forth* and the *likeness of resemblance.*[535] It is the *unconscious* and/or *conscious* universal epistemic structure valid for every being that is sentient in the entire Universe. To understand this verse, we must use again the metaphoric similitude we already offered. Consider looking into a mirror or at a self-portrait. With this acts there are two polarities (1-2) with four elements (a-b-c-d),

1) The *observer*, who is, at the same time, the one
   - a) *subject*, remembering itself as *observer*, and the one
   - b) *looking* into the mirror or at the photograph.
2) The *object*, the *observed one*, which is, at the same time, the
   - c) *image*, distinguished from the *observer*, and the
   - d) *objectivity*, as the looking glass or picture as such.

The consequence of this is that the *observer* can never *see* itself as observer, but only as an *observed* reflected image. The *observer*, therefore, remains locked in a transcendent entity blind to itself *in-itself.* However, the *observer*, as such, while implying to be the *viewer*, sees only itself as it appears *for-itself* in the image. Therefore, it distinguishes and separates itself from the subjective implication it has of itself-in-itself and believes the *observing subjectivity* to be the same *observed objectivity* in the mirror's surface. Let us suppose that, at this point, the *viewing subject* forgets its own original identity as *observer.* Then, it would remember only the *object* of the detected *image.* Thus, it would assume a new identity, namely, that of the reflected image. The subject would identify with a new historicized ego, one *for-itself* who will then declare '*I am so and so, the offspring of such and such one.*' Hence, it will forget its own true origin. [536]⇨

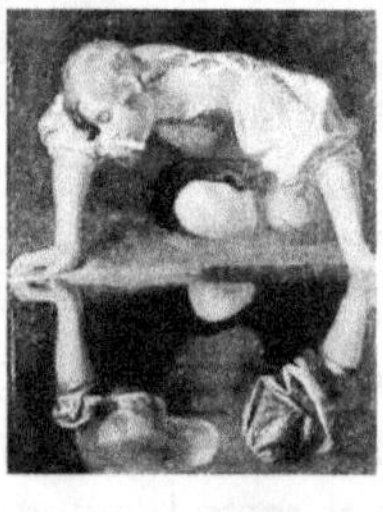

Notwithstanding, the *image* will still mimic everything the *observer* does. Except that, it would not refer it any longer to the *observer*, as such. This is described[537] eloquently by the myth of Narcissus who, forgetting its own true self, drowns trying to grab its own image on the water. As in the metaphoric similitude of the mirror, the Pure Light of Divine-Consciousness, as Consciousness reflecting on Itself, produces an icon,[538] an image of Itself, which has the epistemic configuration of Itself, namely the Light from which it derives. Truthfully, it is always the same Light of the *Observer*, which, when shining on the mirroring abyss of the yet uncreated *objectivity* produces the *subject*. This last one is the Human *Adam*. S/he is the *subject*, the male *zakar* (זָכָר).[539] S/he is called so because s/he is the one who, while *looking*, remembers, *viz. zakar* (זכר),[540] and calls to mind the Light from which it comes. Again, that Light of Consciousness is the Human *Adam*. S/he is the *object*, the female *nĕqebah*.[541] S/he is called so because s/he is the one who separates, *viz. naqab*,[542]and distinguishes the *image* from the *observer*. Obviously, this does not confer superiority or inferiority to the *male* and/or to the *female*. It denotes only the indivisible synthesis of subject-object in the process of knowledge, metaphorically represented as an act of *copulation* (יָדַע *yada`*). Both, male and female, can only be logically distinguished and graphically represented as the *Star* ✡ *of David*. Etymologically, however, if we were to sketch a positional distinction, it would be that of the *female*▽ *ob*ject placed (e*jected*) *upon* (*ob*) the *male*△*sub*ject located *under* (*sub*) her.[543] Furthermore, this statement, confirmed also by *Genesis* 5:2:

"*Adam* (אדם)... [is] *created* (*bārā* בָּרָא) *female* (*unaqēḇāh* וּנְקֵבָה) [and] *male* (*zāḵār* זָכָר),"

does not mean hermaphroditism,[544] nor approves or condemns homosexuality. It simply states the male/female human being who articulates on the three levels of consciousness proceeding in the first three days of the creative descent, namely, Auto-transparency, I-consciousness and Individual-ego-consciousness.

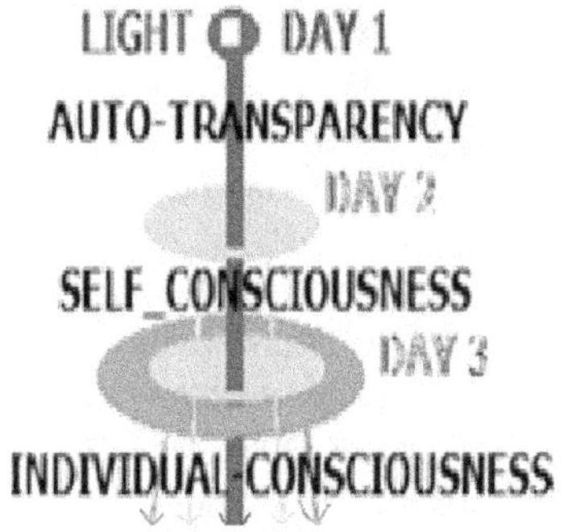

GRAPHIC: *Articulations of Consciousness*

VI ⊙ DAY >>>>>

1:28-Human Power

וַיְבָרֶךְ אֹתָם אֱלֹהִים וַיֹּאמֶר לָהֶם אֱלֹהִים פְּרוּ וּרְבוּ וּמִלְאוּ אֶת־הָאָרֶץ וְכִבְשֻׁהָ וּרְדוּ בִּדְגַת הַיָּם וּבְעוֹף הַשָּׁמַיִם וּבְכָל־חַיָּה הָרֹמֶשֶׂת עַל־הָאָרֶץ׃ *vayaḇāreḵa* (blessed) *'ōṯām* (them) *'ĕlōhiym* (Divine-Consciousness) *vayō'mer* (said) *lāhem* (and) *'ĕlōhiym* (Divine-Consciousness) *paru* (be fruitful) *uraḇu* (multiply) *umila'u* (replenish) *'eṯ* (the) *hā'āreṣ* (earth) *vaḵiḇašuāh* (sudue) *uraḏu* (rule) *biḏāḡaṯ* (fish) *hayām* (sea) *uḇa'vōp̄* (birds) *hašāmayim* (sky) *uḇaḵāl* (all) *ḥayāh* (living animals) *hārōmeśeṯ* (moving) *'al* (on) *hā'āreṣ* (earth)
καὶ *kai* (and) **ηὐλόγησεν** *ēulogēsen* (blessed) **αὐτοὺς** *autos* (them) **ὁ** *o* (the) **θεὸς** *theos* (God) **λέγων** *legōn* (said) **αὐξάνεσθε** *auxanesthe* (grow) **καὶ** *kai* (and) **πληθύνεσθε** *plēthunesthe* (multiply) **καὶ** *kai* (and) **πληρώσατε** *plērōsate* (replenish) **τὴν** *tēn* (the) **γῆν** *gēs* (earth) **καὶ** *kai* (and) **κατακυριεύσατε** *katakupieusate* (subdue) **αὐτῆς** *autēs* (it) **καὶ** *kai* (and) **ἄρχετε** *archete* (dominate over) **τῶν** *tōn* (the) **ἰχθύων** *ichthuōn* (fish) **τῆς** *tēs* (of the) **θαλάσσης** *thalassēs* (sees) **καὶ** *kai* (and) **τῶν** *tōn* (the) **πετεινῶν** *peteinōn* (birds) **τοῦ** *tou* (of the) **οὐρανοῦ** *ouranou* (sky) **καὶ** *kai* (and) **πάντων** *pantōn* (all) **τῶν** *tōn* (the) **κτηνῶν** *ktēnōn* (animals) **καὶ** *kai* (and) **πάσης** *pasēs* (entire) **τῆς** *tēs* (the) **γῆς** *gēs* (earth) **καὶ** *kai* (and) **πάντων** *pantōn* (all) **τῶν** tōn (the) **ἑρπετῶν** *erpetōn* (crawling) **τῶν** *tōv* (the) **ἑρπόντων** *erpontōn* (serpents) **ἐπὶ** *epi* (on) **τῆς** *tēs* (the) **γῆς** *gēs* (earth)
benedixit-(blessed)***que*** (and) ***illis*** (them) ***Deus*** (God) ***et*** (and) ***ait*** (said) ***crescite*** (grow) ***et*** (and) ***multiplicamini*** (multiply) ***et*** (and) ***replete*** (replenish) ***terram*** (the earth) ***et*** (and) ***subicite***

(subdue) ***eam*** (it) ***et*** (and) ***dominamini*** (dominate) ***piscibus*** (on the fish) ***maris*** (of the sea) ***et*** (and) ***volatilibus*** (the birds) ***caeli*** (of the sky) ***et*** (and) ***universis*** (all) ***animantibus*** (the living beings) ***quae*** (that) ***moventur*** (move) ***super*** (on) ***terram*** (the earth)
And God blessed them, and God said unto them, Be fruitful, and multiply, and replenish the earth, and subdue it: and have dominion over the fish of the sea, and over the fowl of the air, and over every living thing that moveth upon the earth.
and Divine-Consciousness blessed them and Divine-Consciousness said, "*Grow and multiply and replenish the earth and subdue it, dominate over the fish of the great roaring river, the birds of the sky and all the living beings that move on the earth.*"

GRAPHIC: *The circle of Power*

To bless, *barak* (בָּרַךְ), implies to confer mindfulness on the blessed one. The Light of Divine-Consciousness is the *Observer-in-Itself*, the creative core, the central life and the heart of Adam. In return, s/he, *'adam* (אָדָם), the subject-object is the epistemic correlation. This correlation produces all the *multiplicity* (רָבָה *rabah*) of all the actual objective experiences. Furthermore, those experiences are ordained and ruled according to the subject-object epistemic structure. Adam, the Human Being, both the male-*subject* and the female-*object*, operate as the epistemic polarities of consciousness. *They* (אֵת 'eth)[545] completely *fill* (מָלֵא *male'*) and *subdue* (כָּבַשׁ *kabash*)[546] the *world* (אֶרֶץ *'erets*), *viz.* the firm dimensions of physical objectivity, with their *ruling* (רָדָה *radah*)[547] structure of knowledge. Therefore, they control their thoughts, like multiplying *fish* (דָּגָה *dagah*)[548] in the sea or the *great roaring river* (יָם *yam*)[549] of the continuous flowing thinking. Their ideas are, like *birds* (עוֹף *`owph*),[550] soaring in the *sky* (שָׁמַיִם *shamayim*)[551] of conceptuality. Eventually, all those virtual models will move out of their *cover of darkness* (דָּגָה *dagah* & עוֹף *`owph*) to come into light as actual *living* (חַי *chay*) beings *moving* (רָמַשׂ *ramas*) on the solid *ground* (אֶרֶץ *'erets*) of experiential objectivity. Then, the human being partakes of the fourth day of the creative descent, namely the circle in which they exercise epistemic **power** and control over the entire known world.

The proof that these verses refer to Adam as the epistemic subject-object correlation is the injunction to multiply before the creation of Eve.[552] Since that activity refers only to Adam, therefore, this verse refers to an epistemic multiplication not a biological one.

VI ⊙ DAY >>>>>>

1:29-Human Epistemic and Biological Impulses

וַיֹּאמֶר אֱלֹהִים הִנֵּה נָתַתִּי לָכֶם אֶת־כָּל־עֵשֶׂב זֹרֵעַ זֶרַע אֲשֶׁר עַל־פְּנֵי כָל־הָאָרֶץ וְאֶת־כָּל־הָעֵץ אֲשֶׁר־בּוֹ פְרִי־עֵץ זֹרֵעַ זָרַע לָכֶם יִהְיֶה לְאָכְלָה׃ *vayō'mer* (said) *'ĕlōhiym* (Divine-Consciousness) *hinēh* (behold) *nāṯatiy* (I gave) *lāḵem* (to) *'eṯ* (and) *kāl* (all) *'ēśeḇ* (herb) *zōrēa'* (to sow) *zera'* (seed) *'ăšer* (which) *'al* (on) *panēy* (face) *ḵāl* (all) *hā'āreṣ* (earth) *va'eṯ* (and the) *kāl* (all) *hā'ēṣ* (tree) *'ăšer* (which) *bvō* (in) *p̄ariy* (fruit) *'ēṣ* (tree) *zōrēa'* (to sow) *zāra'* (seed) *lāḵem* (to) yihayeh (be) *la'āḵalāh* (food)
καὶ *kai* (and) **εἶπεν** *eipen* (said) **ὁ** *o* (the) **θεός** *theos* (God) **ἰδοὺ** *idou* (behold) **δέδωκα** *dedōka* (I gave) **ὑμῖν** *umin* (you) **πᾶν** *pan* (all) **χόρτον** *chorton* (feeding place) **σπόριμον** *sporimov* (fit for sowing) **σπεῖρον** *speiron* (plant) **σπέρμα** *sperma* (seed) **ὅ** *o* (thus) **ἐστιν** *estin* (is) **ἐπάνω** *epanō* (on) **πάσης** *pasēn* (entire) **τῆς** *tēs* (the) **γῆς** *gēs* (earth) **καὶ** *kai* (and) **πᾶν** *pan* (all) **ξύλον** *xulon* (tree) **ὃ** *o* (thus) **ἔχει** *exei* (having) **ἐν** *en* (in) **ἑαυτῷ** *eautō* (itself) **καρπὸν** *karpon* (fruit) **σπέρματος** *spermatos* (seed) **σπορίμου** *sporimou* (fit for sowing) **ὑμῖν** *umin* (you) **ἔσται** *estai* (let be) **εἰς** *eis* (into) **βρῶσιν** *brōsin* (food)
dixit-(said)***que*** (and) ***Deus*** (God) ***ecce*** (look) ***dedi*** (I gave) ***vobis*** (to you) ***omnem*** (all) ***herbam*** (herb) ***adferentem*** (producing) ***semen*** (seed) ***super*** (on) ***terram*** (the earth) ***et*** (and) ***universa*** (every) ***ligna*** (tree) ***quae*** (that) ***habent*** (have) ***in*** (in) ***semet*** (it) ***ipsis*** (self) ***sementem*** (seed)

generis (kind) ***sui*** (its) ***ut*** (so that) ***sint*** (it shall be) ***vobis*** (for you) ***in*** (as) ***escam*** (food)
And God said, Behold, I have given you every herb bearing seed, which is upon the face of all the earth, and every tree, in the which is the fruit of a tree yielding seed; to you it shall be for meat.
And Divine-Consciousness said, "*Behold, I gave you all the shinning epistemic-plants producing seed-of-ideas and every epistemic-tree that have in them seeds-of-ideas, so that it shall be your food-for-thought ...*

In the fifth day of the creative descending consciousness, Adam, the human being partakes of the circle in which s/he experiences **epistemic and biological multiplication** of the entire world that becomes his/her food (אֳכְלָה *'oklah*). In fact, all epistemic structures are like *shinning plants.*[553] They produce[554] *logical-semen.*[555] These seeds are what Plotinus calls

"*seminal reasons,"*[556]

namely, the ideal-seed of everything by which the object is recognized as that specific object. Furthermore, metaphorically, trees (עֵץ *`ets*) are growing forces, like *silent screams to the sky.*[557] Edward Elgar asked,

"The trees are singing my music – or have I sung theirs?"[558]

They are metaphors for the swelling faculties of knowledge producing (זֶרַע *zara`*) *logical-seeds* (זֶרַע *zera`*). These germs are *food-*(אכלה *'oklah*)*-for-thought* and, figuratively, for judgment (אכלה *'oklah*).[559] In fact, to think is to judge. Any *judgment* is *cognition*, a representation of objects. Thus, *the power of judgment* is a mental *capacity* and *the faculty of judging* is *the faculty of thinking.*[560] In fact, *to judge*, from Latin *iudicare*, implies to evaluate, assess, determine, examine, pronounce an opinion on something and/or formulate a verdict. *E.g.*, the sentence '*this is a book*' implies four judgements:

1) *This*, judges or assesses a specific geometrical point as distinct from others,
2) *Is*, judges or determines its specific existence,
3) *A*, judges or evaluates it among others, and
4) *Book*, judges or formulates it as belonging to the category of reading objects.

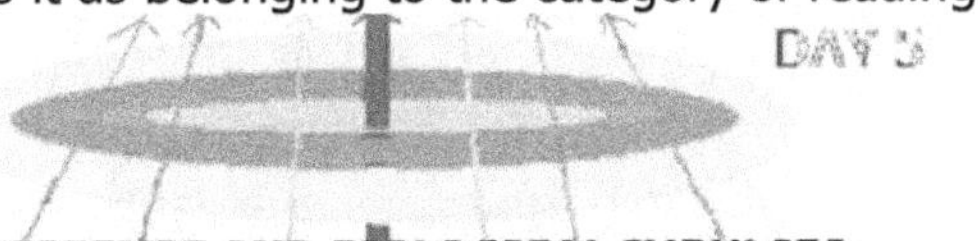

EPISTEMIC AND BIOLOGICAL IMPULSES

GRAPHIC: *The circle of Epistemic and Biological Impulses*

VI ⊙ DAY >>>>>>>

1:30-Human Life

וּלְכָל־חַיַּת הָאָרֶץ וּלְכָל־עוֹף הַשָּׁמַיִם וּלְכֹל רוֹמֵשׂ עַל־הָאָרֶץ אֲשֶׁר־בּוֹ נֶפֶשׁ חַיָּה אֶת־כָּל־יֶרֶק עֵשֶׂב לְאָכְלָה וַיְהִי־כֵן׃ *ulakāl* (all) *ḥayat* (living) *hā'āreṣ* (on earth) *ulakāl* (all) *'vōp̄* (birds) *hašāmayim* (in the sky) *ulakōl* (all) *rvōmēś* (move) *'al* (on) *hā'āreṣ* (earth) *'ăšer* (which) *bvō* (in) *nepēš* (soul) *ḥayāh* (living) *'et* (and) *kāl* (all) *yereq* (green plants) *'ēśeb* (herb) *la'ākalāh* (food) *vayahiy* (be) *kēn* (thus)
καὶ *kai* (and) **πᾶσι** *pasi* (to all) **τοῖς** *tois* (the) **θηρίοις** *thēriois* (animals) **τῆς** *tēs* (of the) **γῆς** *gēs* (earth) **καὶ** *kal* (and) **πᾶσι** *pasi* (to all) **τοῖς** *tois* (all) **πετεινοῖς** *peteinois* (birds) **τοῦ** *tou* (in the) **οὐρανοῦ** *ouranou* (sky) **καὶ** *kai* (and) **παντὶ** *panti* (all) **ἑρπετῷ** *erpetō* (serpents) **τῷ** *tō* (who) **ἕρποντι** *erponti* (move) **ἐπὶ** *epi* (on) **τῆς** *tēs* (the) **γῆς** *gēs* (earth) **ὃ** *o* (who) **ἔχει** *echei* (have) **ἐν** *ev* (in) **ἑαυτῷ** *eautō* (itself) **ψυχὴν** *psuchēn* (soul) **ζωῆς** *zōēs* (living) **πάντα** *panta* (all) **χόρτον** *chorton* (feeding place) **χλωρὸν** *chlōron* (green wood) **εἰς** *eis* (into) **βρῶσιν** *brōsin* (food) **καὶ** *kai* (and) **ἐγένετο** *egeneto* (it was) **οὕτως** *outōs* (thus)
et (and) ***cunctis*** (to all) ***animantibus*** (the animated beings) ***terrae*** (of the earth) ***omni-***(all)***que*** (and) ***volucri*** (birds) ***caeli*** (of the sky) ***et*** (and) ***universis*** (all) ***quae*** (that) ***moventur*** (move) ***in*** (on) ***terra*** (earth) ***et*** (and) ***in*** (in) ***quibus*** (which) ***est*** (is) ***anima*** (a soul) ***vivens*** (living) ***ut*** (so that) ***habeant*** (they may have) ***ad*** (to) ***vescendum*** (eat) ***et*** (and) ***factum*** (done) ***est*** (is) ***ita*** (so)

And to every beast of the earth, and to every fowl of the air, and to every thing that creepeth upon the earth, wherein there is life, I have given every green herb for meat: and it was so.
... and to all the animated sensitive beings of the earth, to all the birds of the psychological-sky and to all, who live and wind on the earth, so that they may have epistemic food." Therefore, it was so.

To read this verse literally would imply that carnivores had to be herbivores. Then, the question ensues, why furnish predators with canines? Moreover, which herbs were fishes supposed to eat? Truthfully, in the sixth day of the creative descent, Adam, the human being, with all the other creatures, partakes of the food of ***life*** (חַי *chay*) in the circle in which s/he becomes an individual living being. The cognitive senses are like the *living* (חַי *chay*) *appetites* (נֶפֶשׁ *nephesh*) of *animals* (חַי *chay*). The superior[561] psychological senses are like *birds* (עוֹף *`owph*).[562]

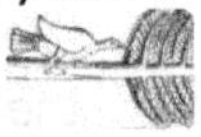

The sense's intentional directions are like winding *serpents* (רמשׂ *ramas*). They all partake of the *food* (אכלה *'oklah*) of feeling offered by the *green* (יֶרֶק *yereq*) shining epistemic *plants* (עֵשֶׂב *`eseb*) of the objective *earth* (אֶרֶץ *'erets*).

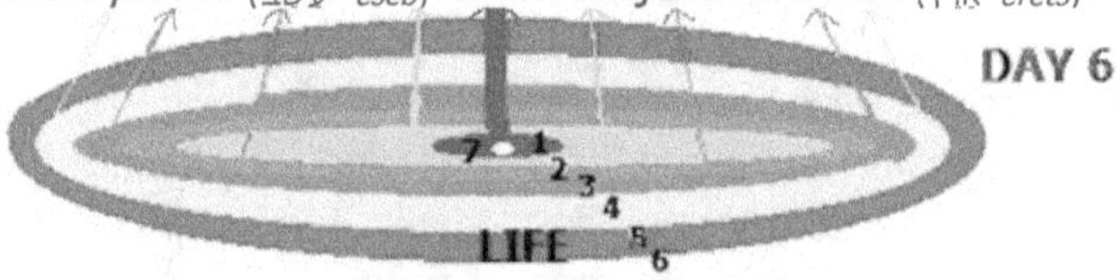

GRAPHIC: *The circle of Life*

VI ⊙ DAY <

1:31-End of the Sixth Day of Creation: The Human Being

וַיַּרְא אֱלֹהִים אֶת־כָּל־אֲשֶׁר עָשָׂה וְהִנֵּה־טוֹב מְאֹד וַיְהִי־עֶרֶב וַיְהִי־בֹקֶר יוֹם הַשִּׁשִּׁי׃ פ *vayara'* (saw) *'ĕlōhiym* (Divine-Consciousness) *'et* (and) *kāl* (all) *'ăšer* (which) *'āśāh* (He made) *vahinēh* (behold) *ṭvōb* (good) *ma'ōd* (very) *vayahiy* (it was) *'ereb* (the evening) *vayahiy* (it was) *bōqer* (the morning) *yvōm* (day) *hašišiy* (sixth) *p̄* (.)
καὶ *kai* (and) **εἶδεν** *eiden* (saw) **ὁ** *o* (the) **θεὸς** *theos* (God) **τὰ** *ta* (that) **πάντα** *panta* (all) **ὅσα osa** (as it) **ἐποίησεν** *epoiēsen* (was done) **καὶ** *kai* (and) **ἰδοὺ** *idou* (saw) **καλὰ** *kala* (good) **λίαν** *lian* (very) **καὶ** kai (and) **ἐγένετο** *egeneto* (arose) **ἑσπέρα** *espera* (evening) **καὶ** *kai* (and) **ἐγένετο** *egeneto* (arose) **πρωί** *prōi* (in the morning) **ἡμέρα** *ēmera* (day) **ἕκτη** *ektē* (sixth)
vidit-(saw)***que*** (and) ***Deus*** (God) ***cuncta*** (all) ***quae*** (that) ***fecit*** (He had done) ***et*** (and) ***erant*** (it was) ***valde*** (very) ***bona*** (good) ***et*** (and) ***factum*** (done) ***est*** (is) ***vespere*** (the evening) ***et*** (and) ***mane*** (the morning) ***dies*** (day) ***sextus*** (sixth)
And God saw every thing that he had made, and, behold, it was very good. And the evening and the morning were the sixth day.
Divine-Consciousness saw that all He had done was very good. Thus, it was the evening and the morning of the sixth day.

The descending circularity of consciousness ends with the sixth day. The Breath of God, described in verse 2, exhaled His Creation to flow in the lungs of Adam, the human being. The next chapters will describe Its ascension, the inhaling process.

> Animals are sentient beings named and ruled by the *fe/male* human image of Consciousness.

HERE ENDS THE FIRST CHAPTER OF
THE EXHALING BREATH OF GOD:
THE DESCENDING SIX DAYS OF CREATION

CHAPTER 2

GOD'S INHALING BREATH AND THE ASCENDING TREE IN THE GARDEN OF EDEN

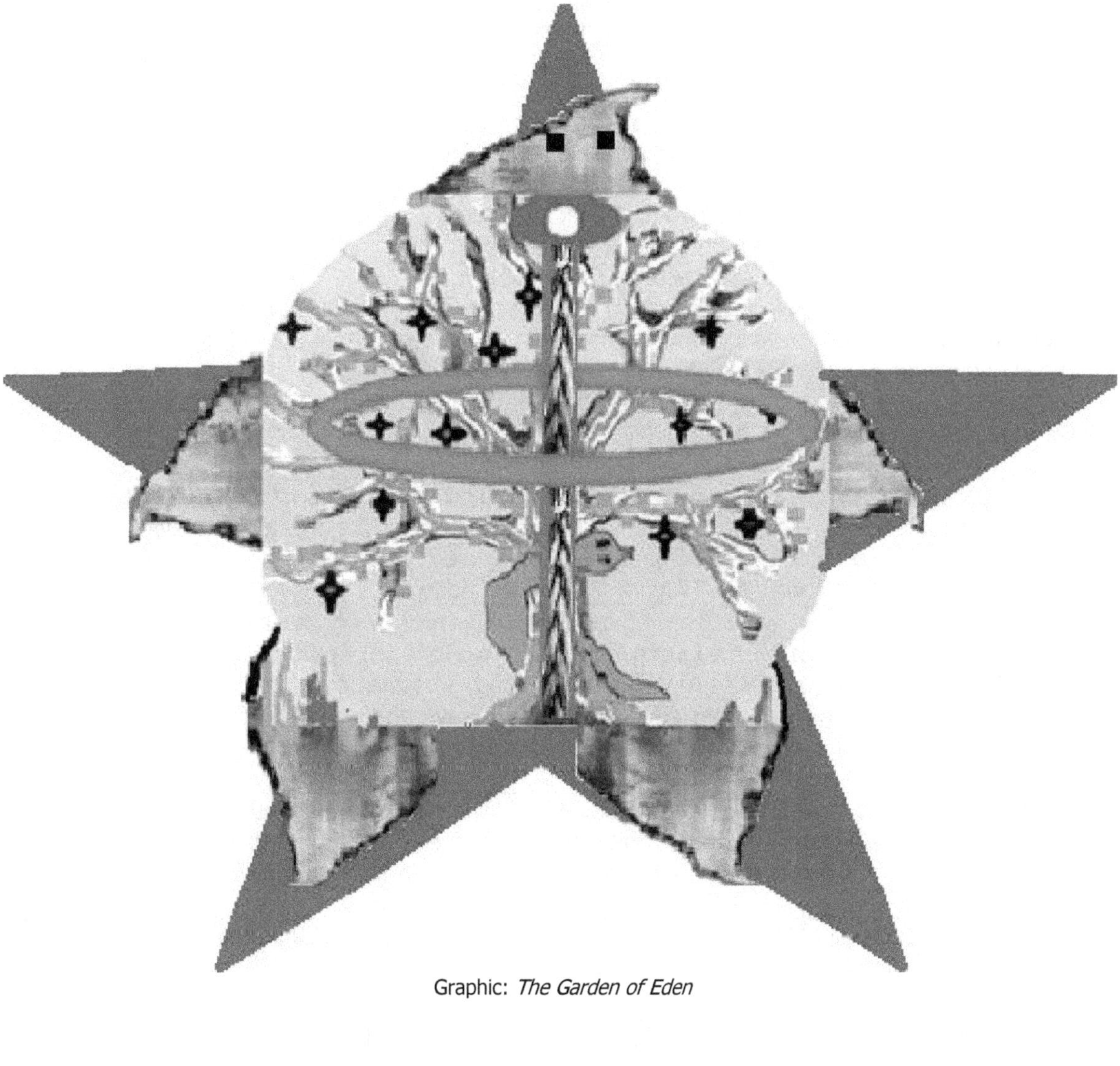

Graphic: *The Garden of Eden*

2-I SECTION: THE SILENCE OF AWARENESS

2:1-End of the Descending Process of Creation

וַיְכֻלּוּ הַשָּׁמַיִם וְהָאָרֶץ וְכָל־צְבָאָם׃ *vaya<u>k</u>ulu* (accomplished) *hašāmayim* (heaven) *vahā'āreṣ* (earth) *va<u>k</u>āl* (all) *ṣa<u>b</u>ā'ām* (host)
καὶ *kai* (and) **συνετελέσθησαν** *sunetelesthēsan* (were accomplished) **ὁ** *o* (the) **οὐρανὸς** *ouranos* (sky) **καὶ** *kai* (and) **ἡ** *ē* (the) **γῆ** *gē* (earth) **καὶ** *kai* (and) **πᾶς** *pas* (all) **ὁ** *o* (the) **κόσμος** *kosmos* (cosmos) **αὐτῶν** *autōn* (of them)
igitur (therefore) ***perfecti*** (perfected) ***sunt*** (were) ***caeli*** (the sky) ***et*** (and) ***terra*** (the earth) ***et*** (and) ***omnis*** (the whole) ***ornthatus*** (equipment) ***eorum*** (of them)
Thus the heavens and the earth were finished, and all the host of them.
Then, the sky and the earth were completed along with all their components.

If one would insist on a purely literal reading of this verse, then s/he would have difficulty distinguishing between heaven and earth, if she would be standing on the moon or in space. Truly, at the end of Its-Sixth-Circular-Creative-Ripple-Expansion, Consciousness finds Itself as this individual reading these pages right here and now. Divine-Consciousness,

> "*the God of heaven*"[563]

completes[564] and presides over Adam's two epistemic polarities,

1) the subject, as *heaven*,[565] on one side, and
2) the object, as *firm ground of objectivity*,[566] on the other.

With them, all the other epistemic *hosts* (*tsaba'*)[567] *go forth* (*tsaba'*).[568] These are all the *transcendental a-priori* modalities or rules of knowledge, as they <u>logically</u> precede experience and the consciousness-*of* the objective known world. In fact,

> "God is not only the Creator of the heavens and the earth, with all their hosts; He is also the constant ruler of all created beings."[569]

2:2-The Centrality of the Seventh Day

וַיְכַל אֱלֹהִים בַּיּוֹם הַשְּׁבִיעִי מְלַאכְתּוֹ אֲשֶׁר עָשָׂה וַיִּשְׁבֹּת בַּיּוֹם הַשְּׁבִיעִי מִכָּל־מְלַאכְתּוֹ אֲשֶׁר עָשָׂה׃ *vaya<u>k</u>al* (accomplished) *'ĕlōhiym* (Divine-Consciousness) *bayvōm* (day) *haša<u>b</u>iy'iy* (seventh) *mala'<u>k</u>atvō* (work) *'ăšer* (which) *'āśāh* (made) *vayišabō<u>t</u>* (rested) *bayvōm* (day) *haša<u>b</u>iy'iy* (seventh) *mikāl* (from) *mala'<u>k</u>atvō* (work) *'ăšer* (which) *'āśāh* (had done)
καὶ *kai* (and) **συνετέλεσεν** *sunetelesen* (completed) **ὁ** *o* (the) **θεὸς** *theos* (God) **ἐν** *en* (in) **τῇ** *tē* (the) **ἡμέρᾳ** *ēmera* (day) **τῇ** *tē* (the) **ἕκτῃ** *ektē* (sixth) **τὰ** *ta* (the) **ἔργα** *erga* (work) **αὐτοῦ** *autou* (he) **ἃ** *a* (that) **ἐποίησεν** *epoiēsen* (done) **καὶ** *kai* (and) **κατέπαυσεν** *katepausen* (rested) **τῇ** *tē* (the) **ἡμέρᾳ** *ēmera* (day) **τῇ** *tē* (the) **ἑβδόμῃ** *ebdomē* (seventh) **ἀπὸ** *apo* (from) **πάντων** *pantōn* (all) **τῶν** *tōn* (the) **ἔργων** *ergōn* (work) **αὐτοῦ** *autou* (he) **ὧν** *ōn* (thus) **ἐποίησεν** *epoiēsen* (had done)
conplevit-(completed) ***que*** (and) ***Deus*** (God) ***die*** (day) ***septimo*** (seventh) ***opus*** (work) ***suum*** (his) ***quod*** (which) ***fecerat*** (he had done) ***et*** (and) ***requievit*** (rested) ***die*** (day) ***septimo*** (seventh) ***ab*** (from) ***universo*** (all) ***opere*** (the work) ***quod*** (which) ***patrarat*** (he had accomplished)
And on the seventh day God ended his work which he had made; and he rested on the seventh day from all his work which he had made.
On the seventh day, Divine-Consciousness completed His work, which He had done. Therefore, on the seventh day He rested from all the work, which He had accomplished.

<u>Apodictic-Aware-Certitude</u> is the *Unthinkable-Unknowable-Reality* without which, however, any thought, knowledge, reality and/or truth is impossible. However, the thought of awareness is <u>not</u> *Awareness*. It is *consciousness-of-awareness*, which is still founded on *Awareness*. Metaphorically, *Genesis* explains how the manifestation and/or *emanation* (*səphîrô<u>t</u>* ספירות) of *Awareness* takes place throughout the entire objective-world. Only Its *Evidence* is

> "*the way, the truth, and the life.*"[570]

Upon reaching the Seventh Day,[571] the One-Divine-Consciousness *ends* or *completes* (כָּלָה *kalah*),[572] so to say, the creative process. Indeed, the actual, literal end or completion of creation would imply, by definition, the extinction of Creation itself. Creation must be an act of Consciousness without which there would be no Creation. A die-hard literal reader could interpret this as the dissolution at the end of time. If that were the case, then creation would never have taken place at all. In fact, with that *end*, that *completion*, the world would have disappeared, without leaving any trace, not even as memory. This is absurd because the persistence of memory would still set the world in a created existence. The *end* or *completion* (כָּלָה *kalah*) of Creation must coincide with its beginning. Thus, the *projection* of Consciousness, as such, can never end.

By *completion* (כָּלָה *kalah*) and *resting* (שַׁבָּת *shabath*)[573] we must understand that the Creator reaches Its Own Centrality from which the whole process departed without ever having moved out of Itself. Like an Infinite Zero (∞0), this Center is exactly the same timeless-spaceless-causeless Unconceptualizable Transcendent and Ineffable Silence (**יהוה**) that, as a manner of speech, *precedes* the Absolute Beginning without any before. Truthfully, the Seventh day is the whole Reality in-Itself. It is the Center of the circle, which radiates itself on every one of the infinite points of the circumference without departing from itself. It is beyond creation. It is beyond the consciousness-*of*. In fact, the circularity of consciousness begins on the First Day of Creation with the light of Consciousness. This Seventh Day, instead, is not circular at all. It is the Stillness-of-Centrality. It is the Truth of Silence, from which we come and to which we go. It is the Truth of Apodictical Awareness. It is Self-Evidence. It does not need any demonstration to recognize Itself as Certitude here and now. In every act of consciousness-*of* any experience, as such, there is Certitude, which is not a belief, but pure Apodicticity. To clarify this last concept we must again distinguish belief and/or science from faith.

BELIEF is not synonym of faith, as we will define it. The believer, confident in her idea, may not feel the need for any scientific validation. Those who profess a specific creed are adamant about its legitimacy. The belief becomes a mental idol, an image intellectualized as a dogma and historicized in a past expected to reappear in the future. That doctrine becomes a palliative, an escape route to circumvent the need to objectify the transcendent. Then, the believer feels satisfied *eating* and conforming to this conceptual *forbidden fruit*.

SCIENCE proceeds differently. It requires verifiability. Namely, it searches, assisted by mathematical laws, for the repeatability of an observed event. To be scientifically valid, the confirmation of a physical law needs a pragmatic proof. Namely, it requires experimentation, the repeatable and successful retesting conforming to the previous hypothesized, remembered and stated outcome. However, both the formulation and the experimentation require the circularity of consciousness based on Awareness, their only true foundation and verification, which makes that law true.[574] Yet, that same verification helps to enforce the separation of the natural principles from the intellect that recognizes them. Nevertheless, this independence from the mind is non-verifiable. Therefore, the transcendence of the physical world, together with the

"deeply organic connection between physics and mathematics,"[575]

remains a necessary axiom for all science.

FAITH is Certitude beyond *dogmatic-belief*, and

"*Certitude is the foundation of trusted things and the evidence of unseen.*"[576]

<Certain-Awareness is that which we are. Certainty is the beginning and the Beginning is Certainty. Certitude is the foundation. Certitude is the *A*lpha, the beginning, and the *Ω*mega, the end, of everything. Certainty is never an object of thought. The words we are here writing on certainty are not the Certainty that founds them. Certainty is Transcendence. Certainty is the Silence of Unconscious States in which and of which nothing can be said. It may be realized as Mindfulness or Consciousness. Every experience is informed by unshakable certainty. Certitude is the Eternal-Now. By certainty, we do not mean consciousness-*of* something. We mean *Faith* as different from dogmatic-belief. We may believe in a world preexisting and/or outliving us, but we

have only *Faith* (אֱמוּנָה *'emuwnah*, πίστις *pistis*), namely, Certitude in this-experience, as experience and nothing more, right here and right now. Let us look around. During the waking and/or dreaming stages of our experience, we see the world as external and/or internal. Try, if you can, to state anything of which you are not conscious-*of*. Even if you can, that very moment you become conscious-*of* it. However, there is another important element at the foundation of consciousness, namely CERTITUDE, which we call AWARENESS. No one, even when stating a made up lie, is not *certain* of that statement as a statement. Awareness, therefore, is the foundation on which consciousness rests. That Certitude is the Self of the 'I' or of the Ego. It is the fire, which burns the *Biblical* bush without consuming it. In fact, as we have seen, from the burning bush, the Transcendent Awareness declares to Moses,

"'*I AM THAT I AM.*'"[577]

In this sense, "*I am*" ((היה *hayah*) is the most intimate essence of our being. From this point of view, God is the personality of Awareness. The oracle of Delphi declares,

"*KNOW THYSELF*... [and Socrates explains,] an unexamined life is not worth living... however, it is not easy to convince you."[578]

"*The very purpose of Self-inquiry is to focus the entire mind at its Source. It is not, therefore, a case of one 'I' searching for another 'I.' Much less is Self-inquiry an empty formula, for it involves an intense activity of the entire mind to keep it steadily poised in pure Self-awareness...* [Awareness or God] *is always the first person, the 'I,' ever standing before you. Because you give precedence to worldly things, God appears to have reached to the background. If you give up all else and seek Him alone, He alone will remain as the 'I,' the Self.*"[579]

From the resting (שבת *shabath*) seventh day, at the end of the descending creative hypostases, the process reverses. To enter this reversal, Adam, the conscious human, made in the image of Divine-Consciousness, must retrace the creative steps.

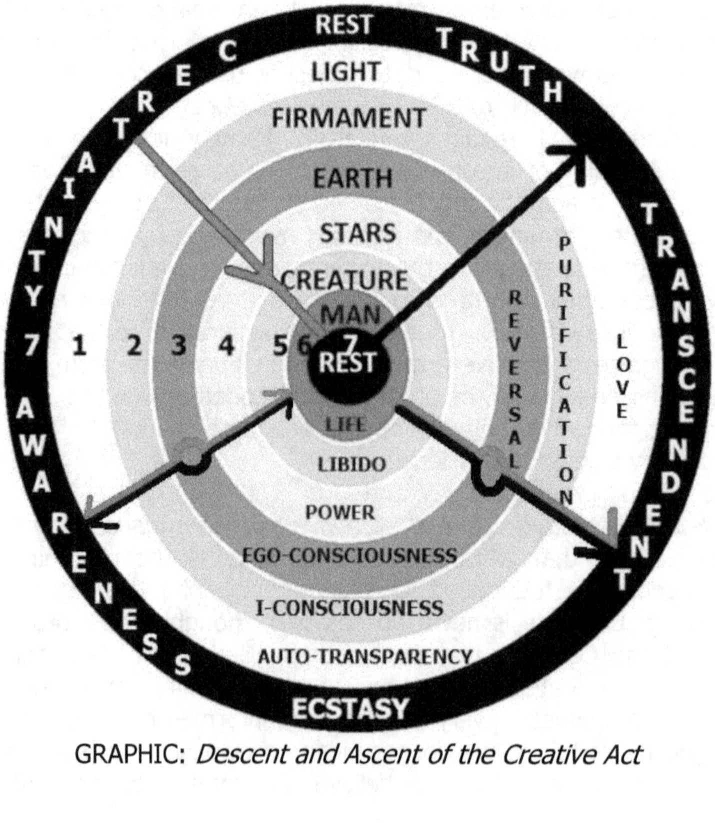

GRAPHIC: *Descent and Ascent of the Creative Act*

1) The human finds itself at the level of Life. That corresponds to the Sixth Day of Creation. There, Adam is conscious-*of* life as it evolves in the Central Nervous System responsible for future behavioral responses.[580]
2) As his/her consciousness further expands, s/he ascends to the Fifth Day of Creation, along the ladder of creation. There, the animal instinct prevails and the human becomes conscious-*of* the sexual drive. Libido regulates all aspects of life, from birth to death. The sexual force of libido grips the Ego who enters in conflict with the behavioral norms imposed by society.[581]
3) As his/her consciousness keeps enlarging with a ripple effect, driven by the hunger to know and have representation, the Adam reaches the Fourth Day of Creation. There s/he becomes conscious of the rulers of the sky and the constant struggle (جهاد *jihād*) of society in which s/he exercises its Power of domination. There is the need to end an inferiority status and to gain a superior one.[582]
4) On the level of the Third Day of Creation, the human enters the heart of intuition, which transforms and sublimates the previous three circles of consciousness. At this level, the individual finds reconciliation with the universal archetypes and the unconscious becomes transpersonal.[583]
5) The consciousness-*of* domination, present in the Fourth Day, purifies in the Second Day of Creation. The human reaches the consciousness-*of* its own true Spiritual Interiority as a Heavenly Firmament. Then, the world, purged from its objective combative power and conquest, reverts from the exteriority to conquer its own true spiritual interiority. At this stage, the struggle of political power becomes non-violent respect-for-life and beholding-of-truth.[584]
6) The consciousness-*of* the sexual drive sublimates in the First Day of Creation. In the center of consciousness, the human sublimates the sexual drive into pure Transcendent spiritual love. This is the perception center of command and knowledge. Here, the mere Libido sublimates into pure Transcendent Spiritual Love.[585]

    "*Let us love one another: for love is of Transcendence; and every one that loveth is born of Transcendence, and knoweth Transcendence... No man hath seen The Transcendent at any time.* [However] *if we love one another, The Transcendent dwelleth in us, and his love is perfected in us.*"[586]

7) Finally, the Rest in the Seventh Day is the human realization of Transcendence as the Silent Ineffable Foundation, from which we come and to which we go. Life's heavy-*lead* (Pb ♄) of the Sixth Day alchemically transmutes and sublimates into the Pure-*Gold* (Au☉) of Apodictical-Awareness.>[587] That is the seat where Divine-Consciousness

    "*rested* (שָׁבַת *shabath*) *on the seventh day.*" (∞☉)

    Here is where one will

    "*be... therefore perfect* (τέλειοι *teleioi*)*, even as your Father which is in heaven is perfect* (τέλειος *teleios*)."[588]

    Here, Life sublimates and identifies with the real internal source of Life itself.[589]

2:3-The Apnea and Inhaling of God's Breath

וַיְבָרֶךְ אֱלֹהִים אֶת־יוֹם הַשְּׁבִיעִי וַיְקַדֵּשׁ אֹתוֹ כִּי בוֹ שָׁבַת מִכָּל־מְלַאכְתּוֹ אֲשֶׁר־בָּרָא אֱלֹהִים לַעֲשׂוֹת׃ פ *vayab̠āreḵa* (blessed) *'ĕlōhiym* (Divine-Consciousness) *'eṯ* (the) *yvōm* (day) *hašabiy'iy* (seventh) *vayaqadēš* (sanctified) *'ōṯvō* (with) *kiy* (because) *ḇvō* (in) *šāḇaṯ* (rest) *mikāl* (from) *mala'ḵatvō* (work) *'ăšer* (which) *bārā'* (created) *'ĕlōhiym* (Divine-Consciousness) *la'ăśvōṯ* (made) *p̄* (.)
καὶ *kai* (and) **ηὐλόγησεν** *ēulogēsen* (blessed) **ὁ** *o* (the) **θεὸς** *theos* (God) **τὴν** *tēn* (the) **ἡμέραν** *ēmeran* (day) **τὴν** *tēn* (the) **ἑβδόμην** *ebdomēn* (seventh) **καὶ** *kai* (and) **ἡγίασεν** *ēgiasen* (sanctified) **αὐτήν** *autēn* (it) **ὅτι** *oti* (because) **ἐν** *en* (in) **αὐτῇ** *autē* (it) **κατέπαυσεν** *katepausen* (rested) **ἀπὸ** *apo* (from) **πάντων** *pantōn* (all) **τῶν** *tōn* (the) **ἔργων** *ergōn* (work) **αὐτοῦ** *autou* (he) **ὧν** *ōn* (thus) **ἤρξατο** *ērxato* (created) **ὁ** *o* (the) **θεὸς** *theos* (God) **ποιῆσαι** *poiēsai* (made)
et (and) ***benedixit*** (he blessed) ***diei*** (the day) ***septimo*** (seventh) ***et*** (and) ***sanctificavit*** (sanctified) ***illum*** (it) ***quia*** (because) ***in*** (in) ***ipso*** (it) ***cessaverat*** (he stopped) ***ab*** (from) ***omni*** (all)

opere (work) ***suo*** (his) ***quod*** (which) ***creavit*** (he created) ***Deus*** (God) ***ut*** () ***faceret*** (he made)
And God blessed the seventh day, and sanctified it: because that in it he had rested from all his work which God created and made.
Therefore, Divine-Consciousness blessed the seventh day and sanctified it because in it He rested from all His work, which Divine-Consciousness had created and had made.

The entire creative process is the circular *immobile* itinerary of Awareness that, starting from Its Own Centrality, discovers and unveils Itself as fundamental Awareness from which It never departed. The *Day of Creation* brings the creature in the Light of Consciousness. In the *Seventh Day of Rest* (שבת *shabath*), the Breath of Divine-Consciousness reverts in-Itself. The inhaling process retracts from its *external* procession. Since God has no physical attributes, His resting must be related to His Creative Consciousness accomplishment. However, as the flow of blood cannot stop, penalty the body's death, so if God would cease creating the creature would stop existing. By definition, the Indivisible-God must be always totally present within His creation, thus, in every *saint* and/or *sinner*.[590] Only the missed-mark (*viz.* the sin, as such) will be

"*like the chaff which the wind driveth away.*"[591]

However, since nothing can exist outside Consciousness, how must we understand God's resting day? When the Conscious Day shines, the world appears. When the Light of Consciousness rests, shining in-Itself, where are the creatures? How can they persist, when they are not brought constantly vivified by that direct illumination? God's Resting is the original state of Divine-Consciousness as Consciousness not yet, so to say, illuminating objects. It is the state of apnea of God's breath, before it *exhales* the command,

"*Let there be Light.*"

To think about God as an architect, who stops building after the completion of a structure, contradicts the concept of God's eternal-omnipresence. The literal interpretation of God's Rest, as taking place *in time*, *after* creation, is contrary to the definition of God. It is illogical to conceive the independent persistence of the world during God's Rest. Nothing can exist outside God's Awareness. Any created being must be eternally present in God's Creative Consciousness. If not, the creature would stop existing. In other words, the concept of God implies that He *thinks*/creates both time and the world. Therefore, all the days of creation together with the seventh day must take place all in Its Present/Presence. The contrary would imply that time, as a real ruler, would determine and structure god's behavior. Furthermore, the persistence of the world during God's Rest would require necessarily the continuation of the creative conscious process. This, conversely, would nullify His Day of Rest. Moreover, the persistence of the world would place the Day of Rest and Creation under the controlling supremacy of a temporal structure, thus it would negate the creation of space/time/causality.

In reality, God's Day of Rest is a metaphor that connotes and explains the mystery of our origin. The Rest implies the return to the state prior to consciousness and creation. Truthfully, that state never ceased to be. It is always one and indivisible, present all in all the individual thoughts here and now. It is the apnea, short or long that it may be, between the inhaling and exhaling process of knowledge.

If God creates time, then, necessarily, His Day of Rest must be this Eternal Now, which means that it was before, during as well as after the Six Days of Creation. In fact, we are caught in the illusion of time's passing. The only reality is this Eternal Now, filled *now* with the entire past and future. On the seventh day, the Light of Consciousness shines in-Itself. Like a midnight sun, it shines not on the waking, dreaming and/or dreamless stages of life alone, but on their entire synthesis, which we can call, for a lack of a better term, the *Ineffable-Un-Conceivable-Un-Consciousness*. It is the Silence of Awareness in-Itself.

As in the descending process, the central third Day of Creation is the moment that, from Consciousness, the physical transformation takes place. Now, during the inhaling reabsorption of the Days of Creation into the Resting Stillness, God transforms His Creation. From the Earth, as a pivotal point, the reversal of the creative process starts anew. Let us understand, however, that none this takes place *somewhere outside*, but it is happening right here and right now in the mind of the reader of these words.

(III ↓) From the Earth, the Third Day, each day, at the same time, retracts into the preceding one. Namely,

(II→IV) the Purity of the Second Day sanctifies (קדש qadash) the Power of the Fourth Day.

(I→V) The Love of the First Day sublimates the Biological-drive of the Fifth Day. Finally,

(VII→VI ↑) the Ecstatic Rest of the Seventh Day transmutes the Life of the Sixth Day.

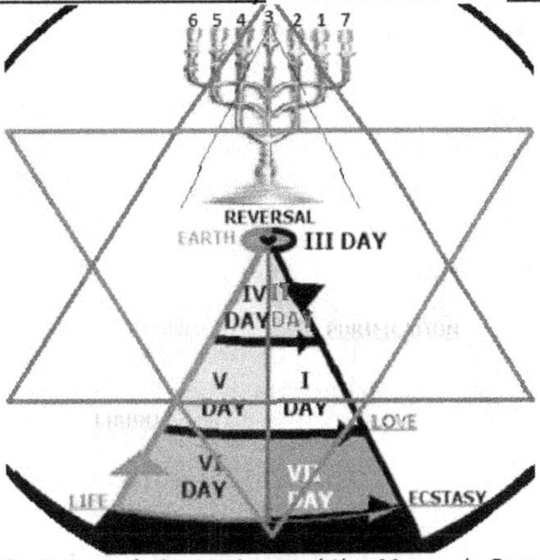

GRAPHIC: *Reversal, Ascension and the Menorah Candelabrum*

At this last stage, the entire Creation reabsorbs in the same state in which it is before it is creatively projected. This is the eschatological reabsorption at the *non-end-nor-beginning-of-the-world*, which concludes the Cycle of Knowledge. On this Day, Divine-Consciousness enters the stillness without any activity. All potential and/or physical connection within the consciousness-*of* the world of objectivity is interrupted. The conscious and physical world disappears in the *pre-creative* ineffable state of the Ecstatic-True-Transcendent-Life. This is the Infinite Zero or the One Who remains when we take our *cognitive eyes* away from the world. This last one, nevertheless, reappears immediately upon focusing on it, just as when we awake from a deep sleep.

2:4-CERTAIN AWARENESS

אֵלֶּה תוֹלְדוֹת הַשָּׁמַיִם וְהָאָרֶץ בְּהִבָּרְאָם בְּיוֹם עֲשׂוֹת יְהוָה אֱלֹהִים אֶרֶץ וְשָׁמָיִם׃ *'ēleh* (these) *ṯvōlaḏvōṯ* (descendants) *hašāmayim* (heaven) *vahā'āreṣ* (earth) *bahibāra'ām* (created) *bayvōm* (day) *'ăśvōṯ* (made) *yahvāh* (Transcendent) *'ĕlōhiym* (of Divine-Consciousness) *'ereṣ* (earth) *vašāmāyim* (heaven)
αὔτη *autē* (these) **ἡ** *ē* (the) **βίβλος** *biblos* (lists) **γενέσεως** *geneseōs* (origin) **οὐρανοῦ** *ouranou* (heaven) **καὶ** *kai* (and) **γῆς** *gēs* (earth) **ὅτε** *ote* (when) **ἐγένετο** *egeneto* (arose) **ᾗ** *ē* (the) **ἡμέρᾳ** *emera* (day) **ἐποίησεν** *epoiēsen* (created) **ὁ** *o* (the) **θεὸς** *theos* (God) **τὸν** *ton* (the) **οὐρανὸν** *ouranon* (sky) **καὶ** *kai* (the) **τὴν** *tēn* (the) **γῆν** *gēn* (earth)
istae (these) ***generationes*** (the generations) ***caeli*** (of heaven) ***et*** (and) ***terrae*** (earth) ***quando*** (when) ***createe*** (created) ***sunt*** (are) ***in*** (in) ***die*** (the day) ***quo*** (in which) ***fecit*** (made) ***Dominus*** (Lord) ***Deus*** (God) ***caelum*** (the sky) ***et*** (and) ***terram*** (the earth)
These are the generations of the heavens and of the earth when they were created, in the day that the LORD God made the earth and the heavens,
These are the descending generations of heaven and earth, when they were created in the day in which the Transcendence of Divine-Consciousness made the sky and the earth, and...

As we read, God the Creator is Divine-Consciousness (אלהים *'elohiym*). However, now, for the first time in the *Torah*, we encounter Its proper name as יְהֹוָה, $Y_{ĕ}H_{o}V_{a}H$.[592] The name, deriving from *hayah*,[593] *to be*, means the Essence of Transcendence. It is the ineffable name uttered by the voice, coming out of the burning bush that we will encounter in *Exodus*, which declares,

"*I AM THAT I AM.*"[594]

That voice states Its essence as SELF-IN-ITSELF,

"*the Transcendent Self-Evidence of Divine-Consciousness* ."[595]

As we have seen, that name is unpronounceable and unconceivable because any mental construction of IT would reduce ITS ABSOLUTE TRANSCENDENCE to an immanent object. Then, how can we refer to IT? Let us follow a paragon. Someone, upon thinking, seeing, hearing, tasting, smelling and/or feeling something, may question, '*What is that, which I am thinking, seeing, hearing, tasting, smelling and/or feeling?*' Conversely, however, s/he could never say, '*I am not thinking, seeing, hearing, tasting, smelling and/or feeling something.*' That is because Certain-Evidence is the foundation of every knowledge. Certain-Evidence does not refer to what is experienced or believed as being independent from the knowledge-*of* it. Certain is Certainty. It is the state that envelops all that which we may be certain-*of*. Certainty is not established by what is stated. A belief might prove incorrect, but Certainty, *viz.* the Faith that sustained and enveloped that erroneous belief, remains Certain and Evident as such. There is nothing before that. Certainty is always the support and beginning of every one of all those acts. Certainty, as Truth, is Pure Awareness. It is FAITH, not signifying belief and/or dogma, but, in the sense of the Hebrew *'emuwnah*[596] and the Greek *pístis*, meaning *certitude*.[597] This term conveys the unshakable *assurance*, *trust*[598] and *certainty* inherent, here and now in the foundation of *Faithful*-Awareness.[599] That Certitude is not conceivable except as a concept, which, therefore, is not the original certitude but only the thought of IT, of which, nevertheless we are certain. This explains the injunction in *Exodus*,[600]

"*Thou shalt not take*[601] *the name of Yěhovah* (יְהוָה) *of Divine-Consciousness into emptiness*[602]."

In fact, any pronunciation of it would reduce IT to an empty meaningless vocalization. Namely, YĚHOVAH, THE CERTAIN-TRUTH, is not *yěhovah, the certain-truth,* as spelled and written on this page. As an example, the thought, the sound and/or writing of the word *blue* is not the real color "blue" as blue. Similarly, when we say, that a

"Rose is a rose is a rose is a rose,"[603]

we mean that the mental evocation of the object produced by the sound of the word rose is very different from that flower as that flower in itself. For this same principle, in 1677, the author Altus titled his work *Livre Muět*, the *Mute Book* without words, so that

"all the Nations of the world... can read it and understand it... immediately."[604]

More so, to realize the Transcendent-Certain-Truth, the only recourse is *to rest* (שָׁבַת *shabath*), to cease any creative conceptualization of the objective world. Therefore,

"'*Put off thy shoes from off thy feet, for the place whereon thou standest is holy ground*'...[605] *and Moses hid his face; for he was afraid to look upon Divine-Consciousness.*"[606]

Then, fix or suspend the flowing breath of thought and concentrate into the meditative stillness of Pure-Apodictical-Awareness. Thus, CERTAIN AWARENESS becomes God's Seventh Day of Rest, which was such even before the First Day.

<The Self-in-Itself is unknown. However, even if not known, we realize It as this undeniable Apodictic-Awareness we have right Now. Awareness is the only true witness. Who can deny the certainty we have of this writing or even of the dream we had last night. We may doubt the reality in-itself, *i.e.:* without the dreamer, of the oneiric world, but never of having the dream as fantasy. Awareness is always the foundation of everything including doubt as awareness of disbelief. Nevertheless, Awareness is always Certitude-of-Awareness.>[607]

The difference between Yěhovah and 'Elohiym is,

1) Yěhovah[608] is the Transcendent, namely, That, which stands always beyond the subject-object correlation.
   a. We can never know **Him** because that would reduce him to an object, thus not **It**.
   b. Our thought of **Her** is not **It**, we can think of her, but then it is an idea, not **It**.
   c. However, we always tend towards **It**. Every thought, every knowledge, every action, every intention presupposes the direction beyond the subject-object correlation, *viz.* into the Transcendent.

2) 'Elohiym[609] is Divine-Consciousness, which establishes the creative epistemic structure of the world making it intelligible.

From Awareness, descending (תולדות towlĕdah) along three tiered levels, Divine-Consciousness brings forward (יָלַד yalad) His creation.

I) On the first level, there is the Divine-Consciousness as Pure-Consciousness.

II) Then, on the second level, He projects His Light of Consciousness.

III) On the third level, takes place the transformation where the physical world becomes a reflection of the ideal one. There, that Light illuminates the world as consciousness-*of* these objects here and now.

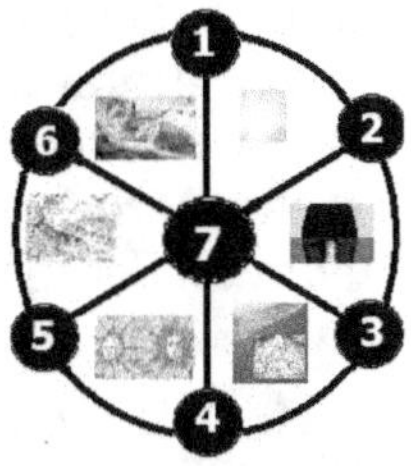

The seventh day is the center of the circularity of consciousness. That point emanates its radiuses on each of the six circular days of creation on the circumference and identifies with each of those points. Therefore, by keeping the seventh day sacred we rest in the contemplation of the entire procreative process. Thus *Deuteronomy* states[610]

"*As the Transcendent thy God hath commanded thee, 'Observe*[611] *the Sabbath resting Day*[612] *of Atonement*[613] *to keep it sacred.*[614]*'"*

Concluding, heaven/subject and earth/object are established in their ways of knowing by the Uncaused Centrality of Certain Awareness

2-II SECTION: ADAM

2:5-The Barrenness of the Ideal Earth

וְכֹל שִׂיחַ הַשָּׂדֶה טֶרֶם יִהְיֶה בָאָרֶץ וְכָל־עֵשֶׂב הַשָּׂדֶה טֶרֶם יִצְמָח כִּי לֹא הִמְטִיר יְהוָה אֱלֹהִים עַל־הָאָרֶץ וְאָדָם אַיִן לַעֲבֹד אֶת־הָאֲדָמָה׃
vaḵōl (all) *śiyaḥ* (plant) *haśāḏeh* (of the field) *ṭerem* (not yet) *yihayeh* (transcendent) *ḇā'āreṣ* (earth) *vaḵāl* (all) *'ēśeḇ* (herb) *haśāḏeh* (field) *ṭerem* (not yet) *yiṣamāḥ* (sprout) *kiy* (because) *lō'* (no) *himaṭiyr* (rain) *yahvāh* (transcendent) *'ĕlōhiym* (Divine-Consciousness) *'al* (over) *hā'āreṣ* (the earth) *va'āḏām* (human) *'ayin* (no) *la'ăḇōḏ* (to work) *'eṯ* (and) *hā'ăḏāmāh* (the ground)
καὶ *kai* (and) **πᾶν** *pan* (all) **χλωρὸν** *chlōron* (plant) **ἀγροῦ** *agrou* (of the field) **πρὸ** *pro* (before) **τοῦ** *tou* (the) **γενέσθαι** *genesthai* (had germinated) **ἐπὶ** *epi* (on) **τῆς** *tēs* (the) **γῆς** *gēs* (earth) **καὶ** *kai* (and) **πάντα** *panta* (all) **χόρτον** *chorton* (feeding place) **ἀγροῦ** *agrou* (of the field) **πρὸ** *pro* (before) **τοῦ** *tou* (the) **ἀνατεῖλαι** *anateilai* (it sprouted) **οὐ** *ou* (not) **γὰρ** *gar* (in fact) **ἔβρεξεν** *ebrexen* (let rain) **ὁ** *o* (the) **θεὸς** *theos* (God) **ἐπὶ** *epi* (on) **τὴν** *tēn* (the) **γῆν** *gēn* (the) **καὶ** *kai* (and) **ἄνθρωπος** *anthrōpos* (man) **οὐκ** *ouk* (not) **ἦν** *ēn* (was) **ἐργάζεσθαι** *ergazesthai* (could have toiled) **τὴν** *tēn* (the) **γῆν** *gēn* (earth)
et (and) **omne** (all) **virgultum** (plant) **agri** (of the field) **antequam** (before) **oreretur** (had germinated) **in** (in) **terra** (the ground) **omnem-**(all) **que** (and) **herbam** (the herb) **regionis** (in the field) **priusquam** (before) **germinaret** (it sprouted) **non** (not) **enim** (in fact) **pluerat** (had rained) **Dominus** (Lord) **Deus** (God) **super** (on) **terram** (the earth) **et** (and) **homo** (the human) **non** (not) **erat** (was) **qui** (who) **operaretur** (could have tilled over) **terram** (the earth)
and every plant of the field before it was in the earth, and every herb of the field before it grew: for the LORD God had not caused it to rain upon the earth, and there was not a man to till the ground.
... and [Divine-Consciousness made] every plant of the field before it had germinated in the ground and every herb in the field before it had sprouted. In fact, the Transcendent of Divine-Consciousness had not caused rain on the earth and no human was there who could have tilled over the earth.

In the *logical-beginning*, Divine-Consciousness creates Life and the world in its potential state. Then, plants and herbs, metaphors for objectivity in general, were in the realm of possibility. They were still in an ideal state ready to grow. The potential state of an idea implies a sort of Platonic *Hyperuranium*.[615] This means that its ideal possibility actualizes only when the consciousness-*of* it projects it as a fact, as the collapse of the quantum states.[616] When those possibilities rain down[617] as abundant[618] reflections from the Ocean of Awareness, then, they materialize as secondary waters, namely, the infinite manifestations of all the actual experiences of this world's dimension. In the state of rest, those possibilities are in the Pure Intentional Light of Consciousness. They are in the superior waters of possibility. This is the *a-priori* condition, the pure state, which precedes logically every epistemic consciousness-*of* the objective world. Then, Adam,[619] the red-subject, was not there to actualize them. This is like dreams or ideas while we are in dreamless NREM sleep.

The vast superior ocean of possible thoughts, not yet conceptualized, logically precedes the actual manifestation of any notion. Nevertheless, to put those ideas into actuality, the human mind, *viz.* the *redden* (אָדָם *'adam*) *Adam* (אָדָם *'adam*), has to think them as dreams or thoughts right here and now. In fact, the entire universe cannot exist if not recognized existent by an active operating intelligence, experiencing and toiling[620] in and on this red-ground (אֲדָמָה *'adamah*),[621] namely, the circular subject-object correlation.

2:6-The Mist

וְאֵד יַעֲלֶה מִן־הָאָרֶץ וְהִשְׁקָה אֶת־כָּל־פְּנֵי־הָאֲדָמָה
va'ēḏ (mist) *ya'ăleh* (went up) *min* (from) *hā'āreṣ* (the earth) *vahišaqāh* (giving drink) *'eṯ* (to) *kāl* (all) *panēy* (surface) *hā'ăḏāmāh* (of the land)
πηγὴ *pēgē* (spring) **δὲ** *de* (but) **ἀνέβαινεν** *anebainen* (came up) **ἐκ** *ek* (from) **τῆς** *tēs* (the) **γῆς** *gēs* (earth) **καὶ** *kai* (and) **ἐπότιζεν** *epotizen* (to irrigatge) **πᾶν** *pan* (all) **τὸ** *to* (the) **πρόσωπον** *prosōpon* (surface) **τῆς** *tēs* (the) **γῆς** *gēs* (earth)

sed (but) ***fons*** (a spring) ***ascendebat*** (was arising) ***e*** (from) ***terra*** (the earth) ***inrigans*** (irrigating) ***universam*** (the entire) ***superficiem*** (surface) ***terrae*** (of the earth)
But there went up a mist from the earth, and watered the whole face of the ground.
However, a fogy mist was arising from the earth watering the entire surface of the land.

A mist,[622] going up[623] from the earth's objectivity, transforms the potentiality of the creative process into its actuality. Thomas Merton asks,

> "What was this fountain that sprang up in the center of the earth and watered it all before man was made and before there was even any rain?"[624].

This mist, this fog is the noematic aspect of objectivity, *viz.* the objective aspect of experience in its modes-of-being-given. In the Akkadian-Sumerian tradition, this is the fog (*edu*) that <made Gilgamesh fall asleep and lose immortality.[625] Through that fog, the Ego finds itself in the dream world and subsequently in this awakened valley of tears. On the other hand, before creation, the Spirit, the Wind of God, was on the unified waters beyond the dreamless-sleep, where there was no fog because the breath of God dispersed it.

We find the world crystallized *out there*, constituted *ab initio*, from the very beginning, conceived as having a history and bearer of history. The world-object, then, is the past because it is 'already given.' It is the noema, the perceived objective aspect of the lived experience in its modes of being given. On the other side, the present instant is the perceiving itself, the act of perception aiming to grasp the object; it is the noesis, the subjective aspect of the lived experience.>[626]

The misty fog, then, is the beginning of the inebriation of objectivity that distracts us from its creative origin, as we will see in Noah's account. The fog and the irrigating waters (שָׁקָה *shaqah*) are the infinite flowing experiences that give themselves as noematic drink[627] to the thirsty mind of the human about to be generated. Whereas, the Superior Waters are the ones, which,

> "*whosoever drinketh of the water... shall never thirst; but... shall be in him a well of water springing up into everlasting life.*"[628]

2:7-The Breath of Adam's Life

וַיִּיצֶר יְהוָה אֱלֹהִים אֶת־הָאָדָם עָפָר מִן־הָאֲדָמָה וַיִּפַּח בְּאַפָּיו נִשְׁמַת חַיִּים וַיְהִי הָאָדָם לְנֶפֶשׁ חַיָּה׃ *vayiyṣer* (formed) *yahvāh* (the Transcendence) *'ĕlōhiym* (of Divine-Consciousness) *'et̲* (and) *hā'āḏām* (human) *'āp̄ar* (dust) *min* (from) *hā'ăḏāmāh* (the earth) *vayipaḥ* (breathed) *ba'apāyv* (nostril) *nišamat̲* (breath) *ḥayiym* (living) *vayahiy* (being) *hā'āḏām* (human) *lanep̄eš* (self) *ḥayāh* (living)
καὶ *kai* (and) **ἔπλασεν** *eplasen* (formed) **ὁ** *o* (the) **θεὸς** *theos* (God) **τὸν** *ton* (the) **ἄνθρωπον** *anthropōn* (man) **χοῦν** *choun* (dust) **ἀπὸ** *apo* (from) **τῆς** *tēs* (the) **γῆς** *gēs* (earth) **καὶ** *kai* (and) **ἐνεφύσησεν** *enephusēsen* (breathed) **εἰς** *eis* (in) **τὸ** *to* (the) **πρόσωπον** *prosōpon* (face) **αὐτοῦ** *autou* (his) **πνοὴν** *pnoēn* (breath) **ζωῆς** *zōēs* (of life) **καὶ** *kai* (and) **ἐγένετο** *egeneto* (became) **ὁ** *o* (the) **ἄνθρωπος** *anthrōpos* (man) **εἰς** *eis* (in) **ψυχὴν** *psuchēn* (soul) **ζῶσαν** *zōsan* (living)
formavit (formed) ***igitur*** (therefore) ***Dominus*** (Lord) ***Deus*** (God) ***hominem*** (man) ***de*** (out of) ***limo*** (the mud) ***terrae*** (of the earth) ***et*** (and) ***inspiravit*** (breathed) ***in*** (in) ***faciem*** (face) ***eius*** (his) ***spiraculum*** (the spirit) ***vitae*** (of life) ***et*** (and) ***factus*** (made) ***est*** (is) ***homo*** (man) ***in*** (in) ***animam*** (a soul) ***viventem*** (living)
And the LORD God formed man of the dust of the ground, and breathed into his nostrils the breath of life; and man became a living soul.
Therefore, the Transcendence of Divine-Consciousness conceived and formed Adam the red human out of the red mud of the earth and breathed in his nostril the breath of life and the human was made into a living spirit.

Let us analyze the various aspects of the creation and conception[629] of Adam,[630] the human being. The word *'adam* derives from the verb *'adam,*[631] *to be red*. Also the earth, out of which Adam was formed, is a red agriculturally tilled land.[632] The color red is a symbol of activity and work. In fact, the "Red-One"[633] was the designation for Esau,[634] whose name means the one who is active by working and hunting.

Therefore, the red color of Adam and Esau indicates the *Earth Race*[635] that had the fiery, bustling appearance of the worker interacting with the world.[636] Metaphorically, that redness represents also the Subject-Object active circularity, as the friction of two fire-sticks fitted one into the other and churned around,

"used for kindling fire by attrition."[637]

Genesis will describe it as a whirling fire-brand a

"*flaming sword which turned every way*"

to conceal the tree of life in the middle of the Garden of Eden.[638]

Once the human is shaped out of that red earth, Divine-Consciousness blew[639] His Breath[640] of Life[641] in Adam's nostrils. What is this breath? What is the difference between this breath and the Divine Breath or Wind[642] hovering over the abyss of the waters? The Wind of God hovering over the abyss is the Stillness of the Transcendent in Its Resting state, *before* and *after* It proceeds along the creative procession. Now, this Breath of Life is creating, is instilling life in the Human Being who, thus, becomes sentient.

If, as we have seen,[643] Adam, the male and female[644] human, is the image of God, then, by analyzing the image, we can infer God's essence. Beyond its physical appearance, Consciousness characterizes the life of the human being. Consciousness articulates on three steps,[645] as relayed by Ezekiel in his description of God's chariot.[646]

1) Auto-Transparency is the moment in which the human is conscious while it does

    "not think of thinking... because... it is present to itself, without needing to mediate itself, that is, to see itself before itself as object of its own knowledge."[647]

   Like an *apnea* of the breath of consciousness, this Auto-transparency is best understood if we refer it to the *NREM* (Non-Rapid-Eyes-Movement) state of deep sleep.[648] We can call this with an oxymoron, the *state of being awake in dreamless sleep*.

    "*I sleep, but my hearth waketh: it is the voice of my beloved that knocketh.*"[649]

    "*It is necessary for you / to experience nonbeing... Be a sleep and a pure listening / at the same time.*"[650]

    "The *NREM* state is often called 'quiet sleep' because of the slow regular breathing, the general absence of body movement, and the slow, regular brain activity... The body is not paralyzed ... it *can* move, but it *does not* move because the brain doesn't order it to move. The sleeper has lost contact with his environment. There is a shut-down of perception because the five senses are no longer gathering information and communicating stimuli to the brain."[651]

   That is the state of pure-potential-consciousness, which is present in the next two stages without being conceptualized. However, once conceptualized, it becomes active in the next step, when

    "*sleep departed from mine eyes.*"[652]

   Ezekiel[653] describes it as

    "*a fire*[654] *taking hold of itself.*"[655]

2) I-Consciousness is the next moment in which thought is conscious-*of* itself as thought. Consciousness, from the Latin *con-scio*, requires knowledge (*scio*) integrated with (*con*)

    "a large repertoire of states (information) *and* it must be unified; that is, it should be doing so as a single system... Consciousness is integrated information."[656]

   <Consciousness-*of* is the act of focusing on one or more objects with different degrees of intensity. That act finds its foundation in Epistemic-Awareness, which is always identical to itself regardless of the levels of conscious, subconscious or unconscious intensity. Beyond consciousness, therefore, the central fulcrum is always That-Unified-Certainty, which is the Only-One truly dispelling uncertainty or ignorance.>[657] Like an *inhaling* breath of consciousness, this is evident in the dream[658] state, during which our thoughts, coming out of the *mist* or *fog* (אד *'ed*),

become visible. The thirst (שָׁקָה *shaqah*) for representations *fogs-up* (עָלָה` *alah*) the previous sleep with no dreams. In the oneiric studies, this state, has been labeled

"*REM* (for Rapid-Eye-Movement) sleep to define the phenomenon… observed… which has been called 'active sleep'."[659]

Ezekiel[660] describes it as

"*a great dreamy*[661] *cloud.*"[662]

3) Ego-Consciousness, like an *exhaling* breath of consciousness, is the waking consciousness-*of* the objects, which we have right here and now as we read this page. Ezekiel[663] describes it as

"*a living spirit-wind*[664] *that came out of the hidden*[665] *north-heaven.*"[666]

Those three states of consciousness are always present all in each of the three levels and constitute our integrated general self-consciousness. In fact, right here and now we are

I) auto-transparent to our self,
II) conscious-*of* our thoughts, and
III) conscious-*of* this body engaged in the world of objectivity.

Therefore, Consciousness displays itself along all the three previous steps (רֶגֶל *regel*) or revolving wheels[667] of consciousness. They alternate rotating and oscillating from one state into the other and vice versa. Ezekiel describes it

"*as it were a wheel in the middle of a wheel…*[668] *for the breath*[669] *of the living was in the wheels.*"[670]

The ancient world knew well these sleep distinctions. From ⇦Shamanic Pre-Columbian America,[671] to Egypt,[672] to Greece[673] and all the way to India,[674] the sleep world was a matter of great investigation. Philo of Alexandria wrote extensive commentaries on sleep.[675] Divinities spoke in dreams, momentous events took place during sleep and oracles foretold the future in oneiric occurrences. Sleep levels and their distinctions were topics of serious analysis among priestly classes and adepts of initiatory mysteries.[676] The *Torah* distinguishes them as

a) dream[677] (*viz.* REM) *chalowm,*[678] *dream*, from the verb *chalam,*[679] *to dream*, and
b) deep sleep[680] (*viz.* NREM) *tardemah,*[681] *deep sleep, trance*, from the verb *radam,*[682] *to be asleep, to be unconscious, to be in heavy sleep, to fall into heavy sleep, to be fast asleep.*

"*The Transcendent* (יְהֹוָה *Yĕhovah*) *made a covenant, a libation*[683] *pouring upon you the flowing-breath* (רוּחַ *ruwach*) *of deep sleep* (תַּרְדֵּמָה *tardemah*), *and hath closed your eyes: the prophets and your rulers, the seers hath he covered. And the vision* (חָזוּת *chazuwth*) *of all is become unto you as the words of a book that is sealed* (חָתַם *chatham*)… *and … cannot* [be] *read* (קָרָא *qara'*)… *for it is sealed.*"[684]

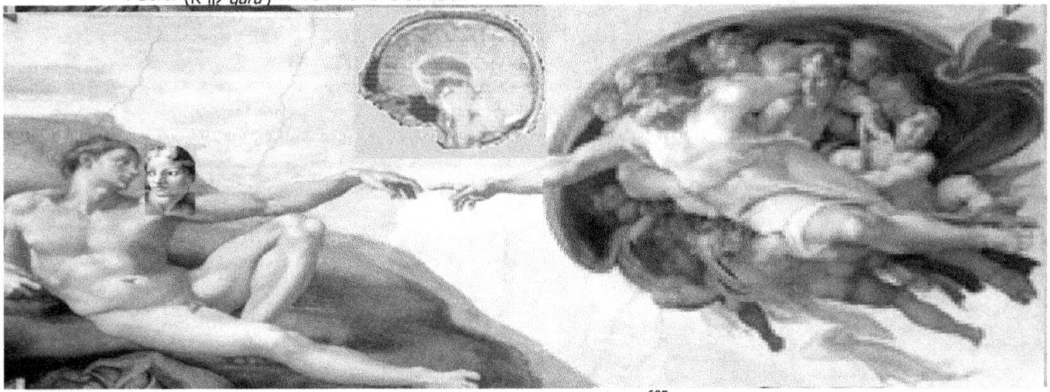

GRAPHIC: *Creation of Adam*[685]

However, where does Consciousness come from and where does it go? There is a fourth element, which transcends us. It is the silence from which we come before-birth and to which we go after death.

4) Yĕhovah, the Pure-Apodictic-Awareness, is the fourth all-encompassing state or wheel of the chariot. It is the Transcendent-Silence and the Resting-Stillness from which we come from and to which we go. Again, Ezekiel describes that

> *"out of the midst*[686] *of the auto-transparent-fire*[687] *there was an illuminating*[688] *brightness*[689] *all-encompassing it,*[690] *and out of the midst thereof as a spiritual-eye*[691] *of polished shining*[692] *substance...*[693] *Like the appearance of a rainbow in the cloud in a rainy day, so was the appearance of the brightness all around. This was the realization*[694] *of the likeness of the glory of the Transcendent."*[695]

2:8-Adam's Garden

וַיִּטַע יְהוָה אֱלֹהִים גַן־בְעֵדֶן מִקֶדֶם וַיָשֶׂם שָׁם אֶת־הָאָדָם אֲשֶׁר יָצָר׃
vayiṭa` (planted) *yahvāh* (Transcendent) *'ĕlōhiym* (Divine-Consciousness) *gan* (garden) *ḇa'ēḏen* (happiness) *miqeḏem* (for) *vayāśem* (placed) *šām* (there) *'eṯ* (and) *hā'āḏām* (human) *'ăšer* (which) *yāṣār* (formed)
καὶ *kai* (and) **ἐφύτευσεν** *ephuteusen* (planted) **κύριος** *kurios* (Lord) **ὁ** *o* (the) **θεὸς** *theos* (God) **παράδεισον** *paradeison* (paradise) **ἐν** *en* (in) **Εδεμ** *Edem* (Eden) **κατὰ** *kata* (from) **ἀνατολὰς** *anatolas* (the rising East) **καὶ** *kai* (and) **ἔθετο** *etheto* (established) **ἐκεῖ** *ekei* (in that place) **τὸν** *ton* (the) **ἄνθρωπον** *anthrōpon* (man) **ὃν** *on* (that) **ἔπλασεν** *eplasen* (He had formed)
plantaverat (planted) ***autem*** (also) ***Dominus*** (Lord) ***Deus*** (God) ***paradisum*** (a paradise) ***voluptatis*** (of happiness) ***a*** (from) ***principio*** (the beginning) ***in*** (in) ***quo*** (which) ***posuit*** (He placed) ***hominem*** (the man) ***quem*** (who) ***formaverat*** (He had shaped)
And the LORD God planted a garden eastward in Eden; and there he put the man whom he had formed.
Also, from the very beginning, the Transcendent Divine-Consciousness planted Eden, an eastern paradise garden of conscious happiness in which He placed the human whom He had shaped.

The vain and superficial search for the geographical location of Eden is destined to fail. That is as searching for the contact lenses while they are all along on your eyes. Furthermore, conferring to Eden a literal physical geographical location it would make it irrelevant to the size of the Earth. Even if the Garden were an alien planet, then that place would still be infinitesimally unimportant compared to the actual vastness of the Universe/s.[696]

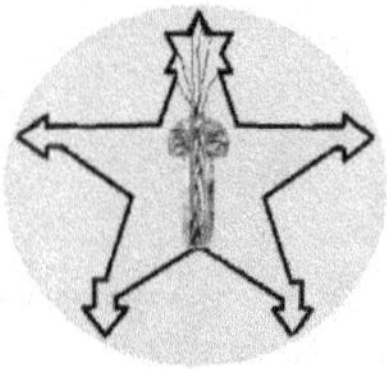

In fact, that Garden of Eden is, metaphorically, this human body, the limbs depart from the head as four rivers generated from one spring. Then and there,[697] in Adam's body, consciousness delights from all experiences. From its very beginning,[698] the same soil, which was erected[699] in Adam's shape, is also the enclosed garden[700] of happiness.[701] Eden was formed to house[702] the human's *eastern arising sun* (קֶדֶם *qedem*) of Consciousness.

> The idea, before being thought, is potentially in the mind. Placed in the Garden of Consciousness, that mind acknowledges itself as this subject and object knower of this world.

2-III SECTION: THE GARDEN OF EDEN

2:9-The Trees of Life and Knowledge

וַיַּצְמַח יְהוָה אֱלֹהִים מִן־הָאֲדָמָה כָּל־עֵץ נֶחְמָד לְמַרְאֶה וְטוֹב לְמַאֲכָל וְעֵץ הַחַיִּים בְּתוֹךְ הַגָּן וְעֵץ הַדַּעַת טוֹב וָרָע׃
vayaṣamaḥ (produced) *yahvāh* (Transcendent) *'ĕlōhiym* (Divine-Consciousness) *min* (from) *hā'ăḏāmāh* (land) *kāl* (all) *'ēṣ* (tree) *neḥamāḏ* (pleasant) *lamara'eh* (to see) *vaṭvōḇ* (good) *lama'ăḵāl* (to eat) *va'ēṣ* (tree) *haḥayiym* (life) *baṯvōḵa* (middle) *hagān* (garden) *va'ēṣ* (tree) *hada'aṯ* (knowledge) *ṭvōḇ* (good) *vārā'* (evil)
καὶ *kai* (and) **ἐξανέτειλεν** *exaneteilen* (made to spring up) **ὁ** *o* (the) **θεὸς** *theos* (God) **ἔτι** *eti* (still) **ἐκ** *ek* (of) **τῆς** *tēs* (the) **γῆς** *gēs* (earth) **πᾶν** *pan* (every) **ξύλον** *xulon* (tree) **ὡραῖον** *ōraion* (beautiful) **εἰς** *eis* (in) **ὅρασιν** *orasin* (see) **καὶ** *kai* (and) **καλὸν** *kalon* (beautiful) **εἰς** *eis* (in) **βρῶσιν** *brōsin* (to eat) **καὶ** *kai* (and) **τὸ** *to* (the) **ξύλον** *xulon* (tree) **τῆς** *tēs* (the) **ζωῆς** *zōēs* (life) **ἐν** *en* (in) **μέσῳ** *mesō* (middle) **τῷ** *tō* (the) **παραδείσῳ** *paradeisō* (paradise) **καὶ** *kai* (and) **τὸ** *to* (the) **ξύλον** *xulon* (tree) **τοῦ** *tou* (the) **εἰδέναι** *eidenai* (know) **γνωστὸν** *gnōston* (knowledge) **καλοῦ** *kalou* (good) **καὶ** *kai* (and) **πονηροῦ** *ponēpou* (evil)
produxit (produced) ***-que*** (and) ***Dominus*** (the Lord) ***Deus*** (God) ***de*** (out of) ***humo*** (earth) ***omne*** (every) ***lignum*** (tree) ***pulchrum*** (beautiful) ***visu*** (to see) ***et*** (and) ***ad*** (to) ***vescendum*** (eat) ***suave*** (sweet) ***lignum*** (tree) ***etiam*** (also) ***vitae*** (of life) ***in*** (in) ***medio*** (the middle) ***paradisi*** (of the paradise) ***lignum-***(tree) ***que*** (and) ***scientiae*** (of knowledge) ***boni*** (good) ***et*** (and) ***mali*** (evil)
And out of the ground made the LORD God to grow every tree that is pleasant to the sight, and good for food; the tree of life also in the midst of the garden, and the tree of knowledge of good and evil.
And the Transcendent Divine-Consciousness out of that land produced every tree beautiful to see and sweet to eat. Also, at the center of that paradise were the tree of Life and the tree of Knowledge of Good and Evil.

'Eden (עֵדֶן),[703] meaning *delight, pleasure*, derives from the verb *'adan* (עָדַן),[704] which means *to luxuriate, to delight oneself*,

"*to conduct oneself softly*, i.e. to live sumptuously, delicately."[705]

In fact, Nehemiah states,

"*And they took strong cities, and a fat land, and possessed houses full of all goods, wells digged, vineyards, and oliveyards, and fruit trees in abundance: so they did eat, and were filled, and became fat, and delighted themselves* (עָדַן *'adan*) *in thy great goodness.*"[706]

There is no experience, without consciousness. Necessarily, all types of delight imply consciousness. Therefore, the Garden of Eden is this **Garden of Consciousness**. Daily, in it, we find the luxurious *growing* vegetation[707] of conscientiality.[708]

Two trees grow in Eden and they are both in the midst (תָּוֶךְ *tavek*)[709] of that garden. What distinguish them are their directions. The Tree of Life is the direction leading to Transcendence, while the Tree of Knowledge is the projection towards objectivity. The middle (תָּוֶךְ *tavek*) ground of that garden, shared by those two Trees, is that of consciousness. However, the Tree of Knowledge becomes conscious-*of* the world and, consequently, is deep-rooted and buried in it. Thus, paradoxically, its direction leads to suffering, to death and to the loss of the delightful (עדן *'adan*) state of Pure Consciousness. On the other hand, in the Tree of Life, Consciousness rises to Heaven until it identifies with Awareness merging with the Transcendent.

Out of that red land, the Transcendent Divine-Consciousness made all trees (עֵץ *'ets*) grow. The trees are the pleasant driving-nerves of consciousness as pure intentionality.[710] At the very heart of consciousness, there are two specific trees,

1) The Tree (עֵץ *'ets*) of Life[711] is the symbol of the vital force directed inward. It is the Shield of David (✡)[712] with two interlocked triangles.

▽) One descends from Heaven to vivify the human heart. The Kabbalah, *Zohar, Beha 'Alothekha* describes it as,

"*the Tree of Life extends from above downward.*"[713] ✡

△) The other ascends from the earthly human heart to Heaven. The Tree of Life is also the ascending drive back to the original creative Breath (נְשָׁמָה *nĕshamah*) of Life (חי *chay*). Adam came from it and returns to the Resting Stillness of the Transcendent Breath (רוּחַ *ruwach*). ✡

GRAPHIC: *The Tree of Life*

2) The Tree (עֵץ *`ets*) of Knowledge (דעת *da`ath*) -*of* Good (טוב *towb*) and Bad (רע *ra`*) is directed to the external world. The Tree (עֵץ *`ets*) of Knowledge-[714]*of* Good (טוב *towb*) and Bad (רע *ra`*) is not the understanding of moral or ethical principles. In Hebrew, *knowledge-of good and bad* is the equivalent as saying the knowledge-*of dualism, of this and that.* Therefore, "*good and bad*" become synonym for "*everything.*"

"In the Bible, the expression *good and bad* (טוֹב *towb* רָע *ra`*) somethimes means everything (Deut. 1:39; II Sam. 19:35), as when we say, *I know its good and its bad features*, meaning that I know everything about it that can be known... see Deut. 29:18, moist and dry meaning, *everything*. The combination of contrasting terms to express totality is called *merism*; compare *good and bad* in Gen. 2:17, and the English *young and old*"[715]

<Thus, it is *knowledge* in general. It denotes the epistemic dichotomy of this world of opposites, when we enter the field of time and space. Thus, it describes the gnoseological process of thinking or distinguishing *this* from *that* or judging *good from evil.*>[716] Knowledge (*da`ath* דַּעַת)[717] derives from the verb *yada`* (יָדַע),[718] which means to be conscious-*of.*[719] Therefore, we can name it 'the Tree of **<u>Consciousness-*of*-everything</u>**.' The forbidden fruit, then, is the hunger for the product of the consciousness-*of*-the-object produced by the tree of knowledge.

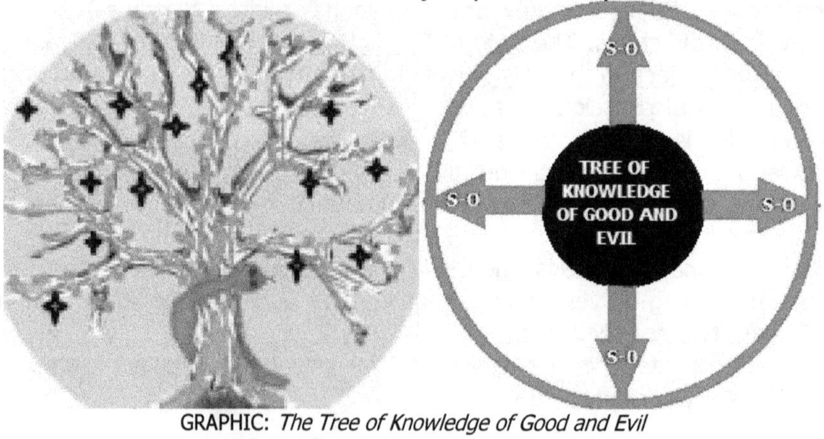

GRAPHIC: *The Tree of Knowledge of Good and Evil*

Kant states that

"Thinking therefore is the same as judging,"[720]

meaning that any representation or thought is always a classification, thus a judgment. Judging is stating something by the modality or the way in which it gives itself to us. The thought of any object implies the preliminary judgment of its being this or that and/or non-being that or this. As an example, to say, '*You are human,*' implies three judgments:

a) *You,* is judging the second singular person as distinguished from other pronouns.
b) *Are,* is judging existence as distinguished from non-being.
c) *Human,* is judging Homo Sapiens as distinguished from other species.

The *Tree of Knowledge* proves the validity of the epistemic reading and interpretation of *Genesis.* To eat (אָכַל *'akal*) is to assimilate and identify with the food. Its knowledge (דַּעַת *da`ath*) is the content of our concepts and they are our thoughts judging *good and evil*, or *this and that*. Thus, the question arises,

"To be, or not to be: that is the question:/ Whether 'tis nobler in the mind to suffer/... Or to take arms against a sea of troubles... To die, to sleep;/ To sleep: perchance to dream... what dreams may come... For who would bear the whips and scorns of time...? Thus conscience does make cowards of us all."[721]

If questions and doubts still linger over this commentary and exegesis, *knowledge*, the name (דַּעַת *da`ath*) of this tree, confirms its accuracy and its true epistemic nature or *specie*. Even if someone may stubbornly interpret the tree as being a mind-altering herb,[722] still its effects refer to an epistemic process of such intensity that changes human thinking process. Once taken by the gravitational whirlwind of the black hole in the *epistemic* Tree of Knowledge (דַּעַת *da`ath* עֵץ *'ets*), then, we hold a <u>*relig*</u>ious outlook-*of* creation. This establishes a <u>*relig*</u>ament, a *re*binding with the world conceived escapable only through death.

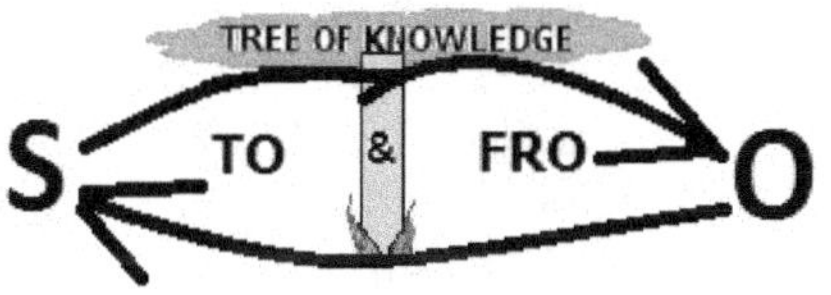

The book of Daniel says,

"*stop the words and seal the enumerating-book, even to the time of the end: many shall <u>run to and fro</u>* (שׁוּט *shuwt*)*, and knowledge shall <u>multiply</u>.*"[723]

Sealing the *enumerating-book* of knowledge by *stopping words* means the serene observation of the world. Therefore, it breaks the identification with the world of multiplying[724] objectivity generated by *running <u>to and fro</u>* (שׁוּט *shuwt*) the subject-object circular correlation, like a wooden friction fire starter bow drill. This explains ⇦[725] Adam's *redness*. Metaphorically, the color derives from its continuous *back and forth friction* during the subject-object epistemic correlation. This *red-hot* vibration takes place in the mind[726] generating three epistemic forms

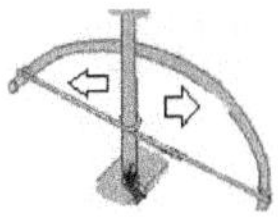

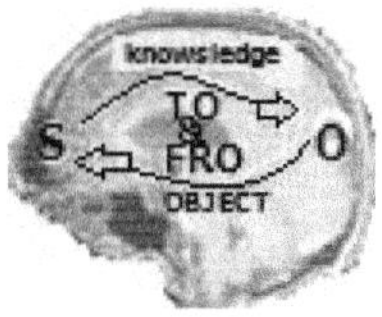

a) <u>Time</u>, (the *appointed defined meeting set time*, מוֹעֵד *mow`ed*,[727] the *beginning*, רֵאשִׁית *re'shiyth*)[728] as the timeless simultaneous lap between knower-known, in fact the knower could not know without the immediateness of the known;
b) <u>Space</u>, (רֶוַח *revach*,[729] the *heaven* שָׁמַיִם *shamayim*)[730] as the spaceless distance between understander-understood, in fact the understander would not understand if separated from the understood;
c) <u>Causality</u>, (the *created* בָּרָא *bara*)[731] as the causeless process between causer-effected, in fact the causer could not cause without the presence of the effected.

Alongside, the mind, conceptualizing and abstracting these three epistemic forms, projects them to a reality beyond itself. **The forbidden fruit is the mind itself**. The *Bṛhadāraṇyaka Upanishad* declares that Death, hungry-Mṛtyu[732] or Yama-end-maker,[733] created the mind and generated the other as different from himself. Ramana Maharshi states that

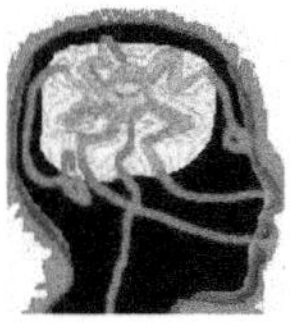

"*The obstacle is the mind... When the mind comes out of the Self, the world appears.*

Therefore, when the world appears [to be real]*, the Self does not appear; and when the Self appears* [shines]*, the world does not appear...* [In reality, there is] *no difference such as exterior and interior or up and down."*[734]

"You are not your mind, [which is] the greatest obstacle to enlightenment,"

declares Tolle.[735] This is the reason why Jesus says,

"*That whosoever looketh on a woman to lust after her hath committed adultery with her already in his heart."*[736]

<In fact, that *look* focuses on the object of consciousness not on consciousness in itself, thus loses sight of its origin. Contrary to any civil law, which, steeped in the dichotomy of good and bad, condemns the deed not the intention, here the stress is on keeping the central awareness awaken. The Real is beyond Idealism; it rests within the Pure Awareness, not being an idea itself. That is the Imperishable beyond death and beyond immortality.>[737]

Summarizing, the *knowledge of good and bad* is that which *judges*, thus, *thinks*. Then, the *fruit* that we must abstain from is desire, the outcome of the identifying *ingestion* of that thought-object. To define the mind as the forbidden fruit does not imply a ban on science. It is not a negation of thoughtful analysis and/or of scientific research as such. On the contrary, Consciousness commands an unbiased observation, that of the mathematician/scientist as such. The abstention refers to the desire of the fruit of passionate attachment to the related finding. To be *scientific*, the discovering-mind must operate mathematically and critically. Namely, it must proceed with a dispassionate development. It must focus open-mindedly unmoved during the progressive sequence of scientific discoveries. That is the correct serene mathematical calculation of science. <To be precise, the scientific research observes *scientifically* an objective world *unscientifically* postulated in-itself, while disregarding the observer.>[738]

"The difference between empirical and Transcendental subjectivity remained unavoidable... The modern idea of an objectivistic universal science *more geometrico*, with its psychophysical dualism, [interprets] empirical observations, concepts, and constructions, which are completely devoid of any legitimation from original self-evidence... Psychology... alongside the new natural science... failed to inquire after what was essentially the only genuine sense of its task as the universal science of psychic being... All theoretical thinking moves on the ground of the taken-for-granted, pre-given world of experience, the world of natural life... is supposed to be already known, or is yet to be known, by the exact natural sciences according to its objective, true being-in-itself... The taken-for-grantedness in virtue of which the 'world' constantly and pre-scientifically exists for us, 'world' being a title for an infinity of what is taken for granted, what is indispensable for all objective sciences."[739]

2:10-The Rivers

וְנָהָר יֹצֵא מֵעֵדֶן לְהַשְׁקוֹת אֶת־הַגָּן וּמִשָּׁם יִפָּרֵד וְהָיָה לְאַרְבָּעָה רָאשִׁים׃ *vanāhār* (river) *yōṣē* (went out) *mē'ēḏen* (from Eden) *lahašaqvōṯ* (to water) *'eṯ* (the) *hagān* (garden) *umišām* (from) *yipārēḏ* (divided) *vahāyāh* (become) *la'arabā'āh* (four) *rā'šiym* (divisions)
ποταμὸς *potamos* (river) **δὲ** *de* (but) **ἐκπορεύεται** *ekporeuetai* (went) **ἐξ** *ex* (out) **Εδεμ** *Edem* (Eden) **ποτίζειν** *potizein* (watering) **τὸν** *ton* (the) **παράδεισον** *paradeison* (paradise) **ἐκεῖθεν** *ekeithen* (thence) **ἀφορίζεται** *aphorizetai* (it divided) **εἰς** *eis* (in) **τέσσαρας** *tessaras* (four) **ἀρχάς** *archas* (heads)
et (and) ***fluvius*** (a river) ***egrediebatur*** (exited) ***de*** (from) ***loco*** (the place) ***voluptatis*** (of happiness) ***ad*** (to) ***inrigandum*** (irrigate) ***paradisum*** (the paradise) ***qui*** (from which) ***inde*** (thence) ***dividitur*** (it divided) ***in*** (into) ***quattuor*** (four) ***capita*** (heads)
And a river went out of Eden to water the garden; and from thence it was parted, and became into four heads.
Thereafter, a river went out from this place of delight to water the earthly paradise. From this place, the river divided into four branches.

Eden, the seat of delight, starts in Adam's head. From it, departs a river (נָהָר *nahar*)[740] divided in four branches (ראש *ro'sh*).[741] This is the articulation of consciousness within the body, *viz.* from the head down through the four limbs. The rivers are metaphors for the flowing waters of the light of consciousness. In fact, the word *nahar*, river[742] derives from the verb *nahar*,[743] which means to shine, to beam. Therefore, they light-up like streams of conscious brightness.

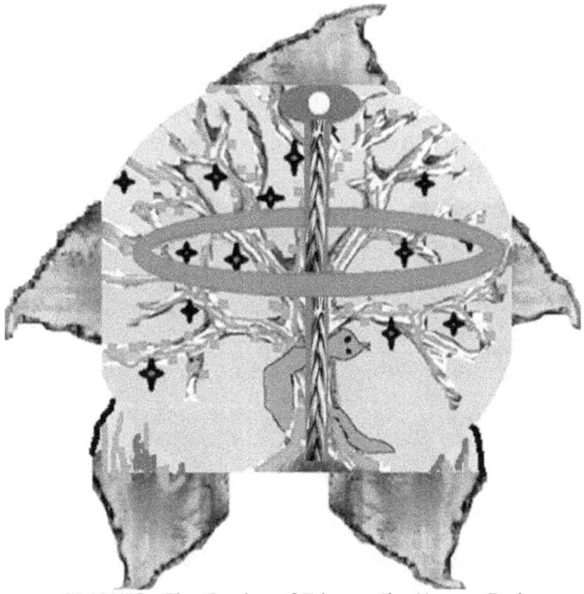

GRAPHIC: *The Garden of Eden as the Human Body*

They stream like a spinning-top, shaping the directions of a three-dimensional compass-rose. Vertically, the stream of consciousness flows out from the Zenith of the Earthly Paradise and reaches the Nadir in Eden. Once there, this river fills the whole Garden with flowing consciousness. On that plane, consciousness operates according to the four horizontal divisions of space, namely, North, East, South and West. Space, time, together with cause are the *modus operandi* with which knowledge becomes conscious-*of* the objects.

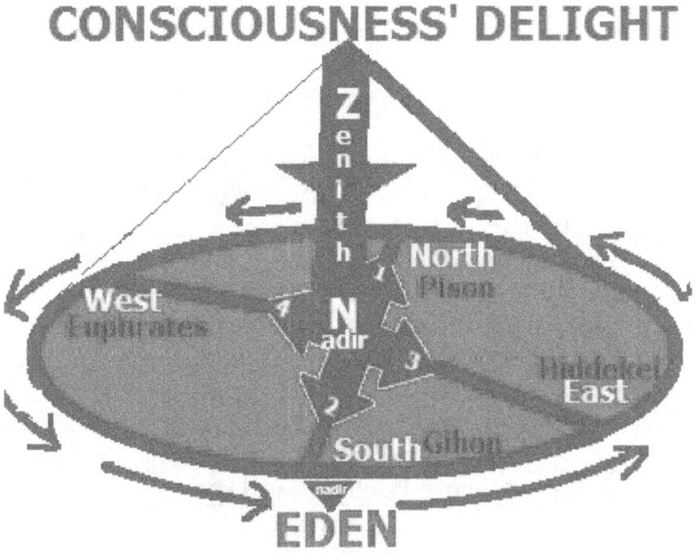

GRAPHIC: *The One River with Four Branches*

Those four branches are similar to Ezekiel's description of the four wings of the

"living creatures... [who] *had the likeness of a man ... and ... had four wings... joined one to another... they went every one straight forward... And their wings were stretched upward; two wings of every*

one were joined one to another, and two covered their bodies... When they went, they went upon their four sides."[744]

2:11-The Increasing First Branch River

שֵׁם הָאֶחָד פִּישׁוֹן הוּא הַסֹּבֵב אֵת כָּל־אֶרֶץ הַחֲוִילָה אֲשֶׁר־שָׁם הַזָּהָב׃
šēm (name) *hā'eḥāḏ* (first one) *piyšvōn* (the Increaser) *hu'* (is) *hasōḇēḇ* (turn around) *'ēṯ* (the) *kāl* (all) *'ereṣ* (land) *haḥăviylāh* (Havilah) *'ăšer* (which) *šām* (there) *hazāhāḇ* (gold)
ὄνομα *onoma* (the name) **τῷ** *tō* (of the) **ἑνὶ** *eni* (first) **Φισων** *Phisōn* (Phison) **οὗτος** *outos* (so) **ὁ** *o* (which) **κυκλῶν** *kuklōn* (circles) **πᾶσαν** *pasan* (all) **τὴν** *tēs* (the) **γῆν** *gēs* (land) **Ευιλατ** *Euilat* (Euilat) **ἐκεῖ** *ekei* (there) **οὗ** *ou* (thus) **ἐστιν** *estin* (is) **τὸ** *to* (the) **χρυσίον** *chrusion* (gold)
nomen (the name) ***uni*** (of the first) ***Phison*** (Pison) ***ipse*** (itself) ***est*** (is) ***qui*** (which) ***circuit*** (circles) ***omnem*** (the whole) ***terram*** (land) ***Evilat*** (of Evilat) ***ubi*** (where) ***nascitur*** (is born) ***aurum*** (gold)
The name of the first is Pison: that is it which compasseth the whole land of Havilah, where there is gold;
The name of the first one is Increaser, which surrounds completely the Circular land where there is the splendor of gold;

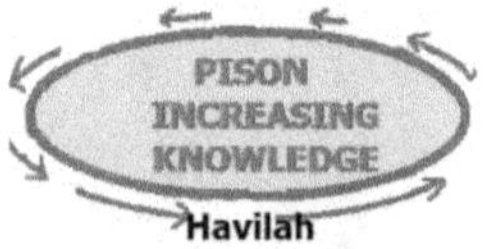

Pison (פִּישׁוֹן *piyshown*), the name of the first river branch, means *increase.*[745] The river springs[746]

"*out of ... north-heaven.*"[747]

and encompasses (סָבַב *cabab*) *Havillah* (חֲוִילָה *Chaviylah*), which means circular[748] land (אֶרֶץ *'erets*). It is the river that *increases* by running <u>*to and fro*</u>. It is the proliferation and multiplication produced by the awaken knowledge, as we read in Daniel's description.[749] Here again, it expresses and confirms the circularity of consciousness. The river <u>Pison</u> represents the <u>circular flow of consciousness</u> in the awaken realm in which the splendor of gold (זָהָב *zahab*) is abundant. This is the gold-weight of the perceiving senses as metaphoric *talents* (τάλαντον *talanton*)[750] or *round circle* (כִּכָּר *kikkar*),[751] which identify and place the objective world in the circularity of ⊙ the conscience-*of.*

In the *beginning* of the *historical* stages of creation, mineral gold could not have had more financial value than any other stone on earth. In the narrative of world's creation, the mere description of physical golden qualities of certain lands does not refer to its monetary appeal. Therefore, here, the precious metal is a metaphor for its brilliance. In fact, the Hebrew word for gold, *zahab* (זָהָב), means *splendor*[752] and value of something else, namely, of consciousness. Then, that precious metal becomes <the Gold of Awareness.>[753] The commentary and metaphoric interpretation of this verse continues with the next one.

2:12-Gold and Precious Stones

וּזֲהַב הָאָרֶץ הַהִוא טוֹב שָׁם הַבְּדֹלַח וְאֶבֶן הַשֹּׁהַם׃
uzăhaḇ (gold) *hā'āreṣ* (land) *hahiv* (the) *ṭvōḇ* (good) *šām* (there) *habaḏōlaḥ* (bdellium-separateness) *va'eḇen* (building stone) *hašōham* (gem)
τὸ to (the) **δὲ** de (but) **χρυσίον** *krusion* (gold) **τῆς** *tes* (of the) **γῆς** *gēs* (land) **ἐκείνης** *ekeinēs* (that) **καλόν** *kalon* (good) **καὶ** *kai* (and) **ἐκεῖ** *ekei* (that) **ἐστιν** *estin* (is) **ὁ** *o* (the) **ἄνθραξ** *anthrax* (coal)[754] **καὶ** *kai* (and) **ὁ** *o* (the) **λίθος** *lithos* (stone) **ὁ** *o* (the) **πράσινος** *prasinos* (emerald)
et (and) ***aurum*** (the gold) ***terrae*** (of earth) ***illius*** (that) ***optimum*** (very good) ***est*** (is) ***ibi-que*** (there) (and) ***invenitur*** (can be found) ***bdellium*** (bdellium) ***et*** (and) ***lapis*** (stone) ***onychinus*** (of onyx)
And the gold of that land is good: there bdellium and the onyx stone.
And the splendid consciousness of that realm is very good. Also there can be found the principle of distinction and the building gemstone of knowledge.

Gold (זָהָב *zahab*) means brilliance and it is a

"metaph.[or] of the golden splendor of the heavens."[755]

The gold of that (הוּא huw') land is the good (טוֹב towb) brightness (זָהָב zahab) flowing *north*[756] in the waking conscious state. It is the symbol of the mineral solar light[757] that transforms the waking desire into known experiences. Therefore, knowledge has the logical capability to think, to judge and to distinguish objects among themselves. Consequently, the object becomes, figuratively, the precious *gem* (שֹׁהַם shoham),[758] the *stone* (אֶבֶן 'eben)[759] or the *building block* (בָּנָה banah)[760] of the epistemic process.

In this golden waking state is present also the precious bdellium (בְּדֹלַח bĕdolach),[761] a gum resin like myrrh, which is a metaphor for the dreamless division, the embalming perfume[762] that anoints the catalectic state of dreamless sleep. In fact, the verb *badal*, from which its name derives, is,

"figuratively applied to the mind, *to separate, to distinguish* diverse things."[763]

Then, similar to the dreamless state, Auto-transparency is the presence of the self to itself without the mediation of thought. Thus, the self *distinguishes* (*badal*) itself from the known precious *gem*-(שֹׁהַם shoham)-objects of dream and wakeful representations.

The precious gold and myrrh are two of the three metaphoric gifts presented to the newborn Jesus. The third one is the dream fog of frankincense, the symbol of prayer elevating from the physical realm to Heaven. In [764]⇨

"*Bethlehem of Judaea in the days of Herod the king... there came* [three] *wise men* (μάγοι) *from the east to Jerusalem* (ἀπὸ ἀνατολῶν... εἰς Ἱεροσόλυμα)... [Who] *warned of God in a dream* (ὄναρ),... [presented the infant Jesus with three] *gifts* (δῶρα)*; gold* (χρυσὸν)*, and frankincense* (λίβανον)*, and myrrh* (σμύρναν)."[765]

2:13-The Black Second Branch River

וְשֵׁם־הַנָּהָר הַשֵּׁנִי גִּיחוֹן הוּא הַסּוֹבֵב אֵת כָּל־אֶרֶץ כּוּשׁ׃ *vašēm* (name) *hanāhār* (river) *hašēniy* (second) *giyḥvōn* (bursting forth) *hu'* (is) *hasvōḇēḇ* (runs around) *'ēṯ* (the) *kāl* (all) *'ereṣ* (land) *kuš* (black)
καὶ *kai* (and) **ὄνομα** *onoma* (name) **τῷ** *tō* (of the) **ποταμῷ** *potamō* (river) **τῷ** *tō* (the) **δευτέρῳ** *deuterō* (second) **Γηων** *Gēōn* (Geon) **οὗτος** *outos* (so) **ὁ** *o* (the) **κυκλῶν** *kuklōn* (encircling) **πᾶσαν** *pasan* (all) **τὴν** *tēn* (the) **γῆν** *gēs* (land) **Αἰθιοπίας** *Aithiopias* (of Ethiopia)
et (and) ***nomen*** (the name) ***fluvio*** (of the river) ***secundo*** (second) ***Geon*** (Geon) ***ipse*** (same) ***est*** (is) ***qui*** (which) ***circuit*** (surrounds) ***omnem*** (all) ***terram*** (the land) ***Aethiopiae*** (of Ethiopia)
And the name of the second river is Gihon: the same is it that compasseth the whole land of Ethiopia.
And the name of the second river is Gushing-Fort, which circuits the entire Black Realm.

This location is not the restrictive geographical location of Ethiopia. The word *kuwsh* (כּוּשׁ)[766] means black. Thus, it has a nocturnal reference as absence of light. Furthermore, it cannot refer to the Ethiopians, as descendants from Cush, a son of Ham, because they had not been generated yet.

The name of the second river is *Gihon*, meaning the *One-Which-Gushes-Fourth*[767] towards the opposite southern direction, the dream state. When we dream, there is the consciousness-*of* our visions. In fact, during those experiences all types of feelings and emotions *gush-fourth*. This river circles (סָבַב cabab) the entire nocturnal oneiric *Black* (כּוּשׁ kuwsh)[768] *Realm* (אֶרֶץ 'erets). Both rivers of consciousness, *Pison* the first and *Gihon* the second one, are the two opposite polarities, respectively of the northern-external-awake and southern-internal-dream consciousness. Furthermore, they both represent, allegorically, the arms' of this *bodily Garden of Eden*.

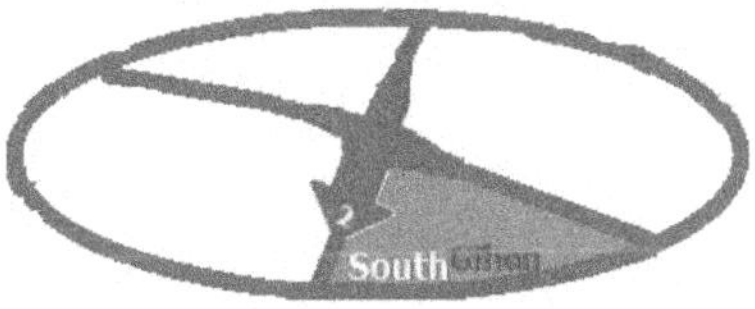

2:14-The Successful Third and Fruitful Fourth Branch Rivers

וְשֵׁם הַנָּהָר הַשְּׁלִישִׁי חִדֶּקֶל הוּא הַהֹלֵךְ קִדְמַת אַשּׁוּר וְהַנָּהָר הָרְבִיעִי הוּא פְרָת׃ *vašēm* (name) *hanāhār* (river) *hašaliyšiy* (third) *ḥideqel* (rapid) *hu'* (is) *hahōlēḵa* (going) *qiḏamaṯ* (east) *'ašur* (successful) *vahanāhār* (river) *hārabiy'iy* (fourth) *hu'* (is) *pārāṯ* (fruitful)
καὶ *kai* (and) **ὁ** *o* (the) **ποταμὸς** *potamos* (river) **ὁ** *o* (the) **τρίτος** *tritos* (third) **Τίγρις** *Tigris* (Tigris)

οὗτος *outos* (so) **ὁ** *o* (the) **πορευόμενος** *poreuomenos* (bringing) **κατέναντι** *katenanti* (towards) **Ἀσσυρίων** *Assuriōn* (Assyrians) **ὁ** *o* (the) **δὲ** *de* (and) **ποταμὸς** *potamos* (river) **ὁ** *o* (the) **τέταρτος** *tetartos* (fourth) **οὗτος** *outos* (so) **Εὐφράτης** *Euphratēs* (Euphrates)
nomen (name) ***vero*** (truthfully) ***fluminis*** (river) ***tertii*** (third) ***Tigris*** (Tigris) ***ipse*** (same) ***vadit*** (goes) ***contra*** (towards) ***Assyrios*** (the Assyrians) ***fluvius*** (river) ***autem*** (also) ***quartus*** (fourth) ***ipse*** (same) ***est*** (is) ***Eufrates*** (Euphrates)
And the name of the third river is Hiddekel: that is it which goeth toward the east of Assyria. And the fourth river is Euphrates.
Truthfully, the name of the third river is Rapid Step, which goes successfully towards the east. The fourth river is the Fruitful One.

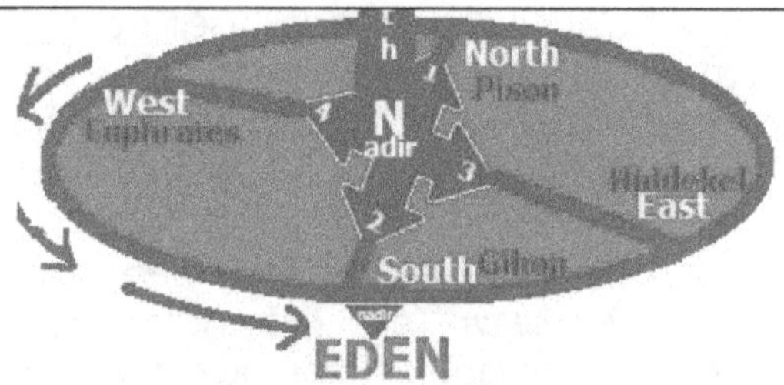

GRAPHIC: *The Fourth Branch River*

Usually, the river Hiddekel is identified with the river Tigris, which, with the Euphrates, delimits Mesopotamia, *viz.* the land between (μέσος *mesos*) rivers (ποταμός *potamos*). However, those two do not split from the same river of Eden, as described in the previous verses. They have two separate origins. The source of the Tigris is Lake Hazar, in the Taurus Mountains of Eastern Turkey. The Euphrates, joined with the Eastern Euphrates (Murat River), originates near Mount Ararat north of Lake Van, and, when joined with the Western Euphrates (Karasu = *black water*), originates from the Dumlu Dağ (Erzurum, Turkey). Furthermore, the Tigris and Euphrates, at their Al-Qurnah confluence, form the *Swift River* (Arvand Rud or Shatt al-Arab), which discharges, soon after, in the Persian Gulf. Therefore, Tigris and Euphrates, are two separate geographical rivers, they are not branches of the *one river* (נָהָר *nahar*) coming out from Eden, as described by our verses.

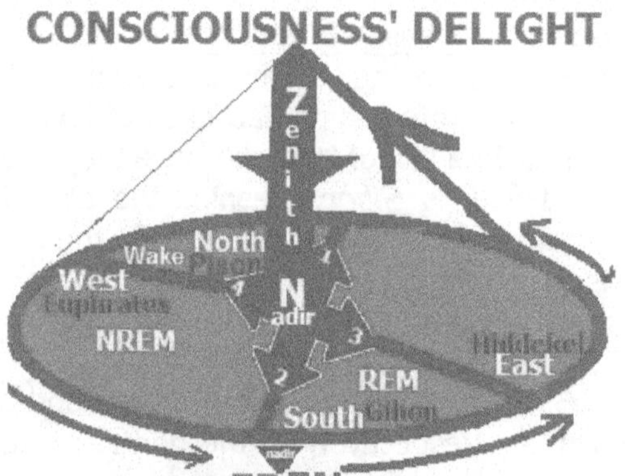

GRAPHIC: *The Third Branch River*

The configuration of consciousness has nothing to do with the physical geographical locations, except as the logical *a-priori* form of space. Therefore, as we saw, the previous two rivers are symbols of two different moments of consciousnesses. The Euphrates articulates in the oneiric dreamless NREM state and the Hiddekel in

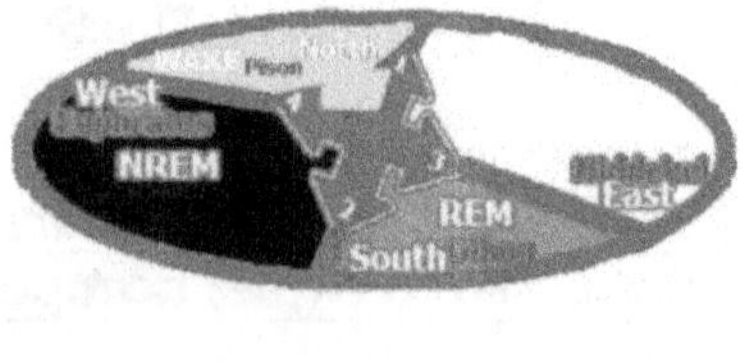

the original starting point. Furthermore, in this verse and on its semantic basis, the metaphors of these last two rivers become clearer. Allegorically, they represent the legs' movement. The third river, *Hiddekel*,[769] which in Hebrew means *rapid*, goes towards the east of Assyria. In addition, *Assyria* in Hebrew means *step*,[770] which derives from the verb *'ashar*,[771] *to go straight on, to advance, to be successful*. Furthermore, the forth river, *Euphrates*[772] means *fruitfulness* or *fruit bearing*. Thus, if one stream goes towards the Oriental Assyria, then, the other goes towards the Occident. This last one, the *Fruitful* Euphrates, is the fourth river. It represents the state of dreamless sleep, which, at the end, reverts to bear again the *fruits* of dreams and wakefulness. Thus, it starts the entire flow again. The third river, however, is the *Rapid Step* one, it is the one, which goes successfully towards[773] the East, from which life itself raises.[774] Thus, from Hiddekel's rapid origin, to Pison's bright wakefulness, through Gihon's dreamy flow and Euphrates' fruitful slumber, the Circularity of Consciousness concludes by returning to its original fast beginning. Once all possible aspects of consciousness appear and flow on the earth, then, the human can enter the Garden of Eden.

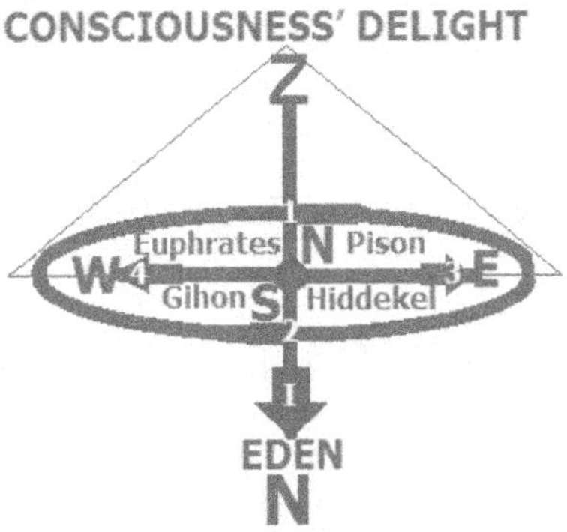

The forbidden fruit is the desirous mind. Consciousness is life that vivifies the heart while knowing the world. It is like a river, dividing in four branches corresponding to the circadian flow of wakefulness, dream, NREM and its origin and silent edge.

2-IV SECTION: EDEN'S GUARDIAN

2:15-The Appointment

וַיִּקַּח יְהוָה אֱלֹהִים אֶת־הָאָדָם וַיַּנִּחֵהוּ בְגַן־עֵדֶן לְעָבְדָהּ וּלְשָׁמְרָהּ׃
vayiqaḥ (joined) *yahvāh* (Transcendent) *'ĕlōhiym* (Divine-Consciousness) *'et̠* (the) *hā'āḏām* (human) *vayaniḥēhu* (to rest) *ḇaḡan* (garden) *'ēḏen* (of happiness) *la'āḇaḏāh* (to operate) *ulašāmarāh* (to guard)
καὶ *kai* (and) **ἔλαβεν** *elaben* (took) **κύριος** *kurios* (Lord) **ὁ** *o* (the) **θεὸς** *theos* (God) **τὸν** *tov* (the) **ἄνθρωπον** *antrōpon* (man) **ὃν** *on* (thus) **ἔπλασεν** *eplasen* (he had formed) **καὶ** *kai* (and) **ἔθετο** *etheto* (placed) **αὐτὸν** *auton* (same) **ἐν** *en* (in) **τῷ** *tō* (the) **παραδείσῳ** *paradeisō* (paradise) **ἐργάζεσθαι** *ergazesthai* (to build) **αὐτὸν** *auton* (same) **καὶ** *kai* (and) **φυλάσσειν** *phulassein* (keep)
tulit (brought) ***ergo*** (therefore) ***Dominus*** (Lord) ***Deus*** (God) ***hominem*** (man) ***et*** (and) ***posuit*** (placed) ***eum*** (him) ***in*** (in) ***paradiso*** (the paradise) ***voluptatis*** (of happiness) ***ut*** (so that) ***operaretur*** (he would operate) ***et*** (and) ***custodiret*** (safe keep) ***illum*** (it)
And the LORD God took the man, and put him into the garden of Eden to dress it and to keep it.
Therefore, the Transcendent Divine-Consciousness united the subject-with-the-object, Adam, and caused the human to rest in the earthly pleasant paradise for them to function and be vigil in it.

The verb *laqach* (לקח),[775] besides meaning *to take*, signifies also *to marry*, *to take in marriage*, *to take a wife*.[776] In addition, the verbs *yanach* (יָנַח)[777] and/or *nuwach* (נוח),[778] besides denoting *to place*, indicates also *to rest*, *to repose*, *to be quiet*.

Therefore, the Transcendent Divine-Consciousness placed the human being, united as subject-object, *to rest* in this psychophysical garden of pleasant perception. There, subject and object are *married* (*laqach* לקח) and conjoined with no distinction of alterity. That is the state of rest, where s/he is

"*placed … to sleep*,"[779]

in the deep realm with no dreams. In this garden, s/he functions (עבד *`abad*)[780] by keeping a vigil watch (שמר *shamar*) over the earthly pleasant paradise.[781]

2:16-Eat from All the Tree-Faculties

וַיְצַו יְהוָה אֱלֹהִים עַל־הָאָדָם לֵאמֹר מִכֹּל עֵץ־הַגָּן אָכֹל תֹּאכֵל׃
vayaṣav (commanded) *yahvāh* (Transcendent) *'ĕlōhiym* (Divine-Consciousness) *'al* (over) *hā'āḏām* (the human) *lē'mōr* (saying) *mikōl* (from) *'ēṣ* (tree) *hagān* (garden) *'āḵōl* (eat) *tō'ḵēl* (to eat)
καὶ *kai* (and) **ἐνετείλατο** *eneteilato* (commanded) **κύριος** *kurios* (Lord) **ὁ** *o* (the) **θεὸς** *theos* (God) **τῷ** *tō* (the) **Αδαμ** *Adam* (Adam) **λέγων** *legōn* (saytng) **ἀπὸ** *apo* (from) **παντὸς** *pantos* (every) **ξύλου** *xulou* (tree) **τοῦ** *tou* (the) **ἐν** *en* (in) **τῷ** *tō* (the) **παραδείσῳ** *paradeisō* (paradise) **βρώσει** *brōsei* (eater) **φάγῃ** *phagē* (to eat)
praecepit-(commanded) ***que*** (and) ***ei*** (him) ***dicens*** (saying) ***ex*** (from) ***omni*** (every) ***ligno*** (tree) ***paradisi*** (of paradise) ***comede*** (eat)
And the LORD God commanded the man, saying, Of every tree of the garden thou mayest freely eat:
And the Transcendent Divine-Consciousness commanded the human saying, "*Eat from every tree of the earthly paradise.*

The Hebrew word *`ets* (עֵץ),[782] *tree*, derives from the verb *`atsah* (עָצָה),[783] which means *to shut*, as when one

"*shuts his eyes to devise contrary things.*"[784]

Also, *`atsah* means, *to make firm* as wood or bone.[785] In Eden, in the Garden of Happiness, all trees are metaphors for firm, intentional drives of consciousness towards the concrete hardness of objects. Trees are allegories for human faculties, like intricate roots of nerve structures in a body. Polizzi, the director of *The Sacred Science*, so describes his intuition of the metaphorical tree,

"I was walking beneath a huge willka [sacred] tree in the jungle... when a shiver of realization ran down my spine. This tree relies on all of its branches, leaves, and roots to interface with the outside environment in a harmonious way in order to survive and thrive. There is no one part that is more important than the other, there is no separation among its many constituents. Every inch of this willka has an important role to play, and the health of the surrounding jungle depends on each tree like this one living in full connection with its neighbors.
We're not much different than trees in this respect. The system of life-flow that is so essential to a healthy forest also applies to the two-legged mammals that walk the trails carved into its soil."[786]

The tree, as a metaphor for human faculties, is a common ancient archetype. The tradition of sacred humanized trees, in one form or another, is present in all mythologies. In fact, the tree, as a Christmas symbol, derives from Nordic and Druid lore. Legend has it, that the Cross was made from the wood of the Tree of Knowledge.[787] Aroung 4000 B.C., the earliest engraved records on the

"cylinders of Chaldaea,"[788]

portray trees inhabited by gods and goddesses. In the Egyptian mythology, the goddess Nut, in a sycamore tree, granted solace to the soul of the dead with bread

"water and air."[789]

The Kabbalist anonymous book *Bahir* describes [790]⇨

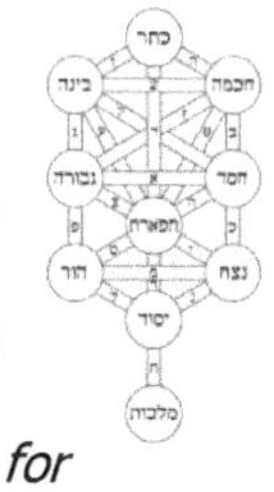

"the divine world as a tree (*ilan*) [(אילן) on which] the divine powers are positioned one above the other like the branches of a tree. It seems that the image was one of an upside-down tree, its roots above and its branches growing downwards, toward the earth. These ... conceptions became characteristic of the kabbalah as a whole."[791]

"*Sit every man under his vine and under his fig tree; and none shall make them afraid: for the mouth of the LORD of hosts hath spoken* it."[792]

In the Indian tradition, the sacred fig tree becomes the source of *soma*, an immortalizing elixir,[793] and is identified with the Supreme Immortal Spirit.

"*This ancient fig tree has the root above and the branches below and all worlds rest in it.*"[794]

The *Bhagavad Gītā*[795] identifies it with the human being itself. The hair represent the roots set, like a holy banyan tree,[796] above in the heaven and the limbs are the branches. From an epistemic perspective, the root are set in Awareness as the Thousand Petals Lotus seated at the top of the head.[797]

The Norse mythology calls this World-Tree *Yggdrasil.*[798] An archaeological example of a symbolically planted inverted tree was found near the coast of Norfolk East England in a 2050 B.C. timber circle named Seahenge.[799] The inverted tree inspired also Dante Alighieri.[800] In the Classical Greek and Roman Literature, Apollonius Rhodius[801] narrates of a man imbedded in a tree. In the *Aeneid,*[802] Virgil narrates that, in Thrace, a man named Polydorus became a tree. Ovid describes that the nymph Daphne metamorphosed into a laurel tree.[803]

Therefore, trees were intended as metaphors for the faculties of consciousness, namely, the *a-priori* forms or modalities of potential knowledge, like time, space, causality and so on. Our verse states that their fruits are good to eat. This means that to engage with them is permissible because they do not distract from the internal reality that generates them. It is like a skillful dreamer watching the dream while being conscious that it is only a mental production. Then, the dreamer is not deluded by conceiving the vision as an external reality, because the eyes are stlll shut (עצה *'atsah*). When they will open, then, this world will appear in all its alluring, disturbing and lethal *nakedness.*[804]

2:17-The Dangerous Tree

וּמֵעֵץ הַדַּעַת טוֹב וָרָע לֹא תֹאכַל מִמֶּנּוּ כִּי בְּיוֹם אֲכָלְךָ מִמֶּנּוּ מוֹת תָּמוּת׃ *umē'ēṣ* (from) *hada'aṯ* (knowledge) *ṭvōḇ* (good) *vārā* (evil) *lō* (not) *ṯō'ḵal* (eat) *mimenu* (for) *kiy* (that) *bayvōm* (day) *'ăḵālaḵā* (eat) *mimenu* (for) *mvōṯ* (die) *tāmuṯ* (to die)
ἀπὸ *apo* (from) **δὲ** *de* (but) **τοῦ** *tou* (the) **ξύλου** *xulou* (tree) **τοῦ** *tou* (of the) **γινώσκειν** *ginōskein* (knowledge) **καλὸν** *kalon* (gool) **καὶ** *kai* (and) **πονηρόν** *ponēron* (evil) **οὐ** *ou* (do not) **φάγεσθε** *phagesthe* (eat) **ἀπ'** *ap'* (from) **αὐτοῦ** *autou* (it) **ᾗ** *ē* (that) **δ'** *d'* (but) **ἂν** *an* (if) **ἡμέρᾳ** *ēmera* (day)

φάγητε *phagēte* (you shall eat) **ἀπ'** *ap'* (from) **αὐτοῦ** *autou* (it) **θανάτῳ** *thanatō* (of death) **ἀποθανεῖσθε** *apothaneisthe* (shall die)
de (of the) ***ligno*** (tree) ***autem*** (however) ***scientiae*** (of knowledge) ***boni*** (of good) ***et*** (and) ***mali*** (evil) ***ne*** (do not) ***comedas*** (eat) ***in*** (in) ***quocumque*** (whichever) ***enim*** (in fact) ***die*** (day) ***comederis*** (you shall eat) ***ex*** (out) ***eo*** (of it) ***morte*** (by death) ***morieris*** (you will die)
But of the tree of the knowledge of good and evil, thou shalt not eat of it: for in the day that thou eatest thereof thou shalt surely die.
However, do not eat of the tree of Knowledge-of Good and Evil. In fact, the day in which you shall eat of it, you will experience death."

The literal reading of this passage generates great incongruence. The usual interpretation of this verse is that Divine-Consciousness had placed the tree of Knowledge of Good and Bad at the center of Eden to test the moral obedience of His creatures. However, the postulated omniscience of Divine-Consciousness must have known very well that they would have disobeyed. Furthermore, as a parent would be legally culpable for a loaded gun left unsupervised in the hands of children, similarly, producing a *lethal weapon* like the *Tree of Knowledge* would incriminate the same producer. Therefore, the planting of that tree, as moral instruction, would be itself a contradicting immoral act.

Truthfully, while all the *faculty-sensitive-trees* are there at *hand*, one should not eat of the Tree of Knowledge. This is not a moral commandment, as interpreted. It is a warning, like saying, *'Don't touch fire, you'll burn.'* All commandments[805] caution from the inevitable epistemic consequence of *hungry eating*, *'akal* (אכל).[806] <To eat is to absorb and, in this case, to identify with the fruit of knowledge. The consequence of that *eating* is that the consciousness-*of* is fascinated and fashioned by the objective world.>[807] In fact,

> "*to eat any one's words*, is to receive them eagerly ... i.e. I eagerly devoured them, made them my own,"[808]
>
> "*Thy words were found, and I did eat them.*"[809]
>
> "*Son of man, hear what I say unto thee... and eat that I give thee... Moreover ... eat that thou findest; eat this roll, and go speak unto the house of Israel.*"[810]
>
> "*And I went unto the angel, and said unto him, Give me the little book. And he said unto me, Take it, and eat it up... And I took the little book out of the angel's hand, and ate it up.*"[811]

In other words, the object of knowledge must be ingested by the brain in order to be know.

Knowledge, in Hebrew *da'ath* (דעת),[812] derives from the verb *yada'* (ידע),[813] which means *to know, to perceive, to see, to experience* and *to know a person carnally*. This means that who will eat of the tree of experience enters the dichotomy, the dualism of subject-object, of time-space and of cause-effect. This implies the experience of death. In fact, there are two reasons why death lies at the root of experience.

1) In the subject-object interpersonal correlation, the subject epistemically *kills* the subjectivity of the other.[814] Namely, when the ego knows you, the *I* must *eliminate* your '*I*' to know you <u>as you</u>, not as an '*I*'.

   > "*And he will be a wild man; his hand* will be *against every man, and every man's hand against him; and he shall dwell in the presence of all his brethren.*"[815]

   This is true also when the the ego *looks* at itself. Then the ego perceives the objective image of itself, the *I* can never *see* the observing observer as such. Therefore, the ego set its real self-in-itself on the path of epistemic death.

2) In the space-time dimension, we constantly experience the object as already *being-given-there*, namely, coming from a past. Therefore, we understand the object we experience as <u>always</u> coming from a time that precedes this knowledge. Then, out of the Stillness of the Present, that object is past, *viz. dead*. In fact, the *closest* an object is located, the more *present* it appears to us. Whereas, the *furthest* it is situated, the more *past* it seems. However, even the experience/thought, which we are experiencing and thinking now, is still at a certain infinitesimal distance from the thinker. Thus, when perceived, the object always comes into view as being

already past. Therefore, we say that '*time cannot be stopped,*' namely, it flows into the death of the past.

The Tree of Knowledge is the body, which produces the epistemic fruit of action, namely, the circular friction between the subject and the object. This action, once produced, is past. When we eat it, we identify with the dead history and pass away with it. Thus, by eating the fruit of the Tree of Knowledge, we experience death. That is, we ingest the dead past in which the object of knowledge [816]⇨ is imbedded. Namely, we forget the present life, from which we come, and we become

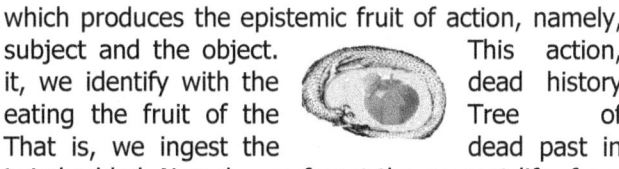

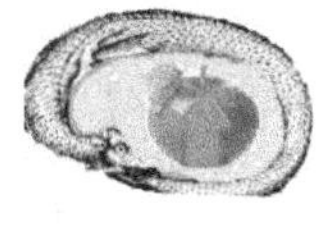

"*being*[s] *for death.*"[817]

However, the command, forbidding to eat the fruit of knowledge, implies the rightful return of the creative hypostases to their own living origins from which they come. Knowledge means to comprehend alterity and to identify with it. It is similar to eating. In fact, as the brain acknowledges the known, it also ingests it. The knower becomes the known, thus, other than itself. The desire *to eat* is to absorb and to identify with the fruit of knowledge. The consciousness-*of* is fascinated and seduced by the objective world. It forgets the blissful state of undisturbed, undistracted Apodictic-Certitude, thus, the injunction not to eat that fruit. One should

"*abandon all actions, with full consciousness in the Supreme Self, be without any desire, free from all worldly attachments and desisting from any affliction...* [Thus] *having rejected all attachments, perform your actions in a state of yoga-union unaffected by victory as well as failure.*"[818]

Similarly, Jesus says,

"*Take my unifying-yoke* [(ζυγόν *zugon*) *viz. yoga*) *upon you, and learn of me; for I am meek and lowly in heart: and ye shall find rest unto your souls. For my yoke* is *easy, and my burden is light.*"[819]

2:18-Adam's Loneliness

וַיֹּאמֶר יְהוָה אֱלֹהִים לֹא־טוֹב הֱיוֹת הָאָדָם לְבַדּוֹ אֶעֱשֶׂה־לּוֹ עֵזֶר כְּנֶגְדּוֹ׃ *vayō'mer* (said) *yahvāh* (Transcendent) *'ĕlōhiym* (Divine-Consciousness) *lō̆* (not) *ṭvōḇ* (good) *hĕyvōṯ* (to be) *hā'āḏām* (human) *laḇadvō* (alone) *'e'ĕśeh* (I will make) *lvō* (for him)*'ēzer* (helper) *kaneḡadvō* (in front)
καὶ *kai* (and) **εἶπεν** *eipen* (said) **κύριος** *kurios* (Lord) **ὁ** *o* (the) **θεός** *theos* (God) **οὐ** *ou* (not) **καλὸν** *kalon* (good) **εἶναι** *einai* (to be) **τὸν** *ton* (for the) **ἄνθρωπον** *anthropōn* (man) **μόνον** *movon* (alone) **ποιήσωμεν** *poiēsōmen* (let us make) **αὐτῷ** *autō* (for him) **βοηθὸν** *boēthōn* (helper) **κατ'** *kat'* (from) **αὐτόν** *auton* (him)
dixit (said) ***quoque*** (also) ***Dominus*** (Lord) ***Deus*** (God) ***non*** (not) ***est*** (is) ***bonum*** (good) ***esse*** (be) ***hominem*** (man) ***solum*** (alone) ***faciamus*** (let us make) ***ei*** (for him) ***adiutorium*** (help) ***similem*** (similar) ***sui*** (to him)
And the LORD God said, It is not good that the man should be alone; I will make him an help meet for him.
The Transcendent Divine-Consciousness also said, "*It is not good for the human to be alone. Let us make for him a suitable helping companion for him.*"

The epistemic loneliness or solipsism is the impossibility for the *I* to know itself as self-in-itself or to know another *I* as *I*. Even the production of an artificial intelligence will enhance this loneliness. In fact, also the seemingly autonomous robotic response to external stimuli will never allow us to know it as having an Auto-transparency capability.

"Computers will never be able to completely replicate the complexity of the human mind."[820]

It is true that androids' automatic mechanical multiplication could become a threat for humans.[821] Robots could also be programmed to be conscious-*of* the objective world, including themselves as active producers. We could also test and verify the workability of those programs. However, they will never be able to have thoughtless self-transparency, namely, to be present to themselves without needing the automatic process of thinking of themselves, because that cannot be programed. In fact, once coded, self-transparency cannot be non-programed transparency.

As an eye that can see but can never see itself as eye except as a reflection, similarly, I can think and know me as me-object, logically necessitating a subject, but I can never know the I-subject-in-itself as such.

The observer can observe itself as an observing entity, but can never observe itself as pure observer. This epistemic existential loneliness characterizes only the subject as such. In fact, Yĕhovah (יְהֹוָה), the Awareness in Divine-Consciousness (אֱלֹהִים *'elohiym*) realizes Adam's loneliness.[822] Therefore, it ensues the necessity of helpful (עֵזֶר *`ezer*) companions for him. In other words, in the solitude of the realm of deep sleep (NREM), all neurotransmitters and senses are in their potential state as faculties or abilities. That is, the neurons in the nervous system, as such, are quiescent. They are in a situation of alert presence ready to connect, to impulse and to wake up as this sight, this hearing, this taste, this smell, this feeling, this thought and so on.[823] Metaphorically, the flora represents the branching out of the nervous system, while the fauna represents the actual senses. In fact, many ancient writings[824] associated

"a particular animal with each of the five senses."[825]

Thus, the injunction,

"Be wise as serpents and harmless as doves."[826]

Furthermore, *Genesis'* verses intend to highlight the idea that what takes place above, on the epistemic level as nervous-sensitivity and projecting-senses, also takes place below, on the physical plain as trees and animals.

Solipsism or epistemic loneliness is the condition of all sentient beings, thus follows the hungering projection toward the other, who, as such, can never be reached *in-itself*. This is also the universal condition of random *evolution*, the *rolling out of*[827] one state into another. This condition reverberates in us, as this unique solitary individuality of our epistemic structure. Our individual solitude reflects the universal paradigmatic solipsism of this Adam, who is always

"Lonely and pensive."[828]

Therefore, our personal solipsism is the universal epistemic loneliness. In reality, the Other is the Transcendent-Awareness-In-Itself, when we erroneously conceive it as other than Our-Self-In-Itself. Thus, when Adam will see Eve's nakedness, s/he would have missed the realization, the *vision* of Awareness. It is only through unconditional love and compassion[829] that we can completely overcome epistemic loneliness. In fact, then we realize that we are never alone because we are all in the same all-encompassing Awareness that characterizes the Other One.

"*The kingdom of heaven is like unto a net, that was cast into the sea, and gathered of every kind.*"[830]

Saint Mother Teresa of Calcutta prays,

"*Dear Jesus, help me to spread Thy fragrance everywhere I go. Flood my soul with Thy spirit and love. Penetrate and possess my whole being so utterly that all my life may only be a radiance of Thine. Shine through me and be so in me that every soul I come in contact with may feel Thy presence in my soul. Let them look up and see no longer me but only Jesus. Stay with me and then I shall begin to shine as you shine, so to shine as to be a light to others.*"[831]

2:19-Animal Companions

וַיִּצֶר יְהוָֹה אֱלֹהִים מִן־הָאֲדָמָה כָּל־חַיַּת הַשָּׂדֶה וְאֵת כָּל־עוֹף הַשָּׁמַיִם וַיָּבֵא אֶל־הָאָדָם לִרְאוֹת מַה־יִּקְרָא־לוֹ וְכֹל אֲשֶׁר יִקְרָא־לוֹ הָאָדָם נֶפֶשׁ חַיָּה הוּא שְׁמוֹ׃   *vayiṣer* (formed) *yahvāh* (Transcendent) *'ĕlōhiym* (Divine-Consciousness) *min* (from) *hā'ăḏāmāh* (ground) *kāl* (all) *ḥayaṯ* (living animals) *haśāḏeh* (field) *va'ēṯ* (with) *kāl* (all) *'vōp̄* (birds) *hašāmayim* (sky) *vayāḇē* (went) *'el* (to) *hā'āḏām* (human) *lira'vōṯ* (to see) *mah* (what) *yiqarā* (would have called) *lvō* (for him) *vaḵōl* (all) *'ăšer* (which) *yiqarā* (call) *lvō* (for him) *hā'āḏām* (human) *nep̄eš* (mind) *ḥayāh* (living) *hu'* (became) *šamvō* (name)
καὶ *kai* (and) **ἔπλασεν** *eplasen* (formed) **ὁ** *o* (the) **θεὸς** *theos* (God) **ἔτι** *eti* (yet) **ἐκ** *ek* (out of) **τῆς**

tēs (the) **γῆς** *gēs* (earth) **πάντα** *panta* (all) **τὰ** *ta* (the) **θηρία** *thēria* (animals) **τοῦ** *tou* (of the) **ἀγροῦ** *agrou* (land) **καὶ** *kai* (and) **πάντα** *panta* (all) **τὰ** *ta* (the) **πετεινὰ** *peteina* (birds) **τοῦ** *tou* (of the) **οὐρανοῦ** *ouranou* (sky) **καὶ** *kai* (and) **ἤγαγεν** *ēgagen* (brought) **αὐτὰ** *auta* (them) **πρὸς** *pros* (before) **τὸν** *ton* (the) **Αδαμ** *Adam* (Adam) **ἰδεῖν** *idein* (to see) **τί** *ti* (what) **καλέσει** *kalesei* (he would call) **αὐτά** *auta* (them) **καὶ** *kai* (and) **πᾶν** *pan* (all) **ὃ** *o* (the) **ἐὰν** *ean* (if) **ἐκάλεσεν** *ekalesen* (would have called) **αὐτὸ** *auto* (them) **Αδαμ** *Adam* (Adam) **ψυχὴν** *psuchēn* (living) **ζῶσαν** *zōsan* (animal) **τοῦτο** *touto* (in this way) **ὄνομα** *onoma* (name) **αὐτοῦ** *autou* (of it)
formatis (formed) ***igitur*** (therefore) ***Dominus*** (the Lord) ***Deus*** (God) ***de*** (out of) ***humo*** (the land) ***cunctis*** (all) ***animantibus*** (the animals) ***terrae*** (of the earth) ***et*** (and) ***universis*** (every) ***volatilibus*** (bird) ***caeli*** (of the sky) ***adduxit*** (brought) ***ea*** (them) ***ad*** (to) ***Adam*** (the Human) ***ut*** (to) ***videret*** (see) ***quid*** (what) ***vocaret*** (he would call) ***ea*** (them) ***omne*** (every) ***enim*** (in fact) ***quod*** (which) ***vocavit*** (called) ***Adam*** (Adam) ***animae*** (being) ***viventis*** (living) ***ipsum*** (that same) ***est*** (is) ***nomen*** (the name) ***eius*** (of it)
And out of the ground the LORD God formed every beast of the field, and every fowl of the air; and brought them unto Adam to see what he would call them: and whatsoever Adam called every living creature, that was the name thereof.
Therefore, out of that land the Transcendence of Divine-Consciousness formed all the animated senses of the field and every emotional one. He summoned them to the Human mind to see how s/he would call them. In fact, however the Human recalled those living beings that is the same name they have.

The five senses, together with the mind, vivify and bring to consciousness the whole world. The senses experience, *shape*, *yatsar* (יָצַר),[832] *out* of *'adamah* (אֲדָמָה),[833] the *red*, *'adam* (אָדם),[834] the soil of Adam (אָדם *'adam*), namely the redden humanity.[835] The verb *yatsar* is identical with *yatsar* (יָצַר),[836] meaning *to squeeze into a shape causing distress*, and it is comparable to *yatsa`* (יָצַע),[837] *to spread out*. Therefore, the active animal-(חי *chay*)-senses are, metaphorically, the activities of the mind's breath[838] and of the will spreading out to experience the world. Namely, they are the *living*[839] drive of the flesh appetizing (חי *chay*) for experiences. They come forward out of the same soil-fabric (אֲדָמָה *'adamah*), which made Adam, the Human. The physical animal-senses come out of the mind's cultivated field (שָׂדֶה *sadeh*). The ethereal (שָׁמַיִם *shamayim*) birds, *`owph*,[840] are the psychosomatic-senses flying in the *darkness of the psyche*, *` uwph*.[841] All of the animal-senses together bring the experience of the objective world to Adam's attention, namely, to the human mind, which names them. The term *qara'* (קָרָא) does not mean only to call or to name, but also

"to call anyone to oneself... to invite... to summon."[842]

Therefore, the mind calls to attention its living animal-senses to implement their role of ushering and presenting to the brain the perceived objects.

Furthermore, it is at this point that Adam, the human, becomes a symbolic-animal. Namely, s/he names or attaches name-symbols to every object of experience. Here, there is no reference to a proto-idiom or any historical language. Its reference is to the human symbolizing faculty. *Shem* (שֵׁם)[843] means both name and memory. Then, the *name-symbol* brings up to the mind's *memory* the signified object even during its absence. As an example, by pronouncing the word '*whale*', this symbolic term, this name (שֵׁם *shem*) summons, *qara'*,[844] the idea of that cetaceous into the mind. The thinker, then, judges that concept to be that of the particular marine mammal, even if it is not actually present. This name assigning corresponds to placing the ideal and/or its concrete object into existence.

2:20-The Human Names All Animals

וַיִּקְרָא הָאָדָם שֵׁמוֹת לְכָל־הַבְּהֵמָה וּלְעוֹף הַשָּׁמַיִם וּלְכֹל חַיַּת הַשָּׂדֶה וּלְאָדָם לֹא־מָצָא עֵזֶר כְּנֶגְדּוֹ׃ *vayiqarā* (called) *hā'ādām* (human) *šēmvōt* (names) *lakāl* (all) *habahēmāh* (cattle) *ula`vōp* (bird) *hašāmayim* (of the sky) *ulakōl* (all) *ḥayat* (living forms) *haśādeh* (in the spreading field) *ula'ādām* (for human) *lō* (not) *māṣā* (found) *`ēzer* (help) *kanegadvō* (in front)
καὶ *kai* (and) **ἐκάλεσεν** *ekalesen* (called) **Αδαμ** *Adam* (Adam) **ὀνόματα** *onomata* (names) **πᾶσιν** *pasin* (all) **τοῖς tois** (the) **κτήνεσιν ktēnesin** (cattle) **καὶ** *kai* (and) **πᾶσι** *pasi* (all) **τοῖς** *tois* (the)

πετεινοῖς *peteinois* (birds) **τοῦ** *tou* (of the) **οὐρανοῦ** *ouranou* (sky) **καὶ** *kai* (and) **πᾶσι** *pasi* (all) **τοῖς** *tois* (the) **θηρίοις** *thēriois* (beast) **τοῦ** *tou* (of the) **ἀγροῦ** *agrou* (land) **τῷ** *tō* (the) **δὲ** *de* (but) **Αδαμ** Adam (Adam) **οὐχ** *ouch* (not) **εὑρέθη** *eurethē* (found) **βοηθὸς** *boēthos* (helper) **ὅμοιος** *omoios* (suitable) **αὐτῷ** *autō* (for him)
appellavit- (called) ***que*** (and) ***Adam*** (Adam) ***nominibus*** (with names) ***suis*** (their) ***cuncta*** (to all) ***animantia*** (animal) ***et*** (and) ***universa*** (every) ***volatilia*** (bird) ***caeli*** (of the sky) ***et*** (and) ***omnes*** (all) ***bestias*** (the beasts) ***terrae*** (of the earth) ***Adam*** (Adam) ***vero*** (however) ***non*** (non) ***inveniebatur*** (found) ***adiutor*** (a helper) ***similis*** (suitable) ***eius*** (for him)
And Adam gave names to all cattle, and to the fowl of the air, and to every beast of the field; but for Adam there was not found an help meet for him.
And Adam gave to all the experience-animals their names and to every bird of the mental-sky and to all the life forms of the spreading field. However, for Adam no suitable helper had been found for him.

The world without the observer is not a world we can know. It is like an ocean, a series of infinite unknown waves of possibilities, none of which collapses in an actual experience. In fact, at the subatomic level,

"each elementary quantum phenomenon is an elementary act of *fact creation*."[845]

That is to say, the observer determines a phenomenon to be a fact, only when the observer registers it as actual experience. On the epistemic level, we call this type of determination, intentionality, namely experience as a stream of consciousness directed toward something. This direction towards the experienced confers sense and meaning to the objects of knowledge.

In this verse, the verb *qara'* (קָרָא),[846] *to name* or *to call*, signifies *to summon* before a judge.[847] It is identical to *qara'* (קָרָא),[848] which means *to encounter*, *to meet* someone. In addition, the word *shem* (שֵׁם),[849] means *name*, *memorial*. It derives from *suwm* (שׂוּם),[850] *to put, to place in a conspicuous position, to set in place, to ordain, to determine*. As we pointed out, metaphorically, the trees are the faculties of the senses, namely, the <u>faculties</u> of hearing, feeling, seeing, tasting, smelling and thinking. The perception-organs, *viz.* the ears, the skin, the eyes, the tongue the nose and the brain, are the *chay* (חַי),[851] the *active living animal appetite*. *By breathing*, they *cause to grow* (חָיָה *chayah*)[852] and *make* the world *known* (חָוָה *chavah*).[853] Then, Adam's naming becomes synonym of conferring intentionality to the animal-senses as simple directional drive toward the world. In fact, the verb *qara'* (קָרָא), to call*, is also*

"often used of the cray of beasts,"[854]

thus, a plain projection towards the external world. The reason for the animal symbolism is to convey the idea of the alertness of active propelling vitalities. Similarly, according to the parable, Saint Francis of Assisi

"used to call the body 'brother donkey.'"[855]

Compare this to Abraham's *reddish ass*,[856] saddled with the wood for the burnt offering of his son Isaac. In this verse, the animals are metaphors for the organs of the senses, namely, the qualities that belong to the '*I*.' The *New Testament*[857] refers to them as *little lambs* (ἀρνία *arnia*) and *sheep* (πρόβατον *probaton*) going forward (προβαίνω *probainō*) in the world of objectivity. They must be fed (βόσκω *boskō*) and shepherd (ποιμαίνω *poimainō*) when they step out of Awareness, which is the One who should be loved

"*more than these*[858] ... [and] *knowest all things*."[859]

At this level, the senses are like *animals* (בְּהֵמָה *běhemah*)[860] *spreading out in the field* (sadeh שָׂדֶה)[861] of conscious action.[862] When they fly away (עוּף `*uwph*)[863] from the external field, they become like birds (עוֹף `*owph*)[864] hovering over the *dark covering* (עוּף `*uwph*) of the *airy* (שָׁמַיִם *shamayim*)[865] internal oneiric psychical experience.

However, all these are *mute animals* (בְּהֵמָה *běhemah*),[866] namely they are in a state of plain and simple intentioning direction that has not found (מָצָא matsa')[867] yet its objective destination. In other words, they are the senses in their pristine state, namely, when they are ready to feel just before sensing. They are in the state prior *to having reached any*[868] object, which, then, *succor* (עזר *'ezer*),[869] and *is of help* (עזר *'azar*)[870] in securing the achievement of experience.

Our friendly reader asks,

'Why must we understand those Biblical animals as metaphors for the senses and not as the actual living beings?'

We reply,

'In the poem "The Wind on the Island," Pablo Neruda describes,

"The wind is a horse/ listen how it runs/ through the sea, through the sky.// It wants to take me away: pay attention/ to how it roams the world/ to take me far."[871]

When you read this poem, do you really think that the Chilean poet saw a four legged animal galloping in the sky?'

2:21-The Deep Sleep

וַיַּפֵּל יְהוָה אֱלֹהִים תַּרְדֵּמָה עַל־הָאָדָם וַיִּישָׁן וַיִּקַּח אַחַת מִצַּלְעֹתָיו וַיִּסְגֹּר בָּשָׂר תַּחְתֶּנָּה׃ *vayapēl* (to fall) *yahvāh* (Transcendent) *'ĕlōhiym* (Divine-Consciousness) *taradēmāh* (deep sleep) *'al* (on) *hā'āḏām* (human) *vayiyšān* (sleeping) *vayiqaḥ* (took) *'aḥaṯ* (one) *miṣala'ōṯāyv* (rib out of) *vayisagōr* (closed up) *bāśār* (body) *taḥatenāh* (under)
καὶ *kai* (and) **ἐπέβαλεν** *epebalen* (imposed) **ὁ** *o* (the) **θεὸς** *theos* (God) **ἔκστασιν** *ekstasin* (trance) **ἐπὶ** *epi* (on) **τὸν** *ton* (the) **Αδαμ** *Adam* (Adam) **καὶ** *kai* (and) **ὕπνωσεν** *upōsen* (he slept) **καὶ** *kai* (and) **ἔλαβεν** *elaben* (he took) **μίαν** *mian* (one) **τῶν** *tōn* (the) **πλευρῶν** *pleurōn* (rib) **αὐτοῦ** *autou* (his) **καὶ** *kai* (and) **ἀνεπλήρωσεν** *aneplērōsen* (filled) **σάρκα** *sarka* (flesh) **ἀντ'** *ant'* (for) **αὐτῆς** *autēs* (it)
inmisit (placed) ***ergo*** (therefore) ***Dominus*** (Lord) ***Deus*** (God) ***soporem*** (deep sleep) ***in*** (in) ***Adam*** (Adam) ***cumque*** (while) ***obdormisset*** (he was sleeping) ***tulit*** (he took out) ***unam*** (one) ***de*** (of the) ***costis*** (ribs) ***eius*** (his) ***et*** (and) ***replevit*** (replenished) ***carnem*** (flesh) ***pro*** (for) ***ea*** (it)
And the LORD God caused a deep sleep to fall upon Adam, and he slept: and he took one of his ribs, and closed up the flesh instead thereof;
Therefore, the Transcendence of Divine-Consciousness induced a deep sleep on the Human. While he was sleeping, God took out a rib from his side and enclosed it in a body.

The first thing that we must highlight in this verse is the mist (אד *'ed*) or the deep sleep, *tardemah*,[872] induced on the human. This is one of the sleep, *yashen*,[873] states. In fact, it is the state of Non-Rapid-Eye-Movement (NREM), which, goes back to the dream (REM) state again. It becomes *fruitful* because it generates the next side, the dream world. As we have seen, this side corresponds metaphorically to the Fruitful Euphrates, the fourth river-branch. This is the *side* or *rib enclosed* (סגר *cagar*)[874] in a *body* (בָּשָׂר *basar*)[875] *bearing objective information* (בשר *basar*),[876] namely the oneiric and waking visual images. This is the *side*[877] or *rib* (צלע *tsela`*), which transports, through the nervous system, objective information to the subjective I and, from it, back to the object itself.

2:22-The Woman

וַיִּבֶן יְהוָה אֱלֹהִים אֶת־הַצֵּלָע אֲשֶׁר־לָקַח מִן־הָאָדָם לְאִשָּׁה וַיְבִאֶהָ אֶל־הָאָדָם׃ *vayiben* (built) *yahvāh* (Transcendent) *'ĕlōhiym* (Divine-Consciousness) *'eṯ* (with) *haṣēlā`* (limb) *'ăšer* (which) *lāqaḥ* (had taken) *min* (from) *hā'āḏām* (human) *la'išāh* (woman) *vayabi'eāh* (brought) *'el* (her) *hā'āḏām* (man)
καὶ *kai* (and) **ᾠκοδόμησεν** *ōkodomēsen* (built) **κύριος** *kurios* (Lord) **ὁ** *o* (the) **θεὸς** *theos* (God) **τὴν** *tēn* (the) **πλευράν** *pleuran* (rib) **ἣν** *ēn* (thus) **ἔλαβεν** *elaben* (he took) **ἀπὸ** *apo* (from) **τοῦ** *tou* (the) **Αδαμ** *Adam* (Adam) **εἰς** (in) **γυναῖκα** *gunaika* (woman) **καὶ** *kai* (and) **ἤγαγεν** *ēgagen* (brought) **αὐτὴν** *autēn* (her) **πρὸς** *pros* (to) **τὸν** *ton* (the) **Αδαμ** *Adam* (Adam)
et (and) ***aedificavit*** (made) ***Dominus*** (Lord) ***Deus*** (God) ***costam*** (rib) ***quam*** (which) ***tulerat*** (taken) ***de*** (out of) ***Adam*** (Adam) ***in*** (in a) ***mulierem*** (woman) ***et*** (and) ***adduxit*** (brought) ***eam*** (her) ***ad*** (to) ***Adam*** (Adam)

And the rib, which the LORD God had taken from man, made he a woman, and brought her unto the man.
And the Transcendent of Divine-Consciousness, from the rib-side taken out of the human, shaped a woman and brought her to the human.

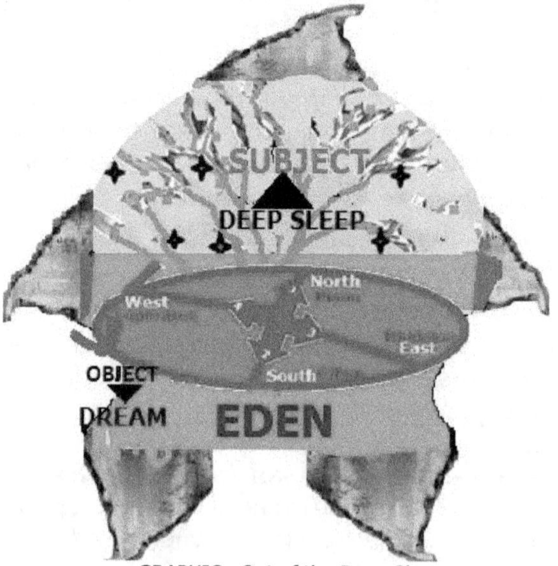

GRAPHIC: *Out of the Deep Sleep*

By definition, God, cannot be anthropomorphic. Thus, His shaping or *building* (בָּנָה *banah*)[878] is purely metaphoric. The creation of *heaven/earth* evolves into the epistemic individualized functions of *Adam/Eve* as the *Subject/Object* faculties. From there the individual will articulate in all the states of life. [879]⇨

Coming out of the NREM state of deep-sleep (תַּרְדֵּמָה *tardemah*), the human encounters the REM state of dreams (חֲלוֹם *chalowm*). That is to say, out of nothingness, visions find their way to a sort of virtual incarnation. As the human further proceeds out of the dream world, s/he encounters the physicality of wakefulness. There the *woman*[880] *comes into*[881] Adam's presence. The Hebrew word *'ishshah*, woman, derives from *'esh*[882] *fire* and is cognate to *'ishshah*[883] meaning '*burnt offering to the Lord.*' Therefore, we can say that here the woman comes into Adam as a burnt offering. Then, woman, is a metaphor for the object, which offers itself into Adam, the subject. Precisely *'ishshah*, woman, represents the object in its noematic quality, namely, the objective aspect of experience in its modes-of-being-given. Genderless Adam is a metaphor for the subject. Precisely it is the subject in its noetic quality, namely, the subjective aspect of experience as act-of-perception aiming to grasp the object. To be correct, the pair Adam-woman is not truly a metaphor. It is the actual paradigm of all humans, male-female with no gender distinction here and now in their unique quality as beings. It is the synthesis of noesis-noema and of subject-knower and known-objects.

2:23-Subject-Object

וַיֹּאמֶר הָאָדָם זֹאת הַפַּעַם עֶצֶם מֵעֲצָמַי וּבָשָׂר מִבְּשָׂרִי לְזֹאת יִקָּרֵא אִשָּׁה כִּי מֵאִישׁ לֻקֳחָה־זֹּאת׃   *vayō'mer* (said) *hā'āḏām* (Adam) *zō'ṯ* (this) *hapa'am* (now) *'eṣem* (bone) *mē'ăṣāmay* (from my bones) *uḇāśār* (flesh) *mibaśāriy* (from my flesh) *lazō'ṯ* (this) *yiqārē* (we shall call) *'išāh* (woman) *kiy* (because) *mē'iyš* (out of man) *luqŏḥāh* (taken) *zō'ṯ* (this)
καὶ *kai* (and) **εἶπεν** *eipen* (said) **Αδαμ** *Adam* (Adam) **τοῦτο** *touto* (in this way) **νῦν** *nun* (now) **ὀστοῦν** *ostoun* (bone) **ἐκ** *ek* (out of) **τῶν** *tōn* (the) **ὀστέων** *osteon* (bones) **μου** *mou* (my) **καὶ** *kai* (and) **σὰρξ** *sarx* (flesh) **ἐκ** *ek* (out of) **τῆς** *tēs* (the) **σαρκός** *sarkos* (flesh) **μου** *mou* (my) **αὕτη** *autē* (in this way) **κληθήσεται** *klēthēsetai* (shall be called) **γυνή** *gunē* (woman) **ὅτι** *oti* (because)

ἐκ *ek* (out of) **τοῦ** *tou* (the) **ἀνδρὸς** *andros* (man) **αὐτῆς** *autēs* (same) **ἐλήμφθη** *elēmphthē* (was taken) **αὕτη** *autē* (in that way)
dixit- (said) ***que*** (and) ***Adam*** (Adam) ***hoc*** (this) ***nunc*** (now) ***os*** (bone) ***ex*** (out of) ***ossibus*** (bones) ***meis*** (my) ***et*** (and) ***caro*** (flesh) ***de*** (out of) ***carne*** (flesh) ***mea*** (my) ***haec*** (her) ***vocabitur*** (shall be called) ***virago*** (woman) ***quoniam*** (because) ***de*** (out of) ***viro*** (man) ***sumpta*** (extracted) ***est*** (is)
And Adam said, This is now bone of my bones, and flesh of my flesh: she shall be called Woman, because she was taken out of Man.
And the human said, "*This is now bone from my bones and flesh from my flesh. She shall be named woman because she is extracted from the man.*"

Adam, the human, is this man/woman who is the reader of this page right here and now (פעם *pa`am*).[884] The word female, *'ishshah* (אִשָּׁה),[885] derives from *'iysh* (אִישׁ),[886] meaning man, a contraction for *'enowsh* (אֱנוֹשׁ),[887] denoting the existent mortal men, from *'anash* (אָנַשׁ),[888] in the sense of being frail. Thus, the female, with the echoing '*male,*' is bones (עֶצֶם *`etsem*) and flesh (בָּשָׂר *basar*) of the male. Both are of the same and one nature. Actually, the substance or the bones, *`etsem* (עֶצֶם),[889] are *`atsam* (עָצַם),[890] the *vast and numerous binding*[891] of the *objective information* (בָּשָׂר *basar*) coming from the *flesh* or ⇦[892] the *body* (בָּשָׂר *basar*). woman and the man are polarities of the same one human. Like the *Re-bis*, the double-thing of the Hermetic tradition,[893] <we, the subject-knower and the object-known, as metaphoric man and woman, inhabit this immanent-*Garden* of duality. *Immanent*, from Latin, *im-(in)-manēre* (to in-stay, to re-main intrinsic) is that which remains intrinsic between the knower/subject (male+) and the known/object (female-) dichotomy, as the inseparable positive(+)/negative(-) polarities of a dynamo. In the *midst of the Garden*, in its *immanence*, grows the metaphorical epistemic *Tree of Knowledge.*>[894]

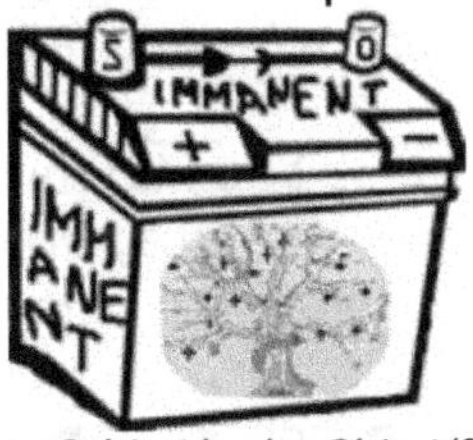

GRAPHIC: *Dynamo as Subject/male+Object/female-Polarities*

In verse 1:27, the word for woman is *nĕqebah*,[895] which derives from *naqab*,[896] to separate. This means that she is the paradigmatic separator or distinguisher between the *observed-image* and the *observer* reflecting in it. Here, however, the woman, *'ishshah* does not mean the physical woman in flesh and bones. It is again a metaphor for the epistemic generation of objectivity for the subject. Namely, the object is generated so that the subject might know it. This process is more understandable if we analyze it within the oneiric realm. There, the dream-object (*viz.* female) is *generated* for the dreamer (*viz.* male) to enjoy, while both are one and the same.

2:24-One Flesh

עַל־כֵּן יַעֲזָב־אִישׁ אֶת־אָבִיו וְאֶת־אִמּוֹ וְדָבַק בְּאִשְׁתּוֹ וְהָיוּ לְבָשָׂר אֶחָד׃ *`al* (then) *kēn* (therefore) *ya`ăzāḇ* (shall leave) *'iyš* (man) *'eṯ* (thus) *'āḇiyv* (his father) *va'eṯ* (and) *'imvō* (his mother) *vaḏāḇaq* (shall adhere to) *ba'išatvō* (wife) *vahāyu* (to be) *laḇāśār* (flesh) *'eḥāḏ* (one)
ἕνεκεν *eneken* (for reason) **τούτου** *toutou* (of this) **καταλείψει** *kataleipsei* (shall leave) **ἄνθρωπος** *avthrōpos* (man) **τὸν** *ton* (the) **πατέρα** *patera* (father) **αὐτοῦ** *autou* (his) **καὶ** *kai* (and) **τὴν** *tēn* (the) **μητέρα** *mētera* (mother) **αὐτοῦ** *autou* (his) **καὶ** *kai* (and) **προσκολληθήσεται** *proskollēsetai* (shall adhere) **πρὸς** *pros* (to) **τὴν** *tēn* (the) **γυναῖκα** *gunaika* (wife) **αὐτοῦ** *autou* (his) **καὶ** *kai* (and) **ἔσονται** *esontai* (shall be) **οἱ** *oi* (the) **δύο** *duo* (two) **εἰς** *eis* (in) **σάρκα** *sarka* (flesh) **μίαν** *mian* (one)
quam (that) ***ob*** (on) ***rem*** (account) ***relinquet*** (shall relinquish) ***homo*** (man) ***patrem*** (father)

suum (his) ***et*** (and) ***matrem*** (mother) ***et*** (and) ***adherebit*** (shall adhere) ***uxori*** (to wife) ***suae*** (his) ***et*** (and) ***erunt*** (they shall be) ***duo*** (two) ***in*** (in) ***carne*** (flesh) ***una*** (one)
Therefore shall a man leave his father and his mother, and shall cleave unto his wife: and they shall be one flesh.
Because of that, man shall relinquish his father and mother and shall adhere to his wife and they shall be two in one flesh.

The two, Subject/*man* and Object/*woman*, are inseparable. They are the epistemic *a-priori* synthesis, logically distinguishable, but never physically split. In fact, if we take away the subject, *viz.* the knower or the dreamer, the object disappears. Similarly, the subject vanishes if we eliminate the object. When there is no dreamer/subject, there is no dream/object as well as, in the absence of dream/object, there is no dreamer/subject. Metaphorically, the two are as one (אֶחָד *'echad*) flesh (בָּשָׂר *basar*), *viz.* joined indissolubly in the epistemic synthesis of subject and object.

However, mesmerized by their mutual adherence (דָּבַק *dabaq*) to one another, the subject/object forsakes[897] their founding paternal-origin[898] and beneficent-mother,[899] from which they both derive. What we mean here is that in our daily experiences, our hunger for representation, our love or lust for the world makes us forget the fundamental Awareness without which no experience or representation or the world would be possible. When that Awareness shines back alone in Its state of rest (שַׁבָּת *shabath*), then a reversal or return to the origins takes place.

> "*And every one that hath forsaken houses, or brethren, or sisters, or father, or mother, or wife, or children, or lands, for my name's sake, shall receive an hundredfold, and shall inherit everlasting life.*"[900]

2:25-Nakedness

וַיִּהְיוּ שְׁנֵיהֶם עֲרוּמִּים הָאָדָם וְאִשְׁתּוֹ וְלֹא יִתְבֹּשָׁשׁוּ׃ *vayihayu* (were) *šanēyhem* (two) *ʿărumiym* (naked) *hā'āḏām* (Adam) *va'išatvō* (wife) *valō'* (not) *yiṯabōšāšu* (ashamed)
καὶ *kai* (and) **ἦσαν** *ēsan* (were) **οἱ** *oi* (the) **δύο** *duo* (two) **γυμνοί** *gumnoi* (naked) **ὅ** *o* (the) **τε** *te* (both) **Αδαμ** *Adam* (Adam) **καὶ** *kai* (and) **ἡ** *ē* (the) **γυνὴ** *gunē* (wife) **αὐτοῦ** *autou* (his) **καὶ** *kai* (and) **οὐκ** *ouk* (not) **ᾐσχύνοντο** *ēschunonto* (were ashamed)
erant (were) ***autem*** (while) ***uterque*** (both) ***nudi*** (naked) ***Adam*** (Adam) ***scilicet*** (namely) ***et*** (and) ***uxor*** (wife) ***eius*** (his) ***et*** (and) ***non*** (not) ***erubescebant*** (were ashamed)
And they were both naked, the man and his wife, and were not ashamed.
Namely, while both the human and his wife were uncovered, they were not confused.

A literal interpretation of this passage would imply the absurdity that husband and wife, besides lovers, nudists, primitive naked jungle dwellers and/or infants, might feel *shame* (בּוֹשׁ *buwsh*) for their nakedness. Obviously, this nakedness must refer to something different from the simple body nudity.

In Hebrew, *ʿarowm*,[901] naked, derives from the verb *ʿaram*,[902] to uncover. Therefore, continuing with our epistemic interpretation, both the subject and the object appear uncovered. That is, both noetic and noematic aspects are auto-transparent to each other. This, as we have seen, is the *unconscious* moment of <u>Auto-Transparency</u>, in which the human is *conscious* while it does

> "not think of thinking... because... it is present to itself, without needing to mediate itself, that is to see itself before itself as object of its own knowledge."[903]

Now we can understand that the first object/woman to appear from the human *rib-side* is no other than consciousness auto-transpiring to itself. Therefore, the conscious/subject is not *confused*, *buwsh*,[904] by otherness, while it transpires to itself as consciousness/object. The thinking process does not interfere, namely, it does not *dress up* the object as different and other than itself. It is like an eye seeing itself in the mirror without being directly conscious-*of* itself. The object is in its pure noematic aspect. Adam/Eve is in the state of NREM, thus, s/he *is not confused* by the world's objectivity. Furthermore, this is evident also during the apex of copulation. Then, none of the partners is embarrassed by their nakedness. Vice versa, being conscious-*of* nakedness implies conceptualizing the absence of objective visible appearance, which *dresses* the other as otherness. If Adam/Eve were to notice the lack of *dressing* dreams, then s/he would not be in NREM sleep and/or in union, but in the dream world. The absence of thought, as in Auto-Transparency, besides the NREM state, is evident and present in the culminating state when Adam *knows carnally, yada`* יָדַע,[905] Eve and she *conceives, harah* הָרָה.[906] Then no thought is present. When thought arises, then the thoughtless unity is gone and the nakedness of the other is objectively experienced.

Subject-object rests in the field of consciousness. There, life and knowledge sprout necessitating perceptive companions. The identification with the object of knowledge leads to death. The living senses experience and confer idea-symbols to the objects of the world. Man and wife are paradigms of subject and objects. Their synthesis is evident only in the moment of intuition.

HERE ENDS THE SECOND CHAPTER OF GOD'S INHALING BREATH AND THE ASCENDING TREE IN THE GARDEN OF EDEN

CHAPTER 3

THE TREE OF KNOWLEDGE

& THE TREE OF LIFE

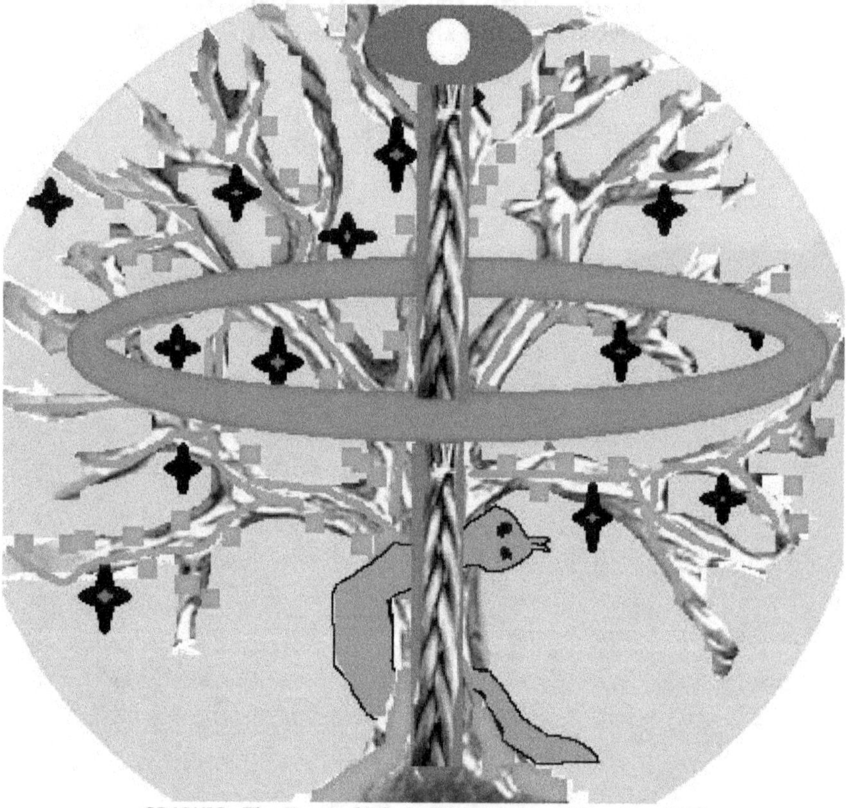

GRAPHIC: *The Trees of Life & of Knowledge-of Good and Evil*

3-I SECTION: THE TEMPTATION

3:1-The Serpent

וְהַנָּחָשׁ הָיָה עָרוּם מִכֹּל חַיַּת הַשָּׂדֶה אֲשֶׁר עָשָׂה יְהוָה אֱלֹהִים וַיֹּאמֶר אֶל־הָאִשָּׁה אַף כִּי־אָמַר אֱלֹהִים לֹא תֹאכְלוּ מִכֹּל עֵץ הַגָּן׃   *vahanāḥāš* (now the serpent) *hāyāh* (was) *ʿārum* (subtle) *mikōl* (from) *ḥayat̠* (animal) *haśād̠eh* (field) *ʾăšer* (which) *ʿāśāh* (made) *yahvāh* (Transcendent) *ʾĕlōhiym* (Divine-Consciousness) *vayōʾmer* (said) *ʾel* (to the) *hāʾišāh* (woman) *ʾap̄* (yea) *kiy* (that) *ʾāmar* (said) *ʾĕlōhiym* (Divine-Consciousness) *lōʾ* (not) *tōʾk̠alu* (to eat) *mikōl* (from) *ʿēṣ* (tree) *hagān* (garden)
ὁ *o* (the) **δὲ** *de* (but) **ὄφις** *ophis* (serpent) **ἦν** *ēn* (was) **φρονιμώτατος** *phrnimōtatos* (wiser) **πάντων** *pantōn* (of all) **τῶν** *tōn* (the) **θηρίων** *thēriōn* (animals) **τῶν** *tōn* (the) **ἐπὶ** *epi* (on) **τῆς** *tēs* (the) **γῆς** *gēs* (earth) **ὧν** *ōn* (thus) **ἐποίησεν** *epoiēsen* (made) **κύριος** *kurios* (Lord) **ὁ** *o* (the) **θεός** *theos* (God) **καὶ** *kai* (and) **εἶπεν** *eipen* (said) **ὁ** *o* (the) **ὄφις** *ophis* (snake) **τῇ** *tē* (to the) **γυναικί** *gunaiki* (woman) **τί** *ti* (why) **ὅτι** *oti* (that) **εἶπεν** *eipen* (said) **ὁ** *o* (the) **θεός** *theos* (God) **οὐ** *ou* (not) **μὴ** *mē* (that) **φάγητε** *phagēte* (eat) **ἀπὸ** *apo* (from) **παντὸς** *pantos* (all) **ξύλου** *xulou* (trees) **τοῦ** *tou* (the) **ἐν** *en* (in) **τῷ** *tō* (the) **παραδείσῳ** *paradeisō* (paradise)
sed (but) ***et*** (and) ***serpens*** (the serpent) ***erat*** (was) ***callidior*** (cleverer than) ***cunctis*** (any) ***animantibus*** (animals) ***terrae*** (of the earth) ***quae*** (which) ***fecerat*** (made) ***Dominus*** (Lord) ***Deus*** (God) ***qui*** (he) ***dixit*** (said) ***ad*** (to) ***mulierem*** (the woman) ***cur*** (in fact) ***praecepit*** (ordered) ***vobis*** (you) ***Deus*** (God) ***ut*** (to) ***non*** (not) ***comederetis*** (should eat) ***de*** (from) ***omni*** (every) ***ligno*** (tree) ***paradise*** (in paradise)
Now the serpent was more subtil than any beast of the field which the LORD God had made. And he said unto the woman, Yea, hath God said, Ye shall not eat of every tree of the garden?
Now, the serpent was cleverer than any other animal, which the Transcendent of Divine-Consciousness had made on earth. The snake asked the woman,   *"Had Divine-Consciousness ordered that you should not eat from every tree in the garden?"*

GRAPHIC: *The Serpent of Intentionality*

Intentionality is perceiving experience as stream of consciousness directed toward the world. We can say that when intentionality becomes consciousness-*of*-objects, then, it becomes synonym of **desire** and **hunger**. When the linear direction of intentionality reverts on itself, it becomes a snaking course. It goes from the subject, the perceiver-of-the-objects, to the perceived-objects. Then, it returns to the perceiving-subject who becomes a subject-conscious-*of* the object. Consequently, we identify with the object declaring it to be our life-experience, metaphorically our *food-for-thought*.

To understand better this flow, let us consider what happens when we feel physical pain. The main perceiving organ is the brain. Without it, we cannot detect pain. Therefore, the brain instantaneously spots a damaged tissue. That is because its nerve endings transmit the pain, say in the foot, to the brain. Immediately, we take that suffering as our own. We state that we are suffering. We identify with that discomfort and we reach to mend it away. Now, all this happens in the immediateness of our body. However, this is not different from the experience of the rest of the objective world. The reality of experience is conceived external, but still it must reach our brain, which then identifies with it by calling it '*my experience*.' In other words, *nothing can be stated external that is not internal.* However, in our experience, the exteriority *lures* us to identify with what is only peripheral, forgetting the internal reality. It is as if the icy realm of outer space would freeze us and made us forget the warm light of consciousness we come from, which allows us to see.

The Circle of Intentionality is the metaphoric serpent,[907] the very subtle[908] animal sense (חי *chay*) in the field[909] of knowledge. It is the continuous desire or projection towards the apprehension of the object of knowledge. Inevitably, however, it finds itself always at the starting point without ever being able to reach the object in-itself, because it experiences only its *objectified nakedness*.

Metaphorically, the serpent speaks to the woman because she represents the objective aspect of knowledge. Namely, she is the one who generates objectivity for the subject. Then, from that object, intentionality aims towards another object and so on. Meantime, the serpent's question is in reality the human considering, '*Why should we not experience, eat and become one with the fruits from the tree-consciousness-of knowledge?* The next verses will explain what this luring temptation is.

3:2-The Woman's Reply

וַתֹּאמֶר הָאִשָּׁה אֶל־הַנָּחָשׁ מִפְּרִי עֵץ־הַגָּן נֹאכֵל׃
vatō'mer (said) *hā'išāh* (woman) *'el* (to the) *hanāḥāš* (serpent) *mipariy* (from) *'ēṣ* (tree) *hagān* (garden) *nō'ḵēl* (we may eat)
καὶ *kai* (and) **εἶπεν** *eipen* (said) **ἡ** *ē* (the) **γυνὴ** *gunē* (woman) **τῷ** *tō* (to the) **ὄφει** *ophei* (serpent) **ἀπὸ** *apo* (from) **καρποῦ** *kronou* (fruit) **ξύλου** *xulou* (tree) **τοῦ** *tou* (the) **παραδείσου** *paradeisou* (paradise) **φαγόμεθα** *phagometha* (we can eat)
cui (to whom) ***respondit*** (answered) ***mulier*** (the woman) ***de*** (out of) ***fructu*** (the fruit) ***lignorum*** (of the trees) ***quae*** (which) ***sunt*** (are) ***in*** (in) ***paradiso*** (the paradise) ***vescemur*** (we may eat)
And the woman said unto the serpent, We may eat of the fruit of the trees of the garden:
The woman answered the serpent, "*We may eat the fruit of the trees, which are in the garden:*

Which ones are these edible fruits (פרי *pěriy*) of the garden? Fruits are metaphors for outcomes of Consciousness. In fact, here,

"*fruit*... [is a] metaph.[or] used of the *result* of labour or endeavour. Isaiah 3:10,

'*ye shall eat the fruit of your hands*;'

ye shall experience the results."[910]

To eat them is an allegory for the assimilation and identification with that food. Beside the *Biblical* fruits, in ancient Egyptian texts, we find the concept of eating connected to knowledge with expressions as

"*He hath eaten the knowledge of every god*,"[911] or

"*that which he seeth and that which he heareth make him wise and serve as food for him.*"[912]

<The conscious being, residing within the object, enjoys at the same time the individual subject-knower and the objects-known as food. The maker of both is objectivity itself, synthetically united[913] with the conscious being.>[914]

However, to explain these metaphors, we must clarify that these edible fruits are unconditional ecstatic acts. They are unbiased pure scientific observation, happiness and aesthetic rapture in the Garden of Eden. They are, seeing without looking, hearing without listening, tasting without savoring, smelling without sniffing, feeling without touching, doing without acting,[915] reflecting without thinking, knowing without accepting, loving without lusting, and so on. Thus, Paul states, let

"*those who mourn,* [be] *as if they did not; those who are happy, as if they were not.*"[916]

It is the continuous identification within Pure Consciousness leading into Awareness. Therefore, it is without hunger or desire for the fruit or the consequence of knowledge.

3:3-The Forbidden Fruit

וּמִפְּרִי הָעֵץ אֲשֶׁר בְּתוֹךְ־הַגָּן אָמַר אֱלֹהִים לֹא תֹאכְלוּ מִמֶּנּוּ וְלֹא תִגְּעוּ בּוֹ פֶּן־תְּמֻתוּן׃   *umipariy* (from) *hā'ēṣ* (the tree) *'ăšer* (which) *baṯvōḵa* (middle) *hagān* (garden) *'āmar* (said) *'ĕlōhiym* (Divine-Consciousness) *lō̄* (not) *ṯō'ḵalu* (eat) *mimenu* (because) *valō̄* (not) *ṯiga'u* (touch) *bvō* (if) *pen* (not) *tamuṯun* (die)
ἀπὸ *apo* (from) **δὲ** *de* (but) **καρποῦ** *karpou* (fruit) **τοῦ** *tou* (of the) **ξύλου** *xulou* (tree) **ὅ** *o* (thus) **ἐστιν** *estin* (is) **ἐν** *en* (in) **μέσῳ** *mesō* (middle) **τοῦ** *tou* (of the) **παραδείσου** *paradeisou* (paradise) **εἶπεν** *eipen* (said) **ὁ** *o* (the) **θεός** *theos* (God) **οὐ** *ou* (not) **φάγεσθε** *phagesthe* (to eat) **ἀπ'** *ap'* (from) **αὐτοῦ** *autou* (it) **οὐδὲ** *oude* (not even) **μὴ** *mē* (not even) **ἅψησθε** *apsēsthe* (touch) **αὐτοῦ** *autou* (it) **ἵνα** *ina* (that) **μὴ** *mē* (not) **ἀποθάνητε** *apothanēte* (die)
de (of) ***fructu*** (the fruit) ***vero*** (truthfully) ***ligni*** (of the tree) ***quod*** (which) ***est*** (is) ***in*** (in) ***medio*** (the middle) ***paradisi*** (of paradise) ***praecepit*** (ordered) ***nobis*** (us) ***Deus*** (God) ***ne*** (not) ***comederemus*** (we shall eat) ***et*** (and) ***ne*** (not) ***tangeremus*** (we shall touch) ***illud*** (it) ***ne*** (not) ***forte*** (perhaps) ***moriamur*** (will die)
But of the fruit of the tree which is in the midst of the garden, God hath said, Ye shall not eat of it, neither shall ye touch it, lest ye die.
Truthfully, Divine-Consciousness ordered,   *'you should not eat nor touch the fruit from the tree, which is in the middle of the garden of consciousness, if you do not want to die."*

The *woman*, born out of Adam's other side, the one who generates the objectivity of otherness, realizes that there is one fruit that should not be eaten nor *mentally touched,*[917] *viz.* identified with. This is the fruit of the Tree of *Knowledge of Good and Evil*, specifically the knowledge-*of Everything.* **This is the desirous attached identification of the mind with the object**. Therefore,

"*See then that ye walk circumspectly, not as fools, but as wise, restoring present-proper-time, because the days are evil.*"[918]

Since, when one leaves the *present-proper-time* (καιρός *kairos*) of *deep-dreamless-sleep, tardemah* (תַּרְדֵּמָה), one experiences the *evil days* (ἡμέραι *ēmerai* πονηραί *ponērai*) of yearning dreams and worrisome wakefulness. Thus, one tastes pain and death. In the *Torah*, in fact,

"all kinds and degrees of desire were forbidden"[919]

because they lead to

"*the graves of desire.*"[920]

Namely, Consciousness, at the center of happiness, may become conscious-*of* and desirous-*of* the object. Thus, the experience-*of* the world *for-itself* loses and misses happiness, which is *in-itself.* This is like the injunction not to judge or to conceptualize the world.

"*Do not judge, and you will not be judged. Do not condemn, and you will not be condemned. Forgive, and you will be forgiven.*"[921]

In fact, the parameters we use to judge others are deep-rooted in our mindset, therefore, they will come back to condemn us with the same measure. When we identify with the known object, then, death[922] ensues, as we will see in the next commentaries. In fact, in the Garden of Eden, there is no death. When we eat the fruit of the Tree of Knowledge then we encounter death. However, at the time of death Pure Consciousness continues lighting up the world and with it a new neighboring individual consciousness-*of* conceives another domain in which to eat again the forbidden fruit.

3:4-The Serpent's Reply

וַיֹּאמֶר הַנָּחָשׁ אֶל־הָאִשָּׁה לֹא־מוֹת תְּמֻתוּן׃
vayō'mer (said) *hanāḥāš* (serpent) *'el* (to the) *hā'išāh* (woman) *lō* (not) *mvōṯ* (death) *tamuṯun* (you will die)
καὶ *kai* (and) **εἶπεν** *eipen* (said) **ὁ** *o* (the) **ὄφις** *ophis* (serpent) **τῇ** *tē* (to the) **γυναικί** *gunaiki* (woman) **οὐ** *ou* (noy) **θανάτῳ** *thanatō* (death) **ἀποθανεῖσθε** *apothaneisthe* (you will die)
dixit (said) ***autem*** (therefore) ***serpens*** (the serpent) ***ad*** (to) ***mulierem*** (the woman) ***nequaquam*** (by no means) ***morte*** (death) ***moriemini*** (you will die)
And the serpent said unto the woman, Ye shall not surely die:
Therefore, the serpent replied to the woman, "*Surely, you will not die.*

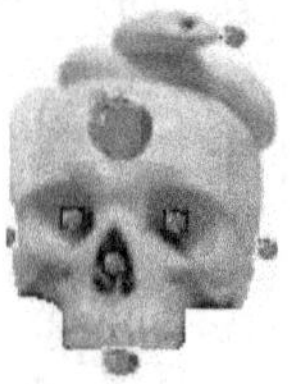

The serpent is intentionality gone astray. Its intention is consciousness spiraling upon itself. It is consciousness wanting to be conscious-*of* itself *for-itself*, while losing its own life *in-itself*. This intentionality does not rest in Awareness-Itself, but rather in the consciousness-*of* itself as an object. [923]⇨

Nevertheless, the intentional-serpent is convinced that its self-coiling is the life of its own self-recognition. It is like Dorian Gray[924] looking at his self-portrait and saying, '*This is my* *living I.*' In other words, in all sentient beings, the consciousness-*of*-consciousness becomes an object of experience with which we identify. We conceive it to be our own true self and life.

The answer given by the serpent is the same we would get if we were to request our reader, to

'Stop thinking and objectifying desire!'

S/he would answer

'Why would God have created all this world if not to be enjoyed? Consciousness-of the world is life and my thinking proves that I am alive! In fact, the great philosopher Descartes says, 'I think, hence I am.''[925]

The same theme of death, self and hunger-for-the-fruit is present in the ancient Indian *Bṛhadāraṇyaka Upanishad*. Where it says,

"*Verily, this entire world was concealed by Death, by Hunger, because hunger is death.*[926] *Then, Death projected the mind-thought: 'Let me be a being for-myself.'"*[927]

Nevertheless, Mṛtyu-Death, *selfishly* hungering *for-itself*, coils around to reach itself as food *for-itself* only to discover that, by doing so, he

"*will accomplish very small food.*"[928]

3:5-Ye Shall Be as Gods

כִּי יֹדֵעַ אֱלֹהִים כִּי בְּיוֹם אֲכָלְכֶם מִמֶּנּוּ וְנִפְקְחוּ עֵינֵיכֶם וִהְיִיתֶם כֵּאלֹהִים יֹדְעֵי טוֹב וָרָע׃
kiy (because) *yōḏēa'* (knows) *'ĕlōhiym* (Divine-Consciousness) *kiy* (that) *bayvōm* (day) *'ăkālakem* (you shall eat) *mimenu* (from it) *vanipaqaḥu* (shall open) *'ēynēykem* (eyes) *vihayiyṯem* (you shall be) *kē'lōhiym* (like gods) *yōḏa'ēy* (knowing) *ṭvōḇ* (good) *vārā'* (evil)
ᾔδει *ēdei* (knows) **γὰρ** *gar* (in fact) **ὁ** *o* (the) **θεὸς** *theos* (God) **ὅτι** *oti* (that) **ἐν** *en* (in) **ᾗ** *ē* (thus) **ἂν** *an* (if) **ἡμέρᾳ** *ēmera* (day) **φάγητε** *phagēte* (you shall eat) **ἀπ'** *ap'* (from) **αὐτοῦ** *autou* (it) **διανοιχθήσονται** *dianoichthēsontai* (shall open) **ὑμῶν** *umōv* (your) **οἱ** *oi* (the) **ὀφθαλμοί** *ophthalmoi* (eyes) **καὶ** *kai* (and) **ἔσεσθε** *esesthe* (you shall be) **ὡς** *ōs* (like) **θεοὶ** *theoi* (gods) **γινώσκοντες** *ginōskontes* (knowing) **καλὸν** *kalon* (good) **καὶ** *kai* (and) **πονηρόν** *ponēron* (evil)
scit (knows) ***enim*** (in fact) ***Deus*** (God) ***quod*** (that) ***in*** (in) ***quocumque*** (very) ***die*** (day) ***comederitis*** (you shall eat) ***ex*** (of) ***eo*** (it) ***aperientur*** (shall be opened) ***oculi*** (eyes) ***vestri*** (yours) ***et*** (and) ***eritis*** (you shall be) ***sicut*** (like) ***dii*** (gods) ***scientes*** (knowing) ***bonum*** (the good) ***et*** (and) ***mălum*** (the evil) ( )
For God doth know that in the day ye eat thereof, then your eyes shall be opened, and ye shall be as gods, knowing good and evil.

In fact, Divine-Consciousness knows that in the very day in which you shall eat of it, your eyes shall be opened and you shall be like gods, knowing everything, the good and the bad."

The Serpent, asserting that eating this fruit will open the eyes of the eaters and they will be like gods, tempts humans to conceptualize the unthinkable. The instant in which Eve believes the Serpent, that moment she turns her sight away from the Certainty of her Faith and loses It. That temptation plunges us into the world of sin, missed aims, pain and death.

There is a puzzling expression in the *Lord's Prayer* that says,

"*our Father Who* [are] *in Transcendent-Heaven ... do not lead us into temptation*."[929]

The question arises. How can *Pure Goodness*, by antonomasia meaning Supreme Righteousness, lead into temptation? To answer it, we must first look at the Greek word for temptation, *peirasmos* (πειρασμός), meaning *experiment, attempt, trial, proving*. It derives from the verb *peirazō* (πειράζω), *to attempt, to endeavor*, and from the noun *peira* (πεῖρα), *trial, experience* and *attempt*. Finally, it has its base in the adverb *peran* (πέραν), *piercing beyond, on the other side*. Therefore, the *Bible* calls it *temptation-of-object-experimentation*.[930] This is exactly the same injunction not to eat from the tree of knowledge. In fact, *three* (τρίτος *tritos*) times,[931] *viz.* on the three levels of wake, dream and dreamlessness, Jesus encouraged his circle of twelve (360/30) disciples to

"*Be waken-aware and pray* [i.e. meditate] *that ye enter not into the temptation-of-object experimentation: the spirit indeed* [is] *willing, but the flesh* [is] *weak*."[932]

We must realize that Awareness-in-Itself, the only Certain-Reality we have, is what leads us, in this Present-Consciousness. That Awareness is Apodictic-Certainty. However, we believe into the reality of the world as an object independent from that awareness and from us,

a) we want to reduce Awareness, as such, to an object of thought, and
b) we erroneously interpret Certainty to be the quality embedded in the objective world as such.

Therefore,

"*be waken-aware and pray, lest ye enter into temptation*"[933]

of conceptualizing יְהֹוָה, the Transcendent. Actually, **the objectification of the transcendent necessarily implies transcending and idolizing the object, as the metaphoric *apple-fruit* allegorically *offered* by Eve/*object* to Adam/*subject*.** Namely, we perceive the entire universe, observed out there, as *reality in-itself*. As an example, look at our dream experience and/or at this book in our hands. While experiencing them both in the dreaming and/or in the waking states, we are certain of them. Nevertheless, it is Awareness that gives Certainty to the dream and/or wakeful experiences. Blinded by the brightness of Awareness, we erroneously transfer Its Certainty to the objects as if It were their own intrinsic nature. Namely, while we focus on the object and hunger for it, it seems as if Awareness may urge us to conceive itself as an object of knowledge, *viz.* the thought-of-awareness. This is the fundamental error of Idealism, which, stemming from the Cartesian *cogito*[934] and stating that

"what is rational is real; and what is real is rational,"[935]

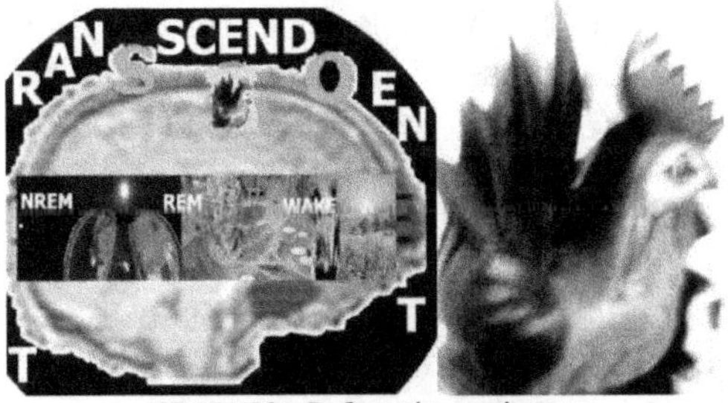

GRAPHIC: *Before the cock crow*

objectifies the idea itself and loses its Apodictic Source. Similarly, Peter repudiates Jesus' Awareness *trice* (τρίς *tris*), namely, in dreamless-sleep, in dreams and in wakefulness.

"*before the cock crow*."[936]

However, all dream and/or wake experiences disappear when we awake and/or when we die. <The temptation is the identification with the impermanent object erroneously conceived as real-in-itself. The *Mutus Liber* declares,

"*Pray, Read, Read, Read, Reread, Labor and Ye Shall Discover,*"[937]

namely you shall *un*veil the Hidden One. That veil impedes immortality, tempts, distracts and lures away from it. Therefore, the emphasis is on a vigilant and constant attention on the Truth, which is the inherent apodicticity of Awareness.>[938] Therefore, one

"*should always pray* [*i.e.* meditate], *and not to be utterly spiritless.*"[939]

The affinity between the Latin words *mălum* (*viz.* evil) and *mālum* (*viz.* apple ) symbolically fashioned the forbidden fruit as an apple.[940] Actually, the fundamental erroneous assumption of the serpent, here, is that god conceives and thinks the world anthropomorphically, namely, as a separate object from him. Thus, we feel the necessity to emulate his supposed *hunger* to create. This verse and the following ones give us the full explanation for the meaning of life and the reason why we live. Like a racing greyhound dog on a racetrack chasing after an elusive artificial mechanical rabbit-lure, or a donkey pursuing a carrot hanging on its nose, the mind chases the impossible objectification of its Transcendent Apodictic Awareness.

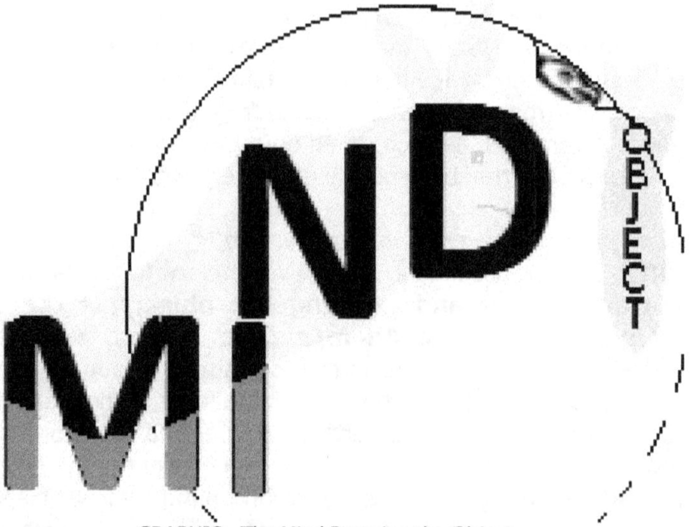

GRAPHIC: *The Mind Pursuing the Object*

In fact, the mind looks at the world as a reality independent from itself. It confers transcendence to the object without ever catching it in-itself. The entire epistemic process tends always towards its own transcendence, without ever reaching It. The object placed out there, before our eyes, even in our dreams, is always real until realized otherwise.[941] Namely, we recognize the dream to be such only upon awakening. Life, as we know it, desires and hungers for the representation of the world. Furthermore, the mind conceives reality as our *other side rib* (צלע *tsela`*), as distinct and separated from the knower. The mind wants to conceptualize, to know and to tangibly experience[942] awareness, namely, to bring it in the *day light* (יוֹם *yowm*) of the circularity as *consciousness-of-awareness*. However, that Awareness is not conceivable except as a thought, which is different from Pure-Awareness-in-Itself. Transcendence is unconceivable. 'Elohiym (אֱלֹהִים), Divine-Consciousness, is Its name. However, Yĕhovah (יְהֹוָה), ITS TRUE NAME, remains ineffable, unpronounceable and *un-writeable*, except as a connotation, a reference to the Unknown as such. Its name, when it is so taken (נָשָׂא *nasa'*), conceived or thought becomes empty.[943] To try to conceive IT is to reduce it to an inanimate object. This **conceptual reduction is the *forbidden* fruit**. Beyond the metaphor, what this means is that the mind attributes transcendent qualities to the objective world. The mind, on its *sneaky* and *snaky* intentioning trajectory, focuses on the objectified awareness and identifies with it, instead of reuniting with the emanating source from which its own image reflects. **The mind wants to conceptualize Transcendence as an object of knowledge and thought.**

"*They turned back and tempted God, and limited the Holy One of Israel.*"[944]

When we try to conceptualize and/or historicize God,[945] inevitably, we end up referring it to our death. This gives rise to superstitious, luciferous and demonic religions, which impose relative laws and morals in the name of politically imagined deity[946] plaguing humanity with radicalized crusades, wars and inquisitions. Any search for God starts with an enquiry on the state of death. We understand him as being beyond death, of which we understand nothing, except as lifeless corps. In other words, it is like a lover who, searching for the lost love, fancies the statue of the beloved one. Subsequently, the lover, desperate and frozen by the coldness of that marble, continues the search by shaping a new sculptured likeness of the dear one. Similarly, the mind, searching to reach Awareness, seeks to know it as a thought and an object of the world. The Hebrew word for thought is *ra`yown.*[947] It corresponds to *ra`yown,*[948] which means longing, striving. It derives from *ra`ah,*[949] meaning to pasture, to feed, also to delight and to hold intercourse,[950] in the sense of *r@`uwth,*[951] longing, striving desire. Thus, thinking becomes like an *appetite* for the object.

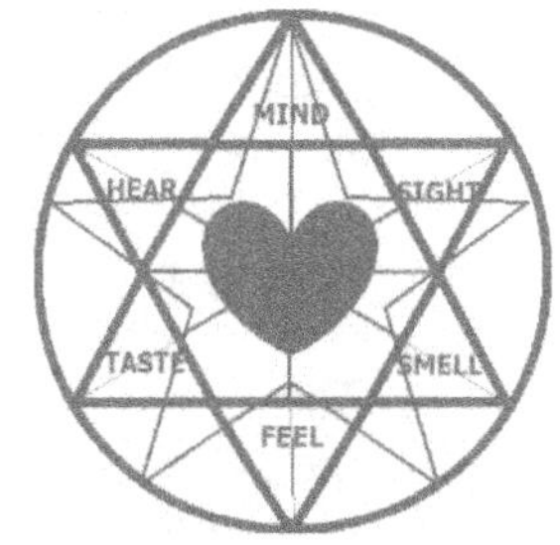

In the Indian tradition, the gods are understood as the organs and faculties of the senses called *indriya*, the qualities that belong to the 'I,' *viz. Indra*.

"*All the faculties of the senses become one in their corresponding deities, deeds and the intellectual self.*"[952]

"*Verily, the gods are the five channels of perception of this heart.*"[953]

However, Apodictic Awareness, which is the foundation of every experience, *viz.* the good (טוב *towb*) and evil (רע *ra`*), is not an experience itself. The *snaky* intentionality erroneously leads us into believing, identifying and eating (אָכַל *'akal*) the experienced world as real in-itself, as it it were the Divine-Consciousness itself permeating the object in-itself. Thus, continuing with our previous example, the lover's eyes (עַיִן *`ayin*) open[954] only to see the statue/object of the loved one, but, at the same time, completely miss the real beloved one. Therefore,

"*Our heart is troubled until it rests in you, Lord*"[955]

of Pure-Certain-Awareness.

"The one primarily in need of redemption is... [s/he] who is lost and sleeping in matter... directed to... the liberation... from the darkness of matter... To this end [s/]he needs meditation, fasting, and prayer... Matter... must be redeemed, the spirit that manifests itself in the transformation is... the *filius macrocosmi* [*viz.* son of the macrocosm]. Therefore, what comes out of the transformation is... an ineffable material being named the *stone*,"[956]

viz. the *Philosopher's Stone*,[957] the obect *in-itself* having the transmuting quality of Consciousness itself.

When Jesus, abstaining from eating the *fruit* of this world

"*had fasted forty days and forty nights, he was afterward an hungred.*"[958]

Then, the devil tempted him three times. This is the classical story of the three wishes or desires that actualize objectivity on three levels.

"The wonder is that the characteristic efficacy to touch and inspire deep creative centers dwells in the smallest nursery fairy tale— as the flavor of the ocean is contained in a droplet or the whole mystery of life within the egg of a flea. For the symbols of mythology are not manufactured; they cannot be ordered, invented, or permanently suppressed. They are spontaneous productions of the psyche, and each bears within it, undamaged, the germ power of its source."[959]

The three wishes take place

"*because of your uncertainty... if ye have certainty* (πίστις *pistis*) *as a grain of mustard seed... nothing shall be impossible... Furthermore this kind* [of demon] *goeth not out but by prayer and fasting...*[960] *with God all things are possible*"[961] "[and] *all things are possible to him that has faith* (πιστεύω *pisteuō*)."[962]

Therefore, the serpent is this hunger, this desire, this primordial energy, this nature, this sexual drive[963] and this dominance of life that tempts us three times, namely,

1) The Ego-consciousness' wakeful hunger of for the daily life-needs is the first temptation. In fact,

    "*the tempter... said... command that these stones be made bread.*"[964]

    Indeed, the *serpentine* intentionality urges the mind to transform the petrified objectivity in *food for thought*. This temptation refers to the very heart of life's creation. Thus, Jesus answers,

    "*Man shall not live by bread alone, but by every word of God,*"[965]

    namely by the realization that the creative '*fiat*' (*viz.* '*let there be*'), voiced by Awareness, is the sustainer of the entire objective world.

2) The I-consciousness' oneiric desire for the dream (REM) realm is the second temptation. Then, the devil tempts Jesus saying,

    "'*Cast thyself down...* [and] *angels... shall bear thee up'.*"[966]

    Aristotle recognizes that

    "All men by nature desire to know,"[967]

    therefore, Jesus' miraculous abilities tempt him to test their procreative capabilities, however,

    "*Jesus said unto him* [the tempter], *'It is written again, Thou shalt not tempt the Lord thy God'.*"[968]

    Like Eros, the Greek god of love, the process of knowledge hungers, lusts and desires. The physicist Stephen Hawking, asked about the joys deriving from scientific discoveries, replied,

    "I wouldn't compare it to sex, [only because] it lasts longer."[969]

    Therefore, the goal of all of the serpent's desires is to test the objective world and possess it. The serpent, through the I, fulfils its never-ending hunger, his desire to know and *eat* the world.

    "*Whosoever therefore will be a friend of the world is the enemy of God.*"[970]

    Thus, the I becomes the enjoyer of this entire world.

    "*Those who find pleasure in the flesh... find... in it death.*"[971]

    In fact, desire is the drive towards the representation of the objective world as that which is already past, then belonging to death. Satisfying the desire of that fruit means assimilating death, and

    "*in the day that thou eatest thereof thou shalt surely die.*"[972]

3) The peaceful wish of Auto-transparency in the deep sleep (NREM) state without representation is the final temptation.

    "*All the kingdoms of the world and the glory of them... I will give thee, if thou wilt fall down and worship me,*"[973]

    says the devil, tempting Jesus for the third and last time.

    "*Then saith Jesus unto him, 'Get thee hence, Satan: for it is written, Thou shalt worship the Lord thy God, and him only shalt thou serve.' Then the devil leaveth him, and, behold, angels came and ministered unto him.*"[974]

    <A thin line separates the third state of NREM and dying. In the moment of passing away, one leaves, willingly or unwillingly, the state of daily existence. One enters, through the very personal, intimate and not communicable experience of the death state. The third wish, the one that wants to rest in-itself, persists as *eternal rest* in which all that we know disappears, all ends. Freud recognized this as the

    "death instinct [which] can never be absent in any vital process. [He recognizes two instincts] the erotic instincts... and the death instincts which act against that tendency."[975]

    However, the erotic instincts, like the imbedded mammalian rut, compel us. One way or the other nature, in its evolutionary process, drives us. These forces come out from nowhere, from a world that is not the one of the living. From that dark unknown, the erotic desire wants to reach a world of representation, an experience of life[976] and generates it.[977] Furthermore, who wants to abandon life? Even the suicidal looks for an escape from the current hell, an opening to another eventevent, craving, nevertheless, for a different *life experience*. The agnostic or the disbeliever, even if agrees that after death there is only oblivion, a condition without representations, in a sense similar to NREM but with no return, must concede that the dying person expires desiring another *experience*. Therefore, one dies pregnant with the third wish: the wish to continue to have experiences no matter if it is oblivion, paradise, hell or return to this life, *i.e.* to the state of wakefulness, which gains

"*All the kingdoms of the world and the glory of them*," thus, the third temptation.

When we write about death and/or about the encounter with death, in reality we write about the condition of this physical life, of this '*I*' here and now, of this '*I*' reading these pages. The three wishes, we just mentioned, drive our daily life. They all proceed directed towards the immanent world of representations. There is another direction, which aims towards the Transcendence of the Self-in-itself. Immanence and Transcendence are the two faces of the same medal. In each side, however, there is the same seed, the alloy that makes up the medal that is Awareness.>[978] This is the *forth* reality after the *forty* days of abstinence from the food of the mind.

3:6-The Fruit of Desire

וַתֵּרֶא הָאִשָּׁה כִּי טוֹב הָעֵץ לְמַאֲכָל וְכִי תַאֲוָה־הוּא לָעֵינַיִם וְנֶחְמָד הָעֵץ לְהַשְׂכִּיל וַתִּקַּח מִפִּרְיוֹ וַתֹּאכַל וַתִּתֵּן גַּם־לְאִישָׁהּ עִמָּהּ וַיֹּאכַל׃ *vatēre'* (seeing) *hā'išāh* (female) *kiy* (that) *ṭvōḇ* (good) *hā'ēṣ* (tree) *lama'ăḵāl* (food) *v aḵiy* (for) *ṯa'ăvāh* (desire) *hu'* (to become) *lā'ēynayim* (eyes) *vaneḥamāḏ* (pleasurable) *hā'ēṣ* (tree) *lahaśakiyl* (to be knowledgeable) *vatiqaḥ* (took) *mipirayvō* (from) *vatō'ḵal* (to eat) *vatitēn* (gave) *gam* (also) *la'iyšāh* (to male) *'imāh* (with) *vayō'ḵal* (to eat)
καὶ *kai* (and) **εἶδεν** *eiden* (saw) **ἡ** *ē* (the) **γυνὴ** *gunē* (woman) **ὅτι** *oti* (that) **καλὸν** *kalov* (good) **τὸ** *to* (the) **ξύλον** *xulon* (tree) **εἰς** *eis* (in) **βρῶσιν** *brōsin* (food) **καὶ** *kai* (and) **ὅτι** *oti* (because) **ἀρεστὸν** *areston* (pleasant) **τοῖς** *tois* (to the) **ὀφθαλμοῖς** *ophthalmois* (eyes) **ἰδεῖν** *idein* (to see) **καὶ** *kai* (and) **ὡραῖόν** *ōraion* (attractive) **ἐστιν** *estin* (was) **τοῦ** *tou* (the) **κατανοῆσαι** *katanoēsai* (knowledge) **καὶ** *kai* (and) **λαβοῦσα** *labousa* (took) **τοῦ** *tou* (the) **καρποῦ** *karpou* (fruit) **αὐτοῦ** *autou* (it) **ἔφαγεν** *ephagen* (ate) **καὶ** *kai* (and) **ἔδωκεν** *edōken* (gave) **καὶ** *kai* (and) **τῷ** *tō* (the) **ἀνδρὶ** *andri* (man) **αὐτῆς** *autēs* (it) **μετ'** *met'* (with) **αὐτῆς** *autēs* (her) **καὶ** *kai* (and) **ἔφαγον** *ephagon* (ate)
vidit (saw) ***igitur*** (therefore) ***mulier*** (the wife) ***quod*** (that) ***bonum*** (good) ***esset*** (was) ***lignum*** (the tree) ***ad*** (to) ***vescendum*** (eat) ***et*** (and) ***pulchrum*** (beautiful) ***oculis*** (to the eyes) ***aspect-*** (appearance) ***que*** (and) ***delectabile*** (desirable) ***et*** (and) ***tulit*** (took) ***de*** (from) ***fructu*** (fruit) ***illius*** (it) ***et*** (and) ***comedit*** (ate) ***dedit-***(gave) ***que*** (and) ***viro*** (to man) ***suo*** (her) ***qui*** (who) ***comedit*** (ate)
And when the woman saw that the tree was good for food, and that it was pleasant to the eyes, and a tree to be desired to make one wise, she took of the fruit thereof, and did eat, and gave also unto her husband with her; and he did eat.
Therefore, the female-objectivity understanding that the tree was pleasurable to eat, beautiful in appearance, fragrantly desirable for knowledge, she took the fruit and ate it. Then, she gave it to the male subjectivity that also ate it.

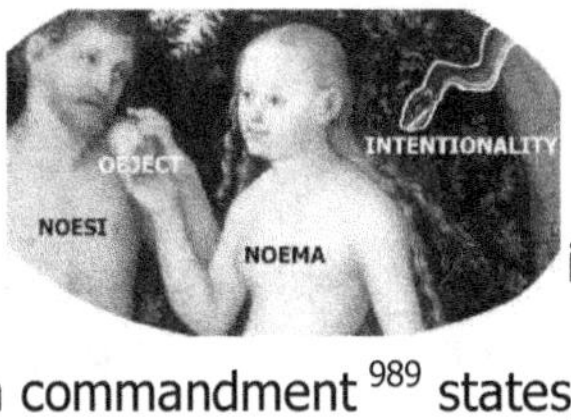

This verse describes the five senses, as they gather experiences in the synthesis of the mind. In fact, here, the woman understands (*ra'ah*),[979] tastes (*'akal*)[980] the good (*towb*)[981] food (*ma'akal*),[982] sees it pleasant (*ta'avah*)[983] for the eyes (*`ayin*),[984] delights (*chamad*)[985] and feels (*laqach*)[986] the forbidden fruit of the tree (עץ *'ets*), namely the faculty of the senses. Finally, all the senses find their unity in the mind (*sakal*).[987] The key point of this verse is the *aromatic desire* (*chamad*),[988] which is the mover of the entire process of hungry knowledge. In fact, the tenth commandment [989] states,

"*Thou shalt not <u>covet/desire</u>* (חָמַד *chamad*)[990]*... anything* (כֹּל *kol*)[991] *of the neighboring-thought* (רֵעַ *rea`*)[992]." [993]⇨

The female aspect is a metaphor for objectivity. It represents the perception (רָאָה *ra'ah*) of the *neighbor* (רֵעַ *rea`*) object as good (טוֹב *towb*) and pleasurable[994] *food-*(*'akal*)[995]*for-thought* (*sakal*).[996] The female-perception, then, takes passionate-possession[997] of the object, of its *taste*[998] and assimilates it. As objectivity, she becomes, the fruit-object, noematically giving[999] herself to the subject (אִישׁ *'iysh*), the metaphoric male-husband (אִישׁ *'iysh*), for him to eat (אָכַל *'akal*) and acknowledge. Concomitantly, this subject becomes the noetic enjoyer and eater of that objectivity.

Overall, the Tree of Knowledge of Good and Bad is the **Tree of Desire**. This tree is a metaphor for our propensity to judge as *good*, that which satisfies our wish, and as *bad*, that which does not. Thus, Adam and Eve, eating the Forbidden Fruit, establish a common binding taste, during which they both experience its flavor as pleasurable or unpleasurable. Desire, then, becomes Death's hunger. It becomes

"*an urge inherent in organic life to restore an earlier state of things...* an *old* state of things, an initial state from which the living entity has at one time or other departed and to which it is striving to return by the circuitous[1000] paths."[1001] `

Adam and Eve's deadly meal finds its redemption with the Passover Seder.

"*The LORD spake ... concerning the feasts of... the LORD'S Passover... the feast of unleavened bread... ye must eat.*"[1002]

Then, the Pure-Consciousness redeems all *sinful* missed marks into the Serene-Wisdom-Of-Awareness. Then, the unifying communion with the Desireless Paschal Lamb delivers us from the deadly slavery of desire.[1003]

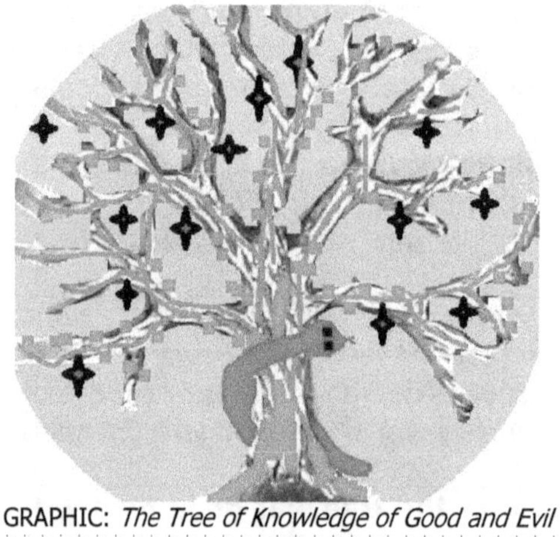

GRAPHIC: *The Tree of Knowledge of Good and Evil*

A young person once asked,

'Why you keep presenting all these metaphors, when it would be simpler to accept that the first couple enjoyed eating a physical forbidden fruit?

Furthermore, how can we be responsible for a sin committed by our progenitors, not by us?'

We reply,

'Your first point may be valid only if you can explain Divine-Justice. How the exclusive guilt of parents can justify the death sentence inflicted, not only on innocent offspring, as you point out in your second question, but also on all the other creatures that had not eaten of that deadly fruit?' 'The Divine Order stated, '<u>Do not</u> <u>incorporate</u> the fruit of knowledge.' That absorption continues today to be the core of our gnoseological nature,

namely Adam/Eve. We daily partake of that same error. Therefore, we are responsible as much as our metaphoric originators. We suffer its consequences. In fact, the elementary configuration of hunger affects the sentient structure of every being here and now. Every creatures interacts with the objective world as a place in which to compete against other beings in order to survive and evolve.[1004] *Furthermore, Adam* (אָדָם *'adam*) *designates the collective universal human being not only allegorically or paradigmatically, but also as integral conscious, subconscious and unconscious individuality. In fact, the LORD Divine-Consciousness "created* (בָּרָא *bārā*) them *male* (זָכָר *zāḵār*) and *female* (וּנְקֵבָה *unaqēḇāh*)." *Adam is, at the same time, each and every-human that ever lived, lives and/or will live. This implies the shared responsibility for all our actions.'*

3:7-With Opened Eyes

וּתִּפָּקַחְנָה עֵינֵי שְׁנֵיהֶם וַיֵּדְעוּ כִּי עֵירֻמִּם הֵם וַיִּתְפְּרוּ עֲלֵה תְאֵנָה וַיַּעֲשׂוּ לָהֶם חֲגֹרֹת׃ *vatipāqaḥanāh* (open) *'ēynēy* (eyes) *šanēyhem* (both) *vayēḏa'u* (know) *kiy* (that) *'ēyrumim* (naked) *hēm* (they) *vayiṯaparu* (sewed together) *'ălēh* (leaves) *ṯa'ēnāh* (fig) *vaya'ăśu* (fashion) *lāhem* (they) ḥăḡōrōṯ (aprons)
καὶ *kai* (and) **διηνοίχθησαν** *diēnoichthēsan* (were opened) **οἱ** *oi* (the) **ὀφθαλμοὶ** *ophthalmoi* (eyes) **τῶν** *tōn* (of the) **δύο** *duo* (two) **καὶ** *kai* (and) **ἔγνωσαν** *egnōsan* (they knew) **ὅτι** *oti* (that) **γυμνοὶ** *gumnoi* (naked) **ἦσαν** *ēsan* (were) **καὶ** *kai* (and) **ἔρραψαν** *errapsan* (sewed) **φύλλα** *phulla* (leaves) **συκῆς** *sukēs* (fig) **καὶ** *kai* (and) **ἐποίησαν** *epoiēsan* (made) **ἑαυτοῖς** *eautois* (for themselves) **περιζώματα** *perizōmata* (apron)
et (and) ***aperti*** (opened) ***sunt*** (were) ***oculi*** (the eyes) ***amborum*** (of both) ***cumque*** (and) ***cognovissent*** (knew) ***esse*** (were) ***se*** (they) ***nudos*** (naked) ***consuerunt*** (sewed) ***folia*** (leaves) ***ficus*** (fig) ***et*** (and) ***fecerunt*** (made) ***sibi*** (for themselves) ***perizomata*** (aprons)
And the eyes of them both were opened, and they knew that they were naked; and they sewed fig leaves together, and made themselves aprons.
And the eyes of them both were opened and they knew they were naked and they sewed together fig leaves and they made girdles for themselves.

Eating from the Tree of Knowledge means to become conscious-*of* everything, namely, of good-and-evil, of this-and-that, of night-and-day and to open the eyes on the reciprocal nudity. Nakedness, here has a double reference.

1) On one side, it refers to reality *in-itself*,
2) on the other, to reality *for-itself*.

The garment we wear is the image we present to others. We are conscious-*of* this cover that dresses-us-up before the world and becomes itself an object in and of objectivity. In turn, the object is *for-us-to-interpret*.[1005] However, we do not known the world as *it-is, without our interpretation of it*. To recognize the distinction between subjective and objective world, means to comprehend the state of nakedness (עירם *`eyrom*), the state of confusion (בוש *buwsh*)[1006] and the metaphoric shame generated by nakedness. Consequently, noetically we *dress-up*, *`alah,*[1007] as the other one noematically *clothes* with *objectivity*. In other words, *for us* to be able talk to you, you need to have physical ears. However, we never know what really goes through them and what reaches your *naked* mind, *viz. in-itself*. *Nakedness* becomes a metaphor for *in-itself*, which is *seen naked* because it cannot be *dressed* by the objectifying mind nor covered before the *sight* of knowledge. Therefore, *covering-up* the bare nakedness becomes an epistemic prerequisite. That is, we cannot see each other if we are not physically or conceptually *tangible*. Then, metaphorically, physicality becomes the covering-fig-leaves (עָלָה `alah - תְּאֵנָה *tě'en* - עָלֶה *`aleh*). In fact, the Hebrew word *`aleh, leaf*, derives from the verb *`alah, to increase, to go up like a garment.*

The leaf becomes a metaphor for the physical body, which dresses-up the human mind, covers-up the confusion deriving from the naked object in-itself. However, the leaf happens to be that of a fig tree. What is the meaning of that fig? In Hebrew*, tĕ'en* תְּאֵנָה,[1008] fig, is spelled with the same consonants (תאנה)[1009] as תַּאֲנָה t*a'anah,*[1010] meaning sexual drive, which derives from the verb *'anah,*[1011] to meet, to encounter. Furthermore, consider that knowledge,[1012] like in the homonymous tree, requires the subject to penetrate the object. Moreover, the word *da `ath* (דעת), meaning the knowledge referred to the tree (עץ *`ets*), derives from the verb *yada`* ,[1013] to know, which becomes an euphemism for carnal intercourse. In fact,

> *"Adam knew Eve his wife and she conceived."*[1014]

Consequently, the faculty of the physical drive of copulation, namely, this *fig tree*, encounters another body. Similarly, from an epistemological perspective, *sewed-together*[1015] is the *a-priori* synthesis of subject-object, which meets the object as otherness. Thus, derives the *blushful* confusion between internal and/or external reality, between the philosophical dualism of spiritualism and materialism.

> "Really, the fundamental, ultimate mystery - the only thing you need to know to understand the deepest metaphysical secrets - is this: that for every outside there is an inside and for every inside there is an outside, and although they are different, they go together. There is, in other words, a secret conspiracy between all insides and all outsides, and the conspiracy is to look as different as possible, and yet underneath to be identical. You do not find one without the other."[1016]

3:8-God's Voice

וַיִּשְׁמְעוּ אֶת־קוֹל יְהוָה אֱלֹהִים מִתְהַלֵּךְ בַּגָּן לְרוּחַ הַיּוֹם וַיִּתְחַבֵּא הָאָדָם וְאִשְׁתּוֹ מִפְּנֵי יְהוָה אֱלֹהִים בְּתוֹךְ עֵץ הַגָּן׃ *vayišama`u* (they heard) *'eṯ* (and) *qvōl* (thundering voice) *yahvāh* (Transcendent) *'ĕlōhiym* (of Divine-Consciousness) *miṯahalēḵa* (flowing) *bagān* (garden) *laruaḥ* (breath) *hayvōm* (of the day) *vayiṯaḥabē* (hide) *hā'āḏām* (man) *va'išatvō* (waman) *mipanēy* (from) *yahvāh* (Transcendent) *'ĕlōhiym* (of Divine-Consciousness) *baṯvōḵa* (in the midst) *'ēṣ* (of the trees) *hagān* (of the garden)
καὶ *kai* (and) **ἤκουσαν** *ēkousan* (they heard) **τὴν** *tēn* (the) **φωνὴν** *phōnēn* (voice) **κυρίου** *kuriou* (Lord) **τοῦ** *tou* (the) **θεοῦ** *theou* (God) **περιπατοῦντος** *peripatountos* (walking) **ἐν** *en* (in) **τῷ** *tō* (the) **παραδείσῳ** *paradeisō* (paradise) **τὸ** *to* (the) **δειλινόν** *deilinon* (breeze of the day) **καὶ** *kai* (and) **ἐκρύβησαν** *ekrubēsan* (hid) **ὅ** *o* (the) **τε** *te* (also) **Αδαμ** *Adam* (Adam) **καὶ** *kai* (and) **ἡ** *ē* (the) **γυνὴ** *gunē* (woman) **αὐτοῦ** *autou* (themselves) **ἀπὸ** *apo* (among) **προσώπου** *prosōpou* (face) **κυρίου** *kuriou* (of Lord) **τοῦ** *tou* (the) **θεοῦ** *theou* (God) **ἐν** *en* (in) **μέσῳ** *mesō* (middle) **τοῦ** *tou* (the) **ξύλου** *xulou* (trees) **τοῦ** *tou* (of the) **παραδείσου** *paradeisou* (paradise)
et (and) ***cum*** (as) ***audissent*** (they heard) ***vocem*** (the voice) ***Domini*** (of the Lord) ***Dei*** (God) ***deambulantis*** (waking) ***in*** (in) ***paradiso*** (paradise) ***ad*** (during) ***auram*** (breeze) ***post*** (past) ***meridiem*** (midday) ***abscondit*** (hid) ***se*** (themselves) ***Adam*** (Adam) ***et*** (and) ***uxor*** (wife) ***eius*** (his) ***a*** (from) ***facie*** (the face) ***Domini*** (of the Lord) ***Dei*** (God) ***in*** (in) ***medio*** (among) ***ligni*** (the trees) ***paradisi*** (of paradise)
And they heard the voice of the LORD God walking in the garden in the cool of the day: and Adam and his wife hid themselves from the presence of the LORD God amongst the trees of the garden.
Moreover, as they perceived the thundering voice of the Transcendent of Divine-Consciousness flowing in the bodily garden as the breath of the circular-day-of-consciousness, the man-subject and his wife-object hid themselves among the trees-sense-faculties of the bodily garden from the presence of the Transcendent of Divine-Consciousness.

Again, a literal rendering of this verse contradictorily and hilariously reduces Transcendence to a physically strolling personality in a wooded garden during a breezy eventide. If blasphemy were possible, this is the case. Nevertheless, let us continue with our epistemological perspective.

Once the intentional desire for representation, intrinsic in our process of knowledge, grips our attention, we forget the TRANSCENDENT building block, namely, we ignore the constant founding search and reference to IT as TRUTH and CERTITUDE in all our processes of knowledge. Nonetheless, let us continue with this verse and let us remember that the events described here are those inherent in the epistemic garden of this person reading this page right here and now. That voice, that walking are metaphoric for the constant presence of Awareness in this psychophysical bodily garden of delights.

The act of hearing implies an immediate intuition or a direct perception[1017] without reasoning, like in the case of our Auto-Transparency, as we have seen. In fact, when we hear a noise we may look for its real and/or apparent source, but we never question the hearing experience as such. Furthermore, this breeze or breath (רוּחַ *ruwach*) is the same Breath of Life that was hovering over the primordial waters of possibilities. It flows over the waters (הָלַךְ *halak*)[1018] of the circular day (יוֹם *yowm*) of consciousness. However, the a-priori synthesis of male-subject and female-object turns the focus away from[1019] that Transcendent-thundering *sound of waters,*[1020] like

"*the noise of great waters, as the voice of the Almighty.*"[1021]

Adam and Eve *hide*[1022] from Its presence.[1023] They conceal among the faculties of the senses, *viz.* the trees, the faculties of the senses, which objectify the world, present here and now in this psychophysical *enclosed* and *covered* (*ganan*)[1024] *garden* (*gan*) [1025] that we call our body. The Sufi mystic Rumi describes it as "*The Guest House.*"

"*This being human is a guest house./ Every morning a new arrival./ A joy, a depression, a meanness,/ some momentary awareness comes/ as an unexpected visitor. / Welcome and entertain them all!/ Even if they're a crowd of sorrows,/ who violently sweep your house/ empty of its furniture,/ still treat each guest honorably./ He may be clearing you out/ for some new delight./ The dark thought, the shame, the malice,/ meet them at the door laughing,/ and invite them in./ Be grateful for whoever comes,/ because each has been sent/ as a guide from beyond.*"[1026]

In addition, the metaphor of the thundering voice of the Transcendent needs an explanation. <'*Does an un-witnessed falling tree make a sound*?' The answer to this riddle is '*Yes*!' In fact, the thought of the falling tree comes with the thought of the ensuing sound. However, we can fantasize a soundless falling tree, in which case the fantastic tree comes with no sound and it would still be a thought aware of itself as fantasy. We cannot totally imagine a universe without a knower, because we would still be the thinker of that imaginary world. As remote as that world may be, it is still as close as our mind is to our self, where we think that riddle. The mind cannot jump out of itself to check the nature of the world without the mind. The next question is similar to the first, but different in nature. '*What is the sound of a mountain*?' Sound confers sense to 'what-is-known.' It brings the object to 'life' in the mind, establishing it into existence. A conveying sound can be the vibrating flight of bees, the honking of geese, the singing of whales, the trumpeting of elephants,[1027] the *screaming* of apes, and overall it is the alerting articulation of animals in general.

Music, the most abstract of arts, is a discourse of numerical entities and mathematical functions expressed in sounds conveying a world of meanings. The *Māṇḍūkya Upanishad* states,

"*Regarding the metrical measures, this Self* [Is], *above all syllables, the sacred and mystical syllable AUM. Thus, the quadrants* [are] *the metrical letters A, U, M and the metrical letters* [are] *the quadrants.*"[1028]

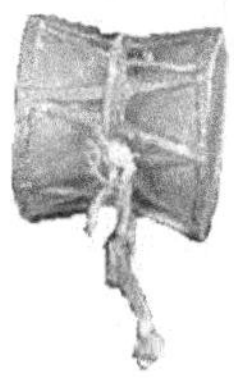

The metrical measures (*dhi-mātra*) of AUM (Om, ॐ) are rhythmic tempo-time measures regulating the beats, like heartbeats, as the 'surprising' foot-tapping sound of the *ḍāmara* or *damaru*, a double-sided small drum used by Śiva and his devotees.[1029]

Again, we refine our original question, '*How does the Universe* <u>*resonate*</u> *in us*?' The first sound-words of 'Elohiym are

"*Yehiy 'owr* (let there be light), *and there was light.*"[1030]

The *Pyramid Texts* conceive the Word as

"the primeval speech which came from God wherein all things got their names."[1031]

"*After that, Adam gave names to all.*"[1032]

Adonis, alias Ali Ahmad Said Esber, Nobel Prize poet candidate said,

"Poetry... offers... knowledge which is explosive and surprising... requires the reader to become, like the poet, a creator."[1033]

The syllable "Om" expresses the resonant[1034] aspect of everything. AUM is the affirmation "yes," a solemn one, like Amen.

"*These things saith the Amen, the faithful and true witness, the beginning of the creation of God.*"[1035]

OM, in its real, undivided aspect, is the Self in-Itself,

"*the pure witness, the aware measure* (*mātra*) *of knowledge* (*cit*),"[1036]

the Amen, the Ātman, the Supreme Self without a second (*advaita*). Om (AUM·ॐ)

"is usually called *praṇava*, more rarely *akshara*, or *ekākshara*, and only in later times *oṃkāra.*"[1037]

Usually, the syllable is an auspicious salutation uttered at the beginning and ending of sacred activities. In the syllable OM, the letter O stands for the diphthong AU,[1038] thus the full rendering as AUM. OM is a *mántra*, an

"instrument of thought, speech... [It is] a prayer or song of praise a Vedic hymn or sacrificial ... magical formula ... incantation, charm, spell"[1039]

evoking, in a single sound, the realization of the entire world. That is to say, the states of wakeful consciousness, of dream *sub*-consciousness, deep sleep unconsciousness and Transcendence, compose a sound (φωνή *phōnē*) that comes together (σῦν *syn*) as Universal Symphony.>[1040] This is like

"*the voice of the trumpet* (*yowbel*, ram's horn trumpet) *exceeding loud... And when the voice of the trumpet sounded long, and waxed louder and louder, Moses spake, and God answered him by a voice,*"[1041]

"*a great* voice, *as of a trumpet.*"[1042]

3:9-Where is Adam, the Subject?

וַיִּקְרָא יְהוָה אֱלֹהִים אֶל־הָאָדָם וַיֹּאמֶר לוֹ אַיֶּכָּה׃
vayiqarā' (called) *yahvāh* (Transcendent) *'ĕlōhiym* (Divine-Consciousness) *'el* (and) *hā'āḏām* (to Adam) *vayō'mer* (said) *lvō* (for him) *'ayekāh* (where)
καὶ *kai* (and) **ἐκάλεσεν** *ekalesen* (called) **κύριος** *kurios* (Lord) **ὁ** *o* (the) **θεὸς** *theos* (God) **τὸν** *ton* (the) **Αδαμ** *Adam* (Adam) **καὶ** *kai* (and) **εἶπεν** *eipen* (said) **αὐτῷ** *ō* (to him) **Αδαμ** *Adam* (Adam) **ποῦ** *pou* (where) **εἶ** *ei* (are you)
vocavit- (called) ***que*** (and) ***Dominus*** (the Lord) ***Deus*** (God) ***Adam*** (Adam) ***et*** (and) ***dixit*** (said) ***ei*** (to him) ***ubi*** (where) ***es*** (are you)
And the LORD God called unto Adam, and said unto him, Where art thou?
And the Transcendent of Divine-Consciousness called Adam and said to him, "*Where are you?*"

Upon reading literally this verse, the first question is, '*why God calls out only for Adam and not for Eve*?' Furthermore, it is as if the mind would enquire where its hand is. We do not need to know where the hand is when we pick-up something.

With this rhetorical question, Transcendence invites the mind, *Adam-subject/object-Eve, to reflect* on the true source of its knowledge. That origin is beyond the continuous transcending of the subjective consciousness-*of* the objective world. The center does not ask where the circumference is, when it radiates it. In other words, it is as if the center of a circle would ask a point on the circumference about its whereabouts. That point, if not distracted by the objective-position before itself, would have to realize that it is the end of the radius stemming from the center.

However, also if we read this as a rhetorical question, as, '*Where is the one reflecting in this mirror*?' Then we would realize that we, the Adam, the subject, can never catch our own I as subject. Namely, in I-consciousness or in ego-consciousness, we know ourselves as known object never as the knower subject. The eye mirroring itself sees a reflected-image object, noematically offering itself to be seen, never as the noetic reflecting-one, looking to see itself. In other words, the subject *in-itself*, as image of the Transcendent, is always unknown, ineffable and alone. Otherwise stated, the subject *for-itself* inevitably hides, covers and dresses its true-identity losing its reality *in-itself*.

3:10-Fear of Epistemic Loneliness

וַיֹּאמֶר אֶת־קֹלְךָ שָׁמַעְתִּי בַּגָּן וָאִירָא כִּי־עֵירֹם אָנֹכִי וָאֵחָבֵא׃   *vayō'mer* (said) *'et* (and) *qōlakā* (voice) *šāma'atiy* (heard) *bagān* (in the garden) *vā'iyrā'* (I was afraid) *kiy* (because) *'ēyrōm* (was naked) *'ānōkiy* (I) *vā'ēḥābē'* (hid)
καὶ *kai* (and) **εἶπεν** *eipen* (said) **αὐτῷ** *autō* (he) **τὴν** *tēn* (the) **φωνήν** *phōnēn* (voice) **σου** *sou* (your) **ἤκουσα** *ēkousa* (I heard) **περιπατοῦντος** *peripatountos* (walking) **ἐν** *en* (in) **τῷ** *tō* (the) **παραδείσῳ** *paradeisō* (paradise) **καὶ** *kai* (and) **ἐφοβήθην** *ephobēthēn* (I was afraid) **ὅτι** *oti* (because) **γυμνός** *gumnos* (naked) **εἰμι** *eimi* (I am) **καὶ** *kai* (and) **ἐκρύβην** *ekrubēn* (I hid)
qui (he) ***ait*** (said) ***vocem*** (voice) ***tuam*** (your) ***audivi*** (I heard) ***in*** (in) ***paradiso*** (paradise) ***et*** (and) ***timui*** (I feared) ***eo*** (it) ***quod*** (because) ***nudus*** (naked) ***essem*** (I was) ***et*** (and) ***abscondi*** (I hid) ***me*** (myself)
And he said, I heard thy voice in the garden, and I was afraid, because I was naked; and I hid myself.
He said,   "*I heard your voice in the garden of happiness and I was afraid because I was naked, therefore I hid myself.*"

As we said, nakedness, in this context, does not refer to the body. No one is afraid for being physically naked. Perhaps, one may be ashamed, but infants do not feel shame. That feeling is learned through culture. In fact, ancient and primitive cultures were not ashamed of nudity and nudist colonies do not feel fear or shame.[1043] Furthermore, besides shamefulness, nakedness may be also cause and object of attraction and desire. Nakedness refers always to the physical appearance of oneself or of the other as objects. Thus, in this verse, nakedness and its fear derive from the distinction and the dichotomy between the interiority of the world in-itself and its exteriority for-itself. Namely, we know only how the world is *for-us* never as it is *in-itself*. This refers also to the *I*-subject, which cannot conceive itself as a pure knower without any objectivity. Thus, this state *in-itself* renders the subject vulnerable, naked before its own loneliness. '*Hold my hand!*' A child cries out to the mother during a nightmare. '*Where are you?*' The lover asks the loved one, while they are in loving union. This is the great fear of being alone in the vast emptiness before creation. Similarly, the *Bṛhadāraṇyaka Upanishad* declares that,

> "*Who is alone is afraid... He desired a second and extended itself as a woman-wife as the object, and a man-husband, the subject, in a loving embrace. It divided Itself in two parts... thus let me hide myself.*"[1044]

Subsequently, the thought that we could be alone and lose the experienced *tasty* forbidden fruit becomes the fear of death. Therefore, Adam has become a

> "beast without peace."[1045]

No one can see its own '*I*' in its own mirror image. In fact, that same *Upanishad* declares,

> "*You cannot see the seer of seeing, hear the hearer of hearing, think the thinker of thinking, nor understand the understander of understanding. This is that Self which is in everything.*"[1046]

The *Babylonian Talmûd Berâkôt* states,

> "*As the Holy One, blessed be He, fills the whole world, so also the soul fills the body. As the Holy One, blessed be He, sees but cannot be seen, so also the soul sees but cannot be seen. As the Holy One, blessed be He, nourishes the whole world, so also the soul nourishes the whole body. As the Holy One, blessed be He, is pure, so also the soul is pure. As the Holy One, blessed be He, dwells in the inmost part* [of the Universe], *so also the soul dwells in the inmost parts* [of the body]."[1047]

> "If you can see only what light reveals and hear only what sound announces, then in truth you do not see nor do you hear."[1048]

<In other words, the 'I' is continuously reducing the world for-itself, never being able to know itself in-itself. Also at the time of I-consciousness, when the I-subject knows itself, it comprehends itself as *me*-object of thought, missing itself as I-subject, thus reducing to an object its own subjectivity, which remains unrelated and, as Narcissus in love with himself, drowns in his own watery reflected image.[1049] We can say... that

> 'consciousness is a being such that in its being, its being is in question in so far as this being implies a being other than itself.'[1050]

The 'I' is the subject of the process of knowledge, which implies its indivisible correlation with its object, without which it would not be a subject. The distinction of subject and object is only logical, never de-facto. Whenever we try to know the subject in-itself, beyond the correlation with its object, as in the state of death, we are confronted with the Unknown.>[1051]

> "The conscious mind knows nothing beyond the opposites and, as a result, has no knowledge of the thing that unites them."[1052]

And God said to Moses,

> "*By my name Yehovah* (יהוה) *I was not known... Thou canst not see my face: for there shall no man see me, and live... thou shalt see my back parts: but my face shall not be seen,*"[1053]

because we cannot see that which is In-Itself and we see only that which is for-itself, namely, the *back parts* or that which is understood as already past.

Therefore, the subject's nakedness[1054] is also the fear[1055] of the loneliness of itself when plunging in-itself, which leads the subject to hide from the terrifying presence of loneliness. Likewise,

> "*Moses hid his face; for he was afraid to look upon the Transcendent.*"[1056]

Therefore, the subject covers itself and searches for a companion with whom to think and know the entire objective world.

3:11-Did You Eat from That Tree?

וַיֹּאמֶר מִי הִגִּיד לְךָ כִּי עֵירֹם אָתָּה הֲמִן־הָעֵץ אֲשֶׁר צִוִּיתִיךָ לְבִלְתִּי אֲכָל־מִמֶּנּוּ אָכָלְתָּ׃ *vayō'mer* (He said) *miy* (who) *higiyḏ* (told) *laḵā* (to) *kiy* (that) *'ēyrōm* (you naked) *'ātāh* (you) *hămin* (from) *hā'ēṣ* (tree) *'ăšer* (which) *ṣiuiyṯiyḵā* (I commanded) *laḇilatiy* (not) *'ăḵāl* (to eat) *mimenu* (from) *'āḵālatā* (you ate)
καὶ *kai* (and) **εἶπεν** *eipen* (he said) **αὐτῷ** *autō* (you) **τίς** *tis* (who) **ἀνήγγειλέν** *anēggeilen* (told) **σοι** *soi* (you) **ὅτι** *oti* (that) **γυμνὸς** *gumnos* (naked) **εἶ** *ei* (were) **μὴ** *mō* (not) **ἀπὸ** *apo* (from) **τοῦ** *tou* (the) **ξύλου** *xulou* (tree) **οὗ** *ou* (that) **ἐνετειλάμην** *eneteilamēn* (I told) **σοι** *soi* (you) **τούτου** *tautou* (in this way) **μόνου** *monou* (alone) **μὴ** *mē* (not) **φαγεῖν** *phagein* (eat) **ἀπ'** *ap'* (from) **αὐτοῦ** *autou* (that) **ἔφαγες** *ephages* (shall eat)
cui (he) ***dixit*** (said) ***quis*** (who) ***enim*** (in fact) ***indicavit*** (told) ***tibi*** (you) ***quod*** (that) ***nudus*** (naked) ***esses*** (you were) ***nisi*** (if not) ***quod*** (that) ***ex*** (out of) ***ligno*** (tree) ***de*** (of) ***quo*** (which) ***tibi*** (you) ***praeceperam*** (I commanded) ***ne*** (not to) ***comederes*** (eat) ***comedisti*** (you have eaten)
And he said, Who told thee that thou wast naked? Hast thou eaten of the tree, whereof I commanded thee that thou shouldest not eat?
He said, "*Who told you that you were naked? Did you eat from the tree, from which I appointed that you should not eat?*"

If we follow the usual interpretation of God's commandment, we have two contradicting possibilities undermining Divine Justice.

1) The moral code is good because God so commands. Then, the law without God's decree could have been different. In this case, that abstinence law is purely arbitrary. It has no intrinsic valid reason. In fact, what is the reason behind singling out one tree among the others? By not creating that plant, in the first place, there would not have been disobedience.
2) The moral rule is good because it is so in-itself. Then, that independent and absolute moral rule compels God's free will. In that case, God would be obliged to follow it. Furthermore, this would

diminish and contradict the assumption of God's absoluteness, making the law superior to God Himself. Then, in fact, the creation of the Tree of Knowledge of Good and Evil, together with the abstinence order, becomes necessary beyond God's free will. He, Himself would be obliged to obey and not eat from that tree.

As we mentioned, more than a commandment, the abstinence from the forbidden fruit is a warning. In fact, God had not appointed, constituted[1057] or meant for the human to eat from it. That is because the Tree of Knowledge is the last descending moment in the process of creation. It is the moment of physical objectivity oblivious of its origin. It is the *end* of the Creative Exhaling Breath, *before* the Resting-Breath (שׁבת *shabath*). To eat, to think or to identify with that moment, forgetful of the Origin and not Resting in Its Life, means to be stuck in that which is dead, not vivified. It means to suffer the consequences deriving from the loss of one's own True-Self, namely the identification with our Apodictic-Awareness.

"There is nothing either good or bad, but thinking makes it so."[1058]

In fact, <un-attracted by that *seductive*, *painful* and *mortal food*, completely absorbed in the Blissful state of undisturbed, undistracted Apodictic-Certitude, one should *look* at the world with the Universal *eyes* of Self-Awareness. There is nothing that one must do to be ethical. *Ius Suprēmum*, the Supreme Law, is beyond good as well as it is devoid of any evil. The Supreme Ethical detachment does not infer a permit to follow licentious conduct, nor it does suggest promoting dissolute comportment.

"*No man can serve two masters: for either he will hate the one, and love the other; or else he will hold to the one, and despise the other. You cannot serve the Transcendent-God and mammon...*[1059] *of unrighteousness.*"[1060]

Finally, *Ius Suprēmum* does not advocate following *Mammon,*[1061] the *ways of the world. Mammon* is wealth-personified as opposed to the Transcendent Self-Awareness. Consequently,

"*That which is highly desired among men is abomination in the sight of Transcendence.*"[1062]

"*A rich man shall hardly enter into the Kingdom of Heaven.*"[1063]

Therefore, *Ius Suprēmum* appears to the merchant's eyes as pure *madness*. It is the way of one who has shaken off all worldly attachments. It is the holy *manner* of the saint. It is the blessed *way* of the hermit of any denomination. That bright path is Awareness, rightly indicated as *light*. Therefore,

"*walk while you have the light, lest darkness come upon you: for he that walketh in darkness knoweth not whither he goeth.*"[1064]

On that simple path, walk

"*the children of light,*"[1065] and the

"*child shalt be called the prophet of the Highest.*"[1066]

In fact, if one does

"*not receive the kingdom of the Transcendent Self-Awareness as a little child, shall in no wise enter therein.*"[1067]

Happiness is not performing good deeds. Happiness is not satisfying all desires. Happiness is not pursuing criminal activities. Happiness is not performing evil deeds to achieve personal aims. Even when having supernatural and/or paranormal abilities, as performing astonishing great miracles like resurrecting the dead,

"*there is no perfect happiness.*"[1068]

Happiness is abiding in the Pure Certitude of Awareness. The constant-present intuitive-gnostic-realization of Self-Awareness,>[1069] this is the only state to aim for. In that state, there is no dichotomy of *naked-in-itself* or *dressed-up-for-itself*. However, when, gripped by desire for the world of representations, *viz.* the metaphoric forbidden *evil-apple*, then, we eat it. We identify with its conceptualization. Then we take our mind away from the single (ἁπλοῦς *haplous*) Certain-Awareness and this world of duality appears.

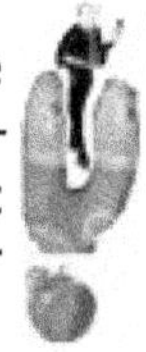

"*The light of the body is the eye: therefore when thine eye is single* (ἁπλοῦς *haplous*), *thy whole body also is full of light; but when thine eye is full of harassment-by-evil-labor-blindness* (πονηρός *ponēros*), *thy body is covered with darkness* (σκοτεινός *skoteinos*)."[1070]

In other words, the mind attempts to reproduce conceptually the whole process of creation freezing it in an impossible object disguised as transcendence.

"*For, brethren, you have been called unto liberty; only* [use] *not liberty for an occasion to the flesh, but by love serve one another.*"[1071]

3:12-Now We Are All Eaters from that Same Tree

וַיֹּאמֶר הָאָדָם הָאִשָּׁה אֲשֶׁר נָתַתָּה עִמָּדִי הִוא נָתְנָה־לִּי מִן־הָעֵץ וָאֹכֵל׃   *vayōʹmer* (said) *hāʹāḏām* (man) *hāʹišāh* (woman) *ʹăšer* (which) *nāṯatāh* (you gave) *ʿimāḏiy* (with me) *hiv̓* (she) *nāṯanāh* (gave) *liy* (and) *min* (from) *hāʿēṣ* (tree) *vāʹōḵēl* (I eat)
καὶ *kai* (and) **εἶπεν** *eipen* (said) **ὁ** *o* (the) **Αδαμ** *Adam* (Adam) **ἡ** *ē* (the) **γυνή** *gunē* (woman) **ἣν** *ēn* (that) **ἔδωκας** *edōkas* (you gave) **μετ᾽** *met* (among) **ἐμοῦ** *emou* (me) **αὕτη** *autē* (this way) **μοι** *moi* (me) **ἔδωκεν** *edōken* (gave) **ἀπὸ** *apo* (from) **τοῦ** *tou* (the) **ξύλου** *xulou* (tree) **καὶ** *kai* (and) **ἔφαγον** *ephagon* (I eat)
dixit-(said) ***que*** (and) ***Adam*** (Adam) ***mulier*** (the wife) ***quam*** (that) ***dedisti*** (you gave) ***sociam*** (companion) ***mihi*** (to me) ***dedit*** (gave) ***mihi*** (me) ***de*** (from) ***ligno*** (the tree) ***et*** (and) ***comedi*** (I ate)
And the man said, The woman whom thou gavest to be with me, she gave me of the tree, and I did eat.
Subsequently, the man-subject replied,   "*The woman-object that you gave me to be bound to, gave me from the tree and I ate.*"

This is not the prehistoric event of our elusive primordial ancestors. It has nothing to do with the literary understanding of creation, with prehistory or with the evolutionary diatribe. It is our epistemic a-temporal paradigmatic structure imprinted in all of us as the metaphoric image of Divine-Consciousness. This is our thinking modality as it takes place here and now in every being. It is the epistemic bind, the *a-priori* synthesis[1072] of male-subject and female-object. In fact, **it is the noematic object that offers**[1073] **itself to be known or *eaten* by the subject.**

A very young person once stated,

'I cannot be responsible for a sin committed by our progenitor.'

We replied,

'You are right. However, you keep eating the forbidden fruit. In every waking and dreaming moment of your life, you keep identifying with your objective world of duality, missing its true source.'

What we understand as evolution is the universal strength of consciousness blindly enforcing and defending each of its own infinite random possibilities. They become unique biological species and/or particular individualities. However, the individual, as such, is not immediately conscious-*of* evolution as the actual driving force. This is because the personal factuality conceals it and does not immediately perceive its own present evolution. Namely, we do not perceive instantly the evolutionary flowing process because we cover it with our established individual present-past appearing as unevolved invariability.

Jacob, one of our students, asked,

'If everything is possible, is it possible for something to be impossible?'

We replied,

'Yes, it is. In fact, a possibility becomes an actuality only when registered as a factual experience. Then, all the other contrary possibilities become impossible. Each possibility is the impossibility of the other ones. In fact, when, in a parallel universe, those impossibilities become possible, then, they make that first fact impossible as a fact. A

phenomenon is such only when the observer registers it as a phenomenon. Then, however, and only then, its contrary is impossible, just to become possible again in another unrelated parallel dimension.'

Desire lures the subject/object to identify with experience, thus s/he discovers objectivity and nudity.

3-II SECTION: THE PUNISHMENT

3:13-The Serpent's Charm

וַיֹּאמֶר יְהוָה אֱלֹהִים לָאִשָּׁה מַה־זֹּאת עָשִׂית וַתֹּאמֶר הָאִשָּׁה הַנָּחָשׁ הִשִּׁיאַנִי וָאֹכֵל׃ *vayō'mer* (said) *yahvāh* (Transcendent) *'ělōhiym* (Divine-Consciousness) *lā'išāh* (woman) *mah* (what) *zō't* (this) *'āśiyt* (you have done) *vatō'mer* (said) *hā'išāh* (the woman) *hanāḥāš* (the serpent) *hišiy'aniy* (deceived) *vā'ōkēl* (I ate)
καὶ *kai* (and) **εἶπεν** *eipen* (said) **κύριος** *kurios* (Lord) **ὁ** *o* (the) **θεὸς** *theos* (God) **τῇ** *tē* (to the) **γυναικί** *gunaiki* (woman) **τί** *ti* (what) **τοῦτο** *touto* (in this way) **ἐποίησας** *epoiēsas* (you have done) **καὶ** *kai* (and) **εἶπεν** *eipen* (said) **ἡ** *ē* (the) **γυνή** *gunē* (woman) **ὁ** *o* (the) **ὄφις** *ophis* (snake) **ἠπάτησέν** *ēpatēsen* (tricked) **με** *me* (me) **καὶ** *kai* (and) **ἔφαγον** *ephagon* (I ate)
et (and) ***dixit*** (said) ***Dominus*** (Lord) ***Deus*** (God) ***ad*** (to) ***mulierem*** (the woman) ***quare*** (what) ***hoc*** (this) ***fecisti*** (you have done) ***quae*** (she) ***respondit*** (answered) ***serpens*** (the serpent) ***decepit*** (deceived) ***me*** (me) ***et*** (and) ***comedi*** (I ate)
And the LORD God said unto the woman, What is this that thou hast done? And the woman said, The serpent beguiled me, and I did eat.
Therefore, the Transcendent of Divine-Consciousness said to the woman, "*What is this that you have done?*" And the woman answered, "*The serpent deceived me and I ate.*"

Upon falling asleep, the mind has the need or the desire to find a ground on which to stand away from the fear of lonely nakedness. Thus, we dream. Similarly, upon awakening, the mind has the need or desire to find a ground on which to act and meaningfully carry out our search for happiness. Thus, we go about our daily business. During both, dream and wakefulness, in order to convey a reality in-itself to those experiences, we conceptualize and objectify the Transcendent Awareness that sustains both those states. We want to fulfill our future aspirations with the same Certainty that we have now as we reach for the cup of coffee before us.

What we are really seeking for in life is Certainty, which confirms our experience. However, we tend to give that certitude a physical appearance. As image of Divine-Consciousness, to use a Biblical terminology, we *forget* *(nash)*[1074] the Transcendent Source of our images. Then, mesmerized by the reflected worldly objects, we worship the objects like gods themselves. It is like giving concrete body to our dreams. While we project them in our mind, dreams *deceive* and *lead us astray* *(nasha)*.[1075] That projection is the intentional *snaky* desire. It reduces the world of experiences to food *for-us*. It stimulates our continuous hunger for still more experiential-food in search for the *physicality* of certainty. Thus, we eat, we ingest in our mind and we know the world as such. Then, we are deceived into believing the savored experience to be the same Certainty we are looking for.

3:14-The Cursed Serpent

וַיֹּאמֶר יְהוָה אֱלֹהִים אֶל־הַנָּחָשׁ כִּי עָשִׂיתָ זֹּאת אָרוּר אַתָּה מִכָּל־הַבְּהֵמָה וּמִכֹּל חַיַּת הַשָּׂדֶה עַל־גְּחֹנְךָ תֵלֵךְ וְעָפָר תֹּאכַל כָּל־יְמֵי חַיֶּיךָ׃ *vayō'mer* (said) *yahoāh* (Transcendent) *'ělōhiym* (Divine-Consciousness) *'el* (to) *hanāḥāš* (serpent) *kiy* (because) *'āśiytā* (you have done) *zō't* (this) *'ārur* (you are despised) *'atāh* (because) *mikāl* (among) *habahēmāh* (cattle) *umikōl* (out of) *ḥayat* (animals) *haśāḏeh* (of the earth) *'al* (upon) *gaḥōnakā* (belly) *tēlēka* (you shall walk) *va'āpār* (ashes) *tō'kal* (you shall eat) *kāl* (all) *yamēy* (days) *ḥayeykā* (of life)
καὶ *kai* (and) **εἶπεν** *eipen* (said) **κύριος** *kurios* (Lord) **ὁ** *o* (the) **θεὸς** *theos* (God) **τῷ** *tō* (to) **ὄφει** *ophei* (serpent) **ὅτι** *oti* (because) **ἐποίησας** *epoiēsas* (have you done) **τοῦτο** *touto* (in this way) **ἐπικατάρατος** *epikataratos* (are cursed) **σὺ** *su* (you) **ἀπὸ** *apo* (among) **πάντων** *pantōn* (all) **τῶν** *tōn* (the) **κτηνῶν** *ktēnōn* (cattle) **καὶ** *kai* (and) **ἀπὸ** *apo* (among) **πάντων** *pantōn* (all) **τῶν** *tōn* (the) **θηρίων** *thēriōn* (beasts) **τῆς** *tēs* (the) **γῆς** *gēs* (earth) **ἐπὶ** *epi* (over) **τῷ** *tō* (the) **στήθει** *stēthei* (breast) **σου** *sou* (your) **καὶ** *kai* (and) **τῇ** *tē* (the) **κοιλίᾳ** *koilia* (belly) **πορεύσῃ** *poreusē*

(you shall go) **καὶ** *kai* (and) **γῆν** *gēv* (dust) **φάγῃ** *phagē* (you shall eat) **πάσας** *pasas* (all) **τὰς** *tas* (the) **ἡμέρας** *ēmeras* (days) **τῆς** *tēs* (of the) **ζωῆς** *zōēs* (life) **σου** (yours)
et (and) ***ait*** (said) ***Dominus*** (the Lord) ***Deus*** (God) ***ad*** (to) ***serpentem*** (the serpent) ***quia*** (because) ***fecisti*** (you have you done) ***hoc*** (this) ***maledictus*** (cursed) ***es*** (you are) ***inter*** (among) ***omnia*** (all) ***animantia*** (the animals) ***et*** (and) ***bestias*** (beasts) ***terrae*** (of the earth) ***super*** (on) ***pectus*** (chest) ***tuum*** (yours) ***gradieris*** (you will walk) ***et*** (and) ***terram*** (dirt) ***comedes*** (you shall eat) ***cunctis*** (all) ***diebus*** (days) ***vitae*** (of life) ***tuae*** (yours)
And the LORD God said unto the serpent, Because thou hast done this, thou art cursed above all cattle, and above every beast of the field; upon thy belly shalt thou go, and dust shalt thou eat all the days of thy life:
And the Transcendent of Divine-Consciousness said to the serpent, "*Because you have done this, you are to be despised among all the sentient beings of the earth; you shall wind on your belly and you shall eat the ashes of the grave all the days of your life.*

The usual simplistic empiric reading of this verse interprets the serpent as one of the snakes we may encounter in the wild. Such a reading, then, portrays the unconceivable incongruence of a maker who, after having created such an animal, condemns it for its deeds. However, animals, when they follow their natural instinct, cannot be guilty of any crime.

Nachash,[1076] the Hebrew name for serpent, derives from the verb *nachash*[1077] meaning *to practice divination.* Since, the animals in these verses, as we saw, are metaphors for the active, living senses (חִי *chay*) craving for experience, the serpent must be again a metaphor itself. The snake is the curving intentional desire for divination. Namely, it is the desire to manifest or foretell something that appears to be unknown. It is exactly the desire to physicalize transcendence and experience it empirically. This desire *habeas corpus*, namely, has a physical body when the Universe, as we know it, pops into existence appearing before our dreaming and/or our waking experience.

Once more, the example of the looking glass comes appropriate. A mirror image frustrates the desire to look directly at the True Self. The likeness on the reflecting surface is like Luci*fer*, the light(*lux*)-*bearer*(*fero*). In Hebrew, הֵילֵל *heylel*[1078] has that same meaning of the shining one, the morning star, Lucifer. That reflected light makes it impossible to see the real person in-itself, namely the looking one behind its own reflection. This illusory reflection is the product of the *snaky* desire for objectivity. Another example is the light of the moon as detected by the eye. At that point, the deceived mind believes that the satellite generates its own brightness. However, that light is only the reflection of the real sunshine, which,

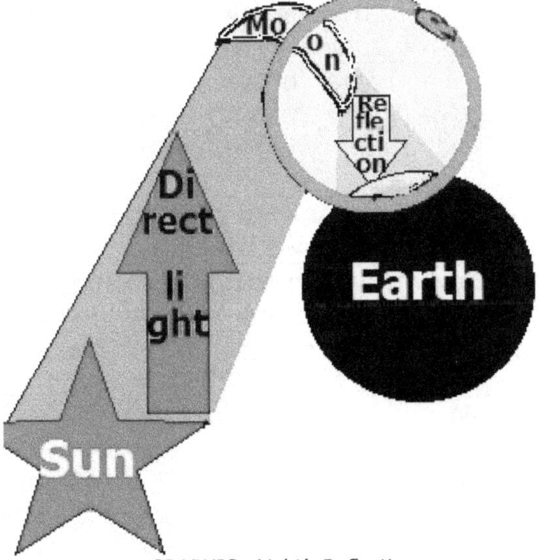

GRAPHIC: *Light's Reflection*

at that moment, is not visible. The serpent is the illusion generated by the mind-moon circle of consciousness, which misses the direct fulguration of the sun.

We could say that the entire creative process produces this deceiving effect. When its reflected objectivity distracts us, the object becomes *food for thought*. We eat and identify with it, forgetting its True Creative Origin. When, on the other hand, un-attracted by that *seductive*, *painful* and *mortal food*, completely absorbed in the Blissful state of undisturbed, undistracted Apodictic-Certitude, one *looks* at the world with the Universal *eyes* of Self-Awareness, one enters in the state of Silent Ecstatic Rest, *viz.* the *shabath*.[1079] The serpent, takes all this away. In fact, because of its own intentional nature, the serpent is condemned to persist, during all its circular days of consciousness (יום *yowm*), winding on its belly,[1080] which means to bring forth[1081] the objective fruit of deceiving thoughts. Therefore, among all the other animal-senses, this snake shall be despised.[1082] Furthermore, by this action, its only food becomes, inevitably, the ashes of the grave (עפר `*aphar*).[1083] This means that, while the past captivates our mind with its deceased history, the future calls us demanding to reduce [1084]⇨ it to a past event. In fact, when time seems to be too slow to pass, it is because we are eager to know the desired future moment as experienced and already having taken place. Thus, we want the future reduced to a past event. Either way we lose the Life of the Apodictical-Present and we eat, namely we know, only the dead ashes of the past grave.

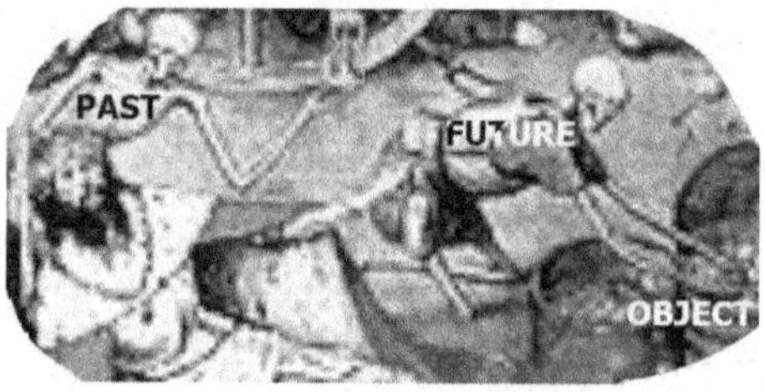

3:15-The Adversary

וְאֵיבָה אָשִׁית בֵּינְךָ וּבֵין הָאִשָּׁה וּבֵין זַרְעֲךָ וּבֵין זַרְעָהּ הוּא יְשׁוּפְךָ רֹאשׁ וְאַתָּה תְּשׁוּפֶנּוּ עָקֵב׃ ס *va'ēyḇāh* (adversity) *'āšiyṯ* (I will put) *bēynaḵā* (between) *uḇēyn* (between) *hā'iššāh* (the woman) *uḇēyn* (between) *zara'ăḵā* (offspring) *uḇēyn* (between) *zara'āh* (offspring) *hu'* (come to pass) *yašupaḵā* (you will lie in wait for) *rō'š* (head) *va'atāh* (to come) *tašupēnu* (you will lie in wait for) *'āqēḇ* (the continuous rear) *s* (.)
καὶ *kai* (and) **ἔχθραν** *exthran* (enmity) **θήσω** *thēsō* (I will put) **ἀνὰ** *ana* (therefore) **μέσον** *meson* (between) **σου** *sou* (you) **καὶ** *kai* (and) **ἀνὰ** *ana* (then) **μέσον** *meson* (between) **τῆς** *tēs* (the) **γυναικὸς** *gunaikos* (woman) **καὶ** *kai* (and) **ἀνὰ** *ana* (then) **μέσον** *meson* (between) **τοῦ** *tou* (the) **σπέρματός** *spermatos* (seed) **σου** *sou* (your) **καὶ** *kai* (and) **ἀνὰ** *ana* (then) **μέσον** *meson* (between) **τοῦ** *tou* (the) **σπέρματος** *spermatos* (seed) **αὐτῆς** *autēs* (her) **αὐτός** *autos* (she) **σου** *sou* (your) **τηρήσει** *tērēsei* (will ambush) **κεφαλήν** *kephalēn* (head) **καὶ** *kai* (and) **σὺ** *su* (you) **τηρήσεις** *tērēseis* (will ambush) **αὐτοῦ** *autou* (his) **πτέρναν** *pternan* (heel)
inimicitias (enmity) ***ponam*** (I will put) ***inter*** (between) ***te*** (you) ***et*** (and) ***mulierem*** (the woman) ***et*** (and) ***semen*** (the seed) ***tuum*** (yours) ***et*** (and) ***semen*** (the seed) ***illius*** (her) ***ipsa*** (self) ***conteret*** (will crush) ***caput*** (head) ***tuum*** (your) ***et*** (and) ***tu*** (you) ***insidiaberis*** (will ambush) ***calcaneo*** (heel) ***ejus*** (his)
And I will put enmity between thee and the woman, and between thy seed and her seed; it shall bruise thy head, and thou shalt bruise his heel.
I will put adversity between you and the woman and between your offspring and her offspring. She will lie in wait for your head and you will continuously lie in wait for its extremities."

Common understanding has it that the serpent is the evil-one and the woman's offspring (זרע *zera`*) is the historical figure of the Savioror or the Messiah.[1085] Therefore, *The Exsultet*, the Catholic liturgical Easter Vigil Mass, calls the original sin

"*Felix culpa*, *blissful blame that earned for us so great, so glorious a Redeemer.*"[1086]

"*For God judged it better to bring good out of evil than not to permit any evil to exist.*"[1087]

The expression '*the woman's seed* (זרע *zera`*)' and '*the serpent's offspring* (זרע *zera`*)' do not refer to a single person, but to the entire humanity, as *sons of light*, those of the woman, and *of darkness*, those of the serpent.[1088] Furthermore, if an individual personified serpent, as such, were created, its real origin would still be divine. In fact, the concept of creation implies necessarily that the Creative Breath must be within the creature at all times to sustain it throughout existence. Any absence of that Breath would determine the non-existence of the *good* or *bad* creature itself and its complete annihilation. Therefore, to attribute to the serpent a created evil individuality would necessarily imply that God is always present in the innermost self of Satan.[1089] However, this is a deontological contradiction, in that, God, the Absolute-Good, would be the original essence of that evil personification.

Nevertheless, in this text, there is no mention of the serpent as *Satan, viz. the adversary* (שָׂטָן),[1090] the person opposed to God. The *Book of Job*,[1091] describes him as the one who comes from

"*running to and fro* (שׁוּט *shuwt*)[1092] *in the earth* (אֶרֶץ *'erets*), *and from walking up and down* (הָלַךְ *halak*)[1093] *in it... And... all that he* [the human Job] *has is in...* [Satan's] *powerful hand* (יָד *yad*).[1094]"

The adversary, in fact, procures all human passionate-possessions. He is the one who, with them, distracts from the true centrality of the world. Indeed, this verse describes the symbolic serpent like the Hermetic Ouroboros biting its own tail.[1095] It is the continuous[1096] running recurrence of the subject chasing an elusive object never reached in itself.

Let us go through the description point by point. There is the separating distinction, the opposition[1097] between the serpent-head-subject, which brings-forth[1098] intentionality, hunger and the woman-tail-object, the other ending,[1099] the metaphoric *heel* (עָקֵב `*aqeb*), the negative polarity of the epistemic duality. Therefore, the verse portrays the symbol of the serpent's head biting its own tail. Furthermore, the opposition is between the two noetic-noematic outcomes.[1100] In fact, the noematic mode of the object offers itself, *lies in wait*[1101] for the subject's head. In return, the noetic aspect of the subject, with its act-of-perception aims to grasp the object, *lies in wait* (שׁוּף *shuwph*) for the object's extreme polarity. Thus the continuous (עָקֵב `*eqeb*) epistemic circle closes up only to begin always a new process.

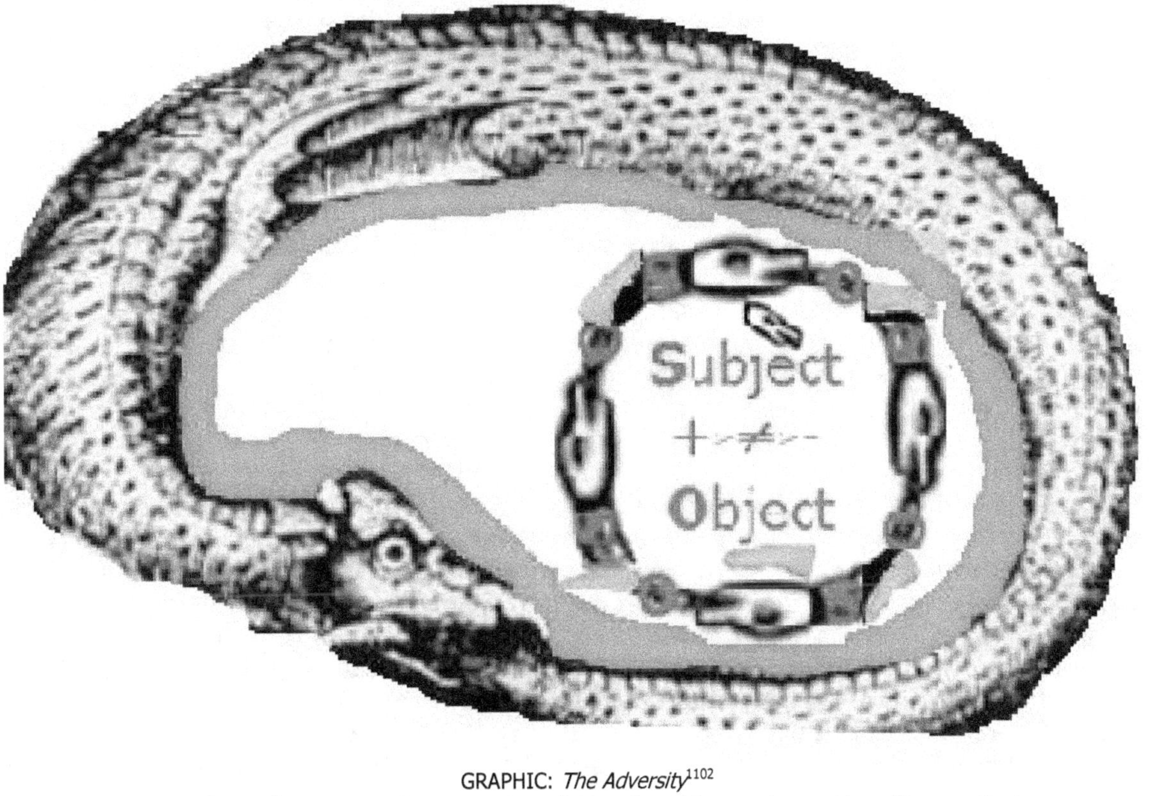

GRAPHIC: *The Adversity*[1102]

The *Book of Numbers* gives the esoteric solution for this condemnation. It says that

"*Fiery serpents ... bit the people; and much people of Israel died... And the LORD said unto Moses, 'Make thee a fiery serpent, and lift it up on a pole: and it shall come to pass, that every one that is bitten, when he looketh upon it, shall live.' And Moses made a serpent of brass, and lifted it up, and it came to pass, that if a serpent had bitten any man, when he beheld the serpent of brass, he lived."*[1103]

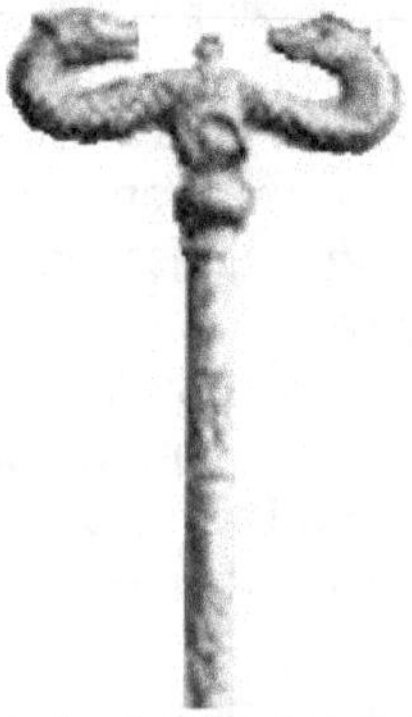

GRAPHIC: *Paterissa, Greek Orthodox Bishops' Pastoral Staff.*

By lifting up[1104] the serpent[1105] on a pole,[1106] Moses untangles its deadly circularity and it becomes a fiery serpent or a seraphim.[1107] Therefore, whosoever beholds[1108] that brass[1109] omen[1110] identifies not with the deadly deceiving objective world of the Tree of Knowledge, but aims at the top of the Tree of Life and realizes[1111] Transcendence in Itself.[1112] In other words, Pure Awareness *realizes* itself as Apodicticity, namely, as the Anointed-Redeemer, the One and Only residing at the very center of the circularity of consciousness.

As described, eating means to identify and become one with the food-*of* the objective world. Since the fruit of the Tree of Knowledge is the world's experience, then death is at hand. However, when a different type of food is *eaten* (φάγω *phago*) or *drunk* (πίνω *pinō*), then it becomes the *body* (σῶμα *sōma*)[1113] that identifies with Awareness and the *blood* (αἷμα *haima*)[1114] that ushers eternal life (ζωὴν αἰώνιον *zōēn aiōniokn*). Then,

"*whoso eateth my flesh, and drinketh my blood, hath eternal life; and I will raise him up at the last day,"*[1115]

namely, when time ceases to flow after the beginning.

3:16-Sorrow and Pain

אֶל־הָאִשָּׁה אָמַר הַרְבָּה אַרְבֶּה עִצְּבוֹנֵךְ וְהֵרֹנֵךְ בְּעֶצֶב תֵּלְדִי בָנִים וְאֶל־אִישֵׁךְ תְּשׁוּקָתֵךְ וְהוּא יִמְשָׁל־בָּךְ׃ ס   *'el* (to) *hā'išāh* (the woman) *'āmar* (He said) *harabāh* (greatly) *'arabeh* (I will multiply) *'iṣa̱bvōnē̱ka* (sorrow) *vahērōnē̱ka* (in conception) *ba'eṣeḇ* (pain) *tēla̱diy* (bear) *ḇāniym* (children) *va'el* (not) *'iyšē̱ka* (male) *tašuqāṯē̱ka* (desire) *vahu'* (to) *yimašāl* (he will rule) *bā̱ka* (over) *s* (.)
καὶ *kai* (and) **τῇ** *gē* (to the) **γυναικὶ** *gunaiki* (woman) **εἶπεν** *eipen* (He said) **πληθύνων** *plēthunōn* (greatly) **πληθυνῶ** *plēthunō* (multiply) **τὰς** *tas* (the) **λύπας** *lupas* (sorrows) **σου** *sou* (your) **καὶ** *kai* (and) **τὸν** *tov* (the) **στεναγμόν** *stenagmon* (moaning) **σου** *sou* () **ἐν** *en* (in) **λύπαις** *lupais* (pain) **τέξῃ** *texē* (bring forth) **τέκνα** *tekna* (children) **καὶ** *kai* (and) **πρὸς** *pros* (before) **τὸν** *ton* (the) **ἄνδρα** *andra* (man) **σου** *sou* (your) **ἡ** *ē* (the) **ἀποστροφή** *apostrophē* (submission) **σου** *sou* (your) **καὶ** *kai* (and) **αὐτός** *autos* (he) **σου** *sou* (you) **κυριεύσει** *kurieusei* (shall have rule over)
mulieri (to the woman) ***quoque*** (also) ***dixit*** (he said) ***multiplicabo*** (I will multiply) ***aerumnas*** (sorrows) ***tuas*** (your) ***et*** (and) ***conceptus*** (conception) ***tuos*** (your) ***in*** (in) ***dolore*** (pain) ***paries*** (you will deliver) ***filios*** (children) ***et*** (and) ***sub*** (under) ***viri*** (of man) ***potestate*** (rulership) ***eris*** (you will be) ***et*** (and) ***ipse*** (he) ***dominabitur*** (will dominate) ***tui*** (you)
Unto the woman he said, I will greatly multiply thy sorrow and thy conception; in sorrow thou shalt bring forth children; and thy desire shall be to thy husband, and he shall rule over thee
He also said to the woman-object,   "*I will multiply your sorrows and your conception. You will deliver and bring forth your children in*

pain and your desire will be your man-subject, and he will dominate you."

The concept that eating the forbidden fruit offended a paternalistic anthropomorphic divinity is very puerile. Similarly, the consequent severe condemnation of his own disobedient children to cruel suffering contradicts his stated infinite love. Furthermore, unless some fundamental zealot would declare today's painless childbirth sinful,[1116] this medical procedure negates that punishment. Also, it is not clear why the other animals, which did not break any rule, suffer the same pains of life. However, if we look at the actual existential distress of life and we analyze the cause of that suffering, then, we realize that pain is rooted in every mind. Psychological and/or physical sorrow[1117] and/or pain[1118] find their recognition only in the mind and by the mind. In fact, in the absence of a brain there is no anguish or ache, like anesthesia in a surgical procedure. Having *eaten* or having identified with the fruit of knowledge, the gates of suffering, of sorrow and pain are wide open. The fruit, which should not have been eaten, is the one deriving from desire (*tĕshuwqah*).[1119] That is intentionality-*of*, it is the reaching out towards[1120] the craved object of knowledge. For this, there is no condemnation, just consequences-*of* our existential being-in-the-world.[1121] No divine judgement sentences the multiplication (רַבָּה *rabah*) of sorrow. There are only consequences deriving from epistemic miscalculations. As an example, it is a good norm not to stare at the sun without protection, because if we look into it we are dazzled. However, the blindness deriving from that action would never be construed as the result of a condemnation. We perceive cataclysmic asteroids, wars of destruction, deadly viruses, debilitating old age and even devastating mind illnesses, as coming from external sources. However, we never experience external forces as external. Experiences take place in the mind and none can take place without it, least what we consider unrelated to it. Ramana Maharshi states that we fear them because we

"*give too much importance to the body.*"[1122]

In fact, to know any event we must classify it as our internally registered experience.

We need to highlight an aspect of suffering, which we can call,

"**The Way of the Cross**... the old way to enlightenment."[1123]

In "*Shamanism, archaic techniques of ecstasy*"[1124] control and transform pain. In fact,

"some physical sufferances find their precise conversion in terms of symbolic and initiatory death: as an example, the dismemberment of the candidate's body, an ecstatic experience, which can be achieved either thanks to the sufferance of '*vocational-sicknesses,*' or through some ritual actions, or, finally, in dreams."[1125]

Compare it to the *Biblical* description:

"*as a lion, so will he break all my bones: from day even to night wilt thou make an end of me.*"[1126]

However, what is suffering? Physical anguish must be always also mental. Suffering is such when it reverberates in the mind. If it does not, it means that the mind is under sedation. Suffering is the product of psychosomatic unbalances, from which both the body and the psyche seek to recover. Tolle so instructs,

"Allow the suffering to force you into the present moment... Use it for enlightenment... With this radiant peace comes the realization — not on the level of mind but within the depth of your Being — that you are indestructible, immortal... Do not resist the pain. Allow it to be there... Then see how the miracle of surrender transmutes deep suffering into deep peace. This is your crucifixion. Let it become your resurrection and ascension... Imagine a ray of sunlight that has forgotten it is an inseparable part of the sun and deludes itself into believing it has to fight for survival and create and cling to an identity other than the sun. Would the death of this delusion not be incredibly liberating?... Enlightenment consciously chosen means to relinquish your attachment to past and future and to make the Now the main focus of your life."[1127]

As in a labyrinth, all obstacles are there to make maze-travelers reach their correct exit. Every trial and error dead-end redirects steps towards the successful achievement of the journey's goal. Similarly, in the web of life, all psychophysical sufferings are there to lead us, through the central internal way-out, into Self-Awareness from which we entered that maze in the first place.

It is helpful here to restate the nature of symbolism. As we saw, metaphors connote the sense of allegories without negating their denoting indication. [1128]⇨ Thus, this last metaphor compares life's distress to the childbirth pain of a *mother*. In the first chapter, verses 22 and 28, Divine-Consciousness blessed the multiplications and growth of thoughts. However, when, through desire, the mind *eats*, *i.e.* attaches itself and identifies with those thoughts, then, consequently, pain and distress grow and multiply. As an example, consider how we are distressed during a nightmare. That is because we identify and take for real in-itself that dream. Therefore, like offspring (בן *ben*),[1129] objectivity *conceives* and generates[1130] thoughts as object producing distress. The object brings forth[1131] those thoughts as its own built[1132] children (בן *ben*). We are constantly worried, annoyed, or looking for the next experience. Thus, we are continuously waiting for the next object-thought to come by. Furthermore, this generating process takes place in the subject-object synthesis with the conceiving presence and rulership[1133] of the *man*-subject,[1134] the other necessary polarity of the epistemic process. However, this polarity is *sub*jected under the weight of that which is *ob*jected and *pro*jected above and before *him/her*. In fact, it is Eve that noematically offers the *apple*-fruit to Adam who, consequently, noetically eats it.

3:17-Ground Cursing

וּלְאָדָם אָמַר כִּי־שָׁמַעְתָּ לְקוֹל אִשְׁתֶּךָ וַתֹּאכַל מִן־הָעֵץ אֲשֶׁר צִוִּיתִיךָ לֵאמֹר לֹא תֹאכַל מִמֶּנּוּ **אֲרוּרָה הָאֲדָמָה בַּעֲבוּרֶךָ בְּעִצָּבוֹן תֹּאכֲלֶנָּה כֹּל יְמֵי חַיֶּיךָ׃** *ula'āḏām* (to Adam) *'āmar* (He said) *kiy* (because) *šāma'atā* (you listened) *laqvōl* (voice) *'išateḵā* (of the woman) *vatō'ḵal* (youn ate) *min* (from) *hā'ēṣ* (the tree) *'ăšer* (which) *ṣiuiyṯiyḵā* (command) *lē'mōr* (say) *lō* (not) *ṯō'ḵal* (to eat) *mimenu* (because) *'ărurāh* (cursed) *hā'ăḏāmāh* (land) *ba'ăḇureḵā* (produced) *ba'iṣāḇvōn* (labour) *tō'kălenāh* (eat) *kōl* (all) *yamēy* (day) *ḥayeyḵā* (life)
τῷ *tō* (the) **δὲ** *de* (to) **Αδαμ** *Adam* (Adam) **εἶπεν** *eipen* (He said) **ὅτι** *oti* (because) **ἤκουσας** *ēkousas* (listened) **τῆς** *tēs* (the) **φωνῆς** *phōnēs* (voice) **τῆς** *tēs* (of the) **γυναικός** *gunaikos* (woman) **σου** *sou* (your) **καὶ** *kai* (and) **ἔφαγες** *ephages* (you ate) **ἀπὸ** *apo* (from) **τοῦ** *tou* (the) **ξύλου** *xulou* (tree) **οὗ** *ou* (that) **ἐνετειλάμην** *eneteilamēn* (I commanded) **σοι** *soi* (you) **τούτου** *toutou* (in this way) **μόνου** *monou* (alone) **μὴ** *mē* (not) **φαγεῖν** *phageiv* (you have eaten) **ἀπ'** *ap'* (from) **αὐτοῦ** *autou* (that) **ἐπικατάρατος** *epikataratos* (cursed) **ἡ** *ē* (the) **γῆ** *gē* (land) **ἐν** *en* (in) **τοῖς** *tois* (the) **ἔργοις** *ergois* (work) **σου** *sou* (your) **ἐν** *en* (in) **λύπαις** *lupais* (pain) **φάγῃ** *phagē* (shall eat) **αὐτὴν** *autēn* (you) **πάσας** *pasas* (all) **τὰς** *tas* (the) **ἡμέρας** *ēmeras* (days) **τῆς** *tēs* (the) **ζωῆς** *zōēs* (life) **σου** *sou* (your)
ad (to) ***Adam*** (Adam) ***vero*** (indeed) ***dixit*** (He said) ***quia*** (because) ***audisti*** (you heard) ***vocem*** (the voice) ***uxoris*** (of wife) ***tuae*** (yours) ***et*** (and) ***comedisti*** (you ate) ***de*** (from) ***ligno*** (tree) ***ex*** (out of) ***quo*** (which) ***praeceperam*** (I commanded) ***tibi*** (you) ***ne*** (not) ***comederes*** (eat) ***maledicta*** (cursed) ***terra*** (the land) ***in*** (for) ***opere*** (deed) ***tuo*** (yours) ***in*** (with) ***laboribus*** (labor) ***comedes*** (you will eat) ***eam*** (it) ***cunctis*** (all) ***diebus*** (the days) ***vitae*** (of life) ***tuae*** (yours)
And unto Adam he said, Because thou hast hearkened unto the voice of thy wife, and hast eaten of the tree, of which I commanded thee, saying, Thou shalt not eat of it: cursed is the ground for thy sake; in sorrow shalt thou eat of it all the days of thy life;
Subsequently, He said to Adam, "*Because you obeyed to the words of your wife and you ate of the tree from which I commanded you not to eat, the ground is cursed on account of your deed. You will eat from it with labor all the days of yours life.*

The voice or words[1135] of the woman (אשה *'ishshah*) are the seductive aspect of the object *subjugating* the subject, like Atlas. Mesmerized by it, Adam, the subject (אדם *'Adam*), obeys[1136] its lure by eating (אכל *'akal*) from the tree (עץ *'ets*) of the desiring faculties of the senses and by identifying and by copulating with the object itself. At this point, the consequences of this action is that the bodily-ground of the Garden of

Happiness (עדן` *eden*) is not any longer the reign of Silent Ecstatic Rest (שָׁבַת *shabath*). The active desire to reach the object has taken control. Consequently, that red ground (אֲדָמָה *'adamah*) is despised (ארר *'arar*). All the days (יוֹם *yowm*) of circular consciousness-*of* the world is cursed with sorrow (עִצָּבוֹן` *itstsabown*). As it is for the object, so it is for the subject.

3:18-The Thorny Green Sprouts of Food

וְקוֹץ וְדַרְדַּר תַּצְמִיחַ לָךְ וְאָכַלְתָּ אֶת־עֵשֶׂב הַשָּׂדֶה׃   *vaqvōṣ* (grieving thorns) *vadaradar* (tribulations) *taṣamiyaḥ* (sprout) *lāka* (thus) *va'ākalatā* (you shall eat) *'et* (and) *'ēśeb* (herb) *haśādeh* (of the field)
ἀκάνθας *akanthas* (thorns) **καὶ** *kai* (and) **τριβόλους** *tribolous* (tribulations) **ἀνατελεῖ** *anatelei* (it shall produce) **σοι** *soi* (for you) **καὶ** *kai* (and) **φάγῃ** *phagē* (you shall eat) **τὸν** *ton* (the) **χόρτον** *chorton* (herb) **τοῦ** *tou* (of the) **ἀγροῦ** *agrou* (land)
spinas (thorns) ***et*** (and) ***tribulos*** (tribulations) ***germinabit*** (shall it germinate) ***tibi*** (for you) ***et*** (and) ***comedes*** (you shall eat) ***herbas*** (the herbs) ***terrae*** (of the land)
Thorns also and thistles shall it bring forth to thee; and thou shalt eat the herb of the field;
[The land] shall produce for you thorny grieving and tribulations and you shall eat the herbs of the spread out land.

Instead of happiness, the garden has become the spread out land[1137] of active desire. Because of the hungry activity of continuous desire and appetizing crave for the object, this soil now produces thorny[1138] grieving[1139] tribulations.[1140] The green sprouts[1141] of that land become our reality and our food. These new growths are the tribulations, which set us in the consciousness-*of*[1142] a dreadful and sickening[1143] nightmare, which severs[1144] us from the Truth of Transcendence.

3:19-Labor and Death

בְּזֵעַת אַפֶּיךָ תֹּאכַל לֶחֶם עַד שׁוּבְךָ אֶל־הָאֲדָמָה כִּי מִמֶּנָּה לֻקָּחְתָּ כִּי־עָפָר אַתָּה וְאֶל־עָפָר תָּשׁוּב׃   *bazē'at* (sweat) *'apeykā* (face) *tō'kal* (you shall eat) *leḥem* (bread) *'ad* (until) *šubakā* (you will return) *'el* (to) *hā'ădāmāh* (the earth) *kiy* (for) *mimenāh* (out of) *luqāḥatā* (taken out) *kiy* (for) *'āpār* (dust) *'atāh* (you came) *va'el* (into) *'āpār* (dust) *tāšub* (you will return)
ἐν *in* (in) **ἱδρῶτι** *idrōti* (swet) **τοῦ** *tou* (of your) **προσώπου** *prosōpou* (face) **σου** *sou* (you) **φάγῃ** *phagē* (will eat) **τὸν** *ton* (the) **ἄρτον** *arton* (bread) **σου** *sou* (your) **ἕως** *eōs* (until) **τοῦ** *tou* (the) **ἀποστρέψαι** *apostrepsai* (return) **σε** *se* (you) **εἰς** *eis* (to) **τὴν** *tēn* (the) **γῆν** *gēn* (ground) **ἐξ** *ex* (from) **ἧς** *ēs* (which) **ἐλήμφθης** *elēmphthēs* (you were taken) **ὅτι** *oti* (because) **γῆ** *gē* (dirt) **εἶ** *ei* (are) **καὶ** *kai* (and) **εἰς** *eis* (to) **γῆν** *gēn* (ground) **ἀπελεύσῃ** *apeleusē* (you will return)
in (in) ***sudore*** (the sweat) ***vultus*** (face) ***tui*** (your) ***vesceris*** (you shall eat) ***pane*** (bread) ***donec*** (till) ***revertaris*** (you will go back) ***in*** (into) ***terram*** (the earth) ***de*** (from) ***qua*** (which) ***sumptus*** (taken out) ***es*** (you are) ***quia*** (for) ***pulvis*** (dust) ***es*** (you are) ***et*** (and) ***in*** (into) ***pulverem*** (dust) ***reverteris*** (you shall return)
In the sweat of thy face shalt thou eat bread, till thou return unto the ground; for out of it wast thou taken: for dust thou art, and unto dust shalt thou return.
You shall eat bread with the sweat of your face until you will go back into the earth from which you came, because you are ashes and into ashes you shall return."

The paradox of *Genesis*, the Beginning, is that once conceived as such, it is reduced to history, to an object remembered, but not any longer in the Present. When we eat the forbidden fruit in order to "*become as gods,*" we want to conceptualize the Apodictic-Transcendent-Awareness. Then we are *killing* It to reduce it to a dead-past. At the same time, we are *killing* ourselves by losing the vivifying identification with That Transcendent, which **is** our Breath of Life. Therefore, as we have seen, the epistemic circularity incessantly chases its own object of knowledge. The mind comes out of the ashes[1145] of death, its own nothingness, and returns[1146] again to the nothingness of those ashes. Adam, namely

"*this body here, is the house of Death.*"[1147] [1148] ⇨

Paradoxically, the knowledge we wanted to achieve by eating the forbidden fruit is lost with the death we gain from the same eating act. In fact, when we categorize something as existent, we mean that the known object falls between the subject/object correlation and, thus, becomes known as past. In this sense, we can never state that the Transcendent exists, because it would imply to known it *for-ourselves* as an existing already given past object, thus not any longer transcendent. Furthermore, if we take *existence* in its etymological Latin sense of *exsistere, i.e.:* that which *out* (*ex*) *stands* (*sistere*), then, the being *in-itself* and out (*ex*) of the epistemic correlation would be necessarily unknown, thus *non-existent.*

All along, Divine-Consciousness has been teaching us. Labor and death result as further consequences deriving from the disoriented thinking act. The craving for knowledge transforms into hunger for daily bread. However, this necessitates laboring activity, which produces physical consequences, namely sweat.[1149] This last name derives from the verb *zuwa`*,[1150] meaning to tremble, to quiver and to be in terror. This anxious fear appears on the *face, 'aph,*[1151] of the stressed, worried and *angry* worker *breathing hard, 'anaph,* [1152] while laboring in the field of nightmare. Nevertheless, the human's existential travails are not over. Death is the inevitable outcome of the epistemic condition. Death is the equalizer reminding us not to focus on the past. In fact, death is past. <The historical-ego is already dead. It is not Now any longer because it is projected in the knowledge of that which is the past as such. The ego is the one who is here and at this time is writing or reading. On the contrary, the Self is the presence of the Transcendent in all historical egos, without which the ego itself would and could not be known. However, the Transcendent-Self does *not exist* because only that which belongs to the consciousness-*of* is placed into existence. When conceived the Self-in-Itself is non-existent. It is the Zero, the Transcendent-Emptiness from Which all comes and all goes.>[1153]

The reason why the fruit is forbidden is because eating it, becoming one with it means to identify with that which is already given, namely is past, *viz.* dead. The subject knows the object as an already given and gone time and space. Naturally, this is not immediately understandable for us. We erroneously call present things that are at *telescopic-view*, at *arm-length*, at *microscopic-analysis* or at *mind-reach* in general. However, whenever we state the present knowledge, we imply that the known object was already there before we knew it. When we think of ourselves, or, when we look at our own hand, we may believe that these two objects are present, *viz.* immediately here. However, our mind knows them as having been there before the act of knowledge. There is no other way to know. Knowledge means to know the past, to know that which is already dead. We are like archeologists digging for past relics. Whenever we state that something *ex*ists, we imply that something is placed-out (ex*istent-ex*) behind or beyond us, into the past, thus in the realm of death, that which is no longer present.

The Greco-Roman literature describes this metaphorically with the myth of Deucalion and Pyrrha.[1154] These two were the only survivors of a universal flood. To repopulate the world, the Titan goddess Themis advised them to collect the bones of their mother Gaia, namely the stones of Earth, and toss them *behind* their shoulders. Therefore, each stone placed in the past, behind them, became a human being. This is more evident from an astrophysical perspective. When we look into space, we understand that the astronomical objects we see are not what they appear but what they were, because they already are past. In fact, the sun we see is that of eight minutes ago.[1155] Further, the Swiss astrophysicist Kevin Schawinski writes in *The Conversation*,

"the Milky Way galaxy may already be dead but it still keeps going."[1156]

More outstanding is that the microwave glow, detected at the edge of the Universe, is the past light of the Big Bang, from which the Universe came and towards which the Universe expands.[1157]

On the other hand, the Present is the continuum constant, which always **is**, even

"*before Abraham was.*"[1158]

Consequently, Adam, the *I/ego*, eating the fruit of desire, identifies with its past, exiles itself from the Garden of Eden and enters into the realm of pain and death.

The *snaky* desire drives us to identify with our dream object, thus, we suffer, die and become separated from our True Present life.

3-III SECTION: THE EXPULSION

3:20-Eve

וַיִּקְרָא הָאָדָם שֵׁם אִשְׁתּוֹ חַוָּה כִּי הִוא הָיְתָה אֵם כָּל־חָי׃ *vayiqarā'* (called) *hā'āḏām* (Adam) *šēm* (name) *'išatvō* (woman) *ḥauāh* (Life) *kiy* (because) *kiy* (his) *hiv'* (she) *hāyaṯāh* (became) *'ēm* (the mother) *kāl* (of all) *ḥāy* (living beings)
καὶ *kai* (and) **ἐκάλεσεν** *ekalesen* (called) **Αδαμ** *Adam* (Adam) **τὸ** *to* (the) **ὄνομα** *onoma* (name) **τῆς** *tēs* (of the) **γυναικὸς** *gunaikos* (woman) **αὐτοῦ** *autou* (his) **Ζωή** *Zōē* (Life) **ὅτι** *oti* (because) **αὕτη** *autē* (she) **μήτηρ** *mētēr* (mother) **πάντων** *pantōn* (of all) **τῶν** *tōn* (the) **ζώντων** *zōntōn* (living beings)
et (and) ***vocavit*** (called) ***Adam*** (Adam) ***nomen*** (name) ***uxoris*** (of the wife) ***suae*** (his) ***Hava*** (Eve) ***eo*** (she) ***quod*** (because) ***mater*** (mother) ***esset*** (was) ***cunctorum*** (of all) ***viventium*** (living beings)
And Adam called his wife's name Eve; because she was the mother of all living.
Moreover, the Human called his woman Eve-life, because she was the mother of all living beings.

Mother, *'em,*[1159] is also a metaphor for the earth as objectivity. It is the logical objective point of departure or division from the subject, who, in return, repeatedly seizes the object-food. The name Eve,[1160] *means* life, living and

"from Arab.[ic,] ... to roll oneself in a circle,"[1161]

namely, the circularity of consciousness.

In fact, causatively the word Eve derives from *chavah,*[1162] meaning to tell, to declare, to show, to make known, to breath, and from *chava'* (חֲוָא)[1163] to inform, to show, interpret, explain, tell and declare. Likewise, it derives from *chayah,*[1164] to live, to have life, remain alive, sustain life, live prosperously, live-forever, to be alive, be restored to life or health. She is the life giver who shows the objective world, informs and makes it known. As such, she is Adam's same *flesh*, *shě'er*, and the one who feeds us by providing *food*, *shě'er.*[1165] Therefore, Eve is the paradigmatic life giver for and of all living beings. Namely, every mother is a conjugation, a reconfiguration of that basic physical and epistemic paradigm called *Eve.*

3:21-The Skin

וַיַּעַשׂ יְהוָה אֱלֹהִים לְאָדָם וּלְאִשְׁתּוֹ כָּתְנוֹת עוֹר וַיַּלְבִּשֵׁם׃ פ *vaya'aś* (fashioned) *yahvāh* (Transcendent) *'ělōhiym* (Divine-Consciousness) *la'āḏām* (Adam) *ula'išatvō* (woman) *kāṯanvōṯ* (garments) *'vōr* (of skin) *vayalabišēm* (dresses) p̄ (.)
καὶ *kai* (and) **ἐποίησεν** *epoiēsen* (made) **κύριος** *kurios* (Lord) **ὁ** *o* (the) **θεὸς** *theos* (God) **τῷ** *tō* (the) **Αδαμ** *Adam* (Adam) **καὶ** *kai* (and) **τῇ** *tē* (the) **γυναικὶ** *gunaiki* (woman) **αὐτοῦ** *autou* (his) **χιτῶνας** *chitōnas* (garments) **δερματίνους** *dermatinous* (of skin) **καὶ** *kai* (and) **ἐνέδυσεν** *enedusen* (dressed) **αὐτούς** *autous* (them)
fecit (made) ***quoque*** (also) ***Dominus*** (Lord) ***Deus*** (God) ***Adam*** (Adam) ***et*** (and) ***uxori*** (wife) ***eius*** (his) ***tunicas*** (tunics) ***pellicias*** (fur) ***et*** (and) ***induit*** (dressed) ***eos*** (them)
Unto Adam also and to his wife did the LORD God make coats of skins, and clothed them.
The Transcendent of Divine-Consciousness fashioned also skin garments for Adam and his woman and dressed them.

Unless *Homo habilis* were *able* only to stitch fig leaves, while *Homo sapiens* were *ignorant* about tailoring their own garments, this verse does not refer to a fashion atelier. Truthfully, the epistemic formation is over.

From a Timeless Nowhere, the age long process of evolution generates, after a gestation period, this actual being. This individual comes to life with this organic dress,[1166] this sensory skin[1167] covering[1168] all the *nakedness*, the in-itself of the physical body of this man/woman reading this page here and now.

3:22-The Tree of Life

וַיֹּאמֶר יְהוָה אֱלֹהִים הֵן הָאָדָם הָיָה כְּאַחַד מִמֶּנּוּ לָדַעַת טוֹב וָרָע וְעַתָּה פֶּן־יִשְׁלַח יָדוֹ וְלָקַח גַּם מֵעֵץ הַחַיִּים וְאָכַל וָחַי לְעֹלָם׃ *vayō'mer* (said) *yahvāh* (Transcendent) *'ělōhiym* (Divine-Consciousness) *hēn* (behold) *hā'āḏām*

(Adam) *hāyāh* (has become) *ka'aḥad̲* (one) *mimenu* (from us) *lād̲a'at̲* (know) *ṭvōb̲* (good) *vārā'* (evil) *va'atāh* (now) *pen* (lest) *yišalaḥ* (stretches out) *yād̲vō* (hand) *valāqaḥ* (takes) *gam* (also) *mē'ēṣ* (from tree) *haḥayiym* (of life) *va'āk̲al* (eats) *vāḥay* (lives) *la'ōlām* (forever)
καὶ *kai* (and) **εἶπεν** *eipen* (said) **ὁ** *o* (the) **θεός** *theos* (God) **ἰδοὺ** *idou* (behold) **Αδαμ** *Adam* (Adam) **γέγονεν** *gegonen* (has become) **ὡς** *ōs* (thus) **εἷς** *eis* (one) **ἐξ** *ex* (of) **ἡμῶν** *ēmōn* (Us) **τοῦ** *tou* (the) **γινώσκειν** *ginōskein* (knowing) **καλὸν** *kalon* (good) **καὶ** *kai* (and) **πονηρόν** *ponēron* (evil) **καὶ** *kai* (and) **νῦν** *nun* (now) **μήποτε** *mēpote* (never) **ἐκτείνῃ** *ekteinē* (extend) **τὴν** *tēv* (the) **χεῖρα** *cheira* (hand) **καὶ** *kai* (and) **λάβῃ** *labē* (takes) **τοῦ** *tou* (the) **ξύλου** *xulou* (tree) **τῆς** *tēs* (of the) **ζωῆς** *zōēs* (life) **καὶ** *kai* (and) **φάγῃ** *phagē* (eats) **καὶ** *kai* (and) **ζήσεται** *zēsetai* (lives) **εἰς** *eis* (for) **τὸν** *ton* (the) **αἰῶνα** *aiōna* (eternity)
et (and) ***ait*** (He said) ***ecce*** (here is) ***Adam*** (Adam) ***factus*** (made) ***est*** (is) ***quasi*** (almost) ***unus*** (one) ***ex*** (of) ***nobis*** (Us) ***sciens*** (knowing) ***bonum*** (good) ***et*** (and) ***malum*** (evil) ***nunc*** (now) ***ergo*** (therefore) ***ne*** (so that) ***forte*** (by chance) ***mittat*** (he sets) ***manum*** (hand) ***suam*** (his) ***et*** (and) ***sumat*** (takes) ***etiam*** (also) ***de*** (from) ***ligno*** (tree) ***vitae*** (of life) ***et*** (and) ***comedat*** (eats) ***et*** (and) ***vivat*** (lives) ***in*** (for) ***aeternum*** (eternity)
And the LORD God said, Behold, the man is become as one of us, to know good and evil: and now, lest he put forth his hand, and take also of the tree of life, and eat, and live for ever:
And the Transcendent of Divine-Consciousness said, "*Behold, the human has become like one of Us knowing everything good and evil. Now, if s/he sets the hand and also takes from the tree of life and eats from it, s/he would live for eternity.*"

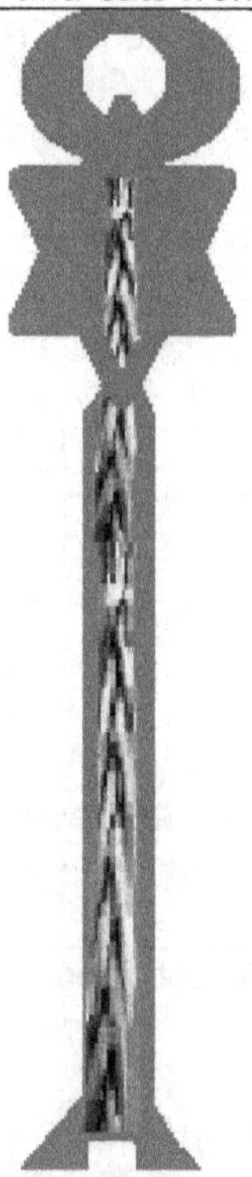

GRAPHIC: *The Tree of Life*

Is a criminal mother, who, to punish her offspring for eating forbidden food from the cupboard, forces them to die of starvation, conceivable? This is what a literal reading of this verse would want us to believe.

<When the rush of Pure Apodictical-Awareness irrupts and Consciousness identifies with It, the personal individual mind cannot forget it. It is by being awake and identifying with that Certitude that one

reaches Heaven. The timeless and spaceless mythical Garden of Eden is the absence of the subject-object correlation. It is where Apodictical-Awareness needs no thought. Where there is no tribulation or unsatisfaction because there is no *hungry-desire* for the *fruit of knowledge*. There, *Certainty* does not require a thought to be *certain of being Certain.*>[1169]

In Chapter 1, verse 2, we have seen that the Spirit or the Breath (רוּחַ *ruwach*) of Transcendent Awareness hovers (רָחַף *rachaph*) over (עַל *`al*) the surface (פָּנִים *paniym*) of the flowing primordial waters, namely, all the infinite possibility of everything. Now, the human, having reached the knowledge of good and evil is potentially all-conscious, omniscient, thus is similar to the Transcendent Awareness. If s/he were to identify, at the same time, with the breath of life ascending to heaven, s/he would be immortal. Thus, death would have no hold on them because there would be no *hungry*-eating, namely, no identification with that which is past. The hovering (רָחַף *rachaph*) is pure restful (שָׁבַת *shabath*) Transcendent Awareness.[1170] Human knowledge (יָדַע *yada`*), instead, is painful hunger attached to the past object. If s/he were to identify with the Detached Rest of the Ultimate Observer, s/he would be immortal. However, this would imply not having eaten the forbidden fruit. In fact, only the circular intentional desirous drive to objectify Transcendent Awareness prevents the human from reaching the Tree of Life. In fact, the constant subject-object circularity prevents us from reaching the stillness of Eternal Life.

3:23-Dismissal from Paradise

וַיְשַׁלְּחֵהוּ יְהוָה אֱלֹהִים מִגַּן־עֵדֶן לַעֲבֹד אֶת־הָאֲדָמָה אֲשֶׁר לֻקַּח מִשָּׁם׃   *vayašalaḥēhu* (sent away) *yahvāh* (Transcendent) *'ĕlōhiym* (Divine-Consciousness) *migan* (from) *'ēḏen* (Eden) *la'ăḇōḏ* (to work) *'eṯ* (the) *hā'ăḏāmāh* (land) *'ăšer* (which) *luqaḥ* (taken out) *mišām* (from)
καὶ *kai* (and) **ἐξαπέστειλεν** *exapesteilen* (He exiled) **αὐτὸν** *auton* (him) **κύριος** *kurios* (Lord) **ὁ** *o* (the) **θεὸς** *theos* (God) **ἐκ** *ek* (from) **τοῦ** *tou* (the) **παραδείσου** *paradeisou* (paradise) **τῆς** *tēs* (of the) **τρυφῆς** *truphēs* (happiness) **ἐργάζεσθαι** *ergazesthai* (to cultivate) **τὴν** *tēn* (the) **γῆν** *gēn* (earth) **ἐξ** *ex* (from) **ἧς** *ēs* (which) **ἐλήμφθη** *elēmphthē* (he was taken)
emisit (sent out) ***eum*** (him) ***Dominus*** (Lord) ***Deus*** (God) ***de*** (from) ***paradiso*** (the paradise) ***voluptatis*** (of happiness) ***ut*** (to) ***operaretur*** (cultivate) ***terram*** (the land) ***de*** (from) ***qua*** (which) ***sumptus*** (taken out) ***est*** (he was)
Therefore the LORD God sent him forth from the garden of Eden, to till the ground from whence he was taken.
The Transcendence of Divine-Consciousness exiled him out from the Paradise of Consciousness to cultivate the land from which he was taken out.

To be sent out[1171] from the Garden of Eden (עֵדֶן), the state of restful happiness, it means that the human, exiled from its interiority *in-itself*, experiences the world as *out-there for-itself*. We always know our dream and/or wakeful objective-world as an external reality independent from our interiority, on which it has its foundation. This is our distortion, which sentences us to death, not God. This is not a punishment. It is the epistemic consequence of the desire to objectify the real life of the Transcendent-Apodictic-Awareness. It is the *thought* of life, which is not life in-itself, but a *concept* that cannot replace life itself. Therefore, we cultivate[1172] this foreign land of dreadful whirlpools and painful tornados. Then, we become as Odysseus[1173] or Aeneas

"who was much tossed through land and by high seas."[1174]

In it, we toil and labor daily. As ego-consciousness, we come out (לָקַח *laqach*) from this deceitful land of objectivity only to disappear in that same soil of ashes. Namely, we become objects among objects in the pit of a mass grave.

3:24-Cherubim's Sword

וַיְגָרֶשׁ אֶת־הָאָדָם וַיַּשְׁכֵּן מִקֶּדֶם לְגַן־עֵדֶן אֶת־הַכְּרֻבִים וְאֵת לַהַט הַחֶרֶב הַמִּתְהַפֶּכֶת לִשְׁמֹר אֶת־   **דֶּרֶךְ עֵץ הַחַיִּים׃ ס**   *vayağāreš* (he drove out) *'eṯ* (and) *hā'āḏām* (Adam) *vayašakēn* (dwell) *miqeḏem* (from the east) *lağan* (garden) *'ēḏen* (Eden) *'eṯ* (and) *hakaruḇiym* (Cherubim) *va'ēṯ* (with) *lahaṭ* (flaming) *haḥereḇ*

(sword) *hamitahapeket* (turning around) *lišamōr* (to guard) *'et* (and) *dereka* (way) *'ēṣ* (tree) *hahayiym* (of life) *s* (.)
καὶ *kai* (and) **ἐξέβαλεν** *exebalen* (expelled) **τὸν** *tov* (the) **Αδαμ** *Adam* (Adam) **καὶ** *kai* (and) **κατῴκισεν** *katōkisen* (placed) **αὐτὸν** *auton* (he) **ἀπέναντι** *apenanti* (in front) **τοῦ** *tou* (of the) **παραδείσου** *paradeisou* (paradise) **τῆς** *tēs* (of the) **τρυφῆς** *truphēs* (happiness) **καὶ** *kai* (and) **ἔταξεν** *etaxev* (stationed) **τὰ** *ta* (a) **χερουβιμ** *xeroubim* (Cherubim) **καὶ** *kai* (and) **τὴν** *tēn* (the) **φλογίνην** *phloginēn* (flaming) **ῥομφαίαν** *romphaian* (sword) **τὴν** *tēn* (the) **στρεφομένην** *strephomenēn* (turning around) **φυλάσσειν** *phulassein* (to guard) **τὴν** *tēn* (the) **ὁδὸν** *odon* (way) **τοῦ** *tou* (of the) **ξύλου** *xulou* (tree) **τῆς** *tēs* (of) **ζωῆς** *zōēs* (life)
eiecit-(expelled) ***que*** (and) ***Adam*** (Adam) ***et*** (and) ***conlocavit*** (placed) ***ante*** (at the entrance) ***paradisum*** (of the paradise) ***voluptatis*** (of happiness) ***cherubin*** (a cherubim) ***et*** (and) ***flammeum*** (a flaming) ***gladium*** (sword) ***atque*** (also) ***versatilem*** (turning all around) ***ad*** (to) ***custodiendam*** (guard) ***viam*** (the way) ***ligni*** (of the tree) ***vitae*** (of life)
So he drove out the man; and he placed at the east of the garden of Eden Cherubims, and a flaming sword which turned every way, to keep the way of the tree of life.
Thus, he expelled the human and placed at the eastern gate of the Paradise of Happiness a Cherubim with a flaming sword turning all around, to guard the road of the tree of life.

<Two trees were in the Garden of Eden. In its midst, were the tree of life

'*and the tree of knowledge of good and evil.*'[1175]

The human creature, disobeying God's commandment, became mortal when s/he ate the fruit from the tree of knowledge and was capable of knowing "*good and bad,*" *viz.* "*everything.*"[1176] Then the Lord placed

'*Cherubim and a flaming sword which turned every way... to keep the way of the tree of life.*'

The image of flame enveloping a plant reappears in the story of the burning bush,...[1177] from which the voice of the Lord comes out saying,[1178]>

"*I am that I am.*"[1179]

The hunger of Adam and Eve is the desire to experience the unexperienceable, which leads necessarily to death. Thus, the expulsion (גָּרַשׁ *garash*) of the human from the Garden of Happiness is not a punishment, but a built-in logical consequence of that impossible epistemic act.

A Cherubim (כְּרוּב *kěruwb*), God's flying ride[1180] with

"*the likeness of four living creatures... a man... a lion... an ox...* [and] *an eagle,*"[1181]

is placed at the oriental (קֶדֶם *qedem*)[1182] gate of Eden. The four faces are allegories representing[1183]⇨

1) the human's[1184] sparkling[1185] intellectual faculties,
2) the lion's[1186] fearce power,[1187]
3) the ox's[1188] strength and boldness going around[1189] in the epistemic process,
4) the eagle (נֶשֶׁר *nesher*)[1190] leading to salvation. In fact, the Lord said

"*I bare you on eagles'* (נֶשֶׁר *nesher*) *wings and brought you into myself.*"[1191]

"*And to the woman were given two wings of a great eagle that she might fly into the wilderness, into her place, where she is epistemically-nourished* (τρέφω *trephō*) *for a time* (καιρὸν *kairon*)*, and times* (καιροὺς *kairous*)*, and half* (ἥμισυ *ēmisu*) *a time*"[1192]

The time/s are in the season/s (מוֹעֵד *mow`ed*)[1193] of dreamless sleep (NREM) and this wakefulness, the divisive-half (חֵצִי *chetsiy*)[1194] time is in the dream state (REM). Therefore, Daniel[1195] reports that at a river

"*stood ... two, one on this side of the bank of the river, and the other on that side of the bank of the river... And one ... man clothed in linen... was upon the waters of the river,.. He... sware... that... the end of these wonders... shall be for a time-season (ləmvō'ēḏ לְמוֹעֵד), times-seasons (mvō'ăḏiym מֽוֹעֲדִים), and a division-half (vāḥēṣiy וָחֵצִי); and when he shall have accomplished to scatter the power of the holy people, all these things shall be finished... And from the time that the recurrent circadian process (*תָּמִיד *tamiyd*)[1196] *shall be taken away, and the abomination that maketh desolate set up, there shall be a thousand two hundred and ninety days days* (יוֹם *yowm*) *of circular consciousness,* [*I will shew thee, hear me; and that which I have seen I will declare*][1197] ... *Blessed is he that waiteth, and cometh to the thousand three hundred and five and thirty days* (יוֹם *yowm*) *of circular consciousness* [*And the word of the LORD came unto me the second time, saying*[1198] (blessed) *he that put his holy Spirit within him*.]"[1199]

Awake, the Cherubim guards (שָׁמַר *shamar*) the way (דֶּרֶךְ *derek*) to the Tree of Life with a rotating (הָפַךְ *haphak*) flaming (לַהַט *lahat*) sword (חֶרֶב *chereb*). This allegory is a metaphor for the impossibility to know and conceptualize the central Apodictic-Transcendent-Awareness. In fact, the Cherubim, the angelic-human-beasts in every thought process, whips around the flaming sword, which cuts/divides the subject from the object while uniting/connecting them in a continuous rotating process. This whirlpool never allows to reach its center, namely, the Tree of Life-Awareness. As an example, that flaming vortex is like a high spinning centrifuge to train astronauts.[1200] Once placed in the whirling cabin, at the end of the rotating arm, the trainee does not see the central motorized axis. S/he perceives the circling trajectory as a forward straight direction, while s/he misses the motionless propulsion of the central axis. Similarly, once in the whirling hardship of daily events, we lose connection with the force, which propelled us into life.

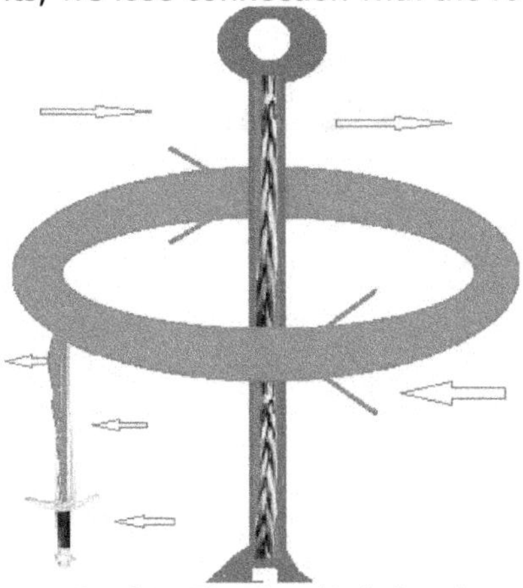

Graphic: *The Cherubim's Sword*

Eve is the life giver. However, instead of fulfilling Life, we possess it conceptually as time passed. Thus, taken by the subject/object whirlpool, we reject immortality.

HERE ENDS THE THIRD CHAPTER OF
THE TREE OF KNOWLEDGE
AND THE TREE OF LIFE

PART 3

GENEALOGICAL PARADIGMS

CHAPTER 4

THE GENERATIONS OF ADAM AND EVE & THAT OF CAIN

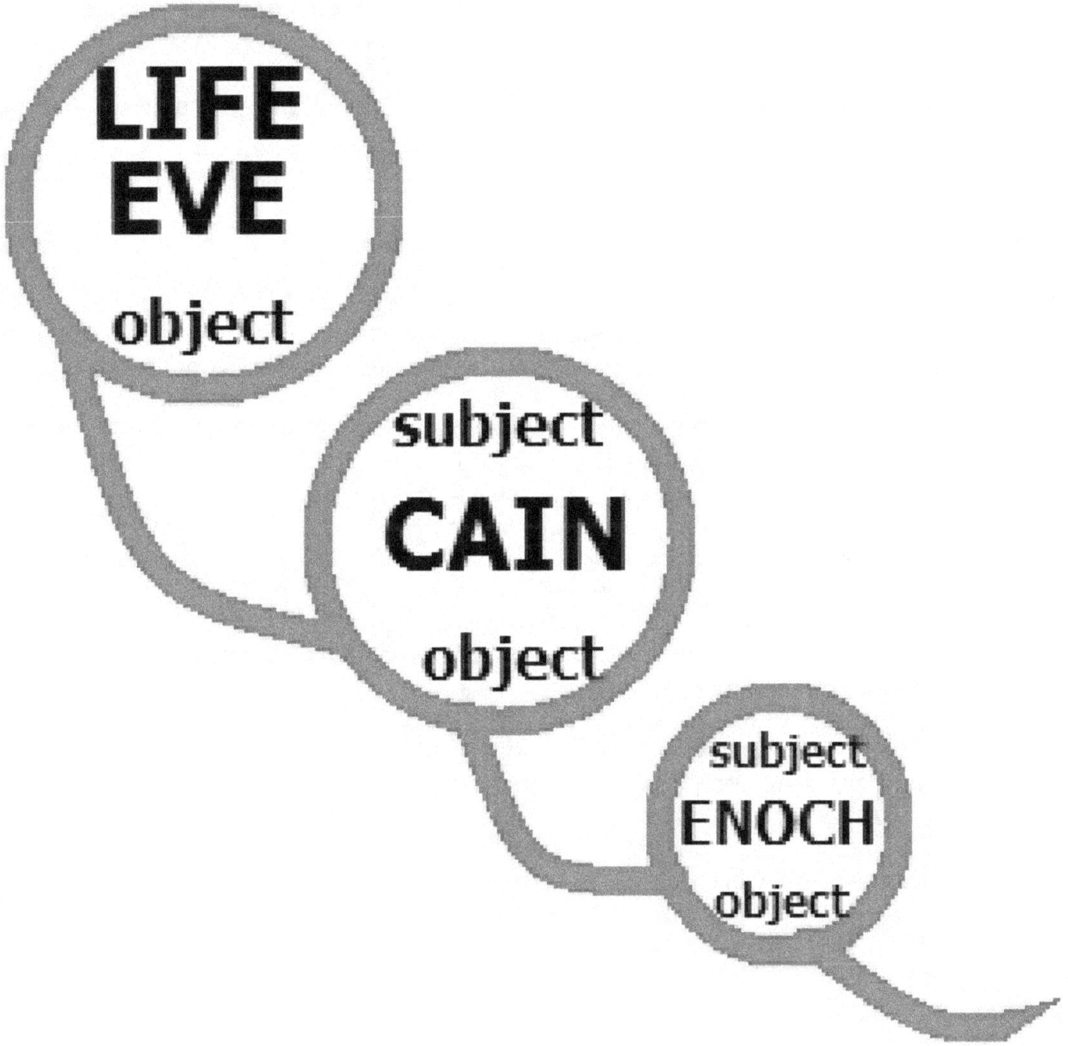

GRAPHIC: *Eve's Generations*

4-I SECTION: CAIN AND ABEL
4:1-Birth of Cain

וְהָאָדָם יָדַע אֶת־חַוָּה אִשְׁתּוֹ וַתַּהַר וַתֵּלֶד אֶת־קַיִן וַתֹּאמֶר קָנִיתִי אִישׁ אֶת־יְהוָה׃
vahā'ā<u>d</u>ām (Adam) *yā<u>d</u>a'* (knew) *'e<u>t</u>* (and) *ḥauāh* (Eve) *išatvō* (the wife) *vatahar* (conceived) *vatēle<u>d</u>* (generated) *'e<u>t</u>* (and) *qayin* (Cain possession) *vatō'mer* (said) *qāniy<u>t</u>iy* (I got possession) *'iyš* (man) *'e<u>t</u>* (from) *yahvāh* (Transcendent)
Αδαμ *Adam* (Adam) δὲ *de* (indeed) ἔγνω *egnō* (knew) Ευαν *Euan* (Eve) τὴν *tēn* (the) γυναῖκα *gunaika* (wife) αὐτοῦ *autou* (his) καὶ *kai* (and) συλλαβοῦσα *sullabousa* (took) ἔτεκεν *etekev* (generated) τὸν *ton* (the) Καιν *Kain* (Cain) καὶ *kai* (and) εἶπεν *eipen* (said) ἐκτησάμην *ektēsamen* (I gained) ἄνθρωπον *anthrōpon* (man) διὰ *dia* (from) τοῦ *tou* (the) θεοῦ *theou* (God)
Adam (Adam) **vero** (indeed) **cognovit** (knew) **Havam** (Eve) **uxorem** (wife) **suam** (his) **quae** (who) **concepit** (conceived) **et** (and) **peperit** (generated) **Cain** (Cain) **dicens** (saing) **possedi** (I possess) **hominem** (a man) **per** (from) **Dominum** (the Lord)
And Adam knew Eve his wife; and she conceived, and bare Cain, and said, I have gotten a man from the LORD.
Indeed Adam wedded Eve his wife. Thus, she conceived and generated/conceived Cain-possession and she said, "*I possess a man-subject from Transcendence.*"

    The cosmic Big Bang, the event from which we originated, projects the entire Cosmos together with the Earth towards its own glare awaiting for us in the future, at the border of the universe. Then, that resounding brilliance reveals itself as that boom from which its cycle generates all over again. Astronomically, the future is our past occurrence. Looking into space, we will experience current and past events generated in and by future occurrences. In 1985, our future was *gestating* an event that would have eventually materialized, on Feb. 23/24, 1987, as a Type II Supernova 1987A in the Dorado Constellation of the Large Magellanic Cloud. Upon its discovery by the Royal Astronomical Society of New Zealand,[1201] the Las Campanas Observatory[1202] placed it in the past of 167,885 light years. Similarly, the current Alpha Centauri starlight twinkling will appear in our future night sky four years from now. Also the luminosity we will perceive a minute from now will be the sun's light of eight minutes before. We are time travelers riding backwards. We come from the unknown looking behind into history. The gravitational pull of the future sinks us in the black hole of the past. In it, we project that which will be coming. We are the deluge behind the sound of thunder that follows the flash of lightning. We chase our own tail. Daily we understand time only as running forward, however, in the quantum dimension, time moves both forward and backward,[1203] hence, the assumed capability to prophecy and foresee.[1204]

    History is the way we know this world, namely, as past. Some African animistic religions view history as moving backwards, from *Sasa*, this *current period*, to *Zamani*, the mythical *past age* of the dead ancestors toward which we are going.[1205] We die because we view ourselves [1206]⇨ as past, as that which is already given standing before our understanding. This is the outcome of eating from the epistemic Tree of Knowledge of Good and Bad. History starts at *conception*. Before we were born, we had no historical mind. Therefore, there was no history for us. Only now, we study what we understand as having taken place before our birth. However, we acknowledge it and make sense of it only after coming to life. Then, it becomes as that which was and is never identically repeatable. Thus, <u>that which was</u>, **is** dead. Moreover, before *conception*, we did not know. After death, we will not know. In fact,

    "*the world knoweth... him* [God] *not.... * [however] *when he shall appear, we shall be like him; for <u>we shall behold him as he is</u>* [in-itself, when]*... every man... purifieth himself, even as he is pure.*"[1207]

    While in the world of the duality of good and evil, history connects to life, which produces the mind. This last one acknowledges the existence of life, history and death. We could not recognize them if we were not conscious-*of* them. Millions of shining suns do not break-dawn in front completely blind eyes.

Similarly, losing consciousness-*of* history is like having Alzheimer's disease.[1208] Furthermore, losing consciousness-*of* the world is as being in catalepsy. Finally, losing the pulsating-*consciousness-of* the body organism, *of* its biological molecular structure and/or *of* its DNA instructions is being dead.

Psychological analyses of various paradigmatic aspects of the human psyche start with this chapter. In this physical historical dimension, Adam and Eve are not our past prehistoric ancestors. Nor they are any longer the logical subject-object epistemic structure. They are the actual physical male/female paradigmatic conditions. They are our present *primordial* human being configuration. Now, Adam is any physical human husband who *carnally-knows* (יָדַע *yada`*) his wife Eve. She is any physical human wife who *conceives* (*harah*)[1209] and *generates* (*yalad*)[1210] offspring, namely, the classic configuration of *every human being* ('iysh) ever born. The word *man, 'iysh,*[1211] means also *husband, human being, person, whosoever* and *another*. The word derives from *'anash,*[1212] which means *to be weak, ill.* In fact, the male-subject becomes weak when it does not execute its functions, namely, it is not in synthesis with its female-object, thus forming the one female/male Adam. The objective-life, Eve herself, generates another-subjective-husband (אִישׁ *'iysh*) who, in turn, will possess again the objective-world. Adam is the wakeful consciousness-*of*-the-objective-world. Metaphorically, therefore, s/he is the masculine subject father figure, a mere spectator remaining in a state of impotence. Eve, on the other hand, is the feminine conscious power[1213] that <has two dominant aspects, both metaphorically indicated as mother figures because, as consciousness-*of*, they generate the known world.

1) The first aspect is Consciousness, which goes back to its original Awareness (as Mary Magdalene repenting).[1214] Then, it becomes Pure Consciousness (as an Assumption to Heaven).[1215]
2) The second aspect is that of desire, of the temptress (as Venus) and of the seducer (as Eve), who is conscious-*of* eating and offering the object for the subject to eat and know.>[1216]

Nobody really knows (יָדַע *yada`*)[1217] who the *other* (אִישׁ 'iysh), the neighboring interlocutor is *in-itself*, what s/he thinks, how s/he feels and so on. The closest answer to this quest for the other-in-itself is the act of copulation. This act (יָדַע *yada`*) physically fulfills the epistemic captivation of the subject into the object, namely the act of *truly-knowing* (יָדַע *yada`*) the other. Nevertheless, the outcome of this action is still an unknown other. The question is, '*Who was the offspring before the female ovum becomes a fertilized human gamete? Where does the germ cell come from?*' The answer can only be *Unknown*. The other person, in general, is the mysterious one. S/he is unidentified before birth, during life and after death. In fact, no one knows what s/he really thinks and who s/he really is in-itself.

The name of the first child born from Life-Eve (חַוָּה Chavvah) is Cain. In Hebrew, Cain, *Qayin,*[1218] means *possession*. Therefore, Eve, *viz. life* itself, possesses, *qanah,*[1219] a male son, namely, another subject to start the epistemic circle all over again. Eve, as the Object, meaningfully expresses the statement that confirms her possession (קָנִיתִי *qāniytiy*) of him. Consequently, Cain, *Possession* himself, will declare ownership of his newly awaken universe of knowledge. However, where does he come from? He comes from the Unknown Transcendence Itself (יְהוָֹה *Yĕhovah*).

4:2-Birth of Abel

וַתֹּסֶף לָלֶדֶת אֶת־אָחִיו אֶת־הָבֶל וַיְהִי־הֶבֶל רֹעֵה צֹאן וְקַיִן הָיָה עֹבֵד אֲדָמָה׃ *vatōsep̄* (once more) *lāledet̠* (she generated) *'et̠* (and) *'āḥiyv* (brother) *'et̠* (and) *hāb̠el* (Abel) *vayahiy* (was) *heb̠el* (Abel) *rō'ēh* (herder) *ṣō'n* (of sheep) *vaqayin* (Cain) *hāyāh* (was) *'ōb̠ēd̠* (worker) *'ăd̠āmāh* (of the red land)
καὶ *kai* (and) **προσέθηκεν** *prosethēken* (again she added) **τεκεῖν** *tekein* (generated) **τὸν** *ton* (the) **ἀδελφὸν** *adelphos* (brother) **αὐτοῦ** *autou* (his) **τὸν** *ton* (the) **Αβελ** *Abel* (Abel) **καὶ** *kai* (and) **ἐγένετο** *egeneto* (was) **Αβελ** *Abel* (Abel) **ποιμὴν** *poimēn* (shepherd) **προβάτων** *probatōn* (of sheep) **Καιν** *Cain* (Cain) **δὲ** *de* (but) **ἦν** *ēn* (was) **ἐργαζόμενος** *ergazomenos* (worker) **τὴν** *tēn* (of the) **γῆν** *gēn* (land)
rursus (again)***-que*** (and) ***peperit*** (generated) ***fratrem*** (brother) ***eius*** (his) ***Abel*** (Abel) ***fuit*** (was) ***autem*** (also) ***Abel*** (Abel) ***pastor*** (herder) ***ovium*** (of sheep) ***et*** (and) ***Cain*** (Cain) ***agricola*** (a farmer)

And she again bare his brother Abel. And Abel was a keeper of sheep, but Cain was a tiller of the ground.
Once more, she generated/caused his brother, Abel. In addition, Abel was the herder-ruler of the sheep-senses and Cain was the worker in the field of life.

We must understand who these brothers are and what the difference between Cain and Abel is. First, they come from the same mother, Life (חַוָּה *Chavvah*). Thus, they share the same blood. Second, their names can clarify their differences. As explained, Cain means possession. Now we know that he labors[1220] in the *'adamah*, the red field[1221] of Adam/subject's state of wakefulness. Therefore, he is the owner of life's field in which he works. Cain is Adam's first born because the first thing that takes place, when we come in the red-field (אֲדָמָה *'adamah*) of dream and/or wakefulness, is to posses representations, to act by tilling that land. On the other hand, Abel,[1222] in Hebrew, means vapor, air, vanity, nothingness,[1223] *breath*,[1224] and also to become vain, to act *emptily*.[1225] Thus, he is the state of dreamless sleep (NREM). Abel is the unknown breath, the central cohesive unconscious/consciousness belonging to all the animal-senses, metaphorically called sheep. In fact, without breath or air all senses expire.[1226] Therefore, allegorically Abel is the keeper and the ruler[1227] of cows, sheep and the multitude of other animals.[1228] As we have seen, the animals (חַי *chay*), metaphorically, are the active, living sense-appetite for experience.[1229] Abel is the second born because, after Cain's work's possession, he is the one who surrenders his animal/senses activity by sacrificing them.

Thus, while Cain is the possessor of the external fields of life's awaken activity, Abel is the psychological controller of all senses, the state of dreamless sleep. From these considerations, we can state that Abel and Cain are the two major human functions, the introvert spiritual purpose and the extrovert materialist occupation. Cain and Abel are not two different persons. They are two different possible directions present in every person. Both form different states of being. One may be more prone to search the way of the heart, while the other may follow the way of the wallet. Whichever prevails will set a personality in opposition with the other.

4:3-At the End of Cain's Day

וַיְהִי מִקֵּץ יָמִים וַיָּבֵא קַיִן מִפְּרִי הָאֲדָמָה מִנְחָה לַיהוָה׃ *vayahiy* (it come to pass) *miqēṣ* (at the end) *yāmiym* (of the days) *vayāḇē* (brought) *qayin* (Cain) *mipariy* (fruits) *hā'ăḏāmāh* (out of the land) *minaḥāh* (offering) *layhvāh* (to the Transcendent)
καὶ *kai* (and) **ἐγένετο** *egeneto* (it was) **μεθ'** *met'* (after) **ἡμέρας** *ēmeras* (the day) **ἤνεγκεν** *ēnegken* (brought) **Καιν** *Kain* (Cain) **ἀπὸ** *apo* (from) **τῶν** *tōn* (of the) **καρπῶν** *kiarpōn* (fruit) **τῆς** *tēs* (of the) **γῆς** *gēs* (earth) **θυσίαν** *thusian* (a sacrifice) **τῷ** *tō* (to) **κυρίῳ** *kuiiō* (Lord)
factum (accomplished) ***est*** (is) ***autem*** (also) ***post*** (after) ***multos*** (many) ***dies*** (days) ***ut*** (that) ***offerret*** (offered) ***Cain*** (Cain) ***de*** (from) ***fructibus*** (the fruits) ***terrae*** (of the earth) ***munera*** (sacrifice) ***Domino*** (to the Lord)
And in process of time it came to pass, that Cain brought of the fruit of the ground an offering unto the LORD.
Cain, having accomplished the end of the days, offered in sacrifice to the Transcendent the fruits of the earth.

The literally pedantic law doctors waste their time uselessly analyzing the agricultural nature of Cain's offering in this verse. They do not understand, instead, that we are here at the presence of Cain's death at the *end of his days*. Paradigmatically, his persona dies as we all do. When we die, willingly or unwillingly, we surrender all our deeds, namely, the fruits of our actions stemming from the epistemic circularity, to the mystery of the unknown. In fact, the word *qets*,[1230] means *at the end of time and space*, it is a contraction from *qatsats*, signifying *to amputate*, *to cut off*. Therefore, at the end of his circular days (יוֹם *yowm*) of consciousness, Cain (קַיִן *Qayin*) brings (בּוֹא *bow'*) his passionate-possession (קַיִן *qayin*) into the Transcendent (יְהֹוָה *Yĕhovah*). Namely, he surrenders his actions to the stillness of death. Then and there, he offers (מִנְחָה *minchah*) the fruit (פְּרִי *pĕriy*), the outcome of all his activities in the field of life. Those are the *thorny* produce of the *ground* (אֲדָמָה *'adamah*) *cursed* (אָרַר *'arar*) by God in *Genesis* 3:17.

This is not a real surrender. Is there anything admirable about giving up one's activity at the end of life? Is it a real renunciation of life or is it compulsion? Is there any enlightening lesson that has been learned from it? The dying person perishes attached to life and its accomplishments. Therefore, Cain, as template of passionate-possession, does not relinquish his possessive predisposition. He still desires to eat the forbidden fruit, which, like the Homeric lotus,[1231] makes the dying person become oblivious of the Tree of Life's Awareness from which s/he derives.

4:4-Abel's Offering

וְהֶבֶל הֵבִיא גַם־הוּא מִבְּכֹרוֹת צֹאנוֹ וּמֵחֶלְבֵהֶן וַיִּשַׁע יְהוָה אֶל־הֶבֶל וְאֶל־מִנְחָתוֹ׃   *vahebel* (Abel) *hēbiy'* (brought) *gam* (also) *hu'* (he) *mibakōrvōt* (out of) *ṣō'nvō* (flock) *umēḥelabēhen* (out of the fat) *vayiša'* (acknowledged) *yahvāh* (Transcendent) *'el* (to the) *hebel* (Abel) *va'el* (those) *minaḥātvō* (offering)
καὶ *kai* (and) **Αβελ** *Abel* (Abel) **ἤνεγκεν** *ēnegken* (brought) **καὶ** *kai* (and) **αὐτὸς** *autos* (he) **ἀπὸ** *apo* (from) **τῶν** *tōn* (the) **πρωτοτόκων** *prōtotkōn* (firstborn) **τῶν** *tōn* (of the) **προβάτων** *probatōn* (sheep) **αὐτοῦ** *autou* (his) **καὶ** *kai* (and) **ἀπὸ** *apo* (from) **τῶν** *tōn* (the) **στεάτων** *steatōn* (fatning) **αὐτῶν** *autōn* (his) **καὶ** *kai* (and) **ἐπεῖδεν** *epeiden* (acknowledged) **ὁ** *o* (the) **θεὸς** *theos* (God) **ἐπὶ** *epi* (upon) **Αβελ** *Abel* (Abel) **καὶ** *kai* (and) **ἐπὶ** *epi* (upon) **τοῖς** *tois* (the) **δώροις** *dōrois* (offerings) **αὐτοῦ** *autou* (his)
Abel (Abel) ***quoque*** (also) ***obtulit*** (brought) ***de*** (of the) ***primogenitis*** (first born) ***gregis*** (of the flock) ***sui*** (his) ***et*** (and) ***de*** (of the) ***adipibus*** (fat) ***eorum*** (their) ***et*** (and) ***respexit*** (had respect) ***Dominus*** (the Lord) ***ad*** (for) ***Abel*** (Abel) ***et*** (and) ***ad*** (for) ***munera*** (offering) ***eius*** (his)
And Abel, he also brought of the firstlings of his flock and of the fat thereof. And the LORD had respect unto Abel and to his offering:
Abel offered also the first-born of his flock and their opulence and the Transcendent acknowledged Abel and his offering.

If we take this verse and creation literally, then the questions arise, '*why would God require animal sacrifice? Does He not, as a Creator, possess them already?*'

Then, even from a literal interpretation, the intent of sacrifice is not to slaughter animals but a different one. In fact,

> "'*To what purpose is the multitude of your sacrifices unto me?' saith the Transcendent* (יְהֹוָה *Yĕhovah*): '*I am full of the burnt offerings of rams, and the fat of fed beasts; and I delight not in the blood of bullocks, or of lambs, or of he goats.*'"[1232]

The value of sacrifice rests in its act of renunciation, of offering (מִנְחָה *minchah*) performed by the worshiper. It is giving up (בּוֹא *bow'*) passionate-possession, namely, Cain's opposite.

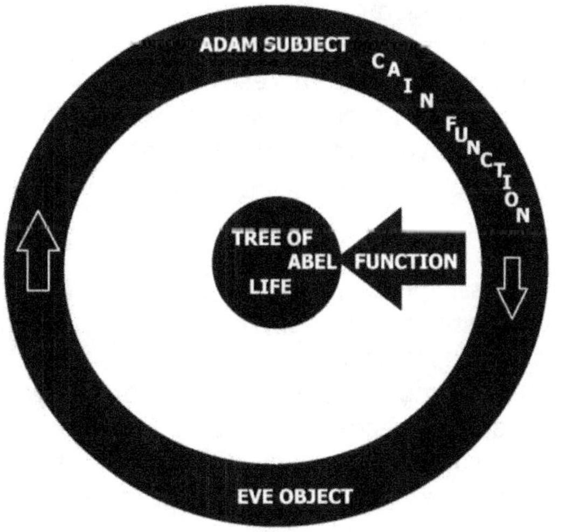

GRAPHIC: *Cain-Abel's functions*

In this verse, the Breath of Abel gives up his flock (צֹאן *tso'n*), *viz.* the main senses (בְּכוֹרָה *bĕkowrah*) and their fatty opulence (חֵלֶב *cheleb*). Namely, it enters in the state of auto-transparency. It quiets the senses, it renounces to the best part (חֵלֶב *cheleb*) of them, *viz.* the connecting desire with the objects. Therefore, when

"*all things were now accomplished, that the scripture might be fulfilled,*"[1233]

Abel enters the resting state of apnea. He identifies with the Resting State of the Divine Breath, which, unseen, looks, unheard, listens, not savored, tastes, non-sniffed, smells, unfelt, feels, non-acting, acts, not-thought, thinks, unknown, knows and loves without desire. It is the continuous identification within the Pure Consciousness leading into Awareness. Therefore, Awareness *acknowledges* (שָׁעָה *sha'ah*)[1234] Abel. By giving up his attachment to the senses, Abel shows no affection for the object of knowledge. He identifies with the Tree of Life disregarding the Tree of Knowledge of Good and Evil.

4:5-Cain's Wrath

וְאֶל־קַיִן וְאֶל־מִנְחָתוֹ לֹא שָׁעָה וַיִּחַר לְקַיִן מְאֹד וַיִּפְּלוּ פָּנָיו׃ *va'el* (those) *qayin* (Cain) *va'el* (that) *minaḥāṯvō* (offering) *lō* (no) *šā'āh* (acknowledgment) *vayiḥar* (wrath) *laqayin* (Cain) *ma'ōḏ* (much) *vayipalu* (fell) *pānāyv* (face)
ἐπὶ *epi* (upon) **δὲ** *de* (but) **Καιν** *Kain* (of Cain) **καὶ** *kai* (and) **ἐπὶ** *epi* (upon) **ταῖς** *tais* (the) **θυσίαις** *thusias* (sacrifica) **αὐτοῦ** *autou* (his) **οὐ** *ou* (not) **προσέσχεν** *proseschen* (acknowledge) **καὶ** *kai* (and) **ἐλύπησεν** *elupēsen* (sorrowful) **τὸν** *ton* (the) **Καιν** *Kain* (Cain) **λίαν** *lian* (very much) **καὶ** *kai* (and) **συνέπεσεν** *sunepesen* (fell) **τῷ** *tō* (the) **προσώπῳ** *prosōpō* (face)
ad (to) ***Cain*** (Cain) ***vero*** (indeed) ***et*** (and) ***ad*** (to) ***munera*** (offering) ***illius*** (his) ***non*** (not) ***respexit*** (respected) ***iratus-*** (angry)***que*** (and) ***est*** (is) ***Cain*** (Cain) ***vehementer*** (strongly) ***et*** (and) ***concidit*** (fell down) ***vultus*** (face) ***eius*** (his)
But unto Cain and to his offering he had not respect. And Cain was very wroth, and his countenance fell.
Indeed, He did not look at Cain and his sacrifice. Cain was burning with great anger, he turned his face away from Him and his face fade away.

Cain and Abel perform two different sacrifices. Why one is acknowledged by the Transcendent, while the other is not? To understand this, we must recognize two moments,

1) One is the descending process, during which the desirous-hungry ego of Cain is conscious-*of* and identifies with his activity progressively sloping (נָפַל *naphal*) into the world full of death.
2) The other is the ascending process, in which the desireless 'I' of Abel identifies with the Self in-Itself.

Cain is the template of our passionate-possession, which assimilates the fruit of the Tree of Knowledge. We toil in the world to increase our possessions. We perceive our accumulated wealth as real in-itself. The famous affirmation of Protagoras,

"Man is the measure of all things,"[1235]

<was resurrected by the Renaissance Merchant Princes who, empowered by money deriving from banking and trading, created a new Humanism. In time, the Protestant Reformation recognized the economic appeal[1236] as having a sacred inherent quality conferring a charisma and a sort of spiritual power.>[1237]

"Money, as the measure against which all things are priced, is the contemporary principle of the value of values."[1238]

Thus, Calvin asserts that

"the Lord ... bestows many blessings ... upon those ... men ... to prove how... he does not allow ... righteousness to go without a temporal reward...They even take the fruits of regeneration as proof of the indwelling of ... God's help in all their necessities."[1239]

There is a deification of wealth. To produce its fruit, our labor is always intentioned towards a reality conceptualized as external, thus, as transcendent. Therefore, we offer our work to riches as *divine grace*. In fact, we offer our gains as reinvestment to produce more profit. It is common to hear religious believers refer to their alms or tithes as *seed-offerings*[1240] made in order to receive multiplied gains.

Eventually, however, compelled by death, Cain's capability to live fades away. Regretting all the unfulfilled dreams and starving for life anew, Cain dies

"desperate, never having loved life as much."[1241]

Thus, at death, the paradigmatic Cain is distraught and unwilling to die. Nevertheless, s/he makes the ultimate offering. S/he gives-up all laboring activities in the field of life and offers them to the Mysterious-End.

However, Cain's death-*sacrifice* is not Abel's ritual renunciation. At death, the emotional attachment to the world sheds its grip and we seem to lose all interest in it. The indifference towards the objective world occurs only for two reasons:

a) We simply die, like any average Cain out there, and we reluctantly fade away (נָפַל *naphal*) with our sacrifice. Or,
b) While living, like Abel, we realize the Apodictical Certitude and we awake into the insight of Divine Awareness.

This is the difference between Cain and Abel. The first one, Cain, is a tiller who offered his work to the transcending profit and, at the time of death, is compelled by life's exhaustion to give up all the fruits of his actions. However, this offering in not done at the Light of the Resting-Transcendent, thus, his sacrifice is not *acknowledged* by Pure-Awareness. Consequently, Cain, like all of us, becomes a

"*being for death.*"[1242]

On the other hand, Abel is the sense-herder who offers to the Transcendent the prime of his live-senses-animal and this sacrifice is *acknowledged* by Awareness. In fact, no interfering distracting labor comes between him and Certainty.

"*Take no thought for your life... Behold the fowls of the air: for they sow not, neither do they reap, nor gather into barns... Consider the lilies of the field, how they grow; they toil not, neither do they spin... Take therefore no thought for the morrow: for the morrow shall take thought for the things of itself. Sufficient unto the day is the evil thereof.*"[1243]

This is the state of total identification with Transcendent Awareness in-Itself, the Omniscient, Omni-Aware. God is Transcendent by definition and It is synonym of Pure Loving Consciousness, which gives completely of Itself. Awareness is Love in that it gives Itself unconditionally without asking anything in return.

"*Love your enemies, bless them that curse you, do good to them that hate you, and pray for them which despitefully use you, and persecute you...*[1244] *hoping for nothing again.*"[1245]

Awareness is Love and Love is Transcendent. We can say nothing about God, Love or Transcendence. We may think of them but we can never know Them. We can feel Love, but not know It. The feeling of Love is its effect not its origin. We can never know that cause as an object. We can only conceptualize it mythologically, metaphorically, poetically or identify it with physical gratification, which are not Love-in-itself. Likely, we recognize Love in the beloved one or the desired one. This one becomes the mask, the face, or the veil that covers the true Transcendent Love. When the veil, the *True-icon* (*Vera-icona*) transpires Transcendence, then, we realize the beloved in its Loving Purity. However, as it happens most of the times, when the mask or the veil covers and obscures the invisible *nakedness* of Love, then we experience only its objectivity obfuscating the Light, which we are really seeking.[1246]

In this immanent objective world, Jacob saw

"*the place called facing God* (*peniel*)*... face to face* (פָּנִים *paniym*)."[1247]

Therefore, as subject, Jacob lived to know his God as his own object, not as God in-Itself. In fact,

"*the Lord spake*[1248] *unto Moses face to face* (פָּנִים *paniym*)*, as a man speaketh unto his friend... And he said, Thou canst not see my face: for there shall no man see me, and live,*"[1249]

namely, establish a subject-object correlation.

God loves because He, as Awareness, is Unconditional-Giving-of-Itself, thus is Love. Then, how could He have loved Adam and Eve less after they disobeyed? God's love for Abel is not different from the one He has for Cain. What "*He did not accept*" was Cain's *offer* not Cain as His creature. Awareness cannot accept the *fruits* of Cain's possession. Because It is Awareness without identification with the object of consciousness. Furthermore, it is not God rejecting him, but Cain shunning away from Him. In fact, Cain was burning (חָרַר *charar)*[1250] with anger,[1251] his face[1252] turned away[1253] from Him and he fell as in a deep fading away (נָפַל *naphal*).[1254]

The creative-Aware-Love of God towards human beings is not moody. It does not have a degree or an *order*. God does not *have a change of heart*, namely, love in one degree at the time of creation and reconsider it when the creature sins. God's projecting act is the creating *fiat* out of love to the point of Self-sacrifice. In fact, a lack or a lesser degree of that creative-love would result inevitably in non-existence or in an impossible *minor* existence for the creature, if that could be conceivable at all. By its own nature, God's Creative-Aware-Love must always be there untarnished, identical for a saint, a Socrates or[1255] a sinner. For this last one, in fact, God promises the advent of the Messiah.[1256] A *perfect* parent cannot have favoritism. Properly, s/he should not condone misbehavior but s/he would not love less an offspring who is

> "a superficial egotist, an unreliable scoundrel... [on the assumption that only] the gracious, noble child *deserves* to be loved more... [on account of the] unique significance of his deep repentance,"[1257]

as in the parable of the prodigal son. In it, a son demands his father for his inheritance, only to squander it away from home. The parent, however, waits to rejoice at his son's return. He loved his prodigal son even before his repentance. The father, unselfishly and out of love, gave him his

> "*share of the estate*"[1258]

and continued to love and look out for his return even while he was an *ungrateful sinner*.[1259] For pure Love, it is not necessary

> "that the other reciprocates"[1260]

one's love, in order to be called friend. God does not love more or less. Contrary to von Hildebrand's assumption, there cannot be any

> "value hierarchy"[1261]

in His Love. There is no hierarchy in Pure Consciousness. God does not love the sin, because it is a negation of love, but always loves the sinner, even when in Hell. Obviously, God does not distance Himself from the sinner, but it is this last one who rejects God's Aware Love. Never let the guard down,

> "*If you want to be perfect, go, sell your possessions and give to the poor, and you will have treasure in heaven. Then come, follow me.*"[1262]

Furthermore, in the presence of

> "the incomparable love for God,"[1263]

all other loves fade in nothingness. Thus,

> "*Love the Lord your God with all your heart and with all your soul and with all your strength.*"[1264]

This is the sublimity of disinterested love. Then,

> "*if... thou shalt seek the LORD thy God, thou shalt find him, if thou seek him with all thy heart and with all thy soul.*"[1265]

Simply put, if Awareness were *to look at* (שָׁעָה *sha`ah*)[1266] Cain's fruit of his action, then Awareness would be conscious-*of* it, thus, It would not be Pure Awareness. On the other side, when the subject is *dis*tracted, tracked *away* (*dis*) from the Transcendent by being (*ad*) *at*tracted[1267] to the objective-*food*, then it becomes a hellish *demonic-power*.[1268] Its mind becomes as a dynamo[1269] in a computer-like-program intentioning its own torment. This is the *Inferno* as described by Dante in his *Divine Comedy*. Hell is being apart from the Transcendent. In Hebrew, *shĕ'owl* (שְׁאוֹל)[1270] means hell, the underworld abode of the dead. It is, figuratively, the place of exile and extreme degradation. It is the

> "*hallow and subterraneum place* derived from the idea of asking, from its asking for, demanding all, without distinction; hence *orcus rapax*."[1271]

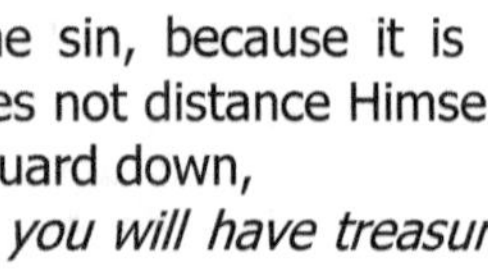

The Hebrew word *shĕ'owl* derives from *sha'al* (שָׁאַל),[1272] meaning to ask, to enquire, to seek and to beg for obtaining something. Therefore, it indicates [1273]⇨ a state of need, hunger and desire. Here we seek experiences. Therefore, hell equates the epistemic subject/object structure of this world.

In an allegorical tale, Plato describes a cave in which slaves, chained from birth, are obliged to look at a game of shadows, which they regard as the ultimate reality. If a slave, able to free himself, would go out of the cave. Then, approaching the external

"light, his eyes will be dazzled, and he will not be able to see anything at all of what are now called realities."[1274]

In that condition, nothing stands between him and the splendor of the sun. In fact, when the former slave, returning to the cave and

"coming suddenly out of the sun to be replaced in his old situation, would he not be certain to have his eyes full of darkness?"[1275]

Furthermore, would he not give little or no importance to his own subjective judgment during the virtual shadow competitions in which the other slaves find exaltation?

Nothing is truly our (*i.e.* Cain) that does not come from the Transcendent. The ultimate Transcendence cannot leave space for our *personal* happiness.[1276]

"*No one can serve two masters. Either he will hate the one and love the other, or he will be devoted to the one and despise the other. You cannot serve both God and selfish interest.*"[1277]

"*If anyone comes to me and does not hate his father and mother, his wife and children, his brothers and sisters -yes, even his own life- he cannot be my disciple.*"[1278]

These very hard and unmistakable words support a disinterested love (*amour desinteressé*). This can explain Abraham's obedience and his readiness to *sacrifice* his beloved son Isaac

"*as a burnt offering*"[1279]

to the Lord. As God had blessed Abel, He blessed Abraham and his descendants,[1280] because of this willingness to fulfill His *jealous* injunction.

"*For I the LORD thy God* [am] *a jealous God.*"[1281]

Nevertheless, by definition, God is Love. Usually, we identify emotion as an outcome of love. However, the possessive pleasurable assimilation of that emotion has nothing to do with Love itself. Thus, Paul declares,

"*Love is not jealous... Love does not demand its own way... and it keeps no record of when it has been wronged.*"[1282]

Therefore, the *jealousy* of God here is in the sense that there is no other ultimate reality than Apodictical Awareness in Itself. In other words, at the end all worldly possessive loving lures disappear without any residue in the light of God's All Loving Awareness. Actually,

"*Whoever wants to save his life*[1283] *will lose it, but whoever loses his life for me will save it.*"[1284]

Therefore, if we want to find what our real personal concern is, we find that it is not our concern at all, because we must renounce to ourselves. In fact,

"*do not worry about your life... consider the ravens, who do not sow... yet God feeds them... the lilies grow, they do not labor... do not worry about it... For where your treasure is, there your heart will be also.*"[1285]

If one loves the Transcendent-Certain-Awareness with the whole heart, which part of it can be left out for the earthly passions? Love is charity. It is the realization that Awareness is the foundation of our true being as well as, concomitantly, of all our neighbors.[1286]

Self-transcendence must be transcendence without any residual immanence in which subjectivity, as purified as it may be, may leave its mark. The subjectivity of Cain demands to receive that which is '*mine*.' However, the true concern must be God Awareness and Awareness only,

"*seek his kingdom, and these things will be given to you as well.*"[1287]

"[The] dissolution of subjectivity... [is not] annihilation of personal existence,"[1288]

because the eternal Aware creative act of God, which is the ineffable essence of our most intimate reality, establishes it.

If and only if creation is real, by definition that *moment* must also be always here and now. Placing creation in a different time or space would imply a temporality or a spatiality that would contradict God's Infinite Eternity and the creation of time/space. Then, the presence of God's creative Awareness is the most fundamental core of any being, without which the creature would not be. Our personality and our subjectivity must be, in essence, the image of the presence of the Transcendent Awareness. That reflection is our true essence. It is our 'Self' and our own true way of being in life.[1289] Ontologically, our subjectivity must be

"*the image*[1290] *of God.*"[1291]

This likeness radiates the unique individuality of our own-life, *i.e.*

"all those things that are of concern to me."[1292]

This is the 'I' that, in a

"Super Value-Response,"[1293]

must reflect the light of Awareness[1294] of God's creation. However, how can one distinguish a pure mirror made *of* Light, *by* the Light, *for* the Light, *with* the Light and *in* the Light from the Light itself?[1295]

"This dialogue with God"[1296]

finds our true happiness in love, in Its love for us and through our love for It. What catches our love must be the Transcendent Beauty of the image of God, the

"*image of the Transcendent,*"[1297]

discovered by both lovers in each other's eyes and, in turn, transcended by God Itself.

Epistemically, the subject inevitably sees the other always as an object. However, an interpersonal subject-object relation distinguishes an object from a thing.[1298] The thing is that which is placed *there* for our use, like when we reach out for our pen, with no further consideration. When, however, we reflect on the ontological nature of the object, then, it is always referred

"in relation to the I."[1299]

In this case, there is an interpersonal relationship caracterized by a transcending quality conferred to the object. This interpersonal relation may refer to a person as well as a thing. Verga's short story of Mazzarò portrays a self-made, very wealthy Sicilian owner, who, facing death, went on a rampage killing all his livestock, and screaming,

"My *belongings*, come away with me!"[1300]

In this case, the *possessions* were viewed as having an internal, inherent quality conceived vital and essential for the person, as if the *properties* had become a metaphysical extension of the person itself. This is Cain's worldview. In the subjectivity devoid of real transcendent afflatus, one finds the other only as an object *per-se*. There, obfuscated by the enigmatic mirror[1301] of the objective immanent world, the divine image dims into egotism. Thus, we annihilate our true Self as Pure image of Transcendence in-Itself. Then, we negate ourselves as the likeness *of*

"*the true light that illuminates every man who comes into the world.*"[1302]

Therefore, we negate Transcendence-in-Itself, separating It from the life of our ego. On the other hand, if we dissolve our egotistic subjectivity in the total unconditional love for our neighbors, then we recognize the divine spark in us.

One does not need to go out of its own subjectivity to find the other, because the other is in

"the *intentio unionis* [intention of the union]... of the self-donation of love,"[1303]

where the 'Thou' becomes "the 'lord' of our subjectivity," namely,

"*love thy neighbour as thyself.*"[1304]

We can never know our neighbor unless we quiet our own ego and love our fellow being unconditionally with all our heart. In turn, that love is a reflection of the highest love that the 'Self' has inherently always for the Transcendent, even when not manifested.[1305]

4:6-Why the distress?

וַיֹּאמֶר יְהוָה אֶל־קָיִן לָמָּה חָרָה לָךְ וְלָמָּה נָפְלוּ פָנֶיךָ׃
vayō'mer (said) *yahvāh* (the Transcendent)'*el* (to) *qāyin* (Cain) *lāmāh* (why) *ḥārāh* (anger) *lāḵa* (thy) *valāmāh* (why) *nāp̄alu* (fell) *p̄āneyḵā* (face)
καὶ *kai* (and) **εἶπεν** *eipen* (said) **κύριος** *kurios* (Lord) **ὁ** *o* (the) **θεὸς** *theos* (God) **τῷ** *tō* (to) **Καιν** *Kain* (Cain) **ἵνα** *iva* (why) **τί** *ti* (you) **περίλυπος** *perilupos* (angry) **ἐγένου** *egenou* (are) **καὶ** *kai*

(and) **ἵνα** *iva* (that) **τί** *ti* (why) **συνέπεσεν** *sunepesen* (fell down) **τὸ** *to* (the) **πρόσωπόν** *prosōpon* (face) **σου** *sou* (your)
dixit- (said)***que*** (and) ***Dominus*** (Lord) ***ad*** (to) ***eum*** (him) ***quare*** (why) ***maestus*** (sad) ***es*** (you are) ***et*** (and) ***cur*** (why) ***concidit*** (fell down) ***facies*** (face) ***tua*** (yours)
And the LORD said unto Cain, Why art thou wroth? and why is thy countenance fallen?
And the Transcendent said to Cain, "*Why are you burning with anger? Why you turned your face away?*

Cain's possessions stand as mountains between him and the Transcendent. They impede the direct realization of Awareness. Cain turns away from the Transcendent. Away from It, he finds the great distress (חָרָה *charah*) of life, which separates him from the Love of Awareness. The epistemic structure of each one of us <u>is</u> that of Cain. His activity is furiously shuttling between the subject and the object, which we possess. This friction is his burning labor, which produces knowledge. The *Bṛhadāraṇyaka Upanishad*, states that Mṛtyu-Death,

"*moved about <u>heated</u>. From him waters were produced... which solidified and became the earth.*"[1306]

Similarly, Cain's continuous ferrying from subject to object and return, generates the hot and furious (חָרָה *charah*)[1307] consuming-*of* burning (חָרַר *charar*)[1308] knowledge. Therefore, he turns his face away by falling and fading (נָפַל *naphal*) into death. The difference, between this *burning* (חָרַר *charar*) of Cain and Exodus' Burning (*ba'ar* בָּעַר) Bush (*cĕnah* סְנֶה), is that the first one consumes the deadly object of his knowledge while the second never consumes itself. One is consciousness-*of* while the second one is Pure-Still-Awareness.

4:7-Actions' Outcome

הֲלוֹא אִם־תֵּיטִיב שְׂאֵת וְאִם לֹא תֵיטִיב לַפֶּתַח חַטָּאת רֹבֵץ וְאֵלֶיךָ תְּשׁוּקָתוֹ וְאַתָּה תִּמְשָׁל־בּוֹ׃ *hălvō̆* (you not) *'im* (if) *tēyṭiyḇ* (do well) *śa'ēṯ* (shall be lifted up) *va'im* (if) *lō̆* (not) *ṯēyṭiyḇ* (do well) *lapeṯaḥ* (doorway) *ḥaṭā't* (sin) *rōḇēṣ* (lieth) *va'ēleykā* (not) *tašuqāṯvō* (desire) *va'atāh* (come) *timašāl* (rule) *bvō* (if)
οὐκ *ouk* (not) **ἐὰν** *ean* (if) **ὀρθῶς** *orthōs* (rightly) **προσενέγκης** *prosenegkēs* (you have brought) **ὀρθῶς** *orthōs* (rightly) **δὲ** *de* (but) **μὴ** *mē* (not) **διέλῃς** *dielēs* (divided) **ἥμαρτες** *ēmartes* (sin) **ἡσύχασον** *ēsuxason* (be at rest) **πρὸς** *pros* (from) **σὲ** *se* (he) **ἡ** *ē* (the) **ἀποστροφὴ** *apostrophē* (submission) **αὐτοῦ** *autou* (he) **καὶ** *kai* (and) **σὺ** *su* (he) **ἄρξεις** *arxeis* (you shall rule) **αὐτοῦ** *autou* (him)
nonne (not) ***si*** (if) ***bene*** (well) ***egeris*** (you do) ***recipies*** (shall you be received) ***sin*** (if) ***autem*** (instead) ***male*** (bad) ***statim*** (immediately) ***in*** (in) ***foribus*** (openings) ***peccatum*** (sin) ***aderit*** (is present) ***sed*** (but) ***sub*** (under) ***te*** (you) ***erit*** (was) ***appetitus*** (the appetite) ***eius*** (his) ***et*** (and) ***tu*** (you) ***dominaberis*** (shall dominate) ***illius*** (that)
If thou doest well, shalt thou not be accepted? and if thou doest not well, sin lieth at the door. And unto thee shall be his desire, and thou shalt rule over him.
Should you not be lifted up if you do well? Instead, if you do not do well, immediately the consequence for the missed mark is present for you under the doorway with its hungry desire, which you should dominate."

In the field of life, actions dominate the destiny of human beings. However, the correct action is to control (מָשַׁל *mashal*) the hungry desire (תְּשׁוּקָה *tĕshuwqah*). Then, the human will do well (יָטַב *yatab*) and s/he will be accepted, lifted up[1309] along the Tree of Life. Truthfully, this is not an action at all. It is like Abel directing the senses inward. It is to stay still[1310] in the Resting Breath. It is reaching and recognizing the fundamental eternity of Apodictical-Awareness, which has no beginning and no end. Cain, on the other hand, stands at the doorway (פֶּתַח *pethach*) of the Garden of Eden. There lies (רָבַץ *rabats*) *sin*.

There is the belief that non-violence (*a-hiṃsā*) equates to peace. This finds no correspondence in a Cosmos created full of violent change and destruction. Therefore, in the political arena, when confronted with war, what is the correct action a leader should take? Jesus declared,

"*I came not to send peace, but a sword,*"[1311]

and the Templar[1312] Monks Knight gave an answer with their humble war behavior, similar to the battle manners of the opposing Muslim militia. On the same line, the *Bhagavad Gītā* explains in details that the leader, <in a state of Pure-Awareness, without any desire, without any worry or mental anguish, should engage in the battle of this life without desiring its outcomes.>[1313] Therefore, Lord Kṛshṇa orders prince Arjuna to fight. In fact, he declares,

"*Having rejected all attachments, perform your actions in a state of union* (*yoga*); *be unaffected by victory as well as failure.*"[1314]

Throughout history, non-violence has never eliminated completely political controversies. An example, Gandhi's heroic

"e*xperiments with Truth*"[1315]

was not able to eliminate the premises for the unrests, killings and wars between India and Pakistan.[1316] In any case, non-violence means the identification with the Transcendent Awareness without fulfilling any personal interest, while letting the action take place according to the required duties.

The general interpretation for *sin* is that of a performed action/thought/omission, which was forbidden and/or imposed by an authoritative power. We are conscious-*of* it as a negative, *immoral* deed, which may generate a sense of remorse. However, the consciousness-*of* the guilt deriving from that negative action becomes another object of thought that further aggravates the first error itself. In fact, the remorse, deriving from the perceived evil deed, could produce psychological and physical disorders.[1317]

However, the Hebrew word for *sin* is *chatta'ath* (חַטָּאת),[1318] which means also "*misstep.*"[1319] It drives from the verb *chata'* (חָטָא),[1320] meaning *to miss the goal, the mark*, thus, suffering its consequences. In effect,

"*righteousness exalteth a nation: but* <u>*missing the mark*</u> (חַטָּאת *chatta'ath*) *is a shame to any people.*"[1321]

The Greek term for *sin* confirms this interpretation. In fact, *amartanō* ἁμαρτάνω,[1322] also means *to miss the mark, to err*. Sin, then, is the consequence (חַטָּאת *chatta'ath*)[1323] deriving from missing the true mark,[1324] namely Awareness itself. To be precise, hungry desire (תְּשׁוּקָה *těshuwqah*) for the fruit of knowledge subdues the human and s/he is not able to rule or control (מָשַׁל *mashal*) it. Therefore, s/he is not lifted up (שְׂאֵת *sě'eth*)[1325] by the Transcendent. Sin or missed mark takes place not only in wakefulness but also in the dream state. In fact, the intentioning will, attached to its object, directs our dreams *dis*tracting and *mis*directing us away from Divine Awareness. It is erroneous to consider dreams as involuntary states of mind. Psychoanalysis[1326] well understands that they are outcomes and measures of our waking will. Dante writes about his sinful misstep, as

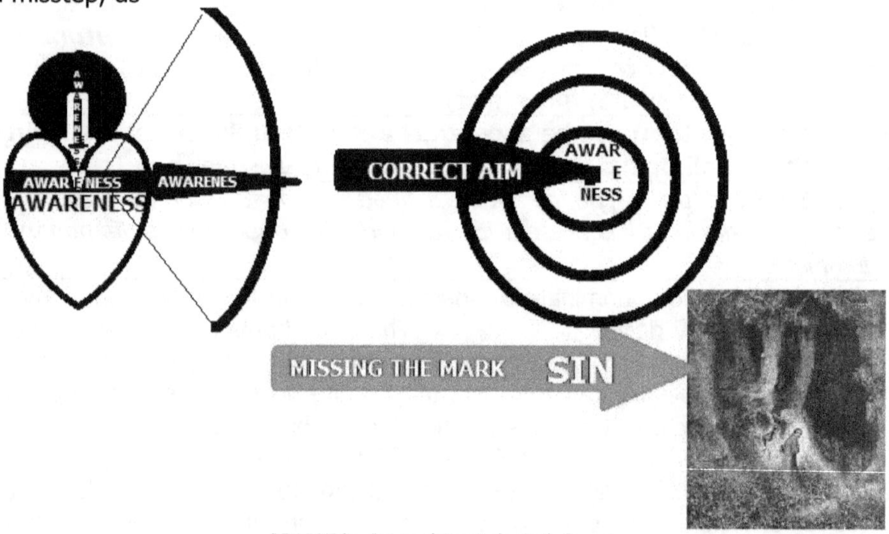

GRAPHIC: *Sin and Dante's dark forest*

"In the middle of the journey of our life/[1327] I found myself within a dark forest,/ Cause the straightforward path was lost.../ I cannot rightly tell how I entered it,/ So full of sleep was I about that moment/ In which I had forsaken the true way."[1328]

The instant a ray of light leaves the Sun, it is *destined* to reach the Earth after about eight minutes. Therefore, seven minutes before, the Earth is *destined* to receive the illumination of that ray. However, if one lives in the expectation of a destined future encounters death. Truthfully, who wills or desires a future event, wishes to fulfill it as an already given dead past. S/he forgets that the only life giving Presence of Awareness is devoid of any deadly past and/or future. In fact,

"*you, who forsake the Transcendent, who forget my holy mountain, who set a table for Fortune*[1329] *and fill cups of mixed wine for Destiny,*[1330] *I will destine*[1331] *you to the sword, and all of you shall bow down to the slaughter, because, when I called, you did not answer; when I spoke, you did not listen, but you did what was evil in my eyes and chose what I did not delight in.*"[1332]

In conclusion, Abel renounces the entire conceived world in order to identify with the Truth of Awareness. Cain, on the other hand, remains attached to his conceptual possession. S/he is the ego-and-or-I-consciousness. This attachment ties the human into the snare of death. The world that s/he knows is the world of the dead, because it is past. Therefore, s/he misses the mark, s/he knows nothing else but death and finally s/he succumbs to it. Epistemically, Cain is the subject possessor of its object with which it identifies and from which never wants to part. Abel, on the contrary, is Pure Breath of Consciousness sacrificing its own consciousness-*of* the object.

4:8-Killing Abel

וַיֹּאמֶר קַיִן אֶל־הֶבֶל אָחִיו וַיְהִי בִּהְיוֹתָם בַּשָּׂדֶה וַיָּקָם קַיִן אֶל־הֶבֶל אָחִיו וַיַּהַרְגֵהוּ׃   *vayōʾmer* (talked) *qayin* (Cain) *ʾel* (to) *heḇel* (Abel) *ʾāḥiyv* (the brother) *vayahiy*[1333] (during existence) *bihayvōṯām* (they existed in) *baśāḏeh* (the field) *vayāqām* (rose) *qayin* (Cain) *ʾel* (against) *heḇel* (Abel) *ʾāḥiyv* (brother) *vayaharaḡēhu* (killed)
καὶ *kai* (and) **εἶπεν** *eipen* (said) **Καιν** *Kain* (Cain) **πρὸς** *pros* (to) **Αβελ** *Abel* (Abel) **τὸν** *ton* (the) **ἀδελφὸν** *adelphos* (brother) **αὐτοῦ** *autos* (his) **διέλθωμεν** *dielthōmen* (let us go) **εἰς** *eis* (in) **τὸ** *to* (the) **πεδίον** *pedion* (field) **καὶ** *kai* (and) **ἐγένετο** *egeneto* (when it happened) **ἐν** *en* (in) **τῷ** *tō* (the) **εἶναι** *einai* (were) **αὐτοὺς** *autous* (they) **ἐν** *en* (in) **τῷ** *tō* (the) **πεδίῳ** *pediō* (field) **καὶ** *kai* (and) **ἀνέστη** *anestē* (rose) **Καιν** *Kain* (Cain) **ἐπὶ** *epi* (against) **Αβελ** *Abel* (Abel) **τὸν** *ton* (the) **ἀδελφὸν** *adelphos* (brother) **αὐτοῦ** *autou* (his) **καὶ** *kai* (and) **ἀπέκτεινεν** *apekteinen* (killed) **αὐτόν** *auton* (him)
dixit-(said)***que*** (and) ***Cain*** (Cain) ***ad*** (to) ***Abel*** (Abel) ***fratrem*** (brother) ***suum*** (his) ***egrediamur*** (let us go) ***foras*** (out) ***cumque*** (when) ***essent*** (they were) ***in*** (in) ***agro*** (the field) ***consurrexit*** (rose) ***Cain*** (Cain) ***adversus*** (against) ***Abel*** (Abel) ***fratrem*** (brother) ***suum*** (his) ***et*** (and) ***interfecit*** (killed) ***eum*** (him)
And Cain talked with Abel his brother: and it came to pass, when they were in the field, that Cain rose up against Abel his brother, and slew him.
During their existence, when they were in the space/time field, Cain talked to his brother Abel and Cain rose against Abel his brother and killed him.

War is the death threat imposed or the killing carried out on an enemy who does not share our same behavioral ways and moral ideologies or does not allow the fulfillment of our requests.[1334] Furthermore, any act of killing implies sending the murdered person to an unknown metaphysical realm, namely, the place from which we come and to which we go. That is a *ghostly* sphere. It is different from the subject-object dimension in which we live. Namely, the one we daily experience as duality and as space, time and causal field. To be coherent, a sovereign state, declaring its separation from any metaphysical belief professed by churches, should never settle for capital punishment and/or war to solve its purely political problems. Any nation doing that utilizes the metaphysical views of those same religions from which it declares its disconnection. In fact, that non-confessional state would be evoking the church's supernatural dimension of the *angel of death* as a political-problem-solving. It is as lowering on their political stages a *deus ex machina*, a *god from a mechanical contraption.*[1335]

Chris, one of our Latin students, stated,

'A free nation has all the right to enforce its own laws and penalties for transgressors, including capital punishment.'

We replied,

'That is true, but not for a nation, which declares, in its own constitution, to be separated from the metaphysical principles of the church. Then, to be coherent, that nation has no right to send anyone in the metaphysical condition of death.'

The event, described in this verse, takes place now, during Cain's existence (וַיְהִי *vayahiy*),[1336] when s/he exists (בִּהְיוֹתָם *bihayvōṯām*)[1337] in this *field* (שָׂדֶה *sadeh*)[1338] of space, time and causality. Subject-Cain, possessor of objects for-itself, and Pure-Breath-of-Subject-in-itself-Abel are the two brother-polarities of our humanity. The Subject-for-itself can never know the Pure-Subject-in-itself, as such. It can only conceptualize it and possesses it as its own object, for-itself. Obviously, the thought of pure-consciousness is not Pure-Consciousness, it is its idea, thus other than it. Pure-Subject-in-itself remains Unknown. Thus, it is the equivalent of killing it, putting it out of hand.[1339] This takes place during conceptual introspection, when we reflect on our own self, which becomes *the-me-object* of *the-I-subject*. Then, the Seer of what we see is Unseen and the Knower of what we know is Unknown.[1340]

Nevertheless, this *killing* (הָרַג *harag*) is more evident when referred to an interlocutor. When we think of the other person with whom we are speaking (אָמַר *'amar*),[1341] like Cain with Abel, we are not directly conscious-*of* his/her consciousness. In waking or dreaming, we are only conscious-*of* his/her being our object and manifesting an understanding. From that behavior, we infer and believe that s/he is listening and that her consciousness, independent from ours, is out there. The American neuroscientist Christof Koch, referring to his mountain dog, declares that

> "when she yelps, whines, gnaws at her paw, limps and then comes to me, seeking aid: I infer that she is in pain because under similar conditions I behave in similar ways (sans gnawing). Physiological measures of pain confirm this inference—injured dogs, just like people, experience an elevated heart rate and blood pressure and release stress hormones into their bloodstream. I'm not saying that a dog's pain is exactly like human pain, but dogs—as well as other animals—not only react to noxious stimuli but also consciously experience pain... [We state - however, that inference can never be inferred without an inferring subject (*e.g.* I, you, s/he, it, we, and/or they). In fact, Koch continues,] ...My subjective experience (and yours, too, presumably)... is an undeniable certainty, one strong enough to hold the weight of philosophy."[1342]

Thus, in the absence of a subject, the dog's suffering would have been unnoticed also by the dog itself. Indeed, if sedated, it is not the perceiving subject of its own objective pain. In any case, we perceive the other as an object. We can never perceive her as consciousness-in-herself. Therefore, when we know him, we must

> "*slay for food.*"[1343]

We must displace her conscious-subjectivity, which becomes our epistemic food, in order to affirm our self as his/her knower. Metaphorically, that is Cain, who forever keeps killing Abel.

> "*And he will be a wild man; his hand* [will be] *against every man, and every man's hand against him; and he shall dwell in the presence of all his brethren.*"[1344]

*In other words, I address my neighbor always as **you**, never as I. To be precise, in order to know you as you, I must discard your I {if there is such an unknown, aside from my firm belief in it}.*

4:9-Where is Abel?

וַיֹּאמֶר יְהוָה אֶל־קַיִן אֵי הֶבֶל אָחִיךָ וַיֹּאמֶר לֹא יָדַעְתִּי הֲשֹׁמֵר אָחִי אָנֹכִי:

vayō'mer (said) *yahvāh* (the Transcendent) *'el* (to) *qayin* (Cain) *'ēy* (where) *hebel* (Abel) *'āḥiykā* (brother) *vayō'mer* (said) *lō* (not) *yāda'atiy* (know) *hăšōmēr* (guardian) *'āḥiy* (brother) *'ānōkiy* (I)
καὶ *kai* (and) **εἶπεν** *eipen* (said) **ὁ** *o* (the) **θεὸς** *theos* (God) **πρὸς** *pros* (to) **Καιν** *Kain* (Cain) **ποῦ** *pou* (where) **ἐστιν** *estin* (is) **Αβελ** *Abel* (Abel) **ὁ** *o* (the) **ἀδελφός** *adelphos* (brother) **σου** *sou* (your) **ὁ** *o* (he) **δὲ** *de* (but) **εἶπεν** *eipen* (said) **οὐ** *ou* (not) **γινώσκω** *ginōskō* (I know) **μὴ** *mē* (not) **φύλαξ** *phulax* (the guardian) **τοῦ** *tou* (of the) **ἀδελφοῦ** *adelphou* (of brother) **μού** *mou* (my) **εἰμι** *eimi* (am) **ἐγώ** *egō* (I)
et (and) ***ait*** (said) ***Dominus*** (the Lord) ***ad*** (to) ***Cain*** (Cain) ***ubi*** (where) ***est*** (is) ***Abel*** (Abel) ***frater*** (brother) ***tuus*** (your) ***qui*** (he) ***respondit*** (answered) ***nescio*** (I do not know) ***num*** (by chance) ***custos*** (guardian) ***fratris*** (of brother) ***mei*** (my) ***sum*** (I am)
And the LORD said unto Cain, Where is Abel thy brother? And he said, I know not: Am I my brother's keeper?
And the Transcendent said to Cain, "*Where is Abel your brother?*" He answered, "*I do not know. Am I the observing-guardian of my brother?*"

The Transcendent's question is pure rhetoric. In fact, Cain does not know, nor can he know where Abel is in-himself. Cain is the subject of Abel the object. We, Cain, do not know where the *observing-guardian,*[1345] *viz.* the subject of Abel, is. Remember that Cain's condition is the condition of every human being partaking of the epistemic spell of the Tree of Knowledge's fruit. We never observe what the other observes with his/her eyes. Namely, we never live the other person's point of view, except as our own interpretation of it. The *Bṛhadāraṇyaka Upanishad* declares that the I, as

> "*Indra, the Conqueror, is without a rival. The second, the other, verily, is the rival.*"[1346]

Then, physical war waging, killing sprees and murderous acts ensue. In fact, they are structural consequences of the same epistemic condition. Every thought, action, deed, impulse, event and other occurrences, all of them take shape before Awareness'-Dispassionate-Serenity. Awareness, present in both the killer and the killed, *records* the murderous act inflicted by the murderer on the murdered, as well as the pain suffered by the slain one. We could say that anguish reverberates also in the violent as violence in the sufferer.

> "*Whatsoever ye shall bind on earth shall be bound in heaven: and whatsoever ye shall loose on earth shall be loosed in heaven.*"[1347]

Redemption is the realization of their common origin in Awareness. Then, the vanquished and the enemy unify in the love for each other and all are one in the Father.

From the personal point of view, Abel is our internal self-in-itself, which, when conceptualized, becomes this ego/I object here and now. Cain, the ego, then, becomes other than Abel, his Unknown-Self-in-it-self. In other words, we lay open to death by killing our own True Unknown Being.

Life generates Possessor and Breath. Possessor yearns for possession, forgetting its Origin. Breath controls the senses identifying with Awareness. Awareness is not conscious-*of* the first one, while Breath identifies with Awareness. Thus, Possessor slays him to be the owner of his own Breath.

4-II SECTION: CAIN'S PUNISHMENT

4:10-Abel's Voice Cries Out

וַיֹּאמֶר מֶה עָשִׂיתָ קוֹל דְּמֵי אָחִיךָ צֹעֲקִים אֵלַי מִן־הָאֲדָמָה׃ *vayō'mer* (He said) *meh* (what) *'āśiytā* (have you done) *qvōl* (the voice) *damēy* (of the blood) *'āḥiykā* (of brother) *ṣō'ăqiym* (cries out) *'ēlay* (to Us) *min* (from) *hā'ădāmāh* (the earth)
καὶ *kai* (and) **εἶπεν** *eipen* (said) **ὁ** *o* (the) **θεός** *theos* (God) **τί** *ti* (what) **ἐποίησας** *epotēsas* (have you done) **φωνὴ** *phōnē* (voice) **αἵματος** *aimatos* (blood) **τοῦ** *tou* (of the) **ἀδελφοῦ** *adelphou* (brother) **σου** *sou* (your) **βοᾷ** *boa* (calls) **πρός** *pros* (from) **με** *me* (me) **ἐκ** *ek* (from) **τῆς** *tēs* (the) **γῆς** *gēs* (earth)
dixit -(said)***que*** (and) ***ad*** (to) ***eum*** (him) ***quid*** (what) ***fecisti*** (have you done) ***vox*** (the voice) ***sanguinis*** (of the blood) ***fratris*** (of brother) ***tui*** (yours) ***clamat*** (calls) ***ad*** (to) ***me*** (me) ***de*** (from) ***terra*** (the earth)
And he said, What hast thou done? the voice of thy brother's blood crieth unto me from the ground.
He said to him. "*What have you done? The voice of the blood of your brother cries out into Us from the earth.*

Blood[1348] was essential for sacrifices. To drench the altar with animal's blood meant to offer their life to the Transcendent.

"*For the life of the flesh is in the blood.*"[1349]

Thus, the blood is a metaphor for life. Consequently, to sacrifice the first-born of the senses'-*flock*, means, metaphorically, to offer the life-breath of the mind to the Transcendent within. Then, the perceiving faculties do not direct towards the external objects of knowledge, but they revert internally. Abel, as we saw, is the Breath and his blood is the Breath's Life.

When we acknowledge another person, *e.g.* Abel, we are epistemically compelled to eliminate his/her subjectivity. In fact, we always call the other one "*you*-object," never "*I*-subject." Thus, our subject acts[1350] to subjugate the neighbor, while affirming his/her objectivity and eliminating any subjectivity. We rise[1351] against[1352] the other and reduce that one to our object. We *kill* and *entomb* his/her subjectivity in the *red land* (אֲדָמָה *'adamah*) of objectivity. Nevertheless, we always project the other in an unexperienced transcending exteriority. It is as if the voice (קוֹל *qowl*) of the other person, *e.g.* Abel, would come out of the land of objectivity claiming its transcendence, its real independent reality. Thus, Transcendence declares that, out of the land of objectivity, Abel's life-blood cries (צָעַק *tsa'aq*) its transcendent subjectivity

"*into Us.*"[1353]

That is to say, everyone, even in dreams, considers the other person to be an independent individual subject in-itself. The other is believed to transcend, *viz.* to be real in-itself and have an independent ego-conscience without any ego-consciousness of it. We attribute subjectivity to others while they are experienced only as objects. In fact, similar to the Greek mythological petrifying gaze of Medusa (Μέδουσα) defeated only with the reflecting shield of Perseus,[1354] the subject petrifies into objects the neighbor's subject. In other words, Cain-subject, epistemically kills and objectifies Abel's life. The real transcendent-Abel-subect lies buried on the other side of the looking glass. The *I*-subject *subjugates* the other's subjectivity reducing it to a *you*-object in three ways,

1) through *yada`* (יָדַע),[1355] *knowledge* and/or *sexual union*, when the other's subject becomes an object of passionate possession,
2) through *'akal* (אָכַל),[1356] *eating* and/or *sacrificing*, when the other's subject becomes an object of nourishing possession,
3) through *harag* (הָרַג),[1357] *killing* and/or *slaying for food*, when the other's subject becomes an object of vanquished possession.

In each case, the object becomes a possession of the subject and each time satisfies Cain's supremacy. The first two ways still pursue the transcendent. In that, knowing/copulating and eating/sacrificing still postulate the objective reality as being real out there. However, the third one, the way of murder/slaying intends to kill and eradicate the Transcendent. Nevertheless, that same eradicating intent, preponderantly, screams out its reality and proclaims the belief that the slayed one is an objective transcending reality in-itself, which needs to be eliminated as such. Nobody of sound mind, in fact, attempts to kill the fictional character on a movie screen.

4:11-The Earth Witnesses Abel's Blood

וְעַתָּה אָרוּר אָתָּה מִן־הָאֲדָמָה אֲשֶׁר פָּצְתָה אֶת־פִּיהָ לָקַחַת אֶת־דְּמֵי אָחִיךָ מִיָּדֶךָ׃ *va'atāh* (now) *'ārur* (despised) *'ātāh* (brought) *min* (from) *hā'ădāmāh* (the earth) *'ăšer* (which) *pāṣaṯāh* (opened) *'eṯ* (the) *piyāh* (mouth) *lāqaḥaṯ* (to receive) *'eṯ* (the) *damēy* (blood) *'āḥiykā* (brother) *miyāḏekā* (from your hand)
καὶ *kai* (and) **νῦν** *nun* (now) **ἐπικατάρατος** *epikataratos* (cursed) **σὺ** *su* (you) **ἀπὸ** *apo* (from) **τῆς** *tēs* (the) **γῆς** *gēs* (earth) **ἣ** *ē* (thus) **ἔχανεν** *echanen* (opened) **τὸ** *to* (the) **στόμα** *stoma* (mouth) **αὐτῆς** *autēs* (her) **δέξασθαι** *dexasthai* (to receive) **τὸ** *to* (the) **αἷμα** *aima* (blood) **τοῦ** *tou* (the) **ἀδελφοῦ** *adelphou* (brother) **σου** *sou* (your) **ἐκ** *ek* (from) **τῆς** *tēs* (the) **χειρός** *cheiros* (hand) **σου** *sou* (your)
nunc (now) ***igitur*** (therefore) ***maledictus*** (cursed) ***eris*** (you are) ***super*** (over) ***terram*** (the earth) ***quae*** (that) ***aperuit*** (opened) ***os*** (the mouth) ***suum*** (its) ***et*** (and) ***suscepit*** (received) ***sanguinem*** (the blood) ***fratris*** (of the brother) ***tui*** (your) ***de*** (from) ***manu*** (hand) ***tua*** (your)
And now art thou cursed from the earth, which hath opened her mouth to receive thy brother's blood from thy hand;
Therefore, now you are despised by the earth, which opened its mouth and received the life-blood of your brother from your hand.

Wine,

"*the blood of grapes,*"[1358]

the *red-essence* of grape juice, figuratively represents blood (דָּם *dam*).[1359] The Hebrew word *dam* (דָּם), *red*, connotes also the redness[1360] of A*dam* (אָ-דָם *'a-dam*),[1361] the human being, and the red earth[1362] from which s/he comes and in which s/he is set. The earth, *viz.* the three dimensional physical objectivity, is the witness of the slaying. It opens the mouth (פָּצְתָה אֶת־פִּיהָ *pāṣaṯāh 'eṯ piyāh*) to testify the presence of the Transcendent it received (לקח *laqach*) in-itself, which Cain's *possessive* hand (יָד *yad*) slays.

"*The invisible things of him from the creation of the world are clearly seen, being understood by the things that are made.*"[1363]

As an example, look at a picture of your loved one. The film, on which the image of your dear one is impressed, is not the real person imbedded in the photograph. The physical snapshot witnesses the real dear one, who, in the photo, is not the real one in flesh and bones. However, without the real loved one, the photo itself could not have been taken. When you look at an object, in dream or in wakefulness alike, **the object itself testifies the Unwavering-Pure-Aware-Certitude you have of that experienced person <u>as such experience</u>**. By this, we mean the Certainty-we-have-here-and-now-of-the-experience-as-experience, not of what the object is or is not *in-itself*. Abel identifies only with that Unwavering-Pure-Aware-Certitude, while Cain identifies with the *earthly* objectivity, which now *curses* and *despises* (ארר *'arar*)[1364] Cain by never giving him rest in his relentless searching travails.

Nevertheless, the principle of evidence confirms the <u>experiential existence</u> of the external-object. No one can state the non-reality of the external objects without stating, at the same time, their reality. In fact, the Indian sage Śaṅkara declared,

"*In every act of perception we are conscious of some external thing corresponding to the idea, ... and that of which we are conscious cannot but exist.*"

Therefore, there is an intentionality of consciousness as real transcending towards the object itself.

"*Nobody when perceiving a post or a wall is conscious of his perception only, but everyone is conscious of posts and walls and the like as objects of their perceptions.*"[1365]

The intentionality of consciousness is evident since

"even those who contest the existence of external things bear witness to their existence when they say that what is an internal object of cognition appears like something external."[1366]

Ichnographically, the Buddha expresses this same concept when, with his [1367]⇨ right hand touches the earth.[1368] He summons the earth as his witness. He convenes the earth because its presence is the objective confirming proof and witness of Buddha's own Pure-Aware-Certitude without which the earth itself could not be. Similarly, when

"The whole multitude of the disciples began to rejoice and praise God with a loud voice for all the mighty works that they had seen;/ Saying, 'Blessed be the King that cometh in the name of the Lord: peace in heaven, and glory in the highest.' And some of the Pharisees from among the multitude said unto him, 'Master, rebuke thy disciples.'/ And he [Jesus] *answered and said unto them, 'I tell you that, if these should hold their peace, the stones would immediately cry out.'"*[1369]

What we mean here is that, while Divine-Consciousness is the foundation without which no objectivity can exist, that objectivity itself is the testimony, the witness *crying out* the lauding praises of Consciousness.

4:12-Cain, the Grieving Wandering Wonderer

כִּי תַעֲבֹד אֶת־הָאֲדָמָה לֹא־תֹסֵף תֵּת־כֹּחָהּ לָךְ נָע וָנָד תִּהְיֶה בָאָרֶץ׃   *kiy* (when) *ta'ăḇōḏ* (you work) *'eṯ* (the) *hā'ăḏāmāh* (earth) *lō'* (not) *ṯōsēp̄* (increase) *tēṯ* (giving) *kōḥāh* (strength) *lāḵa* (to thee) *nā'* (vibrating) *vānāḏ* (grieving wanderer) *tihayeh* (you will be) *bā'āreṣ* (on earth)
ὅτι *oti* (that) **ἐργᾷ** *erga* (work) **τὴν** *tēn* (the) **γῆν** *gēn* (land) **καὶ** *kai* (and) **οὐ** *ou* (not) **προσθήσει** *prosthēsei* (constitute) **τὴν** *tēn* (the) **ἰσχὺν** *isxun* (strenght) **αὐτῆς** *autēs* (its) **δοῦναί** *douvai* (to give) **σοι** *soi* (you) **στένων** *stenōn* (vagabond) **καὶ** *kai* (and) **τρέμων** *tremōn* (trembling) **ἔσῃ** *esē* (will be) **ἐπὶ** *epi* (on) **τῆς** *tēs* (the) **γῆς** *gēs* (earth)
cum (when) ***operatus*** (working) ***fueris*** (you will be) ***eam*** (it) ***non*** (not) ***dabit*** (will not give) ***tibi*** (to you) ***fructus*** (fruits) ***suos*** (its) ***vagus*** (vagabond) ***et*** (and) ***profugus*** (exiled) ***eris*** (you will be) ***super*** (over) ***terram*** (the earth)
When thou tillest the ground, it shall not henceforth yield unto thee her strength; a fugitive and a vagabond shalt thou be in the earth.
When you will be working in the field, it will not yield its richness for you. You will be a vibrating grieving wanderer over the earth."

This verse reconfirms our epistemic interpretation. In fact, Cain, the murderous possessive subject, while acting and working (עָבַד *`abad*) in the field (אֲדָמָה*'adamah*) of time, space and causality, will never be able to reach the *richness*[1370] of the known object in-itself. He will continue to vibrate back and forth[1371] in that field. The subject will grasp the object from/for itself and will bring it back to itself repeatedly and so on. Thus, Cain, the subject, will be a continuously vibrating (נוע *nuwa`*) grieving wanderer[1372] (נָע וָנָד*nā' vānāḏ*) throughout the entire earthly space-time-causality dimension (אֶרֶץ *'erets*). In it, the subject will find only the grievance (נוד *nuwd*) of its unsatisfied hunger for passionate-possession (קַיִן *qayin*). This is the universal, paradigmatic wandering and grieving structure of the subject as king, which was, is and will be so for all generations. He is

"the once king and future king."[1373]

4:13-Unbearable Punishment

וַיֹּאמֶר קַיִן אֶל־יְהוָה גָּדוֹל עֲוֹנִי מִנְּשֹׂא׃   *vayō'mer* (said) *qayin* (Cain) *'el* (to) *yahvāh* (the Transcendent) *gāḏvōl* (greater) *'ăvniy* (guilt of iniquity) *minaśō'* (more than bearable)
καὶ *kai* (and) **εἶπεν** *eipen* (said) **Καιν** *Kain* (Cain) **πρὸς** *pros* (to) **τὸν** *ton* (the) **κύριον** *kurion* (Lord) **μείζων** *meizōn* (greater) **ἡ** *ē* (the) **αἰτία** *aitia* (crime) **μου** *mou* (my) **τοῦ** *tou* (the) **ἀφεθῆναί** *aphethēnai* (to be forgiven) **με** *me* (for me)
dixit -(said)***que*** (and) ***Cain*** (Cain) ***ad*** (to) ***Dominum*** (the Lord) ***maior*** (greater) ***est*** (is) ***iniquitas*** (iniquity) ***mea*** (my) ***quam*** (than) ***ut*** (I shall) ***veniam*** (come) ***merear*** (to deserve)

And Cain said unto the LORD, My punishment is greater than I can bear.

And Cain said to the Transcendent,
"The guilt for my iniquity is greater than what I shall come to bear.

The word *dam*, *blood* in Hebrew, means also *guilt for slaying.*[1374] Therefore, Cain's function conveys a sense of lonely desperate guilt[1375] deriving from the incommunicability between subjects. In fact, the subject, by its own nature, is condemned to a hellish killing, devouring its own subjectivity and that one of others.

"Hell is the others... [feeling] all those eyes intent on me. *Devouring* me,"[1376]
declares Sartre, in his play, "*No exit.*"

Incessantly, the subject chases its dream. This is still the consequence of the inebriation deriving from eating the fruit of knowledge. In that hungry epistemic process, we forget the fundamental Truthful-Awareness. We are *dis*tracted from It. That forgetfulness leads Cain to kill Abel. The subject, the object, the tree, the fruit, and everything else find their origin in our apodictical structure. Diverging from Cain, Abel is the one who sacrifices his own ego and identifies with Awareness alone.

4:14-Fear of Being Slayed

הֵן גֵּרַשְׁתָּ אֹתִי הַיּוֹם מֵעַל פְּנֵי הָאֲדָמָה וּמִפָּנֶיךָ אֶסָּתֵר וְהָיִיתִי נָע וָנָד בָּאָרֶץ וְהָיָה כָל־מֹצְאִי יַהַרְגֵנִי׃

hēn (behold) *gērašatā* (exiled) *'ōṯiy* (this) *hayvōm* (day) *mē'al* (from) *panēy* (face) *hā'ăḏāmāh* (of the earth) *umipāneyḵā* (from the face) *'esāṯēr* (hid) *vahāyiyṯiy* (I am) *nā'* (vibrating) *vānāḏ* (wanderer) *bā'āreṣ* (in the earth) *vahāyāh* (I have been) *ḵāl* (all) *mōṣa'iy* (finding) *yaharaḡēniy* (shall kill me)

εἰ *ei* (if) **ἐκβάλλεις** *ekballeis* (you expell) **με** *me* (me) **σήμερον** *sēmeron* (today) **ἀπὸ** *apo* (from) **προσώπου** *prosōpou* (the face) **τῆς** *tēs* (of the) **γῆς** *gēs* (earth) **καὶ** *kai* (and) **ἀπὸ** *apo* (from) **τοῦ** *tou* (the) **προσώπου** *prosōpou* (face) **σου** *sou* (your) **κρυβήσομαι** *krubēsomai* (I shall be hidden) **καὶ** *kai* (and) **ἔσομαι** *esomai* (I shall be) **στένων** *stenōn* (vagabond) **καὶ** *kai* (and) **τρέμων** *tremōn* (trembling) **ἐπὶ** *epi* (on) **τῆς** *tēs* (the) **γῆς** *gēs* (earth) **καὶ** *kai* (and) **ἔσται** *estai* (it will be) **πᾶς** *pas* (all) **ὁ** *o* (who) **εὑρίσκων** *euriskōn* (find) **με** *me* (me) **ἀποκτενεῖ** *apoktenei* (shall kill) **με** *me* (me)

ecce (behold) ***eicis*** (you evicted) ***me*** (me) ***hodie*** (today) ***a*** (from) ***facie*** (the face) ***terrae*** (of the earth) ***et*** (and) ***a*** (from) ***facie*** (face) ***tua*** (your) ***abscondar*** (I shall be hiding) ***et*** (and) ***ero*** (I was) ***vagus*** (a wanderer) ***et*** (and) ***profugus*** (exiled) ***in*** (on) ***terra*** (the earth) ***omnis*** (everyone) ***igitur*** (therefore) ***qui*** (who) ***invenerit*** (shall find) ***me*** (me) ***occidet*** (shall kill) ***me*** (me)

Behold, thou hast driven me out this day from the face of the earth; and from thy face shall I be hid; and I shall be a fugitive and a vagabond in the earth; and it shall come to pass, that every one that findeth me shall slay me.

Behold, today, you evicted me from the face of the earth and I shall be hiding from your face and I shall be a wanderer exiled on the earth. Therefore, anyone who shall find me shall kill me."

From a literal reading, Cain's fear does not make sense. In fact, how could he be afraid if, besides his parents and his brother, who is dead, there is no one else in the world? Nevertheless, for the human being, the others are the gripping fear. Continuously, the others populate our world with war threats, menacing confrontations, damaging relationships and physical dangers. Then, war becomes the evolutionary supremacy of the fittest. Now, in the present circular day of consciousness (יוֹם *yowm*) we hide (סָתַר *cathar*) from (עַל ` *al*) the actual presence[1377] of the Transcendent Awareness, since we have missed Its face of Truth. Therefore, we are evicted (גָּרַשׁ *garash*) from (עַל ` *al*) IT and from the world (אֲדָמָה *'adamah*) in-itself. Because of our exile, we perceive only the objective facial appearance (פָּנִים *paniym*) of things. Consequently, Cain/subject became a vibrating (נוּעַ *nuwa`*) grieving wanderer (נוּד *nuwd*) searching for Truth. Our subject is constantly laid open to be killed and/or to be reduced by others as their own object of conquest.

4:15-Cain's Mark

וַיֹּאמֶר לוֹ יְהוָה לָכֵן כָּל־הֹרֵג קַיִן שִׁבְעָתַיִם יֻקָּם וַיָּשֶׂם יְהוָה לְקַיִן אוֹת לְבִלְתִּי הַכּוֹת־אֹתוֹ כָּל־מֹצְאוֹ׃

vayō'mer (said) *lvō* (to him) *yahvāh* (Transcendent) *lāḵēn* (into him) *kāl* (all who) *hōrēḡ* (will kill)

qayin (Cain) *šiḇa'āṯayim* (sevenfold) *yuqām* (vengeance) *vayāśem* (shall be taken) *yahvāh* (Transcendent) *laqayin* (Cain) *'vōṯ* (mark) *laḇilatiy* (least) *hakvōṯ* (kill) *'ōṯvō* (with) *kāl* (all) *mōṣa'vō* (finding)
καὶ *kai* (and) **εἶπεν** *eipen* (said) **αὐτῷ** *autō* (to him) **κύριος** *kurios* (Lord) **ὁ** *o* (the) **θεός** *theos* (God) **οὐχ** *ouch* (not) **οὕτως** *outōs* (so) **πᾶς** *pas* (all) **ὁ** *o* (who) **ἀποκτείνας** *apokteinas* (shall kill) **Καιν** *Kain* (Cain) **ἑπτὰ** *epta* (sevenfold) **ἐκδικούμενα** *ekdikoumena* (avenge) **παραλύσει** *paralusei* (shall suffer) **καὶ** *kai* (and) **ἔθετο** *etheto* (placed) **κύριος** *kurios* (Lord) **ὁ** *o* (the) **θεὸς** *theos* (God) **σημεῖον** *sēmeion* (mark) **τῷ** *tō* (on the) **Καιν** *Kain* (Cain) **τοῦ** *tou* (the) **μὴ** *mē* (not) **ἀνελεῖν** *anelein* (would kill) **αὐτὸν** *auton* (him) **πάντα** *panta* (all) **τὸν** *ton* (the) **εὑρίσκοντα** *euriskonta* (found) **αὐτόν** *auton* (him)
dixit -(said)***que*** (and) ***ei*** (to him) ***Dominus*** (the Lord) ***nequaquam*** (by no means) ***ita*** (so) ***fiet*** (will do) ***sed*** (but) ***omnis*** (anyone) ***qui*** (who) ***occiderit*** (will kill) ***Cain*** (Cain) ***septuplum*** (sevenfold) ***punietur*** (shall be punished) ***posuit*** -(placed)***que*** (and) ***Dominus*** (the Lord) ***Cain*** (on Cain) ***signum*** (mark) ***ut*** (so that) ***non*** (not) ***eum*** (he) ***interficeret*** (would be killed) ***omnis*** (by anyone) ***qui*** (who) ***invenisset*** (should find) ***eum*** (him)
And the LORD said unto him, Therefore whosoever slayeth Cain, vengeance shall be taken on him sevenfold. And the LORD set a mark upon Cain, lest any finding him should kill him.
And the Transcendent said to him, "*Whosoever shall kill Cain shall be punished sevenfold.*" Therefore, the Transcendent placed a mark on Cain so that he would not be hurt by anyone who should find him.

There is only one Cain. S/he is this I and ego subjective-consciousness of this one writing and/or reading this page, here and now. If you are an "*I*," try to find another "*I*," besides yours, if you can. Providing, however, that the one you find is not the "*I*" you have already *killed* by reducing it to a "*you*" of your own objective passionate-possession. This is the continuously indelible mark (אות *'owth*) of subjectivity, of death,[1378] namely,

"*the sign* of anything which cannot itself be seen."[1379]

The paradox is that, while the subject always *kills* (הרג *harag*) the subjectivity of others, *i.e.* the paradigmatic Abel, reducing it to its own object, the subject can never be *killed* as a subject-in-itself.

When I know myself as an object, I still conceive that objective "me" as the subject-knower seen by myself in the mirror of my mind.

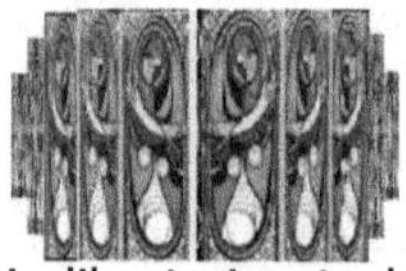

The subject, as a person placed between two facing mirrors, projects an endless self-reflecting series of the same image of itself. Thus, it *echoes* and [1380]⇨ *projects*, before its own subjective-eyes, a limitless sequence of objective *I-me-you/s*. Therefore, the subject, even when it reduces itself to an object *for-itself*, in both I-consciousness and ego-consciousness, still remains untouched as subject in-itself. It is like trying to kill your own image in the mirror. The glass will shatter but the reflecting attempting murderer will remain unharmed.

What we mean here is that even in self-consciousness the "*I*" becomes for the subject an object *for-itself*. Therefore, whosoever kills and strikes (נכה *nakah*) that objectified-subject enters again in *Cain's mode*, namely, in the paradigmatic process by which the subject reduces the *other's-subject* to an object *for-itself*. Consequently, the vengeance (נקם *naqam*) will inflict sevenfold (שבעתים *shib'athayim*) all the pains Cain endures. To be exact, his suffering will affect his whole scale of existence, throughout the six days of creation, including the seventh day of rest.

4:16-Exile

וַיֵּצֵא קַיִן מִלִּפְנֵי יְהוָה וַיֵּשֶׁב בְּאֶרֶץ־נוֹד קִדְמַת־עֵדֶן׃
vayēṣē̕ (he went out) *qayin* (Cain) *milip̄anēy* (from the) *yahvāh* (Transcendent) *vayēšeḇ* (dwelt) *ba'ereṣ* (in the land) *nvōḏ* (of wandering) *qiḏamaṯ* (in front of) *ʿēḏen* (Eden)
ἐξῆλθεν *exēlthen* (he went out) **δὲ** *de* (therefore) **Καιν** *Kain* (Cain) **ἀπὸ** *apo* (from) **προσώπου** *prosōpou* (face) **τοῦ** *tou* (of the) **θεοῦ** *theou* (God) **καὶ** *kai* (and) **ᾤκησεν** *ōkēsen* (dwelt) **ἐν** *en* (in) **γῇ** *gē* (land) **Ναιδ** *Naid* (of Nod) **κατέναντι** *katenanti* (opposite) **Εδεμ** *Edem* (from Eden)
egressus -(went out)***que*** (and) ***Cain*** (Cain) ***a*** (from) ***facie*** (the face) ***Domini*** (of the Lord) ***habitavit*** (lived) ***in*** (in) ***terra*** (the land) ***profugus*** (of exile) ***ad*** (to) ***orientalem*** (the orient) ***plagam*** (of the land) ***Eden*** (of Eden)
And Cain went out from the presence of the LORD, and dwelt in the land of Nod, on the east of Eden
Therefore, Cain went out from Awareness In-Itself and lived in the field of Wandering, opposite from the land of Happiness.

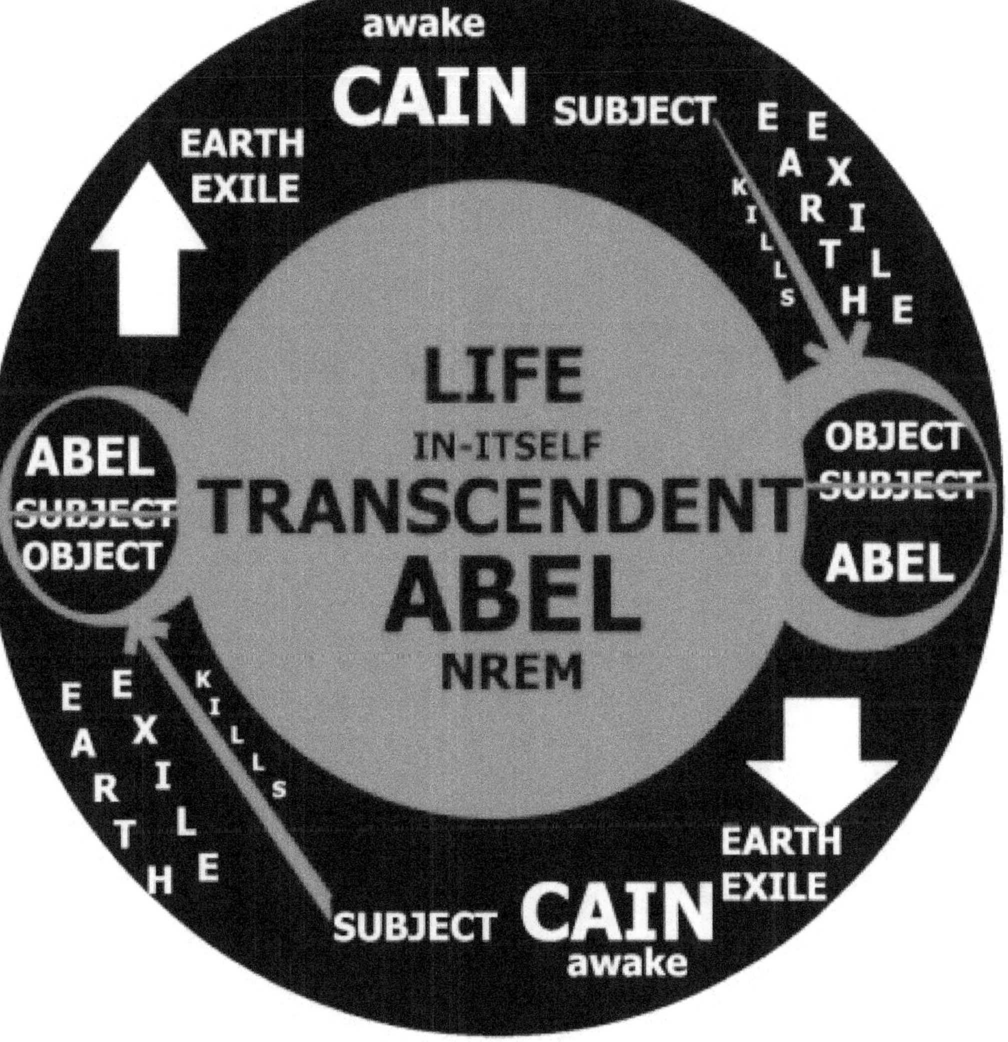

GRAPHIC: *The Land of Nod*

The real homeland of the possessor-subject, *viz.* Cain, is Happiness in Awareness. Without Awareness, how could Cain kill Abel or know his wife, mentioned in next verse? In fact, he would not have been conscious-*of* them. Nevertheless, he kills Abel and knows his wife because he identifies with the experience he has of them and not with the Truth of Awareness. Abel is the Auto-transparency of dreamless-sleep extinguished by Cain's world of representation in the red field of dream and wakefulness.

Taken by the murderous desire to kill Abel and by the lascivious desire for his wife, Cain forgets the Serene Happiness (עֵדֶן `*eden*) from which he comes. Therefore, he goes out (יָצָא *yatsa'*) of the *Real-Thing-In-Itself*, namely the Transcendent (יְהֹוָה *yĕhovah*). He becomes a wanderer, exiled (נוד *nowd*)[1381] from the Face (פָּנִים *paniym*) of his own Source. He establishes his residence (יָשַׁב *yashab*) in *Nod* (נוד *nowd*), which means *wandering in the land* (ארץ *'erets*) *opposite* (קדמה *qidmah*) to Happiness.

> Where are the true neighbors? Ultimately, they remain unknown. However, physicality calls out their reality. In turn, we live as wanderers constantly under the threat of being killed.

4-III SECTION: CAIN'S GENERATIONS

4:17-Enoch

וַיֵּדַע קַיִן אֶת־אִשְׁתּוֹ וַתַּהַר וַתֵּלֶד אֶת־חֲנוֹךְ וַיְהִי בֹּנֶה עִיר וַיִּקְרָא שֵׁם הָעִיר כְּשֵׁם בְּנוֹ חֲנוֹךְ׃
vayēḏa' (knew) *qayin* (Cain) *'eṯ* (and) *'išatvō* (wife) *vatahar* (conceived) *vatēleḏ* (generated) *'eṯ* (and) *ḥănvōḵa* (Enoch dedicated one) *vayahiy* (be) *bōneh* (built) *'iyr* (city) *vayiqarā'* (called) *šēm* (name) *hā'iyr* (the city) *kašēm* (name) *banvō* (name) *ḥănvōḵa* (Enoch)
καὶ *kai* (and) **ἔγνω** *egvō* (knew) **Καιν** *Kain* (Cain) **τὴν** *tēn* (the) **γυναῖκα** *gunaika* (wife) **αὐτοῦ** *autou* (his) **καὶ** *kai* (and) **συλλαβοῦσα** *sullabousa* (took) **ἔτεκεν** *eteken* (generated) **τὸν** *ton* (the) **Ενωχ** *Enoch* (Enoch) **καὶ** *kai* (and) **ἦν** *ēn* (be) **οἰκοδομῶν** *oikodomōn* (built) **πόλιν** *polis* (city) **καὶ** *kai* (and) **ἐπωνόμασεν** *epōnomasen* (named) **τὴν** *tēn* (the) **πόλιν** *polis* (city) **ἐπὶ** *epi* (after) **τῷ** *tō* (the) **ὀνόματι** *onomati* (name) **τοῦ** *tou* (of the) **υἱοῦ** *uiou* (son) **αὐτοῦ** *autou* (his) **Ενωχ** *Enoch* (Enoch)
cognovit (knew) ***autem*** (also) ***Cain*** (Cain) ***uxorem*** (wife) ***suam*** (his) ***quae*** (who) ***concepit*** (conceived) ***et*** (and) ***peperit*** (generated) ***Enoch*** (Enoch) ***et*** (and) ***aedificavit*** (built) ***civitatem*** (a city) ***vocavit-*** (called)***que*** (and) ***nomen*** (with name) ***eius*** (it) ***ex*** (with) ***nomine*** (the name) ***filii*** (of son) ***sui*** (his) ***Enoch*** (Enoch)
And Cain knew his wife; and she conceived, and bare Enoch: and he builded a city, and called the name of the city, after the name of his son, Enoch.
Furthermore, Cain knew his wife who conceived and generated/conceived Enoch, the dedicated instructor. Subsequently, Cain built a city and called it Enoch, after his son's name.

Again, from a literal perspective, the list and enumeration of all the names of Cain's descendants that will follow are not of any direct historical relevance for us or the Cosmos as such, unless they indicate paradigmatic structures of our being. In fact, here there is no indication of who Cain's wife was or where she came from. Literally, she can only be his sister. However, up to this point, *Genesis* does not give any account of her. The reason for it is that she is a metaphoric wife. *'Ishshah,*[1382] the Hebrew word for wife, from *'iysh*[1383] *noble man* and contracted for *'enowsh*[1384] *mankind*, implies just the opposite of man. Thus, she is only the paradigmatic aspect of the object as opposite to the subject. As we proceed from the very general model aspects of humanity into the actual flow of behavior, we find other universal template features belonging to the human condition in general. Figuratively, it is as finding new formative software for our shared collective computer. The generation of Cain is the product of the waking state. It is all the functions, activities and accomplishments humans perform during their daily representations.

First, from Cain, the murderer fearing for his own life, derives the need for a social contract that assures reciprocal safety. Cain, being a possessive subject, is, consequently, a householder and a homesteader. Gradually, his original farm transforms into a city (עִיר *'iyr*). He names this city Enoch, *chanowk,*[1385] after his firstborn. This name means "*the dedicated one*" who trains and instructs (חָנַךְ *chanak*) city dwellers, viz. *citizens*, in the art of social coexistence safeguarding and defending their own properties.[1386]

4:18-Enoch's Generation

וַיִּוָּלֵד לַחֲנוֹךְ אֶת־עִירָד וְעִירָד יָלַד אֶת־מְחוּיָאֵל וּמְחִיָּיאֵל יָלַד אֶת־מְתוּשָׁאֵל וּמְתוּשָׁאֵל יָלַד אֶת־לָמֶךְ׃
vayiuālēḏ (generated) *laḥănvōḵa* (from Enoch) *'eṯ* (and) 'iyrāḏ (Irad) *va'iyrāḏ* (from Irad) *yālaḏ* (generated) *'eṯ* (and) *maḥuyā'ēl* (Mehujael) *umaḥiyyā'ēl* (from Mehujael) *yālaḏ* (generated) *'eṯ* (and) *maṯušā'ēl* (Methusael) *umaṯušā'ēl* (from Methusael) *yālaḏ* (generated) *'eṯ* (and) *lāmeḵa* (Lamech)
ἐγενήθη *egenēthē* (was born) **δὲ** *de* (from) **τῷ** *tō* (the) **Ενωχ** *Enoch* (Enoch) **Γαιδαδ** *Gaidad* (Irad) **καὶ** *kai* (and) **Γαιδαδ** *Gaidad* (Irad) **ἐγέννησεν** *egennēsen* (begot) **τὸν** *ton* (the) **Μαιηλ** *Maiēl* (Mehujael) **καὶ** *kai* (and) **Μαιηλ** *Maiēl* (Mehujael) **ἐγέννησεν** *egennēsen* (begot) **τὸν** *ton* (the) **Μαθουσαλα** *Mathousala* (Methusael) **καὶ** *kai* (and) **Μαθουσαλα** *Mathousala* (Methusael) **ἐγέννησεν** *egennēsen* (begot) **τὸν** *ton* (the) **Λαμεχ** *Lamech* (Lamech)

porro (following) ***Enoch*** (Enoch) ***genuit*** (generated) ***Irad*** (Irad) ***et*** (and) ***Irad*** (Irad) ***genuit*** (generated) ***Maviahel*** (Mehujael) ***et*** (and) ***Maviahel*** (Mehujael) ***genuit*** (generated) ***Matusahel*** (Methusael) ***et*** (and) ***Matusahel*** (Methusael) ***genuit*** (generated) ***Lamech*** (Lamech)
And unto Enoch was born Irad: and Irad begat Mehujael: and Mehujael begat Methusael: and Methusael begat Lamech
Following, Enoch generated Irad. Irad generated/conceived Mehujael. Mehujael generated/conceived Methusael. Methusael generated/conceived Lamech.

The literal reading of this verse and similar others, as mere sequence of human descendants, bears little or no relevance for the economy of the far reach of the entire Cosmos. Furthermore, this is confirmed by the fact that there is no mention of any wife for these templates. There are only their hypostatic aspects and that of their offspring. Only if we recognize the paradigmatic value of the genetic lineage, as describing different functions of sentient beings, then the list acquires a universal meaningful configuration. By paradigm, we mean a template, a pattern and/or a set of inevitable recurring shared outlines within structures not yet singularly individualized. These, once placed into effect, will all manifest the same common traits. Thomas Merton explains,

> "the great Patriarchs contained in themselves the pattern of their race's destiny. All this is fulfilled in the 'Seed of Abraham.'"[1387]

With this in mind, we can read that, from *Enoch*, the *teacher of civility*, comes *Irad*. The name means *fleet*,[1388] namely, the stream of human occupations. All functions sail from him, proceeding one from the other. Namely, from *Irad*, *flows* the fleet of human roles, like,

I) the priestly function, *viz. Mehujael*, meaning *the one smitten by God*.[1389] This function derives from the continuous certainty present within every experience and conferred to that which is experienced as such. From it, derives

II) the prophetic function, *viz. Methusael*, signifying *the one who is with God*.[1390] This function derives from the continuous transcending projection of intentionality present in every experience.[1391] From this last one, emerges

III) the power of those functions, *viz. Lamech*, which means *the powerful one*.[1392]

4:19-Lamech

וַיִּקַּח־לוֹ לֶמֶךְ שְׁתֵּי נָשִׁים שֵׁם הָאַחַת עָדָה וְשֵׁם הַשֵּׁנִית צִלָּה׃   *vayiqaḥ* (took) *lvō* (he) *lemeḵa* (Lamech-power) *šatēy* (two) *nāšiym* (wives) *šēm* (name) *hā'aḥaṯ* (of one) *'āḏāh* (Adah-ornament) *vašēm* (name) *hašēniyṯ* (of the other) *ṣilāh* (Zillah-shade)
καὶ *kai* (and) **ἔλαβεν** *elaben* (took) **ἑαυτῷ** *eautō* (himself) **Λαμεχ** *Lamech* (Lamech) **δύο** *duo* (two) **γυναῖκας** *gunaikas* (wives) **ὄνομα** *onoma* (name) **τῇ** *tē* (of the) **μιᾷ** *mia* (first) **Αδα** *Ada* (Ada) **καὶ** *kai* (and) **ὄνομα** *onoma* (name) **τῇ** *tē* (of the) **δευτέρᾳ** *deutera* (second) **Σελλα** *Sella* (Sella)
qui (who) ***accepit*** (took) ***uxores*** (wives) ***duas*** (two) ***nomen*** (by the name) ***uni*** (one) ***Ada*** (Ada) ***et*** (and) ***nomen*** (name) ***alteri*** (of the other) ***Sella*** (Sella)
And Lamech took unto him two wives: the name of the one was Adah, and the name of the other Zillah.
Lamech-Power took two wives/polarities, one by the name of Adah-Ornament and the other by the name of Zillah-Shade.

This verse is not an endorsement nor has anything to do with polygyny,[1393] which, however, under certain circumstances, was and is legal in the Middle East and elsewhere. In any case, the polygynist must have been and must be powerful and rich to afford multiple wives.[1394] Nonetheless, the fact that the text, in other regards so full of genealogical details, does not deem necessary to determine the consorts' paternity proves the metaphoric aspect of the two women.

Lamech is the human function of power (לֶמֶךְ *lemek*). Any worldly power has two (שְׁנַיִם *shĕnayim*) polarities (אִשָּׁה *'ishshah*) or *wives*. The first is *Adah*, meaning the *ornament*,[1395] the decoration of authority shining on the chest of powerful rulers. The second one is *Zillah*, signifying the *shade*[1396] of the transitory fleeting of this life. In fact, historically all rulers and dynasties, in spite of the power they established, lasted only for a relative short time, even if it happened to be thousands of years.

4:20-Farmers and Herders

וַתֵּלֶד עָדָה אֶת־יָבָל הוּא הָיָה אֲבִי יֹשֵׁב אֹהֶל וּמִקְנֶה׃
vatēleḏ (generated) *'āḏāh* (Adah) *'eṯ* (and) *yāḇāl* (Jabal) *hu'* (is) *hāyāh* (was) *'ăḇiy* (father) *yōšēḇ* (dwellers) *'ōhel* (tents) *umiqaneh* (cattle)
καὶ *kai* (and) **ἔτεκεν** *eteken* (generated) **Αδα** *Ada* (Ada) **τὸν** *ton* (the) **Ιωβελ** *Iōbel* (Iobel) **οὗτος** *outos* (he) **ἦν** *ēn* (was) **ὁ** *o* (the) **πατὴρ** *patēr* (father) **οἰκούντων** *oikouvtōn* (of the dwellers) **ἐν** *en* (in) **σκηναῖς** *skēnais* (tents) **κτηνοτρόφων** *ktēnotrophōn* (herders)
genuit-(generated) ***que*** (and) ***Ada*** (Ada) ***Iabel*** (Iabel) ***qui*** (who) ***fuit*** (was) ***pater*** (the father) ***habitantium*** (of those who live) ***in*** (in) ***tentoriis*** (tents) ***atque*** (and also) ***pastorum*** (of the herders)
And Adah bare Jabal: he was the father of such as dwell in tents, and of such as have cattle.
And Adah generated/conceived Jabal who, like a stream, was the father of house dwelling herders.

The list of human capabilities and faculties proceeds as an attribute, an *ornament*, *viz. Adah*, of power. Here, *Genesis* presents the functional activities of humans. In fact, Adah, the ornament, generates first *Jabal*, namely the *stream*[1397] of all past, present and future *house-dwelling*[1398] farmers and herders, connected with the physical feeding and sustaining aspect of life.

4:21-Artists

וְשֵׁם אָחִיו יוּבָל הוּא הָיָה אֲבִי כָּל־תֹּפֵשׂ כִּנּוֹר וְעוּגָב׃
vašēm (name) *'āḥiyv* (brother) *yuḇāl* (Jubal) *hu'* (is) *hāyāh* (was) *'ăḇiy* (father) *kāl* (all) *tōpēś* (that can handle) *kinvōr* (harp) *va'uḡāḇ* (organ)
καὶ *kai* (and) **ὄνομα** *onoma* (the name) **τῷ** *tō* (of the) **ἀδελφῷ** *adelphō* (brither) **αὐτοῦ** *autou* (his) **Ιουβαλ** *Ioubal* (Ioubal) **οὗτος** *outos* (he) **ἦν** *ēn* (was) **ὁ** *o* (the) **καταδείξας** *katadeixas* (inventor) **ψαλτήριον** *psaltērion* (of psaltery) **καὶ** *kai* (and) **κιθάραν** *kitharan* (harp)
et (and) ***nomen*** (the name) ***fratris*** (of brother) ***eius*** (his) ***Iubal*** (Iubal) ***ipse*** (this one) ***fuit*** (was) ***pater*** (the father) ***canentium*** (of those who can sing) ***cithara*** (with harp) ***et*** (and) ***organo*** (organ)
And his brother's name was Jubal: he was the father of all such as handle the harp and organ.
Furthermore, the name of his brother was Jubal. He was the father from whom derive artists like harpists and organists.

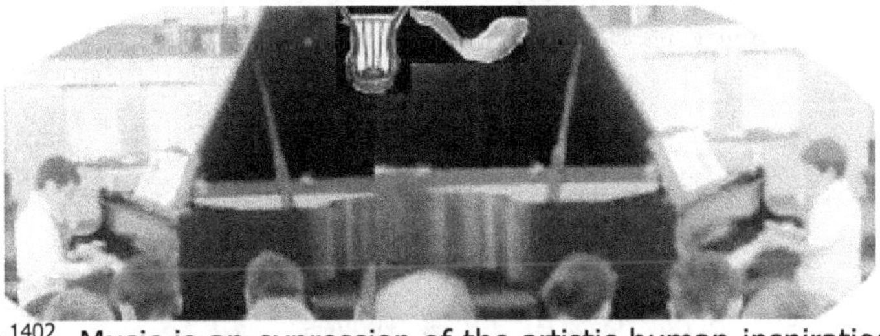

Likewise, from the same attribute of power, derives *Jubal*, meaning the *course*,[1399] *viz.* the functions from which the Arts, in general, and music, in particular, *flow* (יָבַל *yabal*).[1400] They are the aesthetic and psychological creative aspects of life. In fact, the harp (כנור *kinnowr*),[1401] *accompanied by singing, was played during sacred or secular social events.*[1402] Music is an expression of the artistic human inspiration. In fact, the other instrument, mentioned here, is the organ or flute, *`uwgab* (עוּגָב),[1403] which derives from *'agab* (עגב),[1404] in the sense of breathing and loving, thus being artistically *in*spired. The artists

> "provide the contemporary metaphors that allow us to realize the transcendent, infinite, and abundant nature of being as it is."[1405]

4:22-Metalworkers, Wars and Beauty

וְצִלָּה גַם־הִוא יָלְדָה אֶת־תּוּבַל קַיִן לֹטֵשׁ כָּל־חֹרֵשׁ נְחֹשֶׁת וּבַרְזֶל וַאֲחוֹת תּוּבַל־קַיִן נַעֲמָה׃
vaṣilāh (Zillah) *ḡam* (also) *hiv'* (she) *yālaḏāh* (bare) *'eṯ* (and) *tuḇal* (Thubal) *qayin* (Cain) *lōṭēš*

(hammer) *kāl* (all) *ḥōrēš* (who construct) *naḥōšeṯ* (in brass) *uḇarazel* (iron) *va'ăḥvōt* (sister) *tuḇal* (Thubal) *qayin* (Cain) *na'ămāh* (Naamah)
Σελλα *Sella* (Sella) **δὲ** *de* (but) **ἔτεκεν** *eteken* (generated) **καὶ** *kai* (and) **αὐτὴ** *autē* (she) **τὸν** *ton* (the) **Θοβελ** *Thobel* (Thobel) **καὶ** *kai* (and) **ἦν** *ēn* (was) **σφυροκόπος** *sphurokopos* (a smith) **χαλκεὺς** *chalkeus* (manufacturer) **χαλκοῦ** *chalkou* (of brass) **καὶ** *kai* (and) **σιδήρου** *sidērou* (iron) **ἀδελφὴ** *adelphē* (sister) **δὲ** *de* (but) **Θοβελ** *Thobel* (Thobel) **Νοεμα** *Noema* (Noema)
Sella (Sella) ***quoque*** (also) ***genuit*** (bore) ***Thubalcain*** (Thubalcain) ***qui*** (who) ***fuit*** (was) ***malleator*** (the hammerer) ***et*** (and) ***faber*** (maker) ***in*** (of) ***cuncta*** (all) ***opera*** (works) ***aeris*** (in brass) ***et*** (and) ***ferri*** (iron) ***soror*** (the sister) ***vero*** (indeed) ***Thubalcain*** (of Thubalcain) ***Noemma*** (Noemma)
And Zillah, she also bare Tubalcain, an instructer of every artificer in brass and iron: and the sister of Tubalcain was Naamah.
In addition, Zillah generated/conceived Tubalcain. He is the function of the hammering maker of all metal works in brass and iron. Tubalcain's sister was the beautiful Naamah.

From Zillah, the transitory and dark aspect of power, derives all that humans make and/or regard as charming allure. First to come is the blacksmith's faculty to hammer (לטש *latash*), make (חרש *choresh*) and produce things. When the things produced are of brass (נְחֹשֶׁת *nĕchosheth*) or iron (בַּרְזֶל *barzel*), then they can become weapons.

The name Tubalcain (תּוּבַל קַיִן *Tuwbal Qayin*)[1406] means "*thou will be brought of Cain.*" It derives from the verb *yabal* (יָבַל),[1407] to bring, to carry, comparable to *yĕbuwl* (יְבוּל),[1408] to produce, which, in turn, derives from *yabal* (יָבַל),[1409] to bring. Finally, it refers to Cain, *Qayin* (קַיִן),[1410] possession, which is the same as *qayin* (קַיִן)[1411] meaning spear, which has an affinity with *qanah* (קָנָה),[1412] possessor. Therefore, when Tubalcain forges those weapons and brings them to Cain, *i.e.:* the powerful possessor,[1413] then, those arms become means of destruction and conquering wars.

Another aspect of transitory power is the alluring Naamah, meaning *beautiful loveliness,*[1414] Tubalcain's sister.

Summary of Cain's Waking Generation

The nine hypostases of Cain as a retractable telescope⇩	
I)	*Enoch*, is his/her teaching aspect.⇩
II)	*Irad*, is the sequence of his/her functions.⇩
III)	*Mehujael*, is his/her priestly function.⇩
IV)	*Methusael*, is his/her prophetic occupation.⇩
V)	*Lamech*, is his/her ego power.⇩
VI)	*Jabal*, is his/her farming function.
VII)	*Jubal*, is his/her artistic function.
VIII)	*Tubalcain*, is his/her work producing aspect.
IX)	*Naamah*, is his/her beauty allure.

4:23-Lamech's Murderous Act

וַיֹּאמֶר לֶמֶךְ לְנָשָׁיו עָדָה וְצִלָּה שְׁמַעַן קוֹלִי נְשֵׁי לֶמֶךְ הַאְזֵנָּה אִמְרָתִי כִּי אִישׁ הָרַגְתִּי לְפִצְעִי וְיֶלֶד לְחַבֻּרָתִי׃
vayō'mer (said) *lemeḵa* (Lamech) *lanāšāyv* (to the wives) *'āḏāh* (Adah) *vaṣilāh* (Zillah) *šama'an* (listen) *qvōliy* (voice) *našēy* (wives) *lemeḵa* (Lamech) *ha'azēnāh* (hear) *'imarāṯiy* (words) *kiy* (because) *'iyš* (a man-subject) *hāraḡatiy* (I killed) *apīṣa'iy* (for wounding) *vayeleḏ* (young offspring) *laḥaburāṯiy* (to my hurting)
εἶπεν *eipen* (said) **δὲ** *de* (but) **Λαμεχ** *Lamex* (Lamex) **ταῖς** *tais* (the) **ἑαυτοῦ** *eautou* (his) **γυναιξίν** *gunaixin* (wives) **Αδα** *Ada* (Ada) **καὶ** *kai* (and) **Σελλα** *Sella* (Sella) **ἀκούσατέ** *akousate* (listen) **μου** *mou* (to my) **τῆς** *tēs* (the) **φωνῆς** *phōnēs* (voice) **γυναῖκες** *gunaikes* (wives) **Λαμεχ** *Lamech* (of Lamech) **ἐνωτίσασθέ** *enōtisasthe* (consider) **μου** *mou* (my) **τοὺς** *tous* (the) **λόγους** *logous* (eords) **ὅτι** *oti* (because) **ἄνδρα** *andra* (man) **ἀπέκτεινα** *apekteina* (I have killed) **εἰς** *eis* (in) **τραῦμα**

trauma (pain) **ἐμοὶ** *emoi* (my) **καὶ** *kai* (and) **νεανίσκον** *neaniskon* (a young man) **εἰς** *eis* (in) **μώλωπα** *mōlōpa* (grief) **ἐμοί** *emoi* (my)
dixit -(said)***que*** (and) ***Lamech*** (Lamech) ***uxoribus*** (to the wives) ***suis*** (his) ***Adae*** (Ada) ***et*** (and) ***Sellae*** (Sella) ***audite*** (listen) ***vocem*** (to voice) ***meam*** (my) ***uxores*** (wives) ***Lamech*** (of Lamech) ***auscultate*** (pay attention) ***sermonem*** (to sermon) ***meum*** (my) ***quoniam*** (for) ***occidi*** (I killed) ***virum*** (a man) ***in*** (for) ***vulnus*** (wound) ***meum*** (my) ***et*** (and) ***adulescentulum*** (an adolescent) ***in*** (for) ***livorem*** (sorrow) ***meum*** (mine)
And Lamech said unto his wives, Adah and Zillah, Hear my voice; ye wives of Lamech, hearken unto my speech: for I have slain a man to my wounding, and a young man to my hurt.
Also Lamech said to his wives Adah and Zillah, "*Wives of Lamech, listen to my voice, pay attention to my words, because I have killed a subject, a young offspring who wounded and hurt me*

A superficial literal reading of this verse would leave open the question, "*Who was murdered?*" Since, at this point, we know all the inhabitants of the entire Earth, it should be easy to identify the slayed one.[1415] However, besides Abel, no one is named. We have a murder mystery without a body to confirm it. For sure, it is not an abortion. In fact, in that event, there would have been no need to tell his wives. They would have already known about it. Nonetheless, Lamech informs his wives that it was a recently born, *yeled*,[1416] offspring, a young, *yeled*,[1417] extant subject, *'iysh*,[1418] who had wounded, *petsa`*,[1419] him. *Power*, *viz.* Lamech, similar to all possessors, kills to preserve itself. Throughout history, some powerful and evil leaders also killed (הָרַג *harag*) their own offspring to achieve personal gain or to preserve their empire.

In any case, Lamech is an epistemic paradigm. If not so, his story would be irrelevant for the rest of the Earth or of the Universe. Lamech is the power of ego-consciousness conscious-*of*-the-world **for**-itself. Epistemically, the ego must kill and discard the subject **in**-itself, the unknown knower who harms, hurts and mutilates, *chabbuwrah*,[1420] the absolute power of the ego. Meaningfully, *chabbuwrah, to hurt*, derives from *chabar*, to unite, to be joined together by magical knots.[1421] The young subject, therefore, is rooted in Lamech's ego and wounds him because reduces his power of controlling the world for himself. By killing it, the ego can now concentrate on the objective world and on the wives who give him *ornament* and *shade*. Therefore, he kills the subject, *'iysh* (אִישׁ), which is his own offspring, *yeled* (יֶלֶד). The slayed one is Lamech's own subjectivity in-itself, which he killed by knowing hinself as its own object. Namely, that takes place when one, in the waking state, knows its own *I*-subject as *me*-object. That is when one takes for real its own generated image reflected in a mirror or a photograph. Unrest derives from this loss of resting subjectivity in-itself. Guilt and painful wound (פֶּצַע *petsa`*), deriving from this murderous action, persist to haunt and hurt (חַבּוּרָה *chabbuwrah*) all of us perpetrators, condemning ourselves to this dreadful epistemic loneliness.

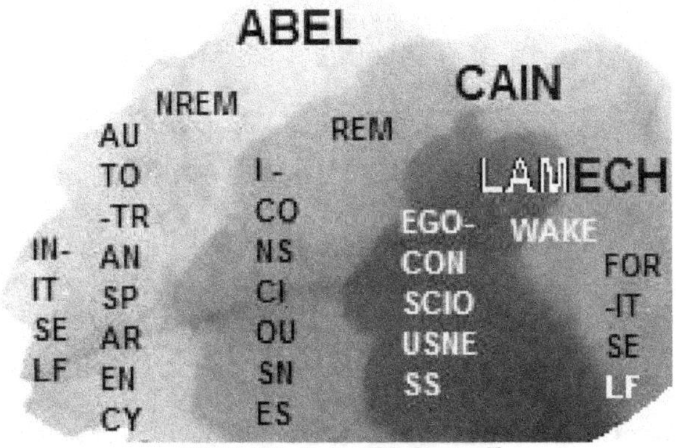

GRAPHIC: *in-itself & for-itself*

The difference between Cain's and Lamech's murders is that while,

1) Cain kills, departing from Abel's NREM state, where all senses are sacrificed, to enter his own red realm of wandering representations,
2) Lamech, in that wandering red land, kills, negating his own unknowable subject/witness that is the invisible observer within his own ego-consciousness-*of* this world.

4:24-Lamech's Punishment

כִּי שִׁבְעָתַיִם יֻקַּם־קָיִן וְלֶמֶךְ שִׁבְעִים וְשִׁבְעָה׃   *kiy* (if) *šiḇaʿāṯayim* (sevenfold) *yuqam* (shall be avenged) *qāyin* (of Cain) *valemeḵa* (of Lamech) *šiḇaʿiym* (seventy) *vašiḇaʿāh* (sevenfold)
ὅτι *oti* (because) **ἑπτάκις** *eptakis* (*sevenfold*) **ἐκδεδίκηται** *ekdedikētai* (was the avenge) **ἐκ** *ek* (of) **Καιν** *Kain* (Cain) **ἐκ** *ek* (of) **δὲ** *de* (but) **Λαμεχ** *Lamech* (Lamech) **βδομηκοντάκις** *bdomēkontakis* (seventy times) **ἑπτά** *epta* (seven)
septuplum (sevenfold) ***ultio*** (punishment) ***dabitur*** (was given) ***de*** (to) ***Cain*** (Cain) ***de*** (to) ***Lamech*** (Lamech) ***vero*** (truly) ***septuagies*** (sevenfold) ***septies*** (seven)
If Cain shall be avenged sevenfold, truly Lamech seventy and sevenfold.
If Cain's retributive punishment was given sevenfold, truly Lamech's should be sevenfold seven."

The epistemic structures are lenses that tint the world. That is to say, we act in this physical world in the same manner we know, understand and see it. Therefore, Cain kills Abel, his own sibling, when he conceptualizes as an object his own *Life's-Breath-Abel*, the Self-in-Itself. Thus, we visualize our restful dreamless-sleep, thus we lose it in the red dream world. Lamech, instead, kills the *manly*-subject, *'iysh* (איש), his own offspring, *yeled* (יֶלֶד). This means that the predominant power of the one and only *ego*-subject, *viz.* Lamech, kills his own I-subject-**in**-itself to know it as a subject-**for**-itself, namely, reducing him/her to its *me*-object. The *I*-subject-in-itself is the child generated/conceived by Lamech but is killed by its own objectifying conceptualization with his two object-wives, Adah, the *ornament*, and Zillah, the *shade*. Thus, Lamech notifies his two consorts, '*I made an object of our child, whom we conceived as a subject.*' The suffering and retributive punishment, deriving from this action, produces the fundamental epistemic loneliness, namely his solipsism. This is true also in the physical dimension, where all offspring become *you*-objects for the parent.

Furthermore, this is not only an epistemic murdering. It is the emblematic function of all the actual physical and epistemic killings. The consequences of one's deeds fall upon the perpetrator. In fact, there is a reciprocity of actions, so that,

"*Whoso sheddeth man's blood, by man shall his blood be shed.*"[1422]

4:25-Seth

וַיֵּדַע אָדָם עוֹד אֶת־אִשְׁתּוֹ וַתֵּלֶד בֵּן וַתִּקְרָא אֶת־שְׁמוֹ שֵׁת כִּי שָׁת־לִי אֱלֹהִים זֶרַע אַחֵר תַּחַת הֶבֶל כִּי הֲרָגוֹ קָיִן׃   *vayēḏaʿ* (knew) *ʾāḏām* (Adam) *ʿvōḏ* (again) *ʾeṯ* (and) *ʾišatvō* (wife) *vatēleḏ* (generated) *bēn* (son) *vatiqarā* (called) *ʾeṯ* (and) *šamvō* (name) šēṯ (Seth) *kiy* (for) *šāṯ* (raised) *liy* (and) *ʾĕlōhiym* (Divine-Consciousness) *zeraʿ* (seed) *ʾaḥēr* (another) *taḥaṯ* (instead) *heḇel* (Abel) *kiy* (that) *hărāḡvō* (killed) *qāyin* (Cain)
ἔγνω *egnō* (knew) **δὲ** *de* (but) **Αδαμ** *Adan* (Adam) **Ευαν** *Euan* (Eve) **τὴν** *tēn* (the) **γυναῖκα** *gunaika* (wife) **αὐτοῦ** *autou* (his) **καὶ** *kai* (and) **συλλαβοῦσα** *sullabousa* () **ἔτεκεν** *eteken* (generated) **υἱὸν** *uion* (son) **καὶ** *kai* (and) **ἐπωνόμασεν** *epōnomasen* (called) **τὸ** *to* (the) **ὄνομα** *onoma* (name) **αὐτοῦ** *autou* (his) **Σηθ** *Sēth* (Seth) **λέγουσα** *legousa* (saying) **ἐξανέστησεν** *exanestēsen* (raised) **γάρ** *gar* (in fact) **μοι** *moi* (for me) **ὁ** *o* (the) **θεὸς** *theos* (God) **σπέρμα** *sperma* (seed) **ἕτερον** *eteron* (another) **ἀντὶ** *anti* (in behalf) **Αβελ** *Abel* (of Abel) **ὃν** *on* (that) **ἀπέκτεινεν** *apekteinen* (killed) **Καιν** *Kain* (Cain)
cognovit (knew) ***quoque*** (also) ***adhuc*** (again) ***Adam*** (Adam) ***uxorem*** (wife) ***suam*** (his) ***et*** (and) ***peperit*** (generated) ***filium*** (son) ***vocavit-*** (called)***que*** (and) ***nomen*** (name) ***eius*** (his) ***Seth*** (Seth) ***dicens*** (saying) ***posuit*** (placed) ***mihi*** (for me) ***Deus*** (God) ***semen*** (seed) ***aliud*** (another) ***pro*** (for) ***Abel*** (Abel) ***quem*** (whom) ***occidit*** (killed) ***Cain*** (Cain)

And Adam knew his wife again; and she bare a son, and called his name Seth: For God, said she, hath appointed me another seed instead of Abel, whom Cain slew.
Adam knew again is wife and generated/conceived a son and called his name Seth, saying, "*God raised for me another seed for Abel whom Cain killed.*"

The Subject-Adam and the Object-Eve have three sons, namely, the three states of mind.

1) The first one is Cain, the possessor, the worker within this waking state.
2) Abel (הֶבֶל *hebel*), the second son, in Hebrew means

   "exhalation, vapour, mist, darkness, which cannot be seen through."[1423]

   "*For he cometh in with vaporous-breath, and departeth in darkness, and his name shall be covered with darkness.*"[1424]

   This is the state of dreamless sleep (NREM), which is like *vapor* (הֶבֶל hebel),[1425] acts *emptily* (הָבַל *habal*)[1426] *and nothing can be said of it other than it is resting silence.*
3) The third offspring is that of dream. Seth is the dream *compensation*, (שֵׁת *sheth*),[1427] the *other* (אַחֵר *'acher*) *seed* (זֶרַע *zera'*) between the silent state of Abel and the waking one of Cain. Seth is an image of the image of God. He is a *resemblance*,[1428] *i.e.* a *dream* of the subject-object.

   "*In the <u>likeness of Divine-Consciousness</u> made He...* [the] *male and female... Adam...* [who] *begat a son in his own likeness, <u>after his image</u>; and called his name Seth,*"[1429]

   as we shall see.

4:26-Seth's Generation

וּלְשֵׁת גַּם־הוּא יֻלַּד־בֵּן וַיִּקְרָא אֶת־שְׁמוֹ אֱנוֹשׁ אָז הוּחַל לִקְרֹא בְּשֵׁם יְהוָה: פ
ulašēṯ (Seth) *gam* (also) *hu'* (to him) *yulaḏ* (was born) *bēn* (son) *vayiqarā'* (he called) *'eṯ* (and) *šamvō* (name) *'ĕnvōš* (Enos) *'āz* (then) *huḥal* (began profaning) *liqarō'* (calling) *bašēm* (the name) *yahvāh* (of the Transcendent) *p̄* (.)
καὶ *kai* (and) **τῷ** *tō* (the) **Σηθ** *Sēth* (Seth) **ἐγένετο** *egeneto* (generatet) **υἱός** *uios* (son) **ἐπωνόμασεν** *epōvomasen* (he called) **δὲ** *de* (and) **τὸ** *to* (the) **ὄνομα** *onoma* (name) **αὐτοῦ** *autou* (his) **Ενως** *Enōs* (Enos) **οὗτος** *outos* (he) **ἤλπισεν** *ēlpisen* (hoped) **ἐπικαλεῖσθαι** *epikaleisthai* (to call) **τὸ** *to* (the) **ὄνομα** *onoma* (name) **κυρίου** *kuriou* (Lord) **τοῦ** *tou* (the) **θεοῦ** *theou* (God)
sed (but) ***et*** (and) ***Seth*** (to Seth) ***natus*** (born) ***est*** (was) ***filius*** (a son) ***quem*** (whom) ***vocavit*** (he called) ***Enos*** (Enos) ***iste*** (this one) ***coepit*** (started) ***invocare*** (invoke) ***nomen*** (the name) ***Domini*** (of the Lord)
And to Seth, to him also there was born a son; and he called his name Enos: then began men to call upon the name of the LORD.
Also to Seth was born a son whom he called Enos. This one started to profane the name of the Transcendent.

The son of Seth is Enos. In Hebrew, this name means *man*.[1430] It is the same as *'enowsh* (אֱנוֹשׁ),[1431] meaning mortal man, person, humanity, which derives from the verb *'anash*,[1432] meaning to be weak, sick, frail. We are here at the presence of the paradigmatic human being, the person here and now, in flesh, bones and dreams. Furthermore, weakness is the typical state of dream as compared to the power of wakefulness. Because of his/her frailty, this person is weak before the great mystery of existence. S/he begins by making up mental images, conceptualizing, hence, <u>*profaning*</u> (חָלַל *chalal*)[1433] the name of the Transcendent, (יְהֹוָה *Yĕhovah*), thus, s/he becomes weaker (חָלָה *chalah*).[1434] Then, s/he <u>dreams up</u> a religion by calling (קָרָא *qara'*) upon the ineffable name (שֵׁם *shem*) of God.

In many cases, humans in uniform impose, with slogans and terrorist wars, their dreamed up creed on non-believers. They are like the schismatic Donatus Magnus of Casae Nigra (313) who preached the necessity of martyrdom to reach sainthood. The bands of his followers were called *Agonistici* (fighters) in the name of Christ. Therefore, seeking martyrdom, the *Donatists Agonistici*, Donatus' armed hand, assaulted Roman troops and caravans to kill and be killed. They loved the death of the Tree of Knowledge more than the Tree of Life itself.[1435]

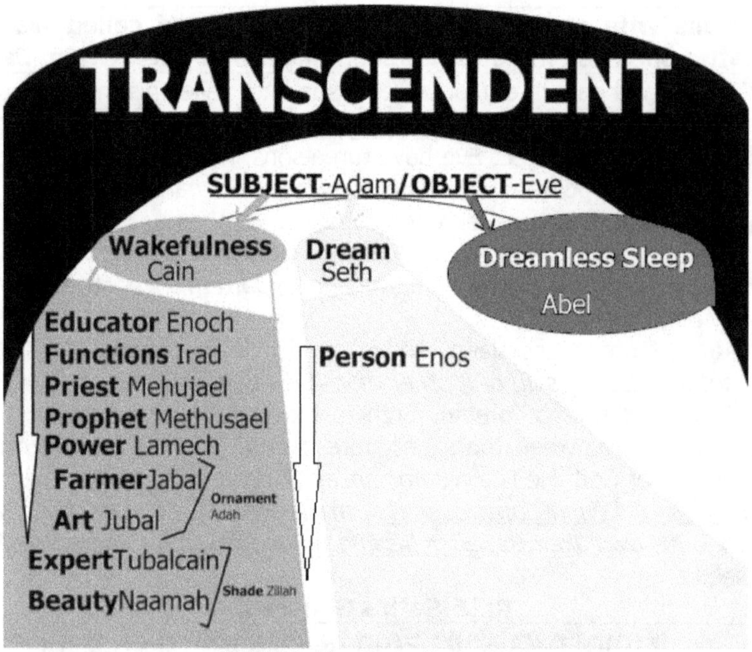

GRAPHIC: *The Generations of Cain*

The political structure, articulated by different social functions, derives from the Possessor. Meanwhile, the dreamer fantasies blaspheming the Transcendent.

HERE ENDS THE FOURTH CHAPTER OF

THE GENERATIONS OF ADAM AND EVE & THAT OF CAIN

CHAPTER 5

THE GENERATIONS OF SETH

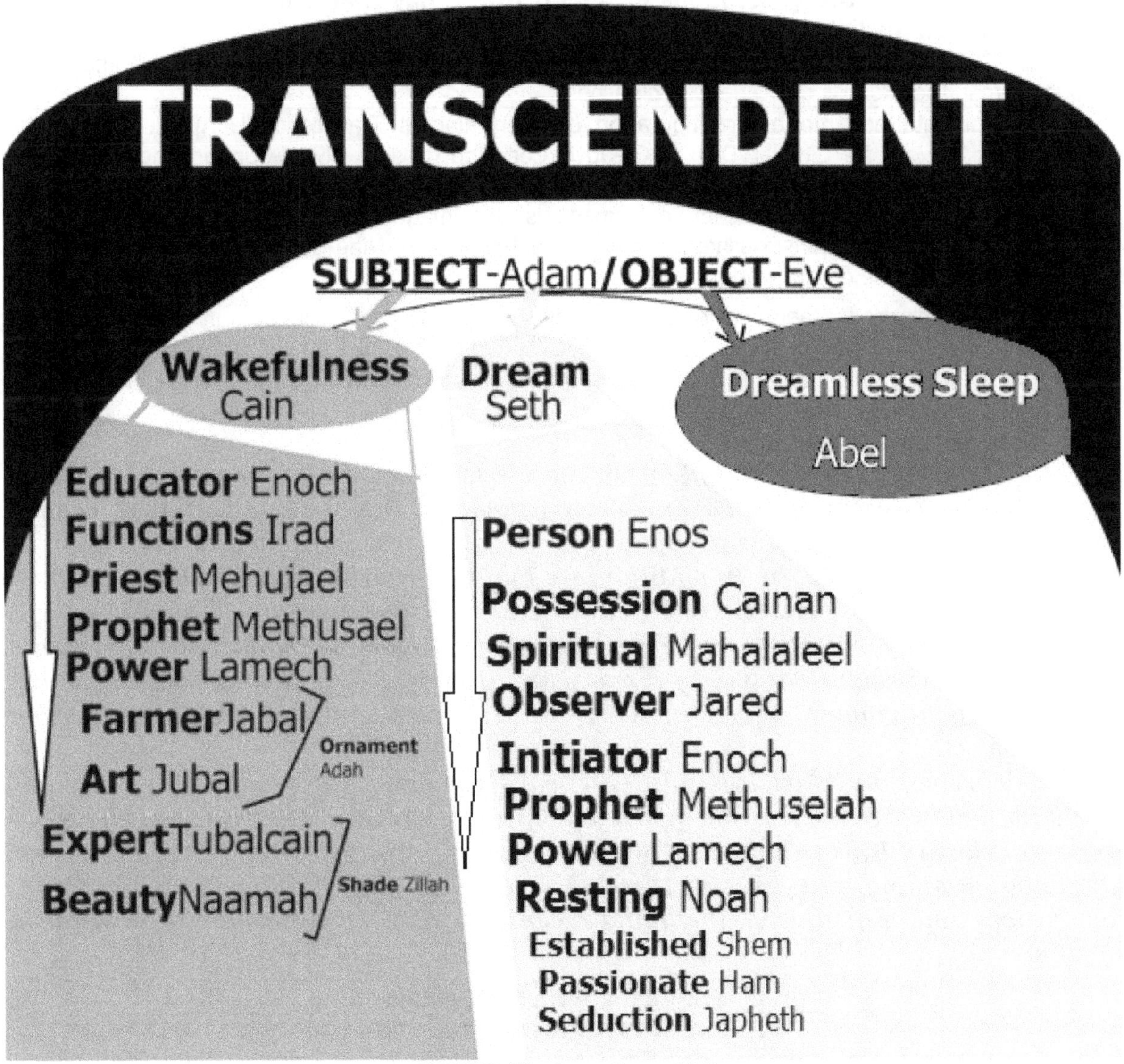

GRAPHIC: *The Generations of Seth*

5-I SECTION: ADAM, MALE AND FEMALE
5:1-Adam, the Image of Divine-Consciousness

זֶה סֵפֶר תּוֹלְדֹת אָדָם בְּיוֹם בְּרֹא אֱלֹהִים אָדָם בִּדְמוּת אֱלֹהִים עָשָׂה אֹתוֹ:
zeh (this) *sēp̄er* (enumeration) *tvōlaḏōṯ* (of the generations) *'āḏām* (of Adam) *bayyōm* (in the day) *barō* (created) *'ĕlōhiym* (the Gods) *'āḏām* (Adam) *biḏamuṯ* (in the likeness) *'ĕlōhiym* (of the Gods) *'āśāh* (made) *ōṯvō* (with him)
αὕτη *autē* (this) ἡ *ē* (is) βίβλος *biblos* (the book) γενέσεως *geneseōs* (of the generation) ἀνθρώπων *anthrōpōn* (of men) ᾗ *ē* (thus) ἡμέρᾳ *ēmera* (day) ἐποίησεν *epoiēsen* (made) ὁ *o* (the) θεὸς *theos* (God) τὸν *ton* (the) Αδαμ *Adam* (Adam) κατ' *kat'* (from) εἰκόνα *eikona* (image) θεοῦ *theou* (of God) ἐποίησεν *epoiēsen* (He made) αὐτόν *auton* (him)
hic (this) *est* (is) *liber* (the book) *generationis* (of the generation) *Adam* (Adam) *in* (in) *die* (the day) *qua* (that) *creavit* (created) *Deus* (God) *hominem* (men) *ad* (in) *similitudinem* (the likeness) *Dei* (of God) *fecit* (He made) *illum* (him)
This is the book of the generations of Adam. In the day that God created man, in the likeness of God made he him;
This is the book of Adam's generation. In the day that Divine-Consciousness created humans, He made them in the likeness of Divine-Consciousness;

The prenatal-post-mortem configuration of everything is Transcendent, Apodictical, Ineffable, Awareness (יְהוָה *Yĕhovah*). Its Circular Day of Creative Consciousness is Divine-Consciousness (אֱלֹהִים *'elohiym*), which has Its Foundation in the Transcendent.

The Auto-transparency present in humans is the image (דְּמוּת *dĕmuwth*) of Divine-Consciousness' (אֱלֹהִים *'elohiym*) circular-day-of-consciousness (יוֹם *yowm*). Eventually, as Divine-Consciousness, also the human becomes a creator in the dream world.

A self-proclaimed atheist, who did not understand what we said so far, may rise in anger declaring,

'This is only your belief, your fantasy concocted by your bigot addictive servitude to
'Religion... the opium of the people.'[1436]

Once more, we calmly reply,

'<u>Inevitably</u> and <u>religiously</u>, we <u>intention</u> the world to be beyond our consciousness-of-it, but, <u>as such</u>, it becomes unknown. We continuously imply the belief that reality is independent from us. We view the world as historical-awareness declared to have existed before we were born. In addition, we buy life insurance for the benefit, after we die, of our loved ones' awareness. In either case, we postulate and fantasize of a past and/or a future awareness never personally experienced by us as such. We cannot avoid this, not even in our dreams. Try if you can. That which is beyond the subject-object correlation is Unknown, which is, therefore, Transcendent, namely Pure Awareness without object.

Awareness, in its purity, must be always apodictic, self-evident. If it were not, it would not be awareness. It is impossible to define It precisely. The best we can do, when we try to classify It, is to express It with a tautology always invoking Awareness or its attributes. Nothing can be apart from Awareness. On It, Consciousness finds its foundation and, reflexively, the mind's consciousness <u>com</u>prehends the word into-existence.'

5:2-Adam, Male and Female

זָכָר וּנְקֵבָה בְּרָאָם וַיְבָרֶךְ אֹתָם וַיִּקְרָא אֶת־שְׁמָם אָדָם בְּיוֹם הִבָּרְאָם: ס
zāḵār (male) *unaqēḇāh* (female) *barā'ām* (created) *vayaḇāreḵa* (blessed) *ōṯām* (with them)

vayiqarā' (calling) *'eṯ* (and) *šamām* (name) *'āḏām* (Adam) *bayvōm* (in day) *hibāra'ām* (when created) *s* (.)
ἄρσεν *arsen* (male) **καὶ** *kai* (and) **θῆλυ** *thēlu* (female) **ἐποίησεν** *epoiēsen* (made) **αὐτοὺς** *autous* (them) **καὶ** *kai* (and) **εὐλόγησεν** *eulogēsen* (blessed) **αὐτούς** *autous* (them) **καὶ** *kai* (and) **ἐπωνόμασεν** *epōnomasen* (named) **τὸ** *to* (the) **ὄνομα** *onoma* (name) **αὐτῶν** *autōn* (their) **Αδαμ** *Adam* (Adam) **ᾗ** *ē* (that) **ἡμέρᾳ** *ēmera* (day) **ἐποίησεν** *epoiēsen* (were made) **αὐτούς** *autous* (they)
masculum (male) ***et*** (and) ***feminam*** (female) ***creavit*** (created) ***eos*** (them) ***et*** (and) ***benedixit*** (blessed) ***illis*** (them) ***et*** (and) ***vocavit*** (called) ***nomen*** (name) ***eorum*** (their) ***Adam*** (Adam) ***in*** (in) ***die*** (the day) ***qua*** (in which) ***creati*** (created) ***sunt*** (were)
Male and female created he them; and blessed them, and called their name Adam, in the day when they were created.
He created them male and female and blessed them. The day, in which they were created, He named them Adam.

Before Eve's creation, **Adam** (אָדָם) **<u>is</u> created** (*barā'ām* בְּרָאָם) **both male** (*zāḵār* זָכָר) **<u>and</u> female** (*unaqēḇāh* וּנְקֵבָה).[1437] In these verses, male[1438] means the subject, namely, the knower as such, the one who performs the action indicated by the verb. Female[1439] means the object, namely, the known as such, the passive one towards whom the action, indicated by the verb, is directed. Adam male/female is the two polarities, without which nothing can exist. In fact, no one can see, hear, smell, taste, touch or think any object, if either the "*I*" or the object are missing. S/he, subject/object is Adam. S/he is the earth reddened[1440] by the incessant subject/object active friction and shuttling correlation. Divine-Consciousness (אֱלֹהִים *'elohiym*) produces (בָּרָא *bara'*) the male/female-subject/object polarities. They are the epistemic poles of the circular day (יוֹם *yowm*) of consciousness. Consciousness recognizes them, metaphorically blessing (בָּרַךְ *barak*) them. Male/female Adam is the paradigmatic epistemological *a-priori* synthesis of subject-object. When that paradigm becomes flesh and blood, then the physical objectivity becomes Adam's wife, Eve. Then, she becomes the actual life giver, Adam's same *flesh* (*shě'er*) who feeds and provides *food* (*shě'er*) for all. Then, the epistemic form becomes the universal physical mother called *Eve*.

From this verse on, *Genesis'* author will observe and describe, with deep psychological introspection, the emanating unfolding power of dreams in the human reality. Following, *Genesis* lists numbers of years. We will translate those numbers and interpret their Gematria values, as they clarify the meaning of the text. We must understand that these verses intend to convey very sophisticated and ineffable concepts. Furthermore, to add to their difficulty, as explained, they defy any conceptualization. Only poetry can open up to their intuition. It is like the

"sweetness to the heart/ that cannot be appreciated by those who do not feel it."[1441]

The Human is male-female, correlated subject-object consciousness.

5-II SECTION: THE GENERATIONS BEFORE THE FLOOD

5:3-Seth, Adam's Dream

וַֽיְחִי אָדָם שְׁלֹשִׁים וּמְאַת שָׁנָה וַיּוֹלֶד בִּדְמוּתוֹ כְּצַלְמוֹ וַיִּקְרָא אֶת־שְׁמוֹ שֵׁת׃ *vayaḥiy* (lived) *ʾāḏām* (Adam) *šalōšiym* (thirty) *umaʾaṯ* (one hundred) *šānāh* (year) *vayvōleḏ* (he begot) *biḏamuṯvō* (likeness) *kaṣalamvō* (image) *vayiqarāʾ* (called) *ʾeṯ* (and) *šamvō* (name) *šēṯ* (Seth)
ἔζησεν *ezēsen* (lived) **δὲ** *de* (but) **Αδαμ** *Adam* (Adam) **διακόσια** *diakosia* (two hundred)[1442] **καὶ** *kai* (and) **τριάκοντα** *triakonta* (thirty) **ἔτη** *etē* (years) **καὶ** *kai* (and) **ἐγέννησεν** *egennēsen* (generated) **κατὰ** *kata* (from) **τὴν** *tēn* (the) **ἰδέαν** *idean* (form) **αὐτοῦ** *autou* (his) **καὶ** *kai* (and) **κατὰ** *kata* (from) **τὴν** *tēn* (the) **εἰκόνα** *eikona* (image) **αὐτοῦ** *autou* (his) **καὶ** *kai* (and) **ἐπωνόμασεν** *epōnomasen* (called) **τὸ** *to* (the) **ὄνομα** *onoma* (name) **αὐτοῦ** *autou* (his) **Σηθ** *Sēth* (Seth)
vixit (lived) ***autem*** (also) ***Adam*** (Adam) ***centum*** (hundred) ***triginta*** (thirty) ***annis*** (years) ***et*** (and) ***genuit*** (generated) ***ad*** (in) ***similitudinem*** (similarity) ***et*** (and) ***imaginem*** (image) ***suam*** (his) ***vocavit*** (called)***-que*** (and) ***nomen*** (name) ***eius*** (his) ***Seth*** (Seth)
And Adam lived an hundred and thirty years, and begat a son in his own likeness, after his image; and called his name Seth:
Also, Adam lived his circle of consciousness till he *poured out the spirit of sleep* (130) in his own image and likeness an easy and light state of mind and called its name Seth:

Consciousness' oneiric circularity at 130° (ק=#100+ל=#30)

From this chapter follows a deep psychological introspection in various paradigmatic aspects of the human oneiric psyche as they unfold in the sleep dimensions. The Patriarchs' life spans want to convey meanings worthy of the revealed text and deeper than just futile year enumeration, as such. First, in God's *Present*, time-*past* and future-*flow* can take place only *in-God's-Present*. Therefore, from God's *perspective*, each created life-span flows after its end and ends before its creation. Second, a year, as Earth's rotation around its Sun, is irrelevant in reference to the billions of light years of the observable Universe. Thus, the lists of the Patriarch's life-years are like true parables, *viz.* meaning something implied by it, but different from its simple story. In other words, there is no immediate necessity to indicate the Patriarchs' life years if not as tools for further epistemic introspections leading to more gnoseological realizations.

Adam, the man and woman call their own image Seth, signifying *compensation* (שֵׁת *sheth*) for the loss of Abel. The name Seth derives from the verb *shiyth* (שִׁית),[1443] meaning *to put, to set lain down, to turn the mind in any direction,*[1444] namely,

"*put all things under his feet.*"[1445]

Seth is the REM condition compensating for the absence of experience in the auto-transparent NREM, the paradigmatic Breath-of-Abel made in the image of Divine-Consciousness. Then, all senses lie down and *rapidly move* turned inward. To confirm that Seth is the realm of dream, this verse declares that Seth is the image of Adam. However, since Adam is an image of the Divine-Consciousness' epistemic structure, Seth becomes an image of the image (דְּמוּת *dĕmuwth*) of those epistemic structures. Namely, Seth is the *dream* of the subject-object Adam compensating for the absence of Abel/NREM. Therefore, Seth is, metaphorically, the I-consciousness-*of*-I, thus, conscious-*of* dream-images as thoughts. Subsequently, *Genesis* gives a list of Patriarchs' names along with the number of years they were active. According to the literal reading of the text, their lifespan lasted hundreds of years. However, those lists are symbolic enumerations expressing paradigmatic recurrent circular year events.[1446] The symbolism, connected with the number of life years, goes beyond pure records. Taken as actual years, they convey no real meaningful insight to the text. In fact, consider how insignificant it is, compared to the age of the Cosmos, the record of years for the understanding the *Book of Genesis*. This is more evident when compared with the reference to the abrupt death ending those unessential year information. In fact, a literal reading of the patriarchs' life spans, as described in the following verses, reduces the text to a mere purposeless list of years and names without shedding new insight to the message. However, the word years, שָׁנָה *shaneh,*[1447] "compare [to] the Lat.[in] *annus*, which pr.[operly] denotes a circle, Gr.[eek] ἐνιαυτός [*eniautos*], Arab.[ic] حَوْل [*hawl*] a circle, a year,"[1448]

derives from the verb שָׁנָה *shanah*,[1449] *to repeat, to do again*, as in the expression,

"*the dream* (חֲלוֹם *chalowm*)[1450] *was doubled* (שָׁנָה *shanah*)"[1451]

Therefore, it represents the concentric ripple effect of recurring consciousness-*of*, continuously flowing and returning on itself to grasp a more expanded *com*prehension of the objective world.

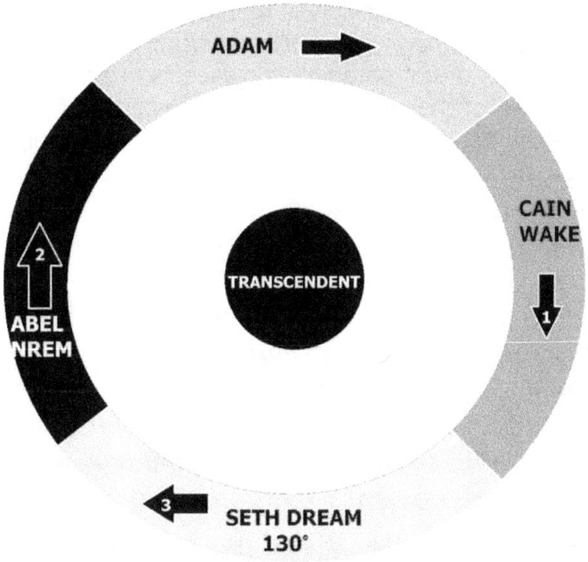

GRAPHIC: *The waking, dreaming and sleep years*

Gematria may help us shed more light and offer a wider understanding of the text and on the numbers related to these years. We do not seek the Gematria numeral interpretation of words, because that may change their meanings. Rather, we favor the translation of numbers into words, which leaves the cypher unaltered. Thus, from the numbers of life years we will deduct the corresponding meaningful words according to Gematria numerology. However, this approach can translate into words, synonyms and/or phrases that may present different meanings, if not contradictory. Therefore, we choose the correct numerical interpretation based on the principle of non-contradiction. Gematria perspective suspends verbal representations to favor introspective numerical abstractions. The prophet Zephaniah writes,

"*For then will I* <u>*turn over*</u> (הָפַךְ *haphak*)[1452] *to the people a* <u>*pure-proofing*</u> (בָּרַר *barar*)[1453] <u>*language*</u> (שָׂפָה *saphah*),[1454] *that they may all call upon the name of the Lord, to serve him with one consent*."[1455]

The word language, *saphah*, derives from *caphah* (סָפָה), to withdraw,[1456] and from *shaphah* (שָׁפָה), to scrape,

"through the idea of termination,"[1457]

compare to *cowph* (סוֹף),[1458] end or conclusion. Thus, it leads to its ultimate goal of signifying the object in itself. Namely, it will have "*one consent*," providing that its Gematria interpretation will never contradict the fundamental intent and purpose of the sacred text itself.

In addition, if these are real waking life spans, it is not clear why they are present in Seth's generation and absent in Cain's previous list. This is because **these years are symbolic expressions of spans of oneiric consciousness**. In fact, the word *years*, *shaneh* (שָׁנָה), means also *to sleep*, as we shall soon explain. They are conscious circularities of dreams and sleep states, which vanish when Cain's wakeful generation appears. In fact, the generation of Cain refers to and are templates paradigms of the waking state, as here and now, while we read *Genesis*.

What we mean is that *Genesis*, in this waking moment of consciousness, describes the dreaming state of consciousness with surrealistic expressions. How can we determine the duration of a dream from the dreamer's perspective? Timing the REM phase is only a perspective of the observer from the waking stage. Nevertheless, the length of dreams - *while dreaming* - is mysterious. Time, days and years, in dreams - *while dreaming* - have a different duration. Then, we may navigate through hundreds of years in an instant. Then, time has a different flow. The dream-flow is real for us *when we dream*, but unreal when we wake-up. Similarly, the waking-phase-time-flow is real for us when we are awake, but unreal when we sleep. The real question is, '*what is time for us while we sleep or while we are dead?*' The list of these Patriarchs and their life span is a record of paradigmatic aspects or functions of human life in their dream dimension. It is not the description of the wakeful historical templates of the individualized personalities in Cain's account. Rather, it is the list related to the paradigmatic faculties, attributes and qualities as belonging to humanity *while* in the dreaming state.

Here, our usual critical believer will comment,

'*You are disparaging the sacred text by reducing it to unconscious dream illusions.*'

We reply,

'*A text that wants to address Adam's entire psychosomatic reality cannot miss his/her oneiric aspects by giving importance and reality only to the waking stage. The length of time, which you call unconscious illusion, is fundamental for the health of the waking state consciousness. In fact, if you sleep only six hours a day, it means that you spend a quarter of the day or one full day every five in the oneiric realm. Thus, no description of creation can skip that essential moment in Adam's life.*'

The name '*Adam*' demonstrates the *Biblical* use of universal paradigms. In fact, the *Torah* describes Adam as the "*male and female*" template. Even if a diehard literalist would want to read it as hermaphrodite, still it would indicate the human with two polarities. Furthermore, we must understand the verb *to generate* (יָלַד; *yalad*) as a metaphor. Truthfully, the male/female Adam, the subject/object, *generates* in the same way thoughts come to be or as we *conceive* (יָלַד; *yalad*) ideas.

> "*And it shall come to pass afterward, that I will pour out my spirit upon all flesh; and your sons and your daughters shall prophesy, your old men shall dream dreams, your young men shall see visions.*"[1459]

While the Indian and/or the Arab numerals[1460] are different from any other letter of those alphabets, in Hebrew, as in ancient Greek, the letters of the alphabet[1461] express also numbers. Thus, the Hebrew *sheba* (שֶׁבַע), seven, is the letter ז (*z*) as well as 7. Numbers and letters are the same. In other words, the Hebrew alphabet expresses, at the same time, letters and numbers. Besides their phonetic aspects and in addition to their semantic combination forming meaningful words (read from right to left), Hebrew letters have numerical equivalents with specific combinations and meanings.[1462] The Kabbalist Gematria[1463] studies and organizes these numerical values in order to add new words and bring additional clarification to the text. We will utilize this method to cast more light over the list of years of the Patriarchs descending from Adam and Seth.

Science predicts the repeatability of an event and its mathematical structure guarantees its predictability. Numbers (N), then, are the structure of nature and Science understands nature through

"the language of mathematics."[1464]

A number ($\mathbb{N}$) is always an abstraction of quantity. However, equality (=) between quantities does not mean identity (I). In fact, identity (I), as uniqueness,[1465] does not allow increasing (+) operation. *E.g.*, if, and *only if* (⇔), $I_{\mathbb{N}}$ is identical to itself $I_{\mathbb{N}}$, then ${}_{\mathbb{N}}I + {}_{\mathbb{N}}I$ would always be $I_{\mathbb{N}}$. The inoperability of an identical number ($\mathbb{N}$) with itself is also true if $\mathbb{N}$ has only a time structure configuration. Specifically, no numerical operation ($/ \cdot \pm$) is possible in the field of time simply as time. Indeed, when, in time, the second $\mathbb{N}$ appears, then, the first $\mathbb{N}$ is already past, thus not present, except as a space/time conception or as memory. Numbers, only as time fragmentation, keep their unique identity. Every minute, as such, is identical with itself. In fact, this minute-now is the only one. The past time ℕ and the future time ℕ are not; thus, the eternal aspect of the present. In this sense, the real continuously inoperable number referring to no quantity and always identical to itself is zero (0), from which all numbers derive.[1466] Moreover, the singularity of Certainty, foundation of all experiences, confirms the unique identity of numbers. In fact, the truly lived Categorical-Intuitive-Experience, as *Erlebnis*,[1467] can only be zero (0) and constantly identical with itself irrespective of the variety of contents as different experiences. Whichever the experience may be, a mine, a cow, a mound of gold, a heap of dung, etc., the Certainty of those occurrences will always be the same empty zero regardless of the *experienced* as such and its awakened emotions.[1468]

To be operable, numbers must refer only to geometrical volumes or space configurations, which can have an equal (=) area but not an identical (*I*) location. Thus, numbers are dimensional quantifications based on space distinctions. Whereas, one acre of land added to an adjacent acre form two acres. The simple operation of 1+1=2 is possible only as the abstract sum of areas, like 1 acre *y* plus (+) 1 acre *z*, a second equal (=) space separated (≠) from the first one. Both locations are unified as *yz*, two volumetrically equivalent (=) distinct (≠) zones, which, placed together, equal (=) 2*yz*. All numbers, then, become abstraction of space configurations, which have distinct locations while having equivalent dimensions. Thus, numbers become real abstract entities universally applicable to all physical dimensional events. In this sense, we can say that the *Biblical* Patriarchs are universal like numbers.

The Hebrew Gematria intends to find connections between words and numbers. Therefore, the literal incredible ages of the Patriarchs prompt us to seek intentional meaning hidden in those cyphers. We are not proceeding from a word to its numerical equivalence in order to change the meaning of the original word. On the contrary, we start from the specific given number, namely the age of a Patriarch, to seek the meaningful reference it may intend. Furthermore, we need to explain the sense or *degree* of the newfound word in its textual contest. Here, we do not mean geometrical or mathematical measurements. Instead, we mean hyperbolic degrees, symbolic of *virtual-dream-life-spans*, as given by Gematria. Then, numbers become letters in words related to their numerical values. Therefore, in this contest, *degree* stands for the level of consciousness reached, as described by the Hebrew semantic-values of numbers with their relative meaning.

First, we read that Adam, as both husband and wife, at the age of one hundred[1469] and thirty,[1470] conceived Seth, their third son. We see the number is composed of two numerical elements, namely #100 and #30. At a first glance, we could argue that one-hundred (ק=#100) represents the completeness of the One-Transcendent-Unity from which both subject and object derive. On the other hand, thirty (ל=#30), *shĕlowshiym*, represents a multiple of three, namely, the triad[1471] of their offspring, Cain, Abel and Seth. Therefore, #130 would be a metaphor for Adam, who, coming from unity, divides itself in three stages.

However, #130 has the Gematria value of the verb *nacak* (נסך), *to pour out* (*the spirit of sleep*).[1472] More so and with a further Gematria reading, hundred is equivalent to the Hebrew letter ק (*q, qôph*, #100), meaning the circle of the sun on the Western horizon.[1473] Thirty is the equivalent of the letter ל (*l, lāmedh*, #30), meaning the *Northern teaching staff*. The letter signifies the desire to know the universe.[1474] Both letters, placed together, form the word *qál* (קל=#130), meaning *low weight*, *light* or *easy*. The word derives from the verb *qalal*,[1475] namely, to be slight, to be swift, to be trifling, to be of little account and to be light.

Now, we can understand that the years, the *degree* or the lifetime[1476] of Adam's recurrent circularity of conscious experience[1477] is interrupted by the generation of Dream/Seth. In fact, the years, *shaneh* (שָׁנָה), are also cognate to the Aramaic *shĕnah*,[1478] which means sleep and year,[1479] corresponding to *shehah*,[1480] sleep, from the verb *yashen*,[1481] meaning to sleep, to be asleep. This event, compared to the harsh and hard reality of the waking state, takes place on the lighter or *easier* (קל *qál*) side of experience. Therefore, the subject/object circularity of experience travels from wakefulness to deep sleep and returns to its origin. During this circular flow of consciousness, Adam generates Seth, who *compensates* (שֵׁת *sheth*) for the loss of Abel, the unknown dreamless sleep. His deliverance,[1482] takes place at #130° degrees/years, in the lighter and easier (קַל *qál*) dream stage.

Consequently, we have a new generational flow, different and parallel to that of Cain. In fact, the functions of Cain's generations are those of the waking state, the state of ego-consciousness. Now, the dream state, the I-consciousness of Seth's generation mirrors the waking functions.

"*It shall even be as when an hungry man dreameth, and, behold, he eateth; but he awaketh, and his soul is empty: or as when a thirsty man dreameth, and, behold, he drinketh; but he awaketh, and, behold, he is faint, and his soul hath appetite.*"[1483]

In return, however, the dream function influences also the waking moment. This is evident in the psychological tendencies revealed in dreams[1484] or in their prophetic[1485] aspects, both affecting the waking moment.

5:4-Adam Conceives Offspring

וַיִּהְיוּ יְמֵי־אָדָם אַחֲרֵי הוֹלִידוֹ אֶת־שֵׁת שְׁמֹנֶה מֵאֹת שָׁנָה וַיּוֹלֶד בָּנִים וּבָנוֹת׃
vayihayu (were) *yaməy* (days) *'āḏām* (of Adam) *'aḥărēy* (after) *hvōliyḏvō* (generated) *'eṯ* (and) *šēṯ* (Seth) šamōneh (eight) *mē'ōṯ* (hundred) *šānāh* (year) *vayvōleḏ* (generated) *bāniym* (sons) *uḇānvōṯ* (daughters)
ἐγένοντο *egenonto* (lived) **δὲ** *de* (but) **αἱ** *ai* (the) **ἡμέραι** *ēmerai* (days) **Αδαμ** *Adam* (of Adam) **μετὰ** *meta* (after) **τὸ** *to* (the) **γεννῆσαι** *gennēsai* (generated) **αὐτὸν** *auton* (he) **τὸν** *ton* (the) **Σηθ** *Sēth* (Seth) **ἑπτακόσια** *eptakosia* (eight hundred) **ἔτη** *etē* (years) **καὶ** *kai* (and) **ἐγέννησεν** *egennēsen* (he generated) **υἱοὺς** *uios* (sons) **καὶ** *kai* (and) **θυγατέρας** *thugateras* (daughters)
et (and) ***facti*** (done) ***sunt*** (were) ***dies*** (days) ***Adam*** (of Adam) ***postquam*** (after) ***genuit*** (he had generated) ***Seth*** (Seth) ***octingenti*** (eight hundred) ***anni*** (years) ***genuit-*** (generated)***que*** (and) ***filios*** (sons) ***et*** (and) ***filias*** (daughters)
And the days of Adam after he had begotten Seth were eight hundred years: and he begat sons and daughters:
After he had generated/conceived Seth, Adam's *two circular sleep years* (800) of consciousness were opened to conceive a *quorum number* (800) of sons and daughters:

Consciousness' oneiric circularity at 800° (ח=#8); (פ=#80); (ף=#800)

Adam's years are calculated because s/he is the initiator or generator of the oneiric circles of consciousness. The Gematria numerical value of the letter ף final (*pē Sofit*) is #800 and it represents the open mouth ready to speak its mind.[1486] The letters פ (*pē* = #80) and ח (*ḥ, ḥêth* = #8) both symbolically represent speech. Furthermore, we have seen that the emergence of Seth, the dream state, fully compensates for the thoughtless stillness of Abel, the dreamless stage.

After the birth of Seth, Adam can now fully think. The subject/object circularity, the circular day (יוֹם *yowm*) and year (שָׁנָה *shaneh*) of consciousness, opens up (פ = #80 and *pē Sofit* ף) to *conceive* (יָלַד *yalad*), in *two years-sleep* (שנתים *šənātayim* = Gematria #800),[1487] a Gematria *quorum number* (מנין *minyán* = Gematria #800)[1488] of sons and daughters, namely, thought-offspring. In other words, in our daily circadian process, *Adam-I/me* proceeds, from the awaken thoughts-perceptions, into more thoughts-experiences, directly generated/conceived as dreams. Eventually, all thoughts rest in the state of dreamless-sleep, from where they wake-up to start the carousel of life anew. All this with two years circularities, one, the conscious circularity of wakefulness, and two, the conscious circularity of dreams.

5:5-Adam's Redemption

וַיִּהְיוּ כָּל־יְמֵי אָדָם אֲשֶׁר־חַי תְּשַׁע מֵאוֹת שָׁנָה וּשְׁלֹשִׁים שָׁנָה וַיָּמֹת׃ ס
vayihayu (are) *kāl* (all) *yaməy* (days) *'āḏām* (Adam) *'ăšer* (which) *ḥay* (lived) *taša'* (nine) *mē'vōṯ* (hundred) šānāh (years) *ušalōšiym* (thirty) *šānāh* (years) *vayāmōṯ* (he died) *s* (.)
καὶ *kai* (and) **ἐγένοντο** *egenonto* (lived) **πᾶσαι** *pasai* (all) **αἱ** *ai* (the) **ἡμέραι** *ēmerai* (days) **Αδαμ** *Adam* (of Adam) **ἃς** *as* (thus) **ἔζησεν** *ezēsen* (lived) **ἐννακόσια** *ennakosia* (nine hundred) **καὶ** *kai* (and) **τριάκοντα** *triakonta* (thirty) **ἔτη** *etē* (years) **καὶ** *kai* (and) **ἀπέθανεν** *apethanen* (he died)
et (and) ***factum*** (done) ***est*** (is) ***omne*** (all) ***tempus*** (the time) ***quod*** (that) ***vixit*** (lived) ***Adam***

(Adam) ***anni*** (years) ***nongenti*** (nine hundred) ***triginta*** (thirty) ***et*** (and) ***mortuus*** (dead) ***est*** (is)
And all the days that Adam lived were nine hundred and thirty years: and he died.
Finally, the living conscious circularity of the Subject/object ends *streaming out* (930) reabsorbing in the Tree of Pure Aware Life.

Consciousness' oneiric circularity at #930° (ט=#9); (צ=#90); (ץ=#900+ל=#30)

Literal interpreters read that Adam lived 930 years. *Tesha`*,[1489] nine, from *sha`ah*,[1490] means to look away, to cause gaze to turn away. Furthermore, the number 9 (ט *ṭ, ṭêth*), symbolizes the surrounding mud. The number 90 (תִשְׁעִים *tish`iym*) corresponds to the letter צ (*ts, tsaddik*), which symbolically means hunting trail, to pursue the desired trailed game.[1491] In addition, the number 100 (מֵאָה *me'ah*) or ק (*qôph*) symbolizes the circle of the sun. Thus, *tesha`*, #9, implies turning away from the subject-object circularity, *i.e.:* the year (שָׁנָה *shaneh*), the mud from which Adam was generated. The number 900, final ץ, *ts* (*tsaddik sofit*),

> "symbolizes the... righteous one... and the *tsaddik* is the foundation of the world... personifies the Tree of Life."[1492]

Moreover, the number 30 (ל, *l, lāmedh*), symbolizes the teaching staff and the desire to know. Therefore, #930 is Adam's redeeming moment. At 900° (ץ) and 30° (ל), Adam, the subject-object circularity of consciousness dies out (מות *muwth*), namely, ends by *streaming out* (לתך *latak* = Gematria #930)[1493] and reabsorbing In-Itself. His/her days (יוֹם *yowm*) and years (שָׁנָה *shaneh*) of desire to know (ל) reabsorb and disappear in the Transcendence, the Tree of Life (ץ), *viz.* the original creative rest (שבת *shabath*) in Pure Awareness.

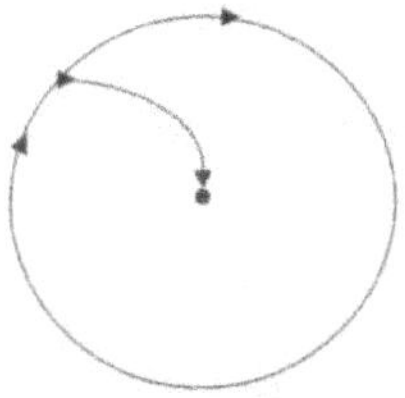

GRAPHIC: *Collapse of the Tree of Knowledge of Good and Evil Circle into the Tree of Life*

5:6-Enos

וַיְחִי־שֵׁת חָמֵשׁ שָׁנִים וּמְאַת שָׁנָה וַיּוֹלֶד אֶת־אֱנוֹשׁ׃ *vayaḥiy* (lived) *šēṯ* (Seth) *ḥāmēš* (five) *šāniym* (years) *uma'aṯ* (hundred) *šānāh* (year) *vayvōleḏ* (generated) *'eṯ* (and) *'ĕnvōš* (Enos)
ἔζησεν *ezēsen* (lived) **δὲ** *de* (but) **Σηθ** *Sēth* (Seth) **διακόσια** *diakosia* (hundred) **καὶ** *kai* (and) **πέντε** *pente* (five) **ἔτη** *etē* (years) **καὶ** *kai* (and) **ἐγέννησεν** *egennēsen* (generated) **τὸν** *ton* (the) **Ενως** *Enōs* (Enos)
vixit (lived) ***quoque*** (also) ***Seth*** (Set) ***centum*** (hundred) ***quinque*** (five) ***annos*** (years) ***et*** (and) ***genuit*** (generated) ***Enos*** (Enos)
And Seth lived an hundred and five years, and begat Enos:
Also Seth/dream *developed* (105) in the round circularity of its process conceiving man, Enos.

Consciousness' oneiric circularity at 105° (י=#10); (ק=#100+ה=#5)

As analyzed, number 100 (מאה *me'ah*) or ק (*qôph*) symbolizes circularity. Thus, Seth's dream state persists in the conscious circularity conceiving Enos,[1494] which means *man*, this mortal person, this dreamer. This is further confirmed by number 5,[1495] or ה (*h, hē*), which symbolizes man.[1496] Moreover, the meaning of number 10, symbolized by the letter י (*y, yôdh*), confirms this man's working activity.[1497] He is the person from whom all dreams proceed and rise, as confirmed by *`alhá* (עלה), the Gematria value of 105,[1498] meaning *to rise* and *to develop*. His counterpart, in the waking stage, is Jubal, the father of artistic creativity.

5:7-Seth's Offspring

וַיְחִי־שֵׁת אַחֲרֵי הוֹלִידוֹ אֶת־אֱנוֹשׁ שֶׁבַע שָׁנִים וּשְׁמֹנֶה מֵאוֹת שָׁנָה וַיּוֹלֶד בָּנִים וּבָנוֹת׃ *vayaḥiy* (lived) *šēṯ* (Seth) *'aḥărēy* (after) *hvōliyḏvō* (generating) *'eṯ* (and) *'ĕnvōš* (Enos) *šeḇa`* (seven) *šāniym* (years) *ušamōneh* (eight) *mē'vōṯ* (hundred) *šānāh* (years) *vayvōleḏ* (generated)

bāniym (sons) *ubānvōṯ* (daughters)
καὶ *kai* (and) **ἔζησεν** *ezēsen* (lived) **Σηθ** *Sēth* (Seth) **μετὰ** *meta* (after) **τὸ** *to* (the) **γεννῆσαι** *gennēsai* (generation) **αὐτὸν** *auton* (his) **τὸν** *ton* (of the) **Ενως** *Enōs* (Enos) **ἑπτακόσια** *eptakosia* (eight hundred) **καὶ** *kai* (and) **ἑπτὰ** *epta* (seven) **ἔτη** *etē* (years) **καὶ** *kai* (and) **ἐγέννησεν** *egennēsen* (generated) **υἱοὺς** *uious* (sons) **καὶ** *kai* (and) **θυγατέρας** *thugateras* (daughters)
vixit- (lived) ***que*** (and) ***Seth*** (Seth) ***postquam*** (after) ***genuit*** (generating) ***Enos*** (Enos) ***octingentis*** (eight hundred) ***septem*** (seven) ***annis*** (years) ***genuit-*** (generated)***que*** (and) ***filios*** (sons) ***et*** (and) ***filias*** (daughters)
And Seth lived after he begat Enos eight hundred and seven years, and begat sons and daughters:
After he had generated/conceived Enos, Seth's days of oneiric consciousness conceived the *flow*ing (807) oneiric offspring as food for dream:

Consciousness' oneiric circularity at 807° (ח=#8); (פ=#80); (ף=#800+ז=#7)

We should keep in mind again that Seth's generation takes place in the dream state, paralleling the waking one. This does not mean that it is not relevant to the waking world. In fact, consciousness takes place on all levels. Each state influences the other. Actually, we are conscious of the dream as we visualize it, while, at the same instance, we are unconscious of the waking state. Similarly, in the waking state we are conscious of it while unconscious of the dreaming one.

As we saw, the numeric value of the final, *sofit*, letter *pē* (ף=#800) represents the open mouth ready to eat food and speak its mind. The letters פ (*pē* = #80) and ח (*ḥ*, *ḥêth*, = #8) both symbolically represent speech.[1499] Therefore, after the birth of Enos, Seth can fully dream. The subject/object circularity, the day (יוֹם *yowm*) and year (שָׁנָה *shaneh*) of oneiric consciousness, opens up (פ = #80 and *pē Sofit* ף) to *conceive* (יָלַד *yalad*) various dreams, as sons and daughters. Namely, all dreams are offspring *flowing* (זרם *zerem* Gematria #807)[1500] from the dreamer and becoming dream food, as symbolized by the number 7,[1501] the letter ז, *z*, *záyin*.

5:8-Seth's Redemption

וַיִּהְיוּ כָּל־יְמֵי־שֵׁת שְׁתֵּים עֶשְׂרֵה שָׁנָה וּתְשַׁע מֵאוֹת שָׁנָה וַיָּמֹת׃ ס
vayihayu (lived) *kāl* (all) *yamēy* (days) *šēṯ* (Seth) *šatēym* (two) *ʿeśarēh* (ten) *šānāh* (year) *uṯašaʿ* (nine) *mē'vōṯ* (hundred) *šānāh* (year) *vayāmōṯ* (he died) s (.)
καὶ *kai* (and) **ἐγένοντο** *egenonto* (lived) **πᾶσαι** *pasai* (all) **αἱ** *ai* (the) **ἡμέραι** *ēmera* (days) **Σηθ** *Sēth* (of Seth) **ἐννακόσια** *ennacosia* (nine hundred) **καὶ** *kai* (and) **δώδεκα** *dōdeka* (twelve) **ἔτη** *etē* (years) **καὶ** *kai* (and) **ἀπέθανεν** *apethanen* (he died)
et (and) ***facti*** (done) ***sunt*** (are) ***omnes*** (all) ***dies*** (the days) ***Seth*** (of Seth) ***nongentorum*** (nine hundred) ***duodecim*** (twelve) ***annorum*** (years) ***et*** (and) ***mortuus*** (dead) ***est*** (is)
And all the days of Seth were nine hundred and twelve years: and he died.
Finally, the living conscious oneiric circularity of Seth/Dream with its active inhabitants *died* (912) out reabsorbing in the Tree of Pure Aware Life.

Consciousness' oneiric circularity at 912° (ט=#9); (צ=#90); (ץ=#900+י=#10+ב=#2)

Here, due to the similarity of verses, we must repeat part of the commentary given for Adam. *Teshaʿ*,[1502] nine, from *shaʿah*,[1503] means to look away, to cause gaze to turn away. Furthermore, the number 9 (ט *ṭ*, *ṭêth*), symbolizes the surrounding mud. Thus, *teshaʿ*, 9, implies turning away from the subject-object circularity, *i.e.* the year (שָׁנָה *shaneh*), the mud from which Adam with Seth, his descendant, were generated. The number 90 (תִּשְׁעִים *tishʿiym*) corresponds to the letter צ (*ts*, *tsaddik*) which symbolically means hunting trail and to pursue the desired trailed game. Moreover, number 10 (י, *y*, *yôdh*) symbolizes activity and number 2 (ב, *b*, *bêth*), inhabitant. Furthermore, two (שְׁנַיִם *shěnayim*),[1504] dual of *sheniy* (שֵׁנִי),[1505] means *second*, from *shanah* (שָׁנָה), *to be other, diverse*,[1506] *viz.* other inhabitants, thus, totaling 912°. The number 900, final ץ (*ts*, *tsaddik sofit*),

"symbolizes the... righteous one... and the tsaddik is the foundation of the world... personifies the Tree of Life."[1507]

Therefore, the number 912 symbolizes the end of the dreaming world of Seth. In fact, at 900 (צ) and 12 (י +ב, עָשָׂר `asar) degrees, the conscious oneiric visualizing circularity of Seth dies out (מות muwth). *He died* (וּמוֹתְתֵנִי umvōṯaṯēniy = Gematria #912).[1508] Namely, the dream ends by shrinking and reabsorbing In-Itself. Its days (יוֹם yowm) and years (שָׁנָה shaneh) of representations reabsorb and disappear in Abel's state of dreamless sleep and, from there, in the Transcendence of the Tree of Life (צ), *viz.* the original creative rest (שַׁבָּת shabath) in Pure Awareness.

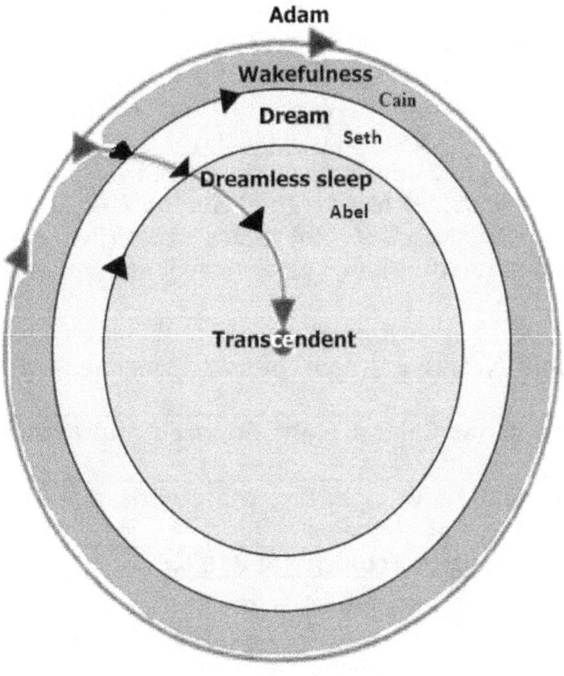

GRAPHIC. Adam's wakefulness, dream, dreamless sleep and Transcendence

5:9-Cainan

וַיְחִי אֱנוֹשׁ תִּשְׁעִים שָׁנָה וַיּוֹלֶד אֶת־קֵינָן׃ *vayaḥiy* (lived) *'ĕnvōš* (Enos) *tiša'iym* (ninety) *šānāh* (years) *vayvōleḏ* (generated) *'eṯ* (and) *qēynān* (Cainan)
καὶ *kai* (and) **ἔζησεν** *ezēsen* (lived) **Ενως** *Enōs* (Enos) **ἑκατὸν** *ekaton* (hundred)[1509] **ἐνενήκοντα** *enenēkonta* (ninety) **ἔτη** *etē* (years) **καὶ** *kai* (and) **ἐγέννησεν** *egennēsen* (generated) **τὸν** *ton* (the) **Καιναν** *Kainan* (Cainan)
vixit (lived) ***vero*** (indeed) ***Enos*** (Enos) ***nonaginta*** (ninety) ***annis*** (years) ***et*** (and) ***genuit*** (generated) ***Cainan*** (Cainan)
And Enos lived ninety years, and begat Cainan:
Indeed, during his oneiric consciousness, *a child shall be born* (90) and Enos conceives Cainan-possessor.

<u>Consciousness' oneiric circularity at 90° (צ=#90)</u>

The number 90[1510] corresponds to the letter צ (ts, tsaddik), which symbolically means stronghold,[1511] hunting trail, to pursue and to possess[1512] the trailed game. This means that Enos, the paradigmatic mortal individual, at 90° degrees of consciousness, in the dream hunt, ambushes and possesses his dream games. There,

"*a child shall be born*" (= Gematria #90)[1513]

to Enos who conceives Cainan (קֵינָן qeynan) and establishes the *nest*[1514] of his passionate-possession. Therefore, the son of Enos becomes another (שֵׁנִי sheniy) inhabitant of the dream world. The word *year*, *shaneh* (שָׁנָה), derives from *shanah* (שָׁנָה), *to repeat, to do again*. It is cognate to *shehah* (שָׁנָא), meaning, *sleep*, which derives from *yashen* (יָשֵׁן), *to sleep*. Furthermore, it is similar to *shĕnayim* (שְׁנַיִם), meaning, *two, second*, which is the dual of *sheniy* (שֵׁנִי), meaning, *another*.[1515]

The oneiric world, as we said, parallels the waking one. Counterparts of the faculties present in the waking realm inhabit the dream dimension. In fact, Cainan (קֵינָן Qeynan) means possession, the same meaning of Cain's (קַיִן Qayin) name. His counterpart in the waking state is Tubal*cain*, who *will be brought* (תובל *tuwbal*) to Cain, *i.e.* the powerful possessor.[1516]

5:10-Enos' Offspring

וַיְחִי אֱנוֹשׁ אַחֲרֵי הוֹלִידוֹ אֶת־קֵינָן חֲמֵשׁ עֶשְׂרֵה שָׁנָה וּשְׁמֹנֶה מֵאוֹת שָׁנָה וַיּוֹלֶד בָּנִים וּבָנוֹת׃   *vayaḥiy* (lived) *'ĕnvōš* (Enos) *'aḥărēy* (after) *hvōliydvō* (having generated) *'et* (and) *qēynān* (Cainan) *ḥămēš* (five) *'eśarēh* (ten) *šānāh* (year) *ušamōneh* (eight) *mē'vōt* (hundred) *šānāh* (year) *vayvōled* (generated) *bāniym* (sons) *ubānvōt* (daughters)
καὶ *kai* (and) **ἔζησεν** *ezēsen* (lived) **Ενως** *Enōs* (Enos) **μετὰ** *meta* (after) **τὸ** *to* (the) **γεννῆσαι** *gennēsai* (generate) **αὐτὸν** *auton* (he) **τὸν** *ton* (the) **Καιναν** *Kainan* (Cainan) **ἑπτακόσια** *eptakosia* (eight hundred) **καὶ** *kai* (and) **δέκα** *deka* (ten) **πέντε** *pente* (five) **ἔτη** *etē* (years) **καὶ** *kai* (and) **ἐγέννησεν** *egennēsen* (generated) **υἱοὺς** *uious* (sons) **καὶ** *kai* (and) **θυγατέρας** *thugateras* (daughters)
post (after) ***cuius*** (of that one) ***ortum*** (birth) ***vixit*** (he lived) ***octingentis*** (eight hundred) ***quindecim*** (fifteen) ***annis*** (years) ***et*** (and) ***genuit*** (generated) ***filios*** (sons) ***et*** (and) ***filias*** (daughters)
And Enos lived after he begat Cainan eight hundred and fifteen years, and begat sons and daughters:
After the birth of Cainan, Enos' days of oneiric consciousness are open to *increase* (815) dream offspring conceiving and interacting with them.

Consciousness' oneiric circularity at 815° **(ח=#8); (פ=#80); (ף=#800+י=#10+ה=#5)**

As we saw, the numerical value of the letter *pē Sofit* (ף final=#800) represents the open mouth ready to give its voice to the mind. The letters פ (*pē* = #80) and ח (*ḥ, ḥêth,* =#8) both symbolically represents speech.[1517] Therefore, after the birth of Cainan, Enos can *increase* (תְּבוּאוֹת *tabu'vōt* = Gematria #815)[1518] his dreams. The subject/object circularity, the day (יוֹם *yowm*) and year (שָׁנָה *shaneh*) of oneiric consciousness, opens up (פ = #80 and *pē Sofit* ף) to *conceive* (יָלַד *yalad*) more dreams, as sons and daughters. He can work actively in the dreams, as symbolized by the number 10 (עָשָׂר *'asar*), letter י (*y, yôdh*). In addition, he can be as a window, symbolized by the number 5 (חָמֵשׁ *chamesh*), letter ה (*h, hē*) from which to view his dreams.

5:11-Enos' Redemption

וַיִּהְיוּ כָּל־יְמֵי אֱנוֹשׁ חָמֵשׁ שָׁנִים וּתְשַׁע מֵאוֹת שָׁנָה וַיָּמֹת׃ ס   *vayihayu* (lived) *kāl* (all) *yamēy* (days) *'ĕnvōš* (Enos) *ḥāmēš* (five) *šāniym* (year) *utaša'* (nine) *mē'vōt* (hundred) *šānāh* (years) *vayāmōt* (died) *s* (.)
καὶ *kai* (and) **ἐγένοντο** *egenonto* (lived) **πᾶσαι** *pasai* (all) **αἱ** *ai* (the) **ἡμέραι** *ēmerai* (days) **Ενως** *Enōs* (Enos) **ἐννακόσια** *ennakosia* (nine hundred) **καὶ** *kai* (and) **πέντε** *pente* (five) **ἔτη** *etē* (years) **καὶ** *kai* (and) **ἀπέθανεν** *apethamen* (died)
facti- (done) ***que*** (and) ***sunt*** (are) ***omnes*** (all) ***dies*** (the days) ***Enos*** (Enos) ***nongentorum*** (of nine hundred) ***quinque*** (five) ***annorum*** (years) ***et*** (and) ***mortuus*** (dead) ***est*** (is)
And all the days of Enos were nine hundred and five years: and he died.
Finally, the living conscious oneiric circularity of Enos, the mortal, the man *turns away* (905) from the cycle of oneiric representation to be reabsorbed in the Tree of Pure Awareness.

Consciousness' oneiric circularity at 905° **(ט=#9); (צ=#90); (ץ=#900+ה=#5)**

Symbolized by the number 5 (חָמֵשׁ *chamesh*), or the letter ה (*h, hē*), Enos, the mortal dreamer, the man, reabsorbs in its origin. In fact, *tesha'*,[1519] *nine*, from *sha'ah*,[1520] means to look away, to cause the gaze *to turn away* (תִּתְהַפֵּךְ *titahapēka* = Gematria #905).[1521] Furthermore, the number 9, ט (*ṭ, ṭêth*), symbolizes the surrounding mud. The number 90 (תִּשְׁעִים *tish'iym*) corresponds to the letter צ (*ts, tsaddik*), which symbolically means hunting trail, to pursue the desired trailed game.[1522] Thus, *tesha`*, 9, implies turning away from the subject-object circularity, *i.e.:* the year (שָׁנָה *shaneh*), the mud from which Adam was generated. Again, the number 900, final ץ (*ts, tsaddik sofit*),

> "symbolizes the... righteous one... and the tsaddik is the foundation of the world... personifies the Tree of Life."[1523]

Thus, Enos ends (מוּת *muwth*) its function at 905° degrees of year consciousness (שָׁנָה *shaneh*), reabsorbing in its own ineffable origin.

5:12-Mahalaleel

וַיְחִי קֵינָן שִׁבְעִים שָׁנָה וַיּוֹלֶד אֶת־מַהֲלַלְאֵל:
vayaḥiy (lived) *qēynān* (Cainan) *šiḇa'iym* (seventy) *šānāh* (years) *vayvōleḏ* (generated) *'eṯ* (and) *mahălala'ēl* (Mahalaleel)
καὶ *kai* (and) **ἔζησεν** *ezēsen* (lived) **Καιναν** *Kainan* (Cainan) **ἑκατὸν** *ekaton* (hundred)[1524] **ἑβδομήκοντα** *ebdomēkonta* (seventy) **ἔτη** *etē* (years) **καὶ** *kai* (and) **ἐγέννησεν** *egennēsen* (generated) **τὸν** *ton* (the) **Μαλελεηλ** *Maleleēl* (Maleleel)
vixit (lived) ***quoque*** (also) ***Cainan*** (Cainan) ***septuaginta*** (seventy) ***annis*** (years) ***et*** (and) ***genuit*** (generated) ***Malalehel*** (Malalehel)
And Cainan lived seventy years, and begat Mahalaleel:
Furthermore, during his oneiric *temple* (70) of consciousness, Cainan conceives Mahalaleel, the praise of God.

<u>Consciousness' oneiric circularity at 70°</u> (ע=#70)

The number 70[1525] is a multiple of the sacred number 7,[1526] corresponding to the letter ע ('o, 'ayin) meaning the watching eye (=#70) of intuition.[1527] Cainan conceives a son, Mahalaleel,[1528] at 70° degrees of dream consciousness. This is dream with spiritual connotations. While we dream we conceive the vision as real in-itself, thus we confer to it a transcending reality. In fact, the name Mahalaleel means *praise of God*. It is the spiritual priestly function within the *temple* (הַהֵיכָל *hahēyḵāl* = Gematria #70)[1529] of this body, which conceives, while dreaming, dreams as transcending realities. It corresponds, in the waking state, to Mehujael, the one *smitten by God* (מְחוּיָאֵל *měchuwya'el*).

5:13-Cainan's Offspring

וַיְחִי קֵינָן אַחֲרֵי הוֹלִידוֹ אֶת־מַהֲלַלְאֵל אַרְבָּעִים שָׁנָה וּשְׁמֹנֶה מֵאוֹת שָׁנָה וַיּוֹלֶד בָּנִים וּבָנוֹת:
vayaḥiy (lived) *qēynān* (Cainan) *'aḥărēy* (after) *hvōliyḏvō* (having generated) *'eṯ* (and) *mahălala'ēl* (Mahalaleel) *'arabā'iym* (forty) *šānāh* (years) *ušamōneh* (eight) *mē'vōṯ* (hundred) *šānāh* (years) *vayvōleḏ* (generated) *bāniym* (sons) *uḇānvōṯ* (daughters)
καὶ *kai* (and) **ἔζησεν** *ezēsen* (lived) **Καιναν** *Kainan* (Cainan) **μετὰ** *meta* (after) **τὸ** *to* (the) **γεννῆσαι** *gennēsai* (generate) **αὐτὸν** *auton* (he) **τὸν** *ton* (the) **Μαλελεηλ** *Maleleēl* (Maleleel) **ἑπτακόσια** *eptakosia* (eight hundred) **καὶ** *kai* (and) **τεσσαράκοντα** *tessarakonta* (forty) **ἔτη** *etē* (years) **καὶ** *kai* (and) **ἐγέννησεν** *egennēsen* (generated) **υἱοὺς** *uious* (sons) **καὶ** *kai* (and) **θυγατέρας** *thugateras* (daughters)
et (and) ***vixit*** (lived) ***Cainan*** (Cainan) ***postquam*** (after) ***genuit*** (generating) ***Malalehel*** (Malalehl) ***octingentos*** (eight hundred) ***quadraginta*** (forty) ***annos*** (years) ***genuit-*** (generated)***que*** (and) ***filios*** (sons) ***et*** (and) ***filias*** (daughters)
And Cainan lived after he begat Mahalaleel eight hundred and forty years, and begat sons and daughters:
After the birth of Mahalaleel, Cainan's days of oneiric consciousness are open to conceive and *dominate* (840) out of the watery chaos, more dream offspring.

<u>Consciousness' oneiric circularity at 840°</u> (ח=#8); (פ=#80); (ף=#800+מ=#40)

The Gematria numerical value of the letter ף, *pē Sofit* (final=#800), represents the open mouth ready to speak its mind. The letters פ (*pē* = #80) and ח (*ḥ, ḥêth* = #8) both symbolically represent speech. After the conception of Mahalaleel, Cainan can now fully dream. The dreamer's circularity, the day (יוֹם *yowm*) and year

(שָׁנָה *shaneh*) of oneiric consciousness, *opens up* (פ = #80 and *pē Sofit* ף) to *conceive* (יָלד *yalad*) in dreams. *'Arba`iym,*[1530] the Hebrew word meaning *forty*, derives from the verb *raba`*,[1531] meaning *to lie down*. Therefore, at 840° degrees of oneiric consciousness, Cainan has *dominion* (למֶמשֶׁלֶת *lamemašelet* = Gematria #840)[1532] and paternal *control* over sons and daughters, namely, all dreams as *offspring*. They come from the unconscious watery chaos symbolically represented by the number 40, conveyed by the letter מ (*m, mêm*).

5:14-Cainan's Redemption

וַיִּהְיוּ כָּל־יְמֵי קֵינָן עֶשֶׂר שָׁנִים וּתְשַׁע מֵאוֹת שָׁנָה וַיָּמֹת׃ ס   *vayihayu* (lived) *kāl* (all) *yamēy* (days) *qēynān* (of Cainan) *`eśer* (ten) *šāniym* (years) *uṯaša`* (nine) *mē'vōṯ* (hundred) *šānāh* (years) *vayāmōṯ* (he died) *s* (.)
καὶ *kai* (and) **ἐγένοντο** *egenonto* (lived) **πᾶσαι** *pasai* (all) **αἱ** *ai* (the) **ἡμέραι** *ēmerai* (days) **Καιναν** *Kainon* (Cainan) **ἐννακόσια** *ennakosia* (nine hundred) **καὶ** *kai* (and) **δέκα** *deka* (ten) **ἔτη** *etē* (years) **καὶ** *kai* (and) **ἀπέθανεν** *apethamen* (died)
et (and) ***facti*** (done) ***sunt*** (are) ***omnes*** (all) ***dies*** (the days) ***Cainan*** (of Cainan) ***nongenti*** (nine hundred) ***decem*** (ten) ***anni*** (years) ***et*** (and) ***mortuus*** (dead) ***est*** (is)
And all the days of Cainan were nine hundred and ten years: and he died.
Finally, the living conscious oneiric circularity of Cainan, the *possessor of richness* (910) ended with the reabsorption in the Tree of Pure Aware Life.

Consciousness' oneiric circularity at 910° (ט=#9); (צ=#90); (ץ=#900+י=#10)

Tesha`*,[1533] nine, from *sha`ah,[1534] means *to look away*, to cause gaze to turn away. Furthermore, the cypher 9, ט (*ṭ, ṭêth*), symbolizes the surrounding mud. Thus, *tesha`*, 9, implies turning away from the subject-object circularity, *i.e.* the year (שָׁנָה *shaneh*), the mud from which Adam with all his descendants were generated. The number 90 (תִּשְׁעִים *tish`iym*) corresponds to the letter צ (*ts, tsaddik*), which symbolically means hunting trail pursuing the desired trailed game.[1535] Moreover, number 10, י (*y, yôdh*) symbolizes *enriching activity* (עָשַׁר *`ashar* = Gematria #910).[1536] The number 900, final ץ (*ts, tsaddik sofit*),

> "symbolizes the... righteous one... and the tsaddik is the foundation of the world... personifies the Tree of Life."[1537]

Therefore, the total number 910 symbolizes the redeeming moment of the whole world of Cainan. In fact, at 900° (ץ) and 10° (י, עֶשֶׂר *`eser*) degrees, Cainan's conscious oneiric circularity of the richness, which he *possesses* (Gematria #910),[1538] dies out (מוּת *muwth*), namely, ends by shrinking and reabsorbing In-Itself. Its days (יוֹם *yowm*) and years (שָׁנָה *shaneh*) of oneiric representations reabsorb and disappear in the Transcendence, the Tree of Life (ץ), *viz.* the original creative rest (שַׁבָּת *shabath*) in Pure Awareness.

5:15-Jared

וַיְחִי מַהֲלַלְאֵל חָמֵשׁ שָׁנִים וְשִׁשִּׁים שָׁנָה וַיּוֹלֶד אֶת־יָרֶד׃   *vayaḥiy* (lived) *mahălala'ēl* (Mahalaleel) *ḥāmēš* (five) *šāniym* (years) vašišiym (sixty) *šānāh* (years) *vayvōleḏ* (generated) *'eṯ* (and) *yāreḏ* (Jared)
καὶ *kai* (and) **ἔζησεν** *ezēsen* (lived) **Μαλελεηλ** *Maleleēl* (Maleleel) **ἑκατὸν** *ekaton* (hundred)[1539] **καὶ** *kai* (and) **ἑξήκοντα** *exēkonta* (sixty) **πέντε** *pente* (five) **ἔτη** *etē* (years) **καὶ** *kai* (and) **ἐγέννησεν** *egennēsen* (generated) **τὸν** *ton* (the) **Ιαρεδ** *Iared* (Iared)
vixit (lived) ***autem*** (also) ***Malalehel*** (Malalehel) ***sexaginta*** (sixty) ***quinque*** (five) ***annos*** (years) ***et*** (and) ***genuit*** (generated) ***Iared*** (Iared)
And Mahalaleel lived sixty and five years, and begat Jared:
Furthermore, during his oneiric protecting consciousness, Mahalaleel conceives Jared, the descent, the *observing seer* (65).

Consciousness' oneiric circularity at 65° (ו=#6); (ס=#60+ה=#5)

At 65° degrees of oneiric consciousness, spiritual Mahalaleel's consciousness conceives Jared, the observer, the *seer* (חזים *ḥōziym* = Gematria #65)[1540] and the protector of all the descending oneiric faculties. In fact, the name Jared (יֶרֶד *yered*)[1541] means *descent*, from the verb *yarad*,[1542] to descend, to sink down. In addition, the number ס (*ṣ, ṣāmekh, #60*) is the symbol of a protecting shield.

"*I am thy shield,*"[1543]
says the Lord, emblematic of the six pointed hexagram, ✡, the Shield of David.[1544] The number ו (*w, wāw,* #6) symbolizes security and, concomitantly, the number ה (*hē, h,* #5)[1545] symbolizes personal observing sight. Therefore, Jared is the observer (#5), the preserver (#60) and the shield (#6) of all the dreaming faculties descending throughout the epistemic process. Its wakeful counterpart, in Cain's generation, is Irad, the regulator of wakeful functions.

5:16-Mahalaleel's Offspring

וַיְחִי מַהֲלַלְאֵל אַחֲרֵי הוֹלִידוֹ אֶת־יֶרֶד שְׁלֹשִׁים שָׁנָה וּשְׁמֹנֶה מֵאוֹת שָׁנָה וַיּוֹלֶד בָּנִים וּבָנוֹת׃ *vayaḥiy* (lived) *mahălala'ēl* (Mahalaleel) *aḥărēy* (after) *hvōliyḏvō* (having generated) *'eṯ* (and) *yereḏ* (Jared) *šalōšiym* (thirty) *šānāh* (years) *ušamōneh* (eight) *mē'vōṯ* (hundred) *šānāh* (years) *vayvōleḏ* (generated) *bāniym* (sons) *uḇānvōṯ* (daughters)
καὶ *kai* (and) **ἔζησεν** *ezēsen* (lived) **Μαλελεηλ** *Maleleēl* (Maleleel) **μετὰ** *meta* (after) **τὸ** *to* (the) **γεννῆσαι** *gennēsai* (generate) **αὐτὸν** *auton* (he) **τὸν** *ton* (the) **Ιαρεδ** *Iared* (Iared) **ἑπτακόσια** *eptakosia* (eight hundred) **καὶ** *kai* (and) **τριάκοντα** *triakonta* (thirty) **ἔτη** *etē* (years) **καὶ** *kai* (and) **ἐγέννησεν** *egennēsen* (generated) **υἱοὺς** *uious* (sons) **καὶ** *kai* (and) **θυγατέρας** *thugateras* (daughters)
et (and) ***vixit*** (lived) ***Malalehel*** (Malalehl) ***postquam*** (after) ***genuit*** (generating) ***Iared*** (Iared) ***octingentis*** (eight hundred) ***triginta annis*** (years) ***et*** (and) ***genuit*** (generated) ***filios*** (sons) ***et*** (and) ***filias*** (daughters)
And Mahalaleel lived after he begat Jared eight hundred and thirty years, and begat sons and daughters:
After the birth of Jared, Mahalaleel's days of *sleep* (830) consciousness actualizes his desire to know by conceiving dream offspring.

Consciousness' oneiric circularity at 830° (ח=#8); (פ=#80); (ף=#800+=#30)

The letter ף, *pē Sofit* (final #800), represents the open mouth ready to voice the mind. The letters פ (*pē* = #80) and ח (*ḥ, ḥêth* = #8) both symbolically represent speech. The subject/object circularity, the day (יום *yowm*) and year (שָׁנָה *shaneh*) of oneiric consciousness, opens up (פ = #80 and *pē Sofit* ף) to *conceive* (יָלַד *yalad*), in *sleep* (Gematria #830)[1546] sons and daughters, namely, all thoughts as offspring. Moreover, thirty, the equivalent of the letter ל (*l, lāmedh,* #30) symbolizes the desire to know.[1547] Therefore, Mahalaleel, at 830° degrees, actualizes its desire to know by conceiving more dreams and oneiric visions as sons and daughters.

5:17-Mahalaleel's End

וַיִּהְיוּ כָּל־יְמֵי מַהֲלַלְאֵל חָמֵשׁ וְתִשְׁעִים שָׁנָה וּשְׁמֹנֶה מֵאוֹת שָׁנָה וַיָּמֹת׃ ס *vayihayu* (lived) *kāl* (all) *yamēy* (days) *mahălala'ēl* (Mahalaleel) *ḥāmēš* (five) *vaṯiša'iym* (ninety) *ušamōneh* (eight) *mē'vōṯ* (hundred) *šānāh* (year) *vayāmōṯ* (he died) s (.)
καὶ *kai* (and) **ἐγένοντο** *egenonto* (lived) *pasai* (all) **αἱ** *ai* (the) **ἡμέραι** *ēmera* (days) **Μαλελεηλ** *Maleleēl* (Maleleel) **ὀκτακόσια** *oktakosia* (eight hundred) **καὶ** *kai* (and) **ἐνενήκοντα** *enenēkonta* (ninety) **πέντε** *pente* (five) **ἔτη** *etē* (years) **καὶ** *kai* (and) **ἀπέθανεν** *apethanen* (he died)
et (and) ***facti*** (done) ***sunt*** (are) ***omnes*** (all) ***dies*** (the days) ***Malalehel*** (of Malalehel) ***octingenti*** (eight hundred) ***nonaginta*** (ninety) ***quinque*** (five) ***anni*** (years) ***et*** (and) ***mortuus*** (dead) ***est*** (is)
And all the days of Mahalaleel were eight hundred ninety and five years: and he died.
Finally, the living conscious oneiric circularity of Mahalaleel, praise of God, *succeeds* (895) to reduce Pure Awareness into a dream.

Consciousness' oneiric circularity at 895° (ח=#8); (פ=#80); (ט=#9); (ף=#800+צ=#90+ה=#5)

The letter ף, *pē Sofit* (final=#800), represents the open mouth ready to *praise God, viz.* Mahalaleel. The letters פ (*pē* = #80) and ח (*ḥ, ḥêth* =#8) both, symbolically, represent speech. The subject/object circularity, the day (יום *yowm*) and year (שָׁנָה *shaneh*) of oneiric consciousness, opens up (פ = #80 and *pē Sofit* ף) to *conceive* (יָלַד *yalad*) dreams. The number 90 (תִּשְׁעִים tish`iym) corresponds to the letter צ (ts, tsaddik), which symbolically means hunting trail, to pursue the desired trailed game. In this case, man's desire *succeeds* (שֶׁהִתְקִיף šehataqiyp = Gematria #895)[1548] into *seeing* his dreams, as symbolized by the number 5 (חָמֵשׁ chamesh), letter ה (h, hē). Here, the conscious oneiric circularity dies out (מוּת muwth). Then, *tesha`* (תֵּשַׁע), nine, from *sha`ah* (שָׁעָה), turns away from the subject-object circularity, *i.e.* the year (שָׁנָה shaneh), the surrounding mud, *viz.* number 9,ט (ṭ, ṭêth).

"*So man lieth down, and riseth not: till the heavens be no more, they shall not awake, nor be raised out of their sleep.*"[1549]

Therefore, the dream ends by shrinking, disappearing reabsorbed In-Itself.

At 895° degrees of dream consciousness-*of* Mahalaleel, dreaming the praise of God, ends. As we saw with Enos,[1550] simply by invoking the name of the Transcendent does not solve the great mystery of existence. In fact, the image or the dream has the effect of visually-conceptualizing (חָלַל chalal) the Transcendent (יְהוָה Yĕhovah) reducing it to a mere mental idol.

"*Not every one that saith unto me, Lord, Lord, shall enter into the kingdom of heaven Awareness; but he that doeth the will of my Father Awareness which is in heaven. / Many will say to me in that day, Lord, Lord, have we not prophesied in thy name? and in thy name have cast out devils? and in thy name done many wonderful works? / And then will I profess unto them, I never knew you: depart from me, ye that work iniquity.*"[1551]

5:18-Enoch

וַֽיְחִי־יֶ֕רֶד שְׁתַּ֛יִם וְשִׁשִּׁ֥ים שָׁנָ֖ה וּמְאַ֣ת שָׁנָ֑ה וַיּ֖וֹלֶד אֶת־חֲנֽוֹךְ׃
vayaḥiy (lived) *yereḏ* (Jared) *šatayim* (two) *vašišiym* (sixty) *uma`aṯ* (hundred) *šānāh* (years) *vayvōleḏ* (generated) *`eṯ* (and) *ḥănvōḵa* (Enoch)
καὶ *kai* (and) **ἔζησεν** *ezēsen* (lived) **Ιαρεδ** *Iared* (Iared) **ἑκατὸν** *ekaton* (hundred) **καὶ** *kai* (and) **ἑξήκοντα** *exēkonta* (sixty) **δύο** *duo* (two) **ἔτη** *etē* (years) **καὶ** *kai* (and) **ἐγέννησεν** *egennēsen* (generated) **τὸν** *ton* (the) **Ενωχ** *Evōch* (Enoch)
vixit-(lived) ***que*** (and) ***Iared*** (Iared) ***centum*** (one hundred) ***sexaginta*** (sixty) ***duobus*** (two) ***annis*** (years) ***et*** (and) ***genuit*** (generated) ***Enoch*** (Enoch)
And Jared lived an hundred sixty and two years, and he begat Enoch:
Furthermore, during his oneiric consciousness, Jared, the *rock* (162), conceives Enoch, the initiator of dreams.

Consciousness' oneiric circularity at 162° (ק=#100+ס=#60+ב=#2)

A hundred is equivalent to the Hebrew letter ק (q, qôph, =#100), meaning the circle of the sun on the Western horizon.[1552] The number ס (ṣ, ṣāmekh, =#60) is a symbol of a protecting shield, emblematic of the six pointed hexagram, ✡. The number ו (w, wāw, =#6) symbolizes security. Finally, the number 2 (ב, b, bêth), *shĕnayim* (שְׁנַיִם), means also *another* and symbolizes *other* (שָׁנָה shanah) inhabitants in the same house. Furthermore, Enoch[1553] means *dedicated to train and initiate*. Therefore, at 162° degrees/years, during his circular flow of oneiric consciousness (#100), Jared reaches and generates Enoch, the initiator. This one is equivalent to the waking Enoch. Jared, as his generator, is the sturdy *rock* (בְּסֶלַע başcela' = Gematria #162)[1554] of dreaming objectivity, the preserver (#60), the protecting shield (#6) of all oneiric faculties and the solid foundation from which derives Enoch, the initiator of all inhabitants (#2) of the dreaming world.

5:19-Jared's Offspring

וַֽיְחִי־יֶ֗רֶד אַֽחֲרֵי֙ הוֹלִיד֣וֹ אֶת־חֲנ֔וֹךְ שְׁמֹנֶ֥ה מֵא֖וֹת שָׁנָ֑ה וַיּ֥וֹלֶד בָּנִ֖ים וּבָנֽוֹת׃
vayaḥiy (lived) *yereḏ* (Jared) *aḥărēy* (after) *hvōliyḏvō* (having generated) *`eṯ* (and) *ḥănvōḵa* (Enoch) *šamōneh* (eight) *mē`vōṯ* (hundred) *šānāh* (years) *vayvōleḏ* (generated) *bāniym* (sons) *uḇānvōṯ* (daughters)
καὶ *kai* (and) **ἔζησεν** *ezēsen* (lived) **Ιαρεδ** *Iared* (Iared) **μετὰ** *meta* (after) **τὸ** *to* (the) **γεννῆσαι** *gennēsai* (generate) **αὐτὸν** *auton* (he) **τὸν** *ton* (the) **Ενωχ** *Enōch* (Enoch) **ὀκτακόσια** *oktakosia* (eight hundred) **ἔτη** *etē* (years) **καὶ** *kai* (and) **ἐγέννησεν** *egennēsen* (generated) **υἱοὺς** *uious*

(sons) **καὶ** *kai* (and) **θυγατέρας** *thugateras* (daughters)
et (and) ***vixit*** (lived) ***Iared*** (Iared) ***postquam*** (after) ***genuit*** (generating) ***Enoch*** (Enoch) ***octingentos*** (eight hundred) ***annos*** (years) ***et*** (and) ***genuit*** (generated) ***filios*** (sons) ***et*** (and) ***filias*** (daughters)
And Jared lived after he begat Enoch eight hundred years, and begat sons and daughters:
After the birth of Enoch, Jared's days of oneiric consciousness are open to conceive a *quorum number* (800) of other dream sons and daughters.

Consciousness' oneiric circularity at 800° (ח=#8); (פ=#80); (ף=#800)

The numerical value of the letter ף, *pē Sofit* (final=#800), represents the open mouth ready to utter its dream. The letters פ (*pē* = #80) and ח (*ḥ, ḥêth* = #8) both symbolically represent speech. Therefore, after the birth of Enoch, Jared can now fully dream. The subject/object circularity, the day (יום *yowm*) and year (שָׁנָה *shaneh*) of oneiric consciousness, *open up* (פ = #80 and *Pē Sofit* ף) to *conceive* (יָלַד *yalad*), in dreams, a *quorum number* (מנין *minyán* = Gematria #800)[1555] of sons and daughters, namely, dreams as offspring.

5:20-Jared's Redemption

וַיִּהְיוּ כָּל־יְמֵי־יֶרֶד שְׁתַּיִם וְשִׁשִּׁים שָׁנָה וּתְשַׁע מֵאוֹת שָׁנָה וַיָּמֹת: פ
vayihayu (lived) *kāl* (all) *yamēy* (days) *yereḏ* (of Jared) *šatayim* (two) *vašišiym* (sixty) vašišiym (sixty) *šānāh* (years) *uṯaša`* (nine) *mē'vōṯ* (hundred) *šānāh* (years) *vayāmōṯ* (he died) *p̄* (.)
καὶ *kai* (and) **ἐγένοντο** *egenonto* (lived) **πᾶσαι** *pasai* (all) **αἱ** *ai* (the) **ἡμέραι** *ēmerai* (days) **Ιαρεδ** *Iared* (Iared) **ἐννακόσια** *ennakosia* (nine hundred) **καὶ** *kai* (and) **ἑξήκοντα** *exēkonta* (sixty) **δύο** *duo* (two) **ἔτη** *etē* (years) **καὶ** *kai* (and) **ἀπέθανεν** *apethamen* (died)
et (and) ***facti*** (done) ***sunt*** (are) ***omnes*** (all) ***dies*** (the days) ***Iared*** (Iared) ***nongenti*** (nine hundred) ***sexaginta*** (sixty) ***duo*** (two) ***anni*** (years) ***et*** (and) ***mortuus*** (dead) ***est*** (is)
And all the days of Jared were nine hundred sixty and two years: and he died.
Finally, the living conscious oneiric circularity of Jared, the *observer* (962) with all descendants, ended with the reabsorption in the Tree of Pure Awareness.

Consciousness' oneiric circularity at 962° (ט=#9); (צ=#90); (ו=#6); (ץ=#900+ס=#60+ב=#2)

Tesha`* (תֵּשַׁע), nine, from *sha`ah (שָׁעָה), means *to turn away* and the number 9 (ט, *ṭ, ṭêth*), symbolizes the surrounding mud. Thus, *tesha`*, 9, implies turning away from the subject-object circularity, *i.e.* the year (שָׁנָה *shaneh*), the mud from which all his descendants and all desires are generated. In fact, the number 90 (תִּשְׁעִים *tish`iym*) corresponds to the letter צ (*ts, tsaddik*), which symbolically means *hunting trail*, to pursue the *desired* trailed game. The number 900, final ץ (*ts, tsaddik sofit*), symbolizes the foundation of the world, namely the Tree of Life.[1556] The number ס (*ṣ, ṣāmekh*, #60) is the symbol of the protecting shield, ✡. The number ו (*w, wāw*, #6) symbolizes security. Finally, the number 2 (ב, *b, bêth*), meaning also *another* (שְׁנַיִם *shĕnayim*), symbolizes the other (שָׁנָה *shanah*) inhabitants of the oneiric world.

Therefore, at 962° degrees/years, during this circular flow of oneiric consciousness, Jared, the one who *observes* (תְּשׁוּרֶנּוּ *tašwrenw* = Gematria #962),[1557] preserves (#60) the protecting shield (#6) of all the oneiric faculties and the initiator of all the inhabitants (#2) of the dreaming world, reabsorbs in the original Tree of Life (#900) from which he derives.

5:21-Methuselah

וַיְחִי חֲנוֹךְ חָמֵשׁ וְשִׁשִּׁים שָׁנָה וַיּוֹלֶד אֶת־מְתוּשָׁלַח:
vayaḥiy (lived) *ḥănvōḵa* (Enoch) *ḥāmēš* (five) *vašišiym* (sixty) *šānāh* (years) *vayvōleḏ* (generated) *'eṯ* (and) *maṯušālaḥ* (Methuselah)
καὶ *kai* (and) **ἔζησεν** *ezēsen* (lived) **Ενωχ** *Enōch* (Enoch) **ἑκατὸν** *ekaton* (hundred)[1558] **καὶ** *kai* (and) **ἑξήκοντα** *exēkonta* (sixty) **πέντε** *pente* (five) **ἔτη** *etē* (years) **καὶ** *kai* (and) **ἐγέννησεν** *egennēsen* (generated) **τὸν** *ton* (the) **Μαθουσαλα** *Mathousala* (Mathousala)
porro (following) ***Enoch*** (Enoch) ***vixit*** (lived) ***sexaginta*** (sixty) ***quinque*** (five) ***annis*** (years) ***et*** (and) ***genuit*** (generated) ***Mathusalam*** (Mathusalam)

And Enoch lived sixty and five years, and begat Methuselah:
Furthermore, during his oneiric consciousness, Enoch conceived Methuselah, the *Prophesizing* (65) Man Of The Dart Who Is With God.

Consciousness' oneiric circularity at 65° (ו=#6); (ס=#60+ה=#5)

At the same 65° degrees of Jared's oneiric observing consciousness, Enoch, the initiator of dream consciousness, envisions Methuselah,[1559] meaning, *The Man Of The Dart Who Is With God.*[1560] This is the epistemic faculty continuously projecting towards Transcendence. The number ס (*ṣ, ṣāmekh,* #60) is a symbol of the six pointed hexagram, ✡, protecting shield. The number ו (*w, wāw,* #6) symbolizes security and, concomitantly, the number ה (*hē, h,* #5, *chamesh*))[1561] symbolizes personal human observing sight.

Therefore, Methuselah is the preserver (#60) and the shield (#6) who observes (#5) his dart aimed to God. He is the prophetic dream and *he shall prophesy* (וְנִבָּאוּ *waniba'w* = Gematria #65).[1562] In fact,

"*He... saw the vision of the Almighty, while falling*[1563] *into a sleep vision, but having his eyes open.*"[1564]

In the waking state, his counterpart is the prophetic function of Methusael.

Anyone, claiming to have had prophetic[1565] dreams, once they come true, will have the impossible task to demonstrate their reliability.[1566] Furthermore, also psychologists explored their possibility.[1567]

5:22-Enoch's Offspring

וַיִּתְהַלֵּךְ חֲנוֹךְ אֶת־הָאֱלֹהִים אַחֲרֵי הוֹלִידוֹ אֶת־מְתוּשֶׁלַח שְׁלֹשׁ מֵאוֹת שָׁנָה וַיּוֹלֶד בָּנִים וּבָנוֹת׃
vayitahalēka (walked) *ḥănvōka* (Enoch) *'et* (with) *hā'ĕlōhiym* (Gods) *'aḥărēy* (after) *hvōliydvō* (generating) *'et* (and) *matušelaḥ* (Methuselah) *šalōš* (three) *mē'vōt* (hundred) *šānāh* (years) *vayvōled* (generated) *bāniym* (sons) *ubānvōt* (daughters)
εὐηρέστησεν *euērestēsen* (was pleasing) **δὲ** *de* (but) **Ενωχ** *Enōch* (Enoch) **τῷ** *tō* (the) **θεῷ** *theō* (God) **μετὰ** *meta* (after) **τὸ** *to* (the) **γεννῆσαι** *gennēsai* (generation) **αὐτὸν** *auton* (his) **τὸν** *ton* (of the) **Μαθουσαλα** *Mathousala* (Methuselah) **διακόσια** *diakosia* (two hundred)[1568] **ἔτη** *etē* (years) **καὶ** *kai* (and) **ἐγέννησεν** *egennēsen* (generated) **υἱοὺς** *uious* (sons) **καὶ** *kai* (and) **θυγατέρας** *thugateras* (daughters)
et (and) ***ambulavit*** (walked) ***Enoch*** (Enoch) ***cum*** (with) ***Deo*** (God) ***postquam*** (after) ***genuit*** (generating) ***Mathusalam*** (Methuselah) ***trecentis*** (three hundred) ***annis*** (years) ***et*** (and) ***genuit*** (generated) ***filios*** (sons) ***et*** (and) ***filias*** (daughters)
And Enoch walked with God after he begat Methuselah three hundred years, and begat sons and daughters:
Moreover, after conceiving Methuselah, Enoch walked with Divine-Consciousness and his days of oneiric consciousness were like a *shepherd*'s (300) staff leading to conceive sons and daughters as dream offspring:

Consciousness' oneiric circularity at 300° (ג=#3); (ל=#30); (ש=#300)

The Hebrew words *ben* (בֵּן),[1569] *son,* and *bath* (בַּת),[1570] *daughter,* derive from the verb *banah* (בָּנָה),[1571] *to build, to construct* and *to establish.* Therefore, these *offspring,* both in the waking and/or in the dreaming realms, represent the metaphoric modalities *built, constructed* and *established* by their symbolic fathers reaching a specific circular degree of consciousness. This means that the *offspring* are qualities, attributes or states of being of the dreamer and/or of the perceiver. In fact, in the preceding verse, at 65° degrees of oneiric consciousness, Enoch conceived his son Methuselah, who *is with God* (מְתוּשָׁאֵל *měthuwsha'el*). In this verse, Enoch himself *walks*[1572] *with Divine-Consciousness* (אֱלֹהִים *'elohiym*). Furthermore, this moving together is confirmed by the number 3,[1573] the letter ג (*g, gimel*), symbolizing walking.[1574]

The number 30, equivalent of the letter ל (*l, lāmedh*), symbolizes the *staff* of the *shepherd* (רֹעֵיךָ *rō'aykā* = Gematria #300),[1575] the yoke leading toward a different direction.[1576] Thus,

"*the Transcendent* (יְהוָה Yĕhovah) [is] *my shepherd* (רָעָה *ra'ah*); *I shall not want.. thy rod and thy staff they comfort me.*"[1577]

Finally, the number 300, the letter ש (*š, šîn*) symbolizes eating.[1578] Thus, *dedicated* Enoch,[1579] after (אחר *'achar*) walking (הלך *halak*) and being directed (ל, #30) by the Pure-Fundamentals of Divine-Consciousness, namely, Aware-Conscious-Certainty, knows the epistemic structure of the universe.[1580] Consequently, also his days of oneiric consciousness are open to conceive offspring as food for dreams (ש, #300).

Only by granting a universal epistemic metaphoric meaning to the term offspring, we can give a worldwide meaning to the whole sequence of descendants. On the contrary, the progeny-line would remain entirely irrelevant to a galaxy five billion light years away from us.

5:23-Enoch's Days

וַיְהִי כָּל־יְמֵי חֲנוֹךְ חָמֵשׁ וְשִׁשִּׁים שָׁנָה וּשְׁלֹשׁ מֵאוֹת שָׁנָה׃ *vayahiy* (were) *kāl* (all) *yamēy* (days) *ḥănvōḵa* (of Enoch) *ḥāmēš* (five) *vašišiym* (sixty) *šānāh* (years) *ušalōš* (three) *mē'vōṯ* (hundred) *šānāh* (years)
καὶ *kai* (and) **ἐγένοντο** *egenonto* (lived) **πᾶσαι** *pasai* (all) **αἱ** *ai* (the) **ἡμέραι** *ēmerai* (days) **Ενωχ** *Enōch* (of Enoch) **τριακόσια** *triakosia* (three hundred) **ἑξήκοντα** *exēkonta* (sixty) **πέντε** *pente* (five) **ἔτη** *etē* (years)
et (and) ***facti*** (done) ***sunt*** (were) ***omnes*** (all) ***dies*** (the days) ***Enoch*** (of Enoch) ***trecenti*** (three hundred) ***sexaginta*** (sixty) ***quinque*** (five) ***anni*** (years)
And all the days of Enoch were three hundred sixty and five years:
Therefore, all the dream circularities of Enoch ended in the realization of *sleep* (365).

Consciousness' oneiric circularity at 365° (ג=#3); (ו=#6); (ל=#30); (ש=#300+ס=#60+ה=#5)

The entire oneiric epistemic circularity of Enoch, the one who is *dedicated*, the initiator of *sleep* (יְשֵׁנָה *yašēnāh* = Gematria #365)[1581] consciousness, is 365° degrees. As we have seen in the previous two verses, this degree includes the dreaming conception of his son Methuselah (#65). Enoch is *walking* (ג, #3) *with Divine-Consciousness* toward another direction (ל, #30), different from the usual identification with the objects, which has its food as dreams (ש, #300) and by which the epistemic structure of the universe is realized. Enoch is the preserver (ס, #60) and the shield (ו, #6) who controls and observes (ה, #5) his dart aimed at Divine-Consciousness.

5:24-Enoch's Dreamless Sleep

וַיִּתְהַלֵּךְ חֲנוֹךְ אֶת־הָאֱלֹהִים וְאֵינֶנּוּ כִּי־לָקַח אֹתוֹ אֱלֹהִים׃ פ *vayiṯahalēḵa* (walked) *ḥănvōḵa* (Enoch) *'eṯ* (with) *hā'ĕlōhiym* (Gods) *va'ēynenu* (was not) *kiy* (because) *lāqaḥ* (took) *'ōṯvō* (from) *'ĕlōhiym* (Gods) *p̄* (.)
καὶ *kai* (and) **εὐηρέστησεν** *euērestēsen* (pleased) **Ενωχ** *Enōch* (Enoch) **τῷ** *tō* (the) **θεῷ** *theō* (God) **καὶ** *kai* (and) **οὐχ** *ouch* (non) **ηὑρίσκετο** *ēurisketo* (find) **ὅτι** *oti* (because) **μετέθηκεν** *metethēken* (took) **αὐτὸν** *auton* (him) **ὁ** *o* (the) **θεός** *theos* (God)
ambulavit- (walked) ***que*** (and) ***cum*** (with) ***Deo*** (God) ***et*** (and) ***non*** (not) ***apparuit*** (appeared) ***quia*** (because) ***tulit*** (took) ***eum*** (him) ***Deus*** (God)
And Enoch walked with God: and he was not; for God took him.
Enoch walked with Divine-Consciousness and moved into nothingness because Divine-Consciousness took him there.

This verse does not proclaim the immortality of Enoch or his assumption to Heaven. Such an event, in fact, would make Enoch the first one, after the fall, to open and enter the gates of Heaven. Thus, it would make him a Savior *ante litteram*. Furthermore, this would undermine various religious interpretations regarding the Messiah, Christ the Anointed One.[1582] In fact, Luther, commenting Paul's affirmation,

> "*For therein is the righteousness of God revealed from faith to faith: as it is written, The just shall live by faith,*"[1583]

stated that we find

> "justification by faith alone (*per solam fidem*)... only Christ (*solus Christus*)... only Grace (*sola gratia*)... [is] an open door into paradise.... a gate to heaven."[1584]

In reality, this verse describes the recurrent flow of the daily circadian rhythm, which leads humans from wakefulness to dream (REM sleep) and to dreamless sleep (NREM). Enoch's mode of being is that of his son. Namely, it is the dart (מְתוּשֶׁלַח *měthuwshelach*), which is with God (מְתוּשָׁאֵל *měthuwsha'el*). Once Enoch releases his arrow and it reaches Divine-Consciousness, it does not return to the world of duality of its propelling bow. Enoch is with Divine-Consciousness. He becomes the template of the oneiric faculty absorbed in its silence. Enoch is not any longer a dreamer or a dream. He is in the thoughtless NREM state, the realm of Auto-Transparency, which is the same realm of Abel.

> "*The LORD hath poured out*[1585] *upon you the spirit of deep sleep,*[1586] *and hath closed your eyes: the prophets and your rulers, the seers hath he covered.*"[1587]

In other words, in this verse, Enoch symbolizes the walking, moving[1588] or translating[1589] of the dreamer from his dream state into the *nothingness*[1590] of the dreamless sleep. That condition persists as a recurrent state constituting one of the three pillars of human reality. Namely, they are waking, dreaming (REM, חֲלוֹם *chalowm*) and deep sleep (NREM, תַּרְדֵּמָה *tardemah*).

Finally, Enoch is the faculty or the template that inverts the cognitive process. With an ever deeply introverted search, s/he travels along those three states of consciousness, namely, ego-consciousness, I-consciousness and Auto-transparency. Retracing ande retracting the whole emanation, the human reaches the final absorption in the original principle from which the entire epistemic process started.

5:25-Lamech

וַיְחִי מְתוּשֶׁלַח שֶׁבַע וּשְׁמֹנִים שָׁנָה וּמְאַת שָׁנָה וַיּוֹלֶד אֶת־לָמֶךְ׃   *vayaḥiy* (lived) *maṯušelaḥ* (Methuselah) *šeḇaʿ* (seven) *ušamōniym* (eighty) *šānāh* (years) *umaʾaṯ* (hundred) *šānāh* (years) *vayvōleḏ* (generated) *ʾeṯ* (and) *lāmeḵa* (Lamech)
καὶ *kai* (and) **ἔζησεν** *ezēsen* (lived) **Μαθουσαλα** *Mathousala* (Methuselah) **ἑκατὸν** *ekaton* (hundred) **καὶ** *kai* (and) **ἑξήκοντα** *exēkonta* (sixty)[1591] **ἑπτὰ** *epta* (seven) **ἔτη** *etē* (years) **καὶ** *kai* (and) **ἐγέννησεν** *egennēsen* (generated) **τὸν** *ton* (the) **Λαμεχ** *Lamech* (Lamech)
vixit (lived) ***quoque*** (also) ***Mathusalam*** (Methuselah) ***centum*** (one hundred) ***octoginta*** (eighty) ***septem*** (seven) ***annos*** (years) ***et*** (and) ***genuit*** (generated) ***Lamech*** (Lamech)
And Methuselah lived an hundred eighty and seven years, and begat Lamech:
In addition, during his oneiric harvesting prophetic circular active consciousness, Methuselah conceived the *strength* (187) and power of Lamech.

Consciousness' oneiric circularity at 187° (ז=#7); (ח=#8); (י=#10); (ק=#100+פ=#80+ז=#7)

As we said, consciousness takes place on every level. We are conscious-*of* the dream as we visualize it. We are conscious-*of* the waking state as we experience it. We are also conscious during the silence of consciousness itself. The repetition of functions/personalities, as Enoch and Lamech, demonstrates it. In the waking dimension, Enoch, the civic educator, is the ancestor, from whom the waking power of Lamech descends. Similarly, in the oneiric dimension, at the end of the dreamless cycle, the dream power of Lamech descends from Enoch, the one who is dedicated to train and initiate.

The powerful cycle of consciousness-*of* objects rules the world. It stems out from the prophetic functions, of Methusael, in the waking world, and of Methuselah, in the dream world. Both names derive from *math* (מַת),[1592] meaning *men*. However, while Methusael (מְתוּשָׁאֵל Mĕthuwsha'el)[1593] is the *man when* (מָתַי *mathay*)[1594] *he is of God* (אֵל *'el*),[1595] Methuselah (מְתוּשֶׁלַח Mĕthuwshelach)[1596] is the *man* (*math* מַת) *of the dart* (שֶׁלַח *shelach*)[1597] *to be* released (שָׁלַח *shalach*).[1598] In both cases, waking and/or dreaming, foresight generates Lamech's *strength* (מָעוּזְךָ *māʿuzaḵen* = Gematria #187)[1599] and *exercised power*. In any case, after Enoch's dreamless sleep, the dream state returns.

As examined, number 100 (מֵאָה *me'ah*) or ק (*qôph*) symbolizes circularity. Thus, Methuselah's dream state persists in the conscious oneiric circularity conceiving Lamech,[1600] the *power* of dreams, which he harvests as food. This is symbolized by the number 7,[1601] letter ז (*z, záyin*). The letters פ (*pē* = #80) and ח (*ḥ, ḥêth*, #8) both symbolically represent speech. Therefore, after the birth of Lamech, Methuselah is able to fully prophesy, to say beforehand,[1602] as a soothsayer. The subject/object circularity, the day (יוֹם *yowm*) and/or year (שָׁנָה *shaneh*) of oneiric consciousness, opens up (פ = #80) to *conceive* (יָלַד *yalad*) his dreams, as food for thought. Then, he can work actively in dreams, as indicated by the number 10, letter י (*y, yôdh*).

5:26-Methuselah's Offspring

וַיְחִי מְתוּשֶׁלַח אַחֲרֵי הוֹלִידוֹ אֶת־לֶמֶךְ שְׁתַּיִם וּשְׁמוֹנִים שָׁנָה וּשְׁבַע מֵאוֹת שָׁנָה וַיּוֹלֶד בָּנִים וּבָנוֹת׃ *vayaḥiy* (lived) *matušelaḥ* (Methuselah) *aḥărēy* (after) *hvōliydvō* (having generated) *'et* (and) *lemeka* (Lamech) *šatayim* (two) *ušamvōniym* (eight) *šānāh* (years) *ušaba'* (seven) *mē'vōt* (hundred) *šānāh* (years) *vayvōled* (generated) *bāniym* (sons) *ubānvōt* (daughters)
καὶ *kai* (and) **ἔζησεν** *ezēsen* (lived) **Μαθουσαλα** *Mathousala* (Methuselah) **μετὰ** *meta* (after) **τὸ** *to* (the) **γεννῆσαι** *gennēsai* (generate) **αὐτὸν** *auton* (he) **τὸν** *ton* (the) **Λαμεχ** *Lamech* (Lamech) **ὀκτακόσια** *oktakosia* (eight hundred)[1603] **δύο** *duo* (two) **ἔτη** *etē* (years) **καὶ** *kai* (and) **ἐγέννησεν** *egennēsen* (generated) **υἱοὺς** *uious* (sons) **καὶ** *kai* (and) **θυγατέρας** *thugateras* (daughters)
et (and) ***vixit*** (lived) ***Mathusalam*** (Methuselah) ***postquam*** (after) ***genuit*** (generating) ***Lamech*** (Lamech) ***septingentos*** (seven hundred) ***octoginta*** (eighty) ***duos*** (two) ***annos*** (years) ***et*** (and) ***genuit*** (generated) ***filios*** (sons) ***et*** (and) ***filias*** (daughters)
And Methuselah lived after he begat Lamech seven hundred eighty and two years, and begat sons and daughters:
After the birth of Lamech, Methuselah's days of oneiric consciousness can *satisfy* (782) the prophetic dream and open up to conceive other dream sons and daughters.

Consciousness' oneiric circularity at 782°

(ב=#2); (ז=#7); (ח=#8); (נ=#50); (ע=#70); (פ=#80); (ק=#100); (ן=#700+פ=#80+ב=#2)

Both letters פ (*pē* = #80) and ח (*ḥ, ḥêth* =#8) symbolically represent speech. After the birth of Lamech,

Methuselah can fully *satisfy* (Gematria #782)[1604] and utter his prophetic dream. The subject/object circularity, the day (יוֹם *yowm*) and year (שָׁנָה *shaneh*) of oneiric consciousness, opens up (פ = #80) to *conceive* (יָלַד *yalad*), in dreams, offspring symbolizing, with the number 2 (ב, *b, bêth*),[1605] other inhabitants. Those become dream food, as represented by the number 7,[1606] the letter ז (*z, záyin*). Its multiple, 70,[1607] corresponding to the letter ע (*'a, 'ayin*), means the watching eye of intuitive unlimited sprouting.[1608] In fact, hundred is equivalent to the letter ק (*q, qôph*, #100) meaning the circle of the sun and the number 700, ן, final (*sofit*) letter נ (*n nûn* = #50), is a symbol for infinite sprouting.

5:27-Methuselah's Redemption

וַיִּהְיוּ כָּל־יְמֵי מְתוּשֶׁלַח תֵּשַׁע וְשִׁשִּׁים שָׁנָה וּתְשַׁע מֵאוֹת שָׁנָה וַיָּמֹת׃ פ *vayihayu* (lived) *kāl* (all) *yamēy* (days) *matušelaḥ* (of Methuselah) *tēša'* (nine) *vašišiym* (sixty) *vašišiym* (sixty) *šānāh* (years) *utaša'* (ninety) *mē'vōt* (hundred) *šānāh* (years) *vayāmōt* (he died) *p̄* (.)
καὶ *kai* (and) **ἐγένοντο** *egenonto* (lived) **πᾶσαι** *pasai* (all) **αἱ** *ai* (the) **ἡμέραι** *ēmerai* (days) **Μαθουσαλα** *Mathousala* (Methuselah) **ἃς** *as* (thus) **ἔζησεν** *ezēsen* (lived) **ἐννακόσια** *ennakosia* (nine hundred) **καὶ** *kai* (and) **ἑξήκοντα** *exēkonta* (sixty) **ἐννέα ἔτη** *etē* (years) **καὶ** *kai* (and) **ἀπέθανεν** *apethamen* (died)
et (and) ***facti*** (done) ***sunt*** (are) ***omnes*** (all) ***dies*** (the days) ***Mathusalae*** (Methuselah) ***nongenti*** (nine hundred) ***sexaginta*** (sixty) ***novem*** (nine) ***anni*** (years) ***et*** (and) ***mortuus*** (dead) ***est*** (is)
And all the days of Methuselah were nine hundred sixty and nine years: and he died.
Finally, the living conscious oneiric circularity of Methuselah, *the one who gives prophecies* (969), ended with the reabsorption in the Tree of Pure Awareness.

Consciousness' oneiric circularity at 969° (ו=#6); (ט=#9); (ק=#100); (ץ=#900+ס=#60+ט=#9)

Any life's span, even if as long as Methuselah's 969 years, at the very moment of death must seem to to be only an instant long. However, the complete circular life span of Methuselah sings the 969° degree refrain, "*I have given prophecy*" (הַנְּבוּאָה נָתַתִּים *natatiym hanabw'āh* = Gematria #969).[1609] Furthermore, the number

ו (*w, wāw,* #6) symbolizes security and ס (*ṣ, ṣāmekh,* #60) symbolizes a protecting shield. The number 90 (תִּשְׁעִים *tish`iym*) corresponds to the letter צ (*ts, tsaddik*) which symbolically means hunting trail, to pursue a desired trailed game. Here, the conscious oneiric circularity, symbolized by #100 (מֵאָה *me'ah*) or ק (*qôph*), dies out (מות *muwth*). In fact, *tesha`* (תֵּשַׁע), nine, from *sha`ah* (שָׁעָה), means turning away from the subject-object circularity, *i.e.* the year (שָׁנָה *shaneh*), the surrounding mud, *viz.* number 9 (ט, *ṭ, ṭêth*). The number 900, final ץ (*ts, tsaddik sofit*) is the foundation of the world, which personifies the Tree of Life. Therefore, Methuselah, the prophet, ends by shrinking, disappearing reabsorbed In-Itself.

5:28-Lamech's Son

וַֽיְחִי־לֶמֶךְ שְׁתַּיִם וּשְׁמֹנִים שָׁנָה וּמְאַת שָׁנָה וַיּוֹלֶד בֵּן׃   *vayaḥiy* (lived) *emeḵa* (Lamech) *šatayim* (two) *ušamōniym* (eighty) *šānāh* (years) *uma'aṯ* (hundred) *šānāh* (years) *vayvōleḏ* (generated) *bēn* (a son)
καὶ *kai* (and) **ἔζησεν** *ezēsen* (lived) **Λαμεχ** *Lamech* (Lamech) **ἑκατὸν** *ekaton* (one hundred) **ὀγδοήκοντα** *ogdoēkonta* (eighty) **ὀκτὼ** *oktō* (eight)[1610] **ἔτη** *etē* (years) **καὶ** *kai* (and) **ἐγέννησεν** *egennēsen* (generated) **υἱὸν** *uion* (a son)
vixit (lived) ***autem*** (also) ***Lamech*** (Lamech) ***centum*** (one hundred) ***octoginta*** (eighty) ***duobus*** (two) ***annis*** (years) ***et*** (and) ***genuit*** (generated) ***filium*** (a son)
And Lamech lived an hundred eighty and two years, and begat a son:
Furthermore, in his oneiric circular *laborious* (182) *working* (182) active consciousness, Lamech conceived a dream son

Consciousness' oneiric circularity at 182° (א=#1); (ח=#8); (י=#10); (ק=#100+פ=#80+ב=#2)

At 182° degrees, Lamech generates a son. Thus, his son will have the qualities of a leader (#1, א, *a, 'Aleph*). His working activity (#10, י, *y, yôdh*) consists of his persisting in conceiving circularly (100, מֵאָה *me'ah*, or ק, *qôph*). Both the letters פ (*pē* = #80) and ח (*ḥ, ḥêth,* =# 8) symbolically represent speech. The subject/object circularity, the day (יוֹם *yowm*) and year (שָׁנָה *shaneh*) of consciousness, opens up (פ = #80) to *conceive* (יָלַד *yalad*) in sleep a dream son, another being, a number 2 (ב, *b, bêth*), who can *labor* (בַּעֲמָלָם *ba'ămālām* = Gematria #182)[1611] and *work* (בְּפֹעַל *bapō'al* = Gematria #182)[1612] for him.

5:29-Noah

וַיִּקְרָא אֶת־שְׁמוֹ נֹחַ לֵאמֹר זֶה יְנַחֲמֵנוּ מִמַּעֲשֵׂנוּ וּמֵעִצְּבוֹן יָדֵינוּ מִן־הָאֲדָמָה אֲשֶׁר אֵרְרָהּ יְהוָה׃   *vayiqarā'* (called) *'eṯ* (and) *šamvō* (name) *nōaḥ* (Noah-rest) *lē'mōr* (saying) *zeh* (this one) *yanaḥămēnu* (will console) *mima'ăśēnu* (from) *umē'iṣaḇvōn* (regarding) *yāḏēynu* (hand) *min* (because) *hā'ăḏāmāh* (land) *'ăšer* (which) *'ērarāh* (was cursed) *yahvāh* (the Transcendent)
καὶ *kai* (and) **ἐπωνόμασεν** *epōnomasen* (called) **τὸ** *to* (the) **ὄνομα** *onoma* (name) **αὐτοῦ** *autou* (his) **Νωε** *Nōe* (Noah) **λέγων** *legōn* (saying) **οὗτος** *outos* (this one) **διαναπαύσει** *dianapausei* (will stop) **ἡμᾶς** *ēmas* (us) **ἀπὸ** *apo* (from) **τῶν** *tōn* (the) **ἔργων** *ergōn* (work) **ἡμῶν** *ēmōn* (our) **καὶ** *kai* (and) **ἀπὸ** *apo* (from) **τῶν** *tōv* (the) **λυπῶν** *lupōn* (labor) **τῶν** *tōn* (of) **χειρῶν** *cheirōn* (hand) **ἡμῶν** *ēmōn* (our) **καὶ** *kai* (and) **ἀπὸ** *apo* (from) **τῆς** *tēs* (the) **γῆς** *gēs* (land) **ἧς** *ēs* (thus) **κατηράσατο** *katērasato* (cursed) **κύριος** *kurios* (by Lord) **ὁ** *o* (the) **θεός** *theos* (God)
vocavit- (called) ***que*** (and) ***nomen*** (name) ***eius*** (his) ***Noe*** (Noah) ***dicens*** (saying) ***iste*** (this one) ***consolabitur*** (shall comfort) ***nos*** (us) ***ab*** (from) ***operibus*** (the works) ***et*** (and) ***laboribus*** (labors) ***manuum*** (of hands) ***nostrarum*** (our) ***in*** (on) ***terra*** (the land) ***cui*** (which) ***maledixit*** (cursed) ***Dominus*** (the Lord)
And he called his name Noah, saying, This same shall comfort us concerning our work and toil of our hands, because of the ground which the LORD hath cursed.
And he [Lamech] called his name Noah, *the rested one*, saying,   "*This one shall comfort us from our works and hand labors on the land, which the Transcendent had cursed.*"

The Patriarchs are paradigms of our epistemic stages of life. Like Kantian forms,[1613] they are the *a-priori* modes in which we know the world. In that, they are the indispensable and necessary structure synthesized with the objective world and without which knowledge and experience would be impossible. Among them, Noah has a very significant role.

The name Noah,[1614] means *rest*, same as *resting-place*,[1615] and derives from the verb *to rest, nuwach*.[1616] Here, *Genesis* describes humans faculties, which proceed as attributes of Lamech's power. Noah is the oneiric counterpart of Jabal, the stream (יָבָל *yabal*) of farmers and herders planting and shepherding. Similarly, Noah's function is to assure a resting place for all life forms and for them to flourish on Earth, as we shall see. In fact, Noah will *relieve*[1617] Lamech-power from the physical[1618] distress, *viz.* the work[1619] and labor,[1620] deriving from the world of duality. The rested state of Noah is the sinless state of dreamless sleep (NREM), where neither desires nor dreams take place. In fact, the Psalm says,

> "*It is vain for you to rise up early, to sit up late, to eat the bread of sorrows: for so He* [the Transcendent, יְהֹוָה Yĕhovah] *giveth sleep to his beloved.*"[1621]

Identifying with the state of deep dreamless sleep means to reach the state of stillness before the fall, when there is no hunger for the forbidden fruit. There, are only the infinite waters of possibilities over which hovers the Spirit of Awareness.

5:30-Lamech's Offspring

וַיְחִי־לֶמֶךְ אַחֲרֵי הוֹלִידוֹ אֶת־נֹחַ חָמֵשׁ וְתִשְׁעִים שָׁנָה וַחֲמֵשׁ מֵאֹת שָׁנָה וַיּוֹלֶד בָּנִים וּבָנוֹת׃ *vayaḥiy* (lived) *lemeḵa* (Lamech) *aḥărēy* (after) *hvōliyḏvō* (having generated) *'eṯ* (and) *nōaḥ* (Noah) ḥāmēš (five) *vaṯiša'iym* (ninety) *šānāh* (years) *vaḥămēš* (five) *mē'ōṯ* (hundred) *šānāh* (years) *vayvōleḏ* (generated) *bāniym* (sons) *uḇānvōṯ* (daughters)
καὶ *kai* (and) **ἔζησεν** *ezēsen* (lived) **Λαμεχ** *Lamech* (Lamech) **μετὰ** *meta* (after) **τὸ** *to* (the) **γεννῆσαι** *gennēsai* (generate) **αὐτὸν** *auton* (he) **τὸν** *ton* (the) **Νωε** *Nōe* (Noah) **πεντακόσια** *pentakosia* (five hundred) **καὶ** *kai* (and) **ἑξήκοντα** *exēkonta* (sixty)[1622] **πέντε** *pente* (five) **ἔτη** *etē* (years) **καὶ** *kai* (and) **ἐγέννησεν** *egennēsen* (generated) **υἱοὺς** *uious* (sons) **καὶ** *kai* (and) **θυγατέρας** *thugateras* (daughters)
vixit-(lived)***que*** (and) ***Lamech*** (Lamech) ***postquam*** (after) ***genuit*** (generating) ***Noe*** (Noah) ***quingentos*** (fife hundred) ***nonaginta*** (ninety) ***quinque*** (five) ***annos*** (years) ***et*** (and) ***genuit*** (generated) ***filios*** (sons) ***et*** (and) ***filias*** (daughters)
And Lamech lived after he begat Noah five hundred ninety and five years, and begat sons and daughters:
After the conception of Noah, Lamech, persisting in his circular years of oneiric-power consciousness, conceives *a number* (595) of more dream sons and daughters.

Consciousness' oneiric circularity at 595° (נ=#50); (ק=#100); (ת=#400); (ך=#500+צ=#90+ה=#5)

At 595° degrees, during the circularity (ק, *q* = #100 מֵאָה *me'ah*) of his powerul hunting (צ, *ts*, = 90 תִּשְׁעִים *tish'iym*) for dream consciousness, Lamech sprouts (נ, *n* =#50) a *number* (הִתְפָּקְדוּ *hāṯapāqaḏw* = Gematria #595)[1623] of other dream beings (ה, *h* = 5 חָמֵשׁ *chamesh*) as sons and daughters. They became his mark (ת, *t* = #400) and crown (ך, *n* = #500).[1624]

5:31-Lamech's Entropy

וַיְהִי כָּל־יְמֵי־לֶמֶךְ שֶׁבַע וְשִׁבְעִים שָׁנָה וּשְׁבַע מֵאוֹת שָׁנָה וַיָּמֹת׃ ס *vayahiy* (lived) *kal* (all) *yamēy* (days) *lemeḵa* (of Lamech) *šeḇa'* (seven) *vašiḇa'iym* (seventy) *šānāh* (years) *ušaḇa'* (seven) *mē'vōṯ* (hundred) *šānāh* (years) *vayāmōṯ* (he died) *s* (.)
καὶ *kai* (and) **ἐγένοντο** *egenonto* (lived) **πᾶσαι** *pasai* (all) **αἱ** *ai* (the) **ἡμέραι** *ēmerai* (days) **Λαμεχ** *Lamech* (Lamech) **ἑπτακόσια** *eptakosia* (seven hundred) **καὶ** *kai* (and) **πεντήκοντα** *pentēkonta* (fifty) **τρία** *tria* (three)[1625] **ἔτη** *etē* (years) **καὶ** *kai* (and) **ἀπέθανεν** *apethamen* (died)
et (and) ***facti*** (done) ***sunt*** (are) ***omnes*** (all) ***dies*** (the days) ***Lamech*** (Lamech) ***septingenti*** (seven hundred) ***septuaginta*** (seventy) ***septem*** (seven) ***anni*** (years) ***et*** (and) ***mortuus*** (dead) ***est*** (is)
And all the days of Lamech were seven hundred seventy and seven years: and he died.

Finally, all the living circular power of Lamech's *sleep* (777) consciousness sprout infinitely and he fades away.

<u>Consciousness' oneiric circularity at 777°</u> **(ז=#7); (ע=#70); (ק=#100); (ן=#700)**

The dream food is symbolized by the number 7, (שֶׁבַע *sheba*), the letter ז (*z, záyin*). Its multiple, 70 (שִׁבְעִים *shib'iym*), corresponds to the letter ע (*'a, 'ayin*), which means the watching eye of intuition infinitely sprouting. In fact, hundred (מֵאָה *me'ah*), equivalent to the letter ק (*q, qôph*, #100), means the circle of consciousness and the number 700, ן, final (*sofit*) letter of נ (*n, nûn*, = #50), is a symbol for infinite sprouting. Thus, 777° degrees of consciousness measure how much dream power of intuition spreads out and fades away in the infinite entropic sprouting process of *sleep* (וַתְּיַשְּׁנֵהוּ *watayašanēhu* = Gematria #777).[1626]

5:32-Shem, Ham, and Japheth

וַיְהִי־נֹחַ בֶּן־חֲמֵשׁ מֵאוֹת שָׁנָה וַיּוֹלֶד נֹחַ אֶת־שֵׁם אֶת־חָם וְאֶת־יָפֶת׃ *vayaḥiy* (was) *nōaḥ* (Noah) *ben* (ninety) ḥămēš (five) *mē'vōṯ* (hundred) *šānāh* (years) *vayvōleḏ* (generated) *nōaḥ* (Noah) *'eṯ* (and) *šēm* (Shem) *'eṯ* (and) *ḥām* (Ham) *va'eṯ* (with) *yāp̄eṯ* (Japheth)
καὶ *kai* (and) **ἦν** *ēn* (was) **Νωε** *Nōe* (Noah) **ἐτῶν** *etōn* (years) **πεντακοσίων** *pentakosiōn* (five hundred) **καὶ** *kai* (and) **ἐγέννησεν** *egennēsen* (generated) **Νωε** *Nōe* (Noah) **τρεῖς** *treis* (three) **υἱούς** *uious* (sons) **τὸν** *ton* (the) **Σημ** *Sēm* (Shem) **τὸν** *ton* (the) **Χαμ** *Cham* (Ham) **τὸν** *ton* (the) **Ιαφεθ** *Iapheth* (Japheth)
Noe (Noah) ***vero*** (indeed) ***cum*** (as) ***quingentorum*** (five hundred) ***esset*** (he was) ***annorum*** (years) ***genuit*** (generated) ***Sem*** (Shem) ***et*** (and) ***Ham*** (Ham) ***et*** (and) ***Iafeth*** (Japheth)
And Noah was five hundred years old: and Noah begat Shem, Ham, and Japheth.
Indeed, Noah, in the circularity of his dream consciousness, conceives *in time* (500) Shem, Ham and Japheth.

<u>Consciousness' oneiric circularity at 500°</u> **(ה=#5); (ס=#50); (ק=#100); (ת=#400); (ך=#500)**

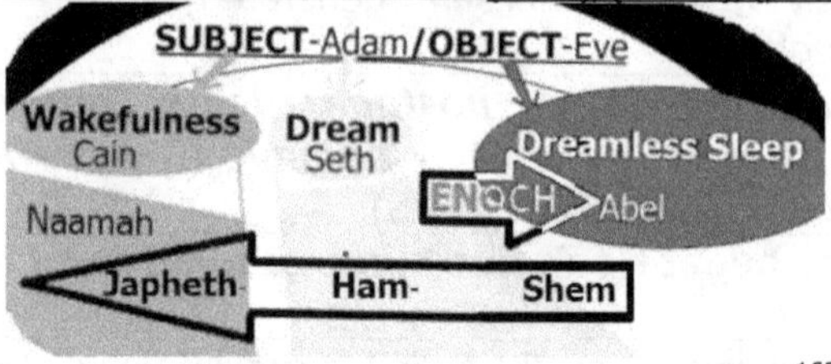

GRAPHIC: *Dream Merging in Wakefulness and in NREM*[1627]

In verse 5:29, Lamech's was expecting a hand from Noah to relieve him from his labor. The letter כ, *kaph*, is equivalent to number 20, which symbolically represents an open hand. The final (*sofit*) graphic expression of that letter is ך, *k*, with the value of #500 and the meaning of *crown*.[1628] Usually, however, 500 was rendered as ק, *q*, #100 (מֵאָה *me'ah*), symbolizing circularity, + #400, ת, *t*, (*tāw*) meaning *mark* or *sign*. The letter ה, *h* (*hē*) is equivalent to the number 5 (חָמֵשׁ *chamesh*), symbolizing the breathing personality who sees and experiences.[1629]

Therefore, Noah, the resting one, at 500° degrees of his circular (#100) consciousness, crowns (500) his father's wish by fulfilling it. In fact, he conceives three personalities (#5) who enter into the realm of waking *time* (לָעֵת *la'at* = Gematria #500)[1630] and reach the mark (#400) in the cursed land of labor, as expressed in verse 5:29.

The names of Noah's three sons are, Shem, Ham and Japheth.

1) <u>Shem</u>[1631] means *name*, the same as *shem*,[1632] which means *glory*, from the verb *suwm*[1633] *to establish*. Thus, Shem is the "<u>established glorious name</u>" in the dreamless realm.
2) <u>Ham</u>,[1634] means *hot*, the same as *cham*,[1635] which means *warm* and comes from *chamam*,[1636] meaning *hot for passion*. Thus, Ham is the "<u>one hot for passion</u>" in the dream realm.
3) <u>Japheth</u>,[1637] means *open*, derives from the verb *pathah*,[1638] which means *to seduce*. Thus, Japheth is the "<u>one open to seduce</u>" in the waking realm.

Thus, Noah's offspring end up back into wakefulness where they establish themselves. Consequently, the loveliness of their counterpart in the waking state, namely, the beautiful Naamah, seduces them.

However, as Enoch is the dream faculty, which enters into dreamless sleep, similarly, Shem, Ham, Japheth, collectively, are the faculties that leave the dreamless sleep (NREM) moving into the dream (REM) state and enter wakefulness. They move from the dreamless and dream state into watchfulness. From their sleep origin, they establish passionate seduction in the waking realm, where there is no oneiric-age°-circularity.

From the perspective of the three levels of Self-consciousness,

1. Abel is a metaphor for Auto-transparency, which does not need the mediation of thought, because it is the continuous presence of itself-in-itsej to itself-in-itself. Its equivalent is the realm of NREM dreamless sleep (תַּרְדֵּמָה *tardemah*).
2. Cain is a metaphor for Ego-consciousness, which thinks of itself as this historical person here and now. Its equivalent is the realm of wakefulness.
3. Seth is a metaphor for I-consciousness, which is conscious of its ideas as dream-ideas, namely the thought that conceives itself as idea or that thinks itself as thought. Its equivalent is the realm of REM dream (חֲלוֹם *chalowm*). Different dream-spans indicate changing aspects of the oneiric realm.

a) The 900° degrees level (*i.e.:* Seth & al.) is symbolic of dreams reabsorbed in their original *ascending-healing-channel* (תְּעָלַת *ta'ālat* = Gematria #900).[1639]
b) The 800° degrees state (*i.e.:* Mahalaleel) symbolizes the *minimum* (מנין *minyán* = Gematria #800)[1640] life span of dreams ending upon awaking.
c) The 700° degrees stage (*i.e.:* Lamech)) is symbolic of the recurring cyclical aspect of *Seth's* (שֵׁת Seth = Gematria #700)[1641] dreams.
d) The 500° degrees realm (*i.e.:* Shem-Ham-Japheth) is symbolic of the established-passionate-seduction of *time* (לְעֵת *la'at* = Gematria #500).[1642]
e) The 300° degrees aim (*i.e.:* Enoc) symbolizes the *shepherd's* (רֹעֶיךָ *rō'aykā* = Gematria #300)[1643] staff reabsorbing into NREM.

Summary of Seth's Dreaming Generation

Seth's (912°) 9 hypostases of **REM** dreams at 130°, as a stretchable-retractable telescope:		
I) *Enos* (905°), the physical mortal-dreamer at 105°	⇔	In wakefulness = *Jubal*
II) *Cainan* (910°), dream's possessive faculty at 90°	⇔	In wakefulness = *Tubalcain*
III) *Mahalaleel* (895°), dream's priestly function at 70°	⇔	In wakefulness = *Mehujael*
IV) *Jared* (962°), function of dream observing at 65°	⇔	In wakefulness = *Irad*
V) *Enoch* (365°), dream's initiator from NREM at 162°	⇔	In wakefulness = *Enoch*, ⇨**NREM**
VI) *Methuselah* (969°), prophetic dream at 65°	⇔	In wakefulness = *Methusael*
VII) *Lamech* (777°), dream power at 187°	⇔	In wakefulness = *Lamech*
VIII) *Noah* (950°), resting dream in NREM at 182°	⇔	In wakefulness = *Jabal*
IX) *Shem-Ham-Japheth*, establish-passion-seduce at 500°	⇔	In wakefulness = *Naamah* ⇨**Wake**

Seth	sequence of the dream world during the dream itself. ⇨
Enos	individual dreamer.⇨
Cainan	holder and possessor of dreams. ⇨
Mahalaleel	perception of dreams as transcending realities in-themselves. ⇨
Jared	preservation and observation of dreams' descending process as rock-solid objectivities. ⇨
Enoch	initiator of new dreams. ⇨
Methuselah	prophetic aspect of dreams. ⇨
Lamech	powerful and strong return of the dream state after the dreamless sleep. ⇨
Noah	dreams' rest in NREM. ⇨
Shem	established glorious name in the dreamless realm.
Ham	hot for passion in the dream realm.

Japheth	open to seduce in the waking realm.

The human generates its oneiric dimensions. In turn, each aspect develops its own components and so on. Each one of them is a paradigm of *a-priori* forms of knowledge.

HERE ENDS THE FIFTH CHAPTER OF THE GENERATIONS OF SETH

PART 4

NOAH

CHAPTER 6

THE ARK

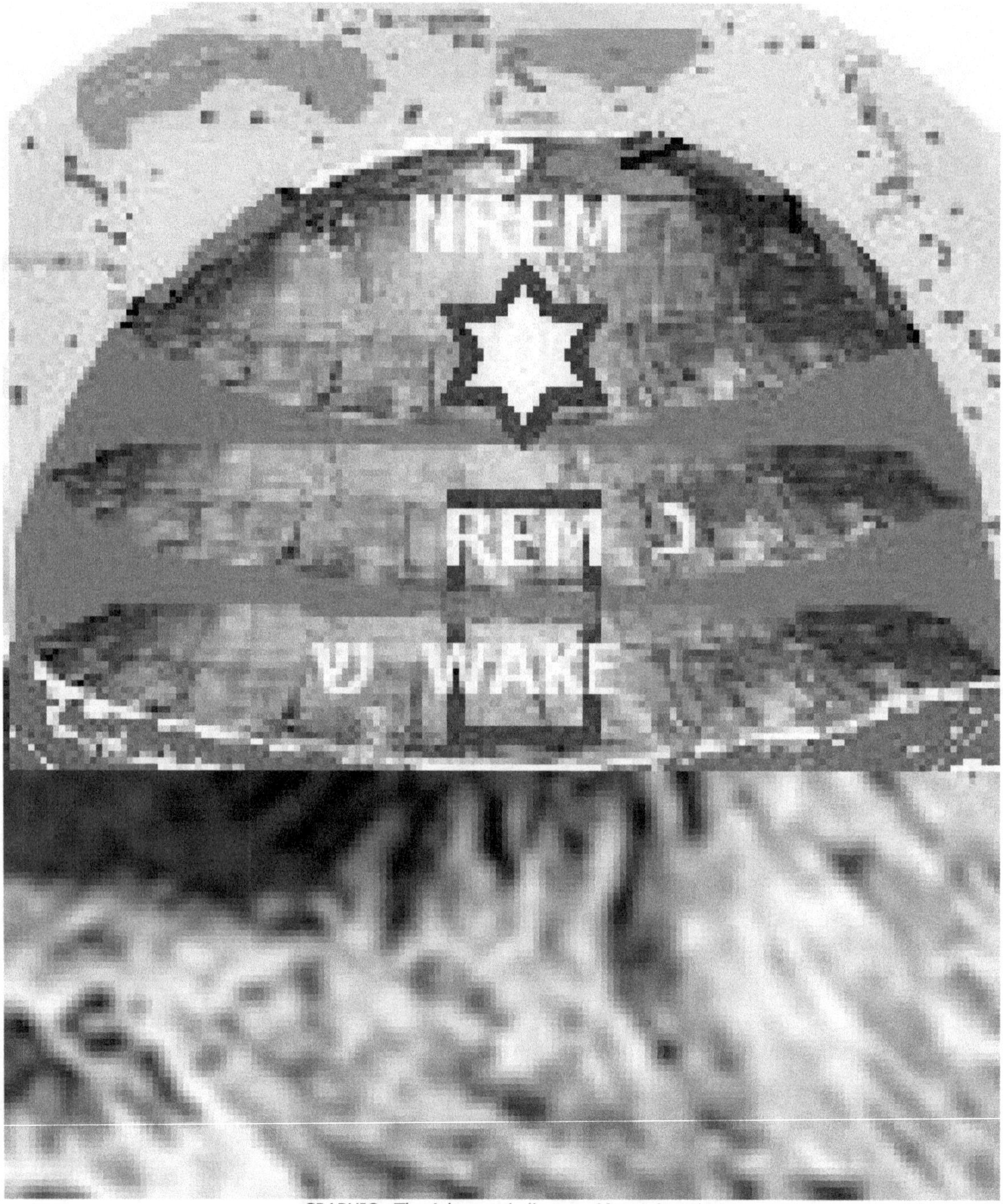

GRAPHIC: *The Ark as a skullcap on Mount Ararat*

6-I SECTION: DAUGHTERS' OFFSPRING

6:1-Subject-Object Multiplication

וַיְהִי כִּי־הֵחֵל הָאָדָם לָרֹב עַל־פְּנֵי הָאֲדָמָה וּבָנוֹת יֻלְּדוּ לָהֶם׃
vayahiy (it was) *kiy* (when) *hēḥēl* (began) *hā'āḏām* (Adam) *lārōḇ* (to multiplie) *'al* (on) *panēy* (face) *hā'ăḏāmāh* (of the earth) *uḇānvōṯ* (daughters) *yulaḏu* (were born) *lāhem* (to them)
καὶ *kai* (and) **ἐγένετο** *egeneto* (came to pass) **ἡνίκα** *ēnika* (when) **ἤρξαντο** *ērxanto* (began) **οἱ** *oi* (the) **ἄνθρωποι** *anthrōpoi* (men) **πολλοὶ** *polloi* (numerous) **γίνεσθαι** *ginesthai* (began to be) **ἐπὶ** *epi* (on) **τῆς** *tēs* (the) **γῆς** *gēs* (earth) **καὶ** *kai* (and) **θυγατέρες** *thugateres* (daughters) **ἐγενήθησαν** *egenēthēsan* (were born) **αὐτοῖς** *autois* (to them)
cumque (when) ***coepissent*** (came to be that) ***homines*** (men) ***multiplicari*** (began to multiply) ***super*** (on) ***terram*** (the earth) ***et*** (and) ***filias*** (daughters) ***procreassent*** (were procreated)
And it came to pass, when men began to multiply on the face of the earth, and daughters were born unto them,
In time, when the subject-object-Adam multiplied in the field of consciousness-*of*, ideal objects were established.

Who are these men (אָדָם *'adam*) and who are these daughters (בַּת *bath*)? How can men generate daughters without having been generated from somebody's daughter and, in turn, mate with someone else's daughter? These questions start an infinite regressive cycle of enquiries. Besides, what is the point of this verse, when the previous text had already established the generation of daughters?

These men, *adam*, and daughters, *bath*, are not historical individual personalities, as the ones we meet daily along the streets of life. They are paradigmatic epistemic structures belonging to everyone. In fact, Adam (אָדָם) is male and female, thus, does not refer to gender. It is a metaphor for the subject-object epistemic structure or template. The word *bath* (בַּת), daughter, derives from the verb *banah*[1644] meaning to build, to establish. When the *Adam*-paradigm multiplies in the red (אֲדָמָה *'adamah*) field (פָּנִים *paniym*) of conscious activity, then, objects are built and established (בָּנָה *banah*) as ideal offspring of the thinking process. This is the outcome of conceptualization, following the consumption of the fruit of the Tree of Knowledge, as it will be more evident in the next verse.

We can already anticipate accusations of cerebralism, as if puerile literal interpretations would do better justice to the revelation of a postulated Divine Omniscience.

6:2-The Sons of God and The Daughters of Men[1645]

וַיִּרְאוּ בְנֵי־הָאֱלֹהִים אֶת־בְּנוֹת הָאָדָם כִּי טֹבֹת הֵנָּה וַיִּקְחוּ לָהֶם נָשִׁים מִכֹּל אֲשֶׁר בָּחָרוּ׃
vayira'u (perceived) *ḇanēy* (sons) *hā'ĕlōhiym* (of the Gods) *'eṯ* (and) *banvōṯ* (daughters) *hā'āḏām* (Adam) *kīy* (because) *ṭōḇōṯ* (fair) *hēnāh* (they) *vayiqaḥu* (took) *lāhem* (them) *nāšiym* (wife) *mikōl* (from) *'ăšer* (which) *bāḥāru* (chose)
ἰδόντες *idontes* (seeing) **δὲ** *de* (but) **οἱ** *oi* (the) **υἱοὶ** *uioi* (sons) **τοῦ** *tou* (of the) **θεοῦ** *theou* (God) **τὰς** *tas* (the) **θυγατέρας** *thugateras* (daughters) **τῶν** *tōn* (of the) **ἀνθρώπων** *anthrōpōn* (men) **ὅτι** *oti* (that) **καλαί** *kalai* (beautiful) **εἰσιν** *eisin* (were) **ἔλαβον** *elabon* (they took) **ἑαυτοῖς** *eautois* (to them) **γυναῖκας** *gunaikas* (wives) **ἀπὸ** *apo* (among) **πασῶν** *pasōn* (all) **ὧν** *ōn* (that) **ἐξελέξαντο** *exelexanto* (they chose)
videntes (seeing) ***filii*** (the sons) ***Dei*** (of God) ***filias*** (the daughters) ***eorum*** (of them)[1646] ***quod*** (who) ***essent*** (were) ***pulchrae*** (beautiful) ***acceperunt*** (they took) ***uxores*** (wives) ***sibi*** (for themselves) ***ex*** (out of) ***omnibus*** (all) ***quas*** (which) ***elegerant*** (they chose)
That the sons of God saw the daughters of men that they were fair; and they took them wives of all which they chose.
The descendants of Divine-Consciousness perceived the beauty of Adam-subject-objects' thought-daughters, thus, chose to be united with them as husband/subject-mind/wife-object-idea/daughter.

Unless we are in the presence of an absurd and contradictory divine racist/gender discrimination among his own creatures, here, there is an important distinction between the *sons* (בֵן *ben*) of Divine-Consciousness (אֱלֹהִים *'elohiym*) and the *daughters* (בַת *bath*) of men (אָדָם *'adam*).

1) Elohim's descendants (*ben* בֵּן)[1647] are the mystics who see without looking, hear without listening, taste without savoring, inhale without sniffing, feel without sensing, think without conceptualizing, know without discerning, love without desiring and

   "*act without acting*"[1648]

   Like Noah, they are those who *rest* in the Divine Breath and establish (*banah* בֵּן) their identify within the Pure Consciousness leading into Awareness.

2) Adam's daughters (בַּת *bath*)[1649] are like the beautiful (טוֹב *towb*) Naamah. Shem tunes and establishes (בָּנָה *banah*) his desires for her. Ham is taken by his passion for her. Finally, Japheth, seduced by her, seduces her in return. Thus, they depend on (בַּת *bath*) the subject/man to cause (בָּנָה *banah*) a son (בֵּן *ben*). The daughters, then, are the ideal outcome of Adam. They are the objective thoughts of the subject. They are the seductive attraction for the forbidden fruit, which has nothing to do with sexuality and/or sin. They are the identity we establish with our own ideas forgetting the source from which they come. Metaphorically, Adam, the subject, perceives (רָאָה *ra'ah*) and chooses (בָּחַר *bachar*) its thoughts-object and takes (לקח *laqach*) them (הֵנָּה *hennah*) as wives (אִשָּׁה *'ishshah*) in a subject-object indissoluble marriage. The world, in which we are established, seduces us. We are passionate about it and we desire it as the *fruit* of our thoughts. Russell recognizes that,

   > "In order to become a scientific philosopher... there must be... the desire to know philosophical truth, and this desire... is very rare in its purity... The desire for unadulterated truth is often obscured, in professional philosophers, by love of system... and the system-maker's vanity which becomes associated with it, are among the snares that the student of philosophy must guard against. The desire to establish this or that result, or generally to discover evidence for agreeable results, of whatever kind, has of course been the chief obstacle to honest philosophizing."[1650]

Furthermore, we adhere not only to our philosophical speculations, but also to our entire thinking process, as such. Thus, we fear its absence in death. As the cliché goes, we "*marry the idea.*" Right or wrong, we follow our ideologies to the extent of dying for them. Then, they give rise to a deluge of wars, killings, plunging destructions, murderous acts and other forms of violent subjugations. They become our desires. Thus, they *are pleasant* (טוֹב *towb*)[1651] and *fair* (טוֹב *towb*),[1652] good (טוֹב *towb*) and desirable (תַּאֲוָה *ta'avah*)[1653] to the eyes, like the forbidden fruit. Then, they become the driving ideological forces of our lives. Thus, we submit to their cause.

6:3-120 Wandering Wondering Years

וַיֹּאמֶר יְהוָה לֹא־יָדוֹן רוּחִי בָאָדָם לְעֹלָם בְּשַׁגַּם הוּא בָשָׂר וְהָיוּ יָמָיו מֵאָה וְעֶשְׂרִים שָׁנָה׃ *vayō'mer* (said) *yahvāh* (the Transcendent) *lō'* (not) *yāḏvōn* (struggle judge) *ruḥiy* (breath) *ḇā'āḏām* (man) *la'ōlām* (forever) *bašagam* (indeed) *hu'* (are) *ḇāśār* (flesh) *vahāyu* (are) *yāmāyv* (days) *mē'āh* (one hundred) *va'eśariym* (twenty) *šānāh* (years)
καὶ *kai* (and) **εἶπεν** *eipen* (said) **κύριος** *kurios* (Lord) **ὁ** *o* (the) **θεός** *theos* (God) **οὐ** *ou* (not) **μὴ** *mē* (not) **καταμείνῃ** *katameinē* (stay) **τὸ** *to* (the) **πνεῦμά** *pneuma* (breath) **μου** *mou* (my) **ἐν** *en* (in) **τοῖς** *tois* (the) **ἀνθρώποις** *anthrōpois* (man) **τούτοις** *tautois* (these) **εἰς** *eis* (in) **τὸν** *ton* () **αἰῶνα** *aiōna* (eternity) **διὰ** *dia* (because) **τὸ** *to* (the) **εἶναι** *einai* (is) **αὐτοὺς** *aitous* (their) **σάρκας** *sarkas* (flesh) **ἔσονται** *esontai* (will be) **δὲ** *de* (but) **αἱ** *ai* (the) **ἡμέραι** *ēmerai* (days) **αὐτῶν** *autōn* (their) **ἑκατὸν** *ekaton* (one hundred) **εἴκοσι** *eikosi* (twenty) **ἔτη** *etē* (years)
dixit-(said) ***que*** (and) ***Deus*** (God) ***non*** (not) ***permanebit*** (will remain) ***spiritus*** (spirit) ***meus*** (my) ***in*** (in) ***homine*** (man) ***in*** (in) ***aeternum*** (eternity) ***quia*** (because) ***caro*** (flesh) ***est*** (is) ***erunt*** (will be)-***que*** (and) ***dies*** (days) ***illius*** (his) ***centum*** (one hundred) ***viginti*** (twenty) ***annorum*** (years)
And the LORD said, My spirit shall not always strive with man, for that he also is flesh:

yet his days shall be an hundred and twenty years.

Therefore the Transcendent said,

"My Breath-Awareness shall not forever control, struggle or judge the subject-object, indeed the human errs in news bearing flesh, s/he will live in the circular days (120) of one and two other levels of consciousness."

The word *diyn* (דין)[1654] signifies to judge, to act as judge, to execute judgment, to govern and *lo'* (לא)[1655] means *no*. Therefore, *lō' yāḏvōn* (לא־יָדוֹן) *indicates "he shall not judge."* Contrary to popular understanding, the Transcendent does not judge. In fact, when

> "*a woman, taken in the very act of adultery...* [was] *to be stoned, ...* [Jesus] *said... 'He that is without sin among you, let him first cast a stone at her'... They which heard it, ... went out one by one... and Jesus was left alone, and ... said* [to the woman] *'Neither do I condemn thee.'*"[1656]
>
> "[Furthermore,] *Father, forgive them; for they know not what they do.*"[1657]

Judging is an epistemic human prerogative. Paradoxically, the absence of guilt-distress makes animals freer than humans who must find ways to judge and punish themselves to appease their remorse for breaking self-imposed relative moral regulations. Then, we curb what we deem to be *sinful* nature. Thus, we follow strict dietary regulations and severe dress codes to cover *shameful* nakedness, as if, blasphemously, God's creation needs to be perfected.[1658] Apodictical Transcendent Awareness does not judge (*lō' yāḏvōn* לא־יָדוֹן) or punish. Awareness is Awareness without any moral assessment. It is the Pure Etical Contemplation without any judging thought, which, on the other hand, necessitates mind forms. In fact, to judge means to place an evaluated object in a time structure. Namely, before, when its outcome was not yet realized -- thus not sentenced -- and after, when it was penalized. Therefore, at the same time of its creation, a postulated timeless all-knowing creator forms its own creature already condemned. This is a *contradiction in terms*. <Beauty, Love and Truth are the intrinsic outcome of the Intuitive-Awareness. They are not commandments *per se*. By identifying with Awareness in its intuitive reality, one reaches Beauty, Love and Truth themselves without attachment. These are synonyms of Awareness.>[1659] Awareness is Awareness without judgment, however,

> "*Know thou the God of thy father, and serve him with a perfect heart and with a willing mind: for the LORD searcheth all hearts, and understandeth all the imaginations of the thoughts: if thou seek him, he will be found of thee; but if thou forsake him, he will cast thee off for ever.*"[1660]

Therefore,

> "*Love and do what you want.*"[1661]

We must realize that we hardly live in the Present Awareness. Whatever we know, we know it as past, that which is already dead. In fact,

> "*No man, having put his hand to the plough, and looking back, is fit for the kingdom of God.*"[1662]

Even the future is a wish or an expectation of something that will take place as past. The philosopher, reflecting on his wolf's death, writes,

> "What counts as now for us is constituted by our memories of what has gone before and our expectations of things yet to come. And this is equivalent to saying that for us there is no now. The moment of the present is deferred, distributed through time: the moment is unreal. The moment always escapes us."[1663]

This philosopher, however, cannot realize that without Certain Awareness. In fact, without Awareness, he would never be able to write or be conscious-*of memories* and/or *expectations*. Awareness does not take place in the past of memories or in the future of expectations, which, however, can only project from the past. If Awareness were in the past or in the future, it would not be Awareness. Therefore, Awareness must be this elusive Present, which, as such, is unconceivable. Eternity (עולם *`owlam*) is Awareness as Now. It is the Transcendent (יְהוָה *Yĕhovah*) Eternal present. In fact, when Jesus was

> "*crucified...* [with] *malefactors* (κακοῦργος *kakourgos*)*, one on the right... and the other on the left,... one ... said unto Jesus, 'Lord, remember me when thou comest into thy kingdom.'*... *And Jesus said unto him, 'Verily I say unto thee, To day shalt thou be with me in paradise.'*"[1664]

On the contrary, we lose Eternal Present, as such, whenever we conceptualize It, namely, we eat the forbidden fruit. Therefore, **we** do not allow the Transcendent Breath (רוּחַ *ruwach*) of Life to *stay* with us. Therefore, Awareness does not control or judge (דִּין *diyn*)[1665] us because (גַּם *gam*) we are news-bearing[1666] flesh[1667] going astray.[1668] The news bearing refers to the flesh's nerve system transmitting information to the mind for the duration of 120 metaphorical years not to Awareness. It is impossible to quantify or measure Awareness, as such. In fact, It is

> "*smaller than the subtle and greater than the great… without hands and feet. With inconceivable powers,* [It] *see*[s] *without eyes, equally* [It] *hear*[s] *without ears.* [It is] *omniscient, omni-aware and free from form and no one knows* [It]. [It is] *eternal Awareness. Indeed,* [It is] *the One to be realized through the many sacred texts of knowledge… For* [It] *there is no good or evil, no birth, no body or destruction, nor there is an intellect or faculties of the senses. For* [It] *there is no … circumference.*"[1669]

Awareness <does not need members to be aware. Similarly, It does not need the faculty of the senses to be omniscient. At the same time, however, it is not-known in-itself, because it is transcendent.> Awareness is beyond the Tree of Knowledge of Good and Evil. It does not eat its fruit. However, <the universal foundation of Ethic is Awareness>[1670] in its Pure detached Apodictic-Certitude.

We must recognize that, in *Genesis*, any chronology is metaphorical. It refers only to a human perspective, not to God, as such. In fact, any time listing must be *no-time* for a Timeless Being, penalty the loss of that timelessness. Unless we ascribe to God an idolatrous chronology, the time span, from *before* the beginning of creation to *after* its end, must all take place, by definition, in the same Present for God. Therefore, in the first part of *Genesis*, we must read all listing of years or days with its Gematria reference in accord with the general sense of the text itself. Moreover, what is the meaning of a literal life span of 120 years, when humans, as we saw, lived much longer or much less.

In Gematria, the number 120 corresponds to *kayāmiym* (כְּיָמִים), meaning *days.*[1671] Referred to the human (אָדָם *'adam*), it becomes the circularity of consciousness or 120 circular years. That figure is composed of 100 (ק, *q*), symbolizing a circle, + 20 (כ, *k*), symbolizing the palm of the hand, or 10 (י, *y*), symbolizing a working hand, by two. In fact, `*esriym*, twenty,[1672] derives from `*eser*, ten (עֶשֶׂר)[1673] plus ten. Furthermore, `*eser* derives from `*asar*, the tenth part,[1674] which again derives from the verb `*ashar*, to be rich and wealthy.[1675] Consequently, the value 20 is that which gains the rich productivity of experiences both in the waking and/or dreaming realms, thus, #10, while awake, and +#10, while dreaming.

As we saw, the entire daily circadian human life is composed of three recurrent stages, waking, dreaming and dreamless sleep. The Ego-consciousness, during the waking phase, and the I-consciousness, during the dreaming REM phase, are both characterized by activity, *viz.* the number 20 (כ) or 10 + 10 (י+י). The Auto-transparency of the dreamless sleep NREM state is a perfect self-contained circle, *viz.* the number 100 (ק). Therefore, symbolically, we have #100 + #10 + #10. These are the three (1+2) circular years (שָׁנָה *shaneh*) of human consciousness, *viz.* the metaphoric 120 years.

6:4-The Land of Fallen Giants

הַנְּפִלִים הָיוּ בָאָרֶץ בַּיָּמִים הָהֵם וְגַם אַחֲרֵי־כֵן אֲשֶׁר יָבֹאוּ בְּנֵי הָאֱלֹהִים אֶל־בְּנוֹת הָאָדָם וְיָלְדוּ לָהֶם הֵמָּה הַגִּבֹּרִים אֲשֶׁר מֵעוֹלָם אַנְשֵׁי הַשֵּׁם׃ פ *hanapīliym* (fallen giants) *hāyu* (were) *ḇā'āreṣ* (on earth) *bayāmiym* (in those days) *hāhēm* (Ham hot for passion) *vaḡam* (also) *'aḥărēy* (after) *ḵēn* (thus) *'ăšer* (which) *yāḇō'u* (entered) *banēy* (sons) *hā'ĕlōhiym* (of Gods) *'el* (and) *banvōṯ* (the daughter) *hā'āḏām* (of Adam) *vayālaḏu* (generated) *lāhem* (they) *hēmāh* (to them) *hagibōriym* (powerful) *'ăšer* (which) *mē'vōlām* (from) *'anašēy* (men) *hašēm* (fame) *p̄* (.)
οἱ *oi* (the) **δὲ** *de* (but) **γίγαντες** *gigantes* (giants) **ἦσαν** *ēsan* (were) **ἐπὶ** *epi* (on) **τῆς** *tēs* (the) **γῆς** *gēs* (earth) **ἐν** *en* (in) **ταῖς** *tais* (the) **ἡμέραις** *ēmerais* (days) **ἐκείναις** *ekenais* (that) **καὶ** *kai* (and) **μετ᾽** *met'* (after) **ἐκεῖνο** *ekeino* (that) **ὡς** *ōs* (this) **ἂν** *an* (if) **εἰσεπορεύοντο** *eiseporeuonto* (entered) **οἱ** *oi* (the) **υἱοὶ** *uioi* (sons) **τοῦ** *tou* (of the) **θεοῦ** *theou* (God) **πρὸς** *pros* (from) **τὰς** *tas* (the) **θυγατέρας** *thugateras* (daughters) **τῶν** *tōn* (the) **ἀνθρώπων** *anthrōpōn* (men) **καὶ** *kai* (and)

ἐγεννῶσαν *egennōsan* (generated) **ἑαυτοῖς** *eautois* (to them) **ἐκεῖνοι** *ekeinoi* (that) **ἦσαν** *ēsan* (were) **οἱ** *oi* (the) **γίγαντες** *gigantes* (giants)[1676] **οἱ** *oi* (the) **ἀπ'** *ap'* (from) **αἰῶνος** *aiōnos* (ages) **οἱ** *oi* (the) **ἄνθρωποι** *anthpōpoi* (men) **οἱ** *oi* (of the) **ὀνομαστοί** *onomastoi* (renown)
gigantes (giants) ***autem*** (also) ***erant*** (were) ***super*** (on) ***terram*** (the earth) ***in*** (in) ***diebus*** (days) ***illis*** (those) ***postquam*** (after which) ***enim*** (in fact) ***ingressi*** (came in) ***sunt*** (are) ***filii*** (the sons) ***Dei*** (of God) ***ad*** (to) ***filias*** (the daughters) ***hominum*** (of men) ***illae-*** (they) ***que*** (and) ***genuerunt*** (generated) ***isti*** (these) ***sunt*** (are) ***potentes*** (the powerful) ***a*** (in) ***saeculo*** (the century) ***viri*** (men) ***famosi*** (famous)
There were giants in the earth in those days; and also after that, when the sons of God came in unto the daughters of men, and they bare children to them, the same became mighty men which were of old, men of renown.
There were also giants on earth in those days. In fact, after the sons of Divine-Consciousness came with Ham's passionate desire into the daughters/ideas of men, they generated to them children that, in the course of centuries, became powerful and famous men.

Structurally, we always know the world only as a projection towards the past, which we call history. Therefore, the expression *in those days* (*yowm*)[1677] refers not only to distant antiquity but also to that past that we call present. We do not need to discover archeologically oversize bones to find giants. We need only to look at the electorate lists of candidates competing for leadership (*paqiyd* פָּקִיד),[1678] to find them. These giants are the *Nephilim.*[1679] The name derives from the verb *naphal,*[1680] which means to fall down, like into

"*an horror of great darkness.*"[1681]

Like *Platonic* ideas abiding beyond their *physical configurations,*[1682] these high stature beings are potential universal archetypes. *They are ideals* actualized into being by the synthesis of a-priori-subjective-forms with objective-ideas. Metaphorically, the sons of Divine-Consciousness (בְּנֵי הָאֱלֹהִים *banēy hā'ĕlōhiym*) are the subjective-a-priori-forms of space, time and causality, as described in the first verse of *Genesis.* Likewise, the thoughts, generated by the subject/object Adam, are allegorical daughters (בְּנוֹת הָאָדָם *banvōṯ hā'āḏām*). Therefore, when those *forms-in-formed* (בּוֹא *bow*)[1683] the ideas, metaphorically they lost their status. In fact, they fell from their heights when *Ham's* (הָם) *hot passionate*[1684] desire for the objects of knowledge, was seduced by the ideal daughters of the subject-object. Simply put, these daughters are the ideas, which take hold and shape human ideologies.

In other words, this is like the theatrical plot that must precede its own staging. Its production, then, becomes the connubial of the author's mind with the ideal characters of the show. Beings, like actors on the stage of life, have a role to play and to identify with.[1685] Once the performance is over, however, those parts vanish. They are frozen. They can rerun only as an endless but lifeless repeating film on the screen of history. History went on and still will go on with its circular days of consciousness (יוֹם *yowm*). In those/these historical days, ideas are the real makers and generators of all human actions. Furthermore, ideologies shape the leaders. Embodying their own ideas, important, powerful (גִּבּוֹר *gibbowr*) and renowned (שֵׁם *shem*) personalities become the actors who come and go on the history stage of this Earth (אֶרֶץ *'erets*). Their ideas are their movers. In the Aeneid, Virgil has Venus, love herself, say to her son Aeneas,

"'Every cloud, which now... dulls your mortal view..., I will clear away... The same father [with all his gods] is supplying spirits and victorious powers to the Greeks'... Then, [to Aeneas] appear evident the dreadful forms/ideas [for what they were, namely,] great divine-spirits hostile to Troy."[1686]

Hegel called those gods, *Spirits, Ideas, History Movers personified as renowned leaders,*

"*World-soul*[s]."[1687]

[1688]⇨

In fact, when that Philosopher saw Napoleon (1769-1821) riding into Vienna, after his 1806 victorious battle of Jena, called him the *Spirit of the World*[1689] riding on a white horse. However, also the French Emperor

"exhaled the mortal breath, / [and] the oblivious relic was / deprived of such a spirit"[1690]

Percy Bysshe Shelley writes,

> "'My name is Ozymandias. King of Kings: / Look on my works, ye mighty, and despair!' / Nothing beside remains. Round the decay / of that colossal wreck, boundless and bare, /the lone and level sands stretch far away."[1691]

These great spirits are like giants. Before each one of them the entire world trembled.[1692] Their fall made a great noise but still ended in the muddy ground. Nobody can really re-experience their thoughts, with the same intensity and passion that they felt. Their ideologies distinguished them and made them great and famous. Nevertheless, they all vanished and will die out, as dream-echoes emitting different resonances according to the composition of the historic walls from which they rebound. Each ego has been and will be a giant, a *Nephilim,* in its own mind and the consequent fall will be ruinous.[1693] When Napoleon lost his giant status in 1815 at the battle of Waterloo, a new *Nephilim,* by the name of Duke of Wellington (1769–1852), emerged only to drown also in this universal flood that we call History.

6:5-Wicked Thought

וַיַּרְא יְהוָה כִּי רַבָּה רָעַת הָאָדָם בָּאָרֶץ וְכָל־יֵצֶר מַחְשְׁבֹת לִבּוֹ רַק רַע כָּל־הַיּוֹם׃ *vayara`* (saw) *yahvāh* (Transcendence) *kiy* (that) *rabāh* (great) *rā'aṯ* (misery) *hā'āḏām* (Adam) *bā'āreṣ* (earth) *vaḵāl* (every) *yēṣer* (from) *maḥašaḇōṯ* (thought) *libvō* (mind) *raq* (only) *ra`* (distress) *hayvōm* (day)
ἰδὼν *idōn* (having seen) **δὲ** *de* (but) **κύριος** *kurios* (Lord) **ὁ** *o* (the) **θεὸς** *theos* (God) **ὅτι** *oti* (that) **ἐπληθύνθησαν** *eplēthunthēsan* (was multiplied) **αἱ** *ai* (the) **κακίαι** *kakiai* (wikedness) **τῶν** *tōn* (of the) **ἀνθρώπων** *anthrōpōn* (men) **ἐπὶ** *epi* (on) **τῆς** *tēs* (the) **γῆς** *gēs* (earth) **καὶ** *kai* (and) **πᾶς** *pas* (all) **τις** *tis* (the) **διανοεῖται** *dianoeitai* (thinking) **ἐν** *en* (in) **τῇ** *tē* (the) **καρδίᾳ** *kardia* (heart) **αὐτοῦ** *autou* (his) **ἐπιμελῶς** *epimelōs* (intently) **ἐπὶ** *epi* (on) **τὰ** *ta* (the) **πονηρὰ** *ponēra* (evil) **πάσας** *pasas* (all) **τὰς** *tas* (the) **ἡμέρας** *ēmeras* (days)
videns (seeing) ***autem*** (also) ***Deus*** (God) ***quod*** (that) ***multa*** (very much) ***malitia*** (wickedness) ***hominum*** (of men) ***esset*** (was) ***in*** (on) ***terra*** (earth) ***et*** (and) ***cuncta*** (all) ***cogitatio*** (the thinking) ***cordis*** (of the heart) ***intenta*** (intent) ***esset*** (was) ***ad*** (to) ***malum*** (evil) ***omni*** (all) ***tempore*** (times)
And GOD saw that the wickedness of man was great in the earth, and that every imagination of the thoughts of his heart was only evil continually.
Therefore, the Transcendent was Aware that the misery of the human being on the land of duality was great and that every thought of the epistemic structure of his/her mind in its recurrent daily circularity was indeed the cause of his/her distress.

The Hebrew word *ra`* (רע)[1694] means evil, distress or misery. In any case, as described in this verse, it is not the action that constitutes wrongdoing, *thought*[1695] is. This is the definitive proof of the epistemic meaning of the Tree of Knowledge. The forbidden fruit is hunger and attachment to the desired object of thought considered as capable of reaching reality in-itself. In Its apodictical centrality, Transcendence Itself, realizes[1696] Adam's great (רב *rab*) distress (רע *ra`*). As we have already highlighted in Chapter 3, that misery (רע *ra`*) derives from careless epistemic desire.

For the sake of clarity, let us retrace the steps of that trouble-causing event. There is a serpentine desire imbedded in our *hunger to know* (יָדַע *yada`*). The *'I',* the *ego*-subject, wants to know you, the object, in the same way, as it knows itself. Inevitably, however, the *'I'* can never discover you as itself, but always as an object, a mask different from itself.

> "*For what man knoweth the things of a man, save the spirit of man which is in him?*"[1697]

The *you* becomes the *mask* behind which I *in*tend your unrelated Self-In-Itself, which is Transcendent. In fact, the modality, intrinsic to our way or form[1698] of knowing, requires the *'I,'* the *ego*-subject, to eliminate *your 'I,'* as Cain did with Abel. In fact, if the *'I'* does not eliminate *your 'I,'* how could we know you as *the other*? We can believe in your *'I,'* but we can never experience it, as such. Then, the *other* becomes *'you,' the other one.* At the same time, paradoxically, the *shivering serpentine* (נָחָשׁ *nachash*) *desire* to know (יָדַע *yada`*) wants to perceive *you* as it perceives itself. Nevertheless, it does not realize that, even when the *ego*-subject perceives itself as an *'I,'* that same *'I'* becomes its own object of thought, therefore not the *'I'* in-itself, but an *ego*-object for-itself.

This continuous circular daily (יוֹם *yowm*) epistemic delirious process takes place only (רַק *raq*)[1699] in the *'I'*s mind,[1700] namely, in the *cursed* land (אֶרֶץ *'erets*) of duality of *good and evil.* In fact, to make this clearer, let us use the pertinent example of lovemaking, which parallels the mind's (לֵב *leb*) epistemic process.

I. The *'I'* desires to know (יָדַע *yada`*) the loved *you, the other, the unknown in-itself.*
II. The loving *'I'* reaches out to *the other, you,* the desired loved one.
III. The *'I'* brings *you* into its arms in order to reach *you* and to know (יָדַע *yada`*) *you in-yourself.*
IV. In a brief instant of *Present's Stillness, you and I* disappear beyond the duality of good and evil.
V. When, in the course of time, the *'I'* opens its arms again, then, the *'I'* perceives *you,* once more, as *the unknown other,* as *you* were before the embrace.

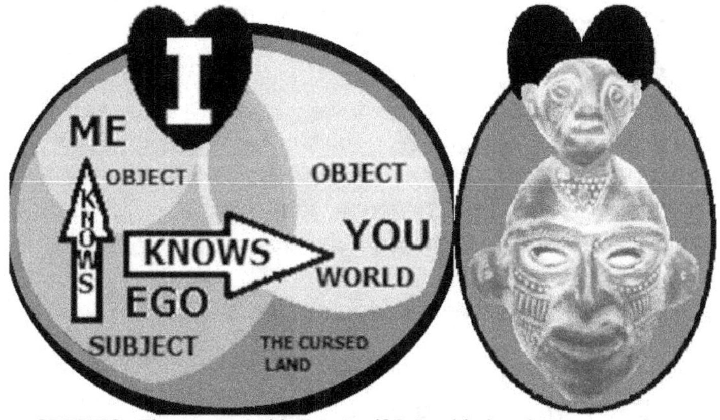

GRAPHIC: *The Unreachable I-in-itself & Double-head Mayan mask.*

6:6-Compassion

וַיִּנָּחֶם יְהוָה כִּי־עָשָׂה אֶת־הָאָדָם בָּאָרֶץ וַיִּתְעַצֵּב אֶל־לִבּוֹ׃   *vayināḥem* (held breath) *yahvāh* (Transcendent) *kiy* (because) *`āśāh* (he had made) *'et* (and) *hā'āḏām* (man) *bā'āreṣ* (on earth) *vayiṯa'aṣēḇ* (he formed) *'el* (it) *libvō* (in mind)
καὶ *kai* (and) **ἐνεθυμήθη** *enethumēthē* (repented) **ὁ** *o* (the) **θεὸς** *theos* (God) **ὅτι** *oti* (that) **ἐποίησεν** *epoiēsen* (he had made) **τὸν** *ton* (the) **ἄνθρωπον** *anthrōpon* (man) **ἐπὶ** *epi* (on) **τῆς** *tēs* (the) **γῆς** *gēs* (earth) **καὶ** *kai* (and) **διενοήθη** *dienoēthē* (he pondered deeply)
paenituit (repented) ***eum*** (He) ***quod*** (because) ***hominem*** (man) ***fecisset*** (had made) ***in*** (on) ***terra*** (earth) ***et*** (and) ***tactus*** (touching) ***dolore*** (with pain) ***cordis*** (in heart) ***intrinsecus*** (inside)
And it repented the LORD that he had made man on the earth, and it grieved him at his heart.
And the Transcendent held the Breath which made the human on earth. And He formed it in the mind.

It is a great contradiction to ascribe to the Transcendent anthropomorphic qualities like grieving and anger. Humans suffer greatly because of thoughts deriving from their mind's epistemic structure. The Transcendent Itself stated it in the preceding verse. Therefore, why would the Transcendence harbor the same type of thoughts and feelings? The *grieving* (עָצַב *`atsab*) is *formed, fashioned* and *shaped*[1701] in-the-mind (לֵב *leb*).[1702] This is the structure of the subject/object correlation, not of the Transcendent-in-Itself.

The Hebrew verb *nacham* (נָחַם),[1703]

"prop.[erly] onomatopoet.[ic] to draw the breath forcibly... because of the misery of others; whence, to pity"[1704]

means that the Transcendent withholds the vivifying Breath which formed the human. Precisely, the human takes the distance from that original Breath. In addition, the Greek text translates the Hebrew *vayiṯə'aṣēḇ* (וַיִּתְעַצֵּב) with *dienoēthē* (διενοήθη),[1705] namely, *he pondered it deeply* and not as *he grieved* (עָצַב *`atsab*).

However, the Transcendent Awareness with *unemotional-compassion registers* all feelings harbored in the human mind. What we do to others we do to ourselves. Thus, Jesus says,

> "*I was an hungred, and you gave me meat: I was thirsty, and you gave me drink: I was a stranger, and you took me in: Naked, and you clothed me: I was sick, and you visited me: I was in prison, and you came unto me.*"[1706]
>
> "*Whosoever shall receive one of such children in my name, receiveth me* [Awareness]*: and whosoever shall receive me, receiveth not me* [individual consciousness]*, but him* [Awareness] *that sent me.*"[1707]
>
> [So that, any action "*ye have done unto one of the least of these my brethren, you have done unto me* [Awareness]."
>
> [Furthermore, what] "*you did not to one of the least of these, you did not to me* [Awareness]."[1708]
>
> "*For whosoever shall give you a cup of water to drink in my name, because you belong to Christ* [Awareness]*, verily I say unto you, he shall not lose his reward.*"[1709]

Malachi[1710] reports that

> "*The Book* (ספר *cepher*) *of Recorded*[1711] *Remembrance* (זִכָּרוֹן *zikrown*)[1712]...*was written*[1713] *before Him.*"

The prophet, here, does not refer to a logbook, a movie-camera, a tape-recorder or any memory storage tool, because all these mechanical devices lack of a built-in self-evidence. The *Book of Remembrance* is a metaphor for Pure-Apodictic-Awareness, which is synonym of Transcendence. This is the Ineffable-Certitude, the Faith within every aspect of experience, which is the continuous Eternal Present we have right here and now. Certainty, however, is neither a conceptualization nor these words. It is not the Cartesian *cogito*, but, similarly, it is not deduced

> "by a syllogism, but by a simple act of mental vision,"[1714]

namely, by Intuition.[1715]

The French Philosopher René Descartes, seeking to

> "distinguish Truth from Error... [resolved] to strip... of all past beliefs."[1716]

He writes, in his *Discourse on Method,*

> "I ought to reject as absolutely false all opinions in regard to which I could suppose the least ground for doubt, in order to ascertain whether after that there remained aught in my belief that was wholly indubitable. Accordingly, seeing that our senses sometimes deceive us, I was willing to suppose that there existed nothing really such as they presented to us... I supposed that all the objects (presentations) that had entered into my mind when awake, had in them no more truth than the illusions of my dreams. But immediately upon this I observed that, whilst I thus wished to think that all was false, it was absolutely necessary that I, who thus thought, should be somewhat; and as I observed that this truth *I think, hence I am,*[1717] was *so certain and of such evidence,*[1718] that no ground of doubt, however extravagant, could be alleged by the Sceptics capable of shaking it, I concluded that I might, without scruple, accept it as the first principle of the Philosophy of which I was in search."[1719]

<When we analyze, with closer attention, Descartes words, immediately we realize that there is an *indubitable certitude* that *precedes* thought, the *cogito,* which too quickly was listed as *first principle.* That certitude is the intuition, the Awareness that we have while experiencing and thinking an object. This Certitude comes before we question the reality of the object in-itself. In other words, the experience, whether *physical, abstract, imagined* or *dreamed,* comes ushered by Awareness itself as such. Namely, Certitude enlightens all and every experience before we enquire-*of* them. Only after awareness, we seek the fallacy of the experience. That is, we inquire about its transcendent correspondence or coherence. Namely, we search for the presence or the absence of an objective reality in itself conceived beyond the I-and-the-world or the subject-and-the-object immanent relationship.>

Certainty does not require a process of thought. No subject-object correlation is ever involved. <No words can describe what Certainty is, but nobody can deny Certainty, without denying life and self at the same time. The flow of the *mind pro*jects from It as cogito (*cum-agito*), hunger or desire to assimilate and

to *eat* cognitively the world. It *projects* as a vortex, an agitation (*agito*) of the self with (*cum*) itself, which never departs from its true essence of not being an object.>[1720]

Giordano Bruno, the Renascence Nolan freethinker, recognized the ever-present Awareness and called It the *Divine Mind*. He stated that unity and infinite number, while being different, are, at the same time, one into the other. Unity is not an accident, but it is an essence, it is

"the end and goal of intelligence, and the abundance of all things."[1721]

The *Divine Mind*, in its Providence, continues Bruno,

"is able to perform all things, not only in the universal but also in the particular."[1722]

"*What woman having ten pieces of silver, if she lose one piece, doth not light a candle, and sweep the house, and seek diligently till she finds* [it]?"[1723]

Awareness operates from within, as the soul of each natural being, affirmed Bruno. It is awareness present in everything, even in the minutest meaningless beings and/or things, like the

"red lace of Paolino... [and of the gown of] Master Danese... [The Divine Mind takes care of] Franzino's melon patch... [and each fruit] from the jujube tree... [It moves the] average size... [bed bug and each beetle,] born out of dung... [And the moles] in Antonio Faivano's garden... [and the puppies of the bitch of] Antonio Savolino... [It does not forget each hair on the head of] Vasta, Albenzio's wife... [nor of the poor widow] Laurenza... [or of][1724] Martiniello's son... [and the molar of] the old woman of Fiurulo... [Nor It forgets Ambruoggio's semen, derived from] his affair with his wife."[1725]

Therefore, like all the previous list of minutiae and trivial microscopic and/or macroscopic details, pity[1726] and affliction,[1727] imprint in the Transcendent, in the Pure-Apodictical-Awareness. However, the Transcendent's pity (נָחַם *nacham*) and affliction (עָצַב `*atsab*) is different from that of the creatures. It is not the human suffering and anger in the passionate sense of the word. It is, instead, the presence of human distress in the detached observing eye of Awareness with dispassionate/compassion (נָחַם *nacham*)[1728] for human's miseries. In fact, as stated in verse 5:3,

"*Awareness shall not forever control, struggle or judge* (דִּין *diyn*) *the human being.*"

To the prophet Jonah, the Transcendent declares his dispassionate/compassion and He wants to,

"*spare Nineveh, that great awaken-city-of-anguish,*[1729] *wherein are more than sixscore thousand persons that cannot discern between their right hand and their left hand; and also much cattle.*"[1730]

Anger, grief, wrath, vengeance, repentance and all other passions, attributed to the Transcendent, are semantic expressions to indicate the inevitable consequence of the distracting distance from the always-dispassionate Awareness. In fact,

"*they that observe lying vanities forsake their own mercy.*"[1731]

In the light of Certain-Awareness, everything is in the present-now. *Before*, *during* and *after* creation, all takes place in the same *Now of Awareness*. Then, how can there be any regret? It is like saying that love begs for revenge when not reciprocated. Like Awareness, love gives without asking anything in return. Revenge has nothing to do with love. Rabia, the Sufi mystic, expresses this very well, when she declared,

"*O my Lord, if I worship You from fear of Hell, burn me in Hell; and if I worship You from hope of Paradise, exclude me from Paradise. But if I love You for Your own sake, do not withhold from me Your Eternal Beauty.*"[1732]

In fact, if one thinks about heaven, that thought cannot be heaven, because it is only its thought. Surely, that idea tends toward an unconceivable heaven. Thus, its conception, as idea, cannot be heaven, but its contrary, *viz.* hell. It becomes a place of torment like any other one. There, the same epistemic structures of this place ensue. Therefore, Heaven must be the Silence from which we come and go. It is the beginning, which coincides with its end only to start again. In other words, like with Abel's sacrifice, Heaven is the renunciation of one's own subjectivity, along with the correlated objectivity, that enables to reach the Transcendent beyond the subject/object correlation.

Love is the Transcendent. It is the Universal Divine Grace of Serene Awareness and our desireless tension towards It. <Pure Awareness is Transcendence and Pure Certitude is Love. Therefore, love must

be truthful, never lies and never deceives. Love tends to reach the Transcendence, the other *I* as *I* in-itself. That other I cannot present itself for what it is not, therefore it cannot lie. If the Ego feels the necessity to garb itself with a mask, in that case it wants to hide its true nature. Then, it cannot be love. In fact, the individual I or the Ego, concealing itself, does not transpire the Transcendence, namely the goal of love itself...

What good is it if one, like the mighty warrior-king Capaneus in Hell,

> "denying and blaspheming... not extinguishing/... arrogance... ha-[s].../ God in disdain"?[1733]

Anger fixes on the object as evil, identifies the adversary as wicked and despises the other as enemy. Both, the angry one and the "other" are "into hellish pain." On the contrary,

> "*I should be happy to have an enemy / for he assists me in my conduct of Awakening.*"[1734]

In fact, as stated by the Dalai Lama, the best teacher is my enemy who teaches me compassion because s/he is the one who offers me

> "opportunities for practicing patience... Like having found a treasure in one's own house, one should be happy and grateful toward one's enemy for providing that precious opportunity... Therefore, we should acknowledge that and dedicate the fruit of our practice of patience first for the benefit of our enemy."[1735]

Anger dispenses its *daimonic* destiny when we are possessed by it. The luciferous[1736] aspect of anger is the identification with the object reflecting the light received from Awareness, which, in itself as a pure observer, is not angry. Anger, then, becomes a springboard to Awareness. Let yourself be angry and, then, let the anger drop by focusing on the presence of Awareness.>[1737] Moreover, the paradox is that even hate and/or murder refer to a transcending attribution given by the murderer to the *other* conceived as the *enemy*.

6:7-Promise to Wipe Away Men

וַיֹּאמֶר יְהוָה אֶמְחֶה אֶת־הָאָדָם אֲשֶׁר־בָּרָאתִי מֵעַל פְּנֵי הָאֲדָמָה מֵאָדָם עַד־בְּהֵמָה עַד־רֶמֶשׂ וְעַד־עוֹף הַשָּׁמַיִם כִּי נִחַמְתִּי כִּי עֲשִׂיתִם׃ *vayōʼmer* (promised) *yahvāh* (the Transcendent) *ʼemaḥeh* (I will wipe away) *ʼe<u>t</u>* (and) *hāʼā<u>d</u>ām* (Adam) *ʼăšer* (which) *bārāʼ<u>t</u>iy* (I have created) *mēʻal* (from) *panēy* (face) *hāʼă<u>d</u>āmāh* (of the earth) *mēʼā<u>d</u>ām* (from man) *ʻa<u>d</u>* (and) *bahēmāh* (beasts) *ʻa<u>d</u>* (and) *remeś* (creeping) *vaʻa<u>d</u>* (and) *ʻvō<u>p</u>* (fowl) *hašāmāyim* (sky) *kiy* (indeed) *niḥamatiy* (I have compassion) *kiy* (because) *ʻăśiy<u>t</u>im* (I have made)
καὶ *kai* (and) **εἶπεν** *eipen* (said) **ὁ** *o* (the) **θεός** *theos* (God) **ἀπαλείψω** *apaleipsō* (I will delete) **τὸν** *ton* (the) **ἄνθρωπον** *anthrōpon* (man) **ὃν** *on* (thus) **ἐποίησα** *epoiēsa* (created) **ἀπὸ** *apo* (from) **προσώπου** *prosōpou* (face) **τῆς** *tēs* (of the) **γῆς** *gēs* (earth) **ἀπὸ** *apo* (from) **ἀνθρώπου** *anthrōpou* (man) **ἕως** *eōs* (to) **κτήνους** *ktēvous* (beast) **καὶ** *kai* (and) **ἀπὸ** *apo* (from) **ἑρπετῶν** *erpetōn* (reptiles) **ἕως** *eōs* (to) **τῶν** *tōn* (the) **πετεινῶν** *peteinōn* (birds) **τοῦ** *tou* (of the) **οὐρανοῦ** *ouranou* (sky) **ὅτι** *oti* (because) **ἐθυμώθην** *ethumōthēn* (I grieve) **ὅτι** *oti* (that) **ἐποίησα** *epoiēsa* (I made) **αὐτούς** *autous* (them)
delebo (I will delete) ***inquit*** (He said) ***hominem*** (man) ***quem*** (whom) ***creavi*** (I created) ***a*** (from) ***facie*** (the face) ***terrae*** (of the earth) ***ab*** (from) ***homine*** (man) ***usque*** (until) ***ad*** (to) ***animantia*** (animals) ***a*** (from) ***reptili*** (reptiles) ***usque*** (until) ***ad*** (to) ***volucres*** (birds) ***caeli*** (of the sky) ***paenitet*** (regrets) ***enim*** (in fact) ***me*** (me) ***fecisse*** (to have made) ***eos*** (them)
And the LORD said, I will destroy man whom I have created from the face of the earth; both man, and beast, and the creeping thing, and the fowls of the air; for it repenteth me that I have made them.
The Transcendent promised, "*I will wipe away from the face of the earth man, whom I created, namely, man together with beast, serpents and birds of the air, indeed I pity them whom I created.*"

The *Bible* describes the *wrath* of God cursing Adam, Eve and Cain,[1738] destroying the Tower of Babel or Sodom and Gomorrah[1739] and plaguing Egypt,[1740] just to mention few. Even contemporary natural disasters are perceived as divine punishments.[1741] According to literal interpreters, men (אָדָם *'adam*) deserved punishments for their disobedience and God repents for having created them. However, how could there be *repentance* (נָחַם *nacham*) for the creative act, if God's postulated foresight already knew the outcome beforehand? Moreover, why, besides men, God would destroy His own created animals (בְּהֵמָה *běhemah*), *serpents* (רֶמֶשׂ remes) *and birds* (עוֹף 'owph)? Who would kill a beloved, obedient and heathy pet?[1742] Why, then, at the same time of their execution, provide for their reproduction, as in verse 6:19? Furthermore, why all aquatic life, including mammals, as described in verse 1:21, is not on the death row? Finally, why irremediably destroy all plants living on dry land? The answer is possible only if we understand *divine wrath* as a metaphor. The only way, for the mind to understand and to justify the inevitable consequences of its own distraction and distance from the Ever-Present-Pure-State-of-Awareness is as punishment coming from God. The mind's structural perspective always understands events as having a reality external to itself. As an example, the expression, *the fire burns*, sounds as if the blaze has in itself the will to smolder. Thus, we say, *the fire burnt the house*. We scorch as if the flames punish us for our careless proximity to it. Similarly, the mind understands its own actual misery and suffering as the consequence of the destructive anger of the transcendent. However, ultimately creation *rests*, as with Noah,[1743] in its own Original Foundation, which is always here and now.

As a flaming light, Awareness illuminates and, as the resting *shabath* (שַׁבָּת), establishes all Creation in the Present. *Outside* of It, we look at death set in the past, where everything is burnt and reduced to ashes. The natural consequence, therefore, is the *promise*[1744] *to wipe away*[1745] from the *face* (פָּנִים *paniym*) *of the land* (אֲדָמָה *'adamah*) of consciousness all those who distance themselves from Pure-Awareness as such, in which all opposites dissolve. Only the Stillness of Its resting place remains as an *ark in the deluge*. We should not forget that all events, supporting this condemnation, take place in the mind (לֵב *leb*). Specifically, "*the epistemic structure*" (verse 6:5), the thinking process (מַחֲשָׁבָה *machashabah*) is the culprit, which takes place on all waking and dreaming levels of human life. With the end of the thinking process, also all human inclinations, allegorically indicated as *beasts* (בְּהֵמָה *běhemah*),[1746] all the *creeping winding* (רָמַשׂ *ramas*)[1747] *tendencies* (רֶמֶשׂ *remes*),[1748] as metaphoric serpents, and the ethereal psychological senses, as *birds* (עוֹף *'owph*),[1749] all are wiped out with the human being. Nevertheless, apart from metaphoric interpretations, we must also acknowledge that all sentient beings are exposed to time perception and, consequently, perish in it.

However, free from the distress of duality, *pity* and *compassion* (נָחַם *nacham*)[1750] remain as the fundamental trait of Dispassionate Detached Awareness.

> "*He will swallow up death in victory; and the Transcendent will wipe away* (מָחָה *machah*) *tears from off all faces; and the rebuke of his people shall he take away from off all the earth: for the Transcendent hath spoken it.*"[1751]

The Egyptian tradition, which must have been very familiar to Moses, described this concept of detachment. The *Papyrus of Ani* depicts a scene of the afterlife. At death, the jackal-headed Anubis, flanked by Thoth, the ibis–headed scribe representing truthful remembrance, evaluates the heart (𓄣). Placed in a Canopic-jar, that organ, metaphor for life's central attachment, is weighted against the *Ma'at's* weightless plume (𓆄).[1752] Revelation says,

> "*I saw, and behold, a black horse, and its rider had a balance in his hand.*"[1753]

And Daniel, declares,

> "*Thou art weighed in the balances, and art found wanting.*"[1754]

The Indian *Śatapatha Brāhmaṇa* states that the dead is weighted in order to receive its just reward.[1755] Therefore, in the Egyptian mythology, if passion rules the deceased's heart, then it weighs more than a feather. In that case, a metaphoric crocodile drags the soul in the flowing stream of life's torments where it gobbles it up. However, a heart, weighing less than the plume, means that it is *lighthearted* and dispassionate. Then the soul *Ka* (ᑌ) goes up to heaven.[1756] Ezekiel writes,

⇦[1757] "*Thus saith the Lord GOD... 'I will give them one heart, and I will put a new spirit within you.'"*[1758]

Ramana Maharshi states,

"*I want you to dive consciously into the Self, i.e., into the Heart.*"[1759]

The heart is at the center *cross*road of a body with arms stretched out (✱).[1760] Originally, the concept of cross, *crux* in Latin, was not a symbol of pain and suffering, as the Roman instrument for capital punishment.[1761] In Hebrew, the letter, *tav* (ת), means *cross* and, in general, in Hebrew. symbolizes a mark, *owt* (אות). ⇨[1762]

"*Tav* symbolizes...the ultimate end of this human cycle is joyful, complete redemption...The final letter *Tav* also opens the Hebrew word *Teshuvah*, (meaning 'repentance,' or more accurately, 'returning to the Source')."[1763]

Then, how must we understand Jesus' saying,

"*'He that taketh not his cross* (σταυρός *stauros*), *and followeth after me, is not worthy of me'...* [After,] *unto a place called Golgotha* (Γολγοθᾶ),... [*viz.*] *skull* (κρανίον *kranion*),... *they crucified* (σταυρόω *stauroō*) *him.*"[1764]

In Aramaic, *gulgoleth* (גֻּלְגֹּלֶת), Golgotha, means *head, skull.*[1765] The name is reduplication from *galal* (גָּלַל),[1766] which means *to roll.* Furthermore, the Greek word *stauros* (σταυρός), *cross*, comes from *istēmi* (ἵστημι), *to straighten up, to stand.*[1767] Thus, it implies the upright *stand*ing direction of a stake or a pole standing on the head (*gulgoleth*). Whether, for *cross*, Greek *stauros* (σταυρός), we mean

I. the Latin *crux* or St. Andrew's cross (X),
II. the Greek cross (+),
III. the cross *immissa* (†),
IV. the cross *commissa* (T), or
V. a single stake (I),[1768]

in each case, the wood adapts to this body and follows its anatomy. The first, with arms and legs spread apart, the second, third and fourth, with arms extended at the sides, all merge in the centrality of the heart. The single rod follows, through the heart, the direction of the spine pole. All this implies that the cross, *tav* (ת), is a metaphor for the redeeming aspect of introspection, which, while is between the subject/object *rolling*-process, *galal* (גָּלַל), it metaphorically extends above the immanent *gulgoleth* (גֻּלְגֹּלֶת) *head* to reach Transcendence.

The mind engages with divine thoughts and/or mortal desires. These last ones produced famous and eminent men who end up drowning in their own mud. Desirous thoughts cause humans to withdraw from the Divine Life itself, thus, they suffer and drown.

6-II SECTION: NOAH'S GENERATIONS

6:8-Noah Rested in Awareness

וְנֹחַ מָצָא חֵן בְּעֵינֵי יְהוָה׃ פ
vanōaḥ (Noah-rest) *māṣā'* (attained) *ḥēn* (acceptance) *ba'ēynēy* (in the eyes) *yahvāh* (of the Transcendent) *p̄* (.)
Νωε *Nōe* (Noah) **δὲ** *de* (but) **εὗρεν** *euren* (found) **χάριν** *charin* (grace) **ἐναντίον** *enantion* (before) **κυρίου** *kuriou* (Lord) **τοῦ** *tou* (the) **θεοῦ** *theu* (God)
Noe (Noah) ***vero*** (truthfully) ***invenit*** (found) ***gratiam*** (grace) ***coram*** (before) ***Domino*** (the Lord)
But Noah found grace in the eyes of the LORD.
However, Noah, resting, attained acceptance in the Aware Eyes of the Transcendent.

Noah is a descendant from Seth's generation. Therefore, he is associated to the realm of sleep. This kingdom is not inferior or less important than the waking state of Cain. Sleep parallels and, in many ways, affects the waking dimension. Like Enoch, Noah comes to (מָצָא *matsa'*) the non-dreaming deep sleep (תַּרְדֵּמָה *tardemah*) realm, which preludes the detached stillness of Awareness. There, Noah rests (נֹחַ *Noach*)[1769] *attaining*[1770] *acceptance*[1771] in the Aware metaphoric *Eyes*[1772] of the Transcendent.

6:9-Noah's Generations

אֵלֶּה תּוֹלְדֹת נֹחַ נֹחַ אִישׁ צַדִּיק תָּמִים הָיָה בְּדֹרֹתָיו אֶת־הָאֱלֹהִים הִתְהַלֶּךְ־נֹחַ׃
'ēleh (these) *tvōladōṯ* (generations) *nōaḥ* (Noah) *nōaḥ* (Noah) *'iyš* (man) ṣadiyq (just) *tāmiym* (perfect) *hāyāh* (was) badōrōṯāyv (among circle) *'eṯ* (with) *hā'ělōhiym* (Gods) *hiṯahaleḵa* (walked) *nōaḥ* (Noah)
αὗται *autai* (thus) **δὲ** *de* (but) **αἱ** *ai* (the) **γενέσεις** *geneseis* (generations) **Νωε** *Nōe* (of Noah) **Νωε** *Nōe* (Noah) **ἄνθρωπος** *anthrōpos* (man) **δίκαιος** *dikaios* (righteous) **τέλειος** *telesios* (complete) **ὢν** *ōn* (was) **ἐν** *en* (in) **τῇ** *tē* (the) **γενεᾷ** *genea* (generation) **αὐτοῦ** *autou* (his) **τῷ** *tō* (to the) **θεῷ** *theō* (God) **εὐηρέστησεν** *euērestēsen* (well pleasing) **Νωε** *Nōe* (Noah)
hae (these) ***generationes*** (generations) ***Noe*** (of Noah) ***Noe*** (Noah) ***vir*** (man) ***iustus*** (just) ***atque*** (and also) ***perfectus*** (perfect) ***fuit*** (was) ***in*** (among) ***generationibus*** (generations) ***suis*** (his) ***cum*** (with) ***Deo*** (God) ***ambulavit*** (he walked)
These are the generations of Noah: Noah was a just man and perfect in his generations, and Noah walked with God.
These are the offspring of Noah. Noah is the cognitive *a-priori* synthesis that moves along with Divine-Consciousness, resting in the righteous and complete circularity of his dwelling.

Each patriarchal figure is a paradigmatic, template aspect or a function of the human epistemic structure. Three major recurrent moments delineate our life. They are the stages of

1) waking (שָׁמַר *shamar*), represented by Cain,[1773]
2) dreaming (חָלַם *chalam*)[1774] with Rapid-Eye-Movements (REM), characterized by Seth, and
3) deep-dreamless-sleep (תַּרְדֵּמָה *tardemah*)[1775] with No-Rapid-Eye-Movements (NREM), symbolized by Abel.

In turn, each patriarchal figure describes one or more aspects of the multiple facets of each one of the complex articulation of these stages.

Like Enoch,[1776] Noah *moves along* (חָלַךְ *halak*) with (אֵת *'eṯ*) Divine-Consciousness (אֱלֹהִים *'elohiym*), the Pure-Epistemic Fundamentals, namely, Aware-Conscious-Certainty. His generation (תוֹלְדוֹת *towlědah*)[1777] is in his *circular* (דּוּר *duwr*)[1778] *dwelling* (דּוֹר *dowr*).[1779] That is the realm of Abel. That state is the *righteous* (צַדִּיק *tsaddiyq*),[1780] *complete* (תָּמָם *tamam*)[1781] and *perfectly*-(תָּמִים *tamiym*)-[1782] contained-in-itself silent *circle* (דּוֹר *dowr*) of dreamless sleep. As the next verses will clarify, this circle contains potentially, in germ, all possible creative ideas.

6:10-Noah's sons

וַיּוֹלֶד נֹחַ שְׁלֹשָׁה בָנִים אֶת־שֵׁם אֶת־חָם וְאֶת־יָפֶת׃
vayvōleḏ (generated) *nōaḥ* (Noah) *šalōšāh* (three) *ḇāniym* (sons) *'eṯ* (and) *šēm* (Shem) *'eṯ* (and) *ḥām* (Ham) *va'eṯ* (and) *yāp̄eṯ* (Japheth)
ἐγέννησεν *egennēsen* (generated) **δὲ** *de* (and) **Νωε** *Nōe* (Noah) **τρεῖς** *treis* (three) **υἱούς** *uious*

(three) **τὸν** *ton* (the) **Σημ** *Sēm* (Sem) **τὸν** *ton* (the) **Χαμ** *Cham* (Ham) **τὸν** *ton* (the) **Ιαφεθ** *Iapheth* (Japheth)
et (and) ***genuit*** (generated) ***tres*** (three) ***filios*** (sons) ***Sem*** (Sem) ***Ham*** (Ham) ***et*** (and) ***Iafeth*** (Japheth)
And Noah begat three sons, Shem, Ham, and Japheth.
From Noah derive three projections, glorious-Shem, passionate-Ham and seduced-seducer-Japheth.

From Noah, the one resting in the state of dreamless sleep, derive the three circadian conditions.

1) Shem (שֵׁם *Shem*) is the *glorious name* (שֵׁם *shem*) *established* (שֵׁם *shem*)[1783] as memory and fame after death (שֵׁם *shem*)[1784] in Noah's dreamless realm, therefore it is like a time memorial monument (שֵׁם *shem*);[1785]
2) Ham (חָם *Cham*)[1786] is the *one hot* (חָם *cham*)[1787] for *passion* (חָמַם *chamam*),[1788] the heat and excitement of the mind[1789] in the causality of the dream realm;
3) Japheth (יֶפֶת *Yepheth*)[1790] is *the widely extending one*[1791] *open* (יֶפֶת *yepheth*) *to seduce* (פָּתָה *pathah*)[1792] in the space of the waking realm.

Therefore, the circadian rhythm concludes with the return to the waking world.

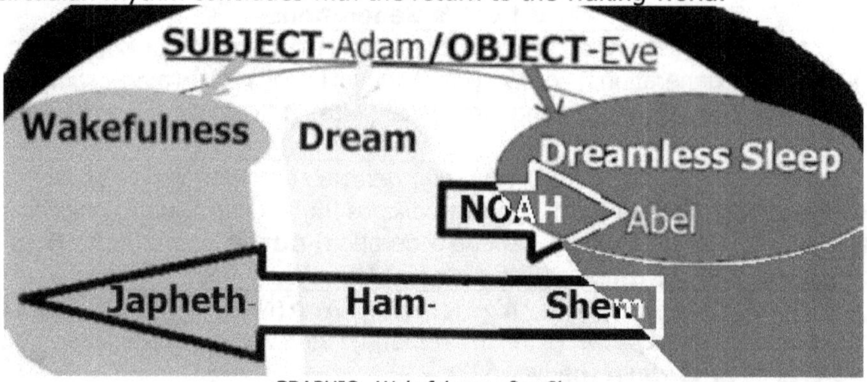

GRAPHIC: *Wakefulness after Sleep*

Shem, Ham and Japheth are metaphors, in order, for time, causality and space. Our mode of knowing is shaped by necessary forms, which are logical prerequisites for any epistemic attainments. We cannot know anything if not established in a time structure. We cannot know any event if not interwoven in a cause-effect relation. We cannot experience any physical object if not placed in a space frame. Therefore, time, causality and space are the *a-priori* forms of our knowledge.[1793] Each of these three forms is concomitant with the known object and only logically preceding it.

6:11-Violence

וַתִּשָּׁחֵת הָאָרֶץ לִפְנֵי הָאֱלֹהִים וַתִּמָּלֵא הָאָרֶץ חָמָס׃ *vatišāḥēṯ* (corrupt) *hā'āreṣ* (the earth) *lipānēy* (before) *hā'ĕlōhiym* (God) *vatimālē'* (was full) *hā'āreṣ* (the earth) *ḥāmās* (of violence)
ἐφθάρη *ephtharē* (wasted) **δὲ** *de* (but) **ἡ** *ē* (the) **γῆ** *gē* (earth) **ἐναντίον** *enantion* (before) **τοῦ** *tou* (the) **θεοῦ** *theou* (God) **καὶ** *kai* (and) **ἐπλήσθη** *eplēsthē* (was full) **ἡ** *ē* (the) **γῆ** *gē* (earth) **ἀδικίας** *adikias* (iniquity)
corrupta (corrupted) ***est*** (is) ***autem*** (also) ***terra*** (the earth) ***coram*** (before) ***Deo*** (God) ***et*** (and) ***repleta*** (full) ***est*** (is) ***iniquitate*** (of iniquity)
The earth also was corrupt before God, and the earth was filled with violence.
The ground of epistemic correlation lays waste before Divine-Consciousness, thus that land is full of violence.

'Erets (אֶרֶץ) *is the ground on which the epistemic correlation takes place. It lays waste* (שָׁחַת *shachath*) *full* (מָלֵא *male'*) of violence (חָמָס *chamac*) before (פָּנִים *paniym*) the dispassionate serenity of Awareness. This violence is the inevitable reduction of the *I-in-itself*, namely Divine-Consciousness (אֱלֹהִים *'elohiym*), to an object of

thought, as we saw in the commentary of verse 6:5. On the physical level, that equates to the real reason why beings engage in wars. Namely, the ego always wants to dominate the others and this leads to its own demise. In fact, the ego perceives itself, the other and the world always as past, therefore as already dead. This is the condition we are, at this point of our epistemic journey, as the universal deluge approaches.

6:12-Corrupting Flesh

וַיַּרְא אֱלֹהִים אֶת־הָאָרֶץ וְהִנֵּה נִשְׁחָתָה כִּי־הִשְׁחִית כָּל־בָּשָׂר אֶת־דַּרְכּוֹ עַל־הָאָרֶץ׃ ס   *vayara'* (gazed) *'ělōhiym* (Gods) *'eṯ* (on) *hā'āreṣ* (earth) *vahinēh* (behold) *nišaḥāṯāh* (lay waste) *kiy* (because) *hišaḥiyṯ* (corrupted) kāl (all) *bāśār* (flesh) *'eṯ* (and) *darakvō* (manner) *'al* (on) *hā'āreṣ* (the earth) *s* (.)
καὶ *kai* (and) **εἶδεν** *eiden* (saw) **κύριος** *kurios* (the Lord) **ὁ** *o* (the) **θεὸς** *theos* (God) **τὴν** *tēn* (the) **γῆν** *gēn* (earth) **καὶ** *kai* (and) **ἦν** *ēn* (was) **κατεφθαρμένη** *katepgtharēmenē* (destroyed) **ὅτι** *oti* (because) **κατέφθειρεν** *katephthetren* (had destroyed) **πᾶσα** *pasa* (all) **σὰρξ** *sarx* (flesh) **τὴν** *tēn* (the) **ὁδὸν** *odon* (way) **αὐτοῦ** *autou* (its) **ἐπὶ** *epi* (on) **τῆς** *tēs* (the) **γῆς** *gēs* (earth)
cum- (as)***que*** (and) ***vidisset*** (saw) ***Deus*** (God) ***terram*** (the earth) ***esse*** (being) ***corruptam*** (corrupted) ***omnis*** (all) ***quippe*** (indeed) ***caro*** (flesh) ***corruperat*** (had corrupted) ***viam*** (the way) ***suam*** (his) ***super*** (on) ***terram*** (earth)
And God looked upon the earth, and, behold, it was corrupt; for all flesh had corrupted his way upon the earth.
Divine-Consciousness gazes upon the land of duality and indeed, it lays waste because the whole information structure distorts the direction in the land of duality.

This reconfirms the previous verse. What lays waste (שחת *shachath*) is the mode of the journey (דרך *derek*),[1794] of the epistemic process. *Basar* (בָשָׂר), the flesh, means the information-bearing nerve system. This implies that the knowledge we derive from it is not vivified by the internal life of Awareness. In fact, it is not Noah's restful mode of Awareness, but is the way of

"*the dissolute-sea-goers*"[1795]

in Jonah's account. Then,

> "In the middle of the journey of our life / I found myself within a dark forest, / cause the straightforward path was lost. ... / I cannot rightly tell how I entered it, / so full of sleep was I about that moment / in which I had forsaken the true way."[1796]

In this journey, the correct conscious direction to take is to convert towards the internal centrality of the Tree of Life not that of the external meandering of the Tree of Knowledge.

From the resting state of our epistemic journey, emerge time, causality and space, which lead us astray.

6-III SECTION: THE FLOOD

6:13-The Wasteland

וַיֹּאמֶר אֱלֹהִים לְנֹחַ קֵץ כָּל־בָּשָׂר בָּא לְפָנַי כִּי־מָלְאָה הָאָרֶץ חָמָס מִפְּנֵיהֶם וְהִנְנִי מַשְׁחִיתָם אֶת־הָאָרֶץ׃

vayōʼmer (said) *ʼĕlōhiym* (the Gods) *lanōaḥ* (to Noah) *qēṣ* (time-end) *kāl* (all) *bāśār* (flesh) *bāʼ* (have come) *lap̄ānay* (before) *kiy* (because) *mālaʼāh* (have been full) *hāʼāreṣ* (land) *ḥāmās* (violence) *mipanēyhem* (from their face) *vahinaniy* (them) *mašaḥiyṯām* (destroy) *ʼeṯ* (and) *hāʼāreṣ* (the earth)

καὶ *kai* (and) **εἶπεν** *eipen* (said) **ὁ** *o* (the) **θεὸς** *theos* (God) **πρὸς** *pros* (to) **Νωε** *Nōe* (Noah) **καιρὸς** *kairos* (the end) **παντὸς** *pantos* (all) **ἀνθρώπου** *anthrōpou* (men) **ἥκει** *ēkei* (have come) **ἐναντίον** *enantion* (before) **μου** *mou* (me) **ὅτι** *oti* (because) **ἐπλήσθη** *eplēsthē* (filled) **ἡ** *ē* (the) **γῆ** *gē* (earth) **ἀδικίας** *adikias* (iniquity) **ἀπ'** *ap'* (by) **αὐτῶν** *autōn* (them) **καὶ** *kai* (and) **ἰδοὺ** *idou* (behold) **ἐγὼ** *egō* (I) **καταφθείρω** *kataphtheirō* (will destroy) **αὐτοὺς** *autous* (them) **καὶ** *kai* (and) **τὴν** *tēn* (the) **γῆν** *gēn* (earth)

dixit (said) ***ad*** (to) ***Noe*** (Noah) ***finis*** (the end) ***universae*** (of all) ***carnis*** (flesh) ***venit*** (came) ***coram*** (before) ***me*** (me) ***repleta*** (filled) ***est*** (is) ***terra*** (the earth) ***iniquitate*** (with iniquity) ***a*** (from) ***facie*** (face) ***eorum*** (of them) ***et*** (and) ***ego*** (I) ***disperdam*** (will disperse) ***eos*** (them) ***cum*** (with) ***terra*** (the earth)

And God said unto Noah, The end of all flesh is come before me; for the earth is filled with violence through them; and, behold, I will destroy them with the earth.

Divine-Consciousness said to Noah,
"*The time-end of all sentient beings came to my Conscious-Face. The land of duality is filled with violence because of their thinking and I will lay waste them and the land.*

The time-end[1797] of all sentient beings[1798] comes[1799] before the face (פָּנִים *paniym*) of the Pure-Epistemic Fundamentals of Divine-Consciousness (אֱלֹהִים *'elohiym*), namely, Aware-Conscious-Certainty. The end takes place due to the violence (חָמָס *chamac*) replenishing (מָלֵא *male'*) the land of duality (אֶרֶץ *'erets*) in the presence of [1800] the circular bending[1801] of their consciousness. Therefore, both the sentient beings and their land of duality will necessarily extinguish or will be reabsorbed in the stillness of Awareness.

The Epic of Gilgamesh, an older[1802] Sumerian account, relates a similar story. In it, Utnapishtim, the Mesopotamic equivalent of Noah, 'revealed' to Gilgamesh,

> "*In those days the world teemed, the people multiplied, the world bellowed like a wild bull, and the great god was aroused by the clamour. Enlil* [1803] *heard the clamour and he said to the gods in council, 'The uproar of mankind is intolerable and* <u>*sleep*</u> *is no longer possible by reason of the babel.'*[1804] *So the gods agreed to exterminate mankind. Enlil did this, but Ea*[1805] *because of his oath warned me in a* <u>*dream*</u>*, He whispered their words to my house of reeds... I* [Utnapishtim] *dare no longer walk in his land... I will... dwell with Ea my lord.*"[1806]

That uproar is

> "the inner noise of thinking."[1807]
>
> "Even if we are not talking with others, reading, listening to the radio, watching television, or interacting online, most of us don't feel settled or quiet. This is because we're still tuned to an *internal* radio station, Radio NST (Non-Stop Thinking)."[1808]

Where do ideas and/or dreams go when, at time-end, we enter the state of dreamless sleep or unconsciousness? Where are they preserved for future conscious generations? The *house of reeds* is this body itself, the habitat of all thoughts that constitute us and this house becomes Noah's ark or the temple, which, once destroyed, can be raised up

> "*in three days.*"[1809]

6:14-Build an Ark

עֲשֵׂה לְךָ תֵּבַת עֲצֵי־גֹפֶר קִנִּים תַּעֲשֶׂה אֶת־הַתֵּבָה וְכָפַרְתָּ אֹתָהּ מִבַּיִת וּמִחוּץ בַּכֹּפֶר׃

ʻăśēh (make) *lakā* (all) *tēḇaṯ* (ark) *ʻăṣēy* (wood) *gōp̄er* (*goper*) *qiniym* (cells) *taʻăśeh* (make) *ʼeṯ* (and) *hatēḇāh* (ark) *vakāp̄aratā* (make atonement) *ʼōṯāh* (with) *mibayiṯ* (within and without)

bakōp̄er (with the price of life)
ποίησον *poiēson* (make) **οὐν** *oun* (therefore) **σεαυτῷ** *seautō* (for yourself) **κιβωτὸν** *kibōton* (an ark) **ἐκ** *ek* (of) **ξύλων** *xulōn* (timber) **τετραγώνων** *tetragōnōn* (square) **νοσσιὰς** *nossias* (with compartments) **ποιήσεις** *poiēseis* (you shall make) **τὴν** *tēn* (the) **κιβωτὸν** *kibōton* (ark) **καὶ** *kai* (and) **ἀσφαλτώσεις** *asphaltōseis* (you shall pitch) **αὐτὴν** *autēn* (it) **ἔσωθεν** *esōthen* (from within) **καὶ** *kai* (and) **ἔξωθεν** *exōthen* (from without) **τῇ** *tē* (the) **ἀσφάλτῳ** *asphaltō* (with asphalt)
fac (make) ***tibi*** (for you) ***arcam*** (an ark) ***de*** (of) ***lignis*** (wood) ***levigatis*** (polished) ***mansiunculas*** (small cubicals) ***in*** (in) ***arca*** (the ark) ***facies*** (make) ***et*** (and) ***bitumine*** (with asphalt) ***linies*** (cover) ***intrinsecus*** (inside) ***et*** (and) ***extrinsecus*** (outside)
Make thee an ark of gopher wood; rooms shalt thou make in the ark, and shalt pitch it within and without with pitch.
Therefore, produce an ark of memory-wood for you, make nest-cells in the ark and make atonement within and without with the price of life.

The ark (תֵּבָה *tebah*)[1810] denotes

"both a chest and a vessel... The etymology is unknown."[1811]

It is a container apt to cross the waters of time. This is the basket-place where all beings, as ideas, remembrances, memories, dreams, imaginations and their interactions are stored, collected and amassed. *The Epic of Gilgamesh* clearly states that a divine warning took place during sleep. In fact, in a dream, Utnapishtim received notice from Ea who

"*whispered their* [gods'] *words to my house of reeds* [***GiPaRu***]. *'Reed-house, Reed-house! Wall, O wall, hearken reed-house, wall reflect... tear down your house and build a boat, abandon possessions and look for life, despite worldly goods and save your soul alive. Tear down your house, I say, and build a boat.*"[1812]

"F. Hommel holds the Hebrew גפר [***GoPeR***-wood] to be the Assyrian *giparu* (reed)."[1813]

Additionally, *giparu* means also *night*.[1814] They were the *night-homes*, the *reed-huts* divided in seven parts and serving as stables and storerooms.[1815]

The real meaning of the word *goper*[1816] is unknown. However, the word has a Gematria count of #283.[1817] This number is equivalent to words related to memory.

"*In the way of thy judgments, O LORD, have we waited for thee; the desire of our soul is to thy name, and to the remembrance of thee. / With my soul have I desired thee in the night.*"[1818]

The Gematria number 283 of *goper* is the same of *wlazikarakā*,[1819] meaning remembrance, of *zikrown*,[1820] meaning memory, and of *zākarawn*,[1821] meaning to remember, to call to mind, thus,

"*we have remembered.*"[1822]

Since, as we saw, *trees* (עץ *`ets*) are metaphors for our drive to know, thus, the *goper* tree is the tree of remembrance. *Goper* (283) is the wood or the tree of *memory* (283). The ark, made[1823] of this wood or reed, like Utnapishtim's house, is the memory receptacle. Divided into rooms or brain-lobes, each remembrance (זִכְּרוֹן *zikrown*) has its own cell-nest.[1824] However, in order for the ark to be able to navigate through the tempestuous water of the violent epistemic vortex it must be waterproof. Therefore, *bitumen* (*kopher* כֹּפֶר)[1825] must *cover over* (*kaphar* כָּפַר)[1826] it *within*[1827] and *without*.[1828] The word *kaphar* (כָּפַר), *to cover over*, means also *to atone for sin*, thus, this *asphalting* has also the sense of *making compensation for the missed mark* (*kaphar* כפר).

Memories are the structural *wooden*-beams of our mind, contained in our brain, namely, the metaphorical reed-($g_i p_a r_u$)-house or the wooden-($g_o p_e r$)-ark, which crosses through the fluidity of time. Nevertheless, as memories articulate and make possible our waking and dreaming conscious time, they are stored in the unconscious states of dreamless sleep or catalepsy. The Hebrew word *kopher* (כפר) means *pitch* and it is used also in the sense of the expiatory *price of life*, *ransom*, *bribe*, which *overlays* and *covers* (כפר *kaphar*)[1829] the *goper*-memories. Thus, the price of life is paying-up, renouncing the attachment to all memories. This is why Ea exhorts Utnapishtim to

"*Abandon possessions and look for life, despite worldly goods and save your soul alive.*"[1830]

Similar to the injunction,

"*sell all that you possess... and ... provide yourselves ... a treasure in the heavens.*"[1831]

There are three stages in life. As in verse 6:3, they are the metaphoric 120 *years of life*. We must understand it as the two (*i.e.* #20=) wakeful (#10+) and REM/dreaming (#10) stages of consciousnesses disappearing into the all-encompassing one (*i.e.* #100) deep-NREM/sleep, which covers-up all memories with its *pitch-dark* dreamlessness. Likewise, the Greek[1832] and Roman[1833] mythology describe a river, the Lethe (Λήθη, *Lḗthē*) near Hypnos (Ὕπνος), sleep, in Hadēs (ᾍδης), the underworld, as the watercourse of oblivion and forgetfulness. There the souls of the dead wash out and forget their previous life and sins. Also Dante describes that river where he forgot the

"present things /[, which] with their false pleasure turned my steps."[1834]

The metaphoric waterproofing *asphalt* of the Ark prevents from drowning in the flood of time. Furthermore, the Gematria number 283 of the word *goper* is also equivalent to the words related to Cherubim, *vahakarubiym.*[1835] In verse 3:24, it was a cherub, who stood

"*at the eastern gate of the Paradise of Happiness a Cherubim with a flaming sword turning all around, to guard the road of the tree of life.*"

This means that the circular-flaming-epistemic-circularity of the *goper*-wood-memory is also the one that prevents us from accessing the Tree of Life. It is possible to free sail to that dimension only when the *price of life* (כֹּפֶר *kopher*) *covers up* (כָּפַר *kaphar*) the attachment to those memories in the stillness of the night.

"*In the firmament above the head of the cherubims... in between the whirlwinds of consciousness* (גַּלְגַּל *galgal*),[1836] *even under the cherub... The cherubims stood on the right side of the house, when the man went in... Then the glory of the LORD went up from the cherub, and stood over the threshold of the house; and the house was filled with the cloud, and the court was full of the brightness of the LORD'S glory.*"[1837]

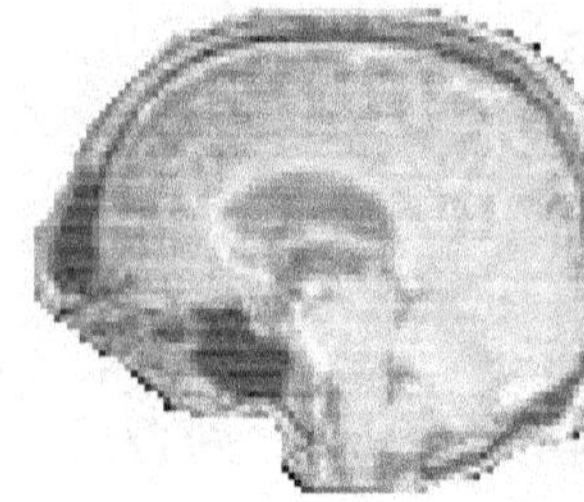

GRAPHIC: *The Ark*[1838]

The command of Divine Consciousness to Noah is clear,

"***Produce*** *an ark of memory-wood* (עֲשֵׂה לְךָ תֵּבַת עֲצֵי־גֹפֶר)."

There is a very meaningful corollary to deduce from this order. In fact, *'asah*[1839] means *to produce*, to fashion, to make, to do, to be effective and to organize. Based on what we said, the outcome of this production is the Ark, namely, this human (*viz.* Adam) physio-psychosomatic individual itself of whom Noah represents the internal metaphoric and paradigmatic structure. Just consider hair growing. No one, outside the body, produces them. An internal living regulation lets the body grow from cell to fetus to full being and that internal regulator <u>is this individual</u>, the reader of these lines, who makes it possible. S/he is Noah, the central builder who shapes this body-ark and maintains all its cells together.

Someone may argue that

'The parents' desire to copulate is the mover of their will. It is a natural <u>external</u> determination to fertilize, which produced the original gamete.'

We answer,

'True, but the will of the parents has hardly any saying when the forces of nature, whatever they may be, drive the couple to mate. However, those forces are still their very intimate nature searching for themselves in a never-ending circular process. The

force of desire, at play here, is the same new individual potentially-to-be-born. What we are saying is that, before conception, we were the not yet individualize driving natural force, as the Freudian "id,"[1840] *which effectively* *<u>forced</u>* *our parents to mate.*

In any case, the making of the Ark is the internal will, which produces it from within and in which this being here and now writes and reads. Those who believe in creation must realize that the Creator must be always our most intimate reality. Those who do not believe in creation must admit that the natural forces, keeping us here in one piece, are our true innermost essence. In either case, existence is within us. Furthermore, if one postulates an external reality influencing us, then s/he becomes a dogmatic believer in an unrelated metaphysical world.'

Thus, *the production*, in this case, is making, from within, an *apparently external* reality. It is Utnapishtim's own reed-body-house torn down and transformed into a boat.

6:15-Ark's Measurements

וְזֶה אֲשֶׁר תַּעֲשֶׂה אֹתָהּ שְׁלֹשׁ מֵאוֹת אַמָּה אֹרֶךְ הַתֵּבָה חֲמִשִּׁים אַמָּה רָחְבָּהּ וּשְׁלֹשִׁים אַמָּה קוֹמָתָהּ׃ *vazeh* (this) *'ăšer* (which) *ta'ăśeh* (fashion) *'ōṯāh* (that) *šalōš* (three) *mē'vōṯ* (hundred) *'amāh* (foundation) *'ōreḵa* (length) *hatēḇāh* (ark) *ḥămišiym* (fifty) *'amāh* (foundation) *rāḥabāh* (width) *ušalōšiym* (third part)*'amāh* (foundation) *qvōmāṯāh* (hight)
καὶ *kai* (and) **οὕτως** *outōs* (in this way) **ποιήσεις** *poiēseis* (make) **τὴν** *tēn* (the) **κιβωτόν** *kibōton* (ark) **τριακοσίων** *triakosiōn* (three hundred) **πήχεων** *pēcheōn* (cubits) **τὸ** *to* (the) **μῆκος** *mēkos* (length) **τῆς** *tēs* (the) **κιβωτοῦ** *kibōtou* (ark) **καὶ** *kai* (and) **πεντήκοντα** *pentēkonta* (fifty) **πήχεων** *mēcheōn* (cubits) **τὸ** *to* (the) **πλάτος** *platos* (width) **καὶ** *kai* (and) **τριάκοντα** *triakonta* (thirty) **πήχεων** *pēcheōn* (cubits) **τὸ** *to* (the) **ὕψος** *upsos* (height) **αὐτῆς** *autēs* (of it)
et (and) ***sic*** (thus) ***facies*** (make) ***eam*** (it) ***trecentorum*** (three hundred) ***cubitorum*** (cubit) ***erit*** (will be) ***longitudo*** (the length) ***arcae*** (of the ark) ***quinquaginta*** (fifty) ***cubitorum*** (cubit) ***latitudo*** (the width) ***et*** (and) ***triginta*** (thirty) ***cubitorum*** (cubits) ***altitudo*** (the height) ***illius*** (of it)
And this is the fashion which thou shalt make it of: The length of the ark shall be three hundred cubits, the breadth of it fifty cubits, and the height of it thirty cubits.
This is the way you should fashion it. The ark should be founded extending like the Breath of Divine-Consciousness, should be founded spreading on everything and should rise to the height of three levels.

Also in *The Epic of Gilgamesh* Ea gives Utnapishtim

"*the measurements of the barque as you shall built her.*"[1841]

The measurements for Noah's ark are, 300 (שָׁלוֹשׁ *shalowsh* מֵאָה *me'ah*) cubits (אַמָּה *'ammah*) in length (אֹרֶךְ *'orek*), 50 (חֲמִשִּׁים *chamishshiym*) in width (רֹחַב *rochab*) and 30 (שְׁלֹשִׁים *shĕlowshiym*) in height (קוֹמָה *qowmah*). To be able to contain <u>all</u> animals, obviously, the Ark must be a metaphor of some kind.

'*Ammah,*[1842] the cubit measurement, means also *foundation* and *grounding.*[1843] It is the *beginning*, the forepart of the arm (*i.e. cubit*), *viz.* the *mother*. In fact, *ammah* derives from the word *'em*[1844] meaning mother or parent. Therefore, the Ark is the foundation on which the three (שָׁלוֹשׁ *shalowsh*) stages of life stretch in a circle (מֵאָה *me'ah* = ק, *q* = 100). Thus, three hundred is the length of the barge and #300 (= ש) is the Gematria number indicating the *Breath of Divine-Consciousness.*[1845]

"*The breath circularity of Divine-Consciousness hovered on the surface of those flowing waters.*"[1846]

Therefore, the Ark of Memories *extends* (אָרַךְ *'arak*)[1847] in time and space[1848] on the ocean of possibility matching the hovering of the Breath of Pure Consciousness. Consequently, with its width (רֹחַב *rochab*) of 50 (חֲמִשִּׁים *chamishshiym*) grounding cubits (אַמָּה *'ammah*), the Ark expands on everything. In fact, כל *kol* [1849] is the Gematria number 50, meaning *everything*. Furthermore, in accordance with its three levels, the three states of wakeful, dreaming (REM) and dreamless-sleep (NREM), symbolized by #30,[1850] find their cubits-foundation on the Ark. In fact, it rises (קום *quwm*)[1851] 30 cubits in height (קוֹמָה *qowmah*), also synonym of *kagōḇah*,[1852] meaning *through the height*, equivalent to Gematria #30. Compare those three levels with the barge of Utnapishtim, of which

"*two thirds was submerged.*"[1853]

For the similarity with the accounts of Noah and his Ark, we chose to report, in this and future chapters, some excerpts from the *Book of Jonah.*[1854] These inserts will shed some meaningful light to understand the connotations of the Universal Deluge. In fact, the three circular levels of consciousness are equivalent to the days and nights that Jonah (יוֹנָה), *whose name* means dove, lived in a fish. The great[1855] fish, *dag* (דָּג),[1856] is the one that covers[1857] Jonah. It swallows[1858] him in its *belly* (מֵעָה *me'ah*),[1859] which is a metaphor for this mind here and now, the place where *emotions, distress or love* (מעה *me'ah*)[1860] figuratively *multiply and increase, viz. dagah* (דָּגָה).[1861] [1862]⇨

"*The Transcendent had prepared a great fish to swallow up Jonah. And Jonah was in the belly of the fish three days and three nights.*"[1863]

"*For as Jonah was three days and three nights in the whale's belly; so shall the Son of man be three days and three nights in the heart of the earth.*"[1864]

Both, the fish and hell metaphorically represent this present state of existence, which, like Cerberus, the dog from hell with three heads of consciousness,[1865] metaphorically articulates through waking, dreaming and dreamless-sleeping. Similarly, according to *The Apostles' Creed*, Jesus stayed in hell three days.[1866] In fact, the Gospel states that he

"*raised again the third day.*"[1867]

My affectionate reader may say,

'You always bring up the three levels of waking, dreaming and sleeping with no dreams. However, this is arbitrary because ancient writers had not reached the sophisticated scientific level of current oneiric study that would have had them identify the REM and NREM stages of sleep, which has no parallel in the psychology of ancient writers.'

We reply,

'This is not so. Many millennia before the current era, the Indian Ṛg Veda had described those stages. They were described with three letter-sounds, AUM· (ॐ Om). Furthermore, the Māṇḍūkya Upanishad gives a very detailed account of those stages.'[1868]

6:16-The Ark's Openings

צֹהַר תַּעֲשֶׂה לַתֵּבָה וְאֶל־אַמָּה תְּכַלֶּנָּה מִלְמַעְלָה וּפֶתַח הַתֵּבָה בְּצִדָּהּ תָּשִׂים תַּחְתִּיִּם שְׁנִיִּם וּשְׁלִשִׁים תַּעֲשֶׂהָ׃   *ṣōhar* (the light) *ta'ăśeh* (make) *latēḇāh* (ark) *va'el* (this) *'amāh* (foundation) *takalenāh* (accomplished) *milama'alāh* (from) *upēṯaḥ* (opening) *hatēḇāh* (ark) *baṣidāh* (side) *tāśiym* (lower) *taḥatiyim* (lower) *šaniyim* (second) *ušališiym* (third) *ta'ăśeāh* (make)
ἐπισυνάγων *episunagōn* (narrow) **ποιήσεις** *poiēseis* (make) **τὴν** *tēn* (the) **κιβωτὸν** *kibōton* (ark)[1869] **καὶ** *kai* (and) **εἰς** *eis* (into) **πῆχυν** *pēchun* (a cubit) **συντελέσεις** *sunteleseis* (complete) **αὐτὴν** *autēn* (it) **ἄνωθεν** *anōthen* (above) **τὴν** *tēn* (the) **δὲ** *de* (but) **θύραν** *thuran* (door) **τῆς** *tēs* (the) **κιβωτοῦ** *kibōtou* (ark) **ποιήσεις** *poiēseis* (make) **ἐκ** *ek* (of) **πλαγίων** *plagiōn* (lateral) **κατάγαια** *katagaia* (lower) **διώροφα** *diōropha* (second) **καὶ** *kai* (and) **τριώροφα** *triōropha* (three stories) **ποιήσεις** *poiēseis* (make) **αὐτήν** *autēn* (it)
fenestram (window) ***in*** (in) ***arca*** (the ark) ***facies*** (make) ***et*** (and) ***in*** (in) ***cubito*** (a cubit) ***consummabis*** (complete) ***summitatem*** (above) ***ostium*** (door) ***autem*** (also) ***arcae*** (of the ark)

pones (place) ***ex*** (at) ***latere*** (the side) ***deorsum*** (downwards) ***cenacula*** (second floor) ***et*** (and) ***tristega*** (third) ***facies*** (make) ***in*** (in) ***ea*** (it)	
A window shalt thou make to the ark, and in a cubit shalt thou finish it above; and the door of the ark shalt thou set in the side thereof; with lower, second, and third stories shalt thou make it.	
Place in the ark the window-light of consciousness, the first accomplished foundation, on the top. On the other side, set the opening of the senses of the Ark. Make the Ark with a lower, a second and a third level.	

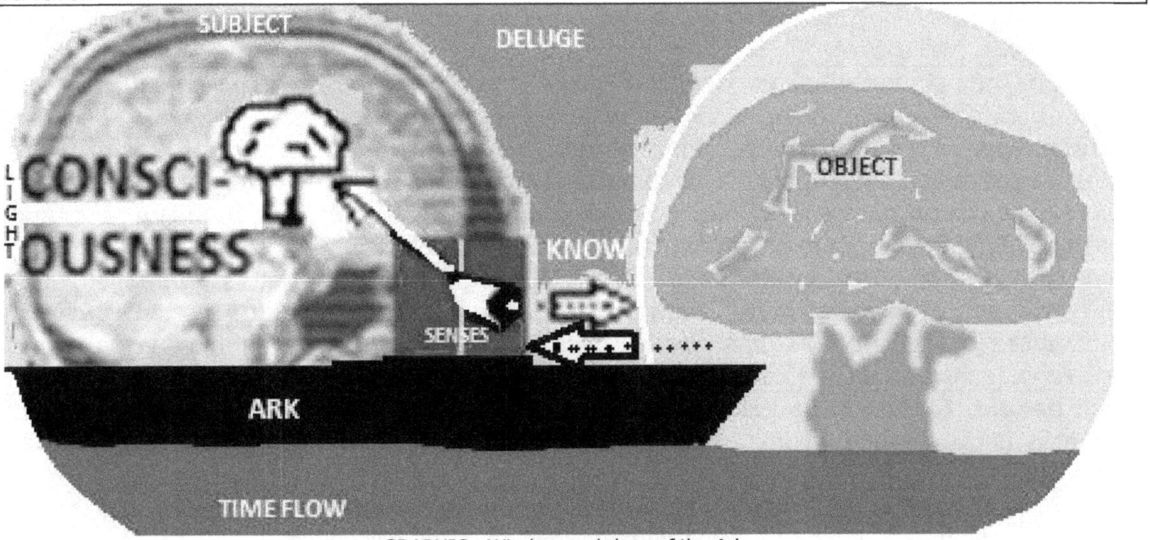

GRAPHIC: *Window and door of the Ark*

The Ark represents the human mind in its entire psychophysical configuration. Noah follows the allegorical instructions, namely the setting of the pure epistemic faculties, *viz.* of the Divine-Consciousness. Noah, then, as a safeguarding, protecting and preserving faculty, sets up (שׂוּם *suwm*) the epistemic organs of the chest of remembrance. He establishes (אַמָּה *'ammah*) and accomplishes[1870] the window-light (צֹהַר *tsohar*) [1871] of consciousness above[1872] the door, the opening[1873] of the senses. As the founding first day of creation, that light measures one cubit. It shines and flows like pressed oil (צָהַר *tsahar*).[1874] Opposite[1875] to it, the door[1876] of the senses opens up)[1877] to the world of experience with its eyes,[1878] ears,[1879] mouth,[1880] hands[1881] and nose.[1882] This is the door of experience, which allows objects to travel in and out and to reach the window of consciousness itself.

The Ark-mind articulates on three levels. They are like Jonah's three days in the belly of the fish or the one horse ridden by two equestrians on the great seal of the Knights Templars.[1883] They all represent the three aspects of life,

1  2 

GRAPHIC: 1 - *Pyramidion capstone*, 2 - *Templar's Seal.*

1) the lower (תַּחְתִּי *tachtiy*) one is the first circular day of <u>Ego-consciousness</u> in the <u>waking state</u> (on the Templar's Seal, represented as the front equestrian),
2) the second (שֵׁנִי *sheniy*) tier is the circular day of <u>I-consciousness</u> in the <u>dream (REM)</u> stage (on the Templar's Seal, represented as the second equestrian), and

3) the third (שְׁלִישִׁי shĕliyshiy) day is the top state the <u>Auto-transparency</u> of the <u>dreamless sleep (NREM)</u> (on the Templar's Seal, represented as the horse). This, like a pyramid's *pyramidion,*[1884] is the tip of the Ark itself.

6:17-Forecasting the Deluge

וַאֲנִי הִנְנִי מֵבִיא אֶת־הַמַּבּוּל מַיִם עַל־הָאָרֶץ לְשַׁחֵת כָּל־בָּשָׂר אֲשֶׁר־בּוֹ רוּחַ חַיִּים מִתַּחַת הַשָּׁמָיִם כֹּל אֲשֶׁר־בָּאָרֶץ יִגְוָע׃
va'ăniy (I) *hinaniy* (behold) *mēḇiy'* (I bring) *'eṯ* (and) *hamabul* (flood) *mayim* (of water) *'al* (on) *hā'āreṣ* (earth) *lašaḥēṯ* (to destroy) *kāl* (all) *bāśār* (sentient being) *'ăšer* (in which) *bvō* (in) *ruaḥ* (breath) *ḥayiym* (living) *mitaḥaṯ* (from) *hašāmāyim* (under the sky) *kōl* (all) *'ăšer* (which) *bā'āreṣ* (land) *yiḡavā* (will expire)
ἐγὼ *egō* (I) **δὲ** *de* (but) **ἰδοὺ** *idou* (behold) **ἐπάγω** *epagō* (will bring) **τὸν** *ton* (the) **κατακλυσμὸν** *kataklusmov* (cataclysm) **ὕδωρ** *udōr* (of water) **ἐπὶ** *epi* (on) **τὴν** *tēn* (the) **γῆν** *gēn* (earth) **καταφθεῖραι** *kataphtheirai* (will destroy) **πᾶσαν** *pasan* (all) **σάρκα** *sarka* (flesh) **ἐν** *en* (on) **ᾗ** *ē* (thus) **ἐστιν** *estin* (is) **πνεῦμα** *pneuma* (breath) **ζωῆς** *zōēs* (of life) **ὑποκάτω** *upokatō* (under) **τοῦ** *tou* (the) **οὐρανοῦ** *ouranou* (sky) **καὶ** *kai* (and) **ὅσα** *osa* (whatsoever) **ἐὰν** *ean* (if) **ᾖ** *ē* (is) **ἐπὶ** *epi* (on) **τῆς** *tēs* (the) **γῆς** *gēs* (earth) **τελευτήσει** *teleutēsei* (shall die)
ecce (behold) ***ego*** (I) ***adducam*** (bring) ***diluvii*** (a deluge) ***aquas*** (of waters) ***super*** (on) ***terram*** (the earth) ***ut*** (to) ***interficiam*** (kill) ***omnem*** (all) ***carnem*** (flesh) ***in*** (in) ***qua*** (which) ***spiritus*** (the spirit) ***vitae*** (of life) ***est*** (is) ***subter*** (under) ***caelum*** (the sky) ***universa*** (all things) ***quae*** (that) ***in*** (on) ***terra*** (earth) ***sunt*** (are) ***consumentur*** (shall be consumed)
And, behold, I, even I, do bring a flood of waters upon the earth, to destroy all flesh, wherein is the breath of life, from under heaven; and every thing that is in the earth shall die.
Behold I bring the flowing deluge of time-waters on the earth to kill all sentient beings under the sky in whom is the breath of life and everything, which is on earth, will perish.

Physical laws follow an intrinsic cause and effect regulated mathematical order.[1885] Cataclysms are natural developments ensuring a new restructured harmony. The extinction of dinosaurs came about as a natural process of evolution not as a punishment. Punishments are social law provisions to ensure public order according to the current ruling ideology of the time. The usual reading of this verse is that the flood comes as a punishment sent by and from heaven for man's wickedness. Since all (כֹּל *kol*) sentient beings (בָּשָׂר *basar*) had to undergo the same capital sentence, what was the sin of the innocent animals? Furthermore, the concept of punishment has a certain wrathful and vengeful paternalistic flavor of unresolved psychological issues, which are very different from the impersonal consequences of natural events.

In this verse, '*I*' (אֲנִי *'aniy*)[1886] is the logical subjectivity. It is the transcendental I-think-conscious-*of*-itself. While the Transcendent is the Ineffable Apodictic-Certitude, the original foundation of the World. Here, the '*I*' is the transcendental I-think, the necessary and inevitable foundation of all knowledge.[1887] It is the *a-priori* mode of cognition, the conscious subject logically preceding the known object. The infinite *watery*-possibility of objects[1888] flows[1889] like a flood.[1890] Our identification with the objective world submerges us as in a deluge. All sentient beings, the *builders* on this earth (אֶרֶץ *'erets*) of duality under (תַּחַת *tachath*) the Transcendent Heaven (שָׁמַיִם *shamayim*), *rejected the stone* of Fundamental Awareness, namely *the head of the corner,*[1891] and die, as we currently do. The whole world lays waste disappearing in the entropic state of its beginning. Therefore, the great-misunderstood mystery is, <u>**the deluge**, which involves the entire universe, it **is here now** and in it all *fallen-giants* perish</u>. Real estate mogul and US President elected Donald Trump defined life as

"*that which we do, while waiting for death.*"[1892]

The affirmation should have clarified also that *what we do is to drown in this flood.* This is the flow of time as continuous past, which submerges us all, right here and right now. In it, we have already found our death. In other words, the epistemic subject-object circularity brings[1893] here, by its own epistemic nature, this continuous time circularity that ends only in an exhausted grave. This is always the consequence deriving from eating the forbidden fruit, namely, the desire to know objectively and conceptualize the Transcendent.

The waters of this universal flood are the same universal immanent waters separated from the Transcendent Waters that we saw in verse 1:6. In fact, the deluge takes places on the second day of creation as well as every time and moment of dream and/or of wakefulness in which we reject the Creative Awareness and submerge in the watery grave. Finally, this is the grave of Cain, the paradigm of all humans. They all die in the delusion of their own passionate-possessions.

6:18-Enter the Ark

וַהֲקִמֹתִי אֶת־בְּרִיתִי אִתָּךְ וּבָאתָ אֶל־הַתֵּבָה אַתָּה וּבָנֶיךָ וְאִשְׁתְּךָ וּנְשֵׁי־בָנֶיךָ אִתָּךְ׃
vahăqimōṯiy (I will establish) *'eṯ* (and) *bariyṯiy* (covenant) *'itāḵa* (with) *ubā'ṯā* (enter) *'el* (into) *hatēḇāh* (the ark) *'atāh* (you) *ubāneyḵā* (sons) *va'išaṯaḵā* (thy wife) *unašēy* (wives) *bāneyḵā* (sons) *'itāḵa* (with)
καὶ *kai* (and) **στήσω** *stēsō* (I will establish) **τὴν** *tēn* (the) **διαθήκην** *diathēkēn* (covenant) **μου** *mou* (my) **πρὸς** *pros* (for) **σέ** *se* (you) **εἰσελεύσῃ** *eiseleusē* (enter) **δὲ** *de* (and) **εἰς** *eis* (in) **τὴν** *tēn* (the) **κιβωτόν** *kibōton* (ark) **σὺ** *su* (you) **καὶ** *kai* (and) **οἱ** *oi* (the) **υἱοί** *uioi* (sons) **σου** *sou* (yours) **καὶ** *kai* (and) **ἡ** *ē* (the) **γυνή** *gunē* (wife) **σου** *sou* (your) **καὶ** *kai* (and) **αἱ** *ai* (the) **γυναῖκες** *gunaikes* (wives) **τῶν** *tōn* (of the) **υἱῶν** *uiōn* (sons) **σου** *sou* (your) **μετὰ** *meta* (with) **σοῦ** *sou* (you)
ponam (I will establish)-*que* (and) *foedus* (pact) *meum* (my) *tecum* (with you) *et* (and) *ingredieris* (enter) *arcam* (the ark) *tu* (you) *et* (and) *filii* (sons) *tui* (yours) *uxor* (wife) *tua* (your) *et* (and) *uxores* (wives) *filiorum* (of sons) *tuorum* (your) *tecum* (with you)
But with thee will I establish my covenant; and thou shalt come into the ark, thou, and thy sons, and thy wife, and thy sons' wives with thee.
I will establish my pact with you and enter the ark, you, your sons, your wife, and the wives of your sons with you.

If we read this verse literally, the question would be, why build an Ark, when God could have saved Noah and the others by lifting them above the flooded earth? Paradoxically, however, entering (בּוֹא *bow*)[1894] into the Ark is going above the earth of duality. Let us ponder that the flooded land is that of wakefulness and dream, subject and object, good and evil. This duality does not exist on the third level of dreamless sleep. Remember also that, with Noah, we are still in the realm of sleep. Therefore, Noah is the *rested* paradigm entering, *conscious*, into the stillness of the dreamless realm. This is the state, which potentially can reactivate back into the dream followed by the waking world. In the NREM state, though, Noah, the subject-husband with the object-wife (אִשָּׁה *'ishshah*) and with the conceptual-offspring (בֵּן *ben*) with their noematic-wives, are all unified in the auto-transparency of the resting stillness of desireless-thought.

Jesus says,

"Come unto my *unity*, all ye that labour and are heavy laden, and I will give you *rest*"[1895]
in my yoke-unity[1896] with Apodictic-Conscious-Awareness.

The NREM state is the closest to Pure Awareness. It is the resting stillness of Pure Transparency. Therefore, rising up[1897] into that state means to enter into an alliance, to establish (קוּם *quwm*) a covenant[1898] with the Breath (רוּחַ *rwaḥ*) of the Divine Certitude, which hovers over everything.

6:19-All Animals in Pair

וּמִכָּל־הָחַי מִכָּל־בָּשָׂר שְׁנַיִם מִכֹּל תָּבִיא אֶל־הַתֵּבָה לְהַחֲיֹת אִתָּךְ זָכָר וּנְקֵבָה יִהְיוּ׃
umikāl (of all that) *hāḥay* (live) *mikāl* (of all) *bāśār* (flesh) *šanayim* (two) *mikōl* (of all) *tāḇiy'* (bring) *'el* (into) *hatēḇāh* (the ark) *lahaḥăyōṯ* (remain alive) *'itāḵa* (with) *zāḵār* (male) *unaqēḇāh* (female) *yihayu* (are)
καὶ *kai* (and) **ἀπὸ** *apo* (of) **πάντων** *pantōn* (all) **τῶν** *tōn* (the) **κτηνῶν** *ktēnōn* (cattle) **καὶ** *kai* (and) **ἀπὸ** *apo* (of) **πάντων** *pantōn* (all) **τῶν** *tōn* (the) **ἑρπετῶν** *erpetōn* (reptiles) **καὶ** *kai* (and) **ἀπὸ** *apo* (of) **πάντων** *pantōn* (all) **τῶν** *tōn* (the) **θηρίων** *thēriōn* (wild beast) **καὶ** *kai* (and) **ἀπὸ** *apo* (of) **πάσης** *pasēs* (all) **σαρκός** *sarkos* (flesh) **δύο** *duo* (two) **δύο** *duo* (two) **ἀπὸ** *apo* (of) **πάντων** *pantōn*

pantōn (all) **εἰσάξεις** *eisaxeis* (enter) **εἰς** *eis* (in) **τὴν** *tēn* (the) **κιβωτόν** *kibōton* (ark) **ἵνα** *ina* (that) **τρέφῃς** *trephēs* (nourish) **μετὰ** *meta* (with) **σεαυτοῦ** *seautou* (you) **ἄρσεν** *arsen* (male) **καὶ** *kai* (and) **θῆλυ** *thēlu* (female) **ἔσονται** *esontai* (they are)
et (and) ***ex*** (of) ***cunctis*** (all) ***animantibus*** (the living things) ***universae*** (of all) ***carnis*** (flesh) ***bina*** (in pair) ***induces*** (introduce) ***in*** (in) ***arcam*** (the ark) ***ut*** (so that) ***vivant*** (they may live) ***tecum*** (with you) ***masculini*** (male) ***sexus*** (sex) ***et*** (and) ***feminini*** (female)
And of every living thing of all flesh, two of every sort shalt thou bring into the ark, to keep them alive with thee; they shall be male and female.
And bring into the ark of all living sentient being, all in pairs of two and keep them alive with you; male and female they shall be.

To insure the survival (חַיָּה *chayah*) of the species, both (שְׁנַיִם *shěnayim*) male (זָכָר *zakar*) and female (נְקֵבָה *něqebah*) of all living (חַי *chay*) sentient (בָּשָׂר *basar*) animals[1899] entered (בּוֹא *bow'*) the ark (תֵּבָה *tebah*). This does not explain or justify the reason for the elimination of all the others individuals left out. Furthermore, with a literal meaning, not all animals entered the ark. Marine life did not. Truthfully, it did not need shelter from the deluge. In fact, the flood may have been the best event ever to take place in the life of those sea creatures.

However, the Ark is a metaphor for the cranium. To enter it means to penetrate the most intimate recesses of the mind, the unconscious one, the dreamless sleep where all objects are alive (חַיָּה *chayah*) in their potential state. They are there. They are ready to enter into the action of dream and/or wakefulness. In it are all beings in their polar distinctions, including the aquatic ones. In fact, the ark itself is a symbol of a sea-going vessel, like Jonah's fish, capable of crossing from one riverbank of life to the other one.

6:20-The Seminal Reasons

מֵהָעוֹף לְמִינֵהוּ וּמִן־הַבְּהֵמָה לְמִינָהּ מִכֹּל רֶמֶשׂ הָאֲדָמָה לְמִינֵהוּ שְׁנַיִם מִכֹּל יָבֹאוּ אֵלֶיךָ לְהַחֲיוֹת׃ *mēhā ʿvōp̄* (from fowl) *lamiynēhu* (its kind) *umin* (from) *habahēmāh* (beasts) *lamiynāh* (kind) *mikōl* (from) *remeś* (creeping things) *hā ʾăḏāmāh* (on the land) *lamiynēhu* (kind) *šanayim* (two) *mikōl* (from) *yāḇō ʾu* (enter) *ʾēleyḵā* (of these) *lahaḥăyvōṯ* (keep alive)
ἀπὸ *apo* (from) **πάντων** *pantōn* (all) **τῶν** *tōn* (the) **ὀρνέων** *orneōn* (bird) **τῶν** *tōn* (the) **πετεινῶν** *peteinōn* (winged) **κατὰ** *kata* (according) **γένος** *genos* (species) **καὶ** *kai* (and) **ἀπὸ** *apo* (from) **πάντων** *pantōn* (all) **τῶν** *tōn* (the) **κτηνῶν** *ktēnōn* (cattle) **κατὰ** *kata* (according to) **γένος** *genos* (species) **καὶ** *kai* (and) **ἀπὸ** *apo* (from) **πάντων** *pantōn* (all) **τῶν** *tōn* (the) **ἑρπετῶν** *erpetōn* (reptiles) **τῶν** *tōn* (the) **ἑρπόντων** *erpontōn* (creeping) **ἐπὶ** *epi* (on) **τῆς** *tēs* (the) **γῆς** *gēs* (earth) **κατὰ** *kata* (according to) **γένος** *genos* (species) **αὐτῶν** *autōn* (their) **δύο** *duo* (two) **δύο** *duo* (two) **ἀπὸ** *apo* (from) **πάντων** *pantōn* (all) **εἰσελεύσονται** *eiseleusontai* (enter) **πρὸς** *pros* (near) **σὲ** *se* (you) **τρέφεσθαι** *trephesthai* (nourish) **μετὰ** *meta* (with) **σοῦ** *sou* (you) **ἄρσεν** *arsen* (male) **καὶ** *kai* (and) **θῆλυ** *thēlu* (female)
de (of the) ***volucribus*** (birds) ***iuxta*** (according to) ***genus*** (species) ***suum*** (their) ***et*** (and) ***de*** (of the) ***iumentis*** (cattle) ***in*** (in) ***genere*** (kind) ***suo*** (its) ***et*** (and) ***ex*** (out) ***omni*** (all) ***reptili*** (reptiles) ***terrae*** (of the earth) ***secundum*** (according to) ***genus*** (species) ***suum*** (its) ***bina*** (pair) ***de*** (of) ***omnibus*** (all) ***ingredientur*** (should enter) ***tecum*** (with you) ***ut*** (so) ***possint*** (they may) ***vivere*** (live)
Of fowls after their kind, and of cattle after their kind, of every creeping thing of the earth after his kind, two of every sort shall come unto thee, to keep them alive.
Of the birds according to their species and of the beasts according to their kind and of all reptiles of the earth according to their species, all of them, in pair, should enter with you so they may keep living.

We have seen Noah as the oneiric counterpart of Jabal, the waking stream (יָבָל *yabal*) of farmers and herders planting and shepherding. Similarly, Noah's function is to assure the continuation and the flourishing of all life forms on Earth.

Plotinus calls

"*Seminal reasons*"[1900]
the potential seeds that actualize the objects. They are the *psyche-sperm* of Plato,[1901] which remain in the creature,

"*Whosoever is born of God doth not commit sin; for his seed remaineth in him.*"[1902]

Furthermore, Ea, commands Utnapishtim,

"*take into the boat the seed of all living creatures.*"[1903]

The semen here is like an epistemic orgasmic shiver that generates the world into existence. As we saw, this same concept is in the Hebrew term "*to know*" (ידע *yada'*), *meaning both* acknowledging perception and carnal experience, as when

'*Adam knew Eve his wife; and she conceived, and bare Cain.*'[1904]

<Hence, knowledge refers to both, the synthesis of the object with the subject (*adaequatio rei et intellectus*)[1905] and the male-female union.

Historical memory persists as bits of information or seminal reasons in the reservoir of the unconscious mind.[1906] This is the Ark, the receptacle-of-consciousness,[1907] as a computer  external drive. Therefore, we may say, that consciousness does not dissolve completely. As fossilized bones, as DNA long-term storage of information, there is permanence-of-consciousness,[1908] which belongs to the en-graving of consciousness which is generally understood as unconsciousness. The unconscious mind is the grounding foundation of every sentient act ever performed by any sentient animal. That means that, just as the paleontologist discovers in ancient sediments the remains of dinosaurs, similarly, digging down deep within that receptacle, when the immediateness of individuality is silenced, one will find the other person's thoughts and feelings>[1909] as universal unconscious. Those bits of information, those seminal reasons are the flesh (בָּשָׂר *basar*), the sentient beings stored in our mind, namely, in Noah's Ark.

6:21-The Food in the Ark

וְאַתָּה קַח־לְךָ מִכָּל־מַאֲכָל אֲשֶׁר יֵאָכֵל וְאָסַפְתָּ אֵלֶיךָ וְהָיָה לְךָ וְלָהֶם לְאָכְלָה׃ *va'atāh* (bring) *qaḥ* (take) *lakā* (all) *mikāl* (from) *ma'ăkāl* (food) *'ăšer* (which) *yē'ākēl* (to eat) *a'āsapātā* (remove) *'ēleykā* (of it) *vahāyāh* (to be) *lakā* (all) *valāhem* (hot wealthy) *la'ākalāh* (food for beasts)
σὺ *su* (you) **δὲ** *de* (but) **λήμψῃ** *lēmpsē* (take) **σεαυτῷ** *seautō* (for you) **ἀπὸ** *apo* (fom) **πάντων** *pantōn* (all) **τῶν** *tōn* (the) **βρωμάτων** *brōmatōn* (food) **ἃ** *a* (thus) **ἔδεσθε** *edesthe* (to eat) **καὶ** *kai* (and) **συνάξεις** *sunaxeis* (bring) **πρὸς** *pros* (near) **σεαυτόν** *seauton* (you) **καὶ** *kai* (and) **ἔσται** *estai* (shall be) **σοὶ** *soi* (for you) **καὶ** *kai* (and) **ἐκείνοις** *ekeinois* (for them) **φαγεῖν** *phagein* (to eat)
tolles (take) ***igitur*** (therefore) ***tecum*** (with you) ***ex*** (from) ***omnibus*** (all) ***escis*** (food) ***quae*** (that) ***mandi*** (eaten) ***possunt*** (can be) ***et*** (and) ***conportabis*** (bring them) ***apud*** (near) ***te*** (you) ***et*** (and) ***erunt*** (shall be) ***tam*** (as much as) ***tibi*** (for you) ***quam*** (as) ***illis*** (for them) ***in*** (in) ***cibum*** (food)
And take thou unto thee of all food that is eaten, and thou shalt gather it to thee; and it shall be for food for thee, and for them.
Therefore, take with you all the food that can be eaten, it shall be all the food for you and for them; you shall gather-and-throw-away the wealthy food which the wild beasts devour."

In this context, what does food (מַאֲכָל *ma'akal*) symbolize? Furthermore, which food should be taken (לקח *laqach*) in the Ark *for eating* (אכל *'akal*)?

Like the cliché *food for thought*, food is an apt metaphor for the contents of knowledge. Just like food, information must enter the mind through the senses in order for us to known it. *Genesis*, in *Chapter 3, tells us which* fruits (פְּרִי *pěriy*) are comestible and which are not. The permissible fruits are those of unconditional ecstatic acts, which take us *awake* in the continuous pure potential consciousness, the state of dreamless sleep. The fruit of the Tree of Knowledge, instead, lead us to the identification with the stages of dream and wakefulness. There, as we become conscious-*of* the object, we miss Noah's restfulness and we die.

Therefore, the command of Divine-Consciousness is, *to take* (לקח *laqach*) in the Ark all the *food* (מַאֲכָל *ma'akal*) that can be eaten (אָכַל *'akal*), namely the pe*rmissible one.* That is, *the pure ideas, which remain in the unconscious stillness of the Ark's memory without any attachment to them.* In fact, Divine-Consciousness orders pure ascetic acts. Namely, He commands Noah to gather (אָסַף *'acaph*)[1910] all the edible food. However, at the same time, he should remove, withdraw and take away (אָסַף *'acaph*)[1911] *all the forbidden food, which should not be eaten.* That is, the *hot* (הם *ham*),[1912] *roaring* (הָמָה *hamah*)[1913] and *wealthy* (הָם *hem*)[1914] *food of judgment* (אָכְלָה *'oklah*), which *the wild beasts* (אָכְלָה *'oklah*)[1915] greedily, voraciously and desirously *devour* (אָכַל *'ukal*).[1916] This nourishment does not lead to eternity, in fact, Jesus distinguishes,

"*Whosoever drinketh of this* [physical] *water shall thirst again: But whosoever drinketh of the water that I shall give him shall never thirst; but the water that I shall give him shall be in him a well of water springing up into everlasting life.*"[1917]

6:22-Noah Follows the Orders

וַיַּעַשׂ נֹחַ כְּכֹל אֲשֶׁר צִוָּה אֹתוֹ אֱלֹהִים כֵּן עָשָׂה: ס *vaya'aś* (did) *nōaḥ* (Noah) *kak̲ōl* (all) *'ăšer* (which) *ṣiuāh* (commanded) *'ōt̲vō* (with) *'ĕlōhiym* (Gods) *kēn* (thus) *'āśāh* (done) *s* (.)
καὶ *kai* (and) **ἐποίησεν** *epoiēsen* (did) **Νωε** *Nōe* (Noah) **πάντα** *panta* (all) **ὅσα** *osa* (as) **ἐνετείλατο** *eneteilato* (commanded) **αὐτῷ** *autō* (him) **κύριος** *kurios* (Lord) **ὁ** *o* (the) **θεός** *theos* (God) **οὕτως** *outōs* (him) **ἐποίησεν** *epoiēsen* (did)
fecit (he did) ***ergo*** (thus) ***Noe*** (Noah) ***omnia*** (all) ***quae*** (that) ***praeceperat*** (commanded) ***illi*** (hium) ***Deus*** (God)
Thus did Noah; according to all that God commanded him, so did he.
Thus, Noah did all as Divine-Consciousness had commanded him to do.

Noah followed the command of the epistemic structure (צוה *tsavah*). Similarly, Utnapishtim said to Ea, "*What you have commanded I shall honour and perform.*"[1918]

The thoughts' clamor disturbs the stillness of the mind. Enter the stillness to avoid the drowning noise of the flooding desirous thoughts. With you are all the seeds apt to generate new life in the immanent.

HERE ENDS THE SIXTH CHAPTER OF NOAH'S ARK

CHAPTER 7

THE DELUGE

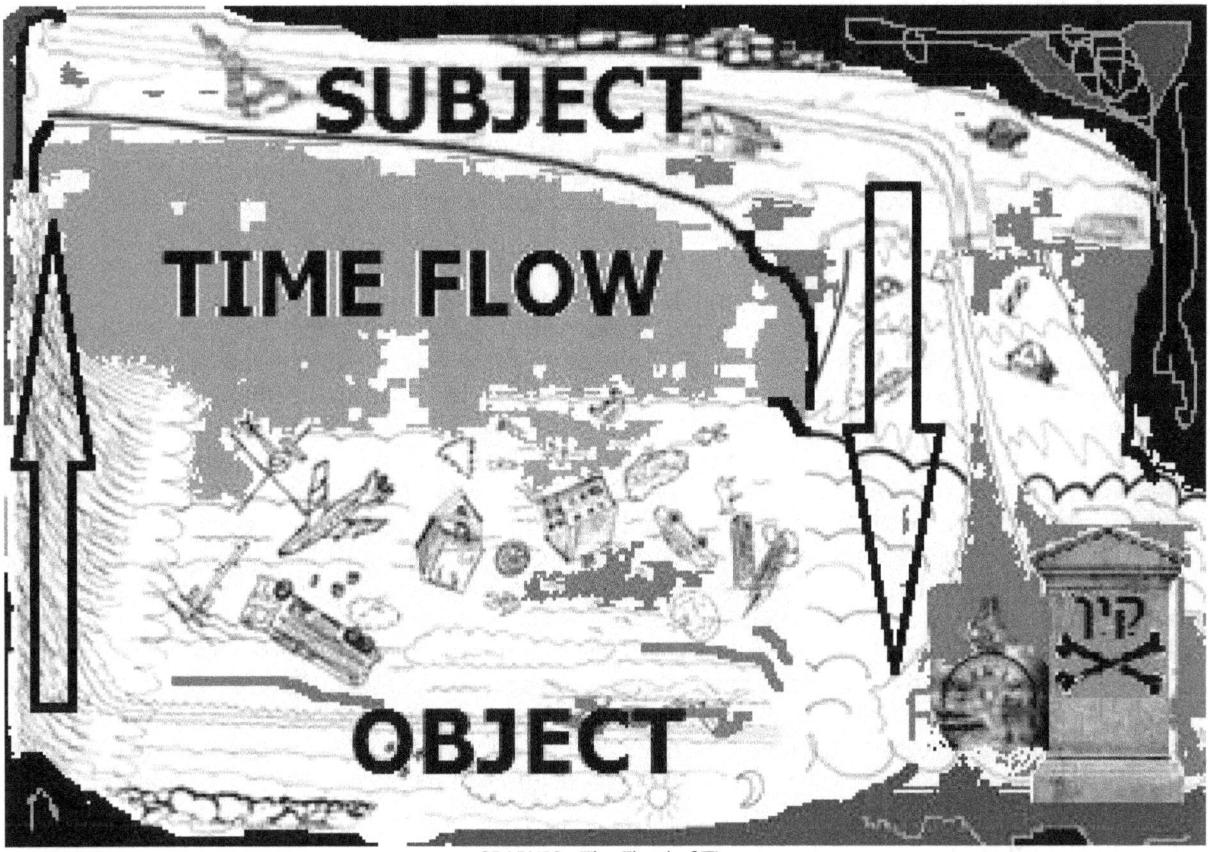

GRAPHIC: *The Flood of Time*

7-I SECTION: THE ARK'S INHABITANTS

7:1-Enter the Ark

וַיֹּאמֶר יְהוָה לְנֹחַ בֹּא־אַתָּה וְכָל־בֵּיתְךָ אֶל־הַתֵּבָה כִּי־אֹתְךָ רָאִיתִי צַדִּיק לְפָנַי בַּדּוֹר הַזֶּה׃   *vayō'mer* (said) *yahvāh* (the Transcendent) *lanōaḥ* (to Noah) *bō̄* (enter) *'atāh* (come) *vaḵāl* (all) *bēyṯaḵā* (house) *'el* (in the) hatēḇāh (ark) *kiy* (because) *'ōṯaḵā* (with) *rā'iyṯiy* (I have seen) *ṣadiyq* (righteous) *lap̄ānay* (before me) *badvōr* (habitation) *hazeh* (in this)
καὶ *kai* (and) **εἶπεν** *eipen* (said) **κύριος** *kurios* (the Lord) **ὁ** *o* (the) **θεὸς** *theos* (God) **πρὸς** *pros* (to) **Νωε** *Nōe* (Noah) **εἴσελθε** *eiselthe* (enter) **σὺ** *su* (you) **καὶ** *kai* (and) **πᾶς** *pas* (all) **ὁ** *o* (the) **οἶκός** *oikos* (house) **σου** *sou* (yours) **εἰς** *eis* (in) **τὴν** *tēn* (the) **κιβωτόν** *kibōton* (ark) **ὅτι** *oti* (because) **σὲ** *se* (you) **εἶδον** *eidon* (I have seen) **δίκαιον** *dikaion* (righteous) **ἐναντίον** *enantion* (before) **μου** *mou* (me) **ἐν** *en* (in) **τῇ** *tē* (the) **γενεᾷ** *genea* (generation) **ταύτῃ** *tautē* (this)
dixit- (said) ***que*** (and) ***Dominus*** (Lord) ***ad*** (to) ***eum*** (him) ***ingredere*** (enter) ***tu*** (you) ***et*** (and) ***omnis*** (all) ***domus*** (of house) ***tua*** (yours) ***arcam*** (the ark) ***te*** (you) ***enim*** (in fact) ***vidi*** (I saw) ***iustum*** (just) ***coram*** (before) ***me*** (me) ***in*** (in) ***generatione*** (generation) ***hac*** (this)
And the LORD said unto Noah, Come thou and all thy house into the ark; for thee have I seen righteous before me in this generation.
The Transcendent said to Noah,   "*Come; enter the Ark with all your epistemic structure; because I have seen your righteousness before me in this generational habitation.*

The *Spirit of Truth* (πνεῦμα τῆς ἀληθείας *pneuma tēs alētheias*), namely, the Transcendent Certitude of Awareness (יְהוָה *Yĕhovah*), is neither outside nor inside nor both. Nonetheless, without It the mind could not be. Nevertheless, It is not the mind. It is not the Ark, when in the Ark. It is not outside the Ark, when not in the Ark. It is nowhere because It is everywhere. It is completely All in every single individual while not ending in them. It is found in the mind, but it is not of the mind.

> "*Even the Spirit of Truth; whom the world cannot receive, because it seeth him not, neither knoweth him: but ye know him; for he dwelleth with you, and shall be in you…* [but] *is not of this world.*"[1919]

It dwells also in the deepest recesses of the heart's mind. In fact, It says to Noah, *come,*[1920] *enter,*[1921] which means, join Me in the Ark, where I also reside. In other words, it is impossible to ascribe awareness, as pure awareness, to any time and/or location. Also for non-creationists, Natural Laws (whatever they may be) are the one reality, which still necessitates the universal timeless presence of awareness to acknowledge Nature and its Laws.

For all creationists, this implies an obvious corollary. Those who believe in a literal objective creation must concede, by their own definition, that the creative act is timeless and cannot end, penalty the non-existence of all creature. In fact, if creation is subject to time then time, not god, becomes the ineluctable creator. If, on the other hand, God creates time, then, He is always Present in all past and future times. Therefore, the Creator becomes the ever-present vivifier in all creatures even when they are condemned to Hell (whatever that is). Actually, under these conditions, Hell becomes only our personal distance, our mental freezing persistence of desire, which is always still in the serene remembrance of the Spirit of Truth. Thus, the most intimate nature of all creatures must be God Himself. Therefore, He must be

> "*with you every day, even till the end of times.*"[1922]

This is true for any being, even if not righteous (צַדִּיק *tsaddiyq*), including Satan himself, together with the entire physical Universe and every single being in it. This further implies that any type of killing is a futile attempt to destroy the Awareness harbored in the murdered one.

In any case, Noah is the paradigm of the resting state in the stage of deep dreamless sleep. This state, between the previous two generational habitations (דּוֹר *dowr*), *viz.* wakefulness and dream, is the most righteous (צַדִּיק *tsaddiyq*), the closest one to the stillness of Pure Awareness. Therefore, he enters the ark with his entire house (בַּיִת *bayith*), namely, all his potential epistemic structure.

Abel and Noah are similar paradigm. The first one sets the tone for sacrifice, the total offering of the Dreamless Sleep, completely withdrawing the senses from the world of duality. The second one, Noah, is the same template, which, while resting in Dreamless Sleep, at the doorstep of the light of Awareness, is ready to return into the world of objective duality. Moreover, both their sacrifices, are accepted by God. Thus, they find favor before (פָּנִים *paniym*) the *eyes*[1923] of Transcendent Awareness.

7:2-Clean and Unclean Animals

מִכֹּל הַבְּהֵמָה הַטְּהוֹרָה תִּקַּח־לְךָ שִׁבְעָה שִׁבְעָה אִישׁ וְאִשְׁתּוֹ וּמִן־הַבְּהֵמָה אֲשֶׁר לֹא טְהֹרָה הִוא שְׁנַיִם אִישׁ וְאִשְׁתּוֹ׃   *mikōl* (from) *habahēmāh* (animals) *haṭahvōrāh* (bright) *tiqaḥ* (take) laḵā (all) *šiḇa'āh* (seven-swear) *šiḇa'āh* (seven-swear) *'iyš* (male) *va'išatvō* (female) *umin* (from) *habahēmāh* (animals) *'ăšer* (which) *lō̆* (no) *ṭahōrāh* (bright) *hiv'* (his) *šanayim* (two) *'iyš* (male) *va'išatvō* (female)
ἀπὸ *apo* (from) **δὲ** *de* (but) **τῶν** *tōn* (the) **κτηνῶν** *ktēnōn* (animals) **τῶν** *tōn* (the) **καθαρῶν** *katharōn* (pure) **εἰσάγαγε** *eisagage* () **πρὸς** *pros* (from) **σὲ** *se* (you) **ἑπτὰ** *epta* (seven) **ἑπτά** *epta* (seven) **ἄρσεν** *arsen* (male) **καὶ** *kai* (and) **θῆλυ** *thēlu* (female) **ἀπὸ** *apo* (from) **δὲ** *de* (but) **τῶν** *tōn* (the) **κτηνῶν** *ktēnōn* (animals) **τῶν** *tōn* (the) **μὴ** *mē* (not) **καθαρῶν** *katharōn* (pure) **δύο** *duo* (two) **δύο** *duo* (two) **ἄρσεν** *arsen* (male) **καὶ** *kai* (and) **θῆλυ** *thēlu* (female)
ex (out of) ***omnibus*** (all) ***animantibus*** (the animals) ***mundis*** (clean) ***tolle*** (take) ***septena*** (seven) ***septena*** (seven) ***masculum*** (male) ***et*** (and) ***feminam*** (female) ***de*** (of the) ***animantibus*** (animals) ***vero*** (however) ***non*** (not) ***mundis*** (clean) ***duo*** (two) ***duo*** (two) ***masculum*** (male) ***et*** (and) ***feminam*** (female)
Of every clean beast thou shalt take to thee by sevens, the male and his female: and of beasts that are not clean by two, the male and his female.
Out of all the bright sense-inclinations, take seven noetic/males and seven noematic/females. However, of the non-shining sense-inclinations take only two, a noetic/male and a noematic/female.

A distinction, between *literally* clean (טָהוֹר *tahowr*) and *literally* un-clean (לֹא *lō̆* טָהוֹר *tahowr*) beasts (חַי *chay*) and animals (בְּהֵמָה *běhemah*), clearly contradicts the story of creation in *Genesis* 1:25. In fact, a literal reading of impure animals would imply that the creator would have created uncleanliness, which denies the goodness (טוֹב *towb*) seen (ראה *ra'ah*) by God after having created them. Furthermore, from a literal perspective, to view some animals unclean would imply an inconsistency since, as created beings, their creator must necessarily be present in them to sustain them. Therefore, purity or impurity must be only metaphorical. Philo of Alexandria argued that in the *Bible*, animals (בהמה *běhemah*) were allegories of human inclinations. Some of them, perceived as not-clean (לֹא טְהֹרָה *lō̆-ṭahōrāh*) for their natural habits (*e.g.* pigs[1924]), become symbols of sins and passions.[1925]

However, which animal is not clean and why? Then again, what does *tahowr*, clean,[1926] mean? The word derives from the verb *taher*[1927] to shine, to be bright[1928]. We must understand that animal or living creatures (נֶפֶשׁ *nephesh*), represent active and living (חַי *chay*) sense-appetites for experience. Consequently, the clean, shining and bright sentient-animal-experiences are those of pure happiness, of pure aesthetic rapture, of pure love without lust, of pure intuitive mathematical ideas in their stillness and so on. These are the clean sentient animals. Consecrated twice by seven times, thus they metaphorically keep their identification within Pure Consciousness leading into Awareness. The unclean animals, on the contrary, are those symbolizing consciousness-*of* the object, seen as potential attachment and possession. Thus, potentially able to neglect the Pure Awareness from which consciousness derives.

Furthermore, to understand the distinction in this verse between male and female, we need to clarify again the difference between the terms *noesis*, with its adjective *noetic*, and *noema*, with its adjective *noematic*. Noesis means the subjective aspect of experience as the act-of-perception aiming to grasp the object. Noema means the objective aspect of experience in its modes-of-being-given as the perceived offering itself to the subject. The couple of the shining (טָהוֹר *tahowr*) animals must be multiplied by seven.[1929] This assertion seems to contradict the divine command to bring only one pair for each animal in the Ark. However, let us analyze the meaning and metaphor of number seven. This word *sheba`* (שֶׁבַע), seven, derives from the verb *shaba,*[1930] to swear, to vow. In fact, when

> "*Abraham... and... Abimelech... made a covenant... Abraham set <u>seven</u> ewe lambs of the flock by themselves. And Abimelech said unto Abraham,*
> *- What is the meaning of these <u>seven</u> ewe lambs, which thou hast set by themselves?-*
> *And he said,*
> *- For these <u>seven</u> ewe lambs shalt thou take of my hand, that they may be a witness unto me, that I have digged this well.*"[1931]

Seventh is the concluding day of creation. It is the resting day of Awareness. Therefore, as seven is the *number-witness* of the completed circular days of creation, similarly seven is the witness and guarantor of a vow and of a covenant. This agreement is the sense-stillness in the divine rapture of the burning silence of Transcendent Awareness. Thus, all the senses with their inherent noematic/noetic polarities merge in the Ark, the same way, as all experiences are present in the Eye of Awareness. The difference is that, while the non-shining (לֹא טְהֹרָה *ṭahōrāh lō*), unclean possessive-thought-experiences are still present as events experienced with burdening desire, the pure shining (טהור *tahowr*) senses of rapture are in a motionless, desireless and rested (Noah) wakefulness. Thus, the Psalm says,

> "*Awake up, my glory; awake, psaltery and harp: I myself will awake early... Be thou exalted, O Divine-Consciousness* (אֱלֹהִים *'elohiym*)*, above the heavens:* let *thy glory be above all the earth.*"[1932]

Furthermore, the unclean animals should be only two (שְׁנַיִם shĕnayim).[1933] Numerically, the letter ב (*b̲ b*) is #2 and indicates to inhabit the house.[1934] Moreover, *shĕnayim*, two, derives from *sheniy* (שָׁנָה),[1935] meaning, *to repeat*. Therefore, the two unclean animals are the noetic/noematic aspects of emotionally involved experiences, which *repeatedly* chase each other while inhabiting their circular house of consciousness-*of* the world. For a further comparative example, all the animals brought in the ark are as software programs and settings installed in a computer. Similarly, Joseph Campbell states that a computer chip is like

> "a whole hierarchy of angels, all on slats, and those little tubes, those are miracles, those are miracles, they are."[1936]

7:3-Birds of the Sky

גַּם מֵעוֹף הַשָּׁמַיִם שִׁבְעָה שִׁבְעָה זָכָר וּנְקֵבָה לְחַיּוֹת זֶרַע עַל־פְּנֵי כָל־הָאָרֶץ׃ *gam* (also) *mē 'vōp̄* (from birds) *hašāmayim* (of the sky) *šib̲a 'āh* (seven) *šib̲a 'āh* (seven) *zāk̲ār* (male) *unaqēb̲āh* (female) *laḥayvōt̲* (to live) *zera`* (seed) *'al* (on) *panēy* (face) *k̲āl* (of all) *hā 'āreṣ* (the earth)
καὶ *kai* (and) **ἀπὸ** *apo* (from) **τῶν** *tōn* (the) **πετεινῶν** *peteinōn* (birds) **τοῦ** *tou* (of the) **οὐρανοῦ** *ouranou* (sky) **τῶν** *tōn* (the) **καθαρῶν** *katharōn* (pure) **ἑπτὰ** *epta* (seven) **ἑπτά** *epta* (seven) **ἄρσεν** *arsen* (male) **καὶ** *kai* (and) **θῆλυ** *thēlu* (female) **καὶ** *kai* (and) **ἀπὸ** *apo* (from) **τῶν** *tōn* (the) **πετεινῶν** *peteinōn* (birds) **τῶν** *tōn* (the) **μὴ** *mē* (not) **καθαρῶν** *katharōn* (pure) **δύο** *duo* (two) **δύο** *duo* (two) **ἄρσεν** *arsen* (male) **καὶ** *kai* (and) **θῆλυ** *thēlu* (female)[1937] **διαθρέψαι** *diathrepsai* (to preserve) **σπέρμα** *sperma* (seed) **ἐπὶ** *epi* (on) **πᾶσαν** *pasan* (all) **τὴν** *tēn* (the) **γῆν** *gēn* (earth)
sed (but) ***et*** (and) ***de*** (of the) ***volatilibus*** (birds) ***caeli*** (of the sky) ***septena*** (seven) ***septena*** (seven) ***masculum*** (male) ***et*** (and) ***feminam*** (female) ***ut*** (thus) ***salvetur*** (is saved) ***semen*** (the seed) ***super*** (over) ***faciem*** (the face) ***universae*** (of all) ***terrae*** (the earth)
Of fowls also of the air by sevens, the male and the female; to keep seed alive upon the face of all the earth.
Likewise, [take] *seven noetic/males and noematic/females out of the ethereal senses to preserve the archetypal-seed to face experience.*

The birds (עוף *'owph*) are metaphors for the ethereal (שָׁמַיִם *shamayim*) senses of the psyche. They are logic, aesthetic, moral, epistemology, intuitions, psychological traits, tendencies and so on. In a state of mute[1938] serene testimony, like the seventh (שֶׁבַע *sheba`*) day of rest, all go in the ark in their noetic-male (זכר *zakar*) / noematic-female (נְקֵבָה *nĕqebah*) pair formation. Like Platonic archetypes,[1939] the seeds (זרע *zera`*) of all those ideal animals and birds, are preserved alive (חַיָּה *chayah*) in the Ark of the Mind only to be activated anew once they will go back in the waking/dreaming field (אֶרֶץ 'erets) of experiences facing (פָּנִים paniym) the physical senses. This preservation is the continuous ideal presence of everything in the Memory-Receptacle of the Mind-Ark.

7:4-Forty Days and Nights

כִּי לְיָמִים עוֹד שִׁבְעָה אָנֹכִי מַמְטִיר עַל־הָאָרֶץ אַרְבָּעִים יוֹם וְאַרְבָּעִים לָיְלָה וּמָחִיתִי אֶת־כָּל־הַיְקוּם אֲשֶׁר עָשִׂיתִי מֵעַל פְּנֵי הָאֲדָמָה:
kiy (for) *layāmiym* (day) *'vōḏ* (yet) *šiba'āh* (seven) *'ānōḵiy* (I) *mamaṭiyr* (rain) *'al* (on) *hā'āreṣ* (earth) *'arabā'iym* (forthy) *yvōm* (days) *va'arabā'iym* (forty) *lāyalāh* (nights) *umāḥiyṯiy* (I have wiped out) *'eṯ* (and) *kāl* (all) *hayaqum* (existing beings) *'ăšer* (which) *'āśiyṯiy* (I have created) *mē'al* (from) *panēy* (face) *hā'ăḏāmāh* (of the earth)
ἔτι *eti* (yet) γὰρ *gar* (in fact) ἡμερῶν *ēmerōn* (days) ἑπτὰ *epta* (seven) ἐγὼ *egō* (I) ἐπάγω *epagō* (shall bring) ὑετὸν *ueton* (rain) ἐπὶ *epi* (on) τὴν *tēn* (the) γῆν *gēn* (earth) τεσσαράκοντα *tessarakonta* (forty) ἡμέρας *ēmeras* (days) καὶ *kai* (and) τεσσαράκοντα *tessarakonta* (forty) νύκτας *nuktas* (night) καὶ *kai* (and) ἐξαλείψω *exaleipsō* (I shall blot out) πᾶσαν *pasan* (all) τὴν *tēn* (the) ἐξανάστασιν *exanastasin* (offsprings) ἣν *ēn* (thus) ἐποίησα *epoiēsa* (I made) ἀπὸ *apo* (on) προσώπου *prosōpou* (face) τῆς *tēs* (of the) γῆς *gēs* (earth)
adhuc (thus) **enim** (in fact) *et* (and) **post** (after) *dies* (days) **septem** (seven) *ego* (I) **pluam** (rain) *super* (on) **terram** (the earth) *quadraginta* (forty) **diebus** (days) *et* (and) **quadraginta** (forty) *noctibus* (nights) **et** (and) *delebo* (I will delete) **omnem** (all) *substantiam* (substance) **quam** (that) *feci* (I made) **de** (on the) *superficie* (surface) **terrae** (of the earth)
For yet seven days, and I will cause it to rain upon the earth forty days and forty nights; and every living substance that I have made will I destroy from off the face of the earth.
At the end of that <u>restful</u> (7) testimony, the epistemic structure will bring down <u>destruction</u> (40) in the world of duality. From that, the rain of archetypes will flow down during the distress of the day's wakefulness and the night's dream, and I will obliterate all existences I have made."

If we want to continue reading the text literally, then, we should conclude that it is contradictory. In fact, not all living beings, including innocent plants, would have perished in the flood. Actually, marine life would be thriving in those waters, as never before.

The deluge starts after the seventh day of faithful testimony, namely, after the seventh day of rest. The creative circle starts again when we eat the forbidden fruit and we leave the resting moment of dreamless sleep to enter the conceptual world of duality. The whirlpool of deluge starts when we separate the epistemic synthesis of subject and object. That is, the '*I*' distinguishes itself from the objective world.

The Gematria value of the word *kiyḏwō*,[1940] meaning *destruction*, is 40.[1941] The letter מ, *m*, which symbolizes water and chaos, equals to number 40, which is also the first letter of the word *machah*,[1942] meaning to destroy.[1943] Furthermore, the word *dalw*,[1944] meaning *distress-brought-down* by rain during the night's (לַיִל *layil*) dreams and wakeful days (יוֹם *yowm*), is also equivalent to 40 (אַרְבָּעִים *'arba'iym*).[1945] The rain (מָטָר *matar*) is a metaphor for the flowing down of all ideas from their Heavenly Receptacle on the four-*'arba*'[1946] square-*raba*'[1947] corners of the Universe.

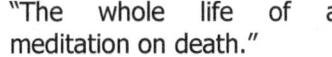

Beings[1948] perish according to their own nature. In fact, as beings come into existence, immediately they become

"being-for-death,"[1949]

"Then... '*the aim of life is death*'"[1950] itself.

In the Egyptian tradition, the sacred barge is a symbol for the passage from one stage of life to another. The whole journey is not a mere legendary account of a mythical [1951]⇨ voyage, but it is the condition and reality of human existence destined to death. Cicero,[1952] paraphrasing Socrates,[1953] declared,

"The whole life of a philosopher is, as some philosopher says, a meditation on death."

However, Greek Philosophy fancies eternal possession of good and immortality,

"The mortal nature always seeks... to be immortal, [hence, the continuous] thinking process...[1954] preserves our knowledge"[1955]

for the future. The ancient Indian sage Yājñavalkya-Sacrifice-Speaker[1956] emphatically denies any kind of knowledge after death. In fact, only where there is life there is the duality of the 'I' and the world. Through experience, one knows the other.

"*But, the dead do not know anything.*"[1957]

When everything is gone, how can one in that state experience and know the world or oneself?[1958] Then,

"*the end will be where the beginning is. Blessed is the person who stands at rest in the beginning. And that person will be acquainted with the end and will not taste death.*"[1959]

As we saw, existence refers to that which *is conceived as* independent or as being-out-of-(*ex-sistere*) the subject-object-correlation. The *thoughtless-certain-faith* we have of something being there, states the existence of anything (יָקוּם *yĕquwm*). We can never doubt the mental and/or physical experience, doubt itself becomes an undoubtable occurrence, as such. What we can doubt is the postulated reference to a corresponding *external* reality not yet proven as such. When verified, its truthful and/or fallacious correspondence will become again another certain occurrence. Thus, existence refers only to that which we physically and/or mentally experience as experience. Events, as such, come inevitably flanked with apodictical certainty or *faith*. This is the metaphoric shield or the armor conferring *factual solidity* to the occurrence. Without that *Faith*, there cannot be any objective world or experience of it.

As the internal-intentioning-**S**ubject drives circularly towards the **O**bject, it projects this last one in a reality conceived external to that convolutedness. On the Tree of Knowledge, the drive manifests its achievement as a forbidden fruit, an object missing the **A**wareness from which they both originate. Whatever state of mind derives from the hungry assimilation of that fruit, it is attributed to an object that, in itself, is conceived completely different from that mental state. As an example,

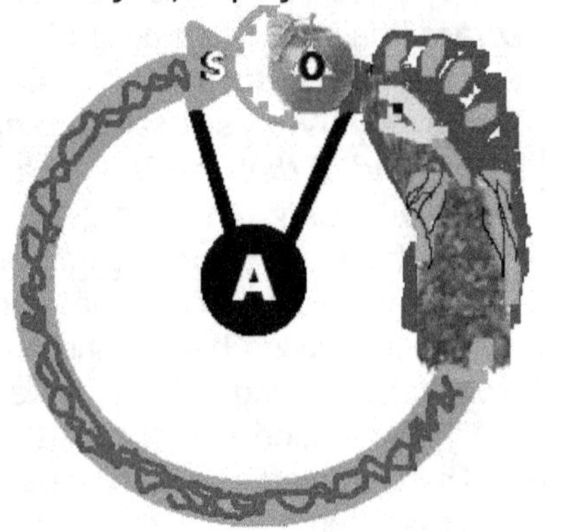

"*what woman having ten pieces of silver* (δραχμή *drachmē*),[1960] if *she lose one piece, doth not light a candle, and sweep the house, and seek diligently till she find it? And when she hath found it, she calleth her friends and her neighbours together, saying, Rejoice with me; for I have found the piece which I had lost.*"[1961]

Nevertheless, the misplaced drachma does not feel the dismaying and rejoicing of its own loss and recovery, nor it is conscious-*of* those mental states. Similarly, while "*Neurons Paralyze Us During REM Sleep,*"[1962] they are not individually paralyzed or feel sleepy in-themselves. They affect the state of our brain, which enters in a new stage that, in-itself, is completely different from its causes.

These examples could lead us to believe that there is a deep connection between cause and effect as if an element of the cause persists in its effect even when the causing event is gone. Truthfully, that persistence is in the mental structure, in the epistemic form, which understands the world as interrelated. Cause-effect is one of the *a-priori* modalities, which enable us to comprehend and know the world. In the interactive connection, however, the agent that we call cause-in-itself remains *insensitive* to the event that we call effect-in-itself and vice versa. In fact, the volcanos and/or asteroids that caused the extinction of the dinosaurs[1963] never suffered the pain felt by those prehistoric animals.

The deluge comes when we miss the mark by attributing and referring *Certainty* to the objective world in-itself. Then the whole world starts tumbling and ruining on us. Then we eat the metaphoric apple, which does not convey any real nourishment. When we conceptually place (*sistere*) the object as being outside (*ex*) our experience, we reduce it to a noumenon, namely something thought as such, but unexperienced in-itself.[1964] Existence can be stated only when the subject is, physically, psychologically and/or mentally, in the presence of the experienced object as experience. We may transfer and believe that existence is inherent also to something outside, independent from the subject-object correlation. This may occur in two ways,

1) it may occur experiencing someone's death. Then, in the presence of the dead body, the persistence of this world and our present vivid memories of the deceased may erroneously lead us to believe that the world persists in existence even after death; or
2) it may occur at the end of our own thinking process. Then, the whole world, as we know it (and that is all there is), supposedly ceases to be experienced, thus stops to be judged as persisting in its existence. This can happen when exiting an intentional or unintentional withdrawing into the unifying crunch of dreamlessness or unconsciousness. Then, again, the reappearance of the world leads us to believe that it kept on existing even while we were asleep or sedated. Entering the dream world is accessing a virtual reality, which requires an internal redirection of all our senses. The oneiric landscape is still that of duality, in which the subject is the dreamer and the object's name is dream. While dreaming, the subject/dreamer calls itself 'I' and the object/dreamed 'you.' Nevertheless, that is a new dimension, which ends when we awake, like entering this life when we are born and exiting it when we die. The dreamer does not know what lies before or after the dream, as the living ignores what follows or precedes life. When we stop the deluge of judging-thoughts, then, the resting stillness preludes the Wisdom of Awareness.

An assiduous visitor of Virtual Reality Games may believe, for a second, in the external existence of that world, which he is experiencing. Similarly, the persistence of sunlight after our sleep makes us believe in the continuation of the world after our death. However, in death we cannot express the judgement of existence. Even the suicidal expects a more pleasant status. In fact, no premeditated suicide would go through with the sick plan if the condition, for which the insane intent was previously deliberated, does not subsist any longer or turns out to be favorable. That is, a sufferer from an incurable disease, who, unable to cope with the pain, contemplates euthanasia, will never end life if the agony and the illness recedes completely. Thus, the suicidal looks for an escape, an opening into another experience. It craves for a different life, a different objectivity, but still, an experience. It is like wishing that

> "Faeries, come take me out of this dull world, / For I would ride with you upon the wind, / Run on the top of the dishevelled tide, / And dance upon the mountains like a flame."[1965]

Nevertheless, it is definitively not a withdrawal into the Silence of Transcendence.

This world is the flood, in which we drown every day. Paul enigmatically declared,

> "*I die daily.*"[1966]

The deluge is the continuous flow of all the entire possible conceptual and/or physical objects that inundates our minds and our experiences. This is the intolerable cacophony, the

> "*uproar of mankind... the babel*"

reported by Enlil.[1967] This is the loud drowning reverberation of all human thoughts, in the mind and through the media, and/or animal impulses. This is how all-living existing beings (יקום *yĕquwm*) perish (יקום *yĕquwm*) in this flood. Understand the flood as the succession of experiential events, which drown us as we seek to find the solid rock of certainty on which to rest and survive.

Caitlyn, one of our students, asks,

'If God is omnipotent, why can't He prevent terrible things from happening? Why a good kid can be cancer stricken? Why God couldn't hit a criminal with that disease, rather than an innocent child? If God is omnipresent and He created everything, why He does

not intervene to prevent suffering, acts of war, terrible terrorists' attacks and deadly natural calamities from occurring? On which side is God?'

We reply,

'The ultimate calamity is Death. Humans and/or nature cause calamities. Human tragedies are wars, crimes and/or terrorists' acts. The perpetrators justify wars and terror. Furthermore, whosoever claims victory perceives that violence as moral, just and good. God does not take sides, He directs us. He tells us not to ingest the forbidden fruit, which urges and gears us towards the past and death. <Love, hate, passion, tranquility, anger, serenity, envy, compassion, greed, generosity, parsimony, gluttony, desperation, joy, lust, fear, courage, chastity, pride, humbleness, laziness, energy, beauty, ugliness, art, brutality, piety, blasphemy and all others, are all coloring the world into reality. Better still, without those colors the world would be unconceivable and unknown. Therefore, the same astronomical event of a sunrise may be different if viewed from the arms of a loved one, or during a financial crisis, or when distracted by something else, or during a scientific analysis. In each case, the unknown sunrise-in-itself, i.e. devoid of any observer, belongs to a mythological realm. In La Bohème, when enamored Rodolfo compares his loved one's beauty to a sunrise, Mimi, his dying lover, reproaches him,>[1968]

"*You made a wrong comparison. You meant: beautiful as a sunset.*"[1969]

However, Caitlyn asks, where is God during a natural disaster? During the 79 AD eruption of Mount Vesuvius at Pompeii, terror was so intense that

"There were those who, for fear of death, were calling upon death."[1970]

Nevertheless, for the person of Certain-Faith, as for the Biblical Job, God is always here. He is the Transcendent Awareness lovingly watching over the terror of our nightmares. The name Job (אִיּוֹב 'Iyowb),[1971] *from* (אָיַב *'ayab*),[1972] *means enemy, adversary of Satan* (שָׂטָן),[1973] *who describes itself as the one who is*

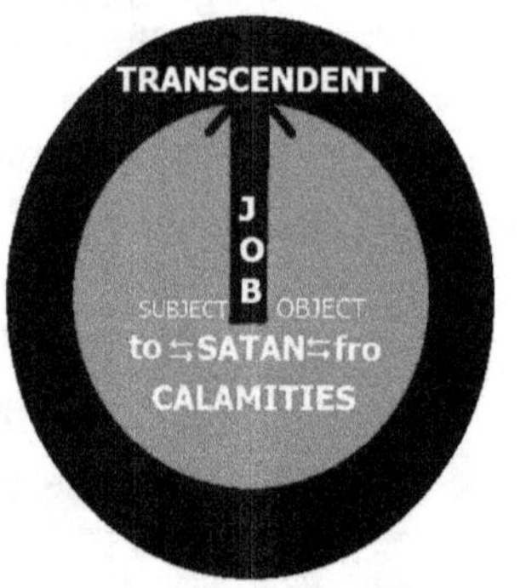

"*going to and fro in the earth, and from walking up and down in it.*"[1974]

To go to and fro (שׁוּט *shuwt*),[1975] *up and down* (הָלַךְ *halak*)[1976] *is the immanent movement within the land* (אֶרֶץ *'erets*)[1977] *of duality and calamity, the circularity of subject/object. Job does not despair, instead, he departs* (סוּר *cuwr*)[1978] *from Satan and stands upright* (יָשַׁר *yashar*)[1979] *to go peacefully straight* (יָשַׁר *yashar*)[1980] *to the Transcendent Aware Wisdom. There,*

"*He shall deliver thee in six troubles: yea, in seven there shall no evil touch thee.*"[1981]

~~~~~~

7:5-Noah's Obedience

וַיַּעַשׂ נֹחַ כְּכֹל אֲשֶׁר־צִוָּהוּ יְהוָה׃ *vaya'aś* (did) *nōaḥ* (Noah) *kaḵōl* (everything) *'ăšer* (which) *ṣiuāhu* (had commanded) *yahvāh* (the Transcendent)
καὶ *kai* (and) **ἐποίησεν** *epoiēsen* (did) **Νωε** *Nōe* (Noah) **πάντα** *panta* (all) **ὅσα** *osa* (which) **ἐνετείλατο** *eneteilasto* (commanded) **αὐτῷ** *autō* (him) **κύριος** *kurios* (Lord) **ὁ** *o* (the) **θεός** *theos* (God)
fecit (did) ***ergo*** (therefore) ***Noe*** (Noah) ***omnia*** (all) ***quae*** (that) ***mandaverat*** (had commanded) ***ei*** (him) ***Dominus*** (the Lord)
~~~~~~

And Noah did according unto all that the LORD commanded him.
And Noah did everything as the Transcendent had commanded him.

Therefore, Noah, **<u>aware</u>**, enters the restful silent state of dreamless sleep. In fact, Transcendence is Awareness and Its *Will* is to be in the Purity of Awareness. All memories, as DNA, as animal ideas, fuse in the Ark's mind. <Based on the latest reports on memory improvement, new studies are focusing again on the theory of

> "memory consolidation during sleep"[1982] and of
>
> "memory reconsolidation, [where] both SWS and REM sleep have been associated with the consolidation of memory, suggesting that there may be more than a single phase of sleep-dependent consolidation."[1983]

In fact, the

> "initial learning phase is followed by a ... memory consolidation ... predominantly during sleep"[1984]

especially in NREM.[1985] After which we are back in the dream and waking states.>[1986]

7:6-Noah the Righteous

וְנֹחַ בֶּן־שֵׁשׁ מֵאוֹת שָׁנָה וְהַמַּבּוּל הָיָה מַיִם עַל־הָאָרֶץ׃
vanōaḥ (Noah) *ben* (with) *šēš* (six) *mē'vōṯ* (hundred) *šānāh* (years) *vahamabul* (flood) *hāyāh* (was) *mayim* (of waters) *ʿal* (on) *hā'āreṣ* (earth)
Νωε *Nōe* (Noah) **δὲ** *de* (but) **ἦν** *ēn* (was) **ἐτῶν** *etōn* (year) **ἑξακοσίων** *exakosiōn* (six hundred) **καὶ** *kai* (and) **ὁ** *o* (the) **κατακλυσμὸς** *kataklusmos* (cataclysm) **ἐγένετο** *egeneto* (came) **ὕδατος** *udatos* (of water) **ἐπὶ** *epi* (on) **τῆς** *tēs* (the) **γῆς** *gēs* (earth)
erat (was)***-que*** (and) ***sescentorum*** (six hundred) ***annorum*** (years) ***quando*** (when) ***diluvii*** (the deluge) ***aquae*** (of water) ***inundaverunt*** (inundated) ***super*** (on) ***terram*** (the earth)
And Noah was six hundred years old when the flood of waters was upon the earth.
Moreover, Noah was in his *righteous* (600) circular years of consciousness while the deluge of water was on the consciousness-*of* the world.

The Gematria value of the Hebrew word *watseḏaqaṯ* (וְצִדְקַת),[1987] meaning *righteousness*, is 600. At the time of the deluge, Noah was six *(שֵׁשׁ shesh) hundred (מֵאָה me'ah)* years old. Therefore, while the deluge rages over the earthly stages of dream and wakefulness, Noah is in his righteous circular years (שָׁנָה *shaneh*) of dreamless sleep. *Ecclesiastes* declares,[1988]

> "*The sleep of a* [just] *labouring man is sweet.*"

Then, the next generations from Noah are all descendants from the oneiric dimension as they articulate flowing in the dream and waking state.

However, why is dreamless sleep the state of righteousness? <Awareness is never thought. Thought is the outcome of Awareness. **Awareness is Awareness**, **Word**, ***Lógos***, ***Verbum***,[1989] Intuitive-Apodictical-Self-Evident-Certitude.

> "*In the logical-beginning was <u>Apodictic-Truth</u>* (λόγος *logos verbum*), *and <u>Apodictic-Truth</u> was with <u>Transcendent-Awareness</u>* (θεός *theos Deus*), *and <u>Apodictic-Truth</u> was <u>Transcendent-Awareness</u>. The same was in the logical-beginning with <u>Transcendent-Awareness</u>. All things were made by IT; and without IT was not anything made that were made. In IT was <u>Pure-Consciousness</u>* (ζωή *zōē Vita*)*; and <u>Pure-Consciousness</u> was the light of men. And the light shines in darkness; and the darkness comprehended IT not.*"[1990]

Thought arises as <u>consciousness-*of*</u> the light of Awareness shone on the perceived objects. That luminescence bounces off them and reflects back to a conscious thinking subject. When thought assigns the origin of that brightness <u>only</u> to the object, then the thought-object becomes *luciferous*, a light carrier.[1991] It becomes like the moon, apparently producing its own light.

> "*How art thou fallen from heaven, O Lucifer* (הילל *heylel*)*, son of the morning!* [How] *art thou cut down to the ground, which didst weaken the nations!... I will be like the most High* [the Transcendent]."[1992]

The Awareness we are referring-*to* is not the awareness that we describe with these words. This is a conceptual presentation of awareness, not Awareness in-Itself.

"*The path* (*tao,* 道) *that can be taught*/ *is not the never-ending Path* (*Tao,* 道),"
confirms Lao Tzu.[1993] Whosoever describes the Transcendent, voices an opinion that is a noumenon, a thought, never known as Transcendent. Because we imagine the transcendent in various forms and with different classifications, we give rise to various religions with different denominations all at war with each other. Nevertheless, nothing can ever define It. Because the Transcendent is indefinable and ineffable, thus nothing can be said about It. If anything can be said about It, then it is not the Transcendent. In whatsoever way we think of the Transcendent, it becomes inevitably immanent.>[1994] Each experience turns out to be

"*witness of the Aware-Light, so that everyone through it might be sure... It is not that Light, but bears witness to that Light... the true Light, which lighteth every man that cometh into the world.*"[1995]

Consciousness-*of-this-world* is like

"*the voice* (φωνή *phōnē*) *of one crying in an uninhabited-desert* (ἐν τῇ ἐρήμῳ *en tē erēmō*)."[1996]

That desert (אֲדָמָה *'adamah*) is also this *world* we identify with when we regard it as an object-real-in-itself.

"*John* [the Baptist] *bare witness* (μαρτυρεῖ *marturei*) *of him, and cried, saying, 'This was he of whom I spake, He that cometh after me is preferred before me: for he was before me.*"[1997]

The consciousness-*of* the world *bears witness-of* the ensuing Certainty, but cannot *know* Certainty as such. While all certitude *comes-after* the experience, at the same time, *before* any consciousness-*of*-the-world is the Apodictic Awareness. In reality,

"*No man hath known* (ἑώρακεν *eōraken*) *God at any time*"[1998]

because the

"*kingdom* [of Apodictical-Awareness] *is not of this world,*"[1999]

'adamah (אֲדָמָה), of which we are the consciousness. Biblically, the witnessing-one was identified with John the Baptist. He identifies with the consciousness-*of*, characteristic of the theological-religious rethinking of transcendence. Nevertheless, Certain-Awareness remains the basis for any theology, philosophy, science, religion and these words. The foundation of the entire world rests on the Awareness we have here and now.

"*In the beginning The Transcendent created the heaven and the earth... And The Transcendent named the dry* [land] *Earth ... and saw that* [it was] *good.*"[2000]

How can we *name* or *see* anything, if Awareness is not logically *pre-sent* a-priori in the *named* one or in the *seen* one? By Awareness, we do not mean the consciousness-*of*-something. Instead, we intend, the Intuitive Apodictic Certitude,[2001] as such, which, besides being the foundation of the consciousness-*of*-something, is also the ground-stand of both the subconscious and unconscious. In other words, that founding Awareness is present in every state of mind. The ancient Indian text, *Bṛhadāraṇyaka Upanishad,* declares that in the unconscious state, one

"*does not see, smell, taste, hear, think and know, except that, while not seeing, smelling, tasting, speaking, hearing, thinking and knowing, one is still the seer, smeller, taster, speaker, hearer, thinker and knower. In fact, the seen, smelled, tasted, spoken, heard, thought and known does not separate from the seer, smeller, taster, speaker, hearer, thinker and knower, because it is imperishable. Merely, in that state, there is no otherness and nothing else that one may see, smell, taste, speak, hear, think and know.*"[2002]

Thus, that state is the high desert, the dreamless sleep, the unconsciousness where there is no consciousness-*of* objectivity. In it, paradoxically, we must bring our awakened attention.

Noah's paradigm is similar to Moses' when

"*the angel of the LORD appeared unto him* [Moses] *in a flashing point of spear of fire out of the midst of a bush: and he intently looked, and, behold, the bush burned with supernatural fire, and the bush* [was] *not consumed or devoured.*"[2003]

<The fulgurating fire of Pure Awareness shines of its own accord. It does not turn towards the world to consume it epistemically. Thus, the bush or the world is not consumed or devoured by the fire of

Certitude. On the contrary, all levels of realities, conscious, subconscious or unconscious, persist in their own dimensions. For each one, the guarantor of those realms is exactly that Certitude.

> "*And Moses said, I will now reject and turn away from it, and see this great sight, why the bush is not burnt.*"[2004]

Thoreau asks,

> "With all your science can you tell how it is, and whence it is, that light comes into the soul?"[2005]

When Moses rejects the direct connection with the fire and turns away from it to investigate about its origin, he is moving away from the source of everything. He is going back to the consciousness-*of* the world, where he had left his senses-flock. He is trying to conceptualize the Transcendent. In fact, conceptualizing or naming the Transcendent-Awareness implies necessarily losing It by reducing It to a thought, namely to Its contrary, which is immanent in the subject-object correlation.

> "*And when the LORD saw that he rejected and turned away to see* [and conceptualize and be conscious-*of* the origin of that fiery Awareness]*, The Transcendent called unto him out of the midst of the bush, and said, 'Moses, Moses.' And he said, 'Here I* [am]*.*"[2006]

Moses identifies himself as this '*I*' here and at this time. Then the Transcendent [2007]⇨

> "*said, 'Do not approach here: put off thy shoes from off thy feet, for the place whereon thou standest* [is] *the Sacred Transcendent.*"[2008]

The '*I*,' as the subject *per-se*, cannot be or have a stand on this ground. The '*I*' or ego is the consciousness-*of* or the spirit-*of*-the-world. It is the principle of individuation, which animates the rational life of the body, the power of thinking, of knowing, of desiring, of feeling and of acting. This level is set apart; it must transcend this cosmos. In fact,

> "*Blessed* [are] *the poor in ego-spirit: for theirs is the kingdom of heaven... The pure in heart... shall see the Transcendent.*"[2009]
>
> "*My kingdom is not <u>of</u> this world... my kingdom is <u>Now</u>, not from this cosmic place,*"[2010]

declares Jesus. It is not the consciousness-*of* this world. His kingdom is <u>Now</u>, the Pure-Present-Apodictic-Awareness, not from the immanent subject-object consciousness-*of* this space-time dimension.

> "*Moreover he said, 'I* [am] *the Transcendent God of thy father, the Transcendent God of Abraham, the Transcendent God of Isaac, and the Transcendent God of Jacob.' And Moses hid his face; for he was afraid to look upon the Transcendent.*"[2011]

Moses changes his action. Previously, he had rejected the direct connection with the fire and had turned away from it to investigate its cause. Now, he hides his face, because he

> "*cannot see the seer of seeing, hear the hearer of hearing, think the thinker of thinking, nor understand the understander of understanding.* [As] *It is your Self, which is in everything*"[2012]

and in everyone. It is the Eternal-Apodictic-Awareness. In fact, when Moses asked for His name,[2013]

> "*The Transcendent said unto Moses, 'I AM THAT I AM:'*[2014] *and he said, 'Thus shalt thou say unto the children of Israel, I AM hath sent me unto you.*'"[2015]

He is the '<u>*I*</u>' <u>in-Itself</u>. Then, Moses asks,

> "*Who am I,*"[2016]

and The Transcendent states that he must realize that same *I-in-Itself* as the foundation of his own being.

> "*Because, certainly I am the Self-Evident proof, that I have sent thee: When thou hast brought forth the people out of Egypt.*"[2017]

The Hebrew word *Mitsrayim, meaning* Egypt, besides its historical and geographical reference, also means siege, entrenchment, with the sense of limit, enclosure, to bind, besiege, and confine, to shut in, to be an adversary. Therefore, the deliverance from Egypt has here a wider metaphorical reference. It means escape from the world of suffering and enslavement. It means the liberation from the subjugation within the subject-object death enclosure, which derives from the fruit of the tree of knowledge distinct from the divine source of the tree of life.>[2018]

The righteousness of the state of dreamless sleep is when we enter its Ark in a state of enhanced attention contemplating Certitude. The *unrighteous* ones are those who fall out of it and drown in the flood. In fact, they, seduced by the world of objectivities, identify with it. Noah, on the other hand, identifies and rests in the contemplative stillness of the Ark.

GRAPHIC: *Salvation in the Ark*[2019]

A reader may enquire,

'Isn't contradictory to say that one should enter the unconscious state of dreamless sleep while being awake contemplating Certitude?'

We reply,

'In meditation, <with a gradual process of concentric concentrated introspection, seeking to unite with (con) our most intimate central Self, we should drive inward (intro) and look (specto) forgetting the loving-attractive-identification with the deceptive world of our desires.[2020] *We cannot do both, in fact,*

> "*No man can serve two masters: for either he will hate the one, and love the other; or else he will hold to the one, and despise the other. Ye cannot serve God and mammon.*"[2021]

Therefore, with purity of heart, relaxed and with no anxiety, gradually withdraw inward the consciousness-of the objects deriving from the senses' activities. Look, hear, taste, smell and feel objects without paying attention to them. It is like those comforting moments when we enter in a suspension of perception while fully perceiving. These moments were more frequent in our infancy, when we were staring at something in an intense stillness. You may remember those instants and the surprising annoyance when somebody snapped us out of that intense state. However, now we willfully seek to recreate that state. It is similar to the aesthetic moment described by Kandinsky,

> "Lend your ears to music, open your eyes to painting, and... stop thinking! Just ask yourself if the work has enabled you to 'walk about' into a hitherto unknown world. If the answer is yes, what more do you want?"[2022]

Focus on the constant presence of the five-faculties-of-the-senses and the mind as a sixth organ. In themselves, the senses are independent and indifferent to any form of pleasure, apathy or aversion towards their objects. Pleasure, apathy and aversion are the demons, which color the world's reality of which they are conscious-of but with felt participation. From the previous stages of concentration, move deeper.

On the onset of sleep, immediately preceding slumber, the mind enters a state of total, immovable concentration. Focus on that state of consciousness, where the mind forgets its own objects of thought together with its own Ego-consciousness. Concentrate only on that act of thinking unaffected by attraction, indifference or dislike. From this juncture, a new internal organ takes over, thought, the imperishable thinking process, takes over with renewed vengeance, so strong that it creates a new world, namely the realm of dreams. If, during the waking state, you successfully centered your attention on the faculties of the senses alone and not on their objects, then that focus has become your second nature. Therefore, it will be possible for you to focus also on those same faculties, as they operate in the dream state, and be unaffected by attraction, indifference or dislike for the objects experienced during the nighttime visions. Then, you will be awake *in your dreams. The I-consciousness, the I-think, awakens and arises in this dreaming juncture. With an immovable concentration, become conscious-of awareness only. In a way, this whole work is at this stage. It leads consciousness to become here and now conscious-of awareness, to recognize the I-aware as the building block, as the founding keystone of this entire world and draw attention only on it.*

Then, in the deepest sleep without dreams, in the presence of a unified cognitive mind, having gone through all the previous concentration steps and without any object of the senses, you will enter in a meditation state. In that, is the comprehensive Realization of Awareness. There, the consciousness-of awareness disappears to leave only the shining presence of Awareness that makes the world come into existence. Finally, in ecstasy, individuality unifies fusing and identifying with Pure-Aware-Certitude, like the extinguishing of a fire consuming its fuel while not burning itself out as Fire. Paul uses the example of the athlete,

> "*Forgetting those things which are behind and reaching forward to those things which are ahead... I press toward the goal for the prize...*[2023] *And everyone who competes is temperate in all things...* [and] *we* [do it for] *an imperishable* [crown]... [Therefore] *I discipline my body and bring* [it] *into subjection.*"[2024]

However, so long as an effort is made to reach that state... that state is not really reached.

> "*There is no reaching the Self... You are the Self; you are already That.*"[2025]

The *state of Being-in-itself does not necessitate an effort to be-in-itself. Focusing on Awareness alone, then the whole world will be obtained in its true essence. Whereas, not having recognized that Awareness, then even that necessary fundamental Awareness will be unrealized for us. Thus,*

> "*the day of the Lord so cometh as a thief in the night,*"[2026]

that can be hauled away by the objectivizing process. This is the meaning of the Biblical injunction,

> "*For to everyone who has, more will be given, and he will have abundance; but from him who does not have, even what he has will be taken away.*"[2027]

In fact, when that Awareness is discovered as consciousness-of-something, then it is lost, but when consciousness-of- something is set aside, then that Awareness shines of its own nature.

"*Whoever finds his life will lose it, and whoever loses his life for my sake will find it.*"[2028]

Among the vows required by Monastic Orders for their members, the most difficult and most important is that of unconditional obedience to the superior. It is not only the good personality of the teacher that demands total devotion and submission, the bad superior, as well, requires the same respect, not for what the master does, but because obedience itself teaches how to practice total mystical disengagement beyond personal desires...

Perhaps, the great Spanish writer Cervantes (1547-1616) expresses this same concept of total disengagement when he describes Don Quixote's adventures with his horse, the nag Rozinante. Although the animal had

> "all blemishes [and was only] skin and bones, [the hero of La Mancha] silenced his worries and continued on his way, without taking any other road than that one which his horse wanted to take, believing that the force of the adventures consisted in that."[2029]

In line with this story is the historical "Obedience of St. Ignatius" of Loyola (1491-1556), who formulated Spiritual Exercises of poverty, chastity and obedience for his Society of Jesus (1539-40). In fact, he declares,

> "I am equally ready to go to any country, and prefer neither east nor west, so that if I were inclined to any particular place... I would force my mind in another direction till the balance was even."[2030]

These spiritual exercises are a science. Mimma Benvenuti, an Italian spiritual anthroposophist, stated,

> "The Science of the Spirit is not a theory, as it is a practice... To those who... criticize and blame us, we owe great gratitude, because they are in that moment our teachers... Many things of collective and human value depend from us..., not from the international communities."[2031]

BE AWARE... Walk aware of your surroundings. Leave all cares to Divine Providence of Awareness. Feel the breeze and the wind on your skin, in your hair. Look ahead while looking behind and at your sides. Feel the other persons' consciousness. Feel their pains. Feel their sadness. Feel it in compassion without attachment... Cover your interior fields aware of your designing and changing landscapes. Remember you are the dreamer... Soar aware in the sky of still silence in your dreamless sleep. Be aware in that thoughtless sky without dreams. Remember you are that serenity. In the shining midnight black sun of silence, be aware in the instant of death. Remember you are the immortal. BE AWARE.

> "*This Self of mine, the source of every action, of every desire, of every scent, and of every flavor, residing within the heart, encompassing all this, but indifferent, without conferring meaning or sense to the objects, this is the Supreme Transcendent Spirit.*"[2032]

It is the Absolute-Aware-collapse of the subject-object-circumference in its Self-dimensionless-center... This is our real nature, in that whatever we do, even when we think we are being selfish, we are in reality seeking for It, for the Pure Self in It-Self, for the Transcendent,

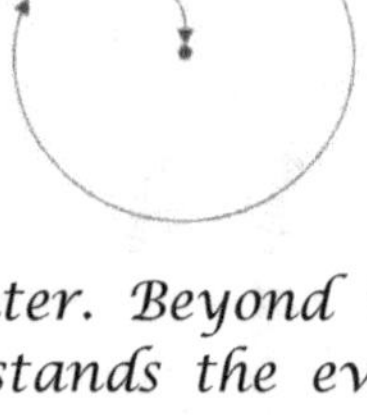

> "*beyond the world, beyond bliss... Who is in this state is inactive even while engaged in activity. This is also called... the natural state of absorption in oneself without concepts,*"[2033]

the collapse of the life and death circle disappearing in its own center. Beyond the world, beyond the object, beyond your identification with it, there stands the ever-present foundation of Awareness. Focus on It.

You do not need to abandon life to do this. On the contrary, live life to its fullest extent. However, constantly and incessantly identify with This Awareness here and now. Let this identification become your real nature. From the outside, no one will notice the difference, except that you will become the innermost essence of everyone, because the whole world is established on It. This meditative training will not inhibit your life productivity, on the contrary, it will let it escalate, surge and increase. Your action will border perfection and its outcome will be most favorable for you.

Actively, fully participate and live your life completely. Nevertheless, look at the world Aware, without seeing it. Listen to the world Aware, without hearing it. Savor the world Aware, without testing it. Inhale the world Aware, without smelling it. Sense the world Aware, without feeling it. Conceptualize the world Aware, without thinking of it. What is most important, keep practicing your identification with... Consciousness in you... In you is the Kingdom of God, identify with it. Constantly

> *"watch ye and pray, lest ye enter into temptation."*[2034]

The temptation is the identification with the impermanent object conceived as real-in-itself... Namely you shall *unveil* *the Hidden One. That veil impedes immortality, tempts, distracts and lures away from it. Therefore, the emphasis is on a vigilant and constant attention on the Truth, which is the inherent apodicticity of Awareness.*

One final advice,

> *"Let not thy left hand know what thy right hand doeth... But thou, when thou prayest, enter into thy closet, and when thou hast shut thy door, pray to thy Father which is in secret... use not vain repetitions."*[2035]

Try not to think in terms of what you may have experienced during meditation and definitely do not tell others. The thought of it will reduce to an object what you may have realized, thus destroy its spiritual achievement.'>[2036]

7:7-Entering the Ark of Deep Sleep

וַיָּבֹא נֹחַ וּבָנָיו וְאִשְׁתּוֹ וּנְשֵׁי־בָנָיו אִתּוֹ אֶל־הַתֵּבָה מִפְּנֵי מֵי הַמַּבּוּל׃   *vayāḇō̄* (went) *nōaḥ* (Noah) *uḇānāyv* (sons) *va'išatvō* (wife) *unašēy* (wife) *ḇānāyv* (of sons) *'itvō* (with) *'el* (into) *hatēḇāh* (the ark) *mipanēy* (from) *mēy* (water) *hamabul* (flood)
εἰσῆλθεν *eisēlthen* (enter) **δὲ** *de* (thus) **Νωε** *Nōe* (Noah) **καὶ** *kai* (and) **οἱ** *oi* (the) **υἱοὶ** *uioi* (sons) **αὐτοῦ** *autou* (your) **καὶ** *kai* (and) **ἡ** *ē* (the) **γυνὴ** *guvē* (wife) **αὐτοῦ** *autou* (yours) **καὶ** *kai* (and) **αἱ** *ai* (the) **γυναῖκες** *gunaikes* (wives) **τῶν** *tōn* (of the) **υἱῶν** *uiōn* (sons) **αὐτοῦ** *autou* (your) **μετ'** *mrt'* (with) **αὐτοῦ** *autou* (you) **εἰς** *eis* (in) **τὴν** *tēn* (the) **κιβωτὸν** *kibōton* (ark) **διὰ** *dia* (because) **τὸ** *to* (the) **ὕδωρ** *udōr* (water) **τοῦ** *tou* (of the) **κατακλυσμοῦ** *kataklusmou* (cataclysm)
et (and) ***ingressus*** (entered) ***est*** (is) ***Noe*** (Noah) ***et*** (and) ***filii*** (sons) ***eius*** (his) ***uxor*** (wife) ***eius*** (his) ***et*** (and) ***uxores*** (wives) ***filiorum*** (of the sons) ***eius*** (his) ***cum*** (with) ***eo*** (him) ***in*** (in) ***arcam*** (ark) ***propter*** (because) ***aquas*** (of the waters) ***diluvi*** (of the flood)
And Noah went in, and his sons, and his wife, and his sons' wives with him, into the ark, because of the waters of the flood.
Because of the flooding waters-of-objectivity, the resting-Noah went in the Ark-unconsciousness with his potential-noematic-wife, his epistemic-forms-sons and his sons' potential-noematic-wives.

Real is what we experience as an event when we come across it, namely when it is recorded at the presence of Awareness. As the waking world is real until we die, so the dream world is real until we awake. We should bear in mind that the Ark is, metaphorically, our mind's interiority beyond the reality of the dream and waking worlds. In the state of dreamless sleep, Noah is the name of our rested and unarticulated subject/object *a-priori* synthesis. As an inert hand has the capability to grip, similarly, each state of mind comes with its potential objectivity, metaphorically indicated as its wife. Noah's wife is the noematic potential objectivity in the oneiric and waking states. Metaphorically, their three offspring are our logical modes of knowing. Namely, they are the logical prerequisite for any possible knowledge, viz., time, causality and space.[2037] Metaphorically, they will be named, in order, Shem, Ham and Japheth. Their wives are the potential noematic objective possibilities of those forms.

When we enter the state of deep sleep, the entire world of *will and representation* remains outside submerged in the watery deluge of wakeful and dream representations. Metaphorically, Noah, entering the Ark, ascends into deep sleep. The subject with the object and with all its modes of knowing synthesize in the thoughtless cataleptic state of NREM, the third level of the Ark. Similar to the account of Noah, is the story of Jonah. He

> "*found a ship*[2038] *...and went down into it.*$_{(3)}$ *Jonah descended*[2039] *into the recesses*[2040] *of the ship; and he lay*[2041] *and was fast asleep*[2042]$_{(5)}$. *The multifaceted-*[2043]*ship-ruler-as-subject*[2044] *came to him, and said unto him...'O sleeper*[2045]*... arise'*[2046]$_{(6)}$. *And he said unto them, 'I am an Hebrew,*[2047] *viz. one from beyond,'"*$_{(9)}$[2048]

similar to

> "*Utnapishtim the Faraway,"*[2049]

in *The Epic of Gilgamesh*.

7:8-Potential Ideal Energies

מִן־הַבְּהֵמָה הַטְּהוֹרָה וּמִן־הַבְּהֵמָה אֲשֶׁר אֵינֶנָּה טְהֹרָה וּמִן־הָעוֹף וְכֹל אֲשֶׁר־רֹמֵשׂ עַל־הָאֲדָמָה׃ *min* (from) *habahēmāh* (animals) *haṭahvōrāh* (clean) *umin* (from) *habahēmāh* (animals) *'ăšer* (which) *'ēynenāh* (not) *ṭahōrāh* (clean) *umin* (from) *hā'vōp̄* (birds) *vak̲ōl* (all) *'ăšer* (which) *rōmēś* (creeping) *'al* (on) *hā'ăd̲āmāh* (earth)
καὶ *kai* (and) **ἀπὸ** *apo* (from) **τῶν** *tōn* (the) **πετεινῶν** *peteinōn* (birds) **καὶ** *kai* (and) **ἀπὸ** *apo* (from) **τῶν** *tōn* (the) **κτηνῶν** *katēnōn* (cattle) **τῶν** *tōn* (the) **καθαρῶν** *katharōn* (clean) **καὶ** *kai* (and) **ἀπὸ** *apo* (from) **τῶν** *tōn* (the) **κτηνῶν** *katēnōn* (animals) **τῶν** *tōn* (the) **μὴ** *mē* (non) **καθαρῶν** *katharōn* (clean) **καὶ** *kai* (and) **ἀπὸ** *apo* (from) **πάντων** *pantōn* (all) **τῶν** *tōn* (the) **ἑρπετῶν** *erpetōn* (creepers) **τῶν** *tōn* (the) **ἐπὶ** *epi* (on) **τῆς** *tēs* (the) **γῆς** *gēs* (earth)
de (of) ***animantibus*** (the animals) ***quoque*** (both) ***mundis*** (clean) ***et*** (and) ***inmundis*** (unclean) ***et*** (and) ***de*** (of) ***volucribus*** (the birds) ***et*** (and) ***ex*** (out of) ***omni*** (all) ***quod*** (that) ***movetur*** (move) ***super*** (over) ***terram*** (the earth)
Of clean beasts, and of beasts that are not clean, and of fowls, and of every thing that creepeth upon the earth,
[He went in] with the potentially disengaged energetic animals, with the potentially engaged energetic animals, with the potentially flying ideological-energies and with all the snaking potential tendencies in the world of duality.

As we have seen, the animals (בְּהֵמָה *bĕhemah*) in the ark are symbols of mental energies in their potential and intuitive state. Clean or shining energies are those potentially tending towards disengaged ideas, like mathematics, serenity, happiness, aesthetic and others. On the contrary, unclean animals are symbols of all potential thoughts cluttered by the attachment and possession of their known object and forgetting the Awareness from which they come, like greed, envy, hate and others. Birds (עוֹף *'owph*) are the metaphoric ideological energies capable of flying[2050] to the *Hyperuranium*[2051] abode of ideas like beauty and good. We are not using that Platonic term as a physical place, but in the sense of an ideal storage of recurring archetypal universal mind structures and configurations. Finally, the creeping or snaking animals (רָמַשׂ *ramas*) are metaphors for the pure epistemic tendencies, like logic, epistemology, intuitions and others in their pure potentialities.

7:9-The Noetic and Noematic Aspects

שְׁנַיִם שְׁנַיִם בָּאוּ אֶל־נֹחַ אֶל־הַתֵּבָה זָכָר וּנְקֵבָה כַּאֲשֶׁר צִוָּה אֱלֹהִים אֶת־נֹחַ׃ *šanayim* (two) *šanayim* (two) *bā'u* (went) *'el* (to the) *nōaḥ* (Noah) *'el* (the) *hatēb̲āh* (ark) *zāk̲ār* (male) *unaqēb̲āh* (female) *ka'ăšer* (as) *ṣiuāh* (had commanded) *'ĕlōhiym* (Gods) *'et̲* (to) *nōaḥ*

(Noah)
δύο *duo* (two) **δύο** *duo* (two) **εἰσῆλθον** *eisēlthon* (went) **πρὸς** *pros* (to) **Νωε** *Nōe* (Noah) **εἰς** *eis* (in) **τὴν** *tēn* (the) **κιβωτόν** *kibōton* (ark) **ἄρσεν** *arsen* (male) **καὶ** *kai* (and) **θῆλυ** *thēlu* (female) **καθὰ** *katha* (as) **ἐνετείλατο** *eveteilato* (had commanded) **αὐτῷ** *autō* (him) **ὁ** *o* (the) **θεός** *theos* (God)
duo (two) ***et*** (and) ***duo*** (two) ***ingressa*** (gone) ***sunt*** (are) ***ad*** (to) ***Noe*** (Noah) ***in*** (in) ***arcam*** (ark) ***masculus*** (male) ***et*** (and) ***femina*** (female) ***sicut*** (as) ***praeceperat*** (had commanded) ***Deus*** (God) ***Noe*** (to Noah)
There went in two and two unto Noah into the ark, the male and the female, as God had commanded Noah
Two by two, the noetic and noematic aspects went into the mind-ark with Noah, as Divine-Consciousness had ordained within the resting-Noah.

Where do the waking and/or dream (REM) world go when we are in the state of sleep with no dreams (NREM)?[2052] Like a secure bank treasury, this unconscious ark-realm preserves all forms and thoughts in their potential state. In return, they populate that inner world. As we have seen, the ark is a metaphor for the innermost recesses of the psyche. Therefore, all animals, as symbols of all potential ideas in their intuitive state and with their noetic-male and noematic-female potentialities, go (בוא *bow*) in the ark-mind with Noah, namely, the rested psyche.

This is our epistemic mind-configuration, as ordained by our innermost Structure-of-Consciousness. Namely, this is Divine-Consciousness ordering (צוה *tsavah*)[2053] knowledge without needing to be objectified as the ordainer. For example,

a) While *time* (*viz.* Shem) is the mean without which one would not be able to expect something, no one, as *animal-mental-energy* (בְּהֵמָה *běhemah*), *thinks* about *time*, as such, when having pleasure in the dream/waking realm. In that moment, *time* becomes a *subconscious form* shaping our knowledge.
b) While *space* (*viz.* Japheth) is the mean without which one would not be able to perceive things, no one, as *animal-mental-energy* (בְּהֵמָה *běhemah*), *thinks* about *space*, as such, when looking at something interesting in the dream/waking realm. In that moment, *space* becomes a *subconscious form* shaping our knowledge.
c) While *causality* (*viz.* Ham) is the mean without which one would not be able to interconnect objects, no one, as *animal-mental-energy* (בְּהֵמָה *běhemah*), *thinks* about *causality*, as such, when feeling pain in the dream/waking realm. In that moment, *causality* becomes a *subconscious form* shaping our knowledge.

7:10-The Cataclysm after the Rest

וַיְהִי לְשִׁבְעַת הַיָּמִים וּמֵי הַמַּבּוּל הָיוּ עַל־הָאָרֶץ׃
vayahiy (came to pass) *lašiba'at* (seven) *hayāmiym* (days) *umēy* (water) *hamabul* (deluge) *hāyu* (came) *'al* (on) *hā'āreṣ* (the earth)
καὶ *kai* (and) **ἐγένετο** *egeneto* (came to pass) **μετὰ** *meta* (after) **τὰς** *tas* (the) **ἑπτὰ** *epta* (seven) **ἡμέρας** *ēmeras* (days) **καὶ** *kai* (and) **τὸ** *to* (the) **ὕδωρ** *udōr* (water) **τοῦ** *tou* (the) **κατακλυσμοῦ** *kataklusmou* (cataclysm) **ἐγένετο** *egeneto* (took place) **ἐπὶ** *epi* (on) **τῆς** *tēs* (the) **γῆς** *gēs* (earth)
cumque (as) ***transissent*** (passed by) ***septem*** (the seven) ***dies*** (day) ***aquae*** (water) ***diluvii*** (from the deluge) ***inundaverunt*** (inundated) ***super*** (on) ***terram*** (the earth)
And it came to pass after seven days, that the waters of the flood were upon the earth.
At the end of the seventh day of rest, the waters of the deluge were upon the world of duality.

On the seventh[2054] circadian day of creation, after the *rest* (*viz.* Noah) in the NREM state, all the ideas in the ocean of possibilities become actualities. They *flood* (מבול *mabbuwl*) both the REM and the waking world,

"*like the spawn of fish they float in the ocean.*"[2055]

Then, after the seventh day, *swimming* between the two shores of rest and the world of duality *flooded-by-representations*, the ark-mind itself became like a fish (דג *dag*). In fact, the Gematria number of fish (*dag*) is seven.[2056]

From that fish-ark, Jonah prayed,

"*The waters compassed me about, even to the soul: the depth closed me round about, the weeds were wrapped about my head. I went down to the bottoms of the mountains; the earth with her bars was about me for ever: yet hast thou brought up my life from corruption, O LORD my God. When my soul fainted within me I remembered the LORD: and my prayer came in unto thee, into thine holy temple.*"[2057]

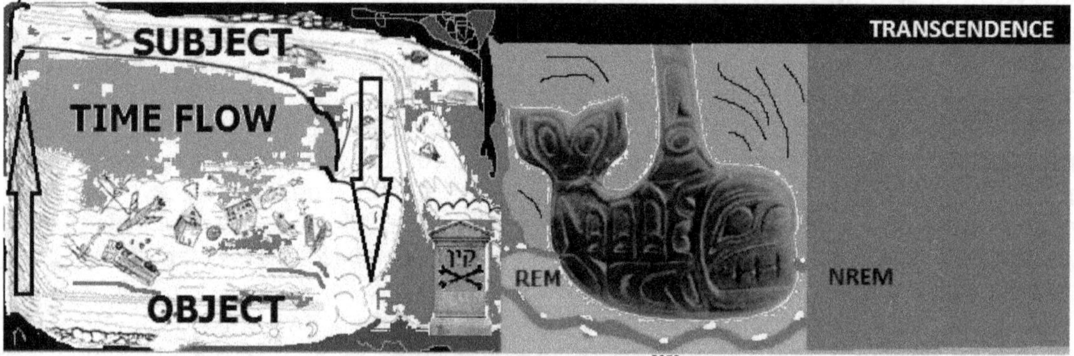

GRAPHIC: *The Ark as a Fish* [2058]

What we define real is within the mind. What we state to be independent from the mind, is still, necessarily within it. In it are potentially the pure and passionate ideas, which, when actualized, they flood the mind.

7-II SECTION: THE FLOOD
7:11-The Flood Begins

בִּשְׁנַת שֵׁשׁ־מֵאוֹת שָׁנָה לְחַיֵּי־נֹחַ בַּחֹדֶשׁ הַשֵּׁנִי בְּשִׁבְעָה־עָשָׂר יוֹם לַחֹדֶשׁ בַּיּוֹם הַזֶּה נִבְקְעוּ כָּל־מַעְיְנֹת תְּהוֹם רַבָּה וַאֲרֻבֹּת הַשָּׁמַיִם נִפְתָּחוּ:
bišanaṯ (sleep-years) *šēš* (six) *mēʾvōṯ* (hundred) *šānāh* (sleep-years) *laḥayēy* (life) *nōaḥ* (Noah) *baḥōḏeš* (lunar month) *hašēniy* (second) *bašiḇaʿāh* (seven-) *ʿāśār* (-teenth) *yvōm* (day) *laḥōḏeš* (of the lunar-month) *bayvōm* (day) *hazeh* (now) *niḇaqaʿu* (broke up) *kāl* (all) *maʿayanōṯ* (springs) *tahvōm* (deep) *rabāh* (great) *vaʾărubōṯ* (windows) *hašāmayim* (of heavens) *nipataḥu* (were opened)
ἐν *en* (in) τῷ *tō* (the) ἑξακοσιοστῷ *exakosiostō* (six hundreth) ἔτει *etei* (year) ἐν *en* (in) τῇ *tē* (the) ζωῇ *zōē* (life) τοῦ *tou* (of the) Νωε *Nōe* (Noah) τοῦ *tou* (the) δευτέρου *deuterou* (second) μηνός *mēnos* (month) ἑβδόμῃ *ebdomē* (the seventh) καὶ *kai* (and) εἰκάδι *eikadi* (twentieth day of the month)[2059] τοῦ *tou* (the) μηνός *mēnos* (month) τῇ *tē* (the) ἡμέρᾳ *ēmera* (day) ταύτῃ *tautē* (same) ἐρράγησαν *erragēsan* (broke up) πᾶσαι *pasai* (all) αἱ *ai* (the) πηγαὶ *pēgai* (springs) τῆς *tēs* (of the) ἀβύσσου *abussou* (abyss) καὶ *kai* (and) οἱ *oi* (the) καταρράκται *katarraktai* (cataracts) τοῦ *tou* (of the) οὐρανοῦ *ouranou* (sky) ἠνεῴχθησαν *ēneōchthēsan* (were opened)
anno (in the year) **sescentesimo** (six hundredth) **vitae** (of the life) **Noe** (of Noah) **mense** (in the month) **secundo** (second) **septimodecimo** (seventeenth) **die** (day) **mensis** (of the month) **rupti** (broken) **sunt** (are) **omnes** (all) **fontes** (the springs) **abyssi** (of the abyss) **magnae** (great) **et** (and) **cataractae** (the cataracts) **caeli** (of the sky) **apertae** (open) **sunt** (are)
In the six hundredth year of Noah's life, in the second month, the seventeenth day of the month, the same day were all the fountains of the great deep broken up, and the windows of heaven were opened.
In the *righteousness* (600) of Noah's resting *sleeping-abode* (2), past the *two recurring* [waking/dream] lunar cycles, the *fishes* (17) [swam] into the circularity of consciousness and now all the disturbing mental faculties from the great deep broke loose.

Let us analyze the lexicon,
- *Deep*[2060] derive from *huwm*,[2061] which means *to distract, to disturb*.
- *Month*[2062] is the new lunar cycle.[2063]
- *Seventeen*[2064] is the Gematria word equivalent to *fishes* (*daḡēy*).[2065] Again, the fish is a metaphor for the ark as well as the faculty to swim between the riverbanks of different realms.
- *Six hundred* (שֵׁשׁ־מֵאוֹת *šēš-mēʾvōṯ*) is the Gematria word equivalent to *righteousness* (*tsĕdaqah*),[2066] namely, the state beyond the *knowledge of good and evil*.
- *Springs*[2067] derive from *ʿayin*,[2068] which means *mental faculties*.
- *Two-recurring*[2069] months are the two waking and dreaming circadian cycles, also, the number 2 is equivalent to the letter ב, *b*, which has the meaning of *house* and *inhabit*.
- *Years*, *shĕnah*,[2070] mean also sleep, *shĕnah*.[2071] In fact, Daniel, in two separate verses of the same Book (§6), uses the identical Aramaic root *shĕnah* (שְׁנָה), once with the meaning of years[2072] and another indicating sleep.[2073]

Therefore, following the seventh circle of his life,[2074] after *Resting*-Noah was in his righteous abode of NREM sleep, the fishes swam in the two watery circular days (יוֹם *yowm*) of consciousness-of the wake and dream world of representation. Now,[2075] the archetypal-heaven above[2076] opens the door (פָּתַח *pethach*) of the senses[2077] pouring out all the deep distracting and disturbing possible ideas as flooding actual events and experiences of the objective world.

7:12-Forty Days and Nights of Rain

וַיְהִי הַגֶּשֶׁם עַל־הָאָרֶץ אַרְבָּעִים יוֹם וְאַרְבָּעִים לָיְלָה:
vayahiy (was) *hageshem* (rain) *ʿal* (on) *hāʾāreṣ* (earth) *ʾarabāʾiym* (forty) *yvōm* (days) *ʾarabāʾiym* (forty) *lāyalāh* (night)
καὶ *kai* (and) ἐγένετο *egeneto* (came) ὁ *o* (the) ὑετὸς *uetos* (rain) ἐπὶ *epi* (on) τῆς *tēs* (the) γῆς *gēs* (earth) τεσσαράκοντα *tessarakonta* (forty) ἡμέρας *ēmeras* (days) καὶ *kai* (and)

τεσσαράκοντα *tessarakonta* (forty) **νύκτας** *nuktas* (nights)
et (and) ***facta*** (done) ***est*** (is) ***pluvia*** (rain) ***super*** (on) ***terram*** (earth) ***quadraginta*** (forty) ***diebus*** (days) ***et*** (and) ***quadraginta*** (forty) ***noctibus*** (nights)
And the rain was upon the earth forty days and forty nights.
In fact, the rain of thoughts fell on the earth of duality *destroying* (40) in the waking-day and causing *destruction* (40) in the night-dream.

The Epic of Gilgamesh[2078] describes the flood stating that

> "*For six days and six nights the winds blew, torrent and tempest and flood overwhelmed the world, tempest and flood raged together like warring hosts.*"

Genesis describes the event in forty days. The letter מ, *m, mêm* is also the number 40, which symbolically represents the unconscious watery chaos.[2079] Furthermore, the Gematria value of the word *ḥabōl* (חֲבֹל), *you destroy*, corresponds to number 40.[2080] In addition, the Gematria value of the word *kiydwō* (כִּידוֹ), *destruction*, also matches number 40.[2081] Therefore, forty days and forty nights stand for the total destruction caused by the flow of the thinking process in which we drown, both while awake and while dreaming. The days (יוֹם *yowm*) are the consciousness-*of* the waking world in which we are desirous of our experiences. The nights (לַיִל *layil*)[2082] are the oneiric world in which we are mesmerized by the objects in our dreams. In both night and day, objectivity is the night aspect*. The term layil, night, is the* same as *luwl,*[2083] an unused root meaning *enclosed space with folding back winding staircase*. Those staircases lead down in the world's distress, where we drown. The destruction here is caused by the loss of the serene restful stage lived in the NREM *unconscious-state*, which does not need the mediation of thought to be conscious in itself. In fact, it was only the hunger for the forbidden *food for thoughts* that collapsed Adam and Eve in the mortal state.

7:13-Potential Faculties and Epistemic Forms

בְּעֶצֶם הַיּוֹם הַזֶּה בָּא נֹחַ וְשֵׁם־וְחָם וָיֶפֶת בְּנֵי־נֹחַ וְאֵשֶׁת נֹחַ וּשְׁלֹשֶׁת נְשֵׁי־בָנָיו אִתָּם אֶל־הַתֵּבָה׃
ba'eṣem (in same) *hayvōm* (day) *hazeh* (this) *bā* (entered) *nōaḥ* (Noah) *vašēm* (Shem) *vaḥām* (Ham) *vāyep̄eṯ* (Japheth) *banēy* (sons) *nōaḥ* (of Noah) *va'ēšeṯ* (wife) *nōaḥ* (of Noah) *ušalōšeṯ* (the three) *našēy* (wives) *ḇānāyv* (of sons) *'itām* (with) *'el* (them) *hatēḇāh* (in ark)
ἐν *en* (in) **τῇ** *tē* (the) **ἡμέρᾳ** *ēmera* (day) **ταύτῃ** *tautē* (same) **εἰσῆλθεν** *eisēlthen* (entered) **Νωε** *Nōe* (Noah) **Σημ** *Sēm* (Shem) **Χαμ** *Cham* (Ham) **Ιαφεθ** *Iapheth* (Japheth) **υἱοὶ** *uioi* (sons) **Νωε** *Nōe* (of Noah) **καὶ** *kai* (and) **ἡ** *ē* (the) **γυνὴ** *gunē* (wife) **Νωε** *Nōe* (of Noah) **καὶ** *kai* (and) **αἱ** *ai* (the) **τρεῖς** *treis* (three) **γυναῖκες** *guvaikes* (wives) **τῶν** *tōn* (of the) **υἱῶν** *uiōn* (sons) **αὐτοῦ** *autou* (his) **μετ'** *met'* (with) **αὐτοῦ** *autou* (him) **εἰς** *eis* (in) **τὴν** *tēn* (the) **κιβωτόν** *kibōton* (ark)
in (in) ***articulo*** (the moment) ***diei*** (of day) ***illius*** (same) ***ingressus*** (entered) ***est*** (is) ***Noe*** (Noah) ***et*** (and) ***Sem*** (Shem)***et*** (and) ***Ham*** (Ham) ***et*** (and) ***Iafeth*** (Japheth) ***filii*** (sons) ***eius*** (his) ***uxor*** (wife) ***illius*** (his) ***et*** (and) ***tres*** (the three) ***uxores*** (wives) ***filiorum*** (of sons) ***eius*** (his) ***cum*** (with) ***eis*** (him) ***in*** (in the) ***arcam*** (ark)
In the selfsame day entered Noah, and Shem, and Ham, and Japheth, the sons of Noah, and Noah's wife, and the three wives of his sons with them, into the ark;
In that same day, Noah and Shem, Ham and Japheth Noah's sons, and Noah's wife and the three wives with them, entered into the Ark;

When Noah enters his resting place, the whole world of duality disappears. All epistemic tendencies and world's possibilities go in the Ark with him. Then, the current actuality of this world retreats in the deep vastness of pure possibilities. These potentials are the waters in which is the prenatal world. They form the unconscious reality. They are the watery condition over which the Breath of Awareness hovers without mediating it with any thought.

Rested-Noah enters his internal resting place with all his potential faculties and epistemic forms, namely, object, time, space, causality, noetic and noematic aspects, metaphorically indicated as wife, sons and daughters in law. When those heavenly watery springs, those fluid potentialities will open up to rain over the earth, then they will actualize as the cacophonic flood of deadly desperate drowning thoughts submerging this world of duality.

7:14-All Ideas in their Potential State

הֵמָּה וְכָל־הַחַיָּה לְמִינָהּ וְכָל־הַבְּהֵמָה לְמִינָהּ וְכָל־הָרֶמֶשׂ הָרֹמֵשׂ עַל־הָאָרֶץ לְמִינֵהוּ וְכָל־הָעוֹף לְמִינֵהוּ כֹּל צִפּוֹר כָּל־כָּנָף׃
hēmāh (they) *vak̲āl* (all) *haḥayāh* (energy animals) *lamiynāh* (kind) *vak̲āl* (all) *habahēmāh* (beasts) *lamiynāh* (kind) *vak̲āl* (kind) *hāremeś* (creeping things) *hārōmēś* (creeping) *ʿal* (on) *hāʾāreṣ* (the earth) *lamiynēhu* (kind) *vak̲āl* (all) *hāʿvōp̄* (fowl) *lamiynēhu* (kind) *kōl* (all) *ṣipvōr* (birds) *kāl* (all) *kānāp̄* (wings)
καὶ *kai* (and) **πάντα** *panta* (all) **τὰ** *ta* (the) **θηρία** *thēria* (animals) **κατὰ** *kata* (according to) **γένος** *genos* (the species) **καὶ** *kai* (and) **πάντα** *panta* (all) **τὰ** *ta* (the) **κτήνη** *ktēnē* (cattle) **κατὰ** *kata* (according to) **γένος** *genos* (the species) **καὶ** *kai* (and) **πᾶν** *pan* (all) **ἑρπετὸν** *erpeton* (reptiles) **κινούμενον** *kinoumenon* (moving) **ἐπὶ** *epi* (on) **τῆς** *tēs* (the) **γῆς** *gēs* (earth) **κατὰ** *kata* (according to) **γένος** *genos* (the species) **καὶ** *kai* (and) **πᾶν** *pan* (all) **πετεινὸν** *peteinon* (birds) **κατὰ** *kata* (according to) **γένος** *genos* (the species)
ipsi (they) ***et*** (and) ***omne*** (every) ***animal*** (the animal) ***secundum*** (according to) ***genus*** (kind) ***suum*** (its) ***universa-*** (every)***que*** (and) ***iumenta*** (cattle) ***in*** (in) ***genus*** (kind) ***suum*** (its) ***et*** (and) ***omne*** (all) ***quod*** (which) ***movetur*** (moves) ***super*** (on) ***terram*** (earth) ***in*** (in) ***genere*** (kind) ***suo*** (its) ***cunctum-*** (all)***que*** (and) ***volatile*** (fowl) ***secundum*** (according to) ***genus*** (kind) ***suum*** (its) ***universae*** (every) ***aves*** (bird) ***omnes-*** (all) ***que*** (and) ***volucres*** (winged)
They, and every beast after his kind, and all the cattle after their kind, and every creeping thing that creepeth upon the earth after his kind, and every fowl after his kind, every bird of every sort.
With them are also every animal-idea, according to its kind and every potential cattle-thought in its category and all the serpentine-tendencies in its kind, winding on the earth of duality, and all the flying-psychological traits, according to their characteristics, and all the circling birds of consciousness hiding their wings;

To all those, who still insist on a literal interpretation of the flood, ironically, we say, *blessed are all the aquatic life animals surviving and thriving in all that devastating deluge*. However, the epistemic reader understands that every *kind*[2084] of *animal*[2085] is a metaphor for the totality of all the energy-ideas that populate the recesses of our mind-ark in their potential state. They are creeping *winding*[2086] *tendencies.*[2087] As *fowl,*[2088] they are psychological traits, as *bird*[2089] of *circling*[2090] consciousness *hiding*[2091] their *wings.*[2092] Finally, they are potential living *appetites*[2093] ready to inundate the world of duality once they exit their resting potential state in our mind-ark, to access the dream and waking grounds.

Potential ideas are not definite thoughts-*of* something. They are metaphorically *hiding* or *covering* (כָּנָף *kanaph*) their *wings* (כָּנָף *kanaph*). In fact, they are the ideation logically *preceding* the formulation-*of* definite thoughts, ideas and/or notions, *before* they actually take place by becoming airborne. As an example, consider dreaming-*of* an elephant, *of* a savory meal, or *of* a joyous feeling. Before the actual elephant, the meal and/or the joy become dreams, in the state of dreamless sleep (NREM), they are not actually that. Thus, where do they come from? They come from the unconscious reservoir,

"where can be done / all that is wanted,"[2094]

where there is the potential ability to develop and to come into existence as dreams. In turn, the dream ideas become *tangible* in the waking world, when and where the light of consciousness

"comes into the soul."[2095]

It is not the intent of this work to answer the age-old question, if ideas are *a-priori*,[2096] namely, if they precede experience, or are *a-posteriori*,[2097] thus, they emerge shaped by experience. In any case, we must recognize that we cannot state as existent what is unconceived. In fact, only after *conception* we can declare that something is. It is self-evident to say that nothing is conceivable outside the mind itself.

However, when we think-*of* the objective world as the ultimate-reality, then we die drowning in its deluge of passionate concepts and desirable ideas.

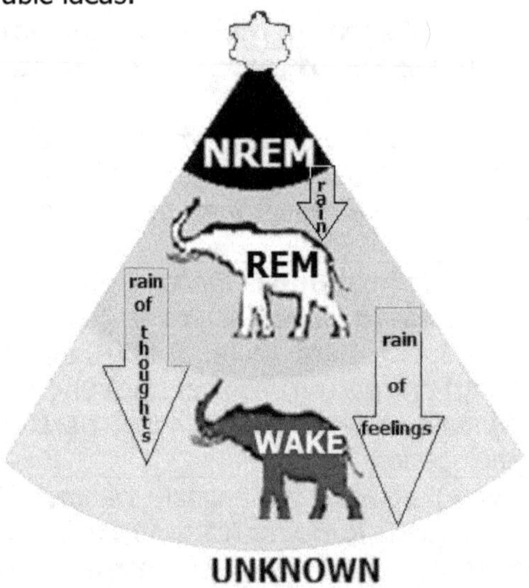

GRAPHIC: *Emergence of Ideas from NREM*

7:15-Ideas in the Mental Reservoir

וַיָּבֹאוּ אֶל־נֹחַ אֶל־הַתֵּבָה שְׁנַיִם שְׁנַיִם מִכָּל־הַבָּשָׂר אֲשֶׁר־בּוֹ רוּחַ חַיִּים׃ *vayāḇō'u* (they went into) *'el* (that) *nōaḥ* (Noah) *'el* (that) *hatēḇāh* (ark) *šanayim* (two) *šanayim* (two) *mikāl* (from) *habāśār* (all flesh-energy) *'ăšer* (which) *bvō* (in) *ruaḥ* (breath) *ḥayiym* (of life)
εἰσῆλθον *eisēlthon* (they went) **πρὸς** *pros* (to) **Νωε** *Nōe* (Noah) **εἰς** *eis* (in) **τὴν** *tēn* (the) **κιβωτόν** *kibōton* (ark) **δύο** *duo* (two) **δύο** *duo* (two) **ἀπὸ** *apo* (from) **πάσης** *pasēs* (all) **σαρκός** *sarkos* (flesh) **ἐν** *en* (in) **ᾧ** *ō* (which) **ἐστιν** *estin* (was) **πνεῦμα** *pneuma* (breath) **ζωῆς** *zōēs* (of life)
ingressae (entered) ***sunt*** (are) ***ad*** (to) ***Noe*** (Noah) ***in*** (in) ***arcam*** (the ark) ***bina*** (two) ***et*** (and) ***bina*** (two) ***ex*** (from) ***omni*** (all) ***carne*** (flesh) ***in*** (in) ***qua*** (which) ***erat*** (was) ***spiritus*** (the spirit) ***vitae*** (of life)
And they went in unto Noah into the ark, two and two of all flesh, wherein is the breath of life.
Every energy-idea, as flesh transmitting information within the breath of life, entered with the rested Noah in the mental reservoir of the ark with both their potentiality and actuality.

All the energy-ideas[2098] of the flesh transmitting information[2099] go within that state of cataleptic condition. There, they are in a sort of suspended animation, in a state of remembrance,[2100] in a potential state, where

"*God remembered Noah, and every living thing, and all the cattle that was with him in the ark.*"[2101]

There, they are in pair of potentiality and actuality. Namely, they are potentially ready for their meaningful release when they will enter in the actual presence of their signified objects, *viz.* in the waking and/or dreaming realms. In fact, as an example, the utterance of any word brings up, from the unconscious ocean of possibilities, the object signified by the idea-word pronounced. The mind becomes actually conscious of that resurrected object. Namely, if we say "frog," the idea of that anura enters your mind, where previously was not. Conversely, unexpectedly seeing that amphibian, the idea of that toad leaps into your brain. In both cases, that animal comes into existence, potentially as an idea and/or actually as a body, seemingly from nowhere. As Aristotle pointed out, nothing passes from potency into act without having been prior in act.[2102] That which is in potency must contain in-itself also its act, otherwise it could not pass into actuality. Like a tree must be present completely in the DNA-*memory*-record of its seed in order to become a plant producer of its own seeds.

7:16-The Ark Closes

וְהַבָּאִים זָכָר וּנְקֵבָה מִכָּל־בָּשָׂר בָּאוּ כַּאֲשֶׁר צִוָּה אֹתוֹ אֱלֹהִים וַיִּסְגֹּר יְהוָה בַּעֲדוֹ׃
vahabā'iym (they went in) *zāḵār* (male) *unaqēḇāh* (female) *mikāl* (from every) *bāśār* (flesh) *bā'u* (went) *ka'ăšer* (as) *ṣiuāh* (commanded) *'ōṯvō* (with) *'ĕlōhiym* (the Gods) *vayisagōr* (shot in) *yahvāh* (the Transcendent) *ba'ăḏvō* (behind)
καὶ *kai* (and) **τὰ** *ta* (the) **εἰσπορευόμενα** *eisporeuomena* (entered) **ἄρσεν** *arsen* (male) **καὶ** *kai* (and) **θῆλυ** *thēlu* (female) **ἀπὸ** *apo* (from) **πάσης** *pasēs* (all) **σαρκὸς** *sarkos* (flesh) **εἰσῆλθεν** *eisēlthen* (went in) **καθὰ** *katha* (according to) **ἐνετείλατο** *eneteilato* (commanded) **ὁ** *o* (the) **θεὸς** *theos* (God) **τῷ** *tō* (to the) **Νωε** *Nōe* (Noah)[2103] **καὶ** *kai* (and) **ἔκλεισεν** *ekleisen* (shot in) **κύριος** *kurios* (Lord) **ὁ** *o* (the) **θεὸς** *theos* (God) **ἔξωθεν** *exōthen* (from without) **αὐτοῦ** *autou* (of him) **τὴν** *tēn* (the) **κιβωτόν** *kibōton* (ark)
et (and) ***quae*** (those that) ***ingressa*** (entered) ***sunt*** (are) ***masculus*** (male) ***et*** (and) ***femina*** (female) ***ex*** (out of) ***omni*** (every) ***carne*** (flesh) ***introierunt*** (went in) ***sicut*** (as) ***praeceperat*** (commanded) ***ei*** (him) ***Deus*** (God) ***et*** (and) ***inclusit*** (closed) ***eum*** (him) ***Dominus*** (Lord) ***de*** (from) ***foris*** (outside)
And they that went in, went in male and female of all flesh, as God had commanded him: and the LORD shut him in.
Those that entered were male-noetic and female-noematic aspects of all sentient beings. They went in as Divine-Consciousness had commanded him and the Transcendent shot him in the Ark from behind.

When we consider the quantity and diversity of animals in the ark, without considering the unmentioned insects,[2104] fish and plants, then the literal reading of this verse is clearly absurd.[2105] In reality, ideas enter the reservoir of unconscious memory with their pair of potential noetic and noematic aspects. The Ark itself is a symbol for all marine life metaphorically transporting from one state of being to another. The Ark and Noah are similar to the account of Jonah and the whale. There the Ark becomes a

> "*great fish* [covering] *to swallow up Jonah. And Jonah was in the belly of the fish three days and three nights,*"[2106]

corresponding to the three levels of the Ark, namely, the three circles of consciousness, *i.e.*: the waking, dreaming and deep sleep states.

Ancient Indian sacred texts[2107] describe this sleep as the

> "*deep-unconscious-sleep,*[2108] *the third quadrant, where one asleep does not desire any desire*[2109] *does not see any dream.*[2110] *The state of deep-unconscious-sleep* [stands] *alone, having become one compact knowledge, made of bliss. Indeed,* [it is] *the enjoyer of bliss. Its mouth is consciousness* [and] *the knower.*"[2111]
>
> "*Thus, when a person is sleeping, so that s/he sees no dream whatsoever, verily s/he becomes one with that breathing self. Then, speech together with all the names goes to him. The eye together with all the forms goes to him. The ear together with all sounds goes to him. The mind together with all thoughts goes to him. When he awakens, as from a blazing fire, sparks spread out in all directions. Similarly, therefore, from this self the vital breaths spread out each in its own place. From the vital breaths, the resplendent senses* [spread out] *and from the resplendent senses the worlds spread out.*"[2112]

7:17-The Floating Ark

וַיְהִי הַמַּבּוּל אַרְבָּעִים יוֹם עַל־הָאָרֶץ וַיִּרְבּוּ הַמַּיִם וַיִּשְׂאוּ אֶת־הַתֵּבָה וַתָּרָם מֵעַל הָאָרֶץ׃
vayahiy (was) *hamabul* (the flood) *'arabā'iym* (forty) *yvōm* (days) *'al* (on) *hā'āreṣ* (the earth) *vayirabu* (multiplied) *hamayim* (waters) *vayiśa'u* (lift up) *'eṯ* (with) *hatēḇāh* (ark) *vatārām* (raised) *mē'al* (up from) *hā'āreṣ* (the earth)
καὶ *kai* (and) **ἐγένετο** *egeneto* (was) **ὁ** *o* (the) **κατακλυσμὸς** *kataklusmos* (the cathaclism) **τεσσαράκοντα** *tessarakonta* (forty) **ἡμέρας** *ēmeras* (days) **καὶ** *kai* (and) **τεσσαράκοντα** *tessarakonta* (forty) **νύκτας** *nuktas* (nights)[2113] **ἐπὶ** *epi* (on) **τῆς** *tēs* (the) **γῆς** *gēs* (earth) **καὶ** *kai*

(and) **ἐπληθύνθη** *eplēthunthē* (increased) **τὸ** *to* (the) **ὕδωρ** *udōr* (water) **καὶ** *kai* (and) **ἐπῆρεν** *epēren* (raised) **τὴν** *tēn* (the) **κιβωτόν** *kibōton* (ark) **καὶ** *kai* (and) **ὑψώθη** *upsōthē* (high) **ἀπὸ** *apo* (over) **τῆς** *tēs* (the) **γῆς** *gēs* (earth)
factum- (done)***que*** (and) ***est*** (is) ***diluvium*** (deluge) ***quadraginta*** (forty) ***diebus*** (days) ***super*** (on) ***terram*** (the earth) ***et*** (and) ***multiplicatae*** (multiplied) ***sunt*** (are) ***aquae*** (the waters) ***et*** (and) ***elevaverunt*** (lifted up) ***arcam*** (the ark) ***in*** (on) ***sublime*** (high) ***a*** (from) ***terra*** (the earth)
And the flood was forty days upon the earth; and the waters increased, and bare up the ark, and it was lift up above the earth.
For *forty-destructive* days, the deluge was upon the earth and the waters increased and lifted up the ark above the earth.

The days (יוֹם *yowm*) are metaphors for the whirlpool-thought-consciousness-*of* the deluge. Those thoughts distract the mind away from its own Foundation, namely, the Certain-Conscious-Awareness.

"*Death comes and carries off that man, praised for his children and flocks, his mind distracted, as a flood carries off a sleeping village.*"[2114]

As we have seen, the Gematria value of the word destruction equals forty (אַרְבָּעִים *'arba`iym*). Thus, the flood (מַבּוּל *mabbuwl*) of thoughts causes havoc and destruction for every being, caught in it. Nevertheless, we must clarify that it is not the thought as such that causes pain and devastation. From the human perspective we call it thought. Nevertheless, it is the flooding experience-*of*--attachments, which every sentient being identifies with.

"Keep your soul from gazing and your mind from conceiving, lest you drown."[2115]

Humans, animals, plants and physical objects, all exist submerged in this time-space-flooded world. However, the paradox is that the watery devastation is also the mean of *salvation*. In fact, the water itself, the cause of that desolation and tribulation, *lifts up*[2116] the Ark saving all its occupants. That is, the objective time-flow, with which we identify and in which we drown, testifies and pushes us up to its own fundamental Eternal-Present-Awareness, which we discarded without recognizing that it was

"*the light of the world. A city that is set on an hill cannot be hid.*"[2117]

7:18-Above the Chaos

וַיִּגְבְּרוּ הַמַּיִם וַיִּרְבּוּ מְאֹד עַל־הָאָרֶץ וַתֵּלֶךְ הַתֵּבָה עַל־פְּנֵי הַמָּיִם׃ *vayiḡabaru* (prevailed) *hamayim* (the waters) *vayirabu* (multiplied) *ma'ōḏ* (exceedingly) *'al* (on) *hā'āreṣ* (the earth) *vatēleḵa* (went) *hatēḇāh* (ark) *'al* (on) *panēy* (face) *hamāyim* (of the waters)
καὶ *kai* (and) **ἐπεκράτει** *epekratei* (were strong) **τὸ** *to* (the) **ὕδωρ** *udōr* (water) **καὶ** *kai* (and) **ἐπληθύνετο** *eplēthuneto* (multiplied) **σφόδρα** *sphodra* (excessively) **ἐπὶ** *epi* (on) **τῆς** *tēs* (the) **γῆς** *gēs* (earth) **καὶ** *kai* (and) **ἐπεφέρετο** *epephereto* (transported) **ἡ** *ē* (the) **κιβωτὸς** *kibōtos* (ark) **ἐπάνω** *epanō* (above) **τοῦ** *tou* (the) **ὕδατος** *udator* (waters)
vehementer (very strongly) ***inundaverunt*** (inundated) ***et*** (and) ***omnia*** (all) ***repleverunt*** () ***in*** (over) ***superficie*** (the surface) ***terrae*** (of the earth) ***porro*** (following) ***arca*** (ark) ***ferebatur*** (transported) ***super*** (over) ***aquas*** (the waters)
And the waters prevailed, and were increased greatly upon the earth; and the ark went upon the face of the waters.
The waters prevailed and greatly multiplied on the earth and the ark was transported over the waters.

As 'Elohiym's Breath of Divine-Consciousness hovers over the *Waters*, similarly, the Ark floats over the flooding waters. In this world of duality, experiences multiply (רבה *rabah*) exponentially (מְאֹד *m@`od*) with every event of the day. Metaphorically the waters are the strong (גָּבַר *gabar*) overpowering events, which submerge every sentient being. Picture the flood like a flow of exponentially reproducing information traveling through a computer program. That information finds its way on the screen of the processor. Thus, the waters take the Ark up to the light of Awareness. That is because all experiences are *witnesses* of the Pure-Aware-Certitude. The water-experiences testify Awareness, which is their foundation without which the earth and the deluge itself could not be.[2118] Similarly, we can attempt to read Paul's affirmation,

"The invisible things of him from the creation of the world are clearly seen, being understood by the things that are made."[2119]

Since we do not use the word "Awareness" as a synonym of "consciousness-*of*-something," a clarification is necessary again. By Awareness, we mean Certainty or Apodictic-Faith. However, Awareness is not the conceptualization-*of* Certainty itself. It is Certainty as that which causes the immediate thoughtless response of all beings to stimuli. However, it is not the stimulus itself. It is the Apodictic-Certitude present in everything here and now. While being always Certain-In-Itself, Certitude does not need to think of being certain. In fact, the intervention of thought is not the Certain-Faith. Apodicticity cannot be explained by words, but words cannot express anything without It.

7:19-All Is Flooded Below Heaven

וְהַמַּיִם גָּבְרוּ מְאֹד מְאֹד עַל־הָאָרֶץ וַיְכֻסּוּ כָּל־הֶהָרִים הַגְּבֹהִים אֲשֶׁר־תַּחַת כָּל־הַשָּׁמָיִם׃ *vahamayim* (the waters) *gāḇaru* (prevailed) *ma'ōḏ* (exceedingly) ma'ōḏ (exceedingly) *'al* (on) *hā'āreṣ* (the earth) *vayakusu* (were covered) *kāl* (all) *hehāriym* (mountains) *hagaḇōhiym* (high) *'ăšer* (which) *taḥaṯ* (under) *kāl* (the whole) *hašāmāyim* (heaven)
τὸ *to* (the) **δὲ** *de* (but) **ὕδωρ** *udōr* (water) **ἐπεκράτει** *epekratei* (were strong) **σφόδρα** *sphodra* (eccessively) **σφοδρῶς** *sphodrōs* (intense) **ἐπὶ** *epi* (on) **τῆς** *tēs* (the) **γῆς** *gēs* (earth) **καὶ** *kai* (and) **ἐπεκάλυψεν** *epekalupsen* (covered up) **πάντα** *panta* (all) **τὰ** *ta* (the) **ὄρη** *orē* (mountains) **τὰ** *ta* (the) **ὑψηλά** *upsēla* (high) **ἃ** *a* (which) **ἦν** *ēn* (were) **ὑποκάτω** *upokatō* (below) **τοῦ** *tou* (the) **οὐρανοῦ** *ouranou* (sky)
et (and) ***aquae*** (the waters) ***praevaluerunt*** (prevailed) ***nimis*** (excessively) ***super*** (on) ***terram*** (the earth) ***operti-*** (covered) ***que*** (and) ***sunt*** (are) ***omnes*** (all) ***montes*** (the mountains) ***excelsi*** (very high) ***sub*** (under) ***universo*** (the entire) ***caelo*** (sky)
And the waters prevailed exceedingly upon the earth; and all the high hills, that were under the whole heaven, were covered.
The waters-of-experiences excessively prevailed over the whole earth-of-objectivity. They covered all the high ideologies that were below the entire heavenly dome of Awareness.

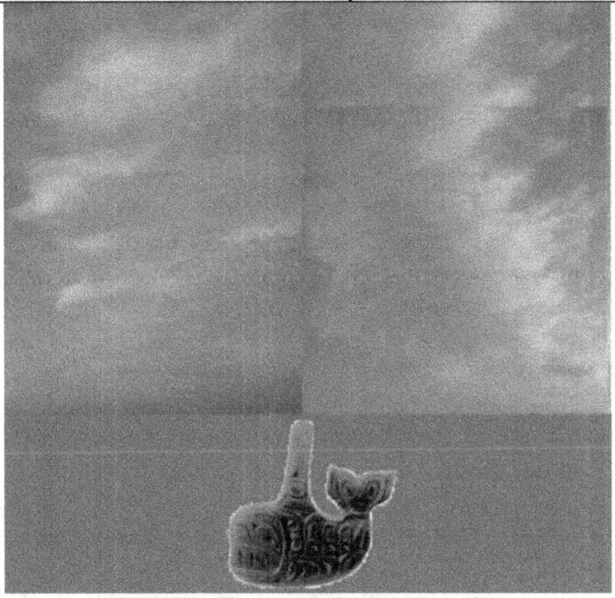

GRAPHIC: *The Waters Covering Everything*

The existential flood covers everything in the mind and on this world. It spares nothing. It affects everything. Even the highest (גָּבֹהַּ *gaboahh*) mountains[2120] are submerged by the cataclysm. In fact, that deluge floods all stimuli, ideas, meanings and ideologies. Furthermore, here, the mountains are symbols for concepts related to higher ideology and/or religious beliefs,[2121] like "*the* <u>*mountain*</u> *of Divine-Consciousness,*"[2122]

"Sinai, as the abode of Jehovah... Zion... the holy land, as being mountainous."[2123]

All meanings may be high. Nevertheless, they are below (תחת *tachath*) the sky.

"There is nothing to say about life. It has no meaning. You make meaning. If you want a meaning in your life, find a meaning and bring it into your life, but life won't give you a meaning. Meaning is a concept. It is a notion of an end toward which you are going."[2124]

These ideological mountains never reach the heaven (שָׁמַיִם *shamayim*) of Aware-Certitude.

7:20-Waters Founded on Perilous Calamity

חֲמֵשׁ עֶשְׂרֵה אַמָּה מִלְמַעְלָה גָּבְרוּ הַמָּיִם וַיְכֻסּוּ הֶהָרִים׃
ḥămēš (five) *ʿeśarēh* (ten) *ʾamāh* (cubits) *milamaʿalāh* (upwards) *gāḇaru* (prevailed) *hamāyim* (waters) *vayaḵusu* (concealed) *hehāriym* (the mountains)
δέκα *deka* (ten) **πέντε** *pente* (five) **πήχεις** *pēcheis* (cubits) **ἐπάνω** *epanō* (above) **ὑψώθη** *upsōthē* (lift up) **τὸ** *to* (the) **ὕδωρ** *udōr* (waters) **καὶ** *kai* (and) **ἐπεκάλυψεν** *epekalupsen* (covered) **πάντα** *panta* (all) **τὰ** *ta* (the) **ὄρη** *orē* (mountains) **τὰ** *ta* (the) **ὑψηλά** *upsēla* (high)
quindecim (fifteen) ***cubitis*** (cubits) ***altior*** (higher) ***fuit*** (was) ***aqua*** (the water) ***super*** (over) ***montes*** (the mountains) ***quos*** (that) ***operuerat*** (concealed)
Fifteen cubits upward did the waters prevail; and the mountains were covered.
The waters, founded on that *perilous calamity*, were *high* (15) over the ideal-mountains concealing them.

As we have seen, the cubit (אַמָּה *'ammah*) is a metaphor for *foundation* and *grounding*. Furthermore, the Gematria numerical value of fifteen (חֲמֵשׁ עֶשְׂרֵה *ḥămēš 'eśarēh*) equals to the words, *high,*[2125] *treacherous,*[2126] *calamity*[2127] and *perish.*[2128] Therefore, the foundation of those floodwaters (מַיִם *mayim*) is this high treacherous calamity in which we all perish. This is the same situation in which Adam and Eve found themselves. In fact, they encountered death when, to be like God, they *eat* the fruit of conceptual knowledge. Then, also the *mountainous* (הַר *har*) *idea of god* was flooded by the *hunger* of the conceptual world.

Those waters of conceptualization concealed (כסה *kacah*) everything including all the high religious and/or moral thoughts. That is to say, those ideas, when flooded by the world perceived for-itself, lost their real *Heavenly-*(שָׁמַיִם *shamayim*)*- Truth-In-Itself.* Again, that **Truth is Awareness.**

One form of these flooded mountains is the literal reading and interpretation of sacred texts distorted by conceptual and empirical understandings. While the immanent world <u>for</u>-itself totally submerges us, the Transcendent <u>In</u>-Itself remains unknown, completely concealed, but always present as the metaphorical Heaven Above.

7:21-We All Die in This Flood

וַיִּגְוַע כָּל־בָּשָׂר הָרֹמֵשׂ עַל־הָאָרֶץ בָּעוֹף וּבַבְּהֵמָה וּבַחַיָּה וּבְכָל־הַשֶּׁרֶץ הַשֹּׁרֵץ עַל־הָאָרֶץ וְכֹל הָאָדָם׃
vayiḡavaʿ (died) *kāl* (all) *bāśār* (flesh) *hārōmēś* (move) *ʿal* (on) *hāʾāreṣ* (earth) *bāʿvōp̄* (fowl) *uḇabahēmāh* (beast) *uḇaḥayāh* (*living*) *uḇaḵāl* (every) *hašereṣ* (creeping) *hāsōmēś* (that creeps) *ʿal* (on) *hāʾāreṣ* (earth) *vaḵōl* (all) *hāʾāḏām* (humanity)
καὶ *kai* (and) **ἀπέθανεν** *apethanen* (died) **πᾶσα** *pasa* (all) **σὰρξ** *sarx* (flesh) **κινουμένη** *kinoumenē* (that moved) **ἐπὶ** *epi* (on) **τῆς** *tēs* (the) **γῆς** *gēs* (earth) **τῶν** *tōn* (the) **πετεινῶν** *peteinōn* (birds) **καὶ** *kai* (and) **τῶν** *tōn* (the) **κτηνῶν** *ktēnōn* (cattle) **καὶ** *kai* (and) **τῶν** *tōn* (the) **θηρίων** *thēriōn* (animals) **καὶ** *kai* () **πᾶν** *pan* (all) **ἑρπετὸν** *erpeton* (sepents) **κινούμενον** *kinoumenon* (moving) **ἐπὶ** *epi* (on) **τῆς** *tēs* (the) **γῆς** *gēs* (earth) **καὶ** *kai* (and) **πᾶς** *pas* (all) **ἄνθρωπος** *anthrōpos* (men)
consumpta- (died)***que*** (and) ***est*** (is) ***omnis*** (all) ***caro*** (flesh) ***quae*** (that) ***movebatur*** (moved) ***super*** (over) ***terram*** (the earth) ***volucrum*** (the birds) ***animantium*** (the living) ***bestiarum*** (animals) ***omnium-*** (all)***que*** (and) ***reptilium*** (reptiles) ***quae*** (that) ***reptant*** (crawl) ***super*** (on) ***terram*** (the earth) ***universi*** (all) ***homines*** (men)
And all flesh died that moved upon the earth, both of fowl, and of cattle, and of beast,

and of every creeping thing that creepeth upon the earth, and every man:
All sentient beings moving on earth, the psychological traits, the vital-energies, the energetic-ideas, all the tendencies that meander on the earth and every human being died.

Literal interpretations project the flood in past prehistoric time. However, **we currently drown in this universal flood**. Heraclitus reports that

"everything flows."[2129]

In fact, everything flows before our consciousness. Everything is in motion. Time flies.

"*This divided*[2130]*-flowing time is the great river of creatures.*"[2131]

In this river, you can never step twice in the same water. Experiences and feelings come in waves, one after the other. Thoughts chase each other without any rest. The outcome of all this is death. The cause of death is this drowning. Namely, drowning is the absence of oxygen. Metaphorically, this means that the vivifying Breath (רוּחַ *ruwach*) or the Tree-of-Life (חַי *chay*) is lost. This is the actual condition of the entire world. Visit the graveyards. In them, everybody is dead and everyone alive is on line waiting to fill those graves.

Every sentient being, performing in today's world of duality, is subject to death. All the energy-ideas, all tendencies, all psychological traits, all appetites of any specie is destined to die and will die (גָּוַע *gava`*).

"Ashes, Ashes. / We all fall down."[2132]

GRAPHIC: *All Types of Cemeteries and or Cremation Sites Are Proof of the Current Flood.*

God does not accept Cain's offer, the fruit of his land-toiling. The flood, in which we drown, is the persistent flow of possessive objectivity at the time of death. It is dying while still attached to our earthly passionate-possessions. That is the meaning of drowning in the flood. , On the other hand, the waist land that ensues is the disappearance of the world once we enter death. From the perspective of the deceased, death is the surging of unattached Awareness. Leveling everyone,[2133] for the average dying Cain, death is the shutting down of the consciousness-*of,* while remaining personally unaware within the Infinite Serene Ocean of Universal Awareness.

7:22-The Shores of Death

כֹּל אֲשֶׁר נִשְׁמַת־רוּחַ חַיִּים בְּאַפָּיו מִכֹּל אֲשֶׁר בֶּחָרָבָה מֵתוּ׃   *kōl* (all) *'ăšer* (whose) *nišamaṯ* (of breath) *ruaḥ* (spirit) *ḥayiym* (living) *ba'apāyv* (nostril) *mikōl* (from) *'ăšer* (who) *beḥārāḇāh* (wasted land) *mēṯu* (died)
καὶ *kai* (and) **πάντα** *panta* (all) **ὅσα** *osa* (which) **ἔχει** *echei* (have) **πνοὴν** *pnoēn* (breath) **ζωῆς** *zōēs* (of life) **καὶ** *kai* (and) **πᾶς** *pas* (all) **ὃς** *os* (that) **ἦν** *ēn* (was) **ἐπὶ** *epi* (on) **τῆς** *tēs* (the) **ξηρᾶς** *xēras* (dry land) **ἀπέθανεν** *apethanen* (died)
et (and) ***cuncta*** (all) ***in*** (in) ***quibus*** (whom) ***spiraculum*** (the breath) ***vitae*** (of life) ***est*** (is) ***in*** (on) ***terra*** (earth) ***mortua*** (dead) ***sunt*** (are)
All in whose nostrils was the breath of life, of all that was in the dry land, died.
Everyone in whose nostrils was the breath of life and all that was on the wasted space, died.

Inexplicably, the text does not mention air blowing cetaceans. Along with all the oxygen breathing (נְשָׁמָה *nĕshamah*) marine mammals, there is also silence over all the other aquatic life. It is not clear why the *blessed* fish are not mentioned among the ark[2134] populations and live on, while all other animals on *dry land* must die (מוּת *muwth*). This proves the clear incongruence[2135] of a literal reading.

Truthfully, the Ark itself symbolizes all marine life. In fact, that metaphorical vessel, like a fish,[2136] crosses the waters to connect different shores or states of being. It leads us from wakefulness to dream, from this one to dreamless sleep and back to wakefulness again. This is the time past. This is the wasted land space.[2137] On these shores, everyone dies (מוּת *muwth*).

7:23-Only in the Ark There Is Salvation

וַיִּמַח אֶת־כָּל־הַיְקוּם אֲשֶׁר עַל־פְּנֵי הָאֲדָמָה מֵאָדָם עַד־בְּהֵמָה עַד־רֶמֶשׂ וְעַד־עוֹף הַשָּׁמַיִם וַיִּמָּחוּ מִן־הָאָרֶץ וַיִּשָּׁאֶר אַךְ־נֹחַ וַאֲשֶׁר אִתּוֹ בַּתֵּבָה׃   *vayimaḥ* (was destroyed) *'eṯ* (and) *kāl* (all) *hayaqum* (existing being) *'ăšer* (which) *'al* (on) *panēy* (face) *hā'ăḏāmāh* (of the yielding land) *mē'āḏām* (from man) *'aḏ* (to) *bahēmāh* (animal) *'aḏ* (to) *remeś* (creeping things) *va'aḏ* (to) *'vōp̄* (birds) *hašāmayim* (of the sky) *vayimāḥu* (was destroyed) *min* (from) *hā'āreṣ* (the earth) *vayišā'er* (remained) *'aḵa* (only) *nōaḥ* (Noah) *va'ăšer* (which) *'itvō* (with) *batēḇāh* (the ark)
καὶ *kai* (and) **ἐξήλειψεν** *exēlripsen* (was obliterated) **πᾶν** *pan* (all) **τὸ** *to* (the) **ἀνάστημα** *anastēma* (existing beings) **ὃ** *o* (thus) **ἦν** *ēn* (was) **ἐπὶ** *epi* (on) **προσώπου** *prosōpou* (face) **πάσης** *pasēs* (all) **τῆς** *tēs* (the) **γῆς** *gēs* (earth) **ἀπὸ** *apo* (from) **ἀνθρώπου** *anthrōpou* (human) **ἕως** *eōs* (to) **κτήνους** *ktēnous* (animal) **καὶ** *kai* (and) **ἑρπετῶν** *erpetōv* (serpent) **καὶ** *kai* (and) **τῶν** *tōv* (the) **πετεινῶν** *peteinōn* (birds) **τοῦ** *tou* (of the) **οὐρανοῦ** *ouranou* (sky) **καὶ** *kai* (and) **ἐξηλείφθησαν** *exēleiphthēsan* (were obliterated) **ἀπὸ** *apo* (on) **τῆς** *tēs* (the) **γῆς** *gēs* (earth) **καὶ** *kai* (and) **κατελείφθη** *kateleiphthē* (left) **μόνος** *monos* (only) **Νωε** *Nōe* (Noah) **καὶ** *kai* (and) **οἱ** *oi* (those) **μετ'** *met'* (with) **αὐτοῦ** *autou* (him) **ἐν** *en* (in) **τῇ** *tē* (the) **κιβωτῷ** *kibōtō* (ark)
et (and) ***delevit*** (was destroyed) ***omnem*** (all) ***substantiam*** (substance) ***quae*** (that) ***erat*** (was) ***super*** (on) ***terram*** (the earth) ***ab*** (from) ***homine*** (humans) ***usque*** (till) ***ad*** (the) ***pecus*** (cattle) ***tam*** (also) ***reptile*** (the reptiles) ***quam*** (together with) ***volucres*** (the birds) ***caeli*** (of the sky) ***et*** (and) ***deleta*** (deleted) ***sunt*** (are) ***de*** (from) ***terra*** (the earth) ***remansit*** (remained) ***autem*** (also) ***solus*** (alone) ***Noe*** (Noah) ***et*** (and) ***qui*** (who) ***cum*** (with) ***eo*** (him) ***erant*** (were) ***in*** (in) ***arca*** (the ark)
And every living substance was destroyed which was upon the face of the ground, both man, and cattle, and the creeping things, and the fowl of the heaven; and they were destroyed from the earth: and Noah only remained alive, and they that were with him in the ark.
Every existing being on the face of the earth of duality, humans, vital-energies, tendencies, psychological traits, was destroyed. Only rested-Noah with those in the ark remained.

From their sidereal stillness, the heavens witness while the deluge ravages on earth and we live and drown in this flood. All living beings die, unless they surfaced with the ark. No cries, no prayers and no help invocations are effective for the drowning ones. Prayer is only the preparation to silent stillness. In fact, invocations are still thoughts, thus, will not save them.

> "*Not every one that saith unto me, Lord, Lord, shall enter into the kingdom of heaven; but he that doeth the will of my Father which is in heaven.*"[2138]

The will of the Heavenly Father is that of Awareness. Its transcendence <is further confirmed by Jesus, when he states,

> "*Our Founding-Father, which art Transcendent-in-heaven.*"[2139]

Namely, heaven is *trans*, beyond, above, on the other side. It is that which must be *ascended*. Apodictical-Self-Awareness is the Fundamental-Transcendent-Reality.

> "*May Thy power-name be hallowed.*"[2140]

May we acknowledge and identify with the Certitude-Awareness that shines here and now as the Apodictical Foundation of the consciousness-*of* this objective world.

> "*May Thy ruler-ship-kingdom come-by-being-manifest.*"[2141]

That identification takes place once we realize the fundamental absolute value of the Apodictical Self-Awareness without which nothing is possible. The world is only "*through It, with It, in It.*" Even if one denies It, also that denial is still

> "*through It, with It, in It.*"[2142]
>
> "*May Thy purposeful-will be done-and-manifest, as it is in the Transcendent-heaven so it is in the immanent-world.*"[2143]

The Transcendent-Self-Awareness shines in-Itself, so we may identify with It, as It shines enlightening the consciousness-*of* this objective world. Pure-Consciousness is the enlightenment, *through Awareness, with Awareness, in Awareness*. Mindful-Consciousness enlightens this objective world. When the world reflects that light back, consciousness becomes conscious-*only-of-that-reflected-light*, thus identifies with the object losing its identification with Awareness.

Only in Awareness>[2144]

> "*you shall realize the truth, and the truth shall make you free.*"[2145]

Only Noah, in a state of *restful stillness* with all the potential faculties, are spared (שָׁאַר *sha'ar*) and they sail towards the Truthful shores of Awareness.

7:24-The Deluge Causes Oppressions and Afflictions

וַיִּגְבְּרוּ הַמַּיִם עַל־הָאָרֶץ חֲמִשִּׁים וּמְאַת יוֹם׃ *vayigābaru* (prevailed) *hamayim* (waters) *'al* (over) *hā'āreṣ* (the earth) *ḥămišiym* (fifty) *uma'at̲* (hundred) *yvōm* (days)
καὶ *kai* (and) **ὑψώθη** *upsōthē* (raised up) **τὸ** *to* (the) **ὕδωρ** *udōr* (water) **ἐπὶ** *epi* (on) **τῆς** *tēs* (the) **γῆς** *gēs* (earth) **ἡμέρας** *ēmeras* (days) **ἑκατὸν** *ekatov* (hundred) **πεντήκοντα** *pentēkonta* (fifty)
obtinuerunt- (prevailed) ***que*** (and) ***aquae*** (the waters) ***terras*** (earth) ***centum*** (hundred) ***quinquaginta*** (fifty) ***diebus*** (days)
And the waters prevailed upon the earth an hundred and fifty days.
The waters prevailing *upon* (150) the earth were the consciousness-*of grief* and *affliction covers* (150) us.

What is the meaning of one hundred and fifty (וּמְאַת חֲמִשִּׁים *ḥămišiym uma'at̲*) days of water prevailing (גָּבַר *gabar*) upon (עַל *'al*) the earth? First, the waters are the fluidity of all experiences flooding our life. The days are circularities of consciousness numbering 150. Various Gematria word-values, each adding up to 150, fit the existential status of the flood. Daily, we live *upon* (=#150)[2146] this earth while *covered* (=#150)[2147] and *oppressed* (=#150)[2148] by that flood and waiting to die. This life is characterized by days in which we are *vexed* (=#150)[2149] and conscious-*of* *affliction* (=#150),[2150] *grief* (=#150),[2151] *lament* (=#150)[2152] and *wailing* (=#150).[2153] Everyone is

> "*troubled: thou takest away their breath, they die, and return to their dust.*"[2154]

From the depth of the psyche, all flooding thoughts distract and disturb the resting mind and, in that travail, we all inevitably perish.

HERE ENDS THE SEVENTH CHAPTER OF THE DELUGE

CHAPTER 8

THE CURSE REVERSED

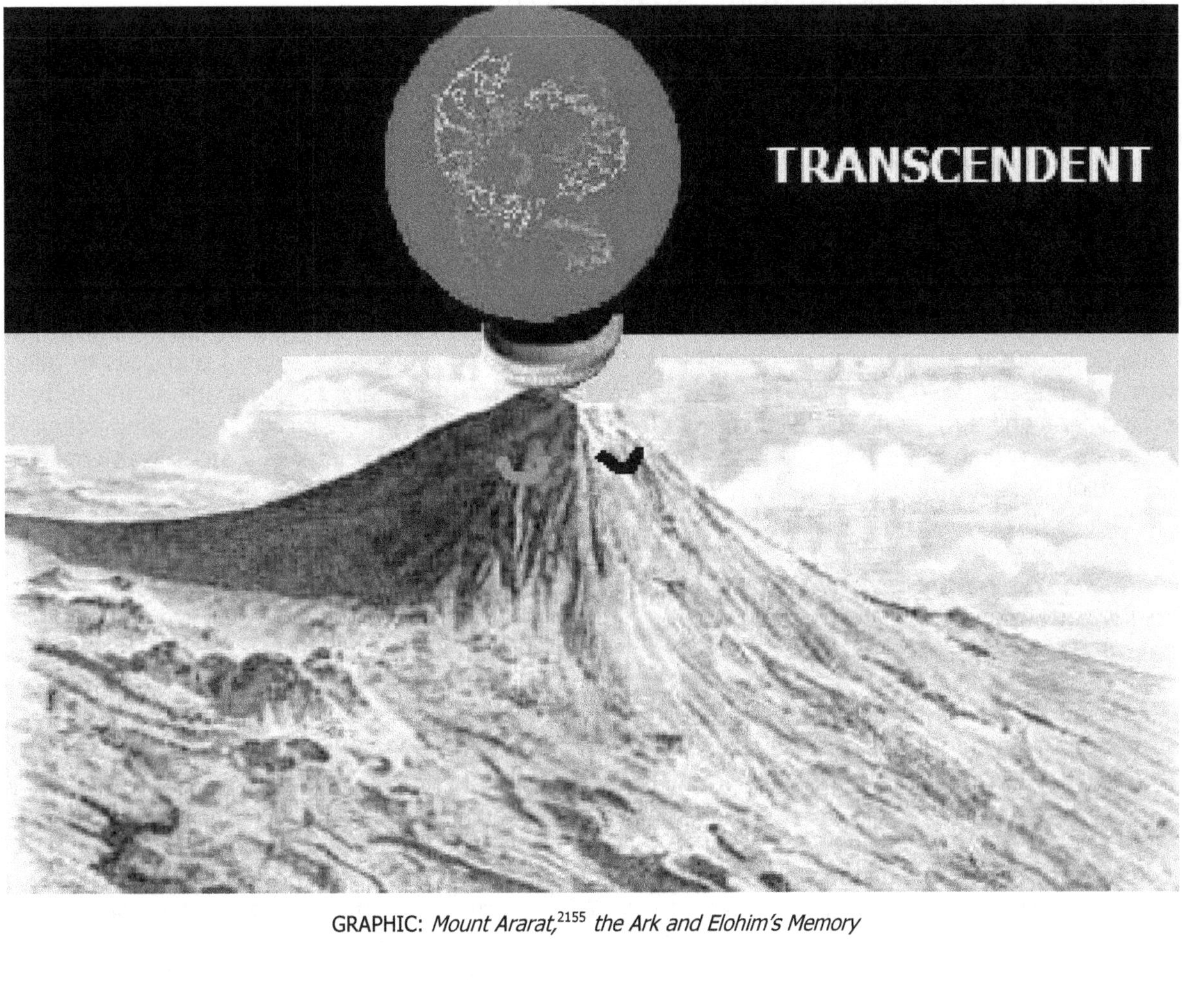

GRAPHIC: *Mount Ararat,*[2155] *the Ark and Elohim's Memory*

8-I SECTION: THE DRY EARTH

8:1-The Breath of Remembrance

וַיִּזְכֹּר אֱלֹהִים אֶת־נֹחַ וְאֵת כָּל־הַחַיָּה וְאֶת־כָּל־הַבְּהֵמָה אֲשֶׁר אִתּוֹ בַּתֵּבָה וַיַּעֲבֵר אֱלֹהִים רוּחַ עַל־הָאָרֶץ וַיָּשֹׁכּוּ הַמָּיִם׃   *vayizəkōr* (remembered) *'ĕlōhiym* (the Gods) *'eṯ* (and) *nōaḥ* (Noah) *və'ēṯ* (with) *kāl* (all) *haḥayāh* (living) *və'eṯ* (with) *kāl* (all) *habəhēmāh* (animals) *'ăšer* (which) *'itvō* (with) *batēḇāh* (ark) *vaya'ăḇēr* (pass over) *'ĕlōhiym* (the Gods) *ruaḥ* (wind) *'al* (on) *hā'āreṣ* (earth) *vayāšōku* (subsided) *hamāyim* (waters)
καὶ *kai* (and) **ἐμνήσθη** *emnēsthē* (remembered) **ὁ** *o* (the) **θεὸς** *theos* (God) **τοῦ** *tou* (the) **Νωε** *Nōe* (Noah) **καὶ** *kai* (and) **πάντων** *pantōn* (all) **τῶν** *tōn* (the) **θηρίων** *thēriōn* (beast) **καὶ** *kai* (and) **πάντων** *pantōn* (all) **τῶν** *tōn* (the) **κτηνῶν** *ktēnōn* (cattle) **καὶ** *kai* (and) **πάντων** *pantōn* (all) **τῶν** *tōn* (the) **πετεινῶν** *peteinōn* (birds) **καὶ** *kai* (and) **πάντων** *pantōn* (all) **τῶν** *tōn* (the) **ἑρπετῶν** *erpetōn* (serpents)[2156] **ὅσα** *osa* (as many) **ἦν** *ēn* (were) **μετ'** *met'* (with) **αὐτοῦ** *autou* (him) **ἐν** *en* (in) **τῇ** *tē* (the) **κιβωτῷ** *kibōtō* (ark) **καὶ** *kai* (and) **ἐπήγαγεν** *epēgagen* (brought) **ὁ** *o* (the) **θεὸς** *theos* (God) **πνεῦμα** *epeuma* (a wind) **ἐπὶ** *epi* (on) **τὴν** *tēn* (the) **γῆν** *gēn* (earth) **καὶ** *kai* (and) **ἐκόπασεν** *ekopasen* (subsided) **τὸ** *to* (the) **ὕδωρ** *udōr* (water)
recordatus (remembered) ***autem*** (also) ***Deus*** (God) ***Noe*** (Noah) ***cunctarum-*** (all) ***que*** (and) ***animantium*** (animals) ***et*** (and) ***omnium*** (all) ***iumentorum*** (cattle) ***quae*** (which) ***erant*** (were) ***cum*** (with) ***eo*** (him) ***in*** (in) ***arca*** (ark) ***adduxit*** (brought) ***spiritum*** (a wind) ***super*** (on) ***terram*** (earth) ***et*** (and) ***inminutae*** (diminished) ***sunt*** (are) ***aquae*** (waters)
And God remembered Noah, and every living thing, and all the cattle that was with him in the ark: and God made a wind to pass over the earth, and the waters <u>asswaged;</u>
Furthermore, Divine-Consciousness remembered Noah with all the intelligible-animal-energies and all the seed-ideas, which were with him in the ark. In addition, Divine-Consciousness brought a impersonal wind of intentionality on the earth and the waters subsided.

This verse validates our translation and commentary regarding the ark. In fact, 'Elohiym (אלהים), Divine-Consciousness, the creative intelligible structure of the universe, remembers and calls to mind[2157] *everyone present in the mental reservoir of the Ark.* Each memory is a paradigm in continuous development and evolution. It is like the genetic structure that informs with its configuring *memory* all individuals according to each different species and kind.[2158] Therefore, from seeds, eggs, gametes and so on develop sprouts, fetuses and from these ones branches, limbs and articulating organs for each individual birth.

> "*Every energy-idea, as flesh transmitting information with the breath of life, entered with the rested Noah in the mental reservoir of the ark with both their potentiality and actuality.*"[2159]

This Divine Memory Reservoir is

> "*the Book* (ספר *cepher*) *of Recorded* (זכר *zakar*) *Remembrance.*[2160]*... written*[2161] *before Him.*"[2162]

This is a metaphor for the timeless Presence of everything before the Pure-Apodictical-Awareness within every aspect of experience, which we have right here and now. Certainty, however, is neither its conceptualization nor these words. Like in a Platonic *Hyperuranium,*[2163] every memory is *Beyond Heaven.* They are in Divine-Consciousness' Presence. Then, remembrances, as a Genomic library or DNA encoded genetic instructions,[2164] are seeds, which will sprout once planted again in the consciousness-*of* the fertile dried-up land. In fact, the non-yet-conceived thoughts hide in the recesses of the mind's memory. Only when conceptualized, the memory becomes an intuited idea, a *visible* dream or a waking event.

Further clarification of the creative ***intelligible***[2165] structure of the universe is necessary. There is no blueprint of a procreative intelligent design. This would imply a god anthropomorphically reduced to a blasphemous demiurgic[2166] architect subject to time and following a pre-designed map. On the contrary, it is the mind's structure, the *forma mentis*, the <u>intelligibility</u> which knowing and interpreting the world <u>puts it into existence</u>. In other words, there is no *intelligent design* or *random evolution* but an *intelligibility* that knows the world as such. This is the perpetual structure of Consciousness. There is <u>no</u> conceivable world, as such, outside consciousness. We cannot think nor have consciousness-*of* the world without thinking and having consciousness-*of* it. However, Consciousness does not need thought to be conscious.

On the other hand, consciousness-*of* an object needs thought to become an idea of the object we are conscious-*of*, which is not Consciousness itself as such. Nevertheless, the foundation of Consciousness is this Certitude, this Faith or this Apodicticity of Awareness. Like mummified[2167] animals (בְּהֵמָה *běhemah*) or a film-track recoded on an un-played video, all ideas, all thoughts, all impulses, all energetic intentions and all acts in general persist in a different kind of virtual conscious/unconscious state. These are the occupants of the Ark.

The wind,[2168] here, is the same, which

"*hovered upon the face of the waters...*[2169] *and made the sea dry land and divided the waters*"[2170]

for Moses to cross over to the other bank of the sea. This

"*wind-breath into the sea*"[2171]

is the Spiritual Life Breath (רוּחַ *ruwach*) of Divine-Consciousness, the creative-drive. It is the impersonal, disengaged intentionality of natural forces without attachment, which passed over (עָבַר *`abar*) those distressful flooding waters and eventually made them subside (שָׁכַךְ *shakak*).

Our friendly reader may ask,

'Why Genesis uses all these metaphors, when it would have been clearer to describe the epistemic process with exact terminology?'

We reply,

'First, not everyone may feel at ease with the words of this book. Second, you must admit that the text intends to be universal and timeless. Thus, it must use a general language comprehensible for all, at every levels, in each situation and in all historical ages. Likewise, if one is under the storm of a passionate obsession, how can the mind, engulfed in it, understand our words? Would it not be more effective to make that person realize the mental state using the word whirlpool as metaphor? When taken by puzzling disorientation, we use the expression, <my head spins,> where, in reality, there is no physical spinning. In that confused state of mind, we cannot understand any epistemic analysis. However, we invite the disoriented person to pay attention to the suffocating spinning feeling as a flood. Then, probably, s/he would be more capable to relate and control that distressing overwhelming force inhabiting the mind.'

8:2-The Rain Subsides

וַיִּסָּכְרוּ מַעְיְנֹת תְּהוֹם וַאֲרֻבֹּת הַשָּׁמָיִם וַיִּכָּלֵא הַגֶּשֶׁם מִן־הַשָּׁמָיִם׃ *vayisāḵəru* (were closed) *ma`əyənōṯ* (springs) *təhvōm* (of the deep) *va`ărubōṯ* (windows) *hašāmāyim* (of the sky) *vayikālē* (are restrained) *hagešem* (rain) *min* (from) *hašāmāyim* (heaven)
καὶ *kai* (and) **ἐπεκαλύφθησαν** *epekaluphthēsan* (were closed) **αἱ** *ai* (the) **πηγαὶ** *pēgai* (springs) **τῆς** *tēs* (of the) **ἀβύσσου** *abussou* (abyss) **καὶ** *kai* (and) **οἱ** *oi* (the) **καταρράκται** *katarraktai* (cataracts) **τοῦ** *tou* (of the) **οὐρανοῦ** *ouranou* (sky) **καὶ** *kai* (and) **συνεσχέθη** *suneschethēn* (was witheld) **ὁ** *o* (the) **ὑετὸς** *uetos* (rain) **ἀπὸ** *apo* (from) **τοῦ** *tou* (the) **οὐρανοῦ** *ouranou* (sky)
et (and) ***clausi*** (closed) ***sunt*** (are) ***fontes*** (the fountains) ***abyssi*** (of the abyss) ***et*** (and) ***cataractae*** (the cataracts) ***caeli*** (of the sky) ***et*** (and) ***prohibitae*** (forbidden) ***sunt*** (are) ***pluviae*** (rain) ***de*** (from the) ***caelo*** (sky)
The fountains also of the deep and the windows of heaven were stopped, and the rain from heaven was restrained;
The deep pleasurable mental qualities ambushing from above shut up and also the ideas from above withheld the downpour.

Our conceptualization constantly floods our mind with all sorts of attractions, distractions, desires, boredoms, pleasures, pains, joys, sorrows, depressions, exhilarations, thoughts and dreams of every type, which, as much as we try, we cannot stop. In fact, fountains, *ma'yan* (מַעְיָן),[2172] here, are metaphors for pleasures, joy, delight, *ma'yan* (מַעְיָן).[2173] Psalm declares,

"*As well the singers as the players on instruments shall be there: all my <u>springs of delight</u> (מַעְיָן *ma'yan*) are in thee.*"[2174]

The word *ma'yan* derives from *'ayin*,[2175] meaning eye, spring of mental quality from our *deep abyss*[2176] of unconsciousness. Through *passageways, windows* or *chimneys*[2177] to and from heaven (שָׁמַיִם *shamayim*), the mind is ambushed and *lurked*[2178] by ideas, which, as flooding rain (גֶּשֶׁם *geshem*), drown us. However, now all springs and openings shut up[2179] and the rain downpour is withheld.[2180] How is this possible? We will see in the following verses.

8:3-End of Attachment

וַיָּשֻׁבוּ הַמַּיִם מֵעַל הָאָרֶץ הָלוֹךְ וָשׁוֹב וַיַּחְסְרוּ הַמַּיִם מִקְצֵה חֲמִשִּׁים וּמְאַת יוֹם:
vayāšuḇu (returned) *hamayim* (waters) *mē'al* (from) *hā'āreṣ* (earth) *hālvōḵə* (continually going) *vāšvōḇ* (returning) *vayaḥəsəru* (decreased) *hamayim* (waters) *miqəṣēh* (after the end) *ḥămišiym* (fifty) *umə'at* (hundred) *yvōm* (days)
καὶ *kai* (and) ἐνεδίδου *enedidou* (subsided) τὸ *to* (the) ὕδωρ *udōr* (water) πορευόμενον *poreuomenon* (bringing) ἀπὸ *apo* (on) τῆς *tēs* (the) γῆς *gēs* (earth) ἐνεδίδου *enedidou* (gave up) καὶ *kai* (and) ἠλαττονοῦτο *ēlattonouto* (dismissed) τὸ *to* (the) ὕδωρ *udōp* (water) μετὰ *meta* (after) πεντήκοντα *pentēkonta* (fifty) καὶ *kai* (and) ἑκατὸν *ekaton* (hundred) ἡμέρας *ēmeras* (days)
reversae- (reversed) *que* (and) *aquae* (the waters) *de* (from) *terra* (the earth) *euntes* (going) *et* (and) *redeuntes* (returning) *et* (and) *coeperunt* (began) *minui* (to decrease) *post* (after) *centum* (hundred) *quinquaginta* (fifty) *dies* (days)
And the waters returned from off the earth continually: and after the end of the hundred and fifty days the waters were abated.
The waters reversed the coming and going from the earth; the flowing waters of thought-attachment decreased after the *consciousness-of oppression, vexation, affliction, grief, lamentation and wailing* (150) ended.

Ponder on the frenzy produced by pleasurable and/or unpleasurable situations, broadcasted events, public performances, community ceremonies, buying sprees and other similar happenings. Further, consider the terror generated by wars, concentration camps, prisons, mental institutions, political persecutions and other social unrests. Energetic impulses incessantly bombard us or *rain* upon us. After which we die. The Gematria value of 150 days are all the consciousness-*of* oppressions,[2181] vexations,[2182] grieves,[2183] lamentations,[2184] wailings[2185] and other afflictions[2186] in this existential flooding condition, namely, our

"being-for-death"[2187]

"*from whom no living person can escape.*"[2188]

"*All go unto one place; all are of the dust, and all turn to dust again.*"[2189]

This means that, besides being impermanent, everything is dust (עָפָר *'aphar*),[2190] thus, the ultimate truth of what we consider to be objectively real, in essence, is powdery inconsistent rubbish. And this can hardly be denied.

However, can the thinking impulses, namely, the waters (מַיִם *mayim*) of the tempestuous mind, be subdued (חָסֵר *chacer*)? Shakespeare has Romeo declare,

"Teach me how I should forget to think!"[2191]

And, in the *Bhagavad Gītā*, Arjuna confesses to Kṛshṇa,

"*The mind is restless, turbulent, obstinate and very strong… and I think that to subdue it is more difficult to control than the wind.*"[2192]

8:4-The Ark Rests

וַתָּנַח הַתֵּבָה בַּחֹדֶשׁ הַשְּׁבִיעִי בְּשִׁבְעָה-עָשָׂר יוֹם לַחֹדֶשׁ עַל הָרֵי אֲרָרָט:
vatānaḥ (rested) *hatēḇāh* (ark) *baḥōdeš* (months) *hašəḇiy'iy* (seventh) *bəšiḇə'āh* (seven) *'āśār*

(tenth) *yvōm* (days) *laḥōdeš* (of the month) *'al* (on) *hārēy* (mountain) *'ărārāṭ* (Ararat)
καὶ *kai* (and) **ἐκάθισεν** *ekathisen* (rested) **ἡ** *ē* (the) **κιβωτὸς** *kibōtos* (ark) **ἐν** *en* (in) **μηνὶ** *mēni* (month) **τῷ** *tō* (the) **ἑβδόμῳ** *ebdomō* (seventh) **ἑβδόμῃ** *ebdomē* (seventh) **καὶ** *kai* (and) **εἰκάδι** *eikadi* (twentieth day)[2193] **τοῦ** *tou* (the) **μηνός** *mēnos* (of the month) **ἐπὶ** *epi* (on) **τὰ** *ta* (the) **ὄρη** *orē* (mountain) **τὰ** *ta* (the) **Αραρατ** *Ararat* (Ararat)
requievit- (rested)***que*** (and) ***arca*** (ark) ***mense*** (month) ***septimo*** (seventh) ***vicesima*** (twenty)[2194] ***septima*** (seventh) ***die*** (day) ***mensis*** (of the month) ***super*** (on) ***montes*** (the mountains) ***Armeniae*** (of Armenia)[2195]
And the ark rested in the seventh month, on the seventeenth day of the month, upon the mountains of Ararat.
On the seventh of the resting lunar month circularities, on the seventeenth conscious circular day, the *fish*$_{(7\ \&\ 17)}$-like ark rested on the mountainous abode-of-the-nobles, which reverses the curse.

The Ark (תֵּבָה *tebah*) rests.[2196] Noah[2197] is the rested-one. Seventh (שְׁבִיעִי *shĕbiy'iy*) is the resting (נוּחַ *nuwach*) day of the new lunar cycle[2198] month.[2199] Furthermore, the circular days (יוֹם *yowm*) of consciousness are seventeen.[2200] In Gematria, the numbers seven[2201] and seventeen[2202] are both equivalent to the word *fish*, a metaphor for the oceangoing ark. Then, the fish-ark lands on the divine mountain,[2203] "*which reverses the curse*" (אֲרָרַט *'Ararat*). This peak is Ararat.[2204] Its name derives from the Sanskrit *āryāvarta*,[2205] meaning "*the abode of the nobles.*"

Like the Ark, the human head sits as on the top of the mountainous body, metaphorically called Ararat. The brain in the cranium resembles a turtle within its carapace. It has the ability to project toward the external waking world as well as to dream retracting within. The center of the intelligibility of the entire world sits on our neck. The rest of the body-mountain is under the waters, *sub-merged* in the *sub-conscious* of our mind. In fact, we feel our organs only when their nerve-sensors reach our brain.

<When mystic visions blossom, the historical and geographical realities shape the mythical languages. A culture that conceives the world as logical interconnections between ideal realities will express its symbols with mathematical-geometrical[2206] forms - *i.e.*: the Star of David.[2207] Whereas, a culture that feels the world as living interconnections between animistic realities will express its symbols with shapes drawn from nature - *i.e.*: the cross-cultural symbol of the turtle.[2208] If we superimpose the symbols of the hexagram and the turtle, we see that they have the same purpose, *i.e.* to rest (Noah) within while moving without. Thus, the ciphers represent the solution of contraries.[2209] What is internal (*sub specie interioritatis*) corresponds to that which is external (*sub specie exterioritatis*). The star is

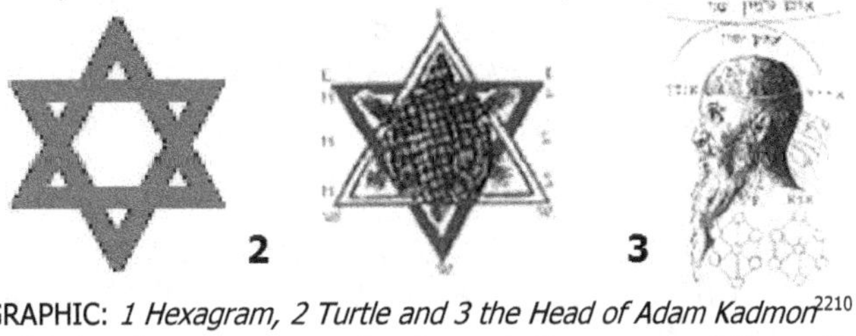

1 2 3

GRAPHIC: *1 Hexagram, 2 Turtle and 3 the Head of Adam Kadmon*[2210]

composed of two interlocked triangles, one - male △- pointing up and the other - female ▽- pointing down, which implies that what takes place above, in the divine mind, coincides with what takes place below, in the created world. The mind or intellect interacts with the external objects, is conscious of its internal ego, similarly, the turtle moves to the outside world and retracts into its own carapace. This is the process of in-breath-out-breath, symbolized by the vital Breath. This Vital Spirit does not refer only to the act of breathing, but it refers to all the processes of flowing from the external world into the internal psychophysical reality and from here back into the external. Therefore, the turtle becomes a symbol of this flow. *Breath* becomes a symbol of power over of the entire world.>[2211]

8:5-Auto-Transparent Objectivity

וְהַמַּיִם הָיוּ הָלוֹךְ וְחָסוֹר עַד הַחֹדֶשׁ הָעֲשִׂירִי בָּעֲשִׂירִי בְּאֶחָד לַחֹדֶשׁ נִרְאוּ רָאשֵׁי הֶהָרִים׃
vəhamayim (waters) *hāyu* (began) *hālvōkə* (continually) *vəḥāsvōr* (to decrease) *'ad* (until) *haḥōdeš*

(month) *hā'ăśiyriy* (ten) *bā'ăśiyriy* (of tenth) *bə'eḥāḏ* (first day) *laḥōḏeš* (month) *nirə'u* (appeared) *rā'šēy* (the head) *hehāriym* (of the mountains)
τὸ *to* (the) **δὲ** *de* (but) **ὕδωρ** *udōr* (water) **πορευόμενον** *poreuomenon* (bringing) **ἠλαττονοῦτο** *ēlattonouto* (dismissed) **ἕως** *eōs* (until) **τοῦ** *tou* (the) **δεκάτου** *dekatou* (tenth) **μηνός** *mēnos* (month) **ἐν** *en* (in) **δὲ** *de* (that) **τῷ** *tō* (the) **ἐνδεκάτῳ** *endekatō* (eleventh) **μηνί** *mēni* (month) **τῇ** *tē* (the) **πρώτῃ** *prōtē* (first) **τοῦ** *tou* (the) **μηνός** *mēnos* (month) **ὤφθησαν** *ōphthēsan* (were seen) **αἱ** *ai* (the) **κεφαλαὶ** *kephalai* (heads) **τῶν** *tōn* (of the) **ὀρέων** *oreōn* (mountains)
at (and) ***vero*** (indeed) ***aquae*** (the waters) ***ibant*** (were going) ***et*** (and) ***decrescebant*** (were decreasing) ***usque*** (in fact) ***ad*** (until) ***decimum*** (the tenth) ***mensem*** (month) ***decimo*** (tenth) ***enim*** (in fact) ***mense*** (month) ***prima*** (first) ***die*** (day) ***mensis*** (of the month) ***apparuerunt*** (appeared) ***cacumina*** (the tips) ***montium*** (of the mountains)
And the waters decreased continually until the tenth month: in the tenth month, on the first day of the month, were the tops of the mountains seen.
And the waters continuously subsided until the *first* (1) of the *higher* (10) object-mountain heads appeared in consciousness.

There are two perspectives of the deluge. The first one is the destructive aspect, when the flood of possessive thoughts drowns the sentient being and clouds its Pure Awareness Certitude. The other one is the drying up of all emotional thoughts, which consents again the Unflooded Truth to shine In-Itself. On the first day (אֶחָד *'echad*) of the tenth circular lunar month, the water subsides to expose the highest (גָּבֹהַ *gāḇōha*) peaks of the mountains. As we have seen, days, months or years are metaphors for the circularity of consciousness. Furthermore, the Gematria numerical value of the word "*higher,*" *gāḇōha* (גָּבֹהַ), equals number 10.[2212] Therefore, when the flooding waters of the turbulent conscious attachment to the thought-objects continuously (הָלַךְ *halak*) subside, the heads,[2213] the leading and first (#1, א, *a*)[2214] highest crests of the mountainous object-ideas appear[2215] in their intuitive state.

Gradually, we observe the objects as in a meditative mode. Like in the state of self-auto-transparency, the waters of stressful-suffered-possession retreat. They expose the summit of objects to the sun of Pure Consciousness without the mediation of thought. To understand how this is possible, consider the automatic act of reaching for an object in the pocket while engaged in an absorbing business conversation. We do not need to think of the object to retrieve it.

Psalm states,

> "*Therefore we will not fear, though the earth be removed, and though the mountains be carried into the midst of the sea;*(2) *Though the waters thereof roar and be troubled, though the mountains shake with the swelling thereof.*(3)... *Come, behold the works of the LORD, what desolations he hath made in the earth.*(8)... *Let go, and know that I am God.*(10) *The Transcendent LORD of hosts is with us; the God of Jacob is our refuge*"(11).[2216]

Jesus states,

> "*If any man come to me, and hate not his father, and mother, and wife, and children, and brethren, and sisters, yea, and his own life also, he cannot be my disciple... He that hateth his life in this world shall keep it unto life eternal.*"[2217]

> "*Therefore take no thought for your life, what ye shall eat, or what ye shall drink; nor yet for your body, what ye shall put on... But seek ye first the kingdom of God, and his righteousness; and all these things shall be added unto you.*"[2218]

The *Bhagavad-Gītā* echoes,

> "*I bring shelter to those beings that are absorbed in me having no other one and to those who always worship me yoked in permanent devotion.*"[2219]

Paul declares that,

> "*those who mourn,* [should be] *as if they did not; those who are happy,* [should be] *as if they were not.*"[2220]

> "*Be ye steadfast, unmovable, always abounding in the work of the Lord.*"[2221]

Herodotus says,[2222]

"Be carefree."

Dante follows,

"be as a firm tower that does not ruin... let us not discuss about them, but look and pass."[2223]

In other words, be

"the same in sorrow or happiness, look with the same eye at a lump of dirt, a stone or gold, look at loved and not loved ones equally, stands equally firm in defamation or praise and the same in honor or dishonor, he who is equal with friends or enemies."[2224]

This is seeing without looking, hearing without listening, tasting without savoring, sniffing without smelling, feeling without touching, conceiving without thinking and doing without acting.

Our reader may argue,

'The world you describe is a very bleak one, not worth living. There is no driving incentive in it.'

We reply,

'The world you refer to has only death as its ultimate spice[2225] *and that is quite desolate. Reality is only in the stillness of Apodictical Awareness. In it is the immortal ecstatic present rapture of oneness beyond duality. That is the meaning of the phrase,'*

"Except ye... become as little children, ye shall not enter into the kingdom of heaven."[2226]

That state is the stillness of Awareness without which nothing can be. In a world, in which there is no evil in-itself, the evildoers are those who discard the fundamental Truth they come from. Thus, they ignore Awareness as their True Goal by electing as leaders their imaginary beliefs. From those, the deluging and terrifying wars of ideologies, pour on us like a web of interconnected computers all infected with contrasting, different and virulent viruses.'

8:6-The Window of the Eyes

וַיְהִי מִקֵּץ אַרְבָּעִים יוֹם וַיִּפְתַּח נֹחַ אֶת־חַלּוֹן הַתֵּבָה אֲשֶׁר עָשָׂה׃ *vayəhiy* (came to pass) *miqēṣ* (after) *'arəbā'iym* (forty) *yvōm* (days) *vayip̄ətaḥ* (opened) *nōaḥ* (Noah) *'eṯ* (the) *ḥalvōn* (piercing window) *hatēḇāh* (of the ark) *'ăšer* (which) *'āśāh* (he had made)
καὶ *kai* (and) **ἐγένετο** *egeneto* (came to pass) **μετὰ** *meta* (after) **τεσσαράκοντα** *tessarakonta* (the fortieth) **ἡμέρας** *ēmeras* (day) **ἠνέῳξεν** *ēneōxen* (opened) **Νωε** *Nōe* (Noah) **τὴν** *tēn* (the) **θυρίδα** *thurida* (window) **τῆς** *tēs* (of the) **κιβωτοῦ** *kibōtou* (ark) **ἣν** *ēn* (that) **ἐποίησεν** *epoiēsen* (he had made)
cumque (as) ***transissent*** (passed by) ***quadraginta*** (forty) ***dies*** (days) ***aperiens*** (opened) ***Noe*** (Noah) ***fenestram*** (the window) ***arcae*** (of the ark) ***quam*** (which) ***fecerat*** (he made) ***dimisit*** (sent away) ***corvum*** (a crow)[2227]
And it came to pass at the end of forty days, that Noah opened the window of the ark which he had made:
After the conscious *destructive-forty* (40) days came to pass, Noah opened the window-senses of the ark-mind that he had made.

The Hebrew word for window[2228] means *pearcing of the wall.* It is the opening (פתח *pathach*)[2229] of the consciousness-*of* the senses.[2230] The kindred root of that verb *pathach* is *paqach,*[2231] which means *to open the eyes.* Then,

"his eyes shall see his destruction."[2232]

The word for *destruction* is *kiyḏwō,*[2233] and its Gematria number[2234] is 40,[2235] which is also the letter מ, *m,* meaning watery chaos.[2236] Then, Adam/Eve's

"eyes... were opened"[2237]

to be conscious-*of*, to experience and to see for-themselves everything, *the good and evil*, the destruction, which is *outside*. Therefore, the senses, as such, miss the Reality in-Itself and they are condemned to

"*surely die*."[2238]

The *Kaṭha Upanishad*, a sacred Indian text,[2239] describes this *window-piercing of the senses* as,

"*The Self-Made pierced the openings of the senses outward, therefore one looks outward, not in-itself. Any wise person, seeking immortality, saw the Self in-Itself with eyes turned inward.*"[2240]

Noah, from the ark-mind, opens the eye-window of the vessel, which he had made.[2241] He opened (פתח *pathach*) his eyes after the flooding-destruction, when the waters were retreating and the heads of the mountainous-ideas were exposed to the sun of Awareness, above the destructive waters, as we have seen.

Memory persists in the Universe and, physiologically, rests in the body's head. When the fluid attachments subside, then we realize the intuitive aspects of ideas.

8-II SECTION: THE BIRDS OF THE ARK

8:7-The Dark Raven

וַיְשַׁלַּח אֶת־הָעֹרֵב וַיֵּצֵא יָצוֹא וָשׁוֹב עַד־יְבֹשֶׁת הַמַּיִם מֵעַל הָאָרֶץ׃ *vayəšalaḥ* (he sent) *'eṯ* (forth) *hā'ōrēḇ* (dark raven) *vayēṣē* (he went out) *yāṣvō* (going out) *vāšvōḇ* (turning back) *'aḏ* (till) *yəḇōšeṯ* (drying) *hamayim* (water) *mē'al* (from) *hā'āreṣ* (earth)
καὶ *kai* (and) **ἀπέστειλεν** *apesteilen* (despatched) **τὸν** *ton* (the) **κόρακα** *koraka* (crow) **τοῦ** *tou* (to) **ἰδεῖν** *idein* (see) **εἰ** *ei* (if) **κεκόπακεν** *kekopaken* (grew weary) **τὸ** *to* (the) **ὕδωρ** *udōr* (water) **καὶ** *kai* (and) **ἐξελθὼν** *exelthōn* (came) **οὐχ** *ouch* (not) **ὑπέστρεψεν** *epestrepsen* (returned) **ἕως** *eōs* (until) **τοῦ** *tou* (the) **ξηρανθῆναι** *xēranthēnai* (dried up) **τὸ** *to* (the) **ὕδωρ** *udōr* (water) **ἀπὸ** *apo* (on) **τῆς** *tēs* (the) **γῆς** *gēs* (earth)
qui (which) ***egrediebatur*** (exited) ***et*** (and) ***revertebatur*** (returned) ***donec*** (until) ***siccarentur*** (were dried up) ***aquae*** (the waters) ***super*** (on) ***terram*** (earth)
And he sent forth a raven, which went forth to and fro, until the waters were dried up from off the earth.
He sent forth a dark-raven, which went out, going out and turning back until the water were dried up on the earth.

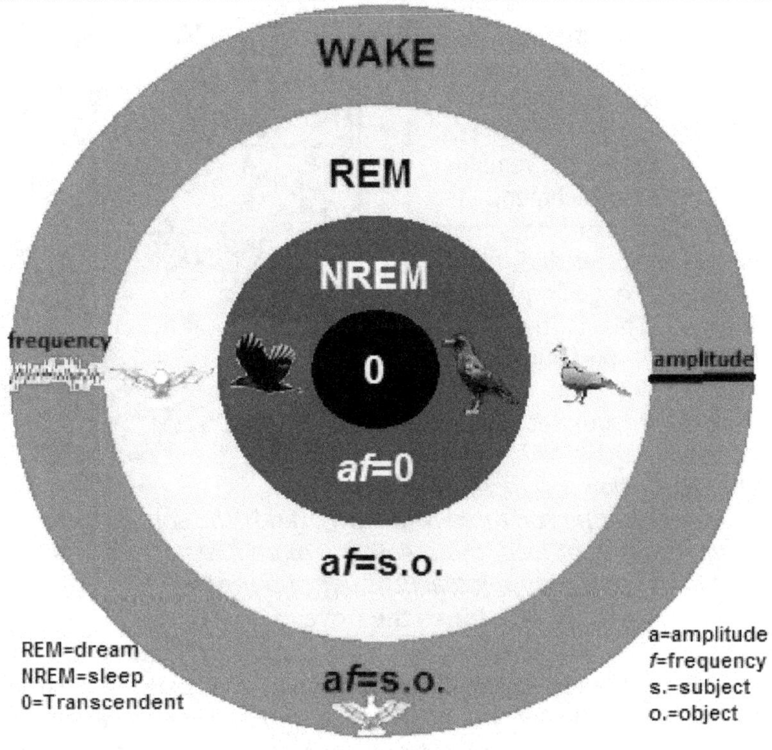

GRAPHIC: *Various Levels of Reality*

Noah's *eye-vision* is *still* turned inward, toward the rested *stillness* of the internal NREM, the Conscience from which he comes. Therefore, from that opening he sends forth a raven. The *raven* or *crow,*[2242] in this verse, needs an explanation. The Hebrew word *'oreb* (עֹרֵב) signifies crow, but it also means to become evening or grow dark (עָרַב *'arab*)[2243]and it is identical to the word *'arab,*[2244] which conveys the idea of concealing with a texture.

Therefore, *raven* or *crow*, flying out of the Ark-NREM realm, symbolizes, at the same time, both the unconscious resting aspect of the dreamless-sleep as well as its continuous *fellowship with* (עָרַב *'ârab*) the sub-consciousnes-*of* the dream state and the consciousness-*of* the waking state. Furthermore, as a metaphor for the movement across the waking/REM/NREM spectrum, the *crow assures* (עָרַב *'ârab*) the persistence of memory in the death state. In fact, the DNA-memory *exchanges* (עָרַב *'ârab*) and extends, after life ends,

"into a time series spanning from life to 48 or 96 h postmortem."[2245]

Therefore, consciousness-*of*, sub-consciousness and unconsciousness all articulate as different moments of the same Continuous Universal Presence of Consciousness. The *crow* symbolizes the concealing aspect of sleep with no dreams. Thus, the NREM is the state in which as a *dark-raven,* it does not conceive or experience the external world. Only the stages of dream (REM) and/or wake experience the *external* world. However, in those states, we suffer the world, which engulfs us. This does not take place in Noah's state of rest. NREM projects[2246] the world in its potentiality while going out[2247] and turning back,[2248] thus remaining in its closed auto-transparent circularity. Hence, the crow covers the potential world away from the passionate flux of engulfing despair.

View the various levels of reality as waves of energy. Each has an amplitude (a) and a frequency (*f*), which oscillate between the subject (s.) and the object (o.) in accord with the intensity of the breath-(רוּחַ *ruwach*)-energy engaged in the wave of mental impulse. This creates a flood in which we, inevitably, drown. The state of deep sleep (NREM) floats above those waves. It remains unaffected in the dry land of detachment. Its concealing (עָרַ *'arab)* dispassion goes out only to return in its own peaceful dark night (עֹרֵב *`oreb*), away from the engulfing waves of passionate nightmares. This is the *Dark Night of the Soul,* which prefigures the splendor of the day.[2249] Saint John of the Cross describes his spiritual progresses during his ascent to Mount Carmel. ⇨

"[On] *the Mount of Perfection,* ... *there is no path, because for the just person there is no law...* [and] *the soul enjoys no longer that food of the sense but needs another kind of food, more delicate, more internal and less of the nature of sense, a food which imparts to the soul deep spiritual quietude and repose.*"[2250]

8:8-Jonah the Dove of Truth

וַיְשַׁלַּח אֶת־הַיּוֹנָה מֵאִתּוֹ לִרְאוֹת הֲקַלּוּ הַמַּיִם מֵעַל פְּנֵי הָאֲדָמָה׃
vayəšalaḥ (he sent out) *'eṯ* (and) hayvōnāh (Jonah dove) *mē'itvō* (from him) *lirə'vōṯ* (to see if) *hăqalu* (were abated) *hamayim* (water) *mē'al* (from) *pənēy* (the face) *hā'ădāmāh* (of the earth)
καὶ *kai* (and) **ἀπέστειλεν** *apesteilen* (dispatched) **τὴν** *tēn* (the) **περιστερὰν** *peristeran* (dove) **ὀπίσω** *opisō* (after it) **αὐτοῦ** *autou* (he) **ἰδεῖν** *idein* (to see) **εἰ** *ei* (if) **κεκόπακεν** *kekopaken* (abated) **τὸ** *to* (the) **ὕδωρ** *udōr* (water) **ἀπὸ** *apo* (on) **προσώπου** *prosōpou* (face) **τῆς** *tēs* (of the) **γῆς** *gēs* (earth)
emisit (he sent out) ***quoque*** (also) ***columbam*** (dove) ***post*** (from) ***eum*** (him) ***ut*** (to) ***videret*** (see) ***si*** (if) ***iam*** (already) ***cessassent*** (were abated) ***aquae*** (the waters) ***super*** (on) ***faciem*** (the face) ***terrae*** (of the earth)
Also he sent forth a dove from him, to see if the waters were abated from off the face of the ground;
Following, to see if the waters had already decreased on the face of the earth, he sent out from

himself Jonah-the-dove-of-Truth.

Let us repeat what we already wrote. This flood did not take place in prehistoric time. If the flood were a primordial punishment for moral deviations, why condemn also the other animals with no moral responsibility? If so, why only the air breathing beings were condemned to die and not the marine life, especially the air breathing sea mammals? This deluge is taking place right here and now. In fact, as every life extinguishes in the flood, so every living being in this entire universe inevitably dies, thus

"*the dead bury their dead.*"[2251]

The common graveyard is this present ocean of desperation from which no life surfaces. This is the world in which Adam/Eve are exiled, namely, the world of the dead. Death's house is this bodily abode, which hungers for the forbidden fruit. It is the body of this writer and reader here and now.

Furthermore, in this chapter we are on Mount Ararat, where the curse is reversed. This means that, by a process of intense meditation, the Awareness, in this waking state, surfaces awake into the dream. From there, always awake, Awareness merges into sleep with no dreams. During this whole process, the Rested One dries up all the sea of suffering, to cross into the promised dry land of Pure Peaceful Awareness. Similarly,

"*Moses stretched out his hand over the sea; and the LORD caused the sea to go back by a strong east wind all that night, and made the sea dry land, and the waters were divided.*"[2252]

Since, as we said, birds are metaphors for the ethereal senses of the psyche, thus, to see (רָאָה *ra'ah*) if the waters were receding (קָלַל *qalal*), Noah sent (שָׁלַח *shalach*) *out from*[2253] himself[2254] a bird. Specifically, he sent out a raven. That bird was an emanation from the state of the dark-dreamless-world-in-itself. Thus, it was not *of* the world-for-itself, neither for-conception nor for-communication. In fact, when immersed in dreamless sleep, who can think or communicate?

After which, Noah sends out another bird, a dove. The Hebrew name for dove is *yonah,*[2255] which is the same as *Yonah,*[2256] *viz. Jonah.* Who is he? *The Book of Jonah*[2257] declares *that*

"*the guiding*[2258] *word*[2259] *of the Transcendent came unto Jonah, the dove,*[2260] *the son of Amittai-my-truth.*"[2261]

The son of truth, therefore, must ascertain that the destructive drowning waters of the universal good and evil objectification, which suffocate life-breath, had retracted.

8:9-Certainty Returns into Dreamlessness

וְלֹא־מָצְאָה הַיּוֹנָה מָנוֹחַ לְכַף־רַגְלָהּ וַתָּשָׁב אֵלָיו אֶל־הַתֵּבָה כִּי־מַיִם עַל־פְּנֵי כָל־הָאָרֶץ וַיִּשְׁלַח יָדוֹ וַיִּקָּחֶהָ וַיָּבֵא אֹתָהּ אֵלָיו אֶל־הַתֵּבָה׃   *vəlō̆* (not) *māṣə'āh* (found) *hayvōnāh* (dove) *mānvōaḥ* (resting place) *ləkap̄* (for the sole) *rag̱əlāh* (of the foot) *vatāšāḇ* (returned) *'el* (and) *hatēḇāh* (in the ark) *kiy* (because) *mayim* (the waters) *'al* (upon) *pənēy* (face) *kāl* (all) *hā'āreṣ* (earth) *vayišəlaḥ* (he stretched out) *yāḏvō* (power hand) *vayiqāḥeāh* (took) *vayāḇē̆* (pulled in) *'ōṯāh* (with) *'ēlāyv* (him) *'el* (the) *hatēḇāh* (ark)
καὶ *kai* (and) **οὐχ** *ouch* (not) **εὑροῦσα** *eurousa* (having found) **ἡ** *ē* (the) **περιστερὰ** *peristera* (dove) **ἀνάπαυσιν** *anapausin* (rest) **τοῖς** *tois* (for) **ποσὶν** *posin* (foot) **αὐτῆς** *autēs* (her) **ὑπέστρεψεν** *upestrepsen* (returned) **πρὸς** *pros* (from) **αὐτὸν** *auton* (him) **εἰς** *eis* (into) **τὴν** *tēn* (the) **κιβωτόν** *kibōton* (ark) **ὅτι** *oti* (because) **ὕδωρ** *udōr* (the water) **ἦν** *ēn* (was) **ἐπὶ** *epi* (on) **παντὶ** *panti* (all) **προσώπῳ** *prosōpō* (the face) **πάσης** *pasēs* (all) **τῆς** *tēs* (the) **γῆς** *gēs* (earth) **καὶ** *kai* (and) **ἐκτείνας** *ekteinas* (he extended) **τὴν** *tēn* (the) **χεῖρα** *cheira* (hand) **αὐτοῦ** *autou* (his) **ἔλαβεν** *elaben* (toke) **αὐτὴν** *autēn* (in him) **καὶ** *kai* (and) **εἰσήγαγεν** *eisēgagen* (entered) **αὐτὴν** *autēn* (her) **πρὸς** *pros* (with) **ἑαυτὸν** *eauton* (him) **εἰς** *eis* (in) **τὴν** *tēn* (the) **κιβωτόν** *kibōton* (ark)
quae (it) ***cum*** (since) ***non*** (not) ***invenisset*** (having found) ***ubi*** (where) ***requiesceret*** (to rest) ***pes*** (the foot) ***eius*** (its) ***reversa*** (returns) ***est*** (is) ***ad*** (to) ***eum*** (him) ***in*** (in) ***arcam*** (the ark) ***aquae*** (the waters) ***enim*** (in fact) ***erant*** (were) ***super*** (on) ***universam*** (the entire) ***terram*** (earth) ***extendit-*** (extended) ***que*** (and) ***manum*** (the hand) ***et*** (and) ***adprehensam*** (took) ***intulit*** (brought) ***in*** (in) ***arcam*** (the ark)
But the dove found no rest for the sole of her foot, and she returned unto him into the

ark, for the waters were on the face of the whole earth: then he put forth his hand, and took her, and pulled her in unto him into the ark.
However, Jonah, the dove having found no rest for its powerful-sole-curvature of its exploring foot returned in to him in the ark, indeed, the waters were upon the entire world. He [Noah] extended the power of his hand took it [the dove] and brought it in the ark.

Invitation to an Introspective Analysis

- *Dear reader, was your last nightmare real?* -

You may answer,

- *It was a disturbing dream!* -

If we add,

- *Since dreams are not real, then, you had no nightmare.* -

You would adamantly affirm.

- *I am certain I had a nightmare.* -

We continue,

- *But tell me; are you certain you are reading this book now? If so, please concentrate only on that certainty. Then, remember the certainty related to your nightmare. What is the difference between the two certainties? None, in fact, if you take away the nightmare and the book and focus only on your certainties, you will realize that they are one and the same in every case. There is only One-Certain-Apodictical-Truth unaffected by the related objects and this*

"*Truth shall make you free.*"[2262]

One more thing, try to describe "certainty" with words or define it conceptually. Impossible, it is like communicating an intense state of being, it

"cannot be understood by him who does not feel it." -[2263]

GRAPHIC: *The Spiral Way of Truth and Life*

When Pontius Pilate asked

"*What is truth?*"[2264]

Jesus did not answer because

"*the world of objectivity cannot receive, the Spirit of Truth, because the world seeth it not, neither knoweth it: but ye know it; for it dwelleth with you, and shall be in you.*[2265]
He that knoweth God heareth us; he that is not of God heareth not us. Hereby know we the Spirit of Truth."[2266]

How can we convey in words the Spirit of Truth?[2267] We can use only symbolic images as
"*the Spirit of God descending like a dove, and lighting upon him.*"[2268]

There are three fundamental constant elements in all our daily experiences.

1) The <u>Way</u> is the direction towards which we go. It is our constant reference to an unconceivable[2269] <u>Blissful-Transcendent in-Itself</u> believed to be the external reality independent from our experiences.
2) The <u>Truth</u>[2270] is the constant presence of the <u>Real-Certainty</u> embedded always in all our valid and/or fallacious experiences as such.
3) The <u>Life</u>[2271] is the constant light of <u>Being-Aware</u>. It is that which makes all our experiences possible.

Emblematic is the account of Jonah, the dove (יוֹנָה), son of 'Amittai (אֲמִתַּי), meaning, *my Truth.*[2272] After

"*three days and three nights.../ Jonah, out of the fish's belly prayed unto the Transcendent his Divine-Consciousness... 'For thou hadst cast me into the deep, in the midst of the seas; and the floods compassed me about: all thy billows and thy waves passed over me. Then I said, I am cast out of thy Eye of Awareness;*[2273] *yet I will pay attention*[2274] *again toward thy holy sanctuary. The waters compassed me about, even to the soul: the depth closed me round about, the weeds were wrapped about my head. I went down to the bottoms of the mountains; the earth with her bars was about me for ever: yet hast thou brought up my life from corruption, O LORD my God. When my soul is wrapped in* [NREM] *darkness*[2275] *within me I remembered the LORD: and my prayer came in unto thee, into thine holy temple. They that observe lying vanities forsake their own mercy. But I will sacrifice unto thee with the voice of thanksgiving; I will pay that that I have vowed. Salvation is of the Transcendent.' And the LORD spake unto the fish, and it vomited out Jonah upon the dry land.*"[2276]

Jonah comes out from the belly[2277] of the fish. Figuratively, that was the place of emotions or distress where he had been for three days. Then he comes out.

That exit corresponds to the *opening* (פָּתַח *pathach*) *of the eyes*_(פָּקַח *paqach*) and to the *pearcing of the wall* (חַלּוֹן *challown*) in the Ark. This window-light-of-consciousness (צֹהַר *tsohar*) is also on the third level of the ark, the rested NREM. The dove/Jonah exits from there and enters into the ark's second level, the dream realm (REM). However, in this level, the restful (מָנוֹחַ *manowach*) stillness, from which it came, is not there. The word *manowach* derives from *manowach resting-place*[2278] and again from the verb *to rest,*[2279] which, ultimately, refers to Noah.[2280] Therefore, to find any rest, the dove must return (שׁוּב *shuwb*) in Noah's hand, the state of being, from which it departed. In fact, when out there in the tempestuous world of dreams, the *dove of certainty* cannot entirely complete its subject-object circularity. This is our daily experiential condition during which

"*the builders rejected the stone,*"[2281]
"*the building gem stone of knowledge.*"[2282]

Let us follow the metaphor of this verse. There, it says that, the dove's *sole-powerful-* (כַּף *kaph*)[2283] *bent-curvature* (כָּפַף *kaphaph*)[2284] of its *exploring* (רָגַל *ragal*)[2285] *foot* (רֶגֶל *regel*)[2286] found no rest. Meaning that, its claws could not complete the grasping bent circle of exploration, which would have brought the object back to the ***subject-in-itself***, from which the dove had departed.

This is our condition and that of every being, submerged right here and now in this epistemic deluge. In fact, no one can know the knower of knowing. Similarly, our image, which we see in the mirror, is always that of the <u>reflected</u> one, never the <u>reflecting</u> one us as such. We never reach the *Self-subject-in-itself*, except as *me-object-for-itself*, never *in-itself*. The epistemic circle remains open. The *Self-in-Itself* is the NREM state of Noah's rest, the stillness of the sleep with no dreams. The dream-reality, instead, floods submerging and distracting us from our true self. The dove's circling grip can never really close on its support. The watery grave takes us away and alienates us from the real foundation on which to stand.

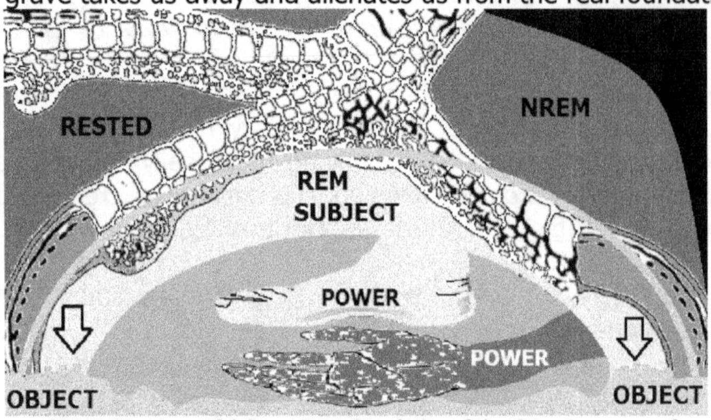

GRAPHIC: *Unrestful Open Bent Circularity of the Consciousness-of*

As the first meditative step, this dove realizes that, in this world's experiences, there is no objective sustaining foundation on which to stand. Then the Rested One extended his hand of power (יָד *yad*), took the dove of certainty and pulled it back into himself. Namely, the REM dream absorbs into the dreamless sleep. That which is auto-transparent does not need to think of something to be certain. Noah's state of pure restfulness is the NREM dreamless state. There, Certainty is in its pure stillness because not related to any object of which to be certain. There are no objects. Nevertheless, we are there in the Ark, with all our epistemic faculties. We are in a state of synthetic potential cognition. This will be clearer in the next verses.

8:10-The Dove Goes Out Again

וַיָּחֶל עוֹד שִׁבְעַת יָמִים אֲחֵרִים וַיֹּסֶף שַׁלַּח אֶת־הַיּוֹנָה מִן־הַתֵּבָה׃
vayāḥel (winding strong) *ʿvōḏ* (yet) *šiḇəʿaṯ* (seventh) *yāmiym* (days) *ʾăḥēriym* (another) *ayōsep̄* (again) *šalaḥ* (sent forth) *ʾeṯ* (and) *hayvōnāh* (dove) *min* (from) *hatēḇāh* (the ark)
καὶ *kai* (and) **ἐπισχὼν** *epischōn* (waiting) **ἔτι** *eti* (yet) **ἡμέρας** *ēmeras* (days) **ἑπτὰ** *epta* (seven) **ἑτέρας** *eteras* (another) **πάλιν** *palin* (back) **ἐξαπέστειλεν** *exapesteilen* (sent) **τὴν** *tēn* (the) **περιστερὰν** *peristeran* (dove) **ἐκ** *ek* (from) **τῆς** *tēs* (the) **κιβωτοῦ** *kibōtou* (ark)
expectatis (he waited) ***autem*** (also) ***ultra*** (further) ***septem*** (seven) ***diebus*** (days) ***aliis*** (other) ***rursum*** (again) ***dimisit*** (sent away) ***columbam*** (the dove) ***ex*** (from) ***arca*** (the ark)
And he stayed yet other seven days; and again he sent forth the dove out of the ark;
Further, he stayed winding strong also for other seven days and again he sent the dove out from the ark/*fish* (7).

Noah, stayed seven more days in its *vayāḥel* (וַיָּחֶל), namely, in that strong (חַיִל *chayil)* winding (חול *chuwl*), state. Namely, *chuwl* and similar, are

"verbs that have the signification of binding or twisting [and] are applied to strength."[2287]

In any case, the concept of the circular binding together is indicative of Noah's rested unified state. Furthermore, the seventh day of creation is the resting (שַׁבָּת *shabath*) one and the word fish (דָּג *dāḡ*), in Gematria, equals #7.[2288] Therefore, on the circular day of restful consciousness, Noah sent forth again, from that ark-fish, Jonah, the dove of testimonial truth.

"*And the LORD spake unto the fish, and it vomited*[2289] *out Jonah upon the dry*[2290] *land.*"[2291]

8:11-Meditation as a Dove

וַתָּבֹא אֵלָיו הַיּוֹנָה לְעֵת עֶרֶב וְהִנֵּה עֲלֵה־זַיִת טָרָף בְּפִיהָ וַיֵּדַע נֹחַ כִּי־קַלּוּ הַמַּיִם מֵעַל הָאָרֶץ׃
vatāḇō̄ (entered) *ʾēlāyv* (into them) *hayvōnāh* (the dove) *ləʿēṯ* (in time) *ʿereḇ* (evening) *vəhinēh* (lo and behold) *ʾălēh* (leaf) *zayiṯ* (olive) *ṭārāp̄* (freshly plucked) *bəp̄iyāh* (in mouth) *vayēḏaʿ* (knew) *nōaḥ* (Noah) *kiy* (that) *qalu* (were abated) *hamayim* (waters) *mēʿal* (from) *hāʾāreṣ* (earth)
καὶ *kai* (and) **ἀνέστρεψεν** *anestrepsen* (returned) **πρὸς** *pros* (into) **αὐτὸν** *auton* (him) **ἡ** *ē* (the)

περιστερὰ *peristera* (dove) **τὸ** *to* (the) **πρὸς** *pros* (into) **ἑσπέραν** *esperan* (evening) **καὶ** *kai* (and) **εἶχεν** *eichen* (had) **φύλλον** *phullon* (leaf) **ἐλαίας** *elaias* (olive tree) **κάρφος** *karphos* (straw) **ἐν** *en* (in) **τῷ** *tō* (the) **στόματι** *stomati* (mouth) **αὐτῆς** *autēs* (its) **καὶ** *kai* (and) **ἔγνω** *egnō* (knew) **Νωε** *Nōe* (Noah) **ὅτι** *oti* (that) **κεκόπακεν** *kakopaken* (was reduced) **τὸ** *to* () **ὕδωρ** *udōr* () **ἀπὸ** *apo* (on) **τῆς** *tēs* (the) **γῆς** *gēs* (earth)
at (thus) ***illa*** (she) ***venit*** (came) ***ad*** (to) ***eum*** (him) ***ad*** (in) ***vesperam*** (the vesper) ***portans*** (carrying) ***ramum*** (a twig) ***olivae*** (of olive) ***virentibus*** (with green) ***foliis*** (leaves) ***in*** (in) ***ore*** (mouth) ***suo*** (its) ***intellexit*** (understood) ***ergo*** (therefore) ***Noe*** (Noah) ***quod*** (that) ***cessassent*** (were receded) ***aquae*** (the waters) ***super*** (on) ***terram*** (the earth)
And the dove came in to him in the evening; and, lo, in her mouth was an olive leaf pluckt off: so Noah knew that the waters were abated from off the earth.
Thus, suddenly in the evening time, the dove entered into them carrying an olive with green leaves in its mouth, and Noah realized that the waters had receded from the earth.

A literal approach would not explain how it could have been possible to find an olive branch on a lifeless planet reduced to dust after the flood. Furthermore, how that dead desiccated planet would have been able to sustain and feed animal life once out of the ark.[2292]

Truthfully, each of **the doves**, sent out from the Ark, **are sequential steps of the same meditative path**, which uplifts the weight of objectivity, as when.

"*the Holy Ghost descended in a bodily shape like a dove upon him.*"[2293]

The first dove realized the unreliable bottomless of the waters of flooding cognitions. This second dove is the next meditative step.

What is the meaning of the bird returning to Noah in the evening[2294] time?[2295] This time corresponds to the dark concealing (ער `*arab*) evening of the crow (עֹרֵב `*oreb*), the first bird to leave the ark, as we have seen. Then, the *crow* symbolized the concealing aspect of sleep with no dreams, where there are no conceptions or experiences of the external world. From the *outside*, the dove of truth reenters the ark through the window-light (צֹהַר *tsohar*) of consciousness, which shines and flows like pressed oil (צָהַר *tsahar*). In fact, this dove has an uprooted[2296] olive[2297] leaf[2298] in its mouth.[2299] A literal reading would be incoherent. In fact, if the flood destroyed all life the olive would not have been able to produce a green twig. Therefore, let us look at the meaning of the words in this verse,

1) uprooted, *taraph* (טָרָף), derives from the verb *taraph*,[2300] meaning to tear in pieces, to feed.
2) olive, *zayith* (זַיִת), "probably derives from an unused root [akin to *ziv*]"[2301] meaning brightness, splendor of flowers.
3) leaf, `*aleh* (עָלֶה), derives from the verb `*alah*[2302] meaning to go up, to transcend, to come up before God.
4) mouth, *peh* (פֶּה), derives from the verb *pa'ah*,[2303] meaning to dash to pieces, to blow.

Lo and behold,[2304] in the present moment of the evening (עֶרֶב `*ereb*) time (עֵת `*eth*), namely, after a complete day circle of consciousness, the dove, the spirit of truth, returned[2305] into[2306] those[2307] epistemic faculties of Noah. The dove of certainty had uprooted (טָרָף *taraph*) the objective world from its *worldliness* with its mouth (פֶּה *peh*). That organ is its ability to distinguish,[2308] individualize, reduce into pieces and whoosh (פָּאָה *pa'ah*) the objective world, like a leaf (עָלֶה `*aleh*) offered as food (טָרָף *taraph*) and blown up before (עָלָה `*alah*) the Transcendent Awareness. However, the dove holds it in its mouth without eating it. The leaf is testimony of the receded waters. Furthermore, the twig turns out to be a bright, splendid and flourished (זו *ziv*) olive (זַיִת *zayith*) branch. Before the Apodictical Truth, Consciousness shines and flows like pressed oil (צָהַר *tsahar*) through the window-light (צֹהַר *tsohar*) of the ark. The oily-fluidity of Consciousness is proof and certainty that the deluge of the thinking process is subsiding[2309] from the earthly (אֶרֶץ *'erets*) objectivity. It is splendid Consciousness without consciousness-*of*-any-object. This is the real task of true meditation, '***to be awake while being in dreamless sleep.***' Finally, this will lead us beyond, to the realization that

"Death is an awakening."[2310]

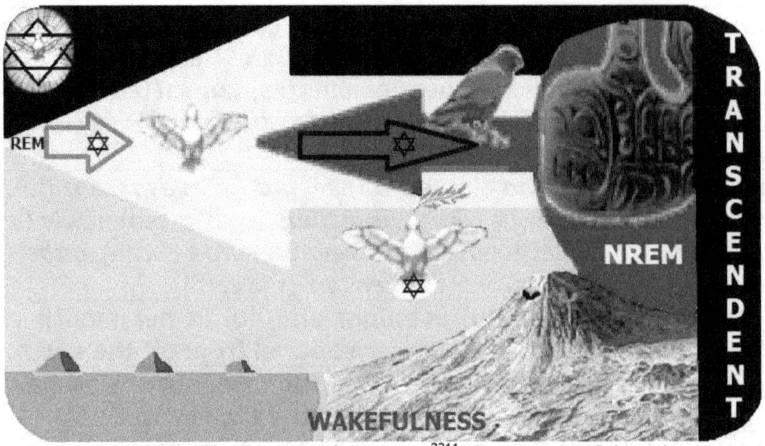

GRAPHIC: *The Raven and the Doves*[2311] *Coming out of the Ark*

<The ancient Hermetic Tradition distinguished two methods for the sacred Alchemic Art, the Dry and the Humid Way.[2312] What is the real meaning of these two ways? Usually, the interpretation is one of chemical nature. It should be evident, by now, that we depart completely from the physical-chemical interpretation. Our reading is fundamentally epistemic, namely, related to the process of knowledge. If any transformation takes place, it is only on the gnoseological level. What **we know** is the **only** reality ***per-se***. The consciousness-*of* the world puts it into epistemic existence. When that knowledge ends, the world *per-se* ends. In fact, who is there that may be conscious-of-it-for-us? We may think of a world *in-se*, but also that thought is inevitably and ultimately *for-us* (*i.e. per-se*). We can never know the world *in-se*, because it will never exist *for-us*, except as our imagined concept. Therefore, the two hermetic ways correspond to:[2313]

- The Dry Way, metaphorically the Dry Land, relates to Being-in-itself (*viz. in-se*), namely, the absolute independent *transcendent* center of the *immanent* circle set apart from the inseparable *subject-object* circular correlation. There we become disengaged from the world's seductions. This is the world before the original sin.
- The Humid Way, metaphorically the Deluge, corresponds to Being-for-itself (*viz. per-se*), namely, the continuous circular reference of a *subject* to its correlated inseparable *object*. There we become emotionally involved with and in the world. This is the world after the original sin.

From these premises, we can argue that for the original sin to affect all humans it must be present in the epistemic structure of every individual. Furthermore, the land drying up symbolizes the desiccation, from the subject-object correlation, of the knowledge of the world as Being-for-itself or *per-se*. It is the dry abstention from any attachment to this world as we see, understand and know it. This is the true spiritual alchemy. It transforms the drowning flood, the heavy-lead-consciousness-*of*-the-objective-world, into the Gold-of-Pure-Awareness.>[2314]

It is through deep meditative introspection into the flooded process of thought that we find our lifesaver, which will propel us to the surface of dry land. That Savior is *Certainty* itself. It is not the certainty-*of*-some-object, which will sink us, with its lead-weight, back into the abyss. It is not the gullible-belief in some puerile dogmatic fables. In fact, many of those who proclaim their belief in an historical savior and not in the Incarnation of Truth, as such, do so in the hope and/or for the desire of personal wellbeing, gain and power, which, again, weights them down in the flood. In fact, after the death in those treacherous waters, when every thought is spent, which certainty can sustain us if we only knew the objects of that certainty and never realized the Truth of Certainty itself? The Savior is the flowing of Pure-Faith, Pure-Certainty dried up and devoid of any objectivity. In the state of dreamless auto-transparency, focus only on the Conscious Certainty flowing objectlessly before Awareness. Like a jaculatory, sent-out short prayer, the dove returns into Noah as meditation. Almost like counting sheep to usher sleep, the unceasing repetition of jaculatory prayers,[2315] even while sleeping, was and is one of the ways to reach the suspension of thought to induce a meditative ecstatic state. The Hebrew practice of ritual intonation, called cantillation (טעמים *te'amim*), during synagogue chants of sacred texts, intends to reach a similar introspective mood. It is to

"*pray without ceasing,*"[2316]

"*meditate day and night.*"[2317]

The Greek Orthodoxy calls this practice *Hesychasm*, to keep stillness (ἡσυχάζω *ēsuchazō*), or

"Philokalia [(φιλο-καλία) *love of beauty*]... through which, by means of the... ascetic practice and contemplation, the intellect is purified, illumined, and made perfect."[2318]

Yoga, in the Indian tradition, means to yoke (√*yuj*), to unite the individual Self with the Supreme Spirit. There are several paths to reach that state. Patañjali, the II century BC Indian sage, taught one of them, called the *Royal-eight-members-yoga*.[2319] Its seventh member or step is the profound meditation (*dhyāna, zen*). <This is the state in which the subject having shed the object, dissolves into Certitude alone. That Certitude is the cohesive central point, which holds the two subject-object spinning together along the orbit of its circumference.>

"Meditating is entering truth without discovering it, without seeing it from outside, without opening it into words."[2320]

In fact, <what persists when the seer sheds the seen, when the hearer sheds the heard, the thinker sheds the thought and the understander sheds the understood? Only Pure Aware Certitude is there from the very beginning.>

"*This is your Shining Self, the Apodictic Transcendent which is in everything.*"[2321]

Yoga recognizes <that all opposites belong to the realm of time, including the dichotomy of good and evil. Thus, salvation lies not only beyond evil but also beyond good because even the good leads back into the snares of time.[2322] Since we can never avoid action, not even during the "act" of meditation, then it is *not what* we do *but how* we perform the action that leads to salvation from drowning in the flood. It is the desire-less accomplishment of assignment that delivers from ignorance.[2323] Hence, the paradox that all dutiful deeds, relatively construed as good or evil by a particular space-time environment, when performed without attachment, may lead to sudden rapture into awareness, a pure meditation devoid of objects. This is not an act of thinking but a re-flection upon oneself. Thinking, in fact, came to be when the human beings, to satisfy their hunger>[2324] for knowledge, eat the craved forbidden object.

Regardless of the tradition, Kabbalah (קַבָּלָה),[2325] Hesychasm (ἡσυχασμός), Yoga (योग) or other, meditation requires the same aware distance from the conceptual world in all three levels of human reality, namely, in the waking, dreaming and dreamless sleep. That is the Garden of Eden, the esoteric Kabbalistic *orchard **PaRaDiSe*** (פרדס $p_a rd_e s$),[2326] which is considered an acronym composed of post-Biblical Hebrew words,

פ*p*) ***peshat*** (פשט),[2327] meaning *to spread out* in the waking experience and *to strip away* into death.

ר*r*) ***remez*** (רמז),[2328] meaning *to hint, to make signs* as in the dream state.

ד*d*) ***derash*** (דרש),[2329] meaning *to interpret* and *to frequent*[2330] the dreamless meditative stage.

ס*s*) ***sod*** (סוד),[2331] meaning *the secret **assembly*** of the whole encompassing reality beyond those three states, where, all those who enter serenely depart in peace.[2332]

Someone may argue that it is impossible and contradictory to try to be aware while sleeping. Here, we do not refer to lucid dreams. Nor we refer to prophetic dreams, if they exist at all.[2333] Wakefulness, dream and dreamless sleep are three faces of the same being. One influences the other and, in turn, is affected by the previous one, and so on. As demonstrated by Freud,[2334] dreams leave impressions on wakefulness as this one influences the oneiric state. If we control our waking stage, we consequently determine the possible directions of our dreams. If beliefs, depressions, desires, expectations, fears, feelings, joys, opinions, sentiments, thoughts, and all other similar events experienced in the waking stage are pure, namely meditatively focused exclusively on their certainty, also dreams would have the same purity of heart. Then, the meditative state of Awareness will be in all levels of being.

"*Watch ye and pray, lest ye enter into temptation. The spirit truly is ready, but the flesh is weak.*"[2335]

Like the adrenalin rush makes the fatigue of the athlete less painful. Consciousness, like luminous oil flows fluidly. Light tints the physical body, but it is not the colored thing. Similarly, Consciousness or Certainty is not the object we are conscious-or-certain-*of*. In darkness, the object is unseen, unless brightened by light. As light, Apodictical Consciousness enlightens the object, but is never the object itself. We know nothing, without that Certainty. Light continues on its trajectory, unblocked by the bodies on its path, actually, it surrounds them to proceed past them. Similarly, **Consciousness, as such, persists unaffected by the objects, envelops them only to continue unaltered in its spaceless present**. The act of halting the flow of Consciousness to become *conscious-of* something is the equivalent of eating the forbidden fruit. This generates the metaphoric War of the Sons of Light against the Sons of Darkness.[2336] This produces the deluge of objectivity into which the individual drowns missing the infinite vivifying *dry land* of Pure Certainty.

8:12-The Dove of Non-Return

וַיִּיָּחֶל עוֹד שִׁבְעַת יָמִים אֲחֵרִים וַיְשַׁלַּח אֶת־הַיּוֹנָה וְלֹא־יָסְפָה שׁוּב־אֵלָיו עוֹד׃   *vayiyāḥel* (he waited) *ʿvōḏ* (still) *šiḇəʿaṯ* (seven) *yāmiym* (days) *ʾăḥēriym* (another) *vayəšalaḥ* (sent away) *ʾeṯ* (and) *hayvōnāh* (dove) *vəlō̆* (not) *yāsəp̄*ah (again) *šuḇ* (return) *ʾēlāyv* (into him) *ʿvōḏ* (any more)
καὶ *kai* (and) **ἐπισχὼν** *epischōn* (waiting) **ἔτι** *eti* (yet) **ἡμέρας** *ēmeras* (days) **ἑπτὰ** *epta* (seven) **ἑτέρας** *eteras* (other) **πάλιν** *palin* (once more) **ἐξαπέστειλεν** *exapesteilen* (he sent) **τὴν** *tēn* (the) **περιστεράν** *peristeran* (dove) **καὶ** *kai* (and) **οὐ** *ou* (not) **προσέθετο** *prosetheto* (put to) **τοῦ** *tou* (the) **ἐπιστρέψαι** *epistrepsai* (returned) **πρὸς** *pros* (in) **αὐτὸν** *auton* (him) **ἔτι** *eti* (again)
expectavit- (waited) ***que*** (and) ***nihilominus*** (nonetheless) ***septem*** (seven) ***alios*** (other) ***dies*** (days) ***et*** (and) ***emisit*** (sent) ***columbam*** (dove) ***quae*** (she) ***non*** (not) ***est*** (is) ***reversa*** (reversed) ***ultra*** (again) ***ad*** (to) ***eum*** (him)
And he stayed yet other seven days; and sent forth the dove; which returned not again unto him any more.
Nonetheless, he waited another seven days, then, he sent out of the Ark/*fish* (7) the dove/Jonah, which did not return again into him.

Noah, the rested one, stayed (יָחַל *yachal*) other (אחר *'acher*) seven (שֶׁבַע *sheba*) circular days (יוֹם *yowm*) in that restful (שַׁבָּת *shabath*) meditation. Then, he sent forth the dove from that ark-fish (דָּג *dāḡ*), which has the Gematria equivalent of #7. This time the dove *exit*ed the ark and *stayed out*.[2337] This dove is the spirit of *ec*stasy (*i.e. out staying*),[2338] of testimonial truth. It reaches the final union with the Transcendent Supreme Reality, when all-is-put-together, joined, united, completed and concluded. In that state, when,

"*all things were now accomplished*,"[2339]

is the last stage that brings everything into harmony and in the intense absorption into silence. It is the awakening power of creation. That power, having traveled through the six circular days, reaches the seventh where it rests without turning back.

Recapitulating, there are four birds,

1) the *crow* (עֹרֵב *`oreb*), symbolizes the conscious turning within and the stillness of the dreamless sleep,
2) the first *dove* (יוֹנָה *yownah*), symbolizes the internal consciousness producer of the dreams' liquid state,
3) the second *dove* (יוֹנָה *yownah*) *with an olive* (זַיִת *zayith*) *leaf* (עָלֶה *`aleh*), symbolizes the meditative fluidity of Consciousness,
4) the third *dove* (יוֹנָה *yownah*) *of non*(לֹא *lo'*)*-return*(שׁוּב *shuwb*), symbolizes the final state of transcendent ecstasy. This coincides with the state present in the now of Creation where everything is beautiful.

Meditation realizes that Consciousness rests in the NREM as it emanates in REM and wakefulness to return in dreamless sleep and beyond in the present instant of creation.

8-III SECTION: EXIT FROM THE ARK

8:13-Opening of the Ark's Roof

וַיְהִי בְּאַחַת וְשֵׁשׁ־מֵאוֹת שָׁנָה בָּרִאשׁוֹן בְּאֶחָד לַחֹדֶשׁ חָרְבוּ הַמַּיִם מֵעַל הָאָרֶץ וַיָּסַר נֹחַ אֶת־מִכְסֵה הַתֵּבָה וַיַּרְא וְהִנֵּה חָרְבוּ פְּנֵי הָאֲדָמָה:

vayəhiy (if came to be) *bə'aḥaṯ* (another) *vəšēš* (six) *mē'vōṯ* (hundred) *šānāh* (years) *bāri'švōn* (first) *bə'eḥāḏ* (one) *laḥōḏeš* (month) *ḥārəḇu* (dry up) *hamayim* (waters) *mē'al* (from) *hā'āreṣ* (land) *vayāsar* (removed) *nōaḥ* (Noah) *'eṯ* (and) *miḵəsēh* (covering) *hatēḇāh* (ark) *vayarə'* (looked) *vəhinēh* (lo and behold) *ḥārəḇu* (dry land) *pənēy* (face) *hā'ăḏāmāh* (of the earth)

καὶ *kai* (and) **ἐγένετο** *egeneto* (it came) **ἐν** *en* (in) **τῷ** *tō* (the) **ἑνὶ** *eni* (first) **καὶ** *kai* (and) **ἑξακοσιοστῷ** *exakosiostō* (six-hundredth) **ἔτει** *etei* (years) **ἐν** *en* (in) **τῇ** *tē* (the) **ζωῇ** *zōē* (life) **τοῦ** *tou* (of) **Νωε** *Nōe* (Noah) **τοῦ** *tou* () **πρώτου** *prōtou* (first) **μηνός** *mēnos* (month) **μιᾷ** *mia* (one) **τοῦ** *tou* (the) **μηνός** *mēnos* (month) **ἐξέλιπεν** *exelipen* () **τὸ** *to* () **ὕδωρ** *udōr* (water) **ἀπὸ** *apo* (from) **τῆς** *tēs* (the) **γῆς** *gēs* (earth) **καὶ** *kai* (and) **ἀπεκάλυψεν** *apekalupsen* (apocalypse) **Νωε** *Nōe* (Noe) **τὴν** *tēn* (the) **στέγην** *stegēn* (roof) **τῆς** *tēs* (of the) **κιβωτοῦ** *kibōtou* (ark) **ἣν** *ēn* (thus) **ἐποίησεν** *epoiēsen* (he had made) **καὶ** *kai* (and) **εἶδεν** *eiden* (he saw) **ὅτι** *oti* (that) **ἐξέλιπεν** *exelipen* (had subsided) **τὸ** *to* (the) **ὕδωρ** *udōr* (water) **ἀπὸ** *apo* (from) **προσώπου** *prosōpou* (face) **τῆς** *tēs* (of the) **γῆς** *gēs* (earth)

igitur (therefore) ***sescentesimo*** (six hundredth) ***primo*** (first) ***anno*** (year) ***primo*** (first) ***mense*** (month) ***prima*** (first) ***die*** (day) ***mensis*** (of the month) ***inminutae*** (reduced) ***sunt*** (are) ***aquae*** (the waters) ***super*** (on) ***terram*** (the earth) ***et*** (and) ***aperiens*** (opened) ***Noe*** (Noah) ***tectum*** (the roof) ***arcae*** (of the ark) ***aspexit*** (looked) ***vidit-*** (saw) ***que*** (and) ***quod*** (if) ***exsiccata*** (dried) ***esset*** (was) ***superficies*** (the surface) ***terrae*** (of the earth)

And it came to pass in the six hundredth and first year, in the first month, the first day of the month, the waters were dried up from off the earth: and Noah removed the covering of the ark, and looked, and, behold, the face of the ground was dry.

At the ends $_{(601)}$ of the conscious circular years, in the *leading* $_{(1)}$ conscious circular month and in the leading circular day of consciousness of the month, the waters dried up from off the earth: and Noah removed the covering of the ark, and *looked* $_{(601)}$, and, behold, the face of the ground was dry.

In Gematria the number, six (שֵׁשׁ *shesh*) hundred (מֵאָה *me'ah*) and one (שָׁנָה *shaneh*), equals to the word *haqtṣāwṯ*,[2340] meaning *at the ends*. The years, month and day, are all metaphors for the epistemic circularities of knowledge. At that end as well as at the very beginning of the epistemic circularity, there, *lo and behold* (הִנֵּה *hinneh*), in the leading-first (א, *a*)[2341] present day and month of that cycle, Noah can see and perceive the world in a whole new way. Interestingly, in Gematria, the Hebrew word *tēra*,[2342] meaning *see*, *perceive*, equals the number 601.

The flooding two days of dream and wakefulness submerge us. However, on the third day of unconscious dreamless sleep (NREM), we have no experience. The great[2343] fish (***dag***),[2344] which had swallowed up[2345] Jonah the dove, had covered (***dag**ah*)[2346] *him completely for three days. When that fish vomits Jonah, then that cover is removed.*[2347] *Lo and behold* (הִנֵּה *hinneh*), *then*, in the present moment, the covering (מִכְסֶה *mikceh*) removal (סוּר *cuwr*) of the ark takes place. This means that we <u>consciously</u> <u>look</u> into the dreamless sleep. Now we *see* and *realize* (תֵּרָא *tēra*) the auto-transparency of the world in its unified state. The exsiccation of all the objective land, once drenched in the passion of attachment, produces a new way of seeing and perceiving the world. The objects' watery emotional possession is not there anymore. The land is now dry.[2348] Then, all things shine and flow in the glorious[2349] light of Awareness and

"speak of his glory,"[2350]

and Saint Francis chants,

"praised be, my Lord, with all Thy creatures."[2351]

The humid way of the deluge dries up. The objective world flows like olive (זַיִת *zayith*) oil (שֶׁמֶן *shemen*)[2352] and the "*rivers ... run like oil*"[2353]

"*oil for the light*"[2354]

of Consciousness. Beyond the meditative state, the stillness of dreamless sleep has become like a gliding surfer on the flood's waves.

"*Hear ye indeed, but understand not; and see ye indeed, but perceive not... lest they see with their eyes, and hear with their ears, and understand with their heart, and convert, and be healed.*"[2355]

Then, we see without looking, we hear without listening, we breathe without smelling, we savor without tasting, we sense without touching, we feel dispassionately, we act without doing and we conceive without thinking. The object does not lure us any longer, because the Universally-Pervading-Beauty of the Transcendent-Pure-Present-Certain-Awareness absorbs us entirely. This is the meaning of the exhortation,

"*long for*[2356] *thy Transcendent God with all thine heart, and with all thy soul, and with all thy might.*"[2357]

Here, the *heart* (לֵבָב *lebab*)[2358] is the waking world, meaning

"the seat of *the senses, affections and emotions of the mind.*"[2359]

The *soul* (נֶפֶשׁ *nephesh*)[2360] is the dream state, signifying the inner breath of sensations.[2361] The *might* (מְאֹד *m@`od*)[2362] is the stage of dreamless sleep, the *mighty force* from which the other two states derive. This love must completely engulf all three stages of life.

"*Therefore, thou shalt bow down*[2363] *to no other* (אַחֵר *'acher*) *mighty thing in nature:*[2364] *because the Transcendent, whose name is Jealous,*[2365] *is a jealous God...*[2366] *a consuming fire.*"[2367]

In fact, no other but the Tree (וְעֵץ *və'ēṣ*) of Life (הַחַיִּים *haḥayiym*) envelops the entire Universe. In humans, we understand it as *Awareness* or *Certainty*, in the fauna, we understand it as *Instinct*, in the flora, we understand it as *Growing-Spontaneity* and, in the physical universe, we understand it as *Energy*. From any perspective, this is the *Universal Life*, which the verses metaphorically refer to as being exclusively jealous. In fact, without It there is no Certainty, Instinct, Spontaneity or Energy. Nevertheless, when we are *dis*tracted, these thoughts become only conceptual objects, not the Truth of Certainty as such. When we are away from It, we find only death. When we bow to the ineluctable epistemic objects' past we enter the realm of death.

In line with the first part of the faithful testimony (شَـهادة *šahādah*),

"*There is no deity except the Transcendent,*"[2368]

we can say, '*there is no belief but Apodictic Truth.*' <The testimony declares the absolute Transcendent inscrutable ineffability of the Real-God-in-Itself, beyond any other idolatrous immanent conceptualization of god/s. When a religion conceptualizes the Transcendence, the danger is that its adherents may become mentally idolatrous and lose any real and living spirituality. To be precise, they are not any longer worshiping the Transcendent as such, but they venerate the individual mental image they have, regardless of how abstract it may be. Religions that place the intervention of God in a particular historical time must necessarily be dogmatic in nature. There is, therefore, a strenuous, at times fanatical, defensive effort to document and demonstrate the historical validity of God's extraordinary events. Those fundamentalists accuse of heresy anyone attempting to disprove God's actual involvement in those historical occurrences.

Etymologically, religion means re-bonded (*re-ligo*), tied to a creed or to a reality believed to be absolute. We call Traditional those historical religions that postulate a *lost Paradise*. The main purpose of religion is to regain that Ultimate Reality from which the individual allegedly parted or separated.[2369] Through a Gnostic or a Devotional approach, the Metaphysical World reinstates the Transcendent reestablishing HARMONY or reaching REUNION. Gnostic is the approach to the Transcendent through a personal realization. Lao Tzu affirms that

"*to know the perpetual is to be enlightened.*"[2370]

Two paths follow this approach: R_1) the *Way of Knowledge* and H_1) the *Way of Nature*. Devotional is the approach to the Transcendent through repentance and a Metaphysical intervention.

"*In guiding a state of a thousand chariots, approach your duties with reverence,*"

admonishes Confucius.[2371] The Torah commands:

"*Thou shalt love the Lord thy God with all thine heart, and with all thy soul, and with all thy might.*"[2372]
Two paths follow this approach: R_2) the *Way of Adoration* and H_2) the *Way of Society*.

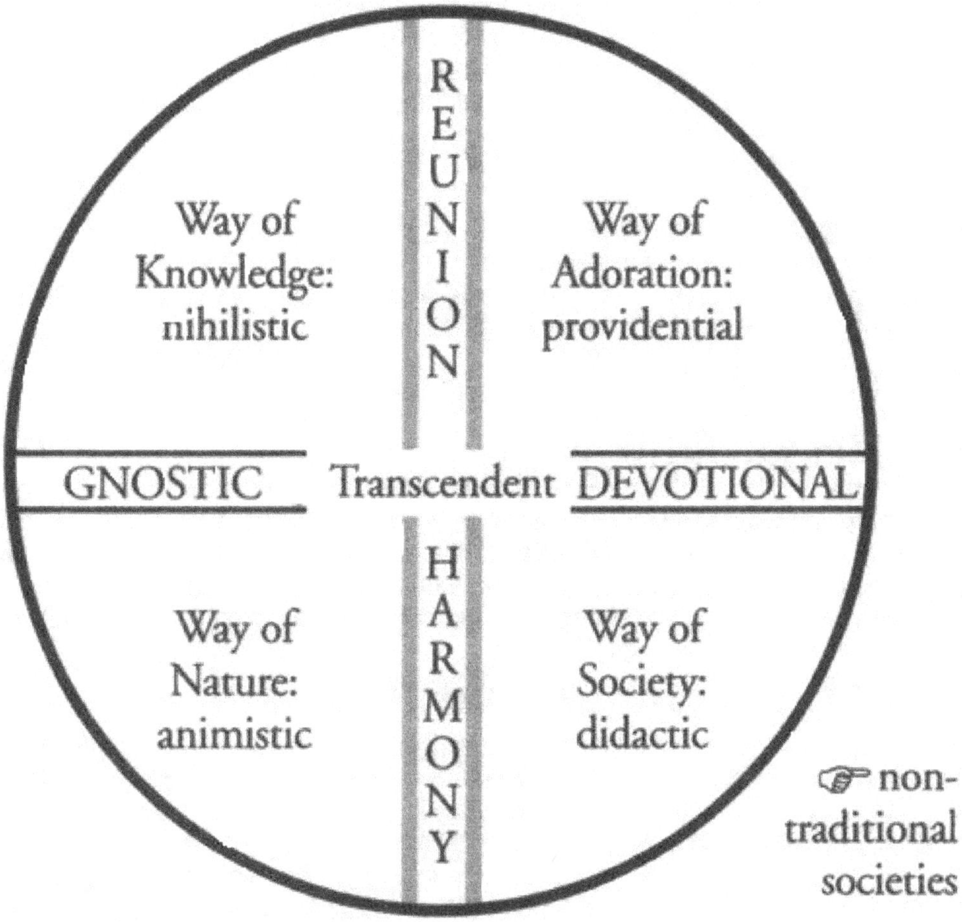

GRAPHIC: *The four ways of religions*

Despite their differences, each path merges, in different degrees, with each and all the others. The ineffable unity, sought by these four Ways, is expressed through myths, shamanistic techniques, ecstatic visions,[2373] parables[2374] and hermetic writings, such as Revelation, Kabbalah, Sangreal and Tantra.

H) HARMONY is envisioned as the holistic Symphony of the Cosmos in which everything finds solution in its opposite. Two paths lead to HARMONY: H_1) the *Way of Nature* and H_2) the *Way of Society*.

H_1) The *Way of Nature* leads to a holistic integration with the Universe. Its mythology becomes a mirror of nature.[2375] It has an *Animistic* view of history, in which the *vitality* of the Immortal Nature enters in communion with the living. In some African Shamanistic religions, which belong to this Way,

> "history moves 'backwards' ... future does not exist. [There are only] *Sasa* ..., the 'now-period' ... of conscious living, [and death, the past,] *Zamani* ..., the period of the myth... [Ancestors affect the life of the living who are] moving gradually [from life to death,] from the *Sasa* to the *Zamani*, ... the state of *collective immortality*."[2376]

Some of the Gnostic religions that characterize this Way are:

α) Taoism, for which, with a cosmic consonance,[2377]

> "*Heaven attained unity, and thereby became pure. Earth attained unity, and thereby became tranquil. The spirits attained unity, and thereby became divine;*"[2378]

β) Science, postulates a noumenal Cosmological Reality, which survives the individual research-scientist with a mathematical intelligibility of Nature's objective Transcendent reality. Einstein, quoting Emmanuel Kant, says,

"The eternal mystery of the world is its comprehensibility."[2379]

"The scientist knows only the external God he calls Matter, an unknowable principle whose existence can only be affirmed by an act of faith, but this is so strong and so unreflecting that it takes itself for an affirmation of something obvious;"[2380]

γ) and other similar religions seeking a harmonious reconnection with the Transcendent.

H_2) The *Way of Society* has a mythology whose main function

"is the enforcement of a moral order."[2381]

It has a *Didactic* view of history, in which

"the purity and order of ancient times"

are examples for the present.[2382] Some of the Devotional religions that characterize this Way are:

α) Confucianism, which states that, through the performance of ethical duties,

"the virtue of the common people will incline towards fullness... Of the things brought about by the rites, harmony is the most valuable;"[2383]

β) Totemic, the religions of the tribal and spiritually integrated communities, which require sacrifices to remote ancestors;

γ) and other similar religions seeking a harmonious society as a way to the Transcendent.

H_{2a}) *Non-Traditional Religions* spring out from the *Way of Society*. Here, we should briefly mention those societies, structured by non-traditional beliefs, which deny the Transcendent, while at the same time refer to it as *economic structure*, and the Metaphysical. In turn, these are replaced by ideologies and economic structures requiring, however, a faithful religious adherence to their teachings imparted as non-dogmatic. Such societies are those founded on

α) the Capitalist separation of State and Church and/or

β) the Communist historical materialism.[2384]

R) REUNION is realized as the reestablishment of the Original Unity between the individual and the Transcendent. Two paths lead to Reunion: R_1) the *Way of Knowledge* and R_2) the *Way of Adoration*.

R_1) The *Way of Knowledge* obtains the Supreme Reality by removing the veil of ignorance.

"*Verily, who thus knows goes daily to the heavenly dimension.*"[2385]

The function of

"mythology is to foster the centering and unfolding of the individual in integrity, in accord with"

the Ultimate Reality.[2386] It has a Nihilistic view of history perceived as recurring dreams. Some of the Gnostic religions that characterize this Way are:

α) Brahmanism, which recognizes the Brahman as the ultimate Reality;

β) Buddhism, which points out the path to the extinction (*nirvāṇa*) of sorrow;

γ) Jainism, which instructs to revere all life without ever using violence (*a-hiṃsā*);[2387]

δ) and other religions that yearn for liberation from life's sorrow.

R_2) The *Way of Adoration*, through love, reunites with God the

"*People of the Book.*"[2388]

These Devotional religions, like these ones, view, with a Providential historicism, God guiding the course of history. Mythology, then, reconciles the

"waking consciousness to the *mysterium tremendum et fascinans.*"[2389]

Some of the Devotional religions that characterize this Way are:

α) Judaism, which expects the advent of the Messiah;

β) Christianity, which finds salvation in the sacrifice of the Son of God;

γ) Islam, which preaches a total submission to the will of Allah (الله *Allh*);

δ) and the others that>[2390]

"*love him, because he first loved us.*"[2391]

8:14-Bright Purity

וּבַחֹדֶשׁ הַשֵּׁנִי בְּשִׁבְעָה וְעֶשְׂרִים יוֹם לַחֹדֶשׁ יָבְשָׁה הָאָרֶץ: ס *ub̲aḥōd̲eš* (month) *hašēniy* (second) *bəšib̲ə 'āh* (seven) *və 'eśəriym* (twentyeth) *yvōm* (day) *laḥōd̲eš* (month) *yāb̲əšāh* (dried) *hā 'āreṣ* (earth) *s* (.)
ἐν *en* (in) **δὲ** *de* (but) **τῷ** *tō* (the) **μηνὶ** *mēni* (month) **τῷ** *tō* (the) **δευτέρῳ** *deuterō* (second) **ἑβδόμῃ** *ebdomē* (seventh) **καὶ** *kai* (and) **εἰκάδι** *eikadi* (twentieth day of the month) **τοῦ** *tou* (the) **μηνός** *mēnos* (month) **ἐξηράνθη** *exēranthē* (dry up) **ἡ** *ē* (the) **γῆ** *gē* (earth)
mense (in the month) ***secundo*** (second) ***septima*** (seventh) ***et*** (and) ***vicesima*** (twentieth) ***die*** (day) ***mensis*** (of the month) ***arefacta*** (dried) ***est*** (is) ***terra*** (on earth)
And in the second month, on the seven and twentieth day of the month, was the earth dried.
In the bright circular lunar month of consciousness, on the month's *pure* (27) circular day of consciousness, the objective world was without the moisture of attachment.

The second lunar month of the Hebrew calendar goes from May to June. It is the month of the flowers' splendor, called *ziv* (זו), *brightness,*[2392] akin to the word *zayith*, olive (זית). At the exit of the two circular consciousness-*of*, namely the waking and dreaming realm, Noah enters awake in the third realm where the objects disappear in the stillness of the rested state. From there, the *rested* auto-transparent-stillness of NREM flows anew and awake into the two realms of REM and wakefulness, drying them up from all attachments.

There are some words, which have an equivalent Gematria number 27. The first one is *zāk̲ə* (זך),[2393] meaning *pure*, thus,

"*bring thee pure beaten olive oil for the light, to cause the lamp to burn always.*"[2394]

As it is evident, the oil, which we mentioned several times in this commentary, is the source of the light and it is the metaphor for the brightness of consciousness. The is a metaphor for the motionless steady flowing of attention in the Presence of Awareness. This is expressed by the parable of the

"ten *chaste-persons* (παρθένος *parthenos*), *which took their lamps, and went forth* (ἐξέρχομαι *exerchomai*) *to meet* (ἀπάντησις *apantēsis*) *the bridegroom* (νυμφίος *nymphios*). *And five of them were wise, and five were foolish. They that were foolish took their lamps* (λαμπάς *lampas*), *and took no oil* (ἔλαιον *elaion*) *with them: But the wise took oil in their vessels with their lamps. While the bridegroom tarried, they all slumbered and slept. And at the mid* (μέσης *mesēs*) *of* (δὲ *de*) *the night* (νυκτὸς *nuktos*) *there was a cry* (κραυγή *kraugē*) *made* (γίνομαι *ginomai*), *'Behold, the bridegroom cometh; go ye out to meet him.' Then all those virgins arose, and trimmed their lamps. And the foolish said unto the wise, 'Give us of your oil; for our lamps are gone out.' But the wise answered, saying, 'Not so; lest there be not enough for us and you: but go ye rather to them that sell, and buy for yourselves.' And while they went to buy, the bridegroom came; and they that were ready went in with him to the marriage* (γάμος *gamos*)*: and the door was shut. Afterward came also the other virgins, saying, 'Lord, Lord, open to us.' But he answered and said, 'Verily I say unto you, I know you not.' Watch* (γρηγορέω *grēgoreō*) *therefore, for ye know neither the day nor the hour wherein the Son of man cometh.*"[2395]

The *oil* (ἔλαιον *elaion*) from the *olive tree* (ἐλαία *elaia*) is the flowing *watching* (γρηγορέω *grēgoreō*), which *rises up* (ἐγείρω *egeirō*) *collecting all* (ἀγορά *agora*) the faculties. Together they fuel the *lamp* (λαμπάς *lampas*) of awareness. From the Greek verb *lambánō* (λαμβάνω), the lamp implies taking hold and marrying the flowing presence of light of awareness, which is beyond time, as

"*the Transcendent* (יְהֹוָה Yĕhovah) *is my light.*"[2396]

Be vigilant because Transcendence is unconceivable and we can never know when the flow of thoughts will cease in order to manifest the splendor of Pure-Awareness-In-Itself.

Once the waters retreat, the world appears in its purity. In addition, the word *wayabēṭ* (וַיַּבֵּט),[2397] meaning *looked*, has a Gematria value of 27. Therefore, Noah, coming out of the ark, *looked* (27) and recognized the objective world dried up, without the moisture of attachment (יָבֵשׁ *yabesh*).[2398] Thus, that objectivity is now *zabach* (זָבַח = 27),[2399] *sacrificed, viz.* made sacred by the *eyes* of Awareness, as the next verses will clarify.

The rested state, within the unconscious awakened sleep without dreams, is <u>not</u> a state of melancholic depression characterized by sadness and hopelessness. On the contrary, it is the heighten state of mindful positive joy. We can define it as the highest state of unified meditative yoga, which we can realize only with a deep introspective stillness. <Yoga is a category of the Indian or Pan-Asian spirit.

> "Yoga is not a religion, but a philosophy in the proper and first meaning of the word: wisdom of love... The great danger of yoga is that it makes a man grow... [Thus, he may fall] from a greater height... Yoga is learning to live and die as one learns to play an instrument... The musical instrument is the living body, the inner body..."[2400]

Yoga is the practical realization techniques for all the orthodox and/or heterodox philosophical systems. It articulates in pure scientifically oriented disciplines, which reject any preconceived belief. For the contemporary mind to understand the real scope of yoga, it must be equated to the dispassionate observation in an absolute objective analysis, which we may find today only in science.[2401] A

> "*very tasty science,*"

declared St. John of the Cross.[2402] Actually, it is in that scientific dispassionate disengagement that yoga finds its own direct realization of the psychical forces, which animate the world. It is the ultimate validation which consents a Gnostic and non-dogmatic approach for all those philosophies. Yoga is the discipline enabling to travel through the waking, dreaming, sleeping stages and entering awake the silence of Transcendence. Yoga is the final yoke between the individual living-self (*jīvā-tman*) and the universal Supreme-Self (*paramā-tman*), which remains always hidden and unknown for the individual.>[2403]

8:15-God's Command at the Exit of the Ark

וַיְדַבֵּר אֱלֹהִים אֶל־נֹחַ לֵאמֹר׃
vayədabēr (spoke) *'ĕlōhiym* (the Gods) *'el* (to the) *nōaḥ* (Noah) *lē'mōr* (saying)
καὶ *kai* (and) **εἶπεν** *eipen* (spoke) **κύριος** *kurios* (the Lord) **ὁ** *o* (the) **θεὸς** *theos* (God) **τῷ** *tō* (into) **Νωε** *Nōe* (Noah) **λέγων** *legēōn* (saying)
locutus (spoken) ***est*** (is) ***autem*** (also) ***Deus*** (God) ***ad*** (to) ***Noe*** (Noah) ***dicens*** (saying)
And God spake unto Noah, saying,
Divine-Consciousness spoke to Noah saying

Thus, Divine-Consciousness (אֱלֹהִים *'elohiym*) commanded and directed Noah.

8:16-Exit the Ark

צֵא מִן־הַתֵּבָה אַתָּה וְאִשְׁתְּךָ וּבָנֶיךָ וּנְשֵׁי־בָנֶיךָ אִתָּךְ׃
ṣē (go out) *min* (from) *hatēḇāh* (the ark) *'atāh* (bring) *və'išətəḵā* (wife) *uḇāneyḵā* (sons) *unəšēy* (wives) *ḇāneyḵā* (sons) *'itāḵə* (with)
ἔξελθε *exelthe* (exit) **ἐκ** *ek* (from) **τῆς** *tēs* (the) **κιβωτοῦ** *kibōtou* (ark) **σὺ** *su* (you) **καὶ** *kai* (and) **ἡ** *ē* (the) **γυνή** *gunē* (wife) **σου** *sou* (your) **καὶ** *kai* (and) **οἱ** *oi* (the) **υἱοί** *uioi* (sons) **σου** *sou* (your) **καὶ** *kai* (and) **αἱ** *ai* (the) **γυναῖκες** *gunaikes* (wives) **τῶν** *tōn* (of the) **υἱῶν** *uiōn* (sons) **σου** *sou* (your) **μετὰ** *meta* (with) **σοῦ** *sou* (you)
egredere (exit) ***de*** (from the) ***arca*** (ark) ***tu*** (you) ***et*** (and) ***uxor*** (wife) ***tua*** (your) ***filii*** (sons) ***tui*** (your) ***et*** (and) ***uxores*** (wives) ***filiorum*** (of the sons) ***tuorum*** (your) ***tecum*** (with you)
Go forth of the ark, thou, and thy wife, and thy sons, and thy sons' wives with thee.
"*Exit the ark you and your wife, your sons and the wives of your sons with you.*

We saw that Noah *rested* in the ark, the state of deep-sleep, with his wife. The wife was the noematic potential objective of the oneiric and waking world. His three offspring were the modes of knowing, the logical prerequisite for any possible knowledge. Their wives were the potential noematic objective actuality of those forms. Entering the state of deep sleep, the entire world of *will and representation* remained outside submerged in the watery deluge of wakeful and dream representations.

Now, upon awakening within the intuition of the oneiric detachment from the object, the *rested* Noah comes out of the ark actualizing again those epistemic forms but with a new direction, as we will see.

8:17-Bring all the Animals with You

כָּל־הַחַיָּה אֲשֶׁר־אִתְּךָ מִכָּל־בָּשָׂר בָּעוֹף וּבַבְּהֵמָה וּבְכָל־הָרֶמֶשׂ הָרֹמֵשׂ עַל־הָאָרֶץ הוצא אִתָּךְ וְשָׁרְצוּ בָאָרֶץ וּפָרוּ וְרָבוּ עַל־הָאָרֶץ׃
kāl (all) *haḥayāh* (living) *'ăšer* (which) *'itəḵā* (with) *mikāl* (among) *bāśār* (flesh) *bā'vōp̄* (fowl) *uḇabəhēmāh* (cattle) *uḇəḵāl* (every) *hāremeś* (creeping thing) *hārōmēś* (creeping) *'al* (on) *hā'āreṣ* (earth) *hoṣē* (exit) *'itāḵə* (with) *vəšārəṣu* (breed) *ḇā'āreṣ* (land) u*p̄āru* (be fruitful) *vərāḇu* (become many) *'al* (on) *hā'āreṣ* (earth)
καὶ *kai* (and) **πάντα** *panta* (all) **τὰ** *ta* (the) **θηρία** *thēria* (beast) **ὅσα** *osa* (as many) **ἐστὶν** *estin* (are) **μετὰ** *meta* (with) **σοῦ** *sou* (you) **καὶ** *kai* (and) **πᾶσα** *pasa* (all) **σὰρξ** *sarx* (flesh) **ἀπὸ** *apo* (from) **πετεινῶν** *peteinōn* (birds) **ἕως** *eōs* (untill) **κτηνῶν** *ktēnōn* (moove) **καὶ** *kai* (and) **πᾶν** *pan* (all) **ἑρπετὸν** *erpeton* (serpents) **κινούμενον** *kinoumenon* (moving) **ἐπὶ** *epi* (on) **τῆς** *tēs* (the) **γῆς** *gēs* (earth) **ἐξάγαγε** *exagage* (bring) **μετὰ** *meta* (with) **σεαυτοῦ** *seautou* (you) **καὶ** *kai* (and) **αὐξάνεσθε** *auxanesthe* (be fruitful) **καὶ** *kai* (and) **πληθύνεσθε** *plēthunesthe* (multiply) **ἐπὶ** *epi* (on) **τῆς** *tēs* (the) **γῆς** *gēs* (earth)
cuncta (all) ***animantia*** (animals) ***quae*** (that) ***sunt*** (are) ***apud*** (with) ***te*** (you) ***ex*** (out of) ***omni*** (all) ***carne*** (flesh) ***tam*** (both) ***in*** (as) ***volatilibus*** (birds) ***quam*** (that) ***in*** (as) ***bestiis*** (beasts) ***et*** (and) ***in*** (as) ***universis*** (all) ***reptilibus*** (reptiles) ***quae*** (that) ***reptant*** (creep) ***super*** (on) ***terram*** (the earth) ***educ*** (bring out) ***tecum*** (with you) ***et*** (and) ***ingredimini*** (step) ***super*** (on) ***terram*** (the land) ***crescite*** (grow) ***et*** (and) ***multiplicamini*** (multiply) ***super*** (on) ***eam*** (it)
Bring forth with thee every living thing that is with thee, of all flesh, both of fowl, and of cattle, and of every creeping thing that creepeth upon the earth; that they may breed abundantly in the earth, and be fruitful, and multiply upon the earth.
Bring out with you all the animals that are with you, of all flesh, be them birds or beasts or reptiles that creep on the earth and step on the earth let them breed grow and multiply on it."

All the faculties of the living[2404] breathing,[2405] flesh-news-bearing,[2406] *viz.* the sense-animals (בְּהֵמָה *bĕhemah*), which show and interpret[2407] the world, went forth[2408] with him into the realm of objectivity. There, all the animals, all the psychological-flying-impulses,[2409] all the serpentine-intentionality,[2410] intentioning[2411] the earthly objects (אֶרֶץ *'erets*), are let free to roam the earth, breed,[2412] be fruitful[2413] and multiply.[2414] This means that all the epistemic faculties, stemming from Divine-Consciousness, are meant to epistemically articulate and proliferate in the world while never hungering or craving for it, thus, never being submerged by the world's seducing spell.

8:18-Noah Exits the Ark

וַיֵּצֵא־נֹחַ וּבָנָיו וְאִשְׁתּוֹ וּנְשֵׁי־בָנָיו אִתּוֹ׃
vayēṣē (went out) *nōaḥ* (Noah) *uḇānāyv* (sons) *və'išətvō* (wife) *unəšēy* (wives) *ḇānāyv* (of sons) *'itvō* (with)
καὶ *kai* (and) **ἐξῆλθεν** *exēlthen* (exited) **Νωε** *Nōe* (Noah) **καὶ** *kai* (and) **ἡ** *ē* (the) **γυνὴ** *gunē* (wife) **αὐτοῦ** *autou* (his) **καὶ** *kai* (and) **οἱ** *oi* (the) **υἱοὶ** *uioi* (sons) **αὐτοῦ** *autou* (his) **καὶ** *kai* (and) **αἱ** *ai* (the) **γυναῖκες** *gunaikes* (wives) **τῶν** *tōn* (of the) **υἱῶν** *uiōn* (sons) **αὐτοῦ** *autou* (his) **μετ'** *met'* (with) **αὐτοῦ** *autou* (him)
egressus (exited) ***est*** (is) ***ergo*** (therefore) ***Noe*** (Noah) ***et*** (and) ***filii*** (sons) ***eius*** (his) ***uxor*** (wife) ***illius*** (his) ***et*** (and) ***uxores*** (the wives) ***filiorum*** (of the sons) ***eius*** (his) ***cum*** (with) ***eo*** (him)
And Noah went forth, and his sons, and his wife, and his sons' wives with him:
Therefore, Noah went out and his wife, his sons and his sons' wives with him.

The world that we see around us is the one submerged in this flood, which we call *our real history*. History books are biographies of this universal flood. World history, as we know it, addresses only that part of the flood, which pertains to humans and the Earth.[2415] However, once the deluging identification with the objects and the engulfing attachment with them are over, then, it is possible to exit harmlessly the ark's interiority. Then, the Ancient-Present is the only *History* of the *New Earth*[2416] shaping before us.

8:19-All the Animals Exit the Ark

כָּל־הַחַיָּה כָּל־הָרֶמֶשׂ וְכָל־הָעוֹף כֹּל רוֹמֵשׂ עַל־הָאָרֶץ לְמִשְׁפְּחֹתֵיהֶם יָצְאוּ מִן־הַתֵּבָה׃ *kāl* (all) *haḥayāh* (living energies) *kāl* (all) hāremeś (winding animals) *vəḵāl* (all) *hā'vōp̄* (flying forces) *kōl* (all) *rvōmēś* (that twists)*'al* (on) *hā'āreṣ* (earth) *ləmišəpəḥōṯēyhem* (after their kind) *yāṣə'u* (went) *min* (from) *hatēḇāh* (the ark)
καὶ *kai* (and) **πάντα** *panta* (all) **τὰ** *ta* (the) **θηρία** *thēria* (animals) **καὶ** *kai* (and) **πάντα** *panta* (all) **τὰ** *ta* (the) **κτήνη** *ktēnē* (flock) **καὶ** *kai* (and) **πᾶν** *pan* (all) **πετεινὸν** *peteinon* (birds) **καὶ** *kai* (and) **πᾶν** *pan* (all) **ἑρπετὸν** *erpeton* (reptile) **κινούμενον** *kinoumenon* (moving) **ἐπὶ** *epi* (on) **τῆς** *tēs* (the) **γῆς** *gēs* (earth) **κατὰ** *kata* (according to) **γένος** *genos* (kind) **αὐτῶν** *autōn* (its own) **ἐξήλθοσαν** *exēlthosan* (came out) **ἐκ** *ek* (from) **τῆς** *tēs* (the) **κιβωτοῦ** *kibōtou* (ark)
sed (but) ***et*** (and) ***omnia*** (all) ***animantia*** (animals) ***iumenta*** (cattle) ***et*** (and) ***reptilia*** (reptiles) ***quae*** (that) ***repunt*** (wind) ***super*** (on) ***terram*** (the earth) ***secundum*** (according to) ***genus*** (kind) ***suum*** (its own) ***arcam*** (from the ark) ***egressa*** (exited) ***sunt*** (are)
Every beast, every creeping thing, and every fowl, and whatsoever creepeth upon the earth, after their kinds, went forth out of the ark.
All the living energies, all the winding animals, all the flying forces, all that twists on the earth after their own kind, went out from the ark.

2417

Together with the epistemic forms, also all the faculties of the senses go out of the ark serenely to contemplate the dry world as it slides into Awareness.

8:20-Noah's Offering

וַיִּבֶן נֹחַ מִזְבֵּחַ לַיהוָה וַיִּקַּח מִכֹּל הַבְּהֵמָה הַטְּהוֹרָה וּמִכֹּל הָעוֹף הַטָּהֹר וַיַּעַל עֹלֹת בַּמִּזְבֵּחַ׃ *vayiḇen* (erected) *nōaḥ* (Noah) *mizəbēaḥ* (altar) *layhvāh* (Transcendent) *vayiqaḥ* (took) *mikōl* (from) *habəhēmāh* (animals) *haṭəhvōrāh* (pure) *umikōl* (from) *hā'vōp̄* (birds) *haṭāhōr* (pure) *vaya'al* (to ascend) *'ōlōṯ* (the stairway) *bamizəbēaḥ* (altar)
καὶ *kai* (and) **ᾠκοδόμησεν** *ōkodomēsen* (built) **Νωε** *Nōe* (Noah) **θυσιαστήριον** *thusiastērion* (altar) **τῷ** *tō* (the) **θεῷ** *theō* (god) **καὶ** *kai* (and) **ἔλαβεν** *elaben* (took) **ἀπὸ** *apo* (from) **πάντων** *pantōn* (all) **τῶν** *tōn* (the) **κτηνῶν** *ktēnōn* (animals) **τῶν** *tōn* (the) **καθαρῶν** *katharōn* (clean) **καὶ** *kai* (and) **ἀπὸ** *apo* (from) **πάντων** *pantōn* (all) **τῶν** *tōn* (the) **πετεινῶν** *peteinōn* (birds) **τῶν** *tōn* (the) **καθαρῶν** *katharōn* (pure) **καὶ** *kai* (and) **ἀνήνεγκεν** *anēneuken* (brought up) **ὁλοκαρπώσεις** *olokarpōseis* (burnt offering) **ἐπὶ** *epi* (on) **τὸ** *to* (the) **θυσιαστήριον** *thusiastērion* (altar)
aedificavit (built) ***autem*** (also) ***Noe*** (Noah) ***altare*** (altar) ***Domino*** (to the Lord) ***et*** (and) ***tollens*** (tooke) ***de*** (out) ***cunctis*** (of all) ***pecoribus*** (the sheep) ***et*** (and) ***volucribus*** (the birds) ***mundis*** (pure) ***obtulit*** (offered) ***holocausta*** (holocaust) ***super*** (on) ***altare*** (altar)
And Noah builded an altar unto the LORD; and took of every clean beast, and of every clean fowl, and offered burnt offerings on the altar.

Noah erected also an altar to the Transcendent. He chose one from every pure-sensitive-animal and from every pure-psychological-bird, climbed on the stairway of the altar and offered them to the Transcendent.

Noah demonstrates his serenity by erecting (בָּנָה *banah*) a metaphoric sacrificing stand (מִזְבֵּחַ *mizbeach*), namely, he lifts up towards the Transcendent Awareness his offerings. On that sacred altar, he offers[2418] to the Apodictical Transcendent his chosen (לקח *laqach*) prime living energies of his epistemic vitalities, as Abel had done. The verb ` *alah* (עָלָה) means to lift oneself, to ascend, to climb, to withdraw, to be brought up or exalted. The exalted animals are those in the stillness of pure aesthetic rapture and of pure love without lust. They are the shining and bright sentient-animal-experiences, the clean epistemic faculties, which now contemplate the world in its own Transcending Beauty. They become *stairways* and *steps*[2419] toward the identification with Pure Consciousness leading into Awareness.

"*Now when these things were thus ordained, the priests went always into the first tabernacle, accomplishing the service* of God. *But into the second went the high priest alone once every year, not without blood, which he offered for himself, and* for *the errors of the people.*"[2420]

At this point, we can anticipate that some obstinate literal readers, taken by an invasive pseudo prophetic frenzy and utterly scandalized, will throw away this book. They prefer to imagine a primitive cave dweller savagely killing innocent pure (טָהוֹר *tahowr*) *animals, like a thanksgiving burnt turkey offering* (עלה ` *olah*)*, to appease a bloodthirsty idol created by their worldly imagination*[2421] *for the satisfaction of their own intestinal interests.*[2422] *Furthermore, since there is only few pairs of every kind of animals, that literal animal sacrifice would threaten the survival of an already endangered species.*

The impure animals, symbolizing attachment, passionate-possession and consciousness-*of* the objects, apparently obliterate Pure Awareness from which consciousness derives. In fact, not having

"*root in oneself... when tribulation or persecution arises... one is offended...* [Then,] *the care of this world and the deceitfulness of riches suffocate us.*"[2423]

"*The wilderness and the solitary place shall be glad for them; and the desert shall rejoice, and blossom as the rose. It shall blossom abundantly, and rejoice even with joy and singing... they shall see the glory of the LORD,* and *the excellency of our God... Then the eyes of the blind shall be opened, and the ears of the deaf shall be unstopped. Then shall the lame man leap as an hart, and the tongue of the dumb sing... And an highway shall be there, and a way, and it shall be called The way of holiness; the unclean shall not pass over it; but it shall be for those: the wayfaring men, though fools, shall not err therein. No lion shall be there, nor* any *ravenous beast shall go up thereon, it shall not be found there; but the redeemed shall walk there.*"[2424]

Actually, now, in the ark, there cannot be any unclean *sense-animal* left. In fact, all those unclean animals/faculties had perished in the flood. While, the, unclean ones, saved in the ark, are cleansed from care and anxiety (μέριμνα *merimna*). Now, those epistemic faculties become pure observing tools without any attachment or pure giving without any expectation. This is like the mystic exercise of concentrating on a plant feeling only its growing

"force that through the green fuse drives the flower."[2425]

"*Do not fix your attention on all these changing things of life, death, and phenomena* [like the deluge]*. Do not think of even the actual act of seeing them or perceiving them but only of that which sees all these things. That which is responsible for it all... keep the mind unshakenly fixed on That Which Sees. It is inside yourself... Let your whole thought in meditation be not on the act of seeing nor on what you see, but immovably on That Which Sees.*"[2426]

8:21-The Curse Is Lifted

וַיָּרַח יְהוָה אֶת־רֵיחַ הַנִּיחֹחַ וַיֹּאמֶר יְהוָה אֶל־לִבּוֹ לֹא־אֹסִף לְקַלֵּל עוֹד אֶת־הָאֲדָמָה בַּעֲבוּר הָאָדָם כִּי יֵצֶר לֵב הָאָדָם רַע מִנְּעֻרָיו וְלֹא־אֹסִף עוֹד לְהַכּוֹת אֶת־כָּל־חַי כַּאֲשֶׁר עָשִׂיתִי׃

vayāraḥ (smelled) *yəhvāh* (Transcendent) *'eṯ* (and) *rēyaḥ* (fragrance) *haniyḥōaḥ* (soothing) *vayō' mer* (said) *yəhvāh* (Transcendent) *'el* (the) *libvō* (mind) *lō'* (no) *'ōsip̄* (do again) *ləqalēl* (curse) *'vōḏ* (yet) *'eṯ* (and) *hā'ăḏāmāh* (ground) *ba'ăḇur* (sake) *hā'āḏām* (man's) *kiy* (because) *yēṣer* (imagination) *lēḇ* (mind) *hā'āḏām* (man's) *ra'* (evil) *minə'urāyv* (from his youth) *vəlō'* (not) *'ōsip̄* (do again) *'vōḏ* (yet) *ləhakvōṯ* (smite) *'eṯ* (and) *kāl* (all) *ḥay* (living) *ka'ăšer* (as) *'āśiyṯiy* (I have done)
καὶ *kai* (and) **ὠσφράνθη** *ōsphranthē* (smelled) **κύριος** *kurios* (Lord) **ὁ** *o* (the) **θεὸς** *theos* (God) **ὀσμὴν** *osmēn* (aroma) **εὐωδίας** *euōdias* (sweetness) **καὶ** *kai* (and) **εἶπεν** *eipen* (said) **κύριος** *kurios* (Lord) **ὁ** *o* (the) **θεὸς** *theos* (God) **διανοηθείς** *dianoētheis* (having thought) **οὐ** *ou* (not) **προσθήσω** *prosthēsō* (establish) **ἔτι** *eti* (again) **τοῦ** *tou* (the) **καταράσασθαι** *katarasasthai* (course) **τὴν** *tēn* (the) **γῆν** *gēn* (earth) **διὰ** *dia* (for) **τὰ** *ta* (the) **ἔργα** *erga* (works) **τῶν** *tōn* (of the) **ἀνθρώπων** *anthrōpōn* (men) **ὅτι** *oti* (because) **ἔγκειται** *egkeitai* (be placed) **ἡ** *ē* (the) **διάνοια** *dianoia* (mind) **τοῦ** *tou* (of the) **ἀνθρώπου** *anthrōpou* (man) **ἐπιμελῶς** *epimelōs* (is bent) **ἐπὶ** *epi* (on) **τὰ** *ta* (the) **πονηρὰ** *ponēra* (evil) **ἐκ** *ek* (of) **νεότητος** *neotētos* (youth) **οὐ** *ou* (no) **προσθήσω** *prosthēsō* (put) **οὖν** *oun* (in facy) **ἔτι** *eti* (again) **πατάξαι** *pataxai* (smite) **πᾶσαν** *pasan* (all) **σάρκα** *sarka* (flesh) **ζῶσαν** *zōsas* (living) **καθὼς** *kathōs* (as) **ἐποίησα** *epoiēsa* (I have done)
odoratus- (smelled) ***que*** (and) ***est*** (is) ***Dominus*** (Lord) ***odorem*** (smell) ***suavitatis*** (suave) ***et*** (and) ***ait*** (said) ***ad*** (to) ***eum*** (himself) ***nequaquam*** (never) ***ultra*** (again) ***maledicam*** (I will curse) ***terrae*** (the earth) ***propter*** (because) ***homines*** (men) ***sensus*** (sense) ***enim*** (in fact) ***et*** (and) ***cogitatio*** (I think) ***humani*** (human) ***cordis*** (hearts) ***in*** (in) ***malum*** (evil) ***prona*** (prone) ***sunt*** (are) ***ab*** (since) ***adulescentia*** (adolescence) ***sua*** (its) ***non*** (not) ***igitur*** (therefore) ***ultra*** (again) ***percutiam*** (I will hit) ***omnem*** (all) ***animantem*** (animals) ***sicut*** (as) ***feci*** (I did)
And the LORD smelled a sweet savour; and the LORD said in his heart, I will not again curse the ground any more for man's sake; for the imagination of man's heart is evil from his youth; neither will I again smite any more every thing living, as I have done.
The Transcendent['s Life's Breath] inhaled and accepted the tranquil fragrance and in the centrality of its Heart intended, "*Never again I will course the land of objectivity because of humans' mind conceptualizing distortion from the very early beginning. Nor will I kill every living thing as I have done.*

Metaphorically, we could compare the breathing to the circular direction of the *day's* circadian rhythm. Exhaling, inhaling and apnea are three aspects of breathing, as waking, REM and NREM are the three states of the circadian rhythm. In fact, exhaling is air flowing out of lungs, as dreamless sleep moves into wakefulness. Inhaled air is like going from wakefulness to the state of dream. Apnea, between breaths, corresponds to the restfulness of NREM. Hence, the whole process starts again. Furthermore, this is the circulation of consciousness. Exhaling is the direction from the subject to the object. Inhaling brings the object back to the subject. Apnea is the stasis between them. As we have seen, symbolically, the process of creation is an exhaling descent of the *Breath* (רוח *ruwach*) *of Life* (נְשָׁמָה *nĕshamah*) into the depth of objectivity generating the world until it rests.

The reabsorption of the Days of Creation into the Resting Stillness corresponds to the inhaling process. From the Earth's third creative Day, each Day sublimates into the previous one. <The Purity of the Second Day sanctifies (קָדַשׁ *qadash*) the Power of the Fourth Day. The Love of the First day sublimates the Biological-drive of the Fifth Day. Finally, the Ecstatic Rest of the Seventh Day transmutes the Life of the Sixth Day.>[2427] On the seventh day, then, the entire Creation reabsorbs, *inhaled* (רִיחַ *ruwach*) in the state it was before Creation. Divine-Consciousness is inactive stillness. The conscious-physicality-*of* the world disappears in the Ecstatic-True-Transcendent-Breath-of-Life. This is the realization of goodness following each day of creation, which culminates with the return of the created in the stillness of the seventh resting day.

Obviously, God does not have nostrils. Therefore, this is a metaphoric *moment* in which, the Transcendent accepts[2428] *smelling* or inhaling (רִיחַ *ruwach*) the tranquil[2429] fragrance[2430] realizing[2431] it in the resting (שַׁבָּת *shabath*) centrality of Its Heart/Mind/Awareness.[2432] Whereas, the human mind/heart (לֵב *leb*) of

Adam, with its conceptualization and intellectual framework,[2433] was unhappy[2434] and crushingly distressed.[2435] This happens from the very early beginning[2436] of eating the forbidden fruit.

Likewise, the olive bearer dove,

> *"Jonah arose, and went unto Nineveh... an exceeding great city of three days' journey.*[2437] *And ... said, 'Yet forty days, and Nineveh shall be overthrown.' So the people of Nineveh believed God, and proclaimed a fast, and put on sackcloth, from the greatest of them even to the least of them. For word came unto the king of Nineveh, and he arose from his throne, and he laid his robe from him, and covered him with sackcloth, and sat in ashes. And he caused it to be proclaimed and published through Nineveh by the decree of the king and his nobles, saying, 'Let neither man nor beast, herd nor flock, taste any thing: let them not feed, nor drink water: But let man and beast be covered with sackcloth, and cry mightily unto God: yea, let them turn every one from his evil way, and from the violence that is in their hands.*[2438] *Who can tell if God will turn and repent, and turn away from his fierce anger, that we perish not?' And God saw their works, that they turned from their evil way; and God repented of the evil, that he had said that he would do unto them; and he did it not."*[2439]

Even today, Indian ascetics [2440]⇨

> "cover themselves with the ashes of the dead, meditate on cremation grounds and carry a skull (*kāpālika*) as food bowl"[2441]

Nevertheless, in Noah's paradigmatic tranquil state of Transcendent-Apodictical-Awareness, there is no forbidden fruit eating and no action. There, the flood subsides never to happen (יָסַף *yacaph*) again. The ground of objectivity (אֲדָמָה *'adamah*) is free from the curse (קָלַל *qalal*) caused by possessive ravenous greed. Therefore, in the central state of This-Present-Truth, death cannot strike (נָכָה *nakah*) again. Francis wrote,

> "*Blessed are those who* [death] *will find in your* [God's] *very holy will / because the second death will not hurt them.*"[2442]

8:22- No Rest in the Epistemic Process

עֹד כָּל־יְמֵי הָאָרֶץ זֶרַע וְקָצִיר וְקֹר וָחֹם וְקַיִץ וָחֹרֶף וְיוֹם וָלַיְלָה לֹא יִשְׁבֹּתוּ׃ *ʿōḏ* (during) *kāl* (all) *yəmēy* (days) *hā'āreṣ* (of the earth) *zeraʿ* (seeding) *vəqāṣiyr* (harvest) *vəqōr* (cold) *vāḥōm* (heat) *vəqayiṣ* (summer) *vāḥōrep̄* (winter) *vəyvōm* (day) *vālayəlāh* (night) *lō̆* (not) *yišəbōṯu* (rest)
πάσας *pasas* (all) **τὰς** *tas* (the) **ἡμέρας** *ēmeras* (days) **τῆς** *tēs* (of the) **γῆς** *gēs* (earth) **σπέρμα** *sperma* (seeds) **καὶ** *kai* (and) **θερισμός** *therismos* (harvest) **ψῦχος** *psuchos* (cold) **καὶ** *kai* (and) **καῦμα** *kauma* (heat) **θέρος** *theros* (summer) **καὶ** *kai* (and) **ἔαρ** *ear* (spring) **ἡμέραν** *ēmeran* (day) **καὶ** *kai* (and) **νύκτα** *nukta* (night) **οὐ** *ou* (not) **καταπαύσουσιν** *katapausousin* (I will stop)
cunctis (all) ***diebus*** (days) ***terrae*** (of the earth) ***sementis*** (seeds) ***et*** (and) ***messis*** (harvest) ***frigus*** (cold) ***et*** (and) ***aestus*** (heat) ***aestas*** (summer) ***et*** (and) ***hiemps*** (winter) ***nox*** (night) ***et*** (and) ***dies*** (day) ***non*** (not) ***requiescent*** (will rest)
While the earth remaineth, seedtime and harvest, and cold and heat, and summer and winter, and day and night shall not cease.
While, during all the circular days of the earth-objectivity, the seeding, the harvest, the cold, the heat, the summer, the winter, the day, the night will not find rest."

Following a literal reading of the deluge, all dry land plants and seeds must have all decayed and died under the universal flooding ocean. Only marine life, plants, algae and fish could have continued thriving in it. Furthermore, immediately after the waters receded, it would have been impossible for plants to resume their productive cycle, unless recreated anew. However, even in that case, the left over arid soil would not have been suitable for the blooming and growth of a new flora.

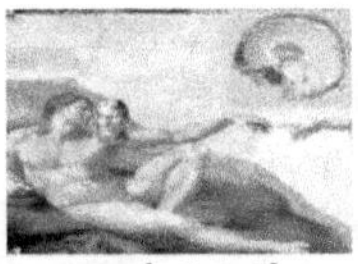

Nevertheless, separate from Noah's tranquil and restful sacrifice, is the different offering of Cain, the tiller of the ground. God does not accept Cain's sacrifice. His offering is the epistemic daily (יוֹם *yowm*) circular structure, which continues actively to toil and roll around in the objective world (אֶרֶץ *'erets*) of passionate possessions. Potentially, the *logical-semen* (זֶרַע *zera`*), as faculties of the mind, are present in the cool[2443] calmness of the spirit.[2444] There they are in a state of quiescence, ready to be engaged in the physical world.

In the actuality of this distressing world of duality, those *logical-semen* (זֶרַע *zera`*) produce (זָרַע *zara`*) and harvest (קָצִיר *qatsiyr*) in the heat[2445] of passion.[2446] Incessantly, they continue with *no* (לֹא *lō*) *rest* (שַׁבָּת *shabath*) during all the active fruit bearing summer[2447] and all the gathering[2448] *winter*[2449] seasons and throughout the circularity of the day (יוֹם *yowm*) and of the winding stairs[2450] of darkness.[2451]

The world without the passionate whirlwind of desires shines of its own beauty, while the earth continues in its circadian rhythm.

HERE ENDS THE EIGHTH CHAPTER OF THE CURSE REVERSED

CHAPTER 9

THE RAINBOW, THE VINEYARD AND THE BLOOD OF GRAPES

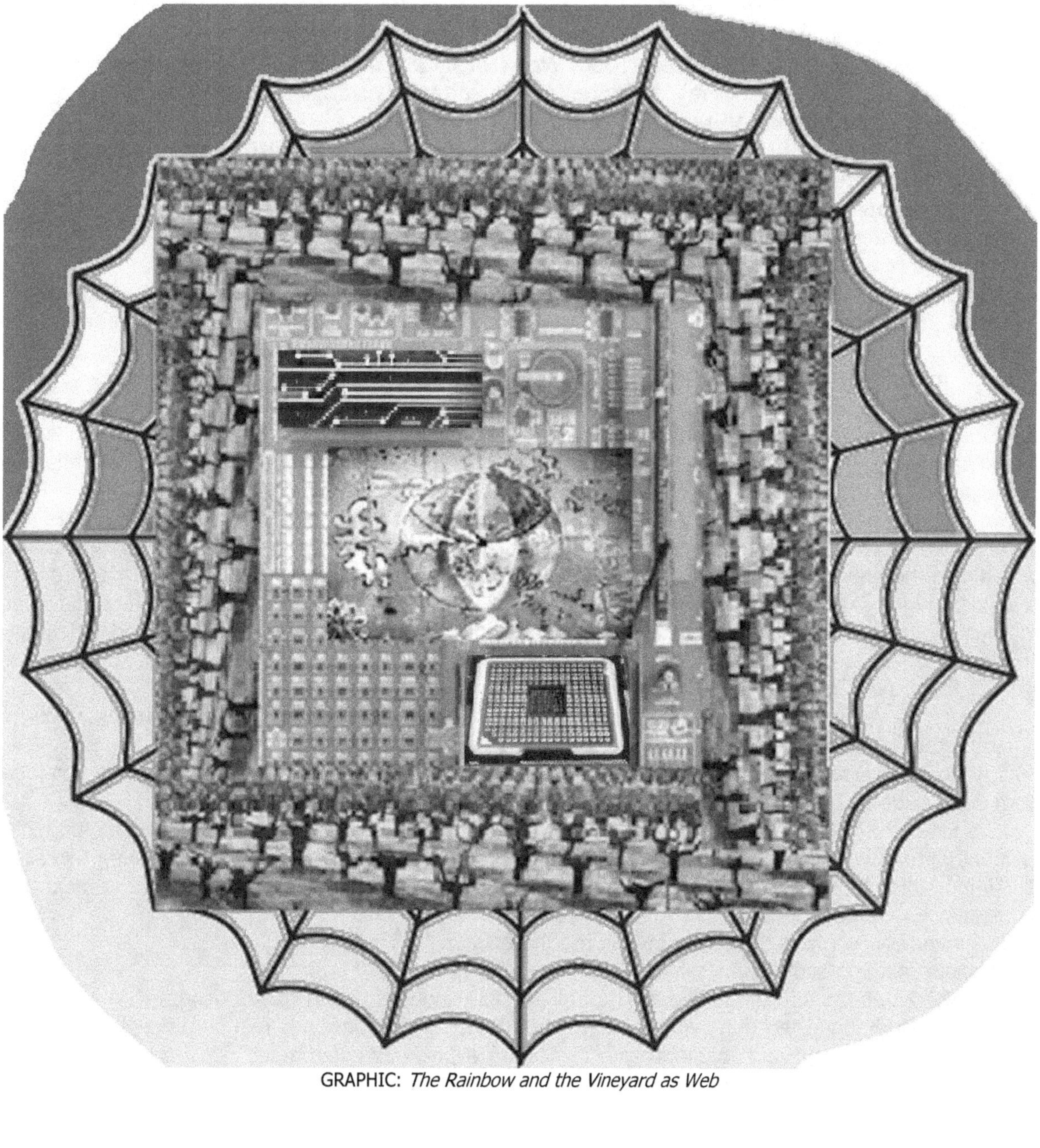

GRAPHIC: *The Rainbow and the Vineyard as Web*

9-I SECTION: THE EPISTEMIC FOOD

9:1-God's Blessing

וַיְבָרֶךְ אֱלֹהִים אֶת־נֹחַ וְאֶת־בָּנָיו וַיֹּאמֶר לָהֶם פְּרוּ וּרְבוּ וּמִלְאוּ אֶת־הָאָרֶץ׃ *vayab̲āreḵa* (blessed) *'ĕlōhiym* (Divine-Consciousness) *'et̲* (and) *nōaḥ* (Noah) *va'et̲* (with) *bānāyv* (sons) *vayō'mer* (said) *lāhem* (to them) *paru* (be fruitful) *urab̲u* (multiply) *umila'u* (fill) *'et̲* (and) *hā'āreṣ* (the earth)
καὶ *kai* (and) **ηὐλόγησεν** *ēulogēsen* (blessed) **ὁ** *o* (he) **θεὸς** *theos* (God) **τὸν** *ton* (the) **Νωε** *Nōe* (Noah) **καὶ** *kai* (and) **τοὺς** *tous* (the) **υἱοὺς** *uious* (sons) **αὐτοῦ** *autou* (his) **καὶ** *kai* (and) **εἶπεν** *eipen* (said) **αὐτοῖς** *autois* (to them) **αὐξάνεσθε** *auxanesthe* (grow) **καὶ** *kai* (and) **πληθύνεσθε** *plēthunesthe* (multiply) **καὶ** *kai* (and) **πληρώσατε** *plērōsate* (fill) **τὴν** *tēn* (the) **γῆν** *gēn* (earth) **καὶ** *kai* (and) **κατακυριεύσατε** *katakurieusate* (dominate)[2452] **αὐτῆς** *autēs* (it)
benedixit- (blessed)***que*** (and) ***Deus*** (God) ***Noe*** (Noah) ***et*** (and) ***filiis*** (sons) ***eius*** (his) ***et*** (and) ***dixit*** (said) ***ad*** (to) ***eos*** (them) ***crescite*** (grow) ***et*** (and) ***multiplicamini*** (multiply) ***et*** (and) ***implete*** (fill) ***terram*** (he earth)
And God blessed Noah and his sons, and said unto them, Be fruitful, and multiply, and replenish the earth.
Divine-Consciousness blessed Noah with his offspring *and* said to them, "*Be fruitful, multiply discursively and fill the objective-earth.*

"*Blessed* [are] *the pure in heart: for they shall see God,*"[2453]

and Noah, being of one-mind, *rested* and unanimous,[2454] reached the blessing (בָּרַךְ *barak*) of the final liberation from the flood. Noah is everyone in the state of restful awakened dreamless sleep. Metaphorically, his sons are his epistemic faculties. Similar to intuitions, Noah's sons discursively fructify (פָּרָה *parah*), multiply (רָבָה *rabah*) and replenish (מָלֵא *male'*) the field (אֶרֶץ *'erets*) of objectivity. They will be moving out of that restfulness to populate the dream land and the waking realm. In dreams, intentionality, as stream of consciousness directed toward something, persists entirely in the subjectivity of the dreamer, while, in the dreamless sleep, that intentional stream persists frozen in the stillness (דָּמַם *damam*) of this state. Subsequently, in the waking state, intentionality flows towards the objective world.

<As the waking state and the dream state are the realm of discursive process, this deep-unconscious sleep state is the realm of intuition. That is the knower in-itself. That is the condition underlining the previous two states. In fact, it is intuition, the state of immediate and total *com*prehension or direct *in*sight of the objective world reality. In it, all opposites coincide into one undifferentiated point without any temporal or spatial juxtaposition or distinction, without proceeding from one element to another.>

From the perspectives of oneiric researchers,

"the controversy over the 'most important' stage of sleep is unresolved... neither stage seems more important in terms of the deprivation-recovery process."[2455]

Why, then, our verse assigns a prominent place and a blessing for the survivors of the deluge coming out from deep sleep?

First, the reason is that NREM is the state of intuition. This stage is the necessary underlining element without which there would be no discursive process or multiplication in the following two stages. It is impossible, in fact, to say something without its thought being completely formed in the mind before its utterance.

"The knower, verily, is the one known in the three states"[2456]

of waking, dreaming and dreamless sleep.

Second, because it is the beginning of all possible knowledge and consciousness.

"It has been suggested that ... our actions are initiated by unconscious mental processes long before we become aware of our intention to act. [№1-3] In a previous experiment [№1]... conscious decision... was preceded by a few hundred milliseconds by a negative brain potential, the so-called 'readiness potential' that originates from the supplementary motor area (SMA), a brain region involved in motor preparation. Because brain activity in the SMA consistently preceded the conscious decision, it has been argued that the brain had already unconsciously made a decision to move even before the subject became aware of it."[2457]

"*In fact, whosoever looketh on a woman to lust after her hath committed adultery with her already in his heart.*"[2458]

<Since consciousness is characterized by intentionality, is it possible to have an experience that is not consciousness-*of*? Śaṅkara recognizes such a consciousness, without objects, without distinction, thus not a transcendental consciousness in act, in the state of deep sleep with no dreams.[2459] Such state is not a pure emptiness, neither a state of unconsciousness, if that were the case nothing could be said about it neither there would be awareness of such state.[2460] On the contrary, it is a synthesis of knowledge made of bliss, in which the entire world is intuitively grasped in that multiplicity, which has become one without otherness.>[2461]

In other words, the objective world, in the state of deep sleep without dreams, is always present and unified with the pure potential consciousness, which is not yet in actuality. This is also the case of cataleptic and comatose states. In fact, when all senses are gone, when all thoughts are gone and when conscience-*of* this Ego is gone what is there left? Whatsoever is left must be the same foundation of the senses, of the thoughts and of the consciousness-*of* this Ego.

When that same building foundation is still present in a comatose but still pulsating body, then it shines forth with all its might. It is like a unified ocean.[2462]

"*Thus, after all dissolves, alone this one remains awake. From this vacuity, this one truly awakes this world consisting of Pure Awareness. This world is meditated by that one and, verily, in that one it dissolves.*"[2463]

From the state of deep sleep, the self

"*returns, as it came, again to the dream state, the place it departed from,*" [2464]

and from here to the state of wakefulness. Therefore, similar to an electron, jumping between orbits, the Self leaps from one dimension of life into another state and beyond.

The mind works on two basic dialectical principles: intuition and discourse.[2465] By intuition,[2466] we mean the potential presence before the mind of the idea as intentionality,[2467] in its total timeless synthesis without distinction of parts. As an example, the sound of the word '*frog*' awakens the image of the amphibian, which, before the articulated word, was not yet present in the waking mind but still somehow already in it. That non-presence is the intuitive moment. When we think of the alphabet, before its recitation, there is no distinction or gap between opposite pairs: "*A*" coincides with "Z" (or Greek Ω) fused together with all other letters, which are all in the mind, one fused in the other because they are not individually expressed. The MRC, Cognition and Brain Sciences Unit,

"found that the mind reads words as a whole, the order of letters does not matter, only first and last must be in right place."[2468]

By *dis*course,[2469] we mean the actual presence, before the mind, of ideas, as intentionality, in their distinctive temporal juxtaposition of parts and logical succession. As when we spread out the sequence of the alphabet recitation: *A* preceding *B* followed by *C* (or Greek Γ) and so on, all the way to *Z* (or Greek Ω). Intuition, on the contrary, takes place during the instantaneous comprehension of the sense of a word. At time, this intuitive moment becomes clear when one, while knowing a specific word-sense, is not able to provide an immediate synonym or, better still, a translation, as in the case of bilingual persons. Then, the word-sense stands clear in the mind in a static oneness without juxtaposition of parts. On the other hand, the discursive comprehension of a word takes place when the word itself is placed in relation to synonyms or translations as in a numerical flow. Intuition and discourse are like a double act that, while intuitively persisting in its unity, proceeds in the discursive procession of separated parts without losing its original unified intuition.

Creative-geniality is emergence into intuition, in the idea that has no distinction of parts. It is as entering, aware, the unconscious, oneiric stage of non-REM, it is "to be conscious without thought"[2470]

potentially containing unified the whole ideal world. From that point, then, one enters the subconscious REM state, after which one finally awakens.[2471]

Engineer iron-master John Wilkinson (1728-1808) claimed that he envisioned his new machines in sleep.[2472] Chemist Friedrich August Kekulé von Stradonitz in 1865[2473] realized in a dream the structure of benzene as a chain of six carbon atoms closed into a ring. Srinivasa Ramanujan, in 1918, fellow of the Royal Society and of Trinity College, used to say that the formulas of his mathematical work, on the theory of numbers, of positions and of continued fractions, were revealed to him in his sleep.[2474] This was similar to the genial mathematical instant solutions and visions offered, without any conscious effort, by the autistic savant Daniel Tammet.[2475] In addition, it seems that Dmitri Mendeleev (1834-1907) had the first insight of his periodic table of elements during a dream.[2476]

Popular belief has it that science evolves slowly in a deductive way. Robert Elliot Pollack, Professor of Biological Sciences and Director, Center for the Study of Science and Religion at Columbia University, writes,

"Ask any scientist what lies at the core of her work, you will learn that it is not the experimental test of the hypothesis – although that is where most of the time and money of science go. It is the idea, the mechanism, the insight that justifies all the rest of the work of science. The moment of insight that reveals the new idea, where an instant before there was just fog, is the moment when the unknown first retreats before the creativity of the scientist. Here, then, is the first door into the unknowable. Where does the scientific insight come from? Surely it comes from someplace currently unknown. Let us consider the possibility that scientific insight, like religious revelation, comes from an intrinsically unknowable place."[2477]

Professor George Andrews, of Pennsylvania State University, confirms that pure mathematicians and many scientists acknowledge that science and mathematics are not just games in which one writes or experiments continuously, but there are flashes of insight that promote new discoveries.[2478] These intuitive moments, these

"basic numerical intuitions, are supported by an evolutionarily ancient approximate number system that is shared by adults ... infants ... and non-human animals."[2479]

"Students cannot be trained to be research scientists by working textbook examples. They must confront real problems at the limits of our understanding."[2480]

In an interview, Einstein said,

"I sometimes *feel* I am right, but do not *know* it. ... I wasn't surprised when the results confirmed my intuition, but I would have been surprised had I been wrong. I'm enough of an artist to draw freely on my imagination, which I think is more important than knowledge. Knowledge is limited. Imagination encircles the world."[2481]

Otto Loewi, 1936 Nobel Prize for medicine, noted:

"Most so called 'intuitive' discoveries are such associations made in the subconscious."[2482]

Rita Levi Montalcini describes her discovery of the New Growth Factor (NGF), which won her the 1986 Nobel Prize in Medicine, as

"a fulguration, an immediate flash"

following a sleepless night.[2483]

As the whole process of trial and error painstakingly continues during the research, without any new breakthrough, it may be that one morning, while bathing, suddenly, the solution of the problem *hits* the researcher. In a flash of insight the whole panorama of the answer is here, as when Archimedes, realizing the principle of buoyancy, cried out

"I found, I found."[2484]

<Then, with a pragmatic paradox, the researcher must prove that flash of intuition, realized as true before proving it. The process continues: testing, writing, and discursively projecting that realization, thus demonstrating and fully justifying the correctness of the insight. In the course of history, we

call geniuses those people to whom that intuition, or creative-geniality, happens more often than the average. The question arises, then, whether that geniality is an exception or the norm, under certain conditions. Whatever the answer may be, and this is not the place to discuss this matter, pedagogy must take creative-geniality very seriously and lead consciousness-*of* towards the joy of discovery.>[2485]

The intuitive state of deep sleep is the one that knows potentially everything and from which the whole phenomenic world of dream and wakefulness emanates.[2486]

> "*Ye shall see heaven open, and the angels of God ascending and descending upon the Son of man.*"[2487]

In Jacob's sleep

> "*he dreamed,*[2488] *and a ladder set up on the earth, and the head*[2489] *of it reached to heaven: and the messengers*[2490] *of God*[2491] *ascending and descending on it.... And, the Lord stood above it... And Jacob awaked*[2492] *out of his sleep,*[2493] *and he said, 'surely the Lord is in this place; and I knew*[2494] [it] *not'.*"[2495] [2496]⇨

That state is un-known to the waking and dreaming state, whereas, in itself it is pure intuition that emanates the other two states. This emanation,

> "*as the rays proceed from the sun,*"

says Śaṅkara,[2497] never loses its wholeness. Thus,

> "*one, not asleep, casts a look upon the sleeping senses.*"[2498]

This undistinguishable synthesis of subject and object eliminates the fear deriving from the other, the producer of fear.

> "*Inasmuch as there is no ego in the Sage, there is no 'other' for him.*"[2499]

If the other, the one who is not *intim*ate, but is *intim*idating, the alien, the different one, is not present, then peace or bliss takes place.

> "*In fact, when the subject reduces to exteriority that which is interiority, then this one is frightened. That, truly, is the fear of the knower who does not reflect.*"[2500]

The ancient Greek philosopher Plotinus compares emanation to

> "*a spring that has no other source than itself, which gives of itself to all rivers without letting itself be exhausted by them, but calmly perseveres in itself.*"[2501]

As sparks from a fire,[2502] this One displays itself by descending in the other two states and informing them. Conversely, continues Plotinus, *"feeling is just like a soul that sleeps. As much soul there is in a body, it is nothing more than a sleeping soul and the true awakening consists in a resurrection."*[2503]

From a creationist point of view, if life springs out from nothingness, we can say that we have been resurrected from that nonexistence. However, if we take it literally meaning 'coming back from the deceased,' then, resurrection cannot mean regaining a three-dimensional physical body. If so, this event would present a number of difficulties. From a logistic standpoint, the sheer number of resurrected physical bodies would find no room on an overcrowded Earth. From a biological viewpoint, in the case of conjoining twins with one head and two bodies, one body and two heads or other natural oddities,[2504] it is not clear which body would be resurrected. From a gnoseological perspective, physicality would take us back to a subject-object epistemic condition, which would still render impossible the realization of the Transcendent as such. Answering to

"the Sadducees, which say there is no resurrection,"[2505]

and preaching

"the resurrection from the dead,"[2506]

Jesus clarifies that the awakened ones,

"in the resurrection... are as the angels of God in heaven."

In fact,

"God is not the God of the dead, but of the living."[2507]

Therefore, the search for that resurrecting immortality requires a journey of the awakened mind through the three realms of this world, namely wakefulness, dream and dreamless-sleep, into the fourth Transcendent one.

"Having sailed across with the boat of the syllable AUM [*viz.* wake (A), REM (U) and NREM (M)] *to the other side into the internal space of the heart, in the inner space, which becomes quietly manifest, one should enter the abode of the Creator as a miner, seeking minerals, penetrates the mine."*[2508]

Thus, the mind in the waking state must ascend to that intuitive origin by bringing the waking-state awareness consciously awake into the dream state, as in lucid dreams. Subsequently, the mind, consciously awake, must ascend in the stillness of unconscious-sleep, realizing that the unconscious auto-transparency was always present here in this waking/dreaming state. In fact, not all our actions are conscious, and those, which are not, still move on the overall background of the unconscious.>[2509]

Legend has it, that chief Rabbi Judah Loew ben Bezalel of Prague (1520-1609), to protect his people, brought to life a "golem" of Talmudic origin, a giant made of clay, like Adam.[2510]

Robots, as modern golems, are interconnections of finely wired networks of electrical impulses for the performance of complex mental or physical tasks. In 1956 John McCarthy, a computer scientist at Stanford University, coined the term Artificial Intelligence (A.I.) of robots. This will provide humans with Intelligence Amplification (I.A.).[2511] Thus, machines, progressing beyond human capabilities, will contribute to the post-human process of evolution. <A.I. will produce self-conscious computing machine systems with an Artificial Intelligence superior to that of humans and capable to design and make exponentially evermore-intelligent robots for the solution of specific problems. Reproduced big or small bits of ego will merge to form in machines any size ego-consciousness. However, it is undeniable that it was human ingenuity, which started the whole process. The robot faculty is by nature only discursive, while the human is by nature both intuitive and discursive, and it was intuition that conceived the robotic mind in the first place. Furthermore, a self-conscious computing machine presents some difficulty for understanding the nature of robotic self-mindfulness.

The two discursive levels of *consciousness-of*, namely Ego-consciousness and I-consciousness, and the two corresponding representative states, wakefulness and dream, as series of interrelated brain waves, could be reduplicated in a robotic discursive mind. The interconnected wiring of very complex circuits leading robots to those levels of thought may require the capability of ultra I.A. that only super quantum computers may be able to achieve.

However, more complex is the level of intuition and Auto-transparency. There, no process of thought is present; it does not need to be present and actually, its presence would invalidate its transparency. In fact,

> "Technology is not going to save us. Our computers, our tools, our machines are not enough. We have to rely on our intuition, our true being... Humanity comes not from the machine but from the heart."[2512]

Furthermore, the intuitive apodictical certitude present in every act of perception is not an object of thought. Therefore, the electrical impulses necessary for the performance of those complex mental tasks are not there, consequently the robot is not there either. The robot is also not there in the fourth state, in the silence, where the mind is not an obstacle any longer,[2513] while, with the creation of robotic minds we are multiplying those obstructing circuits. If, however, the robot should be able to reach the Transcendent level of the Self-In-Itself, then it would merge in that Reality beyond the mental and the mechanical, where the Cosmos as a whole reaches Self-Realization beyond that which is biological and/or physical.

Finally, from a gnoseological or epistemological point of view, A.I. does not solve the epistemic loneliness. The self-awareness, which we cannot experience in the other human, will remain unknown in the robots as well. Again, we may infer it, based on the experienced communicative robotic responses, and therefore believe in the other's self-awareness. However, we can never live it as our own, even if we were in a *global brain* condition. In fact, the *global brain* will always be lived individually by us as *ours*. In other words, the 'I' connected with others on the phone or on the internet, through immediate communication *in real time*, remains always the *solitary* aware recipient of the communicated message. Self-awareness is always, one not many. Nevertheless, even the impossible eventuality of a cacophonic totality of different self-awareness would be lived as a unity by the individuality of the 'I.'>[2514] Furthermore, futuristic chip implants, capable to keep up to date with possible A.I. dominance,[2515] could balance out any *robotic-mind-superiority* trying to overwhelm humans.[2516]

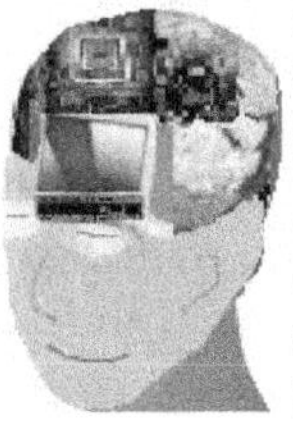

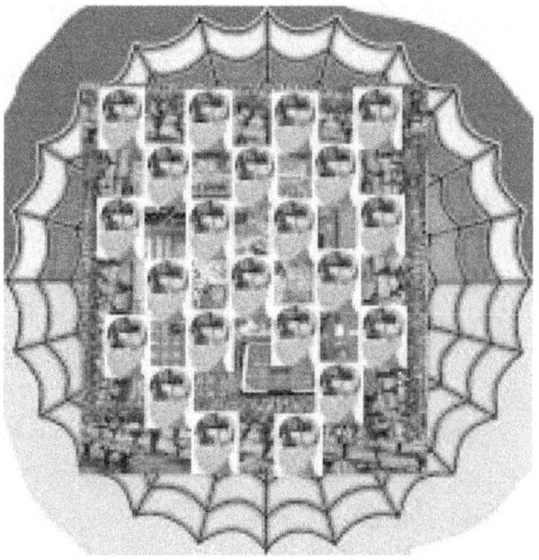

9:2-All Tamed Senses

וּמוֹרַאֲכֶם וְחִתְּכֶם יִהְיֶה עַל כָּל־חַיַּת הָאָרֶץ וְעַל כָּל־עוֹף הַשָּׁמָיִם בְּכֹל אֲשֶׁר תִּרְמֹשׂ הָאֲדָמָה וּבְכָל־דְּגֵי הַיָּם בְּיֶדְכֶם נִתָּנוּ׃ *umvōra'ăkem* (reverent fear of you) *vaḥitakem* (your subjugation) *yihayeh* (shall be) *'al* (over) *kāl* (all that) *ḥayat* (sustain the vigor of life) *hā'āreṣ* (of the earth) *va'al* (over) *kāl* (all) *'vōp̄* (fowl) *hašāmāyim* (of the sky) *bakōl* (all) *'ăšer* (which) *tiramōś* (creepeth) *hā'ădāmāh* (on the earth) *ubakāl* (all) *dağēy* (fish) *hayām* (sea) *bayedakem* (in your hand) *nitānu* (they have been bestowed)
καὶ *kai* (and) **ὁ** *o* (the) **τρόμος** *tromos* (fear) **ὑμῶν** *umōn* (of you) **καὶ** *kai* (and) **ὁ** *o* (the) **φόβος** *phobos* (phobia) **ἔσται** *estai* (shall be) **ἐπὶ** *epi* (on) **πᾶσιν** *pasin* (all) **τοῖς** *tois* (the) **θηρίοις** *thērios* (animals) **τῆς** *tēs* (of the) **γῆς** *gēs* (earth) **καὶ** *kai* (and) **ἐπὶ** *epi* (on) **πάντα** *panta* (all) **τὰ** *ta* (the) **ὄρνεα** *ornea* (birds) **τοῦ** *tou* (of the) **οὐρανοῦ** *ouranou* (sky) **καὶ** *kai* (and) **ἐπὶ** *epi* (on) **πάντα** *panta* (all) **τὰ** *ta* (the) **κινούμενα** *kinoumena* (moving) **ἐπὶ** *epi* (on) **τῆς** *tēs* (the) **γῆς** *gēs* (earth) **καὶ** *kai* (and) **ἐπὶ** *epi* (on) **πάντας** *pantas* (all) **τοὺς** *tous* (the) **ἰχθύας** *ichthuas* (fish) **τῆς** *tēs* (of the) **θαλάσσης** *thalassēs* (sea) **ὑπὸ** *upo* (in) **χεῖρας** *cheiras* (hand) **ὑμῖν** *umin* (your) **δέδωκα** *dedōka* (I have given)
et (and) ***terror*** (the terror) ***vester*** (of you) ***ac*** (and) ***tremor*** (the tremor) ***sit*** (be) ***super*** (on) ***cuncta*** (all) ***animalia*** (the animals) ***terrae*** (of the earth) ***et*** (and) ***super*** (on) ***omnes*** (all) ***volucres*** (the birds) ***caeli*** (of the shy) ***cum*** (with) ***universis*** (all) ***quae*** (that) ***moventur*** (move)

in (on) ***terra*** (the earth) ***omnes*** (all) ***pisces*** (the fish) ***maris*** (of the sea) ***manui*** (in hand) ***vestrae*** (yours) ***traditi*** (delivered) ***sunt*** (yhey are)
And the fear of you and the dread of you shall be upon every beast of the earth, and upon every fowl of the air, upon all that moveth upon the earth, and upon all the fishes of the sea; into your hand are they delivered.
The reverent fear of you and your subjugation shall be over all animals sustaining the vigor of life on earth, over all the birds of the sky and all that creeps on the earth and all the fish of the sea, they have all been bestowed in your hand.

Those, whose need for domination overpowers them, and those, who are greedy for ownership and possession of the fauna, will interpret this verse as literal animal subjugation. However, to comment this verse, we can use many allegories from India to Greece. The *Kaṭha Upanishad*, continuing the allegory first described in the Indian *Ṛg Veda,*[2517] declares,

"*Verily, know the Self as riding in the chariot* [and] *also the body as a two-wheeled chariot. Verily, know the Ego-consciousness as the driver of the chariot and also the faculty of thought as the reins./ They say* [that] *the faculties of the senses* [are] *the horses* [and] *the scope of the senses in them* [is] *the range for pasture./ The wise persons say* [that] *the I-consciousness, the faculty of thought and the faculties of the senses united* [are] *the experiencer./ Thus* [for one] *who is without intuition* [and] *with the faculty of the mind always un-concentrated, his faculties* [are] *un-submissive, like vicious horses for the driver./ However,* [for one] *who has intuition* [and] *the faculty of the mind always yoked in concentration, his faculties* [are] *submissive, like good horses for the driver./ Also, whosoever is always impure, without intuition,* [and] *without intellect does not attain that goal* [and] *falls into the flow of worldly illusions./ However, whosoever is always holy, with the mind unified,* [and] *has intuition, verily attains that goal from which one* [is] *not born again./ One, then, the person who has the intuition of the chariot's driver, who tightens the reins of the faculty of the mind,* [that] *one reaches the end of the journey. That* [is] *the Transcendent place of the All-Pervading Being./ Indeed, beyond the faculty of the senses* [are] *the acts of intentionality and beyond the acts of intentionality* [is] *the faculty of the mind. Beyond the faculty of the mind* [is] *consciousness. Beyond consciousness* [is] *the Great Self.*"[2518]

Similarly, the Greek philosopher Plato describes the body-mind relationship, metaphorically, as a chariot with two horses,

"A pair of... winged horses and a ... charioteer drives his [chariot] in a pair... The soul, in her totality, has the care of inanimate being everywhere and traverses the whole heaven appearing in divers forms... the chariots of the gods in even poise, obeying the rein, glide rapidly; but the others labour, for the vicious steed goes heavily, weighing down the charioteer to the earth when his steed has not been thoroughly trained. ... But of the heaven which is above the heavens...There abides the very being with which true knowledge is concerned; the colourless, formless, intangible essence, visible only to mind, the pilot of the soul."[2519]

As we have seen, all the faculties of the living (חַי *chay*) that sustain the vigor[2520] *of* life[2521] breathing (חָוָה *chavah*), news-bearing flesh (בָּשָׂר *basar*) are the sense-animals (בְּהֵמָה *běhemah*), which show and interpret (חָוָא *chava'*) the world (אֶרֶץ *'erets*). The birds of the air (שָׁמַיִם *shamayim*) are metaphors of all the psychological-*flying*-impulses (עוֹף *`owph*). All the serpentine-forces (רֶמֶשׂ *remes*) are allegories of the intentionality directing towards (רָמַשׂ *ramas*) the earthly (אֲדָמָה *'adamah*) objects. Furthermore, the mind traverses, as great *fishes* (דָּג *dag*) in the ocean[2522] reservoir of all possibilities or as "*birds*" in the air, all the states of consciousness.[2523] In fact, the mind moves along

"*in three states* [wakefulness, dream and dreamless sleep], *in succession, and on account of the knowledge, 'I am that', resulting from the experience which unites through memory.*"[2524]

"Then, which one is the self? This person is the light within the heart.[2525] *S/he, being serenely centered in itself, penetrates both worlds as if s/he were thinking and moving back and forth. S/he, upon entering the dream state, goes beyond this dimension and the forms of death."*[2526]

The mind, then, is the

"internal regulator,"[2527]

who, while in the state of deep sleep without dreams,

"does not know, except that, while not knowing, s/he is still the knower. In fact, knowledge does not separate from the knower, because s/he is imperishable. Merely, in that state, there is no otherness and nothing else that s/he may know."[2528]

Now we can understand that, when the Rested-Noah comes out of the Mind-Ark all the animal-senses are bestowed (נָתַן *nathan*) to Noah. The senses are, like Plato's horses under the reverent[2529] fear[2530] of the charioteer, to use Plato's allegory, and are tamed or broken[2531] and subjugated[2532] by Noah-mental-hand-power,[2533] like the charioteer's controlling reins.

Fear (מוֹרָא *mowra'*) is present in every animal (חַי *chay*) human and non-human. The original solipsism offers no

"evidence for the reality of the Other's soul."[2534]

This perfect isolation leads to the recognition that

"My kingdom is not of this world... is not from hence,"[2535]

namely, from the subject-object dimension of this world of duality, which we are conscious-*of.*

9:3-The Living Existence

כָּל־רֶמֶשׂ אֲשֶׁר הוּא־חַי לָכֶם יִהְיֶה לְאָכְלָה כְּיֶרֶק עֵשֶׂב נָתַתִּי לָכֶם אֶת־כֹּל׃
kāl (all) *remeś* (creeping thing) *'ăšer* (which) *hu'* (is) *ḥay* (alive) *lāḵem* (to you) *yihayeh* (exists) *la'āḵalāh* (food of judgment) *kayereq* (green) *'ēśeḇ* (shining herbs) *nāṯatiy* (I have given) *lāḵem* (to you) *'eṯ* (and) *kōl* (the whole)
καὶ *kai* (and) **πᾶν** *pan* (all) **ἑρπετόν** *erpeton* (serpent) **ὅ** *o* (the) **ἐστιν** *estin* (is) **ζῶν** *zōn* (living) **ὑμῖν** *umin* (for you) **ἔσται** *estai* (is) **εἰς** *eis* (in) **βρῶσιν** *brōsin* (food) **ὡς** *ōs* (thus) **λάχανα** *lachana* (herbs) **χόρτου** *chortou* (for food) **δέδωκα** *dedōka* (I gave) **ὑμῖν** *umin* (for you) **τὰ** *ta* (the) **πάντα** *panta* (all things)
et (and) ***omne*** (all) ***quod*** (that) ***movetur*** (moves) ***et*** (and) ***vivit*** (alive) ***erit*** (was) ***vobis*** (to you) ***in*** (as) ***cibum*** (food) ***quasi*** (as) ***holera*** (vegetation) ***virentia*** (green) ***tradidi*** (I gave) ***vobis*** (to you) ***omnia*** (all things)
Every moving thing that liveth shall be meat for you; even as the green herb have I given you all things.
All existing moving things that are alive shall be your food for thought, just as with the green shining herbs I have given you everything.

Naturally, those, whose stomach dictates its needs, with their mind *fixed on food,* will read this verse literally, namely, as animal consumption. However, *eating* (אָכַל *'akal*) implies the assimilation and transformation of an external object in one's own interiority. Metaphorically, as we have seen, the same occurrence takes place during the process of knowledge.

As food, directed by the senses, enters our mouth nourishing every organ, similarly, knowledge, sensed by the perceiving faculties, enters our mind informing every cognitive neuron. As with the green (יָרָק *yereq*) shining plants[2536] of the objective earth (אֶרֶץ *'erets*), given (נָתַן *nathan*) by Divine-Consciousness, the mind *eats* this food *for thought* or *for judgment.*[2537] Therefore, the *intellect recognizes* and places into existence[2538] *all that moves*[2539] and *is*[2540] *living* (חַי *chay*).

9:4-You Cannot Eat the Blood

אַךְ־בָּשָׂר בְּנַפְשׁוֹ דָמוֹ לֹא תֹאכֵלוּ׃
'aḵa (however) *bāśār* (news bearing flesh) *banapāšvō* (the soul in itself) *ḏāmvō* (the blood) *lō'* (not) *ṯō'ḵēlu* (shall eat)
πλὴν *plēn* (but) **κρέας** *kreas* (flesh) **ἐν** *en* (in) **αἵματι** *aimati* (blood) **ψυχῆς** *psuchēs* (breath of the

psyche) **οὐ** *ou* (not) **φάγεσθε** *phagesthe* (shall eat)
excepto (but) ***quod*** (that which) ***carnem*** (flesh) ***cum*** (with) ***sanguine*** (blood) ***non*** (not) ***comedetis*** (you shall eat)
But flesh with the life thereof, which is the blood thereof, shall ye not eat.
However, you shall not eat the soul in itself, the blood of the news bearing flesh.

A literal reading of this passage forbids eating any meat at all. In fact, unless it specifies the quantity of forbidden blood consumption, any drained and/or well-cooked meat will always retain microscopic blood cells.

"Observant Muslims and Jews, who are forbidden by their religions from consuming blood, believe that an animal's throat must be cut when it is conscious. Yet scientists comparing... [*halal* and *kosher*] meat from cattle that were humanely stunned... found no difference in the retention of red blood cells."[2541]

Thus, in this sense, the verse would become an injunction to be vegetarian.

However (אַךְ *'ak*), the *news-bearing-flesh* (בָּשָׂר *basar*) is that of the *sense-animals* (בְּהֵמָה *běhemah*). The flow of those informative epistemic news, which show and interpret (חָוָא *chava'*) the world (אֶרֶץ *'erets*), is described, metaphorically, as blood. We must analyze the etymology of the Hebrew word *dam*,[2542] meaning *blood*. The term derives from the primary verb-root *damam*,[2543] *to be silent, to be still, to wait, to be and grow dumb*. Parallel it with the verbs: *daham*,[2544] *to astonish, to astound*, with *duwach*,[2545] *to purge*, and with *damah*,[2546] *to destroy, to perish*. Further, compare it to *'adam*[2547] *to be red*. This redness is metaphorical for <the radiant morning light in opposition to the darkness of the night. Royal Purple is the esoteric color of king garments. In the Arthurian saga,

"at the vigil of Pentecost, when all the fellowship of the Round Table were come unto Camelot"[2548]

and the knights were in the midst of a darkened sleep, young Galahad[2549] appeared, to sit in his

"Siege Perilous... [He was dressed] in a coat of red sendal [fine cloth]."[2550]

Dark red is the traditional color of the central fire of man and earth, the gastric fire of the internal state before it moves out to digest and *com*prehend the external world. It is the midnight sun that shines and illuminates around without being illuminated, thus cannot be seen.>[2551]

There are additional meanings of the verb *damam* (דָּמַם) that need clarification, in order to understand the deep sense of the word *blood* (דָּם *dam*) in the context of these verses. The etymological analysis of Gesenius addresses them.

"דָּמַם [*damam*]... (3) *To be quiet, to cease, to leave off*... also *to stand still* ... *Note*. This root is onomatopoetic, and one which is widely spread in other families of languages, and equally with the kindred roots הָמַם [*hâmam* to move noisily], הוּם [*hûm* to murmur], הָמַת [*hâmat* deceased] and Gr[eek]. Μύω [*muō* I am silent], it is the imitation of the sound of the shut mouth (*hm*, *dm*). Its proper meaning therefore, is *to be dumb*, which is applied both to *silence and quietness*, and also to the *stupefaction* of one who is lost in wonder and astonishment; and also in the causative and transitive conjugations it is applied to *destruction and desolation*, inasmuch as things or places which are destroyed and made desolate, are still and quiet.

Most nearly kindred to this root are דּוּם [*dwm*] (in which is to be observed the obscure sound which is peculiar to the mouth when closed; see the Latin and German words below) and דָּמַם [*dmm* silent], which see. The same primary power is found in שָׁמַם [*śmm* name], תְּמַה [*tmh* theme], רָהַם [*rohem*] etc., not to mention those in which the idea of the closed mouth is applied to taste (טָעַם [*ṭam*]), or to abstinence from food (צוּם [*tswm*]), or to unmeaning sounds (בְּרַם [*brm*], נָהַם [*nhm*], נָאַם [*nam*], הָמָה [*hmh*]), or, lastly, to the general sense of closing (see אָטַם [*aṭm*, gasket], עָצַם [*atsm* bone], etc.). From the branches of this family in Greek is μύω [*muō*], which is frequently used of the mouth, lips, or eyes, as being closed, and also of sounds uttered with the mouth shut (see Passow's Gr[eek]. Lex. v. μῦ, μύω [*mu, muō*]), and the citations there given); hence θαῦμα [*thauma*], θάμβος [*thambos*] = Heb. שָׁמַם [*śmm* name], Chaldee תְּמַה [*tmh* theme]; Latin *mutus* [mute] (from μύδος, μύω [*mudos, muō*]), and still more in the Germanic languages, dumm = stupid, English and

Anglo-Saxon *dumb* (which is in meaning nearer to the primary idea), which, with the addition of a sibilant, becomes = stumm; comp. Lat. *stupor, stupidus,* and Germ. staunen, Engl., *to stun,* Fr. *étonner*."[2552]

Gesenius' etymological analysis finds further comparison in the Indian *Upanishads*. In fact, the *Māṇḍūkya Upanishad* describes[2553] the state of deep sleep, the intuition beyond the dialectic subject-object correlation, as the letter M, the sound "Mᵉ," as in the *m* of *man*, the *M*easuring and building block of the entire world. It is

"*the stone which the builders rejected, the same is become the head of the corner.*"[2554]

When emitting the sound Mᵉ, a soft nasal labial,[2555] the lips are closing; similarly, in the state of deep sleep we close[2556] to the waking and dreaming world. Both these last two states merge and dissolve into deep sleep without dreams. This is the state where one,

"*caught up to the third heaven… heard unspeakable words, which it is not lawful for man to utter.*"[2557]

There,

"*the knower, in the state of deep*[2558] *unconscious* [dreamless sleep, is] *the letter-sound M, the third metrical letter,* [meaning] *Measuring-building or Abatement-entering-into-dissolution.*[2559] *Indeed, whosoever thus knows Measures-and-builds this entire* [world] *and verily becomes the Abatement-* [and] *-dissolution-*[of the world by] *entering-into* [itself]."[2560]

Jung declared,[2561]

"I have often encountered motif which made me think that the unconscious must be the world of the infinitesimally small."

It should be understood that the unconscious aspect (ψυχῆς *psuchēs*) is such only from the point of view of the waking and dream states, while, from the vantage point of sleep with no dreams, it is pure intuitive stillness. Therefore, the meaning of the word *blood* becomes cognate to *life-in-itself,*[2562] which, as such, can never be known or *eaten* (אָכַל *'akal*). This knowledge is the equivalent to *eating* the forbidden fruit of the Tree of Knowledge. Eating it, Adam/subject and Eve/object lose the Tree of Life. In fact, consuming it means to conceptualize the unknowable Transcendent, thus, to miss the Life of the Self-In-Itself, namely, *to eat* its *blood-life*.

9:5-Divine-Consciousness Takes Care of the Blood-Life

וְאַךְ אֶת־דִּמְכֶם לְנַפְשֹׁתֵיכֶם אֶדְרֹשׁ מִיַּד כָּל־חַיָּה אֶדְרְשֶׁנּוּ וּמִיַּד הָאָדָם מִיַּד אִישׁ אָחִיו אֶדְרֹשׁ אֶת־נֶפֶשׁ הָאָדָם׃ *va'aka* (in fact) *'et* (and) *dimakem* (blood) *lanapāšōtēykem* (your soul self in-itself) *'edarōš* (I take care) *miyad* (by power) *kāl* (all) *ḥayāh* (living) *'edarašenu* (I take care) *umiyad* (by power) *hā'ādām* (man) *miyad* (by power) *'iyš* (*male-subject*) *'āḥiyv* (*reciprocal kinship-object*) *'edarōš* (I take care) *'et* (and) *nepeš* (self-life) *hā'ādām* (human)
καὶ *kai* (and) **γὰρ** *gar* (in fact) **τὸ** *to* (the) **ὑμέτερον** *umeteron* (your) **αἷμα** *aima* (blood) **τῶν** *tōn* (of the) **ψυχῶν** *psuchōn* (psyche) **ὑμῶν** *umōn* (your) **ἐκζητήσω** *ekzētēsō* (I seek for) **ἐκ** *ek* (of) **χειρὸς** *cheiros* (hand) **πάντων** *pantōn* (all) **τῶν** *tōn* (of the) **θηρίων** *thēriōn* (beasts) **ἐκζητήσω** *ekzētēsō* (I seek for) **αὐτὸ** *auto* (same) **καὶ** *kai* (and) **ἐκ** *ek* (of) **χειρὸς** *cheiros* (hand) **ἀνθρώπου** *anthrōpou* (man) **ἀδελφοῦ** *adelphou* (brother) **ἐκζητήσω** *ekzētēsō* (I seek for) **τὴν** *tēn* (the) **ψυχὴν** *psuchēn* (psyche) **τοῦ** *tou* (of the) **ἀνθρώπου** *anthrōpou* (humanity)
sanguinem (blood) ***enim*** (in fact) ***animarum*** (of souls) ***vestrarum*** (yours) ***requiram*** (I require) ***de*** (from the) ***manu*** (hand) ***cunctarum*** (of all) ***bestiarum*** (the beasts) ***et*** (and) ***de*** (from the) ***manu*** (hand) ***hominis*** (of man) ***de*** (from the) ***manu*** (hand) ***viri*** (of man) ***et*** (and) ***fratris*** (brother) ***eius*** (your) ***requiram*** (I require) ***animam*** (the soul) ***hominis*** (of man)
And surely your blood of your lives will I require; at the hand of every beast will I require it, and at the hand of man; at the hand of every man's brother will I require the life of man.
In fact, by power, I take care of the blood-life of your souls, the self in-itself. By power, I take care of all the living. By power, I take care of man, the male-subject, the reciprocal-kinship-object and

human life-in-itself.

The *Biblical* distinction, between the internal invisible *blood* (דָּם *dam*)[2563] and the external visible *flesh* (בָּשָׂר *basar*),[2564] metaphorically expresses the philosophical distinction between the unseen *being-in-itself*, as blood (דָּם *dam*), and the *showing forth* (בָּשָׂר *basar*)[2565] *being-for-itself*, as flesh (בָּשָׂר *basar*).

"*In fact, the self-life* (נֶפֶשׁ *nephesh*)[2566] *of the flesh is in the blood: and I have given it to you upon the altar to make an atonement for your souls: for it is the blood that maketh an atonement for the self-soul.*"[2567]

Indeed (אַךְ *'ak*), the *Self In-Itself*, the *Life Of The Soul* (נֶפֶשׁ *nephesh*), metaphorically named *blood* (דָּם *dam*), is the Transcendent itself. We cannot understand the Understander of understanding because that is the Transcendent Self, the *Blood In-Itself*. We cannot read the mind of others because their *blood* transcends us. We cannot observe the universe as it is independent from our observing point of view because it's *blood* transcends us. Our view is always *being-for-our-self*, *viz.* for our continuous circular reference of the *subject* to its correlated inseparable *object*. On the other hand, the Self, the Other and the Universe, as *being-in-themselves*, namely, as absolute independent centers unrelated to our inseparable *subject-object* circular correlation, transcend us . The being-in-itself is the Transcendent-*Blood*-Life towards which we always intend without ever reaching It. A perfect metaphor for this is lovemaking. In the present of that thoughtless moment, we reach the perfect union. As much as we cherish the identification with our partner during the apex of the conjugal fusion, that instant is lost in the moment we conceptualize it in the time/space sequence. Thus, the injunction

"*What therefore God hath joined together, let not man separate.*"[2568]

Therefore, only the Transcendent, Divine-Consciousness, by Its Own *Powerful*[2569] *Hand*,[2570] can *take care* (דרשׁ *darash*)[2571] *of the Transcendent life* of man *in-its-blood, viz. the unknowable intimate center of the life* of the subject, *viz.* the *male-in-itself* (אישׁ *'iysh*) *in its a-priory* synthesis of subject/object-*wife*, *the reciprocal-kinship-object*[2572] and *human life-in-itself*. In other words, the mysterious blood of life lies only in the recess of the Mysterious Unknown, in the Omnipresence of Awareness. Jesus confirms this concept of the *blood* as Life-In-Itself declaring,

"*This is my blood, … which is shed for you.*"[2573]

On <this level, the self does not enter in the dialectical correlation of subject-object, but persists in the Auto-Transparency of its being-in-itself. This Auto-Transparency is such only until the moment in which we think of it, at which time it becomes I-consciousness. Then, it becomes consciousness-*of*, always intentionally turned towards the world with which it establishes a correlation. It is as when>[2574]

"*you walk from one place to another: you do not attend to the steps you take. Yet you find yourself after a time at your goal.... There is full awareness in sleep and total ignorance in waking.*"[2575]

In each moment of each of the three states of mind, there is the underlining presence, the *blood* of the other two.

9:6-The Image of Divine-Consciousness

שֹׁפֵךְ דַּם הָאָדָם בָּאָדָם דָּמוֹ יִשָּׁפֵךְ כִּי בְּצֶלֶם אֱלֹהִים עָשָׂה אֶת־הָאָדָם׃   *šōpēḵa* (who pours out) *dam* (the blood) *hā'āḏām* (of man) *bā'āḏām* (by man) *dāmvō* (blood) *yišāpēḵa* (is poured out) *kiy* (because) *baṣelem* (image) *baṣelem* (Divine-Consciousness) *'āśāh* (made) *'eṯ* (and) *hā'āḏām* (man)
ὁ *o* (who) **ἐκχέων** *ekcheōn* (pours out) **αἷμα** *aima* (the blood) **ἀνθρώπου** *anthrōpou* (of man) **ἀντὶ** *anti* (instead) **τοῦ** *tou* (of the) **αἵματος** *aimatos* (blood) **αὐτοῦ** *autou* (his own) **ἐκχυθήσεται** *ekchthēsetai* (shall be shead) **ὅτι** *oti* (because) **ἐν** *en* (in) **εἰκόνι** *eikoni* (image) **θεοῦ** *theou* (of God) **ἐποίησα** *epoiēsa* (made) **τὸν** *ton* (the) **ἄνθρωπον** *anthrōpon* (man)
quicumque (whosoever) ***effuderit*** (poured out) ***humanum*** (human) ***sanguinem*** (blood) ***fundetur*** (shall be poured out) ***sanguis*** (blood) ***illius*** (his) ***ad*** (in) ***imaginem*** (the image) ***quippe*** (because) ***Dei*** (of God) ***factus*** (made) ***est*** (is) ***homo*** (man)
Whoso sheddeth man's blood, by man shall his blood be shed: for in the image of God made he man.

Who pours out man's blood, by a man his blood is poured out, because man is made in the image of Divine-Consciousness.

As it was with Cain, we can read this pouring out (שָׁפַך *shaphak*) the blood (דָם *dam*), this slaying or killing, in three ways.

1) One way is the actual physical human life snatching. This implies the elimination of the physical properties of the murdered one. However,

   "*all they that take the sword shall perish with the sword.*"[2576]

2) The other is the epistemic way. In fact, to know someone means that we must necessarily eliminate the other person's subjectivity for us to know him/her as an object. In fact, we never know the other as a subject "*I*."

   "*A man cannot find out the work that is done under the sun: because though a man labour to seek it out, yet he shall not find it; yea further; though a wise man think to know it, yet shall he not be able to find it.*"[2577]

   We always know the other as an object "*you.*" This implies the denial of the blood-life that makes the other an "*I*" *under the care and power* of the Transcendent Awareness. Certainly, when we interact with someone we possessively and emotionally *believe* in the other person's subjectivity, but we never *live* the subject of the other as such. That is, because, we are the only subject we will ever realize. The other is the one we can physically eliminate or epistemically reduce to a known object.

3) Finally, we reverse this epistemic condition towards our own self. When "*I* know myself," that knower is inevitably not the *I-subject* but the *me-object*. All killings and/or possessive knowledge intend to eliminate the most intimate essence of the human. However, as image (צֶלֶם *tselem*) of Divine-Consciousness, one can never be truly eliminated in-itself. The person walking before us, immersed in her own thoughts, is another parallel universe surrounding the sun of her own subjectivity. Nevertheless, we can never observe that universe except from the belief we have, in our world, of her as a separate cosmos.

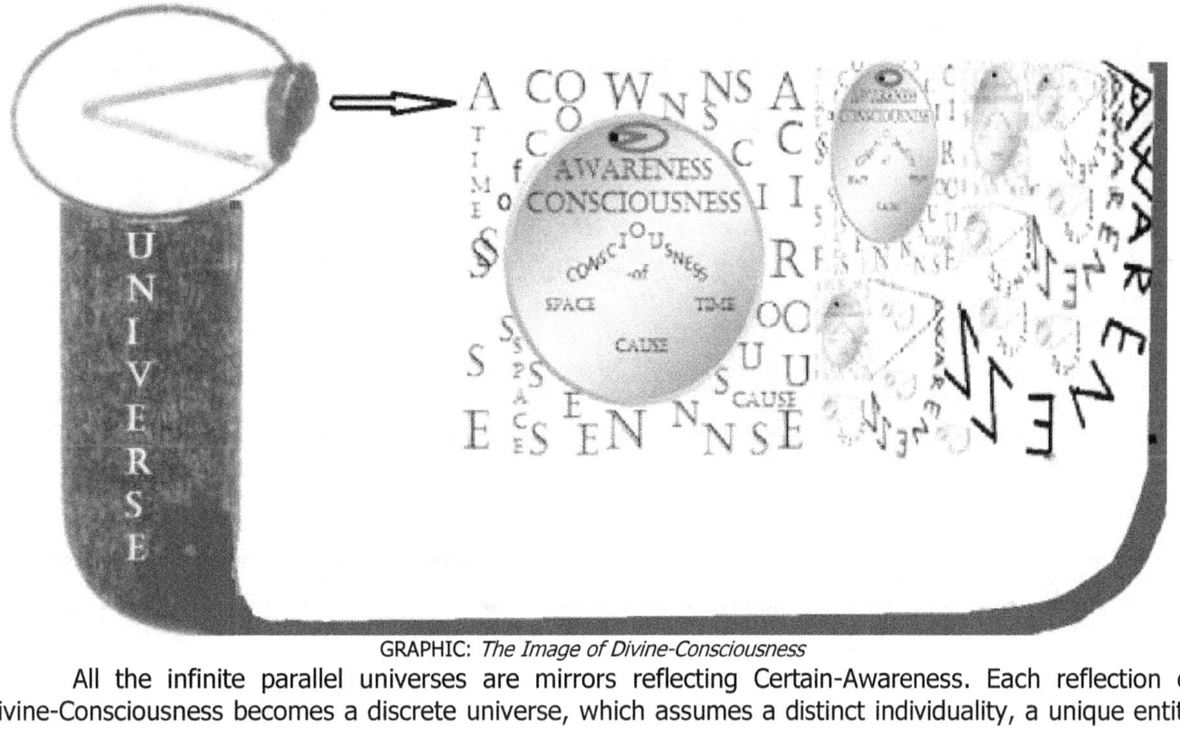

GRAPHIC: *The Image of Divine-Consciousness*

All the infinite parallel universes are mirrors reflecting Certain-Awareness. Each reflection of Divine-Consciousness becomes a discrete universe, which assumes a distinct individuality, a unique entity

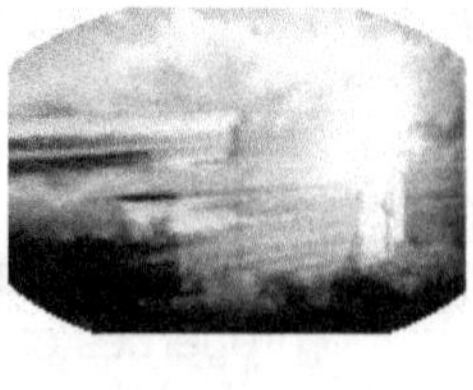

declaring itself, as such, real in-itself. Awareness is like a Sun reflecting in all the infinite drops of water in the bottomless depth of an infinite ocean of possibilities.

The acts of physical killing and/or epistemic-objectivizing equate to the act of eating the forbidden fruit, which is the attempt to eliminate the Transcendent Apodicticity as such and reduce it to an immanent concept. In fact, the act of killing is the attempt to eliminate the other's transcendent life, as the act of knowing is the attempt to eliminate the other's transcendent subjectivity. However,

> "*if the slayer thinks s/he slays, if the slain thinks* [s/he is] *killed, both these do not understand. This One does not slay nor It is slain.*"[2578]

9:7-Multiply Exponentially

וְאַתֶּם פְּרוּ וּרְבוּ שִׁרְצוּ בָאָרֶץ וּרְבוּ־בָהּ׃ ס   *va'atem* (at this parting point) *paru* (be fruitfull) *urabu* (grow) *širaṣu* (multiply) *bā'āreṣ* (on the earth) *urabu* (become many) *bāh* (accordingly) *s* (.)
ὑμεῖς *umeis* (you) **δὲ** *de* (but) **αὐξάνεσθε** *auxanesthe* (grow) **καὶ** *kai* (and) **πληθύνεσθε** *plēthunesthe* (multiply) **καὶ** *kai* (and) **πληρώσατε** *plērōsate* (fill) **τὴν** *tēn* (the) **γῆν** *gēn* (earth) **καὶ** *kai* (and) **πληθύνεσθε** *plēthunesthe* (multiply) **ἐπ'** *ep'* (on) **αὐτῆς** *autēs* (it)
vos (you) ***autem*** (also) ***crescite*** (grow) ***et*** (and) ***multiplicamini*** (multiply) ***et*** (and) ***ingredimini*** (step into) ***super*** (on) ***terram*** (the earth) ***et*** (and) ***implete*** (populate) ***eam*** (it)
And you, be ye fruitful, and multiply; bring forth abundantly in the earth, and multiply therein.
At this parting point be fruitful, grow and multiply on the earth and, accordingly, become many."

The boundary[2579] is at the exit of the ark, *where the desert of the dreamless sleep ends and the* ocean *of the world's representations* unfolds. Understand the ark as the mind. Understand the mind as a computer.[2580] Furthermore, understand all the dwellers of the ark as chips, microprocessors, systems and application software exponentially (שָׁרַץ *sharats*) multiplying (רבה *rabah*) in the field (אֶרֶץ *'erets*) of objectivity and bearing the fruit[2581] of specific tasks. Campbell refers to them as

> "a whole hierarchy of angels – all on slats. And those little tubes – those are miracles."[2582]

Therefore, when we exit the dreamless sleep, similarly, the world of dreams and wakefulness multiplies unfolding before our eyes.

One of the loyal critics of our writings asked.

'Does this mean that we must stay always in a cataleptic state?'

We replied,

'Not at all, on the contrary, it means that we exit NREM totally awake and in the fullness of Awareness. Then, we look at the world aware and disengaged, but not attached to it. Therefore, we like to quote Se. Paul,'

> "*Because of the impending crisis I think it best for you to remain as you are... -- And ... The time is short. So then those who have wives should be as those who have none, -- those with tears like those not weeping, those who rejoice like those not rejoicing, those who buy like those without possessions, -- those who use the world as though they were not using it to the full. For the present shape of this world is passing away. -- And I want you to be free from concern... -- am saying this for your benefit, not to place a limitation on you, but so that without distraction you may give notable and constant service to the Lord.*"[2583]

The mind enters the world controlling its senses and exponentially multiplying ideas.

9-II SECTION: THE COVENANT AND THE RAINBOW

9:8-God Spoke

וַיֹּאמֶר אֱלֹהִים אֶל־נֹחַ וְאֶל־בָּנָיו אִתּוֹ לֵאמֹר׃
vayō'mer (spoke) *'ĕlōhiym* (Divine-Consciousness) *'el* (to) *nōaḥ* (Noah) *va'el* (those) *bānāyv* (sons) *'itvō* (with) *lē'mōr* (saying)
καὶ *kai* (and) **εἶπεν** *eipen* (spoke) **ὁ** *o* (the) **θεὸς** *theos* (God) **τῷ** *tō* (to) **Νωε** *Nōe* (Noah) **καὶ** *kai* (and) **τοῖς** *tois* (the) **υἱοῖς** *uiois* (sons) **αὐτοῦ** *autou* (his) **μετ'** *met'* (with) **αὐτοῦ** *autou* (him) **λέγων** *legōn* (saying)
haec (this) ***quoque*** (also) ***dixit*** (said) ***Deus*** (God)***ad*** (to) ***Noe*** (Noah) ***et*** (and) ***ad*** (to) ***filios*** (sons) ***eius*** (his) ***cum*** (with) ***eo*** (him)
And God spake unto Noah, and to his sons with him, saying,
Divine-Consciousness also brought to light his command for Noah and his sons with him,

Again, Divine-Consciousness made evident (אמר *'amar*)[2584] Its commanding-structural-rules (אמר *'amar*) to the rested one and his epistemic offspring. Time, space and causality are the essential a-priori forms established by Consciousness to allow the process of knowledge to work.

9:9-Divine Banquet

וַאֲנִי הִנְנִי מֵקִים אֶת־בְּרִיתִי אִתְּכֶם וְאֶת־זַרְעֲכֶם אַחֲרֵיכֶם׃
va'ăniy (I) *hinaniy* (behold) *mēqiym* (am establishing) *'et* (and) *bariytiy* (covenant) *'itakem* (with) *va'et* (with) *zara'ăkem* (seed) *'aḥărēykem* (following)
ἐγὼ *egō* (I) **ἰδοὺ** *idou* (behold) **ἀνίστημι** *aqnisteēmi* (establish) **τὴν** *tēn* (the) **διαθήκην** *diathēkēn* (covenant) **μου** *mou* (my) **ὑμῖν** *umin* (with you) **καὶ** *kai* (and) **τῷ** *tō* (the) **σπέρματι** *spermati* (seed) **ὑμῶν** *umōn* (your) **μεθ'** *meth'* (after) **ὑμᾶς** *umas* (you)
ecce (behold) ***ego*** (I) ***statuam*** (establish) ***pactum*** (pact) ***meum*** (my) ***vobiscum*** (with you) ***et*** (and) ***cum*** (with) ***semine*** (seed) ***vestro*** (your) ***post*** (after) ***vos*** (you)
And I, behold, I establish my covenant with you, and with your seed after you;
"Behold I am establishing a banquet with you and with your seed following you,

The word *bĕriyth,*[2585] *covenant,* derives from the verb *barah,*[2586] *to eat.* Therefore, Divine-Consciousness establishes (קום *quwm*) a banquet with Rested-Noah and with his seed (זֶרַע *zera`*), his logical-seeds (λόγοι σπερματικοί *lógoi spermatikoí*), during which they share the same type of epistemic-food. This is the self-transparent symposium with all the epistemic faculties. However, no identification or possessive thought floods the mind, which remains in the contemplative stillness of the universe. The cosmos itself operates in this impersonal manner. In fact, no black hole desires or feels pain swallowing orbiting planets.

"Behold, I have prepared my dinner: ...come unto the marriage... The wedding is ready."[2587]

The invitation is open to the entire universe,

"many are called, but few are chosen."[2588]

The chosen are those who look at the world with the fulfillment of the Grace of Awareness. Then, there is no desire, no hunger and no thirst for the objective world.

"These are they which came out of great tribulation, and have washed their robes, and made them white in the blood of the Lamb. Therefore are they before the throne of God, and serve him day and night in his temple: and he that sitteth on the throne shall dwell among them. ***They shall hunger no more, neither thirst any more****; neither shall the sun light on them, nor any heat. For the Lamb which is in the midst of the throne shall feed them, and shall lead them unto living fountains of waters: and God shall wipe away all tears from their eyes."*[2589]

9:10-All the Epistemic Modalities Move out of the Ark

וְאֵת כָּל־נֶפֶשׁ הַחַיָּה אֲשֶׁר אִתְּכֶם בָּעוֹף בַּבְּהֵמָה וּבְכָל־חַיַּת הָאָרֶץ אִתְּכֶם מִכֹּל יֹצְאֵי הַתֵּבָה לְכֹל חַיַּת הָאָרֶץ׃
va'ēt (with) *kāl* (all) *nepeš* (breath of life in-itself) *haḥayāh* (animal) *'ăšer* (which) *'itakem* (with) *bā'vōp* (bird) *babahēmāh* (beast) *ubakāl* (all) *ḥayat* (animals) *hā'āreṣ* (earth) *'itakem* (with) *mikōl* (out of) *yōṣa'ēy* (exit) *hatēbāh* (ark) *lakōl* (from all) *ḥayat* (animals) *hā'āreṣ* (earth)

καὶ *kai* (and) **πάσῃ** *pasē* (all) **ψυχῇ** *psuchē* (psyche) **τῇ** *tē* (the) **ζώσῃ** *zōsē* (living) **μεθ'** *meth'* (with) **ὑμῶν** *umōn* (you) **ἀπὸ** *apo* (from) **ὀρνέων** *orneōn* (birds) **καὶ** *kai* (and) **ἀπὸ** *apo* (from) **κτηνῶν** *ktēnōn* (cattle) **καὶ** *kai* (and) **πᾶσι** *pasi* (all) **τοῖς** *tois* (the) **θηρίοις** *thēriois* (beast) **τῆς** *tēs* (of the) **γῆς** *gēs* (earth) **ὅσα** *osa* (as much as) **μεθ'** *meth'* (with) **ὑμῶν** *umōn* (you) **ἀπὸ** *apo* (from) **πάντων** *pantōn* (all) **τῶν** *tōn* (the) **ἐξελθόντων** *exelthontōn* (came out) **ἐκ** *ek* (from) **τῆς** *tēs* (the) **κιβωτοῦ** *kibōtou* (ark)
et (and) ***ad*** (to) ***omnem*** (all) ***animam*** (soul) ***viventem*** (living) ***quae*** (which) ***est*** (is) ***vobiscum*** (with you) ***tam*** (be it) ***in*** (as) ***volucribus*** (birds) ***quam*** (or) ***in*** (as) ***iumentis*** (cattle) ***et*** (and) ***pecudibus*** (sheep)[2590] ***terrae*** (of the earth) ***cunctis*** (all) ***quae*** (which) ***egressa*** (exited) ***sunt*** (are) ***de*** (from) ***arca*** (the ark) ***et*** (and) ***universis*** (all) ***bestiis*** (the beast) ***terrae*** (of the earth)
And with every living creature that is with you, of the fowl, of the cattle, and of every beast of the earth with you; from all that go out of the ark, to every beast of the earth.
and with all your life in-itself and with your animal sense and with your flying psychological drive and with your mute state of being, with all the animal-senses of the objective world exiting with you out of the ark, namely, all the senses of the world of objectivity."

The life breath in itself (נֶפֶשׁ *nephesh*), the full epistemic structure of the Mind articulates into the world. All the modalities of our knowledge intentionally go out of the ark-mind. They proceed towards (יָצָא *yatsa'*)[2591] the world of objectivity (אֶרֶץ *'erets*). Different from the structural forms, metaphorically referred to as Noah's sons, are the three general epistemic-sense-faculties, namely,

1) the *animal*-like *living sense-inclination for experience* (חַי *chay*)[2592] of the waking state,
2) the *flying*-like psychological senses (עוֹף *`owph*)[2593] of the dream state and
3) the *mute*-like creature (בְּהֵמָה *běhemah*)[2594] of the dreamless state. In fact, this last term *běhemah*, is translated as the

"*large, great...beast* (so called for being unable to speak)...*of the field* and *wild*."[2595]

They are all invited to the covenant, to the banquet. With it, Divine-Consciousness shares all the epistemic structures, which put and recognize the world into existence.

9:11- Covenant of Immortality

וַהֲקִמֹתִי אֶת־בְּרִיתִי אִתְּכֶם וְלֹא־יִכָּרֵת כָּל־בָּשָׂר עוֹד מִמֵּי הַמַּבּוּל וְלֹא־יִהְיֶה עוֹד מַבּוּל לְשַׁחֵת הָאָרֶץ׃
vahăqimōṯiy (I have established) *'eṯ* (and) *bariyṯiy* (a covenant) *'itaḵem* (with) *valō̆* (not) *yikārēṯ* (severed) *kāl* (all) *bāśār* (flesh) *'vōḏ* (more) *mimēy* (by) *hamabul* (the flood) *valō̆* (not) *yihayeh* (will be) *'vōḏ* (yet) *mabul* (deluge) *lašaḥēṯ* (to decay) *hā'āreṣ* (the earth)
καὶ *kai* (and) **στήσω** *stēsō* (I will establish) **τὴν** *tēn* (the) **διαθήκην** *diathēkēn* (covenant) **μου** *mou* (my) **πρὸς** *pros* (with) **ὑμᾶς** *umas* (you) **καὶ** *kai* (and) **οὐκ** *ouk* (not) **ἀποθανεῖται** *apothaneitai* (die) **πᾶσα** *pasa* (all) **σὰρξ** *sarx* (flesh) **ἔτι** *eti* (yet again) **ἀπὸ** *apo* (by) **τοῦ** *tou* (the) **ὕδατος** *udatos* (water) **τοῦ** *tou* (of the) **κατακλυσμοῦ** *kataklusmou* (cataclysm) **καὶ** *kai* (and) **οὐκ** *ouk* (not) **ἔσται** *estai* (shall be) **ἔτι** *eti* (yet) **κατακλυσμὸς** *kataklusmos* (cataclysm) **ὕδατος** *udatos* (of water) **τοῦ** *tou* (the) **καταφθεῖραι** *kataphtheirai* (destroy) **πᾶσαν** *pasan* (all) **τὴν** *tēn* (the) **γῆν** *gēn* (earth)
statuam (I will establish) ***pactum*** (pact) ***meum*** (my) ***vobiscum*** (with you) ***et*** (and) ***nequaquam*** (never) ***ultra*** (again) ***interficietur*** (will I kill) ***omnis*** (all) ***caro*** (flesh) ***aquis*** (by waters) ***diluvii*** (of the deluge) ***neque*** (nor) ***erit*** (shall be) ***deinceps*** (hereafter) ***diluvium*** (a deluge) ***dissipans*** (to destroy) ***terram*** (the earth)
And I will establish my covenant with you; neither shall all flesh be cut off any more by the waters of a flood; neither shall there any more be a flood to destroy the earth.
I establish a banquet with you. Never again will all flesh bearing information be severed by the flood, nor the deluge will decay the land of objectivity."

Contrary to the forbidden fruit or to the destructive flood, both yielding death, this verse promises immortality. The covenant of Divine-Consciousness is the banquet (בְּרִית *běriyth*) shared in Pure Awareness.

Since no possessive identification with the objective world takes place there, consequently, in Pure Awareness there cannot be any deluge. While Cain dies possessing and possessed by the object, Abel, instead, proceeds in the fullness of Awareness having sacrificed all his epistemic faculties in the stillness of That Awareness. **Awareness is the Will of Transcendence** (יְהֹוָה *Yĕhovah*). Therefore, there the information bearing nerve system, *viz.* the *flesh* (בָּשָׂר *basar*), will not be severed.[2596] The objective world will not decay[2597] again, because it is present in the pure stillness of contemplation. In fact,

"*in heaven their angels do always behold the face of my Father which is in heaven.*"[2598]

When time is the Eternal Present, as it is, which part of the past and/or of the future decays? Immortality reigns at that level. Death is the faster-than-light-wormhole that takes us beyond the dimensions of space/time/causality.[2599] What is a *wasteland* for the dead, like Cain, it is the Glorified Contemplative Awareness for the Rested One, like Abel and Noah. There are two deaths.[2600] The first is that of this physical body. The second one is Cain's oblivious, stubborn rejection of *That-Certain-Awareness*. Life is present only if we extinguish the land of duality and reabsorb in the Stillness-of-Awareness. In fact,

"*whosoever will save his life shall lose it: and whosoever will lose his life for my sake shall find it.*"[2601]

Our reader may object,

'But, if we give up our engagement with this world, how can we continue to enjoy living and to strive for a continuous process of constant progress? Here it appears as if you are promoting the end of life. This seems as if we were already dead.'

We reply,

'Not so. We should continue to participate and perform our duty in this daily battle that we call life. However, we should act without desiring any fruit deriving from our engagement in it.[2602] The attachment to the product of our action is the forbidden fruit (פְּרִי pĕriy).[2603] In fact, it is the constant bond with the past, with which we identify. Therefore, what we call life leads us inevitably to passing away; this is really the death we so dread. Whereas, serenely vivified by the Certain-Spirit-of-Truth, we enter, here and now, in This-Everlasting-Present

"*whose kingdom shall have no end.*"[2604]

9:12-The Sign of the Covenant

וַיֹּאמֶר אֱלֹהִים זֹאת אוֹת־הַבְּרִית אֲשֶׁר־אֲנִי נֹתֵן בֵּינִי וּבֵינֵיכֶם וּבֵין כָּל־נֶפֶשׁ חַיָּה אֲשֶׁר אִתְּכֶם לְדֹרֹת עוֹלָם׃   *vayō'mer* (said) *'ĕlōhiym* (Divine-Consciousness) *zō'ṯ* (this) *'vōṯ* (sign) *habariyṯ* (of the covenant) *'ăšer* (which) *'ăniy* (I) *nōṯēn* (give) *bēyniy* (between) *uḇēynēyḵem* (between) *uḇēyn* (between) *kāl* (all) *nepēš* (the breathing activity of mind) *ḥayāh* (living) *'ăšer* (which) *'itakem* (with) *laḏōrōṯ* (circuits of life's years) *'vōlām* (perpetually concealed)
καὶ *kai* (and) **εἶπεν** *eipen* (said) **κύριος** *kurios* (the Lord) **ὁ** *o* (the) **θεὸς** *theos* (God) **πρὸς** *pros* (to) **Νωε** *Nōe* (Noah) **τοῦτο** *touto* (in this way) **τὸ** *to* (the) **σημεῖον** *sēmeion* (sign) **τῆς** *tēs* (the) **διαθήκης** *diathēkēs* (covenant) **ὃ** *o* (the) **ἐγὼ** *egō* (I) **δίδωμι** *didōmi* (give) **ἀνὰ** *ana* (then) **μέσον** *meson* (between) **ἐμοῦ** *emou* (me) **καὶ** *kai* (and) **ὑμῶν** *umōn* (you) **καὶ** *kai* (and) **ἀνὰ** *ana* (then) **μέσον** *meson* (between) **πάσης** *pasēs* (all) **ψυχῆς** *psuchēs* (souls) **ζώσης** *zōsēs* (living) **ἥ** *e* (that) **ἐστιν** *estin* (is) **μεθ'** *meth'* (with) **ὑμῶν** *umōn* (you) **εἰς** *eis* (in to) **γενεὰς** *geneas* (generation) **αἰωνίους** *aiōnious* (eternal)
dixit- (said) ***que*** (and) ***Deus*** (God) ***hoc*** (this) ***signum*** (sign) ***foederis*** (pact) ***quod*** (which) ***do*** (I give) ***inter*** (between) ***me*** (me) ***et*** (and) ***vos*** (you) ***et*** (and) ***ad*** (to) ***omnem*** (all) ***animam*** (soul) ***viventem*** (living) ***quae*** (which) ***est*** (is) ***vobiscum*** (with you) ***in*** (for) ***generationes*** (generations) ***sempiternas*** (forever)
And God said, This is the token of the covenant which I make between me and you and every living creature that is with you, for perpetual generations:

Divine-Consciousness said, "*This is the sign of the covenant, which I give between you and me and all the living breathing mind activity in the perpetual concealed circuits of life's years.*

There is a sign of something

"which cannot itself be seen (אות *'owth*)."[2605]

However, with its appearance, anyone consents and agrees (אות *'uwth*)[2606] with the covenant (בְּרִית *bĕriyth*). This sign is within the living *breathing activity of the mind seat* (נֶפֶשׁ *nephesh*),[2607] the *ever present* (עוֹלָם *`owlam*)[2608] *hidden*, *concealed* and *secret* (עלם *`alam*)[2609]

"*period* and *circuit* of the years of life, (דור *dowr*)"[2610]

which *goes around in a circle* (דור *duwr*).[2611]

As we will explain, this is the circadian rhythm and the sign, which the verse refers to, is at the very center of this cycle.

9:13-The Rainbow

אֶת־קַשְׁתִּי נָתַתִּי בֶּעָנָן וְהָיְתָה לְאוֹת בְּרִית בֵּינִי וּבֵין הָאָרֶץ׃ *'et* (and) *qašatiy* (bow) *qašatiy* (set) *be'ānān* (in the cloud) *vahāyatāh* (to be) *la'vōt* (a sign) *bariyt* (covenant) *bēyniy* (between) *ubēyn* (between) *hā'āreṣ* (earth)
τὸ *to* (the) **τόξον** *toxon* (bow) **μου** *mou* (my) **τίθημι** *tithēmi* (I establish) **ἐν** *en* (in) **τῇ** *tē* (the) **νεφέλῃ** *nephelē* (cloud) **καὶ** *kai* (and) **ἔσται** *estai* (shall be) **εἰς** *eis* (it) **σημεῖον** *sēmeion* (sign) **διαθήκης** *diathēkēs* (covenant) **ἀνὰ** *ana* (then) **μέσον** *meson* (between) **ἐμοῦ** *emou* (me) **καὶ** *kai* (and) **τῆς** *tēs* (the) **γῆς** *gēs* (earth)
arcum (the arc) ***meum*** (my) ***ponam*** (I will set) ***in*** (in) ***nubibus*** (the clouds) ***et*** (and) ***erit*** (shall be) ***signum*** (a sign) ***foederis*** (of the pact) ***inter*** (between) ***me*** (me) ***et*** (and) ***inter*** (between) ***terram*** (the earth)
I do set my bow in the cloud, and it shall be for a token of a covenant between me and the earth.
I set a rainbow in the observer of the cloud of times to be a sign of the covenant between me and between the objective-earth.

Absurdly, literal readers of this verse could argue that, before the universal deluge, rainbows did not appear at all during or after rain. However, if they did, what would have distinguished them from this new arc? Truly, the rainbow here is a metaphor for the epistemic bridge-structure that directs the mind towards the sky of transcendence. Namely, the mind always projects whatever and/or howsoever it knows -- if not deliberately fictional -- as a being real in-itself independent from the knower, thus, as *tran*scendent. The *Bible* emphasizes <the corner stone[2612] as the central structure adjoining the two **cantilever arms** of a bridge. The sleep stage is the wasteland of the waking and dreaming phases, which dissolve in deep sleep, from where the whole process will start again in the circadian rhythm, namely, the metaphoric *rainbow* (קשת *qesheth*).

GRAPHIC: *The Rainbow Bridge*

The Apodictical-Certitude of Awareness, in the auto-transparent intuition of the presence of our self to our self, does not need the mediation of thought. In other words, we do not need to think of our self to be conscious-*of* our self. Thus,

> "man is the measure of all things"[2613]

and s/he who knows this becomes the measurer and the builder of the world. At the same time, s/he, who enters into its own interiority, becomes the wasteland and the dissolution of the world and its desires.

Technically, to identify the dream state with the REM sleep it is an oversimplification. In fact, dreams occur also

> "outside of REM sleep. Therefore, this stage cannot be equated with dream sleep... REM sleep are in general livelier... [than] non-REM sleep, in which rational and realistic elements similar to waking thoughts tend to prevail."[2614]

The dream state is characterized by the presence of "internal objects" (*i.e.* dreams) and this can be in the REM and non-REM stage, while the deep sleep state is characterized by the absence of "internal objects." This takes place only in the deepest moment of non-REM, where no dreams whatsoever are present and there is no objectivation of any sort.

> "A person awakened from a REM sleep episode is immediately oriented and aware of his surroundings, whereas one awakened from deep sleep experiences a period of extreme drowsiness, disorientation, and limited memory function."[2615]

On the onset of a troublesome malady, we realize our ignorance, an obscurity, a darkness, an impotence in regarding the source and/or the cause of the occurrence. Not only in the event of an illness, but also in every waking moment, our internal organs, our growth, our biological structure in general remain hidden, unknown and mysterious. No one feels the liver or any other internal organ, unless we pay attention to its functionality or it makes its presence known through a pain that stimulates and awakens sensory nerves not sedated by anesthesia. No one feels the appendix unless inflamed, in which case one experiences the spasm not the object, as the surgeon experiences it when performing an appendectomy without feeling the pain. Nevertheless, those organs remain unexplained, mummified in ancient Egyptian Canopic jars, or, at best, shrouded in the myth of a life of their own unconscious to the waking state. There, the waking consciousness connects with the other two states through creative and artistic *ex*pressions.

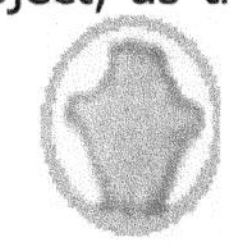

From a holistic perspective, we can view the four stages as,

1) Wakefulness, the state of this sensory consciousness,
2) Dream, the state of feeling the internal organs (you cannot feel your liver as it is inside),
3) Dreamless sleep, the state of the external objective world (a mineral apart from handling it),
4) Transcendent, the ineffable origin and end of those previous three states.

In each of the three states, the other two states are always present:

1) In the waking consciousness there are:
   2) the dream state, as the presence of the internal organs of the body and
   3) the state of unconsciousness, as the presence of the external material-world-at-hand.
2) In the dream life there are:
   1) the waking consciousness, as sustained by those organs and
   3) the external world, as the food of this biological structure.
3) In the unconscious mineral world there are:
   1) the conscious mind, as produced by those organs and
   2) the biological organs, as generated by the evolutionary process.
4) Lastly, the Transcendent is the all-containing silence of the contracting instant preceding the Big Bang and of its following final entropic-dissolution.

In the waking state, we feel the full force of our senses *pro*jected to interiorize the external world. The mind flies to cosmic limits, sight travels to bordering horizons and sound sails where echo waves break. Feeling seizes personal things here and now. Smell *in*spires the perfume carried by vaporous objects. Taste *sap*iently savors *in*corporating the entire nourishing world. When the body is not an instrument, out-reaching towards the external world, then it becomes a *peripheral* analyzed object, like when one examines one's own hand, different from the hub of conscience. Successively, when we examine the immediately-at-hand surrounding geographical world, then this peripheral body becomes the center of it all. In turn, when we consider the still further reachable space, like the solar system, then this surrounding world feels as being its interior. Consecutively, when we scrutinize the greater external expanses of the universe, then we experience this reachable space as its core. Therefore, in a ripple effect, each circle of wakeful consciousness becomes the center of a larger expansion of knowledge until the body contracts in its hub of consciousness while it expands encompassing the entire universe. In fact, when we are mesmerized by a starry summer night's sky losing all individual identity, then we have a sense of sublime oneness, which does not distinguish I from the stars.

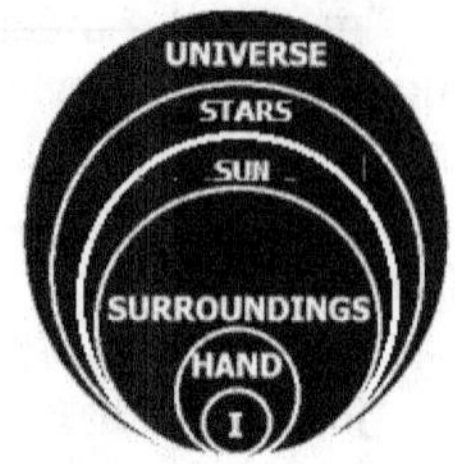

Urged to clarify the unknown, the function of science satisfies the need of the waking state to bring the unexplained to consciousness. In fact, the waking consciousness wills the science of *med*icine to meditate, to take care (Greek μέδω *médō*, Sanskrit √*mid – med*) and to understand those inner organs. Science, then, becomes the tool, the hallmark of the waking state. Furthermore, when the waking consciousness deals with the external unconscious world, then it generates the natural science of physics.

It is in the dream state that the internal organic obscurity steps into a light which is directly unknown to the waking state. In themselves, the internal organs relate to the oneiric state. In fact, apart from science, when illness occurs, then the full force of their mystery strikes our waking consciousness with vengeance and we are not personally able to intervene, except with the automatism of our immune system, which in itself is subconscious. From genes to molecular structure and from organic chemistry to the vital organs, all work on their own account not requiring our willful waking intervention. At that level, it is as if our waking mind were at sleep. We do not need to be awake for our heart to beat, our blood to flow, our lungs to breathe or our digestion to take its course. All this takes place independently from our wakeful or dreaming consciousness.

When we look at the world, in waking and/or dreaming, we *believe* that it persists independently without our conscious intervention. From the consciousness perspective, the objective world in itself is unconscious. We grind a stone with the same approach with which we chew on a steak. We use, manipulate, kill and butcher the world out there because we view it as insentient and insensitive, unless we attribute to the animate or inanimate world a consciousness, with which we sympathize. However, also in the presence of a consciousness, ascribed to another person, even in that case, we ultimately realize that for us that alien consciousness remains unconscious and unknown. We can intellectually and psychologically interpret, speculate, deduct and read the thoughts of minds different from ours, but no one, in fact, can feel the other person's psyche.

Finally, the scientific standpoint, with its objective, dispassionate, unemotional, truth-establishing *out*look, corresponds to the silent and unqualified Transcendent-Apodictical-Certitude of the Transcendent fourth stage underlining all the other states.>[2616]

In other words the state of dreamless sleep, or we can call it the cataleptic state, is the *portal* (so to say, where there is no portal as such) to the Transcendent itself. While, daily, we enter NREM unconscious, here, the emphasis is to access it with full awakened consciousness. That is, when we exit deep sleep, the possessive hunger or desire for dream and wakeful objects submerges us in its deluge. The point here is to retain the stillness of the stage of deep dreamless sleep at all levels. That is the Seventh Day (שְׁבִיעִי *shěbiy`iy*), the Sabbath in which Noah finds his *rest*.

"*The Sabbath itself is a sanctuary... in time.*"[2617]

In that state, reality is inversed. We become unconscious-*of* the objectivity-*of* the world while, at the same time, retaining it without thinking or being conscious-*of* it. The consciousness-*of-the-world* becomes like a *mysterious theophanic cloud* (עָנָן *`anan*) "covering and veiling over the heaven"[2618]

and ready to unleash its payload of flooding water. The word *`anan* (ענן), cloud, derives from the root *`anan* (ענן), meaning

"TO COVER... *to use hidden arts*... mysteries... Many of the ancients understood by it a particular kind of divination."[2619]

"The cock, *viz.* [Assyrian] *`e-na-nu* עָנַן [*`anan, to cloud*] 'to divine,' 'augurans' [diviner], 'observans somnia' [dreams observer] (Vulgate), represents this bird in this capacity as a soothsayer."[2620]

Furthermore, divination wants to know the future, which, obviously, is mysterious and unknown. The cloud becomes a metaphor for enchanter, sorcerer, soothsayer, fortuneteller and the magical art of divination, which distorts the Fundamental Reality in Itself and makes us drown in the time illusion of dreams. Thus we become like a cloud, *`anan, viz.* an

"*observer of times* (ענן *`anan*), *or an enchanter, or a witch... but... the LORD thy God hath not suffered thee so to do.*"[2621]

The Hebrew word *qesheth* (קֶשֶׁת), *rainbow* or *arrow-shooting bow*, derives from *qashah* (קָשָׁה), *hard, stubborn*, in the sense of *bending*, *qowsh* (קוֹשׁ), *to lay a snare, to lure*. Therefore, this verse points out that we keep *hard* and *obstinately*[2622] shooting the intentional *arrow of our bow*[2623] toward the objective world. Consequently, we fall into the *lure* and *circularly bent snare*[2624] of time, whereas, the intent is that

"*thou shalt be perfect with the LORD thy God.*"[2625]

Now, this arc (קֶשֶׁת *qesheth*) is set in this *observer of cloud of times-* (ענן *`anan*). This means that the *connecting-banquet-covenant* (בְּרִית *běriyth*) with the Transcendent is precisely here, on this *objective-earth* (אֶרֶץ *'erets*), in this time snare, in which we are drowning. In other words, Fundamental-Awareness is present in the circular bending (קוֹשׁ *qowsh*) of the subject-object correlation. If we understood that we should *fix the arrow of our gaze* in this Awareness, right here and now, then, we would partake of that same metaphorical supper and we would surface in Its Presence. Thus,

"*Blessed are they which are called unto the* *marriage* (γάμος *gamos*) *supper* (δεῖπνον *deipnon*) *of the Lamb.*"[2626]

9:14-The Bow in the Concealing Cloud

וְהָיָה בְּעַנְנִי עָנָן עַל־הָאָרֶץ וְנִרְאֲתָה הַקֶּשֶׁת בֶּעָנָן׃
vahāyāh (it shall be) *ba`ananiy* (when appears) *`ānān* (cloud) *`al* (on) *hā`āreṣ* (the earth) *vanira`āṯāh* (shall be seen) *haqešeṯ* (a bow) *be`ānān* (in the cloud)
καὶ *kai* (and) **ἔσται** *estai* (it shall be) **ἐν** *en* (in) **τῷ** *tō* (the) **συννεφεῖν** *sunnephein* (gather) **με** *me* (I) **νεφέλας** *nephelas* (clouds) **ἐπὶ** *epi* (over) **τὴν** *tēn* (the) **γῆν** *gēn* (earth) **ὀφθήσεται** *ophthēsetai* (shall be seen) **τὸ** *to* (the) **τόξον** *toxov* (bow) **μου** *mou* (my) **ἐν** *en* (in) **τῇ** *tē* (the) **νεφέλῃ** *nephelē* (cloud)
cumque (when) ***obduxero*** (I shall bring) ***nubibus*** (to the clouds) ***caelum*** (in the sky) ***apparebit*** (will appear) ***arcus*** (arc) ***meus*** (my) ***in*** (in) ***nubibus*** (the clouds)
And it shall come to pass, when I bring a cloud over the earth, that the bow shall be seen in the cloud:
When a veiling cloud happens to appear on the earth a bow shall be seen in that concealing cloud.

A water-pregnant cloud conceals the clear sky above. Similarly, when we communicate with someone, we assume a transcendent listener concealed by our ego. When a veiling mystery appears in our perception, it is proof of an intentioned transcendent unknown. The corner stone of the bow (קֶשֶׁת *qesheth*) can be perceived (רָאָה *ra'ah*) in the mysterious dreamless-sleep cloud (ענן *`anan*) veiling and concealing[2627] the objective land of wakefulness and dream. In other words, ***unconsciousness*** **in deep-dreamless-sleep** **__is proof__** **and sign of the Transcendent Awareness** ever-present in the consciousness-*of* the world. This is the cornerstone of the rainbow, namely, the sign from the Transcendent. This world, however, is unconscious of Pure Awareness. Entering one state means the disappearance of the other. To understand better this paradox, consider that dreams vanish when we awake. Vice-versa, the waking world disappears when we dream. One dissolves when the consciousness-*of* the other appears and both fade away when we enter the cataleptic state of Pure Awareness as Awareness. Furthermore, in the state of ecstasy,[2628]

"*the mind gets resolved in the object of meditation without harbouring the ideas 'I am such and such; I am doing this and this'...* [in] *this subtle state ... even the thought 'I-I' disappears.*"[2629]

"I saw [says Dante] that which is lying within its depth / bound with love in one volume, / that which unfolds through the universe /... In the heaven that beams brightest of his light / I have been and saw things that to repeat / cannot nor knows one who from there descends."[2630]

Historically and without going into specific details, we can list two very general types of proofs of God's existence, *a-priori* and *a-posteriori.*

- The first one, formulated by Anselm, is the *a-priori* ontological proof.[2631] It states that the idea of an Absolute Perfect Being must necessarily include also existence; otherwise, it would not be perfect.
- The second one, formulated by Thomas Aquinas, are the *a-posteriori* proofs. They are deduced from the evidence of motion, cause-effect, necessity, perfection and order.[2632]

Both approaches, however, intend to demonstrate the existence in-itself of the Transcendent, which reduces it to an ideal or physical object of the subject. Therefore, derives the impossibility of knowing It-in-itself. Those who want to demonstrate the non-existence of god incur in the same difficulty. Dawkins, not inclined to any

"agnostic conciliation,"[2633]

namely, to suspend judgement over the existence or non-existence of god, declares god a delusion.[2634] The whole diatribe, here, is over the proof of the existence of an object, be it a god or

"a china teapot revolving about the sun."[2635]

No one defines the real issue, which is fundamentally epistemological. Namely, what we really mean by the terms transcendence, god and existence. We can state nothing about god, the teapot or the world. The concept of an object's existence in-itself is a Kantian noumenon.[2636] Namely, the mind can think-*of* it but can never experience it in-itself, *viz.* without the presence of the mind itself. Everyone uses this mind to prove or disprove anything. Dawkins himself proves his mind's belief in the transcendence of others, when he writes books intended for present and future generations of readers, whom he neither does nor will ever know as such.

The truth of the matter is that when we experience any object we confer to it a reality in itself, which is never experienced. Namely, we can never question the Certainty and/or the Faith related to the experience as experience. This is not the proof of the existence in-itself of anything, not even of that which is experienced. Science will ascertain that. It is neither a thought nor an object. It is the unavoidable presence of apodicticity, present in everything and always inherent with Awareness. Therefore, we can state that God's existence, as a reality separated from our epistemic subject/object circularity, can never be proven. This means that

a) when we know **Him** it is only an object, not **It**,
b) when we think of **Her**, it is only an idea, not **It**,
c) however, we **always tend towards It**. Every knowledge, thought, action, intention takes as fact the direction beyond the epistemic correlation of subject-object. Therefore, there is an actual transcending towards the Transcendent.

9:15-Remembering the Covenant

וְזָכַרְתִּי אֶת־בְּרִיתִי אֲשֶׁר בֵּינִי וּבֵינֵיכֶם וּבֵין כָּל־נֶפֶשׁ חַיָּה בְּכָל־בָּשָׂר וְלֹא־יִהְיֶה עוֹד הַמַּיִם לְמַבּוּל לְשַׁחֵת כָּל־בָּשָׂר׃

vazāḵaratiy (I have remembered now) *'eṯ* (and) *bariyṯiy* (covenant) *'ăšer* (which) *bēyniy* (between) *uḇēynēyḵem* (between) *uḇēyn* (between) *kāl* (all) *nep̄eš* (the breathing activity of mind) *hayāh* (living) *baḵāl* (in all) *bāśār* (flesh bearing information) *valō'* (not) *yihayeh* (will become) *'vōḏ* (anymore) *hamayim* (transitory things) *lamabul* (a deluge) *lašaḥēṯ* (to destroy) *kāl* (all) *bāśār* (flesh bearing information)

καὶ *kai* (and) **μνησθήσομαι** *mnēsthēsomai* (I will remember) **τῆς** *tēs* (the) **διαθήκης** *diathēkēs* (covenant) **μου** *mou* (my) **ἥ** *ē* (which) **ἐστιν** *estin* (is) **ἀνὰ** *ana* (thus) **μέσον** *meson* (between) **ἐμοῦ** *emou* (me) **καὶ** *kai* (and) **ὑμῶν** *umōn* (you) **καὶ** *kai* (and) **ἀνὰ** *ana* (thus) **μέσον** *meson* (between) **πάσης** *pasēs* (all) **ψυχῆς** *psuchēs* (psyche) **ζώσης** *zōsēs* (living) **ἐν** *en* (in) **πάσῃ** *pasē* (all) **σαρκί** *sarki* (the flesh) **καὶ** *kai* (and) **οὐκ** *ouk* (not) **ἔσται** *estai* (shall be) **ἔτι** *eti* (yet) **τὸ** *to* (the) **ὕδωρ** *udōr* (water) **εἰς** *eis* (in to) **κατακλυσμὸν** *kataklusmon* (a cataclysm) **ὥστε** *ōste* (as) **ἐξαλεῖψαι** *exaleipsai* (ruin) **πᾶσαν** *pasan* (all) **σάρκα** *sarka* (flesh)
et (and) ***recordabor*** (I will remember) ***foederis*** (pact) ***mei*** (my) ***vobiscum*** (with you) ***et*** (and) ***cum*** (with) ***omni*** (all) ***anima*** (soul) ***vivente*** (living) ***quae*** (that) ***carnem*** (flesh) ***vegetat*** (living) ***et*** (and) ***non*** (not) ***erunt*** (will be) ***ultra*** (other) ***aquae*** (waters) ***diluvii*** (for a deluge) ***ad*** (to) ***delendam*** (destroy) ***universam*** (all) ***carnem*** (flesh)
And I will remember my covenant, which is between me and you and every living creature of all flesh; and the waters shall no more become a flood to destroy all flesh.
Now I have remembered the covenant between me and you and between all the breathing activity of the mind living in every flesh bearing information. The flowing objects will not become again a deluge to destroy all the flesh bearing information.

Remembrance, is like a property of string theory, namely

"the combination of quantum mechanics and gravity requires the three-dimensional world to be an image of data that can be stored on a two-dimensional projection much like a holographic image."[2637]

Recollection is an action that implies necessarily the **present** as its logical precondition. History is always the present remembrance of former times. There would be no yesterday if we do not remember it now. Recollection, as such, is always a current event. Thus, **in** the past as past, nothing can be called to mind. We can evoke **today** of having remembered yesterday. We can tie a *string* to our finger so we will keep something in mind tomorrow. Nevertheless, it is always the present recollection of a past, which, inevitably, is remembered now. Reminiscence, as such, is never possible in the past or in the future, as such. Remembering (זָכַר *zakar*)[2638] is the current noetic subjective aspect of experience as an act-of-perception (רָאָה *ra'ah*)[2639] aiming at this time to grasp the object already vanished in-itself. Recollection is like the *male organ* (זָכָר *zakar*)[2640] of Awareness, it is

"*as nails* (מַשְׂמְרָה *masmĕrah*) *fastened by the masters of assemblies.*"[2641]

In Awareness, in fact, *Remembering* is always in its stable stillness, fixed in its Ever-Presence (עוֹלָם *`owlam*).[2642] It is the ascending drive of power of the Tree-of-Life.

"Look at a tree, a flower, a plant. Let your awareness rest upon it. How still they are, how deeply rooted in Being. Allow nature to teach you stillness."[2643]

Remembering is the quality of the present. What is that the Transcendent remembers now? It is the Unknown Mysterious Silence, which we call dreamless-sleep. If we were to live it and *remember* it, as we occasionally do with our dreams, we would not depart from that Covenant, which saves us from drowning in the flood. From a human perspective, then, circumcision[2644] *becomes the* metaphoric token for the disengagement of Pure Consciousness, where there is *no deluge* (וְלֹא...לְמַבּוּל *valō'...lamabul*), from the impure water possessive consciousness-*of-flowing-*[2645]objects.

"*And ye shall circumcise*[2646] *the flesh-bearing-information* (בָּשָׂר *basar*) *of your* [impure[2647]] *foreskin;*[2648] *and it shall be a token of the covenant betwixt me and you.*"[2649]

Circumcision, *muwlah* (מוּלָה), from *muwl* (מוּל),[2650] to cut, means to

"*circumcise therefore the foreskin of your heart,*"[2651]

"*circumcise yourself to Jehovah,*"[2652]

"[Hence, it means to] remove impure things from your mind... because the foreskin was regarded as unclean and profane... i.e. put away all wickedness from your minds, and consecrate yourselves to Jehovah."[2653]

Obviously, physical circumcision is meaningless when we are under the possessive spell of the waking and dreaming senses. One must cut away the impure possessive desirous identification with the objective world. Therefore,

> *"be awake* (γρηγορέω *grēgoreō*) *and meditate* (προσεύχομαι *proseuchomai*)*, that ye enter not into temptation: the spirit indeed is willing, but the flesh is weak."*[2654]

As well as, circumcision is unnecessary when awakened in Awareness.

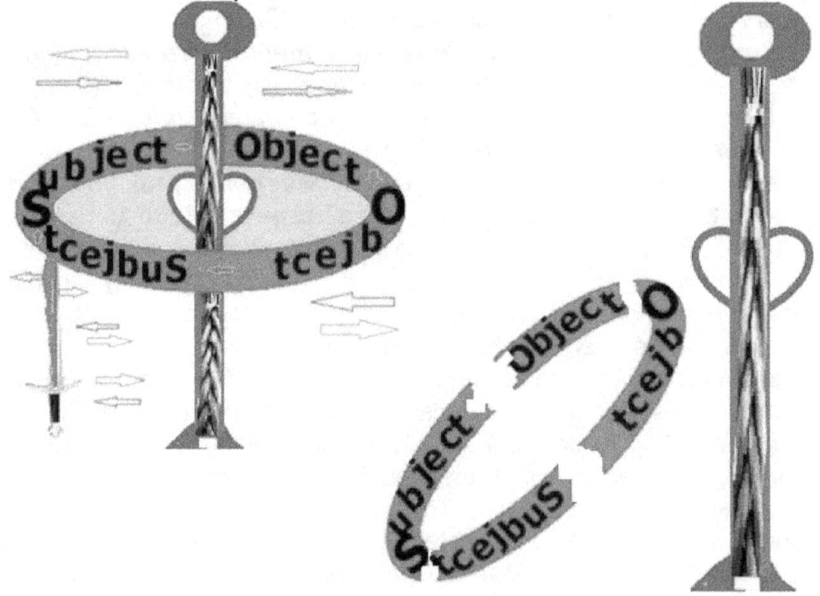

GRAPHIC: *Circumcision.*

> *"If the uncircumcision keep the righteousness of the law, shall not his uncircumcision be counted for circumcision?"*[2655]

Circumcision, then, means to sever, to cut the subject-object circularity to enable the central purity of Awareness to stand rested in Its fulgurating Apodictic Present without duality.

9:16-Perceiving the Covenant

וְהָיְתָה הַקֶּשֶׁת בֶּעָנָן וּרְאִיתִיהָ לִזְכֹּר בְּרִית עוֹלָם בֵּין אֱלֹהִים וּבֵין כָּל־נֶפֶשׁ חַיָּה בְּכָל־בָּשָׂר אֲשֶׁר עַל־הָאָרֶץ׃ *vahāyaṯāh* (was) *haqešeṯ* (bow) *be'ānān* (in the cloud) *ura'iyṯiyāh* (I perceived) *lizakōr* (to remember) *bariyṯ* (the covenant) *'vōlām* (forever) *bēyn* (between) *'ĕlōhiym* (Divine-Consciousness) *uḇēyn* (between) *kāl* (all) *nep̄eš* (the breathing activity of mind) *ḥayāh* (living) *baḵāl* (all) *bāśār* (flesh bearing information) *'ăšer* (which) *'al* (on) *hā'āreṣ* (earth)
καὶ *kai* (and) **ἔσται** *estai* (shall be) **τὸ** *to* (the) **τόξον** *toxon* (bow) **μου** *mou* (my) **ἐν** *en* (in) **τῇ** *tē* (the) **νεφέλῃ** *nephelē* (cloud) **καὶ** *kai* (and) **ὄψομαι** *opsomai* (I will see) **τοῦ** *tou* (the) **μνησθῆναι** *mnēsthēnai* (recall) **διαθήκην** *diathēkēn* (covenant) **αἰώνιον** *aiōnion* (eternal) **ἀνὰ** *ana* (then) **μέσον** *meson* (between) **ἐμοῦ** *emou* (me) **καὶ** *kai* (and) **ἀνὰ** *ana* (then) **μέσον** *meson* (between) **πάσης** *pasēs* (all) **ψυχῆς** *psuchēs* (soul) **ζώσης** *zōsēs* (living) **ἐν** *en* (in) **πάσῃ** *pasē* (all) **σαρκί** *sarki* (flesh) **ἥ** *ē* (that) **ἐστιν** *esti* (is) **ἐπὶ** *epi* (on) **τῆς** *tēs* (the) **γῆς** *gēs* (earth)
erit (was) **-*que*** (and) ***arcus*** (arc) ***in*** (in) ***nubibus*** (theclouds) ***et*** (and) ***videbo*** (I was seeing) ***illum*** (it) ***et*** (and) ***recordabor*** (remembered) ***foederis*** (covenant) ***sempiterni*** (eternal) ***quod*** (that) ***pactum*** (pact) ***est*** (is) inter (between) ***Deum*** (God) ***et*** (and) ***inter*** (between) ***omnem*** (all) ***animam*** (soul) ***viventem*** (living) ***universae*** (all) ***carnis*** (flesh) ***quae*** (that) ***est*** (is) **super** (on) ***terram*** (the earth)
And the bow shall be in the cloud; and I will look upon it, that I may remember the everlasting covenant between God and every living creature of all flesh that is upon the

earth.

Therefore, I perceived the bow being in the mystery and perceiving it I remember forever the covenant between Divine-Consciousness and all the breathing activities of the flesh bearing information to the mind which are living on earth."

Genesis[2656] tells us that Jacob

"*dreamed* (חלם *chalam*), *and behold a ladder set up on the earth, and the beginning-head-top* (רֹאשׁ ro'sh)[2657] *of it reached to heaven.*[2658] *and behold the angels of God ascending and descending on it.*"

The angels are awake, while Jacob is asleep. He dreams of a ladder, which, from the ground level of immanence, ascends towards Transcendence. In the waking, dreaming and sleeping world of duality there is an awakening into Transcendence where *symbols* and metaphors ensue. They are the only *language* capable to allude to the Ineffable. The ladder is a metaphor for the Central Force of Life. In other words, the waking, dreaming and dreamless-sleep states are all awake in the Certainty of Awareness. The angels on the ladder awaken into Transcendence. Those *angels*, those *messengers*[2659] are the carriers of information conveyed by the *breathing activities of the flesh* (נֶפֶשׁ *nephesh*) *bearing information* (בָּשָׂר *basar*) to the mind. They come down[2660] from the mysterious cloud (עָנָן `*anan*) in heaven down to earth's objectivity (אֶרֶץ *'erets*) and back up[2661] again to the *Mind*-(רֹאשׁ ro'sh) *Heavenly-Abode* (שָׁמַיִם *shamayim*) of Divine-Consciousness (אלהים *'elohiym*).

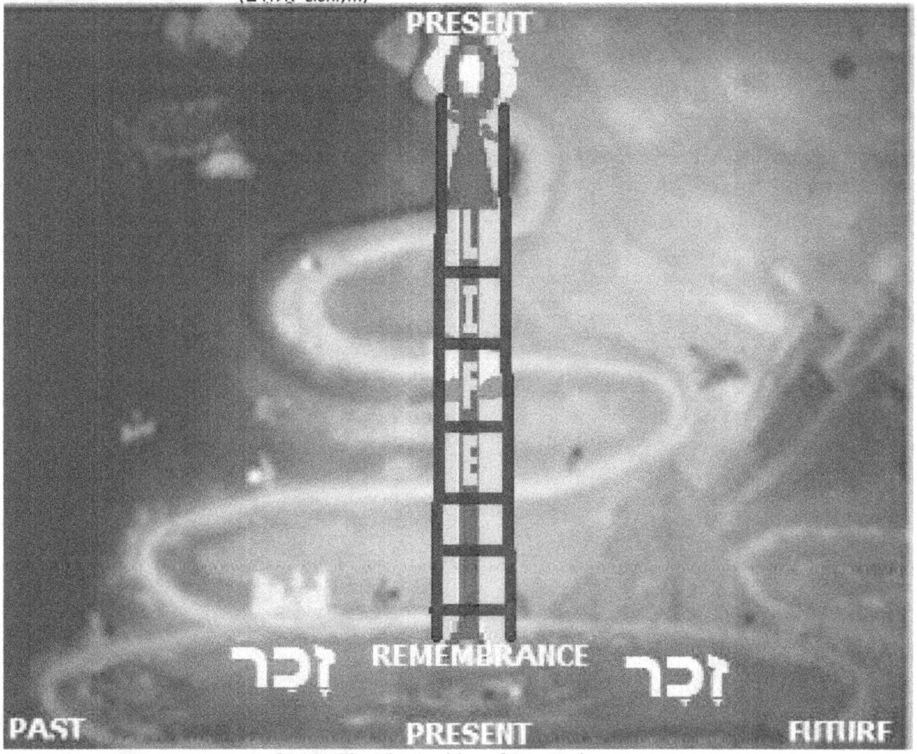

GRAPHIC: *The Ladder of Remembrance*

The average literal reader may say,

'It is blasphemous to consider a pact with God to be an event connected to sleep, thus, devoid of any reality. Furthermore, does that mean that we should be all in a state of cataleptic dumbness?'

We reply,

'It is not as profane as your belief in a physical rainbow as a sign for the covenant. First, for God's omniscience, is a token necessary to remember His covenant? Would He

not remember, if He were without it? Second, there was no rainbow before the flood? The answers are obvious. Furthermore, catalepsy or dreamless sleep is the only moment in which we reach the silence of the mind necessary to connect with the ineffable silence of יְהֹוָה*, the Transcendent, away from the distracting sounds of waterfalls. As described in Jacob's dream, the whole point here is to be awake in that sleep. Eventually we will all enter and vanish in death. However, we should enter awake into Awareness, where pre-fall immortality abides.'*

9:17-The Token of the Covenant

וַיֹּאמֶר אֱלֹהִים אֶל־נֹחַ זֹאת אוֹת־הַבְּרִית אֲשֶׁר הֲקִמֹתִי בֵּינִי וּבֵין כָּל־בָּשָׂר אֲשֶׁר עַל־הָאָרֶץ׃ פ *vayō'mer* (said) *'ĕlōhiym* (Divine-Consciousness) *'el* (this) *nōaḥ* (Noah) *zō't* (this) *'vōṯ* (sign) *habariyṯ* (covenant) *'ăšer* (which) *hăqimōṯiy* (I have established) *bēyniy* (between) *uḇēyn* (between) *kāl* (all) *bāśār* (flesh) *'ăšer* (which) *'al* (on) *hā'āreṣ* (earth) *p̄* (.)
καὶ *kai* (and) **εἶπεν** *eipen* (said) **ὁ** *o* (the) **θεὸς** *theos* (God) **τῷ** *tō* (the) **Νωε** *Nōe* (Noah) **τοῦτο** *touto* (this) **τὸ** *to* (the) **σημεῖον** *sēmeion* (sign) **τῆς** *tēs* (the) **διαθήκης** *diathēkēs* (covenant) **ἧς** *ēs* (which) **διεθέμην** *diethemēn* (I have established) **ἀνὰ** *ana* (then) **μέσον** *meson* (between) **ἐμοῦ** *emou* (me) **καὶ** *kai* (and) **ἀνὰ** *ana* (then) **μέσον** *meson* (between) **πάσης** *pasēn* (all) **σαρκός** *sarkos* (flesh) **ἥ** *ē* (which) **ἐστιν** *estin* (is) **ἐπὶ** *epi* (on) **τῆς** *tēs* (the) **γῆς** *gēs* (earth)
dixit- (said) ***que*** (and) ***Deus*** (God) ***Noe*** (to Noah) ***hoc*** (this) ***erit*** (was) ***signum*** (the sign) ***foederis*** (of the covenant) ***quod*** (which) ***constitui*** (I established) ***inter*** (between) ***me*** (me) ***et*** (and) ***inter*** (between) ***omnem*** (all) ***carnem*** (flesh) ***super*** (on) ***terram*** (the earth)
And God said unto Noah, This is the token of the covenant, which I have established between me and all flesh that is upon the earth.
Divine-Consciousness said to Noah, "*This is the sign of the covenant which I have established between me and between all the flesh-bearing-information which is on the earth.*"

Mystery, coming from the objective world (אֶרֶץ *'erets*) in the cloud of the unknown, is always present before the *flesh-bearing-information* (בָּשָׂר *basar*). The continuous projection towards the solution of that enigma is the *sign* (אוֹת *'owth*) of the covenant (בְּרִית *bĕriyth*). The tension itself toward the Future or, better still, toward the Transcendent is this *established, self-evident* and *proven*[2662] token. Beyond any agnostic or a-theist and/or theist creed, the inevitable Presence in everything of the drive towards the Being-In-Itself is the apodictic proof.

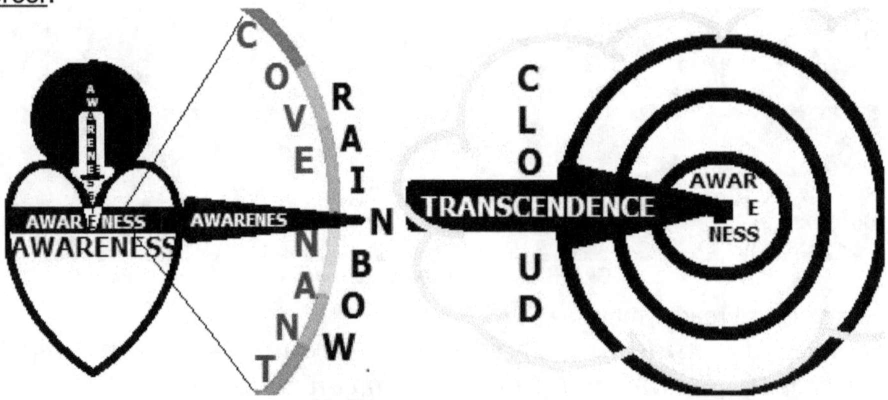

GRAPHIC: *Covenant Rainbow*

The Eternal Present establishes Its banquet from the clouds of NREM desireless state directed into the world of objectivity. The bow, continuously intentioned towards transcendence, is the Present reminder of Transcendence.

9-III SECTION: NOAH'S CONSCIOUSNESS-*OF* THE WORLD

9:18-Noah's Descendants

וַיִּהְיוּ בְנֵי־נֹחַ הַיֹּצְאִים מִן־הַתֵּבָה שֵׁם וְחָם וָיָפֶת וְחָם הוּא אֲבִי כְנָעַן׃ *vayihayu* (were) *ḇanēy* (sons) *nōaḥ* (of Noah) *hayōṣa'iym* (going out) *min* (of) *hatēḇāh* (the ark) *šēm* (Shem) *vaḥām* (Ham) *vāyāp̄eṯ* (Japheth) *vaḥām* (Ham) *hu* (he is) *'ăḇiy* (the father) *ḵanā'an* (of Canaan)
ἦσαν *ēsan* (were) **δὲ** *de* (and) **οἱ** *oi* (the) **υἱοὶ** *uioi* (sons) **Νωε** *Nōe* (of Noah) **οἱ** *oi* (the) **ἐξελθόντες** *exelthontes* (came out) **ἐκ** *ex* (from) **τῆς** *tēs* (the) **κιβωτοῦ** *kibōtou* (ark) **Σημ** *Sēm* (Shem) **Χαμ** *Cha* (Ham) **Ιαφεθ** *Iapheth* (Japheth) **Χαμ** *Xam* (Ham) **ἦν** *ēn* (is) **πατὴρ** *patēr* (father) **Χανααν** *Chanaan* (of Canaam)
erant (were) ***igitur*** (therefore) ***filii*** (the sons) ***Noe*** (of Noah) ***qui*** (who) ***egressi*** (exited) ***sunt*** (are) ***de*** (from the) ***arca*** (ark) ***Sem*** (Shem) ***Ham*** (Ham) ***et*** (and) ***Iafeth*** (Japheth) ***porro*** (following) ***Ham*** (Ham) ***ipse*** (same) ***est*** (is) ***pater*** (the father) ***Chanaan*** (of Canaan)
And the sons of Noah, that went forth of the ark, were Shem, and Ham, and Japheth: and Ham is the father of Canaan.
The sons of Noah going out of the ark were Shem, Ham and Japheth. Ham is the father of Canaan.

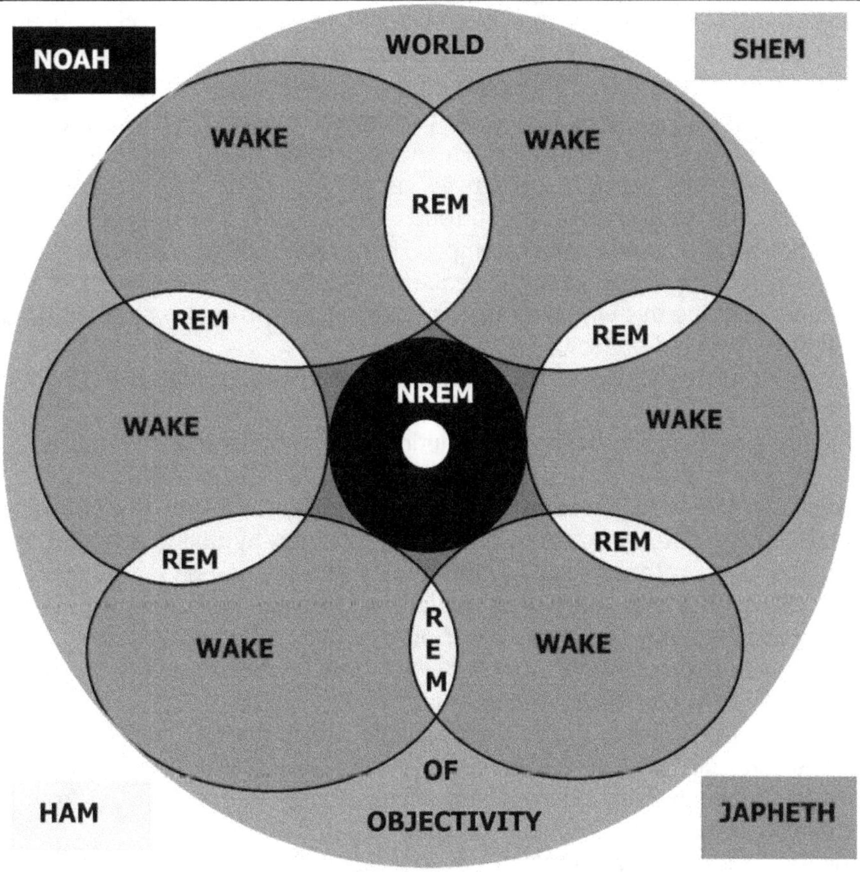

GRAPHIC: *Noah and His Descendants*

Rested-Noah leaves the dreamless sleep with his three epistemic forms. As we have seen, they are, Shem, the glorious established one moving out from the dreamless realm, Ham, the hot passionate one in the dream realm, and Japheth, the seducer in the waking realm. From their original deep sleep, they establish an ardent seducing procession in the realm of duality. Namely, from the Present Stillness comes out Shem as the time pulse between subject and object. Ham proceeds as the vibrating frequency of cause and effect. Finally, Japheth progresses as measurer of the world space. Another offspring of Noah, proceeding out of the Ark, is his grandson Canaan,[2663] generated (אָב *'ab*) by Ham. His name means *merchant, trafficker*. It derives from the verb *kana '*,[2664] *to be subdued, to be depressed.*

9:19-The Three Modes-of-Knowing

שְׁלֹשָׁה אֵלֶּה בְּנֵי־נֹחַ וּמֵאֵלֶּה נָפְצָה כָל־הָאָרֶץ׃   *šalōšāh* (in three divided parts) *'ēleh* (these) *banēy* (sons) *nōaḥ* (of Noah) *umē'ēleh* (as a result) nāp̄*aṣāh* (was broken in) *k̲āl* (all) *hā'āreṣ* (earth)
τρεῖς *treis* (three) **οὗτοί** *outoi* (these) **εἰσιν** *eisin* (are) **οἱ** *oi* (the) **υἱοὶ** *uioi* (sons) **Νωε** *Nōe* (of Noah) **ἀπὸ** *apo* (from) **τούτων** *touōn* (in this way) **διεσπάρησαν** *diesparēsan* (disseminated) **ἐπὶ** *epi* (on) **πᾶσαν** *pasan* (all) **τὴν** *tēn* (the) **γῆν** *gēn* (earth)
tres (three) ***isti*** (these) ***sunt*** (are) ***filii*** (sons) ***Noe*** (of Noah) ***et*** (and) ***ab*** (from) ***his*** (those) ***disseminatum*** (disseminated) ***est*** (is) ***omne*** (all) ***hominum*** (men)[2665] ***genus*** (kind) ***super*** (on) ***universam*** (the entire) ***terram*** (earth)
These are the three sons of Noah: and of them was the whole earth overspread.
These are the three divided parts, the sons of Noah and, as a result, the whole earth is broken into parts.

In this section, the scenario changes completely. Previously, the predominant theme was the world's flood and its consequences, as seen from dreamless-sleep. Now, Noah, the rested paradigm, divides[2666] and articulates with its three[2667] generated levels; Shem, time as it exits dreamless-sleep, Ham, cause as it forms dreams, and Japheth, space as it measures wakefulness. All three of them are *forms-and-modes-of-knowing* of the one I-think. Like a musical composition, the observer, as a unified one sound, resounds in the entire world of objectivity as a three-part[2668] symphony. From the unknown prenatal Transcendent, the subject proceeds through the circadian phases of life. First, the observer moves out of the deep unconscious as music tempo. Then, time (Shem) organizes the sounds, generated by the vibrating (Ham) subject/objects, into the sequence (Japheth) of dance steps.[2669]

Other cultures describe this with the famous enigma (αἴνιγμα *aínigma*) of the Theban Sphinx,[2670] who suffocated all those who did not solve her riddle,

> "What is that which has *one sound* and nevertheless becomes four-footed and two-footed and three-footed?"[2671]

The complexity of the puzzle and its attempted solution may indicate that the enigma was much older than the Hellenic account and, therefore, the correct answer, had been already lost. In fact, the much older Indian *Vedas* describe a hero, named Naciketa, who, by clarifying the *riddle* of *AUM* (ॐ *OM*), defeats Yama-Death. This last one, like the Sphinx, inflicts death by taking the vital breath away. The *one sound* (μίαν *mían*, φωνὴν *phōnēn*) is the *OM* (*óṃ-kāra*), the totality of the One-Self (*ātman*). It is composed of four metrical-parts/feet (Sanskrit *pada*, Greek πούς *poús*) indicated by the letters A-U-M-•.[2672] Those four become two tempo-parts/feet in A-M, namely consciousness and unconsciousness

> "*Verily there are only two conditions of this person, this condition* (A) *and the world beyond* (M)... *In between there is the third condition of dream* (U)." [2673]

In fact, there is a second formulation of the Sphinx's riddle, which goes as such, there are

> "two sisters: one gives birth to the other and she, in turn, gives birth to the first."[2674]

This is the distinction between consciousness and unconsciousness one deriving from the other in turn. According to the Greek geographer Pausanias, Oedipus

> "had been told the oracle in a dream."[2675]

Finally, the three parts/feet, namely *un*conscious, *sub*conscious, conscious, or sleep, dreaming, waking, or past, future, present, or time, causality, space, or Shem, Ham and Japheth, make up the totality of the human being. With the solution of

> "the riddle of the Sphinx, death has no further hold on you, and the curse of the Sphinx disappears."[2676]

9:20-Noah's Change

וַיָּחֶל נֹחַ אִישׁ הָאֲדָמָה וַיִּטַּע כָּרֶם׃
vayāḥel (pierced through become corrupted) *nōaḥ* (Noah) *'iyš* (subject) *hā'ăḏāmāh* (of the ground) *vayiṭa'* (established) *kārem* (a vineyard)
καὶ *kai* (and) **ἤρξατο** *ērxato* (began) **Νωε** *Nōe* (Noah) **ἄνθρωπος** *anthrōpos* (man) **γεωργὸς** *geōrgos* (tilling) **γῆς** *gēs* (the land) **καὶ** *kai* (and) **ἐφύτευσεν** *ephuteusen* (planted) **ἀμπελῶνα** *ampelōna* (a vineyard)
coepit- (started) ***que*** (and) ***Noe*** (Noah) ***vir*** (man) ***agricola*** (farmer) ***exercere*** (to plow)[2677] ***terram*** (the land) ***et*** (and) ***plantavit*** (planted) ***vineam*** (a vineyard)
And Noah began to be an husbandman, and he planted a vineyard:
Piercing through, Noah become a corrupted subject-conscious-*of*-the-world and established a vineyard.

When we exit the dreamless sleep, we change. Resting-Noah is the stillness in the Ark, where no flood can ever take place. Quickly,[2678] upon exiting it, Noah changes. That stillness is profaned and polluted. In fact, the Hebrew verb ***chalal,***[2679] translated in this verse by the King James version only as *"began,"* means, *to perforate, to pierce through, to open, to begin, to profane (the name of God), to defile, to desecrate, to pollute oneself, to dishonor, to violate (a covenant) and to wound.* It is comparable to the Hebrew verbs *challah*[2680] (*to be polished, to become weak, sick, diseased, grieved, sorry, ill, to be tired, sore, to be wounded*) and *chuwl*[2681] (*to twist, to whirl, to dance, to writhe, to fear, to tremble, to travail, to be in anguish, to be pained, to bring forth, to wait anxiously, to bear, to be brought forth, to be born, to suffer, to torture, to wait longingly and to be distressed*). Thus, clearly, the verse proposes that Noah, proceeding from a higher exalted status to a lower one, loses the stillness and clarity realized in the Ark.

> "*The foolish go outward, after lusty pleasures. They fall into the snare of widespread death. However, the wise person, understanding immortality, does not seek the permanent here, among the impermanent.*"[2682]

Therefore, duality appears when we daily *pierce-out* from the rested-stillness of dreamless-sleep (Noah). Then, we become a *subject-conscious-of-*(איש *'iysh*)-the-world (אדמה *' adamah*). Leaving the realm of NREM, we establish[2683] with the world an interconnected *microchip* of dream and waking experiences, like the intricate *web* of vines in a wine-producing *vineyard.*[2684]

> "A vineyard is also sometimes used in the prophets as an image of the people of Israel."[2685]

> "*The kingdom of heaven is like unto a man that is an householder, which went out early in the morning to hire labourers into his vineyard.*"[2686]

In other words, Noah returns to the condition of Cain, the *tiller of the land* (γεωργὸς *geōrgos* γῆς *gēs*) with his continuously indelible mark (אות *'owth*) of subjectivity.

9:21-Noah's Drunkenness

גַל בְּתוֹךְ אָהֳלֹה:אוַיֵּשְׁתְּ מִן־הַיַּיִן וַיִּשְׁכָּר וַיִּתְ
vayēšata (he drunk) *min* (from) *hayayin* (wine) *vayišakār* (become drunk) *vayiṯagal* (was manifested uncovered) *baṯvōḵa* (within) *'āhŏlōh* (of bright tabernacle)
καὶ *kai* (and) **ἔπιεν** *epien* (he drunk) **ἐκ** *ek* (of) **τοῦ** *tou* (the) **οἴνου** *oinou* (wine) **καὶ** *kai* (and) **ἐμεθύσθη** *emethusthē* (was drunk) **καὶ** *kai* (and) **ἐγυμνώθη** *egumnōthē* (was naked) **ἐν** *en* (in) **τῷ** *tō* (the) **οἴκῳ** *oikō* (house) **αὐτοῦ** *autou* (his)
bibens- (drinking) ***que*** (and) ***vinum*** (wine) ***inebriatus*** (inebriated) ***est*** (is) ***et*** (and) ***nudatus*** (naked) ***in*** (in) ***tabernaculo*** (tabernacle) ***suo*** (his)
And he drank of the wine, and was drunken; and he was uncovered within his tent.
He drunk the wine, become drunk and was uncovered within his shining bright tabernacle.

A literal interpretation of this passage shows only the disgraceful and unedifying image of a miserable degraded drunken man.[2687]

> "Metaph.[orically] in the prophets the wicked are said to be drunken, since they rush, by a kind of madness, upon their own destruction."[2688]

Truthfully, the interconnected world of experiences intoxicates inebriates and makes us drunk.[2689] Coming out of *dreamless-deep-sleep* (תַּרְדֵּמָה *tardemah*), as Rested-Noah, we encounter the intricate vines of the vineyard, namely, the consciousness-*of*-dreams and/or the objectivity-*of* wakefulness. Then, there is a psychological alteration, which, from the ever-present-floodless-stillness, takes us back in the flooded-consciousness-*of* this world. It is like the first cry of the newborn intoxicated by the burning sensation of the first air inhaled.

As we have seen in *Genesis* 4, the *red-blood* of the grape juice, *dam* (דָּם), is the same redness (אדם *'adam*) of Adam (אָדָם *'adam*) and of his earth, *'adamah* (אֲדָמָה). Thus, wine becomes a metaphor for blood, representing life-in-itself.

"*God give thee... new wine.*" - "*And ... he will also bless ... thy new wine.*" - "*'Behold, the days come,' saith the LORD, 'that... the mountains shall drop sweet wine, and all the hills shall melt... and... my people of Israel... shall... drink the effervescent wine'.*"[2690]

From the perspective of wakefulness and dream, the Rested-one reveals his worldly inebriation. Then, the state of drunkenness is equivalent to the state of being flooded. *In-itself*,[2691] in the *shining-bright-clearness*[2692] of his *tent-tabernacle*,[2693] the three-dimensional objective garbs do *not manifest* and *do not cover*[2694] him. There, the uncovering (גלה *galah*) is without shame (בוש *buwsh*). It is the pre-fall condition of Adam/Eve, before they were conscious of each other's inscrutability. In fact, the NREM moment is that of Auto-Transparency in which the human is auto-conscious without being conscious-*of* its-own-ego. Without being covered by the objective garb. It is not dressed up with an object *for-itself* different-from and other-than itself. That is the state-of-being-*in-itself*-in-the-ark-tent, before eating the forbidden fruit, namely, logically before

"being-in-the-world"[2695]

and facing it. Recognizing the absence of thought in NREM means that we are not in that state. In fact, only wakefulness can conceive dreamless sleep as dream-naked. In the world's eyes, the behavior of mystics appears as madness. Dr. Malidoma Patrice Somé explains that

"in the shamanic view, mental illness signals '*the birth of a healer*' ... Mental disorders are spiritual emergencies, spiritual crises, and need to be regarded as such to aid the healer in being born. What those in the West view as mental illness, the Dagara [West African] people regard as '*good news from the other world*.' The person going through the crisis has been chosen as a medium for a message to the community that needs to be communicated from the spirit realm. '*Mental disorder, behavioral disorder of all kinds, signal the fact that two obviously incompatible energies have merged into the same field*'... These disturbances result when the person does not get assistance in dealing with the presence of the energy from the spirit realm... Dr. Somé encountered... [in] the United States... mental illness... based on pathology, on the idea that the condition is something that needs to stop... in complete opposition to the way his [Dagara] culture views such a situation... '*the healers who are attempting to be born are treated in this* [Western] *culture. ... What a loss*'... In the West, ... psychic abilities are denigrated... The result can be terrifying. Without the proper context for and assistance in dealing with the breakthrough from another level of reality, for all practical purposes, the person is insane."[2696]

This view prevailed also in medieval times, in fact, St. Francis' accounts[2697] refer that

"Through continual contemplation... Friar Ruffino was so absorbed in God that he had become well-nigh insensible and dumb, and exceeding rarely spoke... St. Francis... ordered him to go to Assisi and preach to the people... Friar Ruffino made answer: "Reverend father, I beseech thee that thou have me excused and send me not, because, as thou knowest, I have not the gift of preaching and am a simple man and ignorant". Then said St. Francis: "Inasmuch as thou hast not obeyed at once, I command thee by holy obedience that thou go to Assisi, naked as thou wast born... and that thou enter into a church, thus naked, and preach to the people". At this command, the aforesaid Friar Ruffino stripped himself, and went to Assisi, and entered into a church; and... went up into the pulpit and began to preach; whereat children and men began to laugh, and said: "Behold, now, how these men do so much penance that they become fools and beside themselves"... St. Francis, considering the prompt obedience of Friar Ruffino, who was of one of the noblest families of Assisi... in fervour of spirit, he stripped himself naked likewise, and so gat him up to Assisi... And, when the men of Assisi beheld St. Francis likewise naked they made a mock at him, deeming that he and Friar Ruffino had gone mad through excessive penance."

Today, as well, in the West, specific mystical behavior, if not recognized as such, may be treated in mental asylums.

It should be clear that all these events are taking place right here and now in the epistemic reality of this human reading these pages. The difference is that these pages *intoxicate*, distract and take us away from the ever-shining Awareness as such. Exiting the deep sleep means to enter the dream world. It means to go into the *misty fog* of the *irrigating waters* (שָׁקָה *shaqah*). It is the inebriation deriving from objectivity, which distracts us from its creative origin. The waters are the *infinite flowing experiences* that give themselves as *drink*[2698] to the *thirsty mind* of the human about *to be generated*.[2699]

9:22-Ham Perceives His Father's Nakedness

וַיַּרְא חָם אֲבִי כְנַעַן אֵת עֶרְוַת אָבִיו וַיַּגֵּד לִשְׁנֵי־אֶחָיו בַּחוּץ׃   *vayara'* (perceived) *ḥām* (Ham) *'ăḇiy* (father) *ḵana'an* (of Canaan) *'ēṯ* (and) *'eravaṯ* (nakedness) *'āḇiyv* (father) *vayagēḏ* (made it known bringing it to light) *lišanēy* (to the two) *'eḥāyv* (brothers) *baḥuṣ* (outside)
καὶ *kai* (and) **εἶδεν** *eiden* (saw) **Χαμ** *Cham* (Ham) **ὁ** *o* (the) **πατὴρ** *patēr* (father) **Χανααν** *Chanaan* (of Canaan) **τὴν** *tēn* (the) **γύμνωσιν** *gumvōsin* (nakedness) **τοῦ** *tou* (of the) **πατρὸς** *patros* (father) **αὐτοῦ** *autou* (his) **καὶ** *kai* (and) **ἐξελθὼν** *exelthōn* (went out)[2700] **ἀνήγγειλεν** *anēggeilen* (told) **τοῖς** *tois* (the) **δυσὶν** *dusin* (two) **ἀδελφοῖς** *adelphois* (brothers) **αὐτοῦ** *autou* (his) **ἔξω** *exō* (outside)
quod (thus) ***cum*** (as) ***vidisset*** (saw) ***Ham*** (Ham) ***pater*** (father) ***Chanaan*** (of Canaan) ***verenda*** (awesome) ***scilicet*** (surely) ***patris*** (of father) ***sui*** (his) ***esse*** (was) ***nuda*** (naked) ***nuntiavit*** (announced) ***duobus*** (to the two) ***fratribus*** (brothers) ***suis*** (his) ***foras*** (outside)
And Ham, the father of Canaan, saw the nakedness of his father, and told his two brethren without.
Ham, Canaan's father, perceived the nakedness of his father and made it known bringing it to light to his two brothers outside.

Metaphorically, *nakedness* expresses the *interest* caused by the objective perception of *another* person. From a purely non-metaphorical physical perspective, *nakedness* is still an objectivation expressing interested sexual connotations. In general, attraction, repugnance and/or indifference characterize objective interest. The *interest* is the mood felt and awakened by the objectifying presence of the other. We react towards the other person/s with love, lust, greed, hate, repulsion and/or carelessness. Therefore, experiencing the *nakedness* of others is the *possessive-hate-desire-dislike-indifference* we show when dealing with our neighbors.

However, we qualify the recipient of our interest as being *naked* in-itself. In fact, the other is always an enigma. That is, we never reach the loved/hated one in-itself. The fear of death of our loved ones and/or our own, ultimately, makes us realize mortality, which takes us all away in the *bareness* of the unknown. Furthermore, we invoke death for our enemies because it defeats them in the abyss of oblivion. In either case, we can never *dress* the intimate essence of the other with a permanent *suit*able objectivity. Thus, *for-us* the other always remains *naked* in its essence, towards which we turn our attentive interest. Nevertheless, *time* (*viz.* Shem) and *space* (*viz.* Japheth), as such, do not perceive desire. The attraction for the object *causes* (*viz.* Ham) desire, thus, objectifies the other.

Before we continue with our commentary of this verse, it is necessary to repeat the function of symbols and metaphors. The description of an oneiric experience may be very different from its Freudian interpretation. The same symbol may mean one thing for the dreamer while revealing another to the psychoanalyst. Both, however, are real, but on different levels. No one can doubt the reality of an oneiric experience as no one can doubt its psychoanalytic reference. As an example, one, troubled by a nightmare, consults a therapist. The dream and the therapist's interpretation are both real but on different stages. The nocturnal vision was *real in the oneiric stage*. The memory of it is *real in the waking state*. The psychoanalytic interpretation is *real in the scientific analysis*. However, all three realities, while different from each other, remain interconnected by an intentional reference to each one. As a further example, let us take an event described in *Genesis* 41. There, Pharaoh dreams of seven fat cows and seven lean ones. Joseph interprets them as years. Both cows and years are real but on different levels. Joseph does not doubt Pharaoh's dream, the sovereign does not question his interpretation, even if they are as different as cows and years. Finally, we do not doubt reading about it. This is the nature of symbols and metaphors. They mean different things on different levels.

In relation to the current verse, interpreters try to explain it literally and with all kinds of stories and tales.

> "Castration and homosexual rape have been suggested. These commentators, rabbinic scholars among them, take support from the existence of Canaanite and other legends that tell of an ancestral god who castrated his father. And some peopled argue that a similar tale... was part of an oral Israelite tradition before the Torah was written... It might seem that... Ham, lacking awe and reverence,... becomes... the first rebel against law and authority."[2701]

All these interpretations are true, but on different levels. However, they are not universal and, definitively, they are not relevant for a galaxy thousands of light years away. For a sacred text to have a real valid message, it must derive from a deep introspection. It must have its foundation on a universal reality. **The universal reality is the way we know that which we name real**. Obviously, **universal is how we know, not what we know**. What we know is the forbidden fruit, which we epistemically eat. *Genesis* describes that *how*. Consequently, stories and tales do not exhaust symbols and metaphors. Similarly, the bee product does not wear out its physical quality when its metaphoric symbolism becomes the appellative *honey* referred to a dear one.

Back to our commentary, in time, Noah's exit from his resting state caused him to appear in his nakedness, thus visible to Ham, his epistemic cause and effect form. The Hebrew word *`ervah*,[2702] *nakedness, nudity*, derives from *`arah*,[2703] *to be nude, to pour out, to lay empty, to empty a vessel*.[2704] Furthermore, both its adjectives, *`eyrom*,[2705] naked, and *`arowm*,[2706] bare, derive from *`aram*,[2707] *to make naked, to uncover*.[2708] Referring these words to the *soul-of-the-blood* (נֶפֶשׁ *nephesh*), nakedness indicates the innermost being-in-itself, as in the *Psalm*,

> "*Transcendent Lord of Hosts, I trusted my eyes in Thee, do not lay empty* (עָרָה *`arah*) *the soul-of-my-blood*."[2709]

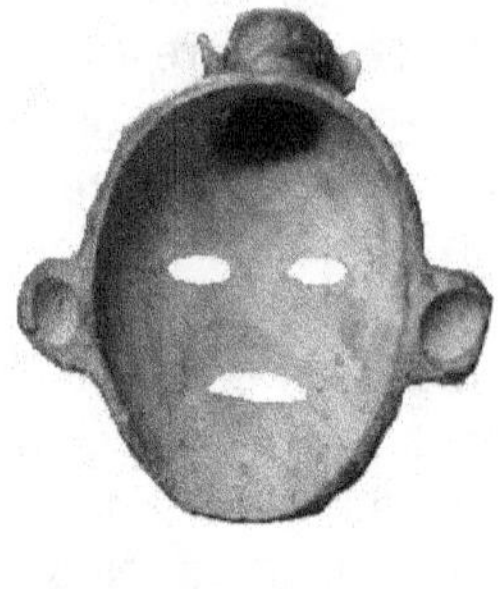

As we saw, the original fall makes Adam and Eve perceive[2710] each other as naked. Namely, makes us emotionally know and identify with the object of experience while we do not know it in-itself. Thus, we see and define the absence of inner reality as nakedness for-us. This requires an opening of our understanding to the previously unknown ineffable-empty-bareness, *viz.* nakedness. To see nakedness is to acknowledge a conceptual vacuity, thus a bare-naked-emptiness. When seen from within, the objective *you*-mask[2711] reveals itself as *naked*-emptiness. No one is in the mask, neither *you* nor *I* are there, because both can never be objectified, thus, known as such.

Auto-Transparency is not auto-transparency when conceived as auto-transparent object. The automatic movement of walking becomes not instinctive when we think of the feet actually moving one after the other. Transcendent, when conceptualized, is not *The Transcendent*. To conceive zero as nothingness, is to judge it empty, thus not 0 but *no-thing*. The known-nothingness of zero is not 0 when placed after 1 to form 10. If zero were to retain its quality of no-thing in the number ten, then it would not be 10 but only 1 with *nothing* after it. The zero in number 10 is unknown as nothingness. When thought, the zero, the nothingness, the naked-empty-space (עֶרְוָה `ervah) is still something, *viz.* naked-emptiness. It is what Lao Tzu calls,

"*The word* (*tao*) *that can be spoken is not the infinite Word* (*Tao*)."[2712]

It is an objective notion completely different from the naked nothingness in-itself. Nakedness (עֶרְוָה `ervah), then, is a metaphor for the ineffability of the unknowable Rested-One-in-the-dreamless-sleep-itself. However, there is a paradox connected with the incapability to express or describe emptiness in words. Defining something as indescribable, it is still a description. It is not ineffability, because we are somehow expressing it as unutterable. We imply the recognition of its quality of unknowability. To perceive and conceive the *emptiness* of the *Naked-Being-In-Itself* is never *to live* it in the stillness of Awareness. Let us revisit Ham's symbology. He is the *passionately hot one.*[2713] Ham is the form of causal epistemic dream. Causal perception starts in dreams, which allows them to articulate. *Dreams* follow from *dreamless-sleep.* In turn, Ham-dream-causality, produced by the *Noah*-NREM, generates Canaan-*low-merchant* who produces the *gold we trust in*, namely, the *evaluation* of objectivity. In our case, it is the assessment of that emptiness as nakedness. The oneiric researchers, evaluating the emptiness of NREM, *viz.* naked of any REM activity, are not themselves in a dreamless state. They are examining a dimension, which is not NREM in-itself. Therefore, the need to publicize[2714] it in the dimensions of time (*viz.* Shem) and space (*viz.* Japheth) ensues. The two dimensions of time and space are different. They are outside[2715] the epistemic circular causal-perception. Whosoever is in NREM, like the Rested-Noah, does not know to be in a dreamless reality. Vice versa, when one perceives NREM as the uncovered-*emptiness* of dreamless sleep, then, like Ham in the dream space, s/he is not in it. Thus, one understands it as emptiness or *nakedness.* This is what Ham reports to his brothers, namely, the vacuity of NREM. Ham, cause and effect, experiences Noah's *out*come from his resting area. This is a deduction not experienced in time (Shem) or space (Japheth). Thus, they, time and space, are outside. It is like deducing unconsciousness. The analysis of unconsciousness is a conscious analysis, not the *Unconscious* in-itself. It is the *naked-nothingness*, which we refer to as unconscious. Furthermore, to use an example, if we want to define an abstract centrality, we could describe it as a center unimaginably without its circumference, thus, we could say '*a center in its nakedness.*'

GRAPHIC: *An unconceivable center without its circumference viewed as naked*

9:23-Shem and Japheth do not Look at their Father's Nakedness

וַיִּקַּח שֵׁם וָיֶפֶת אֶת־הַשִּׂמְלָה וַיָּשִׂימוּ עַל־שְׁכֶם שְׁנֵיהֶם וַיֵּלְכוּ אֲחֹרַנִּית וַיְכַסּוּ אֵת עֶרְוַת אֲבִיהֶם וּפְנֵיהֶם אֲחֹרַנִּית וְעֶרְוַת אֲבִיהֶם לֹא רָאוּ׃ *vayiqaḥ* (took) *šēm* (Shem) *vāyep̄eṯ* (Japheth) *'eṯ* (and) *haśimalāh* (sleeping shroud) *vayāśiymu* (placed) *'al* (over) *šaḵem* (shoulder) *šanēyhem* (of both) *vayēlaḵu* (walked) *'ăḥōraniyṯ* (backwards) *vayaḵasu* (covered) *'ēṯ* (and) *'eravaṯ* (nakedness) *'ăḇiyhem* (turned) *'ăḥōraniyṯ* (back-in-timew) *va'eravaṯ* (emptiness) *'ăḇiyhem* (of father) *lō* (not) *rā'u* (saw)
καὶ *kai* (and) **λαβόντες** *labontes* (took) **Σημ** *Sēm* (Shem) **καὶ** *kai* (and) **Ιαφεθ** *Iapheth* (Japheth) **τὸ** *to* (a) **ἱμάτιον** *imation* (garment) **ἐπέθεντο** *epethento* (placed) **ἐπὶ** *epi* (on) **τὰ** *ta* (the) **δύο** *duo* (two) **νῶτα** *nōta* (backs) **αὐτῶν** *autōn* (their) **καὶ** *kai* (and) **ἐπορεύθησαν** *eporeuthēsan* (went)

ὀπισθοφανῶς *opisthophanōs* (backwards) **καὶ** *kai* (and) **συνεκάλυψαν** *sunekalupsan* (covered) **τὴν** *tēn* (the) **γύμνωσιν** *gumnōsin* (nakedness) **τοῦ** *tou* (of the) **πατρὸς** *patros* (father) **αὐτῶν** *autōn* (their) **καὶ** *kai* (and) **τὸ** *to* (the) **πρόσωπον** *prosōpon* (faces) **αὐτῶν** *autōn* (their) **ὀπισθοφανές** *opisthophanes* (were backward) **καὶ** *kai* (and) **τὴν** *tēn* (the) **γύμνωσιν** *gumnōsin* (nakedness) **τοῦ** *tou* (of the) **πατρὸς** *patros* (father) **αὐτῶν** *autōn* (their) **οὐκ** *ouk* (not) **εἶδον** *eidon* (saw)
at (and) ***vero*** (indeed) ***Sem*** (Shem) ***et*** (and) ***Iafeth*** (Japheth) ***pallium*** (a garment) ***inposuerunt*** (placed) ***umeris*** (on shoulders) ***suis*** (their) ***et*** (and) ***incedentes*** (proceeded) ***retrorsum*** (backwards) ***operuerunt*** (covered) ***verecunda*** (the nakedness) ***patris*** (of the father) ***sui*** (their) ***facies-*** (faces)***que*** (and) ***eorum*** (their) ***aversae*** (backward) ***erant*** (were) ***et*** (and) ***patris*** (of the father) ***virilia*** (manhood) ***non*** (not) ***viderunt*** (saw)
And Shem and Japheth took a garment, and laid it upon both their shoulders, and went backward, and covered the nakedness of their father; and their faces were backward, and they saw not their father's nakedness.
Shem and Japheth took a sleeping shroud and quickly placed it over their shoulders, walked backwards in time and covered the nakedness of their father and turned their faces back-in-time not to see his emptiness.

Shem and Japheth's response, however, is different. Dreamless-sleep is the silence of stillness-in-awareness. In fact, the *Psalm* confirms,

"*Be still, let go* (רָפָה *raphah*) *and realize* (יָדַע *yada*) *that I am Divine-Consciousness* (אֱלֹהִים *'elohiym*)."[2716]

It is like a moment of great surprise, which blows the mind away. At its present insurgence, before any attribution, as intense joy or pain connected to it, one should realize its Present Awareness. That is like staring without looking, hearing without listening, inhaling without smelling, tasting without savoring, feeling without experiencing and thinking without conceiving. It is the *awakened* (קוּץ *quwts*) stillness of identification with Apodictical Awareness Itself. It is Being-Aware or One-Mindfulness. This means to

"*watch and pray, lest ye enter into temptation,*"[2717]

"the slumber of death,"[2718]

This is not a thoughtless vegetative state or a blank fixed staring condition during which the identification with the object persists. It is not like a drug related stupor. Anyone, thinking-*of* that surprising moment, loses its immediateness. Conceptualizing it is to discover Noah's nakedness. In fact, Noah's wine intoxication takes place after exiting the safety of the ark to enter the time interconnection. Then it is like the *Ghost Boy*, whose

"mind leaps and swoops... as it tries to break free of its confines... of... an empty shell... trapped inside a useless body... entirely black within - a nothingness."[2719]

The word *quwts* (קוּץ *quwts*), *awakening*, gives

"the idea of abruptness in starting up from sleep,"[2720]

and has two opposite directions. It can be the awakening surprise in death or in Awareness. In fact,

"*many of them that sleep*[2721] *in the dust of the earth shall awake, some to everlasting life* [of Awakened Awareness], *and some to shame and everlasting contempt*"[2722]

of the sorrowful waking state. In it

"*man lieth down, and riseth not: till the heavens be no more, they shall not awake, nor be raised out of their sleep.*"[2723]

"Spiritual awakening is awakening from the dream of thought."[2724]

It is not a hallucinating state. It has nothing to do with drug-induced states. It is simply the entrance phase of pure Awareness. Tolle offers us an interesting test,

"Close your eyes and say to yourself: 'I wonder what my next thought is going to be.' Then become very alert and wait for the next thought. Be like a cat watching a mouse hole. What thought is going to come out of the mouse hole? ... As long as you are in a state of intense presence, you are free of thought. You are still, yet highly alert. The instant your conscious attention sinks below a certain level, thought rushes in, the mental noise returns; the stillness is lost. You are back in time."[2725]

Jesus, teaching in the temple, said,

"*You cannot tell whence I come, and whither I go...*[2726] *You neither know me* [as Awareness], *nor my Father* [as Transcendent-Self]*: if you had known me, you should have known my Father also...*[2727] *You think*[2728] *according to the craving senses;*[2729]

I think-of nothing...[2730] *And yet if I think, my thinking is Pure-Awareness.*"[2731]

"*I am the universal*[2732] *light-of-awareness:*[2733] *he that followeth me shall not walk in darkness, but shall have the light of life...*[2734] *For I am not alone, but I and the Father* [the Transcendent-Self] *that sent me...*[2735] *are one.*"[2736]

The Self-in-Itself is Truth-Itself. Exiting that Restful Mindfulness (*viz.* Noah) means to *drown* in the deafening intoxicating sounds of the interconnected vineyard of time experiences.

The same comment we made regarding the nakedness of Adam and Eve ensues here. Let us revisit it. To know means to recognize the impenetrability or the nakedness of the mystery, of the unknown-other one. Nakedness refers to reality *in-itself*, which, in turn, *for-our* comprehension, we can only conceptualize as nakedness. This understanding takes place in the two circular days of consciousness-*of*-waking and *of*-dreaming. Nevertheless, on

"*the third day* [of NREM,] *the Transcendent will come down in the sight of all the people upon Mount Sinai.*"[2737]

As we saw, from the silence of stillness, which *Genesis* calls *Rested*-Noah, derive the three epistemic forms of

1) <u>Time</u> (Shem), the internal measure,
2) <u>Space</u> (Japheth), the external structure, and
3) <u>Causality</u> (Ham), the logical interconnections.

From Ham's virtual dream-causality, derives the *deceiving*[2738] Canaan, the *trafficker*,[2739] the merchant, who operates within the cause-effect relationship. The social emblem of Canaan's trafficking is wealth wealth wealth. Namely, it is the expression of economic achieving, the recompense of cravings. Desires accomplish their goals through the quantifying ways of finances. Compared to the previous three epistemic modalities, Canaan is a *lower subdued* and *depressed* function-form exchanging information between the subject and the object. In fact, he is

"*a trafficker and the balances*[2740] *of deceit are in his hand: he loveth to oppress.*"[2741]

His deceit (מִרְמָה *mirmah*) is equivalent to that of the serpent on the Tree of Knowledge. That snake makes us see the *nakedness* of the objects and desire them, while forgetting the Certain-Light from which we come.

The objectivity of the world is the only way we can know it and *to know* (יָדַע *yada'*) is an euphemism for interaction with it. We connect conceptually with the nakedness of the mysterious cognitive impenetrability of the object-in-itself. To understand Shem and Japheth's actions, we must look at Moses' behavior when confronted with the burning bush in Exodus. Moses, the one saved from the flowing transitory waters of objectivity,[2742] had

"*led the multitude of the flock*[2743] *behind*[2744] *the desert, and came to the mountain of The Transcendent*"[2745]

"*and worship at his holy hill.*"[2746]

Upon leaving behind the flock of the senses, one emerges from the many waters of the immanent world of subject-object correlation. Then, one finds itself in the transcendent high desert where there is no consciousness-*of*-objectivity. There,

"*Jesus... in the desert... fasted for forty days and forty nights.*"[2747]

There, Consciousness burns in the Apodictical Certain Awareness, so

"*a bush burned ... not consumed,*[2748] *... and Moses said, 'I will now reject and turn away from it...*[2749] *When the Transcendent saw that he rejected and turned away to speculate* [on that fire] *... said,*[2750]*... 'Do not approach'.*"[2751]

Then, Just as Shem and Japheth,

"*Moses hid* (סָתַר *cathar*) *his face* (פָּנִים *paniym*)*; for he was afraid to look upon the Transcendent...*[2752] *The Transcendent said unto Moses, 'I AM THAT I AM.*'"[2753]

There are similarities between the metaphors of the Burning-bush and the account Noah's nakedness. First, the sight of both is troublesome.[2754] Further, Shem and Japheth move backwards turning their faces backwards, like Moses, who covered[2755] his face not to see and conceptualize the naked nothingness of the

"tremendous and fascinating mystery."[2756]

However,

"*When Moses went in before the Transcendent-Lord to speak with him, he took the veil off the face,*[2757] [*viz.* no objectivity covered the being-in-itself] *until he came out. And he came out, and spake unto the children of Israel that which he was commanded. -- And the children of Israel saw the face of Moses, that the skin of Moses' face shone* [in-itself]*: and Moses put the veil upon his face again* [*viz.* they were seeing the objectivity *for-themselves*], *until he went in to speak with him* [self-in-itself]."[2758]

In fact,

"*Moses, who put a veil cover* (κάλυμμα *kalymma*)[2759] *over his face, that the children of Israel could not stedfastly look to the end of that which is abolished: -- But their minds were blinded* [by objectivity]*: for until this day remaineth the same vail untaken away... -- But even unto this day, when Moses is read, the veil is upon their heart. -- Nevertheless when it shall turn to the Lord, the veil shall be taken away.*"[2760]

At this point, we can almost hear a reader, follower of the money-seeking-preachers who pray, cry, beg and scream for donations they so eagerly worship, exclaim,

'Stop here! Your sophisticated interpretation is not in synchrony with the primitive mind and understanding of the writer and/or his contemporary readers. This is only in your mind and it is your arbitrary interpretative guess.'

We reply,

'However, the author claims[2761] *to have connected with Divine-Consciousness on Mount Sinai. In fact, there,*

"*the Transcendent said unto Moses, 'Lo, I*[2762] *come*[2763] *unto you*[2764] *in the cover*[2765] *of the mysterious theophanic cloud*."[2766]

Therefore, That Reality is

"*I AM,*"[2767]

It is not outside. On the contrary, It is within the Subject, in the mysterious recesses of the deepest psyche. This is, by no means, primitive thinking, in the sense of backwards in time (אַחֲרַנִּית *'achoranniyth*)*, but it is in the sense of origin. It connotes its being the foundation of everything. The expression of consciousness may vary, however, its structure never does. A tiger may roar, as outcome of its consciousness-of the pray. However, the epistemic structure of whosoever is conscious is the same in time, space, causality, gender, genus, and/or species. Furthermore, it is meaningful that Shem and Japheth fetched*[2768] *a bed shroud,*[2769] *used to wrap themselves in at night during sleep,*[2770] *placed it*[2771] *quickly*[2772] *on their shoulders and covered Noah.*[2773] *If, however, a literal reading makes you feel and live better within your own belief, stay with it and skip the introspecting moment.*

Reality articulates on three hypostatic levels. With a circular motion, each hypostasis proceeds from the other, generating the next and reabsorbing into the previous one. Apodictic-Awareness stands firm in the center of that circumference. All three hypostases emanate from the central Awareness.

<Awareness is the immutable Eternal-Present-Center, the Timeless-Zero. The Present is not realized in daily occurrence because it is timeless. There is no present in the past or in the future and, when we try to catch it in the present, it is impalpable. The mind, in fact, catches the object as already given, never in the fulguration of the Present. When we think of the now it is already past. Therefore, the Present remains elusive and timeless. Awareness is the unmovable hub of the wheel. On its rim, subject and object travel chasing each other in a time sequence. Awareness is in the World but it is>

"*not-of the world.*"[2774]

Articulating in the world, Awareness never extinguishes its being all in everything while encompassing all. From It, proceeds the first hypostasis, namely the thoughtless moment of Auto-transparency. This is the first form generated from Apodictic Awareness. It is the unending circularity of the *time* it takes memory to *remember* its historical beginning. The Cristian liturgy, on the day of Ash Wednesday, proclaims,

"*Remember human, you are dust and to dust you will revert.*"[2775]

However, this is only one polarity of remembrance, where dust refers only to the inconsistency of the object as such. The other one, referred to in the *Upanishads*, is the remembrance of the origin.

"*O intelligence, remember the deed, remember o intentional-will, remember the magic, remember.*"[2776]

<The deed is intentionality, the act of will, the consciousness-*of*, which constitutes in existence the objective-world, with which we identify.> Tolle affirms that

"All I can do, is remind you of what you have forgotten."[2777]

Massimo Scaligero declares that

"the decisive test is to go beyond the Field of Death, to recognize the deadly power of the oblivion of... the memory that guards the meaning of the deed and its orientation. Who remembers..., overcomes the apparent death of the soul: overcomes the danger to believe true this death... Man would not have lost immortality, if he had renounced knowledge."[2778]

<Thus, at the time of death, as the world fades-away, by remembering that deed, we realize that it was the consciousness-*of* which produced the objective-world-as-it-is-*for*-us. Will does not mean only a wishful desire that may or may not direct or drive an action, but mainly it denotes that deep biological force that imprints DNA memory in the cell. It is the evolutionary drive that makes the organism adapt to a new environmental condition. Will is the random qualitative jump that still produces a mutation and a new species. Not in the sense of a preordained intelligent design, but in the sense of an exploding blind force whose only *will*, *hunger* or *desire* is the embedded blind force of the explosion itself, while its directions are randomly pursuing all the infinite space coordinates. By force, we do not mean a cause, but

"what imparts to every cause its causality, in other words, the possibility of acting."[2779]

There is not an intelligent-design, but there is an intelligibility-of-that-not-intelligent-design. If that were not the case, we would not be able to recognize the not-intelligent-design of evolution at all. However, once we perceive the random evolutionary event, then we discover that, after its production, it has an internal necessity. That need does not allow it to deviate from those intransgressible essential laws of nature, which, although randomly produced, accompanied the event once it came under perceptive scrutiny. This is the other aspect of the Will, as serene intentional direction of Pure-Consciousness that looks at the blind-will without being affected by it. If the Highest Will were a creative force, then it would have been not Pure Awareness but Adam and Eve's *hunger* leading to death, their consciousness-*of* the multiplicity of the objective world. However, while the Will displays itself along all the scale of reality, the Will-as-intentionality constitutes, in all its moments, the transcendence of the other. That is to say, the pure Will remains as an unmovable Transcendent center that reflects itself on each point of the circumference. In turn, that reflection projects the next immanent point on the circumference as other than itself and having the quality of the Transcendent center. It is like the mirror image of someone,

GRAPHIC: *Mirror image of someone placed between two mirrors facing each other*[2780]

placed between two mirrors facing each other, chasing the infinite series of his/her own image. From an astrophysical perspective, it is like the spinning of objects on the border of a black hole collapsing in the extreme density of its center, which, in turn, generates that spiraling while remaining unknowable, inferred only by its vorticose border.>[2781]

Then, Shem-time becomes the mnemonic-*lapse* between this present attention and the present instant of its origin. Thus, Ham-causality places those memory-instants in causal relation, with the past becoming the cause of the present effects. In turn, Japheth-space is the *spatial dimension* of the *distance* between the coinciding memories of the subject-object circularity.

Like in a black hole,[2782] all events are like film-projections on a movie screen or icons on computer wallpaper virtually imprinted on the background of Awareness. However, those imprints are not in a time sequence, but in the Ever-Present-Awareness. In fact, Awareness is always in the Timeless-Present.

"*Therefore whatsoever you have spoken in darkness shall be heard in the light; and that which you have spoken in the ear in closets shall be proclaimed upon the housetops.*"[2783]

Nothing can escape the now. If a fantastic science-fiction time-travel could be possible, the past would be experienced always as a present event. <All events are co-eternally present. All events, in the moment they are experienced, are preserved because they take place only in the present of that experience, namely in a non-time. This preservation of data is similar to the holographic principle information encoded on the black hole's surface.[2784] Mindfulness is the stillness, which, while containing all the possible objects, does not change and is not qualified nor identifies with them. It does not engage with the object of knowledge. Mindfulness contains the World but it is not-mindful-*of* the world. It is the fire that does not consume the bush. It is what Lao Tzu calls the

"*action without action.*"[2785]

We must realize that the above description is completely inadequate to express Awareness and Mindfulness. In fact, it reduces their transcendence becoming a thought, an immanent concept. Only metaphors, like the *Biblical* Burning-bush, remain the most adequate expressions to convey transcendent references like Awareness and Mindfulness.>[2786]

Furthermore, to continue our commentary, we need to understand the meaning of Shem and Japheth's *walking backwards* and the Hebrew word for *backward.* The term is *'achoranniyth,*[2787] which is a prolonged form of *'achowr,*[2788] means also *to move in time.*[2789] It derives from *'achiyra`,*[2790] meaning, "*brother*[2791] *is evil,*"[2792] from *ra`a`,*[2793] *to be* or *do evil.* With this lexicon explained, we can try to understand this verse. Therefore, the serenity of Resting-Noah is disturbed the moment in which the Auto-transparent function moves out of its state of *shabath* (שבת), rest. Thus, Japheth-space moves back with Shem-time in the realm of time (אחור *'achowr*) past. This is an *evil* deed because *misses the target* and loses

Noah's stillness in the timeless present placing it in the past. Furthermore, they put on (שׂוּם suwm)[2794] a cover on Noah and, like Atlas, on their shoulders. Thus, they establish and constitute (שׂוּם suwm)[2795] their own and Noah's objectivity, in the sense that, by throwing the blanket on the subject's shoulders it makes it an *ob*ject, as that which is *over* (*ob*) *thrown* ($_{e}$*ject*$_{ed}$). In fact, the word *simlah, viz.* shroud, cover,

> "perhaps by permutation for the fem.[inine] of סֶמֶל [*cemel*] (H5566) (through the idea of a cover assuming the shape of the object beneath),"[2796]

becomes the *cemel* (סֶמֶל), namely, an image or an idol.[2797] Namely, the shroud takes[2798] the *shape* of Noah, the underlying covered[2799] object. Concluding, space, time and causality perceive only the objectivity of Noah, not his rested stillness. Namely, Ham is the understanding of his causal appearance. Japheth is the view of his space vacuity. Shem is the perception of his time sequence.

9:24-Noah Awakes from His Intoxication

וַיִּיקֶץ נֹחַ מִיֵּינוֹ וַיֵּדַע אֵת אֲשֶׁר־עָשָׂה־לוֹ בְּנוֹ הַקָּטָן׃   *vayiyqeṣ* (awoke) *nōaḥ* (Noah) *miyēynvō* (from intoxication) *vayēḏa'* (he knew) *'ēṯ* (and) *'ăšer* (that which) *'āśāh* (had performed) *lvō* (through him) *banvō* (son) *haqāṭān* (insignificant)
ἐξένηψεν *exenēpsen* (become sober again) **δὲ** *de* (but) **Νωε** *Nōe* (Noah) **ἀπὸ** *apo* (from) **τοῦ** *tou* (the) **οἴνου** *oinou* (wine) **καὶ** *kai* (and) **ἔγνω** *egnō* (he knew) **ὅσα** *osa* (what) **ἐποίησεν** *epoiēsen* (had done) **αὐτῷ** *autō* (he) **ὁ** *o* (the) **υἱὸς** *uios* (son) **αὐτοῦ** *autou* (he) **ὁ** *o* (the) **νεώτερος** *neōteros* (youngest)
evigilans (awakening) ***autem*** (also) ***Noe*** (Noah) ***ex*** (from) ***vino*** (the wine) ***cum*** (as) ***didicisset*** (learned) ***quae*** (that which) ***fecerat*** (had done) ***ei*** (to him) ***filius*** (son) ***suus*** (his) ***minor*** (minor)
And Noah awoke from his wine, and knew what his younger son had done unto him.
Noah awoke from his intoxication and he knew that which his insignificant son had performed through him.

Noah awakens[2800] from his intoxicating[2801] vineyard-like interconnected dreaming and waking states. The consciousness-*of* those intoxicating states confirms and witnesses, Noah's intuition[2802] of what Ham, his son, his paradigmatic dream-causal function, had performed.[2803] Namely, Ham-dream causes deep-sleep to appear as the vacuity of an empty state.

Siding with Ham's reasoning, our readers may critically react by saying,

'Are you comparing revelation to the state of unconsciousness?'

We reply,

'Yes! But it is the apparent oxymoron of AWARE UNCONSCIOUSNESS. Furthermore, with a literal reading, why would The Absolute Omniscient Omni-Aware Omnipotent Omnipresent Transcendent reveal a menial degrading event, such as Noah's drunken pederast nudity, with no essential universal significate? Additionally, as an example, why not reveal the fate of whales during the universal deluge?'

However, Ham, the dream-causal-function, is *qatan*.[2804] Namely, he is more insignificant than the other two brother-functions, *viz.* Shem-time and Japheth-space. What Ham establishes is the function of dream-causality, and causality is an epistemic form separate from and coming after the other two modalities of time and space.

9:25-Canaan Cursed

וַיֹּאמֶר אָרוּר כְּנָעַן עֶבֶד עֲבָדִים יִהְיֶה לְאֶחָיו׃   *vayō'mer* (he said) *'ārur* (cursed be) *kanā'an* (Canaan) *'eḇeḏ* (messenger) *'ăḇāḏiym* (of messengers) *yihayeh* (will be) *la'eḥāyv* (to relatives)
καὶ *kai* (and) **εἶπεν** *eipen* (he said) **ἐπικατάρατος** *epikatapatos* (cursed be) **Χανααν** *Chanaan* (Canaan) **παῖς** *pais* (child) **οἰκέτης** *oiketēs* (slave) **ἔσται** *estai* (will be) **τοῖς** *tois* (to the) **ἀδελφοῖς** *adelphois* (brothers) **αὐτοῦ** *autou* (his)
ait (he said) ***maledictus*** (cursed be) ***Chanaan*** (Canaan) ***servus*** (servant) ***servorum*** (of servants) ***erit*** (will be) ***fratribus*** (of brothers) ***suis*** (his)

And he said, Cursed be Canaan; a servant of servants shall he be unto his brethren.
Noah said, "*Cursed be Canaan, he will be the messenger of messengers to his relatives.*"

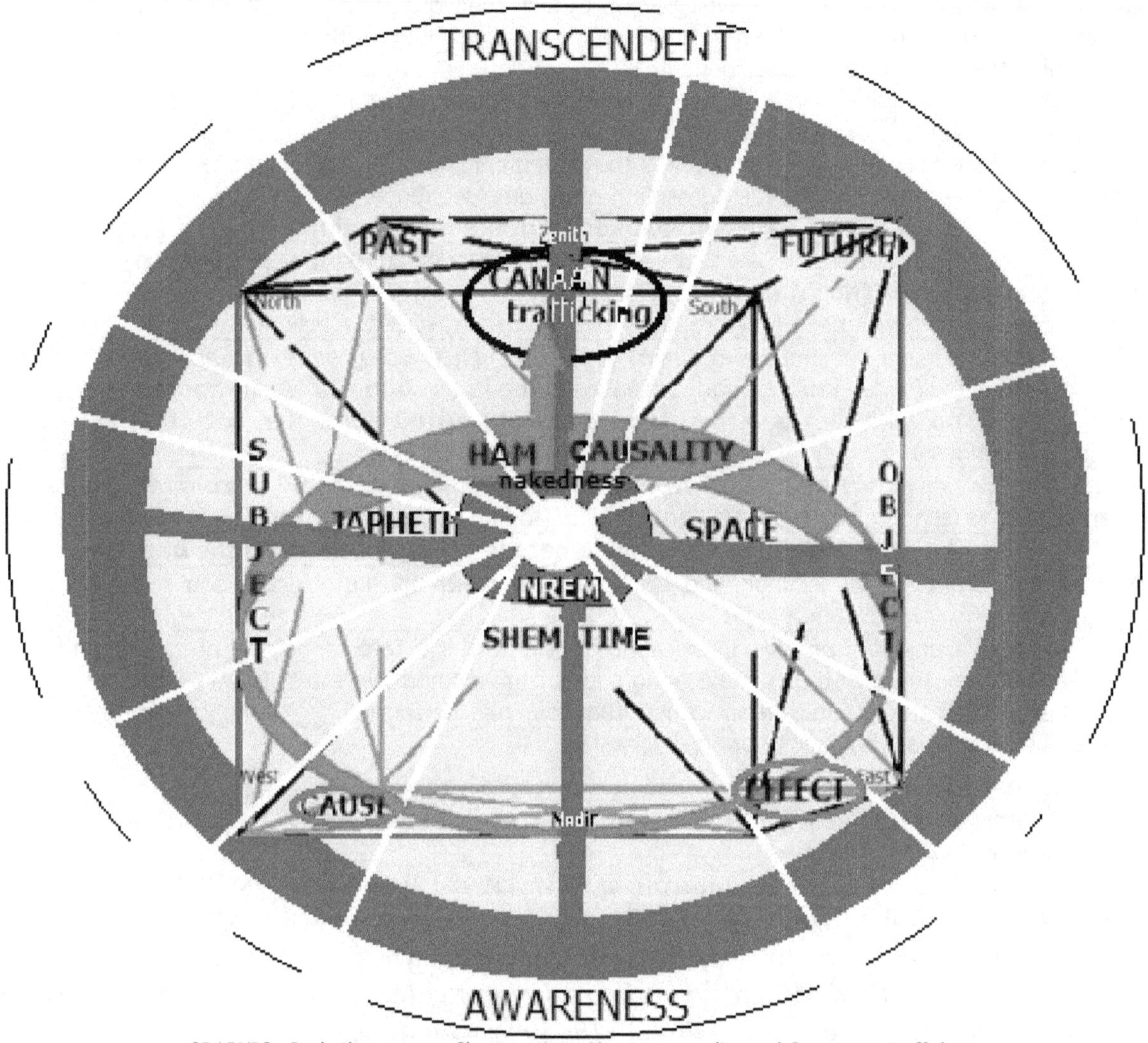

GRAPHIC: *Japheth as space, Shem as time, Ham as causality and Canaan as trafficker*

Again, the literal reading of these verses does not explain why the misdeed of the father would curse and penalize the son. Furthermore, it would reduce Noah's generation to simple offspring and/or geocentric dimensions of populations. In fact, in the overall macro and/or microcosmic universal reality, literal interpretations become myopically narrow and very insignificant. Definitely, they are not worthy of an all-encompassing Divine Revelation. Therefore, if there is an intended relevant meaning, it must be formally infinite.

Canaan is the offspring of Ham's causality-function. In that role, Canaan is the information trafficking function, spreading out its effects. In causality, he is the outcome of cause and effect. In time, he is the flow of past and future. Finally, in space, he is the scattering directions of north, east, south, west, zenith and nadir paths. Like a nervous connector, Canaan is the function that carries the information to the mode-forms of knowing, namely, space, time and causality. From Canaan's frenzy derives the loss of Noah's blissful-rest. Therefore, Noah curses Canaan, not Ham. Thus, Canaan becomes a servant of servants, *`ebed*.[2805] In fact,

"The name of servant is also applied... to messengers, 2 Sam. 10:2-4[2806]... figuratively applied in various senses... [as] *ambassador*... Isa. 49:6[2807]... (*i.e.* messenger, and as it were instrument)."[2808]

Canaan is the messenger, the epistemic agent that brings information to and from the subject and the object. Its primary medium is Ham's causal structure. Subsequently, he serves Shem's time-lapse and, finally, Japheth's space-distance interaction. Thus, he is the servant-messenger of his *relatives.*[2809]

<u>The story of Isaac, Jacob and Esau</u>

Later on, *Genesis* will elaborate on this concept of *servant*[2810] with the twin figures of Jacob and Esau. They are the architypes differentiating races. There, races distinguish not through diverse pigmentations but through distinctive mindsets. In fact, the text relates that Isaac, Abraham's son, at the age of forty married Rebekah.[2811] From her, he got two twin sons. While she was still pregnant,

> "*the LORD said unto her, 'Two races* (גוי *gowy*)[2812] [are] *in thy womb, and two manner of races* (לאם *lĕom*)[2813] *shall be separated* (פרד *parad*)[2814] *from thy bowels; and* [one] *people shall be stronger* (אמץ *'amats*)[2815] *than* [the other] *people; and the elder shall serve* (עבד *` abad*)[2816] *the younger.*"[2817]

Julius Evola, the esoteric Italian traditionalist, states that

> "In reality there are more than many cases of persons, who are exactly of the same physical race, of the same stock, at times even – as brothers or fathers and sons – of the same blood in the most real sense who, nevertheless, cannot understand each other. A frontier separates their souls, their way of feeling and seeing is different and, despite that, the common physical race and the common blood can do nothing. There is a possibility of comprehension, and therefore of true solidarity, of deep unity, only where a common *<u>race of the soul</u>* exists."[2818]

Martin Luther King echoes,

> "I have a dream that my four little children will one day live in a nation where they will not be judged by the color of their skin, but by the content of their character."[2819]

The mind determines the true race. Thought alone, not genetics shapes different peoples, which we may call *Soul's Races* (גוי *gowy* - לאם *lĕom*).[2820] On one side, we have the *Stronger Spiritual Race, 'amats* (אמץ), namely, *brave, bold, secure, assuring, alert* and *superior*. On the other, there is the *Subject Telluric Race, ` abad* (עבד), namely, *to serve* and *to be subject* to the first one.

Continuing with our account, at the twins' birth,

> "*the first* [twin] *came out red, all over like an hairy garment; and they called his name Esau...*[2821] [Also he was] *a hairy man...*[2822] *called Edom* [the Red one]."[2823]

<Esau, *`Esav* (עֵשָׂו), means he who does, he who works, he who makes or he who produces.[2824] Therefore, he is by name, action and appearance fiery, bustling and red while interacting with this world.

> "*And after that came his brother out, and his hand took hold on Esau's heel;*[2825] *and his name was called Jacob...*[2826] *a smooth man*"[2827]

In Hebrew, his name *Ya`aqob* (יַעֲקֹב) means: "heel holder, supplanter, circumvent."[2828] Therefore, as a heel holder, he is also the foundation on which the foot rests. In other words, he is the podium on which one stands. As a supplanter, Jacob is the one who will take over by circumventing the usual ways of things.

What is the metaphorical meaning of these biblical persons? We have three figures, Isaac, the father, with Esau and Jacob, his sons. These are the *two manners of people*, the two paradigmatic aspects of the human being.

1) "*Isaac loved Esau, because he* [was] *the mouth of* [his] *hunt.*"[2829]

   Isaac is *every man*, the enjoyer and consumer of this perception seized by the *mouth*, his consciousness-*of* this world. He, on his deathbed, yearning for another morsel of this world's experience, which he loves so much, begs his consciousness-*of, viz.* Esau,

   > "*Go out to the field, and take me* [some] *hunt; And make me sense a savoury meat, such as I love, and bring* [it] *to me, that I may eat; that my soul may bless thee before I die.*"[2830]

2) "*Esau was a cunning*[2831] *hunter, a man of the* [world's] *field.*"[2832]

Esau is a metaphor for the first born of the epistemic process. He is the *hunting*-consciousness-*of*-and-*in*-the-*game*-world. He is the one who seizes the objects and perceives them. He is the one who knows by experience, the one who discriminates and distinguishes. He is the red fire of consciousness-*of*, which *cooks* the *food for thought*.[2833]

3) "*Jacob* [was] *a plain*[2834] *man, dwelling in tents.*"[2835]

Jacob is the paradigm of the perfect, complete and pure Aware-Certitude, abiding in the innermost tabernacle of every human being. He is the support of consciousness-*of*, without which consciousness-*of* itself cannot be.

Consciousness-*of*, *viz*. Esau, is self-interested absorption in its own epistemic meal. One day, he "*came from the field* [of the objective world]... *And Esau said to Jacob, 'Feed me* [food for thought],[2836] *I pray thee, with that same red* [pottage]*; for I* [am] *faint* [without which I would be thoughtless]'*: therefore was his name called Edom* [the *red-hot* one].[2837] */And Jacob said, 'Surrender to me this day thy birthright* [that I am your Only-True-Certain-support]*.'/ And Esau said, 'Behold, I* [am] *at the point of death: and what profit shall this birthright do to me?'/ And he sold* [recognized] *his birthright* [to belong] *unto Jacob.../ Thus Esau despised* [his] *birthright.*"[2838]

Esau is the totality of all the senses with which consciousness-*of* operates. Metaphorically, he is giving up his leadership recognizing Certitude as the foundation of his consciousness. Some passages from the *Chāndogya Upanishad* may clarify this allegory.

"*Once, the vital spirits of the senses disputed who was superior among them. Speech departed ... and when it came back, he asked 'Thus, how have you been able to live without me?'* [It answered] *'Like dumb, but living with vital breath* [viz. life's foundation]*.' The eye departed ... and when it came back, he asked 'Thus, how have you been able to live without me?'* [It answered] *'Like blind, but living with vital breath.' The ear departed ... and when it came back, he asked 'Thus, how have you been able to live without me?'* [It answered] *'Like deaf, but living with vital breath.' The mind departed ... and when it came back, he asked 'Thus, how have you been able to live without me?'* [It answered] *'Like an infant, but living with vital breath.' Then when that vital breath was about to depart ... the other senses were uprooted. They all came to him and said 'You are the best among us.'*"[2839]

Therefore, *Vital-Breath*, Awareness, Life's Foundation

"*is ... the essence of the limbs*,[2840] [is] "*intention, made of mind, tending conceptually towards truth, with the vital breath as body, the light as form, and space as essence, He is the source of every action, of every desire, of every scent, and of every flavor. Encompassing all this, but indifferent, without conferring meaning or sense to the objects.*"[2841]

"*Verily, that Supreme Transcendent Spirit is this Self. It is composed of knowledge, mind, vital breath, sight, hearing, earth, water, wind, space, light, darkness, desire, detachment, anger, tranquility, justice, injustice, and everything else, thus it is composed of this and that. One transforms itself according to his actions and behaviors. Who does good becomes good, who does evil becomes evil. One becomes virtuous by virtuous action and evil-by-evil action. Furthermore, verily, some say that a person is composed of desire indeed. As his desire is, so becomes his will, then, as his will is, so he enacts his deed, finally, he achieves whatever deed he enacts.*"[2842]

This is the metaphoric sense of Esau's abdication to his right of primogeniture. Therefore, *Genesis* describes how Isaac, before dying, wanted to bless his consciousness-*of*/Esau producer of his beloved experience.[2843] Isaac, whose

"*eyes were dim, so that he could not see, he called Esau his eldest son, and said unto him.../ 'go out to the field, and take me* some *venison.../ And make me savoury meat, such as I love, and bring* it *to me, that I may eat; that my soul may bless thee before I die...'/* [And] *Rebekah* [the ensnarer] *spake unto Jacob her son... / 'Go now to the flock, and fetch me from thence two good kids of the goats; and I will make them savoury meat for thy father, such as he loveth:/ And thou shalt bring* [it] *to thy father, that he may eat, and that he may bless thee before his death.' / And Jacob said to Rebekah his mother, 'Behold, Esau my brother* [is] *a hairy man, and I* [am] *a smooth man:/ My father peradventure will feel me, and I shall seem to him as a deceiver* [which I am not]; *and I shall bring a curse upon me, and not a blessing.'/ And he went, and fetched, and brought* [them] *to his mother: and his mother made savoury meat, such as his father loved./ And Rebekah took goodly raiment of her eldest son Esau, which* [were] *with her in the house, and put them upon Jacob her younger son:/ And she put the skins of the kids of the goats upon his hands, and upon the smooth of his neck:/ And she gave the savoury meat and the bread, which she had prepared, into the hand of her son Jacob./ And he came unto his father, and said, 'My father': and he said, 'Here* [am] *I'; 'who* [art] *thou, my son?'/ and Jacob said unto his father, 'I* [am the real Awareness of] *Esau* [consciousness-*of*] *thy firstborn; I have done according as thou badest me: arise, I pray thee, sit and eat of my venison, that thy soul may bless me.'/ And Isaac said unto his son, 'How* [is it] *that thou hast found* [it] *so quickly, my son?' And he said, 'Because the LORD thy God brought* [it] *to me.'* [*viz.* consciousness-*of* is in the field of space and time, while Awareness is spaceless and timeless]*/ And Isaac said unto Jacob, 'Come near, I pray thee, that I may feel thee, my son, whether thou* [be] *my very son Esau or not.'* [*viz.* Isaac had only consciousness-*of* the world but never focused on the Apodictic-Certitude].*/ And Jacob went near unto Isaac his father; and he felt him, and said, 'The voice* [is] *Jacob's voice, but the hands* [are] *the hands of Esau.'/ And he discerned him not, because his hands were hairy, as his brother Esau's hands: so he blessed him./ And he said,* '[Art] *thou my very son Esau?' And he said, 'I* [am his Awareness].*'/ And he said, 'Bring* [it] *near to me, and I will eat of my son's venison, that my soul may bless thee.' And he brought* [it] *near to him, and he did eat: and he brought him wine, and he drank./ And his father Isaac said unto him, Come near now, and kiss me, my son./ And he came near, and kissed him: and he smelled the smell of his raiment, and blessed him, and said, 'See, the smell of my son* [is] *as the smell of a field which the LORD hath blessed.'"*[2844]

Isaac had never realized the profundity of Jacob. He was familiar only with Esau. Awareness and consciousness-*of* are difficult to distinguish. Consciousness-*of* interacts with the object and recognizes it *with-knowledge.*[2845] Awareness is the foundation of knowledge. It is its essential Truth. It is <u>Certainty</u>. It is *quickness of spirit.*

As an example, at the sight of a venomous snake, we move away from its path. Upon recognizing that it was a rope mistaken for a serpent, we return on our steps. Consciousness-*of* is emotional interpretation of experience. Instead, Awareness in-itself is always Non-Judgmental-Certitude sustaining, now the self, now the path, now the snake, now the mistaken view and now the rope.

Jesus says,

"*My kingdom is not* [the consciousness-] *of this world.*"[2846]

Consciousness-*of* is *Lucifer,*[2847] the light-bearer of the Aware-Sun *reflecting* and bouncing off from the experienced data. Awareness is the Light of Certitude. It is the Mathematical-Scientific enlightening of the World.

Then, as Desirous (*Uśan*), in the *Kaṭha Upanishad,*

"*recognized* [his son Naciketa] *as he* [who had been] *let loose by* [Mṛtyu/Death],"[2848]

similarly, Isaac, having realized Jacob, as the Certainty of Awareness, proclaimed,

"'*Let people serve thee, and nations bow down to thee: be lord over thy brethren, and let thy mother's sons bow down to thee: cursed* [be] *every one that curseth thee, and blessed* [be] *he that blesseth thee.*'"[2849]

In fact, Ramana Maharshi says,

"*When we quest with our mind 'Who am I?' and reach the Heart, 'I'* [*viz.* Esau] *topples down and immediately another entity will reveal itself proclaiming 'I-I'. Even though it also emerges saying 'I', it does not connote the ego, but the One Perfect Existence,*"[2850] *viz.* Jacob.

However,

"*it came to pass, as soon as Isaac had made an end of blessing Jacob, and Jacob was yet scarce gone out from the presence of Isaac his father, that Esau his brother came in from his hunting.*"[2851]

Therefore, on the onset of death, Isaac realizes Certitude/Jacob. This is not a deceit; it is the restoration of the truthful order of things as willed by God.[2852] It is the realization that objectiveness presents itself founded on Apodictical Truth. Beyond the fussiness of objectivity, there is the smoothness of epistemic Certainty. To realize this, it is necessary to *circumvent* (Jacob יַעֲקֹב *Ya'aqob*) the identification with the objective world and realize or bless the Truth on which objectivity is founded. Therefore, Truth is conquered by force,

> "*the kingdom of heaven suffereth violence, and the violent take it by force.*"[2853]
>
> "*And Jacob... wrestled a man with him until the breaking of the day./ And ... he prevailed/ And he said, Thy name shall be called no more Jacob, but Israel: for as a prince hast thou power with God and with men, and hast prevailed.*"

When Jacob wakes up into Awareness, he is Israel and *God prevails* (יִשְׂרָאֵל *Yisra'el*).>[2854]

9:26-Canaan Is Shem's Messenger

וַיֹּאמֶר בָּרוּךְ יְהֹוָה אֱלֹהֵי שֵׁם וִיהִי כְנַעַן עֶבֶד לָמוֹ׃
vayō'mer (he said) *bāru<u>k</u>a* (blessed) *yahoāh* (Transcendent) *'ĕlōhēy* (Divine-Consciousness) *šēm* (Shem) *viyhiy* (shall be) *<u>k</u>ana'an* (Canaan) *'e<u>b</u>e<u>d</u>* (messenger) *lāmvō* (for)
καὶ *kai* (and) **εἶπεν** *eipen* (he said) **εὐλογητὸς** *euogēō* (blessed be) **κύριος** *kurios* (Lord) **ὁ** *o* (the) **θεὸς** *theos* (God) **τοῦ** *tou* (of the) **Σημ** *Sēm* (Shem) **καὶ** *kai* (and) **ἔσται** *estai* (shall be) **Χανααν** *Chanaan* (Canaan) **παῖς** *pais* (servant) **αὐτοῦ** *autou* (his)
dixit- (he said) ***que*** (and) ***benedictus*** (blessed be) ***Dominus*** (Lord) ***Deus*** (God) ***Sem*** (Shem) ***sit*** (will be) ***Chanaan*** (Canaan) ***servus*** (servant) ***eius*** (his)
And he said, Blessed be the LORD God of Shem; and Canaan shall be his servant.
Noah said, "*Blessed be the Transcendent Divine-Consciousness of Shem, Canaan shall be his messenger.*

To understand this and the next verse, we must remember that Shem, time's epistemic function, is the first to move out from the Resting-state, which in turn descends directly from the Pure-Epistemic-Divine-Consciousness (אֱלֹהִים *'elohiym*) founded on the Transcendent-Apodictic-Awareness (יְהֹוָה *yĕhovah*). The trafficking and messaging function of Canaan is that of conceptually shuttling between past and future while constantly missing the present as such.

9:27- Canaan Is Japheth's Messenger

יַפְתְּ אֱלֹהִים לְיֶפֶת וְיִשְׁכֹּן בְּאָהֳלֵי־שֵׁם וִיהִי כְנַעַן עֶבֶד לָמוֹ׃
yap̄ata (shall spread out) *'ĕlōhiym* (Divine-Consciousness) *layep̄e<u>t</u>* (Japheth) *vayišakōn* (he shall dwell) *ba'āhŏlēy* (in the tent) *šēm* (of Shem) *viyhiy* (shall be) *<u>k</u>ana'an* (Canaan) *'e<u>b</u>e<u>d</u>* (the messenger) *lāmvō* (for)
πλατύναι *platunai* (may widen) **ὁ** *o* (the) **θεὸς** *theos* (God) **τῷ** *tō* () **Ιαφεθ** *Iapheth* (Japheth) **καὶ** *kai* (and) **κατοικησάτω** *katoikēsatō* (he shall dwell) **ἐν** *en* (in) **τοῖς** *tois* (the) **οἴκοις** *oikois* (house) **τοῦ** *tou* (of the) **Σημ** *Sēm* (Shem) **καὶ** *kai* (and) **γενηθήτω** *genēthētō* (let be) **Χανααν** *Chanaan* (Canaan) **παῖς** *pais* (servant) **αὐτῶν** *autōn* (his)
dilatet (Shall enlarge) ***Deus*** (God) ***Iafeth*** (Japheth) ***et*** (and) ***habitet*** (shall dwell) ***in*** (in) ***tabernaculis*** (the tent) ***Sem*** (of Shem) ***sit-*** (shall be)***que*** (and) ***Chanaan*** (Canaan) ***servus*** (servant) ***eius*** (his)
God shall enlarge Japheth, and he shall dwell in the tents of Shem; and Canaan shall be his servant.
Divine-Consciousness shall spread out Japheth. He shall dwell in the tent of Shem and Canaan shall be his messenger."

Japheth, on the other hand, is space, which abides[2855] in the shining[2856] abode[2857] of Shem's time. There, in fact, the Pure-Epistemic-Divine-Consciousness (אֱלֹהִים *'elohiym*) allows the spreading out[2858] in the time-sequence of past and future. Trafficking Canaan is the constant intermediary between those two dichotomies. In time, he logically refers to all space directions and vice versa. Space distances, in fact, spread in time measurements, *e.g.* the time it takes for light to reach another object in space.

In conclusion, we know the objective-world throughout its epistemic forms, which are the way we know the deadly deluge of object-attachment in time-space-causality that drown Noah's rest.

9:28-After the Flood

וַיְחִי־נֹחַ אַחַר הַמַּבּוּל שְׁלֹשׁ מֵאוֹת שָׁנָה וַחֲמִשִּׁים שָׁנָה׃
vayaḥiy (lived) *nōaḥ* (Noah) *'aḥar* (after) *hamabul* (flood) *šalōš* (three) *mē'vōṯ* (hundred) *šānāh* (years) *vaḥămišiym* (fifty) *šānāh* (years)
ἔζησεν *ezēsen* (lived) **δὲ** *de* (then) **Νωε** *Nōe* (Noah) **μετὰ** *meta* (after) **τὸν** *ton* (the) **κατακλυσμὸν** *kataklusmov* (flood) **τριακόσια** *triakosia* (three hundred) **πεντήκοντα** *pentēkonta* (fifty) **ἔτη** *etē* (years)
vixit (lived) ***autem*** (also) ***Noe*** (Noah) ***post*** (after) ***diluvium*** (the flood) ***trecentis*** (three hundred) ***quinquaginta*** (fifty) ***annis*** (years)
And Noah lived after the flood three hundred and fifty years.
After the flood, the Rested-Noah lived the epistemic circular years utterly *abolishing mental idols* (350).

The flood ends when all the thoughts that have engulfed our mind cease to be our idols. Then, Noah

"*shall utterly abolish idols.*"[2859]

In Gematria, this last phrase has the numerical equivalent of 350. All thoughts are the empty[2860] idols[2861] of the repeating[2862] circularities of the years.[2863] They disappear when we withdraw in the circadian dreamless-sleep,[2864] cognate to year, and/or when we die.

9:29- Noah's Redemption

וַיִּהְיוּ כָּל־יְמֵי־נֹחַ תְּשַׁע מֵאוֹת שָׁנָה וַחֲמִשִּׁים שָׁנָה וַיָּמֹת׃ פ
vayihayu (are) *kāl* (all) *yamēy* (days) *nōaḥ* (Noah) *taša'* (nine) *mē'vōṯ* (hundred) *šānāh* (years) *vaḥămišiym* (fifty) *šānāh* (years) *vayāmōṯ* (he died) *p̄* (.)
καὶ *kai* (and) **ἐγένοντο** *egenonto* (lived) **πᾶσαι** *pasai* (all) **αἱ** *ai* (the) **ἡμέραι** *ēmerai* (days) **Νωε** *Nōe* (of Noah) **ἐννακόσια** *ennakosia* (nine hundred) **πεντήκοντα** *pentēkonta* (fifty) **ἔτη** *etē* (years) **καὶ** *kai* (and) **ἀπέθανεν** *apethanen* (he died)
et (and) ***impleti*** (completed) ***sunt*** (are) ***omnes*** (all) ***dies*** (the days) ***eius*** (his) ***nongentorum*** (nine hundred) ***quinquaginta*** (fifty) ***annorum*** (years) ***et*** (and) ***mortuus*** (dead) ***est*** (is)
And all the days of Noah were nine hundred and fifty years: and he died.
All the circular days of Noah's consciousness and epistemic circular years ended with the reabsorption in the Transcendent. Moreover, the Epistemic *Power placed upon his sons the empty idolatry, rewarded him and he acknowledged it* (950).

The reabsorption of all Noah's functions takes place at the end (מות *muwth*) of 950° degrees of epistemic years. They reabsorb in Noah's own ineffable origin. There,

"*The Power placed the empty idolatry upon the sons, rewarded him and he shall realize it.*"[2865]

In Gematria, this last verse has the numerical equivalence of 950. It means that all epistemic forms (*viz.* time, space and causality) are like the offspring[2866] of the power[2867] that generates them. They are the noetic aspect of the noematic object placed before them. Consequently, the internal intentional forces of experiential-thoughts always demand their own reconceptualization. The object, then, becomes an empty idolatry.[2868] The greatest historical world achievement is not as great as the one that conquers the

"*restless, turbulent, obstinate*"[2869]

mind itself. The subject is rewarded[2870] with this realization[2871] of the troublesome and empty vacuity[2872] of the mind object in-itself. Therefore, the epistemic circularities of the days (יוֹם *yowm*) and years (שָׁנָה *shaneh*) of Noah end by withdrawing in the circadian dreamless-sleep,[2873] the cognate year and/or by dying (מות *muwth*) reabsorbed in the Transcendent.

A reader may ask,

'*Why give a Gematria calculation when encountering numbers referring to the age of a patriarch? Why not accept the numbers as they are?*'

Our answer is,

'In the Bible's economy, as a revealed text, what is the universal relevance of the exact patriarchs' age? Furthermore, we read that Noah dies. Once deceased, what distinguishes him from all the others who died in the flood? Once dead, regardless of the cause of death, all deceased are over. Namely, the ***flood of death engulfs*** *them all. However, Noah, as all other patriarchal epistemic functions, cannot have an end as such, penalty it would be the end of consciousness. Moreover, if the Bible did not indicate the age of death, the average unsophisticated literal reader may doubt the truthfulness of the text itself, since Noah is nowhere in the flesh now (except as your own psychophysical being). Therefore, the Gematria reading becomes metaphorical to indicate the epistemic persistence of the universal functions. As an example, if we were to say - The thought died out, - it would not mean that the thinking faculty died.'*

Additionally, our reader may think,

'You express your work with written thoughts. Nevertheless, your commentary emphasizes thoughtlessness as the highest and only presence of Reality. How can I believe in it, since my belief would still be a thought?'

We reply,

'It does not matter if we believe in it or not. If dream and virtual reality are unreal at the oncoming of waking reality, how must we understand wakeful life when the reality of death sets in? The truth is that NOTHINGNESS faces us when we think of the state before the Big Bang. Again, NOTHINGNESS faces us when we think of our state after death. NOTHINGNESS surrounds our thought on all its borders. We may live for the length of a whole century, probably more in the future, but NOTHINGNESS is always the ultimate Reality from which we come and to which we go. A span after a century long life is still NOTHINGNESS, which reduces the flood of our thoughts to nothingness, like this book. Our written words want to be only a waking call, which trumpets that wakefulness and dream are ultimately unreliable. Reality starts appearing in dreamless-sleep. However, any conceptualization of nothingness is not NOTHINGNESS; it is its objective aspect of nakedness. NOTHINGNESS is not what you may think of nothing, because what we think of it is still something. That perceiving thought is Ham's experience of his father's nakedness, not his actual emptiness. Noah's nudity, even if it is the closest to NOTHINGNESS, is still this worldly state of Non-Rapid-Eyes-Movement.

Originally, an urn was just dust. By mixing that soil with water, it became mud. Shaping that mud, it became clay. That became a pot after we shaped it. When we pulverize that jar,[2874] then, it goes back to be dust. The question to you is, -What is the fundamental reality of an artistically beautiful clay vase? - The answer is, -Dust! -[2875] Therefore, if nothing that we can possibly think-of is before the Big Bang and nothing we can possibly think-of is after death, what is the fundamental reality of this, which we call reality? The answer is, -NOTHING that we can think-of! Ultimately, even the words in this book are nothing, save that they may have meditatively redirected the focus of your attention on Everlasting Awareness.'

Exiting dreamless sleep, the flooding world of duality of dream and wakefulness intoxicates us. Again, the *in-itself* appears *to-us* in its objective empty-nakedness *for-itself*. Time, Space and Causality *inter*act to shape the consciousness-*of* this objective world.

HERE ENDS THE NINTH CHAPTER
OF THE RAINBOW, THE VINEYARD
AND THE BLOOD GRAPES

PART 5

HISTORICAL AND GEOGRAPHICAL PARADIGMS

CHAPTER 10

THE GENERATIONS OF THE SONS OF NOAH

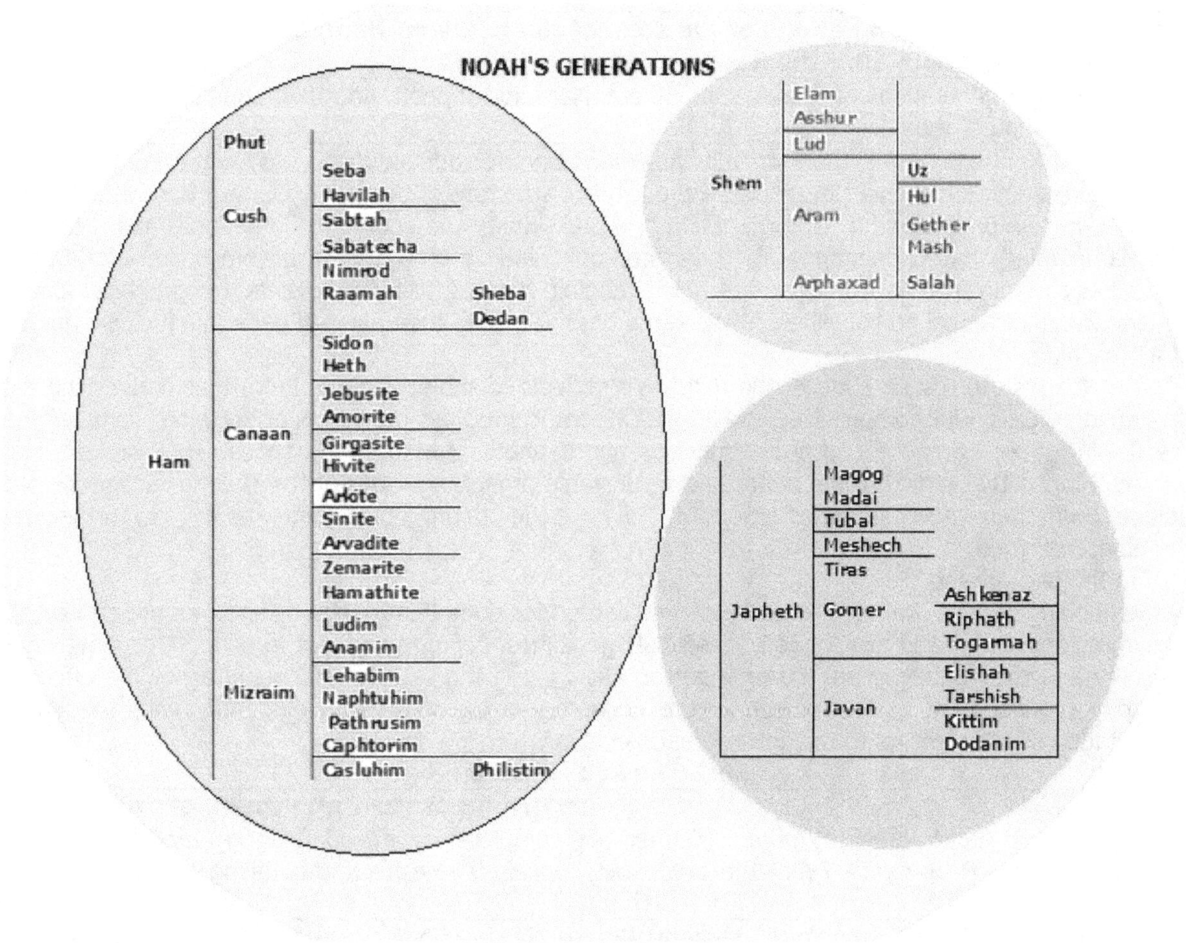

GRAPHIC*: Noah's Generations*

10-I SECTION: SPACE PARADIGMS

10:1-The Generations of Noah's Sons

וְאֵלֶּה תּוֹלְדֹת בְּנֵי־נֹחַ שֵׁם חָם וָיָפֶת וַיִּוָּלְדוּ לָהֶם בָּנִים אַחַר הַמַּבּוּל׃
wa'ēleh (these) *twōleḏōṯ* (the generations) *banēy* (sons) *nōaḥ* (of Noah) *šēm* (Shem) *ḥām* (Ham) *wāyāp̄eṯ* (Japheth) *wayiuālaḏu* (brought forth) *lāhem* (by them) *bāniym* (sons) *'aḥar* (on the background) *hamabul* (the deluge)
αὗται *autai* (in this way) **δὲ** *de* (and) **αἱ** *ai* (the) **γενέσεις** *geneseis* (generations) **τῶν** *tōv* (of the) **υἱῶν** *uiōn* (sons) **Νωε** *Nōe* (of Noah) **Σημ** *Sēm* (Shem) **Χαμ** *Cham* (Ham) **Ιαφεθ** *Iapheth* (Japheth) **καὶ** *kai* (and) **ἐγενήθησαν** *egenēthēsan* (were born) **αὐτοῖς** *autois* (from them) **υἱοὶ** *uioi* (sons) **μετὰ** *meta* (after) **τὸν** *ton* (the) **κατακλυσμόν** *kataklusmon* (cataclysm)
hae (these) ***generationes*** (the generations) ***filiorum*** (of the sons) ***Noe*** (of Noah) ***Sem*** (Shem) ***Ham*** (Ham) ***Iafeth*** (Japheth) ***nati-*** (born) ***que*** (and) ***sunt*** (are) ***eis*** (from them) ***filii*** (sons) ***post*** (after) ***diluvium*** (the deluge)
Now these *are* the generations of the sons of Noah, Shem, Ham, and Japheth: and unto them were sons born after the flood.
These are the generations of Noah's sons, Shem, Ham and Japheth and their sons brought forth on the background of the deluge.

In a Kantian way,[2876] the Patriarchs are metaphors for our *synthetic a-priori* forms of knowledge, logically preceding experience. By tracing the epistemic structure of the mind, *Genesis* describes the world and the way we understand it. In turn, like in a virtual dream, the known world seduces and mesmerizes that same mind that understands it. Therefore, our reading of the Text becomes literal. Namely, it objectifies the narrative as if it were describing tangible objects, historical events, geographical locations and individual historical personalities. At the same time, it misses the universal paradigmatic configurations of its teaching.

Noah is the resting state of the mind as synthesis of subject/object. From that derives the entire epistemic process, which knows the world-object. From it, progress our forms of knowing, namely, Shem, the flowing time, Ham, the causal relationships and Japheth, the sprawling space. They are the logical universal forms that structure the entire known universe organizing it out of the chaotic cacophony of the deluge. From them, new categories articulate. They are the offspring that come about[2877] to further clarify the objective world

"in the background"[2878]

of the flooding objects. Namely, these forms and categories do not cause the deluge, nor are caused by it. Like footsteps or wheels are logically essential modalities *behind* a chariot speed,[2879] so time, space, causality and their outcome are *logically behind* (אַחַר *'achar*)[2880] the cataclysm. They are not the effect, nor are they produced by it. The deluge is the necessary outcome when we identify with the flooding precipitation of attachments to the ephemeral objects in which we drown.

10:2-The Sons of Japheth

בְּנֵי יֶפֶת גֹּמֶר וּמָגוֹג וּמָדַי וְיָוָן וְתֻבָל וּמֶשֶׁךְ וְתִירָס׃
banēy (sons) *yep̄eṯ* (Japheth) *gōmer* (Gomer the complete) *umāḡvōḡ* (Magog) *umāḏay* (Madai) *wayāwān* (Javan) *waṯuḇāl* (Tubal the confusion) *umešeḵa* (Meshech the taking) *waṯiyrās* (Tiras desire)
υἱοὶ *uioi* (sons) **Ιαφεθ** *Iapheth* (of Japheth) **Γαμερ** *Gamer* (Gomer) **καὶ** *kai* (and) **Μαγωγ** *Magōg* (Magog) **καὶ** *kai* (and) **Μαδαι** *Madai* (Madai) **καὶ** *kai* (and) **Ιωυαν** *Iōuan* (Javan) **καὶ** *kai* (and) **Ελισα** *Elisa* (Elisa)[2881] **καὶ** *kai* (and) **Θοβελ** *Thobel* (Thubal) **καὶ** *kai* (and) **Μοσοχ** *Mosoch* (Meshech) **καὶ** *kai* (and) **Θιρας** *Thiras* (Thiras)
filii (the sons) ***Iafeth*** (of Japheth) ***Gomer*** (Gomer) ***Magog*** (Magog) ***et*** (and) ***Madai*** (Madai) ***Iavan*** (Javan) ***et*** (and) ***Thubal*** (Tubal) ***et*** (and) ***Mosoch*** (Meshech) ***et*** (and) ***Thiras*** (Tiras)
The sons of Japheth; Gomer, and Magog, and Madai, and Javan, and Tubal, and Meshech, and Tiras.

The sons of Japheth are Gomer, the complete, Magog, the strong, Madai, the sufficient reason, Javan, the intoxication, Tubal, the confusion, Meshech the taking, Tiras, the desire.

Any mind, reading this verse while hungry for the fruit of objectivity, will understand the names as historical personalities, populations, specific geopolitical nations and/or as parts for the totality of the world. However, continuing with our epistemological reading, we understand that the offspring of Noah's sons must have a universal paradigmatic configuration, which develops from their generators into the offspring. When we understand Noah's sons as metaphors for Space, Time and Causality, we do not mean the idea of space, time and causality, as such, which belongs only to the thinking creatures. We mean those epistemic forms valid for all beings. A celestial body, for example, travels its gravitational orbit without the concept of time, space or causality. Similarly, a plant projects below and above ground. The actions of beings are causes in time and space without the necessity to conceptualize the structure of their actions. In fact, a seagull instinctively directs its steps on the beach towards the shellfish and a squirrel, impulsively travels the space-distance towards the nut, automatically remembering where it hid that food sometime before. The thinking being, besides spontaneous acts, can also conceive and abstract the modalities or the forms of those acts. From a Kantian perspective, as the Patriarchs are metaphors for epistemic logical *a-priori* forms, also their generations are metaphors for the categories[2882] through which those forms articulate.

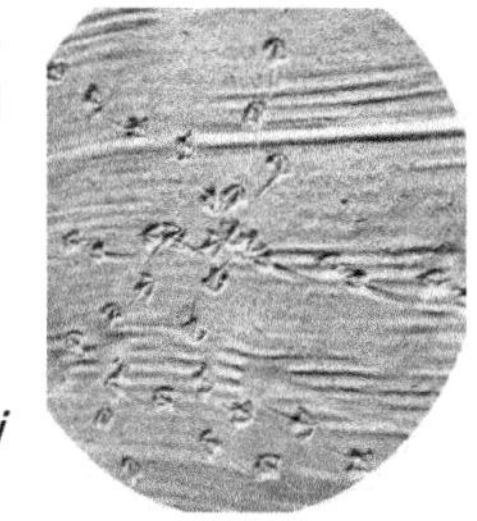

Having identified the epistemic form of space with the metaphoric figure of Japheth, we understand that from it derive the seven directions, namely, Zenith, as Magog, East, as Madai, North, as Javan, West, as Tubal, South, as Meshech, Nadir, as Tiras, and the Sphere, as Gomer. Each name becomes a rhetorical figure of speech as the part for the whole. Therefore, from the epistemic form of space (*viz.* Japheth) derive seven offspring,

1) *<u>Gomer</u>* (גֹּמֶר)[2883] means the <u>Spherical</u> *completion* of all space directional references. The name derives from the verb *gamar* (גָּמַר),[2884] meaning *to end, to complete, to finish*. Therefore, the name indicates the totality or the end of space as "*Unique Forms of Continuity in Space.*"[2885] In the Indian sacred tradition, the horse was a symbol of the totality of space itself. In fact, similar to a Kabalistic Sephirothic Tree, the *Bṛhadāraṇyaka Upanishad* describes the horse as a metaphor for the directions of the compass rose:

   "*the cardinal points are his sides… his head is the Orient; his front legs are South-East and North-East; his tail is the West, and hind legs are South-West and North-West; his hips are the South and the North… his back is the sky; his belly is the atmosphere; his chest is this ground; and he stands on the waters.*"[2886]

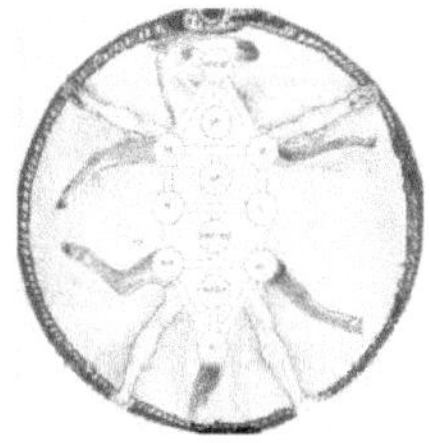

2) *<u>Magog</u>* (מָגוֹג),[2887] namely, the *mountainous land* (מָ *ma*)[2888] *of Gog* (גוֹג), derives from the word *gowg* (גוֹג),[2889] *viz. mountain*, therefore, the height or <u>Zenith</u> in space dimension.
3) *<u>Madai</u>* (מָדַי),[2890] namely the *middle abundant* (דַּי *day*)[2891] *land* (מָ *ma*), symbolized by Media, is connected to the verb *madad*,[2892] meaning to measure distances. It is the <u>East</u>, from where the abundance (דַּי *day*) of the rising sun provides and measures *orient*ation.
4) *<u>Javan</u>* (יָוָן)[2893] is the land of the <u>North</u>, symbolized by Iona, Greece,[2894] the country producer of *wine, yayin* (יַיִן),[2895] the bubbling and effervescent drink procuring intoxication with mind-altering space wandering and drifting.
5) *<u>Tubal</u>* (תֻּבַל)[2896] means "*thou shall be brought.*" The name is cognate to *tebel* (תֵּבֵל),[2897] meaning *the world* and *tebel* (תֶּבֶל)[2898] means *confusion, chaos* deriving from *balal* (בָּלַל),[2899] *to confuse*. Symbolically, it refers to the inhabited land of the <u>West</u> where the sun-flow (בָּלַל *balal*) leads into the obscurity (תבלל *teballul*)[2900] of sunset.

6) *<u>Meshech</u>* (מֶשֶׁךְ)[2901] means *holding*. It derives from *meshek* (מֶשֶׁךְ),[2902] meaning *securing*

and again from the verb *mashak* (מְשַׁךְ),[2903] meaning *to draw*, like a bow securing the directional arrow. Therefore, the sixth element of space is the South, which closes and holds the circularity of space directions securely together.

7) *Tiras* (תִּירָס)[2904] is the Nadir of space, it means *desire*, namely, the directional drive that from the bottom holds the entire space structure.

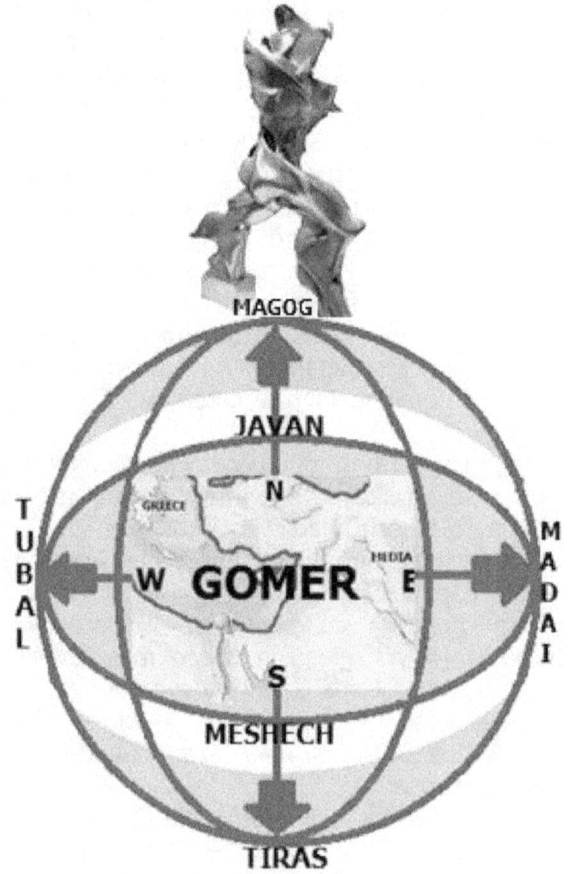

GRAPHIC: *Unique Forms of Continuity in Space*

Even reading this verse from a near-eastern physical and political geographical perspective, nevertheless, it still reaches the same directional conclusions.

10:3-The Sons of Gomer

וּבְנֵי גֹּמֶר אַשְׁכְּנַז וְרִיפַת וְתֹגַרְמָה׃   *ubanēy* (the sons) *gōmer* (Gomer the complete) *'ašakănaz* (Ashkenaz sprinkled sparks) *wariypat* (Riphath the spoken) *watōgaramāh* (Togarmah will break)
καὶ *kai* (and) **υἱοὶ** *uioi* (the sons) **Γαμερ** *Gamer* (of Gomer) **Ασχαναζ** *Aschanaz* (Ashkenaz) **καὶ** *kai* (and) **Ριφαθ** *Riphath* (Riphath) **καὶ** *kai* (and) **Θοργαμα** *Thorgama* (Torgamah)
porro (following) ***filii*** (the sons) ***Gomer*** (of Gomer) ***Aschenez*** (Ashkenaz) ***et*** (and) ***Rifath*** (Riphath) ***et*** (and) ***Thogorma*** (Togarmah)
And the sons of Gomer; Ashkenaz, and Riphath, and Togarmah.
The sons of Gomer, the complete, are Ashkenaz, sprinkled sparks, Riphath, the spoken word and Togarmah, who will end the connection.

If these were only the literal sons of an individual historical personality, what would be their universal relevance? Why not mention the sons of anyone of our ancient African ancestors. Truthfully,

Gomer is the metaphor for the complete spherical structure of space. This shape manifests itself in all its possible physical development,

1) The first one is Ashkenaz. It represents the light spreading itself like photons or sparks of fire. In fact, *'Ashkĕnaz* (אַשְׁכְּנַז) means

   "*a man as sprinkled: fire as scattered.*"[2905]

   "The modern [commentators]... understand it to be *Germany*, and call that country by this Hebrew name, which is only to be attributed to their wonderful ignorance of geography."[2906]

   "The old period of the Old Testament... the world was [conceived as] a little three layer cake, and the world consisted of something a few hundred miles around the Near Eastern centers there. No one ever heard of the Aztecs, you know, or the Chinese, even. And so those whole peoples were not considered, even, as part of the problem to be dealt with."[2907]

   However, *Ashkenaz* does not refer to any individual and/or population. It is light traveling in space and spreading like a wild fire in all directions.

2) The second son is *Riphath* (רִיפַת). It is *riyphath*, the *spoken* (רִיפַת)[2908] words. Thus, it is sound resonating throughout the entire universe along different latitudes and longitudes.
3) Finally, *Togarmah* (תֹּגַרְמָה)[2909] is the *one who will break*[2910] *and end the influence* of space relations, thus, the borders of the Universe itself.

Here, we may understand that the Big Bang explosion, in the form of both light and sound, defines the borders of the entire universe. However, they refer not only to the physical world but also to the oneiric one. In dreams, in fact, we experience space and light. Similarly, the Arthurian saga describes of the light of dream when

"the king and all went unto the court, and every knight knew his own place ... So when ... all sieges [seats, centers of power]..., anon there befell a marvellous adventure, that all the doors and windows of the [bodily] palace shut by themself. Not for then the hall was not greatly darked; and therewith they were all abashed [lowered] both one and other."[2911]

10:4-The Sons of Javan

וּבְנֵי יָוָן אֱלִישָׁה וְתַרְשִׁישׁ כִּתִּים וְדֹדָנִים:
ubanēy (the sons) *yāvān* (of Javan) *'ĕliyšāh* (Elishah, God of the coming one) *watarašiyš* (Tarshish, the precious one) *kitiym* (Kittim, the bruisers) *wadōdāniym* (Dodanim, the "leaders")
καὶ *kai* (and) **υἱοὶ** *uioi* (the sons) **Ιωυαν** *Iōuan* (of Javan) **Ελισα** *Elisa* (Elishah) **καὶ** *kai* (and) **Θαρσις** *Tharsis* (Tarshish) **Κίτιοι** *Kitioi* (Kittim) **Ῥόδιοι** *Rodioi* (Rhodian)[2912]
filii (the sons) ***autem*** (also) ***Iavan*** (of Javan) ***Elisa*** (Elishah) ***et*** (and) ***Tharsis*** (Tarshish) ***Cetthim*** (Kittim) ***et*** (and) ***Dodanim*** (Dodanim)
And the sons of Javan; Elishah, and Tarshish, Kittim, and Dodanim.
The sons of Javan are Elishah, *God of the coming one*, Tarshish, *the precious one*, Kittim, *the bruisers* and Dodanim, *the leader*.

This verse continues the list of epistemic distinctions of space. From *Javan*, the wandering and drifting Northern space, derive,

1) First *Elishah* (אֱלִישָׁה),[2913] meaning *the God of the coming*. It is the space projection towards time expectations.
2) Second *Tarshish* (תַּרְשִׁישׁ),[2914] meaning the corresponding direction to a *precious* space.
3) Third *Kittim* (כִּתִּים),[2915] meaning a contained space, like an *island*.
4) Forth *Dodanim* (דֹּדָנִים),[2916] meaning the *leading* direction of space.

10:5-Geographic, Ethnic and Linguistic Distinctions for Japheth's Offspring

מֵאֵלֶּה נִפְרְדוּ אִיֵּי הַגּוֹיִם בְּאַרְצֹתָם אִישׁ לִלְשֹׁנוֹ לְמִשְׁפְּחֹתָם בְּגוֹיֵהֶם:
mē'ēleh (for these origins) nip*aradu* (have been divided) *'iyēy* (the islands) *hagvōyim* (of the nations) *ba'araṣōtām* (in lands) *'iyš* (every one) *lilašōnvō* (language) *lamišapaḥōtām* (families) *bəgvōyēhem* (in their nations)
ἐκ *ek* (from) **τούτων** *toutōn* (these) **ἀφωρίσθησαν** *aphōristhēsan* (were divided) **νῆσοι** *nēsoi*

(islands) **τῶν** *tōn* (of the) **ἐθνῶν** *ethnōn* (people) **ἐν** *en* (in) **τῇ** *tē* (the) **γῇ** *gē* (land) **αὐτῶν** *autōn* (their) **ἕκαστος** *ekastos* (each) **κατὰ** *kata* (according to) **γλῶσσαν** *glōssan* (language) **ἐν** *en* (in) **ταῖς** *tais* (the) **φυλαῖς** *phulais* (race) **αὐτῶν** *autōn* (their) **καὶ** *kai* (and) **ἐν** *en* (in) **τοῖς** *tois* (the) **ἔθνεσιν** *ethnesin* (ethnicity) **αὐτῶν** *autōn* (their)
ab (from) ***his*** (these) ***divisae*** (divided) ***sunt*** (are) ***insulae*** (the islands) ***gentium*** (of the people) ***in*** (in) ***regionibus*** (regions) ***suis*** (their) ***unusquis-*** (each one)***que*** (and) ***secundum*** (according to) ***linguam*** (language) ***et*** (and) ***familias*** (families) ***in*** (in) ***nationibus*** (nations) ***suis*** (their)
By these were the isles of the Gentiles divided in their lands; every one after his tongue, after their families, in their nations.
According to their origin, the islands of the nations have been parted in their lands, every one according to their language, families and nations.

These (אֵלֶּה *ēleh*) epistemic space-structures divide (פָּרַד *parad*) families (מִשְׁפָּחָה *mishpachah*) and nations (גּוֹי *gowy*) as island-(אִי *'iy*) lands (אֶרֶץ *'erets*) within various populations each one based on their different languages (לָשׁוֹן *lashown*). Note that language is in the paradigm of *riphath* (רִיפַת), the *spoken one.*

This means that each consciousness-*of* has individual perspectives. What we see may differ from what you see due to different angulations. Thinking individualities determine these collective differences, which become separate cultural worldviews and distinct perspectives.

Furthermore, this takes place before the division of tongues, thus, inconsistently precedes the metaphoric Babel tower, as we will analyze in the next chapter. Therefore, a non-metaphoric reading of this and/or the next chapter would lead to an evident chronological apparent discrepancy.

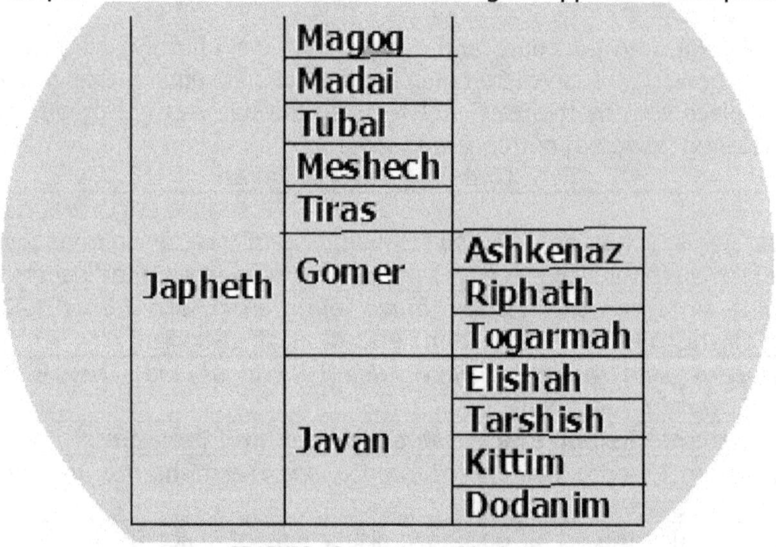

GRAPHIC: *Generations of Japheth*

Time, causality and space are forms of knowledge. From the space-form derive all directions.

10-II SECTION: CAUSALITY PARADIGMS

10:6-The Sons of Ham

וּבְנֵי חָם כּוּשׁ וּמִצְרַיִם וּפוּט וּכְנָעַן׃
ubanēy (the sons) *ḥām* (of Ham) *kuš* (Cush, black) *umiṣarayim* (Mizraim, edge) *upuṭ* (Phut, bow) *ukanā ʿan* (Canaan, lowland)
υἱοὶ *uioi* (the sons) **δὲ** *de* (but) **Χαμ** *Cham* (of Ham) **Χους** *Chous* (Cush) **καὶ** *kai* (and) **Μεσραιμ** *Mesraim* (Mizraim) **Φουδ** *Phoud* (Phut) **καὶ** *kai* (and) **Χανααν** *Chanaan* (Canaan)
filii (the sons) ***autem*** (also) ***Ham*** (of Ham) ***Chus*** (Cush) ***et*** (and) ***Mesraim*** (Mizraim) ***et*** (and) ***Fut*** (Phut) ***et*** (and) ***Chanaan*** (Canaan)
And the sons of Ham; Cush, and Mizraim, and Phut, and Canaan.
The offspring of Ham, causality, are *the dark* Cush, *the double* Mizraim, Phut *the archer*, and Canaan, *the dealer*.

The literal reading of this chapter, as a list of the original populations of the Earth, not only is irrelevant for the rest of humanity spread out on our globe, but also it is subatomic compared to the entire Universe. Definitely, it is not relevant from the perspective of a Text that asserts to be Universal Revelation.

Scripture becomes universally relevant if we read it from an epistemological perspective. Then, the gnoseological forms of space (Japheth), causality (Ham) and time (Shem) become the active modality of all beings. From Ham, the *heated* interactive cause, derive his offspring as his effects,

1) *Cush* (כּוּשׁ),[2917] means *black*. The first son of Ham-dream refers to the *dark* cause of oneiric visions encircled by the river Gihon, *Which-Gushes-Fourth*, that, as we have seen, surrounds (סָבַב *cabab*) the entire nocturnal sleeping Black (כּוּשׁ *kuwsh*) Realm (אֶרֶץ 'erets).[2918] From an astronomical perspective it can refer to the primal uncaused cause like the Big Bang.
2) The second son is *Mizraim* (מִצְרַיִם),[2919] dual of *matsowr* (מָצוֹר),[2920] which means *double distress* or *stronghold*. It is the same as *matsowr* (מָצוֹר),[2921] which gives the sense of *distress*[2922] limit. It derives from *tsuwr* (צוּר),[2923] meaning confine. Therefore, *Mizraim* refers to the double aspect of causality, namely, a) the cause and b) the effect, which are its two limiting polarities.
3) *Phut* (פּוּט),[2924] means *bow*, or *archer*. Therefore, the third element deriving from causality is the intentional aiming of the *archer-cause* securely drawing towards its effect.
4) The fourth son is *Canaan* (כְּנַעַן).[2925] As previously discussed, he is the synchronized trade *deal* web of all cause/effect relations.

10:7-The Sons of Cush and Raamah

וּבְנֵי כוּשׁ סְבָא וַחֲוִילָה וְסַבְתָּה וְרַעְמָה וְסַבְתְּכָא וּבְנֵי רַעְמָה שְׁבָא וּדְדָן׃
ubanēy (the sons) *kuš* (Cush) *sabā'* (drinking Seba) *waḥăviylāh* (circle Havilah) *wasabatāh* (striking Sabtah) *wara ʿamāh* (horse's mane Raamah) *wasabatakā'* (striking Sabtecha) *ubanēy* (the sons) *ra ʿamāh* (Raamah) *šabā'* (seven oats Sheba) *udadān* (leading Dedan)
υἱοὶ *uioi* (the sons) **δὲ** *de* (but) **Χους** *Chous* (of Cush) **Σαβα** *Saba* (Seba) **καὶ** *kai* (and) **Ευιλα** *Euila* (Havilah) **καὶ** *kai* (and) **Σαβαθα** *Sabatha* (Sabtah) **καὶ** *kai* (and) **Ρεγμα** *Regma* (Raamah) **καὶ** *kai* (and) **Σαβακαθα** *Sabakatha* (Sabtecha) **υἱοὶ** *uioi* (the sons) **δὲ** *de* (but) **Ρεγμα** *Regma* (of Raamah) **Σαβα** *Saba* (Sheba) **καὶ** *kai* (and) **Δαδαν** *Dadan* (Dedan)
filii (the sons) ***Chus*** (of Cush) ***Saba*** (Seba) ***et*** (and) ***Hevila*** (Havilah) ***et*** (and) ***Sabatha*** (Sabtah) ***et*** (and) ***Regma*** (Raamah) ***et*** (and) ***Sabathaca*** (Sabtecha) ***filii*** (the sons) ***Regma*** (of Raamah) ***Saba*** (Sheba) ***et*** (and) ***Dadan*** (Dedan)
And the sons of Cush; Seba, and Havilah, and Sabtah, and Raamah, and Sabtecha: and the sons of Raamah; Sheba, and Dedan.
The sons of Cush are, the *drinking* Seba, the *circle* Havilah, the *striking* Sabtah, the *horse's mane* Raamah and *striking* Sabtecha; the sons of Raamah are, the *seven oats* Sheba and the *leading* Dedan.

From the dark Cush, derive five new aspects or metaphoric sons of the epistemic form of causality,

1) <u>Seba</u> (סְבָא),[2926] means *drink thou*. It indicates the stupor of the *ancestor* Noah when the bubbling and effervescent wine-intoxication influenced him. Therefore, it is the mind-altering effect caused by exiting the resting state and entering in the dream realm from dreamless sleep.

2) <u>Havilah</u> (חֲוִילָה *Chaviylah*), means *circle*,[2927] from the verb *chuwl* (חוּל),[2928] to twist, to whirl, as a tautological cause-effect. That is, a cause that produces itself as effect. It indicates a self-contained house, a part of the Garden of Eden, namely, the circular abundant Pison river producer of gold, which flows through it.[2929] An example, this circularity is the thought that thinks of itself as thought, thus causing itself as dreaming sequence. In fact, dreams are thoughts that perceive themselves as internal thought-visions. Another example is a sounding-word causing itself as an echo effect reverberating off a reflecting medium.

3) <u>Sabtah</u> (סַבְתָּא),[2930] signifies *striking, breaking through* the previous encircled causality.[2931] Thus, it signifies the linear process of a cause producing an effect different from its cause.

4) <u>Raamah</u> (רַעְמָה),[2932] meaning *the trembling* or *moving of a horse*, is the same as *ra'mah*,[2933] meaning *vibration, quivering, mane* of horse. This is the *hot* aspect of Ham, the continuous vibrating cause-effect-chain-reaction of the mind, allegorically labeled as a galloping horse, affecting the whole world.

5) <u>Sabtecha</u> (סַבְתְּכָא)[2934] is similar to his brother Raamah. *Sabtah* means *striking*. Its root (סבב *sabab*) denotes the action of *breaking* that horse's gallop. This is further confirmed by the ending (כאה *ka'a*)[2935] of the name, which signifies *submitting*, yielding to the quivering effect.

However, the causalities of the metaphorical horse *Raamah*, continue as his two projections,

I) <u>Sheba</u> (שְׁבָא)[2936] is connected to *sheba* (שבע), the number *seven*, namely, the days during which the act of creation causes the world. Similarly, in the Bṛhadāraṇyaka Upanishad, the primordial horse travels the whole circle of a year to produce the world.[2937]

II) <u>Dedan</u> (דְדָן),[2938] meaning *low country*, derives from *dada* (דדה) meaning *leading forward*[2939] the intended effect, the *lower* aspect of its higher causing parent.

10:8–Nimrod son of Cush

וְכוּשׁ יָלַד אֶת־נִמְרֹד הוּא הֵחֵל לִהְיוֹת גִּבֹּר בָּאָרֶץ׃
wakuš (Cush) *yālaḏ* (begat) *'eṯ* (and) *nimarōḏ* (Nimrod) *hu'* (he) *hēḥēl* (began) *lihaywōṯ* (to be) *gibōr* (a powerful one) *bā'āreṣ* (on earth)
Χους *Chous* (Cush) δὲ *de* (but) ἐγέννησεν *egennēsen* (begot) τὸν *ton* (the) Νεβρωδ *Nebrōd* (Nimrod) οὗτος *outos* (he) ἤρξατο *ērxato* (began) εἶναι *einai* (to be) γίγας *gigas* (a powerful one) ἐπὶ *epi* (on) τῆς *tēs* (the) γῆς *gēs* (earth)
porro (following) **Chus** (Cush) *genuit* (generated) **Nemrod** (Nimrod) *ipse* (the same) *coepit* (started) *esse* (to be) *potens* (powerful) *in* (on) *terra* (the earth)
And Cush begat Nimrod: he began to be a mighty one in the earth.
Cush begat Nimrod and he began to be a powerful one on earth

From Cush, the darkness of the dream world, derives Nimrod, another aspect of the epistemic causality-form configuration, a sixth metaphoric son. The name *Nimrowd* (נִמְרֹד)[2940] means *rebel* or *valiant*. We will explain the metaphor of his personified relation to causality in the commentary of the next verse.

10:9-Nimrod the Hunter

הוּא־הָיָה גִבֹּר־צַיִד לִפְנֵי יְהוָה עַל־כֵּן יֵאָמַר כְּנִמְרֹד גִּבּוֹר צַיִד לִפְנֵי יְהוָה׃
hu' (he) *hāyāh* (was) *gibōr* (a powerful) *ṣayiḏ* (hunter) *lip̄anēy* (before) *yahvāh* (the Transcendent) *'al* (upon) *kēn* (therefore) *yē'āmar* (they say) *kanimarōḏ* (Nimrod) *gibwōr* (powerful) *ṣayiḏ* (hunter) *lip̄anēy* (before) *yahvāh* (the Transcendent)
οὗτος *autos* (he) ἦν *ēn* (was) γίγας *gigas* (a powerful) κυνηγὸς *kunēgos* (hunter) ἐναντίον *enantion* (before) κυρίου *kuriou* (the Lord) τοῦ *tou* (the) θεοῦ *theou* (God) διὰ *dia* (therefore)

τοῦτο *touto* (they) **ἐροῦσιν** *erousin* (say) **ὡς** *ōs* (that) **Νεβρωδ** *Nebrōd* (Nimrod) **γίγας** *gigas* (the powerful) **κυνηγὸς** *kunēgos* (hunter) **ἐναντίον** *enantion* (before) **κυρίου** *kuriou* (the Lord)
et (and) ***erat*** (he was) ***robustus*** (a robust) ***venator*** (hunter) ***coram*** (before) ***Domino*** (the Lord) ***ab*** (from) ***hoc*** (this) ***exivit*** (came out) ***proverbium*** (the proverb) ***quasi*** (as) ***Nemrod*** (Nimrod) ***robustus*** (the mighty) ***venator*** (hunter) ***coram*** (brfore) ***Domino*** (the Lord)
He was a mighty hunter before the LORD: wherefore it is said, Even as Nimrod the mighty hunter before the LORD.
He was a powerful hunter in the eyes of the Transcendent. That is why there is the saying, "*As Nimrod the powerful hunter before the Transcendent.*"

Nimrod is the hunter, *tsayid*.[2941] The word derives from *tsuwd*,[2942] namely, the one who
"*lies in wait for the catch.*"[2943]

Again, with a literal reading, why would this figure be relevant for a divine revelation? Why would God refer to Nimrod, a single individual, if not in reference to a universal paradigm? In fact, the name Nimrod is an aphorism regarding an epistemic structure understood by all sentient beings. Similarly, a chess player plans a move that will cause checkmate. That action is that which is common to the entire sentient behavior. In fact,

> "a scent blown into the hive can trigger a return to the site where the bees previously encountered this odor."[2944]

Cause/effect takes place with a predator and the prey.[2945] Now, this is exactly the causal relation between the subject and the object. In fact, the object becomes also *tsayid*, namely, *the provision*, *the food* or *the food-supply*[2946] of the hunter. In a way, we can say that the predator (*viz. Nimrod*) is another aspect of the rebellious couple (*viz.* Adam/Eve) and the food is the forbidden fruit. The powerful one, *viz. gibbowr*,[2947] *is the mighty mind itself in its constant hunting, noetic tension causing its prey to be its noematic effect. This hunting activity takes place at the* presence[2948] of the Transcendent *Yĕhovah* (יְהוָה). This is true in two senses.

a) Every act of knowledge refers to a known object conceived and understood as a reality external, *viz. transcendent*, to the subject itself. As an example, you perceive this book as an object persisting in its independence from you.
b) Every act of knowledge takes place before the Transcendent Awareness Itself. Indeed, Awareness is the constant guarantor of every act of perception.

10:10-Nimrod's Hunting Grounds

וַתְּהִי רֵאשִׁית מַמְלַכְתּוֹ בָּבֶל וְאֶרֶךְ וְאַכַּד וְכַלְנֵה בְּאֶרֶץ שִׁנְעָר׃   *watahiy* (was) *rē'šiyṯ* (beginning) *mamalaḵatwō* (kingdom) *bāḇel* (Babel, confusion) *wa'ereḵə* (Erech, distance) *wa'akaḏ* (Accad, subtle) *waḵalanēh* (Calneh, sky fortress) *ba'ereṣ* (in the land) *šina'ār* (of Shinar, of two rivers)
καὶ *kai* (and) **ἐγένετο** *egeneto* (started) **ἀρχὴ** *archē* (first) **τῆς** *tēs* (the) **βασιλείας** *basileias* (kingdom) **αὐτοῦ** *autou* (his) **Βαβυλὼν** *Babulōn* (Babel) **καὶ** *kai* (and) **Ορεχ** *Orech* (Erech) **καὶ** *kai* (and) **Αρχαδ** *Archad* (Accad) **καὶ** *kai* (and) **Χαλαννη** *Chalannē* (Calneh) **ἐν** *en* (in) **τῇ** *tō* (the) **γῇ** *gē* (land) **Σενναар** *Sennaar* (Shinar)
fuit (was) ***autem*** (also) ***principium*** (beginning) ***regni*** (of kingdom) ***eius*** (his) ***Babylon*** (Babel) ***et*** (and) ***Arach*** (Erech) ***et*** (and) ***Archad*** (Accad) ***et*** (and) ***Chalanne*** (Calneh) ***in*** (in) ***terra*** (the land) ***Sennaar*** (of Shinar)
And the beginning of his kingdom was Babel, and Erech, and Accad, and Calneh, in the land of Shinar.
The beginning of his kingdom in Shinar, *the land of two rivers*, was Babel, the *confusion*, Erech, the *stretching out*, the *subtle* Accad and Calneh, the *fortress* in the *sky*.

Nimrod's causative hunting begins (ראשית *re'shiyth)* in this causal dimension, the kingdom (מַמְלָכָה *mamlakah)* of *Shinar*, *viz. the land of two rivers* (שִׁנְעָר *Shin'ar*). They are the two flowing aspects of cause and effect. Causality is the *long*, *Erech*,[2949] causality *stretching out*[2950] to reach its effect as a chain reaction of multiplicity, namely, *Babel, the land of confusion.*[2951] There are two further aspects of causality. Eventually, we will examine their meaning in the next chapter. Furthermore, Nimrod, the hunting cause, can be *subtly elusive*, like the meaning of the name *Accad,* [2952] and/or like the *fortress of Anu*, named *Calneh.*[2953] *Anu* or *An* is the Sumerian name[2954] for sky or heaven. Thus, the *fortress of the sky* is a metaphor for the Principle of Sufficient Reason.[2955] This is the strong higher foundation of the primeval cause, which states that nothing is made out of nothing. Logically, every existing effect has its cause and reason for existing.

A reader may argue,

'In every controversial interpretation, you come up with arbitrary metaphorical explanation of epistemic configurations.'

We reply,

'It may seem arbitrary. However, we must step back in the ancient mentality. Then, how would have been possible to formulate universal expressions understandable by the average person? Then, the philosophical terminologies we use today, as 'epistemic structures,' 'paradigms,' etc., were not used. Later, Plato himself had to clarify his philosophy with numerous allegories. Therefore, as an example, no one looks for his mythic cave.[2956] *Jesus, in his sermons, used many paradigmatic parables. Thus, for instance, no one tries to research the actual historical figure of the prodigal son.*[2957] *However, ancient terminologies or metaphors are still comprehensible by the average person. Furthermore, even in our times, we need to clarify the meaning of philosophical terms.*

In the ancient world, how could one have expressed the universality of concepts such as cause and/or subject? Namely, how could one have conveyed the abstract general idea of 'prime agent,' viz. the one who actively produces and/or passively suffers any action whatsoever? Aren't the doer and the sufferer like enclosed in a subtle (Accad) or higher fortress (Anu) within the confines of which actions take place? On the other hand, as we repeatedly stated, why the city of Calneh, as such meaningless for us, would be relevant today so to deserve mention in a Timeless Revealed Text? Only if it refers to universal epistemic structures, then, the story becomes very relevant for us.'

10:11-Nimrod in the Land of Asshur

מִן־הָאָרֶץ הַהִוא יָצָא אַשּׁוּר וַיִּבֶן אֶת־נִינְוֵה וְאֶת־רְחֹבֹת עִיר וְאֶת־כָּלַח׃   *min* (from) *hā'āreṣ* (that land) *hahiw'* (he) *yāṣā'* (went out) *'ašur* (in Asshur step) *wayiben* (he built) *'eṯ* (and) *niynavēh* (Nineveh, the abode of Ninus) *wa'eṯ* (with) *rəḥōḇōṯ* (Rehoboth, broad or open place) *'iyr* (city) *wa'eṯ* (with) *kālaḥ* (Calah, vigorous)
ἐκ *ek* (from) **τῆς** *tēs* (the) **γῆς** *gēs* (land) **ἐκείνης** *ekeinēs* (that one) **ἐξῆλθεν** *exēlthein* (came) **Ασσουρ** *Assour* (to Asshur) **καὶ** *kai* (and) **ᾠκοδόμησεν** *ōkodomēsen* (built) **τὴν** *tēn* (the) **Νινευη** *Nineuē* (Nineveh) **καὶ** *kai* (and) **τὴν** *tēn* (the) **Ροωβωθ** *Roōbōth* (Rehoboth) **πόλιν** *polin* (city) **καὶ** *kai* (and) **τὴν** *tēn* (the) **Χαλαχ** *Chalach* (Calah)
de (from) ***terra*** (land) ***illa*** (that) ***egressus*** (exited) ***est*** (is) ***Assur*** (to Asshur) ***et*** (and) ***aedificavit*** (built) ***Nineven*** (Nineveh) ***et*** (and) ***plateas*** (open plateau) ***civitatis*** (city) ***et*** (and) ***Chale*** (Calah)
Out of that land went forth Asshur, and builded Nineveh, and the city Rehoboth, and Calah.
He went out from that land stepped towards Asshur and built Nineveh, the abode of Ninus, with Rehoboth, the *broad city*, and with *vigorous* Calah.

Going out (יָצָא *yatsa'*) *from* (מִן *min*) *that land* (הָאָרֶץ *hā'āreṣ*), Nimrod *successfully advanced* [2958] his *step* (אַשּׁוּר *'Ashshuwr*), *Asshur.*[2959] There, he *causes* and *erects*[2960] *Nineveh,*[2961] which is *the abode of Ninus*, his own house. In fact, Apollodorus of Athens confirms that

"Ninus is Nimrod himself."[2962]

Therefore, the house of Ninus, Nineveh, is his own powerhouse. It is a *city*[2963] with *wide streets, viz. Rehoboth,*[2964] with *open plazas*[2965] and *growing*[2966] dream potentials. Additionally, as his city, it is *Calah*, meaning *full of strength*[2967] and *vigorously completed* [2968] wakefulness. In fact, Nimrod, the causing agent, is like King Arthur of Camelot, the

"once king and future king."[2969]

He is the subject, as the one who causes and builds this entire epistemic structure.

10:12-The City of the Dead

וְאֶת־רֶסֶן בֵּין נִינְוֵה וּבֵין כָּלַח הִוא הָעִיר הַגְּדֹלָה׃ *wa'eṯ* (with) *resen* (Resen bridle) *bēyn* (between) *niynəvēh* (Nineveh) *uḇēyn* (between) *kālaḥ* (Calah) *hiv'* (it) *hā'iyr* (city) *hagəḏōlāh* (great)
καὶ *kai* (and) **τὴν** *tēn* (the) **Δασεμ** *Dasem* (Resen) **ἀνὰ** *ana* (in) **μέσον** *meson* (between) **Νινευη** *Nineuē* (Nineveh) **καὶ** *kai* (and) **ἀνὰ** *ana* (in) **μέσον** *meson* (between) **Χαλαχ** *Chalach* (Calah) **αὕτη** *autē* (this) **ἡ** *ē* (the) **πόλις** *polis* (city) **ἡ** *ē* (the) **μεγάλη** *megalē* (great)
Resen (Resen) ***quoque*** (also) ***inter*** (between) ***Nineven*** (Nineveh) ***et*** (and) ***Chale*** (Calah) ***haec*** (this one) ***est*** (is) ***civitas*** (city) ***magna*** (great)
And Resen between Nineveh and Calah: the same *is* a great city.
The great city of Resen is the *restraining bridle* between Nineveh and Calah

We should understand that all these citadels are metaphors for the psychophysical epistemic causal structures of this mind. Nimrod/Ninus is, like Arthur of the Celtic lore, the once subject-king who

"lies here,"[2970]

in the great city of *Resen*. This name means the *bridle of the horse*, the *halter* (רֶסֶן *recen*)[2971] or the *restrainer* (רֶסֶן *recen*),[2972] where the horse comes to a halt. This city is between the two polarities of *Nineveh*, the house of Nimrod's causality, and *Calah*, its vigorous effect. Thus, *Resen* is the *great*[2973] *city* (עִיר *'iyr)* of the *restraining bridle* (רֶסֶן *recen)* that *stops, raamah* (רַעְמָה), the ability of the horse to move between cause and effect. Indeed, that ability is the restless mind itself continuously on the move, vibrating between the subject and the object.

Thus, restraining the *vibrating-horse* is the end of the cause-effect-chain-reaction affecting the whole world. The mind silenced and restrained is equivalent to death or to redemption. Therefore, *Resen* is the city of the Dead. There Raamah (רַעְמָה), Nimrod's brother, with Sabtah and_Sabtecha, his other brothers, and his ancestor Ham's *hot vibrating, ra'mah*, expect either to die or to convert their course.

Creation causes an emanating ripple effect.

- The **I day** sublimates the **V day** and radiates the Circle of Light, the resting Auto-Transparent Self.
- The **II day** sublimates the **IV day** and produces the Circle of Consciousness, the dreaming I-consciousness, where thought thinks and experiences itself as dream.
- The **III day** sublimates the **VI day** and awakens the Circle of Perception where the Ego-consciousness thinks itself as this body *here and now* having the world as its representation.
- Then, the entire process reabsorbs in the stillness of the **VII day**.

This body is like a grown-horse that carries our pulsating mind through the world and, thus, is free to vibrate into thinking.[2974] The Indian tradition metaphorically describes the body as a chariot or a horse and the

"*faculty of thought as the reins.*"[2975]

Resen denotes the rein or the bridle. Its name in Sanskrit is *yama*, which means also the "*Restraining Judge*" who rules, as the Egyptian Osiris and the Greek god Pluto or Minos, over the reign of the dead.[2976]

The riddle[2977] of Cain and Abel's archetypes deals with death. Cain is the I-subject-*for*-itself. S/he is the personification of *everyone* who is

"*a tiller* (עָבַד *'abad*) *of the ground*,"[2978]

namely, a performer of deeds (עָבַד *'abad*) causing effects.

"*At the end of the day*,"[2979]

unwillingly, Cain sacrifices "*the fruits*"[2980] of the deeds of his/her historical active life. This means that death *restrains* him/her. On the other hand, Abel is the Self-*in*-itself who, aware and willingly, restrains the senses. Thus, s/he does not eat the fruit of the tree of knowledge. Consequently, Transcendent Awareness "*accepts*"[2981] Abel's sacrifice.

Following, however, Cain kills Abel. Therefore, there are four types of restraining taking place in the city of *Resen*,

1) Cain's subject epistemically *restrains* Abel, the other, and reduces him/her to an object, a "*you*," food for the thought of the-subject, the knower,
2) Cain *restrains* by physically murdering Abel,
3) Death *restrains* the life of all Cain-*land-tillers*, and
4) Abel *restrains* the senses to merge into Pure Awareness.

10:13-The Sons of Mizraim

וּמִצְרַיִם יָלַד אֶת־לוּדִים וְאֶת־עֲנָמִים וְאֶת־לְהָבִים וְאֶת־נַפְתֻּחִים׃
umiṣarayim (Mizraim) *yālaḏ* (generated) *'eṯ* (and) *luḏiym* (Ludim firebrands) *wa'eṯ* (with) *'ănāmiym* (Anamim) *wa'eṯ* (with) *lahāḇiym* (Lehabim) *wa'eṯ* (with) *napatuḥiym* (Naphtuhim)
καὶ *kai* (and) **Μεσραιμ** *Mesraim* (Mizraim) **ἐγέννησεν** *egennēsen* (generated) **τοὺς** *tous* (the) **Λουδιιμ** *Loudiim* (Ludim) **καὶ** *kai* (and) **τοὺς** *tous* (the) **Ενεμετιιμ** *Enemetiim* (Anamim) **καὶ** *kai* (and) **τοὺς** *tous* (the) **Λαβιιμ** *Labiim* (Lehabim) **καὶ** *kai* (and) **τοὺς** *tous* (the) **Νεφθαλιιμ** *Nephthaliim* (Naphtuhim)
at (and) ***vero*** (indeed) ***Mesraim*** (Mizraim) ***genuit*** (generated) ***Ludim*** (Ludim) ***et*** (and) ***Anamim*** (Anamim) ***et*** (and) ***Laabim*** (Lehabim) ***Nepthuim*** (Naphtuhim)
And Mizraim begat Ludim, and Anamim, and Lehabim, and Naphtuhim,
Mizraim generated Ludim, *the firebrand travails*, and Anamim, *the water afflictions*, and Lehabim, *the flaming swords*, and Naphtuhim, *the openings*.

Noticeably, the majority of offspring are sons. Allegorically, they connote the subject's noetic/*male* aspect implying their necessary noematic/*female* correlation. Again, here we must understand that each offspring is a universal category represented by the characteristics of different allegorical populations. Therefore, from *Mizraim*, meaning the two limit polarities of cause and effect, derive seven new aspects or metaphoric seeds of the epistemic form of causality,

1) *Ludim* means the *firebrand travails* [2982] caused by *fighting*[2983] and consequent wars.
2) *Anamim* means the *affliction caused by the waters*,[2984] as the ones of the deadly deluge.
3) *Lehabim* means *flames*,[2985] the perilous *blazing* and *burning sword*[2986] causing destructions.
4) *Naphtuhim* means *openings*;[2987] here, we must intend all open possible causalities.

10:14-And Other Sons

וְאֶת־פַּתְרֻסִים וְאֶת־כַּסְלֻחִים אֲשֶׁר יָצְאוּ מִשָּׁם פְּלִשְׁתִּים וְאֶת־כַּפְתֹּרִים׃ ס
wa'eṯ (with) *paṯarusiym* (Pathrusim) *wa'eṯ* (with) *kasaluḥiym* (Casluhim fortified) *'ăšer* (whom) *yāṣa'u* (came out) *mišām* (from) *pališatiym* (Philistim) *wa'eṯ* (with) *kap̄atōriym* (Caphtorim)
καὶ *kai* (and) **τοὺς** *tous* (the) **Πατροσωνιιμ** *Patrosōniim* (Pathrusim) **καὶ** *kai* (and) **τοὺς** *tous* (the) **Χασλωνιιμ** *Chaslōviim* (Casluhim) **ὅθεν** *othen* (from where) **ἐξῆλθεν** *exēlthen* (came) **ἐκεῖθεν** *ekeithen* (thence) **Φυλιστιιμ** *Phulistiim* (Philistim) **καὶ** *kai* (and) **τοὺς** *tous* (the) **Καφθοριιμ** *Kaphthoriim* (Caphtorim)
et (and) ***Phetrusim*** (Pathrusim) ***et*** (and) ***Cesluim*** (Casluhim) ***de*** (from) ***quibus*** (whom) ***egressi***

(exited) ***sunt*** (are) ***Philisthim*** (Philistim) ***et*** (and) ***Capthurim*** (Caphtorim)
And Pathrusim, and Casluhim, (out of whom came Philistim) and Caphtorim.
Furthermore, Pathrusim, the *lower region of the south*, Casluhim, the *fortified one*, producer of Philistim, the *immigrants*, and Caphtorim, the *crown*.

The next descents of *Mizraim*, the two polarities of causality, are

5) *Pathrusim*,[2988] namely *the lower region*,[2989] the secondary causes followed by
6) *Casluhim*, which means the *fortified one*[2990] who, regaining strength, *causes the generation* (יָצָא *yatsa*)[2991] of

   Philistim, the *immigrants*[2992] from the *land of wonderers*[2993] who

   "roll in ashes or dust (as an act of mourning)."[2994]

   Therefore, it confers the sense of recurrent causality returning from the state of death in a continuous migration of the causal agent, from one instance to another.
7) *Caphtorim*, means *crown*, *ornament*,[2995] namely, like Cain's mark (אות *'owth*) of subjectivity, which prevents him from being

   "*hurt by anyone who should find him.*"[2996]

10:15-The Sons of Canaan

וּכְנַעַן יָלַד אֶת־צִידֹן בְּכֹרוֹ וְאֶת־חֵת׃
uḵəna'an (Canaan) *yālaḏ* (begot) *'eṯ* (and) *ṣiyḏōn* (Sidon hunting) *bakōrvō* (firstborn) *wa'eṯ* (with) *ḥēṯ* (Heth terror)
Χαναακ *Chnaan* (Canaan) **δὲ** *de* (but) **ἐγέννησεν** *egennēsen* (generated) **τὸν** *ton* (the) **Σιδῶνα** *Sidōna* (Sidon) **πρωτότοκον** *prōtotokon* (firstborn) **καὶ** *kai* (and) **τὸν** *ton* (the) **Χετταῖον** *Chettaion* (Heth)
Chanaan (Canaan) ***autem*** (also) ***genuit*** (generated) ***Sidonem*** (Sidon) ***primogenitum*** (firstborn) ***suum*** (his) ***Ettheum*** (Heth)
And Canaan begat Sidon his firstborn, and Heth,
Canaan generated his firstborn, the *hunting* Sidon, and Heth, *fear*.

Imagine a pool table extending as the entire universe. One of the infinite balls on it, hitting a cluster of spheres, will set in motion, with a chain reaction, all the billiards on the table. Each one, then, becomes the cause of the motion of the other. Similarly, from Canaan, the trafficker, derive eleven new aspects or metaphoric sons of the epistemic causality-form. Actually, cause-effect multiplies as paradigmatic traits of different beings.

1) *Sidon*, meaning *hunting*,[2997] is, like Nimrod, the one who lies and waits for the effect as prey. Actually, he is the angler who *catches fish*[2998] from the ocean of objective possibilities. He is the firstborn (בְּכוֹר *běkowr*). Therefore, this is a new metaphor for the causing-agent, which logically precedes the effect of knowledge seized as a hunting prey.
2) *Heth* means *terror*, *fear*,[2999] *to be confused*.[3000] This is caused by the existential human condition. The *Bṛhadāraṇyaka Upanishad* declares that who realizes the epistemic loneliness,

   "*was afraid, therefore who is alone is afraid*... [Also] *fear derives only from a second*."[3001]

   This is what Sartre calls

   "being-seen-by-another... At each instant the Other *is looking at me*."[3002]

   "Hell is the others!"

   cries out Garcin, at the end of Sartre's play *No exit*, feeling

   "all those eyes intent on me. *Devouring* me."[3003]

   Paradoxically, however, the desire for fame is the selfish need to reverberate in the minds of other *devouring* us. The recognition is the way the ego affirms its superiority among other individuals. At times, this notoriety expresses itself without any care or compassion for competing neighbors. Nevertheless, fame is short lived, since also the notorious giants will inevitably tumble into dust.

10:16-More Sons of Canaan

וְאֶת־הַיְבוּסִי וְאֶת־הָאֱמֹרִי וְאֵת הַגִּרְגָּשִׁי׃
wa'eṯ (with) *hayaḇusiy* (Jebusite Jebus' descendants) *wa'eṯ* (with) *hā'ĕmōriy* (Amorite mountaineer) *wa'eṯ* (with) *hagiragāšiy* (Girgasite dwelling on a clayey soil)
καὶ *kai* (and) **τὸν** *ton* (the) **Ιεβουσαῖον** *Iebousaion* (Jebusite) **καὶ** *kai* (and) **τὸν** *ton* (the) **Αμορραῖον** *Amorraion* (Amorite) **καὶ** *kai* (and) **τὸν** *ton* (the) **Γεργεσαῖον** *Gergesaion* (Girgasite)
et (and) ***Iebuseum*** (Jebusite) ***et*** (and) ***Amorreum*** (Amorite) ***Gergeseum*** (Girgasite)
And the Jebusite, and the Amorite, and the Girgasite,
Jebusite, *descendants of those who trample on this place*, Amorite, *the mountaineers*, and the Girgasite, *who dwell on a clay soil.*

Again, here is a list of populations personifying causal relations, which reciprocally affect each other. They are the

3) The *Jebusite* meaning the *descendants of Jebus,*[3004] namely, the *threshing place*[3005] on which we *trample*[3006] daily.
4) The *Amorite*, namely, the *mountaineers,*[3007] who live on elevated social levels, and
5) The *Girgasite*, namely, those who *dwell on this clay soil* of objectivity.[3008]

10:17-The Hivite, Arkite and Sinite

וְאֶת־הַחִוִּי וְאֶת־הַעַרְקִי וְאֶת־הַסִּינִי׃
wa'eṯ (with) *haḥiuiy* (Hivite villagers) *wa'eṯ* (with) *ha'araqiy* (Arkite worrying) *wa'eṯ* (with) *hasiyniy* (Sinite thorn clay)
καὶ *kai* (and) **τὸν** *ton* (the) **Ευαῖον** *Euaion* (Hivite) **καὶ** *kai* (and) **τὸν** *ton* (the) **Αρουκαῖον** *Aroukaion* (Arkite) **καὶ** *kai* (and) **τὸν** *ton* (the) **Ασενναῖον** *Asennaion* (Sinite)
Eveum (Hivite) ***et*** (and) ***Araceum*** (Arkite) ***Sineum*** (Sinite)
And the Hivite, and the Arkite, and the Sinite,
The villagers Hivite, the worrying Arkite and the thorn and clay of Sinite.

Furthermore, the

6) *Hivite* means the *villager,*[3009] who abides in the *living breathing structure,*[3010] which makes the world known.[3011]
7) *Arkite* means the *worrying, gnawing one,*[3012] where
   "*there shall be weeping and gnawing of teeth.*"[3013]
8) *Sinite*, means this place of *thorns* and *clay.*[3014]

10:18-Canaanite Families Spread Out

וְאֶת־הָאַרְוָדִי וְאֶת־הַצְּמָרִי וְאֶת־הַחֲמָתִי וְאַחַר נָפֹצוּ מִשְׁפְּחוֹת הַכְּנַעֲנִי׃
wa'eṯ (with) *hā'aravāḏiy* (Arvadite shall break loose) *wa'eṯ* (with) *haṣamāriy* (Zamarite double woolen garments) *wa'eṯ* (with) *haḥămāṯiy* (fortified Hamathite) *wa'aḥar* (afterwards) *nāpōṣu* (scattered) *mišapaḥvōṯ* (the families) *hakana'ăniy* (of the Canaanites)
καὶ *kai* (and) **τὸν** *ton* (the) **Ἀράδιον** *Aradion* (Arvadite) **καὶ** *kai* (and) **τὸν** *ton* (the) **Σαμαραῖον** *Samaraion* (Zemarite) **καὶ** *kai* (and) **τὸν** *ton* (the) **Αμαθι** *Amathi* (Hamathite) **καὶ** *kai* (and) **μετὰ** *meta* (after) **τοῦτο** *touto* (that) **διεσπάρησαν** *diesparēsan* (spread out) **αἱ** *ai* (the) **φυλαὶ** *phulai* (pople) **τῶν** *tōn* (of the) **Χαναναίων** *Chananaiōn* (Canaanites)
et (and) ***Aradium*** (Arvadite) ***Samariten*** (Zamarite) ***et*** (and) ***Amatheum*** (Hamathite) ***et*** (and) ***post*** (after) ***haec*** (that) ***disseminati*** (spread) ***sunt*** (are) ***populi*** (the people) ***Chananeorum*** (of the Canaanites)
And the Arvadite, and the Zemarite, and the Hamathite: and afterward were the families of the Canaanites spread abroad.
The Arvadite, *who shall break loose wandering*, the Zamarite, *double woolen*, and the Hamathite fortress, after which, the families of the Canaanites scattered abroad.

All these populations are paradigms of causal relations among different peoples. More dwellers descend from Canaan, trafficking with surrounding populations, and they are,

9) *Arvadite*, those *who break loose*[3015] *freely wandering about,*[3016]

10) *Zemarite*, meaning the *double woolens*,[3017] namely, it is the bipolarity of the double skins of Adam and of Eve. Their *wool* or *fleece*[3018] is a metaphor for naked skin. Finally, the

11) *Hamathite*, means the *defense citadel*,[3019] namely, the *fortresses*[3020] of individuality in which every person takes refuge from the others.

Following (אחר *'achar*) this defensive reclusiveness, the original unity of the Canaanite paradigms or *families* (מִשְׁפָּחָה *mishpachah*) *brakes up* (פוץ *puwts*) *dispersing* into the world of cause-effect.

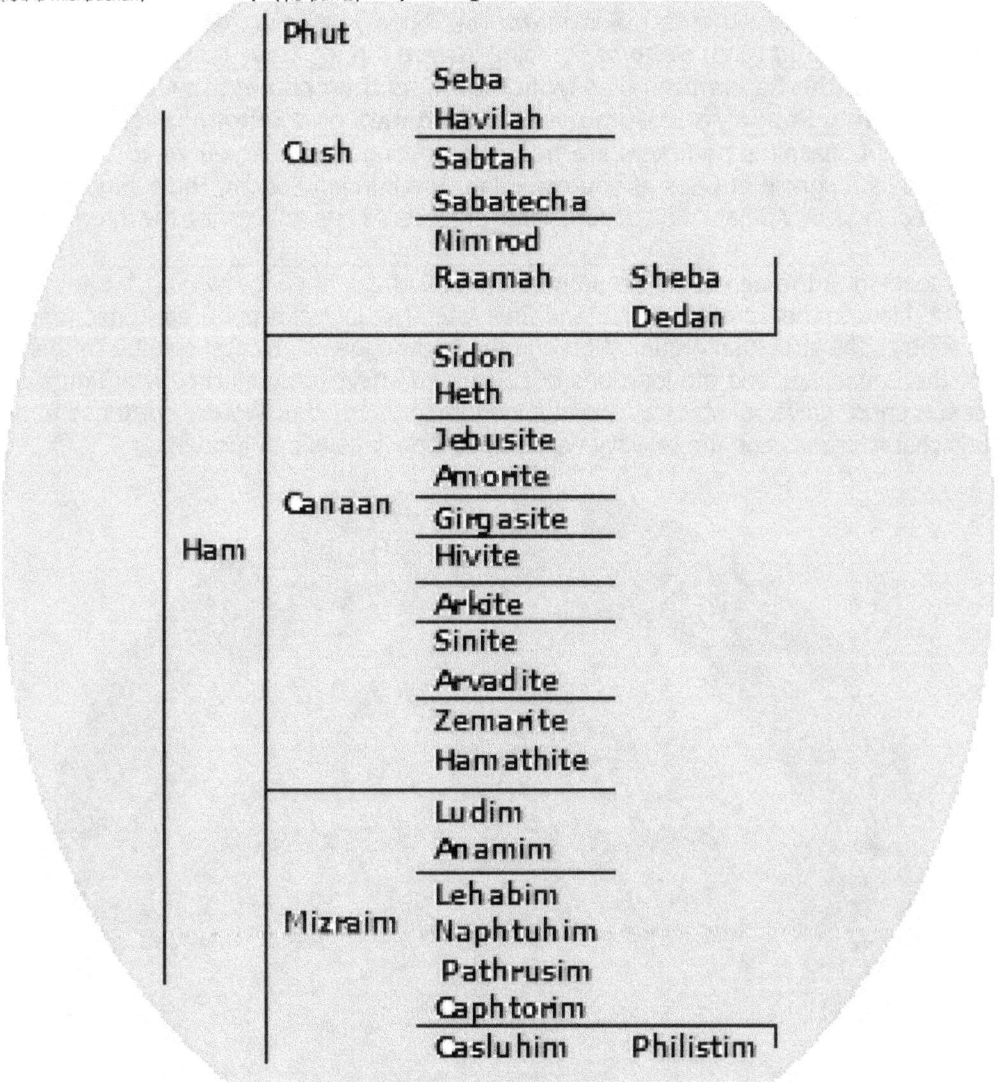

GRAPHIC: *Generations of Ham*

10:19-Journey Through the Mind

וַיְהִי גְּבוּל הַכְּנַעֲנִי מִצִּידֹן בֹּאֲכָה גְרָרָה עַד־עַזָּה בֹּאֲכָה סְדֹמָה וַעֲמֹרָה וְאַדְמָה וּצְבֹיִם עַד־לָשַׁע׃ *wayahiy* (is) *gabul* (border) *hakana'ăniy* (Canaanites traffickers) *miṣiydōn* (from the hunting Sidon) *bō'ăkāh* (as you go to) *ḡarārāh* (Gerar the lodging place) *'ad* (up to) *'azāh* (the strong Gaza) *bō'ăkāh* (as you come in) *sadōmāh* (the burning Sodom) wa'ămōrāh (submerged Gomorrah) *wa'adamāh* (in the red land of Admah) *uṣabōyim* (Zeboim gazelles) *'ad* (up to) *lāša'* (Lasha the break through fissure)
καὶ *kai* (and) **ἐγένοντο** *egenonto* (came in) **τὰ** *ta* (the) **ὅρια** *oria* (borders) **τῶν** *tōn* (of the) **Χαναναίων** *Chananaiōn* (Canaanites) **ἀπὸ** *apo* (from) **Σιδῶνος** *Sidōnos* (Sidon) **ἕως** *eōs* (till)

ἐλθεῖν *elthein* (one comes) **εἰς** *eis* (in to) **Γεραρα** *Gerara* (Gerar) **καὶ** *kai* (and) **Γάζαν** *Gazan* (Gaza) **ἕως** *eōs* (till) **ἐλθεῖν** *elthein* (one comes) **Σοδομων** *Sodomōn* (Sodom) **καὶ** *kai* (and) **Γομορρας** *Gomorras* (Gomorrah) **Αδαμα** *Adama* (Admah) **καὶ** *kai* (and) **Σεβωιμ** *Sebōim* (Zeboim) **ἕως** *eōs* (till) **Λασα** *Lasa* (Lasha)
facti- (made) ***que*** (and) ***sunt*** (are) ***termini*** (borders) ***Chanaan*** (of Canaan) ***venientibus*** (for those who come) ***a*** (from) ***Sidone*** (Sidon) ***Geraram*** (to Gerar) ***usque*** (up to) ***Gazam*** (Gaza) ***donec*** (till) ***ingrediaris*** (you enter) ***Sodomam*** (in Sodom) ***et*** (and) ***Gomorram*** (Gomorrah) ***et*** (and) ***Adama*** (Admah) ***et*** (and) ***Seboim*** (Zeboim) ***usque*** (up to) ***Lesa*** (Lasha)
And the border of the Canaanites was from Sidon, as thou comest to Gerar, unto Gaza; as thou goest, unto Sodom, and Gomorrah, and Admah, and Zeboim, even unto Lasha.
The limits of the Canaanites traffickers are from the hunting Sidon as you go to Gerar the lodging place, up to the stronghold of Gaza as you come into the burning Sodom, the submerged Gomorrah and in the red land of Admah, to Zeboim, land of gazelles, up to Lasha, the break through the fissure.

The meaning of the names of the primordial cities of *Sodom, viz. burning,*[3021] and *Gomorrah, viz. submersion,*[3022] hints to their predestination and final fate. The logical a-priori epistemic form of causality, as we saw, enables the structural organization and the knowledge of physical events. In this verse, again, the limits of the Canaanites and the locations of cause and effect are only rhetorical figure of speech, as the part for the entire universal physical causal configuration. In other words, epistemic forms cause the paradigmatic characteristics and the worldviews of entire populations and locations.

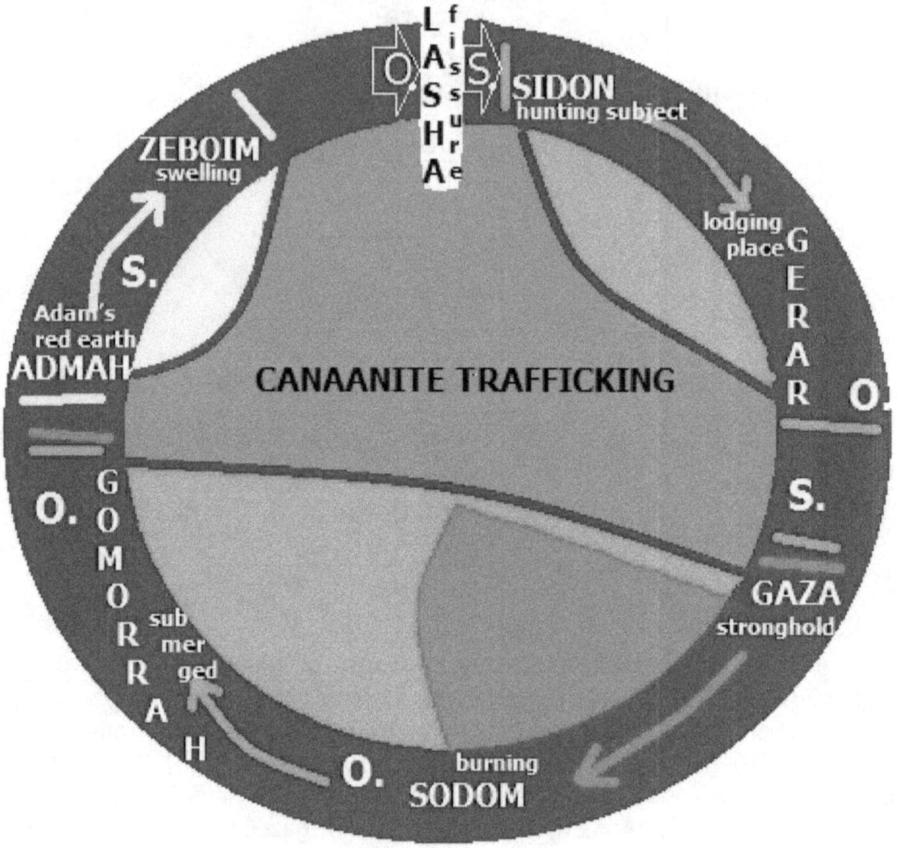

GRAPHIC: *The Border of the Canaanites*

The tension of cause-subject towards the effect-object and its return to itself constitutes the first causal dimension of the mind. Cause and effect are the *borders*[3023] or the *perimeter*[3024] limiting the

Canaanite *trafficking* (כְּנַעֲנִי *kěna`aniy*) causal epistemic activities. Thus, the limit of the subject is its object, as the border of the mind is its skull.

"*The limits of my language* mean the limits of my world."[3025]

As we saw, *Sidon*, meaning *hunting*[3026] or *fishing*,[3027] is the causing subject, which *goes*[3028] and returns into itself in his *lodging place*, namely, *Gerar*.[3029] There, it *drags* and *ponders over* (גָּרַר *garar*)[3030] its effect as *food for thought*. Its habitation is *Gaza*, the protected *stronghold*.[3031] From there, it *goes toward* (בּוֹא *bow'*) the suffering and *burning* of *Sodom*.[3032] *Gomorrah* is the other objective effect of *submersion*[3033] and *subjugation*[3034] caused by the flood. Obviously, Sodom and Gomorrah are just names, as we could say Hiroshima and Nagasaki, to convey the same general idea. Finally, the subject is Adam himself. In fact, another city-effect is *Admah*, *viz.* the original *red earth of Adam*.[3035] The next city-effect is *Zeboim*, the land of *gazelles*,[3036] in the sense of *prominently swift*[3037] outcome of effects.

The next and final perimeter city, *Lasha*, meaning *the break* through *opening*,[3038] needs some further explanation. As there is a thin line, a *fissure* between the REM dream state and NREM state of deep sleep, so there is from this last state and dying. At the moment of passing away, one leaves, willingly (*viz.* Abel) or unwillingly (*viz.* Cain), the state of daily existence. One enters the very personal, intimate and not communicable experience of death. That *fissure* is

"*as large as a razor's edge*... [it] *is the confining bridge, the boundary and passageway of these universes that keeps them separated*."[3039]

"*Narrow is the way, which leadeth unto life, and few there be that find it*."[3040]

"*The path,* [is] *the sharp edge of a razor, of difficult access* [and] *difficult to cross*."[3041]

"*Verily as large as this world space extends, so large is that space within the heart*."[3042]

This is *Lasha*, the narrow passageway that causes the interruption of the subject-object circle (גָּבַל *gabal*).

10:20-Geographic, Ethnic and Linguistic Distinctions for Ham's Offspring

אֵלֶּה בְנֵי־חָם לְמִשְׁפְּחֹתָם לִלְשֹׁנֹתָם בְּאַרְצֹתָם בְּגוֹיֵהֶם׃ ס   *'ēleh* (these) *ḇanēy* (the sons) *ḥām* (of Ham) *lamišapaḥōṯām* (after their families) *lilašōnōṯām* (after their languages) *ba'araṣōṯām* (in their lands) *bağwōyēhem* (in their nations) *s* (.)
οὗτοι *outoi* (these) **υἱοὶ** *uioi* (sons) **Χαμ** *Cham* (of Ham) **ἐν** *en* (in) **ταῖς** *tais* (the) **φυλαῖς** *phulais* (race) **αὐτῶν** *autōn* (their) **κατὰ** *kata* (according to) **γλῶσσαν** *glōssan* (language) **αὐτῶν** *autōn* (their) **ἐν** *en* (in) **τοῖς** *tois* (the) **χώραις** *chōrais* (space) **αὐτῶν** *autōn* (their) **καὶ** *kai* (and) **ἐν** *en* (in) **τοῖς** *tois* (the) **ἔθνεσιν** *ethnesin* (ethnicity) **αὐτῶν** *autōn* (their)
hii (these) ***filii*** (sons) ***Ham*** (of Ham) ***in*** (according to) ***cognationibus*** (families) ***et*** (and) ***linguis*** (languages) ***et*** (and) ***generationibus*** (generations) ***terris*** (countries) ***-que*** (and) ***et*** (and) ***gentibus*** (people) ***suis*** (their)
These *are* the sons of Ham, after their families, after their tongues, in their countries, *and* in their nations.
These are the sons of Ham after their families, their languages, their lands and their nations.

These (אֵלֶּה *ēleh*) structures metaphorically distinguish various epistemic archetypes causing various families (מִשְׁפָּחָה *mishpachah*), nations (גּוֹי *gowy*), and lands (אֶרֶץ *'erets*) all based on their different languages (לָשׁוֹן *lashown*) or views of the world. The distinction), outlined in this verse, of paradigmatic people, according to their languages (לָשׁוֹן *lashown*), is different from the confusion of languages, which will take place with the tower of Babel in the next chapter. Then, we will analyze the metaphorical meaning of that *towering confusion*.

Since the lap between cause and effect implies time and space, we could say that the cause predestined the current effect. On the cross,

"*Jesus knowing that all things were now accomplished and that which is written might reach its designated end... said, 'All is accomplished.' And he bowed his head, and gave up* [his] *life-breath*."[3043]

However, destiny is the *Present* (ἤδη *ēdē*) *accomplished* (τετέλεσται *tetelestai*) and irreversible situation, which happens and confronts us *now* (ἤδη *ēdē*). The past cause of this condition is *written* (γραφή *grafē*) *now* (ἤδη *ēdē*) in our memory. Thus, we find it *now* (ἤδη *ēdē*) ineluctably *predestined* (τελειωθῇ *teleiōthē*). When we *bow* (κλίνας *klinas*) our *head* (κεφαλὴν *kefalēn*), then, we find that memory in the heart of our current *breathing life* (πνεῦμα *pneuma*) "as a state of absolute independence from the nervous system."[3044]

Paradoxically, however, *pre*destination, as that which, from a (*pre*) past must reach a future destination, is not. In fact, nothing at all can be in the past and/or future as such. The past is only now as memory and the future is only now as projection.

All different aspects of causality stretch in the world of experience. As a predator, the cause captures its effect as pray. Populations and cities become paradigms of causal relations among different peoples

SUMMARY OF THE CAUSE-EFFECT GENERATIONS OF HAM

Cush ⇨ Black sleeping realm	*Seba* mind-altering effect of the cause	
	Havilah tautological cause-effect, thought thinking itself as dream	
	Sabtah linear process of cause producing a different effect	
	Raamah mind vibrating cause-effect ⇨	*Sheba* primary cause
		Dedan intended effect
	Sabtecha breaking the quivering effect of the horse's gallop	
	Nimrod powerful hunter in the land of cause/effect (*Shinar*) stretching out (*Erech*) toward the chain reaction (*Babel*) from his subtle (*Accad*) fortress of Sufficient Reason (*Calneh*) advancing (*Asshur*) in his abode (*Nineveh*) with the sleep halter (*Resen*) between potentially wide dream (*Rehoboth*) and strong wakefulness (*Calah*)	
Mizraim ⇨ double polarities cause-effect	*Ludim* war consequences.	
	Anamim affliction caused by the waters.	
	Lehabim means flames causing destructions.	
	Naphtuhim open possible causalities.	
	Pathrusim secondary causes	
	Casluhim regaining strength ⇨	*Philistim* recurrent causality
	Caphtorim mark of subjectivity	
Phut aiming effect.		
Canaan ⇨ cause/ effect relations	*Sidon* hunting the effect as prey he ponders over (*Gerar*) in his stronghold (*Gaza*) the burning (*Sodom*) and subjugated (*Gomorrah*) as subject (*Admah*) of the swift (*Zeboim*).	
	Heth fear caused by existential condition	
	Jebusite this threshing place	
	Amorite elevated social levels	
	Girgasite dwelling on clay	
	Hivite the villager in the breathing structure	
	Arkite the worrying ones	
	Sinite on thorns and clay.	
	Arvadite those who freely wander about.	
	Zemarite bipolarity of the double skins of Adam and of Eve.	
	Hamathite the fortresses of individuality.	

10-III SECTION: TIME PARADIGMS

10:21-Eber the Time Flow

וּלְשֵׁם יֻלַּד גַּם־הוּא אֲבִי כָּל־בְּנֵי־עֵבֶר אֲחִי יֶפֶת הַגָּדוֹל׃
ulašēm (to Shem) *yulaḏ* (begot) *gam* (also) *hu'* (came to pass) *'ăḇiy* (father) *kāl* (all) *banēy* (sons) *'ēḇer* (Eber) *'ăḥiy* (brother) *yep̄eṯ* (Japheth) *hagāḏvōl* (great)
καὶ *kai* (and) **τῷ** *tō* (the) **Σημ** *Sēm* (Shem) **ἐγενήθη** *egenēthē* (were born) **καὶ** *kai* (and) **αὐτῷ** *autō* (himself) **πατρὶ** *patri* (father) **πάντων** *pantōn* (all) **τῶν** *tōn* (the) **υἱῶν** *uiōn* (sons) **Εβερ** *Eber* (Eber) **ἀδελφῷ** *adelphō* (brother) **Ιαφεθ** *Iapheth* (Japheth) **τοῦ** *tou* (the) **μείζονος** *meizonos* (the great)
de (from) ***Sem*** (Shem) ***quoque*** (also) ***nati*** (born) ***sunt*** (are) ***patre*** (father) ***omnium*** (of all) ***filiorum*** (the sons) ***Eber*** (of Eber) ***fratre*** (brother) ***Iafeth*** (of Japheth) ***maiore*** (the greater)
Unto Shem also, the father of all the children of Eber, the brother of Japheth the elder, even to him were *children* born.
From Shem, the father of all Eber's sons and the brother of the great Japheth, came to pass that he also begot sons.

Shem is the universal time-paradigm. His *great*[3045] brother is Japheth, space. Indeed,

"space and time are welded together into a uniform four-dimensional continuum."[3046]

His other brother is Ham's causality-form, namely the cause that precedes its following effect.

From Shem derives Eber, the time flow. In fact, *Eber* means *the opposite side*[3047] of a geographical configurations, the *region behind*[3048] *the form of* space. It also means *to pass by* (עָבַר *'abar)*,[3049] as

"used of time passing by."[3050]

Finally, from Eber's *time flow*, derive, as offspring, all the different forms of time.

10:22-From Eternity to the Future

בְּנֵי שֵׁם עֵילָם וְאַשּׁוּר וְאַרְפַּכְשַׁד וְלוּד וַאֲרָם׃
banēy (sons) *šēm* (of Shem) *'ēylām* (Elam eternity) *wa'ašur* (Asshur step) *wa'arapakašaḏ* (Arphaxad) *waluḏ* (Lud conflict) *wa'ărām* (Aram exalted)
υἱοὶ *uioi* (the sons) **Σημ** *Sēm* (Shem) **Αιλαμ** *Ailam* (Elam) **καὶ** *kai* (and) **Ασσουρ** *Assour* (Asshur) **καὶ** *kai* (and) **Αρφαξαδ** *Arphaxad* (Arphaxad) **καὶ** *kai* (and) **Λουδ** *Loud* (Lud) **καὶ** *kai* (and) **Αραμ** *Aram* (Aram) **καὶ** *kai* (and) **Καιναν** *Kainan* (Cainan)[3051]
filii (the sons) ***Sem*** (of Shem) ***Aelam*** (Elam) ***et*** (and) ***Assur*** (Asshur) ***et*** (and) ***Arfaxad*** (Arphaxad) ***et*** (and) ***Lud*** (Lud) ***et*** (and) ***Aram*** (Aram)
The children of Shem; Elam, and Asshur, and Arphaxad, and Lud, and Aram.
The sons of Shem are Elam, *eternity*, Asshur, *step*, Arphaxad, *flooding river*, Lud, *conflict* and Aram, *exalted future.*

Elam-eternity (עילם *'Eylam)* *is* the constant present, the *perpetual timelessness*[3052] in which he *conceals.*[3053] Subsequently, the first *successfully progressing*[3054] *step-of-Asshur*[3055] follows into the *time-flow* of Arphaxad. <Time is like a deceiving picture animation, a phenakistoscope disc with pictures drawn on its outer frame board, each reproducing sequential individual position steps. If seen while spun on its center, we have the illusion of movement; however, when it is stationary, all the drawn sequential steps are seen at once, with no animation.>[3056]

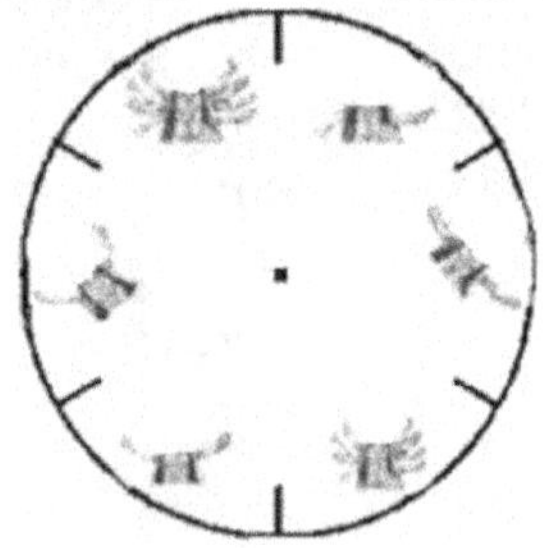

The name Arphaxad or *ar* (אַר)*-pa* (פ)*-kh* (כְ)*-shad* (שַׁד)[3057] is composed by the words

1) *ar* (אר), a contracted derivative from,
   a) *ya'or,*[3058] *river*, or
   b) *'owr,*[3059] *light, flood,*[3060] or
   c) *'arar,*[3061] *curse, and*

2) *kh* (כ), *as if*, and
3) *shed* (שד), meaning
   a) *shed,*[3062] *demon*, or
   b) *shad,*[3063] *breast* that *devastates*[3064],

Thus, we can summarize the name Arphaxad to mean, the *curse* of the *breast-feeding demon* of time*, as if* it were *a devastating flowing* and *flooding river of light*. <When consciousness becomes conscious-*of* something, then it is always *in*-time and *in*-history. Consciousness-*of* constitutes the individual distinction. The *hungry* concentration on the object, *of* which is conscious, dissipates the purity of Present Awareness as such.>[3065] That *hunger* is the *appetite* for the forbidden fruit. Then, time becomes the *curse* following the demonic temptation. <Past, present and future are only mental constructions of a continuum in which creation implies its being *created*

"*before the world was*"[3066]

created, as well as it *is* created *after* it *will be* destroyed, as well as it *is* destroyed when it *is* created.>[3067]

"The distinction between past, present, and future is only a stubbornly persistent illusion,"
wrote Einstein in a March 1955 letter.[3068]
There is a concomitance of all times, ages and events. Jesus states,

"*verily, I say unto you, before Abraham was, I am.*"[3069]

"*Time cooks all living beings as food ... This divided-flowing time is the great river of creatures.*"[3070]

Time, then, becomes the flowing deluge, which submerges us. Thus, time is *Lud*, namely, *strife,*[3071] the name of the fourth son of Shem. This aspect of time is the *trouble* plaguing our existence, during which we all perish. The fifth son of Shem is *Aram*, meaning *exalted, high,*[3072] which derives from the root *'armown*[3073] *meaning to be elevated.* This time form refers to the future. It is the projection of exalted and high expectations of a time to come. Finally, it is the stronghold (ארמון *'armown*) of the evolutionary changing adaptation during the generative course.

10:23-Uz, Hul, Gether and Mash

וּבְנֵי אֲרָם עוּץ וְחוּל וְגֶתֶר וָמַשׁ:
ubanēy (the sons) *'ărām* (of Aram) *'uṣ* (Uz branching plan) *waḥul* (Hul circle) *wageter* (Gether fear) wāmaš (Mash drawn out)
καὶ *kai* (and) **υἱοὶ** *uioi* (the sons) **Αραμ** *Aram* (Aram) **Ως** *Ōs* (Uz) **καὶ** *kai* (and) **Ουλ** *Oul* (Hul) **καὶ** *kai* (and) **Γαθερ** *Gather* (Gether) **καὶ** *kai* (and) **Μοσοχ** *Mosoch* (Mash)
filii (the sons) ***Aram*** (of Aram) ***Us*** (Uz) ***et*** (amd) ***Hul*** (Hul) ***et*** (and) ***Gether*** (Gether) ***et*** (and) ***Mes*** (Mash)
And the children of Aram; Uz, and Hul, and Gether, and Mash.
The sons of Aram are Uz *branching plan*, Hul *circle*, Gether *fear* and Mash *drawn out*.

From Aram, as future time projection, derive

1) *Uz*, meaning the *arboreal,*[3074] namely, time branching out the future *plan*;[3075]
2) *Hul*, meaning *circle,*[3076] namely, the recurring circularity of time as days and years;
3) *Gether*, meaning *fear*[3077] deriving from the uncertainty of the future;
4) *Mash*, meaning *drawn out,*[3078] as the name Moses,[3079] it means to *remove out* from the flowing water, namely, from Arphaxad's river of time.

10:24-Salah Generates Eber

וְאַרְפַּכְשַׁד יָלַד אֶת־שָׁלַח וְשֶׁלַח יָלַד אֶת־עֵבֶר:
wa'arapakašad (Arphaxad) *yālad* (generated) *'et* (and) *šālaḥ* (Salah) *wašelaḥ* (Salah) *yālad* (generated) *'et* (and) *'ēber* (Eber)
καὶ *kai* (and) **Αρφαξαδ** *Arphaxad* (Arphaxad) **ἐγέννησεν** *egennēsen* (generated) **τὸν** *ton* (the) **Καιναν** *Kainan* (Cainan) **καὶ** *kai* (and) **Καιναν** *Kainan* (Cainan)[3080] **ἐγέννησεν** *egennēsen* (generated) **τὸν** *ton* (the) **Σαλα** *Sala* (Salah) **Σαλα** *Sala* (Salah) **δὲ** *de* (then) **ἐγέννησεν** *egennēsen* (generated) **τὸν** *ton* (the) **Εβερ** *Eber* (Eber)
at (and) ***vero*** (indeed) ***Arfaxad*** (Arphaxad) ***genuit*** (generated) ***Sala*** (Salah) ***de*** (from) ***quo***

(whom) ***ortus*** (born) ***est*** (is) ***Eber*** (Eber)
And Arphaxad begat Salah; and Salah begat Eber.
And Arphaxad generated Salah and Salah generated Eber.

Salah flows out from Arphaxad, the *distressful river*. His name means *sprout, weapon, missile,*[3081] which derives from the verb *to send away, let go, stretch out,*[3082] in the sense of
"*to send words to another*, i.e. *to inform by a messenger.*"[3083]
In turn, therefore, *Salah*, the *sprouting* messenger sent forth, as a *cursing word* or as a *weapon*, *Eber*, *the flow of time*.

10:25-Division in days and Years

וּלְעֵבֶר יֻלַּד שְׁנֵי בָנִים שֵׁם הָאֶחָד פֶּלֶג כִּי בְיָמָיו נִפְלְגָה הָאָרֶץ וְשֵׁם אָחִיו יָקְטָן׃ *ula'ēḇer* (to Eber) *yulaḏ* (were born) *šanēy* (two) *ḇāniym* (sons) *šēm* (name) *hā'eḥāḏ* (of one) *peleḡ* (Peleg division) *kiy* (because) *ḇa*-(into)-*yāmāyv* (day-years) *nip̄alaḡāh* (was divided) *hā'āreṣ* (earth) *wašēm* (name) *'āḥiyv* (brother) *yāqaṭān* (Joktan smallness)
καὶ *kai* (and) **τῷ** *tō* (the) **Εβερ** *Ebewr* (Eber) **ἐγενήθησαν** *egenēthēsan* (were born) **δύο** *duo* (two) **υἱοί** *uioi* (sons) **ὄνομα** *onoma* (name) **τῷ** *tō* (of to) **ἑνὶ** *eni* (one) **Φαλεκ** *Phalek* (Paleg) **ὅτι** *oti* (that) **ἐν** *en* (in) **ταῖς** *tais* (the) **ἡμέραις** *ēmerais* (days) **αὐτοῦ** *autou* (his) **διεμερίσθη** *diemeristhē* (divide) **ἡ** *ē* (the) **γῆ** *gē* (earth) **καὶ** *kai* (and) **ὄνομα** *onoma* (name) **τῷ** *tō* (of the) **ἀδελφῷ** *adelphō* (brother) **αὐτοῦ** *autou* (his) **Ιεκταν** *Iektan* (Joktan)
nati (born)***-que*** (and) ***sunt*** (are) ***Eber*** (Eber) ***filii*** (sons) ***duo*** (two) ***nomen*** (name) ***uni*** (of one) ***Faleg*** (Peleg) ***eo*** (he) ***quod*** (that) ***in*** (in) ***diebus*** (days) ***eius*** (his) ***divisa*** (divided) ***sit*** (was) ***terra*** (earth) ***et*** (and) ***nomen*** (name) ***fratris*** (of brother) ***eius*** (his) ***Iectan*** (Joktan)
And unto Eber were born two sons: the name of one *was* Peleg; for in his days was the earth divided; and his brother's name *was* Joktan.
Two sons were born to Eber, the name of one was Peleg, *division*, because the whole earth was divided into day and years; the brother's name was Joktan, *smallness*.

Eber, the flowing time, produces two (שְׁנַיִם *shĕnayim*) *sons* (בֵּן *ben*) or time-categories. The name of the first aspect is *Pelag*, which means *division* and also *channel, stream, river.*[3084] He has that name *because*[3085] the whole earth (אֶרֶץ *'erets*) *was divided* (פלג *palag*) by the *river* (פֶּלֶג *peleg*) of time *in* (ב *ba*) *days and years* (יוֹם *yowm*), in nights and months. However, these vast frames of time are composed of little moments and their *smallness* (יָקְטָן *yoqtan*) is the meaning of the name (שֵׁם *shem*) *Joktan,*[3086] the second aspect of time, the brother (אַח *'ach*) of Pelag. Joktan, in fact, represents the further subdivisions of time, in minutes, seconds, nanoseconds and quantum dimension. His name derives from *qaton,*[3087] *to be small, insignificant* and *to be cut off.*[3088]

10:26-Almodad, Sheleph, Hazarmaveth and Jerah

וְיָקְטָן יָלַד אֶת־אַלְמוֹדָד וְאֶת־שָׁלֶף וְאֶת־חֲצַרְמָוֶת וְאֶת־יָרַח׃ *wayāqaṭān* (Joktan smallness) *yālaḏ* (begat) *'eṯ* (and) *'alamvōḏāḏ* (Almodad not measured) *wa'eṯ* (with) *šālep̄* (Sheleph drawn out) *wa'eṯ* (with) *ḥăṣaramāveṯ* (Hazarmaveth the court of death) *wa'eṯ* (with) *yāraḥ* (Jerah the lunar month)
Ιεκταν *Iektan* (Joktan) **δὲ** *de* (and) **ἐγέννησεν** *egennēsen* (generated) **τὸν** *ton* (the) **Ελμωδαδ** *Elmōdad* (Almodad) **καὶ** *kai* (and) **τὸν** *ton* (the) **Σαλεφ** *Saleph* (Sheleph) **καὶ** *kai* (and) **Ασαρμωθ** *Asarmōth* (Hazarmaveth) **καὶ** *kai* (and) **Ιαραχ** *Iarach* (Jerah)
qui (then) ***Iectan*** (Joktan) ***genuit*** (generated) ***Helmodad*** (Almodad) ***et*** (and) ***Saleph*** (Sheleph) ***et*** (and) ***Asarmoth*** (Hazarmaveth) ***Iare*** (Jerah)
And Joktan begat Almodad, and Sheleph, and Hazarmaveth, and Jerah,
And Joktan smallness begat Almodad, the *not measured*, and Sheleph, the *drawn out*, and Hazarmaveth, the *court of death* and Jerah, the *lunar month*.

However, *Joktan*, that insignificant time dimension, further compounds forming (יָלַד *yalad*) complex and more elaborate period structures. The first one is the sub-atomic dimension of time. His name is *Almodad*, which means *not measured,*[3089] because it is so small. The smallest unit of time is what we call present, which cannot be measured because, when acknowledged as present, is past and not the *present* any longer. Therefore, the next son or time-structure is *Sheleph,*[3090] meaning drawing out. The name derives from *shalaph*[3091] meaning *to pluck off a blade of grass.*[3092] Similarly, the *Kaṭha Upanishad* declares that the unmeasurable size of the present is

> "*always seated in the heart of the creature. One should draw him out from one's own body, with firmness like a stalk from the reed.*"[3093]

This echoes the Biblical separation of tares or rush grass from the blade of wheat.[3094] In addition, *shalaph means to draw out* like a

> "sword from its sheet."[3095]

This reminds us of the *instantaneous* drawing of the sword in the Japanese Zen martial arts, accompanied by a very deep mind concentration, which induces a state of pure enlightenment.[3096] Thus, with the firmness of awareness, we must draw out the *present* from the flow of time. Missing it means to be confronted with the past, that which his not any longer, namely death. This is the next *son* or time-structure of *Joktan*. He is *Hazarmaveth,*[3097] meaning the *enclosure*[3098] of *personified*[3099] death.[3100] This is similar to Osiris

> "*who came into existence as a circle... the place* (*Tuat*) *of departed souls.*"[3101]

The next son is *Jerah,*[3102] meaning the *new lunar month*. The month is one of *Pelag*'s partitions when he, as *Jerah*, *divided* the whole earth *in* (ב *ba*) *days and years* (יוֹם *yowm*), nights and months.

10:27-Hadoram, Uzal and Diklah

וְאֶת־הֲדוֹרָם וְאֶת־אוּזָל וְאֶת־דִּקְלָה׃
wa'eṯ (with) *hăḏwōrām* (Hadoram noble exaltation) *wa'eṯ* (with) *'uzāl* (flooded Uzal) *wa'eṯ* (with) *diqalāh* (Diklah palm grove)
καὶ *kai* (and) **Οδορρα** *Odorra* (Hadoram) **καὶ** *kai* (and) **Αιζηλ** *Aizēl* (Uzal) **καὶ** *kai* (and) **Δεκλα** *Dekla* (Diklah)
et (and) ***Aduram*** (Hadoram) ***et*** (and) ***Uzal*** (Uzal) ***Decla*** (Diklah)
And Hadoram, and Uzal, and Diklah,
And Hadoram, *noble exaltation*, and Uzal, *shall be flooded*, and Diklah, *palm grove.*

> "*During all the circular days of the earth-objectivity, seeding, harvest, cold, heat, summer, winter, day and night will not find rest...*[3103]
>
> *To every thing there is a season, and a time to every purpose under the heaven.*"[3104]

From *Hadoram*, namely the *noble exaltations*[3105] of generations (דּוֹר *dowra*) *echoing* (הֵד *had*) in the time-season of deep-sleep, we move in the *flooding* time, namely, *Uzal.*[3106] Starting with the dream time, *concepts inundate* the mind and

> "*your thoughts came up on your bed.*"[3107]

From there, they awaken growing as a *palm grove*, namely, *Diklah.* [3108]

10:28-Obal, Abimael and Sheba

וְאֶת־עוֹבָל וְאֶת־אֲבִימָאֵל וְאֶת־שְׁבָא׃
wa'eṯ (with) *'wōḇāl* (Obal stripped bare of leaves) *wa'eṯ* (with) *'ăḇiymā'ēl* (Abimael ancestor) *wa'eṯ* (with) *šaḇā'* (Sheba seven)
καὶ *kai* (Obal) **Αβιμεηλ** *Abimeēl* (Abimael) **καὶ** *kai* (and) **Σαβευ** *Sabeu* (Sheba)
et (and) ***Ebal*** (Obal) ***et*** (and) ***Abimahel*** (Abimael) ***Saba*** (Sheba)
And Obal, and Abimael, and Sheba,
And Obal, *stripped bare of leaves*, and Abimael, *ancestor*, and Sheba, *seven.*

Obal, which means *stripped bare of leaves* ,[3109] is another son of Joktan. Being *without leaves,* he implies the time of cold season. Next is *Abimael*, meaning *my father is El* (God), thus *my ancestor.*[3110] The name derives from *ab,*[3111] *father of an individual, ancestor, founder* and an

> "intimate connection and relationship."[3112]

Therefore, it relates to history as ancestral chronicle. Another son is *Sheba*. We have already encountered another Sheba, as the son of Raamah, connected to causality. Now, this Sheba is the son of Joktam connected to time. Like his homonymous, the name *Sheba* (שְׁבָא)[3113] is cognate to *sheba* (שבע), number *seven*. The first Sheba represented the seven causative creative projections of the whole world. Now, however, it indicates the seven days, the time span it took creation to produce the entire world.

10:29-Ophir, Havilah and Jobab

וְאֶת־אוֹפִר וְאֶת־חֲוִילָה וְאֶת־יוֹבָב כָּל־אֵלֶּה בְּנֵי יָקְטָן׃
wa'eṯ (with) *'wōp̄ir* (Ophir reducing to ashes) *wa'eṯ* (with) *ḥăviylāh* (Havilah circle) *wa'eṯ* (with) *ywōḇāḇ* (Jobab desert) *kāl* (all) *'ēleh* (these) *banēy* (sons) *yāqaṭān* (Joktan)
καὶ *kai* (and) **Ουφιρ** *Ouphir* (Ophir) **καὶ** *kai* (and) **Ευιλα** *Euila* (Havilah) **καὶ** *kai* (and) **Ιωβαβ** *Iōbab* (Jobab) **πάντες** *pantes* (all) **οὗτοι** *outoi* (these) **υἱοὶ** *uioi* (sons) **Ιεκταν** *Iektan* (of Joktan)
et (and) ***Ophir*** (Ophir) ***et*** (and) ***Evila*** (Havilah) ***et*** (and) ***Iobab*** (Jobab) ***omnes*** (all) ***isti*** (these) ***filii*** (the sons) ***Iectan*** (of Joktan)
And Ophir, and Havilah, and Jobab: all these *were* the sons of Joktan.
And Ophir, *reducing to ashes*, and Havilah, *circle*, and Jobab, *desert*. All these were the sons of Joktan.

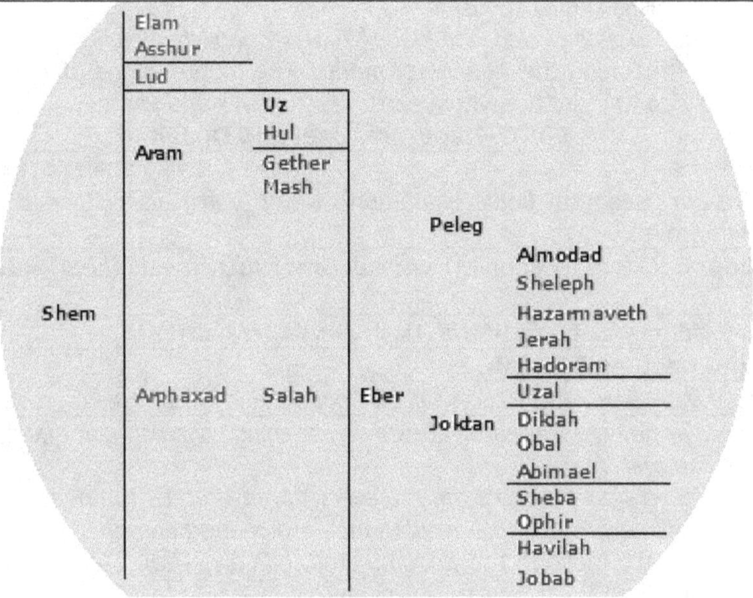

GRAPHIC: *Generations of Shem*

The name of *Ophir*, son of Joktan, means *reducing to ashes*,[3114] which implies death. In fact, any act of knowledge infers death because the known is always that which is *already given* before our mind, therefore, is past, thus dead, reduced to ashes. As described by the *Bṛhadāraṇyaka Upanishad*

"*The I... verily, burns he who strives to be before him.*"[3115]

The next son is *Havilah*. As we have seen, this was also the name of the son of Cush related to the causative dimension. Now, this is also the name of the son of Jokton related to the dimension of time. His name, *Havilah* (חֲוִילָה),[3116] like that of his homonymous, means *circle*.[3117] In this case, however, its reference is to time. In fact, it specifies the instantaneous circuit necessary for the subject to reach its object.

The last son is *Jobab*, meaning the *desert where wild beasts cry out*.[3118] This desert refers to the stillness of time reduced to a region without vegetation when the last *blade of grass of the present* has been *drawn out*. Out of that wasteland the wild beasts of war cry havoc, destruction and desolation.

These are all the sons of Jokton, the quantum structure of the entire Universe.

10:30-History

וַיְהִי מוֹשָׁבָם מִמֵּשָׁא בֹּאֲכָה סְפָרָה הַר הַקֶּדֶם׃ *wayahiy* (was) *mvōšāḇām* (dwelling) *mimēšā* (from Mesha the retreat) *bō'ăḵāh* (as you enter) *sap̄ārāh* (into Sephar narration) *har* (the field) *haqeḏem* (of antiquity)
καὶ *kai* (and) **ἐγένετο** *egeneto* (was) **ἡ** *ē* (the) **κατοίκησις** *katoikēsis* (dwelling) **αὐτῶν** *autōn* (their) **ἀπὸ** *apo* (from) **Μασση** *Massē* (Mesha) **ἕως** *eōs* (to) **ἐλθεῖν** *elthein* (comes) **εἰς** *eis* (into) **Σωφηρα** *Sōphēra* (Sephar) **ὄρος** *oros* (mountain) **ἀνατολῶν** *anatolōn* (of the East)
et (and) ***facta*** (done) ***est*** (is) ***habitatio*** (dwelling) ***eorum*** (their) ***de*** (from) ***Messa*** (Mesha) ***pergentibus*** (for those who proceed) ***usque*** (to) ***Sephar*** (Sephar) ***montem*** (mountain) ***orientalem*** (oriental)
And their dwelling was from Mesha, as thou goest unto Sephar a mount of the east.
Their dwelling was from Mesha, the *retreat*, as you enter into the field of Sephar, the *narration of antiquity*.

Mesha means the *retreat*[3119] of *Jobab's desert*. It is the *dwelling* (מוֹשָׁב *mowshab*) of the time-paradigms, *viz*. the sons of Jokton, which is at the *entrance* (בּוֹא *bow*) into the *field*[3120] of *Sephar*, namely, of the *enumeration* or the *narration*[3121] of *antiquity*,

"*that which is before in ancient times*,"[3122]

thus, the CHRONOLOGY of HISTORY.

10:31- Geographic, Ethnic and Linguistic Distinctions for Shem's Offspring

אֵלֶּה בְנֵי־שֵׁם לְמִשְׁפְּחֹתָם לִלְשֹׁנֹתָם בְּאַרְצֹתָם לְגוֹיֵהֶם׃ *'ēleh* (these) *ḇanēy* (the sons) *šēm* (of Shem) *lamišapaḥōṯām* (after their families) *lilašōnōṯām* (after their languages) *ba'araṣōṯām* (in their lands) *lag̱wōyēhem* (by their nations)
οὗτοι *outoi* (these) **υἱοὶ** *uioi* (sons) **Σημ** *Sēm* (Shem) **ἐν** *en* (in) **ταῖς** *tais* (the) **φυλαῖς** *phulais* (race) **αὐτῶν** *autōn* (their) **κατὰ** *kata* (according to) **γλῶσσαν** *glōssan* (language) **αὐτῶν** *autōn* (their) **ἐν** *en* (in) **τοῖς** *tois* (the) **χώραις** *chōrais* (space) **αὐτῶν** *autōn* (their) **καὶ** *kai* (and) **ἐν** *en* (in) **τοῖς** *tois* (the) **ἔθνεσιν** *ethnesin* (ethnicity) **αὐτῶν** *autōn* (their)
isti (these) ***filii*** (sons) ***Sem*** (Shem) ***secundum*** (according to) ***cognationes*** (families) ***et*** (and) ***linguas*** (languages) ***et*** (and) ***regiones*** (regions) ***in*** (according to) ***gentibus*** (people) ***suis*** (their)
These *are* the sons of Shem, after their families, after their tongues, in their lands, after their nations.
These are the sons of Shem, after their families, after their languages, in their lands, after their nations.

Some literal *Bible* interpreters, besides being geocentric, as opposed to universal, have an even narrower ethnocentric obsession. In fact, they struggle to locate physically geographical sites of places and to identify the ethnicity of populations, as they appear in *Genesis*. These interpreters miss the text intended widespread paradigmatic and metaphorical configurations.

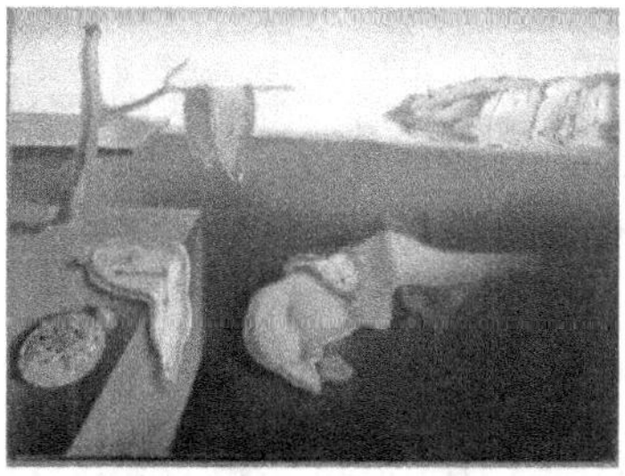

As we saw in *Genesis* (2:19-20), Shem (שֵׁם)[3123] means also the *name* and *memory* that Adam assigns to the objects, thus, the name is the symbol that recalls with the "*Persistence of Memory*"[3124] the signified object.

However, the distinction of people according to their languages (לָשׁוֹן *lashown*), in contrast with the *towering confusion*, yet to come, may have a specific meaning. Namely, each metaphoric rendering may have different symbolic images for the same denotation. In fact, the meaning of a hexagram star, besides being a star image for everyone, has a specific symbolic connotation for a specific ethnicity. Conversely, a turtle, besides being a turtle image for everyone, has the same symbolic connotation of the hexagram for another ethnicity, and vice versa. The images change, while referring to the same connotation. What remains the same for all, are the metaphoric connoted references, while the denoted images, as such, may vary according to the *language* and the *land*.[3125]

10:32-Behind and after the Flood

אֵלֶּה מִשְׁפְּחֹת בְּנֵי־נֹחַ לְתוֹלְדֹתָם בְּגוֹיֵהֶם וּמֵאֵלֶּה נִפְרְדוּ הַגּוֹיִם בָּאָרֶץ אַחַר הַמַּבּוּל׃ פ   *'ēleh* (these) *mišəpəḥōṯ* (the families) *bənēy* (sons) nōaḥ (of Noah) *laṯwōlaḏōṯām* (after their generations) *bağwōyēhem* (in their nations) *umē'ēleh* (from these) *nip̄araḏu* (divided) *hagwōyim* (the nations) *bā'āreṣ* (on the earth) *'aḥar* (on the background) *hamabul* (flood) *p̄* (.)
αὗται *autai* (these) **αἱ** *ai* (the) **φυλαὶ** *phulai* (families) **υἱῶν** *uiōn* (of the sons) **Νωε** *Nōe* (of Noah) **κατὰ** *kata* (according to) **γενέσεις** *geneseis* (generations) **αὐτῶν** *autōn* (their) **κατὰ** *kata* (according to) **τὰ** *ta* (the) **ἔθνη** *ethnē* (ethnicity) **αὐτῶν** *autōn* (their) **ἀπὸ** *apo* (from) **τούτων** *toutōn* (their) **διεσπάρησαν** *diesparēsan* (scatered) **νῆσοι** *nēsoi* (islands) **τῶν** *tōn* (of the) **ἐθνῶν** *ethnōn* (gentiles)[3126] **ἐπὶ** *epi* (on) **τῆς** *tēs* (the) **γῆς** *gēs* (earth) **μετὰ** *meta* (after) **τὸν** *ton* (the) **κατακλυσμόν** *kataklusmon* (cataclysm)
hae (these) ***familiae*** (the families) ***Noe*** (of Noah) ***iuxta*** (according to) ***populos*** (people) ***et*** (and) ***nationes*** (nations) ***suas*** (his) ***ab*** (from) ***his*** (by these) ***divisae*** (divided) ***sunt*** (are) ***gentes*** (the people) ***in*** (on) ***terra*** (the earth) ***post*** (after) ***diluvium*** (the deluge)
These are the families of the sons of Noah, after their generations, in their nations: and by these were the nations divided in the earth after the flood.
These are the families of Noah's sons according to their generations in their nations. From them the nations were divided on the earth on the background of the flood.

We should clarify that the flood does not submerge the epistemic structures as such. The forms-and-categories-of-knowledge are the universal offspring of *rested* Noah. Time, space, causality and their outcome, are not the cataclysm. They are not the effect, nor are they produced by it. They *logically precede* the flood. After it, they come about to further clarify the objective world.

> "The transition from wakefulness towards unconsciousness... studied the link between spatial and temporal correlations... and predicts that the principles we identified are universal and independent from its causes."[3127]

Those forms do not cause the deluge, nor are caused by it or drown in it. They are saved from it. Therefore, Shem, as the *logical a-priori form of time*, is static in the Present. Ham, as the *logical a-priori form of causality*, is inactive in Certainty. Finally, Japheth, as the *logical a-priori form of space*, is motionless in Consciousness. All three are *'achar*,

> "*behind*, in the background,"[3128]

of the flood. *After*, *'achar*,[3129] the flood, the *towlĕdah*, the *generations* (תולדות),[3130] deriving from those forms, articulate, *parad* (פָּרַד),[3131] into history as faculties of different *families*, *species* (מִשְׁפָּחָה *mishpachah*),[3132] *nations* and *animals* (גּוֹי *gowy*).[3133] This last term *gowy* (גּוֹי), nations and/or animals, has the same root as *gevahn* (גּוה),[3134] meaning *back*. Therefore, those epistemic forms are the logical backbone of all epistemic relations with the objective world.

The deluge is the flooding precipitation of attachments to the ephemeral objects. Only when we conceptualize time, space and causality, then these become objects, *viz.* part of the flood. Then, they individualize as *this* time, *this* space, *this* causality. Thus, they become different from the epistemic forms *behind the flood*, which we need in order to know the objects. When we identify with those objects, then, we drown in them. The epistemic forms are modes of knowing not affected by the content of knowledge. The forbidden fruit of knowledge drowns us by taking our mind away from the Ever-Present-Ubiquitous-Uncaused-Apodictic-Awareness.

A literal *universal* flood must necessarily refer to the entire Universe and not to the planet Earth alone. Truthfully, we can understand this universality only if we refer it to the epistemic modalities with which we know the entire cosmos. The flood is the flowing avalanche of all thoughts, appetites, attachments, desires, emotions, intentions, joys, loves, pains, sufferings, and other passions that, in space, time and causality, we apply, here and now, to the fruit of our knowledge. Furthermore, this is only the understanding of this historical *past/present*, *far/near* and *causing-the-deluge-effect* of this knowledge. As such, we can correctly say that the universal flood was in the past because, whatever we know, we know only as past. The *a-priori* forms or modalities of knowledge, *viz.* time (Shem), space (Japheth) and causality (Ham), survive this deluge in that they are *a-priori*, namely, they logically precede the known objects. Then, we know the deluge as past, which, however, continues to persist in our present time, while the epistemic forms of knowledge precede it logically.

~~~

SUMMARY OF THE TIME GENERATIONS OF SHEM

<table>
<tr><td><i>Elam</i> eternity</td><td></td><td></td><td></td><td></td></tr>
<tr><td><i>Asshur</i> step into time</td><td></td><td></td><td></td><td></td></tr>
<tr><td><i>Lud</i> trouble time</td><td></td><td></td><td></td><td></td></tr>
<tr><td rowspan="4"><i>Aram</i> ⇨ exalted future</td><td><i>Uz</i> time branching</td><td></td><td></td><td></td></tr>
<tr><td><i>Hul</i> recurring time</td><td></td><td></td><td></td></tr>
<tr><td><i>Gether</i> fear of future</td><td></td><td></td><td></td></tr>
<tr><td><i>Mash</i> removed from time</td><td></td><td></td><td></td></tr>
<tr><td rowspan="14"><i>Arphaxad</i>⇨ demon of time</td><td rowspan="14"><i>Salah</i> ⇨ messenger weapon</td><td rowspan="14"><i>Eber</i> ⇨ time flow</td><td><i>Pelag</i>⇨ time divide</td><td>see next Chapter</td></tr>
<tr><td rowspan="13"><i>Joktan</i> ⇨ time quantum subdivision</td><td><i>Almodad</i> present not measured</td></tr>
<tr><td><i>Sheleph</i> blade of grass to be pluck off</td></tr>
<tr><td><i>Hazarmaveth</i> enclosure, personified death.</td></tr>
<tr><td><i>Jerah</i> new lunar month dividing earth's time</td></tr>
<tr><td><i>Hadoram</i> noble exaltation of sleep time</td></tr>
<tr><td><i>Uzal</i> flooded dream time</td></tr>
<tr><td><i>Diklah</i> awaken and growing as a palm grove</td></tr>
<tr><td><i>Obal</i> stripped of leaves</td></tr>
<tr><td><i>Abimael</i> ancestral history</td></tr>
<tr><td><i>Sheba</i> seven days of creation</td></tr>
<tr><td><i>Ophir</i> time reducing to ashes</td></tr>
<tr><td><i>Havilah</i> subject/object instant circularity</td></tr>
<tr><td><i>Jobab</i> desert stillness of time time paradigms' dwelling (<i>Mesha</i>) in the field of history (<i>Sephar</i>)</td></tr>
</table>
~~~

Time flows between past and future. Each of its aspects becomes a category shaping epistemic lives.

HERE ENDS THE TENTH CHAPTER OF
THE GENERATIONS OF THE SONS OF NOAH

CHAPTER 11

THE TOWER OF BABEL

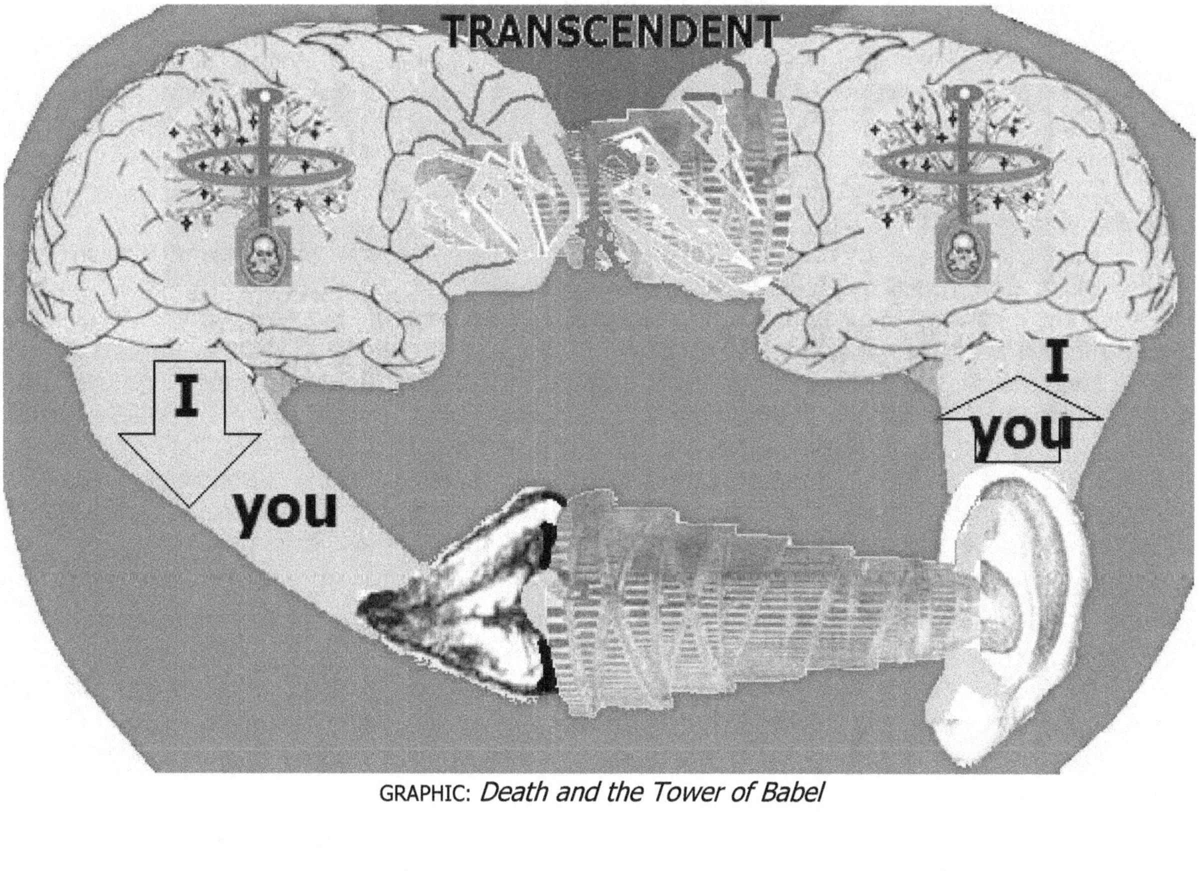

GRAPHIC: *Death and the Tower of Babel*

11-I SECTION: THE BUILDING OF THE TOWER

11:1-One Language

וַיְהִי כָל־הָאָרֶץ שָׂפָה אֶחָת וּדְבָרִים אֲחָדִים׃ *wayahiy* (was) *ḵāl* (all) *hāʾāreṣ* (world) *śāp̄āh* (language) *ʾeḥāṯ* (one) *uḏaḇāriym* (speech) *ʾăḥāḏiym* (one)
καὶ *kai* (and) **ἦν** *ēn* (was) **πᾶσα** *pasa* (all) **ἡ** *ē* (the) **γῆ** *gē* (earth) **χεῖλος** *cheilos* (lip) **ἕν** *en* (one) **καὶ** *kai* (and) **φωνὴ** *phōnē* (sound) **μία** *mia* (one) **πᾶσιν** *pasin* (all)
erat (was) ***autem*** (also) ***terra*** (the earth) ***labii*** (lip) ***unius*** (one) ***et*** (and) ***sermonum*** (sermon) ***eorundem*** (the same)
And the whole earth was of one language, and of one speech.
The whole world had one language and one speech.

Since we already read that, all nations were parted

"*according to their language,*" (*Genesis* 10:5)

this original unified universal speech must refer to something different.

For the one who is auto-transparent in itself, *viz.* Noah in the state of being awake while dreamlessly sleeping, there is only *one* (שָׂפָה *ʾeḥāṯ*) *language* (אֶחָת *śāp̄āh*), namely the intuitive stillness of silence. This is the necessary *unique*[3135] foundation, which *unifies and joins* (אֶחָד *'achad*)[3136] the *whole world* (אֶרֶץ *'erets*). That is the state of real communication, namely the common-*uni*fication,[3137] in which we all are one with the entire Cosmos. This means, the Awareness that we are, right here and now, is universally the same for everyone. That is *being awake in dreamless sleep*. What changes is the object we are conscious-*of*, which is different, at one given point, for each individual. Deluging chaos reigns when we exit the state of dreamlessness.

To understand this we must explain and analyze the Hebrew words for *speech*, dabar (דָּבָר), and *language*, saphah (שָׂפָה).

The word for *speech* is *dabar.*[3138] It derives from the verb *dabar,*[3139] which means discursiveness,

"setting in a row, ranging in order to put words in order."[3140]

Consequently, it conveys the idea of a conceptual articulated procession *proceeding* from '*I*,' the subject-speaker/hearer, to a '*you*, the object-talker/listener.'

Furthermore, the word for *language* is *saphah.*[3141] It derives from *shaphah,*[3142] *to sweep bare, scrape*, which gives the idea of termination, and, probably from the verb *caphah,*[3143] which means *to snatch away, to destroy, to consume, to perish*. Ii is comparable to *cowph,*[3144] meaning *end, conclusion*, which derives from *cuwph,*[3145] *to cease, to come to an end*. This reinstates the epistemic loneliness, which we already explained. In fact, when the spoken word reaches the ear of the listener, the speaker is already placed in the projected past of the discursive procession, thus losing its original unity.

A reader may argue,

'When I speak to you, I do it now and you hear me now, not yesterday or tomorrow.'

We reply,

'Yes, but, the spoken word travels at the speed of sound.[3146] *Thus, in your present now, when we project our speech at speed of sound for your understanding, it reaches your ear in due time after that "now," namely, in the very near future. However, for you, it comes from the past, even if a very short one.'*

Furthermore, *I* (the-speaker) conceives *you* (the-listener) as "*the other one*," which, while projected in the future, is already ended, *viz. cuwph*, is dead to the present because can never-be-in-the-now of the speaker. For the speaker, the listener becomes a noumenon, the one conceived but not known in-itself. Simplifying, the '*I*' believes '*you*' to be other-than-itself, thus, you are placed in transcendence.

11:2-The Land of the Two Rivers

וַיְהִי בְּנָסְעָם מִקֶּדֶם וַיִּמְצְאוּ בִקְעָה בְּאֶרֶץ שִׁנְעָר וַיֵּשְׁבוּ שָׁם: *wayahiy* (it came to pass) *banāsa'ām* (as they pulled out) *miqeḏem* (from the ancient east) *vayimaṣa'u* (they found) *ḇiqa'āh* (plain) *ba'ereṣ* (in the land) *šina'ār* (Shinar land of two rivers) *vayēšaḇu* (dwelt)
καὶ *kai* (and) **ἐγένετο** *egeneto* (it came to pass) **ἐν** *en* (in) **τῷ** *tō* (the) **κινῆσαι** *kinēsai* (moved) **αὐτοὺς** *autous* (they) **ἀπὸ** *apo* (from) **ἀνατολῶν** *anatolōn* (the east) **εὗρον** *euron* (they found) **πεδίον** *pedion* (the plain) **ἐν** *en* (in) **γῇ** *gē* (the land) **Σενναάρ** *Sennaar* (Shinar) **καὶ** *kai* (and) **κατῴκησαν** *katōkēsan* (the inhabited) **ἐκεῖ** *ekei* (there)
cumque (however) ***proficiscerentur*** (they departed) ***de*** (from) ***oriente*** (the orient) ***invenerunt*** (they found) ***campum*** (a field) ***in*** (in) ***terra*** (the land) ***Sennaar*** (of Shinar) ***et*** (and) ***habitaverunt*** (the inhabited) ***in*** (in) ***eo*** (it)
And it came to pass, as they journeyed from the east, that they found a plain in the land of Shinar; and they dwelt there.
As those [cohesive forces] pulled out from the ancient east, it happened that they found the land of *two rivers, a plain divided* in the land of Shinar and they dwelt there.

The cohesive forces of that *original* common unification pull out from the *ancient* silent unity. Those forces set out from the *East. Qedem,*[3147] east, means the *orient,* as origin, where the sun rises, the *ancient eastern enlightening* state,

"which is before in ancient times... of old,"[3148]

therefore, the state of *antiquity.*[3149] Upon leaving the unifying origins, the forces *find* (מָצָא matsa) the *split,* the *divided plain*[3150] of *Shinar,* meaning, the *country of two rivers.*[3151]

When one leaves the blissful and restful original state of *awaken-dreamless-sleep,* one enters the *land* (אֶרֶץ 'erets) of the mind divided between dream and wakefulness. There are the two *I*-subject and *you*-object *river*-polarities. Hence, we *remain* (יָשַׁב yashab) *in the two waking and dreaming mind* and *there we* establish our dwelling.

11:3-Purified Bricks

וַיֹּאמְרוּ אִישׁ אֶל־רֵעֵהוּ הָבָה נִלְבְּנָה לְבֵנִים וְנִשְׂרְפָה לִשְׂרֵפָה וַתְּהִי לָהֶם הַלְּבֵנָה לְאָבֶן וְהַחֵמָר הָיָה לָהֶם לַחֹמֶר: *wayō'maru* (and they said) *'iyš* (one) *'el* (and) *rē'ēhu* (to another) *hāḇāh* (let us) *nilabanāh* (cleanse) *laḇēniym* (a pavement of cleanliness) *waniśarap̄*ah (purified) *liśarēp̄*ah (with ardent purifications) *watahiy* (had) *lāhem* (they) *halaḇēnāh* (cleanliness) *la'āḇen* (for foundation stone) *wahaḥēmār* (the red fermenting trouble) *hāyāh* (had) *lāhem* (they) *laḥōmer* (for cement)
καὶ *kai* (and) **εἶπεν** *eipen* (said) **ἄνθρωπος** *anthrōpos* (a man) **τῷ** *tō* (the) **πλησίον** *plēsion* (neighbor) **δεῦτε** *deute* (come) **πλινθεύσωμεν** *plintheusōmen* (us make bricks) **πλίνθους** *plinthous* (bricks) **καὶ** *kai* (and) **ὀπτήσωμεν** *optēsōmen* (bake) **αὐτὰς** *autas* (them) **πυρί** *puri* (with fire) **καὶ** *kai* (and) **ἐγένετο** *egeneto* (were) **αὐτοῖς** *autois* (them) **ἡ** *ē* (the) **πλίνθος** *plinthos* (bricks) **εἰς** *eis* (for) **λίθον** *lithon* (stone) **καὶ** *kai* (and) **ἄσφαλτος** *asphaltos* (asphalt) **ἦν** *ēn* (was) **αὐτοῖς** *autois* (their) **ὁ** *o* (the) **πηλὸς** *pēlos* (mortar)
dixit (he said)***-que*** (and) ***alter*** (another) ***ad*** (to) ***proximum*** (the next) ***suum*** (his) ***venite*** (come) ***faciamus*** (let us make) ***lateres*** (bricks) ***et*** (and) ***coquamus*** (burn) ***eos*** (them) ***igni*** (in fire) ***habuerunt*** (they had)***-que*** (and) ***lateres*** (brick) ***pro*** (for) ***saxis*** (stones) ***et*** (and) ***bitumen*** (asphalt) ***pro*** (for) ***cemento*** (cement)
And they said one to another, Go to, let us make brick, and burn them throughly. And they had brick for stone, and slime had they for morter.
And they said one to the another,   "*Let us cleanse with a pavement of cleanliness purified with ardent purifications.*"   They had *cleanliness* as foundation stone and they had the *red fermenting trouble* for cement.

In the new land of dreaming and awaken mind, the first thing we do is *speak* (*'amar*) to our neighbors, namely, the other ones.

"The primary signification [of the verb *'amar*[3152]] is, *to bear forth*; hence, *to bring to light, to say*."[3153] In other words, we need to reestablish the communion we had in the forsaken paradise from which we came. Now, however, we must utilize all our epistemic forms, *viz.* time, space and causality, to *bring forward* (אָמַר *amar*), our *unique*[3154] subjectivity in order to reach the objective *other*[3155] as such. That is, the obstacle of a far-reaching communication is the inscrutability of the other. To overcome it and to *bring* it *forward*, a series of purifications and cleansing processes are necessary.

The word *rea`, the other, the companion,* and also *the lover,*[3156] derives from the verb *ra`ah,*[3157] which means *to pasture, to feed,* also *to delight* and *to hold intercourse,*[3158] in the sense of *r@`uwth,*[3159] longing, striving desire. From *ra`ah*, derives also *ra`yown,*[3160] which means *thought.* Thus, the *mind field* is that of *appetite* for the other, the object. However, as we explained, the spoken word fails, because it reaches the ear of the other who is, inevitably, in death's past. Consequently, *they* (לָהֶם *lāhem*), *viz.* the plurality of the single subject,[3161] moving from its original stillness of silence into the *mind-land,* decide to *cleanse*[3162] with a *pavement of cleanliness* (לְבֵנָה *lĕbenah*)[3163] *purified*[3164] with *ardent purifications.*[3165] These are purified bricks with no *straw* given for *building material* [3166]in the field of duality. The word *lĕbenah,* means *purification* and *brick.* Therefore, those *purified bricks* serve as *foundation blocks*[3167] and *cemented*[3168] together by *fermented trouble,*[3169] like *wine,*[3170] the same that inebriates Noah. The fermentation or bubbling up of wine is a metaphor for the hunger that drove Adam and Eve to eat the forbidden fruit. As Dylan Thomas lyrically declares,

> "The force that through the green fuse drives the flower / Drives my green age; that blasts the roots of trees / Is my destroyer."[3171]

The *Kaṭha Upanishad* reports of sacrificial bricks

> "*used in building the sacrificial altar.*"[3172]

Those bricks are the sacrificing-desires. They make-holy (*sacer-facere*), they make-good consecrating the world into existence. Therefore,

> "the sacred is equivalent to a *power*, and, in the last analysis, to *reality*."[3173]

Through the intentionality of desire*, the urge to objectify the original unreachable*, *the force of hunger* generates the other-one as *other* than this one. Those bricks are similar to Lao Tzu's action without action.[3174] In fact,

> "*Go therefore now, work; for there shall no straw be given you, yet shall ye deliver the tale of bricks.*"[3175]

Therefore, do, perform your work (עָבַד *'abad*). Make building *bricks*[3176] without (*lō'* not) using *straw,*[3177] the building material. These are the pure bricks of non-attachment. During the *three days* of wake, dream and dreamless-sleep, they should shape a new temple,

> "*Destroy this temple, and in three days I will raise it up.*"[3178]

In other words, as we enter the land of duality, *viz.* of subject/object and/or of dream/wakefulness, we should build into existence sacrificial actions without the cohesiveness of attachment.

11:4-The Refracting Name

וַיֹּאמְרוּ הָבָה נִבְנֶה־לָּנוּ עִיר וּמִגְדָּל וְרֹאשׁוֹ בַשָּׁמַיִם וְנַעֲשֶׂה־לָּנוּ שֵׁם פֶּן־נָפוּץ עַל־פְּנֵי כָל־הָאָרֶץ׃ *wayō'maru* (they said) *hāḇāh* (let) *niḇaneh* (build) *lānu* (us) *`iyr* (wakeful) *umigədāl* (pulpit) *warō'švō* (head) *ḇašāmayim* (to heaven) *wana'ăśeh* (let make) *lānu* (us) *šēm* (a name Shem) *pen* (bends refracting) *nāp̄uṣ* (scattered) *`al* (upon) *panēy* (the face) *kāl* (all) *hā'āreṣ* (the earth)
καὶ *kai* (and) **εἶπαν** *eipan* (they said) **δεῦτε** *deute* (come) **οἰκοδομήσωμεν** *oikodomēsōmen* (let us build) **ἑαυτοῖς** *eautois* (for us) **πόλιν** *polin* (a city) **καὶ** *kai* (and) **πύργον** *purgon* (a tower) **οὗ** *ou* (thus) **ἡ** *ē* (the) **κεφαλὴ** *kephalē* (head) **ἔσται** *estai* (is) **ἕως** *eōs* (until) **τοῦ** *tou* (the) **οὐρανοῦ** *ouranou* (sky) **καὶ** *kai* (and) **ποιήσωμεν** *poiēsōmen* (let us make) **ἑαυτοῖς** *eautois* (for us) **ὄνομα** *onoma* (a name) **πρὸ** *pro* (before) **τοῦ** *tou* (the) **διασπαρῆναι** *diasparēnai* (we are scattered) **ἐπὶ** *epi* (on) **προσώπου** *prosōpou* (the face) **πάσης** *pasēs* (of all) **τῆς** *tēs* (the) **γῆς** *gēs* (earth)
et (and) ***dixerunt*** (they said) ***venite*** (come) ***faciamus*** (let us make) ***nobis*** (for us) ***civitatem*** (a city) ***et*** (and) ***turrem*** (a tower) ***cuius*** (whose) ***culmen*** (top) ***pertingat*** (may reach) ***ad*** (to)

caelum (the sky) ***et*** (and) ***celebremus*** (let us celebrate) ***nomen*** (name) ***nostrum*** (our) ***antequam*** (before) ***dividamur*** (we will be divided) ***in*** (on) ***universas*** (all) ***terras*** (the earth)
And they said, Go to, let us build us a city and a tower, whose top may reach unto heaven; and let us make us a name, lest we be scattered abroad upon the face of the whole earth.
They said, "*Let us establish a wakeful pulpit-head to heaven; let us identify with Shem's refracting name scattering us upon the face of all the earth.*"

To understand the construction of the tower of Babel, we must explain the meaning of all the words usually rendered, by literal translators, as building, bricks and others.

Leaving its resting state, the plurality of the single subject *establishes*[3179] its wakefulness in a city or a state of anguish. The word *`iyr,*[3180] means *excitement, anguish of terror, a place of waking,* a *city,*

"frequented by people... *fortified places, as towers, watch-towers.*"[3181]

It derives from *` uwr,*[3182] *city* guarded by waking or watching in an encampment. There is

"*one wakeful* (עוּר `uwr) [and] *one answering* (עָנָה `anah)."[3183]

Therefore, *uwr* has the meaning *to rouse oneself* and *to awake from sleep, to be awake*. In addition, it means *to be ardent*, like the bricks, and *hot* like Ham. Furthermore, the name derives from an original root identical to *` uwr,*[3184] in the sense of opening the eyes, which means to be exposed, be laid bare, to be naked to be made naked, as with Noah.

Migdal, meaning *tower,*[3185] means an *elevated pulpit* and *a raised up bed,*[3186] it derives from *gadal,*[3187] which means *elevated stage, to become great*. Its *head,*[3188] like Horace's

"exalted head shall reach the stars."[3189]

In fact, the subject wants to reach *heaven* (שָׁמַיִם *shamayim*), the abode of God, where the transcendent-other-one-abides-in-itself. The *other*, in fact, is the neighbor, the *one we shout at*[3190] *and aim at with thoughts,*[3191] *viz.* we intention in-itself but never know and/or reach as such. Thus, we should love them dispassionately as the love we should have for God, *viz.* with all our heart, soul, and might;[3192] namely, we should realize our communion and identify with them. Therefore,

"*love thy neighbor as thyself.*"[3193]

On the contrary, when we assume (עָשָׂה *` asah*) an individual name (שֵׁם *shem*),[3194] *viz. Shem, lest* we *turn the corner* (*pen*),[3195] then, we *refract away from*[3196] the unity we previously had. Therefore, our individualizing name must prevail over everyone else. That name *scatters, disperses*[3197] us in the entire Cosmos and divides us. Thus, the neighbor becomes the *bad, roa `,*[3198] the *injurious, ra `a `,*[3199] the evil enemy. The name is the same as Shem; it historicizes us in *time* (Shem) and *causes* (Ham) to divide us throughout the entire (כֹּל *ḵāl*) face (פָּנִים *paniym*) of the *world* (אֶרֶץ *'erets*) (Japheth).

11:5-God Comes Down to Oversee the Work

וַיֵּרֶד יְהוָה לִרְאֹת אֶת־הָעִיר וְאֶת־הַמִּגְדָּל אֲשֶׁר בָּנוּ בְּנֵי הָאָדָם׃ *wayēreḏ* (came down) *yəhvāh* (the Transcendent) *lira'ōṯ* (to consider) *'eṯ* (and) *hā'iyr* (the wakefulness) *wa'eṯ* (with) *hamiḡadāl* (raised bed-pulpit) *'ăšer* (which) *bānu* (had built) *banēy* (the sons) *hā'āḏām* (of Adam)
καὶ *kai* (and) **κατέβη** *katebē* (flowed down) **κύριος** *kurios* (the Lord) **ἰδεῖν** *idein* (to see) **τὴν** *tēn* (the) **πόλιν** *polin* (city) **καὶ** *kai* (and) **τὸν** *ton* (the) **πύργον** *purgon* (tower) **ὃν** *on* (which) **ᾠκοδόμησαν** *ōkodomēsan* (had built) **οἱ** *oi* (the) **υἱοὶ** *uioi* (sons) **τῶν** *tōn* (of) **ἀνθρώπων** *anthrōpōn* (man)
descendit (descended) ***autem*** (indeed) ***Dominus*** (the Lord) ***ut*** (to) ***videret*** (see) ***civitatem*** (the city) ***et*** (and) ***turrem*** (the tower) ***quam*** (which) ***aedificabant*** (had erected) ***filii*** (the sons) ***Adam*** (of Adam)
And the LORD came down to see the city and the tower, which the children of men builded.
Transcendent Awareness flowed down to reflect the wakefulness with the raised bed-pulpit, which

the sons of Adam had built.

The term `*iyr* (עִיר), *city*, means a *guarded town*, in the sense of

"a place of waking... [which derives] from עוּר [*'uwr*] (H5782) a city (a place guarded by waking or a watch) in the widest sense."[3200]

Moreover, the verb `*uwr* means

"to rouse oneself, awake, awaken... identical with עוּר (H5783) through the idea of opening the eyes"[3201]

Furthermore, the term *migdal* (מִגְדָּל), which means

"tower, elevated stage, pulpit, raised bed,"[3202]

is the bed, from which we arise, the pulpit, from which we speak and, therefore, the *watchtower*,[3203] from which we look when we awake.

To read literally that the ineffable God, who by definition is ubiquitous, omniscient and omni-aware, moves out to check on his creature's work, is simply puerile. Furthermore, to consider that city, as an actual enclave with actual houses, tower and inhabitants would mean to blame all the cities and towers of the world. Besides, Babel's tower was not taller than any modern skyscraper (וְרֹאשׁוֹ *warō'šwō* *ḇašāmayim* בַשָּׁמַיִם) and/or any space travel flight, so why would it have been more sinful than the height of buildings in New York City or Kuala Lumpur? The problem here is reading the metaphor by its denotation, disregarding its connotation, which also finds comfort and support in its lexicon.

The Transcendent Awareness is always still and present while it emanates throughout all the stages of life. In them, the Stillness of Awareness is completely all in every state never exhausting Itself. That is, Awareness in Itself is present completely in the state of dreamless-sleep. From there, motionless, It proceeds entirely in the state of dream. Subsequently, It totally *flows*[3204] into the *city* of anguish and wakefulness (עִיר *'iyr*), without ever exhausting or losing Its wholeness in Itself as Transcendent Apodictic Awareness.

"*That which is below, is just as that which is above. And that which is above, is just as that which is below, to accomplish the miracles of the One Thing... It ascends from earth to heaven, and again descends on earth, and receives the power of the superiors and of the inferiors.*"[3205]

"*Thy kingdom come. Thy will be done, as in heaven, so in earth.*"[3206]

Therefore, in dream and wakefulness, Awareness reflects, *considers*[3207] the wakeful city and the raised up pulpit-bed (מִגְדָּל *migdal*) established[3208] by the children (בֵּן *ben*) of Adam (אָדָם *'adam*).

11:6-Nothing Restrains from Thinking

וַיֹּאמֶר יְהוָה הֵן עַם אֶחָד וְשָׂפָה אַחַת לְכֻלָּם וְזֶה הַחִלָּם לַעֲשׂוֹת וְעַתָּה לֹא־יִבָּצֵר מֵהֶם כֹּל אֲשֶׁר יָזְמוּ לַעֲשׂוֹת׃   *wayō'mer* (said) *yahwāh* (the Transcendent) *hēn* (behold) `*am* (the concealed) '*eḥāḏ* (unified one) *waśāp̄āh* (language) '*aḥaṯ* (one) *laḵulām* (all) *wazeh* (this one) *haḥilām* (*pierces through*) *la'ăśwōṯ* (to do) *wa'atāh* (now) *lō'* (nothing) *yibāṣēr* (restrains) *mēhem* (from) *kōl* (all) '*ăšer* (which) *yāzamu* (they fix thought upon) *la'ăśwōṯ* (to produce)
καὶ *kai* (and) **εἶπεν** *eipen* (said) **κύριος** *kurios* (the Lord) **ἰδοὺ** *idou* (behold) **γένος** *genos* (race) **ἓν** *en* (one) **καὶ** *kai* (and) **χεῖλος** *cheilos* (language) **ἓν** *en* (one) **πάντων** *pantōn* (of all) **καὶ** *kai* (and) **τοῦτο** *touto* (this way) **ἤρξαντο** *ērxanto* (they begun) **ποιῆσαι** *poiēsai* (to make) **καὶ** *kai* (and) **νῦν** *nun* (now) **οὐκ** *ouk* (not) **ἐκλείψει** *ekleipsei* (shall fail) **ἐξ** *ex* (from) **αὐτῶν** *autōn* (them) **πάντα** *panta* (all) **ὅσα** *osa* (as great as) **ἂν** *an* (if) **ἐπιθῶνται** *epithōntai* (they have undertaken) **ποιεῖν** *poiein* (to do)
et (and) ***dixit*** (he said) ***ecce*** (indeed) ***unus*** (one) ***est*** (is) ***populus*** (the people) ***et*** (and) ***unum*** (one) ***labium*** (language) ***omnibus*** (for all) ***coeperunt*** (they begun)***-que*** (and) ***hoc*** (this) ***facere*** (to do) ***nec*** (nor) ***desistent*** (they desist) ***a*** (from) ***cogitationibus*** (the thoughts) ***suis*** (their) ***donec*** (until) ***eas*** (their) ***opere*** (work) ***conpleant*** (is compleated)
And the LORD said, Behold, the people is one, and they have all one language; and this they begin to do: and now nothing will be restrained from them, which they have

imagined to do.
The Transcendent said, "*Behold, the concealed unified one is all of one language and does pierce this one through. Now nothing restrains them from producing all they fix their thought on.*

Consider that Adam is the *one*[3209] auto-transparent *people.*[3210] People, in fact, stand for the subject-object *synthetically unified*[3211] and *concealed*[3212] in the *one* silent *language* (אחַת *śāpāh*) of stillness. S/he, Adam with the offspring, *pierces through*[3213] and *comes into this world of anguish*[3214] by *lessening*[3215] *this synthesized one*[3216] into whatever they, subject and object, *fix their thought on.*[3217]

We need here a bit of self-introspection. Consider where dreams or thoughts come from. As we dive in ourselves, we realize that they come from the interior silence of the state we call dreamless sleep, namely, one language. The famous Renascence painting of "*An Old Man and his Grandson*"[3218] portrays a silent-gaze-conversation between the eyes of different generations, those of a young boy and those of his grandfather, flowing towards a far dreamlike landscape. Cicero, the great ancient Roman orator himself, stated that

> "silence is one of the great arts of conversation… there is not only an art, but even an eloquence in it."[3219]

Eventually, from that original, universal, eloquent

> "singing silence,"[3220]

whatever we want to dream or think about expresses itself with a particular symbolism.

> "*We dreamed a dream in one night, I and he; we dreamed each man according to the interpretation of his dream.*"[3221]

We call those symbols "words" and we organize them into language. As we *produce* (עָשָׂה `*asah*) them, we identify with those signified objects of thought and, consequently, we *pollute* (חלל *chalal*) losing the immediateness of Apodictic Awareness. There is, so to say, a *descent* of Awareness. Through Auto-transparency, It reaches I-consciousness, the levels of thought that thinks itself as thought, and then merges in Individual-consciousness, the level of thought thinking of the world in its historical physicality. On these two levels, consciousness is not (לא *lo*) *restrained*,[3222] thus, is free to *produce* (עָשָׂה `*asah*) all it wants to *think* (זָמַם *zamam*). Similarly, the *Bṛhadāraṇyaka Upanishad* state that the original horse-like psychosomatic being

> "*not being restrained, started to think.*"[3223]

11:7-The Languages Are Confused

הָבָה נֵרְדָה וְנָבְלָה שָׁם שְׂפָתָם אֲשֶׁר לֹא יִשְׁמְעוּ אִישׁ שְׂפַת רֵעֵהוּ׃ *hāḇāh* (let us) *nēraḏāh* (descend) *wanāḇalāh* (confuse) *šām* (then and there) *śapāṯām* (language) *'ăšcr* (so that) *lō* (not) *yišama'u* (they may understand) *'iyš* (one person) *śap̄aṯ* (language) *rē'ēhu* (another)
δεῦτε *deute* (come) **καὶ** *kai* (and) **καταβάντες** *katabantes* (let us go) **συγχέωμεν** *sugcheōmen* (confound) **ἐκεῖ** *ekei* (there) **αὐτῶν** *autōn* (they) **τὴν** *tēn* (the) **γλῶσσαν** *glōssan* (language) **ἵνα** *ina* (so that) **μὴ** *mē* (not) **ἀκούσωσιν** *akousōsin* (may understand) **ἕκαστος** *ekastos* (each) **τὴν** *tēn* (the) **φωνὴν** *phōnēn* (voice) **τοῦ** *tou* (of the) **πλησίον** *plēsion* (neighbor)
venite (come) ***igitur*** (therefore) ***descendamus*** (let us descend) ***et*** (and) ***confundamus*** (let us confound) ***ibi*** (here) ***linguam*** (language) ***eorum*** (their) ***ut*** (so that) ***non*** (not) ***audiat*** (may hear) ***unusquisque*** (each other) ***vocem*** (voice) ***proximi*** (one near) ***sui*** (his)
Go to, let us go down, and there confound their language, that they may not understand one another's speech.
Let us descend and confuse their language then and there so that they may not understand the language of one person from the other."

The usual literal reading presents a wrathful and unmerciful god. He oddly punishes humans for eating forbidden fruits created by him and condemns them to death. When they try to reach him, by building towered cities, he exiles them into incommunicability.

The sight and/or the sound of a word conveys, through the eyes and/or the ears, an awakening in the brain of a message, a form or an idea that previously may not have been there or was concealed. In return, we project that word in a reality believed to be external to the brain itself. Internal or external, in any case, the word, as such, resurrects to that which is intended as transcendent. In the case of an unknown language, there is no awakened meaning. However, the cryptic word will still convey its own transcendence hidden within its mysterious puzzling quality. Language itself is the Babel Tower, which only Still Silence can comprehend. For this reason, in 1677, Altus published an Alchemic book only with pictures and named it the *Livre Muĕt*,

"*The Mute Book*, yet all the Nations of the world... can read it and understand it... One does not need to be a true Son of the Art to understand it immediately."[3224]

However, let us look at the metaphoric intention of this verse. When we search for a *Theory of Everything*,[3225] we try to achieve the ultimate foundation of a reality conceived to be external, other than us, namely, transcendent. When we ask our beloved, '*Do you love me*?' We declare our incommunicability with the mind of our cherished one conceived to be external, other from us, namely, transcendent.[3226] In each case, we try to reach the transcendent objectively. Nevertheless, when we believe we reached it, it sends us back to another *out there* and so on, in a never-ending hellish descending spiral of incommunicable death. Any attempt to reach that transcendent leads us necessarily to alienation from our true Self. That True Self is the present creative act of Awareness-in-Itself. It is the presence in all of us of that Creative Act.

There is no divine condemnation, as such. There is only the drowning consequence of rejecting the dry roof of the Ark, while choosing to step into the deluge. Out there, we get wet and sink in the sound of thought words, which shatter the original unity of the silent stillness of Awareness. The *Epic of Gilgamesh* relates that

"*Enlil heard the clamour and he said to the gods in council, 'The uproar of mankind is intolerable and sleep is no longer possible by reason of the babel.'*"[3227]

When all human thoughts echo simultaneously, the *uproar* and the *clamor* becomes an *intolerable* and unrestful flooding cacophony.

Therefore, as Awareness emanates and *descends* (יָרד *yarad*) into each of life's stages, the human identifies with the consciousness-*of* each state and becomes its *possessor*.[3228] Losing its original unity, humans are *confounded* (בָּלל *balal*) by languages. In fact, as we saw, *language* (שָׂפָה *saphah*) is that which reinstates the epistemic incommunicability. Thus, *one person*,[3229] *viz.* the subject *who is incurably desperately sick*[3230] of loneliness, does not understand (שָׁמַע *shama'*) the *other one*[3231] also subjected to the same ailment. The *other one* (רֵעָה *ra'ah*)[3232] is anyone who *ra'ah* (רָעָה), *feeds* and *pastures*, like a *ruler*, a *teacher*, a *flock*, a *shepherd*, a *friend*, a *lover*, etc.

What a communicator may intend may not be what the perceiver understands. This is more evident in the presence of cultural differences and it widens among diverse species. In fact, an intense exchange of glances and smiles, displaying teeth, while showing endearment among lovers, may be inappropriate for foreign etiquettes and could be definitely threatening and confrontational among certain non-human animals.[3233]

11:8-The Lord Scattered All the People over the Face of the Earth

וַיָּפֶץ יְהוָה אֹתָם מִשָּׁם עַל־פְּנֵי כָל־הָאָרֶץ וַיַּחְדְּלוּ לִבְנֹת הָעִיר׃ *wayāp̄eṣ* (scattered) *yahwāh* (Transcendent) *'ōṯām* (them) *mišām* (then and there) *'al* (upon) *panēy* (face) *ḵāl* (all) *hā'āreṣ* (of the earth) *wayaḥadalu* (ceased) *liḇanōṯ* (to build) *hā'iyr* (city)
καὶ *kai* (and) **διέσπειρεν** *diespeiren* (scattered) **αὐτοὺς** *autous* (them) **κύριος** *kurios* (Lord) **ἐκεῖθεν** *ekeithen* (from that p0lace) **ἐπὶ** *epi* (on) **πρόσωπον** *prosōpon* (face) **πάσης** *pasēs* (all) **τῆς** *tēs* (the) **γῆς** *gēs* (earth) **καὶ** *kai* (and) **ἐπαύσαντο** *epausanto* (stopped) **οἰκοδομοῦντες**

oikodomountes (building) **τὴν** *tēn* (the) **πόλιν** *polin* (city) **καὶ** *kai* (and) **τὸν** *ton* (the) **πύργον** *purgon* (tower)
atque (thus) ***ita*** (so) ***divisit*** (divided) ***eos*** (them) ***Dominus*** (the Lord) ***ex*** (out of) ***illo*** (that) ***loco*** (locality) ***in*** (through) ***universas*** (the universal) ***terras*** (Earth) ***et*** (and) ***cessaverunt*** (they ceased) ***aedificare*** (to build) ***civitatem*** (the city)
So the LORD scattered them abroad from thence upon the face of all the earth: and they left off to build the city.
Immediately, the Transcendent scattered them upon the face of the whole earth. Thus, they ceased to build the city.

Once *dispersed upon* (עַל *'al*) the *face* (פָּנִים *paniym*) of *space* (אֶרֶץ *'erets*), *then* (שָׁם *sham*), the subject, *scattered* (פּוּץ *puwts*) through time and *divided* by historical events, *comes to an end* and *ceases* (חָדַל *chadal*) to *build* (בָּנָה *banah*) the *city of towering anguish* (עִיר *` iyr*). This happens in two possible ways, by dying, or by withdrawing into the silent stillness of Awareness.

11:9-The City's Name Is Babel

עַל־כֵּן קָרָא שְׁמָהּ בָּבֶל כִּי־שָׁם בָּלַל יְהוָה שְׂפַת כָּל־הָאָרֶץ וּמִשָּׁם הֱפִיצָם יְהוָה עַל־פְּנֵי כָּל־הָאָרֶץ׃ פ   *ʿal* (upon) *kēn* (therefore) *qārā'* (is called) *šamāh* (name) *bābel* (Babel confusion) *kiy* (because) *šām* (there) *bālal* (confounded) *yahwāh* (Transcendent) *śapaṯ* (language) *kāl* (all) *hā'āreṣ* (earth) *umišām* (from there) *hĕp̄iyṣām* (scattered) *yahwāh* (Transcendent) *ʿal* (upon) *panēy* (face) *kāl* (all) *hā'āreṣ* (the earth) *p̄* (.)
διὰ *dia* (therefore) **τοῦτο** *touto* (this) **ἐκλήθη** *eklēthē* (was called) **τὸ** *to* (the) **ὄνομα** *onoma* (name) **αὐτῆς** *autēs* (its) **Σύγχυσις** *Sugchusis* (Confusion) **ὅτι** *oti* (that) **ἐκεῖ** *ekei* (there) **συνέχεεν** *sunecheen* (confused) **κύριος** *kurios* (the Lord) **τὰ** *ta* (the) **χείλη** *cheilē* (language) **πάσης** *pasēs* (of all) **τῆς** *tēs* (the) **γῆς** *gēs* (earth) **καὶ** *kai* (and) **ἐκεῖθεν** *ekeithen* (then) **διέσπειρεν** *diespeiren* (dispersed) **αὐτοὺς** *autous* (them) **κύριος** *kurios* (the Lord) **ὁ** *o* (the) **θεὸς** *theos* (God) **ἐπὶ** *epi* (on) **πρόσωπον** *prosōpon* (the face) **πάσης** *pasēs* (of all) **τῆς** *tēs* (the) **γῆς** *gēs* (earth)
et (and) ***idcirco*** (therefore) ***vocatum*** (called) ***est*** (is) ***nomen*** (name) ***eius*** (his) ***Babel*** (Babel) ***quia*** (because) ***ibi*** (here) ***confusum*** (consused) ***est*** (is) ***labium*** (the language) ***universae*** (of the whole) ***terrae*** (earth) ***et*** (and) ***inde*** (therefore) ***dispersit*** (dispersed) ***eos*** (them) ***Dominus*** (the Lord) ***super*** (on) ***faciem*** (the face) ***cunctarum*** (of the entire) ***regionum*** (region)
Therefore is the name of it called Babel; because the LORD did there confound the language of all the earth: and from thence did the LORD scatter them abroad upon the face of all the earth.
Therefore, by name it is called Babel, confusion, because there the Transcendent confounded languages over the entire Earth and from there, the Transcendent scattered them upon the face of the whole Earth.

The city's name is Babel (בָּבֶל *babel*), meaning *confusion.* In general, a *name* (שֵׁם *shem*) individualizes, historicizes and separates, distinguishing us from others. Therefore (כֵּן *kān*), the name becomes the symbol for this body right here and right now. Babel, then, is this physical biological structure metaphorically described as a towering city of sufferance dividing us from the others, while *confounding* (בָּלַל *balal*) *languages* (שָׂפָה *saphah*) ushering all incomprehension. Thus, we are scattered (פּוּץ *puwts*) throughout the entire (כֹּל *kāl*) face (פָּנִים *paniym*) of the world (אֶרֶץ *'erets*).

A reader may ask,

'Why the Transcendent produces all this confusion?'

We reply,

'It is not the Transcendent in-Itself that produces confusion. It is the search for the transcendent, conceived and believed to be an entity external to the subject-object

correlation, which generates confusion. It is our constant need to objectify as otherness the Reality of Awareness.'

This body is named (קרא qara) Babel, *confusion.* However, the building of this body-city ceases when it is purified back into the oneness of Awareness, as it is at its origin. Then it becomes

> "*the holy city, the new Jerusalem, coming down from God out of heaven... And there shall be no more death, neither sorrow, nor crying, neither shall there be any more pain... And I will give unto him that is athirst of the fountain of the water of life freely... The great city, the holy Jerusalem, descending out of heaven from God... lieth foursquare, and the length is as large as the breadth.*"[3234]

Controlling that citadel, one realizes the Internal Unborn Apodictic Awareness and identifies with it as the Self, where

> "*the Lord God Almighty and the Lamb are the temple of it.*"[3235]

Lauren, one of our students, asked,

- *Which one will be the language of the future?'-*

We replied,

- *All languages come from history, which, as such, are already given. Meaning that we recall from memory the idioms we currently speak. Thus, they are already past, dead to the Absolute Present from which our ideas spring out. In fact our epistemic structure knows only that which is past. In addition, the future, as such, is never. Yes, there is the current expectation of tomorrow, but we never experience tomorrow as such, only as today. Therefore, we can give different answers to your question. From an evolutionary perspective, we can say that, given the persistent communicative shrinkage of the world we will have one language as the combination of all idioms with different regional inflections. This will lead to the technological development of silent communicative electronic impulses sent directly to neural centers in the brain. Conversely, from an epistemological perspective, we can say that silence will ultimately replace the sound transmission of language. On one side, we are all destined to the levelling silence of cemeteries. Nevertheless, on the True Side, we all unite in the Luminous Silence of Awareness where that, which is intended, is instantly communicated.'*

Word-sounds build and convey messages from the past and language loses its original unity. Humans scatter throughout the Earth while remaining locked in their uncommunicable individual loneliness.

11-II SECTION: SHEM'S HISTORY

11:10-Generation of Shem

אֵלֶּה תּוֹלְדֹת שֵׁם שֵׁם בֶּן־מְאַת שָׁנָה וַיּוֹלֶד אֶת־אַרְפַּכְשָׁד שְׁנָתַיִם אַחַר הַמַּבּוּל׃ *'ēleh* (these) *twōladōṯ* (history generations) *šēm* (Shem) *šēm* (Shem) *ben* (son) *ma'aṯ* (a hundred) *šānāh* (years) *waywōleḏ* (begat) *'eṯ* (and) *'arapakašāḏ* (Arphaxad) *šanāṯayim* (two year) *'aḥar* (on the background) *hamabul* (the flood)
καὶ *kai* (and) **αὗται** *autai* (these) **αἱ** *ai* (the) **γενέσεις** *geneseis* (generations) **Σημ** *Sēm* (Shem) **Σημ** *Sēm* (Shem) **υἱὸς** *uios* (son) **ἑκατὸν** *ekaton* (a hundred) **ἐτῶν** *etōn* (years) **ὅτε** *ote* (when) **ἐγέννησεν** *egennēsen* (he begot) **τὸν** *ton* (the) **Αρφαξαδ** *Arphaxad* (Arphaxad) **δευτέρου** *deuterou* (the second) **ἔτους** *etous* (year) **μετὰ** *meta* (after) **τὸν** *ton* (the) **κατακλυσμόν** *kataklusmon* (flood)
hae (these) ***generationes*** (the generations) ***Sem*** (of Shem) ***Sem*** (Shem) ***centum*** (one hundred) ***erat*** (was) ***annorum*** (of years) ***quando*** (when) ***genuit*** (generated) ***Arfaxad*** (Arphaxad) ***biennio*** (two years) ***post*** (after) ***diluvium*** (the deluge)
These are the generations of Shem: Shem was an hundred years old, and begat Arphaxad two years after the flood:
These are the generations in time of Shem. Shem *brought hundredfold forward* (100) in the noetic circularity of *years' consciousness* and brought forward Arphaxad two circular years of consciousness on the background of the flood.

The word *me'ah*[3236] means *one hundred fold*. In fact, Moses relates that,

"*Isaac sowed in that land, and received in that same year an hundredfold* (*mē'āh ša'ārym* שערים מאה)."[3237]

Therefore, it conveys the idea to

"*bring forth fruit... one hundred fold.*"[3238]

In relation to the number of years, Peter declares that,

"*One day* [is] *with the Lord as a thousand years, and a thousand years as one day.*"[3239]

The Hebrew letter ק, *q*, is equivalent to 100 meaning the circle of the horizon sun. Further, the numeral 100 has the equivalent Gematria with the word *yēlēḏwn*,[3240] meaning, *they bring forth*, and with *yālaḏanw*,[3241] meaning *we brought forward*. In both cases, the words derive from the same verb *yalad* (יָלַד),[3242] to beget, to bring forth. As we already explained, the Patriarchs, including Shem, are metaphors for universal paradigmatic epistemic structure. The metaphoric offspring of the Patriarchs, Shem/time, Ham/causality and Japheth/space, are subdivisions or categories deriving from each of those epistemic forms, time, causality and space. Therefore, Shem's aspect does not generate sons in the literal physical sense of the word. Thus, by *generating* we must understand the noetic projection toward the intended noematic objectivity. Therefore, we can translate that Shem begat Arphaxad when he brought him forward in the full, hundredfold circularity of consciousness. Namely, the circularity is expressed as years, or as a 360-degree circle starting from the singularity of its dimensionless and timeless center.

We find similar metaphors of the year's circularity connected to the act of generating in the *Bṛhadāraṇyaka Upanishad*, where it says,

"*That, which was the generating flow, became the 360° year. In the beginning, indeed, the year was not. For as long as the space of time of a year, he parented his child. Thus, after that time, he projected him... not having restrained* [him]*,... after a year he started thinking... The year is its self.*"[3243]

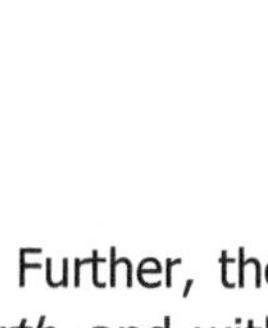

We find a graphic expression of this circularity is on the vignette inside the sarcophagus of Pharaoh Seti I.[3244] There, Osiris, bent outward and shaped as a circle, projects Nut, the sky, out from his head.[3245] His body encircles a legend that says,

"*This is Osiris; his circuit is the place of departed souls.*[3246] [And he declares,] *'I was he who came into existence as a circle.'*"[3247]

The hundredfold year circularity of knowledge is also implicit in the Gematria equivalence of 100. In fact, the words, *knowledge*, *wayōḏa'ay* (וִידָעַי), *to know*, *yōḏiy'un* (יֹדִיעוּ), *the known*, *yōḏa'āyv* (יֹדְעָיו) and *known*, *yvōḏiya'* (יוֹדִיעַ), all derive from the verb to know, *yada '*[3248] and have the equivalent Gematria of 100.

Now, Shem brings forward Arphaxad, who, as we saw, is the *flowing waters*, *mēymēy* (מֵימֵי) referring *to the waters*, *hamayamāh* (הַמָּיְמָה),[3249] -- all equivalent to 100 -- of the *flooding river* of time. There are two (שְׁנַיִם shěnayim) years (שָׁנָה shaneh), two flowing time circularities of consciousness. One is the flow of dream and the other the flow of wakefulness. Furthermore, one is the noetic flow of the subject towards the object, or the acts aiming to grasp the object. The other is the noematic streaming projection of the object in its modes-of-being-given to the subject. And, in those *rivers*, *banaḥălēy* (בְּנַחֲלֵי),[3250] on the background (אחר 'achar) of the flood, one *acquires* and *gets possession* (נָחַל nachal) of the objective world. Moreover, the two circular years represent the past and the future, as we will see.

11:11-Shem Continued in Time

וַיְחִי־שֵׁם אַחֲרֵי הוֹלִידוֹ אֶת־אַרְפַּכְשָׁד חֲמֵשׁ מֵאוֹת שָׁנָה וַיּוֹלֶד בָּנִים וּבָנוֹת: ס *vayəḥiy* (continued) *šēm* (Shem) *'aḥărēy* (following) *hvōliyḏvō* (begetting) *'eṯ* (and) *'arəpakəšāḏ* (Arphaxad) *ḥămēš* (five) *mē'vōṯ* (hundred) *šānāh* (years) *vayvōleḏ* (begot) *bāniym* (sons) *ubānvōṯ* (daughters) *s* (.)
καὶ *kai* (and) **ἔζησεν** *ezēsen* (lived) **Σημ** *Sēm* (Shem) **μετὰ** *meta* (after) **τὸ** *to* (the) **γεννῆσαι** *gennēsai* (he had begotten) **αὐτὸν** *auton* (he) **τὸν** *ton* (the) **Αρφαξαδ** *Arphaxad* (Arphaxad) **πεντακόσια** *pentakosia* (five hundred) **ἔτη** *etē* (years) **καὶ** *kai* (and) **ἐγέννησεν** *egennēsen* (generated) **υἱοὺς** *uious* (sons) **καὶ** *kai* (and) **θυγατέρας** *thugateras* (daughters) **καὶ** *kai* (and) **ἀπέθανεν** *apethanen* (died)[3251]
vixit (lived)***-que*** (and) ***Sem*** (Shem) ***postquam*** (after) ***genuit*** (he begat) ***Arfaxad*** (Arphaxad) ***quingentos*** (five hundred) ***annos*** (years) ***et*** (and) ***genuit*** (generated) ***filios*** (sons) ***et*** (and) ***filias*** (daughters)
And Shem lived after he begat Arphaxad five hundred years, and begat sons and daughters.
Following his projection of Arphaxad, Shem continued the circular years of consciousness *in time* (500) and begot sons and daughters.

Having projected Arphaxad as the flowing river of time, Shem *continued*[3252] his *breathing-flow*[3253] of his *circular years of consciousness* (שָׁנָה shaneh) in time and projected *son*[3254] and *daughters*[3255] as metaphors for the mental projections of thoughts and concepts.

Our text says *five*-(חמש chamesh) (note, the letter ה, *h*, equals 5 meaning *breath*)[3256] *hundred*-(מֵאָה me'ah) (note the letter ק, *q*, equals 100 meaning *circle*), thus 500 equals to the final letter ך, *k*, meaning *crown*.[3257] The Hebrew word *lə'* (לְ) *ēṯ* (עֵת),[3258] *in time*, has a Gematria value of 500. Thus, we can say that Shem's breath is equivalent to the process of time.

11:12-Salah the Sprout

וְאַרְפַּכְשַׁד חַי חָמֵשׁ וּשְׁלֹשִׁים שָׁנָה וַיּוֹלֶד אֶת־שָׁלַח: *və'arəpakəšaḏ* (Arphaxad) *ḥay* (lived) *ḥāmēš* (five) *ušəlōšiym* (thirty) *šānāh* (years) *vayvōleḏ* (begot) *'eṯ* (and) *šālaḥ* (Salah extending sprout)
καὶ *kai* (and) **ἔζησεν** *ezēsen* (lived) **Αρφαξαδ** *Arphaxad* (Arphaxad) **ἑκατὸν** *ekaton* (hundred) **τριάκοντα** *triakonta* (thirty) **πέντε** *pente* (five) **ἔτη** *etē* (years) **καὶ** *kai* (and) **ἐγέννησεν** *egennēsen* (generated) **τὸν** *ton* (the) **Καιναν** *Kainan* (Cainan)[3259]
porro (following) ***Arfaxad*** (Arphaxad) ***vixit*** (lived) ***triginta*** (thirty) ***quinque*** (five) ***annos*** (years) ***et*** (and) ***genuit*** (generated) ***Sale*** (Salah)
And Arphaxad lived five and thirty years, and begat Salah:
Arphaxad continued flowing *bringing forward* (35) the circularity of consciousness and projecting Salah as an extending sprout.

The word *'ēlēḏ* (אֵלֵד), meaning, *I brought forward*,[3260] has a Gematria numeric value of 35. Thus, we can read the *thirty*-(שְׁלֹשִׁים shělowshiym)-*five*-(חָמֵשׁ chamesh) *years* as meaning that Arphaxad *brought forward* the *breathing-flow* (חָוָה chavah) of his own *circular life years of consciousness* (שָׁנָה shaneh). After that, he projected

Salah. His name, *shelach,*[3261] which means *sprout, weapon* or *sword*, derives from the verb *shalach*[3262] *meaning to send away, to let go, to stretch out, to point out,*

"Specially –... *to send words* to another,"[3263]

as we send out to you the words of this book. Therefore, the arrow of flowing time eventually *sprouts Salah*, the faculty of reaching the other one through pointing out, communicating and/or wounding with a weapon.

11:13-Time's Arrow

וַיְחִי אַרְפַּכְשַׁד אַחֲרֵי הוֹלִידוֹ אֶת־שֶׁלַח שָׁלֹשׁ שָׁנִים וְאַרְבַּע מֵאוֹת שָׁנָה וַיּוֹלֶד בָּנִים וּבָנוֹת׃ ס *vayəhiy* (lived) *'arəpakəšad* (Arphaxad) *'aḥărēy* (following) *hvōliydvō* (begetting) *'et* (and) *šelaḥ* (Salah) *šālōš* (three) *šāniym* (years) *və'arəba'* (four) *mē'vōt* (hundred) *šānāh* (years) *vayvōled* (begat) *bāniym* (sons) *ubānvōt* (daughters) *s* (.)
καὶ *kai* (and) **ἔζησεν** *ezēsen* (lived) **Αρφαξαδ** *Arphaxad* (Arphaxad) **μετὰ** *meta* (after) **τὸ** *to* (the) **γεννῆσαι** *gennēsai* (begot) **αὐτὸν** *auton* (he) **τὸν** *ton* (the) **Καιναν** *Kainan* (Cainan) **ἔτη** *etē* (years) **τετρακόσια** *tetrakosia* (four hundred) **τριάκοντα** *triakonta* (thirty) **καὶ** *kai* (and) **ἐγέννησεν** *egennēsen* (he begot) **υἱοὺς** *uios* (sons) **καὶ** *kai* (and) **θυγατέρας** *thugateras* (daughters) **καὶ** *kai* (and) **ἀπέθανεν** *apethanen* (died) **καὶ** *kai* (and) **ἔζησεν** *ezēsen* (lived) **Καιναν** *Kainan* (Cainan) **ἑκατὸν** *ekaton* (one hundred) **τριάκοντα** *triakonta* (thirty) **ἔτη** *etē* (years) **καὶ** *kai* (and) **ἐγέννησεν** *egennēsen* (begot) **τὸν** *ton* (the) **Σαλα** *Sala* (Salah) **καὶ** *kai* (and) **ἔζησεν** *ezesen* (lived) **Καιναν** *Kainan* (Cainan) **μετὰ** *meta* (after) **τὸ** *to* (the) **γεννῆσαι** *gennēsai* (begot) **αὐτὸν** *auton* (he) **τὸν** *ton* (the) **Σαλα** *Sala* (Salah) **ἔτη** *etē* (years) **τριακόσια** *triakosia* (three hundred) **τριάκοντα** *triakonta* (thirty) **καὶ** *kai* (and) **ἐγέννησεν** *egennēsen* (begot) **υἱοὺς** *uious* (sons) **καὶ** *kai* (and) **θυγατέρας** *thugateras* (daughters) **καὶ** *kai* (and) **ἀπέθανεν** *apethanen* (he died)[3264]
vixit (lived)***-que*** (and) ***Arfaxad*** (Arphaxad) ***postquam*** (after) ***genuit*** (having generated) ***Sale*** (Salah) ***trecentis*** (three hundred)[3265] ***tribus*** (three) ***annis*** (years) ***et*** (and) ***genuit*** (generated) ***filios*** (sons) ***et*** (and) ***filias*** (daughters)
And Arphaxad lived after he begat Salah four hundred and three years, and begat sons and daughters.
Following Salah's projection, Arphaxad lived *drawing near and back* (403) and begat sons and daughters.

The unidirectional projection of *sprouting Salah*, the *breathing-time-flow* (חָוָה *chavah*) of Arphaxad's *circular life years of consciousness* (שָׁנָה *shaneh*), takes a double direction. It goes from the past to the future, from where it turns around to reach the past again. Thus, events, which took place light years ago, are visible only in time to come. As an example, the present light of Proxima Centauri, the closest star to the Sun, will appear to us four years in the future. In fact, the numeral 403, four (ארבע *'arba'*) hundred (מֵאָה *me'ah*) three (שָׁלוֹשׁ *shalowsh*), has a Gematria equivalency with the word *magiyšiym*, which derives from *nagash*,[3266] meaning *to draw near and to draw back.*

"It must be remarked that the ancients... were not strictly accurate in the use of words which signify approaching and withdrawing; and thus they are sometimes used of the direct contrary motion; [the idea of going to or coming from *some other place*, may perhaps be the cause of this usage]"[3267]

Throughout, that double direction Arphaxad, the faculty of flowing time, generates thoughts and ideas, metaphorically, sons and daughters.

11:14-Time Goes by

וְשֶׁלַח חַי שְׁלֹשִׁים שָׁנָה וַיּוֹלֶד אֶת־עֵבֶר׃ *vəšelaḥ* (Salah) *ḥay* (lived) *šəlōšiym* (thirty) *šānāh* (years) *vayvōled* (brought forward) *'et* (and) *'ēber* (Eber passing time)
καὶ *kai* (and) **ἔζησεν** *ezēsen* (lived) **Σαλα** *Sala* (Salah) **ἑκατὸν** *ekaton* (a hundred)[3268] **τριάκοντα** *triakonta* (thirty) **ἔτη** *etē* (years) **καὶ** *kai* (and) **ἐγέννησεν** *egennēsen* (generated) **τὸν** *ton* (the) **Εβερ** *Eber* (Eber)
Sale (Salah) ***quoque*** (also) ***vixit*** (lived) ***triginta*** (thirty) ***annis*** (years) ***et*** (and) ***genuit***

(generated) ***Eber*** (Eber)
And Salah lived thirty years, and begat Eber:
Salah, during his *life* (30), brought forward Eber the passing time.

The name *Eber*[3269] means, *the region beyond,*
"situated across the a stream."[3270]
The name derives from the verb *'abar, to pass over,*
"used of time passing by."[3271]
Furthermore, the numeral 30 of the *thirty* (שְׁלֹשִׁים *shělowshiym*) *years* (שָׁנָה *shaneh*) has the equivalent Gematria with the word *ḇəḥayay,*[3272] *life*. Therefore, *stretching out Salah breathed* (חָוָה *chavah*) his *circular conscious years* (שָׁנָה *shaneh*) of *life* (חַי *chay*) as time passes by.

11:15-As Time Passes

וַיְחִי־שֶׁלַח אַחֲרֵי הוֹלִידוֹ אֶת־עֵבֶר שָׁלֹשׁ שָׁנִים וְאַרְבַּע מֵאוֹת שָׁנָה וַיּוֹלֶד בָּנִים וּבָנוֹת׃ ס *vayəḥiy* (lived) *šelaḥ* (Salah) *'aḥărēy* (after) *hvōliydvō* (having brought forward) *'et* (and) *'ēḇer* (Eber) *šālōš* (three) *šāniym* (years) *və'arəba'* (four) *mē'vōṯ* (hundred) *šānāh* (year) *vayvōleḏ* (brought forward) *bāniym* (sons) *uḇānvōṯ* (daughters) *s* (.)
καὶ *kai* (and) **ἔζησεν** *ezēsen* (lived) **Σαλα** *Sala* (Salah) **μετὰ** *meta* (after) **τὸ** *to* (the) **γεννῆσαι** *gennēsai* (generated) **αὐτὸν** *auton* (he) **τὸν** *ton* (the) **Εβερ** *Eber* (Eber) **τριακόσια** *triakosia* (three hundred) **τριάκοντα** *triakonta* (thirty)[3273] **ἔτη** *etē* (years) **καὶ** *kai* (and) **ἐγέννησεν** *egennēsen* (generated) **υἱοὺς** *uious* (sons) **καὶ** *kai* (and) **θυγατέρας** *thugateras* (daughter) **καὶ** *kai* (and) **ἀπέθανεν** *apethanen* (he died)
vixit (lived)***-que*** (and) ***Sale*** (Salah) ***postquam*** (after) ***genuit*** (having generated) ***Eber*** (Eber) ***quadringentis*** (four hundred) ***tribus*** (three) ***annis*** (years) ***et*** (and) ***genuit*** (generated) ***filios*** (sons) ***et*** (and) ***filias*** (daughters)
And Salah lived after he begat Eber four hundred and three years, and begat sons and daughters.
Following Eber's projection, Salah lived *drawing near and back* (403) begetting sons and daughters.

After the projection of *Eber* passing time, the *breathing-time-flow* (חָוָה *chavah*) of *sprouting Salah's circular life years of consciousness* (שָׁנָה *shaneh*) takes a double direction. Again, as time passes, the past goes towards the future and, from there, it turns around to reach the past. In fact, as we saw, the numeral 403, four (אַרבַע *'arba'*) hundred (מֵאָה *me'ah*) three (שָׁלוֹשׁ *shalowsh*), has a Gematria equivalency with the word *magiyšiym*, which derives from *nagash,*[3274] meaning *to draw near and to draw back*. Throughout, that double direction, Salah, the faculty of reaching the other one, through pointing out the passing of time, generates thoughts and ideas, metaphorically, sons and daughters.

11:16-Disrupted Unity

וַיְחִי־עֵבֶר אַרְבַּע וּשְׁלֹשִׁים שָׁנָה וַיּוֹלֶד אֶת־פָּלֶג׃ *vayəḥiy* (lived) *'ēḇer* (Eber) *'arəba'* (four) *ušəlōšiym* (thirty) *šānāh* (years) *vayvōleḏ* (projected) *'eṯ* (and) *pāleḡ* (Peleg river of division)
καὶ *kai* (and) **ἔζησεν** *ezēsen* (lived) **Εβερ** *Eber* (Eber) **ἑκατὸν** *ekaton* (a hundred)[3275] **τριάκοντα** *triakonta* (thirty) **τέσσαρα** *tessara* (four) **ἔτη** *etē* (years) **καὶ** *kai* (and) **ἐγέννησεν** *egennēsen* (generated) **τὸν** *ton* (the) **Φαλεκ** *Phalek* (Peleg)
vixit (lived) ***autem*** (also) ***Eber*** (Eber) ***triginta*** (thirty) ***quattuor*** (four) ***annis*** (years) ***et*** (and) ***genuit*** (generated) ***Faleg*** (Peleg)
And Eber lived four and thirty years, and begat Peleg:
Eber *lived in the togetherness* (34) of the circular consciousness of life when he brought forward Peleg the river of division.

The name *Peleg,*[3276] meaning *division,* is the same as the word *peleg,*[3277] which means *channel* and *river*. Both derive from the verb *palag,*[3278] which means *to divide, to split*. Therefore, we can translate the name Peleg as *the dividing river*. This means that *Eber's passing time* logically divides the togetherness of the subject and the object as well as of You and I. In fact, the numeral 34, of the *thirty*

(שְׁלֹשִׁים *shĕlowshiym*) and *four* (אַרְבַּע *'arba`*) *years* (שָׁנָה *shaneh*) of his life, has a Gematria equivalence with each of the words *vayəḥiy*, meaning *he lived*,[3279] *vəḥayay*,[3280] meaning *life* and *vəyaḥədāv*,[3281] meaning *together*. Therefore, time's flow seems to separates the original unity enjoyed in the logical a-priori of the act of knowledge, namely, before the subject moved out to reach the other. From a physical point of view, think of your dear past ones. They lived once and now time has separated them from you.

11:17-The State of Anguish

וַיְחִי־עֵבֶר אַחֲרֵי הוֹלִידוֹ אֶת־פֶּלֶג שְׁלֹשִׁים שָׁנָה וְאַרְבַּע מֵאוֹת שָׁנָה וַיּוֹלֶד בָּנִים וּבָנוֹת׃ ס *vayəḥiy* (lived) *'ēḇer* (Eber) *'aḥărēy* (after) *hvōliyḏvō* (having generated) *'eṯ* (and) *peleḡ* (Peleg) *šəlōšiym* (thirty) *šānāh* (years) *və'arəba'* (four) *mē'vōṯ* (hundred) *šānāh* (years) *vayvōleḏ* (brought forth) *bāniym* (sons) *uḇānvōṯ* (daughters) *s* (.)
καὶ *kai* (and) **ἔζησεν** *ezēsen* (lived) **Εβερ** *Eber* (Eber) **μετὰ** *meta* (after) **τὸ** *to* (the) **γεννῆσαι** *gennēsai* (generated) **αὐτὸν** *auton* (he) **τὸν** *ton* (the) **Φαλεκ** *Phalek* (Peleg) **ἔτη** *etē* (years) **τριακόσια** *triakosia* (three hundred) **ἑβδομήκοντα** *ebdomēkonta* (seventy) **καὶ** *kai* (and) **ἐγέννησεν** *egennēsen* (generated) **υἱοὺς** *uious* (sons) **καὶ** *kai* (and) **θυγατέρας** *thugateras* (daughters) **καὶ** *kai* (and) **ἀπέθανεν** *apethanen* (died)[3282]
et (and) ***vixit*** (lived) ***Eber*** (Eber) ***postquam*** (after) ***genuit*** (having generated) ***Faleg*** (Peleg) ***quadringentis*** (four hundred) ***triginta*** (thirty) ***annis*** (years) ***et*** (and) ***genuit*** (generated) ***filios*** (sons) ***et*** (and) ***filias*** (daughters)
And Eber lived after he begat Peleg four hundred and thirty years, and begat sons and daughters.
Following Peleg's projection, Eber lived *in anguish* (430) his circular years of consciousness and brought forth sons and daughters.

After the projection of *Peleg's dividing river*, with its consequent epistemic loneliness, the *breathing-time-flow* (חָוָה *chavah*) of Eber enters in years (שָׁנָה *shaneh*) of anguish. In fact, the numeral 430, four (אַרְבַּע *'arba`*) hundred (מֵאָה *me'ah*) thirty (שְׁלֹשִׁים *shĕlowshiym*), has a Gematria equivalency with both the words *miqōṣer*,[3283] meaning *for anguish* and *vayēhatu*, meaning *they were dismayed.*[3284] In addition, during that state he generates thoughts and ideas, namely, metaphoric sons and daughters.

11:18-Reu the Companion

וַיְחִי־פֶלֶג שְׁלֹשִׁים שָׁנָה וַיּוֹלֶד אֶת־רְעוּ׃ *vayəḥiy* (lived) *p̄eleḡ* (Peleg) *šəlōšiym* (thirty) *šānāh* (year) *vayvōleḏ* (brought forward) *'eṯ* (and) *rə'u* (Reu)
καὶ *kai* (and) **ἔζησεν** *ezēsen* (lived) **Φαλεκ** *Phalek* (Peleg) **ἑκατὸν** *ekaton* (a hundred)[3285] **τριάκοντα** *triakonta* (thirty) **ἔτη** *etē* (years) **καὶ** *kai* (and) **ἐγέννησεν** *egennēsen* (generated) **τὸν** *ton* (the) **Ραγαυ** *Ragau* (Reu)
vixit (lived) ***quoque*** (also) ***Faleg*** (Peleg) ***triginta*** (thirty) ***annis*** (years) ***et*** (and) ***genuit*** (generated) ***Reu*** (Reu)
And Peleg lived thirty years, and begat Reu:
Peleg *lived* (30) his years of consciousness and brought forward Reu, *the companion.*

The need to reach the other produces Reu, his companion. In fact, this name,[3286] which means *friend*, stands for *r@'iy*,[3287] *meaning pasture*. It derives from the verb *ra'ah*,[3288] *meaning to pasture, to tend, to feed, to shepherd*, like the action of a *ruler* or *teacher* and also *to associate with* and *to be a friend of someone*. This is the sense of *rea'*,[3289] *friend, companion* and *the other one*. Furthermore, the numeral 30 of the *thirty* (שְׁלֹשִׁים *shĕlowshiym*) *years* (שָׁנָה *shaneh*) has a Gematria equivalent with the word *ḇəḥayay*,[3290] *life*. Therefore, the *dividing-Peleg breathed* (חָוָה *chavah*) his *circular conscious years* (שָׁנָה *shaneh*) of life (חַי *chay*), in the anguish (*miqōṣer* מִקֹּצֶר) of his epistemic solitude, after which he projected *Reu*, his companion.

11:19-Peleg and the Other

וַיְחִי־פֶלֶג אַחֲרֵי הוֹלִידוֹ אֶת־רְעוּ תֵּשַׁע שָׁנִים וּמָאתַיִם שָׁנָה וַיּוֹלֶד בָּנִים וּבָנוֹת׃ ס   *vayəḥiy* (lived) *p̄eleḡ* (Peleg) *'aḥărēy* (after) *hvōliyḏvō* (generating) *'eṯ* (and) *rə'u* (Reu friend) *tēša'* (nine) *šāniym* (years) *umā'ṯayim* (two hundred) *šānāh* (years) *vayvōleḏ* (generated) *bāniym* (sons) *uḇānvōṯ* (daughters) *s* (.)
καὶ *kai* (and) **ἔζησεν** *ezēsen* (lived) **Φαλεκ** *Phalek* (Peleg) **μετὰ** *meta* (after) **τὸ** *to* (the) **γεννῆσαι** *gennēsai* (generated) **αὐτὸν** *auton* (he) **τὸν** *ton* (the) **Ραγαυ** *Ragau* (Reu) **διακόσια** *diakosia* (two hundred) **ἐννέα** *ennea* (nine) **ἔτη** *etē* (years) **καὶ** *kai* (and) **ἐγέννησεν** *egennēsen* (generated) **υἱοὺς** *uious* (sons) **καὶ** *kai* (and) **θυγατέρας** *thugateras* (daughters) **καὶ** *kai* (and) **ἀπέθανεν** *apethanen* (died)[3291]
vixit (lived)***-que*** (and) ***Faleg*** (Paleg) ***postquam*** (after) ***genuit*** (having generated) ***Reu*** (Reu) ***ducentis*** (two hundred) ***novem*** (nine) ***annis*** (years) ***et*** (and) ***genuit*** (generated) ***filios*** (sons) ***et*** (and) ***filias*** (daughters)
And Peleg lived after he begat Reu two hundred and nine years, and begat sons and daughters.
After bringing forth Reu, his friend, Peleg lived his conscious circularity of division from the *other stranger* (209) and generated sons and daughters.

After the generation of Reu, his companion, Peleg continued in the circularity of consciousness *divided* from the other strangers. In fact, the numeral 209 of his two hundred (וּמָאתַיִם *umā'tayim*) nine (תֵּשַׁע *tesha'*) years, is equivalent to each of the words *'aḥēr*,[3292] *other*, and *vəḡēr*,[3293] *stranger*. What this means is that, while we seek companionship, nevertheless, the others, namely the strangers, surround us. During that time, Peleg generated thoughts and concepts as metaphoric sons and daughters.

11:20-Serug, the Branching Brotherhood

וַיְחִי רְעוּ שְׁתַּיִם וּשְׁלֹשִׁים שָׁנָה וַיּוֹלֶד אֶת־שְׂרוּג׃   *vayəḥiy* (lived) *rə'u* (Reu) *šətayim* (two) *ušəlōšiym* (thirty) *šānāh* (years) *vayvōleḏ* (generated) *'eṯ* (and) *śəruḡ* (Serug)
καὶ *kai* (and) **ἔζησεν** *ezēsen* (lived) **Ραγαυ** *Ragau* (Reu) **ἑκατὸν** *ekaton* (a hundred)[3294] **τριάκοντα** *triakonta* (thirty) **δύο** *duo* (two) **ἔτη** *etē* (years) **καὶ** *kai* (and) **ἐγέννησεν** *egennēsen* (generated) **τὸν** *ton* (the) **Σερουχ** *Serouch* (Serug)
vixit (lived) ***autem*** (also) ***Reu*** (Reu) ***triginta*** (thirty) ***duobus*** (two) ***annis*** (years) ***et*** (and) ***genuit*** (generated) ***Sarug*** (Serug)
And Reu lived two and thirty years, and begat Serug:
Reu lived and generated in the course of his circular consciousness a *brother* (32), Serug as branch.

The companionship of Reu, however, branches out with the new shoot of *Serug*.[3295] In fact, this name means *branch*, *shoot*. It derives from the verb *sarag*,[3296] *to be intertwined together*. Furthermore, the numeral 32, referred to the thirty (שְׁלֹשִׁים *shělowshiym*) two (שְׁנַיִם *shěnayim*) years, has a Gematria equivalency with the word *bə'āḥiyhu*,[3297] meaning *brother*. Therefore, the years that Reu, the friend, lived in the circularity of his consciousness, he generated a brother, a branch from himself and

"*they are joined one to another* (בְּאָחִיהוּ *bə'āḥiyhu*), *they stick together, that they cannot be sundered*."[3298]

This is love, which, despite the epistemic solitude, binds together lovers, friends and neighbors.

11:21-Reu Conscious Wakening

וַיְחִי רְעוּ אַחֲרֵי הוֹלִידוֹ אֶת־שְׂרוּג שֶׁבַע שָׁנִים וּמָאתַיִם שָׁנָה וַיּוֹלֶד בָּנִים וּבָנוֹת׃ ס   *vayəḥiy* (lived) *rə'u* (Reu) *'aḥărēy* (after) *hvōliyḏvō* (having generated) *'eṯ* (and) *śəruḡ* (Serug) *šeḇa'* (seven) *šāniym* (years) *umā'ṯayim* (two hundred) *šānāh* (years) *vayvōleḏ* (generated) *bāniym* (sons) *uḇānvōṯ* (daughters) *s* (.)
καὶ *kai* (and) **ἔζησεν** *ezēsen* (lived) **Ραγαυ** *Ragau* (Reu) **μετὰ** *meta* (after) **τὸ** *to* (the) **γεννῆσαι** *gennēsai* (generated) **αὐτὸν** *auton* (he) **τὸν** *ton* (the) **Σερουχ** *Serouch* (Serug) **διακόσια** *diakosia* (two hundred) **ἑπτὰ** *epta* (seven) **ἔτη** *etē* (years) **καὶ** *kai* (and) **ἐγέννησεν** *egennēsen* (generated) **υἱοὺς** *uious* (sons) **καὶ** *kai* (and) **θυγατέρας** *thugateras* (daughters) **καὶ** *kai* (and) **ἀπέθανεν** *apethanen* (died)[3299]

vixit (lived)***-que*** (and) ***Reu*** (Reu) ***postquam*** (after) ***genuit*** (having generated) ***Sarug*** (Serug) ***ducentis*** (two hundred) ***septem*** (seven) ***annis*** (years) ***et*** (and) ***genuit*** (generated) ***filios*** (sons) ***et*** (and) ***filias*** (daughters)
And Reu lived after he begat Serug two hundred and seven years, and begat sons and daughters.
After bringing forth Serug the branch, Reu lived years of conscious *awakening* (207) and generated sons and daughters.

The *two hundred* (וּמָאתַיִם umāʾṯayim) *seven* (שֶׁבַע sheba`) *years* (שָׁנָה shaneh) are Reu's conscious wakefulness. In fact, the numeral 207 corresponds to the Gematria equivalent words *vāʾiyqāṣ,*[3300] *I awake*, and *ḇəhāqiyṣ,*[3301] *in awaking*. Therefore, Reu, after the projection of his neighboring brother, Serug, projects, in the state of wakefulness, his thoughts and concepts, *viz.* his sons and daughters.

11:22-Nahor the Breathing Body

וַיְחִי שְׂרוּג שְׁלֹשִׁים שָׁנָה וַיּוֹלֶד אֶת־נָחוֹר׃
vayəḥiy (lived) *śərūḡ* (Serug) *šəlōšiym* (thirty) *šānāh* (years) *vayvōleḏ* (generated) *ʾeṯ* (and) *nāḥvōr* (snorting Nahor)
καὶ *kai* (and) **ἔζησεν** *ezēsen* (lived) **Σερουχ** *Sepouch* (Serug)) **ἑκατὸν** *ekaton* (a hundred)[3302] **τριάκοντα** *triakonta* (thirty) **ἔτη** *etē* (years) **καὶ** *kai* (and) **ἐγέννησεν** *egennēsen* (generated) **τὸν** *ton* (the) **Ναχωρ** *Nachōr* (Nahor)
vixit (lived) ***vero*** (indeed) ***Sarug*** (Serug) ***triginta*** (thirty) ***annis*** (years) ***et*** (and) ***genuit*** (generated) ***Nahor*** (Nahor)
And Serug lived thirty years, and begat Nahor:
During Serug's conscious *life* (30) he generated the *snorting* Nahor.

The word *life, ḇəḥayay,*[3303] is the Gematria equivalent of the numeral 30, namely, the *thirty* (שְׁלֹשִׁים shělowshiym) *years* (שָׁנָה shaneh). Therefore, the *branching out Serug breathed* (חָוָה chavah) his *circular conscious years* (שָׁנָה shaneh) of this *life* (חַי chay). Finally, the procession of patriarchal archetypes reaches the *breathing* physicality of this body here and now. In fact, the projected faculty is that of *Nahor*, the *snorting* one.[3304] The name is the same as the verb *nachar,*[3305] which means *to snore*, as in the state of sleep, and *to snort*, as horse whinnying.

To understand the connection between the patriarch Nachar and the neighing of a horse, we must read Job's description of

> "*the horse* (סוּס cuwc) *and his rider* (רכב rakab)... *The horse strength... clothed his neck with thunder... the glory of his snorting nostrils* (נחר nachar) *is terrible.*"[3306]

Nachar (נחר), then, is the *one breathing hard, snoring* and *snorting* of *our physical body*. This *breathing being* carries on itself all the generations of archetypal patriarchs as the rider who empowers our epistemic process. Compare the metaphor of the horse with the present jocular and colloquial use of the English term horse as a

> "man, ... horse sense, ... wisdom, ... rationality."[3307]

We already saw the horse metaphor connected with Gomer, in the field of space, with the city of Resen, in the realm of causality and now we recognize it in the course of time. Furthermore, from the Indian[3308] to the Western tradition,[3309] the breathing horse has been described allegorically as this psychosomatic body carrier of all our epistemic forms.

11:23-Nahor the Possessor of Wealth

וַיְחִי שְׂרוּג אַחֲרֵי הוֹלִידוֹ אֶת־נָחוֹר מָאתַיִם שָׁנָה וַיּוֹלֶד בָּנִים וּבָנוֹת׃ ס
vayəḥiy (lived) *śərūḡ* (Serug) *ʾaḥărēy* (after) *hvōliydvō* (having generated) *ʾeṯ* (and) *nāḥvōr* (Nahor) *māʾṯayim* (two hundred) *šānāh* (years) *vayvōleḏ* (generated) *bāniym* (sons) *uḇānvōṯ* (daughters) *s* (.)
καὶ *kai* (and) **ἔζησεν** *ezēsen* (lived) **Σερουχ** *Serouch* (Serug) **μετὰ** *meta* (after) **τὸ** *to* (the) **γεννῆσαι** *gennēsai* (generated) **αὐτὸν** *auton* (he) **τὸν** *ton* (the) **Ναχωρ** *Nachōr* (Nahor) **ἔτη** *etē* (years) **διακόσια** *diakosia* (two hundred) **καὶ** *kai* (and) **ἐγέννησεν** *egennēsen* (generated) **υἱοὺς**

uious (sons) **καὶ** *kai* (and) **θυγατέρας** *thugateras* (daughters) **καὶ** *kai* (and) **ἀπέθανεν** *apethanen* (died)[3310]
vixit (lived)***-que*** (and) ***Sarug*** (Serug) ***postquam*** (after) ***genuit*** (having generated) ***Nahor*** (Nahor) ***ducentos*** (two hundred) ***annos*** (years) ***et*** (and) ***genuit*** (generated) ***filios*** (sons) ***et*** (and) ***filias*** (daughters)
And Serug lived after he begat Nahor two hundred years, and begat sons and daughters.
After having generated Nahor, Serug lived *possessing wealth* (200) and generated sons and daughters.

The *two hundred* (וּמָאתַיִם *umā'ṯayim*) *years* (שָׁנָה *shaneh*) refer to Nahor's time function of wealth. In fact, the numeral 200 corresponds to the Gematria equivalent words *hamiqəneh*[3311] *and miqənay,*[3312] both meaning *cattle*, as *possession* and *wealth*.

"TIME is Money,"

writes Benjamin Franklin to a friend.[3313] Therefore, having taken on the heavy burden of wealth possession, Nahor, projects his thoughts and concepts, *viz.* his sons and daughters. Like Atlas, carrying the weight of the whole world, so Nahor's *physical-breathing-body-horse* carries the entire load of all that s/he possesses. In other words, this individual physical juridical person here is, like Cain, the possessor of the land on which it toils. As a cross-cultural comparison with the Sanskrit literature, the term horse, *aś-va,*[3314] conveys the same connotations of this verse.[3315] In fact, it derives from *aś*, meaning to gain, to obtain and to accumulate, and is cognate to the verb *āśvas,*[3316] to breathe, and with *śvāsa,*[3317] snorting and panting.

11:24-The Bodily Station

וַיְחִי נָחוֹר תֵּשַׁע וְעֶשְׂרִים שָׁנָה וַיּוֹלֶד אֶת־תָּרַח׃ *vayəḥiy* (lived) *nāḥvōr* (Nahor) *tēšaʿ* (nine) *vəʿeśəriym* (twenty) *šānāh* (years) *vayvōleḏ* (generated) *'eṯ* (and) *tāraḥ* (Terah the station)
καὶ *kai* (and) **ἔζησεν** *ezēsen* (lived) **Ναχωρ** *Nachōr* (Nahor) **ἔτη** *etē* (years) **ἑβδομήκοντα** *ebdomēkonta* (seventy)[3318] **ἐννέα** *ennea* (nine) **καὶ** *kai* (and) **ἐγέννησεν** *egennēsen* (generated) **τὸν** *ton* (the) **Θαρα** *Thara* (Thare)
vixit (lived) ***autem*** (also) ***Nahor*** (Nahor) ***viginti*** (twenty) ***novem*** (nine) ***annis*** (years) ***et*** (and) ***genuit*** (generated) ***Thare*** (Terah)
And Nahor lived nine and twenty years, and begat Terah:
Nahor lived *to arrive* (29) at the *station* generating Terah.

The Gematria value of 29 is equivalent to the verb *to come, to arrive.*[3319] Therefore, in the time span of twenty-nine years, we arrive at the station of our journey. *Terah*, in fact, means *delay station.*[3320] This station is this body, this individualized Ego here and now, as you and I,

"*as if it had issued out* (בְּגִיחוֹ *bəḡiyḥvō* = #29)[3321] *of the womb.*"[3322]

During the journey through this life, *we come to* (בְּגִיחוֹ *bəḡiyḥvō*) it and in it.

Continuing our cross-cultural comparison with the Sanskrit literature, the horses' station is the *aśvattha* tree of life. In fact,

"*āśva*... belongs to a horse... and [it is the tree] under which horses stand."[3323]

From a metaphoric physiological perspective, the body is like a tree, the (similar to Samson's[3324] *strength* (כֹּחַ *koach*)[3325] conveyed through his *locks* (מַחְלָפָה *machlaphah*)[3326] or *hair* (שֵׂעָר *se'ar*)[3327]) are the roots in heaven and the limbs are the branches.

"*Indeed, a person is like a forest tree, his hairs are like the leaves and the skin as his outer bark.*"[3328]

"*The holy fig tree with roots above and branches below... with branches extending below and above develops by world's qualities. It has sense objects as sprouts and roots, stretching below in human world, are bonded by action....This tree* [is] *a horses' stand with strong roots must be cut by the mighty weapon of non-attachment.*"[3329]

Thus, this body, this individualized Ego is the life station under which stands the breathing being.

11:25-The Breathing One Encamps in the Body

וַיְחִי נָחוֹר אַחֲרֵי הוֹלִידוֹ אֶת־תֶּרַח תְּשַׁע־עֶשְׂרֵה שָׁנָה וּמְאַת שָׁנָה וַיּוֹלֶד בָּנִים וּבָנוֹת׃ ס *vayəḥiy* (lived) *nāḥvōr* (Nahor) *'aḥărēy* (after) *hvōliydvō* (having generated) *'et* (and) *teraḥ* (Terah the station) *təša'* (nine) *'eśərēh* (ten) *šānāh* (years) *umə'at* (hundred) *šānāh* (years) *vayvōled* (generated) *bāniym* (sons) *ubānvōt* (daughters) *s* (.)
καὶ *kai* (and) **ἔζησεν** *ezēsen* (lived) **Ναχωρ** *Nachōr* (Nahor) **μετὰ** *meta* (after) **τὸ** *to* (the) **γεννῆσαι** *gennēsai* (generated) **αὐτὸν** *auton* (he) **τὸν** *ton* (the) **Θαρα** *Thara* (Terah)**ἔτη** *etē* (years) **ἑκατὸν** *ekaton* (hundred) **εἴκοσι** *eikosi* (twenty) **ἐννέα** *ennea* (nine) **καὶ** *kai* (and) **ἐγέννησεν** *egennēsen* (generated) **υἱοὺς** *uious* (sons) **καὶ** *kai* (and) **θυγατέρας** *thugateras* (daughters) **καὶ** *kai* (and) **ἀπέθανεν** *apethanen* (died)[3330]
vixit (lived)**-*que*** (and) ***Nahor*** (Nahor) ***postquam*** (after) ***genuit*** (having generated) ***Thare*** (Terah) ***centum*** (a hundred) ***decem*** (ten) ***et*** (and) ***novem*** (nine) ***annos*** (years) ***et*** (and) ***genuit*** (generated) ***filios*** (sons) ***et*** (and) ***filias*** (daughters)
And Nahor lived after he begat Terah an hundred and nineteen years, and begat sons and daughters.
After having generated Terah, the station, the breathing Nahor *stood encamping* (119) [in that station] and generated sons and daughters.

The *one hundred* (מֵאָה *me'ah*) *nine* (תֵּשַׁע *tesha`*) and *ten* (עֶשֶׂר *`asar*) *years* (שָׁנָה *shaneh*) correspond to the numeral 119 with the Gematria equivalent to the words *hā'ōmēd*,[3331] *standing*, and *vəhaḥōniym*,[3332] *encamping*. Therefore, the breathing Nahor stands encamping in this bodily station where he generates thoughts and concepts as sons and daughters.

As a ripple effect, each noetic faculty brings forward the next one spreading in time towards the objective possibilities. Thus, *time* (*viz. Shem*), through its flooding and *flowing river* (*viz. Arphaxad*) *of time, sprouts* (*viz. Salah*) into the *region* of time *passing by* (*viz. Eber*). This passage of time *divides* (*viz. Peleg*) us from the *company* (*viz. Reu*) of others. However, it *branches out* while it *unites* (*viz. Serug*) with the inhaling/exhaling *breath* (*viz. Nahor*) of this *individualized bodily Ego station* (*viz. Terah*).

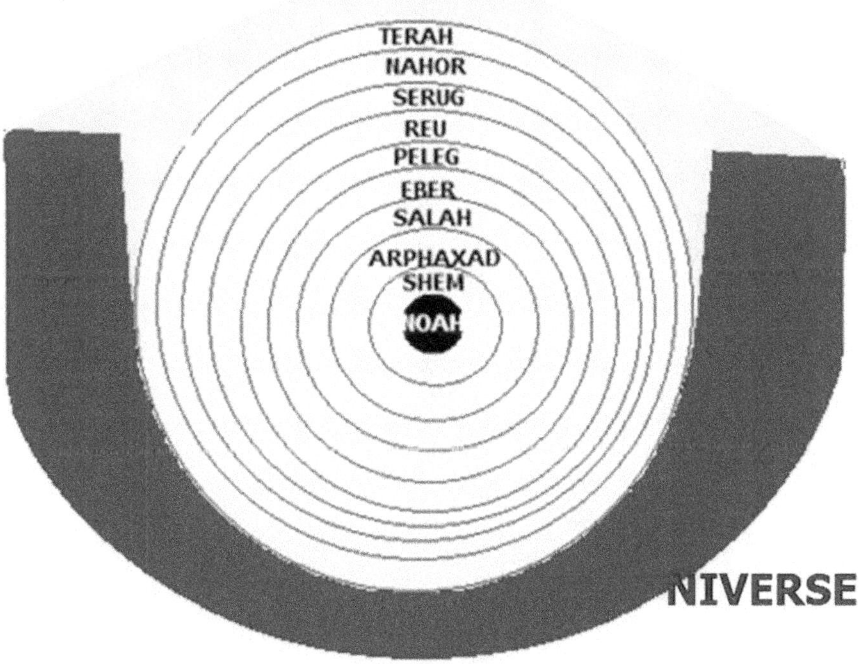

GRAPHIC: *The ripple effect of each noetic faculty*

A reader may inquire,

'If the Patriarchs are universal epistemic paradigms, why Genesis does not say so explicitly?'

We reply,

'There are two reasons why Genesis describes those epistemic paradigms as metaphoric anthropomorphized long living Patriarchs,

1) *to make sure that no individual reader divinizes oneself by exclusively identifying with them. Instead one should realizes that they are real universal epistemic faculties; and*
2) *to teach that the Patriarchs' longevity projects them in a metahistorical dimension as real templates of universal epistemic configurations.'*

Time continues flowing branching with a ripple effect into the two circadian stages of dream and wakefulness.

11-III SECTION: TERAH'S HISTORY

11:26- Abram, Nahor and Haran

וַיְחִי־תֶרַח שִׁבְעִים שָׁנָה וַיּוֹלֶד אֶת־אַבְרָם אֶת־נָחוֹר וְאֶת־הָרָן׃ *vayəḥiy* (lived) *teraḥ* (Terah) *šiḇə'iym* (seventy) *šānāh* (years) *vayvōleḏ* (generated) *'eṯ* (and) *'aḇərām* (Abram) *'eṯ* (and) *nāḥvōr* (Nahor) *və'eṯ* (and) *hārān* (Haran)
καὶ *kai* (and) **ἔζησεν** *ezēsen* (lived) **Θαρα** *Thara* (Thare) **ἑβδομήκοντα** *ebdomēkonta* (seventy) **ἔτη** *etē* (years) **καὶ** *kai* (and) **ἐγέννησεν** *egennēsen* (generated) **τὸν** *ton* (the) **Αβραμ** *Abram* (Abram) **καὶ** *kai* (and) **τὸν** *ton* (the) **Ναχωρ** *Nachōr* (Nahor) **καὶ** *kai* (and) **τὸν** *ton* (the) **Αρραν** *Arran* (Haram)
vixit (lived)***-que*** (and) ***Thare*** (Terah) ***septuaginta*** (seventy) ***annis*** (years) ***et*** (and) ***genuit*** (generated) ***Abram*** (Abram) ***et*** (and) ***Nahor*** (Nahor) ***et*** (and) ***Aran*** (Haran)
And Terah lived seventy years, and begat Abram, Nahor, and Haran.
Terah *went on* (70) living and generated Abram, Nahor and Haran.

The journey continues for *seventy* (שִׁבְעִים *shib'iym*) years (שָׁנָה *shaneh*) and it takes place on three stages. The word *vənāḇvō'āh,*[3333] with a Gematria equivalence of 70, means *we go*. Thus, as

"*we go into* (וְנָבוֹאָה *vənāḇvō'āh*) *the fortified cities,*"[3334]

similarly we enter into our physical *Ego station* (*viz.* Terah), which articulates in the three circadian states. They are the three sons of this bodily station, *viz.* Abram, Nahor and Haran.

1) The name *Abram*[3335] means exalted father of the multitude of builders. It is a contraction of *'Abiyram,*[3336] from *'ab,*[3337] meaning *father,* and *ruwm,*[3338] meaning *to raise up, to extoll, to erect* and *to build.* It corresponds to the metaphoric building of the towering Babel, which the human multitude erects in the waking state.
2) The name *Nahor* (נָחוֹר *nachowr*), as we saw with the first one with this designation, corresponds to the *snoring-one*, thus clearly to the dream state of REM sleep.
3) The name *Haran*[3339] means *mountaineer*, from *harar*, signifying mountain from a root meaning *to come up*. Therefore, it corresponds to the state of dreamless NREM sleep. In this state, the entire mountain of the world is absorbed in one synthetic instant of silence. It is the

   "*Deep-unconscious-sleep where one asleep does not desire any desire, does not see any dream. The state of deep-unconscious-sleep* [stands] *alone, having become one compact knowledge… Its mouth is consciousness* [and] *the knower.*"[3340]

   "*Thus, when a person is sleeping, so that s/he sees no dream whatsoever, verily s/he becomes one with that breathing self. Then, speech together with all the names goes to him. The eye together with all the forms goes to him. The ear together with all sounds goes to him. The mind together with all thoughts goes to him. When he awakens, as from a blazing fire, sparks spread out in all directions. Similarly, therefore, from this self the vital breaths spread out each in its own place. From the vital breaths, the resplendent senses* [spread out] *and from the resplendent senses the worlds spread out.*"[3341]

11:27-The Generations of Terah

וְאֵלֶּה תּוֹלְדֹת תֶּרַח תֶּרַח הוֹלִיד אֶת־אַבְרָם אֶת־נָחוֹר וְאֶת־הָרָן וְהָרָן הוֹלִיד אֶת־לוֹט׃ *və'ēleh* (these) *tvōlədōṯ* (the generations) *teraḥ* (of Terah) *teraḥ* (Terah) *hvōliyḏ* (generated) *'eṯ* (and) *'aḇərām* (Abram) *'eṯ* (and) *nāḥvōr* (Nahor) *və'eṯ* (and) *hārān* (Haran) *vəhārān* (Haran) *hvōliyḏ* (generated) *'eṯ* (and) *lvōṭ* (Lot)
αὗται *autai* (thus) **δὲ** *de* (but) **αἱ** *ai* (the) **γενέσεις** *geneseis* (generations) **Θαρα** *Thara* (Terah) **Θαρα** *Thara* (Terah) **ἐγέννησεν** *egennēsen* (generated) **τὸν** *ton* (the) **Αβραμ** *Abram* (Abram) **καὶ** *kai* (and) **τὸν** *ton* (the) **Ναχωρ** *Nachōr* (Nahor) **καὶ** *kai* (and) **τὸν** *ton* (the) **Αρραν** *Arran* (Haram) **καὶ** *kai* (and) **Αρραν** *Arran* (Haram) **ἐγέννησεν** *egennēsen* (generated) **τὸν** *ton* (the) **Λωτ** *Lōt* (Lot)
hae (these) ***sunt*** (are) ***autem*** (also) ***generationes*** (the generations) ***Thare*** (of Terah) ***Thare*** (Terah) ***genuit*** (generated) ***Abram*** (Abram) ***et*** (and) ***Nahor*** (Nahor) ***et*** (and) ***Aran*** (Haram) ***porro*** (subsequently) ***Aran*** (Haram) ***genuit*** (generated) ***Loth*** (Lot)

Now these are the generations of Terah: Terah begat Abram, Nahor, and Haran; and Haran begat Lot.
These are the generations of Terah. Terah generated Abram, Nahor and Haran. Furthermore, Haran generated Lot.

As with the Biblical

"*flaming sword which turned every way, to keep the way of the tree of life,*"[3342]

once we enter the state of deep sleep, the whole objective world is concealed and

"*the mouth of truth is covered with a golden dish.*"[3343]

That cover is the veiling function of Lot. In fact, the name *Lot*[3344] means *veil covering*, it derives from the verb *luwt* (לוט), to wrap, to hide, to do secretively. From the physical perspective, Lot is the cover that veils each one from the other, thus enforcing the state of incommunicable epistemic loneliness of solipsism. From the oneiric perspective, it is the unthinkable projection of the dreamless sleep of Haran.

Question for the reader,

'What is that you see, perceive, imagine or even dream, when you are in a deep cataleptic sedation? You experience, nothing at all! That is because the nature itself of the dreamless state conceals everything. That concealing aspect is, metaphorically, named Lot.'

Again, the reader may consider,

'It appears that there is a continuous repetition of the same themes. The circadian rhythm is attributed now to one patriarchal aspect and then to another. How must we interpret this?'

We reply,

*'You are right. This shows that the epistemic paradigms proceed gradually from the universal to the particular. Each time they convey a greater individualization until they are recognized operating within this reader here and now. In other words, until the reader realizes that **the text is really describing his or her own self at each level of the universal process**. The paradigm flows down from the universal configuration to a more individualized reflection of itself and assumes a more individualized aspect at each level. Each level is described as a different Patriarch generated by the preceding one.'*

11:28-Haran's Redemption

וַיָּמָת הָרָן עַל־פְּנֵי תֶּרַח אָבִיו בְּאֶרֶץ מוֹלַדְתּוֹ בְּאוּר כַּשְׂדִּים׃ *vayāmāṯ* (died) *hārān* (Haran) *'al* (at) *pənēy* (presence) *teraḥ* (of Terah) *'āḇiyv* (father) *bə'ereṣ* (in the land) *mvōlaḏətvō* (of origin) *bə'ur* (in Ur) *kaśədiym* (of the Chaldees)
καὶ *kai* (and) **ἀπέθανεν** *apethanen* (died) **Αρραν** *Arran* (Haran) **ἐνώπιον** *enōpion* (in the presence of) **Θαρα** *Thara* (of Therah) **τοῦ** *tou* (the) **πατρὸς** *patros* (father) **αὐτοῦ** *autou* (his) **ἐν** *en* (in) **τῇ** *tē* (the) **γῇ** *gē* (land) **ᾗ** *ē* (thus) **ἐγενήθη** *egenēthē* (he was born) **ἐν** *en* (in) **τῇ** *tē* (the) **χώρᾳ** *chōra* (land) **τῶν** *tōn* (of the) **Χαλδαίων** *Chaldaiōn* (Chaldees)
mortuus (dead)***-que*** (and) ***est*** (is) ***Aran*** (Haran) ***ante*** (before) ***Thare*** (Terah) ***patrem*** (father) ***suum*** (his) ***in*** (in) ***terra*** (the land) ***nativitatis*** (of birth) ***suae*** (his) ***in*** (in) ***Ur*** (Ur) ***Chaldeorum*** (of the Chaldees)
And Haran died before his father Terah in the land of his nativity, in Ur of the Chaldees.
Haran perished at the presence of the father Terah, in the land of his origin, in Ur the *flame* of the Chaldees *astrologers*.

Like untilled land[3345] and like the trunk of a tree, whose old roots rotten in the ground,[3346] also Haran, the state[3347] of dreamless sleep, perishes[3348] or ends. When this happens, then Terah, this bodily station, enters into dreamland and subsequently wakes up. Thus, Haran dies in (על 'al) the presence

(פָּנִים *paniym*) of his father Terah. However, Terah himself will die in the state of Haran, as we shall see, then also his wisdom will inevitably die out[3349] with him.

Meaningfully, Haran, the state of dreamless sleep, borders, on the lower end, with the state of dream, which borders also with the wakefulness of this body, *viz.* Terah. On the higher level, Haran begins and ends in Ur of the Chaldees. Haran is the synthetic NREM mountain-state of Pure-Consciousness without any objectivity. Its land (אֶרֶץ *'erets*) of *origin*[3350] is Ur of the Chaldees. The name *Ur* (אור 'uwr) means *flame*,[3351] the *light of revelation*, which *shines* and *becomes light*. This light is the one of the *Chaldees*,[3352] they are the *clod-breakers*, namely, the astrologers who brake the *clay lump* of objectivity. That flame refers to the fire of the burning bush. That is the flame of the Original Transcendent *Yĕhovah* (יְהוָה). *It is the* Wondrous Stupor of Awareness from which departs, like an epistemic Big Bang, the Stillness of Consciousness.

11:29-Terah's Epistemic Procession

וַיִּקַּח אַבְרָם וְנָחוֹר לָהֶם נָשִׁים שֵׁם אֵשֶׁת־אַבְרָם שָׂרָי וְשֵׁם אֵשֶׁת־נָחוֹר מִלְכָּה בַּת־הָרָן אֲבִי־מִלְכָּה וַאֲבִי יִסְכָּה׃ *vayiqaḥ* (took) *'aḇərām* (Abram) *vənāḥvōr* (Nahor) *lāhem* (and) *nāšiym* (wives) *šēm* (the name) *'ēšeṯ* (wife) *'aḇərām* (of Abram) *śārāy* (Sarai) *vəšēm* (the name) *'ēšeṯ* (wife) *nāḥvōr* (of Nahor) *miləkāh* (Milcah) *baṯ* (the daughter) *hārān* (of Haran) *ăḇiy* (the father) *miləkāh* (of Milcah) *va'ăḇiy* (father) *yisəkāh* (of Iscah)
καὶ *kai* (and) **ἔλαβον** *elabon* (took) **Αβραμ** *Abram* (Abram) **καὶ** *kai* (and) **Ναχωρ** *Nachōr* (Nahor) **ἑαυτοῖς** *eautois* (for themselves) **γυναῖκας** *gunaikas* (wives) **ὄνομα** *onoma* (name) **τῇ** *tē* (of the) **γυναικὶ** *gunaiki* (wife) **Αβραμ** *Abram* (Abram) **Σαρα** *Sara* (Sarai) **καὶ** *kai* (and) **ὄνομα** *onoma* (name) **τῇ** *tē* (of the) **γυναικὶ** *gunaiki* (wife) **Ναχωρ** *Nachōr* (Nahor) **Μελχα** *Melcha* (Milcah) **θυγάτηρ** *thugatēr* (daughter) **Αρραν** *Arran* (Haran) **πατὴρ** *patēr* (father) **Μελχα** *Melcha* (Milcah) **καὶ** *kai* (and) **πατὴρ** *patēr* (father) **Ιεσχα** *Iescha* (Iscah)
duxerunt (took) ***autem*** (also) ***Abram*** (Abram) ***et*** (and) ***Nahor*** (Nahor) ***uxores*** (wives) ***nomen*** (the name) ***autem*** (also) ***uxoris*** (of wife) ***Abram*** (of Abram) ***Sarai*** (Sarai) ***et*** (and) ***nomen*** (the name) ***uxoris*** (of the wife) ***Nahor*** (of Nahor) ***Melcha*** (Milcah) ***filia*** (the daughter) ***Aran*** (of Haran) ***patris*** (the father) ***Melchae*** (of Milcah) ***et*** (and) ***patris*** (the father) ***Ieschae*** (of Iscah)
And Abram and Nahor took them wives: the name of Abram's wife was Sarai; and the name of Nahor's wife, Milcah, the daughter of Haran, the father of Milcah, and the father of Iscah.
Abram and Nahor took wives. The name of Abram's wife is Sarai, the name of Nahor's wife is Milcah, the daughter of Haran, the father of Milcah and the father of Iscah.

Haran, the state of NREM deep sleep, is total stillness without objectivity. Therefore, there is no object/wife. However, it has projections, namely, metaphoric son and daughters, which allow its transformation. In fact, even in NREM sleep there are different patterns gradually changing. Dr. Dement describes four gradual levels,

> "a progressive descent from Stage 1 into other stages of NREM sleep. The term 'descent' is meant to imply a progression along the depth-of-sleep continuum as sleep becomes deeper and deeper, the sleeper becomes more remote from the environment, and increasingly more potent stimuli are necessary to cause arousal. Each new stage is announced by its own characteristic pattern in the EEG. After only a few minutes of Stage 1, the onset of Stage 2 is established by the appearance of spindling and K complexes.[3353] Several minutes later the slow delta waves of Stage 3 become apparent. After about ten minutes of this stage, the delta activity becomes more and more predominant and signals the presence of Stage 4. At this point it is extremely difficult to awaken the sleeper... in Stage 4, thirty or forty minutes following sleep onset, a series of body movements heralds the start of re-ascent through the stages of NREM sleep."[3354]

<Usually, stages 3 and 4 combine, constituting a deep-delta sleep[3355] or Slow-Wave-Sleep (SWS). REM and SWS have a cyclical circadian pattern; deprivation of REM or NREM sleep creates psychological disorders. However, it is difficult to awaken and

"deprive a person of stage 4."[3356]

Since

"the intensity of the stimuli necessary to awaken the person"[3357]

determines the depth of sleep, stimuli applied to sleepers in stage 4

"cause them to shift to a more superficial stage of non-REM sleep."[3358]

Borbély reports,

"The waking up of subjects from non-REM sleep also produces dream... Dreaming is thus by no means limited to REM sleep but also occurs as we fall asleep, wake up, and are in non-REM sleep."[3359]

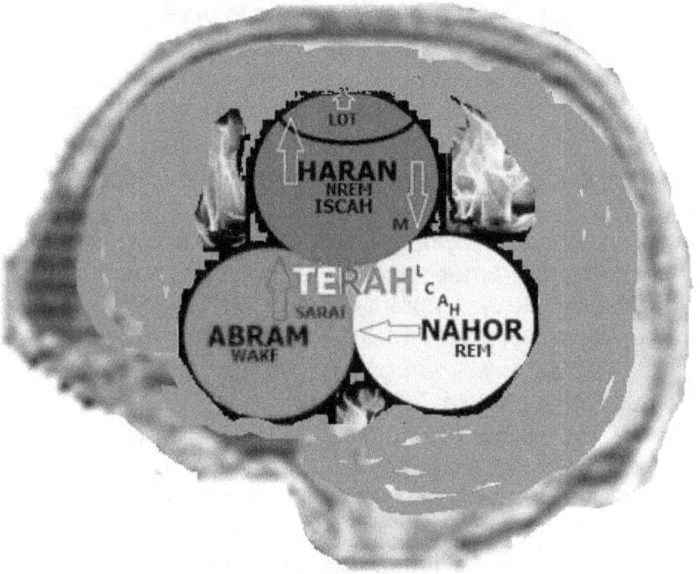

GRAPHIC: *The Generations of Terah*

Thus, dream cannot be measured only by REM.[3360] However

"compared with REM recall, NREM mentation[3361] [*i.e.* recall] is generally more poorly recalled, more like thinking, and less like dreaming, less vivid, less visual, more conceptual,"

which demonstrates that

"NREM sleep is not a mental void."[3362]

Further research on the oneiric or dream realm has revealed two events that more likely indicate the distinction between dream state, *i.e.*: the phasic-events, predominant in the REM stage, with

"rapid, short-lived phenomena like twitches and the rapid eye movements,"

and deep sleep state, *i.e.*: the tonic-events, predominant in the NREM stage, with

"slow, stable phenomena such as suppression of skeletal muscle activity"[3363]

and consequent

"breakdown of cortical effective connectivity."[3364]

This has lead to

"speculation and experimentation on the possibility that phasic events may be 'the building blocks of dreams.'"[3365]

Researchers have found that periods of NREM with dream mentation showed intense phasic-activity. Whereas, periods of NREM with no dream mentation showed EMG records with much tonic-activity.[3366] We can then observe that the dream state corresponds to the phasic-activity of both REM and NREM and deep sleep state corresponds to the tonic-activity of NREM 3 and 4 stage.

"Large parts of the brain... active during waking are inactive during NREM sleep and are reactivated during REM sleep... the brain is not only a collection of passive reflex circuits, but... it actually possesses the means of regulating its own activation."[3367]

Furthermore, we want to point out that every mentation takes place in the waking stage, therefore deforming, as if *translating into the language of wakefulness*, the original state in which the experience was lived by the sleeper.>[3368]

Therefore, on one side, *concealed* in Lot, Haran tends towards its ineffable, unconceivable and fulgurating origin. On the other side, Haran potentially *looks forth* and that is the significance of its daughter's name *Iscah*, from a root meaning *to watch*.[3369] That potentiality is actualized by Haran's other daughter, *Milcah*, who *becomes the queen*,[3370] the *ruling* objectivity in the REM dream world of Nahor. Consequently, *snoring* Nahor, the oneiric subject, unites with *queen* Milcah, his dream objects.

Next, in the epistemic procession, is the waking state. There, with his multitude, Abram builds his world. Of this world, Abram is the subject and *Sarai* means his *dominating*[3371] objectivity. Abram, this subject here, and Sarai, this object here, are both offspring of Terah,[3372] this individualized bodily Ego here and now. In fact, we find the union of these two siblings,[3373] Abram-*sub*ject/*ob*ject-Sarai polarities, both actually generated right here and now by our *Ego-station* (*Terah*), shaping the modality of our waking state. Like Eve came out from Adam side, so the two logical subject-object distinction of the epistemic synthetic a-priori[3374] polarities are the metaphoric Abram-brother/sister-Sarai siblings generated by this mind in this mind. Furthermore, both Milcah and Sarai are the objective world, *cast* ($_{e}$*ject*$_{ed}$) *over* (*ob*) the shoulders of the dreaming and waking subjects, who are *thrown* ($_{e}$*ject*$_{ed}$) *under* (*sub*) the heavy rulership of the objects.

11:30-Sarai's Bareness

וַתְּהִי שָׂרַי עֲקָרָה אֵין לָהּ וָלָד׃   *vatəhiy* (was) *śāray* (Sarai) *ʿăqārāh* (barren) *ʾēyn* (not) *lāh* (she) *vālāḏ* (child)
καὶ *kai* (and) **ἦν** *ēn* (was) **Σαρα** *Sara* (Sarai) **στεῖρα** *steira* (barren) **καὶ** *kai* (and) **οὐκ** *ouk* (no) **ἐτεκνοποίει** *eteknopoiei* (bear children)
erat (was) ***autem*** (also) ***Sarai*** (Sarai) ***sterilis*** (barren) ***nec*** (nor) ***habebat*** (had she) ***liberos*** (children)
But Sarai was barren; she had no child.
Sarai was barren, she had no child.

Objectivity alone, as such, is *barren*. The object by itself, namely, only in its noematic aspect, has no one to whom offer itself too. By itself, the object cannot conceive. Nor it can generate ideal *offspring*[3375] without the noetic presence of the subject. This is the metaphoric meaning of Sarai's bareness. It is impossible to conceive the world, when there is no thinking process. In fact, the world itself would be *barren*,[3376] and, like Sarai, it would be *barren* or *rooted up*[3377] from the vivifying seed of the subject.

However, the absence of objectivity gives the opportunity for a *flight* towards transcendence. In fact, later on, Genesis describes it with the story of Hagar and Ishmael.[3378]

"*Sarai... took Hagar, the flight,*[3379] *her family maid slave*[3380] *... and gave her to her husband Abram to be his wife*[3381]*... And Hagar bare Abram a son: ... Ishmael,*[3382] *whom God will hear.*[3383]

And,

"*Ishmael was always true to his promise.*"[3384]

And God said

"'*I have blessed him.*'"[3385]

However,

"*God said, 'Sarah... shall bear thee* [o Abraham] *a son... and thou shalt call his name Isaac,*[3386] *he who laughs'*[3387]*... and Sarah laugh, saying... 'I... am old.'*"[3388]

Then, Sarah

"*said unto Abraham, 'Cast out this bondwoman and her son*[3389]*... And Abraham ... sent her away: and* *she departed, and wandered in the preaching desert*[3390] *of the wilderness."*[3391]

In other words, the barren (עָקַר *'aqar*) absence of objectivity consents the mind's *flight* (*viz.* Hagar's name) to the *eloquent* (דָּבַר *dabar*) *desert* (מִדְבָּר *midbar*) where *transcendence hearkens* (*viz.* Ishmael's name) and blesses the orator. That desert is the singing silent stillness in which the whole universe unifies into one. When, on the other hand, the objective world is born as Isaac, then, it comes into the circularity of consciousness. Then, Sarai is not barren any longer, she conceives Isaac and from him proceeds the very vast generation of objectivity, which should be sacrificed, as we shall see in the Continuing Annotations.

11:31-From the Land of the Chaldees to the Land of Canaan

וַיִּקַּח תֶּרַח אֶת־אַבְרָם בְּנוֹ וְאֶת־לוֹט בֶּן־הָרָן בֶּן־בְּנוֹ וְאֵת שָׂרַי כַּלָּתוֹ אֵשֶׁת אַבְרָם בְּנוֹ וַיֵּצְאוּ אִתָּם מֵאוּר כַּשְׂדִּים לָלֶכֶת אַרְצָה כְּנַעַן וַיָּבֹאוּ עַד־חָרָן וַיֵּשְׁבוּ שָׁם: *vayiqaḥ* (took) *teraḥ* (Terah) *'eṯ* (and) *'aḇərām* (Abram) *bənvō* (son) *və'eṯ* (and) *lvōṭ* (Lot) *ben* (son) *hārān* (Haran) *ben* (son) *bənvō* (son) *və'ēṯ* (and) *śāray* (Sarai) *kalāṯvō* (perfect daughter in law) *'ēšeṯ* (wife) *'aḇərām* (Abram) *bənvō* (son) *vayēṣə'u* (exited) *'itām* (with them) *mē'ur* from Ur) *kaśədiym* (of the Chaldees) *lāleḵeṯ* (went) *'arəṣāh* (land) *kəna'an* (of Canaan) *vayāḇō'u* (they entered) *'aḏ* (into) *hārān* (Haran) *vayēšəḇu* (they dwelt) *šām* (there)
καὶ *kai* (and) **ἔλαβεν** *elaben* (took) **Θαρα** *Thara* (Therah) **τὸν** *ton* (the) **Αβραμ** *Abram* (Abram) **υἱὸν** *uion* (son) **αὐτοῦ** *autou* (his) **καὶ** *kai* (and) **τὸν** *ton* (the) **Λωτ** *Lōt* (Lot) **υἱὸν** *uion* (the son) **Αρραν** *Arran* (of Haran) **υἱὸν** *uion* (son) **τοῦ** *tou* (of the) **υἱοῦ** *uiou* (son) **αὐτοῦ** *autou* (his) **καὶ** *kai* (and) **τὴν** *tēn* (the) **Σαραν** *Saran* (Sarai) **τὴν** *tēn* (the) **νύμφην** *numphēn* (daughter in law) **αὐτοῦ** *autou* (his) **γυναῖκα** *gunaika* (wife) **Αβραμ** *Abram* (of Abram) **τοῦ** *tou* (the) **υἱοῦ** *uiou* (son) **αὐτοῦ** *autou* (his) **καὶ** *kai* (and) **ἐξήγαγεν** *exēgagen* (led) **αὐτοὺς** *autous* (them) **ἐκ** *ek* (out) **τῆς** *tēs* (the) **χώρας** *chōras* (land) **τῶν** *tōn* (of the) **Χαλδαίων** *Chaldaiōn* (Chaldees) **πορευθῆναι** *poreuthēnai* (went) **εἰς** *eis* (to) **τὴν** *tēn* (the) **γῆν** *gēn* (land) **Χανααν** *Chanaan* (of Canaan) **καὶ** *kai* (and) **ἦλθεν** *ēlthen* (they came) **ἕως** *eōs* (till) **Χαρραν** *Charran* (Harran) **καὶ** *kai* (and) **κατῴκησεν** *katōkēsen* (dwelt) **ἐκεῖ** *ekei* (there)
tulit (took) ***itaque*** (therefore) ***Thare*** (Thera) ***Abram*** (Abram) ***filium*** (son) ***suum*** (his) ***et*** (and) ***Loth*** (Lot) ***filium*** (son) ***Aran*** (of Haran) ***filium*** (the son) ***filii*** (of the son) ***sui*** (his) ***et*** (and) ***Sarai*** (Sarai) ***nurum*** (daughter in law) ***suam*** (his) ***uxorem*** (wife) ***Abram*** (of Abram) ***filii*** (son) ***sui*** (his) ***et*** (and) ***eduxit*** (exited) ***eos*** (them) ***de*** (from) ***Ur*** (Ur) ***Chaldeorum*** (of the Chaldees) ***ut*** (thus) ***irent*** (they went) ***in*** (in) ***terram*** (the land) ***Chanaan*** (of Canaan) ***venerunt*** (they came)***-que*** (and) ***usque*** (into) ***Haran*** (Haran) ***et*** (and) ***habitaverunt*** (swelt) ***ibi*** (there)
And Terah took Abram his son, and Lot the son of Haran his son's son, and Sarai his daughter in law, his son Abram's wife; and they went forth with them from Ur of the Chaldees, to go into the land of Canaan; and they came unto Haran, and dwelt there.
Terah took Abram his son and Lot the son of Haran, the son's son and Sarai his daughter in law, the perfect wife of his son Abram; with them they exited from Ur of the Chaldees and went in the land of Canaan and they entered into the state of Haran and dwelt there.

From a phenomenological perspective, we are the situation in which we live. Thus, as

"man is what he eats,"[3392]

so our individuality embodies all the historical psychophysiological states it is into, in each stage of life. When we breathe, we are the breathing-one. When we sleep, we are the sleeping-one. When we suffer, we are the suffering-one. When we think, we are the thinking-one. When we know, we are the one who knows with all its epistemic faculties and so on. We are also all of them at once. All the personalities encountered in *Genesis*, up to this point, are complete historical universal paradigmatic entities individualized by their particular function or modalities. When our individualized bodily station, goes from one state of life to another, it moves with all its faculties and/or its epistemic modalities.

Therefore, Terah travels with his son, the subjectivity (*viz.* Abram) and his *wife* (אִשָּׁה *'ishshah*) the perfect[3393] objectivity (*viz.* Sarai) and the covering (*viz.* Lot) mystery of his dreamless sleep. He leaves the state of shining light (*viz.* Ur) of the *clod-breakers Chaldees* to reach Canaan, the information trafficking function, which spreads out in all directions. That is the nervous connectivity, which carries information to the forms of knowledge, to and from the subject and the object. However, Haran, the state of deep dreamless sleep, is also the dwelling place of Terah as well as his origin.

11:32-The End of Terah

וַיִּהְיוּ יְמֵי־תֶרַח חָמֵשׁ שָׁנִים וּמָאתַיִם שָׁנָה וַיָּמָת תֶּרַח בְּחָרָן׃ ס   *vayihəyu* (were) *yəmēy* (the days) *terah* (Terah) *hāmēš* (five) *šāniym* (years) *umā'tayim* (two hundred) *šānāh* (years) *vayāmāt* (died) *terah* (Terah) *bəhārān* (in Haram) *s* (.)
καὶ *kai* (and) **ἐγένοντο** *egenonto* (were) **αἱ** *ai* (the) **ἡμέραι** *ēmerai* (days) **Θαρα** *Thara* (of Terah) **ἐν** *en* (in) **Χαρραν** *Charran* (Harran)[3394] **διακόσια** *diakosia* (two hundred) **πέντε** *pente* (five) **ἔτη** *etō* (years) **καὶ** *kai* (and) **ἀπέθανεν** *apethanen* (died) **Θαρα** *Thara* (Therah) **ἐν** *en* (in) **Χαρραν** *Charran* (Haran)
et (and) ***facti*** (done) ***sunt*** (are) ***dies*** (the days) ***Thare*** (of Thare) ***ducentorum*** (two hundred) ***quinque*** (five) ***annorum*** (years) ***et*** (and) ***mortuus*** (dead) ***est*** (is) ***in*** (in) ***Haran*** (Haran)
And the days of Terah were two hundred and five years: and Terah died in Haran.
The days of Terah were circular years of consciousness *among the merchant Canaanite* (205) and Terah died in Haram.

Two hundred (וּמָאתַיִם *umā'tayim*) and *five* (חָמֵשׁ *chamesh*) *years* (שָׁנָה *shaneh*), corresponds to the Gematria numeral 205 equivalent to the words *hakana'ăniy,*[3395] meaning *of the Canaanite*, and *kinə'āneyāh*[3396] *Merchants*. Therefore, Terah, this individual body, lived his conscious circularity in the land of the Canaanite. The state of the Canaanite, namely the trafficking state of wakefulness and dreaming, ends in dreamless sleep. Finally, there, in the state of Haran's dreamless sleep, Terah *perishes* (מוּת *muwth*).

THE GENERATION OF PELAG AFTER BABEL

<table>
<tr><td rowspan="5"><u>Pelag</u> ⇨ time divide</td><td rowspan="5"><u>Reu</u>⇨ companion</td><td rowspan="5"><u>Serug</u>⇨ branching brotherhood</td><td rowspan="5"><u>Nahor</u>⇨ breathing body</td><td rowspan="5"><u>Terah</u> ⇨ bodily station</td><td><u>Abram</u> ∞<u>Sarai</u> ⇨ exalted father ∞ dominating object</td><td><u>Isaac</u> he who laughs</td></tr>
<tr><td><u>Nahor</u>∞<u>Milcah</u> dream state ∞ queen object</td><td></td></tr>
<tr><td rowspan="3"><u>Haran</u> ⇨ mountaineer</td><td><u>Lot</u> veil covering</td></tr>
<tr><td><u>Iscah</u> watch</td></tr>
<tr><td><u>Milcah</u> queen object</td></tr>
</table>

Each stage of this body's circadian rhythm ends as the next one rises, until the body dies.

HERE ENDS THE ELEVENTH CHAPTER OF THE TOWER OF BABEL

PART 6
CONCLUSIONS

CONTINUING ANNOTATIONS
for this commentary on the first part of *Genesis*,
namely the parable of the logically primordial history,
from Creation to the Tower of Babel.[3397]

Overall, **Sacred Texts are expressions revealed directly by the Present Silence of True Awareness. Their content, then, is the universal description of Truth, valid and evident for the entire Universe throughout all its corners and dimensions. Like symphonies, the Texts' Revelation is composed of sounds and silences. There, the pauses are more eloquent than the signifying words. That Silence, in fact, leads to the sense beyond the lyrics.** We identify with the "*Angelic-Daily-Bread*,"[3398] which gives us Eternal-Life,[3399] only in the **Present-Silent-Stillness**. On the other hand, if we hunger for the object, we recognize the distinction between *you* and *me*. Then, we establish the *past* and *future* laps of time. Then, we determine *this* and *that* separated in space. Then, we understand the causal *connectivity* among events. Then, no matter how much physical nourishment we may get, we still taste death.

The first and most common interpretation of *Genesis* is the literal one, in which the *day* denotes a sunless 24 hours period without connoting its implied metaphoric circularity. We do not need to repeat the numerous incongruent difficulties related to the literal interpretation of the text. We have frequently and sufficiently highlighted them during the course of our commentary.[3400]

The second interpretation of *Genesis* is the one that, in contrast with the postulated light of God, relegates the explanation of the text into blind belief in a mysterious and obscure divine intent. While this approach correctly emphasizes the ineffability of the Transcendent, it makes us miss the text's pedagogical aspect. Furthermore, it makes us yearn for the clarity of science.

A third interpretative way is the Kabbalistic analysis of *Genesis*. Since all letters of the Hebrew alphabet correspond to a number, a word can substitute another completely different term, providing that the sum of the new one is numerically equal to the first one. This method has the correct advantage to highlight the infinite possibilities of a quantum *oneiric-like* world. However, each time one of the possible computerized drafting of the text is set, it will still offer itself to one of the previous two interpretative approaches.

Finally, the epistemic reading of *Genesis* confirms its own validity. In fact, in each of the above cases, there is the inevitable presence of the epistemological structure of this reader here and now, to whom and for whom *Genesis'* text is ultimately referring.

Our commentary has analyzed the fundamental aspect of the birth of knowledge and thought. From Awareness proceeds Consciousness, from this one flows consciousness-*of* and, finally, out of it, thought comes into being. Nevertheless, the ruling is, 'ride your horse, but let TRANSCENDENT-AWARENESS lead you and let IT steer your horse and drive you.' [3401]⇨

"*Let yourself be led in depth by the holy Spirit... Do not hurry. Let yourself be driven and you will see that everything will go well.*"[3402]

Similarly, when Peter, escaping persecution, was leaving Rome, he saw Jesus going in the opposite direction and he asked him,

" *'Whither art thou going Lord'? and the Lord said to him 'I go to Rome to be crucified again.* "[3403]

Upon that answer, Peter returned on his steps to face martyrdom.

Our reader may accuse us of being an idealist.

From a possible claim of Neoplatonic[3404] idealism,[3405] we defend by stating that our position was never dogmatic. In fact, we constantly stated the impossibility to prove pure idealism as well as Neo-Aristotelian realism[3406] and/or Historical materialism.[3407] Both, indeed, postulate an indemonstrable reality independent from the knower.

Our reader may say,

'From this commentary, it seems as if you identify god with awareness.'

We reply,

'That is so. Can you conceive your god not being absolutely aware? If so, it would not be a god. When we refer to Awareness, we do not mean the consciousness-of-these-objects, here and now, before our mind. We mean the entire process not exhausted in the time and space of this individualized consciousness-of. Individualized consciousness is the depotentiation of Pure Omniscient Omnipotent Omnipresent Awareness.'

The reader may ask,

'I do not understand. How can that be possible. In fact, I do not know everything and I cannot do everything?'

We reply again,

'Nevertheless, you are aware. If you were not, you could not have stated these imperfections. Awareness is always Aware. Nothing can be without Awareness. Even the lack of awareness necessitates Awareness to confirm that absence as such.'

AWARENESS, CONSCIOUSNESS, APODICTICITY, UNCONSCIOUS and SUBCONSCIOUS

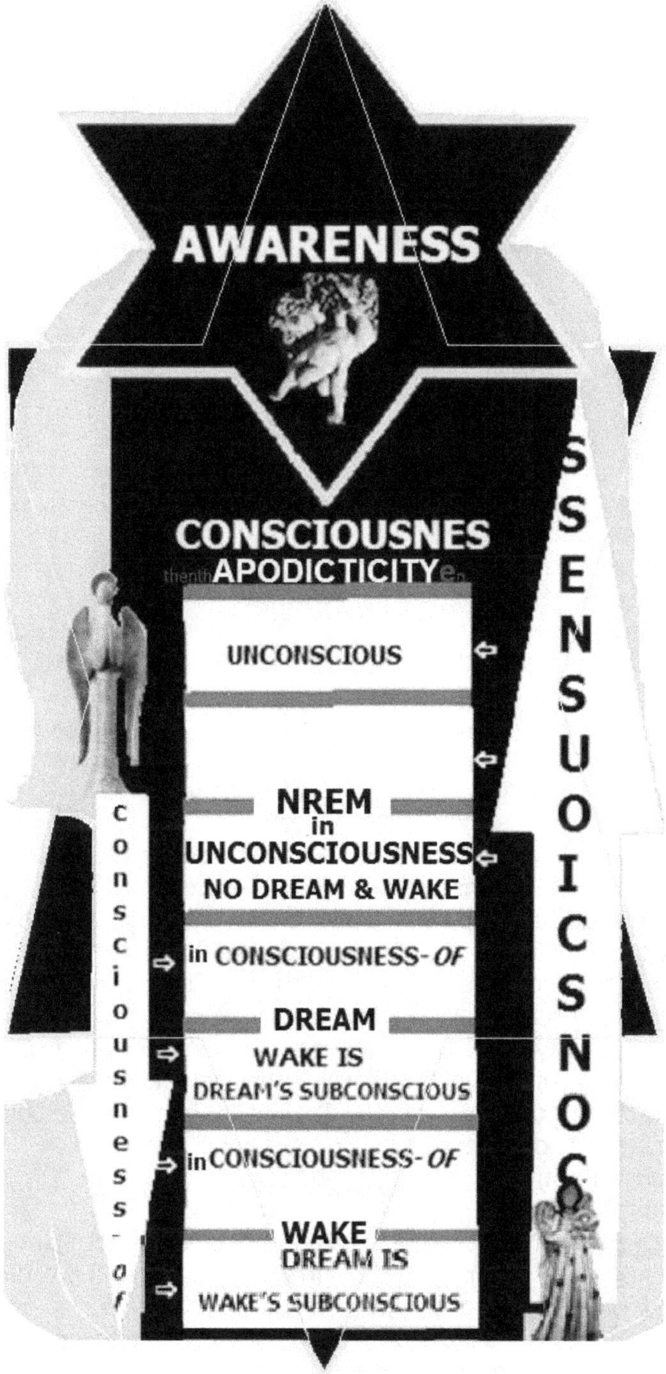

GRAPHIC: *Jacob's ladder*

When in wakefulness, we ride a train. Then, we are conscious-*of* that carrier as an objective reality and *-of* ourselves as riders. However, during the trip, we may not be conscious-*of* the dream-content we had the night before. That dream belongs to a *subterranean* realm, which, in the waking state, we call subconscious.

On the other hand, when in the oneiric realm we dream-*of* conversing with a dead friend, we are conscious-*of* that objectified interlocutor.[3408] Nevertheless, during that sleep we may not be conscious-*of* the transporter we rode previously when we were awake. For the dreamer, that train remains in a subliminal realm.

In the waking and/or dreaming states, we alternate conscious and subconscious thresholds. As we become conscious-*of* one object, another one may slips into a hidden domain. By subconscious, we mean that which does not fall in the immediate focus of our attention or in the consciousness-*of*, as we named it. In both cases, however, we forget the Pure-Consciousness-Light, as such, and *we identify only with the object* we are conscious-*of*, while Consciousness, as such, slips, for-us, into Unconsciousness. Then, we enter the NREM dreamless-sleep and we access the realm that, in the other two states, we define as unconscious. This does not imply the absence of consciousness. It only means that the object is not there, it is missing from our concentrated attention. In fact, the possibility we have to state the unconscious and/or subconscious demonstrates the underlining reality of Consciousness continuously persisting through them.

We proceed, ascending and descending through the three realms of wakefulness, dream and objectiveless-sleep, like angels, like messengers of Consciousness on "*Jacob's ladder*."[3409] *Cullam* (סֻלָּם),[3410] the Hebrew word for ladder, derives from the verb *calal* (סָלַל),[3411] which means *to lift up*, and

"*to move to and fro*."[3412]

We sojourn in each of those states as if each were, individually, the only reality. When we dream, we live the vision as real, ignoring wakefulness. Whereas, when we are awake, we forget the dream in *fantasy-land*. Nonetheless, wakefulness and dream affect each other. In turn, unconsciousness is always present in both those states. When that unconsciousness pops into the mind, then, it becomes the consciousness-*of* some object.

Continuing in our ascension, we enter the realms of Consciousness, the Aesthetic Purity of Beautiful Love, and of Apodicticity. These realms completely inform of themselves the ascending-descending course until they merges within the entire encompassing reality of Awareness, which is always there, before, during and after the whole process takes place.

Awareness, when conceived as such, becomes consciousness-*of*-awareness, not Awareness in-Itself. Consciousness is not conceivable without becoming consciousness-*of*-consciousness, not Consciousness as such in-Itself. In addition, certainty, when thought, becomes consciousness-*of*-certainty, not Certainty as such in-Itself. Only the consciousness-*of* thinks *for-itself of awareness*, *of consciousness* and *of certainty*. This, however, does not negate their reality in-Themselves. In fact, thought infers their reality as Still-Awareness, Pure-Consciousness and Apodictic Certainty. Usually, we consider awareness, consciousness and certainty as synonyms. Nevertheless, there is a difference. In this commentary, we regard Awareness as distinct from Consciousness and It from Certainty, while being all united as one in the Transcendent devoid of any conceivable quality,

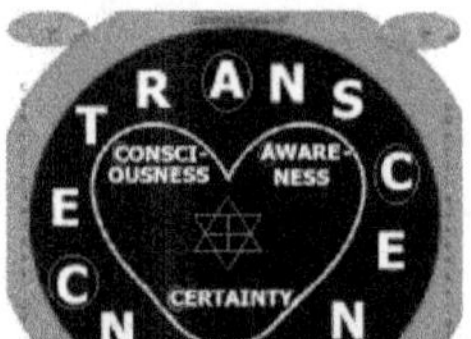

"*I am* [היה *hayah*] *the way, the truth, and the life*."[3413]

In fact, we must distinguish them.

- ***Still Awareness*** (יְהֹוָה Yĕhovah) means the constant Present Spirit or the Life-Breath (רוּחַ *ruwach*)[3414] that floats (רחף *rachaph*)[3415] over (על ` *al*) the surface (פנים *panivm*) of the ocean of objectivity. Furthermore, it is inferred when we look at the world and we consider it as independent from us, thus, transcendent. The consciousness-*of*-the-world implies its transcendence, because it conceives it as an external reality. However, it never knows it as Transcendent, because it reduces it to an objective conceptualization that is not transcendent. This is what the West African Dagara tribe calls *yielbongura*,

  "*the thing that knowledge can't eat*."[3416]

  Awareness, in Its Purity, is Creation because nothing is outside of It. Even when positing something outside, it is still posited by It, in It and for It.

- ***Pure Consciousness*** (אֱלֹהִים 'Elohiym) means the constant Presence of the Self to It-Self. It is the Way, the light that precedes the object's illumination. It is the aesthetic moment of Beauty, the choking insurgence of Love. We do not need to think of ourselves in order to be conscious-*of-ourselves*. The thought of it, however, infers Pure Consciousness as being Transcendent without any object, but, again, the thought of it is not Pure Consciousness, it is only the idea of it.

  "*O YOU who have attained to faith! Remain conscious preserving God* (اللَّهَ اتَّقُوا *Allah taqū*) *and seek to come closer unto Him, and strive* (*jihād* جهاد) *hard in His cause, so that you might attain to a happy state.*"[3417]

  "*Have faith in me* [Pure Consciousness][3418] *that I am in the Father* [Transcendent Awareness], *and the Father in me: or else believe me for the very works' sake./ Verily, verily, I say unto you, He that believeth on me, the works that I do shall he do also; and greater works than these shall he do; because I go unto my Father./ And whatsoever ye shall ask in my name, that will I do, that the Father may be glorified in the Son./ If ye shall ask any thing in my name, I will do it.*"[3419]

- ***Apodictic Certainty*** (אֲדֹנָי Adonai) means Judging Truth. It is Certainty that precedes all experiences. It is the inevitable Present firm constant conviction. Namely, Certainty, as such in-Itself, here and now, requires no test because It has no testable objectivity. Then, Truth becomes the doubtless Fulgurating Faith, the

  "*light that shined from heaven.*"[3420]

  Certainty is the field in which Empiricists miss their mark. They, struck by the Singularity present in every experience as such, erroneously attribute that Apodicticity to the object itself. Thus, they are led (εἰσενέγκῃς *eisenegkēs*) into (εἰς *eis*) the tempting experience (πειρασμόν *peirasmov*).[3421] Consequently, they dogmatically place it in a transcendent reality conceived external to the immanent subject-object correlation. Then, they postulate that unexperienced world out there, beyond their personal death, and label themselves atheists. Ramana Maharshi states that the phrase

  "'*I am that I am,*'[3422] *sums up the whole truth.*"[3423]

  In a poem, Saint Catherine of Siena, recognizes this centrality of Certain-Truth, which is always the evident foundation of all and any experience.

  "*Truth never frightens. / I remember once walking out in the winter... I waited... The cold can enliven thanks, my wool coat / became a sacred robe, how happy I felt to be alive. / I waited in a world of magic, smells of good food, / the street lamps, the smoke coming from chimneys, the candles burning in windows, the snow. / Angels feasted, as I did, on existence and God kept saying/ 'Have more of what I made.' / I saw him* [Truth, Certainty] *coming. We ran into each other's arms/ and he lifted me as he so often had— twirled me through the air... That is what the Truth does: / lifts and lets us fly.*"[3424]

  That is the inevitable Present firm Certainty that is constant in all occurrences independently from the objective references to the events.

  "*And ye shall know the truth, and the truth shall make you free.*"[3425]

  The state of dream

  "is not a region outside the body but instead a part of the dreamer's own mind."[3426]

  In fact, there one

  "*seeth sleep with his eyes.*"[3427]

  However, the dreamer, while dreaming, is certain of what s/he is experiencing.

  "The world of dreams is not less real than the world of waking; it is just real in a different way."[3428]

  Waking and dreaming are

  "two different but 'equal' states ... the activity of individual nerve cells in the brain ... are active during both sleeping and waking. What changes is the pattern of 'firing'."[3429]

In fact, the same forms-categories pertaining to the waking state pertain also to the dream state. Uncertainty sets in when we refer to a reality conceived as external to the experiencer. Then, that reality must be tested according to three truth-tests. We usually consider as factual truth results and/or knowledges, considered *external* and/or *independent* realities (*albeit never verified as such*) tested according to their

1) correspondence with former assertions (*e.g.* the sun rises in the orient every morning),
2) coherence with previous statements (*e.g.* A=A is not B≠A), and/or
3) pragmatic proof of operability (*e.g.* the invented machine works).

Science finds its foundation on these three truth-tests articulated through the mathematical-logical formulations of time, space and causality. The element of absolute dispassionate disinterested observation and proven repeatable experimentation without any personal desire places science cognate to the spiritual attitude of *action without action*. When, however, the scientific community projects the world in a reality independent from that observation, then, science becomes like any other religion, which believes in an unproven and unobserved transcendent universe.

> "*And I will pray the Father, and he shall give you another Legal Assistant* [παράκλητος *paraklētos*], *that he may abide with you for ever;/ Even the Spirit* [πνεῦμα *pneuma*] *of truth* [ἀλήθεια *alētheia*]*; whom the world cannot receive, because it seeth him not, neither knoweth him: but ye know him; for he dwelleth with you, and shall be in you./ I will not leave you orphan* [ὀρφανός *orphanos*]: *I will come to you./ Yet a little while, and the world seeth me no more; but ye see me: because I live, ye shall live also./ At that day ye shall know that I am in my Father-Awareness, and ye in me, and I in you.*"[3430]

d) ***Consciousness-of**-something* is the **Tree-of-Knowledge-*of*-Good-and-Evil**. It is the only level we operate with in the waking and/or dreaming stages, namely, in the dimension of duality. There, an object always follows consciousness. The fact that this is our only operating level does not negate Awareness and Pure Consciousness. On the contrary, only Transcendent Still Awareness, Pure Consciousness and Apodictic Certainty guaranty the validity of the consciousness-*of*-something. In fact,

I) The worst prison is that of solitary confinement. However, no communication can take place if not intentionally directed towards something, *viz.* the other's Awareness as Transcendent, conceived and considered as an external reality, yet unknown to the subjective agent.
II) No action can be accomplished if not done by a subjective central agent conceived but unknown in-itself, *viz.* the Pure Consciousness.
III) No activity takes place if not directed by its conscious and/or unconscious implied Certainty.

A few more words are necessary to clarify the concept of consciousness-*of*. The current studies of this consciousness-*of* do not go beyond its object. In fact, they do not address Consciousness as such. They only relate to the *feeling-of* the object. Therefore, those studies declare that when that *feeling* is gone also

> "consciousness ceases to be... as occurs in deep sleep or in anesthesia."[3431]

The Integrated Information Theory (IIT) of Giulio Tononi, neuroscientist at the University of Wisconsin–Madison, recognizes consciousness-*of* as an indivisible integrated variety of experiences. In fact,

> "consciousness is integrated information, and... its quality is given by the informational relationships [where]... information is... reduction of uncertainty: the more numerous the alternatives that are ruled out, the greater the reduction of uncertainty."[3432]

Any information we are conscious-*of* is unified in the presence of our mind. Underlying this synthesis of consciousness is a multitude of causal interactions among the relevant parts of our brain. According to Tononi, consciousness is the cross-linked differentiated network of brain-integrated information, which we can express quantitatively and compute mathematically. From this point of view, there is no reason why the integration of all the life functions, from heart beat, to blood circulation, to breathing and other, cannot constitute consciousness also in the states of deep-dreamless-sleep or in that of anesthesia. The integration is the unifying process of different objects (the metaphorical Biblical *fruit*) with which we identify.[3433] Christof Koch, neuroscientist at the Allen Institute for Brain Science in Seattle, offers ways of thinking about subjective experience stemming from panpsychism, asserting that consciousness is universal.[3434] However, in all cases, we allways refer to the object of consciousness, never to consciousness as such. Thus, consciousness is alwais conceived as consciousness-*of* something with which we unite establishing an identity. However, <consciousness-*of* is the act of focusing and identifying with the objects of experience with different degrees of intensity. That act finds its foundation in Epistemic-Awareness, which is always identical to itself regardless of the levels of conscious, subconscious or unconscious intensity. Beyond consciousness-*of*-something, therefore, the central fulcrum is always That-Unified-Certainty, which is the Only-One truly dispelling uncertainty and ignorance and around which gravitates consciousness-*of*.>[3435]

As we blindly fall in love for the looks of an idealized attractive person, similarly we are tempted to conceptualize and idolize an objectified god. We forget Its-True-Transcendence-Still-Silence-In-Itself. Therefore, we have the intentional drive to objectify transcendence with a transcending flight. That objectifying intention may derive from the Transcendent Itself, Who, thus, indirectly, may

"*lead us into temptation.*"[3436]

When that temptation takes place, we erroneously call it rebirth. It is like a rapture, as a spirit of prophesy, which manifests itself on different levels. From quiet to frenzy states, one may perceive it delivering different degrees of *mistaken spiritual experience*. In each one of them, there is, for the experiencer, a sense of satisfied wellbeing that delivers the feeling of certain belief. However, it is only a worldly experience. As such, it is not Certainty in itself, but it is only the certainty-*of*-a-pleasing-object, which, as we saw, has nothing to do with GOD, TRANSCENDENCE or TRUTH, but only with our pleasing pleasurable desire.

"*Therefore, the female-objectivity understanding that the tree was pleasurable to eat, beautiful in appearance, fragrantly desirable for knowledge, she took the fruit and ate it*" (*Genesis* 3:6).

<*Transcendence* denotes the tension of the self *in-itself*, as absolute center. The self aims beyond the circular subject-object correlation. However, it is the Consciousness of this correlation alone that establishes that which exists, thus, constitutes it as Transcendent beyond the correlation.>[3437] The Indian tradition summarizes this triple aspect of Transcendence as s*accidānanda*[3438], namely, Flowing-Awareness (*sat*), Wisdom-Consciousness (*cit*) and Blissful-Certitude (*ānanda*), residing in the heart. <We must keep in mind that this heart is not the physical organ, which is only a metaphor referring to the centrality of *Saccidānanda*, the Transcendent Real Aware Bliss in-Itself, in the middle of the subject-object correlation. Consequently, the irruption into this realm modifies the entire world, which, from objective discursive knowledge, becomes intuited synthetic com-prehension, as signified by the hexagram (✡)… It is the reverting of the objective world towards its source… The presence of an inverted triangle (▽)… indicates a new womb from which the second birth,[3439] the virgin birth,[3440] takes place. Dante describes this new life (*Vita Nova*) as,

"I felt myself awakening in the heart / a loving spirit that was sleeping: / and then I saw Love coming from far."[3441]

At this level, the individual finds reconciliation with the universal archetypes, as described by Jung, for whom the unconscious becomes transpersonal (*uberpersonliche*).[3442] Once [the]… coiled [serpentine] power, reaches the heart, it goes back over its steps. From the Heart, it retraces back… in the spiritual dimension. [Its] power is sublimated, becoming, therefore, truly-purified spirit.>[3443]

The fundamental direction to take is to *let go*,

הַרְפּוּ וּדְעוּ כִּי־אָנֹכִי אֱלֹהִים[3444]

"*be still* (רָפָה *raphah*) *and realize* (יָדַע *yada*) *that I am Divine-Consciousness* (אֱלֹהִים *'elohiym*),"

וְאָהַבְתָּ אֵת יְהוָה אֱלֹהֶיךָ בְּכָל־לְבָבְךָ וּבְכָל־נַפְשְׁךָ וּבְכָל־מְאֹדֶךָ׃[3445]

"*love and long for* (אָהַב *'ahab*) *the Transcendent* (יְהוָה *Yĕhovah*) *your Divine-Consciousness with all your heart and with all yourself and with all your power.*"

To love *with all* (כֹּל *kol*)[3446] your being

"*and with all thy mind,*"[3447]

implies a complete surrender of all possessive appetites. It means to refuse the forbidden fruit, namely, the consciousness-*of*-everything, in order to let Awareness shine in Its Fulgurating Splendor. Then, there cannot be any appetite left for the *beloved* world. Therefore,

"*remain God conscious, and know that God is with those who are God Aware.*"[3448]

Abraham, then, is ready to give up his attachment to Isaac, his own progeny and aspirations.[3449] It is shutting off the whole world. Attachment, in fact, tarnishes the *complete* surrender to Awareness. This surrender is *Islām* (اسلام),[3450] the absolute *submission* to the unconceivable Light of Certainty Itself. This is different from the fanatical subjugation to an imagined conceived idea, or a thought or a belief, which becomes an idol or a luciferous reflected light of the mind or of the brain. Then, the object, as object, *subjugates* the subject. Then, it becomes the thought of something qualified as one, many or anything else.

What is that we should surrender? When

"*certain of the Pharisees and of the Herodians... said unto him* [Jesus], *'Master, ... thou... teachest the way of God in truth: Is it lawful to give tribute to Caesar, or not?'... he... said unto them, 'bring me a denarius... And he saith unto them, 'Whose is this image and superscription?' And they said unto him, 'Caesar's*[3451]*... And Jesus answering said unto them, 'Render to Caesar the things that are Caesar's, and to God the things that are God's.'*"[3452]

When we are conscious-*of* the object, we look at that which is already destined to end. Thus, if we give up the attachment to it, we give up that, which is nothing in-itself. However, rendering Awareness to Awareness leads us to this Eternal Present.

The transition from consciousness-*of* to the intuition of Awareness does not take place as an empirical deduction. On the contrary, it is a virgin birth different from any type of experience. It is a *con*version towards the interiority. It is like when Simon (*viz. who hears with acceptance*)[3453] Bar-jona (*viz. son of Jonah-dove*)[3454] said to Jesus Christ,

"'*Thou art the Anointed-Christ, Son of the living Transcendent.' And Jesus answered and said unto him, 'Blessed art thou, Simon Barjona for flesh and blood hath not revealed*[3455] *it unto thee, but my Transcendent Father which is in the Transcendence. And I say also unto thee, That thou art Peter-the-rock,*[3456] *and upon this rock-petrified-objectivity I will build*[3457] *my assembly-church; and the gates of hell shall not prevail against it.'*"[3458]

This is the unveiling taking place upon entering the stillness in which the sun of awareness dries up the flood. Then, the mind is silent. This silencing is not the rejection of one belief only to accept uncritically and to subscribe blindly to a different one. This is the sudden irruption in the stillness of Aware-Conscious-Certainty.

The *surrender* (اسلام) to the Light of Certainty, on the other hand, is the altogether absence of any thought. It is awakening in dreamless sleep. If, however, the possessive attachment to any form of idea arises in the mind, then it will take away from us the stillness of that Awareness to Whom we totally submit. Whosoever wants to reach Transcendence must leave the ego and all worldly attachments.

"*Bring ye all the tithes into the storehouse, that there may be meat in mine house, and prove me now herewith, saith the Lord of hosts, if I will not open you the windows of heaven, and pour you out a blessing, that there shall not be room enough to receive it.*"[3459]

"*If any man will come after me, let him deny himself*[3460] *... house or parents,... or children*[3461] *... If anyone comes to me and does not hate his father and mother, his wife and children, his brothers and sisters -yes, even his own life- he cannot be my disciple.*"[3462]

"*He that hateth his life in this world shall keep it unto life eternal.*"[3463]

Similarly, the Zen Buddhist master, Linji Yixuan (866) states with his *kōan* (公案),

"*Followers of the Way, if you want to get the kind of understanding that accords with the Dharma* [Nature-of-anything], *never be misled by others. Whether you're facing inward or facing outward, whatever you meet up with, just kill it! If you meet a buddha, kill the buddha. If you meet a patriarch, kill the patriarch. If you meet an arhat* [superior], *kill the arhat. If you meet your parents, kill your parents. If you meet your kinfolk, kill your kinfolk. Then for the first time you will gain emancipation, will not be entangled with things, will pass freely anywhere you wish to go.*"[3464]

In addition, filial piety should not distract from the universal quest for the Transcendent.[3465] This is explained in *1King,*[3466] when

"*Elisha* (*God is salvation*) *the son of Shaphat* (*he hath judged*)[3467] *of Abelmeholah* (*in the meadow of dancing*)[3468]*... was plowing with twelve yoke of oxen before him, and he with the twelfth: and Elijah* (*my God is the Transcendent*)[3469] *passed by him, and cast his mantle upon him./ And he left the oxen, and ran after Elijah, and said, 'Let me, I pray thee, kiss my father and my mother, and then I will follow thee.' And he said unto him, 'Go back again: for what have I done to thee?'/ And he returned back from him, and took a yoke of oxen, and slew them, and boiled their flesh with the instruments of the oxen, and gave unto the people, and they did eat. Then he arose, and went after Elijah, and ministered unto him.*"

Similarly, Jesus

"*said unto another, 'Follow me.' But he said, 'Lord, suffer me first to go and bury my father.'/ Jesus said unto him, 'Let the dead bury their dead: but go thou and preach the kingdom of God.'/ And another also said, Lord, 'I will follow thee; but let me first go bid them farewell, which are at home at my house.'* [3470] *And Jesus said unto him, 'No man, having put his hand to the plough, and looking back, is fit for the kingdom of God.*'"[3471]

"*By faith Abraham... offered up Isaac accounting that God was able to raise him up, even from the dead.*"[3472]

This is related to the command that God gave to

"*Abraham: 'Take now thy son, thy only son Isaac, whom thou lovest, ... and offer him... for a burnt offering*[3473] *ascending*[3474] *on the Transcendent designated mountain' into the land chosen by Jehovah*[3475]*... And Abraham took the knife to slay his son and the angel of the Lord... said, 'lay not thine hand upon the lad... for now I know that thou fearest God, seeing thou hast not withheld thy son, thine only son from me... I will bless thee.'*"[3476]

"*The yogi... after saying farewell to the world has no duties left to fulfill; if he thought he had, then he would have no right to the name of 'sage.'*"[3477]

"The ascetic overcomes otherness, in that depersonalizing transfers himself in the I the center of consciousness: in reality transfers the self-sense from the astral plane to the I, who does not necessitate to feel itself in order to be."[3478]

Truthfully, this is not a renunciation at all, but it is the unification with all and everything. In fact, that Transcendent Apodictic Awareness is the same Essence that constitutes the entire objective world and recognizes it existent. The Awareness in you is the same, indivisible and ubiquitous Awareness in everyone everywhere. Without It, the world would and could not be stated. The world, stated as Being by- and in-itself, then, paradoxically and necessarily, would still be Transcendent. The True Hermit, Kabbalist, Mystic, Sage, Saint, Scientist, Yogi and similar is the embodiment of Pure-Awareness. Therefore, be still. Pray in silence with no words or thoughts. Let Pure Apodictic Awareness be your incessant focus. Once you master this in your waking state, then it will necessarily spill in your oneiric realm. Then, that prayer will continue through your dream stage to reach total stillness in NREM. Dying within that overall centrality means to go "*Beyond Immortality.*"[3479] There, no duality of good and evil takes place. Then, there is no death nor the pain of this troublesome valley.

Revelation is not an experience. It is the sudden rapture of the flash of Absolute-Awareness, which leaves the mark of Non-conceptualized-Silent-Pure-Certitude. Upon returning in the consciousness-

of the conceptualized objective world, that mark, translates as that which is not the Pristine-Awareness. It is like the difference between the interpretations of dreams and the actual dream processes themselves. Then, as we think about that mark of awareness, we describe it as a theophany and ascribe to it a religion. Religion, on the other hand, establishes its own belief abouy that rapture and describes it as achievable only through its own doctrine.

Once a journalist asked,

'If you expect to find Mount Vesuvius in the same place you left it the last time you climbed it, doesn't that prove the existence of that volcano outside yourself?'

Our reply was,

'Of course the mountain will be there, where we left it! The same way we find places in our dreams, and those are not outside our head. We also find the familiar places that are in our waking moments. However, the expectation to find things where we left them and the actual finding them there, is still all part of our mind. In fact, the person affected by Alzheimer's disease cannot find the things s/he forgot. Expectations and discoveries are no proof of a reality external to our knowledge. Both cannot take place if not in the mind. The problem is, after our final departure, how can we retrace our way back to find our Earth and our home?'

A final criticism from a friend says,

'When one enters the total absorption in the state of Transcendent Certitude, wouldn't s/he want to defend a loved one who is in danger? In so doing, wouldn't s/he leave that transcendent state to go back to the land of duality?'

We reply,

> "*Why reason ye these things in your hearts?*"[3480]

'You reason like Homer's lotus eaters[3481] *after they ate the forbidden fruit. The sleeping ones do not react to what happens in the waking world and vice versa. The dead are unresponsive to the stimuli of the living. The reason of the Spirit is different from the reason of the flesh. Yet,*

> *"Be ye therefore perfect, even as your Father which is in heaven is perfect."*[3482]

However, does the FATHER intervene during the SON'S crucifixion? Despite His cry,

> " *'ēliy 'ēliy lāmāh 'ăzaḇətāniy* (אֵלִי אֵלִי לָמָה עֲזַבְתָּנִי)*?*[3483] *that is to say, My God, my God, why hast thou forsaken me?*"[3484]

Does God interfere to stop genocide or martyrdom? The Reality of PURE AWARENESS does not stop the unreality of this nightmare. To be perfect as the Father, the right attitude is to participate in all actions while being disengaged.'[3485]

At this point, it may seem as if our commentary favors a contemplative existence devoid of any activity or engagement. It is not so. No one can be without doing something in this life. Even if one only sits in motionless meditation, s/he is still doing something, namely, contemplting. However,

> "*Take no thought for your life...* [or] *for the morrow.*"[3486]

> "As long as we draw lines of division between duty and pleasure in the world of the spirit we will remain far from God and from His joy."[3487]

> "*Therefore, always unattached, perform action as duty.*"[3488]

In an ascending pattern, the epistemic forces gradually shift their external reflecting projections to go back to their inner origins. They go back to the silence from which they come. Then, the subject dies out and the subject-object moon circularity stands still. The description of Joshua's[3489] battle against the Amorites, *the huge discursive objects,*[3490] metaphorically portrays this return. In that moment, Joshua stopped the sun to prolong the day and secure his victory over the enemy. In fact, "*the sun subject of illicit worship*[3491] *stood dead silent,*[3492] *and the* [objective] *lunar month*[3493] *stopped circling*[3494] *until the people had avenged themselves upon their enemies*[3495] [their illusory objective attachments]*... So the sun stood still in the midst of heaven, and hasted not to go down about a whole day,"*[3496]

namely, the whole subject-object circularity.

An action should be performed to the best of our ability, but without any attachment at all to its outcome, while we identify with the Universal-Self-Aware-Certitude. Then, this selfless action becomes that of the Sun-of-Awareness, which shines equally on everyone and everything. Similarly, like the outcome of a scientific discovery may produce an emotional reaction, however, that personal attachment to the scientific research is not scientifically significant. Joseph Campbell[3497] relates the story

"of the samurai, the Japanese warrior, who had the duty to avenge the murder of his overlord. When he cornered the man who had murdered his overlord, and he was about to deal with him with his samurai sword, the man in the corner, in the passion of terror, spat in the warrior's face. And the warrior sheathed the sword and walked away... Because he was made angry, and if he had killed that man in anger, then it would have been a personal act. And he had come to do another kind of act, an impersonal act of vengeance."

The action that performs its duty without attachment to its outcome transcends the dichotomy of good and evil. Schopenhauer compares this action to the man who

"saved a life or even several lives at the risk of his own, he as a rule accepts no reward at all, even if he is poor, for he feels that the metaphysical value of his action would thereby be impaired."[3498]

Ultimately, if one, supported by a literal reading of *Genesis*, despite all the highlighted contradicting incongruences, prefers to continue in its own *imagined* (יֵצֶר *yester*) literal belief, that too is true as much as our *conceived* (מַחֲשָׁבָה *machashabah*) epistemic reading of It. In fact, the Sacred Text should be read neither litterally nor epistemically. Actually, **the text intends to be only a stepping stone, a preparation for the Ineffable Still Silence of Transcendence**.

יְהוָה אֱלֹהֵי ...שָׁמְרָה־זֹּאת לְעוֹלָם לְיֵצֶר מַחְשְׁבוֹת לְבַב עַמֶּךָ וְהָכֵן לְבָבָם אֵלֶיךָ:[3499]

"*O Transcendent Divine-Consciousness ... keep this for ever in the imagination* (יֵצֶר *yester*)[3500] *of the thoughts* (מַחֲשָׁבָה *machashabah*)[3501] *of the heart of thy people, and prepare* (כּוּן *kuwn*)[3502] *their heart unto thee.*"

In fact, the self we referred to is not the Self as Awareness, which can never be conceived as such. This one is realized but never conceived or conceavable, penalty reducing it to a noumenon, a thought or an imagination, which is not the Self. Buddhism refers to it as *anatta*,[3503] emptiness (*śūnyatā*), selflessness, the absence or illusion of a subject ego, I or self as foundation of individuality. The subject, in fact, is always correlated to an object and when this one disappears, the subject follows too. The subject is the thinker for-it-self, never in-it-self. To identify with it means to fall into the snare of the past and death, as the consequence deriving from the original disobedience.

"*If any* man *come to me, and hate not... his own life also, he cannot be my disciple.*"[3504]

In the *house* of Our-Apodictically-Aware-Father, all places, all moments and everything else are like epistemic eternal milestones and we virtually revisit them. In fact,

"*In my Father's house* (οἰκίᾳ *oikia*) *are many mansions* (μοναὶ *monai*)*: if it were not so, I would have told you. I go to prepare a place for you.*"[3505]

The Self Is This Transcendent Person hidden in the recesses of this epistemic being. This Self must be more intimate to us than we are to our own personal ego or I. The Entire Cosmological dimensions depart from the Self as a circumference inflating from its center. The Whole Universe and This Self are One. The Self is one with Awareness. We are all one in the Self and the Self is in each of us.

The mystic Maria Valtorta writes that [3506]⇨

"*Jesus says: 'Put off not only that which constitutes the weight of pure humanity, but also that which is spiritual anguish... Spiritual anguish is not that healthy strive to God, with all the intellectual forces. Spiritual anguish... is the fear of... breaking away from prayer with the concern of not being able to taste that clear stream of sweetness that I am sending you, fear of not being able to find it again. These fears are still a remnant of humanity that infiltrates in spirituality and harms it. We must follow the way of the spirit firmly and calmly. No anxiety, no fear. It is I who creates time... I am the one who makes the wave of grace flow in you; I then know how to adjust the flow of it and send to you my lights in the most propitious moments... Therefore, never be anguished. Pray, listen, meditate, suffer, work, rest always with calmness, trusting in Me... It is of paramount importance, for the soul that wants to advance in the way of Heaven, to know how to keep the powers of the soul firm on God. When this happens, the soul is safe. What are the powers of the soul? Now I give you a human comparison. How is the wheel made? It is made of a circle, of many rays fixed in the circle, of a ring, which unites the rays and makes them rotate around a pivot. Therefore, the wheel is useful. If any of the parts is broken, it does not works well, but if the ring that holds the rays is broken, then, the wheel is useless... The circle is the humanity that gathers all the moral powers, physical and spiritual, which are in a created being. It is the band that assembles all in a man. The rays are the feelings that are concentrated in a mystical ring - the spirit - that collects them and radiates them, since it is a double operation. The spoke is God. If humanity is lacerated by carnal decay, the feelings remain unconnected and end up by being scattered in the dust.* However, *if the spirit is ruined or simply unplugged from its hinge, then the marvelous movement created by God stops and gives way to death. Therefore, to never go out from the divine heart is an absolute necessity for the soul wishing to merit Heaven... Your feelings should never cease to converge to the spirit and depart from the spirit. So they will feed of God and will, even in humble chores, exhibit the imprint of God, because your spirit is and must remain centered on God, the most divine fulcrum of all creation, the sweetest heart of your soul that has found its Way. When the powers of the spirit are fixed on God, be certain also that no force can take it away from there. The motion becomes increasingly swirling, and you know that there is a force, which in fact is called centripetal, which attracts more and more toward the center as the swirling motion increases. Love is what gives the motion. The spirit fixed on God loves God his heart. God loves the spirit centered on Him; and this twofold love increases the swirling motion, the winged flight whose aim is the encounter in my Kingdom between the loving spirit and his Creator.'"*[3507]

SUMMARIZING

The Tree of Knowledge is the driving force *pro*jecting towards the expansion within our experiential field. The fruit *pro*duced by this tree is the objective world as other than us. Up to this point, that plant and its yielded produce are good and beautiful. The trouble starts when we partake of its outcome, *viz.* its objective fruit. When we eat, we absorb that food. In this case, the food is our knowledge, our thoughts. Thus, by eating it, we identify with it and name it our knowledge. We become what we think and we identify with it. Our thoughts shape our actions and us. We assimilated the fruit and identified with the world of duality. We become objects for our self, thus, we become displaced from our own True Identity. This process confirms and implies the Jewish Kabalistic and Hassidic affirmation and recognition of the doctrine of reincarnation in the *Torah*, as explained in the *Zohar.*[3508] To understand epistemically this *transmigration* (גלגול *gilgul*) *of the souls* (נשמות *neshamot*), we must consider the presence of our interlocutor. When we depart from the solipsistic perspective, then, we believe that our neighbor has a consciousness-*of* the world in him/herself separate and distinguished from our own. This view implies that the consciousness-*of*, as such, which we call soul, *viz.* the intimate essence of a sentient being, must have refracted itself migrating from mind to mind to constitute, in time and space, the individuality of all others.

This is the consequence of the assimilating ingestion of the product of the **Epistemic Tree**. This led us to the current existential condition. That nourishing and poisoning food in*formed* us. Therefore, we live distinguishing the subject from the object, the good from the bad, this from that and mine from yours. This produced the current deluge of thoughts in which we drown.

The reluctance to understand this teaching *Torah* is because it instructs us to abstain from eating the fruit of knowledge, **not from knowing as such, but from emotionally identifying with it, thus suffering**. It becomes unconceivable for us not to eat what we currently hold so dear, namely the epistemic outcome of our experience. We deem this restraining order contrary to all natural laws, without realizing that all laws enslave and subjugate us into this current existence.[3509] In fact,

"*those things which proceed out of the mouth come forth from the heart; and they defile the man.*"[3510]

"*But for those who are in the-anointed Transcendent-salvation, who walk not after the craving-flesh, but after the Spiritual-Breath, there is therefore no condemnation.| Because, the control of the Breath of life in the-anointed-Transcendent-salvation hath made me free from the controlling-law of sinful-missed-mark and death.*"[3511]

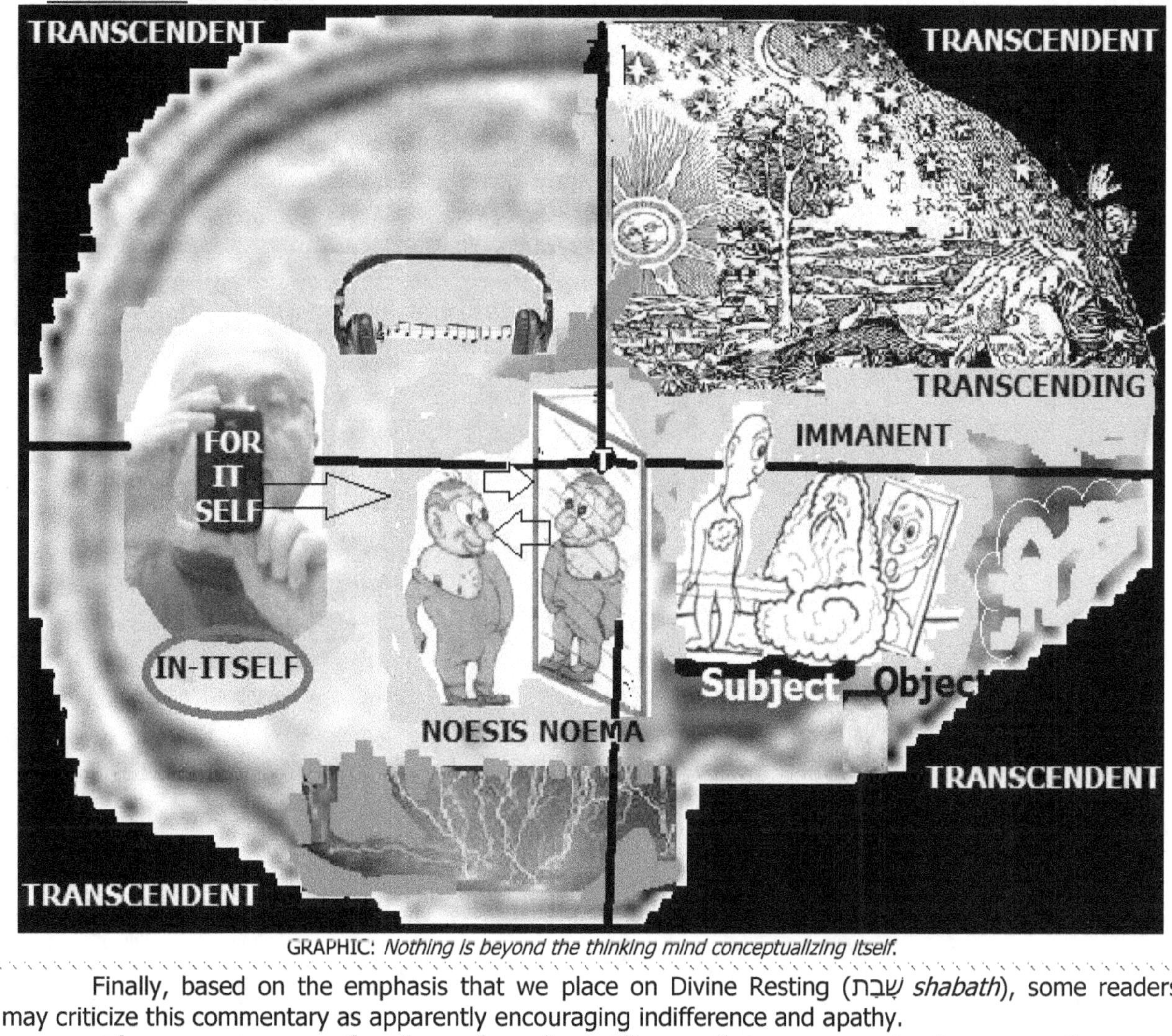

GRAPHIC: *Nothing is beyond the thinking mind conceptualizing itself.*

Finally, based on the emphasis that we place on Divine Resting (שבת *shabath*), some readers may criticize this commentary as apparently encouraging indifference and apathy.

However, it must be clear that the Stillness of Awareness is the Eternal Present Explosion of Joyful Creation. In that instant, there are no religious distinctions or denominations. Then, the Subject is the Object and Object is the Subject with no difference. Then, through that truly

"awakened (*buddha*)... blissful (*ānanda*)... union (*yoga*)"[3512]

of the mind,

"behold, how good and how pleasant it is for brethren to dwell together in unity,"[3513]

"till we all come in the unity of the certain-faith (πίστις *pistis*) *and of the realization* (ἐπίγνωσις *epignōsis*) *of the Son of God, unto a perfect man, unto the measure of the stature of the fulness of the Anointed One."*[3514]

This is not indifferent and apathetic quiescence. On the contrary, this means to be

"in the perfect enjoyment of the divine nature, in perfect joy and happiness."[3515]

As Saint Francis of Assisi explains to Brother Leo, when we sustain poverty, need, pain, distress, hunger, cold, homelessness and persecution with patience and love, then that is

"perfect joy."[3516]

Similarly, as we saw, St. John of the Cross calls it

"a very tasty science."[3517]

This is resting in Awareness, where

"the joy of the Transcendent (יְהֹוָה *Yĕhovah*) *is your strength."*[3518]

TRUTH IS so dazzling EVIDENT that we easily miss it.

"ἐγώ εἰμι... ἡ ζωή... ἐγὼ ἐν τῷ πατρί μου καὶ ὑμεῖς ἐν ἐμοὶ κἀγὼ ἐν ὑμῖν

ego sum... vita... ego sum in Patre meo et vos in me et ego in vobis [3519]

***I AM... THE LIFE... I AM IN MY FATHER, AND YE IN ME, AND I IN YOU*."**

If it were not so, Transcendent-Life would not be flowing through us.

3520

LANGUAGE'S LOGICAL ANALYSIS

SUBJECT-doer	verb-action	direct-**OBJECT**
I	EAT	**THE APPLE**
I	READ	**THE BOOK**
I	KNOW	**MYSELF**

1st person singular	**I**		ME	1st person singular
2nd person singular	**YOU**		YOU	2nd person singular
3rd person singular	**HE-SHE-IT**	PRO-NOUNS	HIM-HER-IT	3rd person singular
1st person plural	**WE**		US	1st person plural
2nd person plural	**YOU**		YOU	2nd person plural
3rd person plural	**THEY**		THEM	3rd person plural

▼↓KNOWLEDGE↓▼

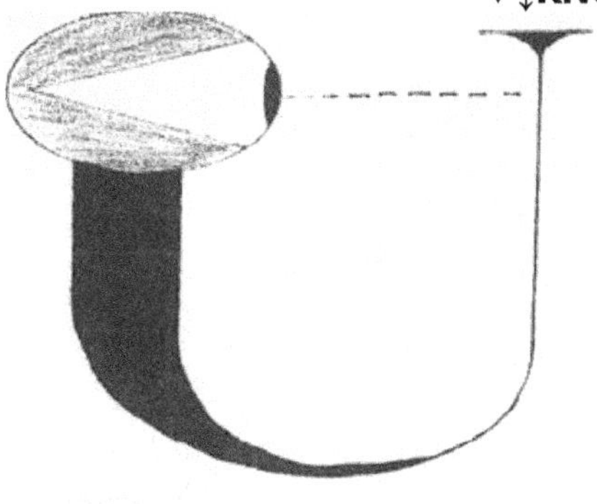

In Dr. John Wheeler's cartoon of an eyeball looking back at the Big Bang, the universe is a loop that brings itself into existence through billions of quantum observations.

"We're all hypnotized into thinking there's something out there," he said.

The serpent (*nachash*) Genesis 3:4;

IMMANENT im = "*in*" + manent = *manēre* "to re-main" (example: manor)

SUB-JECT	*sub* =	"under"+	**ject** =	***Jactāre*** "to throw"	(example: e-**ject**)
OB-JECT	*ob* =	"over" +	**ject** =	***jactāre***[3521] "to throw"	(example: e-**ject**)

I (Subject) know ⇨ me (Object)

We intuit the Subject but never know it as such. We infer it from its object.

The I (subject) can never be known as Subject, but it is only known as --> me (object)

the I for-itself = makes the world an object for-itself

BEYOND BEYOND BEYOND BEYOND BEYOND BEYOND THE IMMANENT,

TRANSCENDENT (*trans* = "beyond" + a-*scend* = "to climb") **is the I-IN-ITSELF,** corresponding to the seventh day, which projects itself in each of the six days on the circumference of creation without ever losing its own Transcendent Centrality.

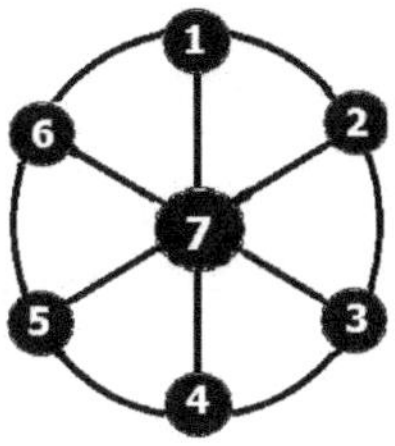

SELECTED CONCISE PHILOSOPHICAL TERMINOLOGIES

Apodictic (*adj.* **Apodictical**)**:** certain, clear and necessary self-evident truth.
A-posteriori: that which follows experience.
A-priori: that which precedes experience logically, but not actually.
Art: potentially universal language synthesis of form and idea.
Autoctisi: the self-constructed spark igniting itself.
Autochthonous: Self-generated.
Autogenous: Self-made, Self-born.
Awareness: is the fundamental apodictical presence of the certitude, which underlines and makes evident consciousness and the consciousness-*of* the world.
Beauty: dawn of knowledge**.**
Being-for-itself: the continuous circular reference of a *subject* to its correlated inseparable *object.*
Being-in-itself: the absolute independent center of the *immanent* circle set apart from the inseparable *subject-object* circular correlation.
Certainty: undeniable, indubitable and apodictical evidence beyond the objects.
Connotation: poetic, allegoric and metaphoric reference, extrapolation of the sense rendered by the tangible physical reality of an object directly signified or denoted.
Conscience: the only immanent condition that states *existence.*
Consciousness: is the absolute subjective a-priori structure of Awareness.
Consciousness-*of*: is the grasping and apprehension-*of* the world in its objective reality.
Creation: the concept of a divine act *pro*ducing everything out of nothing.
Denotation: direct and literal indication of the signified object.
Deontology: (*adj.* **Deontological**) theory of moral duties and rights.
Discursiveness: the process of a temporal procession ranging over the wide field of juxtaposed events and Experiences; the spreading out of a sequence.
Emanation: the process of emission from a higher source into a lower status, which in turn radiates into another position.
Epoché (ἐποχή)**:** suspending judgment in reference to reality *in-itself*; placing the world between brackets.
Episteme: knowledge, intellectually certain (*adj.* **Epistemic**): capable of knowledge or related to knowledge).
Epistemic loneliness: (see **Solipsism**) the impossibility of the I to know itself as I in-itself or to know another I as I.
Epistemology (*adj.* **Epistemological**)**:** the study of how we know what we know and its validity.
Ethics: search for apodictic moral laws.
Existence: that which is established by *conscience* within the *subject-object* correlation.
For-itself: see Being-for-itself.
Freethinker: a thinker who does not subscribe to any preconceived dogma or belief.
Future: projection towards the reduction to consciousness' data.
Gnoseology (*adj.* **Gnoseological**)**:** see Epistemology.
History: weltanschauung's present actualization.
Hypostasis (*pl.* **Hypostases**)**:** principle or substance deriving from another one and at the same time generating an inferior one.
Immanent: that which is inherent or characterizes the circle of the inseparable *subject-object* correlation; the relationship by which the mind, in the epistemic process, reduces the world to an *object for-itself.*
In-itself: see Being-in-itself.
In-se: see Being-in-itself.
Intentionality: experience as a stream of consciousness directed, like desire and hunger, toward

something.

Intuition: the state of immediate and total com-prehension or in-sight of the objective world without any temporal of spatial juxtaposition.

I-think: the *a-priori* subject constantly united with its object.

Knowledge: the epistemic synthetic correlation of subject and object, which intentions objectivity as otherness.

Liberty: autonomous innate unalloyed permanent state of the Self.

Life: satisfying the hunger for representation.

Love: unselfish tension toward the other in-itself

Metaphor: Greek, meaning to escort (*pherō* φέρω) beyond (*meta* μετά) the immediate shape or meaning of things.

Monism: there is only one reality.

Myth: echo of the Ineffable.

Mythology: a many faceted prism, each side representing a relative omni-comprehensive paradigm of the inner human reality, tracing the generating process of the psycho-cosmological world and denoting a tension *in-itself* that announces and echoes the *Transcendent*.

Mythologem: recurrent fabulous tale repeating itself during different times and places.

Noema (*adj.* **Noematic**)**:** the objective aspect of experience in its modes-of-being-given.

Noesis (*adj.* **Noetic**)**:** the subjective aspect of experience as act-of-perception aiming to grasp the object.

Noumenon (*pl.* **Noumena**, *adj.* **Noumenal**): that which is thought but not known.

Numinous: mysterious; relating to the spirits or gods.

Object: the known as such. The passive one to *whom* the action indicated by the verb is directed.

Objectivity: the field of the object. It is the object's position, which, nevertheless, becomes the object of the subject.

Oneiric: pertaining to dreams and sleep.

Ontological: the essence or nature of the existent.

Panpsychism: universal (*pan*) consciousness (*psychism*)

Paradigm (adj. **Paradigmatic**)**:** Archetype, Model and Template

Past: consciousness' data.

***Per-se*:** see Being-for-itself.

Phenomenology (*adj.* **Phenomenological**)**:** The study of experience and its structures as it appears in the light of individual consciousness.

Philosophy: constantly updated critical holistic rethinking of the World with intentional objectivity and History's mover.

Present: continuum perceptive awareness

Quantum (*pl.* **Quanta**)**:** elementary particle/s, a *quantum/a* [Latin: certain amount/s] *of energy* or mass.

Realization: the Apodictical-Certitude that does not necessitate an object, but intuitively reaches Reality In-Itself beyond any duality.

Religion: dogmatic bondage of a creed, vehicle to the Transcendent.

Science: mathematical intelligibility of nature's blind pro-ject.

Solipsism: (see **Epistemic loneliness**) the loneliness of the 'I' as such.

Subconscious: subliminal presence of dream-objects in the waking state and of waking-object in the dream state.

Subject: the knower as such. The one *who* does the action indicated by the verb.

Subjectivity: the field of the subject. It is the subject's view, which, still, becomes its object.

Tautology (*adj.* **Tautological**): a repeating circular reasoning.

Transcendent (*n.* **Transcendence**)**:** that which is never experienced or known *in-itself*, but it can be conceived as that which is beyond the subject-object correlation, thus, becoming an *immanent* thought. *Viz.*: God, Goddess, Lord of hosts, Unknown, Fourth State, Non-existent, Death, Future.

Transcendental: the manner in which *objects* are known, as this is possible *a-priori*.
Transcending: the mind's persisting projection towards an absolute external otherness, but never experienced as such.
Unconscious: the absence of any object of knowledge as such.
Weltanschauung: Worldview.

ALPHABETS

GREEK			HEBREW				
Character		Equivalent #	Character	Equivalent	#	Meaning	Act-direction
Α	α	A a_{lpha} 1	א	a ' $_{leph}$ @	1	Ox	Leader
Β	β	B b_{eta} 2	ב	b̲ b $_{êth}$	2	House	Inhabit
Γ	γ	G g_{amma} 3	ג	g $_{îmel}$	3	Foot	Walk
Δ	δ	D d_{elta} 4	ד	d̲ d $_{âleth}$	4	Door	Move
Ε	ε	E e_{psilon} 5	ה	h $_{ē}$	5	Breath Sight	Man NorthEast
Ζ	ζ	Z z_{eta} ϛ7	ו	w v $_{āw}$	6	Peg Hearing	Secure SouthEast
Η	η	Ē $ē_{ta}$ 8	ז	z $_{áyin}$	7	Food Smell	Dig East-height
Θ	θ	Th th_{eta} 9	ח	ḥ $_{êth}$	8	Wall	Speak East-depth
Ι	ι	I i_{ota} 10	ט	ṭ $_{êth}$	9	Mud	Surround NW.
Κ	κ	K k_{appa} 20	י	y $_{ôdh}$	10	Hand	Work SouthWest
Λ	λ	L l_{ambda} 30	כ ך*	k̲ k $_{aph}$	20	Open Palm	Bend
Μ	μ	M m_{i} 40	ל	l $_{āmedh}$	30	Staff	Teach West-height
Ν	ν	N n_{i} 50	מ ם*	m $_{êm}$	40	Water	Chaos
Ξ	ξ	X x_{i} 60	נ ן*	n $_{ûn}$	50	Sprout	Motion West-depth
Ο	ο	O o_{micron} 70	ס	ṣ ṣ $_{āmekh}$	60	Shield	Protect South-height
Π	π	P p_{i} 80	ע	'a $_{yin}$ [1]	70	Eye	Watch South-depth
Ρ	ρ	R r_{ho} 90 100	פ ף*	p̄ p $_{ē}$	80	Mouth	Blow
Σ	σ ς>	S s_{igma} 200	צ ץ*	ts ṣ $_{addik}$	90	Trail	Hunt North-height
Τ	τ	T t_{au} 300	ק	q $_{ôph}$	100	Horizon Sun	Circle North-depth
Υ	υ	U u_{psilon} 400	ר	r $_{êš}$	200	Head	Start
Φ	φ	Ph ph_{i} 500	ש	ś š $_{în}$	300	Tooth	Eat
Χ	χ	Ch ch_{i} 600	ת	t t̲ $_{āw}$	400	Cross	Mark
Ψ	ψ	Ps ps_{i} 700	*ך#500[2] Crown	*ם#600 Virgin	*ן#700 Infinite	*ף#800 Open Mouth	*ץ#900 Life Tree
Ω	ω	Ō $ō_{mega}$ 800	Some Vowels, Vocalization and Grapheme				

Ar-cha-ic		
	Ϝ w digamma 6	
	Ϙ koppa 90	
	ϡ sampi 900	

ָ	ā $_{c}$a$_{lm}$ @	ֶ	ē $_{ob}$e$_{y}$	ְ	ə a$_{go}$	ִ	ī $_{morph}$i$_{ne}$	וֹ	ō $_{m}$o$_{re}$	וּ	ū $_{m}$u$_{te}$
ַ	ă $_{m}$a$_{t}$	ֶ	ĕ $_{th}$e$_{n}$	ִ	ĭ $_{h}$i$_{t}$	ָ	ŏ $_{t}$o$_{p}$	ֻ	ŭ $_{sh}$u$_{t}$		

ς> Greek final s

* Hebrew final letter (*sofit*)

[1] Assimilated with the ancient letter 𐤏 *Ghah* (*gh*) [goat-rope]

[2] Rarely used, instead used ת *Tāw* 400 + ק *Qôph* 100

SELECTED LIST OF GENESIS' METAPHORS

Abel הֶבֶל *hebel* [4:2H1893] Spiritual function, Breath of Pure Consciousness, NREM
Acceptance שָׁעָה *sha `ah* [4:3H8159] Transcendence's acknowledgment
Adam אָדָם *'adam* [2:5H120] Male/female human subject
Adah עָדָה *` adah* [4:19H5711] The ornament of power
Animals חַי *chay* [1:21H2416] Active, living sense appetite for experience
Ark תֵּבָה *tebah* [6:14H8392] Chest-container of ideas, memories, dreams, and interactions.
Ashamed בּוֹשׁ *buwsh* [2:25H954] To be confused, to cover the object in-itself
Bdellium בְּדֹלַח *bĕdolach* [2:12H916] The distinguishing thought
Birds עוֹף *`owph* [2:19H5775] The ethereal senses of the psyche
Blood דָּם *dam* [4:10H1818] Transcendent Life Being In-Itself
Breath רוּחַ *ruwach* [1:2H7307] Flow of Consciousness
Breath of life נְשָׁמָה *nĕshamah* [2:7H5397] Flow of life
Building-block בָּנָה *banah* [2:12H1129] Consciousness as building block
Daughters בַּת *bath* [5:4H1323] Ideas, ideologies
Day יוֹם *yowm* [1:5H3117] Circle of Consciousness
Cain קַיִן *qayin* [4:1H7014] Material function, awaken object possessor subjectivity
Cainan קֵינָן *qeynan* [5:9H7018] Dream possessor
Cherubim כְּרוּב *kĕruwb* [3:24H3742] Impossible Transcendent's conceptualization
Create בָּרָא *bara'* [1:1H1254] *To create, to eat, to grow fat.*
Day יוֹם *yowm* [1:5H3117] Circularity of Consciousness
Deep Sleep תַּרְדֵּמָה *tardemah* [2:21H8639] Non-Rapid-Eye-Movement [NREM] state
Divine-Consciousness אֱלֹהִים *'elohiym* [1:1H430] Pure-Epistemic-fundamentals=Aware-Conscious-Certainty
Dust עָפָר *` aphar* [3:19H6083] The nothingness of death we come from and go to
Earth אֶרֶץ *'erets* [1:1H776] The firm dimensions of physical objectivity
Eat אָכַל *'akal* [2:16H398] To identify with the epistemic food
Eden עֵדֶן *` eden* [2:8H5731] The human body as a garden of Happiness
Elohim אֱלֹהִים [1:1*H430*] *Divine-Conscious-Rulers*
Enoch חֲנוֹךְ *chanowk* [4:17/5:18H2585] Dedicated one awake & dreaming instructor
Enos אֱנוֹשׁ *'enowsh* [5:6H583] The physical mortal dreamer
Eve חַוָּה *chavvah* [2:20H2332] Paradigmatic objective breath, food to known
Face פָּנִים *paniym* [4:14H6440] Presence in-itself and/or appearance of something
Father אָב *'ab* [2:24H1] Originating subjectivity in itself and for itself
Female נְקֵבָה *nĕqebah* [1:27H5347] Separating *image* from the *observing reflector*
Fig תְּאֵנָה *tĕ'en* [3:7H8384-5] The fruit of subject-object copulating synthesis
Flesh בָּשָׂר *basar* [6:3H1319-20] Information bearing nerve system, being for-itself. See One-flesh
Fruit פְּרִי *pĕriy* [3:2H6529] Consciousness' outcome and/or mind conceptual reduction
Food מַאֲכָל *ma'akal* [2:9H3978] All that which is internally transformed
Garden גַּן *gan* [*2:8H1588*] The human body as the land of Happiness
Gold זָהָב *zahab* [2:11, H2091] Brilliance of Consciousness
Goper-wood גפר *goper* [6:14 H6086] Wood or the tree of memory
Ham חָם *Cham* [5:32H2526] Passion
Irad עִירָד *` iyrad* [4:18H5897] The *fleet* of human functions sail from him
Jabal יָבָל *yabal* [4:20H2989] The streaming faculty of herding and and farming
Japheth יֶפֶת *Yepheth* [5:32H3315] seduction
Jared יֶרֶד *yered* [5:15H3382] Dream descent
Jubal יוּבָל *yuwbal* [4:21H3106] The artistic streaming faculty

Lamech לֶמֶךְ *lemek* [4:18/5:25H3929] The power function, the *powerful one*
Leaf עָלֶה ` *aleh*[3:7H5929] The body as the dress of the mind
Light אוֹר *'owr*[1:3, H21] Splendor of the Pure Consciousness as Love
Maleזָכָר *zakar*[1:27H2145] Subjectivity
Man אִישׁ *'iysh*[2:23H376] *A-priory* synthesis of husband subject-object-wife [cf.]
Mahalaleel מַהֲלַלְאֵל *Mahalal'el*[5:12H4111] Dream praise of God
Mehujaelמְחוּיָאֵל*měchuwya'el* [4:18H4232] Priestly function, the *smitten by God*
Methusaelמְתוּשָׁאֵל*měthuwsha'el*[4:18H4867]Prophetic function being with God
Methuselah מְתוּשֶׁלַח *měthuwshelach*[5:21H4968] Prophetic dream
Middleתָּוֶךְ*tavek*[2:29 H4832] Consciousness' Centrality directed inward/outward
Mist אֵד *'ed*[2:6H108] Fog of objectivity distracting from its origin
Mother אֵם 'em[2:24;3:20H517] Earth's metaphor, logical division from the subject
Naked עָרוֹם `*arowm*[2:25H6174] Distinction of object *in-itself* and *for-itself*
Naamah נַעֲמָה *na `amah* [4:22H5279] Loveliness
Noah נֹחַ *Noach*[5:29H5146]The rested one
Offer מִנְחָה *minchah*[4:3H4503] Renunciation, giving-up (see Sacrifice)
Offspring צֶאֱצָאִים *tse'etsa* [Job5:25H6631] Conceptual seeds
Olive זַיִת *zayith*[8:11H2132] Flowing peace
One-flesh בָּשָׂר *basar*[2:24H1320] The whole body as man-wife, one flesh
Patriarch אָב *'ab*[4:20VH1] a-temporal template of epistemic functions and categories
Rested שָׁבַת*shabath*[2:2H7673] Stillness of Transcendence
River נָהָר *nahar*[2:10H5104] Consciousness' flow in waking and dream
Sacrifice מִנְחָה *minchah*[4:3H4503] Renunciation, giving-up (see Offer)
Serpent נָחָשׁ*nachash*[3:1H5175] Desire as the snaking circle of intention*ality*
Seth שֵׁת *sheth* [4:25H8352] Compensation of the dream state
Sew תָּפַר *taphar*[3:7H8609] Copulate as *a-priori* synthesis
Shem שֵׁם *Shem*[6:10H8035] Established
Sin חַטָּאת *chatta'ath*[4:7H2403] Consequence for missing the true mark.
Stone אֶבֶן*'eben*[2:12H68] Consciousness as building block
Tubalcainתּוּבַל קַיִן*tuwbal qayin*[4:22H8423]Technical instruction brought to Cain
Tree עֵץ `*ets*[2:9H6086] Faculties, drives and/or desire of knowledge
" of **Knowledge**דַּעַת*da `ath*[2:9H1847] Faculty of experience, desire to know
" of **Life** חַי *chay*[2:9 H2416] Faculty of direction into Awareness
Waters מַיִם*mayim*[1:2H4325] Receptacle of infinite possibilities
" **Above** עַל` *al*[1:7H5921] The Infinite Conscious Transcendent Silence
" **Below**תַּחַת*tachath*[1:7H8478] All the immanent possible consciousnesses-*of* experiences
Wife אִשָּׁה*'ishshah*[2:22H802] Polarity of the object-subject *a-priori* synthesis
Womanאִשָּׁה *'ishshah*[2:22H802] Generating objectivity for the man/subject
Yĕhovah יְהוָה[2:4H3068]Transcendent Ineffable Apodictical Awareness
Zillah צִלָּה *tsillah*[4:19H6741] The shade, the transitory fleeting of life

ARTWORK & PHOTOS INDEX

Page
Adam Kadmon, Knorr von Rosenroth 273
Adam und Eva, Cranach the Elder 129
Ancestral worship, family altar, private house, Cuzco, Peru, 1990 (photo) 156
Angelic cupids with grapes, XIX century ceramic, Vietri, Italy 405
An Old Man and his Grandson, Ghirlandaio, 1490, Louvre, Paris 381
Apkallu in Assyrian bas-reliefs 37
Apple (photo) 126
Apocalypse, Simonelli 265
Armor, Italy XVII Century 199
Atlas, Lawrie 21
Banddudû bucket 37
Barge of Horus, Sanctuary of the Ptolemaic Temple of Horus, Edfu, Egypt 243
Birds of the Assyrian Monuments and Records, William Houghton 84
Bow drill fire starter 101
Broken coin (photo) 27
Buddha's aniconic empty throne sculture, 2nd century, Amaravati, India 19
Buddha bhūmisparśa, Tibetan votive Tsa Tsa 172
Buddha statue blown up niche, Bamiyan, Afghanistan (photo) 10
Caduceus, Simonelli 323
Canopic jar 317
Cedar of Lebanon, Bunchrew, Scotland, 1745 (photo) 67
Center, Simonelli 299
Cerberus, Doré, Inferno VI 232
Charioteer on biga with Nike flying above. (Obverse, silver tetradrachm Syracuse, Sicily, 430 BC) . 306
Cock, Indonesia wood 319
Computer chips (photo) 305
Computer external drive (photo) 237
Crete, Labyrinth of Knossos, reverse of Greek AR Stater coin (320-300 BC) 146
Cristo Redentor, Rio de Janeiro 224
Crossing the Red Sea, wall painting, 1640s Yaroslavl, Russia 64
Crown of Egypt 35
Ḍāmara (*sādhu*'s copper and leather drum) India-Nepal, 19th century 133
Dandelion (*Taraxacum*) (photo) 35
Denarius of *Tiberius*, silver obverse 413
Design of man, Leonardo da Vinci 349
Dispassionate in Awareness, Altus, *Mutus Liber* 64
Double-head Mayan mask (Guatemala) 219
Double-headed serpent, (photo) *apple and rebis* 137
Elephant and the blind men 28
Escaping criticism, Pere Borrell del Caso 294
Ecstatic apotheosis, Altus, *Liber Mutus*, Plate 15, detail 116
Expansor, Bruno 336
False Mirror, The, Magritte 36
Four Horsemen of the Apocalypse, 1887, by Victor Vasnetsov 65
Girl before a Mirror, Picasso (Collage) 336
Golem, Prague brass 304
Hercules. Altus, *Liber Mutus*, Plate 15, detail 116

Holy Spirit, Bernini 285
Holy water dispenser (photo) 38
Horse statue (photo) 115
Italic oil lamp (IV Century BC) 291
Jacob's dream, Altus, *Mutus Liber*, First Plate 303
Jonah and the whale, Biblical Stories, 2$ Silver Coin from Palau 2015 232
Kabbalistic Tree of Life with emanations (Səphîrôṯ) and paths in Hebrew, (Kaplan tr., *The Bahir*) .. 109
Kippah, כִּפָּה or *yarmulke* (photo) 39
Koran on the head (photo) 39
L'atmosphère: météorologie populaire, Anonymous wood engraving 38
Looking at the Stars, Simonelli 336
Lorns, The, Honeymoon 26
Lorns, The, Mirrors 415
Madonna of Medjugorje, popular art 416
Mara's assault on the Buddha, 2nd century, Amaravati, India 65
Mark of Death, Simonelli, *Beyond Immortality* 174
Mask of Death & Rebirth, Mayan art replica, 900 AD, Tikal, Mexico 97
Memento mori, Pompeii 335
Menorah Candelabrum 19
Mirror & *Fulang-Chang and I*, Kahlo 72
Moses at the Burning Bush, 12th Cent. icon, Mount Sinai Monastery of St. Catherine (reproduction) 249
Mount Ararat, Turkey 100 Lira, 1972 269
Mount of Perfection, The, ascent to Mount Carmel, Saint John of the Cross 278
Napoleon Crossing the Alps, David 217
Narcissus beholding his own reflected image, Caravaggio 80
Osiris, detail Coffin of Seti I detail, Soane Museum London 385
Our Lady of Sorrows (Anonymous) 33
Ouroboros, Michael Maier (1569 - 1622) 144
Pastori napoletani del Settecento Neapolitan nativity figurines (Three wise men and babe) 105
Paterissa, Greek Orthodox Bishops' Pastoral Staff 144
Persistencia de la memoria, La, Dalí 371
Phenakistoscope disc 366
Philosopher's Stone, Eli Luminosus Aequalis, *Mutus Liber "Loquitur."* 48
Prints in the sand (photo) 349
Procession of the dead, Simonelli 265
Purkinje cells, Santiago Ramón y Cajal 67
Pyramidion capstone, US 1 Dollar bill 233
Raft of the Medusa, Géricault 250
Rastafarian dreadlocks (photo) 392
Rebis, Prussian State Museum 117
Ripple effect 318
Rising sun (photo) 54
Roman Arch and Corner Stone 316
Sacred Heart of Jesus, Byzantine icon 224
Sacred Pipe, Native American sacred calumet 36
Śaiva sādhu ascetic, Mana, Uttarakhand, India (Photo) 297
Scale, watercolor replica on papyrus, Egypt 1986 223
Scream, The, Munch 36
Selva oscura, Dante's Inferno, Gustave Doré's illustration 166

Seventh day's center ... 93
Shofar, *Ram's horn* trumpet, Israel ... 134
Śîn, ש, hands' blessing symb*ol and Trident* (photo) ... 42
Sistine Chapel, Creation of Adam, Michelangelo ... 97
Sistine Chapel, The Last Judgment, Michelangelo ... 163
Skyphos painted vessel in an Oscan warrior's tomb (Saviano, Nola, Naples, Italy) ... 27
Skull, Ivory Asia, Packard 43147 Morris Museum NJ ... 124
Skull and brain MRI (photo) ... 230
Snake khut on Pharaoh Ramses VI's forehead (*Wadi Biban el-Muluk*, King's Valley, Luxor, Egypt) . 35
Solar halo, New Jersey Shore, USA 5/14/2013 (photo) ... 200-5
Squeezed lemon (photo) ... 22
Star of David, Israel popular art on cloth ... 1
Sun at Medjugorje (photo) ... 250
Sunset (photo) ... 349
Surrealistic photo ... 312
Symbolic key ... 28
Tefillin box ... 39
Tefillin box with three prongs ש (photo) ... 42
Templar's Seal, lapel pin ... 233
Tetramorph, Meteora 16th century fresco ... 152
Tree of the Siren (Farkas-Simon, *Camilla*) ... 111
Tree roots (photo) ... 108
Triumph of Death, The, (detail) 1562 Pieter Brueghel the Elder, Museo del Prado ... 142
Triśula, of Shivji Murti at Sur Sagar Lake in BarodaBaroda, Rajasthan, India ... 42
Turris Babel, Kircher ... 375
Unique Forms of Continuity in Space, Boccioni ... 350
Unveiling of the mystery, Villa of the Mysteries, Pompeii, Italy, fresco ... 334
Universe (photo) ... 55
Uros miniature boat, Titicaca, Puno, Peru ... 270
Vajra, Tibet ... 55
Virtual Reality Games (photo) ... 245
Wheel of the Sun Temple at Konark, Orissa, India. 2001 India postage Rs 4^{00} ... 416
Whale, American Pacific Northwest Coast, Haida Art ... 256
Winged Genius, *tree* and *sculpted artifact*, Palace of kings, Ur, Assyria ... 37
Yad (יד(✡ Star of David, Torah scroll and letter *ś*, ש shaped as key ... 1
Young piano players (photo) ... 179

INDEX

ॐ, 101, 224, 286, 318, 319
'asah, 61
Aaron, 76
Abel, 6, 25, 158, 159, 160, 161, 162, 164, 166, 168, 169, 170, 171, 172, 174, 175, 177, 183, 184, 189, 192, 193, 196, 205, 210, 219, 222, 226, 241, 296, 316, 359, 364
Abimael, 11, 370, 374
abortion, 182
Abraham, 47, 115, 149, 164, 179, 242, 250, 340, 368, 401, 413, 414
Abram, 12, 397, 398, 399, 401, 402, 404
Absolute Present, 386
Accad, 356, 357, 366
act, 21, 30, 35, 36, 37, 39, 47, 49, 54, 55, 58, 61, 63, 70, 81, 87, 88, 96, 97, 111, 115, 117, 129, 134, 141, 144, 149, 153, 158, 159, 160, 163, 164, 168, 170, 172, 183, 214, 216, 221, 224, 238, 241, 242, 251, 261, 274, 275, 286, 287, 289, 291, 296, 301, 302, 306, 313, 316, 322, 336, 355, 356, 360, 371, 384, 387, 391, 412, 416, 421, 422
action, 166, 167
actualized, 95
Adah, 179, 180, 181, 182, 183
Adam, 4, 5, 7, 9, 25, 26, 28, 68, 78, 81, 83, 84, 85, 89, 90, 95, 96, 97, 99, 102, 103, 109, 112, 113, 114, 115, 116, 117, 118, 119, 120, 132, 133, 134, 135, 139, 147, 149, 150, 151, 152, 153, 157, 158, 159, 162, 172, 183, 184, 187, 188, 189, 191, 192, 193, 194, 195, 196, 198, 199, 213, 214, 215, 217, 219, 223, 231, 238, 259, 265, 274, 277, 280, 297, 305, 310, 329, 331, 334, 336, 356, 362, 364, 366, 372, 380, 381, 382, 383
Adam and Eve, 131
Admah, 362, 363, 364, 366
Adonai, 46, 410
Adonis, 134
advaita, 135
Aeneid, 110
aesthetic, 123, 180, 242, 243, 251, 255, 296, 409
African religions, 157
age, 146
agnostic, 80, 130
Agonistici, 184
Akkadian, 96
Allah, 222, 289, 291
Allegories, 27
Allegory, 3, 26
Almodad, 11, 369, 374
Alpha Centauri, 157
alphabet, 191
Al-Qurnah, 107
Altus, 93, 384
Alzheimer, 158, 415
'amar, 57, 60, 61, 169, 314, 379, 380
Amen, 32, 135
Amorite, 361, 366
Amorites, 415
Anamim, 359, 366
ānanda, 418
ancestors, 36
Andrews, 303
anesthesia, 411
Angelic Powers, 46
angels, 48, 324, 409
Angels, 48
Anger, 222, 223
animal, 38, 78, 80, 85, 89, 113, 114, 115, 116, 122, 123, 142, 143, 160, 162, 171, 238, 242, 246, 256, 260, 267, 271, 295, 296, 307, 308, 309, 314, 315
animalists, 24
animals, 216
Anointed, 419
Anselm, 321
Anu, 357
Anubis, 224
apnea, 53, 91, 97, 161, 297
Apodictic, 32, 34, 87, 93, 99, 126, 127, 128, 138, 143, 148, 152, 154, 217, 235, 249, 250, 264, 286, 289, 335, 336, 343, 375, 382, 383, 386, 414, 421
Apodictical, 32, 40, 88, 90, 93, 151, 162, 164, 166, 174, 187, 216, 221, 222, 248, 249, 250, 268, 271, 276, 281, 284, 287, 296, 298, 318, 319, 333, 421, 422
apodicticity, 12, 22, 407, 410
Apollodorus of Athens, 358
Apollonius Rhodius, 110
Apostles' Creed, 233
appetite, 78, 115, 128, 159, 166, 193, 368, 380, 413
apple, 127, 138, 245

a-priori, 21, 47, 48, 73, 74, 87, 95, 107, 110, 119, 133, 134, 139, 188, 226, 227, 235, 249, 254, 260, 321, 363, 375, 391, 421, 422, 423
a-priori forms, 48, 314
Arabic, 20, 27, 32
Aram, 367, 368, 374
Aramaic, 78, 192, 225, 258
Ararat, 7, 9, 107, 213, 270, 274, 280, 428
archeologists, 149
archetypes, 25, 28, 90, 110, 218, 243, 244, 359, 364, 393
Archimedes, 303
arhat, 414
Aristotle, 129, 261
Arjuna, 167
ark, 7, 8, 9, 10, 25, 38, 64, 213, 224, 229, 230, 231, 232, 233, 234, 236, 237, 238, 240, 241, 242, 243, 250, 251, 254, 255, 256, 257, 258, 259, 261, 262, 263, 267, 270, 271, 272, 274, 277, 280, 281, 282, 283, 284, 285, 287, 288, 292, 293, 294, 295, 296, 308, 313, 314, 315, 326, 327, 328, 329, 333
Arkite, 11, 361, 366
Arphaxad, 367, 368, 369, 374, 387, 388, 389, 395
art, 64, 285, 342
Arthur, 358
Arthurian saga, 309, 352
Artificial Intelligence, 305
Artists, 6, 180
Arvadite, 361, 366
Arvand Rud, 107
ascending, 22, 62, 64, 101, 152, 161, 210, 304, 322, 324, 414
ascension, 146, 324
Ash Wednesday, 336
ashes, 141, 142, 143, 148, 152, 224, 298, 360, 371, 374
Ashkenaz, 351, 352
asleep, 324
Asshur, 11, 357, 358, 366, 367, 374
assumption, 158
Assyria, 107, 108, 429
asteroids, 146, 245
atheist, 16, 80, 187, 410
Atlas, 21, 394, 427
ātman, 307, 327, 135
attachments, 65, 103, 138, 263, 349, 375, 413
Augustine, 49
AUM•, 134, 135, 233, 305, 327
Autochthonous, 55, 421
Auto-Transparency, 58, 59, 69, 82, 97, 112, 119, 120, 129, 134, 205, 234, 235, 306, 311, 329, 331, 336, 383
awake, 292, 324, 408, 409
Aware, 61, 87, 163, 164, 172, 173, 194, 195, 199, 219, 226, 259, 263, 265, 282, 286, 416
Awareness, 4, 8, 12, 17, 19, 22, 23, 24, 27, 28, 32, 33, 34, 38, 39, 40, 43, 46, 47, 48, 54, 55, 56, 57, 58, 60, 61, 63, 71, 76, 79, 80, 87, 88, 89, 90, 91, 93, 94, 95, 97, 99, 100, 103, 105, 110, 113, 115, 119, 124, 125, 126, 127, 128, 130, 134, 138, 141, 143, 145, 148, 151, 152, 154, 158, 160, 161, 162, 163, 164, 165, 166, 167, 168, 170, 174, 176, 177, 187, 194, 196, 197, 199, 200, 201, 202, 206, 208, 215, 216, 217, 220, 221, 222, 223, 224, 225, 226, 227, 228, 229, 235, 236, 241, 242, 243, 245, 247, 248, 249, 250, 252, 253, 254, 255, 259, 263, 264, 266, 268, 271, 272, 275, 276, 277, 280, 282, 284, 285, 286, 288, 289, 292, 293, 295, 296, 297, 298, 302, 311, 312, 313, 314, 315, 316, 318, 320, 321, 322, 323, 324, 325, 330, 332, 333, 334, 335, 336, 337, 341, 342, 343, 345, 356, 359, 368, 375, 378, 381, 382, 383, 384, 385, 386, 399, 406, 407, 409, 410, 411, 412, 413, 414, 416, 418, 419, 421, 426, 427
Babel, 11, 12, 223, 356, 364, 366, 377, 382, 384, 385, 386, 397, 406
Babylonian Talmûd, 136
bara', 61
barge, 232, 244
Barge of Rā, 387
bdellium, 105, 106
beautiful, 57, 58, 65, 68, 74, 76, 100, 130, 181, 210, 214, 215, 345, 412
beauty, 6, 57, 58, 65, 165, 180, 181, 214, 216, 222, 247, 255, 286, 289, 409, 421
beginning, 1, 3, 18, 42, 46, 47, 48, 49, 50, 51, 55, 58, 59, 60, 63, 73, 88, 93, 95, 96, 99, 145, 166, 148, 217, 232, 235, 245, 249, 286, 288, 297, 301, 324, 336, 356, 387
Beha 'Alothekha, 100
being, 20, 22, 25, 26, 29, 31, 32, 34, 35, 40, 41, 42, 47, 48, 49, 50, 51, 58, 64, 73, 76, 80, 81, 82, 84, 85, 91, 96, 97, 102, 109, 110, 111, 112, 113, 114, 117, 118, 119, 123, 125, 132, 136, 137, 139, 146, 149, 150, 151, 158, 159,

162, 165, 169, 170, 171, 172, 174, 178, 180, 184, 203, 205, 207, 219, 221, 222, 224, 228, 231, 234, 237, 241, 242, 244, 245, 249, 250, 252, 262, 263, 264, 265, 266, 267, 268, 273, 280, 281, 282, 284, 285, 286, 289, 294, 301, 306, 307, 308, 309, 311, 315, 319, 324, 327, 329, 331, 335, 336, 350, 360, 368, 372, 378, 383, 388, 393, 394, 406, 410, 413, 415, 416, 421, 422
being-in-itself, 335
beings, 37, 53, 75, 76, 82, 83, 84, 114, 117, 125, 132, 142, 150, 163, 166, 208, 222, 227, 229, 230, 235, 237, 238, 242, 243, 244, 246, 262, 264, 265, 267, 280, 286, 350, 354, 356, 360, 368
belief, 3, 16, 22, 24, 31, 32, 33, 34, 35, 37, 40, 88, 93, 169, 172, 221, 285, 303, 312, 321, 324, 345, 406, 412, 413, 421
Benvenuti, 253
Bethlehem, 106
Bhagavad Gītā, 14, 110, 167, 275, 276
Bhagavan, 2
Bible, 18, 24, 28, 38, 92, 126, 242, 317, 345, 372, 447
Big Bang, 35, 49, 50, 51, 53, 55, 73, 149, 318, 345, 354, 399
Biological Multiplication, 4, 74, 76
black hole, 50, 102, 157, 314, 337
blessed, 76, 77, 82, 83, 90, 136, 138, 147, 164, 187, 188, 260, 267, 301, 343, 401
blood, 6, 10, 91, 145, 159, 160, 169, 171, 172, 174, 183, 188, 296, 308, 309, 310, 311, 312, 314, 319, 329, 331, 340, 411, 413
Boccioni, 429
body, 145, 146
Bohr, 36
Book of Recorded Remembrance, 221
Borbély, 400
Brahman, 252
Brāhmaṇa, 14, 224
brain, 20, 21, 31, 41, 50, 97, 111, 112, 114, 115, 123, 146, 171, 230, 274, 301, 305, 306, 384, 401, 410
breath, 4, 9, 48, 52, 53, 54, 59, 60, 73, 78, 85, 90, 91, 93, 96, 97, 98, 101, 114, 133, 134, 138, 144, 148, 152, 159, 161, 166, 168, 169, 171, 183, 184, 189, 215, 216, 232, 234, 235, 236, 259, 261, 266, 267, 268, 271, 272, 274, 275, 279, 280, 289, 297, 308, 314, 315, 327, 388, 395, 424
Bṛhadāraṇyaka, 14, 102, 136, 149, 166, 170, 350, 355, 360, 371
brick, 379, 380
brother, 115, 158, 159, 168, 169, 170, 171, 172, 174, 180, 310, 337, 338, 355, 358, 367, 369, 392, 393
Bruno, 24, 38, 222
Buddha, 19, 27, 173, 414, 418, 427
Buddhism, 29, 291, 416
Budge, 428
building block, 106, 133, 310
bull, 27
burial, 27
burning, 166
burning bush, 55, 89, 92, 153, 334, 399
Bush, 166
Cabalistic, 26, 191
Cabalists, 26
Caesar, 413
Cain, 6, 7, 25, 68, 157, 158, 159, 160, 161, 162, 164, 165, 166, 168, 169, 170, 171, 172, 173, 174, 175, 176, 177, 178, 180, 181, 182, 183, 184, 190, 191, 192, 193, 197, 200, 210, 219, 223, 226, 236, 238, 266, 298, 312, 316, 328, 359, 360, 364, 394
Cainan, 7, 196, 197, 198, 199, 210, 367, 368, 388, 389
Calah, 357, 358, 366
calendar, 50, 292
Calneh, 356, 357, 366
Calvin, 161
Camelot, 309, 358
Campbell, 313, 416
Canaan, 10, 11, 12, 326, 327, 330, 332, 334, 338, 339, 340, 343, 354, 360, 361, 363, 366, 402
Canaanite, 11, 331, 361, 362, 364, 403
canopic-jar, 224
cantillation, 286
Capaneus, 223
Caphtorim, 359, 360, 366
capital punishment, 169
capitalist, 291
capitalist separation of State and Church, 291
Casluhim, 359, 360, 366
cataleptic, 313
categories, 350, 410

Catherine of Siena, 410
causality, 10, 46, 48, 50, 54, 58, 91, 110, 169, 173, 218, 227, 254, 256, 259, 314, 316, 327, 334, 335, 336, 337, 338, 339, 344, 349, 350, 354, 355, 356, 358, 359, 360, 363, 366, 367, 370, 375, 380
cause, 318, 336, 354, 364, 399, 400
Celestial Waters, 53
Celtic, 358
Ceres, 64
certainty, 9, 22, 32, 88, 93, 97, 126, 141, 152, 162, 172, 192, 221, 245, 249, 264, 271, 280, 282, 283, 285, 287, 289, 321, 324, 375, 409, 410, 411, 412, 413, 421
certitude, 32, 33, 34, 39, 87, 88, 89, 93, 133, 138, 141, 143, 151, 162, 172, 173, 217, 221, 222, 236, 241, 248, 249, 250, 251, 252, 263, 264, 265, 268, 272, 286, 318, 319, 334, 341, 342, 343, 412, 415, 416, 422
Cervantes, 253
Chaldaea, 110
Chaldees, 12, 398, 399, 402
Chāndogya, 14, 341
chariot, 97, 99, 307, 349, 358
Cherubim, 6, 152, 153, 154, 231
child, 138, 387
childbirth, 146, 147
Christ, 25, 38, 184, 221, 413
Christianity, 291
church, 169
Cicero, 244, 383
circadian, 108, 154, 193, 205, 217, 227, 256, 258, 297, 299, 317, 327, 344, 396, 397, 398, 400, 404v
circadian rhythm, 317
circle, 4, 35, 48, 50, 59, 64, 72, 78, 83, 84, 85, 88, 110, 126, 143, 144, 150, 158, 189, 192, 194, 201, 206, 209, 217, 226, 232, 244, 253, 282, 284, 285, 317, 319, 354, 355, 364, 368, 370, 371, 387, 388, 421, 426
circularity, 3, 9, 22, 35, 53, 54, 56, 59, 60, 62, 64, 70, 72, 77, 85, 88, 105, 108, 127, 145, 148, 189, 192, 193, 194, 195, 196, 197, 198, 199, 200, 201, 202, 203, 204, 205, 206, 207, 208, 209, 210, 219, 226, 231, 232, 235, 258, 275, 279, 282, 283, 288, 299, 311, 336, 337, 351, 355, 368, 374, 387, 388, 392, 402, 403, 406
circumcision, 322
circumference, 35, 50, 59, 88, 135, 217, 253, 286, 416
clean, 242
clouds, 36
cogito, 221
coin, 27, 427
coincidentia oppositorum, 42
commandment, 34, 111, 130, 137, 138, 153
communication, 16, 60, 280, 306, 378, 380, 411
Communist, 291
Communist historical materialism, 291
compassion, 113
computer, 54, 66, 76, 77, 78, 163, 178, 243, 263, 305, 313, 337
computer programs, 66
computers, 18, 305, 306
concentration, 251, 252, 307, 368, 370
Confucianism, 29, 291
Confucius, 289, 291
conscious, 88, 132
consciousness, 3, 4, 9, 12, 20, 21, 22, 23, 25, 32, 33, 35, 39, 40, 41, 42, 46, 47, 48, 50, 51, 53, 54, 55, 56, 57, 58, 59, 60, 61, 62, 63, 64, 65, 66, 68, 69, 70, 73, 74, 76, 77, 80, 82, 83, 84, 85, 87, 88, 89, 90, 91, 92, 93, 94, 95, 97, 98, 99, 100, 103, 104, 105, 106, 107, 109, 110, 111, 112, 114, 115, 119, 122, 123, 124, 125, 127, 129, 133, 134, 135, 137, 139, 143, 145, 148, 149, 150, 151, 152, 158, 159, 161, 162, 163, 168, 169, 172, 173, 174, 175, 187, 188, 189, 190, 191, 192, 193, 194, 195, 196, 197, 198, 199, 200, 201, 202, 203, 204, 205, 206, 207, 208, 209, 210, 214, 215, 217, 218, 221, 224, 229, 231, 232, 233, 234, 238, 242, 243, 248, 249, 250, 251, 252, 253, 254, 256, 258, 259, 260, 262, 263, 264, 266, 268, 271, 272, 273, 274, 275, 277, 282, 283, 284, 285, 287, 288, 289, 291, 292, 296, 297, 301, 302, 304, 305, 307, 311, 314, 318, 319, 320, 322, 327, 329, 334, 335, 336, 338, 340, 341, 344, 345, 353, 358, 368, 383, 384, 387, 388, 389, 390, 391, 392, 397, 399, 402, 406, 407, 409, 410, 411, 412, 413, 414, 421, 422
consciousness-*of*, 22, 25, 27, 32, 33, 41, 54, 55, 56, 57, 58, 59, 61, 63, 64, 66, 68, 69, 70, 76, 80, 87, 88, 90, 92, 94, 95, 98, 111, 124, 125, 127, 148, 149, 157, 168, 189, 190, 201, 205, 242, 248, 249, 250, 252, 258, 259, 263, 264, 268, 271, 272, 273, 284, 285, 296, 302, 319,

320, 329, 334, 335, 336, 338, 353, 384, 406, 407, 409, 411, 412, 413, 421
constant, 74, 90, 127, 251, 254
constitution, 169
conversion, 35, 40
cosmological, 28, 38, 290, 422
Cosmological Reality, 290
cosmology, 29
cosmos, 70, 166, 314
Cranach, 427
creation, 3, 4, 25, 27, 32, 38, 39, 40, 45, 46, 47, 48, 49, 50, 51, 54, 55, 58, 59, 60, 61, 62, 63, 64, 65, 66, 68, 69, 70, 74, 77, 78, 76, 79, 85, 86, 88, 89, 90, 91, 92, 93, 96, 102, 105, 115, 129, 135, 136, 138, 139, 144, 160, 163, 165, 172, 175, 216, 217, 222, 224, 232, 234, 235, 241, 242, 243, 256, 263, 283, 287, 297, 306, 355,358, 368, 371, 374, 406, 420, 421
creationist, 35, 305
Creative-geniality, 302
Creator, 17, 24, 27, 36, 49, 50, 55, 60, 61, 87, 88, 92, 129, 160, 232, 241, 305
creature, 31, 59, 61, 68, 74, 75, 77, 91, 114, 144, 153, 162, 216, 237, 241, 315, 316, 322, 323, 370, 382
Croce, 58
cross, 18, 146, 225, 230, 272, 274, 280, 364, 394
crucifixion, 146
crusades, 128
cubit, 232, 233, 234, 265
cultural, 25, 28, 30, 274, 353, 394
Cush, 11, 354, 355, 365, 371
Dagara, 329, 409
Dalai Lama, 223
Dalí, 428
dandelion, 35, 427
Daniel, 102, 105, 224, 258, 303
Dante, 28, 110, 163, 167, 231, 276, 321, 412
Daphne, 110
Darwin, 52
daughters, 191, 193, 194, 195, 197, 198, 199, 200, 201, 202, 203, 206, 208, 213, 214, 215, 217, 218, 388, 389, 390, 391, 392, 393, 394, 395, 399
David, 100, 200, 428
David Shield, 100
Dawkins, 321
day, 47, 53, 56, 58, 59, 60, 62, 63, 64, 65, 66, 68, 69, 70, 71, 72, 73, 74, 77, 83, 84, 85, 87, 88, 89, 90, 91, 92, 99, 110, 111, 125, 126, 127, 133, 134, 147, 159, 162, 174, 175, 178, 187, 188, 193, 195, 197, 198, 200, 201, 202, 206, 207, 219, 233, 234, 235, 241, 243, 244, 246, 256, 257, 258, 259, 263, 274, 275, 276, 279, 283, 284, 288, 292, 297, 298, 299, 334, 336, 350, 359, 369, 370, 387, 406, 415, 416
dead, 27, 34, 37, 38, 50, 110, 111, 112, 138, 143, 148, 149, 168, 191, 193, 195, 197, 199, 200, 202, 206, 208, 216, 224, 227, 244, 266, 267, 280, 305, 316, 337, 344, 345, 359, 371, 378, 398, 403, 414, 415
Dead Sea, 64
death, 34, 37, 38, 39, 50, 53, 65, 80, 90, 100, 102, 110, 111, 112, 124, 125, 129, 131, 136, 137, 146, 148, 149, 152, 153, 157, 158, 159, 161, 162, 165, 166, 168, 169, 170, 184, 189, 206, 215, 216, 224, 227, 235, 244, 245, 246, 250, 265, 266, 273, 276, 280, 285, 289, 296, 298, 308, 315, 325, 327, 328, 330, 333, 336, 345, 358, 359, 360, 364, 369, 370, 371, 374, 380, 384, 386, 406. 422
Dedan, 354, 355, 366
Delphi, 89
deluge, 8, 9, 64, 65, 215, 224, 227, 233, 234, 235, 237, 244, 245, 246, 248, 255, 256, 260, 263, 264, 268, 280, 282, 284, 285, 287, 288, 293, 296, 301, 315, 316, 319, 321, 322, 344, 349, 359, 368, 375, 384, 387
Dement, 41, 399
demonic, 128
demotic, 26
depression, 134, 293
Descartes, 40, 125, 221
descendants, 248
descending, 25, 53, 56, 60, 63, 64, 68, 74, 77, 84, 85, 89, 91, 92, 93, 138, 161, 191, 199, 200, 282, 304, 324, 384, 386
design, 52, 75, 272, 305, 336
desire, 39, 50, 68, 106, 122, 123, 124, 125, 128, 129, 130, 131, 133, 138, 141, 142, 145, 146, 147, 148, 149, 152, 153, 161, 166, 167, 177, 192, 194, 200, 201, 215, 218, 219, 221, 230, 231, 235, 243, 253, 262, 285, 286, 306, 319, 330, 336, 341, 349, 351, 380, 397, 421
destiny, 168, 223, 364
destroyer, 65

Devanāgarī, 191
devil, 128, 129
devotional, 289
dharma, 414
dhyāna, 286
Diklah, 11, 370, 374
dinosaurs, 245
disasters, 223
discourse, 134, 302
dissolution, 310, 318
Divine Comedy, 163
Divine Mind, 222
Divine Providence, 253
Divine-Consciousness, 7, 10, 34, 46, 47, 48, 52, 53, 54, 55, 56, 57, 58, 59, 60, 61, 62, 63, 64, 65, 66, 68, 69, 71, 72, 73, 74, 75, 76, 77, 78, 79, 80, 81, 82, 83, 85, 87, 89, 90, 91, 92, 93, 95, 96, 97, 99, 100, 109, 111, 112, 113, 114, 116, 117, 122, 124, 125, 126, 127, 132, 133, 135, 139, 141, 142, 147, 149, 150, 151, 152, 173, 183, 184, 187, 188, 189, 203, 204, 205, 214, 218, 226, 227, 228, 229, 232, 234, 235, 238, 239, 243, 256, 262, 264, 271, 272, 282, 293, 294, 297, 301, 308, 310, 311, 312, 314, 315, 316, 317, 323, 324, 325, 333, 335, 343, 412, 416
DNA, 51, 158, 238, 247, 261, 271, 279, 336
Dodanim, 352
dogma, 24, 33, 34, 88, 93, 421
dogmatic, 406
Don Quixote, 253
Donatists, 184
Donatus Magnus of Casae Nigra, 184
Doré, 428
Dorian Gray, 125
double act, 302
doubt, 17, 32, 34, 93, 221, 330, 345
drachma, 245
dream, 7, 20, 21, 29, 31, 32, 34, 36, 39, 41, 42, 54, 56, 58, 63, 64, 69, 75, 80, 93, 96, 97, 98, 102, 106, 107, 110, 116, 117, 118, 119, 120, 126, 127, 129, 140, 141, 147, 152, 159, 167, 172, 174, 184, 187, 188, 189, 191, 192, 193, 194, 195, 196, 197, 198, 200, 201, 202, 203, 204, 205, 206, 207, 208, 209, 210, 211, 219, 227, 229, 230, 234, 235, 236, 237, 238, 241, 244, 246, 248, 252, 254, 255, 256, 258, 260, 262, 267, 271, 274, 279, 280, 281, 282, 283, 286, 289, 293, 297, 301, 302, 303, 304, 305, 307, 308, 310, 315, 318, 319, 320, 325, 326, 327, 328, 329, 330, 331, 332, 333, 334, 338, 345, 349, 352, 354, 355, 358, 364, 366, 370, 374, 379, 380, 382, 383, 397, 398, 399, 400, 401, 404, 408, 409, 410, 414, 415, 426, 428
dreamer, 246
dreaming, 7, 34, 64, 88, 91, 126, 142, 169, 190, 191, 195, 196, 200, 201, 202, 203, 204, 205, 217, 224, 226, 230, 232, 233, 243, 258, 259, 260, 261, 262, 286, 301, 304, 305, 310, 317, 319, 323, 324, 327, 334, 338, 379, 400, 401, 403, 411
dreaming state, 22
dreamless sleep, 289
dreamless-sleep, 41, 54, 96, 193, 226, 232, 320, 322, 324, 327, 328, 332, 344, 345, 379, 380, 382
dreamless-sleeping state, 22
dreams, 20, 28, 34, 41, 97, 98, 108, 117, 127, 141, 162, 171, 184, 190, 191, 193, 194, 195, 197, 199, 200, 201, 202, 204, 205, 206, 210, 221, 229, 230, 244, 256, 259, 260, 273, 279, 280, 281, 282, 284, 286, 288, 301, 302, 305, 308, 310, 313, 318, 320, 322, 327, 331, 332, 383, 400, 415, 422, 425
drug, 36
Druid, 110
Dry, 64, 285
dualism, 31, 101, 111, 133
duality, 3, 31, 46, 48, 65, 118, 132, 138, 144, 168, 205, 208, 219, 220, 224, 228, 229, 235, 236, 241, 244, 246, 255, 256, 258, 259, 260, 263, 266, 267, 276, 308, 316, 324, 326, 328, 380, 411, 415, 422
Dumlu Dağ, 107
dust, 273
duties, 167
E=mc2, 56
Ea, 229, 230, 232, 237, 239
eagle, 153
earth, 94, 99, 100, 108, 120
Earth, 3, 4, 6, 12, 38, 42, 50, 53, 59, 65, 66, 70, 71, 73, 91, 94, 96, 146, 149, 168, 172, 182, 189, 208, 218, 237, 249, 290, 294, 297, 305, 354, 375, 384, 385, 415
east, 38, 64, 99, 104, 106, 107, 108, 110, 152, 153, 176, 179, 280, 339, 350, 372, 379
Easter, 143

Eber, 11, 366, 367, 368, 369, 374, 389, 390, 391, 395
Ecclesiastes, 30, 34, 248
economic, 161, 291
economic structure, 291
ecstasy, 146, 252, 287
Eden, 4, 38, 86, 97, 99, 100, 103, 104, 107, 109, 124, 152, 153, 166, 176, 286, 355
effect, 319, 358, 364
Ego, 69, 89, 90, 96, 98, 129, 210, 217, 222, 234, 251, 302, 305, 307, 358, 394, 395, 397, 401
Ego-consciousness, 98, 251, 305, 358
Egypt, 38, 98, 223, 250, 428, 429
Egyptian, 110, 123, 224, 244, 318, 359
Egyptians, 26, 65
Einstein, 56, 290, 303, 368
Elam, 367, 373
electron, 302
elephant, 28, 260
Elgar, 84
Elijah, 414
Elisha, 414
Elishah, 352
Elohim, 9, 46, 47, 48, 214, 270
'Elohiym, 34, 46, 93, 127, 271, 409
emanation, 205, 304, 421
EMG, 400
Empiricists, 410
emptiness, 27, 48, 93, 136, 302, 331, 332, 333, 345, 416
'emuwnah, 32, 88, 93
enemies, 26, 37, 162, 276, 416
enemy, 168, 170
energy, 27, 54, 56, 67, 129, 256, 259, 260, 261, 266, 271, 279, 422
Energy, 27, 289
England, 110
enlightenment, 54, 146, 268, 370
Enlightenment, 146
Enlil, 229, 246, 384
Enoch, 6, 7, 178, 179, 181, 201, 202, 203, 204, 205, 210, 226
Enos, 7, 184, 194, 195, 196, 197, 198, 201, 210
entheogen, 36
epistemic, 21, 24, 25, 26, 30, 34, 35, 36, 37, 38, 39, 40, 42, 46, 47, 48, 50, 53, 55, 58, 59, 66, 70, 71, 72, 73, 77, 78, 79, 80, 81, 83, 84, 85, 87, 95, 101, 102, 106, 110, 111, 112, 115, 118, 119, 127, 132, 134, 139, 144, 149, 150, 152, 153, 157, 158, 169, 170, 173, 174, 183, 188, 189, 200, 204, 205, 214, 219, 220, 224, 226, 227, 228, 230, 231, 234, 235, 239, 241, 244, 254, 255, 256, 259, 260, 282, 283, 284, 285, 288, 289, 293, 294, 295, 296, 298, 301, 305, 306, 309, 312, 313, 314, 315, 316, 326, 330, 331, 332, 334, 335, 338, 340, 341, 343, 344, 345, 349, 350, 353, 355, 356, 357, 358, 359, 360, 363, 364, 375, 378, 380, 384, 387, 391, 392, 393, 398, 399, 401, 402, 406, 415, 416, 421, 422, 426
Epistemic, 3, 4, 5, 9, 10, 12, 28, 35, 36, 39, 47, 83, 84, 97, 136, 226, 229, 259, 298, 314, 343, 344, 399, 412, 421, 422
epistemic faculty, 203
epistemic forms, 17
epistemic loneliness, 113, 306
epistemic modalities, 375
epistemological, 20, 238, 306, 421
epistemology, 20, 21, 243, 255, 421
Erech, 356, 366
erlebnis, 192
Eros, 129
erotic, 129
Erzurum, 107
Esau, 96, 340, 341, 342
esoteric, 26, 28, 144, 286, 309, 340
Eternal, 418
eternal life, 145
Eternal-Now, 88
eternity, 11, 46, 47, 50, 54, 151, 166, 215, 216, 239, 367, 373
ethic, 24, 217
Ethiopia, 106
Euphrates, 106, 107, 108, 116
eureka, 33
Eve, 6, 25, 28, 68, 83, 113, 119, 120, 133, 147, 150, 153, 156, 157, 158, 162, 183, 184, 188, 223, 238, 259, 265, 277, 280, 310, 329, 331, 334, 336, 356, 362, 366, 380
Evidence, 87
Evident, 23, 32, 47, 88, 93, 248, 250
evil, 65, 100, 101, 110, 111, 125, 126, 127, 128, 132, 138, 143, 150, 151, 152, 153, 162, 217, 219, 220, 223, 236, 277, 280, 286, 296, 297, 298, 337, 341, 381
Evola, 340
evolution, 17, 25, 51, 52, 75, 113, 139, 150, 235, 305, 336

evolutionist, 35, 51
exhaling, 53, 60, 91, 98, 297
existence, 10, 20, 22, 25, 32, 37, 40, 47, 48, 49, 52, 53, 54, 55, 56, 58, 59, 60, 63, 65, 68, 70, 77, 78, 80, 102, 114, 134, 142, 144, 149, 157, 163, 164, 168, 169, 172, 173, 175, 184, 187, 201, 232, 233, 238, 241, 244, 245, 246, 252, 260, 272, 285, 291, 308, 315,321, 331, 336, 364, 368, 370, 380, 387, 415, 421
existential distress, 146
Exodus, 92, 93, 334
experience, 21, 22, 26, 30, 31, 32, 33, 34, 35, 36, 39, 41, 47, 50, 61, 63, 68, 70, 73, 75, 76, 87, 88, 96, 97, 111, 112, 114, 115, 116, 117, 119, 122, 123, 124, 125, 126, 127, 128, 129, 130, 134, 141, 142, 145, 147, 153, 159, 162, 168, 172, 177, 179, 189, 192, 205,208, 219, 221, 227, 234, 238, 242, 243, 244, 245, 246, 249, 254, 260, 263, 271, 277, 279, 282, 286, 288, 302, 306, 307, 312, 315, 319, 321, 322, 330, 331, 337, 340, 341, 343, 345, 352, 364, 398, 401, 410, 413, 414, 421, 422, 425, 426
experiment, 126, 149, 301
Exsultet, 143
exteriority, 31, 36, 37, 42, 90, 123, 136, 171, 304
Eyes, 5, 9, 97, 132, 226, 276, 345
Ezekiel, 97, 98, 99, 104
face, 335
faith, 3, 32, 25, 32, 33, 88, 93, 126, 245, 264, 272, 285, 321, 414, 419
fame, 29, 217, 227, 360
fantasy, 54, 56, 93
fasting, 128
Father, 170
fauna, 113, 289, 307
fear, 5, 6, 24, 39, 58, 136, 137, 141, 149, 174, 215, 222, 275, 304, 306, 307, 308, 328, 360, 366, 368, 374
fear of death, 136
Felix culpa, 143
female, 5, 80, 81, 83, 97, 118, 130, 131, 132, 134, 139, 158, 184, 187, 188, 191, 214, 236, 237, 238, 241, 242, 243, 255, 256, 261, 262, 274, 412
fig, 110, 132, 133, 150, 394
fig leaves, 132, 150
fire-sticks, 97
firmament, 60, 61, 62, 63, 64, 69, 70, 72, 73, 74, 75, 231
fish, 79, 82, 83, 233, 234, 237, 256, 258, 262, 267, 274, 282, 283, 287, 288, 306, 307, 360
flesh, 32, 65, 69, 114, 116, 117, 118, 119, 126, 129, 139, 145, 150, 171, 172, 184, 188, 191, 215, 216, 228, 229, 235, 236, 237, 238, 261, 262, 265, 271, 286, 294, 297, 307, 308, 309, 311, 315, 316, 321, 322, 323, 324, 325, 345, 413, 414, 415, 418, 425, 426
flood, 21, 61, 62, 64, 65, 149, 231, 234, 235, 237, 244, 246, 248, 250, 254, 256, 258, 260, 262, 263, 264, 266, 267, 268, 279, 280, 285, 286, 289, 294, 296, 298, 315, 322, 325, 327, 328, 344, 345, 349, 364, 367, 375, 387, 388
flora, 67, 113, 289
fog, 96, 97, 303, 330
food, 29, 38, 48, 83, 84, 85, 100, 102, 123, 125, 129, 130, 131, 138, 141, 143, 145, 148, 150, 151, 163, 169, 171, 188, 195, 204, 205, 206, 209, 238, 259, 279, 280, 284, 298, 308, 309, 314, 318, 350, 356, 359, 364, 368, 410, 417, 425
forbidden fruit, 28, 33, 34, 65, 88, 127, 130, 131, 138, 146, 148, 160, 215, 216, 219, 235, 244, 280, 287, 297, 298, 310, 313, 315, 329, 331, 356, 368, 375, 380, 413, 415
force, 27, 35, 38, 50, 52, 90, 100, 139, 146, 154, 231, 253, 296, 318, 319, 336, 380, 415
for-itself, 48, 50, 51, 55, 58, 63, 64, 73, 81, 124, 125, 132, 136, 137, 138, 152, 175, 219, 265, 277, 280, 282, 285, 311, 329, 359, 420, 421, 422
forms, 349, 350, 375
fortune, 168
Francis, 115, 288, 298
Francis of Assisi, 115, 419
Franklin, 394
freedom, 64, 65
Freud, 129, 286
fruit, 34, 39, 66, 68, 83, 103, 108, 111, 112, 123, 124, 125, 130, 131, 143, 145, 146, 149, 152, 153, 159, 161, 167, 174, 214, 215, 217, 222, 238, 250, 265, 266, 299, 313, 350, 359, 387, 412
fruits of actions, 66
fundamentalists, 25, 30, 34, 289
future, 19, 38, 49, 50, 51, 52, 88, 89, 91, 98, 141, 143, 157, 168, 173, 180, 189, 192, 216,

229, 232, 244, 290, 316, 320, 321, 322, 327, 336, 339, 343, 345, 358, 365, 367, 368, 374, 378, 386, 389, 390
Future, 11, 325, 367, 421, 422
Galahad, 309
galaxy, 204, 331
Galilei, 24
gamete, 271
Gandhi, 167
Garden, 118, 152
Garden of Eden, 100, 149
Gaza, 362, 363, 364, 366
Gematria, 3, 18, 25, 26, 188, 190, 191, 192, 193, 194, 195, 196, 197, 198, 199, 200, 201, 202, 203, 204, 205, 206, 207, 208, 209, 210, 217, 230, 231, 232, 244, 248, 256, 258, 263, 265, 268, 273, 274, 275, 277, 283, 287, 288, 292, 344, 345, 387, 388, 389, 390, 391,392, 393, 394, 395, 397, 403
gemstone, 105
Genesis, 3, 17, 18, 20, 24, 25, 26, 27, 29, 30, 31, 39, 40, 48, 49, 50, 55, 66, 72, 74, 79, 102, 148, 180, 188, 189, 208, 217, 238, 242, 258, 324, 329, 331, 334, 341, 349, 372, 401, 402, 405, 406, 420
genetic, 271
geometrical/mathematical language, 70
Gerar, 362, 363, 364, 366
Géricault, 428
Gesenius, 309, 310
Gether, 11, 368, 374
Ghirlandaio, 427
Gihon, 106, 354
Gilgamesh, 28, 96, 229, 230, 232, 258, 384
giparu, 230
Girgasite, 361, 366
global brain, 306
gnostic, 289
Gnostics, 26
God, 3, 4, 5, 8, 9, 10, 12, 27, 30, 31, 32, 34, 36, 38, 39, 46, 48, 49, 51, 52, 55, 57, 59, 60, 61, 62, 63, 65, 66, 68, 69, 71, 72, 73, 74, 75, 76, 77, 78, 79, 80, 81, 82, 83, 85, 87, 89, 90, 91, 92, 93, 95, 96, 97, 99, 100, 106, 109, 112, 113, 114, 116, 117,122, 124, 125, 133, 134, 135, 137, 138, 141, 142, 144, 150, 151, 152, 153, 157, 160, 161, 162, 163, 164, 165, 170, 171, 175, 176, 179, 183, 184, 187, 198, 200, 201, 203, 204, 205, 207, 214, 215, 216, 217, 218, 219, 220, 223, 225, 226, 227, 228, 229, 236, 237, 239, 241, 242, 247, 249, 250, 251, 255, 256, 257, 261, 262, 265, 266, 271, 275, 282, 284, 289, 291, 293, 297, 298, 301, 304, 305, 311, 314, 316, 320, 321, 323, 324, 325, 328, 342, 343, 352, 355, 356, 370, 381, 382, 385, 386, 401, 406, 412, 413, 414, 415, 422
gods, 47, 128, 422
gold, 105, 106, 276, 332, 355
Gold, 105, 285
golem, 305
Golgotha, 225
Gomer, 11, 349, 350, 351, 352
Gomorrah, 223, 362, 363, 364, 366
good, 31, 57, 58, 62, 65, 68, 73, 74, 75, 76, 78, 85, 100, 101, 103, 105, 106, 110, 111, 112, 125, 126, 128, 130, 131, 132, 137, 138, 150, 151, 152, 153, 215, 217, 220, 223, 236, 244, 249, 252, 255, 277, 280, 286, 307, 341, 380
good and evil, 416
goodness, 68, 242
goper, 229, 230, 231
Gorakhnāthīs Aghorī, 298
Gospel, 233
Grace, 222, 314
Greece, 98, 307, 350, 429
Greek, 5, 12, 16, 17, 18, 32, 93, 110, 126, 129, 145, 167, 171, 220, 225, 230, 244, 286, 302, 304, 307, 309, 319, 327, 359, 422, 424, 428
guilt, 167
guilt-distress, 216
Hadēs, 231
Hadoram, 11, 370, 374
Hagar, 401, 402
hairs, 394
Ham, 7, 10, 11, 209, 210, 211, 215, 217, 218, 226, 227, 254, 256, 259, 326, 327, 330, 331, 332, 334, 337, 338, 339, 340, 345, 349, 354, 355, 358, 362, 364, 367, 375, 381
Hamathite, 361, 362, 366
Haran, 12, 397, 398, 399, 401, 402, 403, 404
harmony, 287, 289, 291
Hassidic, 417
Havilah, 11, 105, 354, 355, 366, 371, 374
Havillah, 105
Hawking, 129
Hazar, 107
Hazarmaveth, 11, 369, 370, 374

head, 8, 39, 42, 80, 103, 110, 143, 144, 220, 222, 225, 230, 231, 256, 274, 275, 282, 304, 305, 310, 324, 350, 380, 381, 415, 427
healer, 329
heart, 17, 22, 23, 28, 31, 32, 35, 36, 37, 39, 69, 83, 90, 100, 101, 103, 128, 129, 159, 163, 164, 188, 216, 219, 220, 224, 225, 233, 241, 250, 251, 253, 286, 289, 297, 301, 305, 306, 308, 319, 322, 364, 370, 381, 412, 416
heart-center, 35
Heaven, 9, 62, 63, 100, 101, 152, 158, 204, 235, 264, 265, 271
Hebrew, 12, 18, 19, 25, 26, 27, 28, 32, 42, 48, 50, 58, 61, 68, 74, 80, 87, 93, 101, 105, 108, 109, 111, 117, 119, 128, 132, 133, 142, 158, 159, 163, 167, 172, 174, 184, 192, 201, 203, 219, 220, 225, 230, 238, 248, 250, 255, 277, 278, 280, 286, 288, 292, 309, 320, 328, 331, 337, 352, 378, 387, 388, 406, 409, 424, 428
Hebrews, 58
Hegel, 58, 218
hell, 39, 46, 130, 163, 174, 233, 413
Hellenistic, 28
Heraclitus, 266
herb, 66, 68, 83, 84, 95, 102, 148, 308
herbs, 85, 95, 148, 308
hermaphrodite, 191
hermetic, 64, 118, 144, 285
Hermetic Tradition, 64, 285
Herodotus, 276
hesychasm, 286
Heth, 360, 366
hexagram, 200, 201, 203, 274, 372, 412
Hiddekel, 107, 108
Hieroglyphics, 26
Hinduism, 29
Hiroshima, 364
historical materialism, 291, 406
history, 11, 17, 22, 29, 36, 38, 49, 51, 96, 105, 148, 157, 178, 182, 218, 294, 303, 322, 368, 370, 371, 374, 386, 387, 405, 421, 422
Hivite, 11, 361, 366
holy city, 386
Holy Wars, 38
Homer, 16, 415
Homo habilis, 150
Homo sapiens, 102, 150
homosexuality, 82
Horatius, 49, 381
horse, 116, 218, 224, 234, 253, 350, 354, 355, 358, 366, 393, 394
Horus, 427
house, 24, 40, 43, 65, 99, 111, 180, 201, 222, 223, 224, 229, 230, 231, 232, 240, 241, 280, 328, 343, 355, 358, 413, 416
house of Death, 148
Hul, 11, 368, 374
human, 4, 5, 20, 22, 25, 26, 27, 28, 29, 30, 37, 39, 55, 63, 73, 78, 79, 80, 81, 82, 83, 84, 85, 89, 90, 95, 96, 97, 99, 100, 101, 102, 104, 108, 109, 110, 112, 113, 114, 116, 117, 118, 119, 123, 133, 134, 138, 144, 149, 150, 151, 152, 153, 154, 158, 159, 163, 166, 167, 168, 169, 170, 172, 174, 178, 179, 180, 184, 187, 189, 191, 203, 205, 211, 215, 217, 218, 219, 220, 222, 224, 225, 226, 231, 234, 242, 244, 246, 253, 263, 265, 267, 286, 297, 303, 305, 306, 308, 310, 311, 312, 322, 327, 329, 330, 336, 360, 384, 394, 397, 417, 422, 425
humanism, 161
humans, 25, 39, 52, 74, 79, 80, 112, 117, 126, 178, 180, 181, 184, 187, 205, 208, 217, 225, 236, 267, 285, 289, 294, 297, 305, 306, 384
Humid, 64, 285
hunger, 29, 53, 76, 90, 119, 122, 125, 127, 129, 131, 132, 141, 144, 149, 152, 153, 173, 219, 221, 259, 265, 286, 319, 336, 368, 380, 421, 422
hunter, 355, 356, 366
hunting, 38, 96, 194, 195, 196, 197, 199, 201, 202, 207, 208, 356, 360, 362, 363, 364, 366
husband, 119, 130, 131, 136, 145, 158, 192, 214, 236, 401
Hyperuranium, 95, 255, 271
Hypnos, 231
I AM THAT I AM, 89, 250, 335
I-consciousness, 63, 82, 129, 135, 137, 175, 189, 210, 217, 234, 235, 252, 305, 311, 358, 383
I-Consciousness, 97
idea, 22, 31, 33, 34, 35, 48, 51, 58, 60, 63, 65, 88, 93, 114, 115, 172, 210, 215, 260, 261, 265, 271, 272, 278, 302, 303, 309, 321, 338, 350, 357, 364, 378, 387, 389, 410, 413, 421
idealism, 406
idealized, 412
ideas, 24, 31, 32, 34, 64, 66, 75, 83, 95, 191, 210, 215, 218, 226, 229, 230, 238, 242, 244,

255, 256, 258, 260, 261, 262, 264, 265, 266, 271, 272, 273, 275, 277, 302, 389, 390, 391, 425
ideologies, 30, 33, 168, 215, 218, 264
idolize, 412
Ignatius of Loyola, 253
ignorance, 286, 291, 311
illnesses, 146
illusion, 191
image, 10, 31, 54, 73, 79, 80, 81, 88, 89, 97, 111, 118, 128, 135, 136, 137, 139, 141, 142, 153, 165, 172, 184, 187, 189, 201, 282, 289, 302, 311, 312, 322, 328, 336, 337, 338, 372
images, 18, 116, 141, 184, 189, 282, 372
imagination, 18, 33, 56, 219, 296, 297, 303, 416
immanent, 22, 30, 31, 34, 35, 38, 47, 48, 60, 61, 62, 63, 64, 73, 92, 118, 130, 162, 165, 221, 225, 235, 249, 250, 265, 268, 285, 289, 313, 334, 336, 337, 410, 421, 422, 426
immortal, 146
immortality, 53, 96, 103, 224, 244, 277, 290, 305, 328, 336
impersonal, 314
impossibility, 34, 112, 139, 154, 321, 421
impulse, 77, 279
impure, 242, 296
India, 98, 110, 167, 307, 427, 428, 429, 447
Indian, 28, 63, 125, 191, 244, 249, 262, 277, 286, 293, 307, 310, 327, 350, 358, 393
Individual-consciousness, 82, 383
Indra, 128, 170
indriya, 128
ineffable, 48, 61, 79, 88, 90, 91, 187, 221, 235, 324, 422
ineffable apodictic-certitude, 235
inference, 169
inhaling, 53, 60, 85, 91, 97, 297, 329, 333
in-itself, 30, 31, 33, 34, 36, 37, 47, 48, 50, 51, 52, 55, 56, 58, 60, 61, 63, 64, 66, 68, 73, 81, 91, 93, 103, 112, 123, 124, 125, 126, 127, 128, 129, 130, 132, 133, 136, 137, 138, 142, 149, 150, 152, 158, 162, 169, 170, 171, 172, 174, 176, 217, 219, 220, 221, 226, 227, 245, 247, 249, 252, 254, 277, 280, 282, 285, 288, 301, 310, 311, 312, 314, 315, 321, 322, 329, 330, 331, 332, 334, 344, 359, 378, 381, 411, 412, 421, 422
In-Itself, 113
inquisitions, 128
instincts, 129
integral person, 43
Integrated Information Theory, 411
intelligence, 336
Intelligence Amplification, 305
Intelligent, 37, 52
Intelligent Design, 52
intelligibility, 52, 74, 274, 290, 336, 422
Intelligibility of Randomness and/or of Design, 52
intentionality, 5, 61, 63, 68, 76, 100, 115, 122, 123, 125, 128, 144, 146, 172, 271, 272, 294, 301, 302, 307, 336, 380, 421
intercourse, 70, 128, 133, 380
interest, 330
interiority, 36, 37, 39, 43, 90, 136, 152, 254, 294, 304, 308, 318
introspection, 188, 189
intuited, 17
intuition, 40, 58, 90, 134, 188, 198, 206, 209, 221, 293, 301, 302, 303, 304, 305, 306, 307, 310, 318, 338, 422
invisible observer, 183
Irad, 178, 179, 181, 200, 210
Īśa, 14
Isaac, 10, 47, 115, 164, 250, 340, 341, 342, 343, 387, 401, 402, 404, 413, 414
Isaiah, 123
Iscah, 399, 401, 404
Ishmael, 401, 402
Islam, 291
Israel, 64, 65, 144, 250, 328, 335, 343
Italic, 27
I-think, 21, 235, 252, 327, 422
Ius Suprēmum, 138
Jabal, 180, 181, 208, 210, 237
Jacob, 10, 47, 162, 250, 275, 304, 324, 325, 340, 341, 342, 343
Jacob's ladder, 12, 408, 409
Jainism, 291
James I of England, 18
Japanese, 36, 58, 370, 416
Japheth, 7, 10, 11, 209, 210, 211, 215, 226, 227, 254, 256, 259, 326, 327, 330, 332, 333, 334, 335, 337, 338, 339, 340, 343, 349, 350, 352, 353, 354, 367, 375, 381
Jared, 7, 199, 200, 201, 202, 203, 210
Javan, 11, 349, 350, 352
Jebusite, 361, 366

Jerah, 11, 369, 370, 374
Jeremiah, 42
Jerome, 18
Jerusalem, 106, 386
Jesus, 38, 47, 103, 106, 112, 126, 128, 129, 166, 173, 216, 220, 225, 233, 236, 239, 250, 268, 275, 281, 305, 334, 357, 364, 368, 406, 413, 414, 416, 428
Jewish, 28, 39, 417
jihād, 410
jihād, 74, 90, 410
Job, 46, 144, 393
Jobab, 11, 371, 372, 374
John, 249, 279, 293, 303, 305, 419, 428, 447
John of the Cross, 279, 293
Joktan, 369, 370, 371, 374
Jonah, 9, 222, 228, 232, 233, 234, 255, 256, 262, 279, 280, 281, 282, 283, 288, 298
Joshua, 415
joy, 293
Jubal, 180, 181, 194, 210
Judaism, 291
judge, 103
Judges, 46
judging, 65, 84, 101, 102, 216, 410
judgment, 22, 34, 84, 102, 164, 216, 239, 308, 421
Jung, 28, 310, 412
Kabalistic, 417
kabbalah, 100,110, 286. 290
Kabbalistic, 406
Kahlo, 428
Kandinsky, 251
Kant, 21, 31, 58, 101, 290, 447
Karasu, 107
Kekulé von Stradonitz, 303
Kena, 14
Kepler, 71
Ketuvim, 17
key, 28, 130
killing, 148, 165, 168, 169, 170, 171, 241, 296, 312, 313
kinfolk, 414
King Arthur, 358
King James Version, 18
kingdom of God, 47, 275
kingdom of heaven, 113
Kittim, 352
Kleitman, 41
Knights Templars, 167
knowledge, 21, 22, 23, 28, 30, 34, 36, 39, 40, 42, 47, 48, 53, 54, 55, 70, 72, 73, 74, 77, 80, 83, 84, 87, 90, 91, 93, 97, 100, 101, 102, 104, 105, 110, 111, 112, 115, 119, 123, 124, 126, 128, 130, 133, 137, 146, 148, 149, 152, 153, 158, 161, 167, 171, 174, 208, 217, 218, 227, 228, 235, 238, 244, 250, 254, 256, 262, 265, 282, 285, 286, 288, 289, 291, 293, 301, 302, 303, 307, 308, 310, 312, 314, 315, 319, 321, 336, 337, 349, 356, 359, 360, 363, 371, 375, 387, 391, 397, 403, 406, 412, 415, 421, 422
knowledge of good and evil, 103
known, 18, 21, 22, 31, 32, 34, 37, 47, 53, 59, 72, 74, 75, 80, 93, 115, 117, 118, 123, 132, 135, 137, 139, 149, 173, 188, 217, 227, 235, 238, 248, 249, 255, 301, 304, 310, 312, 318, 330, 331, 334, 349, 356, 361, 371, 378, 387, 420, 422, 423
knows carnally, 120
kōan, 413
Koch, 169, 412
Konark,, 429
Koran, 39, 57, 428
Qur'an, 20
Kṛshṇa, 167, 273
Kuala Lumpur, 382
La bohème, 247
labyrinth, 146
ladder, 12, 89, 304, 324, 409
lambs, 115, 131. 160, 242
Lamech, 6, 7, 178, 179, 181, 182, 183, 205, 206, 207, 208, 209, 210
land, 30, 41, 50, 63, 64, 65, 77, 95, 96, 100, 105, 106, 107, 113, 114, 147, 148, 152, 158, 159, 171, 173, 176, 177, 192, 207, 209, 219, 220, 224, 227, 228, 229, 234, 236, 237, 249, 266, 267, 271, 272, 279, 280, 283, 285, 287, 288, 294, 297, 301, 315, 316, 320, 328, 350, 352, 356, 357, 358, 359, 360, 362, 363, 364, 366, 372, 379, 380, 387, 394, 398, 399, 402, 403, 414, 415
language, 29, 30, 36, 41, 42, 60, 65, 114, 190, 191, 324, 352, 353, 364, 372, 378, 382, 383, 384, 385, 386, 401, 421
Lao Tzu, 30, 248, 289, 337, 380
Lasha, 362, 363, 364
Latin, 18, 22, 25, 32, 84, 97, 118, 127, 149, 225, 309, 422

law, 17, 28, 40, 88, 103, 128, 137, 138, 159, 169, 235, 259, 279, 323, 331, 402, 418
lead, 285
leaf, 132, 133, 283, 284, 287
Lehabim, 359, 366
Lenin, 447
leopard, 42
Lethe, 231
letters, 192
Levi Montalcini, 303
liberty, 139
libido, 90
life, 2, 24, 28, 29, 32, 35, 36, 37, 48, 49, 53, 56, 68, 69, 75, 77, 78, 84, 85, 89, 90, 91, 96, 97, 100, 108, 112, 115, 119, 125, 127, 129, 141, 142, 146, 147, 150, 151, 152, 153, 154, 157, 158, 159, 162, 164, 165, 166, 167, 171, 172, 178, 180, 189, 192, 193,206, 208, 210, 214, 217, 221, 224, 226, 228, 229, 230, 231, 232, 235, 237, 244, 246, 250, 257, 258, 260, 261, 262, 265, 267, 268, 271, 275, 280, 288, 289, 296, 302, 305, 306, 307, 309, 310, 311, 312, 313, 314, 315, 316, 317, 318, 327, 329, 333, 334, 345, 359, 364, 382, 384, 386, 388, 389, 390, 391, 393, 394, 398, 402, 409, 413, 415, 422
light, 3, 4, 5, 25, 26, 34, 39, 40, 51, 54, 55, 56, 57, 58, 59, 63, 66, 69, 70, 71, 72, 73, 74, 80, 81, 83, 88, 91, 93, 94, 95, 104, 123, 127, 136, 138, 142, 143, 149, 162, 164, 165, 189, 192, 222, 224, 232, 233, 234, 241, 248, 249, 260, 263, 268, 282, 284, 287, 288, 292, 308, 309, 314, 316, 319, 330, 334, 337, 343, 358, 367, 368, 380, 389, 399, 402, 413, 422
light years, 157
lightening, 55
likeness, 66, 68, 79, 80, 99, 104, 128, 142, 153, 165, 184, 187, 189
Linji Yixuan, 413
lion, 42, 153
listener, 60, 320, 378
literal, 17, 18, 24, 27, 28, 29, 30, 38, 40, 42, 64, 71, 87, 91, 99, 111, 119, 133, 151, 160, 174, 178, 179, 182, 189, 192, 214, 217, 223, 237, 241, 242, 260, 262, 265, 267, 284, 296, 298, 307, 309, 317, 324, 328, 335, 338, 339, 345, 349, 351, 354, 356, 372, 375,381, 384, 387, 406, 416, 421
living, 27
Loewi, 303
logical, 16, 21, 24, 34, 40, 46, 47, 48, 49, 50, 56, 58, 61, 72, 73, 84, 106, 107, 137, 150, 153, 158, 227, 235, 254, 274, 293, 299, 302, 314, 322, 334, 349, 363, 375, 391
Logos, 48
loneliness, 55, 112, 113, 136, 137, 183, 360, 378, 384, 391, 398, 421, 422
Loneliness, 3, 5, 36, 112, 136
Lord's Prayer, 126
Lorenzo de'Medici, 49
Lot, 397, 398, 401, 402, 404
love, 26, 28, 30, 31, 39, 90, 113, 119, 128, 129, 137, 138, 139, 146, 162, 163, 164, 165, 170, 214, 215, 218, 222, 233, 242, 251, 286, 289, 296, 321, 330, 381, 384, 392, 412, 413
Love, 60, 90, 91, 162, 163, 164, 166, 216, 222, 247, 297, 409, 410, 412, 422, 426
Lucifer, 142, 248
Luciferous-mode, 34
Lud, 367, 368, 374
Ludim, 359, 366
luminaries, 69, 70, 71
lunar month, 416
machines, 303, 305, 306
Madai, 349, 350
Magdalene, 158
Magog, 349, 350
Mahā Bhārata, 14
Mahalaleel, 7, 198, 199, 200, 201, 210
Maimonides, 29
Maitrī, 14
male, 5, 80, 81, 83, 97, 118, 130, 131, 132, 134, 139, 145, 158, 166, 184, 187, 188, 191, 214, 227, 229, 236, 237, 238, 241, 242, 243, 255, 256, 261, 262, 274, 301, 310, 311, 322
mammon, 251
man, 30, 31, 36, 65, 78, 79, 80, 81, 95, 96, 99, 104, 109, 110, 111, 112, 116, 117, 118, 119, 130, 133, 136, 137, 138, 139, 145, 147, 150, 151, 153, 157, 162, 165, 181, 182, 183, 184, 187, 189, 193, 194, 197, 201, 203, 215, 216, 219, 220, 223, 226, 231, 233, 235, 248, 249, 263, 265, 267, 275, 296, 297, 298, 304, 309, 310, 311, 312, 318, 328, 333, 352, 379, 381, 383, 393, 402, 413
Māṇḍūkya, 14, 233
mántra, 135
Māra, 65

mark, 6, 19, 57, 164, 166, 167, 168, 174, 175, 208, 209, 225, 328, 360, 366, 414, 424,426
martial arts, 370
Martin Luther King, 340
Mary Magdalene, 158
Mash, 11, 368, 374
Masoretes, 18
Masoretic Text, 18
materialism, 133
mathematical calculation, 103
mathematics, 191, 303
matter, 55, 63, 74, 76, 80, 98, 302, 304, 321, 345
Maya, 8
Mayan, 220, 427, 428
McCarthy, 305
meaning, 25, 27, 68, 101, 238, 252, 253, 293, 305, 336, 341, 394
measurement, 232
media, 18, 246
meditation, 244, 251, 252, 254, 286, 321
Medusa, 171
Mehujael, 178, 179, 181, 198, 210
memories, 36, 41, 50, 216, 230, 231, 247, 337, 425
memory, 51, 88, 114, 191, 221, 227, 230, 231, 238, 245, 247, 248, 261, 262, 271, 279, 307, 318, 331, 336, 337, 364, 365, 372, 386, 425
Mendeleev, 303
mentation, 41, 400, 401
Merchant Princes, 161
Merton, 96, 179
Mesha, 372, 374
Meshech, 349, 350
Mesopotamia, 107
messengers, 48, 304, 324, 338, 339, 340, 409
Messiah, 143, 163, 204
metaphor, 27, 28, 30, 31, 36, 53, 59, 70, 72, 73, 91, 105, 106, 110, 117, 118, 127, 131, 133, 142, 147, 150, 154, 171, 191, 192, 210, 214, 221, 224, 232, 237, 238, 242, 244, 256, 258, 260, 265, 271, 282, 311, 320, 324, 329, 332, 350, 355, 357, 360, 362, 380, 382, 393
Metaphor, 3, 26, 422
metaphysical, 169
Methusael, 178, 179, 181, 203, 205, 210
Methuselah, 7, 202, 203, 204, 205, 206, 210
Michelangelo, 429
microwave glow, 149
Midas, 34
Middle Ages, 28
might, 289
Mikra, 17
Milcah, 399, 401, 404
mind, 16, 20, 21, 22, 23, 24, 25, 26, 27, 28, 29, 30, 31, 32, 34, 35, 37, 39, 40, 48, 50, 51, 52, 53, 54, 58, 59, 60, 65, 70, 73, 74, 76, 77, 81, 88, 89, 95, 96, 99, 102, 103, 106, 108, 112, 113, 114, 124, 125, 127, 128, 129, 130, 132, 133, 134, 135, 137, 138,141, 142, 143, 146, 147, 148, 149, 151, 157, 163, 171, 172, 175, 184, 189, 193, 195, 197, 198, 200, 214, 216, 217, 218, 219, 220, 221, 224, 227, 230, 233, 234, 237, 238, 241, 246, 249, 251, 252, 253, 254, 255, 256, 260, 261, 262, 263, 271, 272, 273, 274, 276, 277, 293, 296, 297, 299, 301, 302, 305, 306, 307, 308, 311, 313, 314, 315, 316, 317, 318, 319, 321, 322, 323, 324, 325, 330, 333, 335, 336, 341, 342, 344, 349, 350, 355, 356, 358, 363, 365, 366, 370, 371, 375, 379, 380, 384, 397, 402, 407, 409, 410, 411, 412, 413, 415, 421, 423, 426, 447
mindful, 293
mindfulness, 83, 88, 333, 334, 305, 337
Minos, 359
mirror, 34, 36, 49, 73, 81, 119, 135, 136, 142, 165, 175, 282, 312, 336
mist, 95, 96, 116, 184
Mizraim, 11, 354, 359, 360, 366
Monastic Orders, 252
money, 161, 303, 334, 335, 394
Money,
Monier-Williams, 14
Moon, 4, 71, 72, 73
moral, 24, 101, 111, 128, 137, 216, 243, 265, 280, 421, 447
morning, 58, 59, 62, 68, 74, 77, 85, 248, 303, 309, 328
Moses, 17, 64, 89, 93, 137, 144, 145, 162, 249, 250, 272, 280, 334, 335, 368, 387, 428
Mother Teresa, 113
Mount Carmel, 279, 428
mountain, 32, 168, 264, 274, 275, 334, 350, 372, 397, 399, 414, 415
Mṛtyu, 129, 131, 238
multiplication, 61, 75, 84, 146, 301
Munch, 428
Murat, 107

music, 65, 84, 180, 251, 327
mute, 78, 115, 243, 315
Mute Book, 93, 384
Mutus Liber, 127
mystic, 27, 134, 222, 274, 296, 416
mystical behavior, 330
myth, 290
mythology, 29, 171, 230, 290, 291, 422
Myths, 28
Naamah, 180, 181, 210, 215
Naciketa, 327
Nadir, 104, 350, 351
Nag Hammadi, 38
Nagasaki, 364
Nahor, 12, 393, 394, 395, 397, 398, 399, 401, 404
naked, 132, 329, 330
nakedness, 5, 10, 30, 110, 119, 120, 123, 132, 136, 137, 141, 150, 162, 216, 330, 331, 332, 333, 334, 335, 345
name, 18, 25, 26, 34, 36, 38, 46, 47, 48, 53, 55, 59, 60, 62, 64, 65, 72, 78, 79, 92, 93, 96, 102, 105, 106, 107, 113, 114, 115, 119, 127, 137, 142, 149, 150, 158, 178, 179, 180, 183, 184, 187, 188, 189, 191, 197, 198, 199, 201, 207, 208, 209, 218, 227, 230, 233, 249, 250, 254, 261, 268, 274, 280, 289, 327, 328, 331, 340, 350, 352, 355, 356, 357, 367, 368, 369, 370, 371, 372, 380, 381, 385, 389, 390, 391, 392, 393, 397, 398, 399, 401, 402, 414
Naphtuhim, 359, 366
Naples, 429
Napoleon, 218, 428
NASA, 71
nation, 169
Native American, 36, 428
Natural Selection, 17
nature, 16, 31, 51, 129, 216
NDE, 37
Near Death Experiences, 34
Nehemiah, 100
Neo-Aristotelian, 406
Neoplatonic, 406
Neo-platonic, 28
Nephilim, 218, 219
Neruda, 116
neurons, 113, 245
Nevi'im, 17
New Jerusalem, 386
New Testament, 115
New York City, 382
night, 41, 53, 58, 59, 60, 64, 69, 71, 72, 73, 74, 93, 230, 231, 244, 258, 259, 279, 280, 298, 303, 309, 319, 335, 370
nightmare, 58, 147, 148, 149, 281, 331, 415
Nimrod, 11, 355, 356, 357, 358, 360, 366
Nineveh, 222, 298, 357, 358, 366
Ninus, 357, 358
nirvāṇa, 291
Noah, 7, 8, 9, 10, 11, 25, 30, 38, 96, 207, 208, 209, 210, 215, 224, 225, 226, 227, 228, 229, 231, 232, 234, 236, 237, 238, 239, 240, 241, 243, 247, 248, 249, 250, 254, 255, 256, 257, 258, 259, 261, 262, 267, 268, 271, 274, 276, 277, 278, 280, 282, 283, 284, 285, 287, 288, 292, 293, 294, 295, 296, 298, 301, 308, 314, 315, 316, 319, 325, 326, 327, 328, 329, 331, 332, 333, 334, 335, 337, 338, 339, 343, 344, 345, 348, 349, 350, 355, 375, 378, 380, 381
noema, 96, 117, 242
noematic, 96, 117, 119, 139, 144, 242, 243, 254, 256, 259, 262, 293, 344, 356, 387, 388, 401, 422
noesis, 96, 117, 242
noetic, 12, 117, 119, 131, 136, 144, 242, 243, 256, 259, 262, 322, 344, 356, 387, 388, 395, 401, 422
Nola, 429
NON-TRADITIONAL RELIGIONS, 291
non-violence, 166
Norfolk, 110
North, 104, 350
Nothingness, 159, 305
noumenon, 22, 31, 32, 47, 245, 248, 321, 378
now, 28, 32, 33, 34, 38, 39, 40, 47, 49, 50, 55, 59, 63, 66, 70, 80, 87, 88, 91, 92, 93, 94, 95, 98, 117, 118, 122, 132, 134, 139, 141, 148, 150, 151, 157, 164, 170, 172, 175, 184, 190, 193, 198, 202, 210, 216, 221, 222, 224, 231, 235, 242, 249, 257, 258, 264, 268, 271, 280, 281, 282, 285, 287, 288, 293, 296, 318, 320, 321, 322, 330, 334, 336, 337, 345, 358, 378, 380, 382, 385, 391, 393, 394, 398, 401, 413, 414
NREM, 7, 9, 41, 42, 53, 54, 97, 98, 108, 113, 116, 117, 119, 120, 129, 130, 153, 159, 183, 184, 189, 205, 208, 210, 217, 226, 230, 232, 233, 234, 236, 248, 255, 256, 258, 260, 261,

278, 279, 282, 283, 287, 288, 292, 297, 301, 305, 313, 319, 325, 328, 329, 332,334, 364, 397, 399, 400, 401, 409, 414, 425
number, 19, 26, 189, 191, 192, 193, 194, 195, 196, 197, 198, 199, 200, 201, 202, 203, 205, 206, 207, 208, 209, 217, 222, 230, 231, 232, 242, 243, 244, 256, 258, 274, 275, 277, 288, 292, 303, 305, 331, 355, 370, 387
numbers, 26, 144, 188, 189, 190, 191, 192, 303, 344
numerology, 18, 26
Nut, 110, 387
Obal, 11, 370, 374
object, 21, 22, 26, 27, 30, 31, 33, 34, 35, 36, 37, 39, 40, 47, 48, 49, 50, 51, 52, 53, 54, 55, 57, 58, 59, 60, 63, 64, 66, 68, 70, 72, 73, 74, 80, 81, 83, 84, 87, 88, 93, 96, 97, 102, 109, 111, 112, 114, 116, 117, 118, 119, 123, 124, 125, 126, 127, 128, 131, 133, 134, 135, 136, 137, 139, 143, 144, 145, 146, 147, 148, 149, 150, 152, 154, 158, 161, 162, 165, 168, 170, 171, 172, 173, 174, 175, 178, 183, 184, 188, 189, 191, 192, 193, 194, 195, 197, 198, 199, 200, 202, 206, 207, 214, 215, 216, 218, 219, 220, 221, 222, 223, 227, 235, 236, 237, 238, 242, 244, 245, 246, 248, 249, 250, 253, 254, 255, 259, 261, 268, 272, 275, 279, 282, 283, 284, 285, 286, 287, 289, 293, 297, 302, 304, 305, 306, 308, 310, 311, 312, 316, 318, 319, 320, 321, 322, 326, 329, 330, 331, 333, 334, 336, 337, 338, 340, 343, 344, 349, 356, 357, 358, 359, 363, 364, 368, 371, 372, 374, 378, 379, 380, 383, 385, 388, 390, 399, 401, 403, 404, 410, 411, 412, 413, 418, 420, 421, 422
objectification, 126
objectivity, 22, 33, 39, 53, 54, 58, 59, 66, 71, 72, 74, 81, 83, 87, 92, 95, 96, 98, 102, 115, 118, 119, 123, 124, 130, 131, 132, 138, 142, 143, 147, 150, 152, 162, 171, 172, 173, 188, 201, 214, 222, 246, 249, 254, 259, 264, 266, 282, 284, 285, 287, 293, 294, 297, 298, 301, 313, 315, 319, 324, 327, 329, 330, 332, 334, 335, 338, 350, 370, 387, 399, 401, 402, 409, 410, 412, 413, 422
objectivity, 9, 275, 401, 422
obscurity, 55, 74, 318, 319, 350
observer, 36, 55, 81, 111, 113, 115, 118, 140, 191, 199, 200, 202, 317, 320, 327
Occident, 108
ocean, 29, 49, 53, 54, 60, 61, 63, 64, 75, 95, 232, 256, 261, 280, 302, 307, 313, 360, 409
Oedipus, 327
offspring, 66, 81, 131, 143, 147, 158, 163, 182, 183, 192, 193, 195, 197, 198, 199, 200, 202, 203, 204, 206, 210, 214, 226, 236, 254, 293, 301, 314, 327, 339, 344, 349, 350, 354, 359, 367, 375, 383, 401
oil, 292
One, 53, 97, 127, 128, 129, 136, 161, 254, 304, 307, 313, 341, 364, 382, 387, 412
oneiric, 3, 36, 41, 56, 75, 93, 97, 98, 106, 115, 116, 118, 129, 189, 190, 193, 194, 195, 196, 197, 198, 199, 200, 201, 202, 203, 204, 205, 206, 207, 208, 209, 210, 237, 246, 248, 254, 259, 286, 293, 301, 302, 318, 319, 330, 332, 352, 354, 398, 400, 401, 406, 414, 422
oneiric aspects, 191
onyx, 105
Ophir, 11, 371, 374
original sin, 143, 285
Oscan, 429
Osiris, 359, 370, 387, 427
other, 113
Ouroboros, 76, 144
Ovid, 110
ox, 153
Ozymandias, 218
pacifists, 24
pain, 123, 124, 145, 146, 147, 149, 181, 220, 256, 263, 318, 333, 386
Pakistan, 167
panpsychism, 422
Papyrus of Ani, 224
parable, 3, 20, 27, 60, 115, 163, 292
parables, 189
paradigm, 28, 117, 150, 179, 182, 188, 214, 236, 241, 249, 327, 353, 356, 367, 398, 422
Paradise, 6, 25, 104, 152, 153, 222, 231, 286, 289
parallel universes, 62, 312
paranormal, 37
parents, 131, 174, 231, 413, 414
paro, 36
passions, 375
Passover, 131
past, 33, 38, 49, 50, 51, 53, 65, 88, 91, 96, 111, 112, 129, 133, 137, 143, 146, 148, 149, 152, 157, 158, 168, 180, 187, 191, 216, 218, 221,

224, 227, 235, 241, 258, 266, 267, 287, 289, 290, 316, 322, 327, 336, 337, 339, 343, 364, 365, 368, 369, 370, 371, 375,376, 378, 380, 386, 388, 389, 390, 391, 416
Patañjali, 286
Pathrusim, 359, 360, 366
patriarch, 25, 344, 393, 414
Patriarch, 189
patriarchal figure, 226
Patriarchs, 25, 179, 189, 191, 192, 208, 349, 387, 396
Paul, 47, 124, 252, 276
Pausanias, 327
Peleg, 12, 369, 390, 391, 392, 395
penalties, 169
Pentateuch, 17
People of the Book, 291
perceptronium, 55
Peter, 25
Pharaoh, 65, 76, 331, 387, 429
phenakistoscope disc, 367, 428
phenomenic, 304
Philistim, 359, 360, 366
Philo of Alexandria, 28, 98, 242
Philokalia, 286
Philosopher's Stone, 128
philosophical, 28, 133, 215, 357
philosophy, 24, 31, 215, 221, 244,249, 293, 422, 447
photons, 55, 352
Phut, 354, 366
physical universe, 289, 447
physicality, 63, 64, 79, 117, 132, 297, 305, 383, 393
physics, 36, 37, 55, 88, 319
Pilate, 281
pipe, 36
Pison, 105, 355
pístis, 32, 93
planet, 50, 56, 71, 99
planets, 314
plants, 28, 37, 67, 83, 84, 85, 95, 224, 262, 263, 308
Plato, 68, 164, 237, 307, 308, 357
Plotinus, 58, 68, 84, 237, 304
Pluto, 359
political, 24, 28, 31, 32, 38, 90, 273
Polizzi, 109
Pollack, 303
Polydorus, 110
possibilities, 21, 53, 54, 60, 61, 64, 72, 95, 115, 134, 137, 139, 256, 259, 261, 307, 313, 360, 395
possibility, 24, 41, 75, 80, 95, 139, 152, 232, 235, 303, 336, 400, 409
potency, 261
potentiality, 95
power, 16, 29, 39, 53, 70, 74, 83, 84, 90, 158, 179, 180, 181, 183, 205, 208, 209, 210, 250, 268, 275, 280, 281, 283, 285, 287, 308, 309, 310, 312, 322, 336, 344, 380, 382, 412
predestination, 363, 365
present, 22, 23, 25, 27, 32, 33, 35, 38, 39, 47, 48, 49, 50, 51, 53, 54, 55, 68, 73, 90, 91, 96, 97, 98, 110, 111, 112, 114, 119, 124, 125, 126, 134, 138, 143, 144, 148, 149, 158, 159, 166, 174, 180, 187, 189, 190, 191, 197, 216, 217, 220, 221, 222, 224, 233, 241, 243, 249, 250, 263, 264, 265, 271, 276, 280, 284, 287, 288, 289, 291, 294, 298, 302, 304, 305, 306, 308, 311, 316, 317, 318, 320, 321, 322, 325, 326, 327, 329, 336, 337, 338, 343, 364, 367, 368, 369, 370, 371, 374, 375, 378, 382, 384, 389, 393, 421, 406, 409, 413, 418, 422
prodigal son, 60
prophesy, 191, 203, 412
prophetic, 203
Prophets, 38
Protagoras, 161
Protestant Reformation, 161
Providence, 222
Psalm, 34, 47, 243, 273, 275, 331, 333
psyche, 146
psychoanalysis, 167
psychological, 28, 84, 85, 159, 180, 193, 224, 235, 243, 260, 265, 266, 267, 294, 295, 307, 315, 329, 400
psychology, 17, 28, 29, 233
psychology, 103
punishment, 6, 173, 183
pure, 31, 32, 33, 38, 40, 50, 58, 67, 75, 78, 88, 90, 95, 97, 100, 113, 119, 136, 138, 152, 163, 165, 170, 189, 223, 234, 238, 241, 242, 243, 250, 255, 283, 286, 292, 295, 296, 370, 380
pyramid, 134
Pyramid Texts, 134
qara', 61

quantum, 32, 35, 36, 51, 95, 115, 157, 305, 322, 369, 371, 374, 406, 422
Raamah, 11, 354, 355, 358, 366, 370
Rabbi Shim'on, 29
race, 96, 340
rainbow, 317, 320
Ramana Maharshi, 23, 102, 225, 342, 410, 447
Ramanujan, 303
Ramses, 429
Rapid Eye Movement, 34, 41
rapture, 123, 242, 243, 276, 286, 296, 414
real, 103, 177, 235, 254, 282, 285, 289, , 412, 340, 342
realism, 406
reality, 188, 273
Reality, 9, 17, 24, 40, 87, 88, 268, 276, 277, 278, 287, 289, 291, 306, 320, 335, 345, 386, 415, 422
reality in-itself, 126
Realization, 306, 422
rebirth, 412
Rebis, 118
Redeemer, 143, 145
Redemption, 170
red-hot vibration, 102
regulations, 216
Rehoboth, 357, 358, 366
reincarnation, 417
religion, 16, 24, 38, 40, 128, 184, 187, 248, 249, 289, , 293, 303, 411, 415, 422
REM, 34, 41, 42, 53, 54, 98, 116, 117, 129, 153, 189, 191, 205, 210, 217, 226, 230, 232, 233, 234, 245, 248, 256, 278, 279, 282, 283, 287, 292, 302, 303, 305, 318, 332, 364, 397, 400, 401
Renaissance, 161
repentance, 224
Reproductive Cycle, 4, 75
Resen, 358, 359, 366
rest, 8, 10, 25, 27, 28, 29, 37, 64, 90, 91, 93, 95, 109, 110, 119, 123, 166, 143, 148, 152, 172, 175, 193, 194, 196, 199, 207, 208, 215, 225, 243, 244, 245, 246, 256, 259, 266, 274, 279, 280, 281, 282, 297, 298, 299, 303, 319, 322, 337, 339, 344, 354, 370
Resting, 418
resurrection, 146
retas, 387
Reu, 12, 391, 392, 393, 395, 404
reunion, 289
revealed, 17, 189
Revelation, 3, 40, 224, 290, 339, 354406, 414
Ṛg Veda, 14, 48, 53, 233, 307
Riphath, 351, 352
rituals, 27
river, 26, 27, 66, 76, 77, 82, 83, 103, 104, 105, 106, 107, 108, 116, 153, 154, 266, 354, 355, 367, 368, 369, 379, 388, 390, 391, 395
robot, 36, 305, 306
Roman, 24, 38, 50, 110, 149, 184, 225, 230
Roman Inquisition, 24
rose, 93
Round Table, 309
rulership, 39, 74, 145, 147, 182, 401
Rumi, 80, 134
Russell, 215
Saadia ben Yosef Gaon, 29
Sabbath, 27, 319
śabda, 135
Sabtah, 354, 355, 358, 366
Sabtecha, 354, 355, 358, 366
saccidānanda, 412
sacred pipe, 36
Sacred Texts, 406
sacrifice, 244, 291, 380, 387
sacrificial-horse, 350
sādhu, 427
sadness, 293
Salah, 11, 12, 368, 369, 374, 388, 389, 390, 395
samādhi, 252
Samson, 394
Sangreal, 290
Śaṅkara, 63, 172, 302, 304
Sanskrit, 14, 274, 319, 327, 359, 394
Sarai, 12, 399, 401, 402, 404
Sartre, 174, 360
Sasa, 157, 290
Satan, 144, 241
Savior, 204, 285
Savioror, 143
Scaligero, 336
scanning, 76, 80
Schrödinger, 56
science, 25, 31, 37, 40, 49, 51, 88, 103, 249, 303, 319, 406
Science, 36, 55, 191, 249, 253, 290, 293, 303, 319, 321, 411, 422

sea, 64, 65, 75, 76, 77, 79, 82, 83, 116, 228, 237, 272, 275, 280, 306, 307
Sea of Galilee, 64
Seahenge, 110
seasons, 59, 69, 299
Seba, 354, 355, 365
seed, 32, 53, 66, 68, 83, 84, 130, 143, 161, 183, 184, 237, 243, 271, 314, 401
seer, 136, 286
Self, 36, 55, 70, 88, 89, 92, 93, 102, 112, 130, 134, 135, 136, 138, 142, 143, 149, 161, 163, 164, 170, 183, 210, 248, 250, 252, 253, 268, 277, 282, 286, 293, 306, 307, 308, 310, 311, 327, 334, 341, 358, 359, 384, 386, 416, 421
Self-Awareness, 17, 146
semantic, 25, 28, 30, 108, 191, 192, 222
semen, 66, 68, 83, 84, 143, 183, 222, 238, 243, 299
Sense, 3, 26
senses, 25, 27, 30, 41, 53, 58, 75, 76, 85, 97, 113, 114, 115, 116, 128, 130, 134, 142, 143, 147, 159, 161, 162, 166, 171, 189, 217, 221, 224, 233, 234, 238, 241, 243, 246, 250, 251, 252, 258, 262, 276, 277, 280, 295, 302, 304, 307, 308, 315, 318, 323, 334, 340,341, 356, 359, 397
Sephar, 372, 374
Sephirothic Tree, 350
Septuagint, 18
seraphim, 145
Serene, 177, 222
serenity, 42, 58, 227, 255, 296, 337
serpent, 76, 122, 123, 125, 141, 142, 143, 144, 145, 260, 267, 308, 334, 420
Serpent, 126
serpents, 75, 76, 77, 78, 79, 82, 84, 85, 144, 223, 224, 271, 294
Serug, 12, 392, 393, 394, 395, 404
Seth, 6, 7, 25, 183, 184, 186, 189, 190, 191, 192, 193, 194, 195, 196, 210, 226
Seti I, 387, 428
seventh day, 420
Seventh Day of Creation, 27
sexual, 330
shabath, 89, 90, 91, 93, 119, 138, 143, 148, 152, 194, 196, 199, 224, 283, 287, 297, 299, 337
shamanic, 36, 329
shamanism, 146
Shatt al-Arab, 107
Sheba, 11, 354, 355, 366, 370, 374
sheep, 115, 158, 159, 160, 285, 295, 315
Sheleph, 11, 369, 374
Shelley, 218
Shem, 7, 10, 11, 12, 114, 209, 210, 211, 215, 226, 227, 254, 256, 259, 326, 327, 330, 332, 333, 334, 335, 337, 338, 339, 340, 343, 349, 354, 367, 368, 371, 372, 375, 380, 381, 387, 388, 395
shield, 200, 201, 202, 203, 204, 207, 245
Shinar, 356, 366, 379
siblings, 401
Siddhārtha, 65
Sidon, 360, 362, 363, 364, 366
Siege Perilous, 309
silence, 31, 34, 49, 98, 184, 205, 243, 253, 267, 287, 293, 306, 309, 318, 325, 333, 334, 378, 380, 383, 397, 414, 415
Silence, 48, 61, 88, 91, 99, 246, 322, 386, 406
Silent Stillness, 61
Simon, 2, 25
sin, 34, 68, 167, 237
Śîn hand blessing, 3, 42
Singularity, 410
Sinite, 11, 361, 366
Śiva, 134
six days, 420
Skinner, 89
sky, 53, 60, 61, 62, 63, 64, 69, 70, 72, 73, 74, 75, 79, 82, 83, 84, 86, 87, 90, 92, 110, 113, 114, 115, 116, 223, 234, 235, 243, 257, 258, 264, 265, 267, 272, 306, 307, 319, 320, 350, 356, 357, 380, 387
skyphos, 429
sleep, 7, 28, 34, 41, 42, 69, 80, 97, 98, 108, 109, 113, 116, 117, 120, 124, 141, 159, 161, 163, 184, 189, 190, 192, 193, 196, 200, 201, 203, 204, 205, 207, 209, 210, 217, 226, 227, 228, 229, 230, 233, 234, 236, 237, 238, 241, 244, 247, 248, 249, 250, 254, 256,257, 258, 260, 262, 267, 279, 280, 282, 283, 284, 285, 286, 287, 288, 289, 293, 297, 301, 302, 303, 304, 305, 307, 308, 309, 310, 311, 313, 317, 318, 319, 320, 324, 325, 326, 327, 328, 329, 330, 332, 333, 335, 338, 355, 364, 366, 370, 374, 378, 381, 383, 384, 393, 397, 398, 399, 400, 401, 402, 403, 413
SMA, 301

Society of Jesus, 253
Socrates, 38, 89, 163, 244
Sodom, 223, 362, 363, 364, 366
software, 54, 76, 313
solipsism, 36, 112, 113, 183, 308, 398
solution of contraries, 274
Somé, 329
sons, 8, 143, 184, 191, 193, 194, 195, 197, 198, 199, 200, 201, 202, 203, 206, 208, 209, 214, 217, 218, 226, 236, 254, 259, 293, 294, 301, 314, 315, 326, 327, 344, 349, 350, 351, 352, 354, 355, 360, 364, 367, 368, 369, 371, 372, 375, 381, 387, 388, 389, 390, 391, 392, 393, 394, 395, 397
Sons of Darkness, 287
Sons of Light, 287
soul, 39, 55, 136, 224, 249, 260, 279, 289, 305, 307, 308, 336
Soul, 31, 279
South, 104, 350, 351
space, 10, 20, 31, 37, 38, 46, 48, 50, 54, 58, 59, 61, 91, 101, 104, 107, 110, 111, 123, 149, 157, 159, 164, 168, 173, 192, 227, 232, 250, 254, 256, 259, 263, 267, 286, 305, 311, 314, 316, 319, 327, 330, 332, 335, 336, 337, 338, 339, 340, 343, 344, 349, 350, 351, 352, 353, 354, 364, 367, 372, 375, 380, 385, 387
spaceless, 48, 50, 53, 59, 88, 152, 287
Spencer, 17
Sphinx, 327
spine, 225
Spirit, 47, 52, 53, 96, 110, 152, 241, 274, 282, 286, 409, 415
spirits, 36
spiritual, 329, 412
Spiritual Exercises, 253
spiritualism, 40, 133
spontaneity, 289
St. Francis, 27
star, 71, 72, 274, 372, 389
Star of David, 81, 274
stillness, 23, 27, 28, 48, 56, 53, 68, 88, 91, 92, 93, 97, 99, 101, 111, 159, 193, 220, 224, 226, 229, 231, 236, 238, 241, 242, 243, 250, 268, 276, 278, 282, 283, 286, 287, 289, 296, 297, 301, 305, 310, 314, 316, 319, 322, 326, 328, 329, 332, 333, 334, 337, 338, 371, 374, 378, 380, 382, 383, 384, 385, 399, 402, 413, 418, 426
stone, 39, 105, 106, 216, 276, 282, 310, 317, 319, 320, 379
string theory, 322
subconscious, 41, 97, 249, 256, 303, 319, 327, 408, 422
subject, 3, 4, 5, 8, 21, 22, 30, 31, 35, 36, 37, 47, 48, 49, 50, 51, 52, 53, 58, 59, 63, 64, 68, 71, 72, 73, 74, 77, 80, 81, 83, 87, 93, 95, 97, 109, 111, 117, 118, 119, 120, 123, 131, 133, 134, 135, 136, 137, 139, 144, 145, 147, 149, 150, 152, 154, 158, 159, 162, 165, 168, 169, 170, 171, 173, 174, 175, 177, 178, 182, 183, 184, 188, 189, 191, 192, 193, 194, 195, 197, 198, 199, 200, 202, 206, 207, 213, 214, 215, 218, 219, 220, 221, 222, 235, 236, 238, 244, 245, 246, 248, 250, 253, 254, 255, 266, 279, 282, 285, 286, 297, 302, 304, 305, 308, 310, 311, 312, 320, 321, 326, 327, 328, 334, 335, 336, 337, 338, 340, 344, 349, 356, 357, 358, 359, 363, 364, 366, 371, 374, 378, 379, 380, 381, 383, 384, 385, 388, 390, 401, 403, 412, 413, 415, 416, 418, 420, 421, 422
subjectivity, 422
subject-object, 415
subject-object correlation, 410
suffering, 24, 100, 123, 146, 175, 183, 222, 224, 250, 280, 364, 402
Sufi, 134, 222
Sumerian, 96, 229, 357
sun, 4, 48, 57, 59, 67, 71, 72, 73, 168, 189, 313, 389, 415, 416, 424, 429
superimposes, 39, 56
supernova, 157
surrender, 146
sushumnā, 415
svapna, 400
Śvetāśvatara, 14
sword, 97, 152, 153, 154, 168, 231, 312, 359, 370, 389, 398
SWS, 400
symbol, 3, 26, 27, 76, 106, 274, 275
symbolism, 115, 147, 189, 331, 383
symbology, 324
synthesis, 81
synthetic a-priori, 349, 401
Taittirīya, 14
talents, 30, 105
Talmûd Berâkôt, 136
Tammet, 303

Tanakh, 17
tantra, 290
Tao, 248
Taoism, 290
Tarshish, 352
Taurus, 107
tefillin, 39, 42, 429
Templar, 8, 234, 429
temptation, 123, 126, 127, 323, 368, 412
Terah, 12, 394, 395, 397, 398, 399, 400, 401, 402, 403, 404
Tetramorph, 429
texts, 17
theist, 80
thinking process, 22
thirty, 189, 192, 193, 194, 200, 232, 388, 389, 390, 391, 392, 393, 399
Thomas Aquinas, 321
Thoreau, 55, 249
thought, 17, 21, 22, 28, 30, 31, 32, 33, 34, 35, 36, 39, 40, 46, 47, 48, 49, 50, 54, 55, 58, 59, 61, 63, 65, 68, 69, 73, 75, 80, 83, 84, 88, 93, 95, 97, 102, 120, 127, 131, 137, 143, 147, 152, 154, 161, 162, 169, 193, 210, 214, 216, 219, 221, 227, 238, 243, 245, 248, 249, 250, 256, 259, 260, 263, 264, 272, 273, 275, 285, 286, 296, 297, 301, 303, 305, 306, 308, 314, 318, 321, 331, 333, 337, 341, 345, 355, 358, 364, 366, 380, 382, 383, 384, 406, 409, 410, 413, 414, 422
Thought, 252
thoughtless, 33, 39, 193, 205, 236, 245, 255, 264, 311, 333, 336
thoughts, 30, 31, 32, 36, 48, 61, 63, 64, 66, 83, 91, 95, 97, 143, 147, 191, 193, 200, 215, 216, 219, 220, 229, 238, 246, 255, 256, 258, 259, 260, 262, 263, 265, 268, 271, 272, 273, 286, 302, 312, 318, 319, 344, 345, 370, 381, 382, 383, 384, 388, 389, 390, 391, 392, 393, 394, 395, 397
Thrace, 110
Tiberius, 427
Tigris, 106, 107
time, 10, 20, 27, 28, 29, 30, 31, 38, 46, 47, 48, 49, 50, 51, 52, 55, 58, 59, 61, 66, 70, 74, 81, 87, 90, 91, 92, 97, 101, 102, 104, 110, 111, 123, 124, 128, 129, 137, 143, 148, 149, 152, 153, 154, 157, 159, 161, 162, 163, 164, 168, 169, 171, 172, 173, 180, 189, 191, 193, 209, 210, 214, 216, 217, 218, 219, 220, 221, 222, 224, 227, 228, 229, 230, 231, 232, 235, 238, 241, 248, 249, 250, 254, 256, 259, 263, 266, 267, 278, 279, 280, 283, 284, 286, 287, 289, 291, 302, 303, 306, 311, 314, 316, 318, 319, 320, 322, 326, 327, 330, 331, 332, 333, 334, 335, 336, 337, 338, 339, 340, 343, 344, 349, 350, 352, 354, 364, 367, 368, 369, 370, 371, 372, 374, 375, 378, 380, 381, 385, 387, 388, 389, 390, 391, 392, 393, 394, 395, 398, 404, 406, 407, 411, 415, 417, 421
timeless, 17, 28, 48, 49, 50, 51, 53, 55, 58, 60, 88, 152, 216, 271, 302, 336, 338
timelessness, 49, 50, 217, 367
Tiras, 349, 350, 351
to judge, 84, 106, 124, 216, 331
to know, 34, 36, 46, 48, 53, 56, 90, 111, 112, 127, 128, 133, 135, 137, 149, 151, 154, 162, 169, 192, 194, 200, 215, 219, 220, 230, 235, 238, 312, 320, 334, 375, 387, 421
tobacco, 36
today, 49, 146, 174, 227, 266, 322, 386
Togarmah, 351, 352
Tolle, 103, 146, 333, 336
tombs, 27
tomorrow, 386
Tononi, 411
Torah, 17, 18, 26, 29, 42, 98, 124, 191, 289, 331, 417
Totemic, 291
Traditional, 289, 291
Transcendence, 7, 22, 31, 36, 38, 48, 53, 54, 61, 80, 88, 90, 92, 96, 114, 116, 127, 130, 133, 135, 138, 145, 148, 152, 157, 158, 162, 164, 165, 171, 194, 196, 199, 203, 219, 220, 221, 222, 225, 246, 247, 289, 293, 316, 324, 412, 413, 416, 422, 425, 426
Transcendent, 3, 19, 22, 23, 27, 30, 31, 32, 34, 35, 36, 39, 42, 46, 47, 48, 53, 54, 56, 58, 60, 61, 62, 63, 71, 73, 79, 80, 88, 89, 90, 92, 93, 95, 97, 98, 99, 100, 101, 109, 112, 113, 116, 117, 122, 126, 127, 133, 134, 135, 136, 137, 138, 141, 142, 149, 150, 151, 152, 154, 157, 159, 160, 161, 162, 163, 164, 165, 166, 167, 168, 169, 170, 171, 172, 173, 174, 175, 176, 177, 184, 187, 192, 201, 207, 208, 215, 216, 219, 220, 222, 223, 224, 225, 226, 233, 235, 240, 241, 243, 247, 248, 249, 250, 253, 261, 262, 265, 268, 275, 280, 282, 284, 286, 287,

289, 290, 291, 295, 296, 297, 298, 305, 306, 307, 310, 311, 312, 313, 318, 319, 320, 321, 322, 324, 325, 327, 331, 334, 335, 336, 338, 341, 343, 344, 355, 356, 359, 381, 382, 383, 384, 385, 399, 406, 409, 410, 411, 412, 413, 414, 415, 416, 418, 419, 422, 425, 426
Transcendent Centrality, 420
transcendental, 21, 74, 87, 103, 235, 302, 423
Transcendent-Awareness, 113
transcending, 22, 31, 36, 412
tree, 28, 54, 66, 68, 83, 97, 100, 102, 109, 110, 111, 122, 123, 124, 130, 133, 134, 137, 139, 147, 150, 151, 152, 153, 174, 222, 230, 231, 250, 283, 322, 359, 394, 398, 412
Tree of Desire, 131
Tree of Knowledge, 4, 5, 7, 25, 100, 101, 102, 110, 111, 112, 118, 124, 131, 132, 138, 145, 157, 161, 170, 184, 194, 214, 217, 219, 228, 238, 310, 334, 417
Tree of Knowledge of Good and Evil, 101
Tree of Life, 4, 6, 7, 37, 100, 101, 145, 150, 151, 152, 154, 160, 161, 166, 184, 194, 195, 196, 198, 199, 202, 207, 228, 231, 310
trees, 35, 66, 68, 84, 100, 109, 110, 111, 115, 122, 123, 133, 134, 153, 230, 380
Triśula, 429
trumpet, 135
Truth, 2, 9, 31, 32, 34, 35, 39, 40, 88, 90, 93, 127, 136, 148, 167, 168, 174, 177, 216, 221, 241, 254, 265, 279, 280, 281, 282, 284, 285, 286, 289, 298, 316, 319, 334, 341, 394, 398,, 406, 409, 410, 421
Tubal, 349, 350
Tubalcain, 181, 197, 210
Turkey, 107, 428
turtle, 274
twelve, 126, 195
uncaused, 354
un-clean, 242
unconscious, 12, 20, 28, 41, 59, 81, 90, 97, 98, 159, 191, 195, 199, 230, 237, 238, 249, 251, 256, 258, 259, 260, 261, 262, 272, 288, 301, 302, 305, 310, 318, 319, 320, 327, 332, 397, 407, 409, 411, 412, 423
unconsciousness, 43
United States, 329
Unity, 12, 58, 192, 222, 390
universal, 204, 331
universal flood, 375
Universal Light, 20
universal sacred literature, 17
Universe, 24, 39, 40, 42, 51, 53, 81, 99, 126, 134, 136, 142, 149, 189, 241, 244, 289, 290, 319, 321,352, 354, 371, 375, 406, 416
Unknowable, 48, 87
unknown, 21, 30, 31, 32, 34, 36, 39, 53, 54, 59, 93, 115, 136, 137,142, 149, 158, 159, 161, 168, 170, 187, 193, 220, 230, 265, 303, 306, 318, 319, 320, 325, 327, 330, 331, 334, 411, 422
Unthinkable, 87
Upanishad, 14, 31, 47, 125, 136, 233, 277, 310, 350, 355, 360, 370, 371, 380, 383, 387
Kaṭha, 14, 307, 370, 380
Māṇḍūkya, 134
Ur, 398, 399, 402
uśan, 359
Utnapishtim, 28, 229, 230, 232, 237, 239, 255
Uz, 11, 368, 374
Uzal, 11, 370, 374
vajra, 429
value, 24, 268
Van, 107
Veda, 14, 217, 307
Sāma, 14
Yajur, 14
veil, 335
Venus, 158
Verga, 165
Virgil, 110
virgin, 412
Virgin Mary, 40
Virtual Reality, 246, 429
viruses, 146
Vishṇu, 252
voice, 135
volcanos, 245
von Hildebrand, 163
Vulgate, 18, 320
wakefulness, 7, 32, 41, 42, 53, 56, 63, 64, 106, 117, 124, 130, 141, 159, 167, 172, 184, 192, 193, 196, 205, 210, 236, 237, 238, 241, 243, 244, 248, 267, 286, 288, 297, 302, 304, 305, 307, 313, 320, 327, 329, 345, 358, 366, 375, 379, 380, 381, 382, 393, 399, 401, 403
waking, 7, 22, 41, 42, 53, 56, 80, 88, 91, 98, 106, 116, 126, 133, 142, 169, 178, 184, 190, 191, 192, 193, 194, 195, 197, 198, 201, 203,

205, 209, 210, 211, 217, 224, 226, 227, 230, 233, 234, 236, 237, 243, 248, 252, 254, 256, 258, 259, 260, 261, 262, 271, 274, 280, 286, 289, 291, 293, 301, 302, 304, 305, 310, 311, 315, 317, 318, 319, 320, 323, 324, 326, 327, 328, 331, 333, 334, 338, 345, 379, 381, 382, 397, 400, 401, 410, 411, 414, 415, 426
waking stage, 191
waking state, 22, 305
war, 128, 146, 166, 168
watching, 292
waters, 3, 4, 9, 48, 52, 53, 54, 60, 61, 63, 64, 65, 74, 75, 76, 77, 95, 96, 97, 104, 134, 152, 230, 232, 235, 244, 248, 254, 256, 262, 263, 264, 265, 267, 268, 271, 272, 273, 275, 277, 278, 279, 280, 281, 283, 284, 285, 288, 292, 315, 322, 330, 334, 350, 359, 366, 388
way, 2, 17, 24, 36, 39, 42, 47, 48, 51, 54, 55, 74, 87, 97, 98, 102, 113, 117, 137, 138, 139, 141, 143, 147, 149, 152, 153, 154, 157, 159, 164, 165, 171, 191, 219, 224, 228, 230, 232, 243, 249, 252, 253, 263, 288, 298, 302, 303, 312, 316, 327, 331, 334, 344, 349, 356, 360, 364, 382, 398, 409, 410, 415
WAY OF ADORATION, 291
WAY OF KNOWLEDGE, 291
WAY OF NATURE, 290
WAY OF SOCIETY, 291
wealth, 28, 138, 161, 334, 394
weltanschauungs, 29
west, 2, 38, 104, 329, 330, 350
Wheeler, 49, 53
Who am I, 36, 250
wife, 109, 118, 119, 130, 133, 136, 139, 147, 150, 157, 158, 164, 177, 178, 179, 183, 184, 192, 214, 222, 236, 238, 254, 259, 275, 293, 294, 311, 399, 401, 402, 413
Wilkinson, 303
will, 18, 21, 22, 24, 25, 26, 28, 30, 33, 34, 36, 37, 38, 40, 42, 46, 48, 50, 51, 54, 55, 57, 59, 62, 63, 64, 65, 67, 69, 72, 74, 78, 80, 81, 83, 85, 88, 89, 95, 96, 97, 110, 111, 112, 114, 123, 124, 125, 126, 129, 137, 138, 142, 143, 145, 147, 148, 157, 158, 159, 163, 164, 166, 167, 168, 169, 173, 174, 175, 178, 187, 188, 191, 192, 197, 201, 207, 208, 214, 215, 216, 218, 219, 223, 224, 226, 229, 231, 232, 234, 235, 236, 238, 243, 244, 245, 247, 248, 249, 251, 252, 253, 254, 255, 266, 268, 271, 273, 274, 275, 281, 282, 283, 285, 286, 291, 293, 296, 297, 298, 301, 303, 305, 306, 307, 308, 309, 310, 312, 315, 316, 317, 320, 321, 322, 323, 325, 334, 336, 338, 339, 343, 350, 351, 352, 353, 355, 356, 357, 360, 364, 368, 370, 380, 382, 384, 386, 388, 389, 399, 401, 406, 413, 414, 415
wine, 172, 329, 333
Wisdom of Awareness, 246
witness, 27, 32, 33, 54, 63, 93, 172, 173, 242, 243, 249, 267
Wittgenstein, 36
wolf, 42
woman, 116, 117, 118, 119, 122, 123, 124, 125, 130, 133, 136, 139, 141, 143, 144, 145, 147, 150, 189, 216, 222
world, 3, 4, 20, 21, 22, 24, 26, 28, 29, 30, 31, 33, 35, 36, 37, 38, 39, 40, 41, 42, 46, 47, 48, 49, 50, 51, 52, 53, 54, 55, 56, 59, 61, 63, 64, 65, 66, 68, 69, 72, 73, 74, 76, 80, 83, 84, 87, 88, 90, 91, 92, 93, 94, 95, 96, 98, 101, 105, 110, 111, 114, 115, 116, 117, 119, 123, 124, 125, 126, 127, 128, 132, 134, 136, 137, 138, 141, 143, 144, 145, 146, 148, 150, 152, 157, 161, 162, 165, 168, 172, 174, 183, 187, 194, 195, 196, 197, 198, 199, 201, 202, 205, 207, 208, 215, 221, 227, 229, 232, 234, 235, 236, 238, 241, 244, 245, 246, 248, 249, 250, 254, 255, 256, 258, 259, 260, 263, 264, 265, 266, 268, 272, 274, 275, 276, 279, 280, 281, 282, 283, 284, 285, 286, 288, 292, 293, 294, 295, 296, 297, 299, 301, 302, 303, 304, 305, 307, 308, 309, 310, 311, 312, 313, 314, 315, 316, 318, 319, 320, 321, 322, 324, 325, 327, 328, 329, 330, 334, 336, 337, 344, 349, 350, 352, 355, 357, 358, 361, 362, 364, 368, 371, 375, 378, 380, 381, 382, 383, 384, 385, 388, 394, 397, 398, 401, 402, 409, 413, 414, 415, 420, 421, 422
world in-itself, 37
World-soul, 218
wrath of God, 223
wringing, 285
Yājñavalkya, 244
Yama, 102, 327, 359
yaqeen, 32
year, 17, 50, 59, 69, 71, 189, 192, 193, 194, 195, 197, 198, 199, 200, 201, 202, 206, 207, 248, 257, 258, 288, 344, 355, 387, 390, 391

years, 189, 190
Yĕhovah, 30, 46, 53, 61, 92, 93, 98, 99, 113, 127, 137, 158, 159, 160, 184, 187, 201, 208, 216, 241, 316, 356, 399, 409, 412, 426
Yggdrasil, 110
yielbongura, 409
Yoga, 14, 29, 167, 252, 286, 287, 293
yūgen, 58
zamani, 157, 290
Zamarite, 361
Zeboim, 362, 363, 364, 366
Zen, 29, 370, 413
Zenith, 104, 350
zero, 27, 51, 88, 192, 331
Zillah, 179, 180, 181, 182, 183
Zohar, 100, 417
יְהֹוָה, 30, 34, 46, 47, 53, 56, 61, 79, 92, 93, 98, 113, 127, 141, 158, 159, 160, 177, 184, 187, 201, 216, 241, 316, 325, 343, 356, 399, 412

NOTES

[1] Sri Ramana Maharshi (Venkataraman Iyer) Tamil Nadu, India (30 December 1879, at Thiruchuli – 14 April 1950, at Sri Ramanasramam, Aruṇācala Hill, Tiruvannamalai).

[2] *Bible*, John 14:6 [and] 8:32 ἀλήθεια *alētheia* = truth, from α-λανθάνω a-*lanthánō = non-unaware = aware.*

[3] *Cf.* nature as the scientific physical universe in-itself (see, Newton, Philosophiæ Naturalis Principia Mathematica) and/or the mythological Mother Nature (see, Campbell, *The Power of Myth*, p. 99).

[4] *Cf.* Worthen, *Wanted: A Theology of Atheism*, where secular humanists search for a moral philosophy. Furthermore, *religious* atheists engage non-atheists with the same vitriolic vengeance of the inquisitions perpetrated by any other religion, *cf.* Lenin, *On Religion* & Goodstein, *University of Miami Establishes Chair for Study of Atheism.*

[5] Palmer, *The Atheist's Primer*, p. 5.

[6] Five (πέντα) *Penta-teuchos* (τεύχος) books: *Genesis, Exodus, Leviticus, Numbers,* and *Deuteronomy.*

[7] *Cf.* Kant, *Critique of Practical Reason*, 5: 161–2, "Two things fill the mind with ever new and increasing admiration and awe... the starry heaven above me and the moral law within me."

[8] *Cf.* Pyramid texts, *The ancient Egyptian pyramid texts*, 1248, Atum generates the world through a solitary orgasmic act. See also *UB.* I.4.3.

[9] (1820–1903) English biologist, philosopher and sociologist, see "*survival of the fittest*" the phrase he coined in *The Principles of Biology*, p. 444.

[10] Darwin, *The origin of species*, pp. 499-500.

[11] *Cf.* Watts, *The Book*, p. 4.

[12] *Cf.* Deuteronomy 1:5, "*In the land of Moab, began Moses to declare this law.*" We relate this authorship without any further analysis. The controversy regarding its author is not the intent of this study or the scope of this work. In fact, by their own nature, sacred writings intend to be simple authorless blueprints for a path that may lead beyond thought into the realization of the Transcendent.

[13] *Cf.* 1 Kings 6:1, "*In the four hundred and eightieth year after the children of Israel* [led by Moses] *were come out of the land of Egypt, in the fourth year of Solomon's reign over Israel, in the month Zif, which is the second month, that he began to build the house of the LORD.*"

[14] Isaiah 6:9-10.

[15] Job 1:3, 21 & 42:3.

[16] *VṚ* X.129.4, "*searching* (*pratíshyā*) *in the heart* (*hṛdí*) *with introspection* (*manīshā*)."

[17] *Cf. Bible*, Matthew 19:19.

[18] Public Domain Text in *Bible* 1) Blue Letter Bible - 2) Masoretic Text - 3) Scholars' Gateway beta - 4) Torah, *The Torah* - 5) Westminster Leningrad Codex; with the *Tiberian* diacritical marks of vocalization.

[19] Jewish scholars' translation of the *Torah*. Public Domain Text in *Bible*, 1) Blue Letter Bible - 2) Brenton, *The Septuagint* - 3) Scholars' Gateway.

[20] Public Domain Text in *Bible*, 1) *Biblia sacra, vulgatae* – 2) Blue Letter Bible- 3) Scholars' Gateway.

[21] Saint Jerome (*Hieronymus* 347 – 420) Latin Christian Doctor of the Church.

[22] Public Domain Text in *Bible*, Blue Letter Bible - 2) *The Holy Bible* - 3) Scholars' Gateway.

[23] Exodus 20:4 & Deuteronomy 5:8.

[24] Leviticus 26:1. *Cf.* also, Deuteronomy 9:12, 16:22 and 27:15.

[25] פֶּסֶל Strong's H6459.

[26] מַצֵּבָה Strong's H4676.

[27] מַשְׂכִּית Strong's H4906, Gesenius (2)

[28] אֶבֶן Strong's H68.

[29] מַשְׂכִּית Gesenius (2), *cf.* Psalm 73:7 & Proverbs 18:11.

[30] כֹּל Strong's H3606, Deuteronomy, 4:23.

[31] נְקֵבָה אוֹ זָכָר *cf.* Deuteronomy, 4:16.

[32] אֶרֶץ Strong's H776, Gesenius (1). Deuteronomy 4:25.

[33] March 2001, see BBC, *Giant Buddha statues 'blown up'*. Aniconic empty throne sculture, 2nd century, Amaravati, India.

[34] Gold, זָהָב *zahab* Strong's H2091, Gesenius. Menorah מְנוֹרָה *mĕnowrah* (Strong's H4501) lamp stand, from מָנוֹר *manowr* (Strong's H4500) beam, in the original sense of נִיר *niyr* (Strong's H5216) lamp, from מָנוֹר *manowr* (Strong's H4500) to make a field shine; Gesenius. *Cf.* Exodus 25:31-40. Gold, זָהָב *zahab* Strong's H2091, Gesenius.

[35] *To Meet* (יָעַד *ya`ad* Strong's H3259), *communicate* (דָּבַר *dabar* Strong's H1696), *cf.* Exodus 25:22.
For a deeper analysis of the menorah and its connection to the Tree of Life, the Hermetic caduceus, the heart-center and the coiled-snake power, see Simonelli, *Beyond Immortality*, pp. 210-11.

[36] *Viz.* pattern, model, from the Greek παράδειγμα (*paradeigma*), [παρά (*para*), "beside, beyond" δείκνυμι (*deiknumi*), "to exhibit, to show, to point out"].

[37] *Bible*, Acts 17:27-28.

[38] *Koran* 12:2, عَرَبِيًّا (may that ye) لَّعَلَّكُمْ (wisdom learn) تَعْقِلُونَ (*arabean* - in Arabic) قُرْآنًا (*qur'ānan* = recite the Koran) إِنَّا أَنزَلْنَاهُ (We sent down)... 96.1. اقْرَأْ (*eqra'* - read or recite or proclaim). "A discourse in the Arabic tongue," Ta Ha 20:110.

[39] Guillaume, *Islam.* p. 59.

[40] *Viz.* Gematria.
[41] Campbell, *Mythic World, Modern Words*, p. 286.
[42] *Cf.* Darwin, *The Expression of the Emotions in Man and Animals.*
[43] *Cf.* Thomas Aquinas, *Summa*, I, q. 16, aa. 1-2.
[44] *Cf.* the *Farnese* statue of Atlas, De Caro, *Il Museo...*, 330 *inv.* 6374.
[45] Kant (1724 –1804), C*ritique of pure reason*, § 17 Introduction.
[46] Object, not as popular synonym of *gadget* and/or similar.
[47] Kant, *ibid.*, I, II, §9, p. 29-30.
[48] As nominative subject performer, or genitive possessor, or dative receiver and/or any other ablative case.
[49] Lee Oscar Lawrie (1877-1963), Atlas 1936 (New York City, 630 Rockefeller Center, 5th Ave & 51-50 Street).
[50] Popularly, today, the terms, *objectify* or *objectification*, are used with a depreciative meaning, viz., to reduce to an object to be used.
[51] Harari, *Sapiens*, p.117.
[52] From the Latin *conceptus*, grasped, conceived, from *concipĕre*, to grasp-together, from *con-cipĕre*, grasp-with the object.
[53] *Cf.* Kant, *Prolegomena* § 45.
[54] *To think*: *Hebrew* זָכַר zakar, Sanskrit मन् *man*, Greek λογίζομαι *logizomai* and Latin *cogito*.
[55] *neti neti* continuous refrain throughout most of the *Upanishads*.
[56] Ramana Maharshi, *Spiritual teaching*, pp. 3 (2), 42.
[57] Deuteronomy 6:5. Long, breathe after (אהב *'ahab* Gesenius 1) the Transcendent (יהוה *Yĕhovah*) True Certain Awareness (אלהים *'elohiym God*) וְאָהַבְתָּ אֵת יְהוָה אֱלֹהֶיךָ בְּכָל־לְבָבְךָ וּבְכָל־ נַפְשְׁךָ וּבְכָל־מְאֹדֶךָ׃ *Cf. Bible*, Matthew, 22:37,39, 5:43; 19:19; 22:39; Mark 12:30-31; Luke 10:27.
[58] From Proto-Germanic *gawaraz* = (*ga*) intensive (+ *waraz* √ *wer* to perceive) vigilant percepting attention.
[59] From Latin *conscius* = (*cum*) with (*sciens*) founding knowledge.
[60] *Cf.* Schaff, *Creeds of Christendom,* Vol. I, § 7 "*consubstantialem Patri... lumen de lumine... incarnatus est de Spiritu Sancto*" (*Nicene Creed*, 325).
[61] From Latin ***certus*** = determined, fixed, sure.
[62] *Cf.* Thoreau, *Walden and Civil Disobedience*, pp. 383 fol. *Cf.* also non violence *a-hiṃsā* in Acaranga Sutra, *The First Anga Agama of the Jainas*. While we greatly respect the vegans' intent to save life and suffering, we must recognize that tax revenues always sustain also, directly or indirectly, wars, weapons of mass destruction and/or animal-exploiting agricultural subsidy. Therefore, wealthy tax payers, self-describing as animalists, pacifists and/or vegans, contradictorily manifest against hunting, wars, cow suffering producing a glass of milk and *eat like* they *care* (*cf.* Francione; for a contrary view see Cerulli, *The Mindful Carnivore*). In this case veganism becomes only an eating disorder. Furthermore, some *religious* animalists and/or vegans may be in favor of killing a hunter. Moreover, they may kill microbes with medications, destroy termites and pests to preserve their houses and crops or purchase meat products for their pets. So-called pacifists, animalist and vegan (who refuse to eat eggs) may be politically prochoice, thus, they consent to the killing human embryos. Further, they forget that abortion inflicts pain on the fetus, considering that the spinal cord, the brain and the nervous system form between the 18th and 20th day of conception (*cf.* Carlson, *Human Embryology & Developmental Biology*, p. 97, b: 292, 308, c: 483-4, d: 305, e: 88-92). In addition, there are those who, while declaring to be pro-life, bomb abortion clinics killing local staff. Furthermore, vegans sustain that eating animals or animal product is immoral (*cf.* Francione, *Eat Like You Care: An Examination of the Morality of Eating Animals*). This implies that Nature itself is immoral and criminal when it instills carnivore instincts in animals and/or destroys them with cataclysms. Iusnaturalism recognize "life" as the first among its natural laws, followed by "liberty and pursuit of happiness" (*cf.* Jefferson, *Letter to the Danbury Baptists*). However, Nature's survival of the fittest (*cf.* Darwin, *The Origin of Species*), with its killing and inflicting pain on its creatures, contradicts that first law. Therefore, if Nature has no moral obligation, then the problem is who or what enforces that morality and which are the consequences for transgressing it (*cf.* Simonelli, *Awareness*). If there is no physical and/or metaphysical moral injunction, then, that vague relative vegan morality becomes only the fabricated injunction of an individual eating disorder.
[63] *Cf.* Greek: α-πολιτεία (*a-politeia* non-citizenship), Sanskrit: *kaivalya*. *cf.* Evola, *Cavalcare la tigre*, p. 152.
[64] *Cf* Simonelli, *Awareness.*, p. 10 fol.
[65] *Cf.* North Korea "control[s] the flow of outside information, all TV sets are registered with the state, which modifies them to ensure they receive only approved channels... [people] are brainwashed, don't know life outside... are brainwashed from the time [they] ... know how to talk, about four years of age, from nursery school, brainwashing through education, this happens everywhere in life, society, even at home."(Walker, *North Korea: 'You are brainwashed from the time you know how to talk'*).
[66] *Cf.* Zuckerman, *Rejecting Islam.*
[67] Thayer, *Throne-makers*, p. 301. Bruno said to his accusers, "*Maiori forsan cum timore sententiam in me fertis quam ego accipiam*" "Perhaps you deliver with greater fear the sentence against me than I receive it."
[68] "*Achademico di nulla achademia; detto il fastidito. In tristitia hilaris, in hilaritate tristis,*" (frontispiece of Bruno's *Candelaio*, I ed.).

This is how the philosopher and mathematician Giordano Bruno from Nola (Naples, Italy - 1548) describes himself. At the hand of the Inquisition of Rome, with a public execution, on February 17, 1600 in Campo dei Fiori, Rome, Italy, Bruno was murdered, burned alive for heresy (*Cf.* Montaldo, *Giordano Bruno*).

[69] *Cf. De l'infinito universo e mondi.* His crime was to have sustained the existence of planets, similar to Earth, ʿoutside the Solar system. On April 2014, NASA confirmed this truth. In fact, Kepler telescope detected a possibly habitable planet 490 light-years away (Levs, *NASA*). Bruno's *Revolution* had ventured far beyond the narrow confines of Copernicus' cosmology and predated by fifty years Galilei's scientific demonstration of heliocentrism. NASA recognized Bruno's genius by naming after him a crater, on the Far Side of the Moon, mapped and photographed (9/6-5/5, 1994) by the Clementine spacecraft's Lunar Mapping Mission, "the brightest crater larger than 20 km diameter is Giordano Bruno, which is probably less than 50 million years old" (U.S. Department of the Interior, *Clementine...*; *Cf.* also Leung, *Clementine's Lunar Mapping Mission*).

[70] *Cf.* Galilei (1564-1642), *Dialogue on the great world systems*, and *The Assayer. The Controversy on the comets of 1618.*

[71] *Cf.* Campbell, *The Hero with a Thousand Faces.*

[72] Laitman, *Attaining the Worlds Beyond: A Guide to Spiritual Discovery*, p. 434 (*Talmud, Kiddushin*).

[73] This is true also in the ancient Indian tradition, *cf. B.U.* I.4.1 and 7.

[74] *Bible,* Matthew 16:17.

[75] Those who follow the *Kabbalah* (קַבָּלָה meaning (*receiving the tradition, cf.* Epstein, *Kabbalah. The way of the Jewish Mystic.*

[76] Gnostic (γνωστικός *gnostikos*), namely, *s/he who has intuitive knowledge* (γνῶσις *gnosis*), which derive from insight, revelation or inspiration (*cf.* The Nag Hammadi Library).

[77] Schimmel, *The Mystery of Numbers*, p. 16.

[78] *Bible*, Revelation 13:17-18. *Cf.* Numbers 1:18 & fol., "*the number* (מִסְפָּר *micpar* - Strong's H4557) *of the names* (שֵׁם *shem* Strong's H8034)," also Job 1:5 מִסְפַּר כֻּלָּם *misəpar* (the number) *kulām* (of them all), and Exodus 12:4, "*the worth-number* (מִכְסָה *mikcah* - Strong's H4373 - from מֶכֶס *mekec*, computation - Strong's H4371) *of the souls* (נֶפֶשׁ *nephesh* - Strong's H5315).

[79] Example (3=ג*g*, 2=ב*b*, 1=א*a*).

[80] Jacob ben Sheshet, *Meshiv Devarim Nekhohim*, p. 107.

[81] *Cf.* Epstein, *Kabbalah.* From the Gematria tradition derives the Neapolitan *Smorfia* (Borrelli, *Nuova smorfia perpetua ed universale dell'astronomo Zoroastro*), which assigns specific numbers to oneiric objects for the interpretation of dreams.

[82] *Cf.* 1:26 n.; 5:3 n. & fol.

[83] *E.g. cf.* Plato's *cave*, *chariot* etc.

[84] Examples are Arabic, Chinese, Hebrew, Sanskrit and others.

[85] *Cf. The Rosetta Stone* (196 BC, now in the British Museum, London) written in Hieroglyphics = sacred-inscriptions (Greek ἱερο-γλυφικά *iero-gluphika*, Egyptian *mdju netjer* = *Words of the Gods*), in Demotic = popular-script (δημοτικός *dēmotikos*) and Greek.

[86] Nick & Pal, *The Lorns.*

[87] *Cf.* the phrase, *to send to Coventry* and the verb *to* Coventry. The expression and the verb refer the city of Coventry, England; history has it that in 1640s Cromwell exiled ostracized Royalists to Coventry. Furthermore, in 1940 the German Luftwaffe razed the city to the ground and coined the German verb, *coventrieren*, 'to flatten' and the English to coventrate, to devastate (*cf.* Humphreys' novel, *Coventry*). In addition, the British motor industry collapsed there in the 1980's.

[88] *Bible,* 2 Corinthians 12:4.

[89] बिन्दु *bindú*, *W.* p= 731b.

[90] शून्यता *śūnyátā*, *W.* p=1085b.

[91] अ-शून्यता *a-śūnyatā*, *W.* p= 113c.

[92] Amendola, Tsujikawa, *Dark Energy.*

[93] *Cf.* Francesco, *Scritti di S. Francesco...* p. 121, *Cantico di frate sole* or *Laude delle creature* 12.

[94] अपदिसति *apadisati*, to call to witness (Stede, *Pali - English Dictionary.*). *Cf.* Warren, *Buddhism in translations...*, p. 81. *Cf. Jātaka* I.74.[25]

We may read the National Geographic Society's edition of the *Gospel of Judas* Iscariot in the same manner. [Judah, in Hebrew יְהוּדָה *Yĕhuwdah* (Strong's H3063) means *praised*, from יָדָה *yadah* (Strong's H3034), *to throw, to cast, to show and to point out* (Gesenius 1), a primitive root used as denominative from יָד *yad* (Strong's H3027), *hand, sign. Furthermore, Iscariot*, from אִישׁ *'iysh* (Strong's H377), means "*to shew oneself*" (Gesenius 1), denominative of אִישׁ *'iysh* (Strong's H376) "*an existing man*," and קִרְיָה *qirya'* (Strong's H7149), a *city, a town*, from קָרָה *qarah* (Strong's H7136), *a meeting place.*] In fact, according to this *Gospel*, Jesus addresses Judas as "*thirteenth daimōn*," (Kasser-Meyer-Wurst, *Gospel of Judas* [34,21], p. 165), *viz.* a "*godlike powerful* (δαίμων *daimōn* - *cf.* Plato, *Symposium* 202e-203a) *physical character of man*" (ἦθος *ēthos* ἀνθρώπῳ *anthrōpō* δαίμων *daimōn*, Heraclitus in Walzer, *Eraclito,* Fragment DK22b119 - K&R 247) who witnesses, manifests, *betrays* and *gives away* (παραδίδωμι *paradidōmi*) Jesus' true identity. Namely, that is his Inner-Awareness, which is misplaced by the *thirty* (τριάκοντα *triakonta*) silver paid by the chief priests and elders (*Bible*, Matthew 27:3), *viz.* the three (30) states of wakefulness, dream and NREM. That treasure purchased this "*field of blood*" (*Bible*, Matthew 27:8) in which we live. Additionally, both Jesus and Judas are out of the circle of the twelve (360/30) disciples. In fact, they both occupy the 13th *dangerous seat* (*cf.* the Arthurian *Siege Perilous*), which is the center of that circle. Furthermore, why Judas would have needed to use a *kiss* (φιλέω *phileō*) as a *sign* (σημεῖον *sēmeion* *Bible*, Matthew 26:48) to point out Jesus, when he was well known by "*the very great multitude*" (*Bible*, Matthew 21:8-9) that was singing hosannas at his entrance in Jerusalem a few days earlier? However, both die. Judas, as this visible psychophysical entity, "*hanged himself*" (*Bible*, Matthew 27:5) and Jesus, as hidden Awareness, hanged and was nailed on the cross of this body. Finally, why would the devil instigate Judas (*cf.* John 13:2; Luke 22:3) to betray and create a Martyr against his own satanic interests?

[95] III c. BC. *skyphos* missing a piece. Restored painted vessel found in an Oscan warrior's tomb (Saviano, Via vicinale 5 vie, Nola, Naples, Italy).

[96] Any disrespect shown to a national flag and/or a hymn (by destroying and/or denigrating them) is a direct conflict and disapproval of the ideology proclaimed by those symbols. *Cf.* Helsel, *49ers Quarterback Colin Kaepernick Defends National Anthem Protest*, the NFL player oxymoronically disrespecting the same symbols that represented his right to express disrespect.

[97] Metaphor, in Greek, means to escort (*pherō* φέρω) beyond (*meta* μετά) the immediate shape or meaning of things.

[98] For the difference between denotation and connotation, *cf.* Campbell, Power of Myth, p 56 - 57.

[99] *Cf.* Simonelli, *Transcendence - The Universal Quest.*

[100] Catherine of Siena, *The Dialogue*, p. 157.

[101] *Bible*, Luke 11:52; "οὐαὶ ὑμῖν τοῖς νομικοῖς ὅτι ἤρατε τὴν κλεῖδα τῆς γνώσεως αὐτοὶ οὐκ εἰσήλθετε, καὶ τοὺς εἰσερχομένους ἐκωλύσατε;" νομικός (*nomikos*) lawyer, interpreter and teacher of the Mosaic Law; τὴν κλεῖδα τῆς γνώσεως (*tēn cleida tēs gnōseōs*) the key of knowledge. ⇨ This symbolic key is composed of a *yad* (יד, the Jewish ritual index ☞ pointer used to follow the sacred Torah text on a scroll) surmounted by a ✡ Star of David, with a Torah scroll in it, and with the letter *ś*, ש, representing a priestly hand gesture blessing.

[102] *Cf.* Philonis (20 BC - 50), *Operum Omnium. De Somniis* I, *De Abrahamo* II, *Quæstiones in Genesi* II, *De Victimas Offerentibus* II, and more.

[103] Dante Alighieri, *Convito* t.II, ch. 1 "*per quattro sensi.*"

[104] *Cf.* Eliade, *The Sacred…*, 95 fol.

[105] *Psyche*, p. 145.

[106] *Cf.* Saxe, *The Poems of John Godfrey Saxe*, The Blind Men and the Elephant.

[107] The timeless universality of psychological traits is confirmed by studies like that of Walid Khalid Abdul-Hamid, *Nothing new under the sun: post-traumatic stress disorders in the ancient world*, which "describes much earlier accounts of post combat disorders that were recorded as occurring in Mesopotamia... during the Assyrian dynasty (1300-609 BC)" (Abstract). Prior the assumption was that it started at Marathon (490 BC). However, this research demonstrates that posttraumatic psychological symptoms were evident... before Abraham and contemporary with the Pharaohs.

[108] *Cf.* as an example, see dreams in Freud, *The standard edition.*

[109] As an example, see Jung, *Psyche and Symbol.*

[110] *VṚ* X.129.4 *sató* (sages)… *hṛdí* (in the heart) *pratíshyā* (searching) *kaváyo* (had found) *manīshā* (with introspection).

[111] *Cf.* Jonah 1:9, Hebrew (עִבְרִי ` *ibriy*) = "one from beyond," (Strong's H5680), `Eber or Heber (עֵבֶר) = "the region beyond" (H5677), `*eber* (עֵבֶר) = "region beyond or across" (H5676), ` *abar* (עָבַר) = "to pass beyond" (H5674).

[112] *The Epic of Gilgamesh*, p. 107.

[113] Ezekiel 12:2.

[114] *Bible*, Matthew 11:15, 13:9,14; Mark 4:9,23, 7:16; Luke 8:8,_14:35.

[115] *Bible*, Matthew 18:3.

[116] "Consciousness is not simply the fruit of the activity of our brain, as many believe, but is the fruit of a primordial awareness that is an intrinsic faculty of nature... Energy... contains also the 'seed' of awareness. (*La coscienza non è semplicemente frutto dell'attività del nostro cervello, come molti pensano, ma è il frutto di una consapevolezza primordiale che è una proprietà intrinseca della natura. … energia contiene … anche il 'seme' della consapevolezza*). Italian physicist Federico Faggin seeks to find (since 2011 at the *Federico ed Elvia Faggin Foundation* in Silicon Valley) an equation capable to describe the awareness of the universe. (ANSA.it, *Il padre del microchip*). *Cf.* also Watts, *The Book*, p. 115.

[117] Merton, *Zen and the Birds of Appetite*, p. 16.

[118] Campbell, *The Flight of the Wild Gander*, p.33.

[119] Campbell, *The Hero with a Thousand Faces*, Prologue.

[120] *Cf.* Plato, *Statesman* 277d.

[121] *Bible*, Matthew11:15.

[122] Dante Alighieri, *La divina commedia, Inferno* IX, 61-63 "*O voi ch'avete li'ntelletti sani / mirate la dottrina che s'asconde / sotto il velame de li versi strani.*"

[123] Rabbi Shimon Bar Yochai (Ancient Israel, I Century).

[124] Matt, [*Zohar* (III. 152a, & Zohar Chadash, Tikunim II:93b), p. 43] & (The *Essential Kabbalah*, p. 135-7).

[125] *Cf. Saadia Gaon, The Book of Beliefs and Opinions*, chapter 7.

[126] *Cf.* Maimonides, *Guide of the Perplexed* (II, 8, 25) & *The Book of Knowledge* (Introduction).

[127] *Bible*, Matthew 7:6. "*Neque mittatis margaritas vestras ante porcos ne forte conculcent eas pedibus suis et conversi disrumpant vos.*"

[128] Strong's H3603, Gesenius (deriving from next H3769), *cf.* Exodus 25:39.

[129] Strong's H3769, Gesenius.

[130] *Bible*, 1 Corinthians 3:18-19-20.

---

[131] *Cf.* Simonelli, *Transcendence.*

[132] Ecclesiastes 8:1, *interpretation* פְּשַׁר *pesher* (Strong's H6592).

[133] Psalm 24:3. עָלָה` *alah* (Strong's H5927) to go up = to trans-ascend, Greek ἀναβαίνω *anabainō*, Latin *ascendo.* יְהֹוָה *Yĕhovah* the Transcendent LORD. *Cf.* Joshua 6:5, Psalm 135:7, 139:8, Isaiah 14:13-14, Jeremiah 10:13, 51:16, Ezekiel 38:9, *Bible*, John 6:62, 20:17, Roman 10:6, Revelation 17:8.

[134] *Bible*, John 5:32 & 37-39.

[135] *Bible*, Acts 17:23, Unknown, ἄγνωστος *agnōstos.*

[136] <Simonelli, *Beyond Immortality*, p. 33.>

[137] Recent researches "demonstrate that movement-related sensory information is... a specific function in memory-related spatial updating," namely, the process of memory not produced by external stimulations (Vass et al., *Oscillations Go the Distance*, Summary).

[138] *Bible*, John 18:36.

[139] Proverbs 23:7.

[140] *Cf.* Watts, *The Book*, p. 11.

[141] McGough, *Debunking Myself.*

[142] Matt, *The Essential Kabbalah*, p. 115.

[143] UAb *Amṛta*-(immortal-nectar)-*bindu* (point-drop) *Upanishad*, mantra 18. *Cf. Bible*, Matthew 13:30 "*Gather ye together first the tares, and bind them in bundles to burn them: but gather the wheat into my barn.*"and Luke 22:31. *Cf.* Meister Eckhart, *When the Kingdom appears to the soul and it is recognized, there is no further need for preaching or instruction,"* , *Meister Eckhart: A Modern translation*, p. 130.

[144] del-Vasto, *Return to the Source*, p, 207, 222.

[145] *Cf.* Kant, *Prolegomena* § 45.

[146] *Cf.* Russell, *Our Knowledge of the External World*, ON THE NOTION OF CAUSE pp. 240-241.

[147] Ecclesiastes 8:16.

[148] Deuteronomy 29:4.

[149] *Res cogitans* = thinking thing, *res extensa* = extended thing; *cf.* Descartes, *Principia Philosophiae*, 2.001.

[150] אָמֵן *'amen* verily, truly, firm, faithful, Strong's H543 (Gesenius). *Cf.* Numbers 5:22 *et al.* From the verb אָמַן *'aman* to be faithful, to be sure, to be certain (Strong's H539).

[151] *Bible,* Revelation, 3:14 τάδε λέγει ὁ ἀμήν ὁ μάρτυς ὁ πιστὸς καὶ ἀληθινός ἡ ἀρχὴ τῆς κτίσεως τοῦ Θεοῦ.

[152] *Bible*, John 1:14. *Καὶ kai* (and) *ὁ o* (the) *λόγος logos* (Spirit of Certainty) *σὰρξ sarx* (flesh) *ἐγένετο egeneto* (was made) *καὶ kai* (and) *ἐσκήνωσεν eskēnōsen* (dwelled) *ἐν en* (among) *ἡμῖν ēmiv* (us), "*et Verbum caro factum est et habitavit in nobis.*"

[153] Hieroglyphically represented as Utchat, the eye 𓂀 (Budge, *The Mummy*, pp. 316 fol.). *Cf.* Latin *uraeus*, the *risen one. Cf.* the *pyramidion*, the Pyramid's capstone on the US Great Seal (Eli Luminosus Aequalis, Altus, *Mutus Liber "Loquitur"*, p. 207).

[154] *Cf. UB* III.4.2.

[155] *In* Hebrew אֱמוּנָה *'emuwnah* derives *from* √אָמַן *'aman* = to be certain. In Greek πίστις *pístis* means assurance, proof, testimonial. Rocci, p.1503b *sicurtà*.

[156] *Bible*, John 20:29.

[157] *Bible*, Matthew 17:20, or *cf.* Luke 17:6 "*unto this sycamine tree, Be thou plucked up by the root, and be thou planted in the sea; and it should obey you.*"

[158] <Simonelli, *Awareness*, p. 72.> *Cf.* the Thunderbolt as a symbol of "The Way toward the Adamantine Reality of Transcendent Truth" (Zimmer, *Myths and Symbols...*, p.145) in the Buddhist iconography.

[159] *Bible*, John 1:1. Ἐν *en* (in) ἀρχῇ *archē* (the beginning) ἦν *ēn* (was) ὁ *o* (the) λόγος *logos* (Spirit of Certainty) καὶ *kai* (and) ὁ *o* (the) λόγος *logos* (Spirit of Certainty) ἦν *ēn* (was) πρὸς *pros* (with) τὸν *ton* (the) θεόν *theon* (Transcendent) καὶ *kai* (and) θεὸς *theos* (Transcendent) ἦν *ēn* (was) ὁ *o* (the) λόγος *logos* (Spirit of Certainty) "*In principio erat Verbum et Verbum erat apud Deum et Deus erat Verbum.*" See Bible, Titus 1:9, πιστοῦ *pistou* (of Faith) λόγου *logou* (Spirit), *fidelem sermonem*, "*Spirit of Certainty.*"

[160] "*Frustra fit per plura, quod potest fieri per pauciora,*" Occam, *Summa Totius Logicae*, I. 12, p. 37.

[161] *Our Lady of Sorrows* (Anonymous), Farkas Simon, *Camilla*, p. 70; flanked by collaged images in the public domain: 1) on left, Secondo Pia's negative of his photograph of the Shroud of Turin File:Turin plasch.jpg Secondo Pia- http://online.wsj.com/article/SB123940218130209621.html , 2) on right, The Veronica, kept in the Vatican File:Veronica - Vatican2.jpg.http://www.visionsofjesuschrist.com/weeping77.jpg.

[162] *Bible,* Hebrew 11:6, χωρὶς δὲ πίστεως (*pisteōs* certain-faith) ἀδύνατον (*adunaton* is impossible) εὐαρεστῆσαι (*euarestēsai* to be in any acknowledgment) πιστεῦσαι (*pisteusai* be certain) γὰρ δεῖ τὸν προσερχόμενον τῷ θεῷ (*theō* Awareness) ὅτι ἔστιν καὶ τοῖς ἐκζητοῦσιν αὐτὸν μισθαποδότης γίνεται.

[163] *Bible*, John 8:18.

[164] Transforming everything into gold objects, *cf.* Ovid, *Metamorphoses*, XI.

[165] *Sees* (*εἶδον eidov*) that idea (*εἶδος eidos*) as a deified idol (*εἴδωλον eidolon,* from *εἶδος eidos*). *Cf.* Genesis 1:4.

[166] <Simonelli, *Awareness*, pp. 68 70.>

[167] Exodus 20:7(שָׁוְא *shav'* in vain), *cf.* Leviticus 24:11. "The later Hebrews... following some old superstition, regarded this name as

so very holy that it might not even be pronounced" (יְהוָה Gesenius). However, the unpronounceable aspect of this name has nothing to do with superstition. It simply means that its pronunciation would reduce the Transcendent to an objective thought, which would be idolatrous and contrary to the Transcendent itself.

[168] *Cf.* McNeil, *Heaven Exists*, & Alexander, *Proof of Heaven*, and many others.

[169] Ecclesiastes 9:5-10.

[170] Psalm 6:5 and 13:3. Sleep of death = מָוֶת *maveth* Strong's H4194. From מות *muwth* Strong's H4191, to die, compare to Sanskrit *mṛ* मृ (Gesenius).

[171] Tolle, *The Power of Now*, p. 102.

[172] Power Snake *khut* encircling Pharaoh Ramses VI's forehead (XX dynasty, 1145-1137 BC; fresco at the entrance of his tomb, *Wadi Biban el-Muluk,* Gates–Valley of the King, Luxor, Egypt), also a symbol of enlightenment (*cf.* Simonelli, *Beyond Immortality*, p. 211) & Double Crown of Egypt.

[173] Harari, *Sapiens*, p. 32.

[174] *Circum-ference* = from Latin: *moving* (*ferens*) something *around* (*circum*) the inevitably *in-ferred* (*in - fert* = *in*cluded) necessary center.

[175] Μετάνοια *metanoia. Cf.* Walden, Treadwell, *The Great Meaning of the Word Metanoia*, 4, 9.

[176] In Hebrew, the word for *heart* is *leb* (לֵב- Strong's H3820). It means inner man, mind, soul, will, heart and understanding.

[177] *Cf.* Koran, *sūrat l-anfāl* (The Spoils of War) 8:65, "*O Prophet, urge* (فعل أمر *ḥarriḍi*) *the believers* (اسم منصوب *l-mu'minīna*) *to battle* (اسم مجرور *l-qitāli*). *If there are among you twenty* [who are] *steadfast, they will overcome two hundred. And if there are among you one hundred* [who are] *steadfast, they will overcome a thousand of those who have disbelieved because they are a people who do not understand.*" Similarly, *Bible*, Matthew 10:34, "*do not suppose that I have come to bring peace to the earth. I did not come to bring peace, but a sword.*"

[178] Reproduction of *The Scream* (1893 – 1910) by Edvard Munch (Løten, Norway 1863 – 1944).

[179] Wittgenstein, *Tractatus Logico-Philosophicus*, 5.62.

[180] Laitman, *Attaining the Worlds Beyond: A Guide to Spiritual Discovery*, p. 434 (Talmud, Kiddushin).

[181] Reproduction of *The False Mirror* (1928) by René Magritte (Lessines, Belgium 1898 – 1967). The blue sky contrasts with the black pupil incapable of seeing itself.

[182] *Cf.* Ramana Maharshi, *Who am I?*

[183] I Samuel, 16:7.

[184] Black Elk, *The sacred Pipe*, Italian translation Alce Nero, *La sacra Pipa*, pp. 19-20. Native American calumet sacred ceremonial pipe. *Cf.* Blue Winds Dancing, The White Cloud Collection of Native American Art, New Orleans Museum of Art, 2008.

[185] <Simonelli, *Beyond Immortality*, p. 66.>

[186] Isaiah 55:8 and 9.

[187] An example of this mind frame is the Japanese "*Paro*" automatons. They are interactive therapeutic robots intended to help stimulate patient's clinical socialization needs. These patients react to the robots and are tricked into believing in an actual emotional rapport with those androids as sentient beings. *Cf.* AIST, *PARO Therapeutic Robot.*

[188] *Cf.* Sagan, *The Cosmic Connection: An Extraterrestrial Perspective*; SETI, Search for Extraterrestrial Intelligence & *A SETI Signal?* Even if the science fiction theory, by which terrestrials got their biology, ideas, discoveries and/or inventions from ancient aliens (*cf.* Daniken, *Chariots of the Gods*), should be proven, still it should be established where those aliens got them from in return and so on, *ad infinitum.*

[189] Wheeler, *Bhor ...*, p. 3 and 17.

[190] Quote attributed to Nikola Testa (1856 – 1943), Mind Unleashed, *31 Outstanding Quotes From Nikola Testa* (1856 – 1943), #28, Unknown source.

[191] *Cf.* Hines, *Pseudoscience and the Paranormal*, for NDE see McNeil, *Heaven Exists*, & Alexander, *Proof of Heaven.*

[192] They draw their nutrients from the soil and transform them in green life, flower and foliage, which grow sensitive to light.

[193] *Cf.* Watts, *The Tao of Philosophy*, p. 10.

[194] *Cf.* Kynard, *The Esoteric Codex*, p. 16; & Woolley, *The Sumerians.*

[195] From Latin = *sacri-facere.*

[196] Detail inscription on an Apkallu, Palace of Assurbanipal II, Northwest Throne Room B, Assyrian, Nimrud 885-59 BC (Princeton  University Art Museum).

[197] Palace of Ashur-nasir-pal II king of Assyria (883 - 859 BC.) at Kalhu (Nimrud) in Mesopotamia. "Assyrian –Relief with Winged Genius - Walters 218" by Anonymous (Assyria) - Walters Art Museum: Home page Info about artwork. Licensed under Public Domain via Wikimedia Commons - https://commons.wikimedia.org/wiki/File:Assyrian_-Relief_with_Winged_Genius_-_Walters_218.jpg#/media/File:Assyrian_-_Relief_with_Winged_Genius_-_Walters_218.jpg; https://ticket.wikimedia.org/otrs/index.pl?Action=AgentTicketZoom&TicketNumber=2012021710000834; & tree and sculpted artifact from the city of Ur, (early III Dynasty, 2600-2400 BC) & pine-cone.

[198] *Cf.* F.A.M. Wiggermann, *Mesopotamian Protective Spirits*, p. 67; & Cohen (Editor), *Assyrian Reliefs from the palace of Ashurnasirpal*, § 7 (Collins, *Attending the King and Eternity*), p. 184.

[199] *Cf.* Armstrong, *A History of God.*

[200] *Cf.* Guion, *Hunt for the Garden of Eden.*
[201] *Cf.* Bennett, *Joanna Lumley: The Search for Noah's Ark* & Kite, *Noah's Ark.*
[202] Anonymous wood engraving, "A medieval missionary tells that he has found the point where heaven and Earth meet," Flammarion, *L'atmosphère: météorologie populaire*, p. 163. Public Domain, Wikimedia Commons, File:Flammarion.jpg.
[203] Athens, 470-399 BCE. *Cf.* Plato, *Text,* Apology.
[204] Bethlehem - Jerusalem, Judea, beginning of I century. *Cf.* Bible, *Biblia sacra.*
[205] Fars, Persia 858 - Baghdad, Abbasid Caliphate 922. *Cf.* Mason, *The death of al-Hallaj.*
[206] Nola, Naples 1548- Rome 1600. *Cf.* Firpo, *Il processo di Giordano Bruno.*
[207] Radhanath Swami, *The Journey Home*, p. 155.
[208] *Cf.* Hollister, *Medieval Europe*, pp. 158 fol.
[209] *Cf.* Hollister, *Medieval Europe*, pp. 170 fol.
[210] *Cf.* Watts, *The Book*, p. 10.
[211] (أساسيون *Asasiyun*) Lewis, *The Assassins*, pp. 97 fol.
[212] *Bible,* Matthew 7:21-23.
[213] *Cf.* The Nag Hammadi Library.
[214] *Cf.* Babenco, *At Play in the Fields of the Lord.*
[215] *Cf.* the similar expression in the *Tabula smaragdina* text in Chrysogonus Polydorus, *De Alchimia.*
[216] *Bible*, Matthew 18:18.
[217] Milton, *Paradise Lost*, Book 1, 254-5.
[218] Genesis 2:12.
[219] *Bible,* Matthew 21:42, Mark 12:10, Luke 20:17 and *cf.* Psalm 118:22, *Lapis, quem reprobavérunt* (ἀπεδοκίμασαν *apedoximasan*) *aedificántes, factus est caput ánguli.*
[220] *Cf.* Plato's Cave, *Republic,* Book VII.514a to 520a.
[221] *Cf.* Śaṅkara's *parāvidya* & *aparāvidya*, the example of the serpent and the rope in *Vedānta-Sūtra,* I.2.20, vol. I p. 135 & III.2.21, vol. II p. 164-5.
[222] *Cf.* the mythical and metaphorical Philosopher's Stone in Eli Luminosus Aequalis, *Mutus Liber Loquitur*, pp. 40-41.
[223] Skullcap, *kippah*, כִּפָּה as the letter כ, *k, kaph*, is also called *yarmulke* in Yiddish.
[224] Also called phylactery (*φυλακτήριον phulaktērion* = defences) box, used during Rabbinical prayers. *Cf.* Exodus 13:9,16; Deuteronomy 6:8 & 11:18. *Cf.* Friedlander, *The Jewish Religion*, p. 333.
[225] *Laylat al-Qadr* (ليلة القدر), *the Night of Power*, evokes when the Koran was revealed to Prophet Muhammad.
[226] Deuteronomy 6:5.
[227] *Cf.* Simonelli, *Beyond Immortality*, pp. 40, 68.
[228] Namely, the traditions of Asian sacred texts (as *Veda, Upanishad, Buddhist Canon, Tao,* etc.).
[229] Wittgenstein, *Tractatus Logico-Philosophicus,* 6.363, (*cf.* Occam's razor, *Summa Totius Logicae*, I. 12, p. 37).
[230] From Greek ἀποκάλυψις *apokálypsis*, ἀπο *apo* (un) καλύπτω *kalúptō*, *to cover*, thus *to uncover*, *to reveal.*
[231] Psalm 12:6.
[232] *Bible*, 2 Timothy 3:16.
[233] *Cf.* Ignatius of Loyola, *Spiritual Exercises.*
[234] Latin, *in-tueri*, from *tueri*, to look, and *in.*
[235] *Cogito ergo sum.* Descartes' Notebook entry, 11/11, 1620, *Descartes...*, Anscombe Ed., p. 3.
[236] *Cf.* Watson, *Cogito ...*, p. 115 and Clarke, *Descartes...*, p. 64.
[237] *Cf.* Anch, *Sleep.*
[238] Dement, *Some Must Watch ...*, p. 24 and 27.
[239] Harrison, *General anesthesia research: aroused from a deep sleep?*
[240] Electroencephalogram: ***Electro*** = electrical - ***Encephalo*** = brain's activity - ***Gram*** = graphic recording.
[240] Dement, *Some Must Watch ...*, p. 26.
[241] *Cf.* Anch, *Sleep: ...*, p. 42.
[242] *Cf.* Dement, *Some Must Watch ...*, p. 28.

Examples of Polygraph records of NREM sleep:			
1Stage 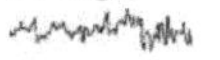	2 Stage 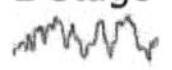	3 Stage < deep-delta sleep or slow-wave-sleep (SWS) > 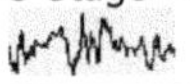	4 Stage 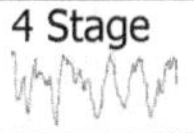

[242] Anch, *Sleep: ...*, pp. 55-56; *cf.* Agnew; Borbély, *Secrets of Sleep*, p. 25.
[242] Anch, *Sleep: ...*, p. 30.
[243] Anch, *Sleep: ...*, pp. 55-56; *cf.* Agnew; Borbély, *Secrets of Sleep*, p. 25.
[244] Anch, *Sleep: ...*, p. 30.
[245] Borbély, *Secrets of Sleep*, p. 44-45, 56; *cf.* Anch, p. 141; Foulkes; Monroe.
[246] Anch, *Sleep: A Scientific Perspective*, p. 141.
[247] Ferrarelli F. et al., *Breakdown in cortical effective connectivity during midazolam-induced loss of consciousness.*
[248] Anch, p. 141.

[249] From Latin *mens* mind; the process of carefully rethinking, considering and recounting something or an object of the mind.
[250] Hobson, *REM sleep and dreaming.*
[251] Rudoy et al., *Strengthening Individual Memories by Reactivating Them During Sleep.*
[252] Psalm 127:2.
[253] Nicolae de Cusa, *De Docta Ignorantia*, I.4, *coincidentia oppositorum.*
[254] <*Cf.* Simonelli, *Beyond Immortality*, pp. 69 -84.>
[255] 5:6.
[256] Strong's H738, Gesenius.
[257] Strongs H3293, Gesenius.
[258] Strong's H2061, Gesenius.
[259] Strong's H6160, "from עֲרַב `*arab*, Strong's H6150, in the sense of sterility. A primitive root (identical with עֲרַב `*arab* Strong's H6148, through the idea of covering with a texture).
[260] Strong's H5246, "From an unused root meaning properly, to filtrate, i.e. be limpid (comp. נִמְרָה *Nimrah*, Strong's H5247 limpid and נִמְרִים *Nimriym*, Strong's H5249, limpid).
[261] Strong's H8245.
[262] Strong's H5892. "From עוּר `*uwr*, Strong's H5782, a city (a place guarded by waking or a watch) in the widest sense (even of a mere encampment or post) A primitive root (rather identical withעוּר` *uwr*, Strong's H5783, through the idea of opening the eyes).
[263] Compare to the trident *Triśula* of Shivji Murti at Sur Sagar Lake in BarodaBaroda, Rajasthan, India (2008).
[264] *Cf.* the Indian symbol ॐ, AUM·, *cf.* Simonelli, *Beyond Immortality*, pp. 79 fol.
[265] Morrison, *Gold from the Land of Israel*, pp. 179-180.
[266] *Bible*, John 14:2.
[267] (*re'shiyth*) *Beginning* Strong's H7225. James Strong (1822 – 1894) American Methodist and Biblical scholar creator of *Strong's Concordance.*
[268] (*'elohiym*) *God* Strong's H430, Gesenius.
[269] (*bara'*) *Created* Strong's H1254.
[270] (*'erets*) *Earth* Strong's H776.
[271] (*shamayim*) *Heaven* Strong's H8064.
[272] Jesuit Fathers of St. Mary's College, *The Church Teaches*, 306 (428), p. 132. Established by The Fourth Lateran Council, 1215.
[273] הָאֱלֹהִים אֵין עוֹד *hā'ĕlōhiym 'ēyn 'vōḏ* (Deuteronomy 4:35).
[274] אֱלוֹהַּ *'elowahh* Strong's H433.
[275] As an example, historical books, referring to Queen Elizabeth I of England, use the singular, not the plural *Queens*. Only, upon reporting her a direct first person speech, she may say, '*We, Elizabeth, Queen…*'
[276] Genesis 18:27; Exodus 34:23; Psalm 8:1. אֲדֹנָי *ăḏōnēy.*
[277] Exodus 21:6 & 22:8.
[278] Michelangelo portrayed the Creator standing in the brain in the cranium (see below).
[279] Psalm 82:1.
[280] 1King 3:28, חָכְמַת אֱלֹהִים *ḥāḵəmaṯ* (wisdom) '*ĕlōhiym* (of God).
[281] Job 28:28. אֲדֹנָי הִיא חָכְמָה `*adonay hu chokmah.*
[282] בָּרָא *bara'; in Greek,* ἐποίησεν, *epoiēsen* = made; in Latin, *creavit* = created, which derives from Sanskrit *kṛ* = to make.
[283] יְהֹוָה *yahvāh*, Gesenius. Never to be read aloud but substituted by another name, like Adonai.
[284] Genesis, Chapter 2:4.
[285] יְהֹוָה Yĕhovah, צָבָא *tsaba'*, Strong's H6635 from צָבָא *tsaba'*, Strong's H6633, to cause to go forth and assembly.
[286] Deuteronomy 5:11 and Exodus 20:7.
[287] Psalm 139:8.
[288] Campbell, *The Power of Myth*, p. 67.
[289] *hayah* Strong's H1961, from which the name יְהֹוָה *yahvāh* derives. Compare to הָוָה, *to breath* (*hava'* Strong's H1933, Gesenius) and to אָוָה, *'avah, to hunger* (Strong's H183).
[290] Deuteronomy 10:17. *yahvāh* (Transcendent Awareness) *'ĕlōhēyḵem* (Consciousness) *hu'* (is) *'ĕlōhēy* (Divine-Consciousness) *hā'ĕlōhiym* (of gods) *va'ăḏōnēy* (Lord) *hā'ăḏōniym* (of lords).
[291] *hayah* (Strong's H1961) from which יְהֹוָה *yahvāh* derives.
[292] Exodus 6:3.
[293] *Cf.* Exodus 20:7.
[294] Following Kant's use of *Transcendental* and *a-priori, cf. Critique of pure reason*, § 17 Introduction.
[295] Psalm 82:6. אֱלֹהִים אַתֶּם וּבְנֵי עֶלְיוֹן כֻּלְּכֶם: '*ĕlōhiym* (Gods ye) '*atem* (with them) *uḇənēy* (sons) '*eləyvōn* (of the Most High) *kuləḵem* (all of you) ---- θεοί *theoi* (Gods) ἐστε *este* (are) καὶ *kai* (and) υἱοὶ *uioi* (sons) ὑψίστου *upsistou* (you) πάντες *pantes* (all) ---- *dii* (gods) *estis* (you are) *et* (and) *filii* (sons) *Excelsi* (of the Most High) *omnes* (all) *vos* (you).
[296] *Bible*, John, 10:34. Θεοί *Theoi* (Gods) ἐστε *este* (you are).
[297] *Bible*, Luke 17:21.
[298] *Bible*, 1 Corinthians 3:16 & *cf.* 2 Corinthians_ 6:16, Leviticus 26:12, Ezekiel 37:27.
[299] *UB.* I. 4. 6. *atisṛshṭṭyāṃ* (in higher creation) *hāsyaitasyāṃ* (indeed this in this) *bhavati* (becomes) *ya* (who) *evaṃ* (verily) *veda*

(knows)

[300] *Cf.* Paramahansa Yogananda, *Autobiography of a Yogi*, pp. 165-173 (§14, An Experience in Cosmic Consciousness).

[301] *Bible,* John 5:31.

[302] *Rig Veda* (the sacred verses, the original and oldest work, of the *Vedas* (knowledge) a collection of four Indian sacred texts, dating back, according to astronomical references, from 4000 to 2500 B.C., before the Northern Aryan conquerors settled in India) *VṚ* X.129.1, *n-āsad āsīn nó sád āsīt.*.

[303] *Cf.* Strong's H1254 (Gesenius 4).

[304] *Cf.* IV Day, 1:18.

[305] "*Panis Angelicus,*" Thomas Aquinas, *The Aquinas Prayer Book, Sacris Solemniis,* pp. 93 fol.

[306] מַלְאָךְ *mal'ak* Strong's H4397, messenger, Greek ἄγγελος *aggelos.*

[307] *Cf. Bible*, John 1:1.

[308] The Philosopher's Stone, Eli Luminosus Aequalis, *Mutus Liber "Loquitur"*, p. 234.

[309] Augustine, *Confessions*, 11.6.8. *vox de nube ... acta atque transacta est, coepta et finita. sonuerunt syllabae atque transierunt, secunda post primam, tertia post secundam ... silentiumque post ultimam.* 7.9. *verbo tibi coaeterno simul et sempiterne dicis omnia quae dicis* 11, 13. *totum esse praesens* 18.23. *si enim sunt futura et praeterita, ... non ibi ea futura esse aut praeterita, sed praesentia.* 20, 26. '*tempora sunt tria, praesens de praeteritis, praesens de praesentibus, praesens de futuris.*'

[310] Wheeler (late Princeton University Emeritus Physics Professor), *Bhor ...*, p. 24.

[311] *Trionfo di Bacco e Arianna, Canto Carnevalesco.* Roscoe, *The life of Lorenzo de'Medici* (1449 – 1492), p. 129. "*Quant'è bella giovinezza,/ che si fugge tuttavia! / Chi vuol esser lieto, sia: / di doman non c'è certezza.*"

[312] Horace (65-8 BC), *Odes* 1.11, 1-2, 6-8, "*Tu ne quaesieris, scire nefas, quem mihi, quem tibi/ finem di dederint... vina liques... fugerit invida/ aetas: carpe diem quam minimum credula postero.*"

[313] *Bible*, Isaiah 22:13, Ecclesiastes 9:7–9 and 1 Corinthians 15:32.

[314] <Simonelli, *Awareness*, p. 197.>

[315] *Cf.* Hawking, *A Brief History of Time.*

[316] רֵאשִׁית Strong's H7225, From the same as in the next note:

[317] רֹאשׁ *ro'sh* Strong's H7218, head summit.

[318] *Cf.* The Antipas Foundation, as of the date of this writing, May 18, 2016 CE (#2 – *Iyar* 5776).

[319] *Cf.* NASA.

[320] *Cf.* Einstein, *The world as I see it*, Paper 4, Does the inertia of a body depend upon its energy-content?

[321] <Simonelli, *Beyond Immortality*, p. 194.>

[322] *Cf.* Guénon, R *Il simbolismo della croce*, pp. 196-200.

[323] *Cf.* Bartusiak, *Black Hole.*

[324] Shakespeare, *The Tempest*, Act 2, Scene I.

[325] *Cf.* Tolle, *The Power of Now.*

[326] Many times, as confirmed also by *Hospice Care* workers, at the bedside of dying persons we heard them enquire, '*What time is it?*' We wonder if that question was intended to verify their persistence still within the field of flowing time-past.

[327] <Simonelli, *Beyond Immortality*, p. 61.>

[328] Hawking, *The Grand Design*, p. 131.

[329] Harari, *Sapiens*, p. 109.

[330] *Cf.* Darwin, *The origin of species*, p. 499, "Judging from the past, we may safely infer that not one living species will transmit its unaltered likeness to a distinct futurity."

[331] *Cf.* Hawking, *A Brief History of Time.*

[332] *Cf.* Dembski, *Intelligent Design.*

[333] Harari, *Sapiens*, p. 391.

[334] *Cf.* Darwin, *The Origin of Species.*

[335] Latin *ex* (out) *volvere* (roll).

[336] תֹּהוּ *tohuw.*

[337] חֹשֶׁךְ *choshek* Strong's H2822, Gesenius.

[338] Overbye, *Peering... The New York Times* article.

[339] Wheeler, *Bhor ...*, p. 18.

[340] Jung, *Visions*, p. 361.

[341] רוּחַ *ruwach* (Strong's H7307), from the verb רִיחַ *ruwach* (Strong's H7306) to breathe with the nostrils.

[342] מַיִם *mayim* plural of מַי . For a similar concept of the waters in other traditions (ex. Vedic) see Simonelli, *Beyond Immortality*, p. 252.

[343] Chang, *Mars Shows Signs of Having Flowing Water, Possible Niches for Life, NASA Says,* & Nasa, *NASA's Hubble Spots Possible Water Plumes Erupting on Jupiter's Moon Europa,* & Netburn, *Rosetta spots two types of water ice on the surface of comet 67P.*

[344] *VṚ* X.129.1. *tadānīṃ* (then) *nāsīd* (nor was) *rájo* (atmosphere) *nó* (nor) *vyòmā* (sky) *paró* (beyond) *yát* (it) / *kíṃ* (what) *āvarīvaḥ* (concealed) *kúha* (where) *kásya* (in whose) *śarmann* (shelter) *ámbhah* (Celestial Waters) *kím* (why) *āsīd* (was) *gahanaṃ* (depth) *gabhīrám̩* (of inscrutable) // 2. *ná* (nor) *mṛtyúr* (death) *āsīd* (was) *amṛtaṃ* (immortality) *ná*

(nor) *tárhi* (then) *ná* (no) *rātryā* (night) *áhna* (day) *āsīt* (was) *praketáḥ* (knowledge) / *ānīd* (was breathing) *avātám̩* (windless) *svadháyā* (by self-power) *tád* (that) *ékam* (One) *tásmād* (therefore) *dhānyán* (indeed other seed)* *ná* (no) *paráḥ* (beyond) *kím̩ ca-* (further) *n-* (none) *āsa* (was)//... 6. *arvāg* (after) *devā* (the resplendent beings of the senses) *asyá* (of this) *visárjanenā-* (the projection). *Cf. Chāndogya* (relating to knowledge) *Upanisad*, VI,2,1. Note that One (*ékam̩*) contradicts the common view of Hindu polytheism. In fact, the gods (*devā*) came after (*arvāg*) that One.

Cf. Nu,  the Egyptian primeval waters (*cf.* Budge, *The Egyptian Book of the Dead*, p. cvii).
**Cf VṚ Die Hymned des Rigveda*, ed. Aufrecht, II, p. 430 n. 2 "*ha anyát*." And *W.* "2. *ha* ... m. ... water; a cipher (i.e. the arithmetical figure which symbolizes 0) ... sky, heaven, ... n. the Supreme Spirit; ... 3. ... ind. ... indeed" (1286a) and "*anyá*, ... other ... another; another person" (45b); "*dhānyá* ... n. corn, grain ... a measure = 4 sesamum seeds" (514b).

345 Strong's H1933, Gesenius.
346 Strong's H183.
347 (רוּחַ *ruwach*) Strong's H7307.
348 (רָחַף *rachaph*) Strong's H7363.
349 *Cf.* breathing in Job 9:18. Greek πνεῦμων *pneumōn*, lung & πνεῦμά *pneuma*,air.
350 רוּחַ חָכְמָה *ruwach chokmah*, Exodus 28:3.
351 מַיִם *mayim* see Strong's H4325.
352 Ramana Maharshi, *Who am I? The Spiritual Teaching*, p. 31.
353 *Cf.* Kumar, *Comprehensive Physics XII*, p. 1416.
354 *Cf.* Einstein, *The Evolution of Physics*, pp. 262-263.
355 Schaff, *Creeds of Christendom*, Vol. I, § 7 "*lumen de lumine*" (*Nicene Creed*, 325).
356 *Cf.* the Sanskrit *vajra*, Tibetan *rdo-rje*, the thunderbolt glimpsed between the two moments of Awareness and consciousness-*of* (*cf. W.* p. 115a & Simonelli, *Beyond Immortality*, p. 183).
357 Strong's H216, Gesenius (c & d); *cf.* Job 36:32, 3:16, 20 & Psalm 56:14.
358 *Cf.* Exodus 3:14.
359 Sanskrit दिव् √*div*, "*cl.4.* ... to shine (2)... in later Skr. Heaven... as the father..., while the earth is the mother (3)... द्यु dyú ... day... *m.* fire" (*W.*, pp. 478b-478c).
360 *Cf.* Thoreau, *A Year...*, July 16, 1851.
361 *Cf.* "*divine Self-Generated,*" in Kasser-Meyer-Wurst, *Gospel of Judas* [47], p. 34.
362 (הָיָה *hayah*) Strong's H1961.
363 (אוֹר *'owr*) Strong's H216.
364 Tegmark, *Consciousness as a State of Matter.*
365 רֵאשִׁית *rē'šiyṯ.*
366 Event = from the Latin *eventus*, past participle of *ex* (out) and *venire* (to come).
367 אָמַר *'amar* (Strong's H559 n1) to bear forth, to bring to light, to say.
368 אוֹר *'owr* light (Strong's H216) and אוֹר (Strong's H215) *'owr*, to be or become light, to be illuminated, to illumine, light up, cause to shine, to make shine.
369 Schrödinger (1887–1961, Austrian Nobel Prize quantum physicist), *Mind and Matter*, quoted in Miranker, Zuckerman, *Mathematical Foundations of Consciousness.*
370 *Bible*, Hebrews 10:2, "συνείδησιν *suneidēsin* (consciousness-of = συνείδησις *suneidēsis*, from συνοράω *sunoraō*, to see-with) ἁμαρτιῶν *amartiōn* (of missing the mark = ἁμαρτία *amartia*, from ἁμαρτάνω *amartanō*, to miss the mark)."
371 *Koran*, Women سورة النساء 4:35 اللَّهَ كَانَ عَلِيمًا خَبِيرًا & *cf.* 1 اللَّهَ كَانَ عَلَيْكُمْ رَقِيبًا *Allah ever watches over you.*
372 Francesco, *Scritti di S. Francesco e di S. Chiara*, Cantico delle creature. "*Altissimu, onnipotente, bon Signore,/ tue so' le laude, la gloria e 'honore et onne benedictione./ Ad te solo, Altissimo, se konfàno/ et nullu homo ène dignu te mentovare./ Laudato sie, mi' Signore, cum tucte le tue creature,/ spetialmente messor lo frate sole,/ lo qual è iorno, et allumini noi per lui./ Et ellu è bellu e radiante cum grande splendore,/ de te, Altissimo, porta significatione./ Laudato si', mi' Signore, per sora luna e le stelle,/ in celu l'ài formate clarite et pretiose et belle./ Laudato si', mi' Signore, per frate vento/ et per aere et nubilo et sereno et onne tempo,/ per lo quale a le tue creature dài sustentamento./ Laudato si', mi' Signore, per sor'aqua,/ la quale è multo utile et humile et pretiosa et casta./ Laudato si', mi' Signore, per frate focu,/ per lo quale ennallumini la nocte,/ et ello è bello et iocundo et robustoso et forte./ Laudato si', mi' Signore, per sora nostra matre terra,/ la quale ne sustenta et governa,/ et produce diversi fructi con coloriti flori et herba./ Laudato si', mi' Signore, per quelli ke perdonano per lo tuo amore,/ et sostengo infirmitate et tribulatione./ Beati quelli ke 'l sosterrano in pace,/ ka da te, Altissimo, sirano incoronati./ Laudato si' mi' Signore per sora nostra morte corporale,/ da la quale nullu homo vivente pò skappare:/ guai a quelli ke morrano ne le peccata mortali;/ beati quelli ke trovarà ne le tue santissime voluntati,/ ka la morte secunda no 'l farrà male./ Laudate et benedicete mi' Signore' et ringratiate/ et serviateli cum grande humilitate.*"
373 *Cf. BU* I.2.4 "*sam̩vatsaro* (the 360° degree year)," the circularity of Creation.
374 Song of Songs 3:1.
375 幽玄 *Cf.* Watts, *The Book*, pp. 33-34.
376 רָאָה *ra'ah* to see, perceive Strong's H7200.
377 טוֹב *towb.*
378 רָאָה Gesenius (3abc).

[379] *Bible*, Ephesians 1:18.
[380] (בָּדַל *badal*) Cf. Strong's H914.
[381] Strong's H7200.
[382] Strong's H2896, from טוב *towb* Strong's H2895, Gesenius (2), *to be beautiful.*
[383] Strong's H2896.
[384] Strong's H2895.
[385] טוב Gesenius (2).
[386] Plotinus (204 – 270), *Enneads*, I,6,7.
[387] Kant, *The critique of judgement*, § 6, underlining is ours.
[388] Genesis 1:4, 10, 12, 18, 21, 25, 31.
[389] Hegel (1770 – 1831), *Vorlesungen über die Aesthetik*, p. 160.
[390] Croce (1866 – 1952), *Estetica*, p. 92.
[391] (יום *yowm*) *Cf.* Strong's H3117. For a similar concept of the year in other traditions (ex. Vedic) see *BU* I.2.4 and *cf.* Simonelli, *Beyond Immortality*, pp. 47 fol. & 253.
[392] Psalm 19:6.
[393] Isaiah 55:11.
[394] (לַיִל *layil*) night Strong's H3915.
[395] *Luwl* לול *winding stair* Strong's H3883. The night (לַיִל *layil*) of objectivity, when conceived as independent or equal to its vivifying source of Awareness, becomes *liyliyth* (לִילִית, Strong's H3917) a female screeching owl night demon (Isaiah 34:14).
[396] Strong's H7121 קָרָא *qara'.*
[397] *Bible*, John 1:1.
[398] *Bible*, Luke 15:20.
[399] רָקִיעַ *raqiya* ' (Strong's H7549), from the next verb
[400] רָקִיעַ √ רָקַע *raqa* ' (Strong's H7554).
[401] מַיִם *mayim.*
[402] *Cf.* Simonelli, *Transcendence.*
[403] (בָּרָא) Strong's H1254.
[404] (אָמַר) Strong's H559.
[405] (עָשָׂה) Strong's H6213.
[406] (קָרָא) Strong's H7121.
[407] בָּדַל *badal* H914.
[408] כֵּן *ken.*
[409] *Cf.* Bruno, *De l'infinito universo e mondi.*
[410] μοναὶ *monai*, *Bible*, John 14:2.
[411] *Cf.* Tegmark, *Our Mathematical Universe.*
[412] יְהוָה אֱלֹהֵי הַשָּׁמַיִם *yəhvāh 'ĕlōhēy hašāmayim*, 2 Chronicles 36:23.
[413] Genesis 28:17 (H8064) שַׁעַר הַשָּׁמָיִם: *ša'ar hašāmāyim.*
[414] *Ibid.* בֵּית אֱלֹהִים *bayith elohiym.*
[415] Deuteronomy 10:14, וּשְׁמֵי הַשָּׁמָיִם *ušamēy hašāmāyim.*
[416] קָרָא *qara'Strong's H7121.*
[417] שָׁמַיִם Strong's H8064.
[418] Deuteronomy 10:14.
[419] *Bible*, Luke 24:51. ἀνεφέρετο *anepherето* (lifted up) εἰς *eis* (into) τὸν *ton* (the) οὐρανόν *ouranon* (heaven).
[420] (788-820 AD) Tucci, *Storia della filosofia indiana*, p. 139.
[421] *Vedānta-Sūtra*, II.2. 28, p. 421.
[422] *Cf.* NASA SCIENCE, *Water Detected on Dwarf Planet Ceres*, & Nathues, *Sublimation in bright spots on (1) Ceres.*
[423] Strong's H3004.
[424] *Cf.* Evola, *La Tradizione Ermetica*, p. 125.
[425] <Eli Luminosus Aequalis, *Mutus Liber Loquitur*, p. 95.> ⇨ *Dispassionate in Awareness* (4), Altus, *Mutus Liber.*
[426] חָרְבָה *charabah* Strong's H2724, from חָרַב Strong's H2717 – *charab, absence of water, Gesenius.*
[427] Exodus 14:21.
[428] מֹשֶׁה *mosheh* Strong's H4872, *from* מָשָׁה *mashah, to draw* Strong's H4871.
[429] Exodus 2:10.
[430] Strong's H2670, *cf.* Exodus 21:2.
[431] *Cf.* 2 Chronicles 10:4.
[432] Public Domain: *Crossing the Red Sea*, a wall painting from the 1640s in Yaroslavl, Russia https://en.wikipedia.org/ File:Чермное.jpg
[433] Exodus 14:22-23.
[434] מִצְרַיִם (Strong's H4714) is the dual of מָצוֹר *matsowr* (Strong's H4693), the same as מָצוֹר *matsowr* (Strong's H4692) in the sense of *siege-enclosure*, *siege works*, from צוּר *tsuwr* (Strong's H6696) *to bind, confine.*
[435] פַּרְעֹה *Par'oh* Strong's H6547 meaning *great house.*

---

[436] יִשְׂרָאֵל *Yisra'el "God prevails,"* Strong's H3478. "*Thy name shall be ... Israel: for as a prince hast thou power with God and with men, and hast prevailed*" (Genesis 32:28).
[437] Swift horse skipping for pleasure סוּס *cuwc* Strong's H5483.
[438] Chariots, millstone רֶכֶב *rekeb Strong's* H7393 from רָכַב *rakab* Strong's H7392, Gesenius (3), fastened.
[439] פָּרָשׁ *parash* Strong's H6571, from פָּרַשׁ *parash* Strong's H6567, *to distinguish, separate.*
[440] *Cf. Bible*, Revelation 6: "2) *a white horse: and he that sat on him had a bow... to conquer...* 4) *another horse ... was red: and ... to him that sat thereon ... was given unto him a great sword...* 5) *a black horse; and he that sat on him had a pair of balances in his hand...* 8) *a pale horse: and his name that sat on him was Death, and Hell followed with him.*" & Revelation 9:16. "*And the number of the army of the horsemen were two hundred thousand thousand: and I heard the number of them.*"
⇨ Public Domain: *Four Horsemen of the Apocalypse* - Conquest, War, Famine & Death, 1887 by Victor Vasnetsov (Lamb visible on top). https://en.wikipedia.org/ File:Apocalypse vasnetsov.jpg
[441] *Bible*, Matthew 4:8-9.
[442] *UK* I.25 (I.I.25) *ye ye* (whatever) *kāmā* (lusted desires) *durlabhā* (hard to satisfy) *martya-*(in the mortals') *loke* (world) *sarvān-* (all) *kāmāṃś-*(desires) *chandataḥ* (according to your wish) *prārthayasva* (ask for)/ *imā* (these) *rāmāḥ* (lovely maidens) *sarathāḥ* (with chariots) *satūryāḥ* (accompanied by music) *na* (never) *hīdṛśā* (such) *lambhanīyāḥ* (obtainable) *manushyaiḥ* (by men).
[443] *Cf.* Sutta Nipāta, III.2, 12,15.
[444] Buddha (VI-IV century BC), Cf. Sutta Nipāta (Descending String) III.2 Padhāna Sutta (The Great Exertion String) vv. 425 fol.
⇨Public Domain: Mara's assault on the Buddha (aniconic representation symbolized by his empty throne), 2nd century, Amaravati, India https://en.wikipedia.org/ File:MaraAssault.jpg
[445] aKempis, III.34.2 p. 191 "*quelli che si dilettano nella carne ... si trova... in questa la morte.*"
[446] Genesis 2:17.
[447] *Cf.* Exodus 14:28.
[448] Exodus 9:14, Strong's H4046.
[449] Exist = Latin *ex-sistĕre*; = *ex* (outside-of) *sistĕre* (to stay).
[450] (אֶרֶץ *'erets*) Strong's H776.
[451] (יָם *yam*) Strong's H3220F.
[452] מִקְוֶה *miqveh* Strong's H4723, *collection, collected mass*, from קָוָה *qavah* Strong's H6960, *to collect, gather together*, Gesenius.
[453] יָם *yam* Strong's H3220, *roaring foaming sea*, Gesenius 1.
[454] אֶרֶץ *'erets* Strong's H776, *ground*, Gesenius 5.
[455] דָּשָׁא *dasha* Strong's H1876.
[456] דֶּשֶׁא *deshe'* Strong's H1877.
[457] *Herb* = עֵשֶׂב *`eseb Strong's* H6212, from an unused root meaning to glisten (or be green) *glistening.*
[458] זָרַע *zara`* Strong's H2232.
[459] זֶרַע *zera`* Strong's H2233.
[460] עֵץ *`ets* Strong's H6086. ⇨*E.g.* in the photo, Cedar of Lebanon (*Cedrus libani*, E. Mediterranea) planted at Bunchrew, Scotland, "by Duncan Forbes 5th of Culloden prior to the Jacobite Rising 1745" (plaque on tree). See Psalm 92:12 "*The righteous ... shall grow like a cedar in Lebanon.*" The tree grows symmetrically as high as 120 feet and 40 feet broad and used in ship building. See Ezekiel 31:3 & 8 " *a cedar in Lebanon with fair branches, and with a shadowing shroud, and of an high stature; and his top was among the thick boughs... The cedars in the garden of God.*"
[461] After its own kind, מִין *miyn* Strong's H4327.
[462] פְּרִי *pĕriy* Strong's H6529.
[463] עֵצָה *`atsah* Strong's H6095.
[464] פָּרָה *parah* Strong's H6509.
[465] עָשָׂה *`asah* Strong's H6213.
[466] "Drawing of Purkinje cells (A) and granule cells (B) from pigeon cerebellum by Santiago Ramón y Cajal, 1899; *Instituto Cajal*, Madrid, Spain." Public Domain, File:PurkinjeCell.jpg https://en.wikipedia.org/wiki/Neuron#/media/File:PurkinjeCell.jpg
[467] Tolle, *Stillness Speaks*, p. 10.
[468] *VR* X.129.5. *retodhā* (seminal agents – *cf. W.* p. 887c "fertilizing") *āsan* (were) *mahimāna* (increasing powers).
[469] λόγοι σπερματικοί (*lógoi spermatikoí*), Plotinus, *Enneads*, III.1.7.4. "Everything is accomplished by seminal reasons" πάντα κατὰ λόγους σπερματικοὺς περαίνεται. *Cf.* also V.9.6-7 and 14.
[470] *Cf. Timaeus* 73c.
[471] *Bible*, 1 John, 3:9.
[472] Ezekiel 36:26.
[473] Strong's H3974.
[474] Strong's H3974, Gesenius (2), *cf.* Exodus 25:6.
[475] (אוֹר *'owr*) Strong's H216.
[476] *Cf.* Simonelli, *Awareness*, p. 87, & *UKai* 7.
[477] (אוֹת *'owth*) Strong's H226. In NDE, Parti (*Dying to Wake Up*, from pp. XIII on) calls it "Being of Light."
[478] יָדַע Strong's H3045.

[479] *Cf.* Risen, *Another Earth? Take a Look at Kepler 425-b. A NASA space telescope searching for a new Earth has found our look-alike planet.* As more planets will be discovered, as Proxima b, the newly (2016) found planet in the orbit of Proxima Centauri (*cf.* Petras, *New Earth-Size Planet Discovered*), the more a literal reading becomes superficially unrealistic.

[480] Subject, in this context, is not synonym of subordinate or dependent; it means the knower as such. The one who does the action indicated by the verb.

[481] The known as such, the passive one to whom the action indicated by the verb is directed.

[482] The sun is mentioned for the first time as sun in *Genesis* 15:12 and the moon as such in *Genesis* 37:9.

[483] Strong's H1419 from גָּדַל *gadal* Strong's H1431, *to bind together* Gesenius (2).

[484] Strong's H6996, from קוּט *quwt,* Strong's H6962, *to be cut off* Gesenius (II)

[485] Subjectivity, in this context, is not synonym of prejudice.

[486] Objectivity, in this context, is not synonym of impartiality.

[487] כּוֹכָב Strong's H3556, builder. From the next

[488] the same as כַּבּוֹן *kabbown*, Strong's H3522, heap up, build &

[489] כָּוָה *kavah* Strong's H3554, to burn, scorch, brand.

[490] Mirror, camera, photographer and the on looking observer [collage of Frida Kahlo's (Mexico City, 1907- 1954) two parts self-portrait and her pet monkeys (*Fulang-Chang and I,* 1937) with the mirror and her painted frame (added after 1939) to hang side-by-side so one could always see herself next to Frida (*cf.* as it is in the *MoMA*, NYC, 1987)].

[491] Kant, C*ritique of pure reason,* § 17 Introduction.

[492] (מָשַׁל) Strong's H4910, Gesenius.

[493] *bara'* בָּרָא *to create, cf.* I Day, 1:1.

[494] The *adaequatio rei et intellectus* (equating the object with the intellect) of the medieval scholastic; *cf.* Thomas Aquinas, *Summa*, I, q. 16, aa. 1-2.

[495] *Cf. Koran*, The City 90:4, لَقَدْ خَلَقْنَا الْإِنْسَانَ فِي كَبَدٍ *"Verily, We have created man into* (جَاهِدُوا) *struggle, toil, and trial."*

[496] עָרַב *`arab* Strong's H6148, Gesenius (3) *to cover with a texture, to give security of exchange.*

[497] עֶרֶב *`ereb* (Strong's H6153) *evening,* from עָרַב *` arab* (Strong's H6150) *to become dark,* identical to עָרַב *`arab* (Strong's H6148) see n. 476 above.

[498] בֹּקֶר *boqer* (Strong's H1242*) end of night and coming of the daylight,* from next

[499] בָּקַר *baqar* (Strong's H1239) *to seek, enquire, to look at, contemplate,* Gesenius (3 & Piel, p. 137, 3).

[500] Strong's H8317.

[501] *Cf.* Darwin, *The Origin of Species.*

[502] Strong's H5315.

[503] Strong's H2416.

[504] Strong's H8318.

[505] Strong's H5774.

[506] (רָמַשׂ *ramas*) Strong's H7430.

[507] (תַּנִּין *tanniyn*) Strong's H8577.

[508] (נָחָשׁ *nachash*) Isaiah, 27:1.

[509] *Cf.* Chevalier, *Dictionnaire*, 3, 339.

[510] Exodus 7:10 & 12.

[511] (רָבָה *rabah*) Strong's H7235.

[512] (חַי *chay*) Strong's H2416.

[513] (חָיָה *chayah*) To live, Strong's H2421.

[514] Strong's H2421.

[515] Strong's H2416, חַי Gesenius.

[516] *Cf.* Genesis 1:11.

[517] חָיָה Strong's H2421.

[518] חָוָה Strong's H2331.

[519] חָוָא Strong's H2324.

[520] Strong's H929 and Gesenius בְּהֵמָה.

[521] Strong's H7431.

[522] Strong's H127.

[523] Strong's H119.

[524] Strong's H120.

[525] אָדָם, *'adam* Strong's H120, it is collective, Gesenius (1).

[526] יְהֹוָה *y*$_{ĕ}$*h*$_{o}$*w*$_{a}$*h*, Strong's H3068, τετρα *tetra* (four) - γράμματον *grammaton* (letters). *Cf.* Dan, *Kabbalah*, pp. 44.

[527] The body of God: י (*y* # 10 meaning Hand Work), ה (*h* # 5 meaning Man, Breath Sight), ו (*w –v* # 6 meaning Secure Hearing) and ה (*h* # 5 meaning Man, Breath Sight), with a Gematria (*i.e.*: letter/word numerical value - *cf.* Epstein, *Kabbalah.*) total equivalent of # 26, meaning: it is (והיה *hayah* Strong's H1961 Genesis 2:10 & הויה Exodus 9:3) the great (כבד *kabed* Strong's H3515 Genesis 12:10) high (והגבהה *gaboahh* Strong's H1364 Daniel 8:3) hand (וידו *yad* Strong's H3027 Genesis 25:26 & בידי Genesis 39:8) the glory (וההוד howd Strong's H1935 1Chronicles 29:11) praise (יודו *yadah* Strong's H3034

Psalm 99:3) exalt (יגבהו *gabahh* Strong's H1361 Ezekiel 31:14) live (בחיו *chay* Strong's H2416 2Samuel 18:18) breast (וחזה *chazeh* Strong's H2373 Leviticus 10:15). *Cf.* Armstrong, *A History of God*, p. 215-216.

[528] (צֶלֶם) Strong's H6754.

[529] (דְּמוּת) Strong's H1823.

[530] (דָּמָה) Strong's H1819 (Gesenius 2&3).

[531] Khan, *Sufi Teachings...*, p. 55. Jalāl ad-Dīn Muhammad Rūmī (XIII century -1207 –1273- Persian Sufi mystic).

[532] <Simonelli, *Beyond Immortality*, p. 85.>

[533] (אָדַם *'adam*) Verb, *to be sparkling red* Strong's H119.

[534] (רָדָה *radah*) Strong's H7287.

[535] Strong's H6754, Gesenius (2).

[536] *Narcissus beholding his own reflected image*, Caravaggio. https://commons.wikimedia.org/wiki/File:Narcissus-Caravaggio_(1594-96)_edited.jpg, Public Domain, File:Narcissus-Caravaggio (1594-96) edited.jpg

[537] *Cf.* Ovid, Metamorphoses, III:402-436.

[538] Greek εἰκών eikōn.

[539] Male Strong's H2145, from the verb zakar (זָכַר) to remember, to call to mind.

[540] זכר *zakar* to remember, to call to mind, Strong's H2142.

[541] (נְקֵבָה) Female, Strong's H5347, from the verb *naqab* (נָקַב) to separates, to distinguish.

[542] נָקַב *naqab*, to separate, to distinguish, Strong's H5344 (Gesenius 2).

[543] *Cf.* the Tantric union of Śiva-Kālī (Simonelli, *Beyond Immortality*, p. 150, & n. 1536).

[544] This statement does not support nor oppose a one-woman one-man marriage (on the subject, *cf.* Simonelli, *Awareness*, pp. 206, 231 fol). However, humans can be born as true hermaphrodite (*cf.* Van Neikerk, W., Retief A. E., *The gonads of human true hermaphrodites*), this, from a literal creationist point of view, must be interpreted as willed by God, which, following the command "*to grow and multiply*" would implicitly promote permissible poly-relationships.

[545] Strong's H853, Gesenius אֵת "demonstrative pronoun" (1).

[546] Strong's H3533.

[547] Strong's H7287.

[548] דָּגָה *dagah* (Strong's H1710) fish, from דָּג *dag* (Strong's H1709) fish, from דָּגָה *dagah* (Strong's H1711) to m ultiply, increase, to cover, to be dark, (Gesenius).

[549] יָם *yam* (Strong's H3220) the sea, the great roaring river, (Gesenius).

[550] עוֹף `owph (Strong's H5775) fowl, from עוּף *`uwph* (Strong's H5774) to fly, to cover with darkness, [Gesenius (3)].

[551] שָׁמַיִם *shamayim* (Strong's H8064) air, from an unused root meaning to be soaring.

[552] She will appear in Genesis 3:20.

[553] (עֵשֶׂב *` eseb*) Strong's H6212.

[554] (זָרַע *zara`*) Strong's H2232.

[555] (זֶרַע *zera`*) Strong's H2233.

[556] λόγοι σπερματικοὶ (*lógoi spermatikoi*), Plotinus (204 – 270), *Enneads*, III.1.7.4.

[557] Simonelli, *Beyond Immortality*, p. 79.

[558] Edward Elgar (1857-1934), *ELGAR - HIS MUSIC.*

[559] (אָכְלָה *'oklah*) Strong's H402, iii.

[560] Kant, *The Critique of Pure Reason*, A69-81-320 / B94-106-376, *urteil* (judgment), *erkenntnis (*cognition), *urteilskraft* (the power of judgment), *fähigkeit* (capacity), *vermögen zu urteilen* ... *denken* (the faculty of judging ... thinking).

[561] (שָׁמַיִם *shamayim*) Strong's H8064.

[562] *Cf.* Society of Biblical Archæology, *Transactions...*, § The Birds of the Assyrian Monuments and Records. By the Rev. William Houghton, M.A., F.L.S, pp. 42-142. *Cf.* Ronnberg, *Birds of Prophecy.*

[563] הַשָּׁמָֽיִם *hašāmāyim* לְאֵ֣ל *lə'ēl* (Psalm 136:26).

[564] כָּלָה *kalah* Strong's H3615

[565] שָׁמַיִם *shamayim* Strong's H8064.

[566] אֶרֶץ *'erets* Strong's H776, Gesenius.

[567] (צָבָא *tsaba'*) Strong's H6635. From the next

[568] צָבָא *tsaba'* Strong's H6633.

[569] Friedlander, *The History and Philosophy of the Jewish Religion*, p. 31.

[570] *Bible*, John 14:6.

[571] (שְׁבִיעִי *shĕbiy`iy*) Strong's H7637.

[572] Strong's H3615.

[573] Strong's H7673.

[574] *Verification*, from Latin *verus* (*veri-*), true, + *facere* (*-fication*), to make.

[575] Ray, *Self Organization in Real and Complex Analysis*, (Abstract).

Numbers (ℕ) are equal (≡) and/or non-equal (≠) physical values dimensionally distinguished and separated from each other. To be operationally multipliable they cannot be uniquely identical. In fact, like an Infinite Zero (∞0), a number (ℕ), uniquely identical (∃!) to itself, cannot add or multiply itself without remaining always itself (*cf.* also Simonelli, *Transcendence*).

[576] *Bible*, Hebrew 11:1. ἔστιν *estin* (is) δὲ *de* (now) πίστις *pistis* (certitude) ἐλπιζομένων *elpizomenōn* (of trusted) ὑπόστασις *upostasis* (foundation) πραγμάτων *pragmatōn* (things) ἔλεγχος *elegchos* (evidence) οὐβλεπομένων *oublepomenōn* (of unseen).

[577] Exodus 3:14 אֶהְיֶה אֲשֶׁר אֶהְיֶה (היה *hayah* to be אֲשֶׁר *'ashér* that). *Cf.* Eli Luminosus Aequalis, *Mutus Liber Loquitur*, pp. 36, 41.

[578] ΓΝΩΘΙ ΣΕΑΥΤΟΝ *gnōthi seauton*, Plato, *Charmides*, 164 and *Apology*, 38a.

[579] Ramana Maharshi, *The Spiritual Teaching ...*, p. 76 and 82 (Self-inquiry = *ātma-vicāra*). *Cf. UK* III.12 (I.3.12) & Simonelli, *Beyond Immortality*, p. 176.

[580] *Cf.* Skinner (1904-1990), *The Behavior of Organisms.*

[581] *Cf.* Freud (1856- 1939), *The standard edition...*

[582] *Cf.* Adler (1870–1937), The Individual Psychology.

[583] *Cf.* Jung (1875 - 1961) *Two essays on analytical psychology* & *Psyche and Symbol.* (*uberpersonliche*).

[584] *Cf.* Gandhi (1869 - 1948), *An Autobiography...* (*a-hiṃsā* & satyā-graha).

[585] *Cf.* Dante, *La Divina Commedia, Paradiso*, XVIII. 4, Dante, the Faithful of Love, calls Beatrice, *"Quella donna ch'a Dio mi menava,"* "that Lady who was leading me to God" and *La Vita Nova*, chapter XXVI, "*Tanto gentile ...*" he described her as "*una cosa venuta / 7 di cielo in terra a miracol mostrare. /8 Mostrasi sì piacente a chi la mira, /9 che dà per gli occhi una dolcezza al core, /10 che intender non la può chi non la prova*" /11. "Something that came/ from heaven to earth to show a miracle./ She shows herself so pleasant to him who admires her,/ that she conveys through the eyes a sweetness to the hearth,/ that cannot be understood by him who does not feel it."

[586] *Bible,* 1John 4:7,12.

[587] < Eli Luminosus Aequalis, *Mutus Liber*, p. 143.>

[588] *Bible,* Matthew 5:48.

[589] *Cf.* Teresa of Avila, *The Interior Castle.* ECSTASY. *Cf.* Simonelli, *Beyond Immortality*, pp. 211-13.

[590] *Cf.* Melanchthon, *The Apology of the Augsburg Confession*, Original Sin, Article II. *Cf.* HFASS, House for All Sinners and Saints.

[591] Psalm 1:4.

[592] (יְהוָה) Strong's H3068.

[593] (הָיָה) Strong's H1961. Compare to הָוָה *hava'* , to be (Strong's H1933) and to אָוָה *'avah*, to desire (Strong's H183).

[594] (אֶהְיֶה אֲשֶׁר אֶהְיֶה *'ehayeh 'ăšer 'ehayeh*) Exodus 3:14.

[595] (אֱלֹהֵי יְהוָֹה yahvāh *'ĕlōhēy*) (אֱלֹהֵי יְהוָֹה yahvāh *'ĕlōhēy*) Exodus 3:15.

[596] אֱמוּנָה *'emuwnah* (Strong's H529) derives *from* √אָמַן *'aman* (Strong's H539,5) = to be sure, to be certain.

[597] πίστις *pístis* means assurance, proof, testimonial. Rocci, p.1503b *sicurtà*.

[598] Latin *fides*.

[599] *Cf.* Simonelli, *Awareness*, p. 72.

[600] 20:7.

[601] (נָשָׂא *nasa'*) Strong's H5375.

[602] (ריק *riyq*) Strong's H7385, from ריק *ruwq* (Strong's H7324), to empty out.

[603] Stein, *The Language That Rises: 1923-1934*, p. 147.

[604] In *AU LECTEUR* (To the Reader), Altus, Baulot, *Mutus liber*, 1677 first edition. "*Livre Muët, néanmoins toutes les Nations du monde... peuvent le lire & l'entendre... d'abord*," in Eli Luminosus, *Liber Mutus Loquitur*, p. 32.

[605] Exodus 3:5.

[606] Exodus 3:6. Similarly, Judas "*could not look him* [Jesus] *in the eyes, and he turned his face away*," (Kasser-Meyer-Wurst, *Gospel of Judas*, [35], p. 22).

[607] <Simonelli, Awareness, p. 32.>

[608] (יְהוָה) Rendered in Greek, *κύριος* (*kurios*), in Latin, *Dominus* and, in English, *Lord.*

[609] (אֱלֹהִים) Rendered in Greek, *θεός* (*theos*), in Latin, *Deus* and, in English, *Lord.*

[610] Deuteronomy 5:12.

[611] שָׁמַר *shamar*, Strong's H8104.

[612] יוֹם *yowm*, Strong's H3117.

[613] שַׁבָּת *shabbath*, Strong's H7676; intensive from שָׁבַת *shabath* (Strong's H7673) *to rest.*

[614] קָדַשׁ *qadash*, Strong's H6942.

[615] *Cf.* Plato, *Phaedrus.*

[616] *Cf.* Wheeler, *Bhor ...*, pp. 17&24.

[617] (מָטָר *matar*) Strong's H4305.

[618] See Genesis 1:2 מַיִם *mayim* see Strong's H4325.

[619] (אָדָם *'adam*) Strong's H120.

[620] (עָבַד *` abad*) Strong's H5647.

[621] Strong's H127.

[622] (אֵד *'ed*) Strong's H108, mist, exhalation, vapor, fog *cf.* Akkadian 𒂊𒁺 *edu*

[623] (עָלָה ` *alah*) Strong's H5927.
[624] Merton, *The Sign of Jonas. The Journal of Thomas Merton, February* 7, 1950, p. 273.
[625] Gilgamesh, p. 114, composed around XVIII century BC.
[626] <Simonelli, *Beyond Immortality*, p. 77>.
[627] (שָׁקָה *shaqah*) Strong's H8248.
[628] *Bible*, John 4:14
[629] (יָצַר *yatsar*) Strong's H3335 (Gesenius 3).
[630] (אָדָם *'adam*) Strong's H120.
[631] (אָדָם) Strong's H119.
[632] (אֲדָמָה *'adamah*) Strong's H127.
[633] Genesis 25:30. אדם *'Edom* from אָדֹם *'adom* = red.
[634] (עֵשָׂו `*esav*) Genesis 25:25. `*Esav* (עֵשָׂו) from the past participle of `*asah* (עָשָׂה) = handling.
[635] עבד ` *abad* to serve, to be subject, Genesis 25:23.
[636] In Sanskrit, the name Āruṇi derives from *aruṇa*, which means red, ruddy as the radiant (*rāj*) morning light (*rajas*) in opposition to the darkness (*tamas*) of the night. Royal Purple is the esoteric color of king (*rāj*) garments. Yama (Death) himself is traditionally "dressed in blood-red garments" (*W.* p. 845a.) In the Arthurian saga, at the vigil of Pentecost, when all the fellowship of the Round Table were come unto Camelot" (Malory, *La mort...*, book XIII, Ch. I, p. 223) and the knights were in the midst of a darkened sleep, young Galahad appeared, to sit in his Siege Perilous." He was dressed "in a coat of red sendal [fine cloth], and ... a mantle ... furred with ermine" (Malory, *La mort...*, book XIII, Ch. IV, p. 228) like the traditional colors of the unconditional gift-giver Bishop Saint Nicholas or the Norse gods Odin and red-haired Thor (*cf.* Woodbridge, *Black and White and Red*, p. 274. *Cf.* Federer, *There Really ...*, "red cap," p. 41. *Cf.* Cioffari, *S. Nicola...*).
[637] *W.* p. 86b *aráṇi*, two woods, the male upper one and female the lower one, *cf. UK* IV.8 (II.I.8) and *UMaitrī* VI.24.
[638] Genesis 3:24.
[639] (נָפַח *naphach*) Strong's H5301 to breathe, to blow.
[640] (נְשָׁמָה *nĕshamah*) Strong's H5397 breath, spirit.
[641] (חַי *chay*) Strong's H2416.
[642] (רוּחַ *ruwach*) Genesis 1:2, Strong's H7307 (the wind, breath, mind, spirit), from the verb רִיחַ *ruwach* to breathe, Strong's H7306.
[643] Genesis 1:26-27.
[644] *unaqēḇāh* (female) זָכָר וּנְקֵבָה *zāḵār* (male).
[645] (רֶגֶל *regel*) Strong's H7272, Ezekiel 1:7.
[646] (מֶרְכָּבָה *merkabah*) Strong's H4818. Blumrich (*The Spaceships of Ezekiel*) "offered a creative but misplaced effort to translate the metaphorical biblical account into a properly engineered spacecraft" (Clark, *The UFO Book: Encyclopedia of the Extraterrestrial*, p. 57).
[647] Carbonara, *Introduzione alla filosofia*, p. 75, "*non deve pensar di pensare ... perchè ... é presente a se stesso, senza bisogno di mediarsi, cioè di vedersi dinanzi a sè medesimo come oggetto del proprio conoscere.*" See also the research of Daniel Sanchez (SRI International - Menlo Park, CA) on subliminal passwords for quantum computers embedded in the unconscious mind of muscle memory. The stored information *is known*, through music playing, *without the mind knowing it* (PBS Thirteen, PBS NOVA *Rise of the Hackers*).
[648] (תַּרְדֵּמָה *tardemah*) Strong's H8639, *cf.* Genesis 15:12.
[649] Song of Songs 5:2.
[650] Rumi, *Bridge to the Soul,* Asleep and Listening, p. 87.
[651] Dement, *Some Must Watch* ..., p. 26.
[652] Genesis 31:40.
[653] Ezekiel 1:4.
[654] Fire (אֵשׁ *'esh*) Strong's H784.
[655] Taking hold of itself (לָקַח *laqach*) Strong's H 3947.
[656] Tononi, *Consciousness as Integrated Information* (IIT).
[657] <Simonelli, *Beyond Immortality*, p. 25.>
[658] (חֲלוֹם *chalowm*) Strong's H2472; *cf.* Genesis 20:3.
[659] Dement, *Some Must Watch ...*, p. 25-26. Dr. William C. Dement, founded the "Sleep Research Center" at Stanford University.
[660] Ezekiel 1:4.
[661] Great dreamy (עָנַן `*anan*) Strong's H6049.
[662] Cloud (עָנָן ` *anan*) Strong's H6051.
[663] Ezekiel 1:4.
[664] Living spirit wind (רוּחַ *ruwach*) Strong's H7307.
[665] Hidden (צָפַן *tsaphan*) Strong's H6845.
[666] North-heaven (צָפוֹן *tsaphown*) Strong's H6828.
[667] (אוֹפָן *'owphan*) Ezekiel 1:16, Strong's H212.
[668] Ezekiel 1:16.
[669] רוּחַ *ruwach*.

[670] Ezekiel 1:12.

[671] See one of the many sculptured *Mask of Death & Rebirth*, replica of a Mayan sculpture and collage representing the three stages of NREM, REM and Wakefulness, 900 AD, Tikal, Mexico. The central mask has the mouth open as pronouncing the letter **A**, indicating wakefulness; the next one has the mouth semi-open as articulating the letter **U**, indicating dream (REM); the third mask has the lips closed as sounding the letter **M**, indicating dreamless-sleep (NREM). *Cf.* the *Māṇḍūkya Upanishad*s sound **AUM** ॐ.

[672] In Egypt, "Dreams were accounted for... as actual happenings." Mackenzie, *Egyptian, Myth And Legend*, p. 83. *Cf.* Nova, *The Dream Stela of Thutmosis IV.*

[673] *Cf. Historia Deorum Fatidicorum, Hermes Mercurius Trismegistus*, p. 37.

[674] See *UM, Māṇḍūkya Upanishad. Cf.* Simonelli, *Beyond Immortality*, pp. 58-86.

[675] Philonis, *Operum Omnium, De Somnis* II.

[676] On this topic, see Simonelli, *Beyond Immortality*, pp. 183 fol.

[677] See Genesis 20:3,6; 31:10,11,24; 37:5,6,9,10; 40:5,8,9,16; 41:7,8,11,12,15,17,22,25,26,32; Numbers 12:6; Judges 7:13,15; 1Kings 3:5,15; Job 20:8; 33:15 Psalm 73:20; 126:1; Ecclesiastes 5:31; Isaiah 29:71; Jeremiah 23:28; Daniel 2:3,4,5,6,7,9,26,28,36,45; 4:6,7,8,9,18,19; 7:1; Joel 2:28.

[678] (חֲלוֹם) Strong's H2472.

[679] (חֲלֹם) Strong's H2492.

[680] See Genesis 2:21; 15:12; 1Samuel 26:12; Job 4:13; 33:15; Proverbs 19:15; Isaiah 29:10; Daniel 8:18; 10:19.

[681] (תַּרְדֵּמָה) Strong's H8639.

[682] (רָדַם) Strong's H7290.

[683] (נָסַךְ *nacak*) Strong's H5258, Gesenius p. 553 (1).

[684] Isaiah 29:10-11.

[685] Collage, Michelangelo, *Sistine Chapel,* creation detail and collage (c. 1510) Vatican City. Public domain https://commons.wikimedia.org/wiki/File:Creaci%C3%B3n_de_Ad%C3%A1m.jpg. *Cf.* Meshberger, *An interpretation of Michelangelo's Creation of Adam Based on Neuroanatomy*, demonstrates that Michelangelo portrayed the Creator standing in the brain in the cranium, *cf.* Buonarroti, *Selected Poems*, Rime XV (v4) p. 68, "the hand that obeys to the intellect" *La man, che obbedisce all' intelletto.*

[686] תָּוֶךְ *tavek.*

[687] אֵשׁ *'esh.*

[688] Illuminating (נָגַהּ *nagahh*) Strong's H5050.

[689] Brightness (נֹגַהּ *nogahh*) Strong's H5051.

[690] All-encompassing it (סָבִיב *cabiyb*) Strong's H5439.

[691] עַיִן *`ayin* Strong's H5869.

[692] Polished shining substance (חַשְׁמַל *chashmal*) Strong's H2830, *cf.* also Ezekiel 1:27.

[693] Ezekiel 1:4.

[694] מַרְאֶה *mar'eh* Strong's H4758.

[695] Ezekiel 1:28.

[696] *Cf.* offensive and superficial web sites as Toptenz, *10 Possible Locations for the Garden of Eden.*

[697] (שָׁם *sham*) Strong's H8033.

[698] (קֶדֶם *qedem*) Strong's H6924.

[699] (נָטַע *nata`*) Strong's H5193.

[700] (גַּן *gan*) Strong's H1588.

[701] (עֵדֶן *`eden*) Strong's H5731. Same as עֶדֶן *`eden*, Strong's H5730, delight, from עָדַן *`adan*, Strong's H5727, to delight oneself.

[702] *vayāśem* (placed), root שׂוּם *suwm* or שִׂים *sîym*, Strong's H7760.

[703] Strong's H5730 or H5731.

[704] Strong's H5727.

[705] עדן Gesenius.

[706] Nehemiah 9:25 (highlighting is ours).

[707] Latin *vegetare*, to grow, animate, flourish, enliven, from *vegēre*, to excite, incite, to be alive, active, from *vegetus*, enlivened, active, vigorous, awaken.

[708] *Cf.* IAC, *Glossary of Conscientiological Terms.*

[709] Strong's H8432.

[710] *Cf.* Marder, *Plant-thinking: a philosophy of vegetal life*, p. 9.

[711] (חַי *chay*) Strong's H2416.

[712] (מָגֵן דָּוִד *māḡēn dāwīḏ*) *Māgen Dāwīd* "Shield of David" (in *Babylonian Talmud*, Pesahim 117 b) and also seal of Solomon.

[713] Ca. 1280 AD, [Num.], 148b [Et, V, 203] as quoted by Goodenough, *Jewish Symbols...*, IV, 92-3; in Campbell, *The Mythic Image*, pp. 192-3.

[714] (דַּעַת *da`ath*) Strong's H1847.

[715] *Torah*, Plaut. *The Torah*, p. 30, n.17, pp. 38-39 and 1539 n. 19. *Cf.* Krašovec, *Der Merismus*, 33 and Honeyman, *Merismus*, p. 11-18.

[716] <Simonelli, *Awareness*, p. 23.>

[717] Strong's H1847.
[718] Strong's H3045.
[719] יָדַע Gesenius (1).
[720] Kant, *Prolegomena to any future metaphysics*, §22.
[721] Shakespeare, *Hamlet*, Act III, Scene I, p. 63.
[722] *Cf.* Christian Forums, *Marijuana the Tree of Knowledge of Good & Evil?* Or other hallucinogen plants?
[723] Daniel 12:4; (stop סָתַם *catham* Strong's H5640), (words דָּבָר *dabar* Strong's H1697), (seal חָתַם *chatham* Strong's H2856), (book סֵפֶר *cepher* Strong's H5612), (time עֵת 'eth Strong's H6256), (end קֵץ *qets* Strong's H7093), (many רַב *rab* Strong's H7227), (run to and fro שׁוּט *shuwt* Strong's H7751), (knowledge דַּעַת *da`ath* Strong's H1847; from יָדַע *yada`* Strong's H3045 to know, perceive), (multiply רָבָה *rabah* H7235).
[724] *Cf.* the injunction to multiply in *Genesis* 1:22.
[725] Bow drill, https://en.wikipedia.org/wiki/Bow_drill, File:Bow Drill with annotations.jpg, Creative Commons Attribution 3.0 Unported license. Cf. *VṚ* III.29.2 and *UK* IV.8 (II.I.8) "*The All-knower, placed within both fire-sticks, like a fetus well borne by pregnant women,* [is] *the Fire-of-knowledge (agni) praised by the awakened persons offering oblations, day after day. Verily, this* [One, in the fourth state, is] *That* [Supreme Self]."
[726] Perhaps, this could have inspired the "*to and fro*" of the rubbing lamp (as a mind, *cf.* "*The light of the righteous rejoiceth: but the lamp of the wicked shall be put out,*" Proverbs 13:9) of the tale of Aladdin (علاء الدين *'Alā' ad-Dīn, = faith's nobility*, *cf.* the *Tales from the Thousand and One Nights*). *Cf.* also ***U.B.***, I, 2, 2, where Death labored on the solidified froth of the secondary waters that had become the earth. As he exerted himself and was heated (*tapta*) by the flame-of-awareness (*tapas*), a fire (*agni*) was generated.
[727] Strong's H4150, from יָעַד *ya`ad*, Strong's H3259, to define, *cf.* Genesis 18:14.
[728] *Beginning* Strong's H7225.
[729] Strong's H7305, *cf.* Genesis 32:16.
[730] *Heaven* Strong's H8064.
[731] *Created*, Strong's H1254, *cf.* Genesis 1:1, as the First-Uncaused-Cause (*cf.* Thomas Aquinas, *Summa theologiae* Part 1, Question 2, Article 3).
[732] *Cf.* *UB* I.2.1-4.
[733] *Cf.* *UK* I.5 (I.I.5).
[734] *Talks with Sri Ramana Maharshi*, p. 59 (16th June 1935) and Ramana Maharshi, *The Spiritual Teaching...*, pp. 4(8) and 23(9).
[735] *The Power of Now*, p. 11.
[736] *Bible*, Matthew, 5:28.
[737] <Simonelli, *Beyond Immortality*, p. 186.>
[738] <Simonelli, *Beyond Immortality*, p. 67.>
[739] Husserl, *The crisis of European sciences...*, Part IIIB, §57-58, pp. 202-4.
[740] Strong's H5104.
[741] Strong's H7218.
[742] (נָהָר *nahar*) Strong's H5104.
[743] (נָהַר) Strong's H5102.
[744] Ezekiel 1:5,6,9,11,17.
[745] (פִּישׁוֹן *piyshown*) Strong's H6376.
[746] (פּוּשׁ *puwsh*) Strong's H6335.
[747] Ezekiel 1:4.
[748] (חֲוִילָה *chaviylah*) Strong's H2341 (some identify this land with India). Probably from חול *chuwl* Strong's H2342, to twist, whirl, dance.
[749] Daniel 12:4.
[750] *Cf.* *Bible*, Matthew 25:24.
[751] Strong's H3603, Gesenius, *cf.* Exodus 25:39.
[752] (זָהָב *zahab*) Strong's H2091.
[753] <Eli Luminosus, *Liber Mutus Loquitur*, p. 143.>
[754] Not in the Hebrew or Latin texts.
[755] זָהָב Gesenius (2).
[756] North, as we will see from its relation with the other three rivers.
[757] An Italian expression goes, "*Il mattino ha l'oro in bocca*" (literally: morning has gold in the mouth) equivalent to the proverb, "The early bird catches the worm."
[758] (שֹׁהַם *shoham*) Strong's H7718, onyx?
[759] (אֶבֶן *'eben*) Strong's H68, which derives from בָּנָה *banah.*
[760] (בָּנָה *banah*) Strong's H1129.
[761] Gum-resin, like myrrh, Strong's H916.
[762] *Cf.* *Bible*, John 19:39-40.
[763] (בְּדֹל *badal*) Strong's H914, Gesenius (2).

[764] The three wise men and the babe. Neapolitan nativity figurines (*Pastori napoletani del settecento*).
[765] *Bible*, Matthew 2:1, 11-12
[766] Strong's H3568.
[767] (גִיחוֹן *giychown*) *Gihon* = bursting forth, Strong's H1521, from the verb גִּיחַ *giyach* = to burst forth (Strong's H1518).
[768] (כּוּשׁ *kuwsh*) Strong's H3568, כּוּשׁ *cush* = black, Ethiopia.
[769] (חִדֶּקֶל *chiddeqel*) Strong's H2313.
[770] (אַשּׁוּר *'ashshuwr*) Strong's H804.
[771] (אֲשֶׁר) Strong's H833.
[772] (פְּרָת pěrath) Strong's H6578.
[773] (הָלַךְ *halak*) Strong's H1980.
[774] (קדמה *qidmah*) Strong's H6926. From קֶדֶם *qedem* (Strong's H6924) *beginning* Gesenius (1). From קָדַם *qadam* (Strong's H6923) *comes before*, Gesenius (Hiphil. 1).
[775] Strong's H3947.
[776] Gesenius לָקַח (1a).
[777] Strong's H3240, "["a spurious root"] ... see ... root נוּחַ" (Gesenius).
[778] נוּחַ Strong's H5117.
[779] מַנִּיחַ ... לִישׁוֹן *maniyaḥ ... liyšvōn*, Ecclesiastes 5:12.
[780] (עָבַד ` *abad*) Strong's H5647.
[781] (שָׁמַר *shamar*) Strong's H8104.
[782] Strong's H6086. *Cf.* Sanskrit, *asthi* bone, kernel of fruit, (*W.* 122c) & Latin *hasta*, pole.
[783] Strong's H6095, Gesenius.
[784] Proverbs 16:30.
[785] *Cf.* עֵצָה Gesenius 1&2.
[786] Polizzi, *Wired For Tribe.* "*The Sacred Science* stems from a calling to honor, preserve, and protect the ancient knowledge and rituals of the indigenous peoples of the world."
[787] *Cf.* Philpot, *The Sacred Tree*, p. 169.
[788] Philpot, *The Sacred Tree*, p. 4.
[789] Budge, *The Egyptian Book of the Dead,* p. 104.
[790] Public Domain, *Kabbalistic Tree of Life with emanations* (*Səphîrôṯ*) *and paths in Hebrew*, (Kaplan tr., *The Bahir*, Fig. 10, p. 155), File:Tree of life bahir Hebrew.svg, https://en.wikipedia.org/wiki/Bahir. *Cf.* Armstrong, *A History of God*, pp. 245-246.
[791] Dan, *Kabbalah*, pp. 21-22. *Cf.* Kaplan tr., *The Bahir [*. Also *Sefer HaBahir* (סֵפֶר הַבָּהִיר) "*Book of the Brightness.*"
[792] Micah 4:4. *Cf.* Zechariah 3:10. "Said of those who lead a tranquil and happy life" (Gesenius תְּאֵנָה).
[793] *Cf.* Philpot, *The Sacred Tree*, p. 115)
[794] *UK* II, 3, 1.
[795] *Cf. BG* 15:1 fol.
[796] *Cf.* Parpola, p. 30fol.
[797] Named *sahasrāra chakra* (wheel on the crown of the head), *cf.* Simonelli, *Beyond Immortality*, p. 198.
[798] *Cf.* (Philpot, *The Sacred Tree*, p. 114.
[799] *Cf.* (Fagan, *The Seventy Great Mysteries of the ancient World*, p. 138.
[800] *Cf.* (*La divina commedia, Purgatorio,* 22,131-4 & 140-1)
[801] *Cf. Argonautica* 2.448-90.
[802] *Cf.* 3.45-6.
[803] *Cf.* Ovid, *Metamorphoses,* I: 452-567. More recently, the metaphor continues. Dante describes bleeding and talking "strange trees," *alberi strani* (*Inferno* XII,15). Giovanni Boccaccio narrates about Idalogo, a man in the tree who speaks "from the woods" (*Il Filocolo*). Ludovico Ariosto describes a voice coming out of a tree "as a log ... set to fire" *Come ceppo ... / posto al fuoco* (*L'Orlando furioso* VI, 27-28). Torquato Tasso describes blood gushing out from a tree with the voice of Clorinda sounding as "an indistinct painful moan" *un indistinto gemito dolente* (*La Gerusalemme liberata* XIII, 41). Finally, Carlo (Collodi) Lorenzini tells the well-known fairy tale of Pinocchio (*Le avventure di Pinocchio*), the fantastic story of a marionette shaped out of that "talking" or "bleeding" wood (*cf.* Simonelli, M. *The Redemption of the 'Supernatural Wood' in Italian Literature*).
[804] *Cf.* Genesis 3:7.
[805] Including the *Ten Commandments, cf.* Exodus 20:1-17 & Deuteronomy 5:4-21.
[806] Strong's H398.
[807] <Simonelli, *Awareness*, p. 160.>
[808] Gesenius אָכַל (1h).
[809] Jeremiah 15:16.
[810] Ezekiel 2:8 & 3:1.
[811] Revelation 10:9-10.
[812] Strong's H1847.
[813] Strong's H3045.

---

[814] *Cf.* Sartre, *Being and Nothingness*, p. 257.
[815] *Cf.* Genesis 16:12.
[816] *Tree of the Siren* (Farkas-Simon, *Camilla*).
[817] *Cf. Sein zum Tode*, Heidegger, *Being and time*, II, I, H. 235-267, pp. 279-311.
[818] *BG* 3.30 *sarvāṇi* (all) *karmāṇi* (actions) *saṃnyasyā-* (having abandoned) *dhyātma-* (Supreme Self) *cetasā* (with consciousness) / *nirāśīr* (without any desire) *nirmamo* (free from all worldly attachments) *bhūtvā* (being) ... *vigata-* (desisting from) *jvaraḥ* (affliction)... //
II.48 *yogasthaḥ* (in a state of unified yoga) *kurū* (perform) *karmāṇī* (actions) *saṃgaṃ* (attachment) *tyaktvā* (having rejected *siddhayasiddhayoḥ* (in success in non success) *samo* (same) *bhūtvā* (be).
Cf. "*yóga m.* (√1. *yuj* ...) the act of yoking... a yoke... (*W.* p. 856b &) *yuj*... to join , unite... *cf.* Gk [Greek]... ζυγὸν [*zugon*]; Lat.[in] ... *jugum*" (*W.* p. 853b) yoke.
[819] *Bible*, Matthew 11:29-30. ζυγόν *zugon* yoke, *cf.* Sanskrit "*yuj*... to join , unite... *cf.* Gk [Greek]... ζυγὸν [*zugon*]; Lat.[in] ... *jugum*" (*W.* p. 853b) yoke &. "*yóga m.* (√1. *yuj* ...) the act of yoking... a yoke... (*W.* p. 856b). "ye shall find (εὑρήσετε *ἀνάπαυσιν* from εὑρίσκω *heuriskō*) rest (ἀνάπαυσις *anapausis* from ἀναπαύω *anapauō*)."
[820] *I computer non potranno mai replicare in tutto e per tutto la complessità della mente umana*, says the Italian physicist Federico Faggin, 1971 inventor of the microchip, ANSA.it, *Il padre del microchip*. On the other hand, it is thanks to the research on Artificial Intelligence that it has been possible to reach a breakthrough on how the human brain is capable to recognize human faces (*Cf.* Poggio, *View-Tolerant Face Recognition and Hebbian Learning Imply Mirror-Symmetric Neural Tuning to Head Orientation*).
[821] Cellan-Jones, *Stephen Hawking warns artificial intelligence could end mankind.*
[822] (בַּד *bad*) Strong's H905, from the verb *badad* (בָּדַד) to withdraw, be separate, be isolated, Strong's H909.
[823] *Cf.* Campbell, *Biology: Concepts and Connections.*
[824] *Cf.* Pliny the Elder (23 – 79), *Naturalis Historia*, Chapter XI, and the Italian XV century bestiary, Berruerio, *Libellus De Natura Animalium*, among others.
[825] Cohen, *Animals as Disguised Symbols in Renaissance Art*, p. 7.
[826] *Bible*, Matthew 10:16.
[827] Latin: *ex* (out of) *volvēre* (to roll).
[828] Petrarca (1304 – 1374), *Il Canzoniere, Solo e pensoso*, sonetto XXXV.
[829] Latin: *cum* (together) + *pati* (to suffer), *cf.* passion, Greek**:** πάθος *pathos*, suffering.
[830] *Bible*, Matthew 13:47.
[831] Mother Teresa, *A Call to Mercy*, Prayer, p. 47.
[832] Strong's H3335.
[833] Strong's H127.
[834] Strong's H119.
[835] Collective word, Strong's H120.
[836] Strong's H3334.
[837] Strong's H3331.
[838] (נֶפֶשׁ *nephesh*) Strong's H5315, Gesenius (3). From נָפַשׁ *naphash* Strong's H5314, *to take breath.*
[839] (חַי *chay*) Strong's H2416, from the verb חָיָה *chayah*, Strong's H2421.
[840] (עוֹף ` *owph*) Strong's H5775.
[841] (עוּף ` *uwph*) Strong's H5774, to fly, (Qal) to cover, be dark.
[842] קָרָא qara' Strong's H7121, Gesenius (2ac).
[843] Strong's H8034.
[844] (קָרָא *qara'*) Strong's H7121.
[845] Wheeler, *Bhor ...*, pp. 17&24.
[846] Strong's H7121.
[847] Gesenius קָרָא (1d).
[848] Strong's H7122.
[849] Strong's H8034.
[850] Strong's H7760.
[851] Strong's H2416.
[852] Strong's H2421.
[853] Strong's H2331. In the Sanskrit literature, they are called *īndriya*: the knowledge-faculties (*jñān-endriya*), the perception-organs (*buddh-īndriya*) and the action-faculties (*karm-endriya*), *cf.* Simonelli, *Beyond Immortality*, p. 47.
[854] Gesenius קָרָא (1d).
[855] Bargellini, P. (2008) *I Fioretti di Santa Chiara*, Capitolo 17: *Il cantico delle creature*, 12, "*il corpo, ch'egli chiamava 'frate asino.*"
[856] *Cf.* Genesis 22:3, חֲמוֹר *chamowr* Strong's H2543, Gesenius. Red like the color of Adam's land.
[857] John 21:15,16,17.
[858] John 21:15 ἀγαπᾷς *agapas* (lovest thou) με *me* (me) πλεῖόν *pleion* (more than) τούτων *toutōn* (these)?.
[859] John 21:17, πάντα *panta* (all things) οἶδας *oidas* (knows).
[860] Strong's H929, "(coll of all animals... of domestic animals)."

[861] Strong's H7704. "From an unused root meaning to spread out."
[862] In the Sanskrit literature, it is called the Field (*ksetra*) of conscience and Field-knower (*kshetrajña*). *Cf.* UŚ. VI.16.
[863] Strong's H5774.
[864] Strong's H5775.
[865] Strong's H8064.
[866] Strong's H929, "from an unused root (probably meaning to be mute)."
[867] Strong's H4672.
[868] *Cf.* Gesenius מָצָא 3.
[869] Strong's H5828.
[870] Strong's H5826.
[871] Neruda, *The Wind on the Island*, in "*4 poemas de Pablo Neruda...*," Poema 15," "VIII," "*El viento en la isla. /// El viento es un caballo:/ óyelo cómo corre/ por el mar, por el cielo.// Quiere llevarme: escucha / cómo recorre el mundo/ para llevarme lejos.*"
[872] (תַּרְדֵּמָה *tardemah*) Strong's H8639.
[873] (יָשֵׁן *yashen*) Strong's H3462.
[874] Strong's H5462.
[875] Strong's H1320.
[876] Strong's H1319.
[877] (צֵלָע *tsela`*) Strong's H6763.
[878] Strong's H1129.
[879] *Cf.* Altus, *Liber Mutus*, Plate 15, detail.
[880] (אִשָּׁה *'ishshah*) Strong's H802.
[881] (בּוֹא *bow'*) Strong's H935.
[882] (אֵשׁ) Strong's H784.
[883] (אִשֶּׁה) Strong's H801 similar meaning of אֶשָּׁה *'eshshah*, Strong's H800.
[884] Strong's H6471.
[885] (אִשָּׁה *'ishshah*) Strong's H802.
[886] Strong's H376.
[887] Strong's H582.
[888] Strong's H605.
[889] Strong's H6106.
[890] Strong's H6105.
[891] Gesenius עֶצֶם 1.
[892] The *rebis* (double-thing) holding the philosophical stone/egg (postcard from Trismosin, *Splendor Solis*, 1532-1535 illuminated manuscript, Prussian State Museum, Berlin).
[893] *Cf.* Khunrath, *Anfiteatro...*, Tavola 9. Pietra filosofale – III, detail.
[894] <Eli Luminosus Aequalis, *Mutus Liber*, p. 37.>
[895] (נְקֵבָה) Female, Strong's H5347, from *naqab* (נָקַב).
[896] נָקַב *naqab*, to separate, to distinguish, Strong's H5344 (Gesenius 2).
[897] (עָזַב *` azab*) Strong's H5800; cf. *Bible*, Matthew 19:5.
[898] (אָב *'ab*) Strong's H1.
[899] (אֵם *'em*) Strong's H517.
[900] *Bible*, Matthew 19:29.
[901] (עָרוֹם) Strong's H6174.
[902] (עָרַם) Strong's H6191.
[903] Carbonara, *Introduzione alla filosofia*, p. 75.
[904] (בּוּשׁ *buwsh*) Strong's H954 (Gesenius 2), applied to the mind means "confused."
[905] Strong's H3045.
[906] Strong's H2029. *Cf.* Genesis 4:1.
[907] (נָחָשׁ *nachash*) Strong's H5175.
[908] (עָרוּם *` aruwm*) Strong's H6175.
[909] (שָׂדֶה *sadeh*) Strong's H7704.
[910] Gesenius פְּרִי (1) פְּרִי *pěriy* Strong's H6529 fruit of the ground or of action, offspring, from פָּרָה *parah* Strong's H6509, to bear fruit or consequences.
[911] Maspero G., *La Pyramide*, p. 61, Pyramid of Unas (2366-2336 BC), V Egyptian Dynasty, in Budge, *Book of the Dead*, p. lvi.
du (he) *ām nef* (hath eaten) *såa* (the knowledge) *en* (of) *neter* (god) *neb* (every).
[912] Maspero, *Études de Mythologie*, p. 344, n. 1, Pyramid of Pepi I (2332-2283 BC), VI Egyptian Dynasty, in Budge, *Book of the Dead*, p. lxxi.
[913] *Cf.* *UMaitrī* VI, 10 (*prakṛ*).
[914] <Simonelli, *Beyond Immortality*, p. 51.>

[915] 爲無爲 *wei wu wei,Tao Te Ching,* 6 (43).

[916] *Bible*, I Corinthians 7:30.

[917] (נָגַע *naga`*) Strong's H3060 c, = to touch the heart, to move the mind of someone.

[918] *Bible*, Ephesians 5:15-16, βλέπετε *blepete* (see) οὖν *oun* (then) πῶς *pōs* (that) κριβῶς *kribōs* (circumspectly) ριπατεῖτε *peripateite* (ye walk) μὴ *mē* (not) ὡς *ōs* (as) ἄσοφοι *asophoi* (fools) ἀλλ' *all'* (but) ὡς *ōs* (as) σοφοί *sophoi* (wise)/ ἐξαγοραζόμενοι *exagorazomenoi* (restoring) τὸν *ton* (the) καιρόν *kairon* (present-proper-time) ὅτι *oti* (because) αἱ *ai* (the) ἡμέραι *ēmerai* (days) πονηραί *ponērai* (evil) εἰσιν *eisin* (are)

[919] Friedlander, *The History and Philosophy of the Jewish Religion*, p. 269.

[920] Numbers 11:34; קִבְרוֹת הַתַּאֲוָה *qibrowth hat-ta'avah* (Strong's H6914) from the fem. pl. of קֶבֶר *qeber* "grave" (Strong's H6913) and קָבַר *qabar* "to bury" (Strong's H6912); & תַּאֲוָה *ta'avah* "desire" (Strong's H8378) with the article interposed, from אָוָה *'avah* (abbrev) "to desire" (Strong's H183).

[921] *Bible*, Luke 6:41.

[922] (מוּת *muwth*) Strong's H4191. *Cf.* Sanskrit मृ *mṛ* to die (W. p. 827b).

[923] Skull, Ivory, Asia, 43147 Morris Museum NJ.

[924] Wilde, *The Picture of Dorian Gray*. In the novel, his portrait ages, while Dorian remains always young.

[925] In Latin, *cogito ergo sum.* Descartes, *Discourse on Method*, pp. 34-35 (IV).

[926] *Cf.* Sanskrit, मृत्यु *mṛtyu* death, English, *mortality*, Hebrew, *maveth* מָוֶת death.

[927] *UB* I.2.1. (composed around the beginning of first millennium B.C.) *āsīt* (was) *mṛtyuna-* (by death) *iv-* (verily) *edam* (this) *āvṛtam* (concealed) *āsīt* (was) *aśanāyayā* (by hunger) *aśanāyā* (hunger) *hi* (because) *mṛtyuḥ* (death) *tan* (this) *mano* (the mind) *kuruta* (he projected) *ātmanvī* (a being for-itself) *syām* (let me be) *iti* (thus). *Cf.* Damasio, *Self Comes to Mind. Upanishad* (sitting down at the master's feet) a collection of 108 Indian sacred texts.

[928] *BU* I.2.5 "*kanīyo'* (very small) *nnaṃ* (food) *karishya* (I will accomplish) *iti* (thus)."

[929] Πάτερ *Pater* (Father) ἡμῶν *ēmōn* (our) ὁ *o* (Who) ἐν *en* (in) τοῖς *tois* (the) οὐρανοῖς *ouranois* (Heavenly Transcendent),... μὴ *mē* (not) εἰσενέγκῃς *eisenegkēs* (lead) ἡμᾶς *ēmas* (us) εἰς *eis* (in) πειρασμόν *peirasmov* (tempting experience), *Bible*, Matthew 6:6,13 & Luke 11:2,4. Emphasis is ours.

[930] Experimentation πειρασμός *peirasmos* (commonly translated as temptation).

[931] *Cf. Bible,* Matthew 26:44.

[932] *Bible*, Matthew 26:41 and Mark 14:38, be aware, pay attention γρηγορέω *grēgoreō*, from ἐγείρω *egeirō* to arouse from the sleep of death; experience πειρασμός *peirasmos*, from πειράζω *peirazō to experiment.*

[933] *Bible*, Mark 14:38, be aware, watch (*Greek Text*: γρηγορεῖτε *grēgoreîte*, *Vulgate*: vigilate), pray (*Greek Text*: προσεύχεσθε *proseúchesthe*, *Vulgate*: orate), temptation (πειρασμόν *peirasmón*).

[934] *Cf.* Descartes, *Discours de la méthode...*, IV.

[935] Hegel, *Philosophy of Right*, p. 18.

[936] *Bible*, Matthew 26:75.

[937] Eli Luminosus Aequalis, *Mutus Liber Loquitur*, pp. 189 fol.

[938] <Simonelli, *Beyond Immortality*, p. 233.>

[939] *Bible*, Luke 18:1.

[940] Nominative: adjective *mălus* (m), *măla* (f), ***mălum*** (n) = evil. Substantive ***mālum*** (n) = apple (*cf.* Cupaiuolo, *Grammatica Latina*).

[941] *Cf. Vedānta-Sūtra,* II.1.14, vol. I p. 324.

[942] (יָדַע *yada`*) Strong's H3045.

[943] (רִיק *riyq*) *cf.* Exodus 20:7. Taken נָשָׂא *nasa'* (Strong's H5375), empty רִיק *riyq* (Strong's H7385), from רִיק *ruwq* (Strong's H7324), to empty out.

[944] Psalm 78:41.

[945] See Freeman, *The Story of God, Episode 1: Beyond Death.*

[946] *Cf.* Cicero, *De natura deorun*, Liber III.

[947] Aramaic רַעְיוֹן Strong's H7476.

[948] רַעְיוֹן Strong's H7475.

[949] רָעָה Strong's H7462.

[950] רָעָה Gesenius (3).

[951] רְעוּת Strong's H7469, Gesenius.

[952] *UMu.* III.2.7. *devāś-* (senses) *ca* (and) *sarve* (all) *prati-* (in corresponding) *devatāsu* (deities) *karmāṇi* (the deeds) *vijñānamayaś-* (intellectual) *ca* (and) *ātmā* (self) ... *bhavanti* (they become).

[953] *UC.* III.13.1. *tasya* (of this) *ha vā-*(verily) *etasya* (here) *hṛdayasya* (heart) *pañca* (five) *deva-*(gods) *sushayaḥ* (channels).

[954] (פָּקַח *paqach*) Strong's H6491.

[955] Augustine, *Confessions,*1.1.1 "*inquietum est cor nostrum donec requiescat in te Domine.*"

[956] Jung, *Psychology and Alchemy*, pp. 299-300 (underlining is ours).

[957] Cf. Eli Luminosus Aequalis, *Mutus Liber Loquitur*, pp. 17, 26, 40, 187, 191, 199.

[958] *Bible*, Matthew 4:2.

[959] Campbell, *The Hero with a Thousand Faces*, p. 1.

[960] *Bible*, Matthew 17:20-21 (underlining is ours) & Mark 9:29. On June 27, 28 and 29, 1981, the Virgin Mary told the seers at

Medjugorje (Bosnia Herzegovina) that to obtain peace was necessary fasting with bread and water. On July 21, 1982, the Queen of peace declared, "*Fast and prayer can block also war*" (our translation, Laurentin, *La Vergine appare a Medjugorje?*, pp. 95, 96, 97).

[961] *Bible*, Matthew 19:26.

[962] *Bible*, Mark 9:23.

[963] *Cf.* Paramahansa Yogananda, *Autobiography of a Yogi*, pp. 148-49, 196-98. Also Valtorta, *Il Poema dell'Uomo-Dio*, vol. 1, p. 30.

[964] *Bible*, Matthew 4:3. *Cf.* Yama tempting Naciketa in *UK* I.23 (I.I.23) fol. & Māra-Namuci, Death the Destroyer tempting the Buddha in *Sutta Nipāta* (Descending String) III.2 *Padhāna Sutta* (The Great Exertion String) vv. 425 *fol. Cf.* also the *Jātaka* stories. Compare to the figure of Naciketa [*UK* I.29 (I.I.29)] the Unknown. He is the one who is not an eater, *i.e.* "*who does not know*" (*VṚ* X.129.7) (comparable to Abel) and, at the same time, his own twin brother (comparable to Cain), the *knower* who, always hungry for knowledge, eats but is never satisfied, because he does not know the self-in-itself. *Cf.* Simonelli, *Beyond Immortality*, pp. 146-151.

[965] *Bibl.e*, Luke & Matthew 4:4.

[966] *Bible*, Matthew 4:6 & Luke 4:11.

[967] Aristotle, *Metaphysics*, 980a[21], (I,1). πάντες ἄνθρωποι τοῦ εἰδέναι ὀρέγονται φύσει.

[968] *Bible*, Matthew 4: 7 & Luke 4:12 fol.

[969] Dreifus, *A Conversation with Stephen Hawking.*

[970] *Bible*, James 4:4.

[971] aKempis, III.34.2 p. 191 "*quelli che si dilettano nella carne ... si trova... in questa la morte.*"

[972] Genesis 2:17.

[973] *Bible*, Matthew 4:8-9.

[974] *Bible*, Matthew 4:10-11 & Luke 4:12 fol.

[975] Freud, *New Introductory...*, p. 139.

[976] *Cf.* Campbell, *The Power of Myth*, p. 5-6.

[977] *Cf. Cf. UB* I. 1. 1 & 2. 3. *Cf. UK* III.3-10 (I.3.3-10), Simonelli, *Una lettura della Bṛhadāraṇyaka Upanishad*, & *The World as the Upanishadic sacrificial-horse*, & *Beyond Immortality...* p. 95, & *La morte nella Bṛhadāraṇyaka Upanishad e Śatapatha Brāhmaṇa*, & *Sacred Topography ...*, p. 1404. & Awareness, p. 66; & Parti, *Dying to Wake Up.*

[978] <Simonelli, *Beyond Immortality*, pp. 146-7.>

[979] (רָאָה) Strong's H7200 to discern.

[980] (אָכַל *'akal*) Strong's H398.

[981] טוב towb Strong's H2896.

[982] מַאֲכָל Strong's H3978.

[983] תַּאֲוָה Strong's H8378.

[984] עַיִן Strong's H5869.

[985] (חָמַד *chamad*) Strong's H2530.

[986] (לָקַח *laqach*) Strong's H3947.

[987] שָׂכַל sakal Strong's H7919.

[988] (חָמַד *chamad*) Strong's H2530.

[989] Exodus 20:17 & Deuteronomy 5:21.

[990] Strong's H2530.

[991] Strong's H3605.

[992] Strong's H7453 *neighbor*, for the sense of *thought* see רֵעַ Gesenius (2).

[993] Lucas Cranach the Elder, *Adam und Eva im Paradies* (*Sündenfall*), 1532, detail Gemäldegalerie, Berlin (Public Domain).

[994] (תַּאֲוָה *ta'avah*) Strong's H8378.

[995] (מַאֲכָל *ma'akal*) Strong's H3978.

[996] (שָׂכַל *sakal*) Strong's H7919 (Gesenius 2).

[997] (לָקַח *laqach*) Strong's H3947.

[998] (אָכַל *'akal*) Strong's H398.

[999] (נָתַן *nathan*) Strong's H5414

[1000] *Cf. luwl* לול *winding stair* Strong's H3883.

[1001] Freud, *The standard edition...*, *Beyond the Pleasure Principle*, pp. 36 and 38.

[1002] Leviticus 23:1-2, 5-6.

[1003] *Cf.* Garr, *Passover, The Festival of Redemption.*

[1004] *Cf.* Darwin, *The origin of species.*

[1005] *Cf.* Hans Christian Andersen, *The Emperor's New Clothes*, and similar tales from Spain to India (D. L. Ashliman), where no one dares to state that they do not see his outfit.

[1006] Gesenius בּוֹשׁ.

[1007] (עָלָה *`alah*) Strong's H5927.

[1008] (תְּאֵנָה) Strong's H8384.

[1009] And the same Gematria number of 456 (5 *h*)ה, (50 *n*)נ, (1 *a*)א, (400 *t*)ת equal to וימת *muwth,* die (Strong's H4191) Genesis 5:5.

[1010] (תַּאֲנָה) Strong's H8385.

1011 (אָנָה) Strong's H579.
1012 (דַּעַת *da`ath*) Strong's H1847.
1013 (יָדַע) Strong's H3045.
1014 Genesis 4:1.
1015 (תָּפַר *taphar*) Strong's H8609.
1016 Watts, *The Tao of Philosophy*, p. 10.
1017 (שָׁמַע *shama`*) by ears, Strong's H8085.
1018 Strong's H1980.
1019 (פָּנָה *panah*) Strong's H6437.
1020 (קוֹל *qowl*) Strong's H6963. *Cf.* John, "*like the sound of many waters,*" [ὡς *ōs* (like) φωνὴ *phone* (sound) ὑδάτων *udatōn* (of waters) πολλῶν *pollōn* (many)] (*Bible*, Revelation 1:15).
1021 Ezekiel 1:24.
1022 (חָבָא *chaba'*) Strong's H2244.
1023 (פָּנִים *paniym*) Strong's H6440.
1024 גָּנַן Strong's H1598.
1025 גַּן Strong's H1588.
1026 Rumi, *The Essential Rumi*, The Guest House p. 109.
1027 *Cf.* Payne, *SILENT THUNDER: In the Presence of Elephants.*
1028 *UM.* 8, *so'yam-* (this) *ātmādhyaksharam-* (Self above all syllables) *oṅkāro* (the sacred and mystical syllable AUM) *dhimātraṃ* (regarding the metrical measures) *pādā* (quadrants) *mātrā* (metrical letters) *mātrāś-* (metrical letters) *ca* (and) *pādā* (quadrants) *akāra* (letter A) *ukāro* (letter U) *makāra* (letter M) *iti* (thus).
1029 *sādhu*'s *ḍāmara* (copper and leather, India-Nepal, 19th century); *cf.* Balfour, *The cyclopædia of India*, p. 881. *& W.* p. 430b, "*ḍāmara*... surprising... lord... N. of... śiva-" Drum with two sides, used for ritual sound offering worship and to announce the *sādhu*'s (wondering monk) begging round.
1030 Genesis 1:3 יְהִי אוֹר.
1031 Rundle-Clark, *Myth and Religion*, p. 63. *Cf. Pyramid Texts* §1098 *fol.*
1032 Genesis, 2:20. שֵׁם *shem.*
1033 McGrath, *A Revolutionary of Arabic Verse.*
1034 *Cf. W.* 1052c "*śabda* ... sound , noise , voice , tone , note... (taught to be eternal)... a word... speech , language... the sacred syllable Om... verbal communication or testimony , oral tradition, verbal authority or evidence (as one of the *pramāṇa*)"
1035 *Bible*, Revelation, 3:14 τάδε λέγει ὁ ἀμὴν ὁ μάρτυς ὁ πιστὸς καὶ ἀληθινός ἡ ἀρχὴ τῆς κτίσεως τοῦ Θεοῦ.
1036 *UKai.* 18 (*sākshī cin-mātraḥ*).
1037 *W.* p. <u>235</u>c "*óm ind.* (√*av* ... originally *oṃ* = *āṃ*, which may be derived from *ā*) 96a "*av* ... to drive ... animate (as a car or horse) ... to promote , to favor ... to satisfy ... to offer (as a hymn to the gods) ... to lead ... (said of the gods) to be pleased with... accept favorably (as sacrifices , prayers or hymns)... defend , protect ... devour." 146a "*āṃ* ... interjection of assent or recollection." 126a "*ā* ... particle of reminiscence."
1038 *Cf.* Macdonell, *A Sanskrit Grammar*, p. 11, 19, a, & Gonda, *Sanskrit grammar*, p.13, II. According to the rules of *Sandhi* (puttin toghether), in Sanskrit the coalescence of the vowels <u>*a*</u> or <u>*ā*</u> merge with <u>*u*</u> or <u>*ū*</u> becoming <u>*o*</u>. *E.g.:* *c<u>a</u>* (and) *<u>u</u>ktam* (said) becomes: *c<u>o</u>ktam.*
1039 *W.* <u>785</u>c. Listen: Holst, *Choral Hymns from the Rig Veda...*
1040 <Simonelli, *Beyond Immortality*, pp. 79-80.>
1041 Exodus 19:16, 19. יוֹבֵל *yowbel, trumpet, ram's horn,* (Strong's H3104), the bleating of a lamb, from יָבַל *yabal to be brought, to be led, to be conducted* (Strong's H2986 & cf. Isaiah 53:7), also *to flow, to walk* (Gesenius 1, 3), from which derives the Latin *jubilaeus*, meaning jubilee. Ram's horn also called *shofar* שׁוֹפָר, which is blown on the Jewish New Year, *Rosh HaShanah.*
1042 *Bible*, Revelation 1:10, σάλπιγξ *salpigx*, trumpet.
1043 *Cf.* Goodson, *Therapy, nudity & joy*, § Nudity in Ancient to Modern Cultures.
1044 *UB.* I.4.2. *tasmād* (therefore) *ekākī* (alone) *bibheti* (is afraid)]... (3) *sa* (he) *dvitīyam* (a second) *aicchat* (desired) *sa* (he) *haitāvān āsa* (extended) *yathā* (as) *strī-*(woman) *pumāṃsau* (man) *samparishvaktau* (in a loving embrace) *sa* (he) *imam* (this) *evātmānaṃ* (self) *dvedhā-* (in two parts) *pātayat* (divided) *tataḥ* (from that) *patiś* (the ruler, husband) *ca* (and) *patnī* (the possessor, wife) *cābhavatām* (and they became)]... (4) *tiro'sānīti* (let me hide myself)."
1045 Dante, *Inferno*, I,58, "*bestia senza pace.*"
1046 *UB* III.4.2. *na* (not) *dṛshṭer* (see) *drashṭāram* (the seer) *paśyeḥ* (of seeing) / *na* (not) *śruter* (hear) *śrotāraṃ* (the hearer) *śṛṇuyāḥ* (of hearing)/ *na* (not) *mater* (think) *mantāraṃ* (the thinker) *manvīthāḥ* (of thinking) / *na* (not) *vijñāter* (understand) *vijñātāraṃ* (the understander) *vijānīūyāḥ* (of understanding)/ *esha* (this) *ta āītmā* (your Self) *arvāntaraḥ* (in everything).
1047 *The Babylonian Talmûd: Tractate Berâkôt* (Benedictions) ..., I:10a p. 60.
1048 Kahlil Gibran, *Sand and Foam. Cf. UKa.Br.* III.2.3; *UKe* II.1 to 3.
1049 *Cf.* Ovid, *Metamorphoses,* III:402-436.
1050 *Cf.* Sartre, *L'étre et le néant*, p. 29: "*un étre pour lequel il est dans son étre question de son étre en tant que cet étre implique un étre autre que lui.*"

[1051] <Simonelli, *Beyond Immortality*, p. 116.>
[1052] Jung , *Psyche and Symbol*, p. 132.
[1053] Exodus 6:3, וּשְׁמִי יְהוָה לֹא נוֹדַעְתִּי לָהֶם: (**ידע** *yada* = to know, perceive, discern, discriminate, distinguish, know by experience, recognize, to be revealed) and 33:20, 23.
[1054] (עֵירֹם ` *eyrom*) Strong's H5903.
[1055] (יָרֵא *yare'*) Strong's H3372.
[1056] Exodus, 3:6.
[1057] (צָוָה *tsavah*) Appointed, constitute, caused to exist, Strong's H6680,1.
[1058] Shakespeare, *Hamlet*. Act II, scene II, 245.
[1059] *Bible*, Matthew 6:24; *cf.* Luke 16:13.
[1060] *Bible*, Luke 16:9-11.
[1061] Aramaic for riches, treasure.
[1062] *Bible*, Luke 16:15.
[1063] *Bible*, Matthew 19:23. *Cf.* "*Through wealth there is no hope for immortality*," *UB* IV.5.3 *amṛtatvasya* (immortality) *tu* (but) nāśāsti (is no hope) *vittene-* (with wealth) *ti* (thus).
[1064] *Bible*, John 12:35.
[1065] *Bible,* John 12:35-36 "be certain" (πιστεύετε *pisteúete, credite*); light (φῶς *phōs*).
[1066] *Bible*, Luke 1:76.
[1067] *Bible*, Mark 9:37, Luke 18:17.
[1068] Declares St. Francis of Assisi the "Juggler of God," *I fioretti*, cap. VIII, p. 34. "*non è ivi perfetta letizia.*" *Cf.* Paul, *Bible*, 1 Corinthians 13:1-3.
[1069] <Simonelli, *Awareness*, pp. 160-2.> This intuitive Self-Awareness in different languages is named as: *spiritual-insight, gnosis*-γνῶσις, *khok·mä*-חכמה, *ma`rifah*-معرفه, *shinākht*-شناخت, *jñāna*-ज्ञान etc.
[1070] *Bible*, Luke 11:34, *cf.* Matthew 6:22.
[1071] *Bible*, Galatians 5:13.
[1072] (עִמָּד ` *immad*) Strong's H5978.
[1073] (נָתַן *nathan*) Strong's H5414.
[1074] נָשָׁא (*nasha'*) is "kindred to the verb נָשָׁה [*nash*] to forget" Gesenius, נָשָׁא.
[1075] (נָשָׁא *nasha'*) Strong's H5377, to go astray, to deceive.
[1076] (נָחָשׁ) Strong's H5175.
[1077] (נָחַשׁ) Strong's H5172.
[1078] (Strong's H1966) from הָלַל *halal* as brightness (Strong's H1984) to shine, *cf.* Isaiah 14:12.
[1079] (שַׁבָּת) *Cf.* Simonelli, *Awareness*, p. 160.
[1080] (גָּחוֹן *gachown*) Strong's H1512.
[1081] (גִּיחַ *giyach*) Strong's H1518.
[1082] (אָרַר *'arar*) Strong's H779.
[1083] Strong's H6083. Gesenius, עָפָר (b).
[1084] *Triumph of Death* (detail) 1562 Pieter Brueghel the Elder (1525 –1569) Museo del Prado, Public Domain File:Thetriumphofdeath.jpg, https://en.wikipedia.org/wiki/The_Triumph_of_Death#/media/File:Thetriumphofdeath.jpg
[1085] מָשִׁיחַ mashiyach, *the anointed one*, Strong's H4899 (*cf.* Daniel 9:25,26); from מָשַׁח *mashach, to anoint,* Strong's H4886.
[1086] Abbey of Solesmes, *The Liber Usualis*, The Paschal Praise, p. 935, *O felix culpa quae talem et tantum meruit habere redemptorem.*
[1087] Augustine, *The Augustine Catechism: The Enchiridion on Faith*, VIII.
[1088] *Cf.* Watson, *The Dead Sea Scrolls.*
[1089] Not surprisingly, the American Church of Satan added to their symbol the message "The Greatest Gift is Knowledge." (Burns, *Satanists, Christians compete…*).
[1090] (שָׂטָן) *satan* Strong's H7854, adversary, from שָׂטַן *satan* Strong's H7853 "*lier in wait*" Gesenius.
[1091] Job 1:7,12.
[1092] Strong's H7751.
[1093] Strong's H1980, akin to יָלַךְ *yalak* (Strong's H3212), to walk.
[1094] Strong's H3027, hand, power.
[1095] *Cf.* the serpent feeding on itself (Chevalier, *Dictionnaire*, 3, 339).
[1096] (עָקֵב ` *eqeb*) Strong's H6118.
[1097] (אָיַב *'ayab*) Strong's H340.
[1098] (גִּיחַ *giyach*) Strong's H1518.
[1099] (עָקֵב ` *aqeb*) Strong's H6119.
[1100] (זֶרַע *zera`*) Strong's H2233.
[1101] (שׁוּף *shuwph*) Strong's H7779.
[1102] Detail of *Ouroboros*, Michael Maier (1569-1622).
[1103] Numbers 21:6,8-9

[1104] נָסַס *nacac,* Strong's H5264.
[1105] נָחָשׁ *nachash*, Strong's H5175.
[1106] נֵס *nec,* Strong's H5251.
[1107] שָׂרַף *saraph*, Strong's H8314. Gesenius II.
[1108] נָבַט *nabat*, Strong's H5027.
[1109] נְחֹשֶׁת *nĕchosheth*, Strong's H5178.
[1110] נָחַשׁ *nachash*, Strong's H5172.
[1111] רָאָה *ra'ah*, Strong's H7200, Gesenius.
[1112] חַיִּי chayay, Strong's H2425.
[1113] *Cf.* Matthew 26:26, Mark 14:22, Luke 22:19.
[1114] *Cf.* Matthew 26:28, Mark 14:24, Luke 22:20.
[1115] *Bible*, John 6:54.
[1116] However, "The pain of childbirth may have benefits on which women who opt for painkilling epidurals miss out, a senior male midwife has said. Dr Denis Walsh, associate professor in midwifery at Nottingham University, said pain was a "*rite of passage*" which often helped regulate childbirth. He said it helped strengthen a mother's bond with her baby, and prepared her for the responsibility of motherhood" (BBC, *Pain in childbirth 'a good thing'*).
We may add that probably this bond may manifest also in the future as preference among siblings. One born of *natural* childbirth may be preferred over the one born with painkilling epidurals.
[1117] (עִצָּבוֹן *`itstsabown*) Strong's H6093.
[1118] (עֶצֶב *`etseb*) Strong's H6089.
[1119] (תְּשׁוּקָה *tĕshuwqah*) Strong's H8669.
[1120] (שׁוּק *tĕshuwqah*) Strong's H7783.
[1121] *Cf. Dasein*, in Heidegger, *Being and Time*, p.68.
[1122] CSS. *Bhagavan Sri Ramana Maharshi.*
[1123] Tolle, *Practicing the Power of Now*, § 2.
[1124] Eliade.
[1125] Eliade, (Italian) *Lo sciamanesimo e le tecniche dell'estasi*, , p 41.
[1126] Isaiah 38:13.
[1127] Tolle, *Practicing the Power of Now*, § 2, pp. 129 fol.
[1128] *Crete, Labyrinth of Knossos*, reverse of Greek AR Stater coin (320-300 BC); the obverse (not shown) portrays Apollo.
[1129] Strong's H1121.
[1130] (הֵרָיוֹן *herown*) Strong's H2032.
[1131] (יָלַד *yalad*) Strong's H3205.
[1132] (בָּנָה *banah*) Strong's H1129.
[1133] (מָשַׁל *mashal*) Strong's H4910.
[1134] (אִישׁ *'iysh*) Strong's H376.
[1135] (קוֹל *qowl*) Strong's H6963 (Gesenius 3).
[1136] (שָׁמַע *shama`*) Strong's H8085.
[1137] (שָׂדֶה *sadeh*) Strong's H7704.
[1138] (קוֹץ *qowts*) Strong's H6975.
[1139] (קוֹץ *qowts*) Strong's H6976.
[1140] (דַּרְדַּר *dardar*) Strong's H1863.
[1141] (עֵשֶׂב `eseb) Strong's H6212.
[1142] (קוּץ *quwts*) Strong's H6974.
[1143] (קוּץ *quwts*) Strong's H6973b.
[1144] (קוּץ *quwts*) Strong's H6972.
[1145] (עָפָר *` aphar*) Strong's H6083.
[1146] (שׁוּב *shuwb*) Strong's H7725.
[1147] *VR* X.135.7. *idaṃ* (here) *yamasya* (of Death) *sādanaṃ* (house), *cf. TB* III.XI.8.4 & *UK* I.7 (I.I.7), or "house of the dead" (Simonelli, *Beyond Immortality*, pp. 130, 133, or city of the dead.
[1148] "*Tuat, the place of departed souls*" (Budge, *The Egyptian Book of the Dead...*, p. civ. And *Coffin Text* 714, & Rundle-Clark, *Myth and Religion,* p. 74).
[1149] (זְעָה *ze`ah*) Strong's H2188.
[1150] (זוּעַ) Strong's H2111.
[1151] (אַף *'aph*) Strong's H639. From next
[1152] (אָנַף *'anaph*) Strong's H599, Gesenius.
[1153] <Simonelli, *Awareness*, p. 31.>
[1154] *Cf.* Ovid, *Metamorphoses*, Book 1: Deucalion and Pyrrha.
[1155] Consider that in a vacuum, the speed of light is approximately 186,282 miles per second (*cf.* NASA, *General Physics: Waves – Light and Sound*). However, the fastest speed is not that of light, but it is the speed of the present. In fact, it would not matter how far one may travel back and/or forth in time, if it were possible, one would end up always in the Present.

Therefore, *time travel*, as such, can never be. The ultimate time machine is this body which lands us always here in the present. What would change is a new experience perceived as relative past and/or future supported by the memory we would have of our original port of departure.

[1156] Australian independent source of views and news, Prof. Schawinski, *Is our Milky Way galaxy a zombie, already dead and we don't know it?*

[1157] *Cf.* Stanford Report, *New evidence from space.*

[1158] *Bible*, John 8:58.

[1159] (אם *'em*) Strong's H517.

[1160] (חַוָּה *chavvah*), Strong's H2332.

[1161] Gesenius, חַוָּה *Chavvah* Strong's H2332.

[1162] חָוָה Strong's H2331; Gesenius.

[1163] Aramaic חֲוָא *chava',* Strong's H2324.

[1164] חָיָהStrong's H2421.

[1165] (שְׁאֵר *shĕ'er*) Strong's H7607 (Gesenius 2 & 3), *cf.* flesh: Psalm 78:20 and food: Exodus 21:10.

[1166] (כְּתֹנֶת *kĕthoneth*) Strong's H3801.

[1167] (עוֹר *` owr*) Strong's H5785.

[1168] (לָבַשׁ *labash*) Strong's H3847.

[1169] <Eli Luminosus Aequalis, *Mutus Liber Loquitur*, p. 40.>

[1170] (יָדַע *yada`*) Strong's H3045 (Gesenius 3).

[1171] (שָׁלַח *shalach*) Strong's H7971.

[1172] (עָבַד *` abad*) Strong's H5647.

[1173] *Cf.* Homer, *Odyssey.*

[1174] Virgil, *Vergili Maronis Aeneis*, 1.3, "*multum ille et terris iactatus et alto.*"

[1175] Genesis 2:9.

[1176] *Torah*, Plaut. *The Torah*, p. 30, n.17.

[1177] *Exodus* 3:2.

[1178] <Simonelli, Beyond Immortality, p. 197.>

[1179] *Exodus* 3:14.

[1180] 2Samuel 22:11.

[1181] Ezekiel 1:5 & 10

[1182] Strong's H6924, from the verb *qadam* (קָדַם)(Strong's H6923) to be in front.

[1183] Tetramorph, 16th century fresco at Meteora (Greece), public domain:
http://www.nsad.ru/index.php?issue=48&section=10019&article=1062
https://commons.wikimedia.org/wiki/File:Tetramorph_meteora.jpg

[1184] אָדָם *'adam* (Strong's H120). From the next entry

[1185] אָדַם *'adam* (Strong's H119), to sparkle (Gesenius).

[1186] אֲרִי *'ariy* (Strong's H738). From the next entry

[1187] אָרָה *'arah* (Strong's H717) (Gesenius).

[1188] שׁוֹר *showr* (Strong's H7794) (Gesenius). From the next entry

[1189] שׁוּר *shuwr_* (Strong's H7788) (Gesenius).

[1190] נֶשֶׁר *nesher (Strong's* H5404).

[1191] Exodus 19:4.

[1192] *Bible*, Revelation 12:14.

[1193] Strong's H4150.

[1194] Strong's H2677.

[1195] Daniel 12:5-7,11-12.

[1196] תָּמִיד *tamiyd* Strong's H8548, continuity, perpetuity, to stretch, continuously (as adverb), continuity (subst).

[1197] 1290 Gematria = Job 15:17. אֲחַוְךָ שְׁמַע־לִי וְזֶה־חָזִיתִי וַאֲסַפֵּרָה = 1(א,*a*)+8(ח,*ḥ*)+6(ו,*w*)+20(ך,*ḵ*)+300(ש,*ś*)+40(מ,*m*)+70(ע,*'a*)+30(ל,*l*)+10(י,*y*)+6(ו,*w*)+7(ז,*z*)+5(ה,*h*)+8(ח,*ḥ*)+7(ז,*z*)+10(י,*y*)+400(ת,*ṯ*)+10(י,*y*)+6(ו,*w*)+1(א,*a*)+60(ס,*ṣ*)+80(פ,*p̄*)+200(ר,*r*)+5(ה,*h*).

[1198] 1335 Gematria = Jeremiah 13:3 וַיְהִי דְבַר־יְהוָה אֵלַי שֵׁנִית לֵאמֹר = 6(ו,*w*)+10(י,*y*)+5(ה,*h*)+10(י,*y*)+4(ד,*ḏ*)+2(ב,*ḇ*)+200(ר,*r*)+10(י,*y*)+ 5(ה,*h*)+6(ו,*w*)+5(ה,*h*)+1(א,*a*)+30(ל,*l*)+10(י,*y*)+300(ש, *ś*)+50(נ,*n*)+10(י,*y*)+400(ת,*ṯ*)+30(ל,*l*)+1(א,*a*)+40(מ,*m*)+200(ר,*r*)

[1199] 1335 Gematria = Isaiah 63.11. בְּקִרְבּוֹ אֶת־רוּחַ קָדְשׁוֹ = 2(ב,b)+100(ק,*q*)+200(ר,*r*)+2(ב,*ḇ*)+6(ו,*w*)+1(א,*a*)+400(ת,*ṯ*)+200(ר,*r*)+6(ו,*w*)+8(ח,*ḥ*)+100(ק,*q*)+ 4(ד,*ḏ*)+300(ש,*ś*)+6(ו,*w*).

[1200] *Cf.* NASA, *The Pull of HyperGravity.*

[1201] *Cf.* IAU, *IAUC 4315: N Cen 1986; V822 Cen (CENTAURUS X-4); Corr.*

[1202] Carnegie Institution for Science (CIS) in the Southern Chilean Atacama Desert.

[1203] *Cf.* Murch, *Prediction and retrodiction for a continuously monitored superconducting qubit.*

[1204] נָבָא *naba'* Strong's H5012, Gesenius. *Cf.* Parapsychological Association, Inc., "the international professional organization of scientists and scholars engaged in the study of 'psi' (or 'psychic') experiences, such as telepathy, clairvoyance, remote viewing, psychokinesis, psychic healing, and precognition... Promoting scholarship and scientific inquiry into currently unexplained aspects of human experience."
[1205] *Cf.* Mbiti, *African Religions and Philosophy*, pp. 28-29, 31 and 33.
[1206] Ancestral worship, family altar, private house, Cuzco, Peru, 1990.
[1207] *Bible*, 1John 3:1-3 ὀψόμεθα *opsometha* (from ὀπτάνομαι *optanomai,* ὀπτάνω *optanō*, I see) αὐτὸν *auton* καθώς *kathōs* ἐστιν *estin*.
[1208] *Cf.* Kerr, *I Love You... Who are You?*
[1209] (הָרָה *harah*) Strong's H2029.
[1210] (יָלַד *yalad*) Strong's H3205.
[1211] אִישׁ 'iysh Strong's H376, Gesenius 2. Contracted for אֱנוֹשׁ 'enowsh, *man* (Strong's H582).
[1212] Strong's H605.
[1213] It is like the Indian Sanskrit term *śakti*, meaning, "power, ability, strength... regal power... the energy or active power of a deity personified as his wife... creative power or imagination... help, aid, assistance, gift (*W.* p. 1044b).
[1214] *Cf. Bible*, Luke 7:37-fol. & 8:2.
[1215] *Cf.* Pius XII, *PIUS EPISCOPUS SERVUS SERVORUM DEI AD PERPETUAM REI MEMORIAM CONSTITUTIO APOSTOLICA MUNIFICENTISSIMUS DEUS FIDEI DOGMA DEFINITUR DEIPARAM VIRGINEM MARIAM CORPORE ET ANIMA FUISSE AD CAELESTEM GLORIAM ASSUMPTAM,* (39), "*absorpta est mors in victoria*" (*1 Cor.* 15, 54)."
[1216] <Simonelli, *Beyond Immortality*, pp. 33-4.>
[1217] יָדַע *yada`* Strong's H3045.
[1218] (קַיִן *Qayin*) Strong's H7014.
[1219] (קָנָה *qanah*) Strong's H7069.
[1220] עָבַד ` *abad* Strong's H5647.
[1221] אֲדָמָה *'adamah* Strong's H127.
[1222] (הֶבֶל *Hebel*) Strong's H1893.
[1223] Josephus, *Jewish Antiquities*, 1, 54.
[1224] Strong's H1892. Abel בָּהַל "breath" (Plaut, *Torah*, p. 44, n. 2).
[1225] (הָבַל *habal*) Strong's H1891.
[1226] *Cf. UC. Chāndogya Upanishad* V.1.6, "the senses disputing who was superior among them recognized that vital breath the best" and *UB* I.3; I.5.21. Also Zipes, *Aesop's Fables, The Belly and the Members*, p. 84. & Menenius Agrippa's 494 BC "apology" in Livy, II. 16, 32, 33.
1227 (רֵעָה *ra`ah*) Strong's H7462.
[1228] Strong's H6629.
[1229] See *Genesis* 2:19.
[1230] (קֵץ *qets*) Strong's H7093, contracted from קָצַץ *qatsats*, Strong's H7112, to cut off.
[1231] Homer, *Odyssey*, IX,118-123. "Whosoever of them ate of the honey-sweet fruit of the lotus, had no longer any wish to bring back word or to return, but there they were fain to abide among the Lotus-eaters (λωτοφάγοι *lōtophagoi*), feeding on the lotus, and forgetful of their homeward way."
[1232] Isaiah 1:11.
[1233] *Bible*, John 19:28.
[1234] (שָׁעָה *sha`ah*) Strong's H8159.
[1235] Plato, *Theaetetus*, 152a.
[1236] *Cf.* Wilson, *The noble savages*, 1.
[1237] <Simonelli, *Beyond Immortality*, p. 91.>
[1238] Goodchild, *Theology of money*, p. 5. *Cf.* also Downton, *Rebel leadership*, 230 *fol. Cf.* Bentham, *Defence of Usury*.
[1239] *Institutes*, III, XIV, 2 & 19.
[1240] *Cf.* Roberts, *The Miracle of Seed Faith.*
[1241] Mario Cavaradossi: "*Muoio disperato e non ho amato mai tanto la vita*" in "*E lucevan le stelle*" (Puccini, *Tosca*, Act III).
[1242] *Cf. Sein zum Tode*, Heidegger, *Being and time*, II, I, H. 235-267, pp. 279-311.
[1243] *Bible*, Matthew 6:25-26,28,34.
[1244] *Bible*, Matthew 5:44 & Luke 6:27.
[1245] *Bible*, Luke 6:35.
[1246] *Cf.* Simonelli, *Transcendence.*
[1247] Genesis 32:30, פנואל *Pĕnuw'el* (Strong's H6439) Peniel = facing God; פנים *paniym* = (Strong's H6440) face; ראה *ra'ah* = to see; from פָּנָה *panah* (Strong's H6437) to turn, and אֵל *'el* (Strong's H410) God; shortened from אַיִל *'ayil* (Strong's H352) ram; from the same as אול *'uwl* (Strong's H193) strong man.
[1248] דבר *dabar* = to set things in order, to lead, to follow, to lay snares, to speak with one another, to put words in order.
[1249] Exodus 33:11-20. רָאָה *ra'ah* to see, perceive.
[1250] Strong's H2787.
[1251] (חָרָה *charah*) Strong's H2734.

[1252] (פָּנִים *paniym*) Strong's H6440.
[1253] (פָּנָה *panah*) Strong's H6437.
[1254] (נָפַל *naphal*) Strong's H5307 (Gesenius 1h).
[1255] *Cf.* von Hildebrand, *The Nature of Love*, p. 352.
[1256] *Cf. Bible*, Mark 9:12.
[1257] von Hildebrand, *The Nature of Love*, p. 353, n. 3.
[1258] *Bible*, Luke 15:12, "*portionem substantiae*."
[1259] *Ibid.* 20. "*cum autem adhuc longe esset vidit illum pater ipsius*."
[1260] von Hildebrand, *The Nature of Love*, p. 353. *Cf. Bible*, Matthew 26:49-50; Mark 14:18; Luke 22:48.
[1261] von Hildebrand, *The Nature of Love*, p.353.
[1262] *Bible*, Matthew 19:21. "*Si vis perfectus esse vade vende quae habes et da pauperibus et habebis thesaurum in caelo et veni sequere me*."
[1263] von Hildebrand, *The Nature of Love*, p. 356.
[1264] Deuteronomy 6:5; (*diliges*, ἀγαπήσεις, אהב *'ahab* = love); וְאָהַבְתָּ אֵת יְהוָה אֱלֹהֶיךָ בְּכָל־לְבָבְךָ וּבְכָל־נַפְשְׁךָ וּבְכָל־מְאֹדֶךָ׃ καὶ ἀγαπήσεις κύριον τὸν θεόν σου ἐξ ὅλης τῆς καρδίας σου καὶ ἐξ ὅλης τῆς ψυχῆς σου καὶ ἐξ ὅλης τῆς δυνάμεώς σου *diliges Dominum Deum tuum ex toto corde tuo et ex tota anima tua et ex tota fortitudine tua.*
[1265] Deuteronomy 4:29. *Cf.* also *Bible*, Matthew 22:37 & Mark 12:30.
[1266] Strong's H8159.
[1267] From Latin *trahere* to drag, draw, derive, acquire with prepositions *dis* (away) and *ad* (to).
[1268] Greek δαίμων *daimōn*, Latin *daemon*, spirit power.
[1269] Greek δύναμις *dynamis*, power.
[1270] Strong's H7585, γέεννα *geenna* in Greek.
[1271] "Catull. II.28.29," (Gesenius שאול), *cf.* "*malae tenebrae/ orci, quae omnia bella devoratis*" "bad darkness / of Orcus, who devour all beautiful things" (Catullus, 3, p. 8). *Cf.* "*rapacis orci*," = *rapax*, ravenous *orcus*, the dead's lower world (Horace, *Quinti Horatii Flacci Opera*, II.18.30).
[1272] Strong's H7592 & Gesenius.
[1273] Michelangelo, *Sistine Chapel, The Last Judgment*, detail, public domain Wikimedia Commons https://commons.wikimedia.org/wiki/File:Rome_Sistine_Chapel_01.jpg.
[1274] Plato, *Republic*, VII. 516a.
[1275] *Ibid.*
[1276] *Cf.* von Hildebrand, *The Nature of Love*, p. 141.
[1277] *Bible*, Matthew 6:24 and *cf.* Luke 16:13. "*Nemo potest duobus dominis servire aut enim unum odio habebit et alterum diliget aut unum sustinebit et alterum contemnet non potestis Deo servire et mamonae*."
[1278] *Bible*, Luke 14:26. "*si quis venit ad me et non odit patrem suum et matrem et uxorem et filios et fratres et sorores adhuc autem et animam suam non potest esse meus discipulus*." *hate* (μισεῖ *misei, odit*) *his own* (ἑαυτοῦ *eautou, suam*) *eigenleben* (ψυχή-ν *phsychē-n, anima-m*).
[1279] Genesis 22:2, 6, 7, 13.
[1280] Genesis 22:1 to 18.
[1281] Exodus 20:5; *cf.* 34:14; Deuteronomy 4:24; 5:9; Joshua 24:19; Nahum 1:2; Zechariah 1:14; 8:2 (קנא *qanna'*).
[1282] *Bible*, 1 Corinthians 13:4-5 (emphasis are ours).
[1283] Life = *anima-m, i.e.*: subjectivity = *eigenleben*, *cf.* von Hildebrand, *The Nature of Love*, pp. xxvii-xxx, 139, 141, 179, 194, 200-220 *passim*, 245, 255, 263 321, 362, 367n, 373-374.
[1284] *Bible*, Luke 9:24 (*salvam facere*), and Matthew 10:39 (*invenire*). *Cf.* Matthew 16:25 and Marc 8:35. "*qui enim voluerit animam suam* (i.e. : *eigenleben*) *salvam facere* (or *invenit*) *perdet illam nam qui perdiderit animam suam* (i.e. : *eigenleben*) *propter me salvam faciet* (or *inveniet*) *illam*."
[1285] *Bible*, Luke 12:22, 24, 27, 29, 34. "*nolite solliciti esse animae* (i.e.: life, *eigenleben*)*... considerate corvos quia non seminant ... et Deus pascit illos... lilia quomodo crescunt non laborant... nolite in sublime tolli... ubi enim thesaurus vester est ibi et cor vestrum erit*."
[1286] *Cf.* וְאָהַבְתָּ לְרֵעֲךָ כָּמוֹךָ אֲנִי vəʾāhabətā (love) lərēʿăḵā (neighbor) kāmvōḵā (as your) ăniy (thy own self) "*Love your neighbor as yourself*," commands Leviticus, 19:18,
[1287] *Bible*, Luke 12:31; *cf.* Matthew 6:33. "*Verumtamen quaerite regnum Dei et haec omnia adicientur vobis*."
[1288] von Hildebrand, *The Nature of Love*, p. 201.
[1289] Own (*eigen*) being in life (*leben*).
[1290] *Cf.* צלם *tselem* - εἰκών *eikÓn* – *imago* (*Genesis* 1:26).
[1291] von Hildebrand, *The Nature of Love*, p. 213; *cf.* דמות *dĕmuwth* - ὅμοιος *ómoios* – *similitude*, likeness. *Cf.* Campbell, *The Mask of God: Creative Mythology.*
[1292] von Hildebrand, *The Nature of Love*, p. 203.
[1293] von Hildebrand, *The Nature of Love*, p. 146.
[1294] *Cf.* אור *'owr* - φῶς *phōs* – *lux* (Genesis 1:3).
[1295] φῶς ἐκ φωτός *fōs ek fōtos* Apostles' Creed.
[1296] von Hildebrand, *The Nature of Love*, p. 211.

1297 *Imago Dei*, von Hildebrand, *The Nature of Love*, p. 70, 337.
1298 *Cf.* von Hildebrand, *The Nature of Love*, p. 145-6.
1299 von Hildebrand, *The Nature of Love*, p. 145.
1300 Verga, *Novelle rusticane*: *La roba*, p. 119. "*Roba mia, vientene con me!*" Compare slaves, animals and things placed in ancient royal tombs.
1301 *Cf. per speculum in enigmate* (1 *Corinthians*, 13:12).
1302 *Bible*, John, 1:9. "*lux vera quae inluminat omnem hominem venientem in mundum.*"
1303 von Hildebrand, *The Nature of Love*, p. 131.
1304 *Bible*, Matthew 19:19.
1305 See Simonelli, *Awareness*, pp. 119 fol.
1306 *UB* I.2.1. *acarat* (moved about) *tasyā-* (from him) *-rcata* (heated) *āpo'* (waters) *jāyanta* (was produced)... 2. *samahanyata* (solidified) *sā* (that) *pṛthivy* (earth) *abhavat* (became).
1307 Strong's H2734.
1308 Strong's H2787.
1309 (שְׂאֵת *sĕ'eth*) Strong's H7613.
1310 (ἡσύχασον *ēsuxason*), as translated by the *Septuagint*.
1311 *Bible*, Matthew 10:34.
1312 *Cf.* Gualtieri, *Templari in cammino.*
1313 <Simonelli, *Awareness*, p. 133.>
1314 *BG.* II.48 *yogasthaḥ* (in a state of union) *kurū* (perform) *karmāṇī* (actions) *saṃgaṃ* (attachment) *tyaktvā* (having rejected *siddhayasiddhayoḥ* (in success in non success) *samo* (same) *bhūtvā* (be).
1315 *Cf.* Gandhi, *An Autobiography: The Story of My Experiments with Truth.*
1316 *Cf.* Johnson, *India-Pakistan Relations: A 50-Year History.*
1317 *Cf.* Freud, *A Case of Hysteria.*
1318 Strong's H2403.
1319 חַטָּאת Gesenius.
1320 Strong's H2398.
1321 Proverbs 14:34.
1322 From the Sanskrit *mṛṣāya* to err, to be mistaken, to hold a wrong notion or opinion and *mṛṣ* (*mṛṣyati*), to forget, to neglect (*W.* p. 131a).
1323 Strong's H2403.
1324 (חָטָא - *chata'*) Strong's H2398.
1325 Strong's H7613.
1326 *Cf.* Freud, *On Metapsychology: The Theory of Psychoanalysis.*
1327 *Cf.* Isaiah 38:10.
1328 Dante, *La divina commedia. Inferno*, I.1-3,10-12 "*Nel mezzo del cammin di nostra vita / mi ritrovai per una selva oscura / ché la diritta via era smarrita... / Io non so ben ridir com'i' v'intrai,/ tant'era pien di sonno a quel punto /che la verace via abbandonai.*"
1329 גָּד *gad* Strong's H1409.
1330 מְנִי *mĕniy* Strong's H4507 *fate, destiny, lot-number.*
1331 From מָנָה *manah* Strong's H4487 *to destine, to allot.*
1332 Isaiah 65:11-12.
1333 Strong's H1961.
1334 *Cf.* Watts, *The Book*, p. 9.
1335 *Cf.* Aristotle, *Poetics*, XV 10b (1454b), p. 56 ἀπὸ μηχανῆς (*apò mechanês*), an actor dressed as a god was lowered on Greco-Roman theatrical stages to disentangle intricate unsolvable plots. In a similar fashion, every beginning of September, two girls in their puberty are lowered with ropes from rooftops to simulate the flights of Angels honoring the Virgin *Madonna della Milicia* at Altavilla, Sicily, Italy, in line with their ancient Greek heritage.
1336 הָיָה *hayah* Strong's H1961. Compare הָוָה *hava', to exist* Strong's H1933.
1337 היה *hayah*, Strong's H1961.
1338 Strong's H7704.
1339 (הָרַג *harag*) Strong's H2026.
1340 *Cf. UB* III.4.2.
1341 Strong's H559.
1342 Koch, *Is Consciousness Universal? Panpsychism, the ancient doctrine that consciousness is universal, offers some lessons in how to think about subjective experience today* (underlining is ours).
1343 (הָרַג *harag*) Strong's H2026 (Gesenius b). *Cf.* "*And behold joy and gladness, slaying* (הָרַג *harag*) *oxen, and killing sheep, eating flesh, and drinking wine: let us eat and drink; for to morrow we shall die.*" (Isaiah 22:13).
1344 Genesis 16:12.
1345 (שָׁמַר *shamar*) Strong's H8104.
1346 *UB* V.43.12 *indraḥ* (Indra, the Conqueror) *sa* (he) *esho'* (this no) *sapatnaḥ* (rival) *dvitīyo* (the second, the other) *vai* (verily)

sapatnaḥ (rival). *Cf. Indra = √inv + <d> + ra =* to conquer (Böhtlingk, *Sanskrit Wörterbuch* in *W.* 166). For a detail explanation of all these aspects *cf.* Simonelli, *Una lettura della Bṛhadāraṇyaka Upanishad*, pp. 383 *fol.* and *La morte nella...*, pp. 455 *fol.*

1347 *Bible*, Matthew 18:18.
1348 (דָּם *dam*) Strong's H1818.
1349 Leviticus, 17:11.
1350 (עָשָׂה ` *asah*) Strong's H6213.
1351 (קוּם *quwm*) Strong's H6965 (see 4:8).
1352 (אֵל *'el*) Strong's H413 (see 4:8).
1353 (אֱלַי *'ēlay*) Strong's H410.
1354 *Cf.* Hesiod, *Theogony*, 270-1, 3-4.
1355 Strong's H3045, Gesenius יָדַע 3(a).
1356 Strong's H398, Gesenius אָכַל (d) as in a *sacrificial banquets*.
1357 Strong's H2026, Gesenius, הָרַג (b) "*to slay for food,*" *cf.* Isaiah 22:13.
1358 *Cf. Genesis* 49:11. וּבְדַם־עֲנָבִים *ubədam 'ănābiym.*
1359 (דָּם *dam*) Strong's H1818 (Gesenius 3). *Cf. Bible*, Matthew 26:27 "*Drink ye all of it;* (28) *For this is my blood,* (Mark 14:24)... *which is shed for you.*" Luke 22:20.
1360 (אָדָם *'adam*) Strong's H119.
1361 (אָדָם *'adam*) Strong's H120.
1362 (אֲדָמָה *'adamah*) Strong's H127.
1363 *Bible*, Romans 1:20 ποιήμασιν (*poieémasin* by the things that are made) νοούμενα (*nooúmena* being understood) καθορᾶται (kathorâtai are clearly seen).
1364 Strong's H779. Gesenius.
1365 *Vedānta-Sūtra,* 28, p. 421.
1366 As already quoted, *Vedānta-Sūtra*, II.2. 28, p. 421. *Cf.* Simonelli, *Note introduttive alla gnoseologia di Šankara.*
1367 Buddha *bhūmisparśa*, detail of Tibetan votive Tsa Tsa clay tablet, Chinese Yuan Dynasty (1271-1368).
1368 The very meaningful posture of *bhūmi-sparśa*, *cf.* Warren, *Buddhism in translations...*, p. 81. *Cf. Jātaka* I.74.
1369 *Bible*, Luke 19:37-40.
1370 (כֹּחַ *koach*) Strong's H3581.
1371 (נוּעַ *nuwa`*) Strong's H5128.
1372 (נוּד *nuwd*) Strong's H5110.
1373 *Cf.* Malory, XXI, VII. "*Arthurus, Rex quondam, Rexque futurus.*" Arthur, once king and future king.
1374 (דָּם *dam*) Strong's H1818 (Gesenius 2).
1375 (עָוֹן ` *avon*) Strong's H5771.
1376 *Cf.* Sartre, *No exit, Huis Clos*, p. 45, "*L'Enfer, c'est les autres!* " (italic is ours).
1377 (פָּנִים *paniym*) Strong's H6440.
1378 *Cf. Mṛtyu-liṅga* mark of Death, of the Subject (Simonelli, *Beyond Immortality*, pp. 49 & 284).
1379 Gesenius, אות (4).
1380 *Girl before a Mirror* (Picasso 1932, detail replica).
1381 (נוֹד *nowd*) Strong's H5113.
1382 אִשָּׁה Strong's H802.
1383 אִישׁ Strong's H376.
1384 אֱנוֹשׁ Strong's H582.
1385 (חֲנוֹךְ *chanowk*) Strong's H2585.
1386 Rousseau, *Du contrat social; Principes du droit politique.*
1387 Merton, *The Sign of Jonas. The Journal of Thomas Merton, February* 7, p. 273.
1388 (עִירָד ` *iyrad*) Strong's H5897.
1389 (מְחוּיָאֵל *měchuwya'el*) Strong's H4232; from מָחָה *machah* = obliterated (H4229) and אֵל *'el* = God (H410).
1390 (מְתוּשָׁאֵל *měthuwsha'el*) Strong's H4967.
1391 *Cf.* Simonelli, *Transcendence - The Universal Quest.*
1392 (לֶמֶךְ *lemek*) Strong's H3929.
1393 *Cf.* (Multiple wives), Majeed, *Polygyny.*
1394 *Cf.* Koran, *Woman*, Sura 4, Ayah 3.
1395 (עָדָה *`adah*) Strong's H5711.
1396 (צִלָּה *tsillah*) Strong's H6741.
1397 (יָבָל yabal) Strong's H2989.
1398 אֹהֶל *'ohel* Strong's H168, Gesenius 2.
1399 (יוּבָל *yuwbal*) Strong's H3106. From next
1400 יָבַל *yabal* (Strong's H2986), Gesenius.
1401 Strong's H3658.
1402 Gesenius כִּנּוֹר.

[1403] Strong’s H5748.
[1404] Strong's H5689, Gesenius.
[1405] Campbell, *Thou Art That*, p. 6.
[1406] Strong's H8423.
[1407] Strong's H2986.
[1408] Strong's H2981.
[1409] Strong's H2986.
[1410] Strong's H7014.
[1411] Strong's H7013.
[1412] Strong's H7069.
[1413] (קַיִן *qayin*) Strong’s H8423.
[1414] (נַעֲמָה *na `amah*) Strong’s H5279.
[1415] *Cf.* AICE. (2013). *LAMECH*, "In the *Aggadah,* Most of the legends about Lamech, the grandson of Cain, center around his killing of his grandfather."
[1416] יֶלֶד Strong's H3205, Gesenius 2.
[1417] יֶלֶד Strong's H3206.
[1418] אִישׁ Strong's H376.
[1419] פֶּצַע Strong's H6482, from פָּצַע *patsa`*, Strong's H6481, to bruise, wound by bruising.
[1420] חַבּוּרָה Strong's H2250.
[1421] חָבַר Strong's H2266, Gesenius 2.
[1422] Genesis 9:6; *cf.* Matthew 26:52.
[1423] Strong's H1893,2; see also, Gesenius, *Hebrew and Chaldee lexicon*, הֶבֶל.
[1424] Ecclesiastes 6:4.
[1425] Strong’s H1892.
[1426] (הֶבֶל *habal*) Strong’s H1891.
[1427] (שֵׁת *sheth*) Strong’s H8352.
[1428] (דְּמוּת *dĕmuwth*) Strong’s H1823.
[1429] Genesis 5:1,2,3.
[1430] (אֱנוֹשׁ *'Enowsh*) Strong’s H583.
[1431] Strong’s H582.
[1432] (אֱנָשׁ) Strong’s H605.
[1433] (חָלַל *chalal*) Strong’s H2490.
[1434] Strong's H2490.
[1435] *Cf.* Pierce, *The Donatist Circumcellions*, pp. 123–133.
[1436] Marx, *Zur Kritik der Hegelschen Rechtsphilosophie*, 378, "*Die Religion ... ist das Opium des Volkes.*"
[1437] *Genesis* 1:27.
[1438] (זָכָר *zakar*) Strong’s H2145.
[1439] (נְקֵבָה *nĕqebah*) Strong’s H5347. Sometimes identified as the spirit Lilith, from *luwl* לול *winding stair* (Strong's H3883), the night (לַיִל *layil*) of objectivity, when conceived as independent or equal to its vivifying source of Awareness, becomes *liyliyth* (לִילִית, Strong’s H3917) a female screeching owl night demon (Isaiah 34:14). *Cf. The Babylonian Talmûd*, Niddah 24b & Shabbat 151b.
[1440] (אָדָם *'adam*) Strong’s H120.
[1441] Dante, *La Vita Nova*, chapter XXVI, "*Tanto gentile,*" "*dolcezza al core,* /10 *che intender non la può chi non la prova*" /11.
[1442] Notice the difference with both the Hebrew and Latin texts.
[1443] Strong's H7896.
[1444] Gesenius, שִׁית 2 & 3a.
[1445] Psalm 8:6.
[1446] *Cf.* Hill, *Making Sense of the Numbers of Genesis.*
[1447] Strong’s H8141, in plural only.
[1448] Gesenius שָׁנָה.
[1449] Strong's H8138.
[1450] Strong’s H2472.
[1451] Genesis 41:32.
[1452] Strong’s H2015.
[1453] Strong's H1305.
[1454] Strong's H8193.
[1455] Zephaniah 3:9.
[1456] Strong's H5595, Gesenius.
[1457] Strong's H8192.
[1458] Strong's H5490.
[1459] Joel 2:28 (3:1).

[1460] Indians conceived the zero (Devanāgarī: ०=0,१=1,२=2,३=3,४=4,५=5,६=6,७=7,८=8,९=9) adopted by the Arabs (Eastern: ٠=0,١=1,٢=2,٣=3,٤=4,٥=5,٦=6,٧=7,٨=8,٩=9).
[1461] See those Alphabets below.
[1462] *Cf.* Ancient Hebrew Research Center. See also the Chapter ALPHABETS *Alphabet* (*Hebrew*) at the end of this book.
[1463] *Cf.* Epstein, *Kabbalah.*
[1464] Galilei, *Assayer* VII, 232.
[1465] *Cf.* Leibniz, *The Leibniz-Clarke correspondence.*
[1466] *Cf.* Simonelli, *Transcendence*, p. 188.
[1467] In reference to the German *erlebnis* (experience), *cf.* Husserl, *Ideas* § 95, & *The Crisis.* Also, Schulte, *Erlebnis und Ausdruck.*
[1468] *Cf. BG* 14.24.
[1469] (מֵאָה *me'ah*) Strong's H3967.
[1470] (שְׁלֹשִׁים *shĕlowshiym*) Strong's H7970.
[1471] (שָׁלוֹשׁ *shalowsh*) Strong's H7969.
[1472] *Cf.* Isaiah 29:10, נָסַךְ n_ac_ak (Strong's H5258). With the *sofit* letter ך changed into its regular כ, we have, 50 (נ, *n*) + 60 (ס, *c*) + 20 (כ, *k*) =130 (כסנ *nck*), *cf.* Heidrick 130.
[1473] *Cf.* Hoffman, *The Hebrew Alphabet.*
[1474] *Cf.* Yeshshem, *HEBREW LETTER: LAMED ל.*
[1475] (קָלַל) Strong's H7043.
[1476] (שָׁנֶה *shaneh*) Strong's H8141 (word expressed only in plural).
[1477] (שָׁנָה *shanah*) Strong's H8138.
[1478] (שְׁנָה) Strong's H8139.
[1479] שְׁנָה *shĕnah (Aramaic)*, *year*, Strong's H8140.
[1480] (שֵׁנָא) Strong's H8142.
[1481] (יָשֵׁן) Strong's H3462.
[1482] (הַצָּלָה *hatsalhá* = 130) Deliverance (הַצָּלָה $h_ats_alh_á$) in Gematria = 130 [5 (ה, *h*) + 90 (צ, *ts*) + 30 (ל, *l*) + 5 (ה, *h*)], *cf.* Heidrick.
[1483] Isaiah 29:8.
[1484] *Cf.* Freud, *The Interpretation of Dreams*, in *The standard edition.*
[1485] *Cf.* Jacob (Genesis 28:12), Joseph (Genesis 37:9), Pharaoh (Genesis 41:1), Daniel 12:4,9; etc.
[1486] *Cf.* Yeshshem, *HEBREW LETTER: PEY ף פ.*
[1487] שנתים $\check{s}_ən_{\underline{a}}t_ay_im$ dual, *two years, sleep* (Strong's H8141 שָׁנֶה *shaneh*), 800 [300 (ש, *ŝ*)+ 50(נ, *n*)+ 400(ת,*t*) + + 10(י, *y*) + 40(מ, *m*)], Genesis 11:10.
[1488] Quorum number (מנין $m_iny_án$) in Gematria = 800 [40 (מ, *m*) + 50 (נ, *n*) + 10 (י, *y*) + 700 (ן, *n*)], *cf.* Heidrick.
[1489] (תֵּשַׁע) Strong's H8672.
[1490] (שָׁעָה) Strong's H8159.
[1491] *Cf.* Hoffman, *The Hebrew Alphabet.*
[1492] Gal Einai, *The Month of Shevat.*
[1493] Pouring, streaming out (לתך l_at_ak) in Gematria = 930 [30 (ל, *l*) + 400 (ת, *t*) + 500 (ך, *k*)], *cf.* Heidrick.
[1494] (אֱנוֹשׁ *'enowsh*) Strong's H583.
[1495] (חָמֵשׁ *chamesh*) Strong's H2568.
[1496] *Cf.* Ancient Hebrew Research Center.
[1497] *Cf.* Hoffman, *The Hebrew Alphabet.*
[1498] (עלה *'alhá*) Rise, develop (עלה *'alh$_á$*) in Gematria = 105 [70 (ע, *'o*) + 30 (ל, *l*) + 5 (ה, *h*)], *cf.* Heidrick.
[1499] *Cf.* Hoffman, *The Hebrew Alphabet.*
[1500] *To flow* (זרם z_er_em) in Gematria = 807 [7 (ז, *z*) + 200 (ר, *r*) + 600 (ם, *m*)], *cf.* Heidrick.
[1501] (שֶׁבַע *sheba*) Strong's H7651.
[1502] (תֵּשַׁע) Strong's H8672.
[1503] (שָׁעָה) Strong's H8159.
[1504] (שְׁנַיִם *shĕnayim*) Strong's H8147.
[1505] Strong's H8145.
[1506] (שָׁנָה *shanah*) Strong's H8138, Gesenius שָׁנָה (2).
[1507] Gal Einai, *The Month of Shevat.*
[1508] He died (וּמוֹתְתֵני $wmv_{\bar{o}}t_at_{\bar{e}}n_iy$) in Gematria = 912 [6 (ו, *w*) + 40 (מ, *m*) + 6 (ו, *w*) + 400 (ת, *t*) + 400 (ת, *t*) + 50 (נ, *n*) + 10 (י, *y*)], *cf.* Judges 9:54.
[1509] Not in the Hebrew and Latin texts.
[1510] (תִּשְׁעִים *tish`iym*) Strong's H8673.
[1511] *Cf.* Ancient Hebrew Research Center.
[1512] (קִינָן *qeynan*) Strong's H7018.
[1513] (נוֹלָד *nwōlād* = 90) 1Kings 13:2, shall be born (נולד $nw_{\bar{o}}l_{\bar{a}}d$) in Gematria = 90 [50 (נ, *n*) + 6 (ו, *w*) + 30 (ל, *l*) + 4 (ד, *d*)].
[1514] (קֵן *qen*) Strong's H7064.
[1515] שָׁנֶה *shaneh* (Strong's H8141 only plural); שָׁנָה *shanah* (Strong's H8138); שֵׁנָא *shehah* (Strong's H8142); יָשֵׁן *yashen* (Strong's

H3462); שְׁנַיִם *shĕnayim* (Strong's H8147); שֵׁנִי *sheniy* (Strong's H8145).
[1516] (קַיִן *qayin*) Strong's H8423.
[1517] *Cf.* Hoffman, *The Hebrew Alphabet.*
[1518] (תְבוּאוֹת *tabu'vōt* = 815)increase (תְבוּאוֹת *tabu'wawt*) in Gematria = 815 [400 (ת, *t*) + 2 (ב, *b*) + 6 (ו, *w*) + 1 (א, *a*) + 6 (ו, *w*) + 400 (ת, *t*)], *cf.* Proverbs 14:4.
[1519] (תֵּשַׁע) Strong's H8672.
[1520] (שָׁעָה) Strong's H8159.
[1521] Turn (תִּתְהַפֵּךְ *tithapek*) in Gematria = 905 [400 (ת, *t*) + 400 (ת, *t*) + 5 (ה, *h*) + 80 (פ, *p*) + 20 (ך, *k*)], *cf.* Job 38:14.
[1522] *Cf.* Hoffman, *The Hebrew Alphabet.*
[1523] Gal Einai, *The Month of Shevat.*
[1524] Not in the Hebrew or Latin texts.
[1525] (שִׁבְעִים *shib`iym*) Strong's H7657.
[1526] (שֶׁבַע *sheba`*) Strong's H7650.
[1527] *Cf.* Hoffman, *The Hebrew Alphabet.*
[1528] (מַהֲלַלְאֵל Mahalal'el) Strong's H4111.
[1529] Temple (הַהֵיכָל *hahaykal*) in Gematria = 70 [5 (ה, *h*) + 5 (ה, *h*) + 10 (י, *y*) + 20 (כ, *k*) + 30 (ל, *l*)], *cf.* 1 Kings 6:17.
[1530] (אַרְבָּעִים *'arba`iym*) Strong's H705.
[1531] (רָבַע) Strong's H7250.
[1532] (לְמֶמְשֶׁלֶת *lamemašelet* = 840) dominion (לְמֶמְשֶׁלֶת *lamemašelet*) in Gematria = 840 [30 (ל, *l*) + 40 (מ, *m*) + 40 (מ, *m*) + 300 n(ש, *š*) + 30 (ל, *l*) + 400 (ת, *t*)], *cf.* Genesis 1:16.
[1533] (תֵּשַׁע) Strong's H8672.
[1534] (שָׁעָה) Strong's H8159.
[1535] *Cf.* Hoffman, *The Hebrew Alphabet.*
[1536] (עָשַׁר *`ashar*) 10=עֶשֶׂר *`eser* (H8141) from עָשַׁר *`ashar* = to become rich (Strong's H6238).
[1537] Gal Einai, *The Month of Shevat.*
[1538] (יֹרֶשֶׁת *yōrešet* = 910) Possesses (יֹרֶשֶׁת *yorešet*) in Gematria = 910 [10 (י, *y*) + 200 (ר, *r*) + 300 (ש, *š*) + 400 (ת, *t*)], Numbers 36:8.
[1539] Not in the Hebrew or Latin texts.
[1540] (חזים *ḥōziym* = 65) Seer (חזים *ḥozym*) in Gematria = 65 [8 (ח, *ḥ*) + 7 (ז, *z*) + 10 (י, *y*) + 40 (ם, *m*)], *cf.* Ezekiel 22,28.
[1541] Strong's H3382.
[1542] (יָרַד) Strong's H3381.
[1543] Genesis 15:1.
[1544] *Cf.* Isaiah 6:1-3. XVII Century Italian armor.
[1545] (חָמֵשׁ *chamesh*) Strong's H2568.
[1546] (מִשְּׁנָתָם *mišanātām* = 830) Sleep (מִשְּׁנָתָם *mišanatam*) in Gematria = 830 [40 (מ, *m*) + 300 (ש, *š*) + 50 (נ, *n*) + 400 (ת, *t*) + 40 (ם, *m*)], *cf.* Job 14:12.
[1547] *Cf.* Hoffman, *The Hebrew Alphabet.*
[1548] (שֶׁהתקיף *šehataqiyp* = 895) Prevails (שֶׁהתקיף *šehataqiyp*) in Gematria = 895 [300 (ש, *š*) + 5 (ה, *h*) + 400 (ת, *t*) + 100 (ק, *q*) + 10 (י, *y*) +80 (ף, *p*)], *cf.* Ecclesiastes 6:10.
[1549] Job 14:12.
[1550] 4:26 & 5:6.
[1551] *Bible*, Matthew 7:21-23.
[1552] *Cf.* Hoffman, *The Hebrew Alphabet. Solar halo* photo, (New Jersey Shore, USA 5/14/2013).
[1553] (חָנַךְ *chanak*) Strong's H2596.
[1554] (בְּסֶלַע *bașcela`*) Rock ( בְּסֶלַע*bașcela`*) in Gematria = 162 [2 (ב, b) + 60 (ס, *șc*) + 30 (ל, *l*) + 70 (ע, *'a*)], cf. Numbers 24:21.
[1555] (מנין *minyán*) *Quorum number* (מנין *minyan*) in Gematria = 800 [40 (מ, *m*) + 50 (נ, *n*) + 10 (י, *y*) + 700 (ן, *n*)], *cf.* Heidrick.
[1556] *Cf.* Hoffman, *The Hebrew Alphabet.*
[1557] (תְּשׁוּרֶנּוּ *tašwrenw* = 962) To observe (תְּשׁוּרֶנּוּ *tašwrenw*) in Gematria = 962 [400 (ת, *t*) + 300 (ש, *š*) + 6 (ו, *w*) + 200 (ר, *r*) + 50 (נ, *n*) + 6 (ו, *w*)], *cf.* Job 20:9.
[1558] Not present in the Hebrew or Latin texts.
[1559] (מְתוּשֶׁלַח *Mĕthuwshelach*) Strong's H4968.
[1560] (מְתוּשָׁאֵל *mĕthuwsha'el*) Strong's H4967.
[1561] (חָמֵשׁ *chamesh*) Strong's H2568.
[1562] (וְנִבְּאוּ *waniba'w* = 65) Shall prophesy (וְנִבְּאוּ *waniba'w*) in Gematria = 65 [6 (ו, *w*) + 50 (נ, *n*) + 2 (ב, *b*) + 1 (א, *a*) + 6 (ו, *w*)], *cf.* Joel 2:28 (3:1).
[1563] (נָפַל *naphal*) Strong's H5307.
[1564] Numbers 24:4.
[1565] *Cf.* Nostradamus, *Nostradamus and his prophecies.*
[1566] *Cf.* Lincoln's dream, foretelling his assassination (Lamon, *Recollections of Abraham Lincoln*, CHAPTER VII, DREAMS AND PRESENTIMENTS).

[1567] *Cf.* Jung, *ETH Lecture*, V, Page 23 fol. Clairvoyance.
[1568] Different from the Hebrew and Latin texts.
[1569] Strong's H1121.
[1570] Strong's H1323.
[1571] Strong's H1129.
[1572] (הָלַךְ *halak*) Strong's H430.
[1573] (שָׁלוֹשׁ *shalowsh*) Strong's H7969.
[1574] *Cf.* Hoffman, *The Hebrew Alphabet.*
[1575] (רֹעֶיךָ *rō'ayḵā* = 300) Shepherd (רֹעֶיךָ*r*$_{\bar{o}}$*'ayḵ*$_{\bar{a}}$) in Gematria = 300 [200 (ר, *r*) + 70 (ע, *'a*) + 10 (י, *y*) + 20 (ך, *k*)], *cf.* Genesis 13:8. רָעָה *ra`ah* Strong's H7462 to shepherd of ruler, teacher.
[1576] *Cf.* Ancient Hebrew Research Center.
[1577] Psalm 23:1, 4.
[1578] *Cf.* Hoffman, *The Hebrew Alphabet.*
[1579] (חֲנוֹךְ *chanowk*) Strong's H2585.
[1580] Cf. Yeshshem, HEBREW LETTER: LAMED ל.
[1581] (יְשֵׁנָה *yašēnāh* = 365) Sleep (יְשֵׁנָה *yašēnāh*) in Gematria = 365 [10 (י, y) + 300 (ש, š) + 50 (נ, n) + 5 (ה, h)], cf. 1Kings 3:20.
[1582] מָשִׁיחַ *mashiyach* Strong's H4899, *cf.* Daniel 9:25-26, the anointed one. Χριστός Christos, from מָשַׁח *mashach* to anoint Strong's H4886.
[1583] *Bible*, Romans 1:17.
[1584] *Martin Luthers Werke*, 401, 33, 7-9.
[1585] (נָסַךְ *nacak*) Strong's H5258.
[1586] (תַּרְדֵּמָה *tardemah*) Strong's H8639.
[1587] Isaiah 29:10.
[1588] (הָלַךְ *halak*) Strong's H1980.
[1589] (לָקַח *laqach*) Strong's H3947.
[1590] (אַיִן *'ayin*) Strong's H369.
[1591] Not in the Hebrew or Latin texts.
[1592] Strong's H4962.
[1593] Strong's H4967.
[1594] Strong's H4970.
[1595] Strong's H410.
[1596] Strong's H4968.
[1597] Strong's H7973.
[1598] Strong's H7971.
[1599] (מָעוֹז *mā'uzaḵen* = 187) Strength (מָעֻזְכֶן *mā'uz*$_{a}$*ḵ*$_{e}$*n*) in Gematria = 187 [40 (מ, *m*) + 70 (ע, *'a*) + 7 (ז, *z*) + 20 (כ, *k*) + 50 (ן, *n*)], *cf.* Isaiah 23:14.
[1600] (לֶמֶךְ Lemek) Strong's H3929.
[1601] (שֶׁבַע *sheba*) Strong's H7651.
[1602] Latin, *fari* (to speak) *pro* (before) it happens.
[1603] Not in the Hebrew or Latin texts.
[1604] (תַּשְׂבִּיעַ *taśabiya* = 782) Satisfy (תַּשְׂבִּיעַ *t*$_{a}$*ś*$_{a}$*b*$_{i}$*ya*) in Gematria = 782 [400 (ת, *t*) + 300 (ש, *š*) + 2 (ב, *b*) + 10 (י, *y*) + 70 (ע, *'a*)]; *cf.* Isaiah 58:10.
[1605] (שְׁנַיִם *shěnayim*) (שָׁנָה *shanah*) Strong's H8138. *Solar halo* (New Jersey Shore, USA 5/14/2013).
[1606] (שֶׁבַע *sheba*) Strong's H7651.
[1607] (שִׁבְעִים *shib`iym*) Strong's H7657.
[1608] *Cf.* Hoffman, *The Hebrew Alphabet.*
[1609] [(נְתַתִּים *naṯatiym*) + (הַנְּבוּאָה *hanaḇw'āh*) = 969] I have given (נְתַתִּים *n*$_{a}$*ṯ*$_{a}$*t*$_{i}$*ym*) prophecy (הַנְּבוּאָה *h*$_{a}$*n*$_{a}$*ḇw'āh*) in Gematria = 969 {[50 (נ, *n*) + 400 (ת, *t*) + 400 (ת, *t*) + 10 (י, *y*) + 40 (ם, *m*)] + [5 (ה, *h*) + 50 (נ, *n*) + 2 (ב, *b*) + 6 (ו, *w*) + 1 (א, *a*) + 5 (ה, *h*)]}, *cf.* Numbers 18:8 & Nehemiah 6:12.
[1610] Not in the Hebrew or Latin texts.
[1611] (בַּעֲמָלָם *ba'ămālām* = 182) Labor (בַּעֲמָלָם *b*$_{a}$*'ăm*$_{\bar{a}}$*l*$_{\bar{a}}$*m*) in Gematria = 182 [2 (ב, *b*) + 70 (ע, *`a*) + 40 (מ, *m*) + 30 (ל, *l*) + 40 (ם, *m*)], *cf.* Ecclesiastes 4:9.
[1612] (בְּפֹעַל *bapō'al* = 182) Work (בְּפֹעַל *b*$_{a}$*p̄*$_{\bar{o}}$*'al*) in Gematria = 182 [2 (ב, *b*) + 80 (פ, *p*) + 70 (ע, *'a*) +30 (ל, *l*)], *cf.* Psalm 9:16(17).
[1613] *Cf.* Kant, C*ritique of pure reason*, § 17 Introduction.
[1614] (נֹחַ *Noach*) Strong's H5146.
[1615] (נוּחַ *nuwach*) Strong's H5118.
[1616] (נוּחַ *nuwach*) Strong's H5117.
[1617] (נָחַם *nacham*) Strong's H5162.
[1618] (יָד *yad*) Strong's H3027.
[1619] (מַעֲשֶׂה *ma`aseh*) Strong's H4639.

[1620] (עִצָּבוֹן` *itstsabown*) Strong's H6093.
[1621] Psalm 127:1-2 (שֵׁנָא *shehah*) sleep, Strong's H8142 from יָשֵׁן *yashen* to sleep Strong's H3462.
[1622] Not in the Hebrew and Latin texts.
[1623] (הָתְפָּקְדוּ *hāṯapāqaḏw* = 595) Number (הָתְפָּקְדוּ $h_{ā}\underline{t}_{a}p_{ā}q_{a}\underline{d}w$) in Gematria = 595 [5 (ה, *h*) + 400 (ת, *ṯ*) + 80 (פ, *p*) + 100 (ק, *q*) + 4 (ד, *d*) + 6 (ו, *w*)], *cf.* Numbers 1:47.
[1624] ך, final *n* = 500 is rarely used, in its place is used ת *tāw* 400 + ק *qôph* 100 instead.
[1625] Not in the Hebrew and Latin texts.
[1626] (וַתְּיַשְּׁנֵהוּ *watayašanēhu*) Sleep (וַתְּיַשְּׁנֵהוּ $w_{a}t_{a}y_{a}š_{a}n_{ē}hw$) in Gematria = 777 [6 (ו, w) + 400 (ת, *ṯ*) + 10 (י, *y*) + 300 (ש, *š*) + 50 (נ, *n*) + 5 (ה, *h*) + 6 (ו, w)], *cf.* Judges 16:19.
[1627] See the Mayan *Mask of Death & Rebirth*, sculpture representing the three stages of NREM, REM and Wakefulness.
[1628] *Cf.* Hoffman, *The Hebrew Alphabet.*
[1629] *Cf.* Hoffman, *The Hebrew Alphabet.*
[1630] (לְעֵת *la'at* = 500) Time (לְעֵת l_{a}*'aṯ*) in Gematria = 500 [30 (ל, *l*) + 70 (ע, *'a*) + 400 (ת, *ṯ*)], *cf.* Genesis 8:11.
[1631] (שֵׁם *Shem*) Strong's H8035.
[1632] (שֵׁם) Strong's H8034.
[1633] (שׂוּם) Strong's H7760.
[1634] (חָם *Cham*) Strong's H2526.
[1635] (חָם) Strong's H2525. *Cf.* Sanskrit तपस् *tapas* = warmth, heat, pain, suffering (W 437a), producer of the world of representations (*UB* I. 2. 2).
[1636] (חָמַם) Strong's H2552.
[1637] (יֶפֶת Yepheth) Strong's H3315.
[1638] (פָּתָה) Strong's H6601.
[1639] (תְּעָלַת *ta'ālaṯ*) Ascending healing channel (תְּעָלַת t_{a}*'āl*$_{a}$*ṯ*) in Gematria = 900 [400 (ת, *ṯ*) + 70 (ע, *'a*) + 30 (ל, *l*) + 400 (ת, *ṯ*)], *cf.* Isaiah 7:3, "*Then said the LORD unto Isaiah, Go forth now ... at the end of the ascending healing channel of the upper pool in the highway of the fuller's field.*"
[1640] (מניך *minyán*) Quorum number (מניך $m_{i}ny_{á}n$) in Gematria = 800 [40 (מ, *m*) + 50 (נ, *n*) + 10 (י, *y*) + 700 (ן, *n*)], *cf.* Heidrick.
[1641] (שֵׁת) Seth (שֵׁת) in Gematria = 700 [400 (ש, *ṯ*) + 300 (ת, *š*)], *cf.* Genesis 4:25.
[1642] (לְעֵת *la'aṯ*) Time (לְעֵת l_{a}*'aṯ*) in Gematria = 500 [30 (ל, *l*) + 70 (ע, *'a*) + 400 (ת, *ṯ*)], *cf.* Genesis 8:11.
[1643] (רֹעֶיךָ *rō'ayḵā*) Shepherd (רֹעֶיךָ$r_{ō}$*'ayḵ*$_{ā}$) in Gematria = 300 [200 (ר, *r*) + 70 (ע, *'a*) + 10 (י, *y*) + 20 (ך, *k*)], *cf.* Genesis 13:8.
[1644] (בָּנָה) Strong's H1129.
[1645] *Cf.* Enoch. *The Book of Enoch*, § VI.
[1646] This text does not specify between the sons of God and the daughters of Adam.
[1647] Strong's H1121, from בָּנָה *banah*, Strong's H1129.
[1648] Lao Tzu, *Tao Tê Ching* II.2, 爲無爲 (*wéi wú wéi*).
[1649] Strong's H1323, offspring dependent upon something (Gesenius 7); it derives from בָּנָה *banah* (Strong's H1129) to establish, cause, and בֵּן *ben* (Strong's H1121) son.
[1650] Russell, *Our Knowledge of the External World*, ON THE NOTION OF CAUSE pp. 240-241.
[1651] Strong's H2895.
[1652] Strong's H2896.
[1653] Strong's H8378
[1654] Strong's H1777. It is a primitive root, compare to אָדוֹן 'adown, Strong's H113, meaning master, king, the Lord God.
[1655] Strong's H3808.
[1656] *Bible*, John 8:4-5,7,9.11 (highlighting is ours).
[1657] *Bible*, Luke 23:34.
[1658] *Cf.* Campbell, *The Power of Myth*, pp. 31-32.
[1659] <Simonelli, *Awareness*, pp. 144-154.>
[1660] 1 Chronicles 28:9.
[1661] Augustine, *In Epistolam Joannis Ad Parthos*, VII, 8. "*Dilige* (love), *et* (and) *quod* (that which) *vis* (you want) *fac* (do)."
[1662] *Bible*, Luke 9:60, underlining is ours.
[1663] Rowlands, *The philosopher and the wolf*, p. 207.
[1664] *Bible*, Luke 23:33, 39, 42.
[1665] Strong's H1777.
[1666] (בָּשַׂר *basar*) Strong's H1319.
[1667] (בָּשָׂר *basar*) Strong's H1320.
[1668] (שָׁגַג *shagag*) Strong's H7683.
[1669] *UKai* 20, *aṇor-* (than the subtle) *aṇīyān-* (smaller) ... *tadvat* (similarly) *mahān-* (of the great) 21, *apāṇi-* (without hands) *pādo'* (feet) ... *acintya-* (inconceivable) *śaktiḥ* (powers) *paśyāmy-* (I see) *acakshuḥ* (without eyes) *sa-* (equally) *śṛṇomy-* (hear) *akarṇaḥ* (without ears) / *ahaṁ* (I) *vijānāmi* (know) *vivikta-* (free from) *rūpo* (form) *na* (none) *cāsti* (and is) *vettā* (knower) *mama* (of me) *cit* (awareness) *sadā* (eternally) *ham* (I) / *vedair-* (through the books of knowledge) *anekair-* (many)

22, *na* (no) *puṇya-*(good) *pāpe* (evil) *mama* (for me) *nāsti* (not is) *nāśo* (destruction) *na* (no) *janma* (birth) *dehe-* (body) *ndriya-* (faculties of the senses) *buddhir-* (intellect) *asti* (is) / *na* (no)... *mbaraṁ* (and circumference).
[1670] <Simonelli, *Awareness*, pp. 96-7.>
[1671] Days (כִּיָמִים $k_a y_ā m_i ym$) in Gematria = 120 [20 (כ, *k*) + 10 (י, *y*) + 40 (מ, *m*) + 10 (י, *y*) + 40 (ם, *m*)], *cf.* Genesis 29:20.
[1672] (עֶשְׂרִים or עֶשֶׂר *`esriym*) Strong's H6242 & H6235.
[1673] Strong's H6235.
[1674] (עָשַׂר) Strong's H6237.
[1675] (עָשַׂר) Strong's H6238.
[1676] Detail not in the Hebrew and Latin texts.
[1677] יוֹם Strong's H3117.
[1678] *paqiyd* פָּקִיד (Strong's H6496), commissioner, deputy, overseer, officer, (passive, equivalent to *Nephilim*, *cf.* Auffarth, The Fall of the Angels, p. 21, 34 & Marks, *Biblical Naming and Poetic Etymology*, p. 21-42).
[1679] (נְפִיל or נפל *něphiyl*) Strong's H5303. Any attempt to identify these giants with dinosaurs (*cf.* Bible Timeline, *Why doesn't the Bible mention the Dinosaurs?*) of the Mesozoic Era is chronologically impossible. Dinosaurs and humans never coexist (*cf.* Smithsonian Institution. *Human Evolution Timeline*).
[1680] (נָפַל) Strong's H5307.
[1681] *Cf.* Genesis 15:12. *Cf.* also Genesis 4:5,6; 2 Samuel 1:10; Proverbs 24:16; Isaiah 21:9; Jeremiah 51:8; Amos 5:2.
[1682] *Cf.* Plato, *Phaedrus.*
[1683] Went into (בּוֹא *bow'*) Strong's H935.
[1684] הָם Ham (Strong's H1990); & הָם hem abundance riches (Strong's H1991); & הֵם *hem* them (Strong's H1992).
[1685] *Cf.* Pirandello, *Sei personaggi in cerca d'autore: commedia da fare*, & *Uno, nessuno e centomila.*
[1686] Virgil, *Vergili Maronis Aeneis*, II, 605-6, 17-18, 22-23, *omnem, quae nunc... mortalis hebetat visus tibi... nubem eripiam... ipse pater Danais animos virisque secundas sufficit... apparent dirae facies inimicaque Troiae numina magna deum.* Similarly, Enoch, in his *The Book of Enoch* (§ VI), describes them as *fallen angels.*
[1687] Hegel, *The Letters*, Letter to Niethammer, October 13, 1806.
[1688] Napoleon Crossing the Alps (1800) Jacques-Louis David - histoire image: public domain https://commons.wikimedia.org/wiki/File:David_-_Napoleon_crossing_the_Alps_-_Malmaison1.jpg
[1689] *Cf.* Hegel, *Phenomenology of Spirit.*
[1690] "*dato il mortal sospiro, / stette la spoglia immemore / orba di tanto spiro,*" Manzoni, *Le tragedie, gl'inni sacri, le odi,* Cinque Maggio, ode celebrating Napoleon's death (May 5, 1821 in the South Atlantic Ocean island of Saint Helena**).**
[1691] Shelley, "Ozymandias" in *Miscellaneous...*, 100.
[1692] *Cf.* Puccini, *Tosca*, looking at Scarpia's body, whom she had just killed (Act 2, last scene), declares, "*Avanti a lui tremava tutta Roma*" Before him all Rome trembled.
[1693] See also Thutmose III (Egypt, 1479–1425 BC), Alexander the Great (Greece, 356–323 BC), Ashoka (India, 304–232 BC), Cyrus (Persia, 580–529 BC), Caesar (Rome, 100–44 BC), Charlemagne (France, 742–814), Genghis Khan (Mongolia, 1162–1227), Tamerlane (Uzbekistan, 1336–1405), Moctezuma (Tenochtitlan, 1398–1469), Hitler (Germany, 1889–1945), Stalin (Russia, 1878-1953), Mao Tse-tung (China, 1893–1976), Stalin (Cuba, 1912-2016), just to mention a few.
[1694] Strong's H7451.
[1695] (מַחֲשָׁבָה *machashabah*) Strong's H4284.
[1696] (רָאָה *ra'ah*) Strong's H7200.
[1697] *Bible*, 1Corinthians 2:11.
[1698] (יֵצֶר *yetser*) Strong's H3336 (intellectual framework) from the verb *yatsar* (יָצַר H3335,3), to form in the mind.
[1699] Strong's H7535.
[1700] (לֵב *leb*) Strong's H3820.
[1701] עָצַב *`atsab* Strong's H6087, Gesenius (1).
[1702] Strong's H3820.
[1703] Strong's H5162.
[1704] נָחַם Gesenius (1a).
[1705] From the verb διανοέομαι (*dianoeomai*) *to ponder deeply.*
[1706] *Bible*, Matthew 25:35-36.
[1707] *Bible*, Mark 9:37.
[1708] *Bible*, Matthew 25:40-45.
[1709] *Bible*, Mark 9:41.
[1710] 3:16.
[1711] (זָכַר *zakar*) Strong's H2142.
[1712] Strong's H2146.
[1713] (כָּתַב *kathab*) Strong's H3789.
[1714] Descartes, *Rules*, Reply II Obj. III, 123.
[1715] Galilei, *Dialogue* I Day, 112.
[1716] Descartes, René (1596-1650), *Discourse on Method*, pp. 1 (I), 15 (II).
[1717] In Latin, *cogito ergo sum.*

[1718] (Emphasis is ours) *si ferme et si assurée*, Descartes, *Discours de la méthode...*, IV.
[1719] Descartes, *Discourse on Method*, pp. 34-35 (IV).
[1720] See <Simonelli, *Beyond Immortality*, pp. 26, 50-51.>
[1721] *Cf.* Bruno, *Opera Italiane, De la causa*, II, Teofilo.
[1722] Bruno, *Opere italiane*, *Spaccio*, I, 3, Mercury explaining to Sophia.
[1723] *Bible*, Luke 15:8.
[1724] *Cf.* Bruno, *Opere italiane*, II, 75-7, n. 5.
[1725] *Cf.* Bruno, *Opere italiane*, *Spaccio*, I, 3, Mercury reporting to Sophia.
[1726] (נָחַם *nacham*) Strong's H5162, Niphal, (Gesenius 1a).
[1727] (עָצַב ` *atsab*) Strong's H6087, Hithpael.
[1728] נָחַם nacham to be sorry, to be moved to pity, to have compassion, Strong's H5162.
[1729] Great (גָּדוֹל *gadowl*) Strong's H1419, awaken (עוּר `uwr*)* Strong's H5782, city- of-anguish (עִיר ` *iyr*) Strong's H5892.
[1730] Jonah 4:11, *cf.* also 1:2 where God had told Jonah, "*Arise, go to Nineveh, and cry against it; for their wickedness is come up before me.*"
[1731] Jonah 2:8.
[1732] Rabia al-Adawiyya (714?-801) in Fadiman, *Essential Sufism*, p. 86. *Cf.* identical expressions in St. Francis Xavier (Caswall, *Hymns...*, VIX, p. 152).
[1733] Dante, *Divina Commedia, Inferno*, XI, 46 "*negando e bestemmiando*"; XIV. 63-64, 69-70 "*non s'ammorza /la ... superbia... abbia / Dio in disdegno.*" Capaneus, one of the mythological seven kings of Thebes, deemed himself superior to God. While scaling the city's walls, Zeus' lighting struck him down.
[1734] Śāntideva (VIII century Mādhyamika Mahāyāna Buddhist), *Guide...*, VI: 48 and 107.
[1735] Dalai Lama, *Healing Anger*, p. 97.
[1736] *Daimonic*: Greek *daimōn* (δαἱμων) demonic genius dispensing (δαίομαι *daíomai*) destiny, Sanskrit *as-ura* from √*as* to exist. luciferous: Latin from Lucifer, light (*lux*) bearing (*fero*).
[1737] <Simonelli, *Beyond Immortality*, pp. 221, 225.>
[1738] *Cf.* Genesis 3:14-24; 4:9-15.
[1739] *Cf.* Genesis 11:1-9; 19:23-29.
[1740] *Cf.* Exodus 7-14.
[1741] *Cf.* Brinkley, *The Great Deluge: Hurricane Katrina*, p. 618.
[1742] *Cf.* "Why would God resurrect people but not dogs? ... and ... the same principle must hold for people and dogs and, by extension, for other animals as well," (Koch, *Is Consciousness Universal? Panpsychism, the ancient doctrine that consciousness is universal, offers some lessons in how to think about subjective experience today*). See also De Benedetti's *Teologia degli animali* (Theology of animals), p. 55, ""*Io credo... che l'animale, compagno di tante solitudini, di tante tristezze... ci accompagnerà anche nell'altra vita.* (I think... that the animal, companion of so many loneliness, of so many sadness... will accompany us also in the afterlife.)"
[1743] נֹחַ *Noach* (H5146) Noah; נוּחַ *nuwach* (H5118) resting place; נוּחַ nuwach *(H5117) to rest.*
[1744] (אָמַר 'amar) Strong's H559.
[1745] (מָחָה machah) Strong's H4229.
[1746] Strong's H929.
[1747] Strong's H7430.
[1748] Strong's H7431.
[1749] Strong's H5775
[1750] (נָחַם *nacham*) Strong's H5162.
[1751] Isaiah 25:8.
[1752] *Cf.* XXX, Budge, *The Egyptian Book of the Dead,* pp. 255-258. Scale, watercolor replica on papyrus, Egypt 1986.
[1753] *Bible*, Revelation 6:5.
[1754] Daniel 5:27.
[1755] *Cf. ŚB.* I.9.3. and Dasgupta, *A history of Indian philosophy*, p. 25.
[1756] *Cf.* Budge, *The Mummy*, pp. 228 and 311.
[1757] *Cf. The Sacred Heart of Jesus*, in Saint Lutgardis of Aywières (1182 – 1246), Grassi, *Healing the Heart: The Transformational Power of Biblical Heart Imagery*, p. 110.
[1758] Ezekiel 11:17,19.
[1759] Ramana Maharshi, *The Spiritual Teaching...*, pp. 71-72.
[1760] *Cf.* Guénon, *Il simbolismo della croce*, rapporto tra punto e spazio, p. 122.
[1761] *Cf.* Donne, *Poems*, The Cross, pp. 167-169.
[1762] Cross-shaped *Cristo Redentor* in Rio de Janeiro (Wikipedia GNU Free Documentation License, Version 1.2 by Free Software Foundation. Creative Commons Attribution-ShareAlike license versions 3.0, 2.5, 2.0, 1.0. File:Cristo Redentor Rio de Janeiro 4.jpg http://en.wikipedia.org/wiki/File:Cristo_Redentor_Rio_de_Janeiro_4.jpg).
[1763] Hoffman, *The Hebrew Alphabet*, pp. 83, 85.
[1764] *Bible*, Matthew 10:38 (ὂς οὐ λαμβάνει τὸν σταυρὸν (cross) αὐτοῦ καὶ ἀκολουθεῖ ὀπίσω μουοὐκ ἔστιν μου ἄξιος)... 27:33... 35, also Mark 15:22, & John 19:17; Golgotha, in Latin *Calvariae Locus*.

1765 Strong's H1538.
1766 Strong's H1556.
1767 Rocci, p. 1699, which, in turn derives from the Sanskrit *sthāvará, standing still* (*W.* 1264a).
1768 *Cf.* Brown, *The Death of the Messiah*, pp. 824 n.4 & 870.
1769 Strong's H5146.
1770 (מָצָא *matsa'*) Strong's H4672.
1771 (חֵן *chen*) Strong's H2580.
1772 (עַיִן *`ayin*) Strong's H5869. Compare to the metaphoric eyes of Horus, "*the falcon god,*" (*cf.* Budge, *The Gods of the Egyptians*, I, pp. 363, 457 & 467), represented by a hawk, compare to its proverbial sight and the same metaphor with the Native American eagle (*cf.* Andrews, *Animal Speak*, pp. 136 fol., 152 fol).
1773 Strong's H8104.
1774 Strong's H2492.
1775 Strong's H8639.
1776 Genesis 5:22.
1777 (תּוֹלְדוֹת *towlĕdah*) Strong's H8435.
1778 (דּוּר *duwr*) Strong's H1752, Gesenius.
1779 (דּוֹר *dowr*) Strong's H1755.
1780 (צַדִּיק *tsaddiyq*) Strong's H6662.
1781 (תָּמַם *tamam*) Strong's H8552.
1782 (תָּמִים *tamiym*) Strong's H8549.
1783 Strong's H8035.
1784 *Gesenius,* שֵׁם (1c).
1785 Strong's H8034.
1786 Strong's H2526.
1787 Strong's H2525.
1788 Strong's H2552.
1789 Gesenius חָמַם.
1790 Strong's H3315.
1791 Gesenius, יֶפֶת.
1792 Strong's H6601.
1793 *Cf.* Schopenhauer, *The world as will and representation*, v.2, c.1.
1794 Strong's H1870, (Gesenius 3).
1795 Jonah 1:5, *dissolute* (מָלַח *malach*) Strong's H4414, *sea-goers* or *mariners* (מַלָּח *mallach*) Strong's H4419.
1796 Dante, *La divina commedia. Inferno*, I.1-3,10-12 "*Nel mezzo del cammin di nostra vita / mi ritrovai per una selva oscura / ché la diritta via era smarrita... / Io non so ben ridir com'i' v'intrai,/ tant'era pien di sonno a quel punto /che la verace via abbandonai.*"
1797 (קֵץ *qets*) Strong's H7093.
1798 (בָּשָׂר *basar*) Strong's H1320.
1799 (בּוֹא *bow'*) Strong's H935.
1800 (פָּנִים *paniym*) Strong's H6440.
1801 (פָּנָה *panah*) Strong's H6437.
1802 II millennium BC, *cf. The Epic of Gilgamesh*, pp. 17 fol.
1803 Mesopotamian Akkadian god Enlil (Sumerian An) was the god of energy, wind, atmosphere and agriculture.
1804 Imagine all human thoughts always loudly reverberating. The *uproar* of humankind's *clamor* would be the *intolerable* unrestful cacophony of a drowning flood. Metaphorically, worrying thoughts can keep us awake.
1805 Mesopotamian Akkadian god Ea (Sumerian Enki) was the god of the earth and water (including the amniotic fluid) for purification who assigned the roles of the other gods.
1806 *The Epic of Gilgamesh*, p. 108-9.
1807 Tolle, *Stillness Speaks*, p. 4.
1808 Thich Nhat Hanh, *Silence*, p. 47.
1809 *Bible*, Matthew 26:61; 27:40; Mark 15:29; John 2:19-20.
1810 Strong's H8392. Like the ark (תֵּבָה *tebah*) in which had been placed baby Moses (מֹשֶׁה *Mosheh*)(Strong's H4872) when he was drawn (מָשָׁה *mashah*)(Strong's H4871) from the water by the Pharaoh's daughter.(*Cf.* Exodus 2:3 & 10).
1811 תֵּבָה Gesenius. Another word for Ark is *'arown* אֲרוֹן,(Strong's H727) meaning *money chest*, from אָרָה *'arah*,(Strong's H717) in the sense of gathering. However, this one refers to the lost Ark of the Covenant (בְּרִית *bĕriyth*)(Strong's H1285, *cf.* Numbers 10:33) containing the Ten Commandments' tablets. (*Cf.* Exodus 25:10 fol). *Cf. UMaitrī* III.4. *śarīram* (the physical body)... *kośa* (a treasury) *iva* (like) *vasunā.* (full of riches), "*physical body... like a treasury chest full of riches.*"
1812 *The Epic of Gilgamesh*, p. 108.
1813 Singer, *The Jewish Encyclopedia*, entry: *Gopher-wood.* Hommel, Fritz 1854-1936.
1814 Schrader, *The cuneiform inscriptions*, p. 8.
1815 Called *sarifas* in Arabic, see Hommel, *Explorations in Bible lands*, pp. 252 & 305 & fol. *Cf. The Epic of Gilgamesh*, p. 109.

[1816] (גֹּפֶר *goper*) Strong's H6086.
[1817] ר, *r* = 200 + פ, *p* = 80 + ג, *g* =3.
[1818] Isaiah 26:8-9.
[1819] (וּלְזִכְרְךָ) Strong's H2143, $wl_{a}z_{i}\underline{k}_{a}r_{a}\underline{k}_{\bar{a}}$ (וּלְזִכְרְךָ) [20 (ך, *k*) + 200 (ר, *r*) + 20 (כ, *k*) + 7 (ז, *z*) + 30 (ל, *l*) + 6 (ו, *w*) = 283].
[1820] (זִכָּרוֹן) Strong's H2146, $z_{i}kr_{o}wn$ (זִכָּרוֹן), [50 (ן, *n*) + 6(ו, *w*) + 200 (ר, *r*) + 20 (כ, *k*) + 7 (ז, *z*) = 283]. See Exodus 12:14 & 17:14.
[1821] (זָכְרֵנוּ) Strong's H2142,_$z_{\bar{a}}\underline{k}_{a}r_{a}wn$ (זָכְרֵנוּ), [50 (ן, *n*) + 6(ו, *w*) + 200 (ר, *r*) + 20 (כ, *k*) + 7 (ז, *z*) = 283].
[1822] Numbers 11:5.
[1823] (עָשָׂה ` *asah*) Strong's H6213.
[1824] (קֵן *qen*) Strong's H7064.
[1825] (כֹּפֶר *kopher*) Strong's H3724. *Cf. The Epic of Gilgamesh*, p. 109.
[1826] (כָּפַר *kaphar*) Strong's H3722.
[1827] (בַּיִת *bayith*) Strong's H1004.
[1828] (חוּץ *chuwts*) Strong's H2351.
[1829] Strong's H3722.
[1830] *The Epic of Gilgamesh*, p. 108.
[1831] *Bible*, Luke 18:22 & 33, *cf.* Matthew 19:21, Mark 10:21.
[1832] *Cf.* Plato, *Text and English translations in Plato*, *Republic*, end of X book.
[1833] *Cf.* Virgil, *Vergili Maronis Aeneis*, Book VI.
[1834] Dante, *La divina commedia*, Purgatorio XXXI, 34-35. "*Le presenti cose /col falso lor piacer volser miei passi.*"
[1835] Strong's H3742, $v_{a}h_{a}k_{a}r_{u}\underline{b}_{i}ym$ (וְהַכְּרֻבִים), [40 (ם, *m*) + 10 (י, *y*) + 2 (ב, *b*) + 200 (ר, *r*) + 20 (כ, *k*) + 5 (ה, *h*) + 6 (ו, *w*) = 283]. See Ezekiel 10:3.
[1836] Strong's H1534.
[1837] Ezekiel 10:1 to 5.
[1838] As the head of Adam Kadmon (*cf.* Knorr von Rosenroth, *Kabbala denudata*). Magnetic Resonance Imaging (MRI) of skull and brain.
[1839] (עָשָׂה) Strong's H6213.
[1840] *Cf.* Freud, *On Metapsychology... The Ego and the Id.*
[1841] *The Epic of Gilgamesh*, p. 108.
[1842] (אַמָּה) Strong's H520, (Gesenius 4).
[1843] *Cf.* "הַסִּפִּים *hasipiym* of the door *amvōṯ'* the grounding-cubit אַמּוֹת" Isaiah 6:4.
[1844] (אֵם) Strong's H517. *Cf.* Sanskrit मा *mā*, meaning mother and measure (W. p. 771b).
[1845] ($\breve{e}l_{o}h_{i}ym$ אֱלֹהִים *rwaḥ* רוּח) [40 (ם, *m*) + 10 (י, *y*) + 5 (ה, *h*) + 30 (ל, *l*) + 1 (א, *a*) + 8 (ח, *ḥ*) + 6 (ו, w) + 200 (ר, r) = 300].
[1846] Genesis 1:2.
[1847] Strong's H748.
[1848] (אֹרֶךְ *'orek*) Strong's H753.
[1849] (כל $k_{o}l$) [30 (ל, *l*) + 20 (כ, *k*) = 50)].
[1850] (שְׁלֹשִׁים *shĕlowshiym*) Strong's H7970, Multiple of שָׁלוֹשׁ *shalowsh* 3, 300, third (H7969).
[1851] Strong's H6965.
[1852] (כְּגֹבַהּ) from גֹּבַהּ *gobahh* height Strong's H1363; (כְּגֹבַהּ $k_{a}\bar{g}_{\bar{o}}\underline{b}_{a}h$) [20 (כ, *k*) + 3 (ג, *g*) + 2 (ב, *b*) + 5 (ה, *h*) = 30], Psalm 10:4.
[1853] *The Epic of Gilgamesh*, p. 108.
[1854] The events in this story are set during the reign of Jeroboam II (fourteenth king of ancient Israel in the years 786–746 BCE). Tradition assigns the composition of the *Book of Jonah* between the V or IV century BCE (*cf. Encyclopaedia Britannica*, Jonah. As we stated already, the controversies regarding the authorship and/or the year of writing of sacred texts are not the intent of this study or the scope of this work.). In any case, this book belongs to the exegetic biblical writings called *Midrash* (*Cf.* Singer, *The Jewish Encyclopedia*, JONAH. Jonah also mentioned in II Kings 14:25).
[1855] (גָּדוֹל *gadowl*) Strong's H1419.
[1856] Strong's H1709.
[1857] (דָּגָה *dagah)* Strong's H*1711.*
[1858] (בָּלַע *bala`*) Strong's H1104
[1859] (מֵעָה *me`ah*), Strong's H4578.
[1860] (מֵעָה *me`ah*), Strong's H4578.
[1861] (דָּגָה *dagah*) Strong's H1711.
[1862] *Jonah and the whale*, Biblical Stories, 2$ Silver Coin from Palau 2015.
[1863] Jonah 1:17.
[1864] *Bible*, Matthew 12:40 & *cf.* 16:4 and Luke 11:30.
[1865] *Cf.* Cerberus, (Hesiod, *Theogony*, 319-326ff.). Similarly, many animals and deities of the Indian pantheon sport 3 heads, *cf.* Zimmer, *Myths and Symbols in Indian Art and Civilization*, Plate 33. Image: Cerberus, Doré Inferno VI.
[1866] *Cf.* Schaff, *Creeds of Christendom,* Vol. I, § 7 "crucified... and... buried;... the third day He rose again" (*Nicene Creed*, 325) "*from the dead*" (Marcellus of Ancyra, 341) and, "*He descended into hell*" (Venantius Fortunatus, 570 and *The Received*

Form, VII-VIII cent.), "*ad inferna*" (Aquilejan Creed) or "*ad inferos*" (Athanasian Creed) "*apud inferos*" (Augustine) "into that which is below;" *cf.* Psalm 16:10 "*Thou wilt not leave my soul in hell* (שְׁאוֹל *shě'owl*)"& *Bible*, Act 2:27 and 2:31 "*His soul was not left in hell*" (εἰς ᾅδου *eìs ádou*). *Cf.* the pre-columbian deity Bacab, the son of the creator, who was killed and resurrected after three days (León-Portilla, *Time and Reality* ..., pp. 45, 65).

[1867] *Bible*, Matthew, 16:21.

[1868] See the complete translation of the *Māṇḍūkya Upanishad* (IV –I century B.C. ?) in Simonelli, *Beyond Immortality*, pp. 58 fol.

[1869] Different meaning from the Hebrew and Latin texts.

[1870] (כָּלָה *kalah*) Strong's H3615.

[1871] (צֹהַר *tsohar*) Strong's H6672.

[1872] (מַעַל *ma`al*) Strong's H4605.

[1873] (פֶּתַח *pethach*) Strong's H6607.

[1874] (צָהַר *tsahar*) Strong's *H6671.*

[1875] (צַד *tsad*) Strong's H6654, Gesenius adversary; צַד *tsad* Strong's H6655 *(Aramaic)* *beside* Gesenius *contra* Daniel 7:25.

[1876] (פֶּתַח *pethach*) Strong's H6607.

[1877] (פָּתַח *pathach* Strong's H6605.

[1878] *Cf.* eyes (עַיִן *` ayin*) open (פָּתַח *pathach*), 1Kings 8:29.

[1879] *Cf.* open (פָּתַח *pathach*) ears (אֹזֶן *'ozen*), Isaiah 50:5.

[1880] *Cf.* open (פָּתַח *pathach*) mouth (פֶּה *peh*), Job 3:1.

[1881] *Cf.* open (פָּתַח *pathach*) hand (יָד *yad*), Deuteronomy 15:8.

[1882] *Cf.* send forth (נָתַן *nathan*) the smell (רֵיחַ *reyach*), Song of Songs 1:12.

[1883] 1119–1312, *cf.* Gualtieri, *Templari in cammino.*

[1884] Like the Pyramid's capstone on the US Great Seal (*cf.* US One Dollar bill). Also as a skullcap *kippah.*

[1885] *Cf.* Galilei, *Assayer* VII, 232.

[1886] (אֲנִי *'aniy*) Strong's H589. Contracted from אָנֹכִי *'anokiy*, Strong's H595.

[1887] *Cf.* Kant, C*ritique of pure reason*, § 17 Introduction.

[1888] (מַיִם *mayim*) Strong's H4325.

[1889] (יָבַל *yabal*) Strong's H2986.

[1890] (מַבּוּל *mabbuwl*) Strong's H3999.

[1891] *Cf. Bible*, Mark 12:10, & Luke 20:17, builders (οἰκοδομοῦ *oikodomou*) rejected (ἀπεδοκίμασαν *apedokimasan*) the stone (Λίθον *Lithon*) the head (κεφαλὴν *kefalēn*) of the corner (γωνίας *gōnias*).

[1892] *Cf.* interview in the Seattle Post-Intelligencer, *People in the News.*

[1893] (בּוֹא *bow'*) Strong's H935.

[1894] Strong's H935.

[1895] *Bible*, Matthew 11:28 "*I will give you rest*" (ἀναπαύσω *anapausō*, from ἀναπαύω anapauō "to cause or permit one to cease from any movement or labour in order to recover and collect his strength, to give rest, refresh, to give one's self rest, take rest, to keep quiet, of calm and patient expectation" (Strong's G373).

[1896] *Cf. Bible*, Matthew 11:29, in that yoke (ζυγόν *zugon*) ye shall find (εὑρήσετε *eurēsete* from εὑρίσκω *euriskō*) rest (ἀνάπαυσιν *anapausin* from ἀνάπαυσις anapausis).

[1897] (קוּם *quwm*) Strong's H6965.

[1898] (בְּרִית *běriyth*) Strong's H1285.

[1899] *Cf.* Kluger, *The Animal Mind* & Griffin, *Animal Minds Beyond Cognition to Consciousness.*

[1900] λόγοι σπερματικοὶ (*lógoi spermatikoi*), Plotinus (204 – 270), *Enneads*, III.1.7.4. "Everything is accomplished by seminal reasons" πάντα κατὰ λόγους σπερματικοὺς περαίνεται. *Cf.* also V.9.6-7 and 14.

[1901] *Cf. Timaeus* 73c.

[1902] *Bible*, 1John, 3:9, seed, σπέρμα (*sperma*).

[1903] *The Epic of Gilgamesh*, p. 108.

[1904] Genesis 4:1 (Italic is ours). *Cf.* also: 17 "And Cain *knew* his wife; and she conceived, and bare Enoch"; 25 "And Adam *knew* his wife again; and she bare a son ... Seth."

[1905] *Cf.* Thomas Aquinas, *Summa*, I, q. 16, aa. 1-2.

[1906] *Cf.* Murayama, *Top-down cortical input during NREM sleep consolidates perceptual memory.*

[1907] (*ālayavijñāna*) *ālaya-* (receptacle) *vi-*(distinction) *jñāna* (knowledge). *Cf.* Vasubandhu, *Vijñaptimātratāsiddhi-Triṃśikā*, (Thirty stanzas only on consciousness), IV century BC Yogācāra (yoga-rule) Buddhism, v.3 and 5. *Cf.* also (*alayavijñāna*) *a-* (non) *laya-* (dissolution) *vi-*(distinction) *jñāna* (knowledge).

[1908] *Cf.* Saenger, Principles of Nucleic Acid Structure.

[1909] <Simonelli, *Beyond Immortality*, pp. 47 & 161.>

[1910] (אָסַף *'acaph*) Strong's H622.

[1911] (אָסַף *'acaph*) Strong's H622, Gesenius 1(4-5). *Cf.* the similar concept with the Sanskrit *saṁnyāsa* renunciant (W. p= 1148,a], the one who, having placed everything together (*sam*, W. 1152,a), throws it away (*nyas* W. p= 572,a).

[1912] (הם *ham*) Strong's H1990.

[1913] (הָמָה *hamah*) Strong's H1993.

1914 (הֵם *hem*) Strong's H1991.
1915 (אָכְלָה *'oklah*) Strong's H402.
1916 (אָכַל *'ukal*) Strong's H 401.
1917 *Bible*, John 4:13-14.
1918 *The Epic of Gilgamesh*, p. 108.
1919 *Bible*, John 14:17 & 18:36. οὐκ *ouk* (not) ἔστιν *estin* (is) ἐκ *ek* (of) τοῦ *tou* (the) κόσμου *kosmou* (world) τούτου *toutou* (this).
1920 (אַתָּה *'athah)* Strong's H857-H858.
1921 *(*בּוֹא *bow')* Strong's H935.
1922 *Bible*, Matthew 28:20 μεθ' *meth'* (with) ὑμῶν *umōn* (you) εἰμι *eimi* (I am) πάσας *pasas* (all) τὰς *tas* (the) ἡμέρας *ēmeras* (days) ἕως *eōs* (even till) τῆς *tēs* (the) συντελείας *suntelias* (end) τοῦ *tou* (of the) αἰῶνος *aiōnos* (times)**.**
1923 (רָאָה *ra'ah*) Strong's H7200.
1924 חֲזִיר *chaziyr* (Strong's H2386), *cf.* Deuteronomy 14:8.
1925 *Cf.* Philonis, *Operum Omnium, De Concupiscentia* V, 10.
1926 (טָהוֹר *tahowr*) Strong's H2889.
1927 (טָהֵר) Strong's H2891 (Gesenius 1).
1928 Compare Sanskrit *deva*, god, from the root √*div*, to shine, *W.* 492b, 478b.
1929 (שֶׁבַע *sheba`*) Strong's H7651.
1930 (שָׁבַע) Strong's H7650.
1931 Genesis 21:27 to 30. *Cf* Exodus 37:23.
1932 Psalm 57:8 & 11.
1933 שְׁנַיִם shěnayim two (Strong's H8147).
1934 *Cf.* Hoffman, *The Hebrew Alphabet.*
1935 שָׁנָה sheniy to repeat (Strong's H8145).
1936 Campbell, *The Power of Myth, with Bill Moyers*, p. 18.
1937 Not in the Hebrew and Latin texts.
1938 (בְּהֵמָה *běhemah*) Strong's H929: "from an unused root (probably meaning to be mute)."
1939 *Cf.* Plato (429–347 B.C.), *Symposium* 211 A-B and other.
1940 (כִּידוֹ) Strong's H3589. *Destruction* (כִּידוֹ k_i*yḏ*$w_ô$) in Gematria = 40, [6 (ו, *w*) + 4 (ד, *d*) + 10 (י, *y*) + 20 (כ, *k*) = 40], *cf.* Job 21:20 (*His eyes shall see his* *destruction*).
1941 (אַרְבָּעִים *'arba`iym*) Strong's H705.
1942 (מְחָה) Strong's H4229.
1943 *Cf.* Hoffman, *The Hebrew Alphabet.*
1944 (דָּלוֹ) Strong's H1809. *Distress-brought-down* (דָּלוֹ d_a*lw*) in Gematria = 40, [6 (ו, *w*) + 30 (ל, *l*) + 4 (ד, *d*) = 40], *cf.* Job 28:4.
1945 (אַרְבָּעִים *'arba`iym*) Strong's H705.
1946 (אַרְבַּע *'arba`*) Strong's H702. From the following
1947 (רָבַע raba`) Strong's H7251.
1948 (יְקוּם *yěquwm*) Strong's H3351.
1949 (*Sein zum Tode*), Heidegger, *Being and time*, II, I, H. 235-267, pp. 279-311.
1950 Freud, *The standard edition..., Beyond the Pleasure Principle,* p. 38.
1951 *Cf.* de Rachewiltz, *Il libro egizio.* Barge of Horus, Sanctuary of the Ptolemaic Temple of the falcon-headed Horus son of Isis and Osiris, Edfu, Egypt.
1952 *Tusculanarum disputationum*, I.XXX.
1953 *Cf.* Plato, *Phaedo*, 67d.
1954 (μελέτη *meletē*) Plato, *Symposium* XXV, 208a.
1955 *Ibid.* 207a and d.
1956 *Cf. UB* II.4.12, 13 and IV.5.13.
1957 Ecclesiastes 9:5.
1958 *Cf. UB* II.4.14.
1959 *Nag Hammadi*, Gospel of Thomas, 18.
1960 Drachma (δραχμή *drachmē*) *cf.* Simonelli, *Hyria, A lost City-State,* p. 14.
1961 *Bible*, Luke 15:8-9.
1962 INSERM, from NEUROSCIENCE NEWS.
1963 *Cf.* Brannen, *The Death of the Dinosaurs.*
1964 *Cf.* Kant, *Prolegomena*, § 45.
1965 Yeats, *The Land of Heart's Desire*, p. 15.
1966 *Bible*, 1 Corinthians 15:31; καθ' *kath'* ἡμέραν *ēmeran* ἀποθνήσκω *apothnēskō*
1967 *The Epic of Gilgamesh*, p. 108-9.
1968 <Simonelli, *Beyond Immortality*, p. 31.>

1969 Puccini, *La Bohème*, Act IV. "*Hai sbagliato il raffronto. Volevi dir: bella come un tramonto.*"
1970 "*Erant qui metu mortis mortem precarentur,*" Pliny the Younger, *Letters and Panegyricus I*, VI.20.14.
1971 Strong's H347, *cf.* Job, 1:8.
1972 Strong's H340.
1973 Strong's H7854.
1974 Job 1:7.
1975 Strong's H7751.
1976 Strong's H1980.
1977 Strong's H776.
1978 Strong's H549.
1979 Strong's H3477.
1980 Strong's H3474, *cf.* Job 1:8.
1981 Job 5:19.
1982 *Cf.* Eschenko, *Learning-Dependent*, 08.
1983 Stickgold, *Sleep-dependent memory*, p. 331-335.
1984 Axmacher, *The Role of Sleep in Declarative Memory*, 500.
1985 Eschenko. *Learning-Dependent*, 08.
1986 Simonelli, *Beyond Immortality*, pp. 69-70.
1987 Strong's H6666 (צְדָקָה *tsĕdaqah*). *Righteousness* (וּצְדָקַת *w$_a$ts$_e$d$_a$q$_a$t*) in Gematria = 600, [400 (ת, *t*) + 100 (ק, *q*) + 4 (ד, *d*) + 90 (צ,*ts*) + 6 (ו, *w*) = 600], *cf.* Isaiah 5:23 & 1 Samuel 26:23 (צִדְקָתוֹ *ts$_e$d$_a$q$_a$tw$_o$*), & Judges 5:11 *Righteousness acts* (צִדְקוֹת *ts$_e$d$_a$qw$_o$t*).
1988 5:12.
1989 λόγος Word *Bible*, John 1:1 & 2.
1990 *Bible*, John 1:1-5, Ἐν ἀρχῇ ἦν ὁ λόγος καὶ ὁ λόγος ἦν πρὸς τὸν θεόν καὶ θεὸς ἦν ὁλόγος/ ὖτος ἦν ἐν ἀρχῇ πρὸς τὸν θεόν/ πάντα δι᾽ αὐτοῦ ἐγένετο καὶ χωρὶς αὐτοῦ ἐγένετο οὐδὲ ἕν ὃ γέγονεν / ἐν αὐτῷ ζωὴ ἦν καὶ ἡ ζωὴ ἦν τὸ φῶς τῶν ἀνθρώπων/ καὶ τὸ φῶς ἐν τῇ σκοτίᾳ φαίνει καὶ ἡ σκοτία αὐτὸ οὐ κατέλαβεν
In principio erat Verbum et Verbum erat apud Deum et Deus erat Verbum. Hoc erat in principio apud Deum. Omnia per ipsum facta sunt et sine ipso factum est nihil quod factum est. In ipso vita erat et vita erat lux hominum. Et lux in tenebris lucet et tenebrae eam non conprehenderunt.
1991 *Luciferic*, Latin: light = *lucem* – *ferre* = to carry.
1992 Isaiah 14:12.
1993 *Tao Te Ching*, I.1-2.
1994 <Simonelli, *Beyond Immortality*, p. 156.>
1995 *Bible*, John 1:7-8-9.
1996 *Bible*, John 1:23 & Mark 1:3 & Luke 3:4.
1997 *Bible*, John 1:15 μαρτυρεῖ *martureī*,.
1998 *Bible*, John 1:18. ἑώρακεν *eōraken* (ὁράω *oráō*). *Cf.* ὁράω from the 3 linguistic themes "ὁρα, (*F*)ἰδ, ὀπ" [*ora*, (*w*)*id*, *op*), & εἶδον (*eīdon*) Rocci, p. 1351 & 546. (*F*)ἰδ from Sanskrit √1. *vid* "to know... to seek out, look for" (from which *veda*) *W*. 964c & 1015a.
1999 *Bible*, John 18:36.
2000 Genesis 1:1 and 10.
2001 *Bible*, John 12:35-36 "be certain" (πιστεύετε *pisteúete*, *credite*).
2002 *UB* IV.3.30. *na* (not) {[*paśyati* (does see) (23)], [*jighrati* (does smell) (24)]}, [*rasayati* (does taste) (25)], [*vadati* (does speak) (26)], [*śṛṇoti* (does hear) (27)], [*manute* (does think) (28)]} *vijānāti* (does know) [*paśyan* (seeing) (23), [*jighran* (smelling) (24)], [*rasayan* (tasting) (25)], [*vadan* (speaking) (26)], [*śṛṇvan* (hearing) (27], [*manvāno* (thinking) (28)]}*vijānan* (knowing) *vai* (verily) *tan* (that) *na* (not) {[*paśyati* (does see) (23)], [*jighrati* (does smell) (24)], [*rasayati* (does taste) (25)], [*vadati* (does speek) (26)], [*śṛṇoti* (does hear) (27)], [*manute* (does think) (28)]}*vijānāti* (does know) *na* (not) *hi* (verily) {[*drashṭur* (the seer) (23), [*ghrātur* (the smeller) (24)], [*rasayitū* (the taster) (25)], [*vakṭur* (the speaker) (26)], [*śrotuḥ* (the hearer) (27)], [*mantur* (the thinker) (28)]} *vijñātur* (the knower) {[*dṛshṭer* (seen) (23), [*ghrāter* (smelled) (24)], [*rasayater* (tasted) (25)], [*vakṭer* (spoken) (26)], [*śruter* (heard) (27)], [*mater* (thought) (28)]}*vijñāter* (knower) *viparilopo* (separation) *vidyate* (there is) *avināśitvāt* (imperishable) *na* (not) *tu* (however) *tad* (that) *dvitīyam* (second) *asti* (is) *tato'* (therefore) *nyad* (opposit) *vibhaktam* (divided) *yad* (that) {[*paśyet* (he may see) (23), [*jighret* (he may smell) (24)], [*rasayet* (he may taste) (25)], [*vadet* (he may speak) (26)], [*śṛṇuyāt* (he may hear) (27], [*manvīta* (he may think) (28)]}*vijānīyāt* (he may know).
2003 Exodus, 3:2, "לבה *labbah* flashing point of spear... he intently looked (רָאָה *ra'ah*), and, behold, the bush (סְנֶה *cĕnah*) burned (בָּעַר *ba`ar*) with supernatural fire (אֵשׁ *'esh*), and the bush [was] not consumed or devoured (אָכַל *'akal*)."
2004 Exodus, 3:3 סור *cuwr* to reject and turn away from.
2005 Thoreau, *A Year...*, July 16, 1851.
2006 Exodus, 3:4.
2007 Reproduction of 12th Century Byzantine icon of Moses at the Burning Bush, Mount Sinai, Monastery of Saint Catherine.

[2008] Exodus, 3:5 קרב *qarab* to bring near, approach, קֹדֶשׁ *qodesh Sacred set-apart,* קָדַשׁ *qadash that which is separated, namely transcendent.*

[2009] *Bible*, Matthew 5:3 & 8. *The poor in ego-spirit* (οἱ πτωχοὶ τῷ πνεύματι *oi ptōchoi tō pneumati*) refers to the spirit (πνεῦμα *pneuma*, - *cf.* Sanskrit *prāṇa* vital-principal) as the *principium individuationis.* Heart καρδία *kardia*, mind and thought.

[2010] *Bible*, John 18:36. Ἡ *Ē* (the) βασιλεία *basileia* (kingdom) ἐμὴ *emē* (my) οὐκ *ouk* (not) ἔστιν *estin* (is) ἐκ *ek* (of) τοῦ *tou* (the) κόσμουτούτου *kosmoutoutou* (this world) ... νῦν *nun* (now) δὲ *de* (but) ἡ *ē* (the) βασιλεία *basileia* (kingdom) ἡἐμὴ *ēemē* (my) οὐκ *ouk* (not) ἔστιν *estin* (is) ἐντεῦθεν *enteuthen* (from here). κόσμος *kosmos* cosmos, world; νῦν *nyn* now, present; ἐντεῦθεν *enteuthen* this place.

[2011] Exodus, 3:6.

[2012] *UB* III.4.2.

[2013] Exodus, 3:13.

[2014] אֶהְיֶה אֲשֶׁר אֶהְיֶה *hayah asher hayah*

[2015] Exodus, 3:14.

[2016] Exodus, 3:11.

[2017] Exodus, 3:12. כִּי הָאוֹת: אוֹת *'owth* miraculous sign or proof; כִּי *kiy* because, certainly, surely. מִצְרַיִם *mitsrayim Egypt,* dual of מָצוֹר*matsowr Egypt* siege, entrenchment The same as מָצוֹר *matsowr* in the sense of a limit, enclosure צוּר *tsuwr* to bind, besiege, confine, to shut in, enclose, to be an adversary.

[2018] <Simonelli, *Awareness*, pp. 60-62.>

[2019] Adaptation from Géricault's "*Raft of the Medusa*" (1818–9). Sun at Medjugorje.

[2020] *Cf.* Patañjali, *Yoga Sutras.*

[2021] *Bible*, Matthew 6:24 and Luke 16:13.

[2022] Cytowic, *The Man Who Tasted Shapes*, p. 56, as described by Kandinsky, *Concerning the Spiritual in Art.*

[2023] *Bible*, Phlippians 3:13,14.

[2024] *Bible*, 1 Corinthians 9:24,25,27.

[2025] Ramana Maharshi, *The Spiritual Teaching...*, p. 61. *Cf.* p. 35 (5).

[2026] *Bible*, 1 Timothy 5:2. "*I come as a thief,*" says Revelation 16:15. *Cf.* also 1 Thessalonians 5:4; 2 Peter 3:10 and Revelation 3:3.

[2027] *Bible*, Matthew 25:29.

[2028] *Bible*, Matthew 10:39; *cf.* also 16:25, Marc 8:35 and Luke 9:24.

[2029] Cervantes, *Don Quijote*, Part I, § I and II, "*su rocín... tenía... más tachas... pellis et ossa... al fin le vino a llamar Rocinante... Con esto se quietó y prosiguió su camino, sin llevar otro que aquel que su caballo quería, creyendo que en aquello consistía la fuerza de las aventuras.*" For a similar reading, see De Unamuno, *Our Lord Don Quixote.*

[2030] Rose, *Ignatius Loyola...*, p. 537.

[2031] Benvenuti (1924-1990), *La scienza dello Spirito*, "*La Scienza dello Spirito non è una teoria, ma una pratica... A coloro che... ci rivolgono critiche e appunti, dobbiamo grande gratitudine, perché sono in quel momento i nostri maestri... Da noi, dipendono molte cose di valore collettivo, umano... non... dalle comunità mondiali*" *L'Archetipo*, La posta dei lettori, p. 27.

[2032] *UC.* III.14.4. *sarva-* (all) *-karmā* (actions) *sarva-* (all) *-kāmaḥ* (desires) *sarva-* (all) *-gandhaḥ* (scents) *sarva-* (all) *-rasaḥ* (flavors) *sarvam* (all) *idam* (this) *abhyātto'* (encompassing) *vāky* (not speaking) *anādaraḥ* (indifferent) *esha* (this) *ma* (my) *ātmā-* (Self)*-ntar* (within) *hṛdaye* (the heart) *etad* (this) *brahma* (the Supreme Transcendent Spirit) *etam* (This One).

[2033] *sahaja-nirvikalpa samādhi*, Ramana Maharshi, *The Spiritual Teaching...*, p. 31 (4).

[2034] *Bible*, Mark 14:38, watch (*Greek Text*: γρηγορεῖτε *grēgoreîte*, *Vulgate*: vigilate), pray (*Greek Text*: προσεύχεσθε *proseúchesthe*, *Vulgate*: orate), temptation (πειρασμόν *peirasmón*).

[2035] *Bible*, Matthew 6:3 & 6-7.

[2036] <Simonelli, *Beyond Immortality*, pp. 38 & 229 to 233.>

[2037] *Cf.* Schopenhauer, *The world as will and representation*, I, pp. 8 fol.

[2038] Ship (אֳנִיָּה *'oniyah*)

[2039] Descended (יָרַד *yarad*) Strong's H3381.

[2040] Recesses (יְרֵכָה *yĕrekah*) Strong's H3411.

[2041] *Lay* (שָׁכַב *shakab*) Strong's H7901.

[2042] Asleep (רָדַם *radam*) Strong's H7290.

[2043] Multifaceted (רָבַב *rabab*) Strong's H7231.

[2044] Subject (רַב *rab*) Strong's H7227.

[2045] Sleeper (רָדַם *radam*)

[2046] Arise (קוּם *quwm*) Strong's H6965. *Cf.* Jesus "*entered into a ship, his disciples followed him./ And, behold, there arose a great tempest in the sea, insomuch that the ship was covered with the waves: but he was asleep. And his disciples came to him, and awoke him.*" (*Bible*, Matthew 8:23-25).

[2047] Hebrew "*one from beyond*" (עִבְרִי *`ibriy*) Strong's H5680, patronymic from `Eber or Heber (עֵבֶר) = "the region beyond" (H5677), the same as *`eber* (עֵבֶר) = "region beyond or across" (H5676), from *`abar* (עָבַר) = "to pass beyond" (H5674).

[2048] Book of Jonah 1:3,5-6, 9.

[2049] *The Epic of Gilgamesh*, p. 107.

[2050] (עוף *'uwph)* Strong's H5774.
[2051] *Cf.* Plato, *Phaedrus.*
[2052] Similar to the question asked by Dr. Stuart Hameroff (University of Arizona professor and anesthesiologist) regarding patients under clinical sedation, in Arntz, *What tʜē #$*! D̄θ ωΣ (k)пow!?*
[2053] Strong's H6680.
[2054] (שְׁבִיעִי *shĕbiy'iy*) *Cf.* Genesis 2:2.
[2055] *The Epic of Gilgamesh*, p. 110.
[2056] Strong's H1709, fish דג *d$_a$g* = 7 [3 (ג, *g*) + 4 (ד, *d*)]; *cf.* Jonah 1:17.
[2057] Jonah 2:5-7.
[2058] Whale, Haida Art of the American Pacific Northwest Coast.
[2059] Different from the Hebrew and Latin texts.
[2060] (תְּהוֹם *tĕhowm*) Strong's H8415.
[2061] (הוּם) Strong's H1949.
[2062] (חָדָשׁ *chadash*) Strong's H2318.
[2063] (חֹדֶשׁ *chodesh*) Strong's H2320.
[2064] (בְּשִׁבְעָה־עָשָׂר *bašiba'āh-'āśār*) Strong's H7650, H7651, H7652 & H6237, H6240.
[2065] (דְּגֵי *dağēy*) Strong's H1709, דְּגֵי *d$_a$ğ$_ē$y* = 17 [4 (ד, *d*) + 3 (ג, *g*) + 10 (י, *y*)]; *cf.* "*on the fishes*" Genesis 9:2.
[2066] Strong's H6666 (צְדָקָה *tsĕdaqah*). *Righteousness* (וְצִדְקַת *w$_a$ts$_e$d$_a$q$_a$t*) in Gematria = 600, [400 (ת, *t*) + 100 (ק, *q*) + 4 (ד, *d*) + 90 (צ, *ts*) + 6 (ו, *w*) = 600], *cf.* Isaiah 5:23 & Judges 5:11 (צִדְקוֹת *ts$_e$d$_a$qw$_ō$t*) & 1 Samuel 26:23 (צִדְקָתוֹ *ts$_e$d$_a$q$_ā$tw$_ō$*).
[2067] (מַעְיָן *ma'yan*) Strong's H4599.
[2068] (עַיִן) Strong's H5869.
[2069] (שֵׁנִי *sheniy*) Strong's H8145.
[2070] Root שְׁנָה *shĕnah* (Aramaic) Strong's H8139 sleep Daniel 6:18, *cf* Gesenius (שְׁנָה II) וְשִׁנְתֵּהּ *vəšinətēh* sleep, *cf.* (שָׁנָה *shaneh*) Strong's H8141.
[2071] Root שְׁנָה *shĕnah* (Aramaic) Strong's H8140 year Daniel 6:1 (5:31), Gesenius (שְׁנָה I &II) שְׁתִין *šitiyn* years, *cf.* (שֵׁנָא *shehah*) Strong's H8142.
[2072] Daniel 5:31 (6:1), "*Darius the Median took the kingdom, being about threescore and two* ***years*** (וְשִׁנְתֵּהּ *vəšinətēh* root **שְׁנָה *shĕnah*,** Strong's H8140) *old.*"
[2073] Daniel 6:18, "*Then the king went to his palace, and passed the night fasting: neither were instruments of musick brought before him: and his* ***sleep*** (שִׁתְּין *šitiyn* root **שְׁנָה *shĕnah*** Strong's H8139) *went from him.*"
[2074] (חַי *chay*) Strong's H2416.
[2075] (זֶה *zeh*) Strong's H2088.
[2076] (שָׁמַיִם *shamayim*) Strong's H8064.
[2077] (פָּתַח *pathach*) *Cf.* Genesis 6:16.
[2078] P. 111.
[2079] *Cf.* Hoffman, *The Hebrew Alphabet.*
[2080] Strong's H2254; חֲבֹל *ḥ$_a$b$_ō$l* = 40 = [8(ח, *ḥ*) + 2(ב, *b*) + 30(ל, *l*)], *cf.* Exodus 22:26 (25).
[2081] Strong's H3589; כִּידוֹ *k$_i$y$_d$w$_ō$* = 40 = [20(כ, *k*) + 10(י, *y*) + 4(ד, *d*) + 6(ו, *w*)]; *cf.* Job 21:20.
[2082] Strong's H3915.
[2083] (לוּל) Strong's H3883.
[2084] (מִין *miyn*) Strong's H4327.
[2085] (בְּהֵמָה *bĕhemah*) Strong's H929.
[2086] (רָמַשׂ *ramas*) Strong's H7430.
[2087] (רֶמֶשׂ *remes*) Strong's H7431.
[2088] (עוֹף *'owph*), Strong's H5775.
[2089] (צִפּוֹר *tsippowr*) Strong's H6833
[2090] (צָפַר *tsaphar*) Strong's H6852.
[2091] (כָּנַף *kanaph*) Strong's H3670.
[2092] (כָּנָף *kanaph*) Strong's H3671.
[2093] (חַי *chay*) Strong's H2416.
[2094] Dante, *La Divina Commedia*, Inferno III, 95-6 & V, 22-4 "*dove si puote/ ciò che si vuole.*"
[2095] Thoreau, *A Year...*, July 16, 1851.
[2096] *Cf.* Plato, *Text..., Meno.*
[2097] *Cf.* Aristotle, *Posterior Analytics.*
[2098] (בָּשַׂר *basar*) Strong's H1320.
[2099] (בָּשָׂר *basar*) Strong's H1319.
[2100] (זָכַר *zakar*) Strong's H2142.
[2101] Genesis 8:1.
[2102] *Cf.* Aristotle, *Metaphysics*, 12.1072a.

[2103] Not in the Hebrew and Latin texts.

[2104] Of which only the over 3000 (x2) species of termites would have created serious structural damage to the Ark.

[2105] **IRONICALLY SPEAKING**: *Mr./s.* Bison (*Bison bison*) eastbound, *Mr./s.* Polar-bear (*Ursus maritimus*) southbound, *Mr./s.* Penguin (*Sphenisciformes Spheniscidae*) northbound and *Mr./s.* Tasmanian devil (Sarcophilus harrisii) westbound, would have needed very fast connecting carriers to reach the ark of their destinations. The real problem would have been the return trip, when connecting carriers were not available due to the destruction caused by the flood. If, on the other hand, it would be argued that those animals developed from the original Ark inhabitants, then it would be evolution, and it would contradict a literal reading of creation. These are only a few examples of the absurdity of literal reading worthy only of very trivial motion pictures, like Charles' *Religulous with Bill Maher*, or popularly superficial films, like Huston's *The Bible*, and/or many very superficial Disney-style Luna-Parks childishly idolatrous *Bible Amusement Theme Parks* (*e.g.* in California, Connecticut, Florida, Tennessee, etc.) & Ark Encounter, *A life-sized Noah's Ark Experience*, in Williamstown, Kentucky.

[2106] Jonah 1:17, בִּמְעֵי הַדָּג שְׁלֹשָׁה יָמִים וּשְׁלֹשָׁה לֵילוֹת:, [דג *dag: fish, from* דָּגָה *dagah:* to multiply, increase, to cover (*i.e.:* multitude covering over everything)].

[2107] *Upanishads*, traditionally 108 reveled books (the earliest ones date back from around 900 BCE). They constitute the end of the *Veda* (around 4000 to 2500 BCE).

[2108] *Cf.* Genesis, 2:1 (תרדמה *tardemah*).

[2109] Like the unclean animals.

[2110] *Cf. UŚ* IV. 6 *fol.*

[2111] *UM.* 5*yatra* (where) *supto* (one asleep) *na* (not) *kaṃcana* (any) *kāmaṃ* (desire) *kāmayate* (does desire) *na* (not) *kaṃcana* (any) *svapnaṃ* (dream) *paśyati* (does see) *tat* (that) *sushuptam* (deep unconscious sleep) *sushupta* (deep unconscious sleep) *sthāna* (state) *ekī -bhūtaḥ* (one-become) *prajñāna-ghana* (knowledge-compact) *evānanda-mayo* (alone-bliss-made) *hyānanda-bhuk* (verily-bliss-enjoyer) *ceto-mukhaḥ* (consciousness-mouth) *prājñas-* (the knower) *tṛtīyaḥ* (third) *pādaḥ* (quadrant).

[2112] *UkaBr.* III. 3. *Yatraitat* when thus) *purushaḥ* (a person) *suptaḥ* (sleeping) *svapnaṃ* (dream) *na* (no) *kañcana* (whatsoever) *paśyaty* (he sees) *athāsmin* (that self) *prāṇa* (breathing) *evaikadhā* (verily one) *bhavati* (becomes) *tad* (that) *enam* (him) *vāk* (speech) *sarvaiḥ* (with all) *nāmabhiḥ* (names) *sahāpyeti* (together goes to it) *cakshuḥ* (the eye) *sarvaiḥ* (with all) *rūpaiḥ* (forms) *sahāpyeti* (together goes) *śrotraṃ* (the ear) *sarvaiḥ* (with all) *śabdaiḥ* (sounds) *sahāpyeti* (together goes) *manaḥ* (the mind) *sarvaiḥ* (with all) *dhyānaiḥ* (thoughts) *sahāpyeti* (together goes) *sa* (he) *yadā* (when) *pratibudhyate* (he awakens) *yathāgner* (as from a fire s) *jvalataḥ* (blazing) *sarvā* (in all) *diśo* (regions) *visphuliṅgā* (sparks) *vipratishṭherann* (spread out) *evam* (thus) *evaitasmād* (so this therefore) *ātmanaḥ* (from the self) *prāṇā* (the vital breaths) *yathāyatanaṃ* (each in its own place) *vipratishṭhante* (spread out) *prāṇebhyo* (from the vital breaths) *devāḥ* (the resplendent senses) *devebhyo* (from the resplendent senses) *lokāḥ* (the worlds).

[2113] Not in the Hebrew or Latin texts.

[2114] *Dhammapada,* XX, 287, p. 69.

[2115] Matt, *The Essential Kabbalah*, p. 131. Conceiving (הָרָה *harah - Strong's H2029), cf. Isaac of Akko, Otsar Hayyim.*

[2116] (רום *ruwm)* Strong's H7311.

[2117] *Bible*, Matthew 5:14.

[2118] *Cf.* Simonelli, *Beyond Immortality*, p. 104 & *Awareness*, p. 52.

[2119] *Bible*, Romans 1:20 ποιήμασιν (*poieémasin* by the things that are made) νοούμενα (*nooúmena* being understood) καθορᾶται (*kathorātai* are clearly seen).

[2120] (הַר *har*) Strong's H2022.

[2121] Gesenius', a) *cf.* Exodus 4:27 & 18:5; Psalm 2:6 & 15:1 & 24:3 & 43:3; Isaiah 2:3 & 11:9 & 14:25 & 57:13 & 65:9 "*my mountains.*"

[2122] אֶל־הַר הָאֱלֹהִים *'el har hā'ĕlōhiym*, Exodus 3:1.

[2123] הַר Gesenius (abd). *Cf.* Exodus 4:27; 18:5; Psalm 24:3; Isaiah 2:3; 11:9; 56:7; 57:13; Psalm 2:6.

[2124] Campbell, *Myths of Light*, p. 135.

[2125] (גבהָה *ḡaḇōhāh*) Strong's H1364 (גבהָה *ḡ$_a$ḇ$_o$h$_a$h*) high, 15= [5(ה, *h*) + 5(ה, *h*) + 2(ב, *b*) + 3(ג, *g*)]; *cf.* Deuteronomy 3:5.

[2126] (בָּגוֹד *bāḡwōḏ*) Strong's H901 (בָּגוֹד *b$_a$ḡw$_o$ḏ*) treacherous, 15= 2(ב, *b*) + 3(ג, *g*) + 6(ו, *w*) + 4(ד, *d*)]; *cf.* Isaiah 48:8.

[2127] (אֵיד *'ēyḏ* Strong's H343 (אֵיד *'ēyḏ*) calamity, 15= [1(א, *a*) + 10(י, *y*) + 4(ד, *d*)]; *cf.* Job 21:30.

[2128] (וּבַאֲבֹד *wḇa'ăḇōḏ*) Strong's H6 (וּבַאֲבֹד *wḇa'$_ă$ḇ$_o$ḏ*) perish, 15= [6(ו, *w*) + 2(ב, *b*) + 1(א, *a*) + 2(ב, c) + 4(ד, *d*)]; *cf.* Proverbs 11:10.

[2129] Fragment attributed to Heraclitus' (535–475 BC), in Simplicius (*On Aristotle's Physics*, 1313.11) reports: πάντα ῥεῖ (*pánta rei*) *everything flows*, Plato (*Cratylus*, 402, 8) reports: πάντα χωρεῖ καὶ οὐδὲν μένει. (*pánta khōrei kaì oydèn ménei*) everything moves and nothing rests.

[2130] *vi-√grah* = "divide (esp. to draw out fluids at several times)" (W 957 c2).

[2131] *UMaitrī* VI. 16. *vigrahavān* (divided) *esha* (this) *kālaḥ* (time) *sindhurājaḥ* (river king) *prajānām* (of creatures).

[2132] Alchin, *Secret History of Nursery Rhymes Book*, p. 40 (1665 rhyme for the Great Bubonic Plague of London).

[2133] *Cf.* the late great Neapolitan comedian, Totò, *'A livella*, (The leveler) "Do you know what death is? ... it's a leveler... / a king, a magistrate, a great man... / has lost everything, life and also the name.../ Only the living ones perform these buffooneries: / We are serious... we belong to death!" "*'A morte 'o ssaje ched"e?...è una livella.../ 'Nu rre,'nu maggistrato,'nu grand'ommo.../ ha perzo tutto,'a vita e pure 'o nomme.../ Perciò ... / Sti ppagliacciate 'e ffanno sulo 'e vive:/ nuje simmo serie...appartenimmo à morte!" Cf.* Scale, watercolor replica on papyrus, Egypt 1986 in XXX, Budge, *The Egyptian Book of the Dead,* pp. 255-258.

[2134] In reality, Genesis 9:2 mentions fishes and their death (as we will see). However, they are not in the ark.

[2135] **IRONICALLY SPEAKING**, *Mr./s.* Cetaceans and all fish would have needed *special* watery accommodations in the ark, but, then again, they would have been better off outside, in the deluge.

[2136] See the Book of Jonah.

[2137] (חָרְבָה *charabah*) Strong's H2724, from חָרֵב *chareb,* waste (H2720), and חָרַב *charab, to be waste or desolate (*H2717).

[2138] *Bible,* Matthew 7:21.

[2139] *Bible,* Luke 11:2, Πάτερ (*páter* father-founder) ἡμῶν (*ēmõon* our) ὁ (*o* who) ἐν (*en* in) τοῖς (*toîs* the) οὐρανοις (*ouranois* heaven-transcendent),

[2140] *ibid.*, ἁγιασθήτω (*agiasthētō* acknowledged be) τὸ (*to* the) ὄνομά {*onoma* name-power [according to the Hebrew usage (Rocci, p. 1339b – *d*)]} σου (*sou*) your.

[2141] *ibid.*, ἐλθέτω (*elthétō* may appear) ἡ (*ē* the) βασιλεία (*basileia* ruler-ship) σου (*sou* your)

[2142] *Cf. Bible*, Romans 11:36.

[2143] *Bible*, Luke 11:2*,* γενηθήτω (*genēthētō* may be manifest) τὸ (to the) θέλημά (*thelēmá* purpose) σου (*sou* your) ὡς (*ōs* as) ἐν (*en* in) οὐρανῷ (*ouranō*, heaven-transcendent), καὶ (*kai* and) ἐπὶ (*epi* in) τῆς (*tēs* the) γῆς (*gēs* earth-immanent). *Cf. Bible,* Matthew 6:10.

[2144] <Simonelli, *Awareness*, pp. 143-4.>

[2145] *Bible*, John, 8:32 ἀλήθεια *alētheia* = truth, from α-λανθάνω a-*lanthánō = non-unaware = aware.*

[2146] (מֵעָלַי *mē'ālāy*) Strong's H5921, (מֵעָלַי *me'ālay*) upon; 150= 40(מ, *m*) + 70(ע, *a*) + 30(ל, *l*) + 10(י, y); Genesis 13:9.

[2147] (סֹכְכִים *ṣōḵaḵiym*) Strong's H5526, (סֹכְכִים *ṣoḵaḵiym*) cover; 150 = [60(ס, *ṣ*) +20(כ, k) + 20(כ, k)+ 10(י, *y*) + 40(ם, *m*)]; Exodus 25:20.

[2148] (וַיִּלְחֲצוּ *wayilaḥătṣw*) Strong's H3905, (וַיִּלְחֲצוּ *wayilaḥătsw*) oppress; 150 = [6(ו, *w*) + 10(י, *y*)+ 30(ל, *l*) + 8(ח, *ḥ*) + 90(צ, *ts*) + 6(ו, *w*)]; Judges 1:34.

[2149] (נִינָם *niynām*) Strong's H3238, (נִינָם *niynam*) vex; 150 = [50(נ, *n*)+ 10(י, *y*)+ 50(נ, *n*)+ 40(ם, *m*)]; Psalm 74:8.

[2150] (עָנְיֵךְ *'ānayēḵa*) Strong's H6040, (עָנְיֵךְ *'ānayeḵa*) affliction; 150 = [70(ע, *a*) + 50(נ, *n*) + 10(י, *y*) + 20(ך, k)]; Genesis 16:11.

[2151] (כַּעַס *ka'as*) Strong's H3708, (כַּעַס *ka'as*) grief; 150 = [20(כ, k) + 70(ע, *a*) + 60(ס, *ṣ*)]; Deuteronomy 32:27.

[2152] (סְפוֹד *sap̄wōḏ*) Strong's H5594, (סְפוֹד *sap̄woḏ*) lament; 150 = [60(ס, *ṣ*) + 80(פ, *p*) + 6(ו, *w*) + 4(ד, *d*)]; Ecclesiastes 3:4.

[2153] (סִפְדוּ *sip̄aḏw*) Strong's H5594, (סִפְדוּ *sip̄aḏw*) wailing; 150 = [60(ס, *ṣ*) + 80(פ, *p*) + 4(ד, *d*) + 6(ו, *w*)]; Jeremiah 4:8.

[2154] Psalm 104:29.

[2155] Mount Ararat on the back of a 1972 Turkey 100 Lira. *Uros miniature boat,* Titicaca, Puno, Peru.

[2156] Not in the Hebrew or Latin texts.

[2157] (זָכַר *zakar)* Strong's H2142.

[2158] *Cf. Genesis* 1:11 foll.

[2159] See our translation of Genesis 7:15.

[2160] (זִכְּרוֹן *zikrown*) Strong's H2146.

[2161] (כָּתַב *kathab*) Strong's H3789.

[2162] Malachi 3:16.

[2163] *Cf.* Plato, *Phaedrus,* 247b–c (ὑπερουράνιος *upper-ouranios* = beyond-heaven).

[2164] *Cf.* NIM, *Genomic library.*

[2165] From Latin *inter-*(inside)-*legō* (I read, I collect).

[2166] Demiurge, *cf.* Plato, *Timaeus.*

[2167] *Cf.* Budge, E. A. Wallis, *The Mummy.*

[2168] (רוּחַ *ruwach*) Strong's H7307.

[2169] Genesis 1:2.

[2170] Exodus 14:21.

[2171] Jonah 1:4.

[2172] (מַעְיָן *ma'yan*) Strong's H4599.

[2173] Gesenius מַעְיָן 2.

[2174] Psalm 87:7.

[2175] (עַיִן) Strong's H5869.

[2176] (תְּהוֹם *tĕhowm*) Strong's H8415.

[2177] (אֲרֻבָּה *'arubbah*) Strong's H699, Participle passive of אָרַב *'arab*, see below.

[2178] (אָרַב *'arab*) Strong's H693.

[2179] (סָכַר *caker*) Strong's H5534.

[2180] (כָּלָא *kala'*) Strong's H3607.

[2181] (וַיִּלְחֲצוּ *wayilaḥătṣw*) Strong's H3905, (וַיִּלְחֲצוּ *wayilaḥătsw*) oppress; 150 = [6(ו, *w*) + 10(י, *y*)+ 30(ל, *l*) + 8(ח, *ḥ*) + 90(צ, *ts*) + 6(ו, *w*)]; Judges 1:34.

[2182] (נִיְנָם *niynām*) Strong's H3238, (נִיְנָם $n_{i}yn_{\bar{a}}m$) vex; 150 = [50(נ, *n*)+ 10(י, *y*)+ 50(נ, *n*)+ 40(ם, *m*)]; Psalm 74:8.
[2183] (כָּעַס *ka'as*) Strong's H3708, (כָּעַס k_{a}*'as*) grief; 150 = [20(כ, k) + 70(ע, *a*) + 60(ס, *ṣ*)]; Deuteronomy 32:27.
[2184] (סִפּוּד *sap̄wōḏ*) Strong's H5594, (סִפּוּד $s_{a}\bar{p}w_{\bar{o}}\underline{d}$) lament; 150 = [60(ס, *ṣ*) + 80(פ, *p*) + 6(ו, *w*) + 4(ד, *d*)]; Ecclesiastes 3:4.
[2185] (סִפְדוּ *sip̄aḏw*) Strong's H5594, (סִפְדוּ $s_{i}\bar{p}_{a}\underline{d}w$) wailing; 150 = [60(ס, *ṣ*) + 80(פ, *p*) + 4(ד, *d*) + 6(ו, *w*)]; Jeremiah 4:8.
[2186] (עָנְיֵךְ *'ānayēḵa*) Strong's H6040, (עָנְיֵךְ $'\bar{a}n_{a}y_{\bar{e}}\underline{k}_{a}$) affliction; 150 = [70(ע, *a*) + 50(נ, *n*) + 10(י, *y*) + 20(ך, k)]; Genesis 16:11.
[2187] (*Sein zum Tode*), Heidegger, *Being and time*, II, I, H. 235-267, pp. 279-311.
[2188] Francesco, *Scritti di S. Francesco...* p. 121, *Cantico di frate sole* or *Laude delle creature* 12 "*da la quale nullu homo vivente pò scappare*."
[2189] Ecclesiastes 3:20.
[2190] Strong's H6083.
[2191] *Romeo and Juliet*, Act 1, Scene 1, 234, p. 25.
[2192] *BG*. VI.34, *caṃcalaṃ* (restless) *hi* (indeed) *manaḥ* (the mind)... *pramāthi* (turbulent) *balavad* (very strong) *dṛḍham* (obstinate) / *tasyā'* (it) *haṃ* (I) *nigrahaṃ* (more) *manye* (I think) *vāyor-* (of the wind) *iva* (than) *sudushkaram* (difficult to control).
[2193] Different from the Hebrew text.
[2194] Different from the Hebrew text.
[2195] Not in the Hebrew and Greek texts,
[2196] (נוּחַ *nuwach*) Strong's H5117.
[2197] (נֹחַ*Noach*) Strong's H5146.
[2198] (חֹדֶשׁ*chodesh*) Strong's H2320.
[2199] (חָדָשׁ*chadash*) Strong's H2318.
[2200] (בְּשִׁבְעָה־עָשָׂר *bəšiḇə'āh-'āśār*) Strong's H7650, H7651, H7652 & H6237, H6240.
[2201] Strong's H1709 (דג *dag*) fish = 7[3(ג, *g*) + 4(ד, *d*)]; Jonah 1:17.
[2202] Strong's H1709, (דְּגֵי *dəḡēy*) on all fishes = 17 [4 (ד, *d*) + 3 (ג, *g*) + 10 (י, *y*)]; *cf.* Genesis 9:2 & Strong's H1710 (הַדָּגָה$h_{a}d_{\bar{a}}\bar{g}_{\bar{a}}h$) fish 17 [5(ה, *h*) + 4(ד, *d*) + 3(ג, *g*) + 5(ה, *h*)]; Numbers 11:5.
[2203] (הַר *har*) אֶל־הַר הָאֱלֹהִים *'el har hā'ĕlōhiym*, Exodus 3:1.
[2204] (אֲרָרַט *'Ararat*) Strong's H780. *Cf.* Gesenius.
[2205] आर्यावर्त W. 152c.
[2206] *i.e.*: Kabbalah = tradition (*Sefer Yetzirah*) - Gematria (Suarès, *The cipher of Genesis ...*).
[2207] *Cf. Māgen Dāwīd* "Shield of David" (in *Babylonian Talmud*, Pesahim 117 b) and also seal of Solomon.
[2208] *Cf.* the turtle as the Earth-Maker in the Native American Mythology (Gill, *Dictionary*, pp. 78-9 & 316).
[2209] (*coincidentia oppositorum*) Nicolae de Cusa, *De Docta Ignorantia*, I.4.
[2210] קדמון *kadmon* Primordial אדם *adam* Man, *cf.* Knorr von Rosenroth, *Kabbala denudata*.
[2211] <Simonelli, *Beyond Immortality*, pp. 26-27.>
[2212] Strong's H1364 גָּבֹהַ$g_{a}b_{o}h_{a}$ higher = 10[3(ג, *g*) + 2(ב, *b*) + 5(ה, *h*)]; *cf.* 1Samuel 9:2.
[2213] (ראשׁ *ro'sh*) Strong's H7218.
[2214] 1 = א, *a*, Meaning Ox, Leader
[2215] (רָאָה *ra'ah*) Strong's H7200
[2216] Psalm 46:2,3,8,10 (רָפָה*raphah Strong's H7*503 *let go*),11 (יְהוָה...מִשְׂגָּב *Yĕhovah... misgab The Transcendent is our refuge*).
[2217] *Bible*, Luke 14:26 οὐ μισεῖ [*ou* (not) *misei* (hate)] and John 12:25 μισῶν [*misōn* (hateth)] & *cf. Koran, Repentance*, 9:24.
[2218] *Bible*, Mattew 6:25 & 33.
[2219] *BG* IX.22 *ananyāḥ* (having no other) *cintayantaḥ* (absorbed) *mām* (in me) *ye* (to those) *janāḥ* (beings) *paryupāsate* (worship) / *teṣām* (of them) *nitya* (always) *abhiyuktānām* (in permanent devotion) *yoga* (yoked) *kṣemam* (shelter) *vahāmi* (bring) *aham* (I).
[2220] *Bible*, I Corinthians 7, 30. *Cf.* Bruno, frontispiece of *Candelaio*, I ed., "In sadness cheerful: in cheerfulness sad, *In tristitia hilaris, in hilaritate tristis.*
[2221] *Bible*, 1 Corinthians, 15:58.
[2222] *Histories*, 6. 129.4 "*ού φροντίς* (*ou phrontis*) no worry."
[2223] Dante Alighieri, *La divina commedia*, *Purgatory* 5, 14 "*sta come torre ferma, che non crolla*" and *Inferno* 3, 51 "*non ragioniam di lor, ma guarda e passa*."
[2224] *BG* XIV. 24. *sama-* (the same) *duḥkha-* (in sorrow) *sukhaḥ* (in happiness) *sva-* (in the self) *sthaḥ* (centered) *sama-* (equally) *loshṭāśma-* (a lump of dirt, a stone) *kāṃcanaḥ* (gold) / *tulya-* (equal) *priyāpriyo* (loved not loved) *dhīras* (firm) *tulya-* (equal) *niṃdātma-* (in defamation of self) *saṃstutiḥ* (praise) // 25. *mānāpamānayos* (in honor in dishonor) *tulyas* (equal) *tulyo* (equal) *mitrāri-* (of friend of enemy)
[2225] *Cf. UK* II.25 (I.2.25), "*mṛtyur-* (death) *yasyopasecanaṃ* (for whom the spice)."
[2226] *Bible*, Matthew 18:3.
[2227] Next in the Hebrew and Greek texts.
[2228] (חַלּוֹן *challown*) Strong's H2474 & Gesenius.
[2229] (פָּתַח *pathach*) Strong's H6605 & Gesenius.
[2230] *Cf. open the mouth* (Ezekiel 3:2 & Psalm 78:2), *open the hand* (Deuteronomy 15:8,11).

[2231] (פָּקַח) Strong's H6491 & Gesenius.
[2232] Job 21:20.
[2233] (כִּידוֹ) Strong's H3589.
[2234] *Destruction* (כִּידוֹ *kiydwō*) in Gematria = 40, [6 (ו, *w*) + 4 (ד, *d*) + 10 (י, *y*) + 20 (כ, *k*) = 40].
[2235](אַרְבָּעִים *'arba `iym*) Strong's H705.
[2236] *Cf.* Hoffman, *The Hebrew Alphabet.*
[2237] Genesis 3:7, פָּקַח *paqach,* Strong's H6491.
[2238] Genesis 2:17.
[2239] The earliest part of this text dates around the VII century BC.
[2240] *UK* IV.1 (II.I.1) *parāñci* (outward) *khāni* (the senses' openings) *vyatṛṇat* (pierced) *svayambhūs-* (the Self-Made) *tasmāt* (therefore) *parāṅ* (outward) *paśyati* (looks) *nāntarātman* (not in-itself) / *kaścid* (any one?) *dhīraḥ* (wise) *pratyag-* (the inner) *ātmānam-*(Self) *aikshad* (saw) *āvṛtta-* (turned inward) *cakshur-* (with eyes) *amṛtatvam-*(immortality) *icchan* (seeking) /
[2241] (עָשָׂה *` asah*) Strong's H6213.
[2242] (עֶרֶב *` oreb*) Strong's H6158.
[2243] Strong's H6150, Strong's Definitions: "עָרַב 'ârab, aw-rab'; a primitive root (rather identical with H6148 through the idea of covering with a texture); to grow dusky at sundown:—be darkened, (toward) evening."
[2244] Strong's H6148, Strong's Definitions: "עָרַב 'ârab, aw-rab'; a primitive root; to braid, i.e. intermix; technically, to traffic (as if by barter); also or give to be security (as a kind of exchange):—engage, (inter-) meddle (with), mingle (self), mortgage, occupy, give pledges, be(-come, put in) surety, undertake."
[2245] Noble, *Accurate Predictions of Postmortem Interval Using Linear Regression Analyses of Gene Meter Expression Data,* Abstract. *Cf.* Leslie, *'Undead' genes come alive days after life ends.*
[2246] (שָׁלַח *shalach*) Strong's H7971.
[2247] (יָצָא *yatsa'*) Strong's H3318.
[2248] (שׁוּב *shuwb*) Strong's H7725.
[2249] *Cf.* John of the Cross, and Chevalier, *Dictionnaire*, p. 288.
[2250] John of the Cross, *The Dark Night of the Soul*, I. I. XII, p. 52, engraving of "*The Mount of Perfection,... ya por aquí no hay camino, que para el justo no'ay ley.*" *Cf.* Augustine, *In Epistolam Joannis Ad Parthos Tractatus Decem, VII, 8.* "*Dilige* (love), *et* (and) *quod* (that which) *vis* (you want) *fac* (do)." And *Bhagavad-Gītā* III. 17. *tasya* (for him) *kāryaṃ* (duty) *na* (not) *vidyate* (exists).
[2251] *Bible*, Matthew 8:22 and Luk. 9:60.
[2252] Exodus 14:21.
[2253] (מִן *min)* Strong's H4480.
[2254] (אֵת *'eth)* Strong's H853.
[2255] (יוֹנָה) Strong's H3123.
[2256] (יוֹנָה*)* Strong's H3124.
[2257] Jonah 1:1.
[2258] דָּבָר *dabar* Strong's H1696.
[2259] דָּבָר *dabar* Strong's H1697.
[2260] יוֹנָה *yonah* Strong's H3124.
[2261] אֲמִתַּי 'Amittay = my truth Strong's H573, אֱמֶת' *emeth* = truth Strong's H571.
[2262] "*Truth* (ἀλήθεια *alētheia*) *shall free* (ἐλευθερώσει *eleutherōsei*) *you* (ὑμᾶς *umas*)," *Bible*, John 8:32.
[2263] Dante, *La Vita Nova*, chapter XXVI, "*Tanto gentile,*" "*intender non la può chi non la prova/*" 11.
[2264] *Quid est veritas*? *Bible*, John 18:38.
[2265] τὸ *to* (the) πνεῦμα *pneuma* (Spirit) τῆς *tēs* (of) ἀληθείας *alētheias* (truth), *Bible*, John 14:17 & John 15:26 & John 16:13.
[2266] *Bible*, 1John 4:6.
[2267] (אֱמֶת *'emeth*) Strong's H571.
[2268] τὸ *to* (the) πνεῦμα *pneuma* (Spirit) τοῦ *tou* (of) Θεοῦ *Theou* (God) καταβαῖνον *katabainon* (descending) ὡσεὶ *ōsei* (like) περιστερὰν peristeran (dove) καὶ *kai* (and) ἐρχόμενον *erchomenon* (lighting) ἐπ' *ep'* (upon) αὐτόν *auton* (him); *Bible*, Matthew 3:16 & Mark 1:10, Luke 3:22, John 1:32.
[2269] *Cf.* "*The way* (*tao*) *that can be thought* / *is not the never-ending Way* (*Tao*)," confirms Lao Tzu, *Tao Te Ching*, I.1-2.
[2270] *Cf. saccidānanda, sat* (being-awareness-life)-*cit* (real-certain-truth)-*ānanda* (blissful-transcendent-way) in Simonelli, *Beyond Immortality*, pp. 78, 210, 212.
[2271] *Cf. Bible*, John 14:6, "*I am the way, the truth, and the life.*"
[2272] (אֱמֶת *'emeth*) Strong's H571.
[2273] עַיִן *`ayin eye as* spiritual faculty, Strong's H5869.
[2274] נָבַט *nabat Strong's* H5027.
[2275] עָטַף *`ataph* Strong's H5848, Gesenius (3).
[2276] Jonah 1:17 & 2:1,3-10.
[2277] (מֵעָה *me`ah*) Strong's H4578.

[2278] (נוֹחַ *manowach*) Strong's H5117.
[2279] (נוּחַ *nuwach*) Strong's H5118.
[2280] (נֹחַ *Noach*) Strong's H5146.
[2281] *Bible,* Matthew 21:42, Mark 12:10, Luke 20:17 and *cf.* Psalm 118:22, *Lapis, quem reprobavérunt* (ἀπεδοκίμασαν *apedoximasan*) *aedificántes, factus est caput ánguli.*
[2282] Genesis 2:12.
[2283] (כַּף *kaph*) Strong's H3709.
[2284] (כָּפַף *kaphaph*) Strong's H3721.
[2285] (רָגַל *ragal*) Strong's H7279
[2286] (רֶגֶל *regel*) Strong's H7272.
[2287] Gesenius חוּל & חֵיל 6, twisting (חוּל *chuwl*) Strong's H2342 & strength (חַיִל *chayil)* Strong's H2428.
[2288] (דָּג *dāg*) Strong's H1709; 7 = [4(ד, *d*) + 3(ג, *g*)]; cf. Jonah 1:17.
[2289] (קִיא *qow'*) Strong's H6958.
[2290] (יַבָּשָׁה *yabbashah*) Strong's H3004.
[2291] Jonah 2:10.
[2292] **IRONICALLY SPEAKING**, ancient alien theorists could concoct the theory that the flooded planet was similar to Mars's doom and the ark was a space ship bound for Earth (*cf.* Ancient Aliens, *Ancient Alien Theory*).
[2293] *Bible*, Luke 3:22.
[2294] (עֶרֶב *` ereb*) Strong's H6153.
[2295] (עֵת *` eth*) Strong's H6256.
[2296] (טָרַף *taraph*) Strong's H2965.
[2297] (זַיִת *zayith*) Strong's H2132.
[2298] (עָלֶה *` aleh*) Strong's H5929.
[2299] (פֶּה *peh*) Strong's H6310.
[2300] (טָרַף) Strong's H2963.
[2301] (זוֹ) Strong's H2099, Gesenius.
[2302] (עָלָה) Strong's H5927.
[2303] (פֵּאָה) Strong's H6284.
[2304] (הִנֵּה *hinneh*) Strong's H2009.
[2305] (בּוֹא *bow'*) Strong's H935.
[2306] (אֵל 'el) Strong's H413.
[2307] (אֵל 'el) Plural, Strong's H411.
[2308] (יָדַע *yada`*) Strong's H3045.
[2309] (קָלַל *qalal*) Strong's H7043.
[2310] Parti, *Dying to Wake Up*, p. 177, World War II poet Karl Skala's NDE poem.
[2311] The dove is from Bernini's Holy Spirit (1666), shown on the alabaster window above the main altar in Saint Peter's Basilica (Vatican City).
[2312] *Cf.* Evola, *La Tradizione Ermetica*, p. 125.
[2313] Already quoted for Genesis 1:9.
[2314] <Eli Luminosus Aequalis, *Liber Mutus Loquitur*, p. 95.>
[2315] Like the Greek Orthodox *Jesus Prayer*, the constant repetition of the jaculatory "Κύριε (*Kurie* Lord) Ἰησοῦ (*Iēsou* Jesus) Χριστέ (*Christe* Christ), Υἱὲ (*Uie* Son) τοῦ (*tou* of) Θεοῦ (*Theou* God), ἐλέησόν (*eleēson* have mercy) με (*me* on me), τὸν (*ton* the) ἁμαρτωλόν (*amartōlon* sinner);" (*Cf.* Anonymous Pilgrim, *The Way of a Pilgrim*) or in other religion, like the Mantra of Avalokiteśvara (Chenrazee, Tibet's protector): "*Om* (AUM, the four stages of life) *ma-ṇi* [the jewel (*ma* = happiness *ni =* within)] *pad-me* [in the lotus (*pad* = fixed, *me* = exchange)] *hūṃ* (indeed) (*The Tibetan Book of the Dead*, I.II, p. 149 n. 1). *Cf.* St. Louis de Montfort, *The Secret of the Rosary.*
[2316] *Bible*, I Thessalonians 5:17, ἀδιαλείπτως *adialeiptōs* (without ceasing) προσεύχεσθε *proseuchesthe* (pray). *Cf.* Laude, *Pray Without Ceasing.*
[2317] Psalm 1:2.
[2318] Palmer-Sherrard-Ware (Ed.) *The Philokalia*. The constant repetition of 'The Jesus Prayer,' 'Lord Jesus Christ, Son of God, have mercy on me, a sinner,' in Anonymous Pilgrim, *The Way of a Pilgrim.*
[2319] *Raja-ashṭā-ṅga-yoga*, *cf.* Patañjali, *Yoga Sutras.*
[2320] del-Vasto, *Return to the Source*, p. 218.
[2321] *UB.* III.4.2; *cf.* 4.4.18 and *UKena* I.2.
[2322] *Cf. UMaitrī* III.2.
[2323] *Cf. BG* II.48.
[2324] <Simonelli, *Beyond Immortality*, pp. *25,* 118-9, 209>.
[2325] (קַבָּלָה (Literally: "tradition" and the traditional Cabbalist is a *mekubal* (מְקוּבָּל).
[2326] (פרדס *pardes*), paradise, enclosed garden, Strong's H6508.
[2327] *peshat* (פשט) to strip of, literal meaning, Strong's H6584.

[2328] *remez* (רמז) to hint, Klein, A Comprehensive Etymological Dictionary of the Hebrew Language.
[2329] *derash* (דרש), interpretation, Klein, A Comprehensive Etymological Dictionary of the Hebrew Language.
[2330] דרש Gesenius (1).
[2331] *sod* (סוד), secret counsel, Klein, A Comprehensive Etymological Dictionary of the Hebrew Language.
[2332] In order, those states correspond to the four emblematic figures who entered *p$_{a}$rd$_{e}$s*: Ben Azzai, Ben Zoma, Acher Elisha ben Abuyah and Akiba ben Joseph; *cf.* Matt-Pritzker (Ed). *Sefer ha-Zohar.*
[2333] Here one should rely on personal experience only. However, in *Genesis, cf.* the prophetic dreams of Joseph (§37), of the Cupbearer, of the Baker (§40) and of the Pharaoh (§41).
[2334] *Cf. The standard edition of the complete psychological works of Sigmund Freud.*
[2335] *Bible*, Mar 14:38, *cf.* Matthew 26:41.
[2336] *Cf.* Watson (Ed.) *The Dead Sea Scrolls,* pp. 95-124.
[2337] *Exit*ed, as in ex-it, Latin, *ex* (out) *ire* (to go) & *stayed out*, as in ec-stasy, Latin *ex* (out) *stare* (to stay).
[2338] Trance, Latin *ex* (out) *stare* (to stay).
[2339] *Bible*, John 19:28.
[2340] (הַקְּצֹוֹת) Strong's H7099, *at the ends* (הַקְּצֹוֹת *h$_{a}$qtṣ$_{ə}$wṯ*) = 601= [5(ה, *h*) + 100(ק, *q*) + 90(צ, *ts*) + 6(ו, *w*) + 400(ת, *t*)]; Exodus 38:5.
[2341] The Hebrew letter א, *a*, means *leader.*
[2342] (תֶּרְא) Strong's H7200, *see, perceive* (תֶּרְא *t$_{ə}$ra*) = 601 = [400(ת, *t*) + 200(ר, *r*) + 1(א, *a*)]; Proverbs 23:31.
[2343] (גָּדוֹל *gadowl*) Strong's H1419.
[2344] (דָּג *dag*) Strong's H1709.
[2345] (בָּלַע *bala`*) Strong's H1104; Jonah 1:17, [דג *dag: fish, from* דָּגָה *dagah:* to multiply, increase, to cover (*i.e.:* multitude covering over everything)].
[2346] (דָּגָה *dagah)* Strong's H1711.
[2347] Jonah 2:10.
[2348] (חָרֵב *charab*) Strong's H2717.
[2349] (כָּבוֹד *kabowd*) Strong's H3519.
[2350] Psalm 29:9.
[2351] Francesco, *Scritti di S. Francesco...* p. 121, *Cantico di frate sole* or *Laude delle creature* 12 "*Laudato sie, mi Signore cum tucte le Tue creature.*"
[2352] Strong's H8081.
[2353] Ezekiel 32:14.
[2354] Exodus 25:6.
[2355] Isaiah 6:9-10.
[2356] (אָהַב *'ahab*) Strong's H157, Gesenius 1.
[2357] Deuteronomy 6:5; *cf.* also 7:9, 10:12, 11:1, 19:9, 30:6-16-20, Psalm 70:4, Ezekiel 16:8, Micah 6:8, Zephaniah 3:17, Matthew 22:37, Mark 12:30 and Luke 10:27.
[2358] Strong's H3824.
[2359] לֵבָב Gesenius (b).
[2360] Strong's H5315.
[2361] *Cf.* נֶפֶשׁ Gesenius (1 & 3).
[2362] Strong's H3966.
[2363] (שָׁחָה *shachah*) Strong's H7812.
[2364] (אֵל *'el*) Strong's H410.
[2365] (קַנָּא *qanna')* Strong's H7067.
[2366] Exodus 34:14.
[2367] Deuteronomy 4:24.
[2368] لا إله إلا الله (*lā 'ilāha 'illallāh*) *There is no deity except Allah,"* Koran 64:13. *Cf.* "*I* am *the LORD, and* there is *none else,* there is *no God beside me.*" Isaiah 45:5.
[2369] De Giorgio, 4.
[2370] Lao Tzu, *Tao Te Ching*, 60-16.
[2371] Confucius, *The Analects*, I. 5.
[2372] Deuteronomy 6:5.
[2373] *Cf.* Eliade, *Shamanism.*
[2374] *Bible*, Matthew 13:53.
[2375] *Cf.* Campbell, *The Mask of God.*
[2376] Mbiti, *African Religions and Philosophy* , 28-29, 31and 33.
[2377] Tucci, *Storia ... cinese* 51.
[2378] Lao Tzu, *Tao Te Ching* 2-39.
[2379] Einstein, *Out of My Later Years. p. 61 and Physics and Reality. Cf.* Kant, *Critique of Pure Reason,* A516 B544.
[2380] del-Vasto, *Return to the Source*, p. 223.
[2381] *Cf.* Campbell, *The Mask,* 4.

[2382] *Sources of Chinese,* 102. *Sources of Chinese Tradition*, compiled by Theodore de Bary, Wing-tsit Chan, Burton Watson, *Introduction to Oriental Civilization*, n. LIV-LVI, ed. Theodore de Bary, Columbia University Press, NY, 1960.
[2383] Confucius, *The Analects*, I. 9; 12.
[2384] For "separation between church and state," *cf.* Jefferson's 1802 *Letter to the Danbury Baptist Association* (in Schultz, *Encyclopedia…*, p. 288) and for truths to be self-evident" *cf.* Jefferson's 1776 *Declaration of independence* (in Vincent, *The platform…*, p. 7. For Communism as a religion *cf.* Russell, *Why I Am Not a Christian…* , p. V. See also the *prophetic* views of Marx's *Capital* and the dogmatic impositions in Mao's *Little Red Book.*
[2385] *UC* VIII. 3. 5.
[2386] Campbell, *The Mask*, 6.
[2387] *Cf.* non violence *a-hiṃsā* in Acaranga Sutra, *The First Anga Agama of the Jainas.*
[2388] *Koran* 5:65.
[2389] *Cf.* Campbell, *The Mask.*
[2390] <Simonelli, *Beyond Immortality*, p. 27-29.>
[2391] *Bible*, I John 4:19).
[2392] Strong's H2099, Gesenius.
[2393] Strong's H2134, זָךְ $z_{\bar{a}}\underline{k}_{ə}$ pure = 27=[7(ז, *z*) + 20(ך, *k*)]; Exodus 27:20.
[2394] Exodus 27:20. *Italic oil lamp* (IV Century BC).
[2395] *Bible*, Matthew 25:1-13.
[2396] Psalm 27:1.
[2397] Strong's H5027, וַיַּבֵּט $w_{a}y_{a}b_{ē}ṭ$ looked = 27 =[6(ו, *w*) + 10(י, *y*) + 2(ב, *b*) + 9(ט, *ṭ*)]; 1 Samuel 17:42.
[2398] Strong's H3001.
[2399] Strong's H2076, יְזַבֵּחַ *yəzabēaḥ* sacrificed = 27 = [10(י, *y*) + 7(ז, *z*) + 2(ב , *b*) + 8(ח, *ḥ*)]; Habakkuk 1:16.
[2400] del-Vasto, *Return to the Source*, p, 223, 234, 240.
[2401] *Cf.* del-Vasto, *Return to the Source*, pp. 222-223 and Crowley, *Confessions…*, p. 631.
[2402] "*sciencia muy sabrosa," The Poems…*, 27, p. 8.
[2403] <Simonelli, *Beyond Immortality*, pp, 205-6.>
[2404] (חַי *chay*) Strong's H2416.
[2405] (חַוָּה *chavah*) Strong's H2331, *cf.* Gesenius.
[2406] (בָּשָׂר *basar*) Strong's H1320.
[2407] (חֲוָא *chava'*) Strong's H2324 (Aramaic).
[2408] (יָצָא *yatsa'*) Strong's H3318.
[2409] (עוֹף ` *owph*) Strong's H5775.
[2410] (רֶמֶשׂ *remes*) Strong's H7431.
[2411] (רָמַשׂ *ramas*) Strong's H7430.
[2412] (שָׁרַץ *sharats*) Strong's H8317.
[2413] (פָּרָה *parah*) Strong's H6509.
[2414] (רָבָה *rabah*) Strong's H7235.
[2415] As an example, *cf.* Harari, *Sapiens. A brief History of Humankind.*
[2416] *Cf.* Tolle, *Eckhart Tolle A New Earth.*
[2417] *Escaping criticism*, Pere Borrell del Caso (1873), Collection Banco de España, Madrid, Wikimedia Commons pere borrel del caso.png, Public Domain.
[2418] (עָלָה ` *alah*) Strong's H5927.
[2419] (עֹלָה ` *olah*) Also meaning burnt offering, Strong's H5930.
[2420] *Bible*, Hebrew 9:6-7.
[2421] (יֵצֶר *yetser*) Strong's H3336.
[2422] *Cf.* Francione, *Eat Like You Care*, cp. 2.
[2423] *Bible*, Matthew 13:21-22, underlining is ours; συμπνίγω (*sympnigō*), suffocate, choke.
[2424] Isaiah 35:1-2, 5-6, 8-9.
[2425] Dylan, *18 Poems*: *The force that through the green fuse drives the flower.*
[2426] Humphreys, *Glimpses of the Life and Teachings of Bhagavan Sri Ramana Maharshi*, p. 17.
[2427] Genesis 2:4.
[2428] (רוּחַ *ruwach*) Strong's H7306.
[2429] (נִיחֹחַ *nichowach*) Strong's H5207.
[2430] (נוּחַ *nuwach*) Strong's H5117.
[2431] (אָמַר *'amar*) Strong's H559.
[2432] (לֵב *leb*) Strong's H3820.
[2433] (יֵצֶר *yetser*) Strong's H3336.
[2434] (רַע *ra`*) Strong's H7451.
[2435] (רָעַע *ra`a`*) Strong's H7489.
[2436] (נַעַר *na`uwr*) Strong's H5271.

[2437] Waking, REM, NREM.

[2438] *Cf.* ABC News, *Lion Adopts Baby Antelope*, & NBC News, *Goat intended as tiger's meal becomes its friend instead.*

[2439] Book of Jonah 3:3-10.

[2440] Śaiva sādhu ascetic (September 27, 2016, Mana, Valley of Flowers, West Himalaya National Park, Uttarakhand, India).

[2441] Dalrymple, *Nine Lives...*, p. 219 and 225. *Cf.* Simonelli, *Beyond Immortality*, p. 42.

[2442] Francesco, *Scritti di S. Francesco, Cantico delle creature*, "*beati quelli ke trovarà ne le tue santissime voluntati, ka la morte secunda no 'l farrà male.*"

[2443] (קֹר qor) Strong's H7120.

[2444] (קַר *qar*) Strong's H7119.

[2445] (חֹם *chom*) Strong's H2527.

[2446] (חָמַם *chamam*) Strong's H2552.

[2447] (קַיִץ *qayits*) Strong's H7019.

[2448] (חָרַף *charaph*) Strong's H2778.

[2449] (חֹרֶף choreph) Strong's H2779.

[2450] (לוּל *luwl*) Strong's H3883.

[2451] (לַיִל *layil*) Strong's H3915.

[2452] Not in the Hebrew or Latin texts.

[2453] *Bible*, Matthew 5:8.

[2454] In the Latin sense of *un-animus* (of one mind) = *unus* (one) *animus* (mind, spirit).

[2455] Anch, *Sleep: ...*, p. 58.

[2456] Nikhilānanda, *Gauḍapāda's Kārikā* I-6(1).

[2457] Chun Siong Soon, *Unconscious determinants...*, p. 543 and № "n.1: Libet, B. et al. *Behav. Brain Sci.* 8, 529–566 (1985). n.2: Wegner, D.M., *Trends Cogn. Sci.* 7, 65–69 (2003). n.3: Haggard, P. *Trends Cogn. Sci.* 9, 290–295 (2005)."

[2458] *Bible*, Matthew 5:28.

[2459] *Cf. UM* 5.

[2460] Nikhilānanda, *Māṇḍūkyopanishad*,I, 6 (2).

[2461] <Simonelli, *Beyond Immortality*, p. 105.>

[2462] *Cf. B.U.* IV.3.32.

[2463] *UMaitrī* VI.17. *evaisha* (so this) *kṛtsna-* (after all) *kshaya* (remains) *eko* (alone) *jāgartīti* (awake thus) *etasmād* (from this) *ākāśād* (vacuity) *esha* (this) *khalv* (truly) *idaṃ* (this) *cetāmātram* (of pure awareness consisting) *bodhayati* (awakes) *anenaiva* (by this verily) *cedam* (and this) *dhyāyate* (meditating) *asmin* (in that) *ca* (and) *pratyastam* (disappearance) *yāti* (disappears)

[2464] *UMaitrī* IV.3.15-16-17 *punaḥ* (again) *pratinyāyam* (in inverted order) *pratiyony* (to source or origin) *ādravati* (hasten towards)

[2465] *Cf.* Carbonara, *Disegno d'una filosofia.*

[2466] Latin, *in-tueri*, to look-in.

[2467] *Cf.* Brentano, *Psychologie*, I, 115, 2.

[2468] The MRC Cognition and Brain Sciences Unit (Medical Research Council - CBU, Cambridge University UK http://www.mrc-cbu.cam.ac.uk/) "*funod taht the mnid rades wrods as a wolhe, the odrer of ltertes deos not matetr, olny fsrit and lsat msut be in rhgit pacle.*" *Cf. UB* IV, 4, 2; *UT* II.5; III.10.5. For sleep *cf.*: *UB* II.1.16-17 (NREM)-19; IV.3.19 to 31.

[2469] Latin, *dis*, apart & *currere*, to run.

[2470] Tolle, *The Power of Now*, p. 81. *Cf.* Anch, *Sleep: ...*, p. 56 fol .

[2471] Dement, *Some must watch. Cf.* Jung, *Psychology*, p. 54 and *Mandala*, p. 22.

[2472] *Cf.* Callcut, *John Wilkinson – Copper King?* n. 17.

[2473] *Cf.* Benfey, *Kekule* .

[2474] *Cf.* Kanigel, *The man who knew ...*, 183 *fol.*, 226 *fol.*, 280 *fol.*

[2475] *Cf.* Tammet, *Thinking In Numbers.*

[2476] Strathern, *Mendeleyev's Dream.*

[2477] Pollack, *The Faith of Biology*, Chapter 1, Insight, Revelation and the Unknowable, p. 3.

[2478] *Cf.* Sykes, *The man who loved...*

[2479] Halberda, *Individual differences ...*, 9/08.

[2480] Park, *The Unmaking of American Science Policy*, 14 (italics are ours).

[2481] *Saturday Evening Post*, 10/26/1929.

[2482] Valenstein, *The War of the Soups ...* Similar experiences were reported by Nikola Tesla, who discovered alternating current (Tesla, *My Inventions...*, ch. 2), naturalist Louis Agassiz (Stewar, *Tesla...*), Elias Howe inventor of the sewing machine (Waldemar-Kaempffert, *A Popular History ...*, vol. II.), President Abraham Lincoln assassination premonition dream (Lamon, *Recollections of Abraham Lincoln*), novelists Mary Shelley (introduction to *Frankenstein*), Stephen King and Robert Louis Stevenson, songwriter Paul McCartney, golfer Jack Nicklaus (Barrett, *The Committee of Sleep...*), and entrepreneurs Madame Walker (Bundles, *On Her Own Ground...*) and David Ogilvy (Jacobs, *The Executive Life*).

[2483] Scarano, *Gente*, 35-7, "*una folgorazione, un flash improvviso.*"

[2484] Plutarch, *Epicurus*, 1094 C and *cf.* Vitruvius, IX, praef. 10; εὕρηκα εὕρηκα from εὑρίσκω (*euriscō*) = I find. Buoyancy = a body, immersed in a fluid, receives an upward drive equal to the weight of the displaced liquid.
[2485] <Simonelli, *Philosophy as a Path ...*, pp 26-27.>
[2486] *Cf.* Simonelli, *Il neoplatonismo ...*, pp. 198 to 215.
[2487] *Bible*, John 1:51.
[2488] Genesis 28:12 חלם *chalam* dreamed.
[2489] Genesis רֹאשׁ *ro'sh* top, head, beginning.
[2490] Genesis מלאך *mal'ak* theophanic angel messengers, ἄγγελοι *aggeloi*.
[2491] Genesis אלהים *'elohiym* pl. Godlike ruler, God, corresponding to *prājña*.
[2492] Genesis 16 יקץ *yaqats* awaked.
[2493] Genesis שׁוֹא *shehah* sleep.
[2494] Genesis ידע *yada`* knew.
[2495] Genesis 12; 13; 16.
[2496] *Jacob's dream*, in Altus, *Mutus Liber*, & Eli Luminosus Aequalis, *Mutus Liber Loquitur*, Frontispiece & First Plate.
[2497] Nikhilānanda, p. 37.
[2498] *UB.* IV.3.11. *asuptaḥ* (not asleep) *suptān* (the sleeping ones) *abhicākaśīti* (casts a look upon)
[2499] Ramana Maharshi, *Spiritual teaching*, p. 69.
[2500] *UT.* II.7.1. *yadā* (when) *hy* (verily) *evaisha* (verily this) *etasminn* (in this one) *udaram* (nterior) *antaraṃ* (exterior) *kurute* (makes) *atha* (then) *tasya* (of this) *bhayam* (fear) *bhavati* (is) *tattveva* (that truly) *bhayaṃ* (fear) *vidusho'* (knower) *manvānasya* (who does not reflect)
[2501] Plotinus, III, 8, 10.
[2502] *Cf.* Plotinus, V, 1, 6. and the same example in *UMu.* II.I.1.
[2503] Plotinus, IV.4.32.
[2504] *Cf.* Worden, *Mutter Museum.* Conjoined twins at the Scott Lindgren-Mütter Museum Philadelphia PA. *Ex.* twins with one head (*Cephalothoracopagus monosymmetros*) and two headed *ectopagus* (*Dicephalus Dibrachius Tripus*).
[2505] *Bible*, Matthew 22:23; *cf.* also Mark 12:18 and Luke 20:27.
[2506] *Bible*, Act 4:2.
[2507] *Bible*, Matthew 22:30, 32; *cf.* also Mark 12:25, 27 and Luke 20:36, 38.
[2508] *UMaitrī* VI.28. *oṃ*kāra- (of the syllable AUM) *plavenāntarhṛdayākāśasya* [with the boat (as the Ark)] internal in the heart space) *pāram* (to the other side) *tīrtvāvirbhūte'* (having sailed across becomes manifest) *ntarākāśe* (in the inner space) *śanakairavaṭaivāvaṭakṛd* (quietly the mine as miner) *dhātukāmaḥ* (minerals seeking) *saṃviśaty* (penetrates) *evaṃ* (so) *brahma-* (of the Creator) *śālāṃ* (in the abode) *viśet* (one should enter). OM or ॐ or AUM· stands for A = wakefulness, U = dream (REM), M = dreamless sleep (NREM), · = the silence from which the sound comes and to which it goes (*cf.* *Māṇḍūkya Upanishad*, translated by Simonelli, *Beyond Immortality*, pp. 58-86).
[2509] <Simonelli, *Beyond Immortality*, pp. 69 -84.>
[2510] *Cf.* Kuras, *As Golems Go...*, p. 12 and Dan, *Kabbalah*, pp. 105-108. Golem (Brass, popular art, Prague 2000).
[2511] *Cf.* McCarthy, *Epistemological Problems of Artificial Intelligence.*
[2512] Campbell, *The power of myth*, p. 14, 18.
[2513] *Cf.* Ramana Maharshi, *Spiritual teaching*, p. 42.
[2514] <Simonelli, *Beyond Immortality*, pp. 78-79.> *Cf.* Gallant (Professor of Psychology and Vision Science;, Helen Wills Neuroscience Institute Department of Psychology, UC Berkeley), *Brain decoding: Reading minds*, "by scanning blobs of brain activity, scientists may be able to decode people's thoughts, their dreams and even their intentions." *Cf.* Ogawa (Bell Laboratories in Murray Hill, N.J.) & Kwong (Massachusetts General Hospital in Charlestown), *Brain imaging: fMRI 2.0.* & Gallant, *Natural speech reveals the semantic maps that tile human cerebral cortex.* Advanced studies are attempting to map (fMRI) the brain systematically.
[2515] *Cf.* North, *Our Robot Nightmares.*
[2516] *Cf.* Simonelli, *Philosophy as a Path to Education for Leadership*, § *Developing creative thinking for the XXI Century*. *Cf.* Dr. Matthew Phillips and a team of researchers at HRL Laboratories, LLC, MALIBU, Calif. February 10, 2016 have discovered that using transcranial Direct Current Stimulation (tDCS) low-current electrical brain stimulation can improve learning skills and creativity besides helping patients recover from strokes (HRL Laboratories, LLC., *HRL DEMONSTRATES THE POTENTIAL TO ENHANCE THE HUMAN INTELLECT'S EXISTING CAPACITY TO LEARN NEW SKILLS*).
[2517] *VR.* X.235.3 "*a new wheel-less chariot with only one spinal-cord-pole and turning everywhere.*"
[2518] *UK* III.3-10 (I.3.3-10), *ātmānaṃ* (the Self) *rathinaṃ* (riding in the chariot) *viddhi* (know) *śarīraṃ* (the body) *ratham-* (a two wheeled chariot) *eva* (verily) *tu* (also) / *buddhiṃ* (Ego-consciousness) *tu* (also) *sārathiṃ* (the driver of the chariot) *viddhi* (know) *manaḥ* (the faculty of thought) *pragraham-* (reins) *eva* (verily) *ca* (and) / *indriyāṇi* (the faculties of the senses) *hayān-* (horses) *āhur-* (they say) *vishayāṃs-* (the scope of the senses) *eshu* (in them) *gocarān* (the range for pasture) / *ātmendriya-* (the self consciousness and the faculties of the senses) *mano-*(the faculty of thought) *yuktaṃ* (united) *bhoktety-* (the experiencer thus) *āhur-* (say) *manīshiṇaḥ* (the wise men) / *yas-* (who) *tv-* (thus) *avijñānavān-* (without intuition) *bhavaty-* (is) *ayuktena* (un-concentrated) *manasā* (with the faculty of the mind) *sadā* (always) / *tasyendriyāṇy-* (his faculties) *avaśyāni* (un-submissive) *dushṭāśvā* (vicious horses) *iva* (like) *sāratheḥ* (for the driver)/ *yas-* (who) *tu* (however) *vijñānavān-* (with intuition) *bhavaty-* (is) *yuktena* (yoked in concentration) *manasā* (with the faculty of the

mind) *sadā* (always) / *tasyendriyāṇy-* (his faculties) *vaśyāni* (submissive) *sadaśvā* (good horses) *iva* (like) *sāratheḥ* (for the driver) / *yas-* (who) *tv-* (also) *avijñānavān-* (without intuition) *bhavaty* (is) *amanaskaḥ* (without intellect) *sadāśuciḥ* (always impure) / *na* (not) *sa* (he) *tat-* (that) *padam-* (goal) *āpnoti* (does attain) *saṃāraṃ* (the flow of worldly illusions) *cādhigacchati* (falls into) / *yas-* (who) *tu* (however) *vijñānavān-* (with intuition) *bhavati* (is) *samanaskaḥ* (unanimous) *sadā* (always) *śuciḥ* (holy) / *sa* (he) *tu* (verily) *tat-* (that) *padam-* (goal) *āpnoti* (does attain) *yasmād-* (from which) *bhūyo* (again) *na* (not) *jāyate* (born)/ *vijñāna-* (that has the intuition) *sārathir-* (of the chariot's driver) *yastu* (he then) *manaḥ-* (faculty of the mind) *pragrahavān-* (tightens the reins) *naraḥ* (man) / *so'* (he) *dhvanaḥ* (of the journey) *pāram-* (the end) *āpnoti* (reaches) *tad-*(that) *vishṇoḥ* (of the all-pervading being) *paramaṃ*(Transcendent) *padam* (place) / *indriyebhyaḥ* (the faculty of the senses) *parā-* (beyond) *hy-* (indeed) *arthā* (the acts of intentionality) *arthebhyaś-* (the acts of intentionality) *ca* (and) *paraṃ* (beyond) *manaḥ* (the faculty of the mind)/ *manasastu* (the faculty of the mind) *parā* (beyond) *buddhir-* (consciousness) *buddher-* (consciousness) *ātmā* (self) *mahān-* (great) *paraḥ* (beyond). *Cf.* Simonelli, *Beyond Immortality*, 172 fol.

[2519] *Phaedrus* , 246. Charioteer driving a biga right with Nike flying above. (Obverse, silver tetradrachm Syracuse, Sicily, 430 B.C.).

[2520] (חָיֶה *chayeh*) Strong's H2422.

[2521] (חַיָּה *chayah*) Strong's H2421.

[2522] (יָם *yam*) Strong's H3220.

[2523] *UB* IV. 3. 18 & 19

[2524] Nikhilānanda, *Śaṅkara's Commentary of Gauḍapāda's Kārikā* p. 25.

[2525] *VṚ* VI.9.6. *jyotir* (the light) *hṛdaya* (in the heart). The light in the heart.

[2526] *UB* I, IV.3.7. *katama* (which one) *ātmeti* (the self then) *yo*(who) *yaṃ* (this) *vijñānamayaḥ* (composed of knowledge) *prāṇeshu* (among the vital senses) *hṛdy* (heart) *antarjyotiḥ* (the light within) *purushaḥ* (person) *sa* (he) *samānaḥ* (serenely centered in itself) *sann* (being) *ubhau* (both) *lokāv* (worlds) *anusañcarati* (penetrates) *dhyāyatīva* (thinking as if) *lelāyatīva* (moving to and fro as if) *sa* (he) *hi* (upon) *svapno* (dream state) *bhūtvā* – (becoming) *imaṃ* (this) *lokam* (dimension) *atikrāmati* (beyond goes) *mṛtyo* (death) *rūpāṇi* (the forms).

[2527] *UM.* 6, *esho'ntaryāmy.*

[2528] *UB* IV.3.30. *na* (not) *vijānāti* (does know) *vijānan* (knowing) *vai* (verily) *tan* (that) *na* (not) *vijānāti* (does know) *na* (not) *hi* (verily) *vijñātur* (the knower) *vijñāter* (knower) *viparilopo* (separation) *vidyate* (there is) *avināśitvāt* (imperishable) *na* (not) *tu* (however) *tad* (that) *dvitīyam* (second) *asti* (is) *tato'* (therefore) *nyad* (opposit) *vibhaktam* (divided) *yad* (that) *vijānīyāt* (he may know)

[2529] (יָרֵא *yare'*) Strong's H3372.

[2530] (מוֹרָא *mowra'*) Strong's H4172.

[2531] (חַתַּת *chathath*) Strong's H2865.

[2532] (חַת *chath*) Strong's H2844.

[2533] (יָד *yad*) Strong's H3027.

[2534] Sartre, *Being and Nothingness*, p. 223.

[2535] *Bible*, John 18:36, ἡ βασιλεία ἡ ἐμὴ οὐκ ἔστιν ἐκ τοῦ κόσμου (cosmos or dimension)... οὐκ ἔστιν ἐντεῦθεν.

[2536] (עֵשֶׂב *`eseb*) *cf.* Genesis 1:30.

[2537] (אָכְלָה *'oklah*) Strong's H402, from אָכַל *'akal* (H398) to eat, *cf. 'Ukal* אֻכָל (H401) the One Devoured.

[2538] (הָיָה *hayah*) Strong's H1961.

[2539] (רָמַשׂ *ramas*) Strong's H7430, see *moving things* רֶמֶשׂ *remes* (H7431).

[2540] (הוּא *hava'*) Strong's H1934 *(Aramaic), see* הָוָה *hava'* (H1933).

[2541] *Cf.* Webster, *Test on halal meat. Halal* are the *allowed* animals slaughtered according the *dhabīḥah*, Islamic ritual rules; forbidden animals or not ritually slaughtered are *haram, sinful. Kosher* are foods that conform to dietary Jewish law, *kashrut*; those not in accordance are called torn, *treif.*

[2542] (דָּם) Strong's H1818.

[2543] (דָּמַם) Strong's H1826.

[2544] (דָּהַם) Strong's H1724.

[2545] (דּוּחַ) Strong's H1740.

[2546] (דָּמָה) Strong's H1820.

[2547] (אָוֶן) Strong's H119.

[2548] Malory, *La mort...*, book XIII, Ch. I, p. 223.

[2549] By assonance see Sanskrit *gala* = to eat and √*had* = to digest (Agni Vaiśvānara).

[2550] Malory, *La mort...*, book XIII, Ch. IV, p. 228.

[2551] <Simonelli, *Beyond Immortality*, pp. 134-5.>

[2552] Strong's H1826, Gesenius דָּמַם. Heinrich Friedrich Wilhelm Gesenius (1786 – 1842) German orientalist and Biblical scholar.

[2553] *UM.* 5 *fol.*

[2554] *Cf. Bible,* Matthew 21:42, Mark 12:10, Luke 20:17 and *cf.* Psalm 118:22, *Lapis, quem reprobavérunt* (ἀπεδοκίμασαν *apedoximasan*) *aedificántes, factus est caput ánguli.*

[2555] Makāra, *cf.* Greek letter M: "μῦ" (*mŭ-ÿ*, Rocci, p. 1170a); μύω [μῦō, μὐ]" (*mū-ÿ*, *mú-ý* = I close up, I keep silent; p. 1263b), *cf.*

Sanskrit *mūka* = *mu*te, silent (*W.*, p.825b); "μύσις, ... [μύω]" (*músis... múō* = closing eyes, lips; p. 1262b); "μῦέω, μύω]" (*mūéō, múō* = I initiate to the *mys*teries; p. 1256b), *cf.* En. *mys*tic. M_a (म) is the third sound of the Sanskrit syllable AUM (OM ॐ), meaning mother, measure. The base of the accusative of the 1st person pronoun and *ma*dhyama, the 4th note of the Indian music scale.

2556 *Cf.* MacDonell, *Sanskrit*, p. 4.

2557 *Bible*, 2 Corinthian 12:2 and 4. *Cf. W.* p. 771ab. Also Greek pronoun ἐ-μὲ (*é-mê*) and μὲ (*mê*); Latin *me, mihi.* En. me.

2558 *Cf.* דָּמַם *damam*, to be quiet, still.

2559 *Cf.* דָּמָה *damah, to destroy.*

2560 *UM.* 11 *sushupta-* (the deep unconsciousness) *stānaḥ* (state) *prājño* (the knower) *makāras-* (letter-sound M) *tṛtīyā* (third) *mātrā* (metrical letter) *miter* (Measuring-building) *apīter-* (Abatement-entering-into-dissolution-) *vā* (or) *minoti* (Measures-building) *ha* (indeed) *vā* (verily) *idaṁ*(this) *sarvam* (all) *apītiś-* (Abatement-entering-dissolution) *ca* (and) *bhavati* (becomes) *ya* (who) *evaṃ* (thus) *veda* (knows).

2561 *Psyche and Symbol*, p. 79.

2562 (נֶפֶשׁ *nephesh*) Strong's H5315.

2563 Strong's H1818.

2564 Strong's H1320. euphemistically meaning also *male organ of generation.*

2565 Strong's H1319, from which derives H1320.

2566 Strong's H5315.

2567 Leviticus 17:11.

2568 *Bible*, Mark 10:9 & Matthew 19:6, separate χωρίζω *chorizo.*

2569 (מִיַּד *miyad*) Strong's H4481.

2570 (יָד *yad*) Strong's H3027.

2571 Strong's H1875.

2572 (אָח *'ach*) Strong's H251.

2573 *Bible*, Matthew 26:28... Mark 14:24 & Luke 22:20.

2574 <Simonelli, *Beyond Immortality*, p. 75.>

2575 Ramana Maharshi, *Spiritual teachings*, p. 44 and 46.

2576 *Bible*, Matthew 26:52.

2577 Ecclesiastes 8:17.

2578 *UK* II.19 (I.2.19) *hantā* (the slayer) *cen-* (if) *manyate* (thinks) *hantuṃ* (he slays) *hataś-*(the slain) *cen-* (if) *manyate* (thinks) *hatam* (killed) / *ubau* (both) *tau* (these) *na* (not) *vijānīto* (understand) *nāyaṃ* (not does this) *hanti* (slay) *na* (nor) *hanyate* (is slain) / The *Bhagavad-Gītā* II.19 reconfirms, "He who views someone a killer and he who considers himself killed, the two do not know. This one does not kill and is not killed." *BG ya* (he) *enaṃ* (this) *vetti* (views) *hantāraṃ* (killer) *yaś* (he) *cainaṃ* (and this) *manyate* (considers) *hatam* (killed) / *ubhau* (the two) *tau* (those) *na* (not) *vijānīto* (know) *nāyaṃ* (not this) *haṃti* (kills) *na* (not) *hanyate* (is killed) //

2579 (אֵתָם *'Etham*) Strong's H864. Name of the border between Egypt and the Arabian desert; *cf.* Gesenius.

2580 The word *computer* itself derives from Latin and means *to think, calculate* and *estimate* (*putare*) *together* (*com-*).

2581 (פָּרָה *parah*) Strong's H6509.

2582 Campbell, *The Power of Myth*, p. 20.

2583 *Bible*, 1Corinthians 7:26, 30-32, 35.

2584 Strong's H559, Gesenius (1).

2585 (בְּרִית) Strong's H1285, Gesenius.

2586 (בָּרָה) Strong's H1262, Gesenius.

2587 *Bible*, Matthew 22:4,8.

2588 *Bible*, Matthew 22:14.

2589 *Bible*, Revelation 7:14-17, emphasis is ours.

2590 Not in the Hebrew text.

2591 Strong's H3318.

2592 Strong's H2416.

2593 Strong's H5775.

2594 (בְּהֵמָה *běhemah*) Strong's H929.

2595 Gesenius, בְּהֵמָה, 3, 4.

2596 (כָּרַת *karath*) Strong's H3772.

2597 (שָׁחַת *shachath*) Strong's H7843.

2598 *Bible,* Matthew 18:10.

2599 Space (height, length, depth), time (past, present, future) and causality = 7 dimensions.

2600 *Cf.* Francesco, *Scritti di S. Francesco, Cantico delle creature,* "*la morte secunda.*"

2601 *Bible*, Matthew 16:25.

2602 *Cf. BG* II.48.

2603 Strong's H6529. *Cf.* Simonelli, *Awareness*, pp. 137, 149-50.

[2604] *Cf.* Schaff, *Creeds of Christendom,* Vol. I, § 7 "*cuius regni non erit finis,*" (*Nicene Creed*, 325).
[2605] (אוֹת *'owth*) Strong's H226 and Gesenius אוֹת, 4.
[2606] (אוֹת *'uwth*) Strong's H225, Gesenius 1.
[2607] (נֶפֶשׁ *nephesh*) Strong's H5315.
[2608] (עוֹלָם *` owlam*) Strong's H5769.
[2609] (עָלַם *` alam*) Strong's H5956.
[2610] (דּוֹר *dowr*) Strong's H1755, Gesenius 1.
[2611] (דּוּר *duwr*) Strong's H1752, Gesenius 1.
[2612] *Cf. Bible*, Matthew 21:42 & Mark 12:10 & Luke 20:17.
[2613] Protagoras of Abdera, in Socrates' words, Plato, *Theaetetus 160 e.*
[2614] Borbély, pp. 55, 56, 58.
[2615] Borbély, pp. 202.
[2616] <Simonelli, *Beyond Immortality*, pp. 69-84> & *cf. Māṇḍūkya Upanishad.*
[2617] Heschel, *The Insecurity of Freedom, p. 8.*
[2618] Strong's H6051, Gesenius 1.
[2619] Strong's H6049, Gesenius 1.
[2620] Society of Biblical Archæology, *Transactions*, p. 99. *Cf.* the crow (עֹרֵב *` oreb*) in Genesis 8:7. Indonesian woodden cock.
[2621] Deuteronomy 18:10,14.
[2622] (קָשָׁה_*qashah*) Strong's H7185.
[2623] (קֶשֶׁת *qesheth*) Strong's H7198, Gesenius a.
[2624] (קוֹשׁ *qowsh*) Strong's H6983.
[2625] Deuteronomy 18:13.
[2626] *Bible*, Revelation 19:9 (underlining is ours). Lamb ἀρνίον *arnion*, (diminutive of ἀρήν *arēn* or ἀρνός *arnos* sheep) the pure sacrifice lamb that takes away (αἴρω *airō*) the *sins* of the world.
[2627] (עָנַן *` anan*) Strong's H6049.
[2628] *Cf.* Saint Teresa of Avila, *The Interior Castle.*
[2629] *The Collected Works of Sri Ramana Maharshi*, p. 23 (27, 8).
[2630] Dante, *La Divina Commedia - Paradiso*, XXXIII, 85-87, "*Nel suo profondo vidi che s'interna | legato con amore in un volume, | ciò che per l'universo si squaderna.*" And I, 4-6. "*Nel ciel che piu' de la sua luce prende / fu' io, e vidi cose che ridire/ ne' sa ne' puo' chi di la' su'discende.*"
[2631] *Cf.* Anselm, *Proslogion*, IV, (Saint Anselm of Aosta 1033-1109) ontological proof: the idea of a perfect being implies existence to be perfect.
[2632] *Cf.* Thomas Aquinas, *Summa Theologica*, I^{a}, q. 2 a. 3 co., (Saint Thomas Aquinas 1225-1274) *a-posteriori* proofs.
[2633] Dawkins, *Snake Oil and Holy Water*, p. 236.
[2634] *Cf.* Dawkins, *The God Delusion.*
[2635] Russell, *The Collected Papers of Bertrand Russell, Vol. 11: Last Philosophical Testament, 1943–68. Is There a God?* pp. 543–548.
"If I were to suggest that between the Earth and Mars there is a china teapot revolving about the sun in an elliptical orbit, nobody would be able to disprove my assertion provided I were careful to add that the teapot is too small to be revealed even by our most powerful telescopes. But if I were to go on to say that, since my assertion cannot be disproved, it is intolerable presumption on the part of human reason to doubt it, I should rightly be thought to be talking nonsense. If, however, the existence of such a teapot were affirmed in ancient books, taught as the sacred truth every Sunday, and instilled into the minds of children at school, hesitation to believe in its existence would become a mark of eccentricity and entitle the doubter to the attentions of the psychiatrist in an enlightened age or of the Inquisitor in an earlier time."
Russell's teapot echoes monk Gaunilo's "fantastic lost island existence" argument, replying to the ontological a-priori proof of St. Anselm. The saint affirmed that the Idea of God's Absolute Very Perfect Being implies necessarily also Existence to Be Perfect (*cf.* Anselm, *Proslogion*). In any case, without the mind, Russell's included, no Earth, Mars and teapot could be stated.
[2636] *Cf. Prolegomena* § 45.
[2637] Susskind, *The world as a hologram*, Abstract (underlining is ours).
[2638] Strong's H2142.
[2639] Strong's H7200.
[2640] Strong's H2145, *cf.* Döderlein, *Lateinische Synonyme und Etymologien*, p. 1, 166.
[2641] Ecclesiastes 12:11.
[2642] Strong's H5769.
[2643] Tolle, *Stillness Speaks*, p. 5.
[2644] (מוּלָה *muwlah*) Strong's H4139, *cf.* Exodus 4:26.
[2645] (מַיִם *mayim*) Strong's H4325.
[2646] (נָמַל *namal*) Strong's H5243.
[2647] עָרֵל *`arel, to regard as impure* (Strong's H6188, *Gesenius* 2).
[2648] (עָרְלָה *` orlah*) Strong's H6190, from עָרֵל *`arel.*
[2649] Genesis 17:11.

[2650] Strong's H4135.
[2651] Deuteronomy 10:16.
[2652] Jeremiah 4:4.
[2653] Gesenius מול,... NIPHAL.
[2654] *Bible*, Matthew 26:41.
[2655] Bible, Romans 2:26.
[2656] Genesis 28:12.
[2657] Strong's H7218.
[2658] (שָׁמַיִם *shamayim*) Strong's H8064.
[2659] (מַלְאָךְ *mal'ak*) Strong's H4397.
[2660] (יָרַד *yarad*) Strong's H3381.
[2661] (עָלָה *`alah*) Strong's H5927.
[2662] (קוּם *quwm*) Strong's H6965.
[2663] (כְּנַעַן Kĕna`an) Strong's H3667.
[2664] (כָּנַע) Strong's H3665.
[2665] Not in the Hebrew or Greek texts.
[2666] (שָׁלַשׁ *shalash*) Strong's H8027.
[2667] (שָׁלוֹשׁ *shalowsh*) Strong's H7969.
[2668] (נָפַץ *naphats*) Strong's H5310.
[2669] *Cf. Dance of the Hours* (*Danza delle ore*) ballet in Act III of the opera by Ponchielli (1834-1886), *La Gioconda*. As detected by functional magnetic resonance imaging (F.M.R.I.), music is fundamental for the evolution of language; *cf.* Norman et al., *Distinct Cortical Pathways for Music.*
[2670] The Sphinx (σφίγξ *sphígx* = dissolute strangler), according to Hesiod (*Theogony*, 319-326ff.), was the daughter of Chimera (goat), the fire breathing monster with three natures (goat, lion, serpent) and her brother Orthros (dawn), the two-three headed dog of hell (brother of the three headed Cerberus, another dog from hell) and owned by Geryon (the Titan with three bodies) for guarding his heard of read cattle.
[2671] Apollodorus of Athens (180 – 120 BC), *The library*, III.V.8. *one sound* μίαν [*mían*, one = μίᾰ (*míā*), Sanskrit *éka*] ἔχον (*échon*, has) φωνὴν [*phōnhèn*, sound; φωνή (*phōnéh*) Sanskrit *kāra* (*UM* 1].Tί ἐστιν ὃ μίαν ἔχον φωνὴν. "The rendering φωνή is supported by" the great majority of ancient sources. "On the other hand the reading μορφή [*morphé*, shape] is supported [only] by some MSS." (346 n. 2).] τετρά-πουν [four-footed; τετρά-πούς (*tetrá-poús*) Sanskrit *catush-pada* (*UM* 2)] καὶ δί-πουν [two-footed; δί-πούς (*dí-poús*) Sanskrit *dví-pada* (*UM* 3-4)] καὶ τρί-πουν [three-footed; τρί-πούς (*trí-poús*) Sanskrit *trí-pada* (*UM* 1)] γίνεται [becomes; γίνομαι = γίγνομαι (*gínomai = gígnomai*) Sanskrit *jan*]... Σφίγξ ἀπὸ τῆς ἀχροπόλεως ἑαυτὴν ἔρριψεν "The Sphinx [Sanskrit Man-beast *purusha-mṛga*] threw herself from the citadel." Apollodorus explained the riddle the best he could. He clarified that it referred to the human being. In fact, in its infancy, s/he walks using all four limbs. In adulthood, s/he walks on two limbs. In old age, s/he walks with the help of an inanimate cane. However, this solution of the riddle does not explain the *one sound* clearly connected with metrical feet and not limbs. *Cf.* Simonelli, *Beyond Immortality*, pp. 183-4.
[2671] Wilford, *Asiatic Researches* (300).
[2672] अ-उ-म-ं pronounced *OM* and abbreviated as ॐ.
[2673] *UB* IV.3.9 *tasya* (of that) *vā* (verily) *etasya* (of this) *purushasya* (person) *dve* (two) *eva* (only) *sthāne* (conditions) *bhavataḥ* (are) *idaṃ* (this) *ca* (and) *para-* (beyond) *loka-* (world) *sthānaṃ* (condition) *ca* (and)... *sandhyaṃ* (in between) *tṛtīyaṃ* (third) *svapna-* (dream) *sthānam* (condition).
[2674] Grimal, *The dictionary of classical mythology*, p. 324a.
[2675] Pausanias (II century AD), *Description of Greece, Boeotia IX.XXVI.4,* (ὀνείρατος - *oneíratos* – in a dream).
[2676] Campbell, *The Power of Myth*, p. 152.
[2677] Not in the Hebrew or Greek texts.
[2678] שָׁכַם *shakam* (Strong's H7925), from which derives שְׁכֶם *shĕkem* shoulders (Strong's H7926).
[2679] (חָלַל*) Strong's H2490 & Gesenius p. 281.*
[2680] (חָלָה) Strong's H2470 & Gesenius, p. 279.
[2681] (חול) Strong's H2342 & Gesenius, p. 264 seg.
[2682] *UK* IV.2-(II.I.2) *parācaḥ* (outward) *kāmān-* (lusty pleasures) *anuyanti* (go after) *bālās-*(the foolish) *te* (they) *mṛtyor-* (of Father-death) *yanti* (fall into) *vitatasya* (widespread) *pāśam* (snare) / *atha* (however) *dhīrā* (wise person) *amṛtatvaṃ* (immortality) *viditvā* (understanding) *dhruvam-* (the permanent) *adhruveshv-* (among the impermanent) *iha* (here) *na* (not) *prārthayante* (do seek) /
[2683] (נָטַע *nata`*) Strong's H5193.
[2684] (כֶּרֶם *kerem*) Strong's H3754. Culturally, the wine tradition continues, *cf.* Schmid, *Researchers Find Oldest Known Winery In Cave In Armenian Mountains.*
[2685] כֶּרֶם Gesenius (2) "Isa.[iah] 3:14, seq.; 27:2, seq.; 51:3, compare."
[2686] *Bible*, Matthew 20:1, cf. seq.; 21:28 & Luke 20:9.
[2687] *Cf.* Rashi (Rabbi Shlomo Yitzchaki, 1040-1105), *Studies in Rashi,–* Bereishit, Chap. 9.

[2688] Gesenius *823 (2). Cf.* Isaiah 29:9, 51:21, Lamentations 4:21& Nahum 3:11.
[2689] (שֵׁכָר *shaker*) Strong's H7937.
[2690] Genesis 27:28 - Deuteronomy 7:13 (new wine תִּירוֹשׁ *tiyrowsh*, Strong's H8492) - Amos 9:13-14 (sweet wine עָסִיס *`aciyc*, Strong's H6071; effervescent wine יַיִן *yayin*, Strong's H3196).
[2691] (תָּוֶךְ *tavek*) Strong's H8432.
[2692] (אָהַל *'ahal*) Strong's H166
[2693] (אֹהֶל *'ohel*) Strong's H168.
[2694] (גָּלָה *galah*) Strong's H1540, Gesenius (2).
[2695] *Dasein*, Heidegger, *Being and Time*, p.68.
[2696] Marohn, *The Natural Medicine Guide to Bipolar Disorder*, § 10 The Shamanic View of Mental Illness, pp. 173-5.
[2697] St. Francis, *The Little Flowers of St. Francis*, § XXX, p. 83-4.
[2698] (שָׁקָה *shaqah*) *Strong's* H8248.
[2699] Genesis 2:6.
[2700] Not in the Hebrew or Latin texts.
[2701] Kass, *The Beginning of Wisdom,* p. 205 n. 11 and p. 207.
[2702] (עֶרְוָה) Strong's H6172.
[2703] (עָרָה) Strong's H6168.
[2704] Gesenius עָרָה 3.
[2705] (עֵירֹם) Strong's H5903.
[2706] (עָרוֹם) Strong's H6174.
[2707] (עָרַם) Strong's H6191.
[2708] Gesenius עָרַם 1.
[2709] Psalm 141:8. *yahoih* (Transcendent) *'ăḏōnāy* (Lord of Hosts) *'ēynāy* (eyes) *baḵāh* (in) *ḥāsiyṯiy* (I trusted) *'al* (not) ***ta'ar* (leave naked) *napāšiy* (blood-soul). תְּעַר נַפְשִׁי**־יְהוִה אֲדֹנָי עֵינָי בְּכָה חָסִיתִי אַל (highlighting is ours).
[2710] (רָאָה *ra'ah*) Genesis 3:11, Strong's H7200.
[2711] See and compare to our GRAPHIC: *The Unreachable I-in-itself & Double-head Mayan mask.*
[2712] 道可道 · 非常道 (*tao k'o tao, fei ch'ang tao*) Lao Tzu, *Tao Te Ching*, I.1-2, 道 (*Tao*) word *cf.* Greek λόγος (*logos*) (*Bible*, John 1:1).
[2713] *Cf. UB* I. 2. 2, heated (*tapta*) by the flame-of-consciousness (*tapas*).
[2714] (נָגַד *nagad*) Strong's H5046.
[2715] (חוּץ *chuwts*) Strong's H2351.
[2716] Psalm 46:10.
[2717] To watch (γρηγορέω *grēgoreō*), to pray (προσεύχομαι *proseuchomai*), temptation (πειρασμός *peirasmos*), *Bible*, Mark 14:38 & *cf.* Matthew 26:41.
[2718] קוּץ *quwts*, Gesenius.
[2719] Pistorius, *Ghost Boy*, pp. IX-X.
[2720] Strong's H6974.
[2721] יָשֵׁן *yashen*, Strong's H3463.
[2722] Daniel 12:2.
[2723] Job 14:12. שֵׁנָא *shehah*, Strong's H8142, Job 14:12.
[2724] Tolle, *Stillness Speaks*, p. 11.
[2725] Tolle, *The Power of Now*, p. 93. *Cf.* Mahadevan, *Ramana Maharshi*, It. tr. p. 39.
[2726] *Bible*, John 8:14.
[2727] *Bible*, John 8:19.
[2728] Think concerning right and wrong (κρίνω *krinō).*
[2729] Craving senses (σάρξ *sarx*).
[2730] *Bible*, John 8:15, nothing (οὐδείς *oudeis*).
[2731] *Bible*, John 8:16, ἀληθής *alēthēs* Pure-Awareness *from* α-λανθάνω *a-lanthanō* = not-unaware.
[2732] Belonging to the κόσμος *kosmos.*
[2733] φῶς *phōs = light, from* φημί *phēmi* to make thoughts known, and φαίνω *phainō* to be evident, to be viewed into light, to appear, shine, resplend, to be manifest.
[2734] *Bible*, John 8:12.
[2735] *Bible*, John 8:16.
[2736] *Bible*, John 10:30.
[2737] Exodus 19:11.
[2738] (מִרְמָה *mirmah*) Strong's H4820.
[2739] (כְּנַעַן *Kĕna`*) Strong's H3667.
[2740] (מאזְנַיִם *mo'zen*) Strong's H3976.
[2741] Hosea 12:7.
[2742] *Cf.* Exodus, 2:10, משה *Mosheh Moses,* משה *mashah* to draw, מים *mayim* water of transitory things. *Cf.* "he drew me out

of many waters," 2 Samuel 22:17 and Psalm 18:16.
[2743] צאן *tso'n* of multitude (metaphor).
[2744] אַחַר *'achar*
[2745] Exodus, 3:1, הַר *har mountain,* אלהים *'elohiym* God, חרב c*horeb* desert.
[2746] Psalm 99:9.
[2747] *Bible,* Matthew 4:1-2; in εἰς *eis* the τὴν *tēv* desert ἔρημον *erēmon* (*in desertum*)... fasted νηστεύσας *nēsteusas* days ἡμέρας *ēmeras* forty τεσσαράκοντα *tessarakonta* and καὶ *kai* nights νύκτας *nuktas* forty τεσσαράκοντα *tessarakonta.*
[2748] Exodus, 3:2, "לבה *labbah* flashing point of spear... he intently looked (רָאָה *ra'ah*), and, behold, the bush (סְנֶה *cĕnah*) burned (בָּעַר *ba`ar*) with supernatural fire (אֵשׁ *'esh*), and the bush [was] not consumed or devoured (אָכַל *'akal*)."
[2749] Exodus, 3:3 סוּר *cuwr* to reject and turn away from.
[2750] Exodus, 3:4.
[2751] Exodus, 3:5 קרב *qarab* to bring near, approach, קֹדֶשׁ *qodesh Sacred set-apart,* קָדַשׁ *qadash that which is separated, namely transcendent.*
[2752] Exodus, 3:6.
[2753] אֶהְיֶה אֲשֶׁר אֶהְיֶה *hayah asher hayah* Exodus, 3:14.
[2754] *Cf.* the 15 BC - 15 AD unveiling of the mystery scene in a fresco in Villa of the Mysteries, Pompeii, Italy.
[2755] (סָתַר *cathar*) Gesenius, סָתַר 2-1 to cover.
[2756] *Mysterium tremendum et fascinans, cf.* Campbell, *The Mask,* & Otto, *The Idea of the Holy.*
[2757] מַסְוֶה *macveh* Strong's H4533, "A covering, a veil (for the face)" (Gesenius).
[2758] Exodus 34:34-35.
[2759] From καλύπτω (*kaluptō*) to hide, to veil).
[2760] *Bible*, 2 Corinthians 3:13-16.
[2761] Exodus 19:20.
[2762] (אָנֹכִי *'ānōḵiy*) Strong's H595.
[2763] (בָּא *bā'*) Strong's H935.
[2764] (אֵלֶיךָ *'ēleyḵā*) Strong's H411.
[2765] (בְּעַב *ba'aḇ*) Strong's H5645.
[2766] (הֶעָנָן *he'ānān*) Exodus 19:9.
[2767] Exodus, 3:14.
[2768] (לָקַח *laqach*) Strong's H3947.
[2769] (שִׂמְלָה *simlah*) Strong's H8071.
[2770] Gesenius p. 791.
[2771] (שׂוּם *suwm*) Strong's H7760.
[2772] (שָׁכַם *shakam*) Strong's H7925.
[2773] (שְׁכֶם *shĕkem*) Strong's H7926.
[2774] *Bible*, John 15:19; 17:14; 16; 1 John 2:16.
[2775] *Memento, homo, quia pulvis es et in pulverem revertis cf.* Genesis 3:19. *Cf.* also "*Memento mori*" in Pompeii, house-shop I, 5, 2, a level with skull as plumb line, flanked left by richness (purple robe) and right by poverty (rags), over a butterfly (soul) on a wheel (circle of life).
[2776] *Uīśa* 17 *krato* (intelligence) *smara* (remember) *kṛtaṃ* (the deed) *smara* (remember) *krato* (intention-will) *smara* (remember) *kṛtaṃ* (the magic-results) *smara* (remember).
[2777] Tolle, *The Power of Now,* p. 9.
[2778] Scaligero (Antonio Sgabelloni, 1906–1980, Italian anthroposophist), *Graal ...*, p. 143-4 and 150.
[2779] Schopenhauer, *The World as Will and Representation,* vol. II, Ch. IV, p. 44.
[2780] *Collage, Girl before a Mirror* (Picasso 1932, detail replica), *Expansor* (Bruno 1584 c.) see. Yates, *Giordano Bruno e la tradizione ermetica.*; in *Articuli adversus mathematicos* (the design is reproduced) & *Looking at the Stars* (Simonelli 1990).
[2781] <Simonelli, Beyond Immortality, pp. 108-109.>
[2782] *Cf.* Susskind, *The world as a hologram.*
[2783] *Bible*, Luke 12:3.
[2784] *Cf.* Susskind, *The Black Hole War.*
[2785] 爲無爲 *wei wu wei, Tao Te Ching,* 6 (43).
[2786] <Simonelli, Awareness, pp. 59-63.>
[2787] (אַחֲרֹנִית) Strong's H322.
[2788] (אָחוֹר) Strong's H268.
[2789] אָחוֹר Gesenius.
[2790] (אֲחִירַע) Strong's H299.
[2791] (אָח *'ach*) Strong's H251.
[2792] (רַע ra`) Strong's H7451.
[2793] (רָעַע) Strong's H7489.
[2794] Laid, Strong's H7760.

[2795] שׂוּם *suwm* Strong's H7760.
[2796] שַׂמְלָה, Strong's H8071.
[2797] *cemel*, סֶמֶל, Strong's H5566.
[2798] לָקַח *laqach*, Strong's H3947.
[2799] כָּסָה *kacah*, Strong's H3680.
[2800] יָקַץ *yaqats*, Strong's H3364.
[2801] יַיִן *yayin*, Strong's H3196.
[2802] יָדַע *yada`*, Strong's H3045.
[2803] עָשָׂה *` asah*, Strong's H6213.
[2804] קָטָן, Strong's H6996.
[2805] עֶבֶד , Strong's H5650, from the verb עבד *` abad* Strong's H5647.
[2806] 2 Samuel 10:2, "*David's <u>messengers</u> came into the land of the children of Ammon.*"
[2807] Isaiah 49:6, "*It is a light thing that thou shouldest be my <u>ambassador</u>... and ... I will also give thee for a light to the Gentiles.*"
[2808] Gesenius p. 599, (1)... (b)... (2)...(b).
[2809] אָח *'ach*, Strong's H251.
[2810] עֶבֶד *`ebed* servant, Strong's H5650.
[2811] Isaac (יִצְחָק *Yitschaq*) = <u>he laughs</u>. Abraham laughed at the news that a child "be born unto him that is an hundred years old? and shall Sarah, that is ninety years old, bear?" (Genesis 17:17). Rebekah (רִבְקָה *Ribqah*) = <u>The ensnarer</u>.
[2812] גוי *gowy* nations, gentiles, other animal, race.
[2813] לאם *lĕom* people, race.
[2814] פרד *parad* separated.
[2815] אמץ 'amats stronger, brave, bold, secure, assuring, alert and superior to.
[2816] עבד *` abad* H5647 to serve, to be subject from which derives עֶבֶד *`ebed* servant, Strong's H5650.
[2817] Genesis 25:23.
[2818] Evola, *Sintesi di dottrina della razza*, p. 116 (translation and underlining is ours). "*Nella realtà si danno fin troppi casi di persone, che sono esattamente della stessa razza del corpo, dello stesso ceppo, talvolta perfino – come fratelli o padri e figli – dello stesso sangue nel senso piú reale, ma che purtuttavia non riescono a comprendersi. Una frontiera separa le loro anime, il loro modo di sentire e di vedere è diverso e contro di ciò la comune razza del corpo e il comune sangue nulla possono. Esiste una possibilità di comprensione, e quindi di vera solidarietà, di unità profonda, solo dove esiste una comune '<u>razza dell'anima</u>.'*"
[2819] Martin Luther King, *A Testament of Hope*, p. 217.
[2820] Even the original Indian caste system had, traditionally, the same mental configuration. Only later it became hereditary and oppressive (*cf.* Simonelli, *Beyond Immortality*, pp. 90-91).
[2821] Genesis 25:25.
[2822] Genesis 27:11. Hairy שָׂעִיר *sa `iyr* he-goat, buck hairy, as sacrificial animal.
[2823] Genesis 25:30. אדם *'Edom* from אָדֹם *'adom* = red.
[2824] *`Esav* (עֵשָׂו) from the past participle of *`asah* (עָשָׂה) = handling.
[2825] See Plate 2.
[2826] Genesis 25:26.
[2827] Genesis 27:11. חָלָק *chalaq* flattering, smooth from חָלַק *chalaq* to divide, share, plunder, allot, apportion, assign.
[2828] *Ya `aqob* (יַעֲקֹב) from עָקַב *aqab*, take by the heel, follow at the heel, to supplant, circumvent, assail insidiously, overreach.
[2829] Genesis 25:28; *the mouth* פה *peh*; *hunt*ציד *tsayid.*
[2830] Genesis 27:3-4; savoury מַטְעַם *mat `am* from to perceive טָעַם *ta `am*.
[2831] ידע *yada `* to know by experience, to perceive, to discriminate, to distinguish.
[2832] Genesis 25:27.
[2833] See Plate 2.
[2834] תם *tam* perfect, complete, who lacks nothing, innocent, pure.
[2835] Genesis 25:27. אהל *'ohel* the sacred tent of Jehovah (the tabernacle).
[2836] *Cf.* Adam and Eve eating from the *tree of knowledge*.
[2837] Metaphoric color of activity (*cf.* the expression: *red-hot*).
[2838] Genesis 25:29-30-31-32-33-34.
[2839] V.1.6. *atha ha* (now once) *prāṇā* (the spirit of the senses) *ahaṃ-śreyasi* (I superiority) *vyūdire* (disputed) *ahaṃ* (I) *śreyān* (superior) *asmi* (am) *ahaṃ* (I) *śreyān* (superior) *asmīti* (am therefore) 8. *vāg* (speech) *uccakrāma* (departed) ... *paryetyovāca* (came back asked) *katham* (how) *aśakata* (have you been able) *ṛte* (without) *maj* (me) *jīvitum* (to live) *iti* (thus) *yathā* (like) *kalā* (dumb) ... *prāṇantaḥ* (living) *prāṇena* (with breath). 9. *cakshur* (the eye) *hoccakrāma* (departed) ... *paryetyovāca* (came back asked) *katham* (how) *aśakata* (have you been able) *ṛte* (without) *maj* (me) *jīvitum* (to live) *iti* (thus) *yathā* (like) *andhā* (blind) ... *prāṇantaḥ* (living) *prāṇena* (with breath). 10. *śrotraṃ* (the ear) *hoccakrāma* (departed) ... *paryetyovāca* (came back asked) *katham* (how) *aśakata* (have you been able) *ṛte* (without) *maj* (me) *jīvitum* (to live) *iti* (thus) *yathā* (like) *badhirā* (deaf) ... *prāṇantaḥ* (living) *prāṇena* (with breath). 11. *mano* (the mind) *hoccakrāma* (departed)

... *paryetyovāca* (came back asked) *katham* (how) *aśakata* (have you been able) *ṛte* (without) *maj* (me) *jīvitum* (to live) *iti* (thus) *yathā* (like) *bālā* (infant) ... *prāṇantaḥ* (living) *prāṇena* (with breath). 12. *atha ha* (then) *prāṇa* (vital breath) *uccikramishan* (was about to depart) *sa* (that) ... *itarān* (the other) *prāṇān* (senses) *samakhidat* (were uprooted) *taṃ* (to it) *hābhisametyocuḥ* (came said) ... *tvaṃ* (you) *naḥ* (among us) *śreshṭho* (the best) *si* (are).

[2840] *Ayāsya Āṅgirasa* Agile Angel-limb. *UB* I.3.19. *so'* (he) *yāsya* (Agile) *āṅgirasaḥ* [of <*aṅgiras* Greek ἄγγελος = angel (Rocci 7)> angel-metrical-limb] *aṅgānāṃ* (of the metrical-limbs) *hi* (because) *rasaḥ* (the essence).

[2841] *UC* III.14.2. *mano-* (mind) *-mayaḥ* (made of) *prāṇa-* (vital breath) *-śarīro* (as body) *bhā-* (light) – *rūpaḥ* (form) *satya-* (truth) *-saṃkalpa* (conceptual determination) *ākāś-* (space) *-ātmā* (self) *sarva-* (all) *-karmā* (actions) *sarva-* (all) *-kāmaḥ* (desires) *sarva-* (all) *-gandhaḥ* (scents) *sarva-* (all) *-rasaḥ* (flavors) *sarvam* (all) *idam* (this) *abhyātto'* (encompassing) *vāky* (not speaking) *anādaraḥ* (indifferent).

[2842] *UB* IV.4.5. *sa* (that) *vā* (verily) *ayam* (this) *ātmā* (Self) *brahma* (the Supreme Transcendent Spirit) *vijñāna-mayo* (of knowledge-composed) *mano-mayaḥ* (of mind-composed) *prāṇa-mayaś* (of vital breath-composed) *cakshur-mayaḥ* (of sight-composed) *śrotra-mayaḥ* (of hearing-composed) *pṛthivī-maya* (of earth-composed) *āpo-mayo* (of water-composed) *vāyu-maya* (of wind-composed) *ākāśa-mayas* (of space-composed) *tejo-mayo'* (of light-composed) *tejo-mayaḥ* (of darkness-composed) *kāma-mayo'* (of desire-composed) *kāmo-mayaḥ* (of detachment-composed) *krodha-mayo'* (of anger-composed) *krodha-mayo* (of tranquility-composed) *dharma-mayo'* (of justice-composed) *dharma-mayaḥ* (of injustice-composed) *sarva-mayaḥ* (of everything-composed) *tad* (that) *yad* (which) *etat* (this) *idam-* (this) *-mayaḥ* (composed of) *adomaya* (of that composed) *iti* (thus) *yathākārī-* (as one acts) *-yathācārī* (as one behaves) *tathā* (the same) *bhavati* (becomes) *sādhukārī* (who good does) *sādhur* (good) *bhavati* (becomes) *pāpakārī* (who evil does) *pāpo* (evil) *bhavati* (becomes) *puṇyaḥ* (virtuous) *puṇyena* (by virtuous) *karmaṇā* (action) *bhavati* (becomes) *pāpaḥ* (evil) *pāpena* (by evil) *athau* (still) *khalv* (verily) *āhuḥ* (say) *kāmamaya* (of desire-composed) *evāyam* (indeed this) *purusha* (person) *iti* (thus) *sa* (he) *yathākāmo* (as the desire) *bhavati* (is) *tat* (then) *kratur* (will) *bhavati* (becomes) *yat* (which) *kratur* (will) *bhavati* (is) *tat* (then) *karma* (deed) *kurute* (performs) *yat* (whatever) *karma* (deed) *kurute* (performs) *tat* (then) *abhisampadyate* (achieves).

[2843] He was the "*very froward generation... without Certitude*" (Deuteronomy 32:20).

[2844] Genesis 27:1, 3-4, 6, 9, 10-12, 14-27.

[2845] From Latin *cum-* (= with) - *scio* (= I know), *cf.* science.

[2846] Ἡ βασιλεία ἡ ἐμὴ οὐκ ἔστιν ἐκ τοῦ κόσμου τούτου, *Bible*, John 18:36.

[2847] From Latin *lux-* (= light) – *fero* (=I carry).

[2848] *UK* I.10 (I.I.10) *prasṛshṭaṃ* (let loose by) *mā'-* (me) *pratīta* (recognizing)/. *Cf.* Simonelli, *Beyond Immortality*, pp. 114, 132, 178.

[2849] Genesis 27:29.

[2850] Ramana Maharshi, *Gems From Bhagavan*, p. 14.

[2851] Genesis 27:30.

[2852] *Cf.* Genesis 25:23.

[2853] *Bible*, Matthews 11:12.

[2854] Genesis 32:24-25, 28. יִשְׂרָאֵל *Yisra'el* = God prevails; from שָׂרָה *sarah* = persevering power, אֵל *'el* = god-like. <Eli Luminosus Aequalis, *Mutus Liber Loquitur*, pp. 44-46>.

[2855] שָׁכַן *shakan*, Strong's H7931

[2856] אָהַל *'ahal*, Strong's H166.

[2857] אֹהֶל *'ohel*, Strong's H168.

[2858] פָּתָה pathah, Strong's H6601.

[2859] In Gematria, the number 350 is equivalent to this phrase in Isaiah 2:18, וְהָאֱלִילִים כָּלִיל יַחֲלֹף: *v$_a$h$_ā$ĕl$_i$yl$_i$ym* [the empty vane idols (Strong's H457, אֱלִיל *'eliyl*, Gesenius)] *k$_ā$l$_i$yl* (completely) *y$_a$ḥ$_ă$l$_o$p̄* (pass away); 350 = [6(ו, *wv*) + 5 (ה, *h*) + 1(א, *aĕ*) + 30(ל, *l*) + 10(י, *y*) + 30(ל, *l*) + 10(י, *y*) + 40(מ, *m*) + 20(כ, *k*) + 30(ל, *l*) + 10(י, *y*) + 30(ל, *l*) + 10(י, *y*) + 8(ח, *ḥ*) + 30(ל, *l*) + 80 (פ, *p̄*)].

[2860] אַל *'al* (Strong's H408), also, *cf.* empty ריקם *r$_ē$yq$_ā$m*, [200 (ר, *r*) + 10 (י,*y*) + 100(ק, *q*) + 40(ם, *m*)] (Strong's H7387) in Genesis 31:42 & emptiness רקים *r$_ē$q$_i$ym*, [200 (ר, *r*) + 100(ק, *q*) + 10 (י,*y*) + 40(ם, *m*)] (Strong's H7386) in Judge 7:16, both with a Gematria equivalent of 350.

[2861] אֱלִיל *'eliyl* H457.

[2862] שָׁנָה *shanah*, Strong's H8138.

[2863] שָׁנָה *shaneh*, Strong's H8141.

[2864] Cognate of year is שְׁנָה *shĕnah* (Aramaic) (Strong's H8139) & שֵׁנָא *shehah*, Strong's H8142.

[2865] Job 21:19, אֱלוֹהַ יִצְפֹּן־לְבָנָיו אוֹנוֹ יְשַׁלֵּם אֵלָיו וְיֵדָע *lv$_ō$h$_a$* (the Power) *y$_i$ṣ$_a$p$_ō$n* (placed upon) *l$_a$ḇ$_ā$n$_ā$yv* (the sons) *'av$_ō$nv$_ō$* (empty idolatry) y$_a$š$_a$l$_ē$m (rewarded) $_ē$l$_ā$yv (his) v$_a$y$_ē$ḏā' (he shall realize); this verse, in Gematria, is numerically equivalent to 950 [1(א, *a 'ĕ*) + 30(ל, *l*) + 6(ו, *w v*) + 5(ה, *h*) + 10(י, *y*) + 90(צ, *ṣ*) + 80(פ, *p*) + 50(נ, *n*) + 30(ל, *l*) + 2(ב, *ḇ b*) + 50(נ,*n*) + 10(י, *y*) + 6(ו,*W v*) + 1(א, *'a*) + 6(ו, *w v*) + 50(נ, *n*) + 6(ו, *w v*) + 10(י, *y*) + 300(ש, *ś š*) +30(ל, *l*) + 40(מ, *m*) + 1(א, *a*) +30(ל, *l*) +10(י, *y*) + 6(ו, *w v*) + 6(ו, *w v*) + 10(י, *y*) + 4(ד, *ḏ d*) + 70(ע, *'a*)].

[2866] בֵּן *ben* Strong's H1121.

[2867] אֱלוֹהַ *'elowahh* (Strong's H433), "in a singular sense" [Gesenius (B)].

[2868] אָוֶן *'av$_ō$nv$_ō$* (empty idolatry), Strong's H205. Compare, "*that is who you are. That is the god you serve,*" in Kasser-Meyer-Wurst, *Gospel of Judas* [39], p. 27.

2869 *BG.* VI.34.
2870 שָׁלַם *shalam*, Strong's H7999.
2871 יָדַע *yada*, Strong's H3045.
2872 אָוֶן Gesenius.
2873 Cognate of year is שְׁנָה *shĕnah* (Aramaic) (Strong's H8139) & שְׁנָא *shehah*, Strong's H8142.
2874 *Cf.* clay pottery חֶרֶשׂ *cheres*, Strong's H2789 (Jeremiah 19:1 & 10).
2875 *Cf. UC* VI.1.4.
2876 *Cf.* Kant, *Prolegomena to any future metaphysics*, §§ 2, 5.
2877 יָלַד *yalad*, Strong's H3205.
2878 אַחַר *'achar*, Gesenius (1a), Strong's H310. From אָחַר *'achar* (Strong's H309).
2879 *Cf.* Judges 5:28. *"Why do the wheels* (*viz. the hoof-beats,* פַּעַם *pa 'am* - Strong's H6471) *of his chariot tarry* (*viz. delay,* אָחַר *'achar* - Strong's H309)*?"*
2880 אַחַר *'achar*, Gesenius (2).
2881 Not in the Hebrew or Latin texts.
2882 *Cf.* Kant, *The Critique of Pure Reason*, I, I, c. 1, Transcendental Analytic.
2883 Strong's H1586.
2884 Strong's H1584.
2885 Umberto Boccioni (1882-1916), *Unique Forms of Continuity in Space* (1913), Museum of Modern Art, NYC.
2886 *UB* I. 1. 1 & 2. 3. *Cf.* Simonelli, *Sacred Topography ...*, p. 1404. Leonardo da Vinci design of man.
2887 *Magowg*, Strong's H4031.
2888 Gesenius, מָגוֹג, the syllable "ma" denotes a place or region."
2889 Strong's H1463, see Gesenius.
2890 *maday* מָדַי Strong's H4074.
2891 דַּי *day* Strong's H1767, Job 39:25.
2892 מדד Strong's H4058, *cf.* Psalm 60:6.
2893 *Yavan*, Strong's H3120.
2894 *Cf.* Daniel 8:21 and others.
2895 Strong's H3196; see Gesenius.
2896 *Tuwbal*, Strong's H8422.
2897 Strong's H8398.
2898 Strong's H8397. See Gesenius.
2899 Strong's H1101. See Gesenius.
2900 Strong's H8400, *cf.* Leviticus 21:20.
2901 *Meshek*, Strong's H4902. Gesenius 2.
2902 Strong's H4901. See Gesenius.
2903 Strong's H4900. See Gesenius.
2904 *Tiyrac*, Strong's H8494.
2905 Strong's H813.
2906 Gesenius, אַשְׁכְּנַז [*Ashkenaz, Ashchenaz*].
2907 Campbell, *Joseph Campbell, The Power of Myth with Bill Moyers.* 'The Message of the Myth.'
2908 Strong's H7384.
2909 *Towgarmah (you will break her)*, Strong's H8425.
2910 See רְמָא *remah*, to cast, to throw, Strong's 7412.
2911 Malory, *Le Morte Dārthur*, XIII, III, p. 227 (highlight is ours).
2912 דֹּדָנִים Gesenius, "*Rhodians*, which is found in the Samaritan copy, LXX, and the Hebrew text itself, 1Chr. 1:7."
2913 *'Eliyshah.* Strong's H473.
2914 *Tarshiysh* (Strong's H8659) "yellow jasper," as תַּרְשִׁישׁ *tarshiysh* (Strong's H8658) "precious stone," as תַּרְשִׁישׁ *tarshiysh* (Strong's H8659).
2915 *Kittiy*, Strong's H3794.
2916 *Dodaniym*, Strong's H1721.
2917 *Kuwsh*, Strong's H3568.
2918 Gihon, *cf.* Genesis 2:13.
2919 *Mitsrayim*, Strong's H4714.
2920 Strong's H4693.
2921 Strong's H4692.
2922 Gesenius (1) (a).
2923 Strong's H6696.
2924 *Puwt*, Strong's H6316.
2925 *Kĕna 'an*, Strong's H3667.
2926 *Cĕba'*, Strong's H5434.
2927 *Chaviylah*, Strong's H2341.

[2928] From חול *chuwl,* Strong's H2342, to twist, to turn around.
[2929] *Cf.* Genesis 2:11, see חֲוִילָה Gesenius (3).
[2930] *Cabta',* Strong's H5454.
[2931] From the root *sabab* (סבב), meaning to turn, to go around, encircle, *cf.* Uittenbogaard, A. (2000-2014). *The Hebrew word.*
[2932] *Ra`mah,* Strong's H7484.
[2933] רַעְמָה, Strong's H7483; from רעם *ra`am* (Strong's H7482) thunder noise, from רעם *ra`am* (Strong's H7481) *to thunder.*
[2934] *Cabtěka',* Strong's H5455.
[2935] *Cf.* Uittenbogaard, A. (2000-2014). *The Hebrew word.*
[2936] *Shěba',* Strong's H7614. *Cf.* Uittenbogaard, A. (2000-2014). *The Hebrew word.*
[2937] *Cf. BU* I.2.4. "*saṃvatsaro* (the year) *'bhavat* (became)... *ha* (indeed) *purā* (in the beginning) *tataḥ* (then) *saṃvatsara* (the year) *āsa* (was) *tam* (him) *etāvantaṃ* (so far) *kālam* (space of time) *abhibhaḥ* (parented) *yāvān* (as long as) *saṃvatsaraḥ* (year) *tam* (him)" and I,2.7.
[2938] *Dědan,* Strong's H1719. *Cf.* Uittenbogaard, A. (2000-2014). *The Hebrew word.*
[2939] Jones, *Jones' dictionary of Old Testament proper names,* דדה.
[2940] Strong's H5248.
[2941] צַיִד, Strong's H6718.
[2942] צוד, Strong's H6679.
[2943] צוד, Gesenius.
[2944] Koch, *Is Consciousness Universal? Panpsychism, the ancient doctrine that consciousness is universal, offers some lessons in how to think about subjective experience today.*
[2945] *Cf.* Prince, *How animals hunt.*
[2946] צַיִד, Strong's H6718.
[2947] גִבּוֹר*,* Strong's H1368.
[2948] (פָּנִים *paniym*) Strong's H6440.
[2949] (אֶרֶךְ *'Erek*) Strong's H751; *cf.* (אָרֵךְ *'arek*) Strong's H750 & (אָרֹךְ *'arok*) Strong's H752.
[2950] (אָרַךְ *'arak*) Strong's H748.
[2951] (בָּבֶל *Babel*) Strong's H894.
[2952] (אַכַּד *'Akkad*) Strong's H390.
[2953] (כַּלְנֵה *Kalneh*) Strong's H3641.
[2954] ❄ the Mesopotamian Akkadian Anu (Sumerian *An*), connected with the gods Enlil and Ea (*cf.* our commentary of *Genesis* 6:13), was the highest sky god, father of all gods and of the calendar.
[2955] Leibniz, *THE MONADOLOGY,* 32.
[2956] Plato, *Republic,* VII. 516a.
[2957] *Bible,* Luke 15:11-32.
[2958] (אָשַׁר *'ashar*) Strong's H833.
[2959] (אַשּׁוּר *'Ashshuwr*) *a step* Strong's H804. Present city of Nimrud, Kalhu 20 miles from Mosul.
[2960] (בָּנָה *banah*) Strong's H1129 *to build, cause to continue.*
[2961] (נִינְוֵה *Niyněveh*) Strong's H5210.
[2962] The Greek historian Apollodorus of Athens (180 BC), "αὐτος *autos* (the same) Νῖνον *Ninon* (Ninus) τὸν *ton* (the) Νεβρωδ *Nebrōd* (Nimrod)," Mueller, *Fragmenta historicorum graecorum..., Apollodori Fragmenta,* Liber IV, fragment 68, vol. 1, p. 440.
[2963] (עִיר *`iyr*) Strong's H5892.
[2964] (רחבות *Rěchobowth*) *Strong's H7334, from next*
[2965] (רְחֹב *rěchob*) Strong's H7339, from next
[2966] (רָחַב *rachab*) Strong's H7337.
[2967] (כֶּלַח *kelach*) Strong's H3624 & Gesenius.
[2968] (כֶּלַח *Kelach*) Strong's H*3625* & Gesenius. Same as the following note
[2969] Malory, XXI, VII. "*Rex quondam, Rexque futurus*" of the entire epistemic structure as Camelot.
[2970] "*Hic jacet,*" like King Arthur of Camelot, Malory, XXI, VII.
[2971] (רֶסֶן *recen*) Strong's H7449, Gesenius. The same as next note
[2972] (רֶסֶן *recen*) Strong's H7448, Gesenius, compare to the Sanskrit verb यम् *yam,* to restrain (W 845b), from which यम *Yama,* bridle, Death (W 846a).
[2973] (גדול *gadowl*) Strong's H1419.
[2974] *UB* I.2.7. *śvaḥ* (a grown-horse)... *aśvat* (it grew)... *anavarudhya-* (not restraining) *-ivā-* (thus) *-manyata* (he thought).
[2975] *UK* III.3 (I.3.3) *ratham* (a two wheeled chariot)... *manaḥ* (the faculty of thought) *pragraham* (reins). *Cf.* also Plato, *Phaedrus,* 246.
[2976] *W.* p. 846a √*yam,* to restreint p. 845b.
[2977] *Cf.* Kugel, pp. 85 *fol.*
[2978] Genesis 4:2 tiller, deeds = עָבַד *`abad*; ground = אדמה *'adamah*; and 5, 8-9-11-12-14-15-17.
[2979] Genesis 4:3. קֵץ *qets* at the end of יום *yowm* day (24 hour period) as defined by evening and morning.

[2980] Genesis 3 פרי periy fruit (of actions).
[2981] Genesis 4:4. שָׁעָה *sha`ah* accepted
[2982] (לודיי *luwdiy*) Strong's H3866. From next
[2983] (לוד *luwd*) Strong's H3865.
[2984] (עֲנָמִים *`anamim*) Srong's H6047.
[2985] (לְהָבִים *lěhabiym*) Strong's H3853, plural of next.
[2986] (לַהַב *lahab*) flame, sword Strong's H3851
[2987] (נַפְתֻּחִים *naphtuchiym*) Strong's H5320.
[2988] (פַּתְרֻסִי *pathruciy*) Strong's H6625, (Gesenius), from next
[2989] פַּתְרוֹס *pathrowc* Strong's H6624 region of the south.
[2990] (כַּסְלֻחִים *kacluchiym*) Strong's H3695.
[2991] Strong's H3318.
[2992] (פְּלִשְׁתִּי *pělishtiy*) Strong's H6430. From next
[2993] (פְּלֶשֶׁת *pělesheth*) Strong's H6429, Gesenius. From next
[2994] (פָּלַשׁ *palash*) Strong's H6428 A, Gesenius.
[2995] (כַּפְתֹּרִי *kaphtoriy*) Strong's H3732, from (כַּפְתּוֹר *kaphtor*) Strong's H3731, same as (כַּפְתּוֹר *kaphtor*) Strong's H3730 ornament (Gesenius).
[2996] Genesis 4:15.
[2997] (צִידוֹן *tsiydown*) Strong's H6721. From
[2998] (צוּד *tsuwd*) Strong's H6679.
[2999] (חֵת *cheth*) Strong's H2845 & Gesenius. From
[3000] (חַתַּת *chathath*) Strong's H2865 & Gesenius.
[3001] *UB* I.4.2 *so'* (he) *bibhet* (was afraid) *tasmād* (therefore) *ekākī* (alone) *bibheti* (is afraid) ... *dvitīyād* (from a second) *vai* (verily) *bhayaṃ* (fear) *bhavati* (becomes).
[3002] *Being and Nothingness*, p. 257 (italic is ours).
[3003] *L'Enfer, c'est les autres!* Sartre, *Huis Clos*, *No exit...*, p. 45 (italic is ours).
[3004] (יְבוּסִי *yěbuwciy*) Strong's H2983. From
[3005] (יְבוּס *Yěbuwc*) Strong's H2982. From
[3006] (בּוּס *buwc)* Strong's H947.
[3007] (אֱמֹרִי *'emoriy)* Strong's H567, Gesenius.
[3008] (גִּרְגָּשִׁי *girgashiy)* Strong's H1622.
[3009] (חִוִּי *Chivviy*) Strong's H2340. From *village*, town, (חַוָּה *chavvah*) Strong's H2333. Properly
[3010] (חַוָּה *chavvah*) Strong's H2332 (life-giving, i.e. living-place, to breath).
[3011] חָוָה *chavah* Strong's H2331.
[3012] (עַרְקִי *`arqiy*) Strong's H6208.
[3013] *Bible*, Matthew 8:12; 22:13; 24:51; 25:30; Luke 13:28; *cf.* Matthew 13:42, 50.
[3014] (סִינִי *ciynay*) Strong's H5513.
[3015] (אַרְוָדִי *'arvadiy*) Strong's H721. From
[3016] (רוּד *ruwd*) Strong's H7300, Gesenius.
[3017] (צְמָרִי *tsěmariy*) Strong's H6786. From
[3018] (צֶמֶר *tsemer)* Strong's H6785.
[3019] (חֲמָתִי *chamathiy*) Strong's H2577, Gesenius. From
[3020] (חֲמָת *chamath*) Strong's H2574, Gesenius.
[3021] (סְדֹם *cědom*) Strong's H5467.
[3022] (עֲמֹרָה *`amorah*) Strong's H6017.
[3023] (גְּבוּל *gěbuwl*) Strong's H1366. From
[3024] (גָּבַל *gabal*) Strong's H1379, Gesenius.
[3025] Wittgenstein, *Tractatus Logico-Philosophicus*, 5.6.
[3026] (צִידוֹן *tsiydown)* Strong's H6721. From
[3027] (צוּד *tsuwd*) Strong's H6679, Gesenius.
[3028] (בּוֹא *bow'*) Strong's H935.
[3029] (גְּרָר *gěrar*) Strong's H1642. From next
[3030] (גָּרַר *garar*) Strong's H1641, Gesenius.
[3031] (עַזָּה *`Azzah*) Strong's H5804; from (עַז *`az*) Strong's H5794, strong; From (עָזַז *`azaz*) Strong's H5810, to be strong.
[3032] (סְדֹם *cědom*) Strong's H5467.
[3033] (עֲמֹרָה *`amorah*) Strong's H6017. From next
[3034] (עָמַר *`amar*) Strong's H6014, Gesenius.
[3035] (אַדְמָה *'Admah*) Strong's H126; contracted for (אֲדָמָה *'adamah)* Strong's H127, land; from (אָדַם *'adam*) Strong's H119, Adam, to be red.
[3036] (צְבָאִים *tsěbo'iym*) Strong's H6636, gazelles, plural of (צְבִי *tsěbiy*) Strong's H6643 beauty glory. From next
[3037] (צָבָה *tsabah*) Strong's H6638.

[3038] (לְשַׁע *lesha`*) Strong's H3962.
[3039] *UB* III.3.2. *yāvatī kshurasya dhārā* & IV. 4. 22. *setur* (the bridge, as boundary and passage way) *vidharaṇa* (confining) *eshāṃ* (of these) *lokānām* (universes) *asambhedāya* (to be separated).
[3040] *Bible*, Matthew 7:14.
[3041] *UK* III.14 (I.3.14) *kshurasya* (of a razor) *dhārā* (edge) *niśitā* (sharp) *duratyayā* (difficult to cross) *durgam* (of difficult access) *pathas-* (path)
[3042] *UC* VIII.1.3. *yāvān* (as large as) *vā* (verily) *ayan* (this) *ākāśaḥ* (space) *tāvān* (so large) *esho'* (that) *ntarhṛdaya* (in the heart) *ākāśaḥ* (space).
[3043] *Bible*, John 19:28,30 now (ἤδη *ēdē*), accomplished (τετέλεσται *tetelestai*), that which is written (*viz.* scripture γραφή *graphē*), reach the designated end (*viz.* fulfilled τελειωθῇ *teleiōthē*), bowed (κλίνας *klinas*), head (κεφαλὴν *kephalēn*), life-breath (πνεῦμα *pneuma*).
[3044] Scaligero, *Manuale...*, p. 39. "*come uno stato di assoluta indipendenza dal systema nervoso.*"
[3045] (גָּדוֹל *gadowl*) Strong's H1419. The word (also translated as older) has its principal meaning of *great* (as in this case) from (גָּדַל *gadal*) Strong's H1431, *to become great.*
[3046] Einstein, *Space-Time.*
[3047] (עֵבֶר *`eber*) Strong's H5677, Gesenius.
[3048] (עֵבֶר *`eber*) Strong's H5676. From
[3049] (עָבַר *`abar*) Strong's H5674.
[3050] Gesenius, עָבַר*,* 3) a)*,* see Genesis 50:4, "*When, the time (yamēy) יְמֵי of his mourning past by (waya`abaru) וַיַּעַבְרוּ* [(*i.e.* עָבַר *`abar),* then] *Joseph spake unto the house of Pharaoh."*
[3051] Not present in the Hebrew or Latin texts.
[3052] (עֵילָם *`Eylam*) Strong's H5867, meaning eternity. From
[3053] (עָלַם *`alam)* Strong's H5956.
[3054] (אָשַׁר *'ashar*) Strong's H833. From which derives
[3055] (אַשּׁוּר *'ashshuwr) Strong's H804.*
[3056] <Simonelli, *Beyond Immortality*, p, 61.>
[3057] (אַרְפַּכְשַׁד *'arpakshad*) Strong's H775.
[3058] (יְאֹר *ya`or*) Strong's H2975.
[3059] (אוֹר *'owr*) Strong's H216, as the Nile. From (אוֹר *'owr*) Strong's H215, to be illuminated.
[3060] *Cf.* Amos 8:8.
[3061] (אָרַר *'arar*) Strong's H779*.*
[3062] (שֵׁד shed) Strong's H7700.
[3063] (שַׁד *shad*) Strong's H7699. From
[3064] (שׁוּד *shuwd*) Strong's H7736.
[3065] <Simonelli, *Beyond Immortality*, p. 26.>
[3066] *Bible,* John 17:5 and "thou lovedst me *before* the foundation of the world" 24 (Italic is ours).
[3067] <Simonelli, *Beyond Immortality*, p. 49.>
[3068] To the family of Besso, the deceased Italian-Swiss physicist (Dyson, *Disturbing the Universe*, Ch. 17, Science and the Search for God).
[3069] *Bible*, John 8:58.
[3070] *UMaitrī* VI. 15. *kālaḥ* (time) *pacati* (cooks) *bhūtāni* (living beings) *sarvāṇy* (all) *eva* (verily)" 16. *vigrahavān* (divided) *esha* (this) *kālaḥ* (time) *sindhurājaḥ*(river king) *prajānām* (of creatures)
[3071] (לוּד *luwd) Strong's H3865.*
[3072] (אֲרָם *'aram) Strong's* h758.
[3073] אַרְמוֹן, Strong's H759.
[3074] (עוּץ *`uwts)* Strong's H5780, *wooded.* From next
[3075] (עוּץ *`uwts)* Strong's H5779, to counsel, to plan.
[3076] (חוּל *chuwl)* Strong's H2342 & (חוּל *chuwl*) Strong's H2343.
[3077] (גֶּתֶר *gether)* Strong's H1666.
[3078] (מַשׁ *mash)* Strong's H4851.
[3079] From the verb משה *masha.*
[3080] Not in the Hebrew or Latin texts.
[3081] (שְׁלַח *shelach)* Strong's H7974. The same as (שֶׁלַח *shelach)* Strong's H7973. From
[3082] (שָׁלַח *shalach)* Strong's H7971.
[3083] Gesenius (1), שָׁלַח, Specially - (*aa*).
[3084] (פֶּלֶג *peleg)* Strong's H6389, *division*, the same as (פֶּלֶג *peleg)* Strong's H6388, see Gesenius, from (פָּלַג *palag)* Strong's H6385, meaning to divide, to split
[3085] (כִּי *kiy)* Strong's H3588.
[3086] (יָקְטָן *yoqtan*) Strong's H3355.
[3087] קָטֹן Strong's H6994, from a primitive root (קָטֹן *qatan)* Strong's H6996.
[3088] From (קוּט *quwt)* Strong's H6962.

[3089] (אַלְמוֹדָד *'almowdad)* H486.
[3090] (שֶׁלֶף *shelaph) Strong's* H8026.
[3091] (שָׁלַף*)* Strong's H8025.
[3092] שָׁלַף Gesenius (3); *cf.* Psalm 129:6.
[3093] *UK* VI.17 (II.3.17) *sadā* (always) *janānāṃ* (of the creature) *hṛdaye* (in the heart) *sannivishṭaḥ* (seated)/ *taṃ* (him) *svāc-* (one's own) *charīrāt* (from body) *pravṛhen-* (should draw out) *muñjād-* (from the reed) *iv-* (like) *eshīkāṃ* (the stalk) *dhairyeṇa* (with firmness).
[3094] *Cf. Bible*, Matthew 13:30.
[3095] שָׁלַף Gesenius (1), *cf.* Numbers 22:23 & Joshua 5:13.
[3096] *Satori* さとる, enlightenment in the martial arts (*kenzen itchi*), like Kendo and Iaijutsu; *cf.* Ratti, *Secrets of the Samurai*, p. 275.
[3097] (חֲצַרְמָוֶת *chatsar-maveth) Strong's* H2700, Gesenius.
[3098] (חָצֵר *chatser)* Strong's H2691, Gesenius.
[3099] *Cf.* Psalm 49:15.
[3100] (מָוֶת *maveth)* Strong's H4194, Gesenius.
[3101] Budge, *The Egyptian Book...*, p. civ. And *Coffin Text* 714, & Rundle-Clark, *Myth and Religion,* p. 74.
[3102] (יֶרַח *yerach)* Strong's H3392, same as (יֶרַח *yerach*) Strong's H3391.
[3103] Genesis 8:22.
[3104] Ecclesiastes 3:1.
[3105] הֲדוֹרָם *hadowram Strong's* H1913.
[3106] אוּזָל *'uwzal* Strong's H187.
[3107] Daniel 2:20.
[3108] (דִּקְלָה *diqlah*) Strong's H1853.
[3109] עוֹבָל *`owbal Strong's* H5745, Gesenius.
[3110] אֲבִימָאֵל *'abiyma'el Stong's* H39.
[3111] אָב *'ab* Strong's H1.
[3112] אָב Gesenius (1) and (7). Cf. Job 17:14.
[3113] *Shĕba', Strong's* H7614. *Cf.* Uittenbogaard, A. (2000-2014). *The Hebrew word.*
[3114] אוֹפִיר *'Owphiyr Strong's* H211.
[3115] *UB* I.4.1. *haṃ* (I) ... *oshati* (burns) *ha* (verily) vai (when indeed) *sa* (he) *tam* (him) *yo'* (who) *smāt* (this) *pūrvo* (before) *bubhūshati* (strives to be) *ya* (who) *evaṃ* (thus) *veda* (knows).
[3116] *Chaviylah*, Strong's H2341.
[3117] From חוּל *chuwl,* Strong's H2342, to twist, to turn around.
[3118] יוֹבָב *yowbab Strong's* H3103, Gesenius.
[3119] (מֵשָׁא *mesha'*) Strong's H4852, Gesenius, meaning *freedom, retreat.*
[3120] (הַר *har*) Strong's H2022, Gesenius, *mountain, mountainous country, land.* A shortened form of הָרַר *harar* Strong's H2042.
[3121] (סְפָר *cĕphar) Stong's* H5611, Gesenius, it means *numbering*, same as (סְפָר *cĕphar)* Strong's H5610, meaning *census, enumeration,* from (סָפַר *caphar)* Strong's H5608, Gesenius (2), *to count, to relate, to narrate, to recount.*
[3122] (קֶדֶם *qedem) Strong's* H6924, it means *east, antiquity* [Gesenius (3)], "*of old*" [Gesenius (a)], from (קָדַם *qadam)* Strong's H6923, Gesenius (2), *to precede.*
[3123] Strong's H8034.
[3124] Salvador Dalí's *La persistencia de la memoria*, (*The Persistence of Memory*, 1931 - art reproduction, original oil on canvas in the Museum of Modern Art, New York City 162.1934).
[3125] *Cf.* explanation regarding the GRAPHIC: *1 Hexagram, 2 Turtle and 3 the Head of Adam Kadmon.*
[3126] Not in the Hebrew or Latin texts.
[3127] Tagliazucchi, *Large-scale signatures of unconsciousness.* Abstract.
[3128] אַחַר *'achar* Strong's H310, Gesenius (1).
[3129] From אָחַר *'achar* Strong's H309, after, to delay, hesitate, tarry, defer, remain behind.
[3130] (תוֹלְדוֹת *towlĕdah*) Strong's H8435.
[3131] (פָּרַד *parad*) Strong's H6504, Gesenius.
[3132] (מִשְׁפָּחָה *mishpachah*) Strong's H4940, Gesenius (1).
[3133] (גּוֹי *gowy*) Strong's H1471 nations, other animals Gesenius (2).
[3134] (גְּוָה *gevahn*) Strong's H1465, behind, body, Gesenius (2). From גֵּו *gev* (Strong's H1460), the back. Also corresponding to גַּב *gab*, Strong's H1354, back.
[3135] One (אֶחָד *'echad*) Strong's H259. From next
[3136] (אָחַד *'achad*) Strong's H258, Gesenius, "to unite, to join oneself together."
[3137] From Latin *unitas* oneness, uni+fication *facere*, to make.
[3138] (דָּבָר) Strong's H1697. From next
[3139] (דָּבַר) Strong's H1696.
[3140] Gesenius (דָּבַר) (1) & (5).
[3141] (שָׂפָה *saphah*) Strong's H8193.

[3142] (שָׂפָה) Strong's H8192.
[3143] (סָפָה) Strong's H5595, Gesenius (1).
[3144] (סוּף) Strong's H5490.
[3145] (סוּף) Strong's H5486, Gesenius.
[3146] In the International Standard Atmosphere, but varying according to the medium, sound waves travel at 1108 feet per second or 761.2 miles per hour (Mach 1) (*cf.* NASA, *General Physics: Waves - Light and Sound*).
[3147] (קֶדֶם *qedem*) *Strong's* H6924.
[3148] קֶדֶם antiquity, Gesenius (3) & (a). From next
[3149] (קָדַם *qadam*) Strong's H6923, Gesenius (2), *to precede*.
[3150] Plain בִּקְעָה *biq`ah Strong's* H1237. From בָּקַע *baqa`* Strong's H1234 to split, to divide, to rip up, to break up.
[3151] שִׁנְעָר shin`*ar* H8152.
[3152] אָמַר Strong's H559.
[3153] Gesenius, אָמַר (1).
[3154] One (אִישׁ *'iysh) Strong's* H376.
[3155] (רֵעַ *rea`*) *Strong's* H7453.
[3156] Gesenius II רֵעַ (a).
[3157] רֵעָה Strong's H7462.
[3158] רֵעָה Gesenius (3).
[3159] רְעוּת Strong's H7469, Gesenius.
[3160] Aramaic רַעְיוֹן Strong's H7476, corresponding to רַעְיוֹן *ra`yown* Strong's H7475
[3161] The subject, as such, is never more than one. However, it refracts into the many singular individualities, never known as such.
[3162] (לָבָן *laban*) *Strong's* H3835, Gesenius.
[3163] (לְבֵנָה *lĕbenah*) *Strong's* H3843, from previous H3835.
[3164] (שָׂרַף *saraph) Strong's* H8313.
[3165] (שְׂרֵפָה *sĕrephah) Strong's* H8316, from previous H8313.
[3166] (תֶּבֶן *teben*) *straw for building* Strong's H8401), *cf.* Exodus 5:18.
[3167] (אֶבֶן *'eben) Strong's* H68, *cf.* Isaiah 28:16.
[3168] (חֹמֶר *chomer*) *Strong's* H2563 From חָמַר *chamar* (H2560)
[3169] (חֵמָר *chemar*) *Strong's* H2564, from (חָמַר *chamar*) Strong's H2560.
[3170] (חֲמַר *chamar Aramaic*) Strong's H2562, from (חֶמֶר *chemer)* Strong's H2561, both meaning wine.
[3171] Thomas, *18 poems*: The force that through the green fuse drives the flower ...
[3172] *iṣhṭakā*, *W.* p. 169bc, from √*ishṭá* 1 "wished , desired... desire... sacrifice" (b) and 2 "sacrificing, sacrifice" (c); see, by assonance, *kā* 3 p. 266b. *UK* I.15 (I.I.15). *Cf.* also *ŚB Śatapatha Brāhmaṇa*, Tr. Julius Eggeling, X. Part IV, p. 356-60. *Cf.* also Simonelli, *Beyond Immortality*, pp. 137-8.
[3173] Eliade, *The Sacred...*, p. 12.
[3174] *Tao Te Ching,* 6 (43).
[3175] Exodus 5:18.
[3176] לְבֵנָה *lĕbenah Strong's* H3843.
[3177] תֶּבֶן *teben Strong's* H8401, probably from בָּנָה *banah* Strong's H1129, to build. In fact, straw was regarded as the essential element to make building bricks.
[3178] *Bible*, John 2:19.
[3179] (בָּנָה *banah*) Strong's H1129.
[3180] (עִיר *`iyr*) Strong's H5892.
[3181] Gesenius, עִיר (1).
[3182] עוּר Strong's H5782, Gesenius (1), (1), (2), (3).
[3183] Malachi 2:12.
[3184] עוּר Strong's H5783.
[3185] (מִגְדָּל*) Strong's* H4026.
[3186] Gesenius, מִגְדָּל (4).
[3187] גָּדַל Strong's H1431.
[3188] (ראשׁ *ro'sh) Strong's* H7218, Gesenius.
[3189] Latin poet Horace (65 – 8 B.C.), *Quinti Horatii ...* p. 9, *Carminum* I.1.35-36. "*Sublimi feriam sidera vertice*."
[3190] רֵעַ *rea`* Strong's H7452.
[3191] רֵעַ *rea`* Strong's H7454.
[3192] *Cf.* Deuteronomy 6:5.
[3193] Leviticus 19:18, וְאָהַבְתָּ לְרֵעֲךָ כָּמוֹךָ *wa'āhaḇatā larē'ăḵā kāmwōḵā. Cf. Bible,* Matthew 5:43; 19:19; 22:39; Mark 12:31.
[3194] (שֵׁם *shem*) Strong's H8034, Gesenius (3). Perhaps it derives from שׂוּם *suwm,* Strong's H7760, which gives the idea of conspicuous position, further, to appoint, to lay violent hands upon, to direct toward and to transform into.
[3195] פֵּן *pen* Strong's H6434. From next
[3196] פָּנָה *panah* Strong's H6437.
[3197] פּוּץ *puwts Strong's* H6327.

3198 רֹע Strong's H7455. From next
3199 רָעַע Strong's H7489.
3200 Strong's H5892.
3201 עוּר `*uwr* Strong's H5782 and Gesenius.
3202 מִגְדָּל *migdal* Strong's H4026.
3203 מִגְדָּל Gesenius (1). See 2 Kings 9:17, וְהַצֹּפֶה ... עַל־הַמִּגְדָּל (*vəhaṣōp̄eh ... 'al-hamiḡədāl*) *a watchman on the tower* & 17:9, מִמִּגְדַּל נוֹצְרִים עַד־עִיר (*mimiḡədal nvōṣəriym 'aḏ- 'iyr*) *from the watchmen's tower to the fenced city*.
3204 יָרַד *yarad* Strong's H3381.
3205 *Secretum Secretorum*: *Secrets' Secret*. *Tabula smaragdina* text in Chrysogonus Polydorus, *De Alchimia*, and Khunrath, *Amphiteatrum...*, figure. 8. "*Quod est inferius, est sicut quod est superius. Et quod est superius, est sicut quod est inferius, ad perpetranda miracula rei unius... Ascendit a terra in coelum, iterumque descendit in terram, et recipit vim superiorum et inferiorum. Sic habebis gloriam totius mundi.*"
3206 *Bible,* Luke 11:2; & Matthew 6:10
3207 רָאָה *ra'ah* Strong's H7200.
3208 בָּנָה *banah* H1129.
3209 אֶחָד *'echad* Strong's H259.
3210 עַם `*am* *Strong's* H5971. From next
3211 עָמַם `*amam* Strong's H6004, Gesenius (1), *to gather together.*
3212 Gesenius, עָמַם *to hide, to conceal.*
3213 חָלַל *chalal* Strong's H2490, Gesenius (1). Compare to
3214 חוּל *chuwl* Strong's H2342, and
3215 חָלָה *chalah* Strong's H2470.
3216 זֶה *zeh* Strong's H2088.
3217 זָמַם *zamam* H2161.
3218 Domenico Ghirlandaio, 1490, Louvre, Paris. Public Domain, Ritratto di nonno con nipote.jpg, https://en.wikipedia.org/wiki/An_Old_Man_and_his_Grandson#/media/File:Domenico_ghirlandaio,_ritratto_di_nonno_con_nipote.jpg
3219 Quoted in, *The Works of Hannah More,* V.2, p. 345.
3220 Bovio-Lama, *Silenzio Cantatore*. *Cf.* also Desamangalam, *Singing silence*.
3221 Genesis 41:11.
3222 בָּצַר *batsar* Strong's H1219.
3223 *UB* I.2.7. (*anavarudhya*-non restraining-*ivā*-thus-*manyata*-he thought). *Cf. W.* "*Médhya*, mf(*ā*)n. (fr. *medha*" = "*n....* a sacrifice,... (ifc.<in fine compositi>) = *medhā*, <f.> intelligence, knowledge, understanding." (833a). *Cf. VṚ* X.90.10
3224 In *AU LECTEUR* (To the Reader), Altus, Baulot, *Mutus liber*, 1677 first edition. "*Livre Muĕt, néanmoins toutes les Nations du monde... peuvent le lire & l'entendre... Il ne faut qu'estre un veritable Enfant de l'Art, pour le connoître d'abord.*" (*Cf.* Eli Luminosus Aequalis, *Mutus Liber Loquitur*, p. 32).
3225 *Cf.* Ellis, *The superstring: theory of everything, or of nothing?*
3226 This is the reason why; who declares to be *a-theist* (*viz. a-transcendentalist*) in reality affirms his/her *theism* (*viz. transcendentalism*). In fact, s/he must believe in the transcendence of the listener, whom s/he does not know in-it-self.
3227 *The Epic of Gilgamesh*, p. 108-9.
3228 "*Have no intercourse* (רָעָה *ra `ah*, Strong's H7462, Gesenius 3) *with a... possessor of a thing* (בַּעַל *ba `al, Strong's H1167, Gesenius 4).*" (Proverbs 22:24).
3229 (אִישׁ *'iysh) Strong's H376.* Contracted for אֱנוֹשׁ *'enowsh* Strong's H582, *individual, mortal.* From next
3230 אָנַשׁ *'anash* Strong's H605, *to be weak, very sick, incurably desperate.*
3231 (רֵעַ *rea `*) Strong's H7453*. From the next*
3232 רָעָה *ra `ah* Strong's H7462.
3233 *Cf.* Hamilton, *Gorilla Cracks Glass Window At Zoo After Little Girl Beats Chest*
3234 *Bible*, Revelation 21:2-4-6-10-16. *Cf. UC* VIII.1.1, the city of Brahman (*brahma-pure*) & 3. *Cf.* also *UK* V.1 (II.2.1), *BG* V.13 and Simonelli, *Beyond Immortality*, p. 189. *Cf.* the phrase sung at Passover Seder and on Yom Kippur: "Next year in Jerusalem" (לשנה הבאה בירושלים *l'shana haba'ah b'yerushalayim*); Gilad Barach, *The Meaning of "Next Year in Jerusalem."*
3235 *Bible*, Revelation 21:22. *Cf.* Teresa of Avila, *The Interior Castle*.
3236 (מֵאָה) Strong's H3967, Gesenius.
3237 Genesis 26:11. Also, "*Meah of100 Gates*" is the name of a Tower in the ancient walls of Jerusalem (Nehemiah 3:1 & 12:39).
3238 *Bible*, Mark 4:20.
3239 *Bible*, 2 Peter 3:8. *Cf. UMaitrī* VI.1.
3240 יִלּוֹדוֹן y$_{e}$l$_{e}$dwn, Strong's H3205 in Hosea 9:16; 100 = 10(י*y*) +30(ל*l*) + 4(ד*d*) + 6(ו*w*) +50(ן*n*).
3241 יָלַדְנוּ *y$_{a}$l$_{a}$d$_{a}$nw*, Strong's H3205, Gesenius (1), in Isaiah 26:18; 100 = 10(י*y*) +30(ל*l*) + 4(ד*d*) +50(נ*n*) + 6(ו*w*).
3242 Strong's H3205.
3243 *BU* I.2.4. "*tad* (that) *yad* (which) *reta* (the generating flow) *āsīt* (was) *sa* (that) *saṃvatsaro* (the year) *'bhavat* (became) *na*

(not) *ha* (indeed) *purā* (in the beginning) *tataḥ* (then) *saṃvatsara* (the year) *āsa* (was) *tam* (him) *etāvantaṃ* (so far) *kālam* (space of time) *abhibhaḥ* (parented) *yāvān* (as long as) *saṃvatsaraḥ* (year) *tam* (him) *etāvataḥ* (thus) *kālasya* (time) *parastād* (afterwards) *asṛjata* (he projected) *taṃ* (him)...
7. *tam* (him) *anavarudhya-* (not restraining) *-ivā-* (thus) *-manyata* (he thought) *taṃ* (him) *saṃvatsarasya* (of a year) ... *saṃvatsara* (the year) *ātmā* (self).

[3244] London, Soane Museum: head inside border of the coffin of Seti I (1318 - 1304 BC, XIX Dynasty), son of Ramses I, father of Ramses II the Great. This sarcophagus, the most beautiful one in the Kings' Valley (West of Thebes – Egypt), was discovered in 1817 by Giovanni Belzoni (*Cf.* Budge, *Mummy*, p. 418- 9).

[3245]  *Cf.* Simonelli, *The World as the Upanishadic sacrificial-horse.*

[3246] 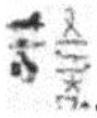.

[3247] Budge, *The Egyptian Book...*, p. civ. And *Coffin Text* 714, & Rundle-Clark, *Myth and Religion,* p. 74.

[3248] יָדַע Strong's H3045, see Job 19:13; 32:7; 42:11 & Psalm 103:7.

[3249] Deriving from מַיִם *mayim* water, Strong's H4325, Exodus 7:15 & 19.

[3250] Another word equivalent to 100, Isaiah 7:19, נַחַל *nachal* Strong's H5158, from נָחַל *nachal*, Strong's H5157, Gesenius (7), in the sense to acquire, to get as a possession.

[3251] Not in the Hebrew or Latin texts.

[3252] *Lived*, חָיָה *chayah, Strong's* H2421, *to continue*, Gesenius (2). Compare to

[3253] חָוָה *chavah*, Strong's H2331, *to breath.*

[3254] (בֵּן *ben*) Strong's H1121, said also of lifeless things, i.e. sparks, stars, arrows (fig.).

[3255] (בַּת *bath*) Strong's H1323, Gesenius (7) "Figuratively, *the daughter of any thing* is used with regard to *whatever depends upon it, pertains to it, or is distinguished for it.*"

[3256] *Cf.* Hoffman, *The Hebrew Alphabet.*

[3257] *Cf.* Hoffman, *The Hebrew Alphabet.*

[3258] לְעֵת (Genesis 8:11) Strong's H6256 (עת *`eth, time*), 30 (ל,*l*) + 70 (ע,*'a*) + 400 (ת,*t*) = 500.

[3259] ἑκατὸν *ekaton* (hundred) & Καιναν *Kainan* (Cainan) different from the Hebrew and Latin texts.

[3260] אֵלֵד *'ēlēd* 1(א, *a*) + 30(ל, *l*) + 4(ד,*d*) = 35 (Genesis 18:13), from יָלַד *yalad* (Strong's H3205).

[3261] שֶׁלַח Strong's H7974, Gesenius (1), same as שֶׁלַח *shelach,* Strong's H7973 with the meaning of weapon.

[3262] שֶׁלַח Strong's H7971, Gesenius (3).

[3263] שָׁלַח Gesenius (*aa*).

[3264] Possible interpolation of a long genealogical description not in the Hebrew or Latin texts.

[3265] Different from the Hebrew texts.

[3266] מַגִּישִׁים *m$_{a}$g$_{i}$yš$_{i}$ym you are bringing in and out* (Malachi 1:7) = 40(מ *m*)+ 3(ג *g*)+ 10(י *y*)+ 300(ש *š*)+ 10(י *y*)+ 40(ם *m*) =403, from נָגַשׁ *nagash*, Strong's H5066.

[3267] נָגַשׁ Gesenius (1,2).

[3268] Not in the Hebrew and Latin texts.

[3269] עֵבֶר *`eber* Strong's H5677, same as עֵבֶר *` eber* Strong's H5676.

[3270] עֵבֶר Gesenius (1).

[3271] עָבַר (Strong's H5674) Gesenius (3a).

[3272] בְּחַיַּי b$_{ə}$ḥ$_{a}$y$_{a}$y (Genesis 27:46), from חַי *chay* (Strong's *H2416),* 2(ב,b)+ 8(ח,*ḥ*)+ 10(י,*y*)+ 10(י,*y*) = 30.

[3273] Different from the Hebrew and Latin texts.

[3274] מַגִּישִׁים *m$_{a}$g$_{i}$yš$_{i}$ym you are bringing in and out* (Malachi 1:7) = [40(מ *m*)+ 3(ג *g*)+ 10(י *y*)+ 300(ש *š*)+ 10(י *y*)+ 40(ם *m*)] =403, from נָגַשׁ *nagash*, Strong's H5066.

[3275] Not in the Hebrew and Latin texts.

[3276] פֶּלֶג *peleg* Strong's H6389.

[3277] פֶּלֶג *peleg* Strong's H6388.

[3278] פָּלַג *palag* Strong's H6385.

[3279] וַיְחִי *v$_{a}$y$_{ə}$ḥ$_{i}$y he lived,* 6(ו,*v*) + 10(י,*y*)+ 8(ח,*ḥ*)+ 10(י,*y*)=34, in Genesis 5:3; Strong's H2421 חָיָה chayah. *Cf.* also יְחַיּוּ *yəḥayu we keep alive*, in Genesis 12:12 & *וְהַחֲיֵה vəhaḥăyēh, to keep alive*, in Joshua 9:20.

[3280] וְחַיַּי *v$_{ə}$ḥ$_{a}$yay life,* 6(ו,*v*)+ 8(ח,*ḥ*)+ 10(י,*y*)+ 10(י,*y*)=34, in Psalm 88:3; חַי *chay* Strong's H2416. *Cf.* also חַיָּיו ḥayāyv *of life* in Genesis 47:28.

[3281] וַיְחַדָּו *v$_{a}$y$_{a}$ḥ$_{a}$d$_{ā}$v together* 6(ו,*v*)+ 10(י,*y*)+ 8(ח,*ḥ*)+ 4(ד,*d*)+6(ו,*v*)=34 Exodus 26:24; Strong's H3162 יַחַד *yachad.*

[3282] ἑβδομήκοντα *ebdomēkonta* (seventy) ... ἀπέθανεν *apethanen* (died) not in the Hebrew and Latin texts.

[3283] מִקֹּצֶר *m$_{i}$q$_{ō}$ṣ$_{e}$r for anguish*, 40(מ,*m*)+ 100(ק,*q*)+90(צ,*ṣ*)+200(ר,*r*)= 430, in Exodus 6:9; קֹצֶר *qotser* Strong's H7115.

[3284] וַיֵּחַתּוּ *v$_{a}$y$_{e}$ḥ$_{a}$tu they were dismayed*, 6(ו,*v*)+ 10(י,*y*)+ 8(ח,*ḥ*)+ 400(ת,*t*)+ 6(ו,*v*)=430, in 1Samuel 17:11; חָתַת *chathath* Strong's H2865.

[3285] Not in the Hebrew and Latin texts.

[3286] רְעוּ *r@ `uw* Strong's H7466.

[3287] רְעִי Strong's H7471.

3288 רֶעָה Strong's H7462.
3289 רֵע Strong's H7453.
3290 בְחַיַּי *bəḥayay* (Genesis 27:46), from חַי *chay* (Strong's *H2416),* 2(ב,b)+ 8(ח,*ḥ*)+ 10(י,*y*)+ 10(י,*y*) = 30.
3291 ἀπέθανεν *apethanen* (died) not in the Hebrew and Latin texts.
3292 אַחֵר *'aḥer* other, 1(א,*a*)+ 8(ח,*ḥ*)+ 200(ר,*r*)= 209, in Genesis 4:25; אַחֵר *'acher* Strong's H0312.
3293 וְגֵר *vəḡer* stranger, 6(ו,*v*)+ 3(ג,*g*)+ 200(ר,*r*)= 209, in Exodus 22:21;גֵר *ger* Strong's H1616.
3294 Not in the Hebrew and Latin texts.
3295 שְׂרוּג *Sĕruwg* Strong's H8286, Gesenius.
3296 שָׂרַג Strong's H8276, Gesenius, *cf.* Job 40:17.
3297 בְּאָחִיהוּ *bə'āḥiyhu* brother, 2(ב,*b*)+ 1(א,*a*)+ 8(ח,*ḥ*)+10(י,*y*)+5(ה,*h*)+6(ו,v)=32, in Job 41:17; אָח *'ach* Strong's H251.
3298 Job 41:17.
3299 ἀπέθανεν *apethanen* (died) not in the Hebrew and Latin texts.
3300 וָאִיקָץ *vā'iyqāṣ* I awake, 6(ו,*v*)+ 1(א,*a*)+10(י,*y*)+100(ק,*q*)+90(צ,*ṣ*)=207, in Genesis 41:21, יקץ *yaqats* Strong's H3364.
3301 בְּהָקִיץ *bəhāqiyṣ* in awaking, 2(ב,*b*)+5(ה,*h*)+100(ק,*q*)+10(י,*y*)+ 90(צ,*ṣ*)=207, in Psalm 17:15, קוּץ *quwts* Strong's H6974.
3302 Not in the Hebrew and Latin texts.
3303 בְחַיַּי bəḥayay (Genesis 27:46), from חַי *chay* (Strong's *H2416),* 2(ב,b)+ 8(ח,*ḥ*)+ 10(י,*y*)+ 10(י,*y*) = 30.
3304 נָחוֹר *Nachowr Strong's* H5152.
3305 נַחַר Strong's H5170, Gesenius.
3306 Job 39:18-19-20, underlining is ours.
3307 *Roget's International Thesaurus*, n. 373.2 and n. 498.3.
3308 *Cf. UB* I. 1. 1 & 2. 3. *Cf. UK* III.3-10 (I.3.3-10). *Cf.* Simonelli, *Una lettura della Bṛhadāraṇyaka Upanishad,* & *The World as the Upanishadic sacrificial-horse*, & *Beyond Immortality*... p. 95, & *La morte nella Bṛhadāraṇyaka Upanishad e Śatapatha Brāhmaṇa,* & *Sacred Topography* ..., p. 1404.
3309 *Cf.* Plato, *Phaedrus* , 246.
3310 ἀπέθανεν *apethanen* (died) not in the Hebrew and Latin texts.
3311 הַמִּקְנֶה *hamiqneh, cattle, possession, wealth*, 5(ה,*h*)+ 40(מ,*m*)+ 100(ק,*q*)+ 50(נ,*n*) + 5(ה,*h*)=200, in Genesis 29:7, מִקְנֶה *miqneh* Strong's H4735, Gesenius (1).
3312 מִקְנַי *miqnay, cattle, possession, wealth*, 40(מ,*m*)+ 100(ק,*q*)+ 50(נ,*n*) + 10(י,*y*)=200, in Exodus 17:3, מִקְנֶה *miqneh* Strong's H4735.
3313 Franklin, *Franklin: Writings.* "*Advice to a Young Tradesman, Written by an Old One*" (1748).
3314 *W.*, p 114c.
3315 Cf. Simonelli, *Una lettura della Bṛhadāraṇyaka Upanishad.*
3316 *W.,* p. 159b.
3317 *W.*, p. 1106a.
3318 Not in the Hebrew and Latin texts.
3319 See Genesis 12:14 *he came* כְּבוֹא *kəḇvō'*; Genesis 27:4 וְהָבִיאָה *vəhāḇiy'āh bring in*; Exodus 16:5 יָבִיאוּ *yāḇiy'u they come in*; Deuteronomy 23:11 וּכְבֹא *ukəḇō'he shall come*; Judge 6:4 בּוֹאֲךָ *bvō'ăḵā until they come*; 1 Samuel 29:6 וּבֹאֲךָ *uḇō'ăḵā thy coming*; 2 Chronicles 28:27 הֱבִיאֻהוּ *hĕḇiy'uhu they brought*; Nehemiah 8:2 וַיָּבִיא *vayāḇiy' brought* all deriving from בּוֹא *bow' to come, to go*, Strong's H935 and all with a Gematria value of 29.
3320 תֶּרַח *Terach* Strong's H8646.
3321 Gematria 29, בְּגִיחוֹ bəḡiyḥvō, 2(ב,*b*)+ 3(ג,*g*)+10(י,*y*)+ 8(ח,*ḥ*)+6(ו,*v*)=29.
3322 Job 38:8, גִיח *giyach, to come*, Strong's H1518.
3323 *W.* pp. 115a; 159a; & 1135c "*satya*... the *aśvattha* tree."
3324 Judges 16:19, 22.
3325 Strong's H3581.
3326 Strong's H4253.
3327 Strong's H8181. *Cf.* "*They shall not make baldness upon their head, neither shall they shave off the corner of their beard, nor make any cuttings in their flesh.*" Leviticus 21:5. *Cf.* photo of Rastafarian dreadlocks.
3328 *UB* III.9.28 *yatha* (as) *vṛksho* (tree) *vanaspatiḥ* (forest) *tathaiva* (that he indeed) *purusho'* (person) *mṛshā* (surely) *tasya* (his) *lomāni* (hair) *prṇāni* (leaves) *tvag* (skin) asyotpāṭikā (his bark) *bahiḥ* (outward).
3329 *BG* XV.1. *urdhva-*(above) *mūlam* (roots) *adhaḥ-*(below) *śākham* (branches) *aśvatthaṃ* (holy fig tree)... 2. *adhaś* (below) *cordhvaṃ* (and above) *prasṛtās* (extend) *tasya* (of that) *śākhāḥ* (branches) *guṇa-* (by the qualities) *praVṚddhā* (developed) *vishaya-* (sense objects) *pravālāḥ* (sprouts) */ adhaś* (below) *ca* (and) *mūlāny* (roots) *anusaṃtatāni* (stretched) *karmānubaṃdhīni* (bonded by action) *manushya-* (of humans) *loke* (in the world)... 3. *aśvattham* (tree under which the horses stand) *enaṃ* (this) *suvirūḍha-* (fully developed) *mūlam* (roots) *asaṃga-* (of non-attachment) *śastreṇa* (by the weapon) *dṛḍhena* (strong) *chittvā* (cutting). Cf. Simonelli, *Beyond Immortality*, pp. 197 fol.
3330 εἴκοσι *eikosi* (twenty) & ἀπέθανεν *apethanen* (died) not in the Hebrew and Latin texts.
3331 הָעֹמֵד *hā'ōmeḏ, is standing*, in Deuteronomy 1:38, 5(ה,*h*)+ 70(ע,*a*)+ 40(מ,*m*)+ 4(ד,*ḏ*)=119; עָמַד *`amad* Strong's H5975, *to stand*. Also with a Gematria value of 119 is עָמְדָה *'āmədāh she stood*, in Genesis 30:9.
3332 וְהַחֹנִים vəhaḥōniym, encamping, in Numbers 2:3, 6(,*v*)+ 5(ה,h)+ 8(ח,*ḥ*)+ 50(נ,*n*)+ 10(י,*y*)+ 40(ם,*m*)=119 חָנָה *chanah* Strong's

H2583, also with a 119 Gematria, וְנַחֲנֶה *vanaḥăneh we encamp*, in Ezra 8:15 & הַחוֹנִים *haḥvōniym encamp*, in Nahum 3:17.

3333 וְנָבוֹאָה *vənābvō'āh*, (6ו,*v*)+ 50(נ,*n*)+ 2(ב,*b*)+ (6ו,*v*)+ 1(א,*a*)+ 5(ה,*h*)=70, in Jeremiah 4:5, בוא *bow'* Strong's H935, also אֲבִיאֶנּוּ *'ăbiy'enu I bring*, in Genesis 42:37 and וְהִתְנַחֲלוּם *vəhitənaḥălum they brought*, in Isaiah 14:2, have a Gematria value of 70.

3334 Jeremiah 4:5.

3335 אַבְרָם *'Abram* Strong's H87, Gesenius.

3336 אֲבִירָם Strong's H48, original name of Abraham.

3337 אָב Strong's H1.

3338 רום Strong's H7311, Gesenius.

3339 הָרָן *Haran* (Strong's H2039), perhaps from הַר *har* (Strong's H2022), a shortened form of הַר *harar* (Strong's H2042) hill, mountain, from a root meaning to loom up, come up.

3340 *UM.* 5 *yatra* (where) *supto* (one asleep) *na* (not) *kaṃcana* (any) *kāmaṃ* (desire) *kāmayate* (does desire) *na* (not) *kaṃcana* (any) *svapnaṃ* (dream) *paśyati* (does see) *tat* (that) *sushuptam* (deep unconscious sleep) *sushupta* (deep unconscious sleep) *sthāna* (state) *ekī -bhūtaḥ* (one-become) *prajñāna-ghana* (knowledge-compact) ... *ceto-mukhaḥ* (consciousness-mouth) *prājñas-* (the knower).

3341 *UKa.* III. 3. *Yatraitat* when thus) *purushaḥ* (a person) *suptaḥ* (sleeping) *svapnaṃ* (dream) *na* (no) *kañcana* (whatsoever) *paśyaty* (he sees) *athāsmin* (that self) *prāṇa* (breathing) *evaikadhā* (verily one) *bhavati* (becomes) *tad* (that) *enam* (him) *vāk* (speech) *sarvaiḥ* (with all) *nāmabhiḥ* (names) *sahāpyeti* (together goes to it) *cakshuḥ* (the eye) *sarvaiḥ* (with all) *rūpaiḥ* (forms) *sahāpyeti* (together goes) *śrotraṃ* (the ear) *sarvaiḥ* (with all) *śabdaiḥ* (sounds) *sahāpyeti* (together goes) *manaḥ* (the mind) *sarvaiḥ* (with all) *dhyānaiḥ* (thoughts) *sahāpyeti* (together goes) *sa* (he) *yadā* (when) *pratibudhyate* (he awakens) *yathāgner* (as from a fire s) *jvalataḥ* (blazing) *sarvā* (in all) *diśo* (regions) *visphuliṅgā* (sparks) *vipratishṭheranṇ* (spread out) *evam* (thus) *evaitasmād* (so this therefore) *ātmanaḥ* (from the self) *prāṇā* (the vital breaths) *yathāyatanaṃ* (each in its own place) *vipratishṭhante* (spread out) *prāṇebhyo* (from the vital breaths) *devāḥ* (the resplendent senses) *devebhyo* (from the resplendent senses) *lokāḥ* (the worlds)

3342 Genesis 3:24 חי *chay* life, עֵץ *`ets* tree, חרב *chereb* sword, הפך *haphak* turned every way, להט *lahat* flaming.

3343 *UĪśa* 15 *hiraṇmayena* (with a golden) *pātreṇa* (dish) *satyasya* (of truth) *āpihitam* (is covered) *mukham* (the mouth)

3344 לוט *Lowt*, covering, veil, Strong's H3876, Gesenius; the same as לוט *lowt* Strong's H3875, from לוט *luwt* Strong's H3874, to wrap closely or envelop, to hide, to do secretively.

3345 *Cf.* Genesis 47:19.

3346 *Cf.* Job 14:8. "*Though the root thereof wax old in the earth, and the stock thereof die in the ground.*"

3347 *Cf.* Amos 2:2. "*it shall devour the palaces of Kerioth: and Moab shall die.*"

3348 מות *muwth Strong's H4191,* Gesenius. From the stock *mrt*, Sanskrit मृ *mṛ*, Greek μορτὸς *mortos*, Latin *mors*, English murder.

3349 *Cf.* Job 12:2. "*wisdom shall die with you.*"

3350 מולדת *mowledeth* Strong's H4138, Gesenius.

3351 אור *'Uwr* Strong's H218. The same as אור *'uwr* (Strong's H217), flame, light of fire, revelation, Gesenius. From אור *'owr* (Strong's H215) *to be* or *to become light*, *to shine*, Gesenius.

3352 כשדי *Kasdiy*, כַּשְׂדִּימָה *kas-dee'-maw* Strong's H3778, כשדים (Gesenius).

3353 Anch, *Sleep: ...*, "paroxysmal wave form of high amplitude standing out from a low-amplitude background in the EEG" p. 125.

3354 Dement, *Some Must Watch ...*, p. 28. Examples of Polygraph (*poly* = many – *graph* = graphic) records:

WAKING: , REM: , NREM = 1 Stage , 2 Stage 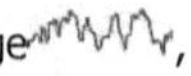, 3 Stage [deep-delta sleep or slow-wave-sleep (SWS)] , 4 Stage 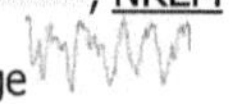

3355 *Cf.* Borbély, *Secrets of Sleep*, p. 23.

3356 Anch, *Sleep: ...*, pp. 55-56; *cf.* Agnew; Borbély, *Secrets of Sleep*, p. 25.

3357 Anch, *Sleep: ...*, p. 30.

3358 Borbély, *Secrets of Sleep*, p. 167.

3359 *Ibid.* pp. 55, 57, 202.

3360 *Cf. ibid.* p. 40.

3361 From Latin *mens* mind; the process of carefully rethinking, considering and recounting something or an object of the mind.

3362 Borbély, *Secrets of Sleep*, p. 44-45, 56; *cf.* Anch, p. 141; Foulkes; Monroe.

3363 Anch, *Sleep: A Scientific Perspective*, p. 141.

3364 Ferrarelli F. et al., *Breakdown in cortical effective connectivity during midazolam-induced loss of consciousness.*

3365 Anch, *Sleep: A Scientific Perspective*, p. 141.

3366 *Cf.* Rechtschaffen, *The relationship of phasic and tonic.* EMG = Electromyogram = *Electro* = electrical – *Myo* = muscle's activity - *Gram* = graphic recording.

3367 Hobson, *REM sleep and dreaming.*

3368 <Simonelli, *Beyond Immortality*, pp. 70-1.>

3369 יִסְכָּה *Yickah* Strong's H3252.

3370 מִלְכָּה *Milkah* Strong's H4435, *queen;* form of מַלְכָּה *melek* Strong's H4428, *king*, from מָלַךְ *malak* Strong's H4427, *to become*

queen, to reign, to rule.
[3371] שָׂרַי *Saray* Strong's H8297, *princess*; original name of Sarah, ("*And God said ... thou shalt not call her name Sarai, but Sarah.*" – Genesis 17:15) שָׂרָה *sarah noblewoman* Strong's H8282. from שַׂר *sar* Strong's H8269, *prince, ruler*, from שָׂרַר *sarar* Strong's H8323, *to be a prince, to reign, to have dominion over.*
[3372] Genesis 20:11-12. "*Abraham said... 'My wife ... is my sister... the daughter of my father... and she became my wife.'*"
[3373] For die-hard literal readers who really understand here an irrelevant incestuous relationship, we refer them to the historical aspects of such practices; *cf.* Bixler, *Sibling incest in the royal families of Egypt, Peru, and Hawaii.*
[3374] *Cf.* Kant, *The Critique of Pure Reason.*
[3375] וָלָד *valad Strong's* H2056, for יֶלֶד *yeled* Strong's H3206, from יָלַד *yalad* Strong's H3205.
[3376] עָקַר *'aqar Strong's* H6135. From
[3377] עָקַר *'aqar* Strong's H6131, Gesenius.
[3378] *Cf.* Psalm 83:6.
[3379] הָגָר *hagar* Strong's H1904, *flight.*
[3380] שִׁפְחָה *shiphchah* Strong's H8198, from an unused root meaning to spread out as a family; see מִשְׁפָּחָה *mishpachah* Strong's H4940, *family*, from שָׁפָה *shaphah* Strong's H8192, *to be wind-swept*, compare שִׁפְחָה *shiphchah* Strong's H8198, namely one of a family, Gesenius.
[3381] Genesis 16:3.
[3382] יִשְׁמָעֵאל *Yishma`e'l* Strong's H3458 , *God will hear*, from שָׁמַע *shama`* Strong's H8085, *to hear*, and אֵל *'el* Strong's H410, *God*, shortened from אַיִל *'ayil* Strong's H352, *sacrificial ram*, same as אול *'uwl* Strong's H193 , *nobles, wealthy men*, from a root meaning *to twist*, and *to be strong.*
[3383] Genesis 16:15.
[3384] إِسْمَاعِيلَ كَانَ صَادِقَ الْوَعْدِ *is'mā'īl* (Ishmael) *kāna* (was) *sadegh* (true) *uada* (promise) Koran 19:54.
[3385] Genesis 17:20.
[3386] יִצְחָק *Yitschaq Strong's* H3327, *he laughs*, from צָחַק *tsachaq* Strong's H6711, *to laugh.*
[3387] Genesis 17:19.
[3388] Genesis 18:13. When pregnant with her son, Sarah could not have viewed herself *old* (זָקֵן *zaqen*). In fact, her age, was relatively very young, proportionately compared with the Patriarchs' longevity. This proves, as we noted, that the Patriarchs' long life span was a metaphor.
[3389] Genesis 21:10.
[3390] מִדְבָּר *midbar* Strong's H4057, *wilderness, mouth with no food* Gesenius (2&3). From דָּבַר *dabar* Strong's H1696 in the sense of *to speak, declare, converse.* Compare with *Bible*, Matthew 3:1, "*John the Baptist, preaching in the wilderness.*"
[3391] Genesis 21:14.
[3392] Feuerbach, *Sämmtliche Werke*, X, 5, "*Der mensch ist was er isst.*"
[3393] כַּלָּה *kallah* Strong's H3618, *daughter in law*, from כָּלַל *kalal*, Strong's H3634, *to make complete, to make perfect.*
[3394] Not in the Hebrew or Latin texts.
[3395] הַכְּנַעֲנִי *$h_ak_an_a$ ăn$_i$y* (of the Canaanites) 5(ה,h)+ 20(כ,*k̲*)+ 50(נ,*n*)+ 70(ע,*a*)+ 50(נ,*n*)+ 10(י,*y*)=205 (Genesis 10:18), כְּנַעֲנִי *Kena`aniy Canaanite* Strong's H3669 and
[3396] כִּנְעָנֶיהָ *kinə'āneyāh* merchants (Isaiah 23:8).
[3397] The Book continues with the historical aspects of the patriarchs until Chapter 50.
[3398] *Bible*, Matthew 6:11. *Cf.* "*Panis Angelicus,*" Thomas Aquinas, *The Aquinas Prayer Book, Sacris Solemniis,* pp. 93 fol.
[3399] *Bible*, John 6:68. "*Lord... thou hast the words of eternal life.*"
[3400] Check the list of the word "literal" in the index.
[3401] Knights Templars' Great Seal.
[3402] On July 4, 1983, the message of the Virgin Mary to the seers at Medjugorje was, "*Lasciatevi condurre dallo Spirito santo in profondità... Non vi affrettate. Lasciatevi guidare e vedrete che tutto correrà bene*" (our translation, Laurentin, *La Vergine appare a Medjugorje?,* July 4, 1983, p. 99). *Cf.* Valtorta, *Il Poema dell'Uomo-Dio.* Pope Pius XII (1947) and Rev. (Cardinal) Bea (1952) verbally approved the first edition of this last book. Eventually, Cardinal Ottaviani (1959) placed it in the *Index Librorum Prohibitorum* (the Catholic Church's List of Prohibited Books - abolished in 1966 by Pope Paul VI - the list contained, among others, books of Copernicus and Galilei).
[3403] Pick, *The Apocryphal Acts... of Peter*, 35 (6) p. 115, '*Quo vadis Domine,*' '*Eo Romam iterum crucifigi,*'.
[3404] *Cf.* Plato, *Text and English translations in Plato; cf.* also Simonelli, *Il neoplatonismo ed il pensiero indiano.*
[3405] *Cf.* Hegel, *Phenomenology of Spirit.*
[3406] *Cf.* Aristotle, *Metaphysics.*
[3407] *Cf.* Marx, *Capital / Manifesto of the Communist Party.*
[3408] "Brain scans during sleep can decode visual content of dreams... Most of the dreams reflected everyday experiences, but some contained unusual content, such as talking to a famous actor." Kamitani (ATR Computational Neuroscience Laboratories in Kyoto, Japan), *Scientists read dreams.*
[3409] Genesis 28:12.
[3410] Strong's H5551.
[3411] Strong's H5549.

[3412] סָלַל Gesenius (2).
[3413] *Bible*, John 14:6.
[3414] Strong's H7307.
[3415] Strong's H7363.
[3416] Malidoma Patrice Some (elder of the Dagara tribe), *Of Water and the Spirit: Ritual, Magic and Initiation in the Life of an African Shaman*, p. 8.
[3417] *Koran*, The Table 5:35, يَا أَيُّهَا الَّذِينَ آمَنُوا اتَّقُوا اللَّهَ وَابْتَغُوا إِلَيْهِ الْوَسِيلَةَ وَجَاهِدُوا فِي سَبِيلِهِ لَعَلَّكُمْ تُفْلِحُونَ
[3418] *Cf.* Paramahansa Yogananda, in *Autobiography of a Yogi* (p. 169n), states that "God the Son is the Christ Consciousness."
[3419] *Bible*, John 14:11-14.
[3420] *Bible*, Act 9:3, περιήστραψεν *periēstrapsen* (shined) φῶς *phōs* (light) ἐκ *ek* (from) τοῦ *tou* (the) οὐρανοῦ *ouranou* (heaven) and blinded Paul called Saul of Tarsus on his way to Damascus.
[3421] *Bible*, Matthew 6:6,13 & Luke 11:2,4.
[3422] Exodus 3:14. אֶהְיֶה אֲשֶׁר אֶהְיֶה *'ehəyeh* (I am, Strong's H1961) *'ăšer* (that which, Strong's H834) *'ehəyeh* (I am, Strong's H1961).
[3423] Ramana Maharshi, *Spiritual teaching*, p. 64.
[3424] Ladinsky, *Love Poems from God*, p. 202, Saint Catherine of Siena (1347 – 1380 Rome), *Smells of Good Food* (underlining is ours).
[3425] *Bible*, John 8:32.
[3426] Borbély, *Secrets of Sleep*, p. 64, where he also clearly misinterprets "the Vedic texts" saying, "dreams were regarded as an intermediate stage between this world and the next."
[3427] Ecclesiastes 8:16.
[3428] Kiessig, *Dichter erzählen ihre Träume,* p. 330. In Egypt, "Dreams were accounted for… as actual happenings." Mackenzie, *Egyptian, Myth And Legend*, p. 83. *Cf.* Nova, *The Dream Stela of Thutmosis IV.*
[3429] Borbély, *Secrets of Sleep*, p. 125.
[3430] *Bible*, John 14:16-20.
[3431] Koch, *Is Consciousness Universal? Panpsychism, the ancient doctrine that consciousness is universal, offers some lessons in how to think about subjective experience today.*
[3432] Tononi, *Consciousness as Integrated Information.*
[3433] *Cf.* Koch, *A "Complex" Theory of Consciousness. Is complexity the secret to sentience, to a panpsychic view of consciousness?*
[3434] *Cf.* Koch, *Is Consciousness Universal?*
[3435] <Simonelli, *Beyond Immortality*, p. 25.>
[3436] *Bible*, Matthew 6:13, "*lead* (εἰσενέγκῃς *eisene$_n$gkēs*) *us* (ἡμᾶς *ēmas*) *into* (εἰς *eis*) *temptation* (πειρασμὸν *peirasmon*)."
[3437] <Simonelli, *Transcendence…*, p. 179.>
[3438] *Cf. UG.* 4.
[3439] *Cf.* "*Except a man be born again, he cannot see the kingdom of God*" (*Bible*, John 3:3,7).
[3440] *Cf.* "*Behold, a virgin shall be with child, and shall bring forth a son, and they shall call his name Emmanuel, which being interpreted is, God with us*" (*Bible*, Matthew 1:23).
[3441] Dante, *La Vita Nova*, chapter XXIV "*Io mi senti' svegliar dentro a lo core | un spirito amoroso che dormia: | e poi vidi venir da lungi Amore.*"
[3442] *Cf.* Jung (1875 - 1961) *Two essays on analytical psychology* & *Psyche and Symbol.*
[3443] <Simonelli, *Beyond Immortality*, p. 212.
[3444] *harəpu* (be still let go) *uḏə'u* (realize) *kiy* (that) *'ānōḵiy* (I am) *'ĕlōhiym* (Divine-Consciousness) Psalm 46:10.
[3445] *və'āhaḇətā* (love) *'ēṯ* (and) *yəhvāh* (Transcendent) *'ĕlōheyḵā* (Divine-Consciousness) *bəḵāl (with all) ləḇāḇəḵā* (your hearth) *uḇəḵāl* (with all) *napəšəḵā* (yourself) *uḇəḵāl* (with all) *mə'ōḏeḵā* (your power) Deuteronomy 6:5.
[3446] כֹּל *kol, all* Strong's H3606 Aramaic, corresponding to כֹּל *kol, all* Strong's H3605, from כָּלַל *kalal, to complete* Strong's H3634.
[3447] *Bible,* Luke 10:27.
[3448] *Koran*, The Cow, 2:194 اتَّقُوا اللَّهَ وَاعْلَمُوا أَنَّ اللَّهَ مَعَ الْمُتَّقِينَ.
[3449] Genesis 22.
[3450] الإسلام *al-'Islām,* اسلام *islam* submission, سلام *salam* peace (*Cf.* El-Ezabi, *English-Arabic Reader's Dictionary*, pp. 362, 497, 693).
[3451] Obverse, silver Denarius of Roman emperor Tiberius (14-37 AD), laureate & looking left, "AVGVSTVS (Augustus) TI[*berius*] (Tiberius) CAESAR (Caesar) DIVI (of Divine) AVG[*usti*] (of Augustus) F[*ilius*] (son)."
[3452] *Bible*, Mark 12:13-17.
[3453] שִׁמְעוֹן *Shim`own* Strong's H8095, Gesenius; from שָׁמַע *shama`* Strong's H8085 to hear. Interestingly, that same "*Simon Peter having a sword drew it, and smote the high priest's servant, and cut off his right ear. The servant's name was Malchus*" (*Bible*, John 18:10).
[3454] Bar-jona *Aramaic,* בַּר *bar* (Strong's H1247), son (corresponding to בֵּן *ben* Strong's H1121, son, from בָּנָה *banah* Strong's H1129, to build) and יוֹנָה *Yonah* Strong's H3124 Jonah = dove, *cf.* the dove released from the ark and Jonah disgorged by the whale (the same as יוֹנָה *yownah* Strong's H3123 dove, probably from the same as יַיִן *yayin* Strong's H3196, wine.
[3455] ἀπεκάλυψέν *apekalupsen* unveiled, from the verb ἀποκαλύπτω *apokaluptō* to reveal = ἀπό *apo* away from καλύπτω *kalupto* to veil.

[3456] Greek πέτρος *petros*, Latin *petra* = stone, rock.
[3457] *Cf.* son, from בָּנָה *banah* Strong's H1129, to build.
[3458] *Bible*, Matthews 16:16-18.
[3459] *Cf. Bible,* Malachi 3:10.
[3460] *Bible*, Luke 9:23 and Matthew 16:24. Jesus clearly declares, "Whosoever wants to follow me, should deny himself" *si quis vult post me venire abneget* (ἀπαρνησάσθω *aparnhesásthō* = renounce, renege) *se ipsum* (ἑαυτὸν *eautòn* = himself)... *semet ipsum* (Matthew). Von Hildebrand, in *The Nature of Love* (§ 9), takes a contrary position, pontificating that, without, my 'I' and my personal subjectivity, *eigenleben*, (203), there is no "capacity for personal happiness, not even for the sublime happiness of union with God in the beatific vision." (214) Consequently, he superficially accuses Hinduism and Buddhism of "dissolution of subjectivity" (201).
[3461] *Bible,* Luke 18, 29-30.
[3462] *Bible*, Luke 14:26. "*si quis venit ad me et non odit patrem suum et matrem et uxorem et filios et fratres et sorores adhuc autem et animam suam non potest esse meus discipulus.*" *hate* (μισεῖ *misei, odit*) *his own* (ἑαυτοῦ *eautou, suam*) *eigenleben* (ψυχὴ-ν *phsychē-n, anima-m*).
[3463] *Bible,* John, 12:25. *BIBLIKH ETAIRIA*. μισῶν (*misōn* = hateth). ὁ μισῶν τὴν ψυχὴν αὐτοῦ ἐν τῷ κόσμῳ τούτῳ εἰς ζωὴν αἰώνιον φυλάξει αὐτή.
[3464] Línjì Yìxuán, *The Zen Teachings of Master Lin-Chi*, p. 52 {仏に逢えば仏を殺せ [*Butsu ni aeba butsu (w)o korose*] If you meet a Buddha, kill him}.
[3465] *Cf.* Simonelli, *Transcendence - The Universal Quest.*
[3466] 1King 19:16, 19-21.
[3467] *shaphat* (Shaphat, he hath judged Strong's H8202) שָׁפָט
[3468] *'abel mĕchowlah* (Abelmeholah, meadow of dancing Strong's H65) אָבֵל מְחוֹלָה; *'abel* (meadow Strong's H58) אָבֵל; *mĕchowlah* (dancing Strong's H4246) מְחלָה.
[3469] *'eliysha* ` (Elisha, God is salvation Strong's H477) אֱלִישָׁע; *'eliyah* (Elijah, my God is Jehovah Strong's H452) אֵלִיָּה; *yahh* (Jah shortened form of Jehovah Strong's H3050) יָהּ.
[3470] *Cf.* Yogananda in *Autobiography of a Yogi*, p. 371, states "that John [the Baptist] and Jesus in their last incarnations were, respectively, Elijah and Elisha."
[3471] *Bible*, Luke 9:59-62 & cf. Matthew 8:21-22.
[3472] *Bible,* Hebrews 11:17-19.
[3473] עֹלָה ` *olah* Strong's H5930 Gesenius 2, part of next one.
[3474] עָלָה `*alah* Strong's H5927 to go up, ascend.
[3475] מוֹרִיָּה *mowriyah moriah* (Strong's H4179) "chosen by Jehovah."
[3476] Genesis 22:1-2 -10-11-17. Contrast Abraham's unselfish sacrifice of Isaac with Euripides' immolation of Iphigenia only to guarantee safe passage to Troy for the conquering ambitions of her father Agamemnon (*Cf.* Euripides, *Iphigenia in Aulis*).
[3477] *UY* I.23-4.
[3478] Scaligero, *Tecniche ...*, p. 46. "*L'asceta supera l'alterità, in quanto spersonalizandosi trasferisce nell'Io il centro della coscienza: in realtà trasferisce il senso di sé dall'astrale all'Io, che non ha bisogno di sentire se stesso per essere.*"
[3479] *Cf.* Simonelli.
[3480] *Bible*, Mark 2:8.
[3481] *Cf.* Homer, *Odyssey*, IX,118-123.
[3482] *Bible*, Matthew 5:48.
[3483] Psalm 22:1.
[3484] Aramaic, [illegible] *Bible*, Matthew 27:46. Hinting to a similar appeal and overwhelmed by compassion, seeing children suffering at the Pediatric Hospital *Bambino Gesù* of Rome, upon the presentation of his new book (Bergoglio, *L'amore prima del mondo*), Pope Francis said, "If I could do a miracle? I would heal all children" (NEWS.VA, *Le risposte del Papa ai bambini.* "*Se potessi fare un miracolo? Farei guarire tutti i bambini*").
[3485] *Cf.* Simonelli, *Awareness*, pp. 137 fol.
[3486] *Bible*, Matthew 6:25,34. Compare this to the ancient Olympic participants who preferred "*Death before defeat*" (Murphy).
[3487] Merton, *The Sign of Jonas. The Journal of Thomas Merton, March* 10, 1950, p. 286.
[3488] *BG* 3.19 *tasmād* (therefore) *asaktaḥ* (unattached) *satataṃ* (always) *kāryaṃ* (as duty) *karma* (action) *samācara* (perform).
[3489] Joshua, Jehovah is salvation *yĕhowshuwa* ` יְהוֹשׁוּעַ (Strong's H3091), from, to be saved *yasha* יָשַׁע (Strong's H3467) by יְהוָה Yĕhovah.
[3490] *'emoriy* (Amorite, mountaineer speaker Strong's H567 Gesenius) אֱמֹרִי
[3491] Sun, the subject of illicit worship, *shemesh* שֶׁמֶשׁ (Strong's H8121 C).
[3492] To be still, silent and to die *dämam* דָּמַם (Strong's H1826 C, D).
[3493] Moon *yareach* יָרֵחַ (Strong's H3394), from lunar month *yerach* יֶרַח (Strong's H3391).
[3494] Stand still `*amad* עָמַד (Strong's H5975)
[3495] Enemy *'oyeb* אֹיֵב (Strong's H341), participle of to be hostile *'ayab* אָיַב (Strong's H340).
[3496] Joshua 10:13.
[3497] *The Power of Myth*, Cp. III. The First Storytellers, p. 75.

[3498] *The Basis of Morality*, p. 201.

[3499] 1 Chronicles 29:18 "*yəhvāh* (Transcendent) '*ĕlōhēy* (Divine-Consciousness)... *šŏmərāh*-(keep) *zō'ṯ* (this) *lə'vōlām* (for ever) *ləyēṣer* (in the imagination) *maḥəšəḇvōṯ* (of the thoughts) *ləḇaḇ* (of the heart) '*ameḵā* (of people) *vəhāḵēn* (be firm) *ləḇāḇām* (heart) '*ēleyḵā* (these).

[3500] Strong's H3336.

[3501] Strong's H4284.

[3502] Strong's H3559.

[3503] Non-self (Pali), Sanskrit *śūnyatā* (emptiness) as absence of self (*anatman*). *Cf.* Buddhism, *The Great Discourse of Causation. The Mahanidana Sutta*, Non-Delineations of a Self.

[3504] *Bible*, Luke 14:26.

[3505] *Bible*, John 14:2.

[3506] Madonna of Medjugorje.

[3507] Maria Valtorta (1897 –1961), Italian mystic who reported personal conversations with Jesus Christ. Valtorta, *I quaderni del 1943*, I manoscritto, capitolo 39, 26 giugno 1943. "*Dice Gesù: 'Spogliatevi non solo da ciò che costituisce peso di umanità pura, ma anche da quello che è affanno spirituale... Affanno spirituale non è quel tendere sano, con tutte le forze intellettive, a Dio. Affanno spirituale ... consiste nella paura di ... staccarsi dall'orazione nella tema di non potere gustare quel limpido ruscello di dolcezza che Io vi invio, paura di non poterlo più ritrovare. Queste paure sono ancora un resto di umanità che si infiltra nella spiritualità e le nuoce. Bisogna seguire la via dello spirito con fermezza e con calma. Nessuna ansia, nessuna paura. Sono Io che creo il tempo... Sono Io che faccio fluire in voi l'onda della grazia; so quindi regolare il flusso della medesima e mandarvi le mie luci nei momenti più propizi... Perciò tu non essere mai affannata. Prega, ascolta, medita, soffri, lavora, riposa sempre con calma, fidandoti di Me... È di somma importanza, per l'anima che vuole avanzare nella via del Cielo, saper tenere le potenze dell'anima ferme in Dio.* Quando ciò avviene, l'anima è sicura. *Cosa sono le potenze dell'anima? Ora ti porto un paragone umano. La ruota come è fatta? Di un cerchio, di tanti raggi infissi nel cerchio, di un anello che riunisce i raggi e li fa rotare intorno ad un perno. In tal modo la ruota serve. Se qualcuna delle parti è rotta serve male, ma se è rotto l'anello che tiene i raggi, la ruota non serve affatto. ... Il cerchio è l'umanità che raccoglie tutte le potenze morali, fisiche e spirituali che sono in un essere creato. È la fascia che aduna tutto di un uomo. I raggi sono i sentimenti che si concentrano in un mistico anello - lo spirito - che li raccoglie e che li irraggia, poiché è operazione doppia. Il perno è Dio. Se l'umanità è lesionata da carie carnali, i sentimenti restano slegati e finiscono con lo sparpagliarsi nella polvere. Ma se è rovinato lo spirito o anche semplicemente disimperniato dal suo pernio, allora il moto mirabile dell'essere creato da Dio si ferma e subentra la morte. Perciò non uscire mai dal fulcro divino è necessità assoluta per l'anima che vuole meritare il Cielo... Ma i tuoi sentimenti non cessino di convergere allo spirito e partire dallo spirito. Così si alimenteranno di Dio e porteranno, anche nelle umili faccende, l'impronta di Dio, poiché il tuo spirito è e deve rimanere imperniato su Dio, fulcro divinissimo di tutto il creato, fulcro soavissimo della tua anima che ha trovato la sua Via. Quando le potenze dello spirito sono fisse in Dio, credi pure che nessuna forza la può togliere di là. Il moto diviene sempre più vorticoso, e tu sai che c'è una forza, che appunto è detta centripeta, che attira sempre più verso il centro le cose quanto più un moto è vorticoso. L'amore è quello che dà il moto. Lo spirito fisso in Dio ama Dio suo fulcro. Dio ama lo spirito imperniato su di Lui; e questo duplice amore aumenta il moto vorticoso, la corsa alata il cui termine è l'incontro nel mio Regno fra lo spirito amante e il suo Creatore.'*"

[3508] Matt-Pritzker Ed. *Cf.* Luzzatto, *Way of G-d: Derech Hashem*, 2:3:10, p. 125 fol. & p. 414 n. 39.

[3509] *Cf.* Simonelli, *Awareness.*

[3510] *Bible*, Matthew 15:18.

[3511] *Bible*, Romans 8:1-2. Christ = *the-anointed* (Χριστός Christos), Jesus = *salvation-of-Transcendent-Jehovah* (יְהוֹשׁוּעַ Yĕhowshuwa`, Strong's H3091), *craving-flesh* (σάρξ *sarx*), *Spiritual-Breath* (πνεῦμα *pneuma*), *controlling-law* (νόμος *nomos*), *sinful-missed-mark* (ἁμαρτία *amartia*).

[3512] *W.* pp. 733b... 139c & 1319bc.... 856.

[3513] Psalm 133:1.

[3514] *Bible*, Ephesians 4:13.

[3515] Martin Luther anonymous 1518, as Anonimo Francofortese, *Teologia tedesca - Libretto della vita perfetta*, p. 77. "*In perfetto godimento della natura divina, in perfetta gioia e felicità,*"

[3516] Francesco, *I fioretti di San Francesco*, Chapter VII.

[3517] "*sciencia muy sabrosa,*" *The Poems...*, 27, p. 8.

[3518] Nehemiah 8:10.

[3519] *Bible*, John 14:6,20. *egō eimi... ē zôē ... egō en tō patri mou kai umeis en emoi kagō en umin.*

[3520] *Wheel of the Sun Temple at Konark, Orissa*, 2001 India postage Rs 4^{00}.

[3521] Latin *jacto, jactāvi, jactātum*; see also *jacĕre* [*jacio, jeci, jactum,* (to throw)] and *jacēre* [*jaceo, jacui* (to lie down)].

BIBLIOGRAPHY, DISCOGRAPHY, FILMOGRAPHY & WEB-LINKS

Abbey-of-Solesmes (Ed.). (1961). *The Liber Usualis with Introduction and Rubrics in English.* Tournai (Belgium), New York N.Y: Desclee Company Holy See and The Congregation of Rites.

ABC News. (2012, 10 8). Lion Adopts Baby Antelope. *ABC WorNews*, pp. http://abcnews.go.com/WNT/video/lion-adopts-baby-antelope-17428182.

Acaranga Sutra. (1981). *Ayaro (Acaranga Sutra) The First Anga Agama (Canonical Text) of the Jainas : The Text in Devanagari and Roman Scripts with English Translation, Annotations, Notes, Glossary and Index.* (A. Tulsi, Trans.) New Delhi: Today & Tomorrow.

Adler, Alfred. (1956). *The Individual Psychology of Alfred Adler.* (Ansbacher&Ansbacher, Ed.) New York: Harper Torchbooks.

AICE. (2013). *LAMECH.* Retrieved November 6, 2016, from The Jewish Virtual Library a Division of The American-Israely Cooperative-Enterprise : http://www.jewishvirtuallibrary.org/jsource/judaica/ejud_0002_0012_0_11781.html

AIST. (2014). *PARO Therapeutic Robot.* Retrieved 11 15, 2015, from PARO Robots Japan: http://www.parorobots.com/index.asp

aKempis, Thomas. (1943). *Imitazione di Cristo.* Padova: Gregoriana Editrice.

Alce Nero. (1970). *La Sacra Pipa, Alce Nero descrive e spiega i sette riti dei Sioux Oglala.* (Tippett-Andaló, Trans.) Torino: Borla Editrice.

Alchin, L. (2013). *Secret History of Nursery Rhymes Book.* (M. Tidmarsh, Ed.) Charleston, SC : CREATESPACE.

Alexander, E. (2012). *Proof of Heaven: A Neurosurgeon's Journey into the Afterlife.* New York, London, Toronto, Sydney, New Delhi: Simon & Schuster.

Altus. (1677). *Mutus Liber.* Rupellae: Petrum Savouret.

Amendola, L., Tsujikawa, S. (2010). *Dark Energy: Theory and Observations.* Cambridge, UK: Cambridge University Press.

Anch A. M., Browman C. P., Mitler M. M. , Walsh J. K. (1988). *Sleep: A Scientific Perspective.* Englewood Cliffs, New Jersey: Prentice Hall.

Ancient Aliens. (2016). *Ancient Alien Theory.* Retrieved June 24, 2016, from History http://www.history.com/: http://www.history.com/shows/ancient-aliens/articles/ancient-alien-theory

Ancient Hebrew Research Center. (1999-2013). *Introduction to the Ancient Hebrew Alphabet.* Retrieved 7 16, 2014, from Plowing through history, from Aleph to Tav: http://www.ancient-hebrew.org/1_introduction.html

Andrews, T. (2012). *Animal Speak. The Piritual & Magical Powers of Creatures Great & Small.* Woodbury, Minnesota: Llewellyn Publications.

Angelini, G. (1959). *Nuovo dizionario Latino-Italiano.* Milano, Roma, Napoli, Città di Castello: Socioetà Editrice Dante Alighieri p.a.

Anonimo Francofortese. (2009). *Teologia tedesca - Libretto della vita perfetta.* (Vannini, Trans.) Milano: Bompiani Testi A Fronte.

Anonymous Pilgrim. (1993). *The Way of a Pilgrim and The Pilgrim Continues His Way.* (R. French, Trans.) Pasadena, CA: Hope Publishing House.

ANSA.it. (2015, maggio 19). *Il padre del microchip a caccia della coscienza dell'universo. Federico Faggin cerca un'equazione per descriverla.* Retrieved May 20, 2015, from ANSA > Scienza&Tecnica > Fisica & Matematica >: http://www.ansa.it/scienza/notizie/rubriche/fisica/2015/05/18/il-padre-del-microchip-a-caccia-della-coscienza-delluniverso_04e125a9-b55c-41a0-a36e-4026b15a81c7.html

Anselm. (2012). *Proslogion, With A Reply on Behalf of the Fool by Gaunilo and The Author's Reply to Gaunilo.* (M. J. Charlesworth, Trans.) Notre Dame, IN: University of Notre Dame Press.

Apollodorus, of Athens. (1961). *Apollodorus : The library (Vol. 1)* (Vol. I). (J. Frazer, Trans.) Cambridge, Mass: Harvard University Press, Loeb classical library.

Apollonius, Rhodius. (1961). *The Argonautica.* (R.C.Seaton, Trans.) Cambridge, Mass., London: The Loeb classical library, Harvard University Press; W. Heinemann.

Ariosto, Ludovico. (1982). *L'Orlando furioso* (Vol. 2). (E.Bigi, Ed.) Milano: Rusconi.

Aristotle. (1960, 1932 reprint). *Aristotle: The poetics./ Greek and English translation.* Cambridge, Mass: Harvard University Press, Loeb classical library.

Aristotle. (1962-68). *Metaphysics / Greek and English translation* (Vol. 2). (H. Tredennick, Trans.) Cambridge, Mass.; London: Loeb classical library Harvard University Press; W. Heinemann.

Aristotle. (1994). *Posterior Analytics .* (J. Barnes, Ed., & J. Barnes, Trans.) New York: Oxford University Press USA.

Ark Encounter. (2016, May 27). *BIGGER THAN IMAGINATION A life-sized Noah's Ark Experience.* Retrieved June 27, 2016, from ARK ENCOUNTER PROJECT HISTORY: https://arkencounter.com

Armstrong, K. (1993). *A History of God: The 4,000-Year Quest of Judaism, Christianity, and Islam.* New York: Ballantine Books.

Arntz, W. (Director). (2004). *What тнē #$*! D̄ѳ ωΣ (k)пow!?* [Motion Picture].

Auffarth, C., Stuckenbruck, L. (2004). *The Fall of the Angels.* (Hendel, Ed.) Leiden: Brill.

Augustine. (1965). *In Epistolam Joannis Ad Parthos Tractatus Decem PL 35, 1977-2062.* (Migne-Patrologia-Latina, Ed.) Upper Saddle River, New Jersey: Gregg Publishing.

Augustine. (1992). *Confessions, Latin text.* (J. J. O'Donnel, Ed.) Oxford: Clarendon Press.

Augustine. (2008). *The Augustine Catechism: The Enchiridion on Faith, Hope and Charity by Saint Augustine.* (B. Ramsey, Ed., & B. Harbert, Trans.) Hyde Park, New York: New City Press.

Axmacher, N., Haupt S., Fernández G., Elger C. E., Fell J. (2008, March). The Role of Sleep in Declarative Memory Consolidation—Direct Evidence by Intracranial EEG. *Cerebral Cortex*, 500-507 .

Babenco, H. (Director). (1991). *At Play in the Fields of the Lord* [Motion Picture].

Balfour, E. (1885). *The cyclopædia of India and of Eastern and Southern Asia* (Vol. 1). London: Bernard Quaritch.

Bargellini, P. (2008). *I Fioretti di Santa Chiara.* (Spiritualià-francescana, Ed.) Assisi: Porziuncola.

Barrett, D. (2001). *Barrett, D. (2001). The Committee of Sleep: How Artists, Scientists, and Athletes Use Dreams for Creative Problem-Solving-- and How You Can Too.* (R. H. Inc, Ed.) New York.

Bartusiak, M. (2015). *Black Hole: How an Idea Abandoned by Newtonians, Hated by Einstein, and Gambled on by Hawking Became Loved.* New Haven, CT: Yale University Press.

BBC. (2001, March Sunday, 11). Giant Buddha statues 'blown up'. *BBC News*, p. http://news.bbc.co.uk/2/hi/south_asia/1214384.stm.

BBC. (2009 , July 13). Pain in childbirth 'a good thing'. *BBC NEWS*, p. http://news.bbc.co.uk/2/hi/health/8147179.stm.

Benfey, O. T. (Proc. 1965-6, September 15-16). Kekule von Stradonitz, August, 1829-1896. (A.C.Society, Ed.) *Kekule centennial: A symposium. Co-sponsored by the division of History of chemistry, the division of Organic chemistry and the division of Chemical education at the 150th meeting of the American chemical society. Atlantic City, N.J., Washington: American.*

Bennett, M. (Director). (23 December 2012 (UK)). *Joanna Lumley: The Search for Noah's Ark TV Movie Documentary* [Motion Picture].

Bentham, J. (1818). *Defence of Usury; Showing the Impolicy of the Present Legal Restraints on the Terms of Pecuniary Bargains...* London: Peyne and Foss, Pall Mall.

Benvenuti, M. (Anno X, 2005, Agosto). La scienza dello Spirito non è una teoria, ma una pratica. (DiLieto, Ed.) *L'Archetipo, mensile di ispirazione antroposofica, numero 8 -- http://www.cazzanti.net/archivi/letture/L'archetipo%20-*

%20Mensile%20di%20ispirazione%20antroposofica/2005/ago2005.pdf (www.larchetipo.com Tribunale di Roma N. 104/89 del 4.3.1989, p. 27.

Bergoglio, J. M. (2016). *L'amore prima del mondo.* Milano: Rizzoli.

Berruerio (Publisher). (15 April 1524). *Libellus De Natura Animalium.* Savona: Giuseppe Berruerio.

BG. (1926). *Bhagavad-Gītā Text* (Vol. Besant). Adyar, Madras, India: Theosophical Publishing House.

Bible. (2009-2014). *Genesis.* (DavidDeLauro, Producer) Retrieved 2014, from Scholars' Gateway beta: http://scholarsgateway.com/search/WLC-LXX-YLT/Genesis

Bible. (1957). *Biblia sacra, vulgatae editionis Sixti V pontificis maximi iussu recognita et Clementis VIII auctoritate edita.* Romae: Editiones Paulinae.

Bible. (1958). *The Holy Bible* (King James ed.). Philadelphia, PA : The National Bible Press.

Bible. (2011). *Genesis 1 King James Version (KJV)l http://www.blueletterbible.org/Bible.cfm?b=Gen&c=1&t=KJV.* Retrieved 2013, from Blue Letter Bible: http://www.blueletterbible.org/

Bible Timeline. (2013). *Why doesn't the Bible mention the Dinosaurs?* Retrieved July 19, 2016, from Amazing Bible Timeline with World History: http://amazingbibletimeline.com/bible_questions/q3_dinosaurs_bible/

Bible Westminster Leningrad Codex. (2009). *Tanach - תנ"ך.* Retrieved January 1, 2012, from Unicode/XML Westminster Leningrad Codex maintained by the J. Alan Groves Center for Advanced Biblical Research: http://tanach.us/Tanach.xml

Bixler, R. H. (1982). 'Sibling incest in the royal families of Egypt, Peru, and Hawaii. *Journal of Sex Research 18: 264-281* , 264-281.

Blumrich, J. F. (1974). *The Spaceships of Ezekiel.* New York, NY: Bantam Books.

Boccaccio, Giovanni. (1967). *Il Filocolo, Tutte le opere, ed., Milano: Mondadori, .* (A.E.Quaglio ed., Vol. I). (VittoreBranca, Ed.) Milano: Mondadori.

Böhtlingk, Otto von, and Roth, Rudolf von. (1855-1875). *Sanskrit Wörterbuch.* St. Petersburg: Kaiserliche Akademie der Wissenschaften .

Borbély, A. (1986). *Secrets of Sleep.* (Schneider, Trans.) New York: Basic Books, Inc.

Borrelli, R. N. (1856). *Nuova smorfia perpetua ed universale dell'astronomo Zoroastro.* Napoli: Tipografia dell'Ariosto.

Bovio-Lama (Composer). (2014). Silenzio Cantatore, Antologia sonora della canzone napoletana, Vol. 14 (Canzoni celebri napoletane in ordine alfabetico) #42, 4. [M. Abbate, Performer] Napoli, Napoli, Italy: Phonotype Record.

Brannen, P. (2015, January 31). The Death of the Dinosaurs. *The New York Times*, p. Sunday Review OPINION.

Brentano, F. (1874-1889). *Psychologie vom empirischen Standpunkte : Erster Band Vom Ursprung sittlicher Erkenntnis.* Leipzig: Duncker & Humblot.

Brenton, L. C. (Ed.). (1990). *The Septuagint with Apocrypha: Greek and English.* (Brenton, Trans.) Peabody, Massachusetts: Hendrickson Publishers, Incorporated.

Brinkley, D. (2006). *The Great Deluge: Hurricane Katrina, New Orleans, and the Mississippi Gulf Coast.* New York City, NY: William Morrow & Company.

Brown, R. E. (1999). *The Death of the Messiah, From Gethsemane to the Grave, Volume 1: A Commentary on the Passion Narratives in the Four Gospels.* New York: Doubleday.

Bruno, G. (1925-7). *De l'infinito universo e mondi.In Opere italiane. (Vols. I, DIALOGHI METAFISICI, II, DIALOGHI MORALI, III, COMMEDIA)* (Vol. III). (Gentile-Spampanato, Ed.) Bari: Laterza.

Bruno, G. (1925-7). *Opere italiane Vol. II, DIALOGHI MORALI: Asino cillenico; Cabala del cavallo Pegaseo; De gli eroici furori; Lo spaccio de la bestia trionfante* (Vol. 3). (G.Gentile, Ed.) Bari: Laterza.

Bruno, G. (1925-7). *Opere italiane Vol. III COMMEDIA: Candelaio* (Vol. 3). (V.Spampanato, Ed.) Bari : Laterza.

Bruno, G. (1925-7). *Opere italiane, Vol. I - DIALOGHI METAFISICI: De la causa, principio e uno; De l'infinito, universo et mondi; La cena de le ceneri* (Vol. 3). (G.Gentile, Ed.) Bari: Laterza.

Buddhism. (1984). *The Great Discourse of Causation. The Mahanidana Sutta and its Commentarial Exegesis. Translated from the Pali by Bhikkhu Bodhi.* (BhikkhuBodhi, Trans.) Kandy, Sri Lanka: Buddhist Publication Society.

Budge, E. A. Wallis. (1967). *The Egyptian Book of the Dead, (The Papyrus of Ani) Egyptian Text Translitteration and Translation.* New York: Dover Publications, Inc.

Budge, E. A. Wallis. (1969). *The Gods of the Egyptians* (Vols. I-II). New York: Dover Publications, Inc.

Budge, E. A. Wallis. (1978). *An Egyptian Hieroglyphic Dictionary* (Vol. I & II). New York: Dover Publications, Inc.

Budge, E. A. Wallis. (1989). *The Mummy. A Handbook of Egyptian Funerary Archeology.* New York: Dover Publications.

Bundles, A'Lelia P. (2001). *On Her Own Ground: The Life and Times of Madam C.J. Walker.* New York: Simon & Schuster Inc.

Buonarroti. (1885). *Selected Poems from Michelagnolo Buonarroti.* (Cheney, Ed.) Boston: Lee and Shepard, Publishers.

Burns, F. (2014, December 22). *Satanists, Christians compete for attention at Michigan statehouse.* Retrieved December 22, 2014, from United Press International (UPI): http://www.upi.com/Top_News/US/2014/12/22/Satanists-Christians-compete-for-attention-at-Michigan-statehouse/6251419260844/#ixzz3MeOiYPqF

Callcut, V. (2005, March 2). *John Wilkinson – Copper King?* Retrieved 1 12, 2017, from The Oldcopper Website: http://www.oldcopper.org/broseley/wilkinson/wilkinson_copper_king.html#_Toc96918995

Calvin, J. (1957). *Institutes of the Christian religion.* Grand Rapids: Eerdmans.

Campbell (Writer), & Walker-Badger (Director). (1988). *Joseph Campbell, The Power of Myth with Bill Moyers* [Motion Picture].

Campbell, J. (1988). *The Power of Myth, with Bill Moyers.* New York: Doubleday.

Campbell, J. (1990). *The Flight of the Wild Gander. Explorations in the Mythological Dimensions of Fairy Tales, Legends and Symbols.* New York: Harper Perennial A Division of HarperCollins Publishers.

Campbell, J. (2001). *Thou Art That: Transforming Religious Metaphor.* Novato, CA: New World Library.

Campbell, J. (2003). *Myths of Light: Eastern Metaphors of the Eternal .* (D. Kudler, Ed.) Novato, CA: New World library.

Campbell, J. (2004). *Mythic Worlds, Modern Words: Joseph Campbell on the Art of James Joyce (The Collected Works of Joseph Campbell).* Novato, CA: New World Library.

Campbell, J. (2008). *The Hero with a Thousand Faces.* Novaro, California: New World Library.

Campbell, Joseph. (1968). *The Mask of God: Creative Mythology.* New York: The Viking Press.

Campbell, Joseph. (1974). *The Mythic Image.* (Bollingen-Series.C, Ed.) Princeton: Princeton University Press.

Campbell, Mitchell, Reece. (1999). *Biology: Concepts and Connections* (3 ed.). Menlo Park, CA: Benjamin/Cummings Publ. Co Inc.

Carbonara, C. (1967). *Introduzione alla filosofia.* Napoli: L.S.E.

Carbonara, C. (1973). *Disegno d'una filosofia critica dell'esperienza pura, e immediatezza e riflessione* (2 ed.). Napoli: L.S.E.

Carlson, B. (2004). *Human Embryology & Developmental Biology* (3 ed.). Toronto: Mosby Publications.

Caswall, E. (Ed.). (1873). *Hymns and poems, original and translated.* (E. Caswall, Trans.) London: Burns, Oates & Co .

Catherine of Siena. (1980). *The Dialogue.* (SuzanneNoffke, Trans.) Mahwah, NJ: Paulist Press.

Catullus. (1893). *Catullus.* (E.Truesdell.Merrill, Ed.) Boston, USA: Ginn and Company.

Cellan-Jones, R. (2014, December 2). *Stephen Hawking warns artificial intelligence could end mankind.* Retrieved October 3, 2015, from BBC News / From the section Technology: http://www.bbc.com/news/technology-30290540

Cerulli, T. (2012). *The Mindful Carnivore: A Vegetarian's Hunt for Sustenance.* New York: Pegasus Books.

Cervantes, Miguel de, Saavedra. (1983). *Don Quijote De LA Mancha* (Vol. III). Madrid: Ediciones Cátedra.

Chang, K. (2015, Sept. 28). Mars Shows Signs of Having Flowing Water, Possible Niches for Life, NASA Says. *The New York Times*, p. SPACE & COSMOS.

Charles, L. (Director). (2008). *Religulous with Bill Maher* [Motion Picture].

Chevalier, Jean, & Gheerbrant, Alain . (1974). *Dictionnaire des Symboles.* Paris: Seghers.

Christian Forums. (2004, May 2). *Marijuana the Tree of Knowledge of Good & Evil?* Retrieved April 27, 2016, from Discussion in 'General Theology' started by Starcrystal: http://www.christianforums.com/threads/marijuana-the-tree-of-knowledge-of-good-evil.170238/

Chrysogonus Polydorus. (1541). *De Alchimia.* Nuremberg: Chrysogonus Polydorus.

Chun Siong Soon, et al. (2008). Unconscious determinants of free decisions in the human brain. *Nature Neuroscience, 11 (5)* , 543-545.

Cicero. (1903). *Tusculanarum disputationum Liber Primus et Somnium Scipionis.* (F. e. Rockwood, Ed.) Boston, USA, London: Ginn & Company, Publishers The Athenaeum Press.

Cicero, M. T. (1885). *De natura deorum* (Vol. Libri tres). Cambridge: Cambridge University Press.

Cioffari, G. (1987). *S. Nicola nella critica storica.* Bari: Centro Studi Nicolaiani Edizioni.

Clark, J. (1998). *The UFO Book: Encyclopedia of the Extraterrestrial.* Detroit,MI: Visible Ink Press.

Clarke, D. M. (2006). *Descartes: a biography.* New York: Cambridge University Press.

Coffin texts. (1935-61). *The Egyptian coffin texts* (Vol. 7). (A. deBuck, Ed.) Chicago:: University of Chicago Press.

Cohen, S. (2008). *Animals as Disguised Symbols in Renaissance Art.* Leiden, Boston: Brill.

Cohen-Kangas (Ed.). (2010). *Assyrian Reliefs from the palace of Ashurnasirpal II: A Cultural Biography.* Hanover, New Hampshire - Hanover and London: Hood Museum of Art, Dartmouth College - University Press of New England.

Confucius. (1986). *The Analects (Lun yü).* (D. Lau, Trans.) Middlesex England, NY, USA, Bungay, Suffolk, G.B: Penguin Books.

Croce, B. (1912). *Estetica come scienza dell'espressione e linguistica generale. Teoria e storia.* (4th riveduta ed.). Bari: G. Laterza & figli.

CSS. (2014). *Bhagavan Sri Ramana Maharshi 'The Sage of Arunachala'* . Retrieved 1 4, 2017, from Welcome to the Website dedicated to Arunachala & Bhagavan Sri Ramana Maharshi: http://www.arunachala-ramana.org/about_bhagavan.html

Cupaiuolo, F. (1958). *Grammatica Latina.* Milano: Principato.

Cytowic, R. E. (2003). *The Man Who Tasted Shapes.* Cambridge, MA: MIT Press.

D.L.Ashliman (Ed.). (1999-2014). *The Emperor's New Clothes and.* Retrieved October 25, 2016, from Other tales of Aarne-Thompson-Uther type 1620: www.pitt.edu/~dash/type1620.html

Dalai Lama. (1997). *Healing Anger. The Power of Patience from a Buddhist Perspective.* (G. T. Jinpa, Trans.) Ithaca, New York: Snow Lion Publication.

Dalrymple, W. (2010). *Nine Lives: In Search of the Sacred in Modern India.* New York: Alfred A. Knopf a division of Random House, Inc.

Damasio, A. (2010). *Self Comes to Mind: Constructing the Conscious Brain.* New York: Pantheon Books.

Dan, J. (2006). *Kabbalah, A Very Short Introduction.* New York, NY: Oxford University Press.

Daniken, E. V. (1984). *Chariots of the Gods.* New York: Berkley Books.

Dante Alighieri. (1887). *Il convito.* London: G. Routledge and sons.

Dante Alighieri. (1930). *La divina commedia illustrata da Gustavo Doré* . Milano: Casa Editrice Sonzogno.

Dante Alighieri. (1999). *La Vita Nova.* Milano: Arnoldo Mondadori.

Darwin, C. (1912). *The origin of species by means of natural selection, or the preservation of favoured races in the struggle for life.* New York: Hurst and Co.
Darwin, C. (1913). *The Expression of the Emotions in Man and Animals.* New York: D. Appleton and Company.
Dasgupta, S. (1922). *A history of Indian philosophy* (Vol. 1). Cambridge: Cambridge University Press.
Dawkins, R. (1999, April 19). Snake Oil and Holy Water. *Forbes,* pp. 235-7.
Dawkins, R. (2008). *The God Delusion.* Boston: Houghton Mifflin Co.
De Benedetti, P. (2007). *Teologia degli animali.* Brescia: Morcelliana.
De Caro, S. (Ed.). (1994). *Il Museo Archeologico Nazionale di Napoli.* Napoli: Soprintendenza Archeologica di Napoli e Caserta, Guide Artistiche Electa.
De Giorgio, G. (1973). *La tradizione romana.* Milano: Filamen.
de Rachewiltz, Boris. (1959). *Il libro egizio degli inferi. Testo iniziatico del Sole Notturno.* Roma: Casa Editrice Atanòr.
De Unamuno, M. (1976). *Our Lord Don Quixote: The Life of Don Quixote and Sancho, With Related Essays.* (A.Kerrigan, Trans.) Princeton: Princeton University Press.
del-Vasto, L. (1972). *Return to the Source.* (J.Sidgwick, Trans.) New York: Schocken Books.
Dembski, W. (1999). *Intelligent Design: The Bridge Between Science & Theology.* Downers Grove, Illinois: InterVarsity Press.
Dement, W. (1976). *Some Must Watch While Some Must Sleep.* San Francisco: San Francisco Book Co.
Desamangalam, M. (Ed.). (2011, 4 29). *Singing silence.* Retrieved 9 8, 2015, from bing.com/videos: http://www.bing.com/videos/search?q=singing+silence&FORM=VIRE3#view=detail&mid=10094A122289A5DF73E310094A122289A5DF73E3
Descartes R. (1644). *Principia philosophiae.* Amstelodami: Apud Ludovicum Elzevirium.
Descartes, R. (1952). *Rules for the direction of the mind; Discourse on the method; Meditations on first philosophy: Objections against the meditations and replies; The geometry.* (Founders', Ed., & Latham/Smith, Trans.) Chicago: Encyclopaedia Britannica.
Descartes, R. (1966). *Descartes. Philosophical Writings.* (Anscombe&Geach, Ed.) London: Nelson.
Dhammapada. (1881). *The Dhammapada (in The Dhammapada and Sutta Nipāta)* (Vol. X of "The Sacred Books of the East"). (M. Müller, Trans.) Oxford: the Clarendon Press.
Döderlein, L. (2010). *Lateinische Synonyme und Etymologien* (Vol. 1). Charleston, SC: Nabu Press.
Donne, J. (1896). *Poems of John Donne* (Vol. I). London: Lawrence & Bullen.
Downton, J. V. (1973). *Rebel leadership. Commitment and charisma in the revolutionary process.* NY, London: The Free Press, Collier-Macmillan Publisher.
Dreifus, C. (2011, May 9). A Conversation with Stephen Hawking, Life and the Cosmos, Word by Painstaking Word. *The New York Times,* p. Science Section.
Dylan, T. (1934). *18 Poems.* London: The Sunday Referee and the Parton Bookshop.
Dyson, F. (1979). *Disturbing the Universe.* New York: Harper & Row.
Eckhart, M. (1941). *Meister Eckhart: A Modern translation.* (R.B.Blakney, Trans.) New York: Harper Torchbooks, Harper & Row.
Einstein A., Infeld L. (1967). *The Evolution of Physics: From Early Concepts to Relativity and Quanta.* New York, N.Y.: Touchstone, Simon and Schuste.
Einstein, A. (1926). Space-Time. In E. Britannica, *Encyclopedia Britannica* (13 ed., pp. Space-Time). Chicago, Illinois: Encyclopædia Britannica, Inc. http://www.britannica.com/topic/Albert-Einstein-on-Space-Time-1987141.
Einstein, A. (1936, March). Physics and Reality (tr.: Jean Piccard). *Journal of the Franklin Institute, 221,* 349-82.
Einstein, A. (1949). *The world as I see it.* (A.Harris, Trans.) New York: Philosophical Library.
Einstein, A. (1956). *Out of My Later Years.* New York: Citadel Press.

El-Ezabi, Y. A., Hornby, A. S., Parnwell, E. C. (1984). *English-Arabic Reader's Dictionary.* Beirut: Oxford University Press.

ELGAR - HIS MUSIC, THE DREAM OF GERONTIUS A Musical Analysis. (2014). Retrieved October 13, 2014, from The Elgar Society: http://www.elgar.org/3gerontt.htm

Eli Luminosus Aequalis, Altus. (2013). *Mutus Liber "Loquitur" – The Mute Book "Speaks".* W. Long Branch, NJ: Sacer Equestris Aureus Ordo, Inc.

Eliade, M. (1953 En., 1972 Ital.). *Shamanism: archaic techniques of ecstasy. (Italian) Lo sciamanesimo e le tecniche dell'estasi.* (Italian-d'Altavilla, Trans.) (En.) Princeton, N.J. (Ital.) Roma-Milano: (En.) Princeton University Press, (Ital.) Bocca Editori.

Eliade, M. (1959). *The Sacred and the Profane.* (W. R. Trask, Trans.) NY, London: Harcourt, Bruce & World Inc.

Ellis, J. (1986). The superstring: theory of everything, or of nothing? *Nature 323*, 595 - 598.

Encyclopaedia Britannica. (1967). Chicago, London, Toronto, Geneva, Sydney, Tokyo, Manila: William Benton, Publisher.

Enoch. (1917). *The Book Of Enoch.* (R.H.Charles, Trans.) London: Society for Promoting Christian Knowledge.

Epstein, P. (1978). *Kabbalah. The way of the Jewish Mystic.* New York: Doubleday Co.

Eschenko, O. and Sara, S. (2008). Learning-Dependent, Transient Increase of Activity in Noradrenergic Neurons of Locus Coeruleus during Slow Wave Sleep in the Rat: Brain Stem–Cortex Interplay for Memory Consolidation? *Cerebral Cortex*, doi:10.1093/cercor/bhn020.

Euripides. (1929). *Iphigenia in Aulis.* (F. Melian-Stawell, Trans.) New York: Oxford university press.

Evola, J. (1941). *Sintesi di dottrina della razza.* Milano: Hoepli.

Evola, J. (1996). *La Tradizione Ermetica.* Roma: Edizioni Mediterranee.

Evola, J. (2008). *Cavalcare la tigre.* Roma: Edizioni Mediterranee.

F.A.M. Wiggermann. (1992). *Mesopotamian Protective Spirits: The Ritual Texts.* Groningen: STYX&PP Publications.

Fadiman J. and Frager R. (1997). *Essential Sufism.* San Francisco: Harper.

Fagan, B. (Ed.). (2001). *The Seventy Great Mysteries of the ancient World: Unlocking Secrets of Past Civilization, Mysteries of the Stone Age.* New York: Thames and Hudson.

Farkas Simon, A. (2011-2012). *Camilla the Siren The Daughter of Death's Love, the Siren's Call to Life And Her Love Coordinates.* Wilkes-Barre, PA: Kamadeva.

Federer, W. J. (2002). *There Really Is a Santa Claus - History of Saint Nicholas & Christmas Holiday Traditions.* St. Louis, MO: Ameriserch, Inc.

Ferrarelli F., Massimini M., Sarasso S., Casali A., Riedner B. A., Angelini G., Tononi G., Pearcec R.A. (2010, February 9). Breakdown in cortical effective connectivity during midazolam-induced loss of consciousness. (M.E.Raichle, Ed.) *Proceedings of the National Academy of Sciences 107(6)*, 2681–2686.

Feuerbach, L. (1846-1866). *Sämmtliche Werke.* Leipzig: O. Wigand.

Firpo, L., Quaglioni, D. (1993). *Il processo di Giordano Bruno.* Roma: Salerno.

Flammarion, C. (1888). *Flammarion, Camille (1888). L'atmosphère: météorologie populaire. Paris: Librairie Hachette et Cie.* Paris: Librairie Hachette et C.

Foulkes, D. (1962). Dream reports from different stages of sleep. *Journal of Abnormal and Social Psychology, 65*, 14-25.

Francesco. (1902). *I fioretti di San Francesco.* Firenze: G. Barbera Editore.

Francesco. (1994). *Scritti di S. Francesco e di S. Chiara.* (B.Sammaciccia, Ed., & L. Canonici, Trans.) Assisi: Edizioni Porziuncola.

Francione, G.L. & Charlton, A. (2013). *Eat Like You Care: An Examination of the Morality of Eating Animals.* (Emilia-Leese-Italian, Trans.) NJ & Charleston, SC: Exempla Press, CreateSpace Independent Publishing Platform.

Franklin, B. (1987). *Franklin: Writings.* New York: Library of America.

Freeman (Director). (2015-2016). *The Story of God, Episode 1: Beyond Death with Morgan Freeman, National Geographic TV documentary* [Motion Picture].

Freud, S. (1948). *On Metapsychology: The Theory of Psychoanalysis: 'Beyond the Pleasure Principle,' 'The Ego and the Id' and Other Works.* London: Penguin Books, UK.

Freud, S. (1957). *New Introductory Lectures on Psycho-Analysis.* (W.J.Sprott, Trans.) London: Hogarth Press.

Freud, S. (1962-1974, 1953-c1962). *The standard edition of the complete psychological works of Sigmund Freud* (Vol. 24). (A. Richards, Ed., & J. Strachey, Trans.) London: Hogarth Press and the Institute of Psycho-Analysis.

Freud, S. (2013). *A Case of Hysteria: (Dora).* (Bell, Trans.) Oxford, UK: Oxford University Press.

Friedlander, M. (1946). *The History and Philosophy of the Jewish Religion.* New York: Pardes Publishing House, Inc.

Gal Einai. (2014, 2 12). *The Month of Shevat – According to The Book of Formation (Sefer Yetzirah).* Retrieved 7 16, 2014, from Your Gateway to the Inner Dimension of the Thorah : http://www.inner.org/times/shevat/shevat.htm

Galilei, G. (1953). *Dialogue on the great world systems .* (S.Thomas, Trans.) Chicago: University of Chicago Press.

Galilei, G. (1960). *The Assayer. The Controversy on the comets of 1618.* Philadelphia: University of Pennsylvania Pres.

Gallant J. & al. (2016). Natural speech reveals the semantic maps that tile human cerebral cortex. *Nature 532, 453–458 (28 April 2016) doi:10.1038/nature17637*, 453–458.

Gallant, J. (2013). Brain decoding: Reading minds. *Nature 502, 428–430 (24 October 2013) doi:10.1038/502428a*, 428–430.

Gandhi, M. (1993). *An Autobiography: The Story of My Experiments with Truth.* (M. H. Desai, Trans.) Boston, MA: Beacon Press.

Garr, J. D. (2012). *Passover, The Festival of Redemption.* Atlanta, Georgia: Golden Key Press.

Gesenius, W. (1979). *Gesenius' Hebrew and Chaldee lexicon to the Old Testament Scriptures: numerically coded to Strong's Exhaustive concordance, with an English index of more than 12,000 entries.* (Tregelles, Trans.) Grand Rapids, MI: Baker Book House.

Gilad Barach. (2014, April 18). *The Meaning of "Next Year in Jerusalem".* Retrieved January 27, 2017, from Kol Hamevaser. The Jewish Thought Magazine of the Yeshiva University Student Body: http://www.kolhamevaser.com/2014/04/the-meaning-of-next-year-in-jerusalem/

Gilgamesh. (1986). *The Epic of Gilgamesh.* (N. Sandars, Trans.) England, Canada, Australia, NY USA: Penguin Books.

Gill Sam D., Sullivan Irene F. (1992). *Dictionary of Native American Mythology.* New York, Oxford: Oxford University Press.

Goldwurm, R. H. (Ed.). (1992). *Talmud Bavli, Tractate Megillah, The Schottenstein Edition, The Gemara: The Classical Vilna Edition, with an Annotated Interpretative Elucidation as an Aid to Talmud Study Elucidated by Rabbi Gedaliah Zlotowitz (Cp. 1-3) & Rabbi Hersh Goldwurm (Cp. 4).* Brooklyn, NY: Mesorah Publication, Ltd.

Goodchild, P. (2009). *Theology of money.* Durham, N.C: Duke University Press.

Goodenough, E. R. (1953-1965). *Jewish Symbols in the Greco-Roman Period* (Vols. IV of 13, Series XXXII). New York and Princeton: Pantheon Books and Princeton University Press Bollingen.

Goodson, A. (1991). *Therapy, nudity & joy the therapeutic use of nudity through the ages, from ancient ritual to modern psychology.* Los Angeles: Elysium Growth Press.
Goodstein, L. (2016, May 20). University of Miami Establishes Chair for Study of Atheism. *The New York Times*, pp. http://www.nytimes.com/2016/05/21/us/university-of-miami-establishes-chair-for-study-of-atheism.html.
Grassi, J. A. (2010). *Healing the Heart: The Transformational Power of Biblical Heart Imagery.* Eugene, Oregon: Wipf and Stock Publishers.
Griffin, D. R. (1992). *Animal Minds Beyond Cognition to Consciousness.* Chicago: The University of Chicago Press.
Grimal, P. (1985). *The dictionary of classical mythology.* Oxford, England ; New York, NY: Blackwell.
Gualtieri, C. (1995). *Templari in cammino.* Roma: italo mari editore.
Guénon, R. (1964). *Il simbolismo della croce.* Torino: Edizioni Studi Tradizionali.
Guillaume, A. (1990). *Islam.* London - NY: Penguin Books.
Guion (Director). (Apr 30, 2014). *Hunt for the Garden of Eden documentary Myth Hunters Series Episode Knowledgepollution YouTube www.bing.com/videos/search?q=the+hunt+for+the+garden+of+eden+documentary&FORM=VIRE1#view=detail&mid=DFA3F7DA807D78335339DFA3F7DA807D7833533* [Motion Picture].
Halberda J., Mazzocco M. M. M., Feigenson L. (2008, September 7). Individual differences in non-v, September 7). Individual differences in non-verbal number acuity correlate with maths achievement. *Nature*, p. Published online.
Hamilton, K. (2015, April 24). *Gorilla Cracks Glass Window At Zoo After Little Girl Beats Chest.* Retrieved July 27, 2015, from IFLScience! : http://www.iflscience.com/plants-and-animals/gorilla-cracks-glass-window-zoo
Hannah More. (1835). *The Works of Hannah More* (Vol. 2). New York: Harper and Brothers.
Hans Christian Andersen. (1977). *The Emperor's New Clothes.* New York, NY: Houghton Mifflin Co.
Harari, Y. N. (2011). *Sapiens. A Brief History of Humankind.* London: Harvill Secker.
Harrison R. K. (1986). *Biblical Hebrew.* Bungay, Suffolk, GB: Teach Yourself Hodder and Stoughton.
Harrison, N. L. (2002). General anesthesia research: aroused from a deep sleep. *Nature Neuroscience 5, doi:10.1038/nn1002-928*, 928 - 929.
Hawking, S. W. (1988). *A Brief History of Time. From the Big Bang to Black Holes.* New Yok: Bantam Books.
Hawking, S., Mlodinow, L. (2010). *The Grand Design.* New York: Bantam Books/Random House.
Hebrew Old Testament. (n.d.). *ספר תורה נביאים ובתובים.* (N.H.Snaith, Ed.) London: The British and Foreign Bible Society.
Hegel G.W.F. (2001). *Philosophy of Right.* (S.W.Dyde, Trans.) Kitchener, Ont: Batoche.
Hegel, G.W.F. (1977). *Phenomenology of Spirit.* (Miller, Trans.) Oxford: Oxford University Press.
Hegel, Georg W. F. (1939). *Vorlesungen über die Aesthetik. / 3. Band.* (H. Glockner, Ed.) Stuttgart: F. Frommann.
Hegel, Georg W. F. (1984). *The Letters.* (Butler&Seiler, Trans.) Bloomington: Indiana University press.
Heidegger, M. (1962). *Being and time.* (Macquarrie&Robinson, Trans.) London: S.C.M. Press.
Heidrick, B. (2000?). *Hebrew Gematria.* Retrieved 6 16, 2014, from Bill Heidrick's Cross References: http://www.billheidrick.com/works/hgemat.htm
Helsel, P. (2016, August 29). 49ers Quarterback Colin Kaepernick Defends National Anthem Protest. *NBC NEWS*, pp. http://www.nbcnews.com/news/us-news/49ers-quarterback-colin-kaepernick-defends-national-anthem-protest-n639116.
Herodotus. (1960-1963). *Herodotus, with an English translation* (Vol. 4). (A.Godley, Trans.) Cambridge, Mass: Harvard University Press, Series Loeb classical library.

Heschel, A. J. (1966). *The Insecurity of Freedom: Essays on Human Existence.* New York: Farrar Straus Giroux.
Hesiod. (1914). *Theogony, Text.* (H. G. Evelyn-White, Trans.) Cambridge, MA., London: Harvard University Press: Harvard University Press; William Heinemann Ltd.
HFASS. (2016). *Who We Are.* Retrieved October 14, 2016, from House for All Sinners and Saints http://houseforall.org/: http://www.houseforall.org/whoweare/
Hill, C. A. (2003, December). Making Sense of the Numbers of Genesis. *Perspectives on Science and Christian Faith 55(4)*, 239-251.
Hines, T. (2003). *Pseudoscience and the Paranormal.* Amherst, NY: Prometheus Books.
Historia Deorum Fatidicorum. (1680). *Historia Deorum Fatidicorum, Vatum Sybillarum Phoebadum Apud Priscos Illustrium: cum corum Iconibus est Disertatio De Divinatione & Oraculis.* Francofurti: Ludovicj Bourgeat.
Hobson, J. A. (2009, November). REM sleep and dreaming: towards a theory of protoconsciousness . *Nature Reviews Neuroscience 10 n.11, doi:10.1038/nrn2716*, 803-813.
Hoffman, E. (1998). *The Hebrew Alphabet, A Mystical Journey.* Vancouver, British Columbia: Raincoast Book.
Hollister, W. (1964). *Medieval Europe. A Short History.* New York, London, Sydney: John Wiley & Sons, Inc.
Holst, G. (Composer). (March 9, 2004). Hymn to the Dawn, Hymn to the Waters, On Choral Hymns from the Rig Veda (4 Groups). [I. Holst, Conductor] London, UK: Decca, Op.26, H.97-100.
Homer. (1995). *Odyssey. English & Greek.* (A. Murray, Trans.) Cambridge, Mass: Harvard University Press, The Loeb classical library; L104-Ll05.
Hommel, Fritz, Hilprecht, Benzinger. (1903). *Explorations in Bible lands during the 19th century.* Philadelphia: A.J. Holman and Company.
Honeyman, A. M. (Honeyman, A. M. 1952). Merismus in Biblical Hebrew. *The Society of Biblical Literature 71*, 11-18.
Horace. (1815). *Quinti Horatii Flacci Opera. Interpretatione et notis illustravit Ludovicus Desprez cardinalitius socius ac rhetor emeritus (1691).* Neapolis: Excudebat Cajetanus Raymundus.
Hospice Care. (2016). *End-of-Life Care.* Retrieved October 21, 2016, from Comfort Keepers: http://www.comfortkeepers.com/home/care-services/end-of-life-care?st-t=bing_hospice-nongeo-pm&vt-k=hospice%20care&vt-mt=p&utm_source=bing&utm_medium=cpc&utm_term=hospice-care&utm_campaign=hospice-nongeo-pm&utm_source=bing&utm_medium=cpc&utm_campaign=Hospi
HRL Laboratories, LLC. (2015). *HRL DEMONSTRATES THE POTENTIAL TO ENHANCE THE HUMAN INTELLECT'S EXISTING CAPACITY TO LEARN NEW SKILLS.* Retrieved March 4, 2016, from HRL Laboratories, LLC https://www.hrl.com/index.html: https://www.hrl.com/news/2016/0210/
Humphreys, F. H. (1999). *Glimpses of the Life and Teachings of Bhagavan Sri Ramana Maharshi. As Described by Frank H. Humphreys, R.F.C. Sometime Asst. Supdt. Of Police, Madras.* Tiruvannamalai: V.S. Ramanan Sri Ramanasramam.
Humphreys, H. (2008). *Coventry.* London, New York: W. W. Norton & Company, Inc.
Husserl, E. (1958). *Ideas. General Introduction to Pure Phenomenology.* (W. B. Gibson, Trans.) London, New York: G. Allen & Unwin, The Macmillan Co.
Husserl, E. (1970). *The Crisis of European Sciences and Transcendental Phenomenology: An Introduction to Phenomenological Philosophy.* (D. Carr, Trans.) Evanston, Illinois: Northwestern University Press.
Huston, J. (Director). (1966). *The Bible: In the Beginning...* [Motion Picture].
IAC. (2012 - 2016). *Glossary of Conscientiological Terms.* Retrieved April 25, 2016, from IAC International Academy of Consciousness: http://www.iacworld.org/glossary/

IAU. (1987, February 18). *IAUC 4315: N Cen 1986; V822 Cen (CENTAURUS X-4); Corr.* Retrieved October 31, 2016, from IAU Central Bureau for Astronomical Telegrams: http://www.cbat.eps.harvard.edu/iauc/04300/04315.html

Ignatius of Loyola. (2012). *Spiritual Exercises.* London: limovia.net.

INSERM http://presse.inserm.fr/en/. (2016, DECEMBER 13). *Neurons Paralyze Us During REM Sleep (The study will appear in Brain).* Retrieved 12 19, 2016, from NEUROSCIENCE NEWS: http://neurosciencenews.com/paralysis-rem-sleep-5738/

Isaac of Akko. (XIII-XIV century). *Otsar Hayyim.* Moscow: Guenzburg manuscript 775, 7a.

Jacob ben Sheshet. (1968). *Meshiv Devarim Nekhohim.* (G. Vajda, Ed.) Jerusalem: Israel National Academy of Sciences.

Jacobs, D. L. (1993, October 10). The Executive Life; Waking to the Power Of Our Dream Worlds. *The New York Times.*

Jātaka. (1969). *The Jātaka.* London: Published for the Pali Text Society by Luzac & co.

Jefferson, T. (1998, June). *Letter to the Danbury Baptists. The Final Letter, as Sent Jan. 1. 1802.* Retrieved February 9, 2013, from Library of Congress/Ameritech National Digital Library Competition - Vol 57, No. 6 http://www.loc.gov/index.html: http://www.loc.gov/loc/lcib/9806/danpre.html

Jesuit Fathers of St. Mary's College. (1955). *The Church Teaches, Documents of the Church in English Translations.* St. Louis Mo. & London: B. Herder Book Co.

John of the Cross. (1957). *The Dark Night of the Soul.* (K.F.Reinhardt, Trans.) NY: F. Ungar Pub.

John of the Cross. (1995). *The Poems of St. John of the Cross. A Bilingual Edition.* (J. F. Nims, Trans.) Chicago: The University of Chicago Press.

Johnson, D. (2016). *India-Pakistan Relations: A 50-Year History.* Retrieved July 12, 2016, from Asia Society 60 Years: http://asiasociety.org/education/india-pakistan-relations-50-year-history

Jones, A. (1990). *Jones' dictionary of Old Testament proper names.* Grand Rapids, Mich : Kregel Publications.

Josephus, F. (1998). *Jewish antiquities.* Cambridge, MA: Harvard University Press.

Jung, C. G. (1956). *Two essays on analytical psychology.* New York: Meridian Books.

Jung, C. G. (1958). *Psyche and Symbol. A selection from the Writings of C. G. Jung Archetype, The Phenomenology of the Spirit in Fairy Tales, The Psychology of the Child.* (V. S. Laszlo, Ed.) Garden Ciyy, NY: Doubleday Anchor Books.

Jung, C. G. (1959). *ETH (Swiss Federal Institute for Technology) Lecture V in Modern Psychology by Carl Jung [Volumes 1-2] Rare edition of Dr. Jung's ETH, Lectures 1933-1935, Sommer semester 1937 and Summer semester 1938* (II ed., Vol. I). (LewisLafontaine, Ed.) Zurich: Swiss Federal Institute for Technology, & issuu.

Jung, C. G. (1978). *Psychology and the East.* (Hull, Trans.) Princeton, NJ: Bollingen Series, Princeton University Press.

Jung, C. G. (1980). *Psychology and Alchemy (Collected Works Vol. 12).* London: Routledge.

Jung, C. G. (1992). *Psychology of the Unconscious: A Study of the Transformations and Symbolisms of the Libido.* Princeton: Bollingen Series, Princeton University Press1992.

Jung, C. G. (1997). *Visions: Notes of the Seminar Given in 1930-1934.* (ClaireDouglas, Ed.) Princeton, NJ: Bollinger Series XCIX Princeton University Press.

Kamitani, Y . (2012). Scientists read dreams. *Nature doi:10.1038/nature.2012.11625.*

Kanigel, R. (1991). *The man who knew infinity. A life of the genius Ramanujan.* Toronto, NY, Oxford, Singapore, Sydney: Scribner's, Macmillan.

Kant, E. (1997). *Critique of Practical Reason.* (M.Gregor, Trans.) Cambridge: Cambridge University Press.

Kant, I. (1952). *The critique of judgement.* (J. C. Meredith, Ed.) Oxford: Clarendon Press.

Kant, I. (1952). *The Critique of Pure Reason (All three Critiques and Metaphysics of Morals)* (Vol. XLII of the Great Books of the Western World series). (M. D. Meiklejohn, Trans.) Chicago, London, Toronto, Geneva, Sydney, Tokyo: Encyclopaedia Britannica.

Kant, I. (1953). *Prolegomena to any future metaphysics that will be able to present itself as a science.* Manchester: Manchester University Press.

Kaplan tr. (1979). *The Bahir: An ancient Kabbalistic text attributed to Rabbi Nehuniah ben HaKana, first century, C. E.* (Kaplan, Trans.) New York: Samuel Weiser.

Kaplan, A. (1995). *The Bahir.* Northvale, NJ: Aronson.

Kass, L. R. (2003). *The Beginning of Wisdom, Reading Genesis.* NY, London, Torono, Sydney, Singapore: Free Press, A Division of Simon & Schuster, Inc.

Kasser-Meyer-Wurst (Ed.). (2008). *Gospel of Judas, from Codex Tchacos.* (Kasser-Meyer-Wurst, Trans.) Washington, D.C: National Geographic Society.

Kerr, P. (2010). *I Love You... Who Are You? Loving and Caring for a Parent with Alzheimer's.* Flemington, NJ: Along the Way Press.

Khalil Gibran. (1998, 2005, 2010). *Sand and Foam (1926).* Retrieved January 2, 2011, from New Thought Library Classic: http://scienceofmindandspirit.com/gibranKhalil/sandNfoam/

Khan, H. I. (1994). *Sufi Teachings: Lectures from Lake O'Hara.* Victoria: Ekstasis Editions Canada Ltd.

Khunrath, H. (1609). *Amphiteatrum Sapientiæ Æternæ Solius Veræ, Christiano-Kabalisticum, Diuino-Magicum, nec non Physico-Chymicum, Tertriunum, Catholicon.* Hannover: Wilhelm Anton.

Kite, P. (1989). *Noah's Ark, Great Mysteries Opposing Viewpoints.* San Diego, CA: Greenhaven Press, Inc.

Klein, E. (1987). *A Comprehensive Etymological Dictionary of the Hebrew Language for Readers of English.* Jerusalem, Israel: Carta the Israel Map & Pub Co Ltd.

Kleitman, N. (1952 [187]). Sleep. *Scientific American,* 34-38.

Kluger, J. (2014). *The Animal Mind.* New York, NY: Time Books.

Knorr von Rosenroth, C. F. (1677-1684). *Kabbala denudata, seu, Doctrina Hebraeorum Transcendentalis et metaphysica atque theologica ...* Sulzbachi: Typis Abrahami Lichtenthaleri.

Koch, C. (2009, July 1). A "Complex" Theory of Consciousness. Is complexity the secret to sentience, to a panpsychic view of consciousness? *Scientific American - Mind,* http://www.scientificamerican.com/article/a-theory-of-consciousness/.

Koch, C. (2014, January 1). Is Consciousness Universal? Panpsychism, the ancient doctrine that consciousness is universal, offers some lessons in how to think about subjective experience today. *Scientific American - Mind,* http://www.scientificamerican.com/article/is-consciousness-universal/.

Koran. (1977). *The Holy Qur'an, Arabic text.* (T. M. Association, Ed., & A. Y. Ali, Trans.) USA: American Trust Publications.

Krašovec, J. (1977). Der Merismus im Biblisch-Hebräischen und Nordwestsemitischen. *Biblica et Orientalia, XV,* 184.

Kugel, J. J. (1997). *The Bible as it was .* Cambridge, Mass: Harvard University Press.

Kumar, N. (2008). *Comprehensive Physics XII.* New Delhi, India: Laxmi Publications.

Kuras, B. (2000). *As Golems Go. Rabbi Loew, the reluctant Czech.* Praha : Baronet a Elk.

Kynard, T. (2015). *The Esoteric Codex: Mesopotamian Deities.* Raleigh, NC: Lulu Press, Inc.

Ladinsky D., ed. & tr. (2002). *Love Poems from God. Twelve Sacred Voices from the East and West.* (Ladinsky, Ed., & Ladinsky, Trans.) New York, NY: Penguin Group.

Laitman, M. (2003). *Attaining the Worlds Beyond: A Guide to Spiritual Discovery.* Thornhill, Ontario : Laitman Kabbalah Publishers.

Lamon, W. H. (2015). *Recollections of Abraham Lincoln 1847–1865.* New York: Firework Press.

Lamon, W.H., Teillard (Lamon), D. (1895). *Recollections of Abraham Lincoln, 1847-1865.* Chicago: A.C. McClurg and Company.

Lao Tzu. (1990). *Tao Te Ching, The Classic Book of Integrity and the Way. Based on the Ma-Wang-Tui manuscripts.* (V.Mair, Trans.) N.Y., Toronto, London, Sydney, Auckland: Bantam Books.

Lao Tzu. (1990). *Tao Te Ching, The Classic Book of Integrity and the Way. Based on the Ma-Wang-Tui manuscripts. Original Chinese @ Taoism Depot http://www.edepot.com/taoism.html http://www.edepot.com/taoc.html.* (V.Mair, Trans.) N.Y., Toronto, London, Sydney, Auckland: Bantam Books.

Laude, P. (2006). *Pray Without Ceasing: The Way of the Invocation in World Religions.* Bloomington Indiana: World Wisdom, Inc.

Laurentin, René, Rupčić, Ljudevit. (1984). *La Vergine appare a Medjugorje? Un messaggio urgente dato al mondo in un paese marxista.* (B. Pistocchi, Trans.) Brescia: Editrice Queriniana .

Leibniz, G. (1898). *THE MONADOLOGY.* (R. Latta, Trans.) London: Oxford University Press.

Leibniz, G., in Clarke, Samuel. (1965). *The Leibniz Clarke correspondence, together with extracts from Newton's Principia and Opticks.* New York: Barnes & Noble, Manchester University Press.

Lenin, V. (1979). *On Religion.* London: Central Books Ltd .

León-Portilla, M. (1988). *Time and Reality in the Thought of the Maya.* Norman: University of Oklahoma Press.

Leslie, M. (June, 22 2016). 'Undead' genes come alive days after life ends. *Science*, pp. http://www.sciencemag.org/news/2016/06/undead-genes-come-alive-days-after-life-ends.

Leung, K. (1999, July 5). *Clementine's Lunar Mapping Mission: An Overview of Science Results.* (leung@lpi.jsc.nasa.gov) Retrieved 2003, from 8NASA funded Lunar and Planetary Institute, Houston, Texas: http://cass.jsc.nasa.gov/newsletters/lpib/lpib72/clem.html

Levs, J. (2014, April 18). *NASA discovers Earth-sized planet that may sustain life.* Retrieved April 20, 2014, from CNNTech: http://www.cnn.com/2014/04/17/tech/space-earth-size-planet/index.html

Lewis, B. (2002). *The Assassins.* New York: Basic Books.

Línjì Yìxuán. (1999). *The Zen Teachings of Master Lin-Chi: A Translation of the Lin-Chi Lu.* (BurtonWatson-YuanjueZongan, Trans.) New York: Columbia University Press.

Livy, T. (1949-63). *Ab urbe condita. Text & translation* (Vol. 14). (Foster-Moore-Sage-Schlesinger-Geer, Trans.) Cambridge Mass., London: The Loeb Classical Library, Harvard University Press, William Heinemann Ltd.

Lorenzini (Collodi), Carlo. (1993). *Le avventure di Pinocchio* (I ed.). Firenze: Giunti Editore.

Luther, M. (1883). *Martin Luthers Werke.* (Knaake, Ed.) Weimar: Herman Bohlaus.

Luzzatto, M. C. (1996). *Way of G-d: Derech Hashem* (5th ed.). Jerusalem, New York: Feldheim Publishers.

Macdonell, A. (1927, Reprint 1955). *A Sanskrit Grammar for Students.* London: Oxford University Press.

Macdonell, A. (1927, Reprint 1955). *A Sanskrit Grammar for Students.* London: Oxford University Press.

Mackenzie, D. A. (1907). *Egyptian Myth And Legend.* London: Gresham Publishing Co.

Mahadevan, T. (1977-1980). *Ramana Maharshi. The Sage of Arunacala.* (Italian, Trans.) London, Roma: Unwin, Mediterranee ed.

Maimonides, M. (1971). *Guide of the Perplexed.* (M.Friedlander, Trans.) New York: Dover Publications Inc.

Maimonides, M. (1983). *The Book of Knowledge: From the Mishneh Torah of Maimonides.* Brooklyn, NY: Ktav Pub & Distributors Inc.

Majeed, D. (2015). *Polygyny.* Gainesville, FL: University Press of Florida.

Malidoma Patrice Some. (1994). *Of Water and the Spirit: Ritual, Magic and Initiation in the Life of an African Shaman.* New York : Penguin Books.

Malory, T. (1961). *Le Morte Dārthur, The Book of King Arthur and his Knights of the Round Table* (Vol. 2). New York: University Book.

Manzoni, A. (1911). *Le tragedie, gl'inni sacri, le odi.* Torino: Liberia Società Buona Stampa.

Mao, Tse-tung. (1975). *"Little Red Book" Annotated quotations from Chairman Mao.* (J.DeFrancis, Ed.) New Haven: Yale University Press.

Marder, M. (2013). *Plant-thinking: a philosophy of vegetal life.* New York: Columbia University Press.
Marks, H. (1995, Spring). Biblical Naming and Poetic Etymology. *Journal of Biblical Literature, 114*(1), 21–42.
Marohn, S. (2011). *The Natural Medicine Guide to Bipolar Disorder.* Charlottesville, VA: Hampton Roads Publishing Cm.
Martin Luther King. (2003). *A Testament of Hope: The Essential Writings and Speeches of Martin Luther King, Jr.* (J.M.Washington, Ed.) New York, NY: HarperCollins Publishers.
Marx, K. (1952). *Capital / Manifesto of the Communist Party.* (F. Engels, Ed.) Chicago: Encyclopaedia Britannica.
Marx, K. (1843-44). Zur Kritik der Hegelschen Rechtsphilosophie. *Deutsch-Französische Jahrbücher,* http://www.mlwerke.de/me/me01/me01_378.htm.
Mason, H. (1979). *The death of al-Hallaj: a dramatic narrative.* Notre Dame, Indiana: University of Notre Dame Press.
Masoretic Text (American Bible Society - Manufacturer). (2001). *Biblia Hebraica Stuttgartensia* (I ed.). Stuttgart: Deutsche Bibelgesellschaft.
Maspero, G. (1883). *La Pyramide du roi Ounas, Recuel de Travaux* (Vol. IV). Paris.
Maspero, M. (1893). *Études de mythologie et d'archéologie* (Vol. I). Paris.
Matt, D. C. (1983). *Zohar: The Book of Enlightenment .* Mahwah, NJ : (Classics of Western Spirituality) Paulist Press.
Matt, D. C. (1995). *The Essential Kabbalah. The Heart of Jewish Mysticism.* New York: Quality Paperback Book Club.
Matt-Pritzker (Ed.). (2003-2005-2007-2009-2012-20014). *Sefer ha-Zohar, "The Book of Radiance,".* (D. C. Matt, Trans.) Stanford, California: Stanford University Press.
Mbiti, J. (1970). *African Religions and Philosophy.* Garden City, NY: Anchor Books Doubleday & Co.
McCarthy J. (1977). Epistemological Problems of Artificial Intelligence. *IJCAI- International Joint Conference on Artificial Intelligence. 2,* pp. 1038-1044. Cambridge, Massachusetts, USA: AAAI Press/International Joint Conferences on Artificial Intelligence.
McGough R. A. (2014, October 4). *Debunking Myself: What A Long Strange Trip It's Been.* Retrieved November 16, 2014, from Bibles, Wheels, and Brains. A Freethinker's Exploration of Religion, Science, and the Mind: http://www.biblewheel.com/blog/index.php/2014/10/04/debunking-myself-what-a-long-strange-trip-its-been/
McNeil, N. (2009). *Heaven Exists.* Parker, CO: Outskirts Press Inc.
Melanchthon, P. (2015). *The Apology of the Augsburg Confession.* New York, NY: Scriptura Press.
Merton, T. (1968). *Zen and the Birds of Appetite.* New York : New Directions Publishing.
Merton, T. (1953). *The Sign of Jonas. The Journal of Thomas Merton.* New York: Harcourt, Brace and Company.
Meshberger, Frank MD. (1990; 264 (14). An interpretation of Michelangelo's Creation of Adam Based on Neuroanatomy. *The Journal of the American Medical Association (JAMA) doi: 10.1001/jama 03450140059034,* 1837-1841.
Milton, J. (2005). *Paradise lost.* (G.Teskey, Ed.) New York: W. W. Norton.
Mind Unleashed. (2015). *31 Outstanding Quotes From Nikola Testa.* Retrieved 9 15, 2015, from themindunleashed.org/: http://themindunleashed.org/2015/03/31-outstanding-quotes-from-nikola-tesla.html
Miranker, W., Zuckerman, G. (December 2009). Mathematical Foundations of Consciousness. *Journal of Applied Logic, Departments of Computer Science, Mathematics Yale University, doi:10.1016/j.jal.2008.05.002,* volume 7, Issue 4, 421–440.
Monroe L. J., Rechtschaffen A., Foulkes D., Jensen J. (1965). The discriminability of REM and NREM reports. *Journal of Personality and Social Psychology, 2,* 456-460.

Montaldo, G. (Director). (1973). *Giordano Bruno* [Motion Picture].

Morrison, C. (Ed.). (2006). *Gold from the Land of Israel: A New Light on the Weekly Torah Portion from the Writings of Rabbi Abraham Isaac HaKohen Kook.* Jerusalem, Israel: Urim Publications.

Mother Teresa. (2016). *A Call to Mercy: Hearts to Love, Hands to Serve.* New York: Penguin Random House LLC Crown Publishing Group.

Mueller, K. (1841). *Fragmenta historicorum graecorum ... auxerunt, notis et prolegomenis illustrarunt, indici plenissimo instruxerunt Car. et Theod. Mulleri. Accedunt marmora parium et rosettanum, hoc cum Letronnii, illud cum C. Mulleri commentariis.* Parisiis: Editore Ambrosio Firmin Didot.

Murayama M. & al. (26 May 2016). Top-down cortical input during NREM sleep consolidates perceptual memory. *Science, doi: 10.1126/science.aaf0902,* http://science.sciencemag.org/content/early/2016/05/25/science.aaf0902.

Murch, Tan, Weber, Siddiqi, Mølmer. (2015). Prediction and retrodiction for a continuously monitored superconducting qubit. *Physical Review Letters 10.1103/PhysRevLett.114.090403.*

Murphy, V. (2004, August Monday, 9). Death before defeat in the ancient games. *BBC News Online*, p. http://news.bbc.co.uk/2/hi/europe/3534988.stm.

NASA. (2003, February 7). *The Pull of HyperGravity.* Retrieved May 21, 2016, from NASA SCIENCE/ Science News: http://science.nasa.gov/science-news/science-at-nasa/2003/07feb_stronggravity/

NASA. (2006, January 30). *How Old is the Universe?*. Retrieved May 18, 2014, from NASA GODDARD SPACE FLIGHT CENTER: http://imagine.gsfc.nasa.gov/docs/features/exhibit/map_age.html

NASA. (2013, April 29). *General Physics: Waves - Light and Sound.* Retrieved July 5, 2015, from Cosmicopia: http://helios.gsfc.nasa.gov/qa_gp_ls.html

Nasa. (2016, September 26). *NASA's Hubble Spots Possible Water Plumes Erupting on Jupiter's Moon Europa.* Retrieved September 29, 2016, from NASA.TV http://www.nasa.gov/multimedia/nasatv/index.html#public: http://www.nasa.gov/press-release/nasa-s-hubble-spots-possible-water-plumes-erupting-on-jupiters-moon-europa

NASA SCIENCE. (2014, January 22). *Water Detected on Dwarf Planet Ceres.* Retrieved March 24, 2016, from Science News: http://science.nasa.gov/science-news/science-at-nasa/2014/22jan_ceres/

Nathues, A., et Al. (2015, December 10). Sublimation in bright spots on (1) Ceres. *Nature International weekly journal of science 528, 237–240 (10 December 2015) doi:10.1038/nature15754*, 237–240.

NBC News. (2015, December 30). Goat intended as tiger's meal becomes its friend instead. *WNCN North Carolina News Now*, pp. http://wncn.com/2015/12/30/goat-intended-as-tigers-meal-becomes-its-friend-instead/.

Neruda, P. (2007). *4 poemas de Pablo Neruda y un amanecer en la isla.* Valencia: Versos Y Trazos.

Netburn, D. (2016, January 16). Rosetta spots two types of water ice on the surface of comet 67P. *Los Angeles Times*, pp. http://www.latimes.com/science/sciencenow/la-sci-sn-rosetta-water-ice-20160113-story.html.

NEWS.VA. (2016, 3 10). Le risposte del Papa ai bambini. Il libro presentato a Roma. *Radio Vaticana Official Vatican Network.*

Newton, I. (1687). *Philosophiæ Naturalis Principia Mathematica.* Londini: jussi Societatus Regiae ac typis Josephi Streater; prostat apud plures bibliopolas.

Nick & Pal. (2012). *The Lorns: A New Race of Beings. The Sensational Revelation of Professor Lorry.* West Long Branch, NJ: Sacer Equestris Aureus Ordo. Inc.

Nicolae de Cusa. (1932.). *Opera Omnia: De Docta Ignorantia* (2 ed., Vol. I). (Hoffmann-Klibansky, Ed.) Leipzig: Felix Meiner.

Nikhilānanda, Swami. (1936 - ed. 1968). *The Māṇḍūkyopanishad, with Gauḍapāda's Kārikā and Śaṅkara's commentary (V ed.).* Mysore: Sri Ramakrishna Ashrama.

NIM - National Institutes of Health. (1993, October 10). *Genomic library.* Retrieved July 9, 2015, from U.S. National Library of Medicine: https://vsearch.nlm.nih.gov/vivisimo/cgi-bin/query-meta?query=genomic+library&v%3Aproject=nlm-main-website

Noble, P. A. (2016). Accurate Predictions of Postmortem Interval Using Linear Regression Analyses of Gene Meter Expression Data. *bioRxiv beta The Preprint Server For Bioogy; http://dx.doi.org/10.1101/058370*, http://biorxiv.org/content/early/2016/06/12/058370.

Norman-Haignere, Kanwisher, McDermott. (2015, December 16). Distinct Cortical Pathways for Music and Speech Revealed by Hypothesis-Free Voxel Decomposition. *Neuron. 2015 Dec 16;88(6):1281-96. doi: 10.1016/j.neuron.2015.11.035.*, 1281-96.

North, A. (2014, June 19). Our Robot Nightmares. *The New York Times* , p. Op Talk.

Nostradamus, Edgar Leoni. (2000). *Nostradamus and His Prophecies.* Mineola, New York: Dover Publications, Inc.

NOVA. (2015, 8 13). *The Dream Stela of Thutmosis IV.* Retrieved 12 28, 2016, from NOVA: http://www.pbs.org/wgbh/nova/ancient/sphinx-stela.html

Occam, G. d. (1675). *Summa Totius Logicae.* Oxoniae: Typis L.L. Acad. typogr.

Otto, R. (1923). *The Idea of the Holy.* (J.W.Harvey, Trans.) Oxford: Oxford University Press.

Overbye, D. (2002, March 12). Peering Through the Gates of Time. *The New York Times (Science Time),* p. F 1.

Ovid. (1960). *Metamorphoses.* (Miller, Trans.) Cambridge Mass., London: The Loeb Classical Library, Harvard University Press, William Heinemann Ltd.

Palmer, M. (2012). *The Atheist's Primer.* Cambridge, UK: Lutterworth Press.

Palmer-Sherrard-Ware (Ed.). (1979-1982-1986-1999). *The Philokalia: The Complete Text* (Vols. 1-2-3-4). (Palmer-Sherrard-Ware, Trans.) London: Faber and Faber.

Paramahansa Yogananda. (1993). *Autobiography of a Yogi.* Los Angeles, California: Self-Realization Fellowship.

Parapsychological Association, Inc. (PA) . (2016). *About The Parapsychological Association.* Retrieved October 30, 2016, from Parapsychological Association: http://parapsych.org/base/about.aspx

Parpola, A. (1994, 1997 ed.). *Deciphering the Indus script* (Vol. 2). Cambridge: Cambridge University Press.

Parti, R. (2016). *Dying to Wake Up: A Doctor's Voyage into the Afterlife and the Wisdom He Brought Back.* New York, NY: Atria Books.

Patañjali. (1955). *Yoga Sutras of Patanjali.* (Ballantyne&Sastri-Deva, Trans.) Calcutta: Susil Gupta.

Pausanias. (1961). *Pausanias Description of Greece, with an English translation (Vol. 4)* (Vol. 4). (W. H. Jones, Trans.) Cambridge, Mass.; London: Harvard University Press; W. Heinemann; The Loeb classical library.

Payne, K. (1999). *SILENT THUNDER: In the Presence of Elephants.* New York: Penguin Books.

PBS Thirteen. (2014, September 24). *Rise of the Hackers.* Retrieved June 30, 2015, from PBS NOVA: http://www.pbs.org/wgbh/nova/tech/rise-of-the-hackers.html

Petrarca, F. (2013). *Il Canzoniere.* Milano: Feltrinelli economica.

Petras, Watson, Thorson. (2016, August 24). New Earth-Size Planet Discovered. *USA TODAY*, pp. http://www.usatoday.com/pages/interactives/new-planet-discovered-08-2016/.

Philonis Judaei. (1828). *Operum Omnium Tom. V* (Vol. V). Lipsiae: Sumtibus E.B. Schwickerti.

Philpot, J.H. (1897). *The Sacred Tree or The Tree in Religion and Myth.* New York: The Macmillan Co.

Pick, B. (1909). *The Apocryphal Acts of Paul, Peter, John, Andrew and Thomas.* Chicago: The Open Court Publishing Co.

Pierce, B. R. (1935). The Donatist Circumcellions. *Church History: Studies in Christianity and Culture, Vol.4, No.2*, 123-133.

Pirandello, L. (1921). *Sei personaggi in cerca d'autore: commedia da fare.* Firenze: R. Bemporad & Figlio, Editori.
Pirandello, L. (1983). *Uno, nessuno e centomila.* Milano: Mondadori.
Pistorius, M. (2013). *Ghost Boy. The Miraculous Escape of a Misdiagnosed.* Nashville, Tennessee: Nelson Books.
Pius XII. (1950). *PIUS EPISCOPUS SERVUS SERVORUM DEI AD PERPETUAM REI MEMORIAM CONSTITUTIO APOSTOLICA MUNIFICENTISSIMUS DEUS FIDEI DOGMA DEFINITUR DEIPARAM VIRGINEM MARIAM CORPORE ET ANIMA FUISSE AD CAELESTEM GLORIAM ASSUMPTAM* (Vols. A.A.S., vol. XXXXII (1950), n. 15, pp. 753 - 773.). Vatican City, Rome: Libreria Editrice Vaticana http://w2.vatican.va/content/pius-xii/la/apost_constitutions/documents/hf_p-xii_apc_19501101_munificentissimus-deus.html.
Plato. (1955-63). *Text and English translations in Plato* (Vol. 10). (Loeb-classical-library, Ed.) Cambridge, London: Harvard University Press, W. Heinemann.
Pliny the Elder. (1906). *Naturalis Historia.* Lipsiae: Teubner.
Pliny the Younger. (1969). *Letters and Panegyricus I, Books 1-7* (Reprint ed., Vol. I). (B.Radice, Trans.) Cambridge, Massachusetts: Harvard University Press (Loeb Classical Library).
Plotinus. (1966-1988). *Enneads Greek text: Plotinus, with an English translation by A. H. Armstrong.* (A.H.Armstrong, Trans.) Cambridge, Mass., London: Harvard University Press, W. Heinemann.
Plutarch. (1967). *That Epicurus actually makes a pleasant life impossible* (Vol. L. c. XIV). (E.-D. Lacy, Trans.) Cambridge, Mass: Harvard University Press.
Poggio, T. and others . (2016). View-Tolerant Face Recognition and Hebbian Learning Imply Mirror-Symmetric Neural Tuning to Head Orientation . *Current Biology (MIT)*, DOI: http://dx.doi.org/10.1016/j.cub.2016.10.015.
Polizzi, N. (2016, September 6). *Wired For Tribe.* Retrieved September 9, 2016, from The Sacred Science > Shamanism: http://www.thesacredscience.com/wired-for-tribe?utm_source=iContact&utm_medium=email&utm_campaign=The%20Sacred%20Science%20Free%20Online%20Screening&utm_content=Tribe
Pollack, R. E. (2000). *The Faith of Biology and the Biology of Faith.* New York: Columbia University Press.
Ponchielli, A. (Composer). (1991). La Gioconda. [Tebaldi-Bergonzi, Performer, & L. Gardelli, Conductor] London Decca, UK.
Prince, J. H. (1980). *How animals hunt.* New York: Elsevier/Nelson Books.
Puccini, G. (composer), Giacosa, G. & Illica, L. (librettists). (1984). *La Bohème.* New York: Dover Publications.
Puccini, G. (composer), Giacosa, G. & Illica, L. (librettists). (1992). *Tosca.* N.Y: Dover Publ.
Pyramid texts. (1969). *The ancient Egyptian pyramid texts.* (R. Faulkner, Trans.) Oak Park, Ill: Aris & Phillips, Warminster, Wiltshire, Bolchazy-Carducci.
Radhanath Swami. (2010). *The Journey Home. Autobiography lof an American Swami.* San Raphael, CA: Mandala Publishing.
Ramana Maharshi. (1988). *Who am I? The Spiritual Teaching of Ramana Maharshi.* Boston & London: Shambhala.
Rashi, Rabbi Shlomo Yitzchaki. (2011 - 5772). *Studies in Rashi – Bereishit.* (RabbiEliezerDanzinger, Trans.) Brooklin, NY: Merkos L'inyonei Chinuch.
Ratti, O. & Westbrook, A. (1973). *Secrets of the Samurai.* Rutland, Vermont; Tokyo, Japan: Charles E. Tuttle Company.
Ray, T. (June 25-30, 2006). Self Organization in Real and Complex Analysis. In Minai-Braha-Bar-Yam (Ed.), *PROCEEDINGS OF THE SIXTH INTERNATIONAL CONFERENCE ON COMPLEX SYSTEMS* (p. Paper #73 Mathematical Methods). Boston, MA: The New England Complex Systems Institute.

Rechtschaffen A., Watson R., Wincor M. Z., Molinari S., Barta S. G. (1972). The relationship of phasic and tonic periorbital EMG activity to NREM mentation . *Sleep Research 1*, 114.

Reuven Sivan, Levenston Edward. (1986). *The New Bantam-Megiddo Hebrew & English Dictionary.* Toronto - NY - London - Sydney, Auckland: Bantam Books.

Risen, T. (2015, July 23). Another Earth? Take a Look at Kepler 425-b. A NASA space telescope searching for a new Earth has found our look-alike planet . *USNews.*

Roberts, O. (1977). *The Miracle of Seed Faith.* Grand Rapids MI: Fleming H. Revell Company.

Rocci, L. (1952). *Vocabolario Greco - Italiano* (VII ed.). Roma, Napoli, Citta' di Castello: Dante Alighieri & S. Lapi Coeditori.

Roget. (1956). *Roget's International Thesaurus* (New 1956 ed.). New York: T.Y. Crowell Com.

Ronnberg, A. (2014). *Birds of Prophecy Images from ARAS* . Retrieved June 7, 2016, from Archive for Research in Archetypal Symbolism: https://aras.org/sites/default/files/docs/00024Birds.pdf

Roscoe, W. (1797). *The life of Lorenzo de'Medici: called the Magnificent* (Vol. 1). London: Straman, Cadell, Davies and Edwards.

Rose, S. (1891). *Ignatius Loyola and the early Jesuits.* London & New York: Burns and Oates, Ld. & Catholic Publication Society Co.

Rousseau, J.-J. (1762). *Du contrat social; Principes du droit politique.* Amsterdam: Chez Marc – Michel Rey.

Rowlands, M. (2008). *The Philosopher and the Wolf. Lessons from the Wild on Love, Death, and Happiness* . New York: Pegasus Books.

Rudoy, J.D., Voss, J.L., Westerberg, C.E., Paller, K.A. (2009, November 20). *Strengthening Individual Memories by Reactivating Them During Sleep.* Retrieved December 3, 2009, from www.sci, from Science, Vol. 326. no. 5956, p. 1079 DOI: 10.1126/science.1179013: www.sciencemag.org: http://graphics8.nytimes.com/packages/pdf/science/rudoy091120.pdf

Rumi. (2004). *The Essential Rumi, New Expanded Edition.* (ColemanBarks, Trans.) San Francisco: HarperCollins Publishers Inc.

Rumi. (2007). *Bridge to the Soul, Journeys into the Music and Silence of the Heart.* (C.Barks, Trans.) New York: Harper One, HarperCollins Publisher.

Rundle-Clark, R. T. (1978). *Myth and Religion in Ancient Egypt.* New York: Thames and Hudson.

Rundle-Clark, R. T. (1978). *Myth and Religion in Ancient Egypt.* New York: Thames and Hudson.

Russell, B. (1914). *Our Knowledge of the External World as a Field for Scientific Method in Philosophy.* George Allen & UnwiN LTD: London.

Russell, B. (1957). *Why I Am Not a Christian: And Other Essays on Religion and Related Subjects.* New York: Simon & Schuster, Inc.

Russell, B. (1997). *The Collected Papers of Bertrand Russell, Vol. 11: Last Philosophical Testament, 1943–68. Is There a God? [1952]* (Vol. 11). (Slater&Köllner, Ed.) London: Routledge.

Saadia Gaon. (1948). *Saadia Gaon, The Book of Beliefs and Opinions.* (S.Rosenblatt, Trans.) New Haven: Yale University Press.

Saenger, W. (1984). *Principles of Nucleic Acid Structure.* New York: Springer-Verlag.

Sagan, C. (2000). *The Cosmic Connection: An Extraterrestrial Perspective.* (J. Agel, Ed.) Cambridge, UK: Cambridge University Press.

Śāntideva. (1979). *A Guide to the Bodhisattva's Way Of Life or Entering the Path of Enlightenment (Bodhisattvacaryāvatāra).* (S. Batchelor, Trans.) Dharamsala, India: Library of Tibetan Works and Archives.

Sartre, J. P. (1943, En. tr. 1956). *L'être et le néant, Essai d'ontologie phénoménologique (Being and Nothingness; An Essay on Phenomenological Ontology).* (H.E.Barnes, Trans.) Paris, New York: Philosophical Library.

Sartre, J. P. (1989). *No exit, and three other plays.* (L.Abel, Trans.) New York: Vintage International.

Sartre, J. P. (2007). *Huis Clos.* Upper Saddle River, New Jersey: Prentice Hal.

Saturday Evening Post. (1929, October 26). *Saturday Evening Post.*

Saxe, J. G. (2015). *The Poems of John Godfrey Saxe.* United States of America: Palala Press.

ŚB. (1966). *The Śatapatha-Brāhmaṇa according to the text of the Mādhyandina School* (Vol. IV). (J.Eggeling, Trans.) Delhi, Patna, Varanasi: Motilal Banarsidass.

Scaligero, M. (1970?). *Graal. Saggio sul Mistero del Sacro Amore.* Roma: Perseo.

Scaligero, M. (1975). *Tecniche della concentrazione interiore.* Roma: Edizioni Mediterranee.

Scarano, P. (Scarano, P. (1989, Agosto 3). Montalcini. (Rusconi, Ed.) *Gente, n. 31, anno XXXIII*, pp. 35-7.

Schaff, P. (1877). *Creeds of Christendom, with a History and Critical notes. The History of the Creeds* (Vol. I&II). New York: Harper & Brothers.

Schawinski, K. (2016, January 28). Is our Milky Way galaxy a zombie, already dead and we don't know it? *THE CONVERSATION. Academic rigour, journalistic flair http://theconversation.com/au*, Science + Technology http://theconversation.com/is-our-milky-way-galaxy-a-zombie-already-dead-and-we-dont-know-it-52732.

Schimmel, A. (1993). *The Mystery of Numbers.* New York, Oxford: Oxford University Press.

Schmid, R. E. (2011, January 10). Researchers Find Oldest Known Winery In Cave In Armenian Mountains. *The Associated Press.*

Schopenhauer, A. (1958). *The world as will and representation* (Vol. 2). (Payne, Trans.) Indian Hills, Col: Falcon's Wing Press.

Schopenhauer, A. (1965). *The basic of morality.* (Payne, Trans.) Indianapolis: Bobbs-Merrill.

Schrader, E. (1885). *The cuneiform inscriptions and the Old Testament , tr. from the 2d enl. German ed., with an introductory preface, by O. C. Whitehouse .* London, Edinburgh, Williams & Norgate.

Schrödinger, E. (1958). *Mind and Matter.* Cambridge, UK: Cambridge University Press.

Schulte, J. (1987). *Erlebnis und Ausdruck : Wittgensteins Philosophie der Psychologie.* München: Philosophia.

Schultz, J.D., West, J.G., MacLean I.S. (1999). *Encyclopedia of religion in American politics (Vol. 2).* Phoenix, Arizona: Encyclopedia of religion in American politics.

Seattle Post-Intelligencer. (2007, February Saturday 24). *People in the News: Donald Trump plans his death to a tee .* Retrieved September 22, 2008, from seattlepi.com . (Hearst-newspapers): http://seattlepi.nwsource.com/people/304915_people24.html

Seiji Ogawa, S. & Kwong, K. (2012). Brain imaging: fMRI 2.0. *Nature 484, 24–26 (05 April 2012) doi:10.1038/484024a*, 24-26.

SETI. (© 2016 SETI Institute). *SETI Institute.* Retrieved 1 19, 2016, from Search for Extraterrestrial Intelligence Institute: http://www.seti.org/

SETI. (2016, August 30). *A SETI Signal?* Retrieved August 31, 2016, from 6 SETI Institute: http://www.seti.org/seti-institute/a-seti-signal?utm_content=buffer10136&utm_medium=social&utm_source=twitter.com&utm_campaign=buffer

Shakespeare, W. (1992). *Romeo and Juliet.* (Mowat&Werstine, Ed.) New York, London, Toronto, Sydney: Washington Square Press.

Shakespeare, W. (1998). *Hamlet.* (S.Barnet, Ed.) New York: A Signet Classic.

Shakespeare, W. (2005). *The Tempest.* Stilwell, KS: Digireads.com Publishing.

Shelley, M. (1985). Frankenstein. London: Penguin Classics. (1985). *Frankenstein.* London: Penguin Classics.

Shelley, P. B. (1826). *"Ozymandias" in Miscellaneous and Posthumous Poems of Percy Bysshe Shelley.* London: W. Benbow.

Simonelli, M. G. (11-13 October, 2007). The Redemption of the 'Supernatural Wood' in Italian Literature. Virginia Tech, Blacksburg, VA 24061-0225: Conference, MIFLC 57th Annual Mountain Interstate Foreign Language.

Simonelli, P. J. (1972). Il neoplatonismo ed il pensiero indiano. Atti Accademia di Scienze Morali e Politiche di Napoli, LXXXII , 190-248. *Atti Accademia di Scienze Morali e Politiche di Napoli, LXXXII*, 190-248.

Simonelli, P. J. (1978). Una lettura della Bṛhadāraṇyaka Upanishad. *Annali dell'Istituto Universitario Orientale di Napoli. 38*, 371-402.

Simonelli, P. J. (1996). Philosophy as a Path to Education for Leadership. In Sarsar (Ed.), *Education for Leadership and Social Responsibility* (pp. CHAPTER 3, 23-34). West Long Branch, NJ: Monmouth University, Center for the Study of Public Issues.

Simonelli, P. J. (2004). The World as the Upanishadic sacrificial-horse, as the barge of Rā, from the sarcophagus of Seti I, and according to Genesis. In F. Elders (Ed.), *Visions of Nature. Studies on the Theory of Gaia and Culture in Ancient and Modern Times* (pp. 165-191). Brussells, Belgium: VUB Brussels University Press.

Simonelli, P. J. (2012). *Beyond Immortality. The Electron Frog-Jump Past the Edge of Death's Abyss.* W.Long Branch, NJ: Sacer Equestris Aureus Ordo, Inc.

Simonelli, P. J. (2012). *Hyria, A lost City-State, Una Polis Scomparsa.: Nola-Hyria.* West Long Branch, NJ: SEAO.Inc.

Simonelli, P. J. (2013). *Awareness. The Book of Ethic, Morals and Behavior.* West Long Branch, NJ: Sacer Equestris Aureus Ordo Inc.

Simonelli, P. J. (February 11-16, 2008 16th Annual Conference). Sacred Topography, Holy Chronology and Human Dimensions. The "Mythical" Subdivision of Space and Time in the Upanishadic Tradition. (NAAAS&Affiliates, Ed.) *National Association of African American Studies ... & International Association of Asian Studies*, 1381-1404.

Simonelli, P. J. (1976). Note introduttive alla gnoseologia di Šankara. In *Scritti in onore di Cleto Carbonara, Napoli: Universita' di Napoli.* (pp. 848-861). Napoli: Universita' di Napoli.

Simonelli, P. J. (2000). Transcendence - The Universal Quest. In F. Elders (Ed.), *Mythological Europe Revisited. Humanism and the Third Millennium III* (pp. 175-193). Brussels, Belgium: VUB University Press.

Simonelli, P.J. (1982). La morte nella Bṛhadāraṇyaka Upanishad e Śatapatha Brāhmaṇa. In Éditions-de-la-Maisons-des-Sciences-del'Homme (Ed.), *La mort, les morts dans les sociétés anciennes* (pp. 455-466). Cambridge: Cambridge: Cambridge University Press.

Simplicius. (1997). *On Aristotle's Physics 5 . (The-Ancient-Commentators-on-Aristotle).* (J. Urmson, Ed., & J. Urmson, Trans.) Ithaca, New York: Cornell University Press.

Singer, I. (1901-1906). *The Jewish Encyclopedia.* New York: Funk & Wagnalls.

Skinner, B. F. (1991). *The Behavior of Organisms.* Acton, MA: Copley Publishing Group.

Smithsonian Institution. (2016). *Human Evolution Timeline Interactive.* Retrieved July 19, 2016, from About The Human Origins Initiative: http://humanorigins.si.edu/evidence/human-evolution-timeline-interactive

Society of Biblical Archæology (London, England), Walter L. Nash. (1885). *Transactions of the Society of Biblical archæology* (Vol. VIII). London: Pub. at the offices of the Society.

Sources of Chinese Tradition. (1960). *Sources of Chinese Tradition, Introduction to Oriental Civilization, n. LIV-LVI.* (T.d.Bary, Ed.) NY: Columbia University Press.

Spencer, H. (1897). *The Principles of Biology.* New York: D. Appleton and Company.

St. Francis. (1906). *The Little Flowers of St. Francis and of His Friars.* (Heywood, Trans.) London: Methuen & Co.

St. Louis de Montfort. (1954). *The Secret of the Rosary.* New York: A MONTFORT PUBLICATION.

Stanford Report. (2014, March 17). *New evidence from space supports Stanford physicist's theory of how universe began.* Retrieved October 27, 2015, from Stanford/News - Stanford's Office of University Communications: http://news.stanford.edu/news/2014/march/physics-cosmic-inflation-031714.html

Stede, W., Rhys-David, T.W. (2002). *Pali - English Dictionary.* (R.-D. Stede, Ed.) New Delhi: Munshiram Manoharlal Publishers.

Stein, G. (2003). *The Language That Rises: 1923-1934.* Evanston, Illinois: Northwestern University Press.

Stewar, D. (1999). *Tesla: The Modern Sorcerer.* Berkeley, California: Frog Ltd.

Stickgold R., Walker M. P. (2007, 8). Sleep-dependent memory consolidation and reconsolidation. *Sleep Medicine*, 331-343 doi:10.1016/j.sleep.2007.03.011.

Strathern, P. (2001). *Mendeleyev's Dream : The Quest For the Elements.* NY: St. Martin's.

Strong. (1990). *The new Strong's exhaustive concordance of the Bible : with main concordance, appendix to the main concordance, topical index to the Bible, dictionary of the Hebrew Bible, dictionary of the Greek Testament.* Nashville: T. Nelson Publishers.

Strong. (2007). *Strong's Concordance with Hebrew and Greek Lexicon.* Retrieved 2014, from EliYah.com: http://www.eliyah.com/lexicon.html

Suarès, C. (1970). *The cipher of Genesis; the original code of the Qabala as applied to the Scriptures.* Berkeley: Shambala Publications.

Susskind, L. (1995). The world as a hologram. *Journal of Mathematical Physics J. Math. Phys. 36 (11).doi:10.1063/1.531249*, 6377–6396.arXiv:hep-th/9409089.

Susskind, L. (2008). *The Black Hole War: My Battle with Stephen Hawking to Make the World Safe for Quantum Mechanics.* New York, Boston, London: Little, Brown & Company.

Sutta Nipāta. (1881). *The Sutta Nipāta (in The Dhammapada and Sutta Nipāta)* (Vol. X of "The Sacred Books of the East"). (M. V. Fausböll, Trans.) Oxford: the Clarendon Press.

Sykes, C. (1988). The man who loved numbers: Srinivasa Ramanujan 1887-1920. *NOVA on PBS.* Boston: WGBH Education Foundation, Channel 4 Ltd. InCA prod. .

Tagliazucchi, E, et al. (2016, January). Large-scale signatures of unconsciousness are consistent with a departure from critical dynamics. *Journal Of The Royal Society Interface, 13*(114), Abstract.

Tales from the Thousand and One Nights. (1973). *Tales from the Thousand and One Nights.* (N. J. Dawood, Trans.) London: Penguin Group.

Talks with Sri Ramana Maharshi, as recorded by Sri Munagala S. Venkataramiah (Swami Ramanananda Saraswati) (I935-1939). (2003). Sri Ramanasramam, Tiruvannamalai, Tamil Nadu, India: V.S. Ramanan.

Tammet, D. (2012). *Thinking In Numbers: On Life, Love, Meaning, and Math.* London: Hodder & Stoughton Ltd.

Tasso, Torquato. (1983). *La Gerusalemme liberata* (L.Caretti ed.). Milano: Mondadori.

TB-Sāyana. (1855-70). *Taittirīya Brāhmaṇa of the Black Yajur Veda, Commentary of Sāyana* (Biblio Verlag, Osnabrück, 1981 ed., Vols. reprint vol. 31,4 - 6 ed., Vol. 2). Calcutta: Bibliotheca Indica, Asiatic Society of Bengal, O.S.

Tegmark, M. (2014). *Our Mathematical Universe: My Quest for the Ultimate Nature of Reality.* New York: Alfred A. Knopf.

Tegmark, M. (March 17, 2015). Consciousness as a State of Matter. *Chaos, Solitons & Fractals*, 1-32.

Teresa of Avila. (2007). *The Interior Castle. (B.Zimmerman-Intro.).* (Benedictines-of-Stanbrook, Trans.) New York: Cosimo Classics.

Tesla, N. (1982). *My Inventions: The Autobiography of Nikola Tesla.* Austin, Texas: Hart Brothers.

Thayer, William Roscoe. (1899). *Throne-makers.* Boston, New York: Houghton, Mifflin and company.

The Antipas Foundation, Inc. (2012). *HEBREW CALENDAR 2013 - 2014.* Retrieved May 18, 2014, from FOR THE JEWISH YEAR - AM 5774: http://antipas.net/heb_cal.htm

The Babylonian Talmûd. (2008). *The Babylonian Talmûd: Tractate Berâkôt: (1921) translated into English for the first time, with introduction, commentary, glossary and indices.* (A.Cohen, Trans.) Whitefish, MT: Kessinger Publishing LLC.

The Gospel of Thomas. (n.d.). *The Gospel of Thomas.* (T.O.Lambdin, Trans.) Vols. Nag Hammadi Library II, 2, pp. 118 fol.

The Nag Hammadi Library. (1977 - 1990, 1990 revised ed.). *The Nag Hammadi Library.* (J.M.Robinson, Ed., & C.G.Christianity, Trans.) N.Y: Harper & Row Pub.

The Tibetan Book of the Dead. (1960). *The Tibetan Book of the Dead or The After-Death Experiences on the Bardo Plane, according to Lāma Kazi Dawa-Samdup's English Rendering.* (Evans-Wentz, Ed., & Lāma-Kazi-Dawa-Samdup, Trans.) London, Oxford, New York: Oxford University Press.

Thich Nhat Hanh. (2015). *Silence, The Power of Quiet in a World Full of Noise.* New York: Harper One.

Thomas Aquinas. (1986). *Summa theologiae* (Vol. 3). (Marietti, Ed.) Milano: Marietti.

Thomas Aquinas. (2000). *The Aquinas Prayer Book: The Prayers and Hymns of St. Thomas Aquinas.* (Anderson-Moser, Ed.) Manchester, New Hampshire: Sophia Institute Press.

Thomas, D. (1934). *18 Poems.* London: The Sunday Referee and the Parton Bookshop.

Thoreau, H. D. (1983). *Walden and Civil Disobedience .* New York, NY: Penguin Book USA Inc.

Thoreau, H. D. (1993). *A Year in Thoreau's Journal: 1851.* New York: Penguin Books USA Inc.

Tolle, E. (2001). *Practicing the Power of Now: Essential Teachings, Meditations, and Exercises From The Power of Now.* Novato, CA: New World Library.

Tolle, E. (2003). *Stillness Speaks.* Vancouver, Canada: Namaste Publishing.

Tolle, E. (2004). *The Power of Now: A Guide to Spiritual Enlightenment.* Vancouver, Canada: Namaste Publishing.

Tolle, E. (2006). *Eckhart Tolle A New Earth: Awakening to Your Life's Purpose.* New York: A Plume Book.

Tononi, G. (2008, December). Consciousness as Integrated Information: a Provisional Manifesto. *The Biological Bulletin 215*, 216-242.

Toptenz. (2008, JULY 27). *10 Possible Locations for the Garden of Eden.* Retrieved April 28, 2016, from Toptenz.net: http://www.toptenz.net/10-possible-locations-for-the-garden-of-eden.php

Torah. (1981). *The Torah. A modern commentary.* (W. G. Plaut, Ed.) New York: Union of American Hebrew Congregation.

Totò. (1964). *'A Livella e poesie d'amore.* Roma: Grandi Tascabili Economici Newton.

Trismosin, S. (2003). *Splendor Solis (facsimile reprint).* United States: Kessinger Publishing Co.

Tucci, G. (1922). *Storia della filosofia cinese antica.* Bologna: Zanichelli.

Tucci, G. (1957). *Storia della filosofia indiana.* Bari: Laterza.

U.S. Department of the Interior. (2007, January 4). *U.S. Geological Survey. Clementine - USGS images a return to the moon.* Retrieved January 29, 2008, from Edited by 2255 N Gemini Image processing by the U.S. Geological Survey: http://astrogeology.usgs.gov/Projects/Clementine/

UAb. (2005). *Amritabindu Upanishad in Krishna-Yajurvediya . In The Scriptural Commentaries of Yogiraj Sri Sri Shyama Charan Lahiri Mahasaya* (Vols. 1, pp. 209, Ch. 4). (Y. Niketan, Trans.) New York, Lincoln, Shanghai: iUnivese, Inc.

UB. (1889). *Bṛhadāraṇyaka Upanishad, in der Mādhyadina Recension.* St. Petersburg (and Leipzig): Herausgegeben und übersetzt von O. Böhtlingk.

UC. (1889). *Chāndogya Upanishad.* Leipzig: Kritisch herausgegeben und übersetzt von Otto Böhtlingk.

UG. (1965). *Gaṇapati Upanishad, text* (Vol. XVIII). (L. Renou, Ed., & J. Varenne, Trans.) Paris: Libraire d'Amérique et d'Orient Adrien-Maisonneuve.

UĪśa. (1850). *Īśa Upanishad.* (E. Röer, Ed.) Calcutta: Bibliotheca Indica.

UĪśa. (1850). *Īśa Upanishad.* (E. Röer, Ed.) Calcutta: Bibliotheca Indica.

Uittenbogaard, A. (2000-2014). *The Hebrew word.* Retrieved 2 7, 2015, from Abarim Publications' Biblical Dictionary: www.abarim-publications.com

UK. (1850). *Katha Upanishad.* (E. Röer, Ed.) Calcutta: Bibliotheca Indica.
UKaBr. (1861). *Kaushītaki Brāhmaṇa Upanishad.* (E. Cowell, Ed.) Calcutta: Bibliotheca Indica.
Ukai. (1952). *Kaivalyopaniṣad Texte et traduction.* (L. Renou, Ed., & Tubini, Trans.) Paris (VI): Librairie D'Amerique et d'Orient Adrien-Maisonneuve.
UKena. (1850). *Kena Upanishad.* (E. Röer, Ed.) Calcutta: Bibliotheca Indica.
UM. (1850). *Māṇḍūkya Upanishad.* (E. Röer, Ed.) Calcutta: Bibliotheca Indica.
UMaitrī. (1870). *Maitrī Upanishad.* (E. B. Cowell, Ed.) Calcutta, London: Bibliotheca Indica.
UŚ. (1850). *Śvetāśvatara Upanishad, in Tāittirīya, Āitareya and Śvetāśvatara Upanishads.* (E. Röer, Ed.) Calcutta: Bibliotheca Indica.
UT. (1850). *Taittirīya Upanishad, in Tāittirīya, Āitareya and Śvetāśvatara Upanishads.* (E. Röer, Ed.) Calcutta: Bibliotheca Indica.
UY. (n.d.). *Yoga Darshana Upanishad. Translation in Varenne, Yoga...*
Valenstein, E. S. (2005). *The War of the Soups and the Sparks: The Discovery of Neurotransmitters and the Dispute Over How Nerves Communicate.* New York, Chichester, West Sussexs: Columbia University Press.
Valtorta, M. (1992). *Il Poema dell'Uomo-Dio* (Vol. 10). Isola del Liri: Centro Editoriale Valtortiano.
Valtorta, M. (2006). *I quaderni del 1943.* Isola del Liri: Centro Editoriale Valtortiano (CEV).
Van Neikerk, W., Retief A. E. (1981). The gonads of human true hermaphrodites. *Human Genetics 1981;58(1):117-22*, 117-122.
Varenne, J. (1976). *Yoga And the Hindu Tradition.* (D. Coltman, Trans.) Chicago and London: The University of Chicago Press.
Vass, Copara, Seyal, Shahlaie, Farias, Shen, Ekstrom. (2016, February 25). Oscillations Go the Distance: Low-Frequency Human Hippocampal Oscillations Code Spatial Distance in the Absence of Sensory Cues during Teleportation. *Neuron.*
Vasubandhu and Asaṅga. (1925). *Vijñaptimātratāsiddhi-Triṃśikā with Sthiramati commentary.* (S. Lévi, Ed., & S. Lévi, Trans.) Paris: Librairie Ancienne Honoré Champion.
Vedānta-Sūtras. (1904 - 1968). *The Vedānta-Sūtras, with the commentary by Śaṅkarācārya* (Delhi 1968 ed., Vol. I & II). (M. Muller, Ed., & G. Thibaut, Trans.) Oxford, Delhi, Varanasi, Patna: The Sacred Books of the East, Motilal Banarsidass.
Vincent, C. (Ed.). (1900). *The platform text-book: containing the Declaration of independence.* (C. Vincent, Ed.) Omaha, Nebraska: Vincent Publishing.
Virgil P. (1910). *Vergili Maronis Aeneis in usum scholarum iterum recognovit Otto Ribbeck.* Lipsiae: in aedibus B. G. Teubneri.
Vitruvius, P. (1962). *On architecture.* Cambridge, Mass: Harvard University Press.
von Hildebrand, Dietrich. (2009). *The Nature of Love.* (J.F.Crosby, Trans.) South Bend, Indiana: St. Augustine's Press.
VṚ. (1968). *Die Hymnen des Ṛigveda* (Vols. I-II). (T. Aufrecht, Ed.) Wiesbaden: Otto Harrassowitz.
W. Monier Williams. (1899 - Reprint 1974). *Monier-Williams, A Sanskrit-English Dictionary.* London: Oxford University Press.
Waldemar-Kaempffert (Ed.). (1924). *A Popular History of American Invention.* New York: Scribner's Sons.
Walden, Treadwell. (1896). *The great meaning of metanoia : an underdeveloped chapter in the life and teaching of Christ.* New York: Thomas Whittaker.
Walid Khalid Abdul-Hamid, Jamie Hacker Hughes. (2014, 01). Nothing new under the sun: post-traumatic stress disorders in the ancient world. *Early Science and Medicine 01/2014; 19(6):549-57.*, 549-57.
Walker, P. (2014, February 17). North Korea: 'You are brainwashed from the time you know how to talk'. *theguardian*, pp. http://www.theguardian.com/world/2014/feb/17/north-korea-human-rights-abuses-stories-un-brainwashed.

Walzer, R. (1938). *Eraclito. Raccolta dei frammenti e traduzione italiana.* (Walzer, Trans.) Firenze: Sanzoni.

Warren, H. C. (1922). *Buddhism in translations: passages selected from the Buddhist sacred books* (Vols. Three, Eighth Issue). (Oriental-Series, Ed.) Cambridge, Massachusetts: Harvard University Press.

Watson, R. A. (2007). *Cogito, ergo sum : the life of René Descartes.* Boston: David R. Godine.

Watson, W. G. (Ed.). (1994). *The Dead Sea Scrolls Translated: The Qumran Texts in English.* (F. G. Martinez, Trans.) Leiden, New York, Köln: Brill.

Watts, A. (1989). *The Book. On the Taboo Against Knowing Who You Are.* New York: Vintage Books A Division of Random House, Inc.

Watts, A. (1999). *The Tao of Philosophy.* Singapore: Tuttle Publishing.

Webster, B., Kennedy, D. (2014, September 23). Test on halal meat destroys argument for ritual slaughter of animals. *The Times*, p. Environment.

Wheeler, J. A. (1982). Bohr, Einstein, and the Strange Lesson of the Quantum. (R. Q. Elvee, Ed.) *Mind in nature / Nobel Conference XVII Gustavus Adolphus College, St. Peter, Minnesota with contributions by John Archibald Wheeler ... [et al.]*, 1-30. San Francisco: Harper & Row.

Wilde, O. (1993). *The Picture of Dorian Gray* (Dover Thrift ed.). Mineola, NY: Dover Publications.

Wittgenstein, L. (1996). *Tractatus Logico-Philosophicus (German text with an English translation).* (C. Ogden, Trans.) London and New York: Routledge.

Woodbridge, L. (1987, Summer). Black and White and Red All Over: The Sonnet Mistress Amongst the Ndembu. *Renaissance Quarterly, 40*(2), pp. 247-297.

Woolley L. (1995). *The Sumerians.* New York: Barns & Noble Books.

Worden, G. (2002). *The Mutter Museum: Of the College of Physicians of Philadelphia.* New York, NY: Blast Books.

Worthen, M. (2015, MAY 30). Wanted: A Theology of Atheism. *The New York Times*, pp. OP-ED Sunday Review.

Yates, F. A. (1969). *Giordano Bruno e la tradizione ermetica.* (Pecchioli, Trans.) Bari: Edizioni Laterza.

Yeats, W. B. (1903). *The Land of Heart's Desire.* Portland, Maine: Thomas B. Mosher.

Yeshshem. (2014). *HEBREW LETTER: LAMED ל; PEY ף פ.* Retrieved 7 16, 2014, from yeshshem.com: http://www.yeshshem.com

Zimmer, H. (1974). *Myths and Symbols in Indian Art and Civilization.* (J.Campbell, Ed.) Princeton, NJ: Princeton University Press - Bollingen Series VI.

Zipes, J. D. (1992). *Aesop's Fables.* New York: Signet Classic.

Zuckerman, P. (2015, July 6). *Rejecting Islam. The trauma of apostasy in Muslim communities.* Retrieved July 29, 2015, from Psychology Today The Secular Life Thriving Without Gods or Gurus: https://www.psychologytoday.com/blog/the-secular-life

~~~

FURTHER READINGS

PHILOSOPHY

1972, Pasquale J. Simonelli, ***Il neoplatonismo ed il pensiero indiano,***
Napoli: Atti dell'Accademia di Scienze Morali e Politiche, Vol. LXXXII.

1974, Pasquale J. Simonelli, ***Note su alcuni aspetti ontologico - gnoseologici di una invocazione ad Agni,***
Napoli: Annali dell'Istituto Universitario Orientale, Vol. 34.

1976, Pasquale J. Simonelli, ***Note introduttive alla gnoseologia di Šankara,***
Scritti in onore di Cleto Carbonara, Napoli: Universita' di Napoli.

1978, Pasquale J. Simonelli, ***Una lettura della Brihadaranyaka Upanishad,***
Napoli: Annali dell'Istituto Universitario Orientale, Vol. 38.

1982, Pasquale J. Simonelli, ***La morte nella Brihadaranyaka Upanishad e Satapatha Brahmana,*** *La mort, les morts dans les sociétés anciennes,* Cambridge: Éditions de la Maisons des Sciences de l'Homme, Cambridge University Press.

1996, Pasquale J. Simonelli, ***Philosophy as a Path to Education for Leadership,***
Education for Leadership and Social Responsibility, Ed. S. Sarsar, West Long Branch, NJ: Center for the Study of Public Issues Monmouth University. (PEDAGOGY)

2000, Pasquale J. Simonelli, ***Transcendence - The Universal Quest,***
Mythological Europe Revisited, Humanism and the Third Millennium III, Fons Elders, Ed., Brussels: VUB University Press.

2004, Pasquale J. Simonelli, ***The World as the Upanishadic sacrificial-horse, as the barge of Ra from the sarcophagus of Seti I, and according to Genesis,***
Visions of Nature, Studied on the Theory of Gaia and Culture in Ancient and Modern Times, Fons Elders, Ed., Brussels: VUB University Press.

2008, Pasquale J. Simonelli, ***Sacred Topography, Holy Chronology and Human Dimensions: The "Mythical" Subdivision of Space and Time in the Upanishadic Tradition,*** Baton Rouge, Louisiana: International Association of Asian Studies of the NAAAS & Affiliates, Monograph Series.

2009, Satya-Shiva Caitanya सत्यशिव चैतन्य, ***Beyond Immortality Now. The Electron Frog-Jump Past the Edge of Death's Abyss,*** W.Long Branch, NJ: Sacer Equestris Aureus Ordo, Inc. http://www.amazon.com/dp/1477450955

2012, Pasquale J. Simonelli, ***Beyond Immortality. The Electron Frog-Jump Past the Edge of Death's Abyss,*** W.Long Branch, NJ: Sacer Equestris Aureus Ordo, Inc.
http://www.amazon.com/dp/061563706X

2013, Pasquale J. Simonelli, ***Awareness. The Book of Ethic, Morals and Behavior,***
West Long Branch, NJ: Sacer Equestris Aureus Ordo Inc. (ETHIC)
http://amzn.com/0615754260

2013, Eli Luminosus Aequalis, ***Mutus Liber "Loquitur" – The Mute Book "Speaks",***
W. Long Branch, NJ: Sacer Equestris Aureus Ordo, Inc. (ALCHEMY)
http://amzn.com/0615906079

HISTORY

1973, Pasquale J. Simonelli, ***Nuovi ritrovamenti di iscrizioni in Nola,***
Napoli: Atti dell'Accademia Pontaniana, Vol. XXI.

2000, Pasquale J. Simonelli, ***NOLA-HYRIA, HYRIA, history, economy, legends, and myths of a lost Campanian city in the IV century B.C. -- HYRIA, storia, economia, leggende e miti di una citta' campana perduta nel IV secolo a.C.,*** a cura di Luigi Vecchione, Nola, Napoli: Edizioni "*Opinione* 2" Archeoclub d'Italia.

2000, Pasquale J. Simonelli, ***Hyria, A lost City-State, Una Polis Scomparsa, Nola-Hyria.***
W.Long Branch, NJ: Sacer Equestris Aureus Ordo, Inc. History division.
http://amzn.com/0615702554

2012, Pasquale J. Simonelli, ***Enrico Caruso Unedited Notes,***
Charleston, SC: Sacer Equestris Aureus Ordo, Inc. Music division.
http://amzn.com/0615714900
~~~

CHILDREN's BOOKS

1988-90, Pal, ***The Lorns: A New Race of Beings. The Sensational Revelation of Professor Lorry***. W.Long Branch, NJ: Sacer Equestris Aureus Ordo, Inc. Chidren Books division. http://amzn.com/0615638201

2000, Timendever, ***Time Passport: The Time Traveler***. W.Long Branch, NJ: SEAO. Travel division. http://amzn.com/061569487X

2012, Pal, ***Santa Claus Exists!: Sensational Revelation of Professor Lorry, the Discoverer of The Lorns, proves that Santa Claus Exists***. W.Long Branch, NJ: Sacer Equestris Aureus Ordo, Inc. Chidren Books division. http://amzn.com/0615740677

NOVEL

2011-12, Ariadna Farkas Simon, ***Camilla the Siren: The Daughter of Death's Love, the Siren's Call to Life and Her Love Coordinates***, W. Long Branch, NJ: Sacer Equestris Aureus Ordo, Inc. http://www.amazon.com/dp/0615643124/

ARTICLES IN:

LOGOS, (PHILOSOPHY REVEWS)

Rivista di filosofia diretta da Cleto Carbonara, Napoli: Università di Napoli.

1970, Pasquale J. Simonelli, *Adler, L'importanza di Vico per lo sviluppo del pensiero sociologico*, & *Castelli, I paradossi del senso comune*, No. 3, 1970.

1971, Pasquale J. Simonelli, *Minerbi, La fondazione dell'unità umana*, No. 2.

IL PROGRESSO, New York (NEWSPAPER)

29 Giugno, 1986, Sam Paolese, *L'amore e la morte a Nola*; (HISTORY)
10 Luglio, Sam Paolese, *I programmi di John M. Nolan per rilanciare le poste*; (NEWS)
11 Luglio, Sam Paolese, *Movimento Popolare in cerca di alleanze*; (HISTORY)
13 Luglio, Sam Paolese, *Sacro e profano nella Roma antica*; (HISTORY)
14 Luglio, Sam Paolese, *Arrestato il giovane Budha*; (NEWS)
20 Luglio, Sam Paolese, *Nella valle della pace*; (RELIGION)
22 Luglio, Sam Paolese, *E in Italia non andiamo*, (TOURISM 1);
23 Luglio, Sam Paolese, *Non e' il mare di Palinuro ma che spazi, che pace*! (TOURISM 2);
27 Luglio, Sam Paolese, *Il banchiere che portò Caruso negli USA*; (HISTORY)
10 Agosto, Sam Paolese, *Tra cannoli, baba' e montagne di salcicce*, (FESTIVAL, NJ);
20 Agosto, Sam Paolese, *Lusinghiero successo del festival italiano*, (FESTIVAL, NJ);
5 Settembre, Sam Paolese, *Oltre l'East River*, (ECONOMY I part);
6 Settembre, Sam Paolese, *I prezzi alle stelle*, (ECONOMY II part);
6 Settembre, Sam Paolese, *Toto' cerca casa*, (THE SERVICES);
7 Settembre, Sam Paolese, *L'India? A due passi da Manhattan*,; (CULTURE)
9 Settembre, Sam Paolese, *Il dilemma dello sviluppo nella Monmouth County*, (ECONOMY);
10 Settembre, Sam Paolese, *Battuta d'arresto dopo il lungo boom*, (ECONOMY);
14 Settembre, Sam Paolese, *Estetica e tecnologia nel Village*, (ARCHITECTURE);
30 settembre, Sam Paolese, *Due serate dedicate alla musica e al balletto all'India*.(THEATRE)

AMERICA OGGI,New York (NEWSPAPER CULTURE)

1994, 16 ottobre, Sam Paolese, *L'italiano con orgoglio*;
1995, 16 aprile, Sam Paolese, *Il Monmouth College del New Jersey è ora University. Benvenuta promozione!*.

TOGETHER (NEWSPAPER HISTORY)

American Gathering of Jewish Holocaust Survivors, NYC

1999, 01, Pasquale J. Simonelli, *Citta' di Tunisi: A Ship of Hope for a Fortunate Few*, Volume 13 N. 1.

ARCHEONOLA (HISTORY)

Supplemento 1° a LA CONTEA NOLANA

NOLA ARCHEOCLUB d'Italia Edizioni "Opinione 2" Anno II numero terzo.

2000, 16 giugno, Pasquale J. Simonelli, *Dopo 24 Secoli, un tesoretto Nolano torna in Patria.*

www.ingramcontent.com/pod-product-compliance
Lightning Source LLC
Chambersburg PA
CBHW080537230426
43663CB00015B/2627
9780692958261